FEDERAL WILDLIFE STATUTES:

TEXTS AND CONTEXTS

By

DALE D. GOBLE
Margaret Wilson Schimke Distinguished Professor of Law
University of Idaho College of Law

ERIC T. FREYFOGLE
Max L. Rowe Professor of Law
University of Illinois College of Law

New York, New York
FOUNDATION PRESS
2002

ISBN 1–58778–401–7

TABLE OF CONTENTS

INTRODUCTION

AN OVERVIEW OF WILDLIFE LAW

This is a collection of federal statutes that regulate conduct in regard to wildlife. They are divided into a two general categories: statutes that conserve species and those that conserve habitat. The division is a matter of emphasis: some statutes prohibit the taking of wild animals by killing or capturing them, while others prohibit taking by restricting activities that degrade habitat; some do more than one thing. Since species cannot exist as other than curios in a zoo without habitat, both types of prohibitions have been present from the beginning of Anglo-American wildlife law.

The statutes in this collection share another commonality with the long line of statutes that stretch back nearly to the Norman Conquest of England: they generally employ a small number of tools. Closed seasons, bag limits, and land-use restrictions have a very long history in Anglo-American law.

This introduction briefly examines this history and the constitutional bases for federal wildlife law.

A. The King and His Heirs: Wildlife Law Prior to the Twentieth Century

i. English and British Antecedents

When William the Bastard conquered England and changed his name, he brought with him a passion for the hunt and a well-developed sense of his prerogative as sovereign. These met in the king's power to declare lands to be royal "forests," lands that were managed to conserve the "five wild beasts of venerie, that are called beastes of Forest ... the *Hart,* the *Hynde,* the *Hare,* the *Boare,* and the *Wolfe,*" and the "5 wilde beasts, that are called beasts of Chase, the Buck, the Doe, the Fox, the Martron, and the Roe."[1] "Forests" were a land-use classification rather than a vegetation description; they contained the mix of habitats that "forest" animals required.[2] As one contemporary writer commented, forests were "in particular places suitable for the purpose."[3] Forest law protected both the particular places (by prohibiting habitat-altering activities) and the game species that lived there (by prohibiting hunting) -- in the language of the time, forest law protected "the vert and Venison," the vegetation and the game:[4]

> by the lawes of the Forest, no man may cut downe his woods, nor destroy any coverts, within the Forest, without the ... license of the Lord Chief Justice in Eyre of the Forest, although that the soile, wherein those woods do grow, be a mans owne freehold.[5]

Similarly,

> Hauking and Hunting in Forests are pastimes of delights and pleasures, ordained and appointed chiefly for the recreation of Kings and Princes, & therefore they are not be used in Forests by every common person, but onely by such, as are Earles, Barons,

& Noble men of the Realme, being thereunto lice[n]sed or authorised by the king.[6] The forest law thus was a pervasive body of law that conserved a limited number of game species.

Legal restrictions were not, however, limited to places particularly suitable as wildlife habitat. The English government imposed a wide variety of hunting and habitat-altering restrictions to conserve wildlife. In 1285, for example, Parliament enacted the Statute of Westminister II which set closed seasons on the taking of salmon.[7] A statute enacted in 1393 strengthened these restrictions and also restricted habitat alteration by mandating that all dams include weirs "of reasonable wideness" to permit the fish to reach upstream spawning areas.[8] Similarly, a 1692 statute for "better preserving the red and black game of grouse" prohibited the burning of "grig, ling, heath, furze, goss, or fern," from February through June.[9] Lawmakers also relied upon bag limits,[10] gear restrictions,[11] and prohibitions on commerce[12] to conserve and to allocate wildlife.

The English and British governments thus employed the full range of "modern" wildlife conservation and allocation measures: they limited the taking of wildlife by prohibiting hunting as well as by imposing restrictions on land-use activities that damaged habitat. But the British government also adopted two other types of game laws that have no modern analogues: (1) qualification statutes restricting the right to hunt to the upper classes[13] and (2) statutes imposing penalties on those who stole deer and other game from the landed gentry's parks and warrens.[14] These restrictions were enforced through severe penalties -- including involuntary transportation to America and death without benefit of clergy.

ii. Wildlife Law in a New World

The New World seemed different. Game was abundant. The equality of opportunity to kill it was an "important symbol[] of liberty in the pictures painted for the purposes of generating settlement and financial backing for colonial ventures."[15] Abundance made taking restrictions unnecessary and a policy of free access was simply assumed. Experience demonstrated, however, that, while wildlife might be renewable, it was not infinitely so. Beginning with Massachusetts Bay in 1694, the colonies adopted restrictions on killing or capturing wildlife. By the Revolution, every colony except Georgia had established limitations on killing deer.[16] As population increased, so did legislative output: gear restrictions, bag limits, and licensing requirements soon followed.

Legislatures also routinely restricted land uses to conserve wildlife habitat.[17] The most common examples were statutes requiring mill owners to install fishways in their milldams.[18] When the Essex Company was incorporated by the Massachusetts legislature in 1845, for example, it was required to construct fish passage facilities in the dam it sought to construct at Bodwell's Falls on the Merrimack River.[19]

But the law in the statute books often differed dramatically from the law in the field. Although the evidence is necessarily anecdotal, the prevalence of poaching is uniformly acknowledged by contemporary commenters. As one historian of the Merrimack River Valley and its anadromous fish runs wrote, "a history of the unlawful fishing at [Amoskeag] Falls would be more voluminous than interesting."[20] In part, the prevalence of poaching reflects the rudimentary nature of the nineteenth-century state:

> both the scope and administrative strength of regulation were limited. Regulation tended to be local, self-sustaining -- as in the fee system -- and conservative in the use of staff.... Basically, the law let private citizens enforce what regulation there was. If no one brought a lawsuit, or complained to the district attorney about some violation, nothing was done. The state did not seriously try to administer, or carry through independently, what the statutes decreed.[21]

Perhaps more fundamentally, the "boys-will-be-boys" air of the reports[22] reflects a cavalier attitude that corroborates an observation by Lawrence Friedman that "a group may be less severe on its own forms of deviance than on the deviance of outsiders .... Juries in America were more tolerant of violations of game laws than the king and his servants would have been."[23]

A similar tale can be told about state efforts to restrict conduct that degraded wildlife habitat. The Atlantic coast's anadromous fish runs -- the salmon, shad, and alewives -- offer the clearest example both of the power of states to regulate use of private property to protect the public's common property in wildlife and of the state's primitive administrative apparatus. The Essex Company's dam at Bodwell's Falls, for example, was a technological marvel, the largest dam in the world at the time -- the period's most famous example of "Yankee ingenuity." But no comparable ingenuity was invested in the fish passage facilities. Although the act of incorporation required the company to construct a fishway to allow the passage of anadromous fish,[24] the fishway failed. As a subsequent legislative committee concluded, "there is not the slightest evidence that even a single fish had passed from the water below the dam to the water above."[25]

The rudimentary state enforcement apparatus, the trivialization of wildlife offenses, and the economic gain to be had from converting public resources into private wealth combined to produce a simple fact: fish runs and game animals were depleted -- often to the point of extinction -- by overharvesting and habitat destruction.[26]

The impotence of state law in the face of the technological and social changes sweeping the nation after the Civil War was made clear by the market hunter who was pushing species into extinction for food, plumes, and other commodities. The massive and wasteful slaughter of wildlife -- buffalos slaughtered by the thousands for their hides and passenger pigeons left to rot when the price made them not worth picking up -- led a coalition of Progressives, scientists, Audubon societies, and hunters to seek to protect migratory birds on a state-by-state basis.[27] Their inability to secure enactment of statutes in every state dramatized the federal problem,[28] and led these conservationists to shift their focus and to lobby Congress to protect migratory birds. But the Supreme Court had held in a line of cases that culminated in *Geer v. Connecticut*[29] that the states "owned" the wildlife within their borders in trust for their residents and the first statute seeking to federalize the conservation of migratory birds[30] was held to be unconstitutional.[31]

B. The Emergence of Federal Authority to Conserve Wildlife and Its Habitat

INTRODUCTION

The Law of Animals: A Treatise on Property in Animals Wild and Domestic and the Rights and Responsibilities Arising Therefrom was written at the turn from the nineteenth to the twentieth century.[32] It was, as the title suggests, a treatise on property law. Its topics included acquisition of property in animals both *ferae naturae* and domestic, transfer of that property by sale and mortgage, bailment and carriage. But its author aspired to comprehensiveness and included a chapter on wildlife law -- or "game law," as he called it. The whole of the chapter amounted to less than 20 of the treatise's more than 700 pages. It began with the then-recent United States Supreme Court decision in *Geer v. Connecticut* and the proposition that the state could control access to game because it was the owner "for the benefit of all the people in common."[33]

But even as John Ingham was writing his treatise, more than its title hearkened back to an earlier era -- his very subject matter was being transformed by the rising concern for conservation.

Traditionally, the states managed fish and wildlife as heirs of the king's common-law powers by mesne conveyance through the colonial governments. This idea -- known as the state ownership doctrine -- can be traced to that amalgam of common and international law that informed the early legal developments in this country. In *Arnold v. Mundy,*[34] for example, the court held that the State of New Jersey held the land beneath navigable waters in trust for its citizens because the king had held title to such lands as sovereign. Relying upon Blackstone's *Commentaries* and Vattel's *The Law of Nations*, the court concluded that this meant that the oysters growing on those lands were also owned by the state in trust.[35] In a subsequent federal circuit court decision, Associate Justice Bushrod Washington -- again relying upon Blackstone and Vattel -- held that state ownership-in-trust meant that oysters were not items of commerce and hence a New Jersey statute prohibiting nonresidents from harvesting oysters did not violate either the Commerce Clause or the Privileges and Immunities Clause.[36] In *Geer v. Connecticut,* the Supreme Court succinctly stated the chain of title at the close of the nineteenth century:

> [the] attribute of government to control the taking of animals *ferae naturae,* which was recognized and enforced by the common law of England, was vested in the colonial governments .... It is also certain that the power which the colonies thus possessed passed to the States with the separation from the mother country, and remains in them at the present day, in so far as its exercise may not be incompatible with, or restrained by, the rights conveyed to the Federal government by the Constitution.[37]

This state power was, the Court reasoned, an equitable property held "in trust for all the people of the State."[38] Proponents of "state's rights" seized upon the opinion's broad language and its conflation of state regulatory power with concepts of property, claiming that states owned the wildlife within their borders.[39] Under the then-prevalent constitutional theory, state and federal governments occupied mutually exclusive spheres. If states owned the wildlife within their borders, the federal government had only a very limited role in the conservation of wildlife.[40]

Congress acknowledged this limited and supportive role in 1900 -- the very year that Ingham's treatise was published -- when it enacted the first national wildlife statute, the Lacey Act.[41] But *Geer* and the original Lacey Act were the apogee of the state ownership doctrine. And even then, the doctrine's foundation was being undermined by the emerging conservation movement. With the enactment of the Weeks-McLean Migratory Bird Act,[42] the federal government embarked on a gradual process of preempting parts of wildlife law.

American constitutional law has always had a core of pragmatism. Oliver Wendell Holmes's famous aphorism -- "The life of the law has not been logic: it has been experience"[43] -- applies to constitutional as well as common law, as Holmes himself well recognized.[44] Overarching theories have meant little to Americans who have long turned to the government that they thought capable of redressing their particular grievance.[45] The episodic nature of federal wildlife law is an example.

i. The Bases of Federal Power: The Treaty Clause

In part the increasing federal regulatory presence reflected the fact that not even the combination of the Lacey Act and the state ownership doctrine could remedy all of the problems facing wildlife. There is, for example, a perverse incentive to overharvest something of value that moves across jurisdictional boundaries; a fish left in the river or a bird in the sky is likely to be killed in the next jurisdiction. The resulting "grim competition"[46] produced the calls for national action to protect wildlife[47] that led to the passage of the Weeks-McLean Migratory Bird Act,[48] in which Congress asserted federal jurisdiction over migratory birds. The Act was immediately challenged and equally quickly declared unconstitutional.[49]

The political pressure on the federal government, however, was sufficient that the United States negotiated a treaty with Great Britain -- acting for Canada -- to protect migratory birds.[50] Congress ratified the Treaty and enacted the Migratory Bird Treaty Act (MBTA) to implement it.[51] The Act was also quickly challenged as unconstitutional. In upholding the constitutionality of the MBTA in *Missouri v. Holland*, Justice Holmes bluntly observed "it is not sufficient to rely upon the States. The reliance is vain."[52] The Court held that the federal government had power under the Treaty Making Power to negotiate the treaty; as such, the statute implementing that treaty was also constitutional:

> by Article II, § 2, the power to make treaties is delegated expressly [to the United States], and by Article VI treaties made under the authority of the United States, along with the Constitution and laws of the United States made in pursuance thereof, are declared the supreme law of the land. If the treaty is valid there can be no dispute about the validity of the statute under Article I, § 8, as a necessary and proper means to execute the powers of the Government.[53]

In sum, the power to negotiate treaties is a source of affirmative power for federal regulation of wildlife. It is a source that has been used recurrently.[54]

Significantly, the Court also stated a broader proposition that substantially undercut the rationale offered in *Geer:* "No doubt it is true that as between a State and its inhabitants the State may regulate the killing and sale of [wildlife], but it does not follow that its authority is exclusive of paramount powers. To put the claim of the State upon title is to lean upon a slender reed."[55]

ii. The Bases of Federal Power: Tho Property Clause

Within a decade of its decision in *Missouri v. Holland,* the Court concluded that the Property Clause[56] was another "paramount power" that delegated the federal government the power to regulate wildlife.

The case that first announced this principle grew out of the most famous example of wildlife "management," the deer herd on the Kaibab Plateau.[57] In 1906, the federal government had made the north rim of the Grand Canyon a game preserve and set out to reverse the decline in the number of deer. Hunting was ended; grazing was reduced; predators were controlled. The deer population rebounded. Because the Kaibab Plateau is an island in the desert, the population could not disperse. Browse conditions deteriorated dramatically. In Aldo Leopold's description, it was "as if someone had given God a new pruning shears, and forbidden Him all other exercise. In the end the starved bones of the hoped-for deer herd, dead of its own too-much, bleach with the bones of the dead sage, or molder under the high-lined junipers."[58] Calls for thinning the herd led to political posturing. The winter of 1924-1925 saw a massive kill, followed by renewed disputes. The Forest Service requested the state to increase the permissible take; the state refused. A test case led to a Supreme Court decision that "the power of the United States to ... protect its lands and property does not admit of doubt ... the game laws or any other statute of the state to the contrary notwithstanding."[59]

Subsequent decisions upheld the power of federal land managers to take wildlife contrary to state law in situations in which the property-protecting justification was less clear.[60] The issue was not, however, finally resolved until the Supreme Court decided *Kleppe v. New Mexico.*[61]

Kleppe was a challenge to the constitutionality of the Wild, Free-Roaming Horses and Burros Act of 1971,[62] which had "directed" the Secretaries of the Interior and Agriculture "to protect and manage wild free-roaming horses and burros as components of the public lands."[63] At the request of a public land rancher under the state Estray Law, the New Mexico Livestock Board removed and sold several unbranded burros at public auction. After the Bureau of Land Management demanded return of the burros, the state sought a declaratory judgment that the Act was unconstitutional. The Supreme Court held that it was not: "the 'complete power' that Congress has over public lands necessarily includes the power to regulate and protect the wildlife living there."[64]

Kleppe settled the constitutional authority of the federal government to regulate wildlife on public lands as an incident of its authority to regulate those lands.[65] The Wild, Free-Roaming Horses and Burros Act, however, directs the Secretary to protect and manage the animals even when they are not located on federal lands. While noting that "it is clear that regulations under the Property Clause may have some effect on private lands not otherwise under federal control,"[66] the Supreme Court specifically left open the question of limits on the power delegated by the clause, stating only that "the Clause, in broad terms, gives Congress the power to determine what are 'needful' rules 'respecting' the public lands."[67]

Relying on this language -- and earlier decisions such as *Camfield v. United States*[68] -- for guidance, other federal courts have concluded that the Clause grants Congress power to regulate uses of non-federal lands if the use "interferes with the designated purpose" of the lands.[69] For example, a conviction for hunting ducks within Voyageurs National Park was upheld even though the hunter was in a boat floating on a navigable lake, the waters and bed of which belonged to the state. Relying on the finding of the district court that "hunting on the waters in the park could 'significantly interfere with the use of the park and the purposes for which it was established,'" the court of appeals upheld the hunting prohibitions as "'needful' prescriptions 'respecting' the public lands."[70] The Property Power, the court held, is sufficiently broad "to include the authority to regulate activities on non-federal public waters in order to protect wildlife and visitors on the [public] lands."[71] Subsequent decisions have upheld bans on commercial fishing on navigable waters within Everglades National Park in Florida[72] and waterfowl hunting regulations on Ruby Lake National Wildlife Refuge in Nevada.[73]

The Property Clause thus provides an additional basis for regulations applicable to wildlife on federal and adjacent non-federal lands.

iii. The Bases of Federal Power: The Commerce Clause

The Commerce Clause[74] has given rise to two bodies of law. The first examines the scope of Congress' power to regulate activity that involves "Commerce ... among the several States." This affirmative Commerce Clause is contrasted with the "dormant" Commerce Clause, a body of caselaw that reflects the conclusion that the federal courts have power under the Commerce Clause to limit the reach of state legislation that affects interstate commerce.

a. *The Dormant Commerce Clause*

Geer and the other cases that developed the state ownership doctrine during the nineteenth century often raised questions of the scope of the dormant Commerce Clause. Their shadow extended over wildlife law long after their analysis was an anomaly. *Geer* reflected the intersection of two strands of Commerce Clause law: first, the judiciary's attempt to maintain rigid lines between "inter-" and "intrastate" commerce in order to preserve completely separate spheres of federal "commerce" power and state "police" power;[75] and, second, the idea that natural resources -- wildlife and water, earth and air -- were owned in common by the people with the state acting as a trustee.[76] As trustee, the state had the power to preserve "its natural advantages" by preventing such natural advantages from ever becoming items of interstate commerce.[77]

Geer quickly became an anomaly. The lines both between inter- and intrastate and between resources that could be hoarded and those that could not became untenable.[78] After *Geer*, the Court consistently refused to extend its holding.[79] The passage of time and the demise of the substantive due process analysis that had given birth to the doctrine, increasingly led to the recognition that "ownership" was "no more than a 19th century legal fiction."[80] Nonetheless, it was not until *Hughes v. Oklahoma,*[81] that the Court formally overruled *Geer.* The Court applied a standard dormant commerce clause analysis in striking down a state statute prohibiting the export of wild minnows from Oklahoma.[82] Wildlife thus is -- in part, at least -- commerce rather than some *sui generis* category beyond the reach of federal power.

b. The Affirmative Commerce Clause

Although the Supreme Court's first Commerce Clause decision -- *Gibbons v. Ogden*[83] -- involved the affirmative Clause, this aspect was relatively unimportant in wildlife law until recently because Congress enacted so few statutes that sought to conserve wildlife. As the Supreme Court was careful to note in its decisions in the various state ownership cases, Congress had not acted and thus there was no issue of federal preemption of state law.[84] It was not until 1977, that the Supreme Court examined the application of the affirmative Commerce Clause to wildlife. The case -- *Douglas v. Seacoast Products, Inc.*[85] -- involved a Virginia statute regulating the menhaden fishery within the state's estuarine and in-shore ocean waters. Relying upon Chief Justice John Marshall's opinion in *Gibbons v. Ogden,* the Court held that a federal license to engage in the mackerel fishery preempts inconsistent state law. As the Court acknowledged, "While [Virginia] may be correct in arguing that at earlier times in our history there was some doubt whether Congress had power under the Commerce Clause to regulate the taking of fish in state waters, there can be no question today that such power exists where there is some effect on interstate commerce."[86] Since the "movement of vessels from one State to another in search of fish, and back again to processing plants, is certainly activity which Congress could conclude affects interstate commerce,"[87] Congress has the power to regulate fishing and thus to preempt inconsistent state law. The Court reinforced this conclusion two years later in *Andrus v. Allard*[88] when it upheld the Migratory Bird Treaty Act as a valid exercise of the Commerce Clause.

With the Court's recent resurgent belief that it can police the national-state boundary has come an increasing number of federalism-based challenges to federal wildlife statutes. Thus far, the Courts of Appeals have consistently rejected such challenges. For example, in *National Association of Home Builders v. Babbitt,*[89] the D.C. Circuit held that land-development restrictions resulting from the presence of a federally listed endangered species did not exceed congressional power under the Clause. Conservation of biodiversity "'substantially affects' interstate commerce," much as the forty bushels of wheat at issue in *Wickard v. Filburn*[90] substantially affected commerce when it was understood cumulatively.[91]

Congress thus has power under the Commerce, Treaty, and Property Clauses to regulate activities that impact wildlife and its habitat. The statutes that follow are based upon one or more of the clauses.

C. Federal Wildlife Agencies

Federal authority over wildlife has been delegated by Congress to several agencies. The most important are the Fish and Wildlife Service (FWS) in the Department of the Interior and the National Marine Fisheries Service (NMFS) in the National Oceanic and Atmospheric Administration (NOAA) in the Department of Commerce.

FWS was created under Reorganization Plan No. 2 of 1939.[92] The Plan transferred the functions of the Bureau of Fisheries from the Department of Commerce[93] and of the Bureau of Biological Survey from the Department of Agriculture to the Department of the Interior. These entities were consolidated and renamed the Fish and Wildlife Service in Reorganization Plan No. 3 of 1940.[94] In 1956, Congress renamed the agency the United States Fish and Wildlife Service and divided it into two bureaus, the Bureau of Sport Fisheries and Wildlife and the Bureau of Commercial Fisheries.[95] Finally, Reorganization Plan No. 4 of 1970[96] transferred the functions of the Bureau of Commercial Fisheries of the Department of the Interior, the functions of the Secretary of the Interior administered through the Bureau, and the responsibilities for migratory marine species to a new agency, NOAA in the Department of Commerce. Functions related to Great Lakes and Missouri River fisheries were excepted from the transfer of functions. As NMFS and FWS subsequently explained the division, "Generally, marine species are under the jurisdiction of the Secretary of Commerce and all other species are under the jurisdiction of the Secretary of the Interior."[97] "Marine species" include anadromous species such as salmon which migrate between freshwater spawning and rearing habitat and saltwater maturing habitat.

The FWS mission is divided between land management and wildlife conservation regulatory authority. The agency's statutory management responsibilities for the National Wildlife Refuge System are set out in Chapter 2. FWS's role in wildlife conservation includes enforcement or management authority not only under the Lacey Act,[98] but also under the Migratory Bird Treaty Act,[99] the Bald and Golden Eagle Protection Act,[100] the Airborne Hunting Act,[101] the Marine Mammal Protection Act for walruses, otters, manatees, and polar bears,[102] the Endangered Species Act for non-marine species,[103] Nonindigenous Aquatic Nuisance Control & Prevention Act,[104] the Wild Bird Conservation Act,[105] and the Neotropical Migratory Bird Conservation Act.[106]

NOAA/NMFS has enforcement and management authority under the Marine Mammal Protection Act for "the order Cetacea [whales] and members, other than walruses, of the order Pinnipedia [seals],"[107] the Magnuson-Stevens Fishery Conservation and Management Act,[108] and the Endangered Species Act for marine and anadromous species.[109]

\- 0 -

CHAPTER 1

CONSERVING SPECIES THROUGH RESTRICTIONS ON TAKE AND COMMERCE

The understanding of the federal structure of the United States during the nineteenth century limited the role of the federal government in conserving wildlife. Because the states "owned" the wildlife within their borders, the power to regulate taking within states was purely "a matter of internal police." Therefore, the few federal statutes that regulated the taking of wildlife were based upon the power that the Property Clause delegated to Congress to manage the territories. In 1868, for example, Congress took steps to extend federal law to the territory recently acquired from Russia; in doing so, it specifically prohibited the killing of "any otter, mink, marten, sable, or fur seal, or other fur-bearing animal" within Alaska.[1] This was followed two years later with "An Act to prevent the Extermination of Fur-bearing Animals in Alaska," which established a leasing system that was designed to regulate the harvest of fur seals.[2] By the end of the nineteenth century, however, pressure on Congress increased to solve two problems that were exacerbated by the federal system: market hunting and the plume trade.

Although there had long been a market for game -- particularly waterfowl and other game birds[3] -- technological advances after the Civil War provided new opportunities for market hunters. The use of the railroad -- with its rapid transportation -- and the refrigerator car -- which prevented spoilage -- opened markets in distant metropolitan areas.[4] Similarly, the fashion of the day relied upon bird plumes for hats and other millinery decorations; hunters responded by slaughtering millions of wading birds. Sportsmen, scientific naturalists, and the conservation-minded individuals who created the Audubon societies forged an uneasy coalition that initially focused on convincing state legislatures to enact statutes ending market hunting and prohibiting the use of feathers on hats.[5] They were more successful in the urban and northern states that were the market for the meat and hats and less so in the rural and southern states that were the source of the commodities.

When the coalition failed to achieve its goals at the state level, it shifted its focus to the federal government. The Lacey Act, the first federal wildlife conservation statute with a national scope, was the result. Although the Act was national in scope, it nonetheless reflected the then-restrictive understanding of the commerce power. Congress did not seek to supplant state law but rather to reinforce it. It did so by criminalizing two types of conduct. First, it prohibited interstate transportation by a common carrier of wildlife taken in violation of state law. Second, it subjected interstate shippers to the laws of the state into which the game was transported. Thus, a shipper was liable under federal law when possession or shipment of the wildlife was illegal under the laws of either the shipping or the receiving state.[6]

Since the Lacey Act simply reinforced state law, it failed to prevent the continuing decline in migratory birds. This decline was traceable in part to the perverse incentives provided by the federal system. As an "ardent sportsman" from Louisiana said, "The birds [snipe] were such migrants, and only in the country for a short time, I had no mercy on them, and killed all I could, for a snipe once missed might never be seen again."[7] Given the continuing problems, the coalition that had successfully lobbied for the Lacey Act continued to press Congress to assert jurisdiction over migratory birds. The first bill to federalize the conservation of migratory birds was introduced in Congress in 1903; ten years later Congress enacted the Weeks-McLean Migratory Bird as a rider to an appropriation bill.[8]

The Lacey Act ruffled no feathers since it only reinforced -- and hence tacitly acknowledged the supremacy of -- state law. Such was not the case with Weeks-McLean: the Act was immediately challenged and declared unconstitutional.[9] The political pressure on the federal government was sufficient, however, that the United States negotiated a treaty with Great Britain -- acting for Canada -- to protect migratory birds.[10] In *Missouri v. Holland,*[11] the Supreme Court upheld the Migratory Bird Treaty Act (MBTA) of 1918[12] which Congress had enacted to implement the treaty. The MBTA put the federal government for the first time in the business of regulating the taking of wildlife.

For the next fifty years, Congress acted only sporadically and generally in an ancillary role. In 1926, for example, it responded to a narrow interpretation of the Lacey Act's "wild animals and birds" by enacting the Black Bass Act.[13] Four years later, it addressed the problem of international commerce in wildlife in the Tariff Act of 1930.[14] Like the Lacey Act, both statutes relied upon the Commerce Clause to reinforce the laws of other governments. It was not until 1940, that Congress again took steps to conserve a species by restricting the taking and commercial activity in a species. Concluded that the bald eagle -- "no longer a mere bird of biological interest but a symbol of American ideals of freedom"[15] -- was threatened with extinction, Congress enacted the Bald Eagle Protection Act.[16] The constitutional basis for the authority to protect a symbolic animal was less clear.[17]

And then in the mid-1960s, in response to a broad social consensus that the "environment" needed protection, Congress began to enact statutes that fundamentally transformed wildlife law by shifting the locus of legislation from the state to the national government. The first of these statutes was the Act of October 15, 1966 -- a statute that was subsequently given two names to reflect its twin concerns: sections 1 to 3 became known as the Endangered Species Preservation Act of 1966 [ESPA],[18] while sections 4 and 5 became the National Wildlife Refuge System Administration Act.[19] The ESPA reflected congressional recognition that "one of the unfortunate consequences of growth and development" is the extermination of native species of fish and wildlife; it enunciated a new, national policy for the "conservation, protection, restoration, and propagation" of native fish and wildlife "that are threatened with extinction."[20] But the conjunction of this goal with the more mundane administrative provisions reflected the fact that the ESPA did very little substantively. It was followed three years later with a more ambitious statute, the Endangered Species Conservation Act [ESCA].[21] In 1971, Congress enacted the Wild Free-Roaming Horses and Burros Act[22] to protect feral horses and burros as the "living symbols of the historic and pioneer spirit of the West."[23] The following year Congress federalized the conservation of marine mammals by enacting the Marine

Mammal Protection Act of 1972.[24] And in 1976, the United States proclaimed sovereignty over the marine resources within the exclusive economic zone (EEZ) extending 200 miles from the coast. The Magnuson Fisheries Conservation and Management Act[25] created a complex structure of regional fisheries management councils to manage the marine fisheries.

Many of these statutes asserted jurisdiction over objects previously left to the states to regulate. The shift led to constitutional challenges -- the Wild Free-Roaming Horses and Burros Act, for example, led to the Supreme Court's decision in *Kleppe v. New Mexico*[26] -- and a re-ordering of political relationships. But the federal actions also redefined what wildlife law encompassed. Wildlife law as practiced by the states was focused on game and commerce; it relied upon bag limits and open seasons to control the "harvest" of a small group of species. Although the federal government also regulated commercial species, it was concerned with non-game species as well: wildlife law lost its exclusive focus on deer and haddock and became concerned with black-footed ferrets and snail darters.

This Chapter contains those federal statutes that seek to conserve species by regulating take and commerce. Statutes that protect wildlife habitat -- either directly or incidentally -- are included in Chapter 2. Statutes that do both -- statutes that seek to or can be used to protect biodiversity -- are set out in Chapter 3.

We begin with the first federal statute with a national scope, the Lacey Act.

LACEY ACT
(16 U.S.C. §§ 701, 3371-3378)

The original version of the Lacey Act had five sections:

§ 1 delegated power to the Secretary of Agriculture to include "the preservation, distribution, introduction, and restoration of game birds and other wild birds."[27] This provision is codified at 16 U.S.C. § 701.

§ 2 prohibited the importation of "any foreign wild animal or bird except under special permit" from the Department of Agriculture. The section also prohibited the importation of certain enumerated animals and birds -- including English Sparrows and Starlings -- and delegated the Secretary the power to expand the list of prohibited species. This section is codified as amended at 18 U.S.C. § 42.[28]

§ 3 prohibited delivery to a common carrier and the interstate transportation by the carrier of wildlife taken in violation of state law.[29]

§ 4 required all packages containing wildlife to be "plainly and clearly marked, so that ... the nature of the contents may be readily ascertained on inspection of the outside of such packages."[30]

§ 5 subjected interstate shippers to the laws of the state into which the game was transported.

Sections 2-4 were repealed and restated by §§ 241-244 of the Criminal Code of 1909.[31] They were modified in subsequent enactments of the federal criminal code in 1935 and 1948.

The Black Bass Act (enacted in 1926) essentially reiterated the Lacy Act's provisions: interstate shipment of fish of taken in violation of state law was prohibited, state laws applied to shipments of fish upon arrival in the state, and packages containing fish were required to be marked.

The scope of the two Acts' prohibitions were steadily expanded. By 1952, it was illegal to ship wildlife -- including birds and fish -- in interstate commerce if the wildlife had been taken in violation of the law of a state, the federal government, or foreign nation or if possession of the wildlife would be illegal in the receiving state.

The Black Bass Act and sections 2 and 5[32] of the Lacey Act were repealed and the Act fundamentally rewritten in 1981.[33] The Lacey Act Amendments of 1981 remain the centerpiece of federal regulation of commercial activities in wildlife.

16 U.S.C. § 701. Game and wild birds; preservation. The duties and powers of the Department of the Interior include the preservation, distribution, introduction, and restoration of game birds and other wild birds. The Secretary of the Interior is authorized to adopt such measures as may be necessary to carry out the purposes of this Act, and to purchase such game birds and other wild birds as may be required therefor, subject, however, to the laws of the various States and Territories. The object and purpose of this Act is to aid in the restoration of such birds in those parts of the United States adapted thereto where the same have become scarce or extinct, and also to regulate the introduction of American or foreign birds or animals in localities where they have not heretofore existed.

The Secretary of the Interior shall from time to time collect and publish useful information as to the propagation, uses, and preservation of such birds.

And the Secretary of the Interior shall make and publish all needful rules and regulations for carrying out the purposes of this Act, and shall expend for said purposes such sums as Congress may appropriate therefor.

[May 25, 1900, ch. 553, § 1, 31 Stat. 187; 1939 Reorganization Plan No. II, § 4(f), 4 Fed. Reg. 2731, 53 Stat. 1433]

16 U.S.C. § 3371. Definitions For the purposes of this Act -- **(a)** The term "fish or wildlife" means any wild animal, whether alive or dead, including without limitation any wild mammal, bird, reptile, amphibian, fish, mollusk, crustacean, arthropod, coelenterate, or other invertebrate, whether or not bred, hatched, or born in captivity, and includes any part, product, egg, or offspring thereof.

(b) The term "import" means to land on, bring into, or introduce into, any place subject to the jurisdiction of the United States, whether or not such landing, bringing, or introduction constitutes an importation within the meaning of the customs laws of the United States.

(c) The term "Indian tribal law" means any regulation of, or other rule of conduct enforceable by, any Indian tribe, band, or group but only to the extent that the regulation or rule applies within Indian country as defined in section 1151 of Title 18.

(d) The terms "law," "treaty," "regulation," and "Indian tribal law" mean laws, treaties, regulations or Indian tribal laws which regulate the taking, possession, importation, exportation, transportation, or sale of fish or wildlife or plants.

(e) The term "person" includes any individual, partnership, association, corporation, trust, or any officer, employee, agent, department, or instrumentality of the Federal Government or of any State or political subdivision thereof, or any other entity subject to the jurisdiction of the United States.

(f) The terms "plant" and "plants" mean any wild member of the plant kingdom, including roots, seeds, and other parts thereof (but excluding common food crops and cultivars) which is indigenous to any State and which is either (A) listed on an appendix to the Convention on International Trade in Endangered Species of Wild Fauna and Flora, or (B) listed pursuant to any State law that provides for the conservation of species threatened with extinction.

(g) The term "Secretary" means, except as otherwise provided in this Act, the Secretary of the Interior or the Secretary of Commerce, as program responsibilities are vested pursuant to the provisions of Reorganization Plan Numbered 4 of 1970 (84 Stat. 2090); except that with respect to the provisions of this Act which pertain to the importation or exportation of plants the term means the Secretary of Agriculture.

(h) The term "State" means any of the several States, the District of Columbia, the Commonwealth of Puerto Rico, the Virgin Islands, Guam, Northern Mariana Islands, American Samoa, and any other territory, commonwealth, or possession of the United States.

(i) The term "taken" means captured, killed, or collected.

(j) The term "transport" means to move, convey, carry, or ship by any means, or to deliver or receive for the purpose of movement, conveyance, carriage, or shipment.

[Pub. L. 97-79, § 2, 95 Stat. 1073 (Nov. 16, 1981); Pub. L. 97-79, § 1, provided: "That this Act may be cited as the 'Lacey Act Amendments of 1981.'"]

16 U.S.C. § 3372. Prohibited acts. (a) Offense other than marking offenses. It is unlawful for any person --

(1) to import, export, transport, sell, receive, acquire, or purchase any fish or wildlife or plant taken, possessed, transported, or sold in violation of any law, treaty, or regulation of the United States or in violation of any Indian tribal law;

(2) to import, export, transport, sell, receive, acquire, or purchase in interstate or foreign commerce --

(A) any fish or wildlife taken, possessed, transported, or sold in violation of any law or regulation of any State or in violation of any foreign law, or

(B) any plant taken, possessed, transported, or sold in violation of any law or regulation of any State;

(3) within the special maritime and territorial jurisdiction of the United States (as defined in section 7 of Title 18) --

(A) to possess any fish or wildlife taken, possessed, transported, or sold in violation of any law or regulation of any State or in violation of any foreign law or Indian tribal law, or

(B) to possess any plant taken, possessed, transported, or sold in violation of any law or regulation of any State; [or]

(4) to attempt to commit any act described in paragraphs (1) through [(3)].

(b) Marking offenses. It is unlawful for any person to import, export, or transport in interstate commerce any container or package containing any fish or wildlife unless the container or package has previously been plainly marked, labeled, or tagged in accordance with the regulations issued pursuant to paragraph (2) of section 7(a) of this Act [16 U.S.C. § 3376(a)(2)].

(c) Sale and purchase of guiding and outfitting services and invalid licenses and permits

(1) Sale. It is deemed to be a sale of fish or wildlife in violation of this Act for a person for money or other consideration to offer or provide --

(A) guiding, outfitting, or other services; or

(B) a hunting or fishing license or permit;

for the illegal taking, acquiring, receiving, transporting, or possessing of fish or wildlife.

(2) Purchase. It is deemed to be a purchase of fish or wildlife in violation of this Act for a person to obtain for money or other consideration --

(A) guiding, outfitting, or other services; or

(B) a hunting or fishing license or permit;

for the illegal taking, acquiring, receiving, transporting, or possessing of fish or wildlife.

(d) False labeling offenses. It is unlawful for any person to make or submit any false record, account, or label for, or any false identification of, any fish, wildlife, or plant which has been, or is intended to be --

(1) imported, exported, transported, sold, purchased, or received from any foreign country; or

(2) transported in interstate or foreign commerce.

[Pub. L. 97-79, § 3, 95 Stat. 1074 (Nov. 16, 1981); Pub. L. 100-653, Title I, § 101, 102 Stat. 3825 (Nov. 14, 1988)]

16 U.S.C. § 3373. Penalties and sanctions. (a) Civil penalties.

(1) Any person who engages in conduct prohibited by any provision of this Act (other than subsections (b) and (d) of [16 U.S.C. § 3372]) and in the exercise of due care should know that the fish or wildlife or plants were taken, possessed, transported, or sold in violation of, or in a manner unlawful under, any underlying law, treaty, or regulation, and any person who knowingly violates section 3(d) [16 U.S.C. § 3372(d)] may be assessed a civil penalty by the Secretary of not more than $10,000 for each such violation: *Provided,* That when the violation involves fish or wildlife or plants with a market value of less than $350, and involves only the transportation, acquisition, or receipt of fish or wildlife or plants taken or possessed in violation of any law, treaty, or regulation of the United States, any Indian tribal law, any foreign law, or any law or regulation of any State, the penalty assessed shall not exceed the maximum provided for violation of said law, treaty, or regulation, or $10,000, whichever is less.

(2) Any person who violates subsection 3(b) of this Act [16 U.S.C. § 3372(b)] may be assessed a civil penalty by the Secretary of not more than $250.

(3) For purposes of paragraphs (1) and (2), any reference to a provision of this Act or to a section of this Act shall be treated as including any regulation issued to carry out any such provision or section.

(4) No civil penalty may be assessed under this subsection unless the person accused of the violation is given notice and opportunity for a hearing with respect to the violation. Each violation shall be a separate offense and the offense shall be deemed to have been committed not only in the district where the violation first occurred, but also in any district in which a person may have taken or been in possession of the said fish or wildlife or plants.

(5) Any civil penalty assessed under this subsection may be remitted or mitigated by the Secretary.

(6) In determining the amount of any penalty assessed pursuant to paragraphs (1) and (2), the Secretary shall take into account the nature, circumstances, extent, and gravity of the prohibited act committed, and with respect to the violator, the degree of culpability, ability to pay, and such other matters as justice may require.

(b) Hearings. Hearings held during proceedings for the assessment of civil penalties shall be conducted in accordance with section 554 of Title 5. The administrative law judge may issue subpoenas for the attendance and testimony of witnesses and the production of relevant papers, books, or documents, and may administer oaths. Witnesses summoned shall be paid the same fees and mileage that are paid to witnesses in the courts of the United States. In case of contumacy or refusal to obey a subpena issued pursuant to this paragraph and served upon any person, the district court of the United States for any district in which such person is found, resides, or transacts business, upon application by the United States and after notice to such person, shall have jurisdiction to issue an order requiring such person to appear and give testimony before the administrative law judge or to appear and produce documents before the administrative law judge, or both, and any failure to obey such order of the court may be punished by such court as a contempt thereof.

(c) Review of civil penalty. Any person against whom a civil penalty is assessed under this section may obtain review thereof in the appropriate District Court of the United States by filing a complaint in such court within 30 days after the date of such order and by simultaneously serving a copy of the complaint by certified mail on the Secretary, the Attorney General, and the appropriate United States attorney. The Secretary shall promptly file in such court a certified copy of the record upon which such violation was found or such penalty imposed, as provided in section 2112 of Title 28. If any person fails to pay an assessment of a civil penalty after it has become a final and unappealable order or after the appropriate court has entered final judgment in favor of the Secretary, the Secretary may request the Attorney General of the United States to institute a civil action in an appropriate district court of the United States to collect the penalty, and such court shall have jurisdiction to hear and decide any such action. In hearing such action, the court shall have authority to review the violation and the assessment of the civil penalty de novo.

(d) Criminal penalties. (1) Any person who --

(A) knowingly imports or exports any fish or wildlife or plants in violation of any provision of this Act (other than subsections (b) and (d) of section 3 [16 U.S.C. § 3372(b), (d)]), or

(B) violates any provision of this Act (other than subsections (b) and (d) of section 3 [16 U.S.C. § 3372]) by knowingly engaging in conduct that involves the sale or purchase of, the offer of sale or purchase of, or the intent to sell or purchase, fish or wildlife or plants with a market value in excess of $350,

knowing that the fish or wildlife or plants were taken, possessed, transported, or sold in violation of, or in a manner unlawful under, any underlying law, treaty or regulation, shall be fined not more than $20,000, or imprisoned for not more than five years, or both. Each violation shall be a separate offense and the offense shall be deemed to have been committed not only in the district where the violation first occurred, but also in any district in which the defendant may have taken or been in possession of the said fish or wildlife or plants.

(2) Any person who knowingly engages in conduct prohibited by any provision of this Act (other than subsections (b) and (d) of [16 U.S.C. § 3372]) and in the exercise of due care should know that the fish or wildlife or plants were taken, possessed, transported, or sold in violation of, or in a manner unlawful under, any underlying law, treaty or regulation shall be fined not more than $10,000, or imprisoned for not more than one year, or both. Each violation shall be a separate offense and the offense shall be deemed to have been committed not only in the district where the violation first occurred, but also in any district in which the defendant may have taken or been in possession of the said fish or wildlife or plants.

(3) Any person who knowingly violates [16 U.S.C. § 3372(d)] --

(A) shall be fined under Title 18, or imprisoned for not more than 5 years, or both, if the offense involves --

(i) the importation or exportation of fish or wildlife or plants; or

(ii) the sale or purchase, offer of sale or purchase, or commission of an act with intent to sell or purchase fish or wildlife or plants with a market value greater than $350; and

(B) shall be fined under Title 18, or imprisoned for not more than 1 year, or both, if the offense does not involve conduct described in subparagraph (A) of this subsection.

(e) Permit sanctions. The Secretary may also suspend, modify, or cancel any Federal hunting or fishing license, permit, or stamp, or any license or permit authorizing a person to import or export fish or wildlife or plants (other than a permit or license issued pursuant to the Magnuson-Stevens Fishery Conservation and Management Act [16 U.S.C. § 1801 *et seq.*]), or to operate a quarantine station or rescue center for imported wildlife or plants, issued to any person who is convicted of a criminal violation of any provision of this Act or any regulation issued hereunder. The Secretary shall not be liable for the payments of any compensation, reimbursement, or damages in connection with the modification, suspension, or revocation of any licenses, permits, stamps, or other agreements pursuant to this section.

[Pub. L. 97-79, § 4, 95 Stat. 1074 (Nov. 16, 1981); Pub. L. 100-653, Title I, § 102, 103, 102 Stat. 3825, 3826 (Nov. 14, 1988); Pub. L. 104-208, Div. A, Title I, § 101(a) [Title II, § 211(b)], 110 Stat. 3009-41 (Sept. 30, 1996)]

16 U.S.C. § 3374. Forfeiture. (a) In general.

(1) All fish or wildlife or plants imported, exported, transported, sold, received, acquired, or purchased contrary to the provisions of section 3 of this Act [16 U.S.C. § 3372] (other than subsection 3(b) [16 U.S.C. § 3372(b)]), or any regulation issued pursuant thereto, shall be subject to forfeiture to the United States notwithstanding any culpability requirements for civil penalty assessment or criminal prosecution included in section 4 of this Act [16 U.S.C. § 3373].

(2) All vessels, vehicles, aircraft, and other equipment used to aid in the importing, exporting, transporting, selling, receiving, acquiring, or purchasing of fish or wildlife or plants in a criminal violation of this Act for which a felony conviction is obtained shall be subject to forfeiture to the United States if (A) the owner of such vessel, vehicle, aircraft, or equipment was at the time of the alleged illegal act a consenting party or privy thereto or in the exercise of due care should have known that such vessel, vehicle, aircraft, or equipment would be used in a criminal violation of this Act, and (B) the violation involved the sale or purchase of, the offer of sale or purchase of, or the intent to sell or purchase, fish or wildlife or plants.

(b) Application of customs laws. All provisions of law relating to the seizure, forfeiture, and condemnation of property for violation of the customs laws, the disposition of such property or the proceeds from the sale thereof, and the remission or mitigation of such forfeiture, shall apply to the seizures and forfeitures incurred, or alleged to have been incurred, under the provisions of this Act, insofar as such provisions of law are applicable and not inconsistent with the provisions of this Act; except that all powers, rights, and duties conferred or imposed by the customs laws upon any officer or employee of the Treasury Department may, for the purposes of this Act, also be exercised or performed by the Secretary or by such persons as he may designate: *Provided*, That any warrant for search or seizure shall be issued in accordance with rule 41 of the Federal Rules of Criminal Procedure.

(c) Storage cost. Any person convicted of an offense, or assessed a civil penalty, under [16 U.S.C. § 3373] shall be liable for the costs incurred in the storage, care, and maintenance of any fish or wildlife or plant seized in connection with the violation concerned.

[Pub. L. 97-79, § 5, 95 Stat. 1076 (Nov. 16, 1981)]

16 U.S.C. § 3375. Enforcement. (a) In general. The provisions of this Act and any regulations issued pursuant thereto shall be enforced by the Secretary, the Secretary of Transportation, or the Secretary of the Treasury. Such Secretary may utilize by agreement, with or without reimbursement, the personnel, services, and facilities of any other Federal agency or any State agency or Indian tribe for purposes of enforcing this Act.

(b) Powers. Any person authorized under subsection (a) of this section to enforce this Act may carry firearms; may, when enforcing this Act, make an arrest without a warrant, in accordance with any guidelines which may be issued by the Attorney General, for any offense under the laws of the United States committed in the person's presence, or for the commission of any felony under the laws of the United States, if the person has reasonable grounds to believe that the person to be arrested has committed or is committing a felony; may search and seize, with or without a warrant, in accordance with any guidelines which may be issued by the Attorney General[:] *Provided,* That an arrest for a felony violation of this Act that is not committed in the presence or view of any such person and that involves only the transportation, acquisition, receipt, purchase, or sale of fish or wildlife or plants taken or possessed in violation of any law or regulation of any State shall require a warrant; may make an arrest without a warrant for a misdemeanor violation of this Act if he has reasonable grounds to believe that the person to be arrested is committing a violation in his presence or view; and may execute and serve any subpena, arrest warrant, search warrant issued in accordance with rule 41 of the Federal Rules of Criminal Procedure, or other warrant of civil or criminal process issued by any officer or court of competent jurisdiction for enforcement of this Act. Any person so authorized, in coordination with the Secretary of the Treasury, may detain for inspection and inspect any vessel, vehicle, aircraft, or other conveyance or any package, crate, or other container, including its contents, upon the arrival of such conveyance or container in the United States or the customs waters of the United States from any point outside the United States or such customs waters, or, if such conveyance or container is being used for exportation purposes, prior to departure from the United States or the customs waters of the United States. Such person may also inspect and demand the production of any documents and permits required by the country of natal origin, birth, or reexport of the fish or wildlife. Any fish, wildlife, plant, property, or item seized shall be held by any person authorized by the Secretary pending disposition of civil or criminal proceedings, or the institution of an action in rem for forfeiture of such fish, wildlife, plants, property, or item pursuant to [16 U.S.C. § 3374]; except that the Secretary may, in lieu of holding such fish, wildlife, plant, property, or item, permit the owner or consignee to post a bond or other surety satisfactory to the Secretary.

(c) Jurisdiction of district courts. The several district courts of the United States, including the courts enumerated in section 460 of Title 28, shall have jurisdiction over any actions arising under this Act. The venue provisions of Title 18 and Title 28 shall apply to any actions arising under this Act. The judges of the district courts of the United States and the United States magistrates may, within their respective jurisdictions, upon proper oath or affirmation showing probable cause, issue such warrants or other process as may be required for enforcement of this Act and any regulations issued thereunder.

(d) Rewards and incidental expenses. Beginning in fiscal year 1983, the Secretary or the Secretary of the Treasury shall pay, from sums received as penalties, fines, or forfeitures of property for any violation of this Act or any regulation issued hereunder (1) a reward to any person who furnishes information which leads to an arrest, a criminal conviction, civil penalty assessment, or forfeiture of property for any violation of this Act or any regulation issued hereunder, and (2) the reasonable and necessary costs incurred by any person in providing temporary care for any fish, wildlife, or plant pending the disposition of any civil or criminal proceeding alleging a violation of this Act with respect to that fish, wildlife, or plant. The amount of the reward, if any, is to be designated by the Secretary or the Secretary of the Treasury, as appropriate. Any officer or employee of the United States or any State or local government who furnishes information or renders service in the performance of his official duties is ineligible for payment under this subsection.

[Pub. L. 97-79, § 6, 95 Stat. 1077 (Nov. 16, 1981); Pub. L. 98-327, § 4, 98 Stat. 271 (June 25, 1984); Pub. L. 100-653, Title I, § 104, 102 Stat. 3826 (Nov. 14, 1988)]

16 U.S.C. § 3376. Administration. (a) Regulations.

(1) The Secretary, after consultation with the Secretary of the Treasury, is authorized to issue such regulations, except as provided in paragraph (2), as may be necessary to carry out the provisions of [16 U.S.C. §§ 3373, 3374].

(2) The Secretaries of the Interior and Commerce shall jointly promulgate specific regulations to implement the provisions of [16 U.S.C. § 3372(b)] for the marking and labeling of containers or packages containing fish or wildlife. These regulations shall be in accordance with existing commercial practices.

(b) Contract authority. Beginning in fiscal year 1983, to the extent and in the amounts provided in advance in appropriations Acts, the Secretary may enter into such contracts, leases, cooperative agreements, or other transactions with any Federal or State agency, Indian tribe, public or private institution, or other person, as may be necessary to carry out the purposes of this Act.

[Pub. L. 97-79, § 7, 95 Stat. 1078 (Nov. 16, 1981)]

16 U.S.C. § 3377. Exceptions. (a) Activities regulated by plan under Magnuson-Stevens Fishery Conservation and Management Act. The provisions of paragraph (1) of [16 U.S.C. § 3372(a)] shall not apply to any activity regulated by a fishery management plan in effect under the Magnuson-Stevens Fishery Conservation and Management Act (16 U.S.C. 1801 *et seq.*).

(b) Activities regulated by Tuna Convention Acts; harvesting of highly migratory species taken on high seas. The provisions of paragraphs (1), (2) (A), and (3) (A) of [16 U.S.C. § 3372(a)] shall not apply to --

(1) any activity regulated by the Tuna Conventions Act of 1950 (16 U.S.C. 951-961) or the Atlantic Tunas Convention Act of 1975 (16 U.S.C. 971-971(h)); or

(2) any activity involving the harvesting of highly migratory species (as defined in paragraph (14) of section 3 of the Magnuson-Stevens Fishery Conservation and

Management Act [16 U.S.C. § 1802(14)]) taken on the high seas (as defined in paragraph (13) of [16 U.S.C. § 1802(13)]) if such species are taken in violation of the laws of a foreign nation and the United States does not recognize the jurisdiction of the foreign nation over such species.

(c) Interstate shipment or transshipment through Indian country of fish, wildlife, or plants for legal purposes. The provisions of paragraph (2) of [16 U.S.C. § 3372(a)] shall not apply to the interstate shipment or transshipment through Indian country as defined in section 1151 of Title 18 or a State of any fish or wildlife or plant legally taken if the shipment is en route to a State in which the fish or wildlife or plant may be legally possessed.

[Pub. L. 97-79, § 8, 95 Stat. 1078 (Nov. 16, 1981); Pub. L. 104-208, Div. A, Title I, § 101(a) [Title II, § 211(b)], 110 Stat. 3009-41 (Sept. 30, 1996)]

16 U.S.C. § 3378. Miscellaneous provisions. (a) Effect on powers of States. Nothing in this Act shall be construed to prevent the several States or Indian tribes from making or enforcing laws or regulations not inconsistent with the provisions of this Act.

(b) Repeals. The following provisions of law are repealed:

(1) The Act of May 20, 1926 (commonly known as the Black Bass Act, 16 U.S.C. 851-856).

(2) Section 5 of the Act of May 25, 1900 [16 U.S.C. § 667e] and sections 43 and 44 of Title 18 (commonly known as provisions of the Lacey Act).

(3) Sections 3054 and 3112 of Title 18.

(c) Disclaimers. ****

[Pub. L. 97-79, § 9(a)-(c), (g), (h), 95 Stat. 1079, 1080 (Nov. 16, 1981)]

\- 0 -

MIGRATORY BIRD TREATY ACT
(16 U.S.C. §§ 703-711)

The Migratory Bird Treaty Act of 1918[34] was enacted to implement the provisions of the 1916 Convention with Great Britain[35] (on behalf of Canada). The Convention established three categories of migratory birds -- migratory game birds, migratory insectivorous birds, and migratory nongame birds -- and established closed seasons on birds in each category. For the final two categories, the closed season is year round.[36] For migratory game birds, the closed season is between March 10 and September 1 with "the High Contracting Powers" further agreeing that the actual open season will be for no more than three and one-half months as each party "may severally deem appropriate and define by law or regulation."[37]

The current version of the MBTA implements not only the 1916 Convention with Great

Britain for the Protection of Migratory Birds, but also treaties with Mexico,[38] Japan,[39] and the Soviet Union.[40] Despite the negotiation of the additional treaties, however, the MBTA has remained largely unchanged since 1918[41] -- in part because the 1918 Act was broadly drafted. It begins, for example, with a broad declaration that "it shall be unlawful to ... take, ... kill, ... possess, ... sell, ... ship, [or] export ... any migratory bird."[42] Federal protection extends to "any product ... which ... is composed in whole or part, of any such bird or any part, nest or egg thereof."[43] The Secretary of the Interior is subsequently delegated power to promulgate regulations "to determine when, to what extent, if at all, and by what means ... to allow hunting, taking, ... possession, sale, purchase, shipment, ... or export" of any bird covered by the conventions.[44] The basic structure of the Act thus is somewhat unusual: rather than prohibiting specific conduct, the MBTA prohibits all taking and commercial activity in migratory birds and authorizes the Secretary to promulgate regulations exempting conduct from this general prohibition.

16 U.S.C. § 703. Taking, killing, or possessing migratory birds unlawful. Unless and except as permitted by regulations made as hereinafter provided, it shall be unlawful at any time, by any means or in any manner, to pursue, hunt, take, capture, kill, attempt to take, capture, or kill, possess, offer for sale, sell, offer to barter, barter, offer to purchase, purchase, deliver for shipment, ship, export, import, cause to be shipped, exported, or imported, deliver for transportation, transport or cause to be transported, carry or cause to be carried, or receive for shipment, transportation, carriage, or export, any migratory bird, any part, nest, or egg of any such bird, or any product, whether or not manufactured, which consists, or is composed in whole or in part, of any such bird or any part, nest, or egg thereof, included in the terms of the conventions between the United States and Great Britain for the protection of migratory birds concluded August 16, 1916 (39 Stat. 1702), the United States and the United Mexican States for the protection of migratory birds and game mammals concluded February 7, 1936, the United States and the Government of Japan for the protection of migratory birds and birds in danger of extinction, and their environment concluded March 4, 1972 and the convention between the United States and the Union of Soviet Socialist Republics for the conservation of migratory birds and their environments concluded November 19, 1976.

[July 3, 1918, ch. 128, § 2, 40 Stat. 755; June 20, 1936, ch. 634, § 3, 49 Stat. 1556; Pub. L. 93-300, § 1, 88 Stat. 190 (June 1, 1974); Pub. L. 101-233, § 15, 103 Stat. 1977 (Dec. 13, 1989)]

16 U.S.C. § 704. Determination as to when and how migratory birds may be taken, killed, or possessed. (a) Subject to the provisions and in order to carry out the purposes of the conventions, the Secretary of the Interior is authorized and directed, from time to time, having due regard to the zones of temperature and to the distribution, abundance, economic value, breeding habits, and times and lines of migratory flight of such birds, to determine when, to what extent, if at all, and by what means, it is compatible with the terms of the conventions to allow hunting, taking, capture, killing, possession, sale, purchase, shipment, transportation, carriage, or export of any such bird, or any part, nest, or egg thereof, and to adopt suitable regulations permitting and governing the same, in accordance with such determinations, which regulations shall become effective when approved by the President.

(b) It shall be unlawful for any person to --

(1) take any migratory game bird by the aid of baiting, or on or over any baited area, if the person knows or reasonably should know that the area is a baited area; or

(2) place or direct the placement of bait on or adjacent to an area for the purpose of causing, inducing, or allowing any person to take or attempt to take any migratory game bird by the aid of baiting on or over the baited area.

[July 3, 1918, ch. 128, § 3, 40 Stat. 755; June 20, 1936, ch. 634, § 2, 49 Stat. 1556; 1939 Reorganization Plan No. II, § 4(f), 4 F.R. 2731, 53 Stat. 1433 (July 1, 1939); Pub. L. 105-312, Title I, § 102, 112 Stat. 2956 (Oct. 30, 1998)]

16 U.S.C. § 705. Transportation or importation of migratory birds; when unlawful. It shall be unlawful to ship, transport, or carry, by any means whatever, from one State, Territory, or district to or through another State, Territory, or district, or to or through a foreign country, any bird, or any part, nest, or egg thereof, captured, killed, taken, shipped, transported, or carried at any time contrary to the laws of the State, Territory, or district in which it was captured, killed, or taken, or from which it was shipped, transported, or carried. It shall be unlawful to import any bird, or any part, nest, or egg thereof, captured, killed, taken, shipped, transported, or carried contrary to the laws of any Province of the Dominion of Canada in which the same was captured, killed, or taken, or from which it was shipped, transported, or carried.

[July 3, 1918, ch. 128, § 4, 40 Stat. 755; June 20, 1936, ch. 634, § 4, 49 Stat. 1556; 1939 Reorganization Plan No. II, § 4(f), 4 Fed. Reg. 2731, 53 Stat. 1433 (July 1, 1939); Pub. L. 91-135, § 10, 83 Stat. 282 (Dec. 5, 1969)]

16 U.S.C. § 706. Arrests; search warrants. Any employee of the Department of the Interior authorized by the Secretary of the Interior to enforce the provisions of this Act shall have power, without warrant, to arrest any person committing a violation of this Act in his presence or view and to take such person immediately for examination or trial before an officer or court of competent jurisdiction; shall have power to execute any warrant or other process issued by an officer or court of competent jurisdiction for the enforcement of the provisions of this Act; and shall have authority, with a search warrant, to search any place. The several judges of the courts established under the laws of the United States, and United States magistrates may, within their respective jurisdictions, upon proper oath or affirmation showing probable cause, issue warrants in all such cases. All birds, or parts, nests, or eggs thereof, captured, killed, taken, sold or offered for sale, bartered or offered for barter, purchased, shipped, transported, carried, imported, exported, or possessed contrary to the provisions of this Act or of any regulation prescribed thereunder shall, when found, be seized and, upon conviction of the offender or upon judgment of a court of the United States that the same were captured, killed, taken, sold or offered for sale, bartered or offered for barter, purchased, shipped, transported, carried, imported, exported, or possessed contrary to the provisions of this Act or of any regulation prescribed thereunder, shall be forfeited to the United States and disposed of by the Secretary of the Interior in such manner as he deems appropriate.

[July 3, 1918, ch. 128, § 5, 40 Stat. 756; 1939 Reorganization Plan No. II, § 4(f), 4 Fed. Reg. 2731, 53 Stat. 1433 (July 1, 1939); Pub. L. 90-578, Title IV, § 402(b)(2), 82 Stat. 1118 (Oct. 17, 1968); Pub. L. 95-616, § 3(h)(1), 92

Stat. 3111 (Nov. 8, 1978)]

16 U.S.C. § 707. Violations and penalties; forfeitures. (a) Except as otherwise provided in this section, any person, association, partnership, or corporation who shall violate any provisions of said conventions or of this Act, or who shall violate or fail to comply with any regulation made pursuant to this Act shall be deemed guilty of a misdemeanor and upon conviction thereof shall be fined not more than $15,000 or be imprisoned not more than six months, or both.

(b) Whoever, in violation of this Act, shall knowingly --

(1) take by any manner whatsoever any migratory bird with intent to sell, offer to sell, barter or offer to barter such bird, or

(2) sell, offer for sale, barter or offer to barter, any migratory bird shall be guilty of a felony and shall be fined not more than $2,000 or imprisoned not more than two years, or both.

(c) Whoever violates section 3(b)(2) [16 U.S.C. § 704(b)(2)] shall be fined under Title 18, imprisoned not more than 1 year, or both.

(d) All guns, traps, nets and other equipment, vessels, vehicles, and other means of transportation used by any person when engaged in pursuing, hunting, taking, trapping, ensnaring, capturing, killing, or attempting to take, capture, or kill any migratory bird in violation of this Act with the intent to offer for sale, or sell, or offer for barter, or barter such bird in violation of this Act shall be forfeited to the United States and may be seized and held pending the prosecution of any person arrested for violating this Act and upon conviction for such violation, such forfeiture shall be adjudicated as a penalty in addition to any other provided for violation of this Act. Such forfeited property shall be disposed of and accounted for by, and under the authority of, the Secretary of the Interior.

[July 3, 1918, ch. 128, § 6, 40 Stat. 756; June 20, 1936, ch. 634, § 2, 49 Stat. 1556; Pub. L. 86-732, 74 Stat. 866 (Sept. 8, 1960); Pub. L. 99-645, Title V, § 501, 100 Stat. 3590 (Nov. 10, 1986); Pub. L. 105-312, Title I, § 103, 112 Stat. 2956 (Oct. 30, 1998)]

16 U.S.C. § 708. State or Territorial laws or regulations. Nothing in this Act shall be construed to prevent the several States and Territories from making or enforcing laws or regulations not inconsistent with the provisions of said conventions or of this Act, or from making or enforcing laws or regulations which shall give further protection to migratory birds, their nests, and eggs, if such laws or regulations do not extend the open seasons for such birds beyond the dates approved by the President in accordance with section 3 of this Act [16 U.S.C. § 704].

[July 3, 1918, ch. 128, § 7, 40 Stat. 756; June 20, 1936, ch. 634, § 2, 49 Stat. 1556]

16 U.S.C. § 709. Omitted

16 U.S.C. § 710. Partial invalidity; short title. ****

16 U.S.C. § 711. Breeding and sale for food supply. Nothing in this Act shall be construed to prevent the breeding of migratory game birds on farms and preserves and the sale of birds so bred under proper regulation for the purpose of increasing the food supply.

[July 3, 1918, ch. 128, § 12, 40 Stat. 757]

- 0 -

TARIFF ACT OF 1930
(19 U.S.C. § 1527)

Congress first addressed the problem of international commerce in wildlife in the Tariff Act of 1930.[45] The Act prohibited the importation of any wild mammal or bird (or part thereof) where the country of origin restricts the taking of the animal. Although the Act was progressive when adopted, it has subsequently been overtaken by the now much broader prohibitions in the amended Lacey Act.

19 U.S.C. § 1527. Importation of wild mammals and birds in violation of foreign law. **(a) Importation prohibited.** If the laws or regulations of any country, dependency, province, or other subdivision of government restrict the taking, killing, possession, or exportation to the United States, of any wild mammal or bird, alive or dead, or restrict the exportation to the United States of any part or product of any wild mammal or bird, whether raw or manufactured, no such mammal or bird, or part or product thereof, shall, after the expiration of ninety days after June 17, 1930, be imported into the United States from such country, dependency, province, or other subdivision of government, directly or indirectly, unless accompanied by a certification of the United States consul, for the consular district in which is located the port or place from which such mammal or bird, or part or product thereof, was exported from such country, dependency, province, or other subdivision of government, that such mammal or bird, or part or product thereof, has not been acquired or exported in violation of the laws or regulations of such country, dependency, province, or other subdivision of government.

(b) Forfeiture. Any mammal or bird, alive or dead, or any part or product thereof, whether raw or manufactured, imported into the United States in violation of the provisions of the preceding subdivision shall be subject to seizure and forfeiture under the customs laws. Any such article so forfeited may, in the discretion of the Secretary of the Treasury and under such regulations as he may prescribe, be placed with the departments or bureaus of the Federal or State Governments, or with societies or museums, for exhibition or scientific or educational purposes, or destroyed, or (except in the case of heads or horns of wild mammals) sold in the manner provided by law.

(c) Section not to apply in certain cases. The provisions of this section shall not apply in the case of --

(1) Prohibited importations. Articles the importation of which is prohibited under the

provisions of this chapter, or of section 42(a) of Title 18, or of any other law;
(2) Scientific or educational purposes. Wild mammals or birds, alive or dead, or parts or products thereof, whether raw or manufactured, imported for scientific or educational purposes;
(3) Certain migratory game birds. Migratory game birds (for which an open season is provided by the laws of the United States and any foreign country which is a party to a treaty with the United States, in effect on the date of importation, relating to the protection of such migratory game birds) brought into the United States by bona fide sportsmen returning from hunting trips in such country, if at the time of importation the possession of such birds is not prohibited by the laws of such country or of the United States.

[June 17, 1930, ch. 497, Title IV, § 527, 46 Stat. 741]

- 0 -

BALD AND GOLDEN EAGLE PROTECTION ACT (16 U.S.C. §§ 668-668d)

In 1940 Congress protected the bald eagle as "a symbol of American ideals of freedom."[46] In 1962, protection was extended to golden eagles.[47]

Initially, the Act criminalized the taking or possession of the species, its parts, nests, or eggs. In 1972, Congress amended the Act in response to a narrow interpretation of its scope by the Department of the Interior, by lessening the degree of culpability required for a conviction: anyone who "shall knowingly, or with wanton disregard for the consequences of his act," was subject to criminal penalties.[48] Congress also added "poisoning" to the definition of "take" in response to the Department's position.

Although the Supreme Court has described the Act as containing "sweepingly framed prohibitions,"[49] there are several exceptions. The significance of the exceptions and the laxness of enforcement -- particularly against western ranching interests -- is suggested by the fact that despite the Act, the bald eagle was listed as an endangered species in 1967.[50]

16 U.S.C. § 668. Bald and golden eagles. (a) Prohibited acts; criminal penalties. Whoever, within the United States or any place subject to the jurisdiction thereof, without being permitted to do so as provided in this Act, shall knowingly, or with wanton disregard for the consequences of his act take, possess, sell, purchase, barter, offer to sell, purchase or barter, transport, export or import, at any time or in any manner, any bald eagle commonly known as the American eagle, or any golden eagle, alive or dead, or any part, nest, or egg thereof of the foregoing eagles, or whoever violates any permit or regulation issued pursuant to this Act, shall be fined not more than $5,000 or imprisoned not more than one year or both: *Provided,* That in the case of a second or subsequent conviction for a violation of this section committed after October 23, 1972, such person shall be fined not more than $10,000 or imprisoned not more than two years, or both: *Provided further,* That the commission of each taking or other act prohibited by this section with respect to a bald or golden eagle shall constitute a separate violation of this section: *Provided further,* That one-half of any such fine, but not to exceed $2,500, shall be paid to the person or persons giving information which leads to conviction: *Provided further,* That nothing herein shall be construed to prohibit possession or transportation of any bald eagle, alive or dead, or any part, nest, or egg thereof, lawfully taken prior to June 8, 1940, and that nothing herein shall be construed to prohibit possession or transportation of any golden eagle, alive or dead, or any part, nest, or egg thereof, lawfully taken prior to the addition to this Act of the provisions relating to preservation of the golden eagle.

(b) Civil penalties. Whoever, within the United States or any place subject to the jurisdiction thereof, without being permitted to do so as provided in this Act, possess, sell, purchase, barter, offer to sell, purchase or barter, transport, export or import, at any time or in any manner, any bald eagle, commonly known as the American eagle, or any golden eagle, alive or dead, or any part, nest, or egg thereof of the foregoing eagles, or whoever violates any permit or regulation issued pursuant to this Act, may be assessed a civil penalty by the Secretary of not more than $5,000 for each such violation. Each violation shall be a separate offense. No penalty shall be assessed unless such person is given notice and opportunity for a hearing with respect to such violation. In determining the amount of the penalty, the gravity of the violation, and the demonstrated good faith of the person charged shall be considered by the Secretary. For good cause shown, the Secretary may remit or mitigate any such penalty. Upon any failure to pay the penalty assessed under this section, the Secretary may request the Attorney General to institute a civil action in a district court of the United States for any district in which such person is found or resides or transacts business to collect the penalty and such court shall have jurisdiction to hear and decide any such action. In hearing any such action, the court must sustain the Secretary's action if supported by substantial evidence.

(c) Cancellation of grazing agreements. The head of any Federal agency who has issued a lease, license, permit, or other agreement authorizing the grazing of domestic livestock on Federal lands to any person who is convicted of a violation of this Act or of any permit or regulation issued hereunder may immediately cancel each such lease, license, permit, or other agreement. The United States shall not be liable for the payment of any compensation, reimbursement, or damages in connection with the cancellation of any lease, license, permit, or other agreement pursuant to this section.

[June 8, 1940, ch. 278, § 1, 54 Stat. 250; Pub. L. 86-70, § 14, 73 Stat. 143 (June 25, 1959); Pub. L. 87-884, 76 Stat. 1246 (Oct. 24, 1962); Pub. L. 92-535, § 1, 86 Stat. 1064 (Oct. 23, 1972)]

16 U.S.C. § 668a. Taking and using of the bald and golden eagle for scientific, exhibition, and religious purposes. Whenever, after investigation, the Secretary of the Interior shall determine that it is compatible with the preservation of the bald eagle or the golden eagle to permit the taking, possession, and transportation of specimens thereof for the scientific or exhibition purposes of public museums, scientific societies, and zoological parks, or for the religious purposes of Indian tribes, or that it is necessary to permit the taking of such eagles for the protection of wildlife or of agricultural or other interests in any particular locality, may authorize the taking of such eagles pursuant to regulations which he is hereby authorized to prescribe: *Provided,* That on request of the Governor of any State, the Secretary of the Interior shall authorize the taking of golden eagles for the purpose of seasonally protecting domesticated flocks and herds in such State, in accordance with regulations established under the provisions of this section, in such part or parts of such State and for such periods as the Secretary determines to be necessary to protect such interests: *Provided further,* That bald eagles may not be taken for any purpose unless, prior to such taking, a permit to do so is procured from the Secretary of the Interior: *Provided further,* That the Secretary of the Interior, pursuant to such regulations as he may prescribe, may permit the taking, possession, and transportation of golden eagles for the purposes of falconry, except that only golden eagles which would be taken because of depredations on livestock or wildlife may be taken for purposes of falconry: *Provided further,* That the Secretary of the Interior, pursuant to such regulations as he may prescribe, may permit the taking of golden eagle nests which interfere with resource development or recovery operations.

[June 8, 1940, ch. 278, § 2, 54 Stat. 251; Pub. L. 87-884, 76 Stat. 1246 (Oct. 24, 1962); Pub. L. 92-535, § 2, 86 Stat. 1065 (Oct. 23, 1972); Pub. L. 95-616, § 9, 92 Stat. 3114 (Nov. 8, 1978)]

16 U.S.C. § 668b. Enforcement provisions. (a) Arrest; search; issuance and execution of warrants and process. Any employee of the Department of the Interior authorized by the Secretary of the Interior to enforce the provisions of this Act may, without warrant, arrest any person committing in his presence or view a violation of this Act or of any permit or regulation issued hereunder and take such person immediately for examination or trial before an officer or court of competent jurisdiction; may execute any warrant or other process issued by an officer or court of competent jurisdiction for the enforcement of the provisions of this Act; and may, with or without a warrant, as authorized by law, search any place. The Secretary of the Interior is authorized to enter into cooperative agreements with State fish and wildlife agencies or other appropriate State authorities to facilitate enforcement of this Act, and by said agreements to delegate such enforcement authority to State law enforcement personnel as he deems appropriate for effective enforcement of this Act. Any judge of any court established under the laws of the United States, and any United States magistrate judge may, within his respective jurisdiction, upon proper oath or affirmation showing probable cause, issue warrants in all such cases.

(b) Forfeiture. All bald or golden eagles, or parts, nests, or eggs thereof, taken, possessed, sold, purchased, bartered, offered for sale, purchase, or barter, transported, exported, or imported contrary to the provisions of this Act, or of any permit or regulation issued hereunder, and all guns, traps, nets, and other equipment, vessels, vehicles, aircraft, and other means of transportation used to aid in the taking, possessing, selling, purchasing, bartering, offering for sale, purchase, or barter, transporting, exporting, or importing of any bird, or part, nest, or egg thereof, in violation of this Act or of any permit or regulation issued hereunder shall be subject to forfeiture to the United States.

(c) Customs laws applied. ****

[June 8, 1940, ch. 278, § 3, 54 Stat. 251; Pub. L. 90-578, Title IV, § 402(b)(2), 82 Stat. 1118 (Oct. 17, 1968); Pub. L. 92-535, § 3, 86 Stat. 1065 (Oct. 23, 1972); Pub. L. 101-650, Title III, § 321, 104 Stat. 5117 (Dec. 1, 1990)]

16 U.S.C. § 668c. Definitions. As used in this Act, "whoever" includes also associations, partnerships, and corporations; "take" includes also pursue, shoot, shoot at, poison, wound, kill, capture, trap, collect, or molest or disturb; "transport" includes also ship, convey, carry, or transport by any means whatever, and deliver or receive or cause to be delivered or received for such shipment, conveyance, carriage, or transportation.

[June 8, 1940, ch. 278, § 4, 54 Stat. 251; Pub. L. 92-535, § 4, 86 Stat. 1065 (Oct. 23, 1972)]

16 U.S.C. § 668d. Availability of appropriations for Migratory Bird Treaty Act. ****

\- 0 -

ACT PROHIBITING THE USE OF AIRCRAFT AND MOTOR VEHICLES TO HUNT FERAL HORSES AND BURROS (1959) (18 U.S.C. § 47)

In 1950, Velma Johnston -- aka, "Wild Horse Annie" -- began a campaign to protect feral horses and burros. Portraying the animals as threatened with extinction through "carnage for financial profit,"[51] Johnson was able to mount a massive letter-writing campaign that employed the mythology of the cowboy and his horse as a symbol of the rugged American West.[52] In 1959, Congress took the first step by enacting a legislation that prohibited the use of aircraft and motor vehicles "to hunt, for the purpose of capturing or killing" any wild horse or burro "running at large on any of the public lands."[53] In addition, the Act prohibited the "pollution of any watering hole ... for the purpose of trapping, killing, wounding, or maiming" horses and burros.

The Act appears to have been among the most successful federal criminal statutes since it has produced no reported prosecutions.

18 U.S.C. § 47. Use of aircraft or motor vehicles to hunt certain wild horses or burros; pollution of watering holes. (a) Whoever uses an aircraft or a motor vehicle to hunt, for the purpose of capturing or killing, any wild unbranded horse, mare, colt, or burro running at large on any of the public land or ranges shall be fined under this Act, or imprisoned not more than six months, or both.

(b) Whoever pollutes or causes the pollution of any watering hole on any of the public land or ranges for the purpose of trapping, killing, wounding, or maiming any of the animals referred to in subsection (a) of this section shall be fined under this Act, or imprisoned not more than six months, or both.

(c) As used in subsection (a) of this section --

(1) The term "aircraft" means any contrivance used for flight in the air; and

(2) The term "motor vehicle" includes an automobile, automobile truck, automobile wagon, motorcycle, or any other self-propelled vehicle designed for running on land.

[Pub. L. 86-234, § 1(a), 73 Stat. 470 (Sept. 8, 1959); Pub. L. 103-322, Title XXXIII, § 330016(1)(G), 108 Stat. 2147 (Sept. 13, 1994)]

- 0 -

AIRBORNE HUNTING ACT (1971)
(16 U.S.C. § 742j-1)

Reports of shooting of eagles and wolves from aircraft prompted Congress in 1971 to enact a statute that imposes a fine of up to $5,000 and a year imprisonment on anyone who uses an aircraft to shoot or harass any "bird, fish, or other animal."[54] The Act, however, contains an exception for any person "operating under a license or permit of, any State, or the United States to administer or protect ... land, water, wildlife, livestock, domesticated animals, human life, or crops."[55] The statute has had only modest impact, in part because some states have abused the permitting exception and in part because the Department of the Interior has been unwilling to invoke the Act's stringent sanctions.

16 U.S.C. § 742j-1. Airborne hunting. (a) Prohibition; penalty. Any person who --

(1) while airborne in an aircraft shoots or attempts to shoot for the purpose of capturing or killing any bird, fish, or other animal; or

(2) uses an aircraft to harass any bird, fish, or other animal; or

(3) knowingly participates in using an aircraft for any purpose referred to in paragraph (1) or (2);

shall be fined not more than $5,000 or imprisoned not more than one year, or both.

(b) Exception; report of State to Secretary.

(1) This section shall not apply to any person if such person is employed by, or is an authorized agent of or is operating under a license or permit of, any State or the United States to administer or protect or aid in the administration or protection of land, water, wildlife, livestock, domesticated animals, human life, or crops, and each such person so operating under a license or permit shall report to the applicable issuing authority each calendar quarter the number and type of animals so taken.

(2) In any case in which a State, or any agency thereof, issues a permit referred to in paragraph (1) of this subsection, it shall file with the Secretary of the Interior an annual report containing such information as the Secretary shall prescribe, including but not limited to--

(A) the name and address of each person to whom a permit was issued;

(B) a description of the animals authorized to be taken thereunder, the number of animals authorized to be taken, and a description of the area from which the animals are authorized to be taken;

(C) the number and type of animals taken by such person to whom a permit was issued; and
(D) the reason for issuing the permit.

(c) "Aircraft" defined. As used in this section, the term "aircraft" means any contrivance used for flight in the air.

(d) Enforcement; regulations; arrest; search; issuance and execution of warrants and process; cooperative agreements. The Secretary of the Interior shall enforce the provisions of this section and shall promulgate such regulations as he deems necessary and appropriate to carry out such enforcement. Any employee of the Department of the Interior authorized by the Secretary of the Interior to enforce the provisions of this section may, without warrant, arrest any person committing in his presence or view a violation of this section or of any regulation issued hereunder and take such person immediately for examination or trial before an officer or court of competent jurisdiction; may execute any warrant or other process issued by an officer or court of competent jurisdiction for the enforcement of the provisions of this section; and may, with or without a warrant, as authorized by law, search any place. The Secretary of the Interior is authorized to enter into cooperative agreements with State fish and wildlife agencies or other appropriate State authorities to facilitate enforcement of this section, and by such agreements to delegate such enforcement authority to State law enforcement personnel as he deems appropriate for effective enforcement of this section. Any judge of any court established under the laws of the United States, and any United States magistrate may, within his respective jurisdiction, upon proper oath or affirmation showing probable cause, issue warrants in all such cases.

(e) Forfeiture. All birds, fish, or other animals shot or captured contrary to the provisions of this section, or of any regulation issued hereunder, and all guns, aircraft, and other equipment used to aid in the shooting, attempting to shoot, capturing, or harassing of any bird, fish, or other animal in violation of this section or of any regulation issued hereunder shall be subject to forfeiture to the United States.

(f) Certain customs laws applied. All provisions of law relating to the seizure, forfeiture, and condemnation of a vessel for violation of the customs laws, the disposition of such vessel or the proceeds from the sale thereof, and the remission or mitigation of such forfeitures, shall apply to the seizures and forfeitures incurred, or alleged to have been incurred, under the provisions of this section ****

[Pub. L. 92-159, § 1, 85 Stat. 480 (Nov. 18, 1971); Pub. L. 92-502, 86 Stat. 905 (Oct. 18, 1972)]

- 0 -

WILD FREE-ROAMING HORSES AND BURROS ACT
(16 U.S.C. §§ 1331-1340)

The Act Prohibiting the Use of Aircraft and Motor Vehicles to Hunt Feral Horses and

Burros did not end the exploitation of the feral populations. In addition, the statute did nothing to reduce the competition with domestic livestock. Led by Wild Horse Annie, proponents of protecting feral horses and burros continued to lobby for active management.[56] The success of this campaign can be seen in the Senate report on the bill that became the Wild Free-Roaming Horses and Burros Act of 1971:[57]

> [Feral horses and burros] have been cruelly captured and slain and their carcasses used in the production of pet food and fertilizer. They have been used for target practice and harassed for "sport" and profit. In spite of public outrage, this bloody traffic continues unabated, and it is the firm belief of the committee that this senseless slaughter must be brought to an end.[58]

Like bald eagles, feral horses and burros are symbolic wildlife for Congress: they "are living symbols of the historic and pioneer spirit of the West."[59]

The Act contained two distinct approaches to protecting these symbols. It both criminalized the capture or harassment of feral horses and burros and also provided for their management on the public lands. Thus, any person who "willfully removes or attempts to remove ... converts ... to private use .. maliciously causes the death or harassment ... processes ... into commercial products the remains ... or sells ... a wild free-roaming horse or burro" is subject to a fine and imprisonment.[60]

The Act's management standard proved more problematic. Congress initially adopted management requirements that were arguably internally inconsistent. On the one hand, the Act directed that the feral animals "be considered ... an integral part of the natural system of the public lands" and hence (seemingly) be managed as one of many multiple-use resources.[61] On the other hand, the Act specified that "[a]ll management activities shall be at the minimum feasible level,"[62] that animals could be killed only when "such action is necessary to preserve and maintain the habitat in a suitable condition for continued use ... [and it is] the only practical way to remove excess animals from the area."[63] These provisions led to inconsistent judicial decisions[64] and amendment of the Act. In 1978, Congress directed the Secretary to "immediately remove excess animals" upon two findings: that excess animals are present and that action is necessary.[65] This was buttressed by the definition of "excess" animals as those that "must be removed ... in order to preserve and maintain a thriving natural ecological balance and multiple-use relationship" in the area.[66]

The Wild Horse and Burro Act is anomalous. The protected animals are feral, an exotic species introduced to the continent by Europeans. As a result, the protected animals cannot always be distinguished from unprotected animals. Furthermore, given their exotic status it is at least somewhat ambiguous how they fit into the "natural ecological balance." Finally, the Act is a prime example of the potential problems of managing charismatic wildlife through public opinion polling.[67]

16 U.S.C. § 1331. Congressional findings and declaration of policy. Congress finds and declares that wild free-roaming horses and burros are living symbols of the historic and pioneer spirit of the West; that they contribute to the diversity of life forms within the Nation and enrich the lives of the American people; and that these horses and burros are fast disappearing from the American scene. It is the policy of Congress that wild free-roaming horses and burros shall be protected from capture, branding, harassment, or death; and to accomplish this they are to be considered in the area where presently found, as an integral part of the natural system of the public lands.

[Pub. L. 92-195, § 1, 85 Stat. 649 (Dec. 15, 1971)]

16 U.S.C. § 1332. Definitions. As used in this Act --
(a) "Secretary" means the Secretary of the Interior when used in connection with public lands administered by him through the Bureau of Land Management and the Secretary of Agriculture in connection with public lands administered by him through the Forest Service;

(b) "wild free-roaming horses and burros" means all unbranded and unclaimed horses and burros on public lands of the United States;

(c) "range" means the amount of land necessary to sustain an existing herd or herds of wild free-roaming horses and burros, which does not exceed their known territorial limits, and which is devoted principally but not necessarily exclusively to their welfare in keeping with the multiple-use management concept for the public lands;

(d) "herd" means one or more stallions and his mares;

(e) "public lands" means any lands administered by the Secretary of the Interior through the Bureau of Land Management or by the Secretary of Agriculture through the Forest Service[; and]

(f) "excess animals" means wild free-roaming horses or burros (1) which have been removed from an area by the Secretary pursuant to applicable law or, (2) which must be removed from an area in order to preserve and maintain a thriving natural ecological balance and multiple-use relationship in that area.

[Pub. L. 92-195, § 2, 85 Stat. 649 (Dec. 15, 1971); Pub. L. 95-514, § 14(b), 92 Stat. 1810 (Oct. 25, 1978)]

16 U.S.C. § 1333. Powers and duties of Secretary. (a) Jurisdiction; management; ranges; ecological balance objectives; scientific recommendations; forage allocation adjustments. All wild free-roaming horses and burros are hereby declared to be under the jurisdiction of the Secretary for the purpose of management and protection in accordance with the provisions of this Act [16 U.S.C. §§ 1331 *et seq.*]. The Secretary is authorized and directed to protect and manage wild free-roaming horses and burros as components of the public lands, and he may designate and maintain specific ranges on public lands as sanctuaries for their protection and preservation, where the Secretary after consultation with the wildlife agency of the State wherein any such range is proposed and with the Advisory Board established in section 7 of this Act [16 U.S.C. § 1337] deems such action desirable. The Secretary shall manage wild free-roaming horses and burros in a manner that is designed to achieve and maintain a thriving natural ecological balance on the public lands. He shall consider the recommendations of qualified scientists in the field of biology and ecology, some of whom shall be independent of both Federal and State agencies and may include members of the Advisory Board established in section 7 of this Act [16 U.S.C. § 1337]. All management activities shall be at the minimal feasible level and shall be carried out in consultation with the wildlife agency of the State wherein such lands are located in order to protect the natural ecological balance of all wildlife species which inhabit such lands, particularly endangered wildlife species. Any adjustments in forage allocations on any such lands shall take into consideration the needs of other wildlife species which inhabit such lands.

(b) Inventory and determinations; consultation; overpopulation; research study: submittal to Congress.

(1) The Secretary shall maintain a current inventory of wild free-roaming horses and burros on given areas of the public lands. The purpose of such inventory shall be to: make determinations as to whether and where an overpopulation exists and whether action should be taken to remove excess animals; determine appropriate management levels of wild free-roaming horses and burros on these areas of the public lands; and determine whether appropriate management levels should be achieved by the removal or destruction of excess animals, or other options (such as sterilization, or natural controls on population levels). In making such determinations the Secretary shall consult with the United States Fish and Wildlife Service, wildlife agencies of the State or States wherein wild free-roaming horses and burros are located, such individuals independent of Federal and State government as have been recommended by the National Academy of Sciences, and such other individuals whom he determines have scientific expertise and special knowledge of wild horse and burro protection, wildlife management and animal husbandry as related to rangeland management.

(2) Where the Secretary determines on the basis of (i) the current inventory of lands within his jurisdiction; (ii) information contained in any land use planning completed pursuant to section 1712 of Title 43; (iii) information contained in court ordered environmental impact statements as defined in section 1902 of Title 43; and (iv) such additional information as becomes available to him from time to time, including that information developed in the research study mandated by this section, or in the absence of the information contained in (i-iv) above on the basis of all information currently available to him, that an overpopulation exists on a given area of the public lands and that action is necessary to remove excess animals, he shall immediately remove excess animals from the range so as to achieve appropriate management levels. Such action shall be taken, in the following order and priority, until all excess animals have been removed so as to restore a thriving natural ecological balance to the range, and protect the range from the deterioration associated with overpopulation:

(A) The Secretary shall order old, sick, or lame animals to be destroyed in the most humane manner possible;

(B) The Secretary shall cause such number of additional excess wild free-roaming horses and burros to be humanely captured and removed for private maintenance and care for which he determines an adoption demand exists by qualified individuals, and for which he determines he can assure humane treatment and care (including proper transportation, feeding, and handling): *Provided,* That, not more than four animals may be adopted per year by any individual unless the Secretary determines in writing that such individual is capable of humanely caring for more than four animals, including the transportation of such animals by the adopting party; and

(C) The Secretary shall cause additional excess wild free-roaming horses and burros for which an adoption demand by qualified individuals does not exist to be destroyed in the most humane and cost efficient manner possible.

(3) For the purpose of furthering knowledge of wild horse and burro population dynamics and their interrelationship with wildlife, forage and water resources, and assisting him in making his determination as to what constitutes excess animals, the Secretary shall contract for a research study of such animals with such individuals independent of Federal and State government as may be recommended by the National Academy of Sciences for having scientific expertise and special knowledge of wild horse and burro protection, wildlife management and animal husbandry as related to rangeland management. The terms and outline of such research study shall be determined by a research design panel to be appointed by the President of the National Academy of Sciences. Such study shall be completed and submitted by the Secretary to the Senate and House of Representatives on or before January 1, 1983.

(c) Title of transferee to limited number of excess animals adopted for requisite period. Where excess animals have been transferred to a qualified individual for adoption and private maintenance pursuant to this Act [16 U.S.C. §§ 1331 *et seq.*] and the Secretary determines that such individual has provided humane conditions, treatment and care for such animal or animals for a period of one year, the Secretary is authorized upon application by the transferee to grant title to not more than four animals to the transferee at the end of the one-year period.

(d) Loss of status as wild free-roaming horses and burros; exclusion from coverage. Wild free-roaming horses and burros or their remains shall lose their status as wild free-roaming horses or burros and shall no longer be considered as falling within the purview of this Act [16 U.S.C. §§ 1331 *et seq.*] --

(1) upon passage of title pursuant to subsection (c) of this section except for the limitation of subsection (c) of this section; or

(2) if they have been transferred for private maintenance or adoption pursuant to this Act [16 U.S.C. §§ 1331 *et seq.*] and die of natural causes before passage of title; or

(3) upon destruction by the Secretary or his designee pursuant to subsection (b) of this section; or

(4) if they die of natural causes on the public lands or on private lands where maintained thereon pursuant to section 4 [16 U.S.C. § 1334] and disposal is authorized by the Secretary or his designee; or

(5) upon destruction or death for purposes of or incident to the program authorized in this [section]; *Provided,* That no wild free-roaming horse or burro or its remains may be sold or transferred for consideration for processing into commercial products.

[Pub. L. 92-195, § 3, 85 Stat. 649 (Dec. 15, 1971); Pub. L. 95-514, § 14(a), 92 Stat. 1808 (Oct. 25, 1978)]

16 U.S.C. § 1334. Private maintenance; numerical approximation; strays on private lands: removal; destruction by agents. If wild free-roaming horses or burros stray from public lands onto privately owned land, the owners of such land may inform the nearest Federal marshall or agent of the Secretary, who shall arrange to have the animals removed. In no event shall such wild free-roaming horses and burros be destroyed except by the agents of the Secretary. Nothing in this section shall be construed to prohibit a private landowner from maintaining wild free-roaming horses or burros on his private lands, or lands leased from the Government, if he does so in a manner that protects them from harassment, and if the animals were not willfully removed or enticed from the public lands. Any individuals who maintain such wild free-roaming horses or burros on their private lands or lands leased from the Government shall notify the appropriate agent of the Secretary and supply him with a reasonable approximation of the number of animals so maintained.

[Pub. L. 92-195, § 4, 85 Stat. 650 (Dec. 15, 1971)]

16 U.S.C. § 1335. Recovery rights. A person claiming ownership of a horse or burro on the public lands shall be entitled to recover it only if recovery is permissible under the branding and estray laws of the State in which the animal is found.

[Pub. L. 92-195, § 5, 85 Stat. 650 (Dec. 15, 1971)]

16 U.S.C. § 1336. Cooperative agreements; regulations. The Secretary is authorized to enter into cooperative agreements with other landowners and with the State and local governmental agencies and may issue such regulations as he deems necessary for the furtherance of the purposes of this Act [16 U.S.C. §§ 1331 *et seq.*].

[Pub. L. 92-195, § 6, 85 Stat. 650 (Dec. 15, 1971)]

16 U.S.C. § 1337. Joint advisory board; appointment; membership; functions; qualifications; reimbursement limitation. ****

16 U.S.C. § 1338. Criminal provisions. (a) Violations; penalties; trial. Any person who --

(1) willfully removes or attempts to remove a wild free-roaming horse or burro from the public lands, without authority from the Secretary, or

(2) converts a wild free-roaming horse or burro to private use, without authority from the Secretary, or

(3) maliciously causes the death or harassment of any wild free-roaming horse or burro, or

(4) processes or permits to be processed into commercial products the remains of a wild free-roaming horse or burro, or

(5) sells, directly or indirectly, a wild free-roaming horse or burro maintained on private or leased land pursuant to section 4 of this Act [16 U.S.C. § 1334], or the remains thereof, or

(6) willfully violates a regulation issued pursuant to this Act [16 U.S.C. §§ 1331 *et seq.*],

shall be subject to a fine of not more than $2,000, or imprisonment for not more than one year, or both. Any person so charged with such violation by the Secretary may be tried and sentenced by any United States commissioner or magistrate designated for that purpose by the court by which he was appointed, in the same manner and subject to the same conditions as provided for in section 3401 of Title 18.

(b) Arrest; appearance for examination or trial; warrants: issuance and execution. ****

[Pub. L. 92-195, § 8, 85 Stat. 650 (Dec. 15, 1971)]

16 U.S.C. § 1339. Limitation of authority. Nothing in this Act [16 U.S.C. §§ 1331 *et seq.*] shall be construed to authorize the Secretary to relocate wild free-roaming horses or burros to areas of the public lands where they do not presently exist.

[Pub. L. 92-195, § 10, formerly § 9, 85 Stat. 651, (Dec. 15, 1971); Pub. L. 94-579, Title IV, § 404, 90 Stat. 2775 (Oct. 21, 1976)]

16 U.S.C. § 1340. Joint report to Congress; consultation and coordination of implementation, enforcement, and departmental activities; studies. ****

- 0 -

MARINE MAMMAL PROTECTION ACT
(16 U.S.C. §§ 1361-1407)

As noted, one of the earliest federal wildlife statutes sought to conserve a marine mammal. "An Act to prevent the Extermination of Fur-bearing Animals in Alaska" established a leasing system to regulate the harvest of fur seals on the Pribilof Islands in the Bering Sea.[68] With the rise of pelagic sealing and the failure of the leasing system to produce a sustainable harvest, the United States, Great Britain (acting for Canada), Japan, and Russia entered into a treaty in 1911 to regulate the seal harvest.[69] After the 1911 treaty expired when Japan withdrew in 1940, a new agreement between Canada, Japan, the Soviet Union, and the United States was not finalized until 1957.[70] In 1988, strong efforts by animal rights groups prevented the United States from ratifying a protocol to extend the 1957 agreement. By then, the seals were covered by the Marine Mammal Protection Act of 1972.[71]

The Marine Mammal Protection Act of 1972 (MMPA) was an ambitious break with previous federal regulatory schemes for wildlife. George Coggins has described it with admirable economy as "a technical and complex effort to restore and protect a variety of wildlife populations living in differing biological communities under a variety of legal conditions."[72]

The MMPA had a number of features that marked a fundamental transition in federal wildlife law. First, unlike previous federal legislation that had at least employed language deferential to state management of wildlife, the MMPA expressly preempted all state law "relating to the taking of any species ... of marine mammal."[73] The Act did mitigate the intrusion into traditional state prerogatives by including procedures and standards under which a state could resume management authority over marine mammals.[74]

Second, the MMPA established a comprehensive federal management program based on the preservation of population stocks, a biological unit smaller than the traditional species-based focus.[75] Central to this program was a moratorium "on the taking and importation of marine mammals and marine mammal products."[76] The Act provided for lifting the moratorium on takings when a stock's population reached certain levels.[77]

Finally, and perhaps most significantly, the MMPA replaced the traditional, economics-based "maximum sustained yield" concept,[78] with a biology-based goal: the "optimum sustainable population." OSP was defined as "the number of animals which will result in the maximum productivity of the population or species, keeping in mind the optimum carrying capacity of the habitat and the health of the ecosystem of which they form a constituent element."[79]

Beyond all of its details, the MMPA was the most important piece of wildlife legislation before the Endangered Species Act because of its audacity: it was an ambitious attempt to protect and restore the populations of a diverse group of species.

The current version of the MMPA is substantially different than the statute that Congress adopted in 1972. The practical difficulties in implementing the 1972 Act and the need to balance the conservation of marine mammals against other interests have combined to produce a statute that contains a bewildering detail of statutory provisions.[80] The moratorium now applies primarily to recreational taking and to importation of marine mammal products for commercial purposes. The Act now contains several new terms -- "potential biological removal levels," "strategic stocks," and "take reduction plans" -- and requirements conditioned upon a "stock assessment" for each species.[81] The stock assessment is used to determine the potential biological replacement levels; stocks for which the human-caused mortality exceeds the replacement level is a strategic stock -- a designation that affects commercial fisheries that incidentally take the stock. If there is an incidental take of a strategic stock, the agency is to develop a take reduction plan.[82] Other provisions of the Act have seen similar modifications.[83]

Title I

16 U.S.C. § 1361. Congressional findings and declaration of policy. The Congress finds that--

(1) certain species and population stocks of marine mammals are, or may be, in danger of extinction or depletion as a result of man's activities;

(2) such species and population stocks should not be permitted to diminish beyond the point at which they cease to be a significant functioning element in the ecosystem of which they are a part, and, consistent with this major objective, they should not be permitted to diminish below their optimum sustainable population. Further measures should be immediately taken to replenish any species or population stock which has already

diminished below that population. In particular, efforts should be made to protect essential habitats, including the rookeries, mating grounds, and areas of similar significance for each species of marine mammal from the adverse effect of man's actions;
(3) there is inadequate knowledge of the ecology and population dynamics of such marine mammals and of the factors which bear upon their ability to reproduce themselves successfully;
(4) negotiations should be undertaken immediately to encourage the development of international arrangements for research on, and conservation of, all marine mammals;
(5) marine mammals and marine mammal products either --
(A) move in interstate commerce, or
(B) affect the balance of marine ecosystems in a manner which is important to other animals and animal products which move in interstate commerce,
and that the protection and conservation of marine mammals and their habitats is therefore necessary to insure the continuing availability of those products which move in interstate commerce; and
(6) marine mammals have proven themselves to be resources of great international significance, esthetic and recreational as well as economic, and it is the sense of the Congress that they should be protected and encouraged to develop to the greatest extent feasible commensurate with sound policies of resource management and that the primary objective of their management should be to maintain the health and stability of the marine ecosystem. Whenever consistent with this primary objective, it should be the goal to obtain an optimum sustainable population keeping in mind the carrying capacity of the habitat.

[Pub. L. 92-522, § 2, 86 Stat. 1027 (Oct. 21, 1972); Pub. L. 97-58, § 1(b)(1), 95 Stat. 979 (Oct. 9, 1981); Pub. L. 103-238, § 3, 108 Stat. 532 (Apr. 30, 1994)]

16 U.S.C. § 1362. Definitions. For the purposes of this Act --
(1) The term "depletion" or "depleted" means any case in which --
(A) the Secretary, after consultation with the Marine Mammal Commission and the Committee of Scientific Advisors on Marine Mammals established under title II of this Act [16 U.S.C. §§ 1401 *et seq.*], determines that a species or population stock is below its optimum sustainable population;
(B) a State, to which authority for the conservation and management of a species or population stock is transferred under section 109 [16 U.S.C. § 1379], determines that such species or stock is below its optimum sustainable population; or
(C) a species or population stock is listed as an endangered species or a threatened species under the Endangered Species Act of 1973 [16 U.S.C. § 1531 *et seq.*].
(2) The terms "conservation" and "management" mean the collection and application of biological information for the purposes of increasing and maintaining the number of animals within species and populations of marine mammals at their optimum sustainable population. Such terms include the entire scope of activities that constitute a modern scientific resource program, including, but not limited to, research, census, law enforcement, and habitat acquisition and improvement. Also included within these terms, when and where appropriate, is the periodic or total protection of species or populations as well as regulated taking.
(3) The term "district court of the United States" includes the District Court of Guam,

District Court of the Virgin Islands, District Court of Puerto Rico, District Court of the Canal Zone, and, in the case of American Samoa and the Trust Territory of the Pacific Islands, the District Court of the United States for the District of Hawaii.

(4) The term "humane" in the context of the taking of a marine mammal means that method of taking which involves the least possible degree of pain and suffering practicable to the mammal involved.

(5) The term "intermediary nation" means a nation that exports yellowfin tuna or yellowfin tuna products to the United States and that imports yellowfin tuna or yellowfin tuna products that are subject to a direct ban on importation into the United States pursuant to section 101(a)(2)(B) [16 U.S.C. § 1371(a)(2)(B)].

(6) The term "marine mammal" means any mammal which (A) is morphologically adapted to the marine environment (including sea otters and members of the orders Sirenia, Pinnipedia and Cetacea), or (B) primarily inhabits the marine environment (such as the polar bear); and, for the purposes of this Act, includes any part of any such marine mammal, including its raw, dressed, or dyed fur or skin.

(7) The term "marine mammal product" means any item of merchandise which consists, or is composed in whole or in part, of any marine mammal.

(8) The term "moratorium" means a complete cessation of the taking of marine mammals and a complete ban on the importation into the United States of marine mammals and marine mammal products, except as provided in this Act.

(9) The term "optimum sustainable population" means, with respect to any population stock, the number of animals which will result in the maximum productivity of the population or the species, keeping in mind the carrying capacity of the habitat and the health of the ecosystem of which they form a constituent element.

(10) The term "person" includes (A) any private person or entity, and (B) any officer, employee, agent, department, or instrumentality of the Federal Government, of any State or political subdivision thereof, or of any foreign government.

(11) The term "population stock" or "stock" means a group of marine mammals of the same species or smaller taxa in a common spatial arrangement, that interbreed when mature.

(12)(A) Except as provided in subparagraph (B), the term "Secretary" means --

(i) the Secretary of the department in which the National Oceanic and Atmospheric Administration is operating, as to all responsibility, authority, funding, and duties under this Act with respect to members of the order Cetacea and members, other than walruses, of the order Pinnipedia, and

(ii) the Secretary of the Interior as to all responsibility, authority, funding, and duties under this Act with respect to all other marine mammals covered by this Act.

(B) in section 118 and title IV [16 U.S.C. §§ 1387, 1421 *et seq.*] (other than section 1421f-1) the term "Secretary" means the Secretary of Commerce.

(13) The term "take" means to harass, hunt, capture, or kill, or attempt to harass, hunt, capture, or kill any marine mammal.

(14) The term "United States" includes the several States, the District of Columbia, the Commonwealth of Puerto Rico, the Virgin Islands of the United States, American Samoa, Guam, and Northern Mariana Islands.

(15) The term "waters under the jurisdiction of the United States" means --

(A) the territorial sea of the United States;

(B) the waters included within a zone, contiguous to the territorial sea of the United States, of which the inner boundary is a line coterminous with the seaward boundary of each coastal State, and the other boundary is a line drawn in such a manner that each point on it is 200 nautical miles from the baseline from which the territorial sea is measured; and

(C) the areas referred to as eastern special areas in Article 3(1) of the Agreement between the United States of America and the Union of Soviet Socialist Republics on the Maritime Boundary, signed June 1, 1990; in particular, those areas east of the maritime boundary, as defined in that Agreement, that lie within 200 nautical miles of the baselines from which the breadth of the territorial sea of Russia is measured but beyond 200 nautical miles of the baselines from which the breadth of the territorial sea of the United States is measured, except that this subparagraph shall not apply before the date on which the Agreement between the United States and the Union of Soviet Socialist Republics on the Maritime Boundary, signed June 1, 1990, enters into force for the United States.

(16) The term "fishery" means --

(A) one or more stocks of fish which can be treated as a unit for purposes of conservation and management and which are identified on the basis of geographical, scientific, technical, recreational, and economic characteristics; and

(B) any fishing for such stocks.

(17) The term "competent regional organization" --

(A) for the tuna fishery in the eastern tropical Pacific Ocean, means the Inter-American Tropical Tuna Commission; and

(B) in any other case, means an organization consisting of those nations participating in a tuna fishery, the purpose of which is the conservation and management of that fishery and the management of issues relating to that fishery.

(18)(A) The term "harassment" means any act of pursuit, torment, or annoyance which --

(i) has the potential to injure a marine mammal or marine mammal stock in the wild; or

(ii) has the potential to disturb a marine mammal or marine mammal stock in the wild by causing disruption of behavioral patterns, including, but not limited to, migration, breathing, nursing, breeding, feeding, or sheltering.

(B) The term "Level A harassment" means harassment described in subparagraph (A)(i).

(C) The term "Level B harassment" means harassment described in subparagraph (A)(ii).

(19) The term "strategic stock" means a marine mammal stock --

(A) for which the level of direct human-caused mortality exceeds the potential biological removal level;

(B) which, based on the best available scientific information, is declining and is likely to be listed as a threatened species under the Endangered Species Act of 1973 [16 U.S.C. § 1531 *et seq.*] within the foreseeable future; or

(C) which is listed as a threatened species or endangered species under the Endangered Species Act of 1973 (16 U.S.C. 1531 *et seq.*), or is designated as depleted under this Act.

(20) The term "potential biological removal level" means the maximum number of animals, not including natural mortalities, that may be removed from a marine mammal stock while

allowing that stock to reach or maintain its optimum sustainable population. The potential biological removal level is the product of the following factors:

(A) The minimum population estimate of the stock.

(B) One-half the maximum theoretical or estimated net productivity rate of the stock at a small population size.

(C) A recovery factor of between 0.1 and 1.0.

(21) The term "Regional Fishery Management Council" means a Regional Fishery Management Council established under section 302 of the Magnuson Fishery Conservation and Management Act [16 U.S.C. § 1852].

(22) The term "bona fide research" means scientific research on marine mammals, the results of which --

(A) likely would be accepted for publication in a referred scientific journal;

(B) are likely to contribute to the basic knowledge of marine mammal biology or ecology; or

(C) are likely to identify, evaluate, or resolve conservation problems.

(23) The term "Alaska Native organization" means a group designated by law or formally chartered which represents or consists of Indians, Aleuts, or Eskimos residing in Alaska.

(24) The term "take reduction plan" means a plan developed under section 118 [16 U.S.C. § 1387].

(25) The term "take reduction team" means a team established under section 118 [16 U.S.C. § 1387].

(26) The term "net productivity rate" means the annual per capita rate of increase in a stock resulting from additions due to reproduction, less losses due to mortality.

(27) The term "minimum population estimate" means an estimate of the number of animals in a stock that --

(A) is based on the best available scientific information on abundance, incorporating the precision and variability associated with such information; and

(B) provides reasonable assurance that the stock size is equal to or greater than the estimate.

(28) The term "International Dolphin Conservation Program" means the international program established by the agreement signed in LaJolla, California, in June, 1992, as formalized, modified, and enhanced in accordance with the Declaration of Panama.

(29) The term "Declaration of Panama" means the declaration signed in Panama City, Republic of Panama, on October 4, 1995.

[Pub. L. 92-522, § 3, 86 Stat. 1028 (Oct. 21, 1972); Pub. L. 93-205, § 13(e)(1), 87 Stat. 903 (Dec. 28, 1973); Pub. L. 94-265, Title IV, § 404(a), 90 Stat. 360 (Apr. 13, 1976); Pub. L. 97-58, § 1(a), (b)(2), 95 Stat. 979 (Oct. 9, 1981); Pub. L. 102-251, Title III, § 304, 106 Stat. 65 (Mar. 9, 1992); Pub. L. 102-523, § 2(c), 106 Stat. 3432 (Oct. 26, 1992); Pub. L. 102-582, Title IV, § 401(a), 106 Stat. 4909 (Nov. 2, 1992); Pub. L. 102-587, Title III, § 3004(b), Nov. 4, 1992, 106 Stat. 5067; Pub. L. 103-238, §§ 12, 16(a), 24(a)(2), 108 Stat. 557 (Apr. 30, 1994), 559, 565; Pub. L. 104-208, Div. A, Title I, § 101(a) [Title II, § 211(b)], 110 Stat. 3009-41 (Sept. 30, 1996); Pub. L. 104-297, Title IV, § 405(b)(2), (3), 110 Stat. 3621 (Oct. 11, 1996); Pub. L. 105-42, § 3, 111 Stat. 1123 (Aug. 15, 1997)]

16 U.S.C. § 1371. Moratorium on taking and importing marine mammals and marine mammal products. (a) Imposition; exceptions. There shall be a moratorium on the taking and importation of marine mammals and marine mammal products, commencing on the effective date of this Act, during which time no permit may be issued for the taking of any marine mammal and no marine mammal or marine mammal product may be imported into the United States except in the following cases:

(1) Consistent with the provisions of section 104 [16 U.S.C. § 1374], permits may be issued by the Secretary for taking, and importation for purposes of scientific research, public display, photography for educational or commercial purposes, or enhancing the survival or recovery of a species or stock, or for importation of polar bear parts (other than internal organs) taken in sport hunts in Canada. Such permits, except permits issued under section 104(c)(5) [16 U.S.C. § 1374(c)(5)], may be issued if the taking or importation proposed to be made is first reviewed by the Marine Mammal Commission and the Committee of Scientific Advisors on Marine Mammals established under Title II of this Act. The Commission and Committee shall recommend any proposed taking or importation, other than importation under section 104(c)(5) [16 U.S.C. § 1374(c)(5)], which is consistent with the purposes and policies of section 2 [16 U.S.C. § 1361]. If the Secretary issues such a permit for importation, the Secretary shall issue to the importer concerned a certificate to that effect in such form as the Secretary of the Treasury prescribes, and such importation may be made upon presentation of the certificate to the customs officer concerned.

(2) Marine mammals may be taken incidentally in the course of commercial fishing operations and permits may be issued therefor under section 104 [16 U.S.C. § 1374] subject to regulations prescribed by the Secretary in accordance with section 103 [16 U.S.C. § 1373], or in lieu of such permits, authorizations may be granted therefor under section 118 [16 U.S.C. § 1387], subject to regulations prescribed under that section by the Secretary without regard to section 103 [16 U.S.C. § 1373]. Such authorizations may be granted under title III of this Act with respect to purse seine fishing for yellowfin tuna in the eastern tropical Pacific Ocean, subject to regulations prescribed under that title by the Secretary without regard to section 103 [16 U.S.C. § 1373]. In any event it shall be the immediate goal that the incidental kill or incidental serious injury of marine mammals permitted in the course of commercial fishing operations be reduced to insignificant levels approaching a zero mortality and serious injury rate. The Secretary of the Treasury shall ban the importation of commercial fish or products from fish which have been caught with commercial fishing technology which results in the incidental kill or incidental serious injury of ocean mammals in excess of United States standards. For purposes of applying the preceding sentence, the Secretary --

(A) shall insist on reasonable proof from the government of any nation from which fish or fish products will be exported to the United States of the effects on ocean mammals of the commercial fishing technology in use for such fish or fish products exported from such nation to the United States;

(B) in the case of yellowfin tuna harvested with purse seine nets in the eastern tropical Pacific Ocean, and products therefrom, to be exported to the United States, shall require that the government of the exporting nation provide documentary evidence that --

(i)(I) the tuna or products therefrom were not banned from importation under this paragraph before the effective date of section 4 of the International Dolphin Conservation Program Act; or

(II) the tuna or products therefrom were harvested after the effective date of section 4 of the International Dolphin Conservation Program Act by vessels of a nation which participates in the International

Dolphin Conservation Program, and such harvesting nation is either a member of the Inter-American Tropical Tuna Commission or has initiated (and within 6 months thereafter completed) all steps required of applicant nations, in accordance with article V, paragraph 3 of the Convention establishing the Inter-American Tropical Tuna Commission, to become a member of that organization;

(ii) such nation is meeting the obligations of the International Dolphin Conservation Program and the obligations of membership in the Inter-American Tropical Tuna Commission, including all financial obligations; and

(iii) the total dolphin mortality limits, and per-stock per-year dolphin mortality limits permitted for that nation's vessels under the International Dolphin Conservation Program do not exceed the limits determined for 1997, or for any year thereafter, consistent with the objective of progressively reducing dolphin mortality to a level approaching zero through the setting of annual limits and the goal of eliminating dolphin mortality, and requirements of the International Dolphin Conservation Program;

(C) shall not accept such documentary evidence if --

(i) the government of the harvesting nation does not provide directly or authorize the Inter-American Tropical Tuna Commission to release complete and accurate information to the Secretary in a timely manner --

(I) to allow determination of compliance with the International Dolphin Conservation Program; and

(II) for the purposes of tracking and verifying compliance with the minimum requirements established by the Secretary in regulations promulgated under subsection (f) of the Dolphin Protection Consumer Information Act (16 U.S.C. § 1385(f)); or

(ii) after taking into consideration such information, findings of the Inter-American Tropical Tuna Commission, and any other relevant information, including information that a nation is consistently failing to take enforcement actions on violations which diminish the effectiveness of the International Dolphin Conservation Program, the Secretary, in consultation with the Secretary of State, finds that the harvesting nation is not in compliance with the International Dolphin Conservation Program.

(D) shall require the government of any intermediary nation to certify and provide reasonable proof to the Secretary that it has not imported, within the preceding six months, any yellowfin tuna or yellowfin tuna products that are subject to a direct ban on importation to the United States under subparagraph (B);

(E) shall, six months after importation of yellowfin tuna or tuna products has been banned under this section, certify such fact to the President, which certification shall be deemed to be a certification for the purposes of section 8(a) of the Fishermen's Protective Act [22 U.S.C. § 1978(a)] for as long as such ban is in effect; and

(F)(i) except as provided in clause (ii), in the case of fish or products containing fish harvested by a nation whose fishing vessels engage in high seas driftnet fishing, shall require that the government of the exporting nation provide documentary evidence that the fish or fish product was not harvested with a large-scale driftnet in the South Pacific Ocean after July 1, 1991, or in any other water of the high seas after January 1, 1993, and

(ii) in the case of tuna or a product containing tuna harvested by a nation whose fishing vessels engage in high seas driftnet fishing, shall require that the government of the exporting nation provide documentary evidence that the tuna or tuna product was not harvested with a large-scale driftnet anywhere on the high seas after July 1, 1991.

For purposes of subparagraph (F), the term "driftnet" has the meaning given such term in section 4003 of the Driftnet Impact Monitoring, Assessment, and Control Act of 1987 (16 U.S.C. § 1822 note), except that, until January 1, 1994, the term "driftnet" does not include the use in the northeast Atlantic Ocean of gillnets with a total length not to exceed five kilometers if the use is in accordance with regulations adopted by the European Community pursuant to the October 28, 1991, decision by the Council of Fisheries Ministers of the Community.

(3)(A) The Secretary, on the basis of the best scientific evidence available and in consultation with the Marine Mammal Commission, is authorized and directed, from time to time, having due regard to the distribution, abundance, breeding habits, and times and lines of migratory movements of such marine mammals, to determine when, to what extent, if at all, and by what means, it is compatible with this Act to waive the requirements of this section so as to allow taking, or importing of any marine mammal, or any marine mammal product, and to adopt suitable regulations, issue permits, and make determinations in accordance with sections 102, 103, 104, and 111 of this Act [16 U.S.C. §§ 1372-1374, 1381] permitting and governing such taking and importing, in accordance with such determinations: *Provided, however,* That the Secretary, in making such determinations, must be assured that the taking of such marine mammal is in accord with sound principles of resource protection and conservation as provided in the purposes and policies of this Act: *Provided further, however,* That no marine mammal or no marine mammal product may be imported into the United States unless the Secretary certifies that the program for taking marine mammals in the country of origin is consistent with the provisions and policies of this Act. Products of nations not so certified may not be imported into the United States for any purpose, including processing for exportation.

(B) Except for scientific research purposes, photography for educational or commercial purposes, or enhancing the survival or recovery of a species or stock as provided for in paragraph (1) of this subsection, or as provided for under paragraph (5) of this subsection, during the moratorium no permit may be issued for the taking of any marine mammal which has been designated by the Secretary as depleted, and no importation may be made of any such mammal.

(4)(A) Except as provided in subparagraphs (B) and (C), the provisions of this Act shall not apply to the use of measures --

(i) by the owner of fishing gear or catch, or an employee or agent of such owner, to deter a marine mammal from damaging the gear or catch;

(ii) by the owner of other private property, or an agent, bailee, or employee of such owner, to deter a marine mammal from damaging private property;

(iii) by any person, to deter a marine mammal from endangering personal safety; or

(iv) by a government employee, to deter a marine mammal from damaging public property,

so long as such measures do not result in the death or serious injury of a marine mammal.

(B) The Secretary shall, through consultation with appropriate experts, and after notice and opportunity for public comment, publish in the Federal Register a list of guidelines for use in safely deterring marine mammals. In the case of marine mammals listed as endangered species or threatened species under the Endangered Species Act of 1973 [16 U.S.C. § 1531 *et seq.*], the Secretary shall recommend specific measures which may be used to nonlethally deter marine mammals. Actions to deter marine mammals consistent with such guidelines or specific measures shall not be a violation of this Act.

(C) If the Secretary determines, using the best scientific information available, that certain forms of deterrence have a significant adverse effect on marine mammals, the Secretary may prohibit such deterrent methods, after notice and opportunity for public comment, through regulation under this Act.

(D) The authority to deter marine mammals pursuant to subparagraph (A) applies to all marine mammals, including all stocks designated as depleted under this Act.

(5)(A) Upon request therefor by citizens of the United States who engage in a specified activity (other than commercial fishing) within a specified geographical region, the Secretary shall allow, during periods of not more than five consecutive years each, the incidental, but not intentional, taking by citizens while engaging in that activity within that region of small numbers of marine mammals of a species or population stock if the Secretary, after notice (in the Federal Register and in newspapers of general circulation, and through appropriate electronic media, in the coastal areas that may be affected by such activity) and opportunity for public comment --

(i) finds that the total of such taking during each five-year (or less) period concerned will have a negligible impact on such species or stock and will not have an unmitigable adverse impact on the availability of such species or stock for taking for subsistence uses pursuant to subsection (b) of this section or section 109(f) [16 U.S.C. § 1379(f)] or, in the case of a cooperative agreement under both this Act and the Whaling Convention Act of 1949 [16 U.S.C. § 916 *et seq.*], pursuant to section 112(c) [16 U.S.C. § 1382(c)]; and

(ii) prescribes regulations setting forth --

(I) permissible methods of taking pursuant to such activity, and other means of effecting the least practicable adverse impact on such species or stock and its habitat, paying particular attention to rookeries, mating grounds, and areas of similar significance, and on the availability of such species or stock for subsistence uses; and

(II) requirements pertaining to the monitoring and reporting of such taking.

(B) The Secretary shall withdraw, or suspend for a time certain (either on an individual or class basis, as appropriate) the permission to take marine mammals under subparagraph (A) pursuant to a specified activity within a specified geographical region if the Secretary finds, after notice and opportunity for public comment (as required under subparagraph (A) unless subparagraph (C)(i) applies), that --

(i) the regulations prescribed under subparagraph (A) regarding methods of taking, monitoring, or reporting are not being substantially complied with by a person engaging in such activity; or

(ii) the taking allowed under subparagraph (A) pursuant to one or more activities within one or more regions is having, or may have, more than a negligible impact on the species or stock concerned.

(C)(i) The requirement for notice and opportunity for public comment in subparagraph (B) shall not apply in the case of a suspension of permission to take if the Secretary determines that an emergency exists which poses a significant risk to the well-being of the species or stock concerned.

(ii) Sections 103 and 104 [16 U.S.C. §§ 1373 and 1374] shall not apply to the taking of marine mammals under the authority of this paragraph.

(D)(i) Upon request therefor by citizens of the United States who engage in a specified activity (other than commercial fishing) within a specific geographic region, the Secretary shall authorize, for periods of not more than 1 year, subject to such conditions as the Secretary may specify, the incidental, but not intentional, taking by harassment of small numbers of marine mammals of a species or population stock by such citizens while engaging in that activity within that region if the Secretary finds that such harassment during each period concerned --

(I) will have a negligible impact on such species or stock, and

(II) will not have an unmitigable adverse impact on the availability of such species or stock for taking for subsistence uses pursuant to subsection (b) of this section, or section 109(f) [16 U.S.C. § 1379(f)] or pursuant to a cooperative agreement under section 119 [16 U.S.C. § 1388].

(ii) The authorization for such activity shall prescribe, where applicable --

(I) permissible methods of taking by harassment pursuant to such activity, and other means of effecting the least practicable impact on such species or stock and its habitat, paying particular attention to rookeries, mating grounds, and areas of similar significance, and on the availability of such species or stock for taking for subsistence uses pursuant to subsection (b) of this section or section 109(f) [16 U.S.C. § 1379(f)] or pursuant to a cooperative agreement under section 119 [16 U.S.C. § 1388],

(II) the measures that the Secretary determines are necessary to ensure no unmitigable adverse impact on the availability of the species or stock for taking for subsistence uses pursuant to subsection (b) of this section or section 109(f) [16 U.S.C. § 1379(f)] or pursuant to a cooperative agreement under section 119 [16 U.S.C. § 1388], and

(III) requirements pertaining to the monitoring and reporting of such taking by harassment, including requirements for the independent peer review of proposed monitoring plans or other research proposals where the proposed activity may affect the availability of a species or stock for taking for subsistence uses pursuant to subsection (b) of this section or section 109(f) [16 U.S.C. § 1379(f)] or pursuant to a cooperative agreement under section 119 [16 U.S.C. § 1388].

(iii) The Secretary shall publish a proposed authorization not later than 45 days after receiving an application under this subparagraph and request public comment through notice in the Federal Register, newspapers of general circulation, and appropriate electronic media and to all locally affected communities for a period of 30 days after publication. Not later than 45 days after the close of the public comment period, if the Secretary makes the findings set forth in clause (i), the Secretary shall issue an authorization with appropriate conditions to meet the requirements of clause (ii).

(iv) The Secretary shall modify, suspend, or revoke an authorization if the Secretary finds that the provisions of clauses (i) or (ii) are not being met.

(v) A person conducting an activity for which an authorization has been granted under this subparagraph shall not be subject to the penalties of this Act for taking by harassment that occurs in compliance with such authorization.

(E)(i) During any period of up to 3 consecutive years, the Secretary shall allow the incidental, but not the intentional, taking by persons using vessels of the United States or vessels which have valid fishing permits issued by the Secretary in accordance with section 204(b) of the Magnuson Fishery Conservation and Management Act [16 U.S.C. § 1824(b)], while engaging in commercial fishing operations, or marine mammals from a species or stock designated as depleted because of its listing as an endangered species or threatened species under the Endangered Species Act of 1973 (16 U.S.C. 1531 *et seq.*) if the Secretary, after notice and opportunity for public comment, determines that --

(I) the incidental mortality and serious injury from commercial fisheries will have a negligible impact on such species or stock;

(II) a recovery plan has been developed or is being developed for such species or stock pursuant to the Endangered Species Act of 1973 [16 U.S.C. § 1531 *et seq.*]; and

(III) where required under 118 [16 U.S.C. § 1387], a monitoring program is established under subsection (d) of such section, vessels engaged in such fisheries are registered in accordance with such section, and a take reduction plan has been developed or is being developed for such species or stock.

(ii) Upon a determination by the Secretary that the requirements of clause (i) have been met, the Secretary shall publish in the Federal Register a list of those fisheries for which such determination was made, and, for vessels required to register under section 118 [16 U.S.C. § 1387], shall issue an appropriate permit for each authorization granted under such section to vessels to which this paragraph applies. Vessels engaged in a fishery included in the notice published by the Secretary under this clause which are not required to register under section 118 [16 U.S.C. § 1387] shall not be subject to the penalties of this Act for the incidental taking of marine mammals to which this paragraph applies, so long as the owner or master of such vessel reports any incidental mortality or injury of such marine mammals to the Secretary in accordance with section 118 [16 U.S.C. § 1387].

(iii) If, during the course of the commercial fishing season, the Secretary determines that the level of incidental mortality or serious injury from commercial fisheries for which a determination was made under clause (i) has resulted or is likely to result in an impact that is more than negligible on the endangered or threatened species or stock, the Secretary shall use the emergency authority granted under section 118 [16 U.S.C. § 1387] to protect such species or stock, and may modify any permit granted under this paragraph as necessary.

(iv) The Secretary may suspend for a time certain or revoke a permit granted under this subparagraph only if the Secretary determines that the conditions or limitations set forth in such permit are not being complied with. The Secretary may amend or modify, after notice and opportunity for public comment, the list of fisheries published under clause (ii) whenever the Secretary determines there has been a significant change in the information or conditions used to determine such list.

(v) Sections 103 and 104 [16 U.S.C. §§ 1373 and 1374] shall not apply to the taking of marine mammals under the authority of this subparagraph.

(vi) This subparagraph shall not govern the incidental taking of California sea otters and shall not be deemed to amend or repeal the Act of November 7, 1986 (Public Law 99-625; 100 Stat. 3500).

(6)(A) A marine mammal product may be imported into the United States if the product --

(i) was legally possessed and exported by any citizen of the United States in conjunction with travel outside the United States, provided that the product is imported into the United States by the same person upon the termination of travel;

(ii) was acquired outside of the United States as part of a cultural exchange by an Indian, Aleut, or Eskimo residing in Alaska; or

(iii) is owned by a Native inhabitant of Russia, Canada, or Greenland and is imported for noncommercial purposes in conjunction with travel within the United States or as part of a cultural exchange with an Indian, Aleut, or Eskimo residing in Alaska.

(B) For the purposes of this paragraph, the term --

(i) "Native inhabitant of Russia, Canada, or Greenland" means a person

residing in Russia, Canada, or Greenland who is related by blood, is a member of the same clan or ethnological grouping, or shares a common heritage with an Indian, Aleut, or Eskimo residing in Alaska; and
(ii) "cultural exchange" means the sharing or exchange of ideas, information, gifts, clothing, or handicrafts between an Indian, Aleut, or Eskimo residing in Alaska and a Native inhabitant of Russia, Canada, or Greenland, including rendering of raw marine mammal parts as part of such exchange into clothing or handicrafts through carving, painting, sewing, or decorating.

(b) Exemptions for Alaskan natives. Except as provided in section 109 [16 U.S.C. § 1379], the provisions of this Act shall not apply with respect to the taking of any marine mammal by any Indian, Aleut, or Eskimo who resides in Alaska and who dwells on the coast of the North Pacific Ocean or the Arctic Ocean if such taking --

(1) is for subsistence purposes; or

(2) is done for purposes of creating and selling authentic native articles of handicrafts and clothing: *Provided,* That only authentic native articles of handicrafts and clothing may be sold in interstate commerce: *And provided further,* That any edible portion of marine mammals may be sold in native villages and towns in Alaska or for native consumption. For the purposes of this subsection, the term "authentic native articles of handicrafts and clothing" means items composed wholly or in some significant respect of natural materials, and which are produced, decorated, or fashioned in the exercise of traditional native handicrafts without the use of pantographs, multiple carvers, or other mass copying devices. Traditional native handicrafts include, but are not limited to weaving, carving, stitching, sewing, lacing, beading, drawing, and painting; and

(3) in each case, is not accomplished in a wasteful manner.

Notwithstanding the preceding provisions of this subsection, when, under this Act, the Secretary determines any species or stock of marine mammal subject to taking by Indians, Aleuts, or Eskimos to be depleted, he may prescribe regulations upon the taking of such marine mammals by any Indian, Aleut, or Eskimo described in this subsection. Such regulations may be established with reference to species or stocks, geographical description of the area included, the season for taking, or any other factors related to the reason for establishing such regulations and consistent with the purposes of this Act. Such regulations shall be prescribed after notice and hearing required by section 103 of this Act [16 U.S.C. § 1373] and shall be removed as soon as the Secretary determines that the need for their imposition has disappeared. In promulgating any regulation or making any assessment pursuant to a hearing or proceeding under this subsection or section 117(b)(2) [16 U.S.C. § 1386(b)(2)], or in making any determination of depletion under this subsection or finding regarding unmitigable adverse impacts under subsection (a)(5) of this section that affects stocks or persons to which this subsection applies, the Secretary shall be responsible for demonstrating that such regulation, assessment, determination, or finding is supported by substantial evidence on the basis of the record as a whole. The preceding sentence shall only be applicable in an action brought by one or more Alaska Native organizations representing persons to which this subsection applies.

(c) Taking in defense of self or others. It shall not be a violation of this Act to take a marine mammal if such taking is imminently necessary in self-defense or to save the life of a person in immediate danger, and such taking is reported to the Secretary within 48 hours. The Secretary may seize and dispose of any carcass.

(d) Good Samaritan exemption. It shall not be a violation of this Act to take a marine mammal if --

(1) such taking is imminently necessary to avoid serious injury, additional injury, or death to a marine mammal entangled in fishing gear or debris;

(2) reasonable care is taken to ensure the safe release of the marine mammal, taking into consideration the equipment, expertise, and conditions at hand;

(3) reasonable care is exercised to prevent any further injury to the marine mammal; and

(4) such taking is reported to the Secretary within 48 hours.

(e) Act not to apply to incidental takings by United States citizens employed on foreign vessels outside the United States EEZ. The provisions of this Act shall not apply to a citizen of the United States who incidentally takes any marine mammal during fishing operations outside the United States exclusive economic zone (as defined in section 3 of the Magnuson-Stevens Fishery Conservation and Management Act (16 U.S.C. 1802)) when employed on a foreign fishing vessel of a harvesting nation which is in compliance with the International Dolphin Conservation Program.

[Pub. L. 92-522, Title I, § 101, 86 Stat. 1029 (Oct. 21, 1972); Pub. L. 93- 205, § 13(e)(2), 87 Stat. 903 (Dec. 28, 1973); Pub. L. 97-58, § 2, 95 Stat. 979 (Oct. 9, 1981); Pub. L. 98-364, Title I, § 101, 98 Stat. 440 (July 17, 1984); Pub. L. 99-659, Title IV, § 411(a), 100 Stat. 3741 (Nov. 14, 1986); Pub. L. 100-711, §§ 4(a), 5(c), (e)(1), 102 Stat. 4765, 4766, 4769, 4771 (Nov. 23, 1988); Pub. L. 101-627, § 901(g), 104 Stat. 4467 (Nov. 28, 1990); Pub. L. 102-582, Title I, § 103, Title IV, § 401(b), 106 Stat. 4903, 4909 (Nov. 2, 1992); Pub. L. 103-238, § 4, 108 Stat. 532 (Apr. 30, 1994); Pub. L. 104-208, Div. A, Title I, § 101(a) [Title II, § 211(b)], 110 Stat. 3009-41 (Sept. 30, 1996); Pub. L. 105-18, Title II, § 2003, 111 Stat. 174 (June 12, 1997); Pub. L. 105-42, § 4(a) to (c), 111 Stat. 1123, 1124 (Aug. 15, 1997)]

16 U.S.C. § 1372. Prohibitions. (a) Taking. Except as provided in sections 101, 103, 104, 109, 111, 113, 114, and 1218 of this title and title IV [16 U.S.C. §§ 1371, 1373, 1374, 1379, 1381, 1383, and 1383a, 1386, and 1421 *et seq.*], it is unlawful --

(1) for any person subject to the jurisdiction of the United States or any vessel or other conveyance subject to the jurisdiction of the United States to take any marine mammal on the high seas;

(2) except as expressly provided for by an international treaty, convention, or agreement to which the United States is a party and which was entered into before the effective date of this Act or by any statute implementing any such treaty, convention, or agreement --

(A) for any person or vessel or other conveyance to take any marine mammal in waters or on lands under the jurisdiction of the United States; or

(B) for any person to use any port, harbor, or other place under the jurisdiction of the United States to take or import marine mammals or marine mammal products; and

(3) for any person, with respect to any marine mammal taken in violation of this Act, to possess that mammal or any product from that mammal;

(4) for any person to transport, purchase, sell, export, or offer to purchase, sell, or export any marine mammal or marine mammal product --

(A) that is taken in violation of this Act; or

(B) for any purpose other than public display, scientific research, or enhancing the survival of a species or stock as provided for under subsection 104(c) [16 U.S.C. § 1374(c)]; and

(5) for any person to use, in a commercial fishery, any means or methods of fishing in contravention of any regulations or limitations, issued by the Secretary for that fishery to achieve the purposes of this Act.

(b) Importation of pregnant or nursing mammals; depleted species or stock; inhumane taking. Except pursuant to a permit for scientific research, or for enhancing the survival or recovery of a species or stock, issued under section 104(c) [16 U.S.C. § 1374(c)], it is unlawful to import into the United States any marine mammal if such mammal was --

(1) pregnant at the time of taking;

(2) nursing at the time of taking, or less than eight months old, whichever occurs later;

(3) taken from a species or population stock which the Secretary has, by regulation published in the Federal Register, designated as a depleted species or stock; or

(4) taken in a manner deemed inhumane by the Secretary.

Notwithstanding the provisions of paragraphs (1) and (2), the Secretary may issue a permit for the importation of a marine mammal, if the Secretary determines that such importation is necessary for the protection or welfare of the animal.

(c) Importation of illegally taken mammals. It is unlawful to import into the United States any of the following:

(1) Any marine mammal which was --

(A) taken in violation of this Act; or

(B) taken in another country in violation of the law of that country.

(2) Any marine mammal product if --

(A) the importation into the United States of the marine mammal from which such product is made is unlawful under paragraph (1) of this subsection; or

(B) the sale in commerce of such product in the country of origin of the product is illegal;

(3) Any fish, whether fresh, frozen, or otherwise prepared, if such fish was caught in a manner which the Secretary has proscribed for persons subject to the jurisdiction of the United States, whether or not any marine mammals were in fact taken incident to the catching of the fish.

(d) Nonapplicability of prohibitions. Subsections (b) and (c) of this section shall not apply --

(1) in the case of marine mammals or marine mammal products, as the case may be, to which subsection (b)(3) of this section applies, to such items imported into the United States before the date on which the Secretary publishes notice in the Federal Register of his proposed rulemaking with respect to the designation of the species or stock concerned as depleted; or

(2) in the case of marine mammals or marine mammal products to which subsection (c)(1)(B) or (c)(2)(B) of this section applies, to articles imported into the United States before the effective date of the foreign law making the taking or sale, as the case may be, of such marine mammals or marine mammal products unlawful.

(e) Retroactive effect. This Act shall not apply with respect to any marine mammal taken before the effective date of this Act, or to any marine mammal product consisting of, or composed in whole or in part of, any marine mammal taken before such date.

(f) Commercial taking of whales. It is unlawful for any person or vessel or other conveyance to take any species of whale incident to commercial whaling in waters subject to the jurisdiction of the United States.

[Pub. L. 92-522, Title I, § 102, 86 Stat. 1032 (Oct. 21, 1972); Pub. L. 93- 205, § 13(e)(3), 87 Stat. 903 (Dec. 28, 1973); Pub. L. 95-136, § 4, 91 Stat. 1167 (Oct. 18, 1977); Pub. L. 97-58, § 3(a), 95 Stat. 981 (Oct. 9, 1981); Pub. L. 4763, 4769, 4771 (Nov. 23, 1988); Pub. L. 102-587, Title III, § 3004(a)(1), 106 Stat. 5067 (Nov. 4, 1992); Pub. L. 103-238, §§ 5(a), 13(c), 24(c)(9), 108 Stat. 536, 558, 566 (Apr. 30, 1994)]

16 U.S.C. § 1373. Regulations on taking of marine mammals. (a) Necessity and appropriateness. The Secretary, on the basis of the best scientific evidence available and in consultation with the Marine Mammal Commission, shall prescribe such regulations with respect to the taking and importing of animals from each species of marine mammal (including regulations on the taking and importing of individuals within population stocks) as he deems necessary and appropriate to insure that such taking will not be to the disadvantage of those species and population stocks and will be consistent with the purposes and policies set forth in section 2 of this Act [16 U.S.C. § 1361].

(b) Factors considered in prescribing regulations. In prescribing such regulations, the Secretary shall give full consideration to all factors which may affect the extent to which such animals may be taken or imported, including but not limited to the effect of such regulations on --

(1) existing and future levels of marine mammal species and population stocks;
(2) existing international treaty and agreement obligations of the United States;
(3) the marine ecosystem and related environmental considerations;
(4) the conservation, development, and utilization of fishery resources; and
(5) the economic and technological feasibility of implementation.

(c) Allowable restrictions. The regulations prescribed under subsection (a) of this section for any species or population stock of marine mammal may include, but are not limited to, restrictions with respect to --

(1) the number of animals which may be taken or imported in any calendar year pursuant to permits issued under section 104 of this Act [16 U.S.C. § 1374];

(2) the age, size, or sex (or any combination of the foregoing) of animals which may be taken or imported, whether or not a quota prescribed under paragraph (1) of this subsection applies with respect to such animals;

(3) the season or other period of time within which animals may be taken or imported;

(4) the manner and locations in which animals may be taken or imported; and
(5) fishing techniques which have been found to cause undue fatalities to any species of marine mammal in a fishery.

(d) Procedure. Regulations prescribed to carry out this section with respect to any species or stock of marine mammals must be made on the record after opportunity for an agency hearing on both the Secretary's determination to waive the moratorium pursuant to section 101(a)(3)(A) [16 U.S.C. § 1371(a)(3)(A)] and on such regulations, except that, in addition to any other requirements imposed by law with respect to agency rulemaking, the Secretary shall publish and make available to the public either before or concurrent with the publication of notice in the Federal Register of his intention to prescribe regulations under this section --

(1) a statement of the estimated existing levels of the species and population stocks of the marine mammal concerned;
(2) a statement of the expected impact of the proposed regulations on the optimum sustainable population of such species or population stock;
(3) a statement describing the evidence before the Secretary upon which he proposes to base such regulations; and
(4) any studies made by or for the Secretary or any recommendations made by or for the Secretary or the Marine Mammal Commission which relate to the establishment of such regulations.

(e) Periodic review. Any regulation prescribed pursuant to this section shall be periodically reviewed, and may be modified from time to time in such manner as the Secretary deems consistent with and necessary to carry out the purposes of this Act.

(f) Report to Congress. Within six months after the effective date of this Act and every twelve months thereafter, the Secretary shall report to the public through publication in the Federal Register and to the Congress on the current status of all marine mammal species and population stocks subject to the provisions of this Act. His report shall describe those actions taken and those measures believed necessary, including where appropriate, the issuance of permits pursuant to this Act to assure the well-being of such marine mammals.

[Pub. L. 92-522, Title I, § 103, 86 Stat. 1033 (Oct. 21 1972)]

16 U.S.C. § 1374. Permits. (a) Issuance. The Secretary may issue permits which authorize the taking or importation of any marine mammal. Permits for the incidental taking of marine mammals in the course of commercial fishing operations may only be issued as specifically provided for in sections 101(a)(5) or 306 [16 U.S.C. §§ 1371(a)(5) or 1416], or subsection (h) of this section.

(b) Requisite provisions. Any permit issued under this section shall --

(1) be consistent with any applicable regulation established by the Secretary under section 103 of this Act [16 U.S.C. § 1373], and
(2) specify --

(A) the number and kind of animals which are authorized to be taken or imported,

(B) the location and manner (which manner must be determined by the Secretary to be humane) in which they may be taken, or from which they may be imported,

(C) the period during which the permit is valid, and

(D) any other terms or conditions which the Secretary deems appropriate.

In any case in which an application for a permit cites as a reason for the proposed taking the overpopulation of a particular species or population stock, the Secretary shall first consider whether or not it would be more desirable to transplant a number of animals (but not to exceed the number requested for taking in the application) of that species or stock to a location not then inhabited by such species or stock but previously inhabited by such species or stock.

(c) Importation for scientific research, public display, or enhancing survival or recovery of species or stock. (1) Any permit issued by the Secretary which authorizes the taking or importation of a marine mammal for purposes of scientific research, public display, or enhancing the survival or recovery of a species or stock shall specify, in addition to the conditions required by subsection (b) of this section, the methods of capture, supervision, care, and transportation which must be observed pursuant to such taking or importation. Any person authorized to take or import a marine mammal for purposes of scientific research, public display, or enhancing the survival or recovery of a species or stock shall furnish to the Secretary a report on all activities carried out by him pursuant to that authority.

(2)(A) A permit may be issued to take or import a marine mammal for the purpose of public display only to a person which the Secretary determines --

(i) offers a program for education or conservation purposes that is based on professionally recognized standards of the public display community;

(ii) is registered or holds a license issued under section 2131 *et seq.* of Title 7; and

(iii) maintains facilities for the public display of marine mammals that are open to the public on a regularly scheduled basis and that access to such facilities is not limited or restricted other than by charging of an admission fee.

(B) A permit under this paragraph shall grant to the person to which it is issued the right, without obtaining any additional permit or authorization under this Act, to --

(i) take, import, purchase, offer to purchase, possess, or transport the marine mammal that is the subject of the permit; and

(ii) sell, export, or otherwise transfer possession of the marine mammal, or offer to sell, export, or otherwise transfer possession of the marine mammal --

(I) for the purpose of public display, to a person that meets the requirements of clauses (i), (ii), and (iii) of subparagraph (A);

(II) for the purpose of scientific research, to a person that meets the requirements of paragraph (3); or

(III) for the purpose of enhancing the survival or recovery of a species or stock, to a person that meets the requirements of paragraph (4).

(C) A person to which a marine mammal is sold or exported or to which possession of a marine mammal is otherwise transferred under the authority of subparagraph (B) shall have the rights and responsibilities described in subparagraph (B) with respect to the marine mammal without obtaining any additional permit or authorization under this Act. Such responsibilities shall be limited to --

(i) for the purpose of public display, the responsibility to meet the requirements of clauses (i), (ii), and (iii) of subparagraph (A),

(ii) for the purpose of scientific research, the responsibility to meet the requirements of paragraph (3), and

(iii) for the purpose of enhancing the survival or recovery of a species or stock, the responsibility to meet the requirements of paragraph (4).

(D) If the Secretary --

(i) finds in concurrence with the Secretary of Agriculture, that a person that holds a permit under this paragraph for a marine mammal, or a person exercising rights under subparagraph (C), no longer meets the requirements of subparagraph (A)(ii) and is not reasonably likely to meet those requirements in the near future, or

(ii) finds that a person that holds a permit under this paragraph for a marine mammal, or a person exercising rights under subparagraph (C), no longer meets the requirements of subparagraph (A)(i) or (iii) and is not reasonably likely to meet those requirements in the near future,

the Secretary may revoke the permit in accordance with subsection (e) of this section, seize the marine mammal, or cooperate with other persons authorized to hold marine mammals under this Act for disposition of the marine mammal. The Secretary may recover from the person expenses incurred by the Secretary for that seizure.

(E) No marine mammal held pursuant to a permit issued under subparagraph (A), or by a person exercising rights under subparagraph (C), may be sold, purchased, exported, or transported unless the Secretary is notified of such action no later than 15 days before such action, and such action is for purposes of public display, scientific research, or enhancing the survival or recovery of a species or stock. The Secretary may only require the notification to include the information required for the inventory established under paragraph (10).

(3)(A) The Secretary may issue a permit under this paragraph for scientific research purposes to an applicant which submits with its permit application information indicating that the taking is required to further a bona fide scientific purpose. The Secretary may issue a permit under this paragraph before the end of the public review and comment period required under subsection (d)(2) of this section if delaying issuance of the permit could result in injury to a species, stock, or individual, or in loss of unique research opportunities.

(B) No permit issued for purposes of scientific research shall authorize the lethal taking of a marine mammal unless the applicant demonstrates that a nonlethal method of conducting the research is not feasible. The Secretary shall not issue a permit for research which involves the lethal taking of a marine mammal from a species or stock that is depleted, unless the Secretary determines that the results of such research will directly benefit that species or stock, or that such research fulfills a critically important research need.

(C) Not later than 120 days after April 30, 1994, the Secretary shall issue a general authorization and implementing regulations allowing bona fide scientific research that may result only in taking by Level B harassment of a marine mammal. Such authorization shall apply to persons which submit, by 60 days before commencement of such research, a letter of intent via certified mail to the Secretary containing the following:

(i) The species or stocks of marine mammals which may be harassed.

(ii) The geographic location of the research.

(iii) The period of time over which the research will be conducted.

(iv) The purpose of the research, including a description of how the definition of bona fide research as established under this Act would apply.

(v) Methods to be used to conduct the research.

Not later than 30 days after receipt of a letter of intent to conduct scientific research under the general authorization, the Secretary shall issue a letter to the applicant confirming that the general authorization applies, or, if the proposed research is likely to result in the taking (including Level A harassment) of a marine mammal, shall notify the applicant that subparagraph (A) applies.

(4)(A) A permit may be issued for enhancing the survival or recovery of a species or stock only with respect to a species or stock for which the Secretary, after consultation with the Marine Mammal Commission and after notice and opportunity for public comment, has first determined that --

(i) taking or importation is likely to contribute significantly to maintaining or increasing distribution or numbers necessary to ensure the survival or recovery of the species or stock; and

(ii) taking or importation is consistent (I) with any conservation plan adopted by the Secretary under section 115(b) of this Act [16 U.S.C. § 1383b(b)] or any recovery plan developed under section 4(f) of the Endangered Species Act of 1973 [16 U.S.C. § 1533(f)] for the species or stock, or (II) if there is no conservation or recovery plan in place, with the Secretary's evaluation of the actions required to enhance the survival or recovery of the species or stock in light of the factors that would be addressed in a conservation plan or a recovery plan.

(B) A permit issued in accordance with this paragraph may allow the captive maintenance of a marine mammal from a depleted species or stock only if the Secretary --

(i) determines that captive maintenance is likely to contribute to the survival or recovery of the species or stock by maintaining a viable gene pool, increasing productivity, providing biological information, or establishing animal reserves;

(ii) determines that the expected benefit to the affected species or stock outweighs the expected benefit of alternatives which do not require removal of animals from the wild; and

(iii) requires that the marine mammal or its progeny be returned to the natural habitat of the species or stock as soon as feasible, consistent with the objectives of any applicable conservation plan or recovery plan, or of any evaluation by the Secretary under subparagraph (A).

The Secretary may allow the public display of such a marine mammal only if the Secretary determines that such display is incidental to the authorized maintenance and will not interfere with the attainment of the survival or recovery objectives.

(5)(A) The Secretary may issue a permit for the importation of polar bear parts (other than internal organs) taken in sport hunts in Canada to an applicant which submits with its permit application proof that the polar bear was legally harvested in Canada by the applicant. Such a permit shall be issued if the Secretary, in consultation with the Marine Mammal Commission and after notice and opportunity for public comment, finds that --

(i) Canada has a monitored and enforced sport hunting program consistent with the purposes of the Agreement on the Conservation of Polar Bears;

(ii) Canada has a sport hunting program based on scientifically sound quotas ensuring the maintenance of the affected population stock at a sustainable level;

(iii) the export and subsequent import are consistent with the provisions of the Convention on International Trade in Endangered Species of Wild Fauna and Flora and other international agreements and conventions; and

(iv) the export and subsequent import are not likely to contribute to illegal trade in bear parts.

(B) The Secretary shall establish and charge a reasonable fee for permits issued under this paragraph. All fees collected under this paragraph shall be available to the Secretary until expended for use in developing and implementing cooperative research and management programs for the conservation of polar bears in Alaska and Russia pursuant to section 113(d) [16 U.S.C. § 1383(d)].

(C)(i) The Secretary shall undertake a scientific review of the impact of permits issued under this paragraph on the polar bear population stocks in Canada within 2 years after April 30, 1994. The Secretary shall provide an opportunity for public comment during the course of such review, and shall include a response to such public comment in the final report on such review.

(ii) The Secretary shall not issue permits under this paragraph after September 30, 1996, if the Secretary determines, based on the scientific review, that the issuance of permits under this paragraph is having a significant adverse impact on the polar bear population stocks in Canada. The Secretary may review such determination annually thereafter, in light of the best scientific information available, and shall complete the review not later than January 31 in any year a review is undertaken. The Secretary may issue permits under this paragraph whenever the Secretary determines, on the basis of such annual review, that the issuance of permits under this paragraph is not having a significant adverse impact on the polar bear population stocks in Canada.

(D) The Secretary of the Interior shall, expeditiously after the expiration of the applicable 30 day period under subsection (d)(2) of this section, issue a permit for the importation of polar bear parts (other than internal organs) from polar bears taken in sport hunts in Canada before April 30, 1994, to each applicant who submits, with the permit application, proof that the polar bear was legally harvested in Canada by the applicant. The Secretary shall issue such permits without regard to the provisions of subparagraphs (A) and (C)(ii) of this paragraph, subsection (d)(3) of this section, and sections 101 and 102 [16 U.S.C. §§ 1371 and 1372]. This subparagraph shall not apply to polar bear parts that were imported before June 12, 1997.

(6) A permit may be issued for photography for educational or commercial purposes involving marine mammals in the wild only to an applicant which submits with its permit application information indicating that the taking will be limited to Level B harassment, and the manner in which the products of such activities will be made available to the public.

(7) Upon request by a person for a permit under paragraph (2), (3), or (4) for a marine mammal which is in the possession of any person authorized to possess it under this Act and which is determined under guidance under section 402(a) [16 U.S.C. § 1421(a)] not to be releasable to the wild, the Secretary shall issue the permit to the person requesting the permit if that person --

(A) meets the requirements of clauses (i), (ii), and (iii) of paragraph (2)(A), in the case of a request for a permit under paragraph (2);

(B) meets the requirements of paragraph (3), in the case of a request for a permit under that paragraph; or

(C) meets the requirements of paragraph (4), in the case of a request for a permit under that paragraph.

(8)(A) No additional permit or authorization shall be required to possess, sell, purchase, transport, export, or offer to sell or purchase the progeny of marine mammals taken or imported under this subsection, if such possession, sale, purchase, transport, export, or offer to sell or purchase is --

(i) for the purpose of public display, and by or to, respectively, a person which meets the requirements of clauses (i), (ii), and (iii) of paragraph (2)(A);

(ii) for the purpose of scientific research, and by or to, respectively, a person which meets the requirements of paragraph (3); or

(iii) for the purpose of enhancing the survival or recovery of a species or stock, and by or to, respectively, a person which meets the requirements of paragraph (4).

(B)(i) A person which has a permit under paragraph (2), or a person exercising rights under paragraph (2)(C), which has possession of a marine mammal that gives birth to progeny shall --

(I) notify the Secretary of the birth of such progeny within 30 days after the date of birth; and

(II) notify the Secretary of the sale, purchase, or transport of such progeny no later than 15 days before such action.

(ii) The Secretary may only require notification under clause (i) to include the information required for the inventory established under paragraph (10).

(C) Any progeny of a marine mammal born in captivity before April 30, 1994, and held in captivity for the purpose of public display shall be treated as though born after April 30, 1994.

(9) No marine mammal may be exported for the purpose of public display, scientific research, or enhancing the survival or recovery of a species or stock unless the receiving facility meets standards that are comparable to the requirements that a person must meet to receive a permit under this subsection for that purpose.

(10) The Secretary shall establish and maintain an inventory of all marine mammals possessed pursuant to permits issued under paragraph (2)(A), by persons exercising rights under paragraph (2)(C), and all progeny of such marine mammals. The inventory shall contain, for each marine mammal, only the following information which shall be provided by a person holding a marine mammal under this Act:

(A) The name of the marine mammal or other identification.

(B) The sex of the marine mammal.

(C) The estimated or actual birth date of the marine mammal.

(D) The date of acquisition or disposition of the marine mammal by the permit holder.

(E) The source from whom the marine mammal was acquired including the location of the take from the wild, if applicable.

(F) If the marine mammal is transferred, the name of the recipient.

(G) A notation if the animal was acquired as the result of a stranding.

(H) The date of death of the marine mammal and the cause of death when determined.

(d) Application procedures; notice; hearing; review. (1) The Secretary shall prescribe such procedures as are necessary to carry out this section, including the form and manner in which application for permits may be made.

(2) The Secretary shall publish notice in the Federal Register of each application made for a permit under this section. Such notice shall invite the submission from interested parties, within thirty days after the date of the notice, of written data or views, with respect to the taking or importation proposed in such application.

(3) The applicant for any permit under this section must demonstrate to the Secretary that the taking or importation of any marine mammal under such permit will be consistent with the purposes of this Act and the applicable regulations established under section 103 of this Act [16 U.S.C. § 1373].

(4) If within thirty days after the date of publication of notice pursuant to paragraph (2) of this subsection with respect to any application for a permit any interested party or parties request a hearing in connection therewith, the Secretary may, within sixty days following such date of publication, afford to such party or parties an opportunity for such a hearing.

(5) As soon as practicable (but not later than thirty days) after the close of the hearing or, if no hearing is held, after the last day on which data, or views, may be submitted pursuant to paragraph (2) of this subsection, the Secretary shall (A) issue a permit containing such terms and conditions as he deems appropriate, or (B) shall deny issuance of a permit. Notice of the decision of the Secretary to issue or to deny

any permit under this paragraph must be published in the Federal Register within ten days after the date of issuance or denial.

(6) Any applicant for a permit, or any party opposed to such permit, may obtain judicial review of the terms and conditions of any permit issued by the Secretary under this section or of his refusal to issue such a permit. Such review, which shall be pursuant to chapter 7 of Title 5, may be initiated by filing a petition for review in the United States district court for the district wherein the applicant for a permit resides, or has his principal place of business, or in the United States District Court for the District of Columbia, within sixty days after the date on which such permit is issued or denied.

(e) Modification, suspension, and revocation. (1) The Secretary may modify, suspend, or revoke in whole or part any permit issued by him under this section --

(A) in order to make any such permit consistent with any change made after the date of issuance of such permit with respect to any applicable regulation prescribed under section 103 of this Act [16 U.S.C. § 1373],

(B) in any case in which a violation of the terms and conditions of the permit is found, or

(C) if, in the case of a permit under subsection (c)(5) of this section authorizing importation of polar bear parts, the Secretary, in consultation with the appropriate authority in Canada, determines that the sustainability of Canada's polar bear population stocks are being adversely affected or that sport hunting may be having a detrimental effect on maintaining polar bear population stocks throughout their range.

(2) Whenever the Secretary shall propose any modification, suspension, or revocation of a permit under this subsection, the permittee shall be afforded opportunity, after due notice, for a hearing by the Secretary with respect to such proposed modification, suspension, or revocation. Such proposed action by the Secretary shall not take effect until a decision is issued by him after such hearing. Any action taken by the Secretary after such a hearing is subject to judicial review on the same basis as is any action taken by him with respect to a permit application under paragraph (5) of subsection (d) of this section.

(3) Notice of the modification, suspension, or revocation of any permit by the Secretary shall be published in the Federal Register within ten days from the date of the Secretary's decision.

(f) Possession of permit by issuee or his agent. Any permit issued under this section must be in the possession of the person to whom it is issued (or an agent of such person) during --

(1) the time of the authorized or taking importation;

(2) the period of any transit of such person or agent which is incident to such taking or importation; and

(3) any other time while any marine mammal taken or imported under such permit is in the possession of such person or agent.

A duplicate copy of the issued permit must be physically attached to the container, package, enclosure, or other means of containment, in which the marine mammal is placed for purposes of storage, transit, supervision, or care.

(g) Fees. The Secretary shall establish and charge a reasonable fee for permits issued under this section.

(h) General permits. (1) Consistent with the regulations prescribed pursuant to section 103 of this Act [16 U.S.C. § 1373] and to the requirements of section 101 of this Act [16 U.S.C. § 1371], the Secretary may issue an annual permit to a United States purse seine fishing vessel for the taking of such marine mammals, and shall issue regulations to cover the use of any such annual permits.

(2) Such annual permits for the incidental taking of marine mammals in the course of commercial purse seine fishing for yellowfin tuna in the eastern tropical Pacific Ocean shall be governed by section 306 [16 U.S.C. § 1416], subject to the regulations issued pursuant to section 303 [16 U.S.C. § 1413].

[Pub. L. 92-522, Title I, § 104, 86 Stat. 1034 (Oct. 21, 1972); Pub. L. 98- 364, Title I, § 102, 98 Stat. 440 (July 17, 1984); Pub. L. 100-711, §§ 4(d), 5(d), 102 Stat. 4767, 4769 (Nov. 23, 1988); Pub. L. 103-238, § 5(b), 108 Stat. 537 (Apr. 30, 1994); Pub. L. 105-18, Title II, § 5004, 111 Stat. 187 (June 12, 1997); Pub. L. 105-42, § 4(d), 111 Stat. 1125 (Aug. 15, 1997); Pub. L. 105-277, Div. A, § 101(e) [Title I], 112 Stat. 2681-238 (Oct. 21, 1998); Pub. L. 106-31, Title V, § 5004(1), 16 Stat. 110 (May 21, 1999)]

16 U.S.C. § 1375. Penalties. (a)(1) Any person who violates any provision of this Act or of any permit or regulation issued thereunder, except as provided in section 118 [16 U.S.C. § 1387], may be assessed a civil penalty by the Secretary of not more than $10,000 for each such violation. No penalty shall be assessed unless such person is given notice and opportunity for a hearing with respect to such violation. Each unlawful taking or importation shall be a separate offense. Any such civil penalty may be remitted or mitigated by the Secretary for good cause shown. Upon any failure to pay a penalty assessed under this subsection, the Secretary may request the Attorney General to institute a civil action in a district court of the United States for any district in which such person is found, resides, or transacts business to collect the penalty and such court shall have jurisdiction to hear and decide any such action.

(2) In any case involving an alleged unlawful importation of a marine mammal or marine mammal product, if such importation is made by an individual for his own personal or family use (which does not include importation as an accommodation to others or for sale or other commercial use), the Secretary may, in lieu of instituting a proceeding under paragraph (1), allow the individual to abandon the mammal or product, under procedures to be prescribed by the Secretary, to the enforcement officer at the port of entry.

(b) Any person who knowingly violates any provision of this Act or of any permit or regulation issued thereunder (except as provided in section 118 [16 U.S.C. § 1387]) shall, upon conviction, be fined not more than $20,000 for each such violation, or imprisoned for not more than one year, or both.

[Pub. L. 92-522, Title I, § 105, 86 Stat. 1036 (Oct. 21, 1972); Pub. L. 97-58, § 3(b), 95 Stat. 982 (Oct. 9, 1981); Pub. L. 103-238, § 13(a), (b), 108 Stat. 558 (Apr. 30, 1994)]

16 U.S.C. § 1375a. Disposition of fines. Hereafter, all fines collected by the United States Fish and Wildlife Service for violations of the Marine Mammal Protection Act (16

U.S.C. §§ 1362 to 1407) and implementing regulations shall be available to the Secretary, without further appropriation, to be used for the expenses of the United States Fish and Wildlife Service in administering activities for the protection and recovery of manatees, polar bears, sea otters, and walruses, and shall remain available until expended.

[Pub. L. 106-113, Div. B, § 1000(a)(3) [Title I], 113 Stat. 1535, 1501A-139 (Nov. 29, 1999)]

16 U.S.C. § 1376. Seizure and forfeiture of cargo. (a) Application of consistent provisions. Any vessel or other conveyance subject to the jurisdiction of the United States that is employed in any manner in the unlawful taking of any marine mammal shall have its entire cargo or the monetary value thereof subject to seizure and forfeiture. All provisions of law relating to the seizure, judicial forfeiture, and condemnation of cargo for violation of the customs laws, the disposition of such cargo, and the proceeds from the sale thereof, and the remission or mitigation of any such forfeiture, shall apply with respect to the cargo of any vessel or other conveyance seized in connection with the unlawful taking of a marine mammal insofar as such provisions of law are applicable and not inconsistent with the provisions of this Act.

(b) Penalties. Any vessel subject to the jurisdiction of the United States that is employed in any manner in the unlawful taking of any marine mammal shall be liable for a civil penalty of not more than $25,000. Such penalty shall be assessed by the district court of the United States having jurisdiction over the vessel. Clearance of a vessel against which a penalty has been assessed, from a port of the United States, may be withheld until such penalty is paid, or until a bond or otherwise satisfactory surety is posted. Such penalty shall constitute a maritime lien on such vessel which may be recovered by action in rem in the district court of the United States having jurisdiction over the vessel.

(c) Reward for information leading to conviction. Upon the recommendation of the Secretary, the Secretary of the Treasury is authorized to pay an amount equal to one-half of the fine incurred but not to exceed $2,500 to any person who furnishes information which leads to a conviction for a violation of this Act. Any officer or employee of the United States or of any State or local government who furnishes information or renders service in the performance of his official duties shall not be eligible for payment under this section.

[Pub. L. 92-522, Title I, § 106, 86 Stat. 1036 (Oct. 21, 1972)]

16 U.S.C. § 1377. Enforcement. (a) Utilization of personnel. Except as otherwise provided in this Act, the Secretary shall enforce the provisions of this Act. The Secretary may utilize, by agreement, the personnel, services, and facilities of any other Federal agency for purposes of enforcing this Act.

(b) State officers and employees. The Secretary may also designate officers and employees of any State or of any possession of the United States to enforce the provisions of this Act. When so designated, such officers and employees are authorized to function as Federal law enforcement agents for these purposes, but they shall not be held and considered as employees of the United States for the purposes of any laws administered by the Director of the Office of Personnel Management.

(c) Warrants and other process for enforcement. The judges of the district courts of the United States and the United States magistrates may, within their respective jurisdictions, upon proper oath or affirmation showing probably cause, issue such warrants or other process, including warrants or other process issued in admiralty proceedings in United States district courts, as may be required for enforcement of this Act and any regulations issued thereunder.

(d) Execution of process; arrest; search; seizure. Any person authorized by the Secretary to enforce this Act may execute any warrant or process issued by any officer or court of competent jurisdiction for the enforcement of this Act. Such person so authorized may, in addition to any other authority conferred by law --

(1) with or without warrant or other process, arrest any person committing in his presence or view a violation of this Act or the regulations issued thereunder;

(2) with a warrant or other process, or without a warrant if he has reasonable cause to believe that a vessel or other conveyance subject to the jurisdiction of the United States or any person on board is in violation of any provision of this Act or the regulations issued thereunder, search such vessel or conveyance and arrest such person;

(3) seize the cargo of any vessel or other conveyance subject to the jurisdiction of the United States used or employed contrary to the provisions of this Act or the regulations issued hereunder or which reasonably appears to have been so used or employed; and

(4) seize, whenever and wherever found, all marine mammals and marine mammal products taken or retained in violation of this Act or the regulations issued thereunder and shall dispose of them in accordance with regulations prescribed by the Secretary.

(e) Disposition of seized cargo. (1) Whenever any cargo or marine mammal or marine mammal product is seized pursuant to this section, the Secretary shall expedite any proceedings commenced under section 105(a) or (b) of this Act [16 U.S.C. § 1375(a) or (b)]. All marine mammals or marine mammal products or other cargo so seized shall be held by any person authorized by the Secretary pending disposition of such proceedings. The owner or consignee of any such marine mammal or marine mammal product or other cargo so seized shall, as soon as practicable following such seizure, be notified of that fact in accordance with regulations established by the Secretary.

(2) The Secretary may, with respect to any proceeding under section 105(a) or (b) of this Act [16 U.S.C. § 1375(a) or (b)], in lieu of holding any marine mammal or marine mammal product or other cargo, permit the person concerned to post bond or other surety satisfactory to the Secretary pending the disposition of such proceeding.

(3)(A) Upon the assessment of a penalty pursuant to section 105(a) of this Act [16 U.S.C. § 1375(a)], all marine mammals and marine mammal products or other cargo seized in connection therewith may be proceeded against in any court of competent jurisdiction and forfeited to the Secretary for disposition by him in such manner as he deems appropriate.

(B) Upon conviction for violation of section 105(b) of this Act [16 U.S.C. § 1375(b)], all marine mammals and marine mammal products seized in connection therewith shall be forfeited to the Secretary for disposition by him in such manner as he deems appropriate. Any other property or item so seized may, at the discretion of the court, be forfeited to the United States or otherwise disposed of.

(4) If with respect to any marine mammal or marine mammal product or other cargo so seized--

(A) a civil penalty is assessed under section 105(a) of this Act [16 U.S.C. § 1375(a)] and no judicial action is commenced to obtain the forfeiture of such mammal or product within thirty days after such assessment, such marine mammal or marine mammal product or other cargo shall be immediately returned to the owner or the consignee; or

(B) no conviction results from an alleged violation of section 105(b) of this Act [16 U.S.C. § 1375(b)], such marine mammal or marine mammal product or other cargo shall immediately be returned to the owner or consignee if the Secretary does not, with[in] thirty days after the final disposition of the case involving such alleged violation, commence proceedings for the assessment of a civil penalty under section 105(a) of this Act [16 U.S.C. § 1375(a)].

[Pub. L. 92-522, Title I, § 107, 86 Stat. 1037 (Oct. 21, 1972); 1978 Reorg. Plan No. 2, § 102 (Jan. 1, 1979), 43 Fed. Reg. 36037, 92 Stat. 3783]

16 U.S.C. 1378. International program. (a) Duties of Secretary. The Secretary, through the Secretary of State, shall --

(1) initiate negotiations as soon as possible for the development of bilateral or multilateral agreements with other nations for the protection and conservation of all marine mammals covered by this Act;

(2) initiate --

(A) negotiations as soon as possible with all foreign governments which are engaged in, or which have persons or companies engaged in, commercial fishing operations which are found by the Secretary to be unduly harmful to any species or population stock of marine mammal, for the purpose of entering into bilateral and multilateral treaties with such countries to protect marine mammals, with the Secretary of State to prepare a draft agenda relating to this matter for discussion at appropriate international meetings and forums;

(B) discussions with foreign governments whose vessels harvest yellowfin tuna with purse seines in the eastern tropical Pacific Ocean, for the purpose of concluding, through the Inter-American Tropical Tuna Commission or such other bilateral or multilateral institutions as may be appropriate, international arrangements for the conservation of marine mammals taken incidentally in the course of harvesting such tuna, which should include provisions for (i) cooperative research into alternative methods of locating and catching yellowfin tuna which do not involve the taking of marine mammals, (ii) cooperative research on the status of affected marine mammal population stocks, (iii) reliable monitoring of the number, rate, and species of marine mammals taken by vessels of harvesting nations, (iv) limitations on incidental take levels based upon the best scientific information available, and (v) the use of the best marine mammal safety techniques and equipment that are economically and technologically practicable to reduce the incidental kill and serious injury of marine mammals to insignificant levels approaching a zero mortality and serious injury rate;

(C) negotiations to revise the Convention for the Establishment of an Inter-American Tropical Tuna Commission (1 U.S.T. 230; TIAS 2044) which will incorporate --

(i) the conservation and management provisions agreed to by the nations which have signed the Declaration of Panama and in the Straddling Fish Stocks and Highly Migratory Fish Stocks Agreement, as opened for signature on December 4, 1995; and

(ii) a revised schedule of annual contributions to the expenses of the Inter-American Tropical Tuna Commission that is equitable to participating nations; and

(D) discussions with those countries participating, or likely to participate, in the International Dolphin Conservation Program, for the purpose of identifying sources of funds needed for research and other measures promoting effective protection of dolphins, other marine species, and the marine ecosystem;

(3) encourage such other agreements to promote the purposes of this Act with other nations for the protection of specific ocean and land regions which are of special significance to the health and stability of marine mammals;

(4) initiate the amendment of any existing international treaty for the protection and conservation of any species of marine mammal to which the United States is a party in order to make such treaty consistent with the purposes and policies of this Act;

(5) seek the convening of an international ministerial meeting on marine mammals before July 1, 1973, for the purposes of (A) the negotiation of a binding international convention for the protection and conservation of all marine mammals, and (B) the implementation of paragraph (3) of this section; and

(6) provide to the Congress by not later than one year after October 21, 1972 a full report on the results of his efforts under this section.

(b) Consultations and studies concerning North Pacific fur seals. (1) In addition to the foregoing, the Secretary shall --

(A) in consultation with the Marine Mammal Commission established by section 201 of this Act [16 U.S.C. § 1401], undertake a study of the North Pacific fur seals to determine whether herds of such seals subject to the jurisdiction of the United States are presently at their optimum sustainable population and what population trends are evident; and

(B) in consultation with the Secretary of State, promptly undertake a comprehensive study of the provisions of this Act, as they relate to North Pacific fur seals, and the provisions of the North Pacific Fur Seal Convention signed on February 9, 1957, as extended (hereafter referred to in this subsection as the "Convention"), to determine what modifications, if any, should be made to the provisions of the Convention, or of this Act, or both, to make the Convention and this Act consistent with each other.

The Secretary shall complete the studies required under this paragraph not later than one year after October 21, 1972 and shall immediately provide copies thereof to Congress.

(2) If the Secretary finds --

(A) as a result of the study required under paragraph (1)(A) of this subsection, that the North Pacific fur seal herds are below their optimum sustainable population and are not trending upward toward such level, or have reached their optimum sustainable population but are commencing a downward trend, and believes the herds to be in danger of depletion; or

(B) as a result of the study required under paragraph (1)(B) of this subsection, that modifications of the Convention are desirable to make it and this Act consistent;

he shall, through the Secretary of State, immediately initiate negotiations to modify the Convention so as to (i) reduce or halt the taking of seals to the extent required to assure that such herds attain and remain at their optimum sustainable population, or (ii) make the Convention and this Act consistent; or both, as the case may be. If negotiations to so modify the Convention are unsuccessful, the Secretary shall, through the Secretary of State, take such steps as may be necessary to continue the existing Convention beyond its present termination date so as to continue to protect and conserve the North Pacific fur seals and to prevent a return to pelagic sealing.

(c) Description of annual results of discussions; proposals for further action. The Secretary shall include a description of the annual results of discussions initiated and conducted pursuant to subsection (a)(2)(B) of this section, as well as any proposals for further action to achieve the purposes of that subsection, in the report required under section 103(f) of this Act [16 U.S.C. § 1373(f)].

[Pub. L. 92-522, Title I, § 108, 86 Stat. 1038 (Oct. 21, 1972); Pub. L. 100-711, § 4(b), (c), 102 Stat. 4766, 4767 (Nov. 23, 1988); Pub. L. 105-42, § 4(e), 111 Stat. 1125 (Aug. 15, 1997)]

16 U.S.C. § 1379. Transfer of management authority. (a) State enforcement of State laws or regulations prohibited without transfer to State of management authority by Secretary. No State may enforce, or attempt to enforce, any State law or regulation relating to the taking of any species (which term for purposes of this section includes any population stock) of marine mammal within the State unless the Secretary has transferred authority for the conservation and management of that species (hereinafter referred to in this section as "management authority") to the State under subsection (b)(1) of this section.

(b) Findings prerequisite to transfer of authority; State program; implementation.

(1) Subject to paragraph (2) and subsection (f) of this section, the Secretary shall transfer management authority for a species of marine mammal to a State if the Secretary finds, after notice and opportunity for public comment, that the State has developed and will implement a program for the conservation and management of the species that --

(A) is consistent with the purposes, policies, and goals of this Act and with international treaty obligations;

(B) requires that all taking of the species be humane;

(C) does not permit the taking of the species unless and until --

(i) the State has determined, under a process consistent with the standards set forth in subsection (c) of this section --

(I) that the species is at its optimum sustainable population (hereinafter in this section referred to as "OSP"), and

(II) the maximum number of animals of that species that may be taken without reducing the species below its OSP, and

(ii) the determination required under clause (i) is final and implemented under State law, and, if a cooperative allocation agreement for the species is required under subsection (d)(1) of this section, such an agreement is implemented;

(D) does not permit the taking of a number of animals of the species that exceeds the maximum number determined pursuant to subparagraph (C)(i)(II), and, in the case of taking for subsistence uses (as defined in subsection (f)(2) of this section), does not permit the taking of a number of animals that would be inconsistent with the maintenance of the species at its OSP;

(E) does not permit the taking of the species for scientific research, public display, or enhancing the survival or recovery of a species or stock, except for taking for such purposes that is undertaken by, or on behalf of, the State;

(F) provides procedures for acquiring data, and evaluating such data and other new evidence, relating to the OSP of the species, and the maximum take that would maintain the species at that level, and, if required on the basis of such evaluation, for amending determinations under subparagraph (C)(i);

(G) provides procedures for the resolution of differences between the State and the Secretary that might arise during the development of a cooperative allocation agreement under subsection (d)(1) of this section; and

(H) provides for the submission of an annual report to the Secretary regarding the administration of the program during the reporting period.

(2) During the period between the transfer of management authority for a species to a State under paragraph (1) and the time at which the implementation requirements under paragraph (1)(C)(ii) are complied with --

(A) the State program shall not apply with respect to the taking of the species within the State for any purpose, or under any condition, provided for under section 101 [16 U.S.C. § 1371]; and

(B) the Secretary shall continue to regulate, under this Act, all takings of the species within the State.

(3) After the determination required under paragraph (1)(C)(i) regarding a species is final and implemented under State law and after a cooperative allocation agreement described in subsection (d)(1) of this section, if required, is implemented for such species --

(A) such determination shall be treated, for purposes of applying this Act beyond the territory of the State, as a determination made in accordance with section 103 [16 U.S.C. § 1373] and as an applicable waiver under section 101(a)(3) [16 U.S.C. § 1371(a)(3)];

(B) the Secretary shall regulate, without regard to this section other than the allocations specified under such an agreement, the taking of the species --

(i) incidentally in the course of commercial fishing operations (whether provided for under section 101(a)(2) or (4) [16 U.S.C. § 1371(a)(2) or (4)]), or in the course of other specified activities provided for under section 101(a)(5) [16 U.S.C. § 1371(a)(5)], in the zone described in section

3(14)(B) [16 U.S.C. § 1362(14)(B)], and

(ii) for scientific research, public display, or enhancing the survival or recovery of a species or stock (other than by, or on behalf of, the State), except that any taking authorized under a permit issued pursuant to section 101(a)(1) [16 U.S.C. § 1371(a)(1)] after October 9, 1981 allowing the removal of live animals from habitat within the State shall not be effective if the State agency disapproves, on or before the date of issuance of the permit, such taking as being inconsistent with the State program; and

(C) section 101(b) [16 U.S.C. § 1371(b)] shall not apply.

(c) Standards with which State process must comply. The State process required under subsection (b)(1)(C) of this section must comply with the following standards:

(1) The State agency with management authority for the species (hereinafter in this section referred to as the "State agency") must make an initial determination regarding the factors described in clause (i) of that subsection. The State agency must identify, and make available to the public under reasonable circumstances, the documentation supporting such initial determination. Unless request for a hearing under paragraph (2) regarding the initial determination is timely made, the initial determination shall be treated as final under State law.

(2) The State agency shall provide opportunity, at the request of any interested party, for a hearing with respect to the initial determination made by it under paragraph (1) at which interested parties may --

(A) present oral and written evidence in support of or against such determination; and

(B) cross-examine persons presenting evidence at the hearing.

The State agency must give public notice of the hearing and make available to the public within a reasonable time before commencing the hearing a list of the witnesses for the State and a general description of the documentation and other evidence that will be relied upon by such witnesses.

(3) The State agency, solely on the basis of the record developed at a hearing held pursuant to paragraph (2), must make a decision regarding its initial determination under paragraph (1) and shall include with the record a statement of the findings and conclusions, and the reason or basis therefor, on all material issues.

(4) Opportunity for judicial review of the decision made by the State agency on the record under paragraph (3), under scope of review equivalent to that provided for in section 706(2)(A) through (E) of Title 5, must be available under State law. The Secretary may not initiate judicial review of any such decision.

(d) Cooperative allocation agreements. (1) If the range of a species with respect to which a determination under paragraph (1)(C)(i) of subsection (b) of this section is made extends beyond the territorial waters of the State, the State agency and the Secretary (who shall first coordinate with the Marine Mammal Commission and the appropriate Regional Fishery Management Council established under section 302 of the Act of April 13, 1976 [16 U.S.C. § 1852]) shall enter into a cooperative allocation agreement providing procedures for allocating, on a timely basis, such of the number of animals, as determined under paragraph (1)(C)(i)(II) of subsection (b) of this section, as may be appropriate with priority of allocation being given firstly to taking for subsistence uses in the case of the State of Alaska, and secondly to taking for purposes provided for under section 101(a) [16 U.S.C. § 1371(a)] within the zone described in section 3(14)(B) [16 U.S.C. § 1362(14)(B)].

(2) If the State agency requests the Secretary to regulate the taking of a species to which paragraph (1) applies within the zone described in section 3(14)(B) [16 U.S.C. § 1362(14)(B)] for subsistence uses or for hunting, or both, in a manner consistent with the regulation by the State agency of such taking within the State, the Secretary shall adopt, and enforce within such zone, such of the State agency's regulatory provisions as the Secretary considers to be consistent with his administration of section 101(a) [16 U.S.C. § 1371(a)] within such zone. The Secretary shall adopt such provisions through the issuance of regulations under section 553 of title 5, and with respect to such issuance the Regulatory Flexibility Act [5 U.S.C. § 601 *et seq.*], the Paperwork Reduction Act [44 U.S.C. § 3501 *et seq.*], Executive Order Numbered 12291, dated February 17, 1981, and the thirty-day notice requirement in subsection (d) of such section 553 shall not apply. For purposes of sections 105, 106, and 107 [16 U.S.C. §§ 1375, 1376, and 1377], such regulations shall be treated as having been issued under this Act.

(e) Revocation of transfer of management authority. (1) Subject to paragraph (2), the Secretary shall revoke, after opportunity for a hearing, any transfer of management authority made to a State under subsection (b)(1) of this section if the Secretary finds that the State program for the conservation and management of the species concerned is not being implemented, or is being implemented in a manner inconsistent with the provisions of this section or the provisions of the program. The Secretary shall also establish a procedure for the voluntary return by a State to the Secretary of species management authority that was previously transferred to the State under subsection (b) (1) of this section.

(2)(A) The Secretary may not revoke a transfer of management authority under paragraph (1) unless --

(i) the Secretary provides to the State a written notice of intent to revoke together with a statement, in detail, of those actions, or failures to act, on which such intent is based; and

(ii) during the ninety-day period after the date of the notice of intent to revoke --

(I) the Secretary provides opportunity for consultation between him and the State concerning such State actions or failures to act and the remedial measures that should be taken by the State, and

(II) the State does not take such remedial measures as are necessary, in the judgment of the Secretary, to bring its conservation and management program, or the administration or enforcement of the program, into compliance with the provisions of this section.

(B) When a revocation by the Secretary of a transfer of management authority to a State becomes final, or the State voluntarily returns management authority to the Secretary, the Secretary shall regulate the taking, and provide for the conservation and management, of the species within the State in accordance with the provisions of this Act (and in the case of Alaskan Natives, section

101(b) [16 U.S.C. § 1371(b)] and subsection (i) of this section shall apply upon such revocation or return of management authority).

(f) Transfer of management authority to State of Alaska. (1) The Secretary may not transfer management authority to the State of Alaska under subsection (b)(1) of this section for any species of marine mammal unless --

(A) the State has adopted and will implement a statute and regulations that insure that the taking of the species for subsistence uses --

(i) is accomplished in a nonwasteful manner,

(ii) will be the priority consumptive use of the species, and

(iii) if required to be restricted, such restriction will be based upon --

(I) the customary and direct dependence upon the species as the mainstay of livelihood,

(II) local residency, and

(III) the availability of alternative resources; and

(B) the State has adopted a statute or regulation that requires that any consumptive use of marine mammal species, other than for subsistence uses, will be authorized during a regulatory year only if the appropriate agency first makes findings, based on an administrative record before it, that --

(i) such use will have no significant adverse impact upon subsistence uses of the species, and

(ii) the regulation of such use, including, but not limited to, licensing of marine mammal hunting guides and the assignment of guiding areas, will, to the maximum extent practicable, provide economic opportunities for the residents of the rural coastal villages of Alaska who engage in subsistence uses of that species.

(2) For purposes of paragraph (1), the term "subsistence uses" means the customary and traditional uses by rural Alaska residents of marine mammals for direct personal or family consumption as food, shelter, fuel, clothing, tools, or transportation; for the making and selling of handicraft articles out of nonedible byproducts of marine mammals taken for personal or family consumption; and for barter, or sharing for personal or family consumption. As used in this paragraph --

(A) The term "family" means all persons related by blood, marriage, or adoption, or any person living within a household on a permanent basis.

(B) The term "barter" means the exchange of marine mammals or their parts, taken for subsistence uses --

(i) for other wildlife or fish or their parts, or

(ii) for other food or for nonedible items other than money if the exchange is of a limited and noncommercial nature.

(g) Environmental impact statement not required. Neither the transfer of management authority to a State under subsection (b)(1) of this section, nor the revocation or voluntary return of such authority under subsection (e) of this section, shall be deemed to be an action for which an environmental impact statement is required under section 102 of the National Environmental Policy Act of 1969 [42 U.S.C. § 4332].

(h) Taking of marine mammals as part of official duties. (1) Nothing in this Act or title

IV of this Act shall prevent a Federal, State, or local government official or employee or a person designated under section 112(c) [16 U.S.C. § 1382(c)] from taking, in the course of his or her duties as an official, employee, or designee, a marine mammal in a humane manner (including euthanasia) if such taking is for --

(A) the protection or welfare of the mammal,

(B) the protection of the public health and welfare, or

(C) the nonlethal removal of nuisance animals.

(2) Nothing in this Act shall prevent the Secretary or a person designated under section 112(c) [16 U.S.C. § 1382(c)] from importing a marine mammal into the United States if such importation is necessary to render medical treatment that is not otherwise available.

(3) In any case in which it is feasible to return to its natural habitat a marine mammal taken or imported under circumstances described in this subsection, steps to achieve that result shall be taken.

(i) Regulations covering taking of marine mammals by Alaskan natives. The Secretary may (after providing notice thereof in the Federal Register and in newspapers of general circulation, and through appropriate electronic media, in the affected area and providing opportunity for a hearing thereon in such area) prescribe regulations requiring the marking, tagging, and reporting of animals taken pursuant to section 101(b) [16 U.S.C. § 1371(b)].

(j) Grants to develop or administer State conservation and management programs. The Secretary may make grants to States to assist them --

(1) in developing programs, to be submitted for approval under subsection (b) of this section, for the conservation and management of species of marine mammals; and

(2) in administering such programs if management authority for such species is transferred to the State under such subsection.

Grants made under this subsection may not exceed 50 per centum of the costs of developing a State program before Secretarial approval, or of administering the program thereafter.

(k) Delegation of administration and enforcement to States. The Secretary is authorized and directed to enter into cooperative arrangements with the appropriate officials of any State for the delegation to such State of the administration and enforcement of this Act: *Provided,* That any such arrangement shall contain such provisions as the Secretary deems appropriate to insure that the purposes and policies of this Act will be carried out.

(l) Authorization of appropriations. ****

[Pub. L. 92-522, Title I, § 109, 86 Stat. 1040 (Oct. 21, 1972); Pub. L. 95- 316, § 1, July 10, 1978, 92 Stat. 380; Pub. L. 97-58, § 4(a), 95 Stat. 982 (Oct. 9, 1981); Pub. L. 100-711, § 5(a), (e)(3), 102 Stat. 4769, 4771 (Nov. 23, 1988); Pub. L. 102-587, Title III, § 3004(a)(2), 106 Stat. 5067 (Nov. 4, 1992); Pub. L. 103-238, § 24(c)(10), 108 Stat. 566 (Apr. 30, 1994)]

16 U.S.C. § 1380. Marine mammal research grants. ****

16 U.S.C. § 1381. Commercial fisheries gear development. ****

(b) Reduction of level of taking of marine mammals incidental to commercial fishing operations. The Secretary, after consultation with the Marine Mammal Commission, is authorized and directed to issue, as soon as practicable, such regulations, covering the twenty-four-month period referred to in section 101(a)(2) of this Act [16 U.S.C. § 1371(a)(2)], as he deems necessary or advisable, to reduce to the lowest practicable level the taking of marine mammals incidental to commercial fishing operations. Such regulations shall be adopted pursuant to section 553 of Title 5....

(c) Reduction of level of taking of marine mammals in tuna fishery. Additionally, the Secretary and Secretary of State are directed to commence negotiations within the Inter-American Tropical Tuna Commission in order to effect essential compliance with the regulatory provisions of this Act so as to reduce to the maximum extent feasible the incidental taking of marine mammals by vessels involved in the tuna fishery. The Secretary and Secretary of State are further directed to request the Director of Investigations of the Inter-American Tropical Tuna Commission to make recommendations to all member nations of the Commission as soon as is practicable as to the utilization of methods and gear devised under subsection (a) of this section.

****

[Pub. L. 92-522, Title I, § 111, 86 Stat. 1041 (Oct. 21, 1972)]

16 U.S.C. § 1382. Regulations and administration. ****

(e) Measures to alleviate impacts on strategic stocks. If the Secretary determines, based on a stock assessment under section 117 [16 U.S.C. § 1386] or other significant new information obtained under this Act, that impacts on rookeries, mating grounds, or other areas of similar ecological significance to marine mammals may be causing the decline or impeding the recovery of a strategic stock, the Secretary may develop and implement conservation or management measures to alleviate those impacts. Such measures shall be developed and implemented after consultation with the Marine Mammal Commission and the appropriate Federal agencies and after notice and opportunity for public comment.

[Pub. L. 92-522, Title I, § 112, 86 Stat. 1042 (Oct. 21, 1972); Pub. L. 96- 470, Title II, § 201(e), 94 Stat. 2241 (Oct. 19, 1980); Pub. L. 102-587, Title III, § 3004(a)(3), 106 Stat. 5067 (Nov. 4, 1992); Pub. L. 103-238, §§ 7(a), 24(c)(11), 108 Stat. 542, 566 (Apr. 30, 1994)]

16 U.S.C. § 1383. Application to other treaties and conventions. ****

16 U.S.C. § 1384. Authorization of appropriations. ****

16 U.S.C. § 1383b. Status review; conservation plans. (a) Determinations by rule;

notice and hearing; findings; final rule on status of species or stock involved.

(1) In any action by the Secretary to determine if a species or stock should be designated as depleted, or should no longer be designated as depleted, regardless of whether such action is taken on the initiative of the Secretary or in response to a petition for a status review, the Secretary shall only make such a determination by issuance of a rule, after notice and opportunity for public comment and after a call for information in accordance with paragraph (2).

(2) The Secretary shall make any determination described in paragraph (1) solely on the basis of the best scientific information available. Prior to the issuance of a proposed rule concerning any such determination, the Secretary shall publish in the Federal Register a call to assist the Secretary in obtaining scientific information from individuals and organizations concerned with the conservation of marine mammals, from persons in any industry which might be affected by the determination, and from academic institutions. In addition, the Secretary shall utilize, to the extent the Secretary determines to be feasible, informal working groups of interested parties and other methods to gather the necessary information.

(3)(A) If the Secretary receives a petition for a status review as described in paragraph (1), the Secretary shall publish a notice in the Federal Register that such a petition has been received and is available for public review.

(B) Within sixty days after receipt of the petition, the Secretary shall publish a finding in the Federal Register as to whether the petition presents substantial information indicating that the petitioned action may be warranted.

(C) If the Secretary makes a positive finding under subparagraph (B), the Secretary shall include in the Federal Register notice, a finding that --

(i) a review of the status of the species or stock will be commenced promptly; or

(ii) a prompt review of the petition is precluded by other pending status determination petitions and that expeditious progress is being made to process pending status determination petitions under this Act.

In no case after making a finding under this subparagraph shall the Secretary delay commencing a review of the status of a species or stock for more than one hundred and twenty days after receipt of the petition.

(D) No later than two hundred and ten days after the receipt of the petition, the Secretary shall publish in the Federal Register a proposed rule as to the status of the species or stock, along with the reasons underlying the proposed status determination. Persons shall have at least sixty days to submit comments on such a proposed rule.

(E) Not later than ninety days after the close of the comment period on a proposed rule issued under subparagraph (D), the Secretary shall issue a final rule on the status of the species or stock involved, along with the reasons for the status determination. If the Secretary finds with respect to such a proposed rule that there is substantial disagreement regarding the sufficiency or accuracy of the available information relevant to a status determination, the Secretary may delay the issuance of a final rule for a period of not more than six months for purposes of soliciting additional information.

(F) Notwithstanding subparagraphs (D) and (E) of this paragraph and section 553 of Title 5, the Secretary may issue a final rule as to the status of a species or stock any time sixty or more days after a positive finding under subparagraph (B) if the Secretary determines there is substantial information available to warrant such final status determination and further delay would pose a significant risk to the well-being of any species or stock. Along with the final rule, the Secretary shall publish in the Federal Register detailed reasons for the expedited determination.

(b) Conservation plans; preparation and implementation. (1) The Secretary shall prepare conservation plans --

(A) By December 31, 1989, for North Pacific fur seals;

(B) by December 31, 1990, for Steller sea lions; and

(C) as soon as possible, for any species or stock designated as depleted under this Act, except that a conservation plan need not be prepared if the Secretary determines that it will not promote the conservation of the species or stock.

(2) Each plan shall have the purpose of conserving and restoring the species or stock to its optimum sustainable population. The Secretary shall model such plans on recovery plans required under section 4(f) of the Endangered Species Act of 1973 [16 U.S.C. § 1533(f)].

(3) The Secretary shall act expeditiously to implement each conservation plan prepared under paragraph (1). Each year, the Secretary shall specify in the annual report prepared under section 103(f) of this Act [16 U.S.C. § 1373(f)] what measures have been taken to prepare and implement such plans.

(4) If the Secretary determines that a take reduction plan is necessary to reduce the incidental taking of marine mammals in the course of commercial fishing operations from a strategic stock, or for species or stocks which interact with a commercial fishery for which the Secretary has made a determination under section 118(f)(1) [16 U.S.C. § 1387(f)(1)], any conservation plan prepared under this subsection for such species or stock shall incorporate the take reduction plan required under section 188 [16 U.S.C. § 1387] for such species or stock.

[Pub. L. 92-522, Title I, § 115, as added Pub. L. 100-711, § 3, 102 Stat. 4763 (Nov. 23, 1988), and amended Pub. L. 103-238, § 8, 108 Stat. 543 (Apr. 30, 1994)]

16 U.S.C. § 1385. Dolphin protection. (a) Short title. This section may be cited as the "Dolphin Protection Consumer Information Act".

(b) Findings. The Congress finds that --

(1) dolphins and other marine mammals are frequently killed in the course of tuna fishing operations in the eastern tropical Pacific Ocean and high seas driftnet fishing in other parts of the world;

(2) it is the policy of the United States to support a worldwide ban on high seas driftnet fishing, in part because of the harmful effects that such driftnets have on marine mammals, including dolphins; and

(3) consumers would like to know if the tuna they purchase is falsely labeled as to the effect of the harvesting of the tuna on dolphins.

(c) Definitions. For purposes of this section --

(1) the terms "driftnet" and "driftnet fishing" have the meanings given those terms in section 4003 of the Driftnet Impact Monitoring, Assessment, and Control Act of 1987 (16 U.S.C. 1822 note);

(2) the term "eastern tropical Pacific Ocean" means the area of the Pacific Ocean bounded by 40 degrees north latitude, 40 degrees south latitude, 160 degrees west longitude, and the western coastlines of North, Central, and South America;

(3) the term "label" means a display of written, printed, or graphic matter on or affixed to the immediate container of any article;

(4) the term "Secretary" means the Secretary of Commerce; and

(5) the term "tuna product" means a food item which contains tuna and which has been processed for retail sale, except perishable sandwiches, salads, or other products with a shelf life of less than 3 days.

(d) Labeling standard. (1) It is a violation of section 5 of the Federal Trade Commission Act (15 U.S.C. 45) for any producer, importer, exporter, distributor, or seller of any tuna product that is exported from or offered for sale in the United States to include on the label of that product the term "dolphin safe" or any other term or symbol that falsely claims or suggests that the tuna contained in the product were harvested using a method of fishing that is not harmful to dolphins if the product contains tuna harvested --

(A) on the high seas by a vessel engaged in driftnet fishing;

(B) outside the eastern tropical Pacific Ocean by a vessel using purse seine nets --

(i) in a fishery in which the Secretary has determined that a regular and significant association occurs between dolphins and tuna (similar to the association between dolphins and tuna in the eastern tropical Pacific Ocean), unless such product is accompanied by a written statement, executed by the captain of the vessel and an observer participating in a national or international program acceptable to the Secretary, certifying that no purse seine net was intentionally deployed on or used to encircle dolphins during the particular voyage on which the tuna were caught and no dolphins were killed or seriously injured in the sets in which the tuna were caught; or

(ii) in any other fishery (other than a fishery described in subparagraph (D)) unless the product is accompanied by a written statement executed by the captain of the vessel certifying that no purse seine net was intentionally deployed on or used to encircle dolphins during the particular voyage on which the tuna was harvested;

(C) in the eastern tropical Pacific Ocean by a vessel using a purse seine net unless the tuna meet the requirements for being considered dolphin safe under paragraph (2); or

(D) by a vessel in a fishery other than one described in subparagraph (A), (B), or (C) that is identified by the Secretary as having a regular and significant mortality or serious injury of dolphins, unless such product is accompanied by a written statement executed by the captain of the vessel and an observer participating in a national or international program acceptable to the Secretary that no dolphins were killed or seriously injured in the sets or other gear deployments in which the tuna were caught, provided that the Secretary determines that such an observer statement is necessary.

(2) For purposes of paragraph (1)(C), a tuna product that contains tuna harvested in the eastern tropical Pacific Ocean by a vessel using purse seine nets is dolphin safe if --

(A) the vessel is of a type and size that the Secretary has determined, consistent with the International Dolphin Conservation Program, is not capable of deploying its purse seine nets on or to encircle dolphins; or

(B)(i) the product is accompanied by a written statement executed by the captain providing the certification required under subsection (h);

(ii) the product is accompanied by a written statement executed by --

(I) the Secretary or the Secretary's designee;

(II) a representative of the Inter-American Tropical Tuna Commission; or

(III) an authorized representative of a participating nation whose national program meets the requirements of the International Dolphin Conservation Program,

which states that there was an observer approved by the International Dolphin Conservation Program on board the vessel during the entire trip and that such observer provided the certification required under subsection (h) of this section; and

(iii) the statements referred to in clauses (i) and (ii) are endorsed in writing by each exporter, importer, and processor of the product; and

(C) the written statements and endorsements referred to in subparagraph (B) comply with regulations promulgated by the Secretary which provide for the verification of tuna products as dolphin safe.

(3)(A) The Secretary of Commerce shall develop an official mark that may be used to label tuna products as dolphin safe in accordance with this [section].

(B) A tuna product that bears the dolphin safe mark developed under subparagraph (A) shall not bear any other label or mark that refers to dolphins, porpoises, or marine mammals.

(C) It is a violation of section 5 of the Federal Trade Commission Act (15 U.S.C. 45) to label a tuna product with any label or mark that refers to dolphins, porpoises, or marine mammals other than the mark developed under subparagraph (A) unless--

(i) no dolphins were killed or seriously injured in the sets or other gear deployments in which the tuna were caught;

(ii) the label is supported by a tracking and verification program which is comparable in effectiveness to the program established under subsection (f) of this section; and

(iii) the label complies with all applicable labeling, marketing, and advertising laws and regulations of the Federal Trade Commission, including any guidelines for environmental labeling.

(D) If the Secretary determines that the use of a label referred to in subparagraph (C) is substantially undermining the conservation goals of the

International Dolphin Conservation Program, the Secretary shall report that determination to the United States Senate Committee on Commerce, Science, and Transportation and the United States House of Representatives Committees on Resources and on Commerce, along with recommendations to correct such problems.

(E) It is a violation of section 5 of the Federal Trade Commission Act (15 U.S.C. 45) willingly and knowingly to use a label referred to in subparagraph (C) in a campaign or effort to mislead or deceive consumers about the level of protection afforded dolphins under the International Dolphin Conservation Program.

(e) Enforcement. Any person who knowingly and willfully makes a statement or endorsement described in subsection (d)(2)(B) that is false is liable for a civil penalty of not to exceed $100,000 assessed in an action brought in any appropriate district court of the United States on behalf of the Secretary.

(f) Regulations. The Secretary, in consultation with the Secretary of the Treasury, shall issue regulations to implement this [section], including regulations to establish a domestic tracking and verification program that provides for the effective tracking of tuna labeled under subsection (d) of this section. In the development of these regulations, the Secretary shall establish appropriate procedures for ensuring the confidentiality of proprietary information the submission of which is voluntary or mandatory. The regulations shall address each of the following items:

(1) The use of weight calculation for purposes of tracking tuna caught, landed, processed, and exported.

(2) Additional measures to enhance current observer coverage, including the establishment of criteria for training, and for improving monitoring and reporting capabilities and procedures.

(3) The designation of well location, procedures for sealing holds, procedures for monitoring and certifying both above and below deck, or through equally effective methods, the tracking and verification of tuna labeled under subsection (d) of this section.

(4) The reporting, receipt, and database storage of radio and facsimile transmittals from fishing vessels containing information related to the tracking and verification of tuna, and the definition of set.

(5) The shore-based verification and tracking throughout the fishing, transshipment, and canning process by means of Inter-American Tropical Tuna Commission trip records or otherwise.

(6) The use of periodic audits and spot checks for caught, landed, and processed tuna products labeled in accordance with subsection (d) of this section.

(7) The provision of timely access to data required under this subsection by the Secretary from harvesting nations to undertake the actions required in paragraph (6) of this [subsection.]

The Secretary may make such adjustments as may be appropriate to the regulations promulgated under this subsection to implement an international tracking and verification program that meets or exceeds the minimum requirements established by the Secretary under this subsection.

(g) Omitted.

(h) Certification by captain and observer. --

(1) Unless otherwise required by paragraph (2), the certification by the captain under subsection (d)(2)(B)(i) of this section and the certification provided by the observer as specified in subsection (d)(2)(B)(ii) of this section shall be that no dolphins were killed or seriously injured during the sets in which the tuna were caught.

(2) The certification by the captain under subsection (d)(2)(B)(i) of this section and the certification provided by the observer as specified under subsection (d)(2)(B)(ii) of this section shall be that no tuna were caught on the trip in which such tuna were harvested using a purse seine net intentionally deployed on or to encircle dolphins, and that no dolphins were killed or seriously injured during the sets in which the tuna were caught, if the tuna were caught on a trip commencing --

(A) before the effective date of the initial finding by the Secretary under subsection (g)(1) of this section;

(B) after the effective date of such initial finding and before the effective date of the finding of the Secretary under subsection (g)(2) of this section, where the initial finding is that the intentional deployment on or encirclement of dolphins is having a significant adverse impact on any depleted dolphin stock; or

(C) after the effective date of the finding under subsection (g)(2) of this section, where such finding is that the intentional deployment on or encirclement of dolphins is having a significant adverse impact on any such depleted stock.

[Pub. L. 101-627, Title IX, § 901(a) to (f), (h), (i), 104 Stat. 4465 (Nov. 28, 1990); Pub. L. 105-42, § 5, 111 Stat. 1125 (Aug. 15, 1997)]

§ 1387. Taking of marine mammals incidental to commercial fishing operations. (a) In general. (1) Effective on the date of enactment of this section [April 30, 1994], and except as provided in section 114 [16 U.S.C. § 1383a] and in paragraphs (2), (3), and (4) of this subsection, the provisions of this section shall govern the incidental taking of marine mammals in the course of commercial fishing operations by persons using vessels of the United States or vessels which have valid fishing permits issued by the Secretary in accordance with section 204(b) of the Magnuson-Stevens Fishery Conservation and Management Act 16 U.S.C. § 1824(b)). In any event it shall be the immediate goal that the incidental mortality or serious injury of marine mammals occurring in the course of commercial fishing operations be reduced to insignificant levels approaching a zero mortality and serious injury rate within 7 years after April 30, 1994.

(2) In the case of the incidental taking of marine mammals from species or stocks designated under this Act as depleted on the basis of their listing as threatened species or endangered species under the Endangered Species Act of 1973 (16 U.S.C. 1531 *et seq.*), both this section and section 101(a)(5)(E) of this Act [16 U.S.C. § 1371(a)(5)(E)] shall apply.

(3) Section 104(h) [16 U.S.C. § 1374(h)] and title III of this Act, and not this section, shall govern the taking of marine mammals in the course of commercial purse seine fishing for yellowfin tuna in the eastern tropical Pacific Ocean.

(4) This section shall not govern the incidental taking of California sea otters and shall not be deemed to amend or repeal the Act of November 7, 1986 (Public Law 99-625, 100 Stat. 3500).

(5) Except as provided in section 101(c) [16 U.S.C. § 1371(c)], the intentional lethal take of any marine mammal in the course of commercial fishing operations is prohibited.

(6) Sections 103 and 104 [16 U.S.C. §§ 1373 and 1374] shall not apply to the incidental taking of marine mammals under the authority of this section.

(b) Zero mortality rate goal. (1) Commercial fisheries shall reduce incidental mortality and serious injury of marine mammals to insignificant levels approaching a zero mortality and serious injury rate within 7 years after April 30, 1994.

(2) Fisheries which maintain insignificant serious injury and mortality levels approaching a zero rate shall not be required to further reduce their mortality and serious injury rates.

(3) Three years after April 30, 1994, the Secretary shall review the progress of all commercial fisheries, by fishery, toward reducing incidental mortality and serious injury to insignificant levels approaching a zero rate. The Secretary shall submit to the Committee on Commerce, Science, and Transportation of the Senate and the Committee on Merchant Marine and Fisheries of the House of Representatives a report setting forth the results of such review within 1 year after commencement of the review. The Secretary shall note any commercial fishery for which additional information is required to accurately assess the level of incidental mortality and serious injury of marine mammals in the fishery.

(4) If the Secretary determines after review under paragraph (3) that the rate of incidental mortality and serious injury of marine mammals in a commercial fishery is not consistent with paragraph (1), then the Secretary shall take appropriate action under subsection (f) of this section.

(c) Registration and authorization. (1) The Secretary shall, within 90 days after April 30, 1994 --

(A) publish in the Federal Register for public comment, for a period of not less than 90 days, any necessary changes to the Secretary's list of commercial fisheries published under section 114(b)(1) [16 U.S.C. § 1383a(b)(1)] and which is in existence on March 31, 1994 (along with an explanation of such changes and a statement describing the marine mammal stocks interacting with, and the approximate number of vessels or persons actively involved in, each such fishery), with respect to commercial fisheries that have --

(i) frequent incidental mortality and serious injury of marine mammals;

(ii) occasional incidental mortality and serious injury of marine mammals; or

(iii) a remote likelihood of or no known incidental mortality or serious injury of marine mammals;

(B) after the close of the period for such public comment, publish in the Federal Register a revised list of commercial fisheries and an update of information required by subparagraph (A), together with a summary of the provisions of this section and information sufficient to advise vessel owners on how to obtain an authorization and otherwise comply with the requirements of this section; and

(C) at least once each year thereafter, and at such other times as the Secretary considers appropriate, reexamine, based on information gathered under this Act and other relevant sources and after notice and opportunity for public comment, the classification of commercial fisheries and other determinations required under subparagraph (A) and publish in the Federal Register any necessary changes.

(2)(A) An authorization shall be granted by the Secretary in accordance with this section for a vessel engaged in a commercial fishery listed under paragraph (1)(A) (i) or (ii), upon receipt by the Secretary of a completed registration form providing the name of the vessel owner and operator, the name and description of the vessel, the fisheries in which it will be engaged, the approximate time, duration, and location of such fishery operations, and the general type and nature of use of the fishing gear and techniques used. Such information shall be in a readily usable format that can be efficiently entered into and utilized by an automated or computerized data processing system. A decal or other physical evidence that the authorization is current and valid shall be issued by the Secretary at the time an authorization is granted, and so long as the authorization remains current and valid, shall be reissued annually thereafter.

(B) No authorization may be granted under this section to the owner of a vessel unless such vessel --

(i) is a vessel of the United States; or

(ii) has a valid fishing permit issued by the Secretary in accordance with section 204(b) of the Magnuson-Stevens Fishery Conservation and Management Act (16 U.S.C. § 1824(b)).

(C) Except as provided in subsection (a) of this section, an authorization granted under this section shall allow the incidental taking of all species and stocks of marine mammals to which this Act applies.

(3)(A) An owner of a vessel engaged in any fishery listed under paragraph (1)(A) (i) or (ii) shall, in order to engage in the lawful incidental taking of marine mammals in a commercial fishery --

(i) have registered as required under paragraph (2) with the Secretary in order to obtain for each such vessel owned and used in the fishery an authorization for the purpose of incidentally taking marine mammals in accordance with this section, except that owners of vessels holding valid certificates of exemption under section 114 [16 U.S.C. § 1383a] are deemed to have registered for purposes of this subsection for the period during which such exemption is valid;

(ii) ensure that a decal or such other physical evidence of a current and valid authorization as the Secretary may require is displayed on or is in the possession of the master of each such vessel;

(iii) report as required by subsection (e) of this section; and

(iv) comply with any applicable take reduction plan and emergency regulations issued under this section.

(B) Any owner of a vessel receiving an authorization under this section for any fishery listed under paragraph (1)(A)(i) or (ii) shall, as a condition of that authorization, take on board an observer if requested to do so by the Secretary.

(C) An owner of a vessel engaged in a fishery listed under paragraph (1)(A)(i) or (ii) who --

(i) fails to obtain from the Secretary an authorization for such vessel under this section;

(ii) fails to maintain a current and valid authorization for such vessel; or

(iii) fails to ensure that a decal or other physical evidence of such authorization issued by the Secretary is displayed on or is in possession of the master of the vessel,

and the master of any such vessel engaged in such fishery, shall be deemed to have violated this Act and for violations of clauses (i) and (ii) shall be subject to the penalties of this Act, and for violations of clause (iii) shall be subject to a fine of not more than $100 for each offense.

(D) If the owner of a vessel has obtained and maintains a current and valid authorization from the Secretary under this section and meets the requirements set forth in this section, including compliance with any regulations to implement a take reduction plan under this section, the owner of such vessel, and the master and crew members of the vessel, shall not be subject to the penalties set forth in this Act for the incidental taking of marine mammals while such vessel is engaged in a fishery to which the authorization applies.

(E) Each owner of a vessel engaged in any fishery not listed under paragraph (1)(A)(i) or (ii), and the master and crew members of such a vessel, shall not be subject to the penalties set forth in this Act for the incidental taking of marine mammals if such owner reports to the Secretary, in the form and manner required under subsection (e) of this section, instances of incidental mortality or injury of marine mammals in the course of that fishery.

(4)(A) The Secretary shall suspend or revoke an authorization granted under this section and shall not issue a decal or other physical evidence of the authorization for any vessel until the owner of such vessel complies with the reporting requirements under subsection (e) of this section and such requirements to take on board an observer under paragraph (3)(B) as are applicable to such vessel. Previous failure to comply with the requirements of section 114 [16 U.S.C. § 1383a] shall not bar authorization under this section for an owner who complies with the requirements of this section.

(B) The Secretary may suspend or revoke an authorization granted under this subsection, and may not issue a decal or other physical evidence of the authorization for any vessel which fails to comply with a take reduction plan or emergency regulations issued under this section.

(C) The owner and master of a vessel which fails to comply with a take reduction plan shall be subject to the penalties of sections 105 and 107 [16 U.S.C. §§ 1375 and 1377], and may be subject to section 106 [16 U.S.C. § 1376].

(5)(A) The Secretary shall develop, in consultation with the appropriate States, affected Regional Fishery Management Councils, and other interested persons, the means by which the granting and administration of authorizations under this section shall be integrated and coordinated, to the maximum extent practicable, with existing fishery licenses, registrations, and related programs.

(B) The Secretary shall utilize newspapers of general circulation, fishery trade associations, electronic media, and other means of advising commercial fishermen of the provisions of this section and the means by which they can comply with its requirements.

(C) The Secretary is authorized to charge a fee for the granting of an authorization under this section. The level of fees charged under this subparagraph shall not exceed the administrative costs incurred in granting an authorization. Fees collected under this subparagraph shall be available to the Under Secretary of Commerce for Oceans and Atmosphere for expenses incurred in the granting and administration of authorizations under this section.

(d) Monitoring of incidental takes. (1) The Secretary shall establish a program to monitor incidental mortality and serious injury of marine mammals during the course of commercial fishing operations. The purposes of the monitoring program shall be to --

(A) obtain statistically reliable estimates of incidental mortality and serious injury;

(B) determine the reliability of reports of incidental mortality and serious injury under subsection (e) of this section; and

(C) identify changes in fishing methods or technology that may increase or decrease incidental mortality and serious injury.

(2) Pursuant to paragraph (1), the Secretary may place observers on board vessels as necessary, subject to the provisions of this section. Observers may, among other tasks --

(A) record incidental mortality and injury, or by catch of other nontarget species;

(B) record numbers of marine mammals sighted; and

(C) perform other scientific investigations.

(3) In determining the distribution of observers among commercial fisheries and vessels within a fishery, the Secretary shall be guided by the following standards:

(A) The requirement to obtain statistically reliable information.

(B) The requirement that assignment of observers is fair and equitable among fisheries and among vessels in a fishery.

(C) The requirement that no individual person or vessel, or group of persons or vessels, be subject to excessive or overly burdensome observer coverage.

(D) To the extent practicable, the need to minimize costs and avoid duplication.

(4) To the extent practicable, the Secretary shall allocate observers among commercial fisheries in accordance with the following priority:

(A) The highest priority for allocation shall be for commercial fisheries that have incidental mortality or serious injury of marine mammals from stocks listed as endangered species or threatened species under the Endangered Species Act of 1973 (16 U.S.C. § 1531 *et seq.*).

(B) The second highest priority for allocation shall be for commercial fisheries that have incidental mortality and serious injury of marine mammals from strategic stocks.

(C) The third highest priority for allocation shall be for commercial fisheries that have incidental mortality or serious injury of marine mammals from stocks for which the level of incidental mortality and serious injury is uncertain.

(5) The Secretary may establish an alternative observer program to provide statistically reliable information on the species and number of marine mammals incidentally taken in the course of commercial fishing operations. The alternative observer program may include direct observation of fishing activities from vessels, airplanes, or points on shore.

(6) The Secretary is not required to place an observer on a vessel in a fishery if the Secretary finds that --

(A) in a situation in which harvesting vessels are delivering fish to a processing vessel, statistically reliable information can be obtained from an observer on board the processing vessel to which the fish are delivered;

(B) the facilities on a vessel for quartering of an observer, or for carrying out observer functions, are so inadequate or unsafe that the health or safety of the observer or the safe operation of the vessel would be jeopardized; or

(C) for reasons beyond the control of the Secretary, an observer is not available.

(7) The Secretary may, with the consent of the vessel owner, station an observer on board a vessel engaged in a fishery not listed under subsection (c)(1)(A)(i) or (ii) of this section.

(8) Any proprietary information collected under this subsection shall be confidential and shall not be disclosed except --

(A) to Federal employees whose duties require access to such information;

(B) to State or tribal employees pursuant to an agreement with the Secretary that prevents public disclosure of the identity or business of any person;

(C) when required by court order; or

(D) in the case of scientific information involving fisheries, to employees of Regional Fishery Management Councils who are responsible for fishery management plan development and monitoring.

(9) The Secretary shall prescribe such procedures as may be necessary to preserve such confidentiality, except that the Secretary shall release or make public upon request any such information in aggregate, summary, or other form which does not directly or indirectly disclose the identity or business of any person.

(e) Reporting requirement. The owner or operator of a commercial fishing vessel subject to this Act shall report all incidental mortality and injury of marine mammals in the course of commercial fishing operations to the Secretary by mail or other means acceptable to the Secretary within 48 hours after the end of each fishing trip on a standard postage-paid form to be developed by the Secretary under this section. Such form shall be capable of being readily entered into and usable by an automated or computerized data processing system and shall require the vessel owner or operator to provide the following:

(1) The vessel name, and Federal, State, or tribal registration numbers of the registered vessel.

(2) The name and address of the vessel owner or operator.

(3) The name and description of the fishery.

(4) The species of each marine mammal incidentally killed or injured, and the date, time, and approximate geographic location of such occurrence.

(f) Take reduction plan. (1) The Secretary shall develop and implement a take reduction plan designed to assist in the recovery or prevent the depletion of each strategic stock which interacts with a commercial fishery listed under subsection (c)(1)(A)(i) or (ii) of this section, and may develop and implement such a plan for any other marine mammal stocks which interact with a commercial fishery listed under subsection (c)(1)(A)(i) of this section which the Secretary determines, after notice and opportunity for public comment, has a high level of mortality and serious injury across a number of such marine mammal stocks.

(2) The immediate goal of a take reduction plan for a strategic stock shall be to reduce, within 6 months of its implementation, the incidental mortality or serious injury of marine mammals incidentally taken in the course of commercial fishing operations to levels less than the potential biological removal level established for that stock under section 117 [16 U.S.C. § 1386]. The long-term goal of the plan shall be to reduce, within 5 years of its implementation, the incidental mortality or serious injury of marine mammals incidentally taken in the course of commercial fishing operations to insignificant levels approaching a zero mortality and serious injury rate, taking into account the economics of the fishery, the availability of existing technology, and existing State or regional fishery management plans.

(3) If there is insufficient funding available to develop and implement a take reduction plan for all such stocks that interact with commercial fisheries listed under subsection (c)(1)(A)(i) or (ii) of this section, the Secretary shall give highest priority to the development and implementation of take reduction plans for species or stocks whose level of incidental mortality and serious injury exceeds the potential biological removal level, those that have a small population size, and those which are declining most rapidly.

(4) Each take reduction plan shall include --

(A) a review of the information in the final stock assessment published under section 117(b) [16 U.S.C. § 1386(b)] and any substantial new information;

(B) an estimate of the total number and, if possible, age and gender, of animals from the stock that are being incidentally lethally taken or seriously injured each year during the course of commercial fishing operations, by fishery;

(C) recommended regulatory or voluntary measures for the reduction of incidental mortality and serious injury;

(D) recommended dates for achieving the specific objectives of the plan.

(5)(A) For any stock in which incidental mortality and serious injury from commercial fisheries exceeds the potential biological removal level established under section 117 [16 U.S.C. § 1386], the plan shall include measures the Secretary expects will reduce, within 6 months of the plan's implementation, such mortality and serious injury to a level below the potential biological removal level.

(B) For any stock in which human-caused mortality and serious injury exceeds the potential biological removal level, other than a stock to which subparagraph (A) applies, the plan shall include measures the Secretary expects will reduce, to the maximum extent practicable within 6 months of the plan's implementation, the incidental mortality and serious injury by such commercial fisheries from that stock. For purposes of this subparagraph, the term "maximum extent practicable" means to the lowest level that is feasible for such fisheries within the 6-month period.

(6)(A) At the earliest possible time (not later than 30 days) after the Secretary issues a final stock assessment under section 117(b) [16 U.S.C. § 1386(b)] for a strategic stock, the Secretary shall, and for stocks that interact with a fishery listed under subsection (c)(1)(A)(i) of this section for which the Secretary has made a determination under paragraph (1), the Secretary may --

(i) establish a take reduction team for such stock and appoint the members of such team in accordance with subparagraph (C); and

(ii) publish in the Federal Register a notice of the team's establishment, the names of the team's appointed members, the full geographic range of such stock, and a list of all commercial fisheries that cause incidental mortality and serious injury of marine mammals from such stock.

(B) The Secretary may request a take reduction team to address a stock that extends over one or more regions or fisheries, or multiple stocks within a region or fishery, if the Secretary determines that doing so would facilitate the development and implementation of plans required under this subsection.

(C) Members of take reduction teams shall have expertise regarding the conservation or biology of the marine mammal species which the take reduction plan will address, or the fishing practices which result in the incidental mortality and serious injury of such species. Members shall include representatives of Federal agencies, each coastal State which has fisheries which interact with the species or stock, appropriate Regional Fishery Management Councils, interstate fisheries commissions, academic and scientific organizations, environmental groups, all commercial and recreational fisheries groups and gear types which incidentally take the species or stock, Alaska Native organizations or Indian tribal organizations, and others as the Secretary deems appropriate. Take reduction teams shall, to the maximum extent practicable, consist of an equitable balance among representatives of resource user interests and nonuser interests.

(D) Take reduction teams shall not be subject to the Federal Advisory Committee Act [5 U.S.C. App. 3 § 1 *et seq.*]. Meetings of take reduction teams shall be open to the public, and prior notice of meetings shall be made public in a timely fashion.

(E) Members of take reduction teams shall serve without compensation, but may be reimbursed by the Secretary, upon request, for reasonable travel costs and expenses incurred in performing their duties as members of the team.

(7) Where the human-caused mortality and serious injury from a strategic stock is estimated to be equal to or greater than the potential biological removal level established under section 117 [16 U.S.C. § 1386] for such stock and such stock interacts with a fishery listed under subsection (c)(1)(A)(i) or (ii) of this section, the following procedures shall apply in the development of the take reduction plan for the stock:

(A)(i) Not later than 6 months after the date of establishment of a take reduction team for the stock, the team shall submit a draft take reduction plan for such stock to the Secretary, consistent with the other provisions of this section.

(ii) Such draft take reduction plan shall be developed by consensus. In the event consensus cannot be reached, the team shall advise the Secretary in writing on the range of possibilities considered by the team, and the views of both the majority and minority.

(B)(i) The Secretary shall take the draft take reduction plan into consideration and, not later than 60 days after the submission of the draft plan by the team, the Secretary shall publish in the Federal Register the plan proposed by the team, any changes proposed by the Secretary with an explanation of the reasons therefor, and proposed regulations to implement such plan, for public review and comment during a period of not to exceed 90 days.

(ii) In the event that the take reduction team does not submit a draft plan to the Secretary within 6 months, the Secretary shall, not later than 8 months after the establishment of the team, publish in the Federal Register a proposed take reduction plan and implementing regulations, for public review and comment during a period of not to exceed 90 days.

(C) Not later than 60 days after the close of the comment period required under subparagraph (B), the Secretary shall issue a final take reduction plan and implementing regulations, consistent with the other provisions of this section.

(D) The Secretary shall, during a period of 30 days after publication of a final take reduction plan, utilize newspapers of general circulation, fishery trade associations, electronic media, and other means of advising commercial fishermen of the requirements of the plan and how to comply with them.

(E) The Secretary and the take reduction team shall meet every 6 months, or at such other intervals as the Secretary determines are necessary, to monitor the implementation of the final take reduction plan until such time that the Secretary determines that the objectives of such plan have been met.

(F) The Secretary shall amend the take reduction plan and implementing regulations as necessary to meet the requirements of this section, in accordance with the procedures in this section for the issuance of such plans and regulations.

(8) Where the human-caused mortality and serious injury from a strategic stock is estimated to be less than the potential biological removal level established under section 117 [16 U.S.C. § 1386] for such stock and such stock interacts with a fishery listed under subsection (c)(1)(A)(i) or (ii) of this section, or for any marine mammal stocks which interact with a commercial fishery listed under subsection (c)(1)(A)(i) of this section for which the Secretary has made a determination under paragraph (1), the following procedures shall apply in the development of the take reduction plan for such stock:

(A)(i) Not later than 11 months after the date of establishment of a take reduction team for the stock, the team shall submit a draft take reduction plan for the stock to the Secretary, consistent with the other provisions of this section.

(ii) Such draft take reduction plan shall be developed by consensus. In the event consensus cannot be reached, the team shall advise the Secretary in writing on the range of possibilities considered by the team, and the views of both the majority and minority.

(B)(i) The Secretary shall take the draft take reduction plan into consideration and, not later than 60 days after the submission of the draft plan by the team, the Secretary shall publish in the Federal Register the plan proposed by the team, any changes proposed by the Secretary with an explanation of the reasons therefor, and proposed regulations to implement such plan, for public review and comment during a period of not to exceed 90 days.

(ii) In the event that the take reduction team does not submit a draft plan to the Secretary within 11 months, the Secretary shall, not later than 13 months after the establishment of the team, publish in the Federal Register a proposed take reduction plan and implementing regulations, for public review and comment during a period of not to exceed 90 days.

(C) Not later than 60 days after the close of the comment period required under subparagraph (B), the Secretary shall issue a final take reduction plan and implementing regulations, consistent with the other provisions of this section.

(D) The Secretary shall, during a period of 30 days after publication of a final take reduction plan, utilize newspapers of general circulation, fishery trade associations, electronic media, and other means of advising commercial fishermen of the requirements of the plan and how to comply with them.

(E) The Secretary and the take reduction team shall meet on an annual basis, or at such other intervals as the Secretary determines are necessary, to monitor the implementation of the final take reduction plan until such time that the Secretary determines that the objectives of such plan have been met.

(F) The Secretary shall amend the take reduction plan and implementing regulations as necessary to meet the requirements of this section, in accordance with the procedures in this section for the issuance of such plans and regulations.

(9) In implementing a take reduction plan developed pursuant to this subsection, the Secretary may, where necessary to implement a take reduction plan to protect or restore a marine mammal stock or species covered by such plan, promulgate regulations which include, but are not limited to, measures to --

(A) establish fishery-specific limits on incidental mortality and serious injury of marine mammals in commercial fisheries or restrict commercial fisheries by time or area;

(B) require the use of alternative commercial fishing gear or techniques and new technologies, encourage the development of such gear or technology, or convene expert skippers' panels;

(C) educate commercial fishermen, through workshops and other means, on the importance of reducing the incidental mortality and serious injury of marine mammals in affected commercial fisheries; and

(D) monitor, in accordance with subsection (d) of this section, the effectiveness of measures taken to reduce the level of incidental mortality and serious injury of marine mammals in the course of commercial fishing operations.

(10)(A) Notwithstanding paragraph (6), in the case of any stock to which paragraph (1) applies for which a final stock assessment has not been published under section 117(b)(3) [16 U.S.C. § 1386(b)(3)] by April 1, 1995, due to a proceeding under section 117(b)(2) [16 U.S.C. § 1386(b)(2)], or any Federal court review of such proceeding, the Secretary shall establish a take reduction team under paragraph (6) for such stock as if a final stock assessment had been published.

(B) The draft stock assessment published for such stock under section 117(b)(1) [16 U.S.C. § 1386(b)(1)] shall be deemed the final stock assessment for purposes of preparing and implementing a take reduction plan for such stock under this section.

(C) Upon publication of a final stock assessment for such stock under section 117(b)(3) [16 U.S.C. § 1386(b)(3)] the Secretary shall immediately reconvene the take reduction team for such stock for the purpose of amending the take reduction plan, and any regulations issued to implement such plan, if necessary, to reflect the final stock assessment or court action. Such amendments shall be made in accordance with paragraph (7)(F) or (8)(F), as appropriate.

(D) A draft stock assessment may only be used as the basis for a take reduction plan under this paragraph for a period of not to exceed two years, or until a final stock assessment is published, whichever is earlier. If, at the end of the two-year period, a final stock assessment has not been published, the Secretary shall categorize such stock under section 117(a)(5)(A) [16 U.S.C. § 1386(a)(5)(A)] and shall revoke any regulations to implement a take reduction plan for such stock.

(E) Subparagraph (D) shall not apply for any period beyond two years during which a final stock assessment for such stock has not been published due to review of a proceeding on such stock assessment by a Federal court. Immediately upon final action by such court, the Secretary shall proceed under subparagraph (C).

(11) Take reduction plans developed under this section for a species or stock listed as a threatened species or endangered species under the Endangered Species Act of 1973 (16 U.S.C. 1531 *et seq.*) shall be consistent with any recovery plan developed for such species or stock under section 4 of such Act [16 U.S.C. § 1533].

(g) Emergency regulations. (1) If the Secretary finds that the incidental mortality and serious injury of marine mammals from commercial fisheries is having, or is likely to have, an immediate and significant adverse impact on a stock or species, the Secretary shall take actions as follows:

(A) In the case of a stock or species for which a take reduction plan is in effect, the Secretary shall --

(i) prescribe emergency regulations that, consistent with such plan to the maximum extent practicable, reduce incidental mortality and serious injury in that fishery; and

(ii) approve and implement, on an expedited basis, any amendments to such plan that are recommended by the take reduction team to address such adverse impact.

(B) In the case of a stock or species for which a take reduction plan is being developed, the Secretary shall --

(i) prescribe emergency regulations to reduce such incidental mortality and serious injury in that fishery; and

(ii) approve and implement, on an expedited basis, such plan, which shall provide methods to address such adverse impact if still necessary.

(C) In the case of a stock or species for which a take reduction plan does not exist and is not being developed, or in the case of a commercial fishery listed under subsection (c)(1)(A)(iii) of this section which the Secretary believes may be contributing to such adverse impact, the Secretary shall --

(i) prescribe emergency regulations to reduce such incidental mortality and serious injury in that fishery, to the extent necessary to mitigate such adverse impact;

(ii) immediately review the stock assessment for such stock or species and the classification of such commercial fishery under this section to determine if a take reduction team should be established; and

(iii) may, where necessary to address such adverse impact on a species or stock listed as a threatened species or endangered species under the Endangered Species Act of 1973 (16 U.S.C. 1531 *et seq.*), place observers on vessels in a commercial fishery listed under subsection (c)(1)(A)(iii) of this section, if the Secretary has reason to believe such vessels may be causing the incidental mortality and serious injury to marine mammals from such stock.

(2) Prior to taking action under paragraph (1)(A), (B), or (C), the Secretary shall consult with the Marine Mammal Commission, all appropriate Regional Fishery Management Councils, State fishery managers, and the appropriate take reduction team (if established).

(3) Emergency regulations prescribed under this subsection --

(A) shall be published in the Federal Register, together with an explanation thereof;

(B) shall remain in effect for not more than 180 days or until the end of the applicable commercial fishing season, whichever is earlier; and

(C) may be terminated by the Secretary at an earlier date by publication in the Federal Register of a notice of termination, if the Secretary determines that the reasons for emergency regulations no longer exist.

(4) If the Secretary finds that incidental mortality and serious injury of marine mammals in a commercial fishery is continuing to have an immediate and significant adverse impact on a stock or species, the Secretary may extend the emergency regulations for an additional period of not more than 90 days or until reasons for the emergency no longer exist, whichever is earlier.

(h) Penalties. Except as provided in subsection (c) of this section, any person who violates this section shall be subject to the provisions of sections 105 and 107 [16 U.S.C. §§ 1375 and 1377], and may be subject to section 106 [16 U.S.C. § 1376] as the Secretary shall establish by regulations.

(i) Assistance. The Secretary shall provide assistance to Regional Fishery Management Councils, States, interstate fishery commissions, and Indian tribal organizations in meeting the goal of reducing incidental mortality and serious injury to insignificant levels approaching a zero mortality and serious injury rate.

(j) Contributions. For purposes of carrying out this section, the Secretary may accept, solicit, receive, hold, administer, and use gifts, devises, and bequests.

(k) Consultation with Secretary of the Interior. The Secretary shall consult with the Secretary of the Interior prior to taking actions or making determinations under this section that affect or relate to species or population stocks of marine mammals for which the Secretary of the Interior is responsible under this Act.

(l) Definitions. As used in this section and section 101(a)(5)(E) [16 U.S.C. § 1371(a)(5)(E)], each of the terms "fishery" and "vessel of the United States" has the same meaning it does in section 3 of the Magnuson-Stevens Fishery Conservation and Management Act 16 U.S.C. § 1802).

[Pub. L. 92-522, Title I, § 118, as added Pub. L. 103-238, § 11, 108 Stat. 546 (Apr. 30, 1994), and amended Pub. L. 104-208, Div. A, Title I, § 101(a) [Title II, § 211(b)], 110 Stat. 3009-41 (Sept. 30, 1996)]

16 U.S.C. § 1388. Marine mammal cooperative agreements in Alaska. ****

16 U.S.C. § 1389. Pacific Coast Task Force; Gulf of Maine. (a) Pinniped removal authority. Notwithstanding any other provision of this Act, the Secretary may permit the intentional lethal taking of pinnipeds in accordance with this section.

(b) Application. (1) A State may apply to the Secretary to authorize the intentional lethal taking of individually identifiable pinnipeds which are having a significant negative impact on the decline or recovery of salmonid fishery stocks which --

(A) have been listed as threatened species or endangered species under the Endangered Species Act of 1973 (16 U.S.C. 1531 *et seq.*);

(B) the Secretary finds are approaching threatened species or endangered species status (as those terms are defined in that Act [16 U.S.C. § 1531 *et seq.*]); or

(C) migrate through the Ballard Locks at Seattle, Washington.

(2) Any such application shall include a means of identifying the individual pinniped or pinnipeds, and shall include a detailed description of the problem interaction and expected benefits of the taking.

(c) Actions in response to application. (1) Within 15 days of receiving an application, the Secretary shall determine whether the application has produced sufficient evidence to warrant establishing a Pinniped-Fishery Interaction Task Force to address the situation described in the application. If the Secretary determines sufficient evidence has been provided, the Secretary shall establish a Pinniped-Fishery Interaction Task Force and publish a notice in the Federal Register requesting public comment on the application.

(2) A Pinniped-Fishery Interaction Task Force established under paragraph (1) shall consist of designated employees of the Department of Commerce, scientists who are knowledgeable about the pinniped interaction that the application addresses, representatives of affected conservation and fishing community organizations, Indian Treaty tribes, the States, and such other organizations as the Secretary deems appropriate.

(3) Within 60 days after establishment, and after reviewing public comments in response to the Federal Register notice under paragraph (1), the Pinniped- Fishery Interaction Task Force shall --

(A) recommend to the Secretary whether to approve or deny the proposed intentional lethal taking of the pinniped or pinnipeds, including along with the recommendation a description of the specific pinniped individual or individuals, the proposed location, time, and method of such taking, criteria for evaluating the success of the action, and the duration of the intentional lethal taking authority; and

(B) suggest nonlethal alternatives, if available and practicable, including a recommended course of action.

(4) Within 30 days after receipt of recommendations from the Pinniped-Fishery Interaction Task Force, the Secretary shall either approve or deny the application. If such application is approved, the Secretary shall immediately take steps to implement the intentional lethal taking, which shall be performed by Federal or State agencies, or qualified individuals under contract to such agencies.

(5) After implementation of an approved application, the Pinniped-Fishery Interaction Task Force shall evaluate the effectiveness of the permitted intentional lethal taking or alternative actions implemented. If implementation was ineffective in eliminating the problem interaction, the Task Force shall recommend additional actions. If the implementation was effective, the Task Force shall so advise the Secretary, and the Secretary shall disband the Task Force.

(d) Considerations. In considering whether an application should be approved or denied, the Pinniped-Fishery Interaction Task Force and the Secretary shall consider --

(1) population trends, feeding habits, the location of the pinniped interaction, how and when the interaction occurs, and how many individual pinnipeds are involved;

(2) past efforts to nonlethally deter such pinnipeds, and whether the applicant has demonstrated that no feasible and prudent alternatives exist and that the applicant has taken all reasonable nonlethal steps without success;

(3) the extent to which such pinnipeds are causing undue injury or impact to, or imbalance with, other species in the ecosystem, including fish populations; and

(4) the extent to which such pinnipeds are exhibiting behavior that presents an ongoing threat to public safety.

(e) Limitation. The Secretary shall not approve the intentional lethal taking of any pinniped from a species or stock that is --

(1) listed as a threatened species or endangered species under the Endangered Species Act of 1973 (16 U.S.C. 1531 *et seq.*);

(2) depleted under this Act; or

(3) a strategic stock.

(f) California sea lions and Pacific harbor seals; investigation and report. (1) The Secretary shall engage in a scientific investigation to determine whether California sea lions and Pacific harbor seals --

(A) are having a significant negative impact on the recovery of salmonid fishery stocks which have been listed as endangered species or threatened species under the Endangered Species Act of 1973 (16 U.S.C. 1531 *et seq.*), or which the Secretary finds are approaching such endangered species or threatened species status; or

(B) are having broader impacts on the coastal ecosystems of Washington, Oregon, and California.

The Secretary shall conclude this investigation and prepare a report on its results no later than October 1, 1995.

(2) Upon completion of the scientific investigation required under paragraph (1), the Secretary shall enter into discussions with the Pacific States Marine Fisheries Commission, on behalf of the States of Washington, Oregon, and California, for the purpose of addressing any issues or problems identified as a result of the scientific investigation, and to develop recommendations to address such issues or problems. Any recommendations resulting from such discussions shall be submitted, along with the report, to the Committee on Merchant Marine and Fisheries of the House of Representatives and the Committee on Commerce, Science, and Transportation of the Senate.

(3) The Secretary shall make the report and the recommendations submitted under paragraph (2) available to the public for review and comment for a period of 90 days.

(4) There are authorized to be appropriated to the Secretary such sums as are necessary to carry out the provisions of this subsection.

(5) The amounts appropriated under section 308(c) of the Interjurisdictional Fisheries Act of 1986 (16 U.S.C. § 4107(c)) and allocated to the Pacific States Marine Fisheries Commission may be used by the Commission to participate in discussions with the Secretary under paragraph (2).

(g) Regionwide pinniped-fishery interaction study. (1) The Secretary may conduct a study, of not less than three high predation areas in anadromous fish migration corridors within the Northwest Region of the National Marine Fisheries Service, on the interaction between fish and pinnipeds. In conducting the study, the Secretary shall consult with other State and Federal agencies with expertise in pinniped-fishery interaction. The study shall evaluate --

(A) fish behavior in the presence of predators generally;

(B) holding times and passage rates of anadromous fish stocks in areas where such fish are vulnerable to predation;

(C) whether additional facilities exist, or could be reasonably developed, that could improve escapement for anadromous fish; and

(D) other issues the Secretary considers relevant.

(2) Subject to the availability of appropriations, the Secretary may, not later than 18 months after the commencement of the study under this subsection, transmit a report on the results of the study to the Committee on Commerce, Science, and Transportation of the Senate and the Committee on Merchant Marine and Fisheries of the House of Representatives.

(3) The study conducted under this subsection may not be used by the Secretary as a reason for delaying or deferring a determination or consideration under subsection (c) or (d) of this section.

(h) Gulf of Maine Task Force. The Secretary shall establish a Pinniped-Fishery Interaction Task Force to advise the Secretary on issues or problems regarding pinnipeds interacting in a dangerous or damaging manner with aquaculture resources in the Gulf of Maine. No later than 2 years from April 30, 1994, the Secretary shall after notice and opportunity for public comment submit to the Committee on Merchant Marine and Fisheries of the House of Representatives and the Committee on Commerce, Science, and Transportation of the Senate a report containing recommended available alternatives to mitigate such interactions.

(i) Requirements applicable to task forces. (1) Any task force established under this section --

(A) shall to the maximum extent practicable, consist of an equitable balance among representatives of resource user interests and nonuser interests; and

(B) shall not be subject to the Federal Advisory Committee Act (5 App. U.S.C.).

(2) Meetings of any task force established under this section shall be open to the public, and prior notice of those meetings shall be given to the public by the task force in a timely fashion.

(j) Gulf of Maine harbor porpoise. (1) Nothing in section 117 [16 U.S.C. § 1386] shall prevent the Secretary from publishing a stock assessment for Gulf of Maine harbor porpoise in an expedited fashion.

(2) In developing and implementing a take reduction plan under section 118 [16 U.S.C. § 1387] for Gulf of Maine harbor porpoise, the Secretary shall consider all actions already taken to reduce incidental mortality and serious injury of such stock, and may, based on the recommendations of the take reduction team for such stock, modify the time period required for compliance with section 118(f)(5)(A) [16 U.S.C. § 1387(f)(5)(A)], but in no case may such modification extend the date of compliance beyond April 1, 1997.

[Pub. L. 92-522, Title I, § 120, as added Pub. L. 103-238, § 23, 108 Stat. 562 (Apr. 30, 1994)]

Title II -- Marine Mammal Commission

16 U.S.C. § 1401. Establishment. (a) Designation. There is hereby established the Marine Mammal Commission (hereafter referred to in this Act [16 U.S.C. §§ 1401 *et seq.*] as the "Commission").

(b) Membership and term of office. (1) Effective September 1, 1982, the Commission shall be composed of three members who shall be appointed by the President, by and with the advice and consent of the Senate. The President shall make his selection from a list of individuals knowledgeable in the fields of marine ecology and resource management, and who are not in a position to profit from the taking of marine mammals. Such list shall be submitted to him by the Chairman of the Council on Environmental Quality and unanimously agreed to by that Chairman, the Secretary of the Smithsonian Institution, the Director of the National Science Foundation and the Chairman of the National Academy of Sciences. No member of the Commission may, during his period of service on the Commission, hold any other position as an officer or employee of the United States except as a retired officer or retired civilian employee of the United States.

(2) The term of office for each member shall be three years; except that of the members initially appointed to the Commission, the term of one member shall be for one year, the term of one member shall be for two years, and the term of one member shall be for three years. No member is eligible for reappointment; except that any member appointed to fill a vacancy occurring before the expiration of the term for which his predecessor was appointed (A) shall be appointed for the remainder of such term, and (B) is eligible for reappointment for one full term. A member may serve after the expiration of his term until his successor has taken office.

(c) Chairman. The President shall designate a Chairman of the Commission (hereafter referred to in this Act [16 U.S.C. §§ 1401 *et seq.*] as the "Chairman") from among its members.

(d) Compensation; reimbursement for travel expenses. ****

(e) Executive Director. The Commission shall have an Executive Director, who shall be appointed ... by the Chairman with the approval of the Commission ....

[Pub. L. 92-522, Title II, § 201, 86 Stat. 1043 (Oct. 21, 1972); Pub. L. 97-389, Title II, § 202, 96 Stat. 1951 (Dec. 29, 1982); Pub. L. 98-364, Title I, § 103(a), 98 Stat. 441 (July 17, 1984)]

16 U.S.C. § 1402. Duties of Commission. (a) Reports and recommendations. The Commission shall --

(1) undertake a review and study of the activities of the United States pursuant to existing laws and international conventions relating to marine mammals, including, but not limited to, the International Convention for the Regulation of Whaling, the Whaling Convention Act of 1949 [16 U.S.C. § 916 *et seq.*], the Interim Convention on the Conservation of North Pacific Fur Seals, and the Fur Seal Act of 1966 [16 U.S.C. § 1151 *et seq.*];

(2) conduct a continuing review of the condition of the stocks of marine mammals, of methods for their protection and conservation, of humane means of taking marine mammals, of research programs conducted or proposed to be conducted under the authority of this Act, and of all applications for permits for scientific research, public display, or enhancing the survival or recovery of a species or stock;

(3) undertake or cause to be undertaken such other studies as it deems necessary or desirable in connection with its assigned duties as to the protection and conservation of marine mammals;

(4) recommend to the Secretary and to other Federal officials such steps as it deems necessary or desirable for the protection and conservation of marine

mammals;

(5) recommend to the Secretary of State appropriate policies regarding existing international arrangements for the protection and conservation of marine mammals, and suggest appropriate international arrangements for the protection and conservation of marine mammals;

(6) recommend to the Secretary such revisions of the endangered species list and threatened species list published pursuant to section 4(c)(1) of the Endangered Species Act of 1973 [16 U.S.C. § 1533(c)(1)] as may be appropriate with regard to marine mammals; and

(7) recommend to the Secretary, other appropriate Federal officials, and Congress such additional measures as it deems necessary or desirable to further the policies of this Act, including provisions for the protection of the Indians, Eskimos, and Aleuts whose livelihood may be adversely affected by actions taken pursuant to this Act.

(b) Consultation with Secretary; reports to Secretary before publication. The Commission shall consult with the Secretary at such intervals as it or he may deem desirable, and shall provide each annual report required under section 204 [16 U.S.C. § 1404], before submission to Congress, to the Secretary for comment.

(c) Availability of reports for public inspection. The reports and recommendations which the Commission makes shall be matters of public record and shall be available to the public at all reasonable times. All other activities of the Commission shall be matters of public record and available to the public in accordance with the provisions of section 552 of Title 5.

(d) Recommendations; explanation for non-adoption. Any recommendations made by the Commission to the Secretary and other Federal officials shall be responded to by those individuals within one hundred and twenty days after receipt thereof. Any recommendations which are not followed or adopted shall be referred to the Commission together with a detailed explanation of the reasons why those recommendations were not followed or adopted.

[Pub. L. 92-522, Title II, § 202, 86 Stat. 1044 (Oct. 21, 1972); Pub. L. 93-205, § 13(e)(4), 87 Stat. 903 (Dec. 28, 1973); Pub. L. 97-58, § 6(1), 95 Stat. 987 (Oct. 9, 1981); Pub. L. 100-711, § 5(e)(4), 102 Stat. 4771 (Nov. 23, 1988)]

16 U.S.C. § 1403. Committee of Scientific Advisors on Marine Mammals. (a) Establishment; membership. The Commission shall establish, within ninety days after its establishment, a Committee of Scientific Advisors on Marine Mammals (hereafter referred to in this Act [16 U.S.C. §§ 1401 *et seq.*] as the "Committee"). Such Committee shall consist of nine scientists knowledgeable in marine ecology and marine mammal affairs appointed by the Chairman after consultation with the Chairman of the Council on Environmental Quality, the Secretary of the Smithsonian Institution, the Director of the National Science Foundation, and the Chairman of the National Academy of Sciences.

(b) Compensation; reimbursement for travel expenses. ****

(c) Consultation with Commission on studies and recommendations; explanation for nonadoption. The Commission shall consult with the Committee on all studies and recommendations which it may propose to make or has made, on research programs conducted or proposed to be conducted under the authority of this Act, and on all applications for permits for scientific research. Any recommendations made by the Committee or any of its members which are not adopted by the Commission shall be transmitted by the Commission to the appropriate Federal agency and to the appropriate committees of Congress with a detailed explanation of the Commission's reasons for not accepting such recommendations.

[Pub. L. 92-522, Title II, § 203, 86 Stat. 1044 (Oct. 21, 1972).)

§ 1404. Omitted.

16 U.S.C. § 1405. Coordination with other Federal agencies. ****

§ 1406. Administration. The Commission, in carrying out its responsibilities under this title, may --

(1) employ and fix the compensation of such personnel;

(2) acquire, furnish, and equip such office space;

(3) enter into such contracts or agreements with, or provide such grants to, other organizations, both public and private;

(4) procure the services of such experts or consultants ...; and

(5) incur such necessary expenses and exercise such other powers, as are consistent with and reasonably required to perform its functions under this title; except that no fewer than 11 employees must be employed under paragraph (1) at any time. ****

[Pub. L. 92-522, Title II, § 206, 86 Stat. 1045 (Oct. 21, 1972); Pub. L. 97-58, § 6(2), 95 Stat. 987 (Oct. 9, 1981); Pub. L. 98-364, Title I, § 103(b), 98 Stat. 442 (July 17, 1984)]

16 U.S.C. § 1407. Authorization of appropriations. ****

- 0 -

MAGNUSON-STEVENS FISHERIES MANAGEMENT AND CONSERVATION ACT (16 U.S.C. §§ 1801-1882)

In 1871, Congress took note that "the most valuable food fishes of the coast and the lakes ... are rapidly diminishing in number ... so as materially to affect the interests of trade and commerce" and directed the President to appoint a Commissioner of Fish and Fisheries to study the problem and report to Congress.[84] Congress could, however, do little more than commission reports. The constitutional jurisprudence that gave rise to the state ownership doctrine -- the idea that states "owned" the wildlife within their borders in trust for their residents -- held that the states owned the lands beneath the territorial sea[85] and that fishing was not commerce.[86] Congress thus was powerless to regulate the fisheries within the three leagues of the shore -- and the oceans beyond this territorial sea were the last great commons[87] -- the final place where the rule of *Pierson v. Post*[88] applied without limit. Any direct federal role was thus precluded.[89]

This traditional, state-based regulatory structure dominated fisheries until relatively recently.[90] Substantive federal involvement did not begin until the twentieth century when the United States began to negotiate treaties to regulate high seas fisheries.[91] International agreements became the dominant regulatory regime in the period following World War II; by the mid-1970s, the United States was party to more than 20 international fishery treaties. The federal role also increased as the United States extended its authority outward beyond the territorial sea.[92] But international agreements and jurisdictional extensions were no match for the belief in the freedom of the seas and by the mid-1970s, "almost 70% of the fish caught off the coast of the United States [was] taken by foreign fishermen."[93]

These approaches were fundamentally transformed in 1976 with the enactment of the Magnuson Fishery Conservation and Management Act.[94] The Act asserted federal jurisdiction over the fisheries within an "exclusive economic zone" (EEZ)[95] within 200 nautical miles of the coast.[96] The Magnuson Act marked the end of the foreign trawler fleets and the rapid expansion of a new, American factory fleet. It did not, however, mark the end of overfishing and the depletion of marine fishery stocks. The stocks of most commercially harvested species are collapsing.[97]

The Magnuson Act embodies potentially contradictory goals: promoting the development of an United States fishing industry[98] while simultaneously conserving and managing the fisheries.[99] To these ends, the Act asserted exclusive federal jurisdiction over the fisheries within the EEZ -- with three exceptions: the Act claimed jurisdiction over anadromous fish[100] throughout their migratory life cycle;[101] it also asserted jurisdiction over all "Continental Shelf fishery resources"[102] -- a groups of species such as corals, crabs, mollusks and sponges;[103] and finally, the Act claimed authority over "highly migratory species," a category defined to include tuna, oceanic sharks, sailfishes, and swordfishes.[104]

The Act established eight regional fishery management councils[105] and empowered them to draft fishery management plans (FMPs) "for each fishery under its authority that requires conservation and management."[106] The plans are to be "consistent" with 10 national standards[107] that emphasize reliance upon "the best scientific information available"[108] to prevent overfishing while obtaining "optimum yield."[109] This key term is defined as

> the amount of fish which --
> (A) will provide the greatest overall benefit to the Nation, particularly with respect to food production and recreational opportunities, and taking into account the protection of marine ecosystems;
> (B) is prescribed on the basis of the maximum sustainable yield from the fishery, as reduced by any relevant social, economic, or ecological factor; and
> (C) in the case of an overfished fishery, provides for rebuilding to a level consistent

with producing the maximum sustainable yield in such fishery.[110]

"Overfishing" -- which is in turn defined in terms of the formally undefined "maximum sustainable yield"[111] -- thus is a crucial limit on harvest. FMPs are enforced through regulations adopted by the Department of Commerce.[112]

Title I

16 U.S.C. § 1801. Findings, purposes and policy. (a) Findings. The Congress finds and declares the following:

(1) The fish off the coasts of the United States, the highly migratory species of the high seas, the species which dwell on or in the Continental Shelf appertaining to the United States, and the anadromous species which spawn in United States rivers or estuaries, constitute valuable and renewable natural resources. These fishery resources contribute to the food supply, economy, and health of the Nation and provide recreational opportunities.

(2) Certain stocks of fish have declined to the point where their survival is threatened, and other stocks of fish have been so substantially reduced in number that they could become similarly threatened as a consequence of (A) increased fishing pressure, (B) the inadequacy of fishery resource conservation and management practices and controls, or (C) direct and indirect habitat losses which have resulted in a diminished capacity to support existing fishing levels.

(3) Commercial and recreational fishing constitutes a major source of employment and contributes significantly to the economy of the Nation. Many coastal areas are dependent upon fishing and related activities, and their economies have been badly damaged by the overfishing of fishery resources at an ever-increasing rate over the past decade. The activities of massive foreign fishing fleets in waters adjacent to such coastal areas have contributed to such damage, interfered with domestic fishing efforts, and caused destruction of the fishing gear of United States fishermen.

(4) International fishery agreements have not been effective in preventing or terminating the overfishing of these valuable fishery resources. There is danger that irreversible effects from overfishing will take place before an effective international agreement on fishery management jurisdiction can be negotiated, signed, ratified, and implemented.

(5) Fishery resources are finite but renewable. If placed under sound management before overfishing has caused irreversible effects, the fisheries can be conserved and maintained so as to provide optimum yields on a continuing basis.

(6) A national program for the conservation and management of the fishery resources of the United States is necessary to prevent overfishing, to rebuild overfished stocks, to insure conservation, to facilitate long-term protection of essential fish habitats, and to realize the full potential of the Nation's fishery resources.

(7) A national program for the development of fisheries which are underutilized or not utilized by the United States fishing industry, including bottom fish off Alaska, is necessary to assure that our citizens benefit from the employment, food supply, and revenue which could be generated thereby.

(8) The collection of reliable data is essential to the effective conservation, management, and scientific understanding of the fishery resources of the United

States.

(9) One of the greatest long-term threats to the viability of commercial and recreational fisheries is the continuing loss of marine, estuarine, and other aquatic habitats. Habitat considerations should receive increased attention for the conservation and management of fishery resources of the United States.

(10) Pacific Insular Areas contain unique historical, cultural, legal, political, and geographical circumstances which make fisheries resources important in sustaining their economic growth.

(b) Purposes. It is therefore declared to be the purposes of the Congress in this Act --

(1) to take immediate action to conserve and manage the fishery resources found off the coasts of the United States, and the anadromous species and Continental Shelf fishery resources of the United States, by exercising (A) sovereign rights for the purposes of exploring, exploiting, conserving, and managing all fish, within the exclusive economic zone established by Presidential Proclamation 5030, dated March 10, 1983, and (B) exclusive fishery management authority beyond the exclusive economic zone over such anadromous species and Continental Shelf fishery resources;

(2) to support and encourage the implementation and enforcement of international fishery agreements for the conservation and management of highly migratory species, and to encourage the negotiation and implementation of additional such agreements as necessary;

(3) to promote domestic commercial and recreational fishing under sound conservation and management principles, including the promotion of catch and release programs in recreational fishing;

(4) to provide for the preparation and implementation, in accordance with national standards, of fishery management plans which will achieve and maintain, on a continuing basis, the optimum yield from each fishery;

(5) to establish Regional Fishery Management Councils to exercise sound judgment in the stewardship of fishery resources through the preparation, monitoring, and revision of such plans under circumstances (A) which will enable the States, the fishing industry, consumer and environmental organizations, and other interested persons to participate in, and advise on, the establishment and administration of such plans, and (B) which take into account the social and economic needs of the States;

(6) to encourage the development by the United States fishing industry of fisheries which are currently underutilized or not utilized by United States fishermen, including bottom fish off Alaska, and to that end, to ensure that optimum yield determinations promote such development in a non-wasteful manner; and

(7) to promote the protection of essential fish habitat in the review of projects conducted under Federal permits, licenses, or other authorities that affect or have the potential to affect such habitat.

(c) Policy. It is further declared to be the policy of the Congress in this Act --

(1) to maintain without change the existing territorial or other ocean jurisdiction of the United States for all purposes other than the conservation and management of fishery resources, as provided for in this Act;

(2) to authorize no impediment to, or interference with, recognized legitimate uses

of the high seas, except as necessary for the conservation and management of fishery resources, as provided for in this Act;

(3) to assure that the national fishery conservation and management program utilizes, and is based upon, the best scientific information available; involves, and is responsive to the needs of, interested and affected States and citizens; considers efficiency; draws upon Federal, State, and academic capabilities in carrying out research, administration, management, and enforcement; considers the effects of fishing on immature fish and encourages development of practical measures that minimize bycatch and avoid unnecessary waste of fish; and is workable and effective;

(4) to permit foreign fishing consistent with the provisions of this Act;

(5) to support and encourage active United States efforts to obtain internationally acceptable agreements which provide for effective conservation and management of fishery resources, and to secure agreements to regulate fishing by vessels or persons beyond the exclusive economic zones of any nation;

(6) to foster and maintain the diversity of fisheries in the United States; and

(7) to ensure that the fishery resources adjacent to a Pacific Insular Area, including resident or migratory stocks within the exclusive economic zone adjacent to such areas, be explored, developed, conserved, and managed for the benefit of the people of such area and of the United States.

[Pub. L. 94-265, § 2, 90 Stat. 331 (Apr. 13, 1976); Pub. L. 95-354, § 2, 92 Stat. 519 (Aug. 28, 1978); Pub. L. 96-561, Title II, § 233, 94 Stat. 3299 (Dec. 22, 1980); Pub. L. 99-659, Title I, § 101(c)(1), 100 Stat. 3707 (Nov. 14, 1986); Pub. L. 101-627, Title I, § 101, 104 Stat. 4437 (Nov. 28, 1990); Pub. L. 102-251, Title III, § 301(a), 106 Stat. 62 (Mar. 9, 1992); Pub. L. 104-297, Title I, § 101, 110 Stat. 3560 (Oct. 11, 1996)]

16 U.S.C. § 1802. Definitions. As used in this Act, unless the context otherwise requires --

(1) The term "anadromous species" means species of fish which spawn in fresh or estuarine waters of the United States and which migrate to ocean waters.

(2) The term "bycatch" means fish which are harvested in a fishery, but which are not sold or kept for personal use, and includes economic discards and regulatory discards. Such term does not include fish released alive under a recreational catch and release fishery management program.

(3) The term "charter fishing" means fishing from a vessel carrying a passenger for hire (as defined in section 2101(a) of Title 46) who is engaged in recreational fishing.

(4) The term "commercial fishing" means fishing in which the fish harvested, either in whole or in part, are intended to enter commerce or enter commerce through sale, barter or trade.

(5) The term "conservation and management" refers to all of the rules, regulations, conditions, methods, and other measures (A) which are required to rebuild, restore, or maintain, and which are useful in rebuilding, restoring, or maintaining, any fishery resource and the marine environment; and (B) which are designed to assure that --

(i) a supply of food and other products may be taken, and that recreational benefits may be obtained, on a continuing basis;

(ii) irreversible or long-term adverse effects on fishery resources and the marine environment are avoided; and

(iii) there will be a multiplicity of options available with respect to future uses of these resources.

(6) The term "Continental Shelf" means the seabed and subsoil of the submarine areas adjacent to the coast, but outside the area of the territorial sea, of the United States, to a depth of 200 meters or, beyond that limit, to where the depth of the superjacent waters admits of the exploitation of the natural resources of such areas.

(7) The term "Continental Shelf fishery resources" means the following:

CNIDARIA

Bamboo Coral -- *Acanella spp.*;
Black Coral -- *Antipathes spp.*;
Gold Coral -- *Callogorgia spp.*;
Precious Red Coral -- *Corallium spp.;*
Bamboo Coral -- Keratoisis *spp.; and*
Gold Coral -- *Parazoanthus spp.*

CRUSTACEA

Tanner Crab -- *Chionoecetes tanneri*;
Tanner Crab -- *Chionoecetes opilio*;
Tanner Crab -- *Chionoecetes angulatus*;
Tanner Crab -- *Chionoecetes bairdi*;
King Crab -- *Paralithodes camtschatica*;
King Crab -- *Paralithodes platypus*;
King Crab -- *Paralithodes brevipes*;
Lobster -- *Homarus americanus*;
Dungeness Crab -- *Cancer magister*;
California King Crab -- *Paralithodes californiensis*;
California King Crab -- *Paralithodes rathbuni*;
Golden King Crab -- *Lithodes aequispinus*;
Northern Stone Crab -- *Lithodes maja*;
Stone Crab -- *Menippe mercenaria;* and
Deep-sea Red Crab -- *Chaceon quinquedens*.

MOLLUSKS

Red Abalone -- *Haliotis rufescens*;
Pink Abalone -- *Haliotis corrugata*;
Japanese Abalone -- *Haliotis kamtschatkana*;
Queen Conch -- *Strombus gigas*;
Surf Clam -- *Spisula solidissima;* and
Ocean Quahog -- *Artica islandica*.

SPONGES

Glove Sponge -- *Spongia cheiris*;
Sheepswool Sponge -- *Hippiospongia lachne*;
Grass Sponge -- *Spongia graminea;* and
Yellow Sponge -- *Spongia barbera*.

If the Secretary determines, after consultation with the Secretary of State, that living organisms of any other sedentary species are, at the harvestable stage, either --

(A) immobile on or under the seabed, or

(B) unable to move except in constant physical contact with the seabed or subsoil,

of the Continental Shelf which appertains to the United States, and publishes notice of such determination in the Federal Register, such sedentary species shall be considered to be added to the foregoing list and included in such term for purposes of this Act.

(8) The term "Council" means any Regional Fishery Management Council established under section 302 [16 U.S.C. § 1852].

(9) The term "economic discards" means fish which are the target of a fishery, but which are not retained because they are of an undesirable size, sex, or quality, or for other economic reasons.

(10) The term "essential fish habitat" means those waters and substrate necessary to fish for spawning, breeding, feeding or growth to maturity.

(11) The term "exclusive economic zone" means the zone established by Proclamation Numbered 5030, dated March 10, 1983. For purposes of applying this Act, the inner boundary of that zone is a line coterminous with the seaward boundary of each of the coastal States.

(12) The term "fish" means finfish, mollusks, crustaceans, and all other forms of marine animal and plant life other than marine mammals and birds.

(13) The term "fishery" means --

(A) one or more stocks of fish which can be treated as a unit for purposes of conservation and management and which are identified on the basis of geographical, scientific, technical, recreational, and economic characteristics; and

(B) any fishing for such stocks.

(14) The term "fishery resource" means any fishery, any stock of fish, any species of fish, and any habitat of fish.

(15) The term "fishing" means --

(A) the catching, taking, or harvesting of fish;

(B) the attempted catching, taking, or harvesting of fish;

(C) any other activity which can reasonably be expected to result in the catching, taking, or harvesting of fish; or

(D) any operations at sea in support of, or in preparation for, any activity described in subparagraphs (A) through (C).

Such term does not include any scientific research activity which is conducted by a scientific research vessel.

(16) The term "fishing community" means a community which is substantially dependent on or substantially engaged in the harvest or processing of fishery resources to meet social and economic needs, and includes fishing vessel owners, operators, and crew and United States fish processors that are based in such community.

(17) The term "fishing vessel" means any vessel, boat, ship, or other craft which is used for, equipped to be used for, or of a type which is normally used for --

(A) fishing; or

(B) aiding or assisting one or more vessels at sea in the performance of any activity relating to fishing, including, but not limited to, preparation, supply, storage, refrigeration, transportation, or processing.

(18) The term "foreign fishing" means fishing by a vessel other than a vessel of the United States.

(19) The term "high seas" means all waters beyond the territorial sea of the United States and beyond any foreign nation's territorial sea, to the extent that such sea is recognized by the United States.

(20) The term "highly migratory species" means tuna species, marlin (*Tetrapturus spp.* and *Makaira spp.*), oceanic sharks, sailfishes (*Istiophorus spp.*), and swordfish (*Xiphias gladius*).

(21) The term "individual fishing quota" means a Federal permit under a limited access system to harvest a quantity of fish, expressed by a unit or units representing a percentage of the total allowable catch of a fishery that may be received or held for exclusive use by a person. Such term does not include community development quotas as described in section 305(i) [16 U.S.C. § 1855(i)].

(22) The term "international fishery agreement" means any bilateral or multilateral treaty, convention, or agreement which relates to fishing and to which the United States is a party.

(23) The term "large-scale driftnet fishing" means a method of fishing in which a gillnet composed of a panel or panels of webbing, or a series of such gillnets, with a total length of two and one-half kilometers or more is placed in the water and allowed to drift with the currents and winds for the purpose of entangling fish in the webbing.

(24) The term "Marine Fisheries Commission" means the Atlantic States Marine Fisheries Commission, the Gulf States Marine Fisheries Commission, or the Pacific States Marine Fisheries Commission.

(25) The term "migratory range" means the maximum area at a given time of the year within which fish of an anadromous species or stock thereof can be expected to be found, as determined on the basis of scale pattern analysis, tagging studies, or other reliable scientific information, except that the term does not include any part of such area which is in the waters of a foreign nation.

(26) The term "national standards" means the national standards for fishery conservation and management set forth in section 301 [16 U.S.C. § 1851].

(27) The term "observer" means any person required or authorized to be carried on a vessel for conservation and management purposes by regulations or permits under this Act.

(28) The term "optimum", with respect to the yield from a fishery, means the amount of fish which --

(A) will provide the greatest overall benefit to the Nation, particularly with respect to food production and recreational opportunities, and taking into account the protection of marine ecosystems;

(B) is prescribed on the basis of the maximum sustainable yield from the fishery, as reduced by any relevant social, economic, or ecological factor; and

(C) in the case of an overfished fishery, provides for rebuilding to a level consistent with producing the maximum sustainable yield in such fishery.

(29) The terms "overfishing" and "overfished" mean a rate or level of fishing mortality that jeopardizes the capacity of a fishery to produce the maximum sustainable yield on a continuing basis.

(30) The term "Pacific Insular Area" means American Samoa, Guam, the Northern Mariana Islands, Baker Island, Howland Island, Jarvis Island, Johnston Atoll, Kingman Reef, Midway Island, Wake Island, or Palmyra Atoll, as applicable, and includes all islands and reefs appurtenant to such island, reef, or atoll.
(31) The term "person" means any individual (whether or not a citizen or national of the United States), any corporation, partnership, association, or other entity (whether or not organized or existing under the laws of any State), and any Federal, State, local, or foreign government or any entity of any such government.
(32) The term "recreational fishing" means fishing for sport or pleasure.
(33) The term "regulatory discards" means fish harvested in a fishery which fishermen are required by regulation to discard whenever caught, or are required by regulation to retain but not sell.
(34) The term "Secretary" means the Secretary of Commerce or his designee.
(35) The term "State" means each of the several States, the District of Columbia, the Commonwealth of Puerto Rico, American Samoa, the Virgin Islands, Guam, and any other Commonwealth, territory, or possession of the United States.
(36) The term "special areas" means the areas referred to as eastern special areas in Article 3(1) of the Agreement between the United States of America and the Union of Soviet Socialist Republics on the Maritime Boundary, signed June 1, 1990. In particular, the term refers to those areas east of the maritime boundary, as defined in that Agreement, that lie within 200 nautical miles of the baselines from which the breadth of the territorial sea of Russia is measured but beyond 200 nautical miles of the baselines from which the breadth of the territorial sea of the United States is measured.
(37) The term "stock of fish" means a species, subspecies, geographical grouping, or other category of fish capable of management as a unit.
(38) The term "treaty" means any international fishery agreement which is a treaty within the meaning of section 2 of article II of the Constitution.
(39) The term "tuna species" means the following:

Albacore Tuna -- *Thunnus alalunga;*
Bigeye Tuna -- *Thunnus obesus;*
Bluefin Tuna -- *Thunnus thynnus;*
Skipjack Tuna -- *Katsuwonus pelamis*; and
Yellowfin Tuna -- *Thunnus albacares.*

(40) The term "United States", when used in a geographical context, means all the States thereof.
(41) The term "United States fish processors" means facilities located within the United States for, and vessels of the United States used or equipped for, the processing of fish for commercial use or consumption.
(42) The term "United States harvested fish" means fish caught, taken, or harvested by vessels of the United States within any fishery regulated under this Act.
(43) The term "vessel of the United States" means --

(A) any vessel documented under chapter 121 of Title 46;
(B) any vessel numbered in accordance with chapter 123 of Title 46 and measuring less than 5 net tons;
(C) any vessel numbered in accordance with chapter 123 of Title 46 and used

exclusively for pleasure; or

(D) any vessel not equipped with propulsion machinery of any kind and used exclusively for pleasure.

(44) The term "vessel subject to the jurisdiction of the United States" has the same meaning such term has in section 1903(c) of Title 46, Appendix.

(45) The term "waters of a foreign nation" means any part of the territorial sea or exclusive economic zone (or the equivalent) of a foreign nation, to the extent such territorial sea or exclusive economic zone is recognized by the United States.

[Pub. L. 94-265, § 3, 90 Stat. 333 (Apr. 13, 1976); Pub. L. 95-354, § 3, 92 Stat. 519 (Aug. 28, 1978); Pub. L. 97-453, § 15(a), 96 Stat. 2492 (Jan. 12, 1983); Pub. L. 99-659, Title I, §§ 101(a), 112, 100 Stat. 3706 (Nov. 14, 1986), 3715; Pub. L. 100-239, § 2, 101 Stat. 1778 (Jan. 11, 1988); Pub. L. 101-627, Title I, § 102(a), Title X, §1001, 104 Stat. 4438 (Nov. 28, 1990), 4468; Pub. L. 102-251, Title III, § 301(b), 106 Stat. 62 (Mar. 9, 1992); Pub. L. 104-297, Title I, § 102, 110 Stat. 3561 (Oct. 11, 1996)]

16 U.S.C. § 1803. Authorization of appropriations. ****

Title II
United States Rights and Authority
Regarding Fish and Fishery Resources

16 U.S.C. § 1811. United States sovereign rights to fish and fishery management authority. (a) In the exclusive economic zone. Except as provided in section 102 [16 U.S.C. § 1812], the United States claims, and will exercise in the manner provided for in this Act, sovereign rights and exclusive fishery management authority over all fish, and all Continental Shelf fishery resources, within the exclusive economic zone.

(b) Beyond the exclusive economic zone. The United States claims, and will exercise in the manner provided for in this Act, exclusive fishery management authority over the following:

(1) All anadromous species throughout the migratory range of each such species beyond the exclusive economic zone; except that that management authority does not extend to any such species during the time they are found within any waters of a foreign nation.

(2) All Continental Shelf fishery resources beyond the exclusive economic zone.

[Pub. L. 94-265, Title I, § 101, 90 Stat. 336 (Apr. 13, 1976); Pub. L. 99-659, Title I, § 101(b), 100 Stat. 3706 (Nov. 14, 1986); Pub. L. 101-627, Title I, § 102(b), 104 Stat. 4438 (Nov. 28, 1990); Pub. L. 102-251, Title III, § 301(c), 106 Stat. 62 (Mar. 9, 1992)]

16 U.S.C. § 1812. Highly migratory species. The United States shall cooperate directly or through appropriate international organizations with those nations involved in fisheries for highly migratory species with a view to ensuring conservation and shall promote the achievement of optimum yield of such species throughout their range, both within and beyond the exclusive economic zone.

[Pub. L. 94-265, Title I, § 102, 90 Stat. 336 (Apr. 13, 1976); Pub. L. 99-659, Title I, § 101(b), 100 Stat. 3707 (Nov. 14, 1986); Pub. L. 101-627, Title I, § 103(a), 104 Stat. 4439 (Nov. 28, 1990); Pub. L. 104-297, Title I, § 104, 110

Stat. 3563 (Oct. 11, 1996)]

16 U.S.C. § 1813. Omitted.

Title III
Foreign Fishing and International Fishery Agreements

16 U.S.C. § 1821. Foreign fishing. (a) In general. After February 28, 1977, no foreign fishing is authorized within the exclusive economic zone, or for anadromous species or Continental Shelf fishery resources beyond the exclusive economic zone, unless such foreign fishing --

(1) is authorized under subsections (b) or (c) of this section or section 204(e) [16 U.S.C. § 1824(e)], or under a permit issued under section 204(d) [16 U.S.C. § 1824(d)];

(2) is not prohibited under subsection (f) of this section; and

(3) is conducted under, and in accordance with, a valid and applicable permit issued pursuant to section 204 [16 U.S.C. § 1824].

(b) Existing international fishery agreements. Foreign fishing described in subsection (a) of this section may be conducted pursuant to an international fishery agreement (subject to the provisions of section 202(b) or (c) [16 U.S.C. § 1822(b) or (c)]), if such agreement --

(1) was in effect on April 13, 1976; and

(2) has not expired, been renegotiated, or otherwise ceased to be of force and effect with respect to the United States.

(c) Governing international fishery agreements. Foreign fishing described in subsection (a) of this section may be conducted pursuant to an international fishery agreement (other than a treaty) which meets the requirements of this subsection if such agreement becomes effective after application of section 203 [16 U.S.C. § 1823]. Any such international fishery agreement shall hereafter in this Act be referred to as a "governing international fishery agreement." Each governing international fishery agreement shall acknowledge the exclusive fishery management authority of the United States, as set forth in this Act. It is the sense of the Congress that each such agreement shall include a binding commitment, on the part of such foreign nation and its fishing vessels, to comply with the following terms and conditions:

(1) The foreign nation, and the owner or operator of any fishing vessel fishing pursuant to such agreement, will abide by all regulations promulgated by the Secretary pursuant to this Act, including any regulations promulgated to implement any applicable fishery management plan or any preliminary fishery management plan.

(2) The foreign nation, and the owner or operator of any fishing vessel fishing pursuant to such agreement, will abide by the requirement that --

(A) any officer authorized to enforce the provisions of this Act (as provided for in section 311 [16 U.S.C. § 1861]) be permitted --

(i) to board, and search or inspect, any such vessel at any time,

(ii) to make arrests and seizures provided for in section 311(b) [16 U.S.C. § 1861(b)] whenever such officer has reasonable cause to believe, as a result of such a search or inspection, that any such vessel or any person has committed an act prohibited by section 307 [16 U.S.C. § 1857], and

(iii) to examine and make notations on the permit issued pursuant to section 204 [16 U.S.C. § 1824] for such vessel;

(B) the permit issued for any such vessel pursuant to section 204 [16 U.S.C. § 1824] be prominently displayed in the wheelhouse of such vessel;

(C) transponders, or such other appropriate position-fixing and identification equipment as the Secretary of the department in which the Coast Guard is operating determines to be appropriate, be installed and maintained in working order on each such vessel;

(D) United States observers required under subsection (h) of this section be permitted to be stationed aboard any such vessel and that all of the costs incurred incident to such stationing, including the costs of data editing and entry and observer monitoring, be paid for, in accordance with such subsection, by the owner or operator of the vessel;

(E) any fees required under section 204(b)(1) [16 U.S.C. § 1824(b)(10)] be paid in advance;

(F) agents be appointed and maintained within the United States who are authorized to receive and respond to any legal process issued in the United States with respect to such owner or operator; and

(G) responsibility be assumed, in accordance with any requirements prescribed by the Secretary, for the reimbursement of United States citizens for any loss of, or damage to, their fishing vessels, fishing gear, or catch which is caused by any fishing vessel of that nation;

and will abide by any other monitoring, compliance, or enforcement requirement related to fishery conservation and management which is included in such agreement.

(3) The foreign nation and the owners or operators of all of the fishing vessels of such nation shall not, in any year, harvest an amount of fish which exceeds such nation's allocation of the total allowable level of foreign fishing, as determined under subsection (e) of this section.

(4) The foreign nation will --

(A) apply, pursuant to section 204 [16 U.S.C. § 1824], for any required permits;

(B) deliver promptly to the owner or operator of the appropriate fishing vessel any permit which is issued under that section for such vessel;

(C) abide by, and take appropriate steps under its own laws to assure that all such owners and operators comply with, section 204(a) [16 U.S.C. § 1824(a)] and the applicable conditions and restrictions established under section 204(b)(7) [16 U.S.C. § 1824(b)(7)]; and

(D) take, or refrain from taking, as appropriate, actions of the kind referred to in subsection (e)(1) of this section in order to receive favorable allocations under such subsection.

(d) Total allowable level of foreign fishing. The total allowable level of foreign fishing, if any, with respect to any fishery subject to the exclusive fishery management authority of the United States, shall be that portion of the optimum yield of such fishery which will not be harvested by vessels of the United States, as determined in accordance with this Act.

(e) Allocation of allowable level. (1)(A) The Secretary of State, in cooperation with the Secretary, may make allocations to foreign nations from the total allowable level of foreign fishing which is permitted with respect to each fishery subject to the exclusive fishery management authority of the United States.

(B) From the determinations made under subparagraph (A), the Secretary of State shall compute the aggregate of all of the fishery allocations made to each foreign nation.

(C) The Secretary of State shall initially release to each foreign nation for harvesting up to 50 percent of the allocations aggregate computed for such nation under subparagraph (B), and such release of allocation shall be apportioned by the Secretary of State, in cooperation with the Secretary, among the individual fishery allocations determined for that nation under subparagraph (A). The basis on which each apportionment is made under this subparagraph shall be stated in writing by the Secretary of State.

(D) After the initial release of fishery allocations under subparagraph (C) to a foreign nation, any subsequent release of an allocation for any fishery to such nation shall only be made --

(i) after the lapse of such period of time as may be sufficient for purposes of making the determination required under clause (ii); and

(ii) if the Secretary of State and the Secretary, after taking into account the size of the allocation for such fishery and the length and timing of the fishing season, determine in writing that such nation is complying with the purposes and intent of this paragraph with respect to such fishery.

If the foreign nation is not determined under clause (ii) to be in such compliance, the Secretary of State shall reduce, in a manner and quantity he considers to be appropriate (I) the remainder of such allocation, or (II) if all of such allocation has been released, the next allocation of such fishery, if any, made to such nation.

(E) The determinations required to be made under subparagraphs (A) and (D)(ii), and the apportionments required to be made under subparagraph (C), with respect to a foreign nation shall be based on --

(i) whether, and to what extent, such nation imposes tariff barriers or nontariff barriers on the importation, or otherwise restricts the market access, of both United States fish and fishery products, particularly fish and fishery products for which the foreign nation has requested an allocation;

(ii) whether, and to what extent, such nation is cooperating with the United States in both the advancement of existing and new opportunities for fisheries exports from the United States through the purchase of fishery products from United States processors, and the advancement of fisheries trade through the purchase of fish and fishery products from United States fishermen, particularly fish and fishery products for which the foreign nation has requested an allocation;

(iii) whether, and to what extent, such nation and the fishing fleets of such nation have cooperated with the United States in the enforcement of United States fishing regulations;

(iv) whether, and to what extent, such nation requires the fish harvested from the exclusive economic zone for its domestic consumption;

(v) whether, and to what extent, such nation otherwise contributes to, or fosters the growth of, a sound and economic United States fishing industry, including minimizing gear conflicts with fishing operations of United States fishermen, and transferring harvesting or processing technology which will benefit the United States fishing industry;

(vi) whether, and to what extent, the fishing vessels of such nation have traditionally engaged in fishing in such fishery;

(vii) whether, and to what extent, such nation is cooperating with the United States in, and making substantial contributions to, fishery research and the identification of fishery resources; and

(viii) such other matters as the Secretary of State, in cooperation with the Secretary, deems appropriate.

(2)(A) For the purposes of this paragraph --

(i) The term "certification" means a certification made by the Secretary that nationals of a foreign country, directly or indirectly, are conducting fishing operations or engaging in trade or taking which diminishes the effectiveness of the International Convention for the Regulation of Whaling. A certification under this section shall also be deemed a certification for the purposes of section 8(a) of the Fishermen's Protective Act of 1967 (22 U.S.C. 1978(a)).

(ii) The term "remedial period" means the 365-day period beginning on the date on which a certification is issued with respect to a foreign country.

(B) If the Secretary issues a certification with respect to any foreign country, then each allocation under paragraph (1) that --

(i) is in effect for that foreign country on the date of issuance; or

(ii) is not in effect on such date but would, without regard to this paragraph, be made to the foreign country within the remedial period;

shall be reduced by the Secretary of State, in consultation with the Secretary, by not less than 50 percent.

(C) The following apply for purposes of administering subparagraph (B) with respect to any foreign country:

(i) If on the date of certification, the foreign country has harvested a portion, but not all, of the quantity of fish specified under any allocation, the reduction under subparagraph (B) for that allocation shall be applied with respect to the quantity not harvested as of such date.

(ii) If the Secretary notified the Secretary of State that it is not likely that the certification of the foreign country will be terminated under section 8(a) of the Fishermen's Protective Act of 1967 (22 U.S.C. 1978(a)) before the close of the period for which an allocation is applicable or before the close of the remedial period (whichever close first occurs) the Secretary of State, in consultation with the Secretary, shall reallocate any portion of any reduction made under subparagraph (B) among one or more foreign countries for which no certification is in effect.

(iii) If the certification is terminated under such section 8(d) [22 U.S.C. § 1978(d)] during the remedial period, the Secretary of State shall return to the foreign country that portion of any allocation reduced under subparagraph (B) that was not reallocated under clause (ii); unless the harvesting of the fish covered by the allocation is otherwise prohibited under this Act.

(iv) The Secretary may refund or credit, by reason of reduction of any allocation under this paragraph, any fee paid under section 204 [16 U.S.C. § 1824].

(D) If the certification of a foreign country is not terminated under section 8(d) of the Fishermen's Protective Act of 1967 [22 U.S.C. 1978(d)] before the close of the last day of the remedial period, the Secretary of State --

(i) with respect to any allocation made to that country and in effect (as reduced under subparagraph (B)) on such last day, shall rescind, effective on and after the day after such last day, any harvested portion of such allocation; and

(ii) may not thereafter make any allocation to that country under paragraph (1) until the certification is terminated.

(f) Reciprocity. Foreign fishing shall not be authorized for the fishing vessels of any foreign nation unless such nation satisfies the Secretary and the Secretary of State that such nation extends substantially the same fishing privileges to fishing vessels of the United States, if any, as the United States extends to foreign fishing vessels.

(g) Preliminary fishery management plans. The Secretary, when notified by the Secretary of State that any foreign nation has submitted an application under section 204(b) [16 U.S.C. § 1824(b)], shall prepare a preliminary fishery management plan for any fishery covered by such application if the Secretary determines that no fishery management plan for that fishery will be prepared and implemented, pursuant to title III [16 U.S.C. §§ 1851 *et seq.*], before March 1, 1977. To the extent practicable, each such plan --

(1) shall contain a preliminary description of the fishery and a preliminary determination as to --

(A) the optimum yield from such fishery;

(B) when appropriate, the capacity and extent to which United States fish processors will process that portion of such optimum yield that will be harvested by vessels of the United States; and

(C) the total allowable level of foreign fishing with respect to such fishery;

(2) shall require each foreign fishing vessel engaged or wishing to engage in such fishery to obtain a permit from the Secretary;

(3) shall require the submission of pertinent data to the Secretary, with respect to such fishery, as described in section 303(a)(5) [16 U.S.C. § 1853(a)(5)]; and

(4) may, to the extent necessary to prevent irreversible effects from overfishing, with respect to such fishery, contain conservation and management measures applicable to foreign fishing which --

(A) are determined to be necessary and appropriate for the conservation and management of such fishery,

(B) are consistent with the national standards, the other provisions of this Act, and other applicable law, and

(C) are described in section 303(b)(2), (3), (4), (5), and (7) [[16 U.S.C. § 1853(b)(2), (3), (4), (5), and (7)].

Each preliminary fishery management plan shall be in effect with respect to foreign fishing for which permits have been issued until a fishery management plan is prepared and implemented, pursuant to title III [16 U.S.C. §§ 1851 *et seq.*] with respect to such fishery. The Secretary may, in accordance with section 553 of Title 5, also prepare and promulgate interim regulations with respect to any such preliminary plan. Such regulations shall be in effect until regulations implementing the applicable fishery management plan are promulgated pursuant to section 305 [16 U.S.C. § 1855].

(h) Full observer coverage program. (1)(A) Except as provided in paragraph (2), the Secretary shall establish a program under which a United States observer will be stationed aboard each foreign fishing vessel while that vessel is engaged in fishing within the exclusive economic zone.

(B) The Secretary shall by regulation prescribe minimum health and safety standards that shall be maintained aboard each foreign fishing vessel with regard to the facilities provided for the quartering of, and the carrying out of observer functions by, United States observers.

(2) The requirement in paragraph (1) that a United States observer be placed aboard each foreign fishing vessel may be waived by the Secretary if he finds that --

(A) in a situation where a fleet of harvesting vessels transfers its catch taken within the exclusive economic zone to another vessel, aboard which is a United States observer, the stationing of United States observers on only a portion of the harvesting vessel fleet will provide a representative sampling of the by-catch of the fleet that is sufficient for purposes of determining whether the requirements of the applicable management plans for the by-catch species are being complied with;

(B) in a situation where the foreign fishing vessel is operating under a Pacific Insular Area fishing agreement, the Governor of the applicable Pacific Insular Area, in consultation with the Western Pacific Council, has established an observer coverage program that is at least equal in effectiveness to the program established by the Secretary;

(C) the time during which a foreign fishing vessel will engage in fishing within the exclusive economic zone will be of such short duration that the placing of a United States observer aboard the vessel would be impractical; or

(D) for reasons beyond the control of the Secretary, an observer is not available.

(3) Observers, while stationed aboard foreign fishing vessels, shall carry out such scientific, compliance monitoring, and other functions as the Secretary deems necessary or appropriate to carry out the purposes of this Act; and shall cooperate in carrying out such other scientific programs relating to the conservation and management of living resources as the Secretary deems appropriate.

(4) In addition to any fee imposed under section 204(b) of this Act [16 U.S.C. §

1824(b)(10)] and section 10(e) of the Fishermen's Protective Act [22 U.S.C. § 1980(e)] with respect to foreign fishing for any year after 1980, the Secretary shall impose, with respect to each foreign fishing vessel for which a permit is issued under such section 204 [16 U.S.C. § 1824], a surcharge in an amount sufficient to cover all the costs of providing a United States observer aboard that vessel. The failure to pay any surcharge imposed under this paragraph shall be treated by the Secretary as a failure to pay the permit fee for such vessel under section 204(b)(10) [16 U.S.C. § 1824(b)(10)]. All surcharges collected by the Secretary under this paragraph shall be deposited in the Foreign Fishing Observer Fund established by paragraph (5).

(5) There is established in the Treasury of the United States the Foreign Fishing Observer Fund. The Fund shall be available to the Secretary as a revolving fund for the purpose of carrying out this subsection. The Fund shall consist of the surcharges deposited into it as required under paragraph (4). All payments made by the Secretary to carry out this subsection shall be paid from the Fund, only to the extent and in the amounts provided for in advance in appropriation Acts. Sums in the Fund which are not currently needed for the purposes of this subsection shall be kept on deposit or invested in obligations of, or guaranteed by, the United States.

(6) If at any time the requirement set forth in paragraph (1) cannot be met because of insufficient appropriations, the Secretary shall, in implementing a supplementary observer program:

(A) certify as observers, for the purposes of this subsection, individuals who are citizens or nationals of the United States and who have the requisite education or experience to carry out the functions referred to in paragraph (3);

(B) establish standards of conduct for certified observers equivalent to those applicable to Federal personnel;

(C) establish a reasonable schedule of fees that certified observers or their agents shall be paid by the owners and operators of foreign fishing vessels for observer services; and

(D) monitor the performance of observers to ensure that it meets the purposes of this Act.

(i) Recreational fishing. Notwithstanding any other provision of this title [16 U.S.C. §§ 1821 *et seq.*], foreign fishing vessels which are not operated for profit may engage in recreational fishing within the exclusive economic zone and the waters within the boundaries of a State subject to obtaining such permits, paying such reasonable fees, and complying with such conditions and restrictions as the Secretary and the Governor of the State (or his designee) shall impose as being necessary or appropriate to insure that the fishing activity of such foreign vessels within such zone or waters, respectively, is consistent with all applicable Federal and State laws and any applicable fishery management plan implemented under section 304 [16 U.S.C. § 1854]. The Secretary shall consult with the Secretary of State and the Secretary of the Department in which the Coast Guard is operating in formulating the conditions and restrictions to be applied by the Secretary under the authority of this subsection.

[Pub. L. 94-265, Title II, § 201, 90 Stat. 337 (Apr. 13, 1976); Pub. L. 95- 354, § 4(1) to (4), 92 Stat. 519 (Aug. 28, 1978), 520; Pub. L. 96-61, § 3(a), 93 Stat. 407 (Aug. 15, 1979); Pub. L. 96-118, § 5, 93 Stat. 860 (Nov. 16, 1979); Pub. L. 96-561, Title II, §§ 230, 231(a), 236, 94 Stat. 3296, 3297, 3299 (Dec. 22, 1980); Pub. L. 97-453, § 2(a),

96 Stat. 2481 (Jan. 12, 1983); Pub. L. 98-623, Title IV, § 404(1), (2), 98 Stat. 3408 (Nov. 8, 1984); Pub. L. 99-386, Title II, § 206(a), 100 Stat. 823 (Aug. 22, 1986); Pub. L. 99-659, Title I, §§ 101(c)(2), 103(a), 100 Stat. 3707 (Nov. 14, 1986), 3708; Pub. L. 101-627, Title I, § 104, 104 Stat. 4439 (Nov. 28, 1990); Pub. L. 102-251, Title III, § 301(d), 106 Stat. 63 (Mar. 9, 1992); Pub. L. 103-236, Title I, § 139(24), 108 Stat. 399 (Apr. 30, 1994); Pub. L. 104-297, Title I, § 105(a), 110 Stat. 3563 (Oct. 11, 1996)]

16 U.S.C. § 1822. International fishery agreements. (a) Negotiations. ****

(e) Highly migratory species agreements. (1) Evaluation. The Secretary of State, in cooperation with the Secretary, shall evaluate the effectiveness of each existing international fishery agreement which pertains to fishing for highly migratory species. Such evaluation shall consider whether the agreement provides for --

(A) the collection and analysis of necessary information for effectively managing the fishery, including but not limited to information about the number of vessels involved, the type and quantity of fishing gear used, the species of fish involved and their location, the catch and bycatch levels in the fishery, and the present and probable future condition of any stock of fish involved;

(B) the establishment of measures applicable to the fishery which are necessary and appropriate for the conservation and management of the fishery resource involved;

(C) equitable arrangements which provide fishing vessels of the United States with (i) access to the highly migratory species that are the subject of the agreement and (ii) a portion of the allowable catch that reflects the traditional participation by such vessels in the fishery;

(D) effective enforcement of conservation and management measures and access arrangements throughout the area of jurisdiction; and

(E) sufficient and dependable funding to implement the provisions of the agreement, based on reasonable assessments of the benefits derived by participating nations.

(2) Access negotiations. The Secretary of State, in cooperation with the Secretary, shall initiate negotiations with respect to obtaining access for vessels of the United States fishing for tuna species within the exclusive economic zones of other nations on reasonable terms and conditions.

****

(h) Bycatch reduction agreements. (1) The Secretary of State, in cooperation with the Secretary, shall seek to secure an international agreement to establish standards and measures for bycatch reduction that are comparable to the standards and measures applicable to United States fishermen for such purposes in any fishery regulated pursuant to this Act for which the Secretary, in consultation with the Secretary of State, determines that such an international agreement is necessary and appropriate.

(2) An international agreement negotiated under this subsection shall be --

(A) consistent with the policies and purposes of this Act; and

(B) subject to approval by Congress under section 203 [16 U.S.C. § 1823].

(3) Not later than January 1, 1997, and annually thereafter, the Secretary, in consultation with the Secretary of State, shall submit to the Committee on Commerce, Science, and Transportation of the Senate and the Committee on Resources of the

House of Representatives a report describing actions taken under this subsection.

[Pub. L. 94-265, Title II, § 202, 90 Stat. 339 (Apr. 13, 1976); Pub. L. 99- 659, Title I, § 101(c)(2), 100 Stat. 3707 (Nov. 14, 1986); Pub. L. 101-627, Title I, §§ 105(a), 120(a), 104 Stat. 4439, 4459 (Nov. 28, 1990); Pub. L. 102-251, Title III, § 301(e), 106 Stat. 63 (Mar. 9, 1992); Pub. L. 104-297, Title I, § 105(b), 110 Stat. 3564 (Oct. 11, 1996)]

16 U.S.C. § 1823. Congressional oversight of international fishery agreements. (a) In general. No governing international fishery agreement, bycatch reduction agreement, or Pacific Insular Area fishery agreement shall become effective with respect to the United States before the close of the first 120 days (excluding any days in a period for which the Congress is adjourned sine die) after the date on which the President transmits to the House of Representatives and to the Senate a document setting forth the text of such governing international fishery agreement, bycatch reduction agreement, or Pacific Insular Area fishery agreement. ****

[Pub. L. 94-265, Title II, § 203, 90 Stat. 340 (Apr. 13, 1976); Pub. L. 103-437, § 6(x), 108 Stat. 4587 (Nov. 2, 1994); Pub. L. 104-297, Title I, § 105(c), 110 Stat. 3564 (Oct. 11, 1996)]

16 U.S.C. § 1824. Permits for foreign fishing. (a) In general. After February 28, 1977, no foreign fishing vessel shall engage in fishing within the exclusive economic zone, or for anadromous species or Continental Shelf fishery resources beyond such zone, unless such vessel has on board a valid permit issued under this section for such vessel.

****

[Pub. L. 94-265, Title II, § 204, 90 Stat. 342 (Apr. 13, 1976); Pub. L. 95- 354, § 4(5) to (8), 92 Stat. 520 (Aug. 28, 1978), 521; Pub. L. 96-470, Title I, § 111(b), Title II, § 208, 94 Stat. 2239, 2245 (Oct. 19, 1980); Pub. L. 96-561, Title II, § 232, 94 Stat. 3298 (Dec. 22, 1980); Pub. L. 97-453, § 3, 96 Stat. 2483 (Jan. 12, 1983); Pub. L. 99-272, Title VI, § 6021, 100 Stat. 123 (Apr. 7, 1986); Pub. L. 99-659, Title I, §§ 101(c)(2), 102, 103(b), 100 Stat. 3707 (Nov. 14, 1986), 3709; Pub. L. 101-627, Title I, §§ 106, 120(b), 104 Stat. 4440 (Nov. 28, 1990), 4459; Pub. L. 102-251, Title III, § 301(f), 106 Stat. 64 (Mar. 9, 1992); Pub. L. 104-297, Title I, § 105(d), 110 Stat. 3565 (Oct. 11, 1996)]

16 U.S.C. § 1825. Import prohibitions. (a) Determinations by Secretary of State. If the Secretary of State determines that --

(1) he has been unable, within a reasonable period of time, to conclude with any foreign nation an international fishery agreement allowing fishing vessels of the United States equitable access to fisheries over which that nation asserts exclusive fishery management authority, including fisheries for tuna species, as recognized by the United States, in accordance with fishing activities of such vessels, if any, and under terms not more restrictive than those established under sections 201(c) and (d) [16 U.S.C. §§ 1821(c), (d)] and section 204(b)(7) and (10) [16 U.S.C. § 1824(b)(7), (10)], because such nation has (A) refused to commence negotiations, or (B) failed to negotiate in good faith;

(2) any foreign nation is not allowing fishing vessels of the United States to engage in fishing for tuna species in accordance with an applicable international fishery agreement, whether or not such nation is a party thereto;

(3) any foreign nation is not complying with its obligations under any existing

international fishery agreement concerning fishing by fishing vessels of the United States in any fishery over which that nation asserts exclusive fishery management authority; or

(4) any fishing vessel of the United States, while fishing in waters beyond any foreign nation's territorial sea, to the extent that such sea is recognized by the United States, is seized by any foreign nation --

(A) in violation of an applicable international fishery agreement;

(B) without authorization under an agreement between the United States and such nation; or

(C) as a consequence of a claim of jurisdiction which is not recognized by the United States;

he shall certify such determination to the Secretary of the Treasury.

(b) Prohibitions. Upon receipt of any certification from the Secretary of State under subsection (a) of this section, the Secretary of the Treasury shall immediately take such action as may be necessary and appropriate to prohibit the importation into the United States --

(1) of all fish and fish products from the fishery involved, if any; and

(2) upon recommendation of the Secretary of State, such other fish or fish products, from any fishery of the foreign nation concerned, which the Secretary of State finds to be appropriate to carry out the purposes of this section.

(c) Removal of prohibition. If the Secretary of State finds that the reasons for the imposition of any import prohibition under this section no longer prevail, the Secretary of State shall notify the Secretary of the Treasury, who shall promptly remove such import prohibition.

(d) Definitions. As used in this section --

(1) The term "fish" includes any highly migratory species.

(2) The term "fish products" means any article which is produced from or composed of (in whole or in part) any fish.

[Pub. L. 94-265, Title II, § 205, 90 Stat. 345 (Apr. 13, 1976); Pub. L. 101-627, Title I, § 105(b)(1), 104 Stat. 4440 (Nov. 28, 1990)]

16 U.S.C. § 1826. Large-scale driftnet fishing. (a) Short title. This section incorporates and expands upon provisions of the Driftnet Impact Monitoring, Assessment, and Control Act of 1987 and may be cited as the Driftnet Act Amendments of 1990.

(b) Findings. The Congress finds that --

(1) the continued widespread use of large-scale driftnets beyond the exclusive economic zone of any nation is a destructive fishing practice that poses a threat to living marine resources of the world's oceans, including but not limited to the North and South Pacific Ocean and the Bering Sea;

(2) the use of large-scale driftnets is expanding into new regions of the world's oceans, including the Atlantic Ocean and Caribbean Sea;

(3) there is a pressing need for detailed and reliable information on the number of

seabirds, sea turtles, nontarget fish, and marine mammals that become entangled and die in actively fished large-scale driftnets and in large-scale driftnets that are lost, abandoned, or discarded;

(4) increased efforts, including reliable observer data and enforcement mechanisms, are needed to monitor, assess, control, and reduce the adverse impact of large-scale driftnet fishing on living marine resources;

(5) the nations of the world have agreed in the United Nations, through General Assembly Resolution Numbered 44-225, approved December 22, 1989, by the General Assembly, that a moratorium should be imposed by June 30, 1992, on the use of large-scale driftnets beyond the exclusive economic zone of any nation;

(6) the nations of the South Pacific have agreed to a moratorium on the use of large-scale driftnets in the South Pacific through the Convention for the Prohibition of Fishing with Long Driftnets in the South Pacific, which was agreed to in Wellington, New Zealand, on November 29, 1989; and

(7) increasing population pressures and new knowledge of the importance of living marine resources to the health of the global ecosystem demand that greater responsibility be exercised by persons fishing or developing new fisheries beyond the exclusive economic zone of any nation.

(c) Policy. It is declared to be the policy of the Congress in this section that the United States should --

(1) implement the moratorium called for by the United Nations General Assembly in Resolution Numbered 44-225;

(2) support the Tarawa Declaration and the Wellington Convention for the Prohibition of Fishing with Long Driftnets in the South Pacific; and

(3) secure a permanent ban on the use of destructive fishing practices, and in particular large-scale driftnets, by persons or vessels fishing beyond the exclusive economic zone of any nation.

(d) International agreements. The Secretary, through the Secretary of State and the Secretary of the department in which the Coast Guard is operating, shall seek to secure international agreements to implement immediately the findings, policy, and provisions of this section, and in particular an international ban on large-scale driftnet fishing. The Secretary, through the Secretary of State, shall include, in any agreement which addresses the taking of living marine resources of the United States, provisions to ensure that --

(1) each large-scale driftnet fishing vessel of a foreign nation that is party to the agreement, including vessels that may operate independently to develop new fishing areas, which operate beyond the exclusive economic zone of any nation, is included in such agreement;

(2) each large-scale driftnet fishing vessel of a foreign nation that is party to the agreement, which operates beyond the exclusive economic zone of any nation, is equipped with satellite transmitters which provide real-time position information accessible to the United States;

(3) statistically reliable monitoring by the United States is carried out, through the use of on-board observers or through dedicated platforms provided by foreign nations that are parties to the agreement, of all target and nontarget fish species, marine mammals, sea turtles, and sea birds entangled or killed by large-scale driftnets used

by fishing vessels of foreign nations that are parties to the agreement;

(4) officials of the United States have the right to board and inspect for violations of the agreement any large-scale driftnet fishing vessels operating under the flag of a foreign nation that is party to the agreement at any time while such vessel is operating in designated areas beyond the exclusive economic zone of any nation;

(5) all catch landed or transshipped at sea by large-scale driftnet fishing vessels of a foreign nation that is a party to the agreement, and which are operated beyond the exclusive economic zone of any nation, is reliably monitored and documented;

(6) time and area restrictions are imposed on the use of large-scale driftnets in order to prevent interception of anadromous species;

(7) all large-scale driftnets used are constructed, insofar as feasible, with biodegradable materials which break into segments that do not represent a threat to living marine resources;

(8) all large-scale driftnets are marked at appropriate intervals in a manner that conclusively identifies the vessel and flag nation responsible for each such driftnet;

(9) the taking of nontarget fish species, marine mammals, sea turtles, seabirds, and endangered species or other species protected by international agreements to which the United States is a party is minimized and does not pose a threat to existing fisheries or the long-term health of living marine resources; and

(10) definitive steps are agreed upon to ensure that parties to the agreement comply with the spirit of other international agreements and resolutions concerning the use of large-scale driftnets beyond the exclusive economic zone of any nation.

(e) Report. ****

(f) Certification. If at any time the Secretary, in consultation with the Secretary of State and the Secretary of the department in which the Coast Guard is operating, identifies any nation that warrants inclusion in the list described under subsection (e)(4) of this section, the Secretary shall certify that fact to the President. Such certification shall be deemed to be a certification for the purposes of section 8(a) of the Fishermen's Protective Act of 1967 (22 U.S.C. 1978(a)).

(g) Effect on sovereign rights. This section shall not serve or be construed to expand or diminish the sovereign rights of the United States, as stated by Presidential Proclamation Numbered 5030, dated March 10, 1983, and reflected in this Act or other existing law.

(h) "Living marine resources" defined. As used in this section, the term "living marine resources" includes fish, marine mammals, sea turtles, and sea birds and other waterfowl.

[Pub. L. 94-265, Title II, § 206, as added Pub. L. 95-6, § 3(1), Feb. 21, 1977, 91 Stat. 15, and amended Pub. L. 99-659, Title I, § 101(c)(2), 100 Stat. 3707 (Nov. 14, 1986); Pub. L. 101-627, Title I, § 107(a), 104 Stat. 4441 (Nov. 28, 1990); Pub. L. 104-297, Title I, § 105(f), 110 Stat. 3569 (Oct. 11, 1996)]

16 U.S.C. § 1826a. Denial of port privileges and sanctions for high seas large-scale

driftnet fishing. (a) Denial of port privileges. ****

(b) Sanctions. ****

(3) Prohibition on imports of fish and fish products and sport fishing equipment. (A) Prohibition. The President --

(i) upon receipt of notification of the identification of a nation under paragraph (1)(A); or

(ii) if the consultations with the government of a nation under paragraph (2) are not satisfactorily concluded within ninety days, shall direct the Secretary of the Treasury to prohibit the importation into the United States of fish and fish products and sport fishing equipment (as that term is defined in section 4162 of Title 26) from that nation.

(B) Implementation of prohibition. With respect to an import prohibition directed under subparagraph (A), the Secretary of the Treasury shall implement such prohibition not later than the date that is forty-five days after the date on which the Secretary has received the direction from the President.

(C) Public notice of prohibition. ****

(4) Additional economic sanctions. (A) Determination of effectiveness of sanctions. Not later than six months after the date the Secretary of Commerce identifies a nation under paragraph (1), the Secretary shall determine whether --

(i) any prohibition established under paragraph (3) is insufficient to cause that nation to terminate large-scale driftnet fishing conducted by its nationals and vessels beyond the exclusive economic zone of any nation; or

(ii) that nation has retaliated against the United States as a result of that prohibition.

****

[Pub. L. 102-582, Title I, § 101, 106 Stat. 4901 (Nov. 2, 1992)]

16 U.S.C. § 1826b. Duration of denial of port privileges and sanctions. ****

[Pub. L. 102-582, Title I, § 102, 106 Stat. 4903 (Nov. 2, 1992)]

16 U.S.C. § 1826c. Definitions. In this title, the following definitions apply:

(1) Fish and fish products. The term "fish and fish products" means any aquatic species (including marine mammals and plants) and all products thereof exported from a nation, whether or not taken by fishing vessels of that nation or packed, processed, or otherwise prepared for export in that nation or within the jurisdiction thereof.

(2) Large-scale driftnet fishing. (A) In general. Except as provided in subparagraph (B), the term "large-scale driftnet fishing" means a method of fishing in which a gillnet composed of a panel or panels of webbing, or a series of such gillnets, with a total length of two and one-half kilometers or more is placed in the water and allowed to drift with the currents and winds for the purpose of entangling fish in the webbing.

(B) Exception. Until January 1, 1994, the term "large-scale driftnet fishing" does not include the use in the northeast Atlantic Ocean of gillnets with a total length not to exceed five kilometers if the use is in accordance with regulations adopted by the European Community pursuant to the October 28, 1991, decision by the Council of Fisheries Ministers of the Community.

(3) Large-scale driftnet fishing vessel. The term "large-scale driftnet fishing vessel" means any vessel which is --

(A) used for, equipped to be used for, or of a type which is normally used for large-scale driftnet fishing; or

(B) used for aiding or assisting one or more vessels at sea in the performance of large-scale driftnet fishing, including preparation, supply, storage, refrigeration, transportation, or processing.

[Pub. L. 102-582, Title I, § 104, 106 Stat. 4903 (Nov. 2, 1992)]

****

16 U.S.C. § 1827. Observer program regarding certain foreign fishing. (a) Definitions. As used in this section --

(1) The term "Act of 1976" means the Magnuson-Stevens Fishery Conservation and Management Act (16 U.S.C. 1801 *et seq.*).

(2) The term "billfish" means any species of marlin, spearfish, sailfish or swordfish.

(3) The term "Secretary" means the Secretary of Commerce.

(b) Observer program. The Secretary shall establish a program under which a United States observer will be stationed aboard each foreign fishing vessel while that vessel --

(1) is in waters that are within --

(A) the fishery conservation zone established under section 101 of the Act of 1976 [16 U.S.C. § 1811], and

(B) the Convention area as defined in Article I of the International Convention for the Conservation of Atlantic Tunas; and

(2) is taking or attempting to take any species of fish if such taking or attempting to take may result in the incidental taking of billfish.

The Secretary may acquire observers for such program through contract with qualified private persons.

(c) Functions of observers. United States observers, while aboard foreign fishing vessels as required under subsection (b) of this section, shall carry out such scientific and other functions as the Secretary deems necessary or appropriate to carry out this section.

(d) Fees. There is imposed for each year after 1980 on the owner or operator of each foreign fishing vessel that, in the judgment of the Secretary, will engage in fishing in waters described in subsection (b) (1) of this section during that year which may result in the incidental taking of billfish a fee in an amount sufficient to cover all of the costs of providing an observer aboard that vessel under the program established under subsection (a) of this section. The fees imposed under this subsection for any year shall be paid to the Secretary before that year begins. All fees collected by the Secretary under this subsection shall be deposited in the Fund established by subsection (e) of this section.

(e) Fund. ****

(f) Prohibited acts. (1) It is unlawful for any person who is the owner or operator of a foreign fishing vessel to which this section applies --

(A) to violate any regulation issued under subsection (g) of this section;

(B) to refuse to pay the fee imposed under subsection (d) of this section after being requested to do so by the Secretary; or

(C) to refuse to permit an individual who is authorized to act as an observer under this section with respect to that vessel to board the vessel for purposes of carrying out observer functions.

(2) Section 308 of the Act of 1976 [16 U.S.C. § 1858] (relating to civil penalties) applies to any act that is unlawful under paragraph (1), and for purposes of such application the commission of any such act shall be treated as an act the commission of which is unlawful under section 307 of the Act of 1976 [16 U.S.C. § 1857].

(g) Regulations. The Secretary shall issue such regulations as are necessary or appropriate to carry out this section.

[Pub. L. 96-339, § 2, 94 Stat. 1069 (Sept. 4, 1980); Pub. L. 96-561, Title II, § 238(b), 94 Stat. 3300 (Dec. 22, 1980); Pub. L. 104-208, Div. A, Title I, § 101(a) [Title II, § 211(b)], 110 Stat. 3009-41 (Sept. 30, 1996)]

Title IV
National Fishery Management Program

§ 1851. National standards for fishery conservation and management. (a) In general. Any fishery management plan prepared, and any regulation promulgated to implement any such plan, pursuant to this title [16 U.S.C. §§ 1851 *et seq.*] shall be consistent with the following national standards for fishery conservation and management:

(1) Conservation and management measures shall prevent overfishing while achieving, on a continuing basis, the optimum yield from each fishery for the United States fishing industry.

(2) Conservation and management measures shall be based upon the best scientific information available.

(3) To the extent practicable, an individual stock of fish shall be managed as a unit throughout its range, and interrelated stocks of fish shall be managed as a unit or in close coordination.

(4) Conservation and management measures shall not discriminate between residents of different States. If it becomes necessary to allocate or assign fishing privileges among various United States fishermen, such allocation shall be (A) fair and equitable to all such fishermen; (B) reasonably calculated to promote conservation; and (C) carried out in such manner that no particular individual, corporation, or other entity acquires an excessive share of such privileges.

(5) Conservation and management measures shall, where practicable, consider efficiency in the utilization of fishery resources; except that no such measure shall have economic allocation as its sole purpose.

(6) Conservation and management measures shall take into account and allow for variations among, and contingencies in, fisheries, fishery resources, and catches.

(7) Conservation and management measures shall, where practicable, minimize costs and avoid unnecessary duplication.
(8) Conservation and management measures shall, consistent with the conservation requirements of this Act (including the prevention of overfishing and rebuilding of overfished stocks), take into account the importance of fishery resources to fishing communities in order to (A) provide for the sustained participation of such communities, and (B) to the extent practicable, minimize adverse economic impacts on such communities.
(9) Conservation and management measures shall, to the extent practicable, (A) minimize bycatch and (B) to the extent bycatch cannot be avoided, minimize the mortality of such bycatch.
(10) Conservation and management measures shall, to the extent practicable, promote the safety of human life at sea.

(b) Guidelines. The Secretary shall establish advisory guidelines (which shall not have the force and effect of law), based on the national standards, to assist in the development of fishery management plans.

[Pub. L. 94-265, Title III, § 301, 90 Stat. 346 (Apr. 13, 1976); Pub. L. 97-453, § 4, 96 Stat. 2484 (Jan. 12, 1983); Pub. L. 98-623, Title IV, § 404(3), 98 Stat. 3408 (Nov. 8, 1984); Pub. L. 104-297, Title I, § 106, 110 Stat. 3570 (Oct. 11, 1996)]

16 U.S.C. § 1852. Regional Fishery Management Councils. (a) Establishment. (1) There shall be established, within 120 days after the date of enactment of this Act [April 13, 1976], eight Regional Fishery Management Councils, as follows:

(A) New England Council. The New England Fishery Management Council shall consist of the States of Maine, New Hampshire, Massachusetts, Rhode Island, and Connecticut and shall have authority over the fisheries in the Atlantic Ocean seaward of such States (except as provided in paragraph (3)). The New England Council shall have 18 voting members, including 12 appointed by the Secretary in accordance with subsection (b)(2) of this section (at least one of whom shall be appointed from each such State).
(B) Mid-Atlantic Council. The Mid-Atlantic Fishery Management Council shall consist of the States of New York, New Jersey, Delaware, Pennsylvania, Maryland, Virginia, and North Carolina and shall have authority over the fisheries in the Atlantic Ocean seaward of such States (except North Carolina, and as provided in paragraph (3)). The Mid-Atlantic Council shall have 21 voting members, including 13 appointed by the Secretary in accordance with subsection (b)(2) of this section (at least one of whom shall be appointed from each such State).
(C) South Atlantic Council. The South Atlantic Fishery Management Council shall consist of the States of North Carolina, South Carolina, Georgia, and Florida and shall have authority over the fisheries in the Atlantic Ocean seaward of such States (except as provided in paragraph (3)). The South Atlantic Council shall have 13 voting members, including 8 appointed by the Secretary in accordance with subsection (b)(2) of this section (at least one of whom shall be appointed from each such State).

(D) Caribbean Council. The Caribbean Fishery Management Council shall consist of the Virgin Islands and the Commonwealth of Puerto Rico and shall have authority over the fisheries in the Caribbean Sea and Atlantic Ocean seaward of such States (except as provided in paragraph (3)). The Caribbean Council shall have 7 voting members, including 4 appointed by the Secretary in accordance with subsection (b)(2) of this section (at least one of whom shall be appointed from each such State).

(E) Gulf Council. The Gulf of Mexico Fishery Management Council shall consist of the States of Texas, Louisiana, Mississippi, Alabama, and Florida and shall have authority over the fisheries in the Gulf of Mexico seaward of such States (except as provided in paragraph (3)). The Gulf Council shall have 17 voting members, including 11 appointed by the Secretary in accordance with subsection (b)(2) of this section (at least one of whom shall be appointed from each such State).

(F) Pacific council. The Pacific Fishery Management Council shall consist of the States of California, Oregon, Washington, and Idaho and shall have authority over the fisheries in the Pacific Ocean seaward of such States. The Pacific Council shall have 14 voting members, including 8 appointed by the Secretary in accordance with subsection (b)(2) of this section (at least one of whom shall be appointed from each such State), and including one appointed from an Indian tribe with Federally recognized fishing rights from California, Oregon, Washington, or Idaho in accordance with subsection (b)(5) of this section.

(G) North Pacific Council. The North Pacific Fishery Management Council shall consist of the States of Alaska, Washington, and Oregon and shall have authority over the fisheries in the Arctic Ocean, Bering Sea, and Pacific Ocean seaward of Alaska. The North Pacific Council shall have 11 voting members, including 7 appointed by the Secretary in accordance with subsection (b) (2) of this section (5 of whom shall be appointed from the State of Alaska and 2 of whom shall be appointed from the State of Washington).

(H) Western Pacific Council. The Western Pacific Fishery Management Council shall consist of the States of Hawaii, American Samoa, Guam, and the Northern Mariana Islands and shall have authority over the fisheries in the Pacific Ocean seaward of such States and of the Commonwealths, territories, and possessions of the United States in the Pacific Ocean area. The Western Pacific Council shall have 13 voting members, including 8 appointed by the Secretary in accordance with subsection (b)(2) of this section (at least one of whom shall be appointed from each of the following States: Hawaii, American Samoa, Guam, and the Northern Mariana Islands).

(2) Each Council shall reflect the expertise and interest of the several constituent States in the ocean area over which such Council is granted authority.

(3) The Secretary shall have authority over any highly migratory species fishery that is within the geographical area of authority of more than one of the following Councils: New England Council, Mid-Atlantic Council, South Atlantic Council, Gulf Council, and Caribbean Council.

(b) Voting members. (1) The voting members of each Council shall be:

(A) The principal State official with marine fishery management responsibility and expertise in each constituent State, who is designated as such by the Governor of the State, so long as the official continues to hold such position, or the designee of such official.

(B) The regional director of the National Marine Fisheries Service for the geographic area concerned, or his designee, except that if two such directors are within such geographical area, the Secretary shall designate which of such directors shall be the voting member.

(C) The members required to be appointed by the Secretary in accordance with paragraphs (2) and (5).

(2)(A) The members of each Council required to be appointed by the Secretary must be individuals who, by reason of their occupational or other experience, scientific expertise, or training, are knowledgeable regarding the conservation and management, or the commercial or recreational harvest, of the fishery resources of the geographical area concerned. Within nine months after the date of enactment of the Fishery Conservation Amendments of 1990 [November 28, 1990], the Secretary shall, by regulation, prescribe criteria for determining whether an individual satisfies the requirements of this subparagraph.

(B) The Secretary, in making appointments under this section, shall, to the extent practicable, ensure a fair and balanced apportionment, on a rotating or other basis, of the active participants (or their representatives) in the commercial and recreational fisheries under the jurisdiction of the Council. On January 31, 1991, and each year thereafter, the Secretary shall submit to the Committee on Commerce, Science, and Transportation of the Senate and the Committee on Merchant Marine and Fisheries of the House of Representatives a report on the actions taken by the Secretary to ensure that such fair and balanced apportionment is achieved. The report shall --

(i) list the fisheries under the jurisdiction of each Council, outlining for each fishery the type and quantity of fish harvested, fishing and processing methods employed, the number of participants, the duration and range of the fishery, and other distinguishing characteristics;

(ii) assess the membership of each Council in terms of the apportionment of the active participants in each such fishery; and

(iii) state the Secretary's plans and schedule for actions to achieve a fair and balanced apportionment on the Council for the active participants in any such fishery.

(C) The Secretary shall appoint the members of each Council from a list of individuals submitted by the Governor of each applicable constituent State. A Governor may not submit the names of individuals to the Secretary for appointment unless the Governor has determined that each such individual is qualified under the requirements of subparagraph (A) and unless the Governor has, to the extent practicable, first consulted with representatives of the commercial and recreational fishing interests of the State regarding those individuals. Each such list shall include the names and pertinent biographical data of not less than three individuals for each applicable vacancy and shall be accompanied by a statement by the Governor explaining how each such individual meets the requirements of subparagraph (A). The Secretary shall review each list submitted by a Governor to ascertain if the individuals on the list are qualified for the vacancy on the basis of such requirements. If the Secretary determines that any individual is not qualified, the Secretary shall notify the appropriate Governor of that determination. The Governor shall then submit a revised list or resubmit the original list with an additional explanation of the qualifications of the individual in question. An individual is not eligible for appointment by the Secretary until that individual complies with the applicable financial disclosure requirements under subsection [(j)].

(D) Whenever the Secretary makes an appointment to a Council, the Secretary shall make a public announcement of such appointment not less than 45 days before the first day on which the individual is to take office as a member of the Council.

(3) Each voting member appointed to a Council by the Secretary in accordance with paragraphs (2) and (5) shall serve for a term of 3 years; except that the Secretary may designate a shorter term if necessary to provide for balanced expiration to terms of office. No member appointed after January 1, 1986, may serve more than three consecutive terms. Any term in which an individual was appointed to replace a member who left office during the term shall not be counted in determining the number of consecutive terms served by that Council member.

(4) Successors to the voting members of any Council shall be appointed in the same manner as the original voting members. Any individual appointed to fill a vacancy occurring prior to the expiration of any term of office shall be appointed for the remainder of that term.

(5)(A) The Secretary shall appoint to the Pacific Council one representative of an Indian tribe with Federally recognized fishing rights from California, Oregon, Washington, or Idaho from a list of not less than 3 individuals submitted by the tribal governments. The Secretary, in consultation with the Secretary of the Interior and tribal governments, shall establish by regulation the procedure for submitting a list under this subparagraph.

(B) Representation shall be rotated among the tribes taking into consideration --

(i) the qualifications of the individuals on the list referred to in subparagraph (A),

(ii) the various rights of the Indian tribes involved and judicial cases that set forth how those rights are to be exercised, and

(iii) the geographic area in which the tribe of the representative is located.

(C) A vacancy occurring prior to the expiration of any term shall be filled in the same manner as set out in subparagraphs (A) and (B), except that the Secretary may use the list from which the vacating representative was chosen.

(6) The Secretary may remove for cause any member of a Council required to be appointed by the Secretary in accordance with paragraphs (2) or (5) if --

(A) the Council concerned first recommends removal by not less than two-thirds of the members who are voting members and submits such removal recommendation to the Secretary in writing together with a statement of the basis for the recommendation; or

(B) the member is found by the Secretary, after notice and an opportunity for a hearing in accordance with section 554 of Title 5, to have committed an act prohibited by section 307(1)(O) [16 U.S.C. § 1857(1)(O)].

(c) Nonvoting members. (1) The nonvoting members of each Council shall be:

(A) The regional or area director of the United States Fish and Wildlife Service for the geographical area concerned, or his designee.

(B) The commander of the Coast Guard district for the geographical area concerned, or his designee; except that, if two Coast Guard districts are within such geographical area, the commander designated for such purpose by the commandant of the Coast Guard.

(C) The executive director of the Marine Fisheries Commission for the geographical area concerned, if any, or his designee.

(D) One representative of the Department of State designated for such purpose by the Secretary of State, or his designee.

(2) The Pacific Council shall have one additional nonvoting member who shall be appointed by, and serve at the pleasure of, the Governor of Alaska.

(d) Compensation and expenses. ****

(e) Transaction of business. (1) A majority of the voting members of any Council shall constitute a quorum, but one or more such members designated by the Council may hold hearings. All decisions of any Council shall be by majority vote of the voting members present and voting.

(2) The voting members of each Council shall select a Chairman for such Council from among the voting members.

(3) Each Council shall meet at appropriate times and places in any of the constituent States of the Council at the call of the Chairman or upon the request of a majority of its voting members.

(4) If any voting member of a Council disagrees with respect to any matter which is transmitted to the Secretary by such Council, such member may submit a statement to the Secretary setting forth the reasons for such disagreement. The regional director of the National Marine Fisheries Service serving on the Council, or the regional director's designee, shall submit such a statement, which shall be made available to the public upon request, if the regional director disagrees with any such matter.

(5) At the request of any voting member of a Council, the Council shall hold a roll call vote on any matter before the Council. The official minutes and other appropriate records of any Council meeting shall identify all roll call votes held, the name of each voting member present during each roll call vote, and how each member voted on each roll call vote.

(f) Staff and administration. ****

(g) Committees and panels. (1) Each Council shall establish and maintain, and appoint the members of, a scientific and statistical committee to assist it in the development, collection, and evaluation of such statistical, biological, economic, social, and other scientific information as is relevant to such Council's development and amendment of any fishery management plan.

(2) Each Council shall establish such other advisory panels as are necessary or appropriate to assist it in carrying out its functions under this Act.

(3)(A) Each Council shall establish and maintain a fishing industry advisory committee which shall provide information and recommendations on, and assist in the development of, fishery management plans and amendments to such plans.

(B) Appointments to a committee established under subparagraph (A) shall be made by each Council in such a manner as to provide fair representation to commercial fishing interests in the geographical area of authority of the Council.

(4) The Secretary shall establish advisory panels to assist in the collection and evaluation of information relevant to the development of any fishery management plan or plan amendment for a fishery to which subsection (a)(3) of this section applies. Each advisory panel shall participate in all aspects of the development of the plan or amendment; be balanced in its representation of commercial, recreational, and other interests; and consist of not less than 7 individuals who are knowledgeable about the fishery for which the plan or amendment is developed, selected from among --

(A) members of advisory committees and species working groups appointed under Acts implementing relevant international fishery agreements pertaining to highly migratory species; and

(B) other interested persons.

(5) Decisions and recommendations made by committees and panels established under this subsection shall be considered to be advisory in nature.

(h) Functions. Each Council shall, in accordance with the provisions of this Act --

(1) for each fishery under its authority that requires conservation and management, prepare and submit to the Secretary (A) a fishery management plan, and (B) amendments to each such plan that are necessary from time to time (and promptly whenever changes in conservation and management measures in another fishery substantially affect the fishery for which such plan was developed);

(2) prepare comments on any application for foreign fishing transmitted to it under section 204(b)(4)(C) or section 204(d) [16 U.S.C. § 1824(b)(4)(C) or 1824(d)], and any fishery management plan or amendment transmitted to it under section 304(c)(4) [16 U.S.C. § 1854(c)(4)];

(3) conduct public hearings, at appropriate times and in appropriate locations in the geographical area concerned, so as to allow all interested persons an opportunity to be heard in the development of fishery management plans and amendments to such plans, and with respect to the administration and implementation of the provisions of this Act (and for purposes of this paragraph, the term "geographical area concerned" may include an area under the authority of another Council if the fish in the fishery concerned migrate into, or occur in, that area or if the matters being heard affect fishermen of that area; but not unless such other Council is first consulted regarding the conduct of such hearings within its area);

(4) submit to the Secretary such periodic reports as the Council deems appropriate, and any other relevant report which may be requested by the Secretary;

(5) review on a continuing basis, and revise as appropriate, the assessments and

specifications made pursuant to section 303(a)(3) and (4) [16 U.S.C. § 1853(a)(3), (4)] with respect to the optimum yield from, the capacity and extent to which United States fish processors will process United States harvested fish from, and the total allowable level of foreign fishing in, each fishery (except as provided in ... subsection (a)(3) of this section) within its geographical area of authority; and
(6) conduct any other activities which are required by, or provided for in, this Act or which are necessary and appropriate to the foregoing functions.

(i) Procedural matters. (1) The Federal Advisory Committee Act (5 U.S.C.App.) shall not apply to the Councils or to the scientific and statistical committees or advisory panels established under subsection (g) of this section.
(2) The following guidelines apply with respect to the conduct of business at meetings of a Council, and of the scientific and statistical committee and advisory panels established under subsection (g) of this section:

(A) Unless closed in accordance with paragraph (3), each regular meeting and each emergency meeting shall be open to the public.

(B) Emergency meetings shall be held at the call of the chairman or equivalent presiding officer.

(C) Timely public notice of each regular meeting and each emergency meeting, including the time, place, and agenda of the meeting, shall be published in local newspapers in the major fishing ports of the region (and in other major fishing ports having a direct interest in the affected fishery) and such notice may be given by such other means as will result in wide publicity. Timely notice of each regular meeting shall also be published in the Federal Register. The published agenda of the meeting may not be modified to include additional matters for Council action without public notice or within 14 days prior to the meeting date, unless such modification is to address an emergency action under section 305(c) [16 U.S.C. § 1855(c)] in which case public notice shall be given immediately.

(D) Interested persons shall be permitted to present oral or written statements regarding the matters on the agenda at meetings. All written information submitted to a Council by an interested person shall include a statement of the source and date of such information. Any oral or written statement shall include a brief description of the background and interests of the person in the subject of the oral or written statement.

(E) Detailed minutes of each meeting of the Council, except for any closed session, shall be kept and shall contain a record of the persons present, a complete and accurate description of matters discussed and conclusions reached, and copies of all statements filed. The Chairman shall certify the accuracy of the minutes of each such meeting and submit a copy thereof to the Secretary. The minutes shall be made available to any court of competent jurisdiction.

(F) Subject to the procedures established under paragraph (4), and the guidelines prescribed by the Secretary under section 402(b) [16 U.S.C. § 1881a(b)], relating to confidentiality, the administrative record, including minutes required under subparagraph (E), of each meeting, and records or other documents which were made available to or prepared for or by the Council, committee, or panel incident to the meeting, shall be available for public inspection and copying at a single location in the offices of the Council or the Secretary, as appropriate.

(3)(A) Each Council, scientific and statistical committee, and advisory panel --

(i) shall close any meeting, or portion thereof, that concerns matters or information that bears a national security classification; and

(ii) may close any meeting, or portion thereof, that concerns matters or information that pertains to national security, employment matters, or briefings on litigation in which the Council is interested.

Subparagraphs (D) and (F) of paragraph (2) shall not apply to any meeting or portion thereof that is so closed.

(B) If any meeting or portion is closed, the Council concerned shall notify local newspapers in the major fishing ports within its region (and in other major, affected fishing ports), including in that notification the time and place of the meeting. This subparagraph does not require notification regarding any brief closure of a portion of a meeting in order to discuss employment or other internal administrative matters.

(4) Each Council shall establish appropriate procedures applicable to it and to its committee and advisory panels for ensuring the confidentiality of the statistics that may be submitted to it by Federal or State authorities, and may be voluntarily submitted to it by private persons; including, but not limited to, procedures for the restriction of Council employee access and the prevention of conflicts of interest; except that such procedures, in the case of statistics submitted to the Council by a State or by the Secretary under section 402(b) [16 U.S.C. § 1881a(b)], must be consistent with the laws and regulations of that State, or with the procedures of the Secretary, as the case may be, concerning the confidentiality of the statistics.

(5) Each Council shall specify those procedures that are necessary or appropriate to ensure that the committees and advisory panels established under subsection (g) of this section are involved, on a continuing basis, in the development and amendment of fishery management plans.

(6) At any time when a Council determines it appropriate to consider new information from a State or Federal agency or from a Council advisory body, the Council shall give comparable consideration to new information offered at that time by interested members of the public. Interested parties shall have a reasonable opportunity to respond to new data or information before the Council takes final action on conservation and management measures.

(j) Disclosure of financial interest and recusal. ****

[Pub. L. 94-265, Title III, § 302, 90 Stat. 347 (Apr. 13, 1976); Pub. L. 95-354, § 5(1), 92 Stat. 521 (Aug. 28, 1978); Pub. L. 96-561, Title II, § 234, 94 Stat. 3299 (Dec. 22, 1980); Pub. L. 97-453, § 5, 96 Stat. 2484 (Jan. 12, 1983); Pub. L. 99-659, Title I, § 104(a)(1), (b), (c), (d), (e)(1), 100 Stat. 3709, 3710 (Nov. 14, 1986); Pub. L. 101-627, Title I, §§ 108(a) to (j), 120(c), 104 Stat. 4444-4446, 4459 (Nov. 28, 1990); Pub. L. 102-582, Title IV, § 403, 106 Stat. 4909 (Nov. 2, 1992); Pub. L. 104-297, Title I, § 107, 110 Stat. 3570 (Oct. 11, 1996); Pub. L. 106-113, Div. B., § 1000(a)(1), [Title II, § 210], 113 Stat. 1535, 1501A-33 (Nov. 29, 1999)]

16 U.S.C. § 1853. Contents of fishery management plans. (a) Required provisions. Any fishery management plan which is prepared by any Council, or by the Secretary, with respect to any fishery, shall--

(1) contain the conservation and management measures, applicable to foreign fishing and fishing by vessels of the United States, which are --

(A) necessary and appropriate for the conservation and management of the fishery, to prevent overfishing and rebuild overfished stocks, and to protect, restore, and promote the long-term health and stability of the fishery;

(B) described in this subsection or subsection (b) of this section, or both; and

(C) consistent with the national standards, the other provisions of this Act, regulations implementing recommendations by international organizations in which the United States participates (including but not limited to closed areas, quotas, and size limits), and any other applicable law;

(2) contain a description of the fishery, including, but not limited to, the number of vessels involved, the type and quantity of fishing gear used, the species of fish involved and their location, the cost likely to be incurred in management, actual and potential revenues from the fishery, any recreational interests in the fishery, and the nature and extent of foreign fishing and Indian treaty fishing rights, if any;

(3) assess and specify the present and probable future condition of, and the maximum sustainable yield and optimum yield from, the fishery, and include a summary of the information utilized in making such specification;

(4) assess and specify --

(A) the capacity and the extent to which fishing vessels of the United States, on an annual basis, will harvest the optimum yield specified under paragraph (3),

(B) the portion of such optimum yield which, on an annual basis, will not be harvested by fishing vessels of the United States and can be made available for foreign fishing, and

(C) the capacity and extent to which United States fish processors, on an annual basis, will process that portion of such optimum yield that will be harvested by fishing vessels of the United States;

(5) specify the pertinent data which shall be submitted to the Secretary with respect to commercial, recreational, and charter fishing in the fishery, including, but not limited to, information regarding the type and quantity of fishing gear used, catch by species in numbers of fish or weight thereof, areas in which fishing was engaged in, time of fishing, number of hauls, and the estimated processing capacity of, and the actual processing capacity utilized by, United States fish processors;

(6) consider and provide for temporary adjustments, after consultation with the Coast Guard and persons utilizing the fishery, regarding access to the fishery for vessels otherwise prevented from harvesting because of weather or other ocean conditions affecting the safe conduct of the fishery; except that the adjustment shall not adversely affect conservation efforts in other fisheries or discriminate among participants in the affected fishery;

(7) describe and identify essential fish habitat for the fishery based on the guidelines established by the Secretary under section 305(b)(1)(A) [16 U.S.C. § 1855(b)(1)(A)], minimize to the extent practicable adverse effects on such habitat caused by fishing, and identify other actions to encourage the conservation and enhancement of such habitat;

(8) in the case of a fishery management plan that, after January 1, 1991, is

submitted to the Secretary for review under section 304(a) [16 U.S.C. § 1854(a)] (including any plan for which an amendment is submitted to the Secretary for such review) or is prepared by the Secretary, assess and specify the nature and extent of scientific data which is needed for effective implementation of the plan;

(9) include a fishery impact statement for the plan or amendment (in the case of a plan or amendment thereto submitted to or prepared by the Secretary after October 1, 1990) which shall assess, specify, and describe the likely effects, if any, of the conservation and management measures on --

(A) participants in the fisheries and fishing communities affected by the plan or amendment; and

(B) participants in the fisheries conducted in adjacent areas under the authority of another Council, after consultation with such Council and representatives of those participants;

(10) specify objective and measurable criteria for identifying when the fishery to which the plan applies is overfished (with an analysis of how the criteria were determined and the relationship of the criteria to the reproductive potential of stocks of fish in that fishery) and, in the case of a fishery which the Council or the Secretary has determined is approaching an overfished condition or is overfished, contain conservation and management measures to prevent overfishing or end overfishing and rebuild the fishery;

(11) establish a standardized reporting methodology to assess the amount and type of bycatch occurring in the fishery, and include conservation and management measures that, to the extent practicable and in the following priority --

(A) minimize bycatch; and

(B) minimize the mortality of bycatch which cannot be avoided;

(12) assess the type and amount of fish caught and released alive during recreational fishing under catch and release fishery management programs and the mortality of such fish, and include conservation and management measures that, to the extent practicable, minimize mortality and ensure the extended survival of such fish;

(13) include a description of the commercial, recreational, and charter fishing sectors which participate in the fishery and, to the extent practicable, quantify trends in landings of the managed fishery resource by the commercial, recreational, and charter fishing sectors; and

(14) to the extent that rebuilding plans or other conservation and management measures which reduce the overall harvest in a fishery are necessary, allocate any harvest restrictions or recovery benefits fairly and equitably among the commercial, recreational, and charter fishing sectors in the fishery.

(b) Discretionary provisions. Any fishery management plan which is prepared by any Council, or by the Secretary, with respect to any fishery, may --

(1) require a permit to be obtained from, and fees to be paid to, the Secretary, with respect to --

(A) any fishing vessel of the United States fishing, or wishing to fish, in the exclusive economic zone or for anadromous species or Continental Shelf fishery resources beyond such zone;

(B) the operator of any such vessel; or

(C) any United States fish processor who first receives fish that are subject to the plan;

(2) designate zones where, and periods when, fishing shall be limited, or shall not be permitted, or shall be permitted only by specified types of fishing vessels or with specified types and quantities of fishing gear;

(3) establish specified limitations which are necessary and appropriate for the conservation and management of the fishery on the --

(A) catch of fish (based on area, species, size, number, weight, sex, bycatch, total biomass, or other factors);

(B) sale of fish caught during commercial, recreational, or charter fishing, consistent with any applicable Federal and State safety and quality requirements; and

(C) transshipment or transportation of fish or fish products under permits issued pursuant to section 204 [16 U.S.C. § 1824];

(4) prohibit, limit, condition, or require the use of specified types and quantities of fishing gear, fishing vessels, or equipment for such vessels, including devices which may be required to facilitate enforcement of the provisions of this Act;

(5) incorporate (consistent with the national standards, the other provisions of this Act, and any other applicable law) the relevant fishery conservation and management measures of the coastal States nearest to the fishery;

(6) establish a limited access system for the fishery in order to achieve optimum yield if, in developing such system, the Council and the Secretary take into account --

(A) present participation in the fishery,

(B) historical fishing practices in, and dependence on, the fishery,

(C) the economics of the fishery,

(D) the capability of fishing vessels used in the fishery to engage in other fisheries,

(E) the cultural and social framework relevant to the fishery and any affected fishing communities, and

(F) any other relevant considerations;

(7) require fish processors who first receive fish that are subject to the plan to submit data (other than economic data) which are necessary for the conservation and management of the fishery;

(8) require that one or more observers be carried on board a vessel of the United States engaged in fishing for species that are subject to the plan, for the purpose of collecting data necessary for the conservation and management of the fishery; except that such a vessel shall not be required to carry an observer on board if the facilities of the vessel for the quartering of an observer, or for carrying out observer functions, are so inadequate or unsafe that the health or safety of the observer or the safe operation of the vessel would be jeopardized;

(9) assess and specify the effect which the conservation and management measures of the plan will have on the stocks of naturally spawning anadromous fish in the region;

(10) include, consistent with the other provisions of this Act, conservation and management measures that provide harvest incentives for participants within each gear group to employ fishing practices that result in lower levels of bycatch or in lower

levels of the mortality of bycatch;

(11) reserve a portion of the allowable biological catch of the fishery for use in scientific research; and

(12) prescribe such other measures, requirements, or conditions and restrictions as are determined to be necessary and appropriate for the conservation and management of the fishery.

(c) Proposed regulations. Proposed regulations which the Council deems necessary or appropriate for the purposes of --

(1) implementing a fishery management plan or plan amendment shall be submitted to the Secretary simultaneously with the plan or amendment under section 304 [16 U.S.C. § 1854]; and

(2) making modifications to regulations implementing a fishery management plan or plan amendment may be submitted to the Secretary at any time after the plan or amendment is approved under section 304 [16 U.S.C. § 1854].

(d) Individual fishing quotas. (1)(A) A Council may not submit and the Secretary may not approve or implement before October 1, 2002, any fishery management plan, plan amendment, or regulation under this Act which creates a new individual fishing quota program.

(B) Any fishery management plan, plan amendment, or regulation approved by the Secretary on or after January 4, 1995, which creates any new individual fishing quota program shall be repealed and immediately returned by the Secretary to the appropriate Council and shall not be resubmitted, reapproved, or implemented during the moratorium set forth in subparagraph (A).

(2)(A) No provision of law shall be construed to limit the authority of a Council to submit and the Secretary to approve the termination or limitation, without compensation to holders of any limited access system permits, of a fishery management plan, plan amendment, or regulation that provides for a limited access system, including an individual fishing quota program.

(B) This subsection shall not be construed to prohibit a Council from submitting, or the Secretary from approving and implementing, amendments to the North Pacific halibut and sablefish, South Atlantic wreckfish, or Mid-Atlantic surf clam and ocean (including mahogany) quahog individual fishing quota programs.

(3) An individual fishing quota or other limited access system authorization --

(A) shall be considered a permit for the purposes of sections 307, 308, and 309 [16 U.S.C. §§ 1857, 1858, and 1859];

(B) may be revoked or limited at any time in accordance with this Act;

(C) shall not confer any right of compensation to the holder of such individual fishing quota or other such limited access system authorization if it is revoked or limited; and

(D) shall not create, or be construed to create, any right, title, or interest in or to any fish before the fish is harvested.

(4)(A) A Council may submit, and the Secretary may approve and implement, a program which reserves up to 25 percent of any fees collected from a fishery under section 304(d)(2) [16 U.S.C. § 1854(d)(2)] to be used, pursuant to section

1104A(a)(7) of the Merchant Marine Act, 1936 (46 U.S.C. App. 1274(a)(7)), to issue obligations that aid in financing the --

(i) purchase of individual fishing quotas in that fishery by fishermen who fish from small vessels; and

(ii) first-time purchase of individual fishing quotas in that fishery by entry level fishermen.

(B) A Council making a submission under subparagraph (A) shall recommend criteria, consistent with the provisions of this Act, that a fisherman must meet to qualify for guarantees under clauses (i) and (ii) of subparagraph (A) and the portion of funds to be allocated for guarantees under each clause.

(5) In submitting and approving any new individual fishing quota program on or after October 1, 2002, the Councils and the Secretary shall consider the report of the National Academy of Sciences required under section 108(f) of the Sustainable Fisheries Act, and any recommendations contained in such report, and shall ensure that any such program--

(A) establishes procedures and requirements for the review and revision of the terms of any such program (including any revisions that may be necessary once a national policy with respect to individual fishing quota programs is implemented), and, if appropriate, for the renewal, reallocation, or reissuance of individual fishing quotas;

(B) provides for the effective enforcement and management of any such program, including adequate observer coverage, and for fees under section 304(d)(2) [16 U.S.C. § 1854(d)(2)] to recover actual costs directly related to such enforcement and management; and

(C) provides for a fair and equitable initial allocation of individual fishing quotas, prevents any person from acquiring an excessive share of the individual fishing quotas issued, and considers the allocation of a portion of the annual harvest in the fishery for entry-level fishermen, small vessel owners, and crew members who do not hold or qualify for individual fishing quotas.

[Pub. L. 94-265, Title III, § 303, 90 Stat. 351 (Apr. 13, 1976); Pub. L. 95-354, § 5(2), (3), 92 Stat. 521 (Aug. 28, 1978); Pub. L. 97-453, § 6, 96 Stat. 2486 (Jan. 12, 1983); Pub. L. 99-659, Title I, §§ 101(c)(2), 105(a)(1), (b), 100 Stat. 3707 (Nov. 14, 1986), 3711; Pub. L. 101-627, Title I, § 109, 104 Stat. 4447 (Nov. 28, 1990); Pub. L. 102-251, Title III, § 301(g), 106 Stat. 64 (Mar. 9, 1992); Pub. L. 104-297, Title I, § 108(a), (c)-(e), 110 Stat. 3574 (Oct. 11, 1996) to 3576; Pub. L. 106-554, § 1(a)(4) [Div. B, Title I, § 144(a)(1), (2)], 114 Stat. 2763, 2763A-238 (Dec. 21, 2000)]

16 U.S.C. § 1854. Action by Secretary. (a) Review of plans. (1) Upon transmittal by the Council to the Secretary of a fishery management plan or plan amendment, the Secretary shall --

(A) immediately commence a review of the plan or amendment to determine whether it is consistent with the national standards, the other provisions of this Act, and any other applicable law; and

(B) immediately publish in the Federal Register a notice stating that the plan or amendment is available and that written information, views, or comments of interested persons on the plan or amendment may be submitted to the Secretary during the 60-day period beginning on the date the notice is published.

(2) In undertaking the review required under paragraph (1), the Secretary shall --

(A) take into account the information, views, and comments received from interested persons;

(B) consult with the Secretary of State with respect to foreign fishing; and

(C) consult with the Secretary of the department in which the Coast Guard is operating with respect to enforcement at sea and to fishery access adjustments referred to in section 305(c) [16 U.S.C. § 1853(a)(6)].

(3) The Secretary shall approve, disapprove, or partially approve a plan or amendment within 30 days of the end of the comment period under paragraph (1) by written notice to the Council. A notice of disapproval or partial approval shall specify --

(A) the applicable law with which the plan or amendment is inconsistent;

(B) the nature of such inconsistencies; and

(C) recommendations concerning the actions that could be taken by the Council to conform such plan or amendment to the requirements of applicable law.

If the Secretary does not notify a Council within 30 days of the end of the comment period of the approval, disapproval, or partial approval of a plan or amendment, then such plan or amendment shall take effect as if approved.

(4) If the Secretary disapproves or partially approves a plan or amendment, the Council may submit a revised plan or amendment to the Secretary for review under this subsection.

(5) For purposes of this subsection and subsection (b) of this section, the term "immediately" means on or before the 5th day after the day on which a Council transmits to the Secretary a fishery management plan, plan amendment, or proposed regulation that the Council characterizes as final.

(b) Review of regulations. (1) Upon transmittal by the Council to the Secretary of proposed regulations prepared under section 303(c) [16 U.S.C. § 1853(c)], the Secretary shall immediately initiate an evaluation of the proposed regulations to determine whether they are consistent with the fishery management plan, plan amendment, this Act and other applicable law. Within 15 days of initiating such evaluation the Secretary shall make a determination and --

(A) if that determination is affirmative, the Secretary shall publish such regulations in the Federal Register, with such technical changes as may be necessary for clarity and an explanation of those changes, for a public comment period of 15 to 60 days; or

(B) if that determination is negative, the Secretary shall notify the Council in writing of the inconsistencies and provide recommendations on revisions that would make the proposed regulations consistent with the fishery management plan, plan amendment, this Act, and other applicable law.

(2) Upon receiving a notification under paragraph (1)(B), the Council may revise the proposed regulations and submit them to the Secretary for reevaluation under paragraph (1).

(3) The Secretary shall promulgate final regulations within 30 days after the end of the comment period under paragraph (1)(A). The Secretary shall consult with the Council before making any revisions to the proposed regulations, and must publish

in the Federal Register an explanation of any differences between the proposed and final regulations.

(c) Preparation and review of Secretarial plans. (1) The Secretary may prepare a fishery management plan, with respect to any fishery, or any amendment to any such plan, in accordance with the national standards, the other provisions of this Act, and any other applicable law, if --

(A) the appropriate Council fails to develop and submit to the Secretary, after a reasonable period of time, a fishery management plan for such fishery, or any necessary amendment to such a plan, if such fishery requires conservation and management;

(B) the Secretary disapproves or partially disapproves any such plan or amendment, or disapproves a revised plan or amendment, and the Council involved fails to submit a revised or further revised plan or amendment; or

(C) the Secretary is given authority to prepare such plan or amendment under this section.

(2) In preparing any plan or amendment under this subsection, the Secretary shall --

(A) conduct public hearings, at appropriate times and locations in the geographical areas concerned, so as to allow interested persons an opportunity to be heard in the preparation and amendment of the plan and any regulations implementing the plan; and

(B) consult with the Secretary of State with respect to foreign fishing and with the Secretary of the department in which the Coast Guard is operating with respect to enforcement at sea.

(3) Notwithstanding paragraph (1) for a fishery under the authority of a Council, the Secretary may not include in any fishery management plan, or any amendment to any such plan, prepared by him, a provision establishing a limited access system, including any individual fishing quota program, unless such system is first approved by a majority of the voting members, present and voting, of each appropriate Council.

(4) Whenever the Secretary prepares a fishery management plan or plan amendment under this section, the Secretary shall immediately --

(A) for a plan or amendment for a fishery under the authority of a Council, submit such plan or amendment to the appropriate Council for consideration and comment; and

(B) publish in the Federal Register a notice stating that the plan or amendment is available and that written information, views, or comments of interested persons on the plan or amendment may be submitted to the Secretary during the 60-day period beginning on the date the notice is published.

(5) Whenever a plan or amendment is submitted under paragraph (4)(A), the appropriate Council must submit its comments and recommendations, if any, regarding the plan or amendment to the Secretary before the close of the 60-day period referred to in paragraph (4)(B). After the close of such 60-day period, the Secretary, after taking into account any such comments and recommendations, as well as any views, information, or comments submitted under paragraph (4)(B), may adopt such plan or amendment.

(6) The Secretary may propose regulations in the Federal Register to implement any plan or amendment prepared by the Secretary. In the case of a plan or amendment to which paragraph (4)(A) applies, such regulations shall be submitted to the Council with such plan or amendment. The comment period on proposed regulations shall be 60 days, except that the Secretary may shorten the comment period on minor revisions to existing regulations.

(7) The Secretary shall promulgate final regulations within 30 days after the end of the comment period under paragraph (6). The Secretary must publish in the Federal Register an explanation of any substantive differences between the proposed and final rules. All final regulations must be consistent with the fishery management plan, with the national standards and other provisions of this Act, and with any other applicable law.

(d) Establishment of fees. (1) The Secretary shall by regulation establish the level of any fees which are authorized to be charged pursuant to section 303(b)(1) [16 U.S.C. § 1853(b)(1)]. The Secretary may enter into a cooperative agreement with the States concerned under which the States administer the permit system and the agreement may provide that all or part of the fees collected under the system shall accrue to the States. The level of fees charged under this subsection shall not exceed the administrative costs incurred in issuing the permits.

(2)(A) Notwithstanding paragraph (1), the Secretary is authorized and shall collect a fee to recover the actual costs directly related to the management and enforcement of any --

(i) individual fishing quota program; and

(ii) community development quota program that allocates a percentage of the total allowable catch of a fishery to such program.

(B) Such fee shall not exceed 3 percent of the ex-vessel value of fish harvested under any such program, and shall be collected at either the time of the landing, filing of a landing report, or sale of such fish during a fishing season or in the last quarter of the calendar year in which the fish is harvested.

(C)(i) Fees collected under this paragraph shall be in addition to any other fees charged under this Act and shall be deposited in the Limited Access System Administration Fund established under section 303(h)(5)(B) [16 U.S.C. § 1855(h)(5)(B)], except that the portion of any such fees reserved under section 303(d)(4)(A) [16 U.S.C. § 1853(d)(4)(A)] shall be deposited in the Treasury and available, subject to annual appropriations, to cover the costs of new direct loan obligations and new loan guarantee commitments as required by section 504(b)(1) of the Federal Credit Reform Act (2 U.S.C. § 661c(b)(1)).

(ii) Upon application by a State, the Secretary shall transfer to such State up to 33 percent of any fee collected pursuant to subparagraph (A) under a community development quota program and deposited in the Limited Access System Administration Fund in order to reimburse such State for actual costs directly incurred in the management and enforcement of such program.

(e) Rebuilding overfished fisheries. (1) The Secretary shall report annually to the

Congress and the Councils on the status of fisheries within each Council's geographical area of authority and identify those fisheries that are overfished or are approaching a condition of being overfished. For those fisheries managed under a fishery management plan or international agreement, the status shall be determined using the criteria for overfishing specified in such plan or agreement. A fishery shall be classified as approaching a condition of being overfished if, based on trends in fishing effort, fishery resource size, and other appropriate factors, the Secretary estimates that the fishery will become overfished within two years.

(2) If the Secretary determines at any time that a fishery is overfished, the Secretary shall immediately notify the appropriate Council and request that action be taken to end overfishing in the fishery and to implement conservation and management measures to rebuild affected stocks of fish. The Secretary shall publish each notice under this paragraph in the Federal Register.

(3) Within one year of an identification under paragraph (1) or notification under paragraphs (2) or (7), the appropriate Council (or the Secretary, for fisheries under section 302(a)(3) [16 U.S.C. § 1852(a)(3)]) shall prepare a fishery management plan, plan amendment, or proposed regulations for the fishery to which the identification or notice applies --

(A) to end overfishing in the fishery and to rebuild affected stocks of fish; or

(B) to prevent overfishing from occurring in the fishery whenever such fishery is identified as approaching an overfished condition.

(4) For a fishery that is overfished, any fishery management plan, amendment, or proposed regulations prepared pursuant to paragraph (3) or paragraph (5) for such fishery shall --

(A) specify a time period for ending overfishing and rebuilding the fishery that shall --

(i) be as short as possible, taking into account the status and biology of any overfished stocks of fish, the needs of fishing communities, recommendations by international organizations in which the United States participates, and the interaction of the overfished stock of fish within the marine ecosystem; and

(ii) not exceed 10 years, except in cases where the biology of the stock of fish, other environmental conditions, or management measures under an international agreement in which the United States participates dictate otherwise;

(B) allocate both overfishing restrictions and recovery benefits fairly and equitably among sectors of the fishery; and

(C) for fisheries managed under an international agreement, reflect traditional participation in the fishery, relative to other nations, by fishermen of the United States.

(5) If, within the one-year period beginning on the date of identification or notification that a fishery is overfished, the Council does not submit to the Secretary a fishery management plan, plan amendment, or proposed regulations required by paragraph (3)(A), the Secretary shall prepare a fishery management plan or plan amendment and any accompanying regulations to stop overfishing and rebuild affected stocks of fish within 9 months under subsection (c) of this section.

(6) During the development of a fishery management plan, a plan amendment, or

proposed regulations required by this subsection, the Council may request the Secretary to implement interim measures to reduce overfishing under section 305(c) [16 U.S.C. § 1855(c)] until such measures can be replaced by such plan, amendment, or regulations. Such measures, if otherwise in compliance with the provisions of this Act, may be implemented even though they are not sufficient by themselves to stop overfishing of a fishery.

(7) The Secretary shall review any fishery management plan, plan amendment, or regulations required by this subsection at routine intervals that may not exceed two years. If the Secretary finds as a result of the review that such plan, amendment, or regulations have not resulted in adequate progress toward ending overfishing and rebuilding affected fish stocks, the Secretary shall--

(A) in the case of a fishery to which section 302(a) [16 U.S.C. § 1852(a)(3)] applies, immediately make revisions necessary to achieve adequate progress; or

(B) for all other fisheries, immediately notify the appropriate Council. Such notification shall recommend further conservation and management measures which the Council should consider under paragraph (3) to achieve adequate progress.

(f) Fisheries under authority of more than one Council. (1) Except as provided in paragraph (3), if any fishery extends beyond the geographical area of authority of any one Council, the Secretary may --

(A) designate which Council shall prepare the fishery management plan for such fishery and any amendment to such plan; or

(B) may require that the plan and amendment be prepared jointly by the Councils concerned.

No jointly prepared plan or amendment may be submitted to the Secretary unless it is approved by a majority of the voting members, present and voting, of each Council concerned.

(2) The Secretary shall establish the boundaries between the geographical areas of authority of adjacent Councils.

(g) Atlantic highly migratory species. (1) Preparation and implementation of plan or plan amendment. The Secretary shall prepare a fishery management plan or plan amendment under subsection (c) of this section with respect to any highly migratory species fishery to which section 302(a)(3) [16 U.S.C. § 1852(a)(3)] applies. In preparing and implementing any such plan or amendment, the Secretary shall --

(A) consult with and consider the comments and views of affected Councils, commissioners and advisory groups appointed under Acts implementing relevant international fishery agreements pertaining to highly migratory species, and the advisory panel established under section 302(g) [16 U.S.C. § 1852(g)];

(B) establish an advisory panel under section 302(g) [16 U.S.C. § 1852(g)] for each fishery management plan to be prepared under this paragraph;

(C) evaluate the likely effects, if any, of conservation and management measures on participants in the affected fisheries and minimize, to the extent practicable, any disadvantage to United States fishermen in relation to foreign competitors;

(D) with respect to a highly migratory species for which the United States is authorized to harvest an allocation, quota, or at a fishing mortality level under a relevant international fishery agreement, provide fishing vessels of the United States with a reasonable opportunity to harvest such allocation, quota, or at such fishing mortality level;

(E) review, on a continuing basis (and promptly whenever a recommendation pertaining to fishing for highly migratory species has been made under a relevant international fishery agreement), and revise as appropriate, the conservation and management measures included in the plan;

(F) diligently pursue, through international entities (such as the International Commission for the Conservation of Atlantic Tunas), comparable international fishery management measures with respect to fishing for highly migratory species; and

(G) ensure that conservation and management measures under this subsection --

(i) promote international conservation of the affected fishery;

(ii) take into consideration traditional fishing patterns of fishing vessels of the United States and the operating requirements of the fisheries;

(iii) are fair and equitable in allocating fishing privileges among United States fishermen and do not have economic allocation as the sole purpose; and

(iv) promote, to the extent practicable, implementation of scientific research programs that include the tagging and release of Atlantic highly migratory species.

(2) Certain fish excluded from "bycatch" definition. Notwithstanding section 3(2) [16 U.S.C. § 1802(2)], fish harvested in a commercial fishery managed by the Secretary under this subsection or the Atlantic Tunas Convention Act of 1975 (16 U.S.C. 971d) that are not regulatory discards and that are tagged and released alive under a scientific tagging and release program established by the Secretary shall not be considered bycatch for purposes of this Act.

(h) Repeal or revocation of a fishery management plan. The Secretary may repeal or revoke a fishery management plan for a fishery under the authority of a Council only if the Council approves the repeal or revocation by a three-quarters majority of the voting members of the Council.

[Pub. L. 94-265, Title III, § 304, 90 Stat. 352 (Apr. 13, 1976); Pub. L. 97-453, § 7(a), 96 Stat. 2487 (Jan. 12, 1983); Pub. L. 99-659, Title I, § 106, 100 Stat. 3712 (Nov. 14, 1986); Pub. L. 101-627, Title I, §§ 110(a), (b)(1), (c), 111(a)(2), 120(d), 104 Stat. 4449 (Nov. 28, 1990) to 4452, 4459; Pub. L. 102-567, Title III, § 303, 106 Stat. 4283 (Oct. 29, 1992); Pub. L. 103-206, Title VII, § 702, 107 Stat. 2446 (Dec. 20, 1993); Pub. L. 104-297, Title I, § 109(a) to (c), (e) to (g), (i), 110 Stat. 3581-3585, 3587 (Oct. 11, 1996)]

16 U.S.C. § 1855. Other requirements and authority. (a) Gear evaluation and notification of entry. (1) Not later than 18 months after October 11, 1996, the Secretary shall publish in the Federal Register, after notice and an opportunity for public comment, a list of all fisheries --

(A) under the authority of each Council and all fishing gear used in such fisheries, based on information submitted by the Councils under section 303(a) [16 U.S.C. § 1853(a)]; and

(B) to which section 302(a)(3) [16 U.S.C. § 1852(a)(3)] applies and all fishing gear used in such fisheries.

(2) The Secretary shall include with such list guidelines for determining when fishing gear or a fishery is sufficiently different from those listed as to require notification under paragraph (3).

(3) Effective 180 days after the publication of such list, no person or vessel may employ fishing gear or engage in a fishery not included on such list without giving 90 days advance written notice to the appropriate Council, or the Secretary with respect to a fishery to which section 302(a)(3) [16 U.S.C. § 1852(a)(3)] applies. A signed return receipt shall serve as adequate evidence of such notice and as the date upon which the 90-day period begins.

(4) A Council may submit to the Secretary any proposed changes to such list or such guidelines the Council deems appropriate. The Secretary shall publish a revised list, after notice and an opportunity for public comment, upon receiving any such proposed changes from a Council.

(5) A Council may request the Secretary to promulgate emergency regulations under subsection (c) of this section to prohibit any persons or vessels from using an unlisted fishing gear or engaging in an unlisted fishery if the appropriate Council, or the Secretary for fisheries to which section 302(a)(3) [16 U.S.C. § 1852(a)(3)] applies, determines that such unlisted gear or unlisted fishery would compromise the effectiveness of conservation and management efforts under this Act.

(6) Nothing in this subsection shall be construed to permit a person or vessel to engage in fishing or employ fishing gear when such fishing or gear is prohibited or restricted by regulation under a fishery management plan or plan amendment, or under other applicable law.

(b) Fish habitat. (1)(A) The Secretary shall, within 6 months of October 11, 1996, establish by regulation guidelines to assist the Councils in the description and identification of essential fish habitat in fishery management plans (including adverse impacts on such habitat) and in the consideration of actions to ensure the conservation and enhancement of such habitat. The Secretary shall set forth a schedule for the amendment of fishery management plans to include the identification of essential fish habitat and for the review and updating of such identifications based on new scientific evidence or other relevant information.

(B) The Secretary, in consultation with participants in the fishery, shall provide each Council with recommendations and information regarding each fishery under that Council's authority to assist it in the identification of essential fish habitat, the adverse impacts on that habitat, and the actions that should be considered to ensure the conservation and enhancement of that habitat.

(C) The Secretary shall review programs administered by the Department of Commerce and ensure that any relevant programs further the conservation and enhancement of essential fish habitat.

(D) The Secretary shall coordinate with and provide information to other Federal agencies to further the conservation and enhancement of essential fish habitat.

(2) Each Federal agency shall consult with the Secretary with respect to any action authorized, funded, or undertaken, or proposed to be authorized, funded, or undertaken, by such agency that may adversely affect any essential fish habitat identified under this Act.

(3) Each Council --

(A) may comment on and make recommendations to the Secretary and any Federal or State agency concerning any activity authorized, funded, or undertaken, or proposed to be authorized, funded, or undertaken, by any Federal or State agency that, in the view of the Council, may affect the habitat, including essential fish habitat, of a fishery resource under its authority; and

(B) shall comment on and make recommendations to the Secretary and any Federal or State agency concerning any such activity that, in the view of the Council, is likely to substantially affect the habitat, including essential fish habitat, of an anadromous fishery resource under its authority.

(4)(A) If the Secretary receives information from a Council or Federal or State agency or determines from other sources that an action authorized, funded, or undertaken, or proposed to be authorized, funded, or undertaken, by any State or Federal agency would adversely affect any essential fish habitat identified under this Act, the Secretary shall recommend to such agency measures that can be taken by such agency to conserve such habitat.

(B) Within 30 days after receiving a recommendation under subparagraph (A), a Federal agency shall provide a detailed response in writing to any Council commenting under paragraph (3) and the Secretary regarding the matter. The response shall include a description of measures proposed by the agency for avoiding, mitigating, or offsetting the impact of the activity on such habitat. In the case of a response that is inconsistent with the recommendations of the Secretary, the Federal agency shall explain its reasons for not following the recommendations.

(c) Emergency actions and interim measures. (1) If the Secretary finds that an emergency exists or that interim measures are needed to reduce overfishing for any fishery, he may promulgate emergency regulations or interim measures necessary to address the emergency or overfishing, without regard to whether a fishery management plan exists for such fishery.

(2) If a Council finds that an emergency exists or that interim measures are needed to reduce overfishing for any fishery within its jurisdiction, whether or not a fishery management plan exists for such fishery --

(A) the Secretary shall promulgate emergency regulations or interim measures under paragraph (1) to address the emergency or overfishing if the Council, by unanimous vote of the members who are voting members, requests the taking of such action; and

(B) the Secretary may promulgate emergency regulations or interim measures under paragraph (1) to address the emergency or overfishing if the Council, by less than a unanimous vote, requests the taking of such action.

(3) Any emergency regulation or interim measure which changes any existing fishery management plan or amendment shall be treated as an amendment to such

plan for the period in which such regulation is in effect. Any emergency regulation or interim measure promulgated under this subsection --

(A) shall be published in the Federal Register together with the reasons therefor;

(B) shall, except as provided in subparagraph (C), remain in effect for not more than 180 days after the date of publication, and may be extended by publication in the Federal Register for one additional period of not more than 180 days, provided the public has had an opportunity to comment on the emergency regulation or interim measure, and, in the case of a Council recommendation for emergency regulations or interim measures, the Council is actively preparing a fishery management plan, plan amendment, or proposed regulations to address the emergency or overfishing on a permanent basis;

(C) that responds to a public health emergency or an oil spill may remain in effect until the circumstances that created the emergency no longer exist, *Provided,* That the public has an opportunity to comment after the regulation is published, and, in the case of a public health emergency, the Secretary of Health and Human Services concurs with the Secretary's action; and

(D) may be terminated by the Secretary at an earlier date by publication in the Federal Register of a notice of termination, except for emergency regulations promulgated under paragraph (2) in which case such early termination may be made only upon the agreement of the Secretary and the Council concerned.

(d) Responsibility of Secretary. The Secretary shall have general responsibility to carry out any fishery management plan or amendment approved or prepared by him, in accordance with the provisions of this Act. The Secretary may promulgate such regulations, in accordance with section 553 of Title 5, as may be necessary to discharge such responsibility or to carry out any other provision of this Act.

(e) Effect of certain laws on certain time requirements. ****

(f) Judicial review. (1) Regulations promulgated by the Secretary under this Act and actions described in paragraph (2) shall be subject to judicial review to the extent authorized by, and in accordance with, chapter 7 of Title 5, if a petition for such review is filed within 30 days after the date on which the regulations are promulgated or the action is published in the Federal Register, as applicable; except that --

(A) section 705 of such Title is not applicable, and

(B) the appropriate court shall only set aside any such regulation or action on a ground specified in section 706(2)(A), (B), (C), or (D) of such Title.

(2) The actions referred to in paragraph (1) are actions that are taken by the Secretary under regulations which implement a fishery management plan, including but not limited to actions that establish the date of closure of a fishery to commercial or recreational fishing.

(3)(A) Notwithstanding any other provision of law, the Secretary shall file a response to any petition filed in accordance with paragraph (1), not later than 45 days after the date the Secretary is served with that petition, except that the appropriate court may extend the period for filing such a response upon a showing by the Secretary of good cause for that extension.

(B) A response of the Secretary under this paragraph shall include a copy of the administrative record for the regulations that are the subject of the petition.

(4) Upon a motion by the person who files a petition under this subsection, the appropriate court shall assign the matter for hearing at the earliest possible date and shall expedite the matter in every possible way.

(g) Negotiated conservation and management measures. (1)(A) In accordance with regulations promulgated by the Secretary pursuant to this paragraph, a Council may establish a fishery negotiation panel to assist in the development of specific conservation and management measures for a fishery under its authority. The Secretary may establish a fishery negotiation panel to assist in the development of specific conservation and management measures required for a fishery under section 304(e)(5) [16 U.S.C. § 1854(e)(5)], for a fishery for which the Secretary has authority under section 304(g) [16 U.S.C. § 1854(g)], or for any other fishery with the approval of the appropriate Council.

(B) No later than 180 days after October 11, 1996, the Secretary shall promulgate regulations establishing procedures, developed in cooperation with the Administrative Conference of the United States, for the establishment and operation of fishery negotiation panels. Such procedures shall be comparable to the procedures for negotiated rulemaking established by subchapter III of chapter 5 of Title 5.

(2) If a negotiation panel submits a report, such report shall specify all the areas where consensus was reached by the panel, including, if appropriate, proposed conservation and management measures, as well as any other information submitted by members of the negotiation panel. Upon receipt, the Secretary shall publish such report in the Federal Register for public comment.

(3) Nothing in this subsection shall be construed to require either a Council or the Secretary, whichever is appropriate, to use all or any portion of a report from a negotiation panel established under this subsection in the development of specific conservation and management measures for the fishery for which the panel was established.

(h) Central registry system for limited access system permits. (1) Within 6 months after October 11, 1996, the Secretary shall establish an exclusive central registry system (which may be administered on a regional basis) for limited access system permits established under section 303(b)(6) [16 U.S.C. § 1853(b)(6)] or other Federal law, including individual fishing quotas, which shall provide for the registration of title to, and interests in, such permits, as well as for procedures for changes in the registration of title to such permits upon the occurrence of involuntary transfers, judicial or nonjudicial foreclosure of interests, enforcement of judgments thereon, and related matters deemed appropriate by the Secretary. Such registry system shall --

(A) provide a mechanism for filing notice of a nonjudicial foreclosure or enforcement of a judgment by which the holder of a senior security interest acquires or conveys ownership of a permit, and in the event of a nonjudicial foreclosure, by which the interests of the holders of junior security interests are released when the permit is transferred;

(B) provide for public access to the information filed under such system, notwithstanding section 402(b) [16 U.S.C. § 1881a(b)]; and

(C) provide such notice and other requirements of applicable law that the Secretary deems necessary for an effective registry system.

(2) The Secretary shall promulgate such regulations as may be necessary to carry out this subsection, after consulting with the Councils and providing an opportunity for public comment. The Secretary is authorized to contract with non-Federal entities to administer the central registry system.

(3) To be effective and perfected against any person except the transferor, its heirs and devisees, and persons having actual notice thereof, all security interests, and all sales and other transfers of permits described in paragraph (1), shall be registered in compliance with the regulations promulgated under paragraph (2). Such registration shall constitute the exclusive means of perfection of title to, and security interests in, such permits, except for Federal tax liens thereon, which shall be perfected exclusively in accordance with the Internal Revenue Code of 1986 (26 U.S.C. 1 *et seq.*). The Secretary shall notify both the buyer and seller of a permit if a lien has been filed by the Secretary of the Treasury against the permit before collecting any transfer fee under paragraph (5) of this subsection.

(4) The priority of security interests shall be determined in order of filing, the first filed having the highest priority. A validly-filed security interest shall remain valid and perfected notwithstanding a change in residence or place of business of the owner of record. For the purposes of this subsection, "security interest" shall include security interests, assignments, liens and other encumbrances of whatever kind.

(5)(A) Notwithstanding section 304(d)(1) [16 U.S.C. § 1854(d)(1)], the Secretary shall collect a reasonable fee of not more than one-half of one percent of the value of a limited access system permit upon registration of the title to such permit with the central registry system and upon the transfer of such registered title. Any such fee collected shall be deposited in the Limited Access System Administration Fund established under subparagraph (B).

(B) There is established in the Treasury a Limited Access System Administration Fund. The Fund shall be available, without appropriation or fiscal year limitation, only to the Secretary for the purposes of --

(i) administering the central registry system; and

(ii) administering and implementing this Act in the fishery in which the fees were collected. Sums in the Fund that are not currently needed for these purposes shall be kept on deposit or invested in obligations of, or guaranteed by, the United States.

(i) Alaska and western Pacific community development programs. ****

[Pub. L. 94-265, Title III, § 305, 90 Stat. 354 (Apr. 13, 1976); Pub. L. 96-561, Title II, § 235, 94 Stat. 3299 (Dec. 22, 1980); Pub. L. 97-453, § 8, 96 Stat. 2490 (Jan. 12, 1983); Pub. L. 101-627, Title I, §§ 110(b)(2), 111(a)(1), (b), 104 Stat. 4451, 4452 (Nov. 28, 1990); Pub. L. 104-297, Title I, §§ 110(a) to (d), 111(a), 110 Stat. 3587-3590, 3592 (Oct. 11, 1996)]

16 U.S.C. § 1856. State jurisdiction. (a) In general. (1) Except as provided in subsection (b) of this section, nothing in this Act shall be construed as extending or diminishing the jurisdiction or authority of any State within its boundaries.

(2) For the purposes of this Act, except as provided in subsection (b) of this section, the jurisdiction and authority of a State shall extend --

(A) to any pocket of waters that is adjacent to the State and totally enclosed by lines delimiting the territorial sea of the United States pursuant to the Geneva Convention on the Territorial Sea and Contiguous Zone or any successor convention to which the United States is a party;

(B) with respect to the body of water commonly known as Nantucket Sound, to the pocket of water west of the seventieth meridian west of Greenwich; and

(C) to the waters of southeastern Alaska (for the purpose of regulating fishing for other than any species of crab) ****

(3) A State may regulate a fishing vessel outside the boundaries of the State in the following circumstances:

(A) The fishing vessel is registered under the law of that State, and (i) there is no fishery management plan or other applicable Federal fishing regulations for the fishery in which the vessel is operating; or (ii) the State's laws and regulations are consistent with the fishery management plan and applicable Federal fishing regulations for the fishery in which the vessel is operating.

(B) The fishery management plan for the fishery in which the fishing vessel is operating delegates management of the fishery to a State and the State's laws and regulations are consistent with such fishery management plan. If at any time the Secretary determines that a State law or regulation applicable to a fishing vessel under this circumstance is not consistent with the fishery management plan, the Secretary shall promptly notify the State and the appropriate Council of such determination and provide an opportunity for the State to correct any inconsistencies identified in the notification. If, after notice and opportunity for corrective action, the State does not correct the inconsistencies identified by the Secretary, the authority granted to the State under this subparagraph shall not apply until the Secretary and the appropriate Council find that the State has corrected the inconsistencies. For a fishery for which there was a fishery management plan in place on August 1, 1996 that did not delegate management of the fishery to a State as of that date, the authority provided by this subparagraph applies only if the Council approves the delegation of management of the fishery to the State by a three-quarters majority vote of the voting members of the Council.

****

(b) Exception. (1) If the Secretary finds, after notice and an opportunity for a hearing in accordance with section 554 of Title 5, that --

(A) the fishing in a fishery, which is covered by a fishery management plan implemented under this Act, is engaged in predominately within the exclusive economic zone and beyond such zone; and

(B) any State has taken any action, or omitted to take any action, the results of which will substantially and adversely affect the carrying out of such fishery management plan;

the Secretary shall promptly notify such State and the appropriate Council of such finding and of his intention to regulate the applicable fishery within the boundaries of such State (other than its internal waters), pursuant to such fishery management plan and the regulations promulgated to implement such plan.

(2) If the Secretary, pursuant to this subsection, assumes responsibility for the regulation of any fishery, the State involved may at any time thereafter apply to the Secretary for reinstatement of its authority over such fishery. If the Secretary finds that the reasons for which he assumed such regulation no longer prevail, he shall promptly terminate such regulation.

(3) If the State involved requests that a hearing be held pursuant to paragraph (1), the Secretary shall conduct such hearing prior to taking any action under paragraph (1).

(c) Exception regarding foreign fish processing in internal waters. (1) A foreign fishing vessel may engage in fish processing within the internal waters of a State if, and only if --

(A) the vessel is qualified for purposes of this paragraph pursuant to paragraph (4)(C) or has received a permit under section 204(d) [16 U.S.C. § 1824(d)];

(B) the owner or operator of the vessel applies to the Governor of the State for, and (subject to paragraph (2)) is granted, permission for the vessel to engage in such processing and the application specifies the species to be processed; and

(C) the owner or operator of the vessel submits reports on the tonnage of fish received from vessels of the United States and the locations from which such fish were harvested, in accordance with such procedures as the Secretary by regulation shall prescribe.

(2) The Governor of a State may not grant permission for a foreign fishing vessel to engage in fish processing under paragraph (1) --

(A) for a fishery which occurs in the waters of more than one State or in the exclusive economic zone, except after --

(i) consulting with the appropriate Council and Marine Fisheries Commission, and

(ii) considering any comments received from the Governor of any other State where the fishery occurs; and

(B) if the Governor determines that fish processors within the State have adequate capacity, and will utilize such capacity, to process all of the United States harvested fish from the fishery concerned that are landed in the State.

(3) Nothing in this subsection may be construed as relieving a foreign fishing vessel from the duty to comply with all applicable Federal and State laws while operating within the internal waters of a State incident to permission obtained under paragraph (1)(B).

(4) For purposes of this subsection --

(A) The term "fish processing" includes, in addition to processing, the performance of any other activity relating to fishing, including, but not limited to, preparation, supply, storage, refrigeration, or transportation.

(B) The phrase "internal waters of a State" means all waters within the boundaries of a State except those seaward of the baseline from which the territorial sea is measured.

(C) A foreign fishing vessel shall be treated as qualified for purposes of paragraph (1) if the foreign nation under which it is flagged will be a party to (i) a governing international fishery agreement or (ii) a treaty described in section 201(b) [16 U.S.C. § 1821(b)] during the time the vessel will engage in the fish processing for which permission is sought under paragraph (1)(B).

[Pub. L. 94-265, Title III, § 306, 90 Stat. 355 (Apr. 13, 1976); Pub. L. 97-191, § 1, 96 Stat. 107 (June 1, 1982); Pub. L. 97-453, § 9, 96 Stat. 2491 (Jan. 12, 1983); Pub. L. 98-623, Title IV, § 404(4), 98 Stat. 3408 (Nov. 8, 1984); Pub. L. 99-659, Title I, § 101(c)(2), 100 Stat. 3707 (Nov. 14, 1986); Pub. L. 101-627, Title I, § 112, 104 Stat. 4453 (Nov. 28, 1990); Pub. L. 104-297, § 112(a) to (c), 110 Stat. 3595, 3596 (Oct. 11, 1996)]

16 U.S.C. § 1857. Prohibited acts. It is unlawful --

(1) for any person --

(A) to violate any provision of this Act or any regulation or permit issued pursuant to this Act;

(B) to use any fishing vessel to engage in fishing after the revocation, or during the period of suspension, of an applicable permit issued pursuant to this Act;

(C) to violate any provision of, or regulation under, an applicable governing international fishery agreement entered into pursuant to section 201(c) [16 U.S.C. § 1821(c)];

(D) to refuse to permit any officer authorized to enforce the provisions of this Act (as provided for in section 311 [16 U.S.C. § 1861]) to board a fishing vessel subject to such person's control for purposes of conducting any search or inspection in connection with the enforcement of this Act or any regulation, permit, or agreement referred to in subparagraph (A) or (C);

(E) to forcibly assault, resist, oppose, impede, intimidate, or interfere with any such authorized officer in the conduct of any search or inspection described in subparagraph (D);

(F) to resist a lawful arrest for any act prohibited by this section;

(G) to ship, transport, offer for sale, sell, purchase, import, export, or have custody, control, or possession of, any fish taken or retained in violation of this Act or any regulation, permit, or agreement referred to in subparagraph (A) or (C);

(H) to interfere with, delay, or prevent, by any means, the apprehension or arrest of another person, knowing that such other person has committed any act prohibited by this section;

(I) to knowingly and willfully submit to a Council, the Secretary, or the Governor of a State false information (including, but not limited to, false information regarding the capacity and extent to which a United States fish processor, on an annual basis, will process a portion of the optimum yield of a fishery that will be harvested by fishing vessels of the United States) regarding any matter that the Council, Secretary, or Governor is considering in the course of carrying out this Act;

(J) to ship, transport, offer for sale, sell, or purchase, in interstate or foreign commerce, any whole live lobster of the species *Homarus americanus,* that --

(i) is smaller than the minimum possession size in effect at the time under the American Lobster Fishery Management Plan, as implemented by regulations published in part 649 of title 50, Code of Federal Regulations, or any successor to that plan implemented under this Act, or in the absence of any such plan, is smaller than the minimum possession size in effect at the time under a coastal fishery management plan for American lobster adopted by the Atlantic States Marine Fisheries Commission under the Atlantic Coastal Fisheries Cooperative Management Act (16 U.S.C. 5101 *et seq.*);

(ii) is bearing eggs attached to its abdominal appendages; or

(iii) bears evidence of the forcible removal of extruded eggs from its abdominal appendages;

(K) to steal or attempt to steal or to negligently and without authorization remove, damage, or tamper with --

(i) fishing gear owned by another person, which is located in the exclusive economic zone, or

(ii) fish contained in such fishing gear;

(L) to forcibly assault, resist, oppose, impede, intimidate, sexually harass, bribe, or interfere with any observer on a vessel under this Act, or any data collector employed by the National Marine Fisheries Service or under contract to any person to carry out responsibilities under this Act;

(M) to engage in large-scale driftnet fishing that is subject to the jurisdiction of the United States, including use of a fishing vessel of the United States to engage in such fishing beyond the exclusive economic zone of any nation;

(N) to strip pollock of its roe and discard the flesh of the pollock;

(O) to knowingly and willfully fail to disclose, or to falsely disclose, any financial interest as required under section 302(j) [16 U.S.C. § 1852(j)], or to knowingly vote on a Council decision in violation of section 302(j)(7)(A) [16 U.S.C. § 1852(j)(7)(A)]; or

(P)(i) to remove any of the fins of a shark (including the tail) and discard the carcass of the shark at sea;

(ii) to have custody, control, or possession of any such fin aboard a fishing vessel without the corresponding carcass; or

(iii) to land any such fin without the corresponding carcass.

For purposes of subparagraph (P) there is a rebuttable presumption that any shark fins landed from a fishing vessel or found on board a fishing vessel were taken, held, or landed in violation of subparagraph (P) if the total weight of shark fins landed or found on board exceeds 5 percent of the total weight of shark carcasses landed or found on board.

(2) for any vessel other than a vessel of the United States, and for the owner or operator of any vessel other than a vessel of the United States, to engage --

(A) in fishing within the boundaries of any State, except --

(i) recreational fishing permitted under section 201(i) [16 U.S.C. § 1821(i)];

(ii) fish processing permitted under section 306(c) [16 U.S.C. § 1856(c)]; or

(iii) transshipment at sea of fish or fish products within the boundaries of any State in accordance with a permit approved under section 204(d) [16 U.S.C. § 1824(d)];

(B) in fishing, except recreational fishing permitted under section 201(i) [16 U.S.C. § 1821(i)], within the exclusive economic zone, or for any anadromous species or Continental Shelf fishery resources beyond such zone, unless such fishing is authorized by, and conducted in accordance with, a valid and applicable permit issued pursuant to section 204(b), (c), or (d) [16 U.S.C. § 1824(b), (c), or (d)]; or

(C) except as permitted under section 306(c) [16 U.S.C. § 1856(c)], in fish processing (as defined in paragraph (4)(A) of such section) within the internal waters of a State (as defined in paragraph (4)(B) of such section);

(3) for any vessel of the United States, and for the owner or operator of any vessel of the United States, to transfer at sea directly or indirectly, or attempt to so transfer at sea, any United States harvested fish to any foreign fishing vessel, while such foreign vessel is within the exclusive economic zone or within the boundaries of any State except to the extent that the foreign fishing vessel has been permitted under section 204(d) [16 U.S.C. § 1824(d)] or section 306(c) [16 U.S.C. § 1856(c)] to receive such fish;

(4) for any fishing vessel other than a vessel of the United States to operate, and for the owner or operator of a fishing vessel other than a vessel of the United States to operate such vessel, in the exclusive economic zone or within the boundaries of any State, if --

(A) all fishing gear on the vessel is not stored below deck or in an area where it is not normally used, and not readily available, for fishing; or

(B) all fishing gear on the vessel which is not so stored is not secured and covered so as to render it unusable for fishing;

unless such vessel is authorized to engage in fishing in the area in which the vessel is operating; and

(5) for any vessel of the United States, and for the owner or operator of any vessel of the United States, to engage in fishing in the waters of a foreign nation in a manner that violates an international fishery agreement between that nation and the United States that has been subject to Congressional oversight in the manner described in section 203 [16 U.S.C. § 1823], or any regulations issued to implement such an agreement; except that the binding provisions of such agreement and implementing regulations shall have been published in the Federal Register prior to such violation.

[Pub. L. 94-265, Title III, § 307, 90 Stat. 355 (Apr. 13, 1976); Pub. L. 95-354, § 5(4), 92 Stat. 521 (Aug. 28, 1978); Pub. L. 97-191, § 2, June 1, 1982, 96 Stat. 107; Pub. L. 97-453, § 15(b), 96 Stat. 2492 (Jan. 12, 1983); Pub. L. 99-659, Title I, §§ 101(c)(2), 107(a), 100 Stat. 3707 (Nov. 14, 1986), 3713; Pub. L. 100-629, § 4, 102 Stat. 3286 (Nov. 7, 1988); Pub. L. 101-224, § 8, Dec. 12, 1989, 103 Stat. 1907; Pub. L. 101-627, Title I, § 113, 104 Stat. 4454 (Nov. 28, 1990); Pub. L. 102-251, Title III, § 301(h), 106 Stat. 64 (Mar. 9, 1992); Pub. L. 104-297, Title I, § 113, Title IV, § 405(b)(1), 110 Stat. 3597, 3621 (Oct. 11, 1996); Pub. L. 106-557, § 3, 114 Stat. 2772 (Dec. 21, 2000)]

16 U.S.C. § 1858. Civil penalties and permit sanctions. (a) Assessment of penalty. Any person who is found by the Secretary, after notice and an opportunity for a hearing in accordance with section 554 of Title 5, to have committed an act prohibited by section 307 [16 U.S.C. § 1857] shall be liable to the United States for a civil penalty. The amount of the civil penalty shall not exceed $100,000 for each violation. Each day of a continuing violation shall constitute a separate offense. The amount of such civil penalty shall be assessed by the Secretary, or his designee, by written notice. In determining the amount of such penalty, the Secretary shall take into account the nature, circumstances, extent, and gravity of the prohibited acts committed and, with respect to the violator, the degree of culpability, any history of prior offenses, and such other matters as justice may require. In assessing such penalty the Secretary may also consider any information provided by the violator relating to the ability of the violator to pay, *Provided*, That the information is served on the Secretary at least 30 days prior to an administrative hearing.

(b) Review of civil penalty. Any person against whom a civil penalty is assessed under subsection (a) of this section or against whom a permit sanction is imposed under subsection (g) of this section (other than a permit suspension for nonpayment of penalty or fine) may obtain review thereof in the United States district court for the appropriate district by filing a complaint against the Secretary in such court within 30 days from the date of such order. The Secretary shall promptly file in such court a certified copy of the record upon which such violation was found or such penalty imposed, as provided in section 2112 of Title 28. The findings and order of the Secretary shall be set aside by such court if they are not found to be supported by substantial evidence, as provided in section 706(2) of Title 5.

(c) Action upon failure to pay assessment. If any person fails to pay an assessment of a civil penalty after it has become a final and unappealable order, or after the appropriate court has entered final judgment in favor of the Secretary, the Secretary shall refer the matter to the Attorney General of the United States, who shall recover the amount assessed in any appropriate district court of the United States. In such action, the validity and appropriateness of the final order imposing the civil penalty shall not be subject to review.

(d) In rem jurisdiction. A fishing vessel (including its fishing gear, furniture, appurtenances, stores, and cargo) used in the commission of an act prohibited by section 307 [16 U.S.C. § 1857] shall be liable in rem for any civil penalty assessed for such violation under this section and may be proceeded against in any district court of the United States having jurisdiction thereof. Such penalty shall constitute a maritime lien on such vessel which may be recovered in an action in rem in the district court of the United States having jurisdiction over the vessel.

(e) Compromise or other action by Secretary. The Secretary may compromise, modify, or remit, with or without conditions, any civil penalty which is subject to imposition or which has been imposed under this section.

(f) Subpoenas. For the purposes of conducting any hearing under this section, the Secretary may issue subpoenas for the attendance and testimony of witnesses and the production of relevant papers, books, and documents, and may administer oaths. Witnesses summoned shall be paid the same fees and mileage that are paid to witnesses in the courts of the United States. In case of contempt or refusal to obey a subpena served upon any person pursuant to this subsection, the district court of the United States for any district in which such person is found, resides, or transacts business, upon application by the United States and after notice to such person, shall have jurisdiction to issue an order requiring such person to appear and give testimony before the Secretary or to appear and produce documents before the Secretary, or both, and any failure to obey such order of the court may be punished by such court as a contempt thereof.

(g) Permit sanctions. (1) In any case in which (A) a vessel has been used in the commission of an act prohibited under section 307 [16 U.S.C. § 1857], (B) the owner or operator of a vessel or any other person who has been issued or has applied for a permit under this Act has acted in violation of section 307 [16 U.S.C. § 1857], (C) any amount in settlement of a civil forfeiture imposed on a vessel or other property, or any civil penalty or criminal fine imposed on a vessel or owner or operator of a vessel or any other person who has been issued or has applied for a permit under any marine resource law enforced by the Secretary has not been paid and is overdue, or (D) any payment required for observer services provided to or contracted by an owner or operator who has been issued a permit or applied for a permit under any marine resource law administered by the Secretary has not been paid and is overdue, the Secretary may --

(i) revoke any permit issued with respect to such vessel or person, with or without prejudice to the issuance of subsequent permits;

(ii) suspend such permit for a period of time considered by the Secretary to be appropriate;

(iii) deny such permit; or

(iv) impose additional conditions and restrictions on any permit issued to or applied for by such vessel or person under this Act and, with respect to foreign fishing vessels, on the approved application of the foreign nation involved and on any permit issued under that application.

(2) In imposing a sanction under this subsection, the Secretary shall take into account --

(A) the nature, circumstances, extent, and gravity of the prohibited acts for which the sanction is imposed; and

(B) with respect to the violator, the degree of culpability, any history of prior offenses, and such other matters as justice may require.

(3) Transfer of ownership of a vessel, by sale or otherwise, shall not extinguish any permit sanction that is in effect or is pending at the time of transfer of ownership. Before executing the transfer of ownership of a vessel, by sale or otherwise, the owner shall disclose in writing to the prospective transferee the existence of any permit sanction that will be in effect or pending with respect to the vessel at the time of the transfer.

(4) In the case of any permit that is suspended under this subsection for nonpayment of a civil penalty or criminal fine, the Secretary shall reinstate the permit upon payment of the penalty or fine and interest thereon at the prevailing rate.

(5) No sanctions shall be imposed under this subsection unless there has been a prior opportunity for a hearing on the facts underlying the violation for which the sanction is imposed, either in conjunction with a civil penalty proceeding under this section or otherwise.

[Pub. L. 94-265, Title III, § 308, 90 Stat. 356 (Apr. 13, 1976); Pub. L. 97-453, § 10, 96 Stat. 2491 (Jan. 12, 1983);

Pub. L. 99-659, Title I, § 108, 100 Stat. 3713 (Nov. 14, 1986); Pub. L. 101-627, Title I, § 114, 104 Stat. 4454 (Nov. 28, 1990), Pub. L. 104 297, Title I, § 114(a) to (c), 110 Stat. 3598, 3599 (Oct. 11, 1996)]

16 U.S.C. § 1859. Criminal offenses. (a) Offenses. A person is guilty of an offense if he commits any act prohibited by --

(1) section 307(1)(D), (E), (F), (H), (I), or (L) [16 U.S.C. § 1857(1)(D), (E), (F), (H), (I), or (L)]; or

(2) section 307(2) [16 U.S.C. § 1857(2)].

(b) Punishment. Any offense described in subsection (a)(1) of this section is punishable by a fine of not more than $100,000, or imprisonment for not more than 6 months, or both; except that if in the commission of any such offense the person uses a dangerous weapon, engages in conduct that causes bodily injury to any observer described in section 307(1)L) [16 U.S.C. § 1857(1)(L)] or any officer authorized to enforce the provisions of this Act (as provided for in section 311 [16 U.S.C. § 1861]), or places any such observer or officer in fear of imminent bodily injury, the offense is punishable by a fine of not more than $200,000, or imprisonment for not more than 10 years, or both. Any offense described in subsection (a)(2) of this section is punishable by a fine of not more than $200,000.

(c) Jurisdiction. There is Federal jurisdiction over any offense described in this section.

[Pub. L. 94-265, Title III, § 309, 90 Stat. 357 (Apr. 13, 1976); Pub. L. 97-453, § 11(a), 96 Stat. 2491 (Jan. 12, 1983); Pub. L. 99-659, Title I, § 107(b), 100 Stat. 3713 (Nov. 14, 1986); Pub. L. 100-66, § 2, 101 Stat. 384 (July 10, 1987); Pub. L. 101-627, Title I, § 115, 104 Stat. 4455 (Nov. 28, 1990)]

16 U.S.C. § 1860. Civil forfeitures. (a) In general. Any fishing vessel (including its fishing gear, furniture, appurtenances, stores, and cargo) used, and any fish (or the fair market value thereof) taken or retained, in any manner, in connection with or as a result of the commission of any act prohibited by section 307 [16 U.S.C. § 1857] (other than any act for which the issuance of a citation under section 311(c) [16 U.S.C. § 1861(c)] is sufficient sanction) shall be subject to forfeiture to the United States. All or part of such vessel may, and all such fish (or the fair market value thereof) shall, be forfeited to the United States pursuant to a civil proceeding under this section.

(b) Jurisdiction of district courts. Any district court of the United States which has jurisdiction under section 311(d) [16 U.S.C. § 1861(d)] shall have jurisdiction, upon application by the Attorney General on behalf of the United States, to order any forfeiture authorized under subsection (a) of this section and any action provided for under subsection (d) of this section.

(c) Judgment. If a judgment is entered for the United States in a civil forfeiture proceeding under this section, the Attorney General may seize any property or other interest declared forfeited to the United States, which has not previously been seized pursuant to this Act or for which security has not previously been obtained under subsection (d) of this section. The provisions of the customs laws relating to --

(1) the seizure, forfeiture, and condemnation of property for violation of the customs law;

(2) the disposition of such property or the proceeds from the sale thereof; and

(3) the remission or mitigation of any such forfeiture;

shall apply to seizures and forfeitures incurred, or alleged to have been incurred, under the provisions of this Act, unless such provisions are inconsistent with the purposes, policy, and provisions of this Act. The duties and powers imposed upon the Commissioner of Customs or other persons under such provisions shall, with respect to this Act, be performed by officers or other persons designated for such purpose by the Secretary.

(d) Procedure. (1) Any officer authorized to serve any process in rem which is issued by a court having jurisdiction under section 311(d) [16 U.S.C. § 1861(d)] shall --

(A) stay the execution of such process; or

(B) discharge any fish seized pursuant to such process;

upon the receipt of a satisfactory bond or other security from any person claiming such property. Such bond or other security shall be conditioned upon such person (i) delivering such property to the appropriate court upon order thereof, without any impairment of its value, or (ii) paying the monetary value of such property pursuant to an order of such court. Judgment shall be recoverable on such bond or other security against both the principal and any sureties in the event that any condition thereof is breached, as determined by such court. Nothing in this paragraph may be construed to require the Secretary, except in the Secretary's discretion or pursuant to the order of a court under section 311(d) [16 U.S.C. § 1861(d)], to release on bond any seized fish or other property or the proceeds from the sale thereof.

(2) Any fish seized pursuant to this Act may be sold, subject to the approval and direction of the appropriate court, for not less than the fair market value thereof. The proceeds of any such sale shall be deposited with such court pending the disposition of the matter involved.

(e) Rebuttable presumptions. (1) For purposes of this section, it shall be a rebuttable presumption that all fish found on board a fishing vessel which is seized in connection with an act prohibited by section 307 [16 U.S.C. § 1857] were taken or retained in violation of this Act.

(2) For purposes of this Act, it shall be a rebuttable presumption that any fish of a species which spawns in fresh or estuarine waters and migrates to ocean waters that is found on board a vessel is of United States origin if the vessel is within the migratory range of the species during that part of the year to which the migratory range applies.

(3) For purposes of this Act, it shall be a rebuttable presumption that any vessel that is shoreward of the outer boundary of the exclusive economic zone of the United States or beyond the exclusive economic zone of any nation, and that has gear on board that is capable of use for large-scale driftnet fishing, is engaged in such fishing.

[Pub. L. 94-265, Title III, § 310, 90 Stat. 357 (Apr. 13, 1976); Pub. L. 97-453, § 12, 96 Stat. 2491 (Jan. 12, 1983); Pub. L. 99-659, Title I, § 109(a), 100 Stat. 3714 (Nov. 14, 1986); Pub. L. 101-627, Title I, § 116, 104 Stat. 4456 (Nov. 28, 1990); Pub. L. 104-297, Title I, § 114(d), 110 Stat. 3599 (Oct. 11, 1996)]

16 U.S.C. § 1861. Enforcement. (a) Responsibility. The provisions of this Act shall be enforced by the Secretary and the Secretary of the department in which the Coast Guard is operating. Such Secretaries may, by agreement, on a reimbursable basis or otherwise, utilize the personnel, services, equipment (including aircraft and vessels), and facilities of any other Federal agency, including all elements of the Department of Defense, and of any State agency, in the performance of such duties.

(b) Powers of authorized officers. (1) Any officer who is authorized (by the Secretary, the Secretary of the department in which the Coast Guard is operating, or the head of any Federal or State agency which has entered into an agreement with such Secretaries under subsection (a) of this section) to enforce the provisions of this Act may --

(A) with or without a warrant or other process --

(i) arrest any person, if he has reasonable cause to believe that such person has committed an act prohibited by section 307 [16 U.S.C. § 1857];

(ii) board, and search or inspect, any fishing vessel which is subject to the provisions of this Act;

(iii) seize any fishing vessel (together with its fishing gear, furniture, appurtenances, stores, and cargo) used or employed in, or with respect to which it reasonably appears that such vessel was used or employed in, the violation of any provision of this Act;

(iv) seize any fish (wherever found) taken or retained in violation of any provision of this Act; and

(v) seize any other evidence related to any violation of any provision of this Act;

(B) execute any warrant or other process issued by any court of competent jurisdiction; and

(C) exercise any other lawful authority.

(2) Subject to the direction of the Secretary, a person charged with law enforcement responsibilities by the Secretary who is performing a duty related to enforcement of a law regarding fisheries or other marine resources may make an arrest without a warrant for an offense against the United States committed in his presence, or for a felony cognizable under the laws of the United States, if he has reasonable grounds to believe that the person to be arrested has committed or is committing a felony. The arrest authority described in the preceding sentence may be conferred upon an officer or employee of a State agency, subject to such conditions and restrictions as are set forth by agreement between the State agency, the Secretary, and, with respect to enforcement operations within the exclusive economic zone, the Secretary of the department in which the Coast Guard is operating.

(c) Issuance of citations. If any officer authorized to enforce the provisions of this Act (as provided for in this section) finds that a fishing vessel is operating or has been operated in violation of any provision of this Act, such officer may, in accordance with regulations issued jointly by the Secretary and the Secretary of the department in which the Coast Guard is operating, issue a citation to the owner or operator of such vessel in lieu of proceeding under subsection (b) of this section. If a permit has been issued pursuant to this Act for such vessel, such officer shall note the issuance of any citation under this subsection, including the date thereof and the reason therefor, on the permit.

The Secretary shall maintain a record of all citations issued pursuant to this subsection.

(d) Jurisdiction of courts. The district courts of the United States shall have exclusive jurisdiction over any case or controversy arising under the provisions of this Act. **** ****

[Pub. L. 94-265, Title III, § 311, 90 Stat. 358 (Apr. 13, 1976); Pub. L. 96-470, Title II, § 209(e), Oct. 19, 1980, 94 Stat. 2245; Pub. L. 97-453, §§ 13, 15(c), 96 Stat. 2491, 2493 (Jan. 12, 1983); Pub. L. 99-659, Title I, §§ 101(c)(2), 109(b), 100 Stat. 3707, 3714 (Nov. 14, 1986); Pub. L. 101-627, Title I, § 117, 104 Stat. 4456 (Nov. 28, 1990); Pub. L. 102-251, Title III, § 301(i), 106 Stat. 64 (Mar. 9, 1992); Pub. L. 102-567, Title IX, § 901, 106 Stat. 4316 (Oct. 29, 1992); Pub. L. 104-297, Title I, § 115, 110 Stat. 3599 (Oct. 11, 1996)]

16 U.S.C. § 1861a. Transition to sustainable fisheries. (a) Fisheries disaster relief.

(1) At the discretion of the Secretary or at the request of the Governor of an affected State or a fishing community, the Secretary shall determine whether there is a commercial fishery failure due to a fishery resource disaster as a result of --

(A) natural causes;

(B) man-made causes beyond the control of fishery managers to mitigate through conservation and management measures; or

(C) undetermined causes.

(2) Upon the determination under paragraph (1) that there is a commercial fishery failure, the Secretary is authorized to make sums available to be used by the affected State, fishing community, or by the Secretary in cooperation with the affected State or fishing community for assessing the economic and social effects of the commercial fishery failure, or any activity that the Secretary determines is appropriate to restore the fishery or prevent a similar failure in the future and to assist a fishing community affected by such failure. Before making funds available for an activity authorized under this section, the Secretary shall make a determination that such activity will not expand the size or scope of the commercial fishery failure in that fishery or into other fisheries or other geographic regions.

(3) The Federal share of the cost of any activity carried out under the authority of this subsection shall not exceed 75 percent of the cost of that activity.

(4) There are authorized to be appropriated to the Secretary such sums as are necessary for each of the fiscal years 1996, 1997, 1998, and 1999.

(b) Fishing capacity reduction program. (1) The Secretary, at the request of the appropriate Council for fisheries under the authority of such Council, or the Governor of a State for fisheries under State authority, may conduct a fishing capacity reduction program (referred to in this section as the "program") in a fishery if the Secretary determines that the program --

(A) is necessary to prevent or end overfishing, rebuild stocks of fish, or achieve measurable and significant improvements in the conservation and management of the fishery;

(B) is consistent with the Federal or State fishery management plan or program in effect for such fishery, as appropriate, and that the fishery management plan --

(i) will prevent the replacement of fishing capacity removed by the program through a moratorium on new entrants, restrictions on vessel upgrades, and other effort control measures, taking into account the full potential fishing capacity of the fleet; and

(ii) establishes a specified or target total allowable catch or other measures that trigger closure of the fishery or adjustments to reduce catch; and

(C) is cost-effective and capable of repaying any debt obligation incurred under section 1111 of title XI of the Merchant Marine Act, 1936 [46 App. U.S.C. § 1279f].

(2) The objective of the program shall be to obtain the maximum sustained reduction in fishing capacity at the least cost and in a minimum period of time. ****

[Pub. L. 94-265, Title III, § 312, as added Pub. L. 104-297, Title I, § 116(a), 110 Stat. 3600 (Oct. 11, 1996)]

16 U.S.C. § 1862. North Pacific fisheries conservation. ****

16 U.S.C. § 1863. Northwest Atlantic Ocean Fisheries Reinvestment Program. ****

Title V
Fishery Monitoring and Research

16 U.S.C. § 1881. Registration and information management. ****

16 U.S.C. § 1881a. Information collection. ****

16 U.S.C. § 1881b. Observers. ****

16 U.S.C. § 1881c. Fisheries research. ****

16 U.S.C. § 1881d. Incidental harvest research. ****

16 U.S.C. § 1882. Fisheries systems research. ****

16 U.S.C. § 1883. Gulf of Mexico red snapper research. ****

- 0 -

NEOTROPICAL MIGRATORY BIRD CONSERVATION ACT (2000)
(16 U.S.C. §§ 6101-6109)

Many of the nearly 800 bird species that occur in the United States are neotropical migrants who winter in Latin America and the Caribbean.[113] The populations of many of these species are declining as a result of habitat loss and degradation. To remedy these problems, Congress enacted the Neotropical Migratory Bird Conservation Act.[114] The Act establishes the Neotropical Bird Conservation Account[115] and authorizes the

Secretary of the Interior to establish a program "to provide financial assistance for projects to promote the conservation of neotropical migratory birds."[116]

16 U.S.C. § 6101. Findings. Congress finds that --

(1) of the nearly 800 bird species known to occur in the United States, approximately 500 migrate among countries, and the large majority of those species, the neotropical migrants, winter in Latin America and the Caribbean;

(2) neotropical migratory bird species provide invaluable environmental, economic, recreational, and aesthetic benefits to the United States, as well as to the Western Hemisphere;

(3)(A) many neotropical migratory bird populations, once considered common, are in decline, and some have declined to the point that their long-term survival in the wild is in jeopardy; and

(B) the primary reason for the decline in the populations of those species is habitat loss and degradation (including pollution and contamination) across the species' range; and

(4)(A) because neotropical migratory birds range across numerous international borders each year, their conservation requires the commitment and effort of all countries along their migration routes; and

(B) although numerous initiatives exist to conserve migratory birds and their habitat, those initiatives can be significantly strengthened and enhanced by increased coordination.

[Pub. L. 106-247, § 2, 114 Stat. 593 (July 20, 2000)]

16 U.S.C. § 6102. Purposes. The purposes of this Act are --

(1) to perpetuate healthy populations of neotropical migratory birds;

(2) to assist in the conservation of neotropical migratory birds by supporting conservation initiatives in the United States, Latin America, and the Caribbean; and

(3) to provide financial resources and to foster international cooperation for those initiatives.

[Pub. L. 106-247, § 3, 114 Stat. 593 (July 20, 2000)]

16 U.S.C. § 6103. Definitions. In this Act:

(1) Account. The term "Account" means the Neotropical Migratory Bird Conservation Account established by section 9(a) [16 U.S.C. § 6108(a)].

(2) Conservation. The term "conservation" means the use of methods and procedures necessary to bring a species of neotropical migratory bird to the point at which there are sufficient populations in the wild to ensure the long-term viability of the species, including --

(A) protection and management of neotropical migratory bird populations;

(B) maintenance, management, protection, and restoration of neotropical migratory bird habitat;

(C) research and monitoring;

(D) law enforcement; and

(E) community outreach and education.

(3) Secretary. The term "Secretary" means the Secretary of the Interior.

[Pub. L. 106-247, § 4, 114 Stat. 593 (July 20, 2000)]

16 U.S.C. § 6104. Financial assistance. (a) In general. The Secretary shall establish a program to provide financial assistance for projects to promote the conservation of neotropical migratory birds.

(b) Project applicants. A project proposal may be submitted by --

(1) an individual, corporation, partnership, trust, association, or other private entity;

(2) an officer, employee, agent, department, or instrumentality of the Federal Government, of any State, municipality, or political subdivision of a State, or of any foreign government;

(3) a State, municipality, or political subdivision of a State;

(4) any other entity subject to the jurisdiction of the United States or of any foreign country; and

(5) an international organization (as defined in section 1 of the International Organizations Immunities Act [22 U.S.C. § 288]).

(c) Project proposals. To be considered for financial assistance for a project under this Act, an applicant shall submit a project proposal that --

(1) includes --

(A) the name of the individual responsible for the project;

(B) a succinct statement of the purposes of the project;

(C) a description of the qualifications of individuals conducting the project; and

(D) an estimate of the funds and time necessary to complete the project, including sources and amounts of matching funds;

(2) demonstrates that the project will enhance the conservation of neotropical migratory bird species in the United States, Latin America, or the Caribbean;

(3) includes mechanisms to ensure adequate local public participation in project development and implementation;

(4) contains assurances that the project will be implemented in consultation with relevant wildlife management authorities and other appropriate government officials with jurisdiction over the resources addressed by the project;

(5) demonstrates sensitivity to local historic and cultural resources and complies with applicable laws;

(6) describes how the project will promote sustainable, effective, long-term programs to conserve neotropical migratory birds; and

(7) provides any other information that the Secretary considers to be necessary for evaluating the proposal.

(d) Project reporting. Each recipient of assistance for a project under this Act shall submit to the Secretary such periodic reports as the Secretary considers to be necessary. Each report shall include all information required by the Secretary for evaluating the progress and outcome of the project.

(e) Cost sharing. (1) Federal share. The Federal share of the cost of each project shall be not greater than 25 percent.

*****

[Pub. L. 106-247, § 5, 114 Stat. 594 (July 20, 2000)]

16 U.S.C. § 6105. Duties of the Secretary. In carrying out this Act, the Secretary shall --

(1) develop guidelines for the solicitation of proposals for projects eligible for financial assistance under section 5 [16 U.S.C. § 6104];
(2) encourage submission of proposals for projects eligible for financial assistance under section 5 [16 U.S.C. § 6104], particularly proposals from relevant wildlife management authorities;
(3) select proposals for financial assistance that satisfy the requirements of section 5 [16 U.S.C. § 6104], giving preference to proposals that address conservation needs not adequately addressed by existing efforts and that are supported by relevant wildlife management authorities; and
(4) generally implement this Act in accordance with its purposes.

[Pub. L. 106-247, § 6, 114 Stat. 595 (July 20, 2000)]

16 U.S.C. § 6106. Cooperation. (a) In general. In carrying out this Act, the Secretary shall --

(1) support and coordinate existing efforts to conserve neotropical migratory bird species, through --
(A) facilitating meetings among persons involved in such efforts;
(B) promoting the exchange of information among such persons;
(C) developing and entering into agreements with other Federal agencies, foreign, State, and local governmental agencies, and nongovernmental organizations; and
(D) conducting such other activities as the Secretary considers to be appropriate; and
(2) coordinate activities and projects under this Act with existing efforts in order to enhance conservation of neotropical migratory bird species.

(b) Advisory group. (1) In general. To assist in carrying out this Act, the Secretary may convene an advisory group consisting of individuals representing public and private organizations actively involved in the conservation of neotropical migratory birds.

(2) Public participation. (A) Meetings. The advisory group shall --
(i) ensure that each meeting of the advisory group is open to the public; and
(ii) provide, at each meeting, an opportunity for interested persons to present oral or written statements concerning items on the agenda.
(B) Notice. The Secretary shall provide to the public timely notice of each meeting of the advisory group.
(C) Minutes. Minutes of each meeting of the advisory group shall be kept by the Secretary and shall be made available to the public.
(3) Exemption from Federal Advisory Committee Act. The Federal Advisory Committee Act (5 U.S.C. App.) shall not apply to the advisory group.

[Pub. L. 106-247, § 7, 114 Stat. 595 (July 20, 2000)]

16 U.S.C. § 6107. Report to Congress. Not later than October 1, 2002, the Secretary shall submit to Congress a report on the results and effectiveness of the program carried out under this Act, including recommendations concerning how the Act might be improved and whether the program should be continued.

[Pub. L. 106-247, § 8, 114 Stat. 596 (July 20, 2000)]

16 U.S.C. § 6108. Neotropical Migratory Bird Conservation Account. (a) Establishment. There is established in the Multinational Species Conservation Fund of the Treasury a separate account to be known as the "Neotropical Migratory Bird Conservation Account", which shall consist of amounts deposited into the Account by the Secretary of the Treasury under subsection (b).

(b) Deposits into the Account. The Secretary of the Treasury shall deposit into the Account --

(1) all amounts received by the Secretary in the form of donations under subsection (d); and

(2) other amounts appropriated to the Account.

(c) Use. (1) In general. Subject to paragraph (2), the Secretary may use amounts in the Account, without further Act of appropriation, to carry out this Act.

(2) Administrative expenses. Of amounts in the Account available for each fiscal year, the Secretary may expend not more than 3 percent or up to $80,000, whichever is greater, to pay the administrative expenses necessary to carry out this Act.

(d) Acceptance and use of donations. The Secretary may accept and use donations to carry out this Act. Amounts received by the Secretary in the form of donations shall be transferred to the Secretary of the Treasury for deposit into the Account.

[Pub. L. 106-247, § 9, 114 Stat. 596 (July 20, 2000)]

16 U.S.C. § 6109. Authorization of appropriations. There is authorized to be appropriated to the Account to carry out this Act $5,000,000 for each of fiscal years 2001 through 2005, to remain available until expended, of which not less than 75 percent of the amounts made available for each fiscal year shall be expended for projects carried out outside the United States.

[Pub. L. 106-247, § 10, 114 Stat. 597 (July 20, 2000)]

- 0 -

WILD BIRDS, ELEPHANTS, RHINOCEROS, TIGERS, AND GREAT APES

The Migratory Bird Treaty Act, the Eagle Protection Act, and the Neotropical Migratory

Bird Conservation Act seek to conserve species found at least part of the year in the United States. The Wild Bird Conservation Act,[117] on the other hand, seeks to conserve "exotic" birds[118] that are marketed in the United States. In this, the Act is an example of several statutes that seek to conserve species that are not native to the United States but for which there is a market in this country: elephants,[119] rhinoceros and tigers,[120] and great apes -- chimpanzees, gorillas, bonobos, orangutans, and gibbons.[121]

Enactment of the Wild Bird Conservation Act reflected recognition that the populations of many species "have declined dramatically due to habitat loss and the public's demand for pet birds"; the United States is the major world market, importing "hundreds of thousands of live birds each year for use as pets, creating approximately $300 million in annual retail sales nationwide."[122] This demand leads to substantial mortality: 30-50% of the wild birds caught for export die before leaving their countries of origin and another 14% die in transit or quarantine.[123] Although this international trade is regulated under the Convention on International Trade in Endangered Species of Wild Fauna and Flora (CITES),[124] Congress concluded that the Convention had been "ineffective in stemming the decline in wild bird populations because many exporting countries lack the resources and/or expertise to perform comprehensive population analyses of their wild bird populations[and] are therefore unable to determine whether existing levels of trade are detrimental to the survival of wild avian populations."[125]

Like CITES, the Act regulates trade. It does so by imposing a moratorium on the importation of any species listed on any of the CITES appendices.[126] The Act also authorizes the Secretary of the Interior to establish moratoria on any species not listed under CITES.[127] These moratoria may be lifted by the Secretary through the inclusion of a species on an "approved list." Species may be added to the approved list if they are captive bred[128] or if each country of origin is complying with cites and is implementing and enforcing a

> scientifically-based management plan for the species ... which --
> (A) provides for the conservation of the species and its habitat and includes incentives for conservation;
> (B) ensures that the use of the species is biologically sustainable ...; and
> (C) addresses factors relevant to the conservation of the species, including illegal trade, domestic trade, subsistence use, disease, and habitat loss.[129]

The Act imposes criminal and civil sanctions on importation of birds in violation of the Act.[130]

In addition to imposing restriction on the importation of wild birds, the Act also seeks to assist exporting countries in conserving wild birds by establishing the Exotic Bird Conservation Fund.[131] The Fund is to be used to help finance conservation projects as well as the development of the management plans.[132]

The other acts are similar. Both the African Elephant Conservation Act and the Rhinoceros and Tiger Conservation Act employ the carrot-and-stick approach. The Act establish funds[133] to provide financial assistance for conservation projects.[134] In addition to these incentives, the acts also restrict the importation and exportation of products made from the designated species; the prohibitions are backed up with criminal and civil penalties.[135] The Asian Elephant Conservation Act and the Great Apes Conservation Act establish conservation funds but do not impose trade restrictions.[136]

WILD EXOTIC BIRD CONSERVATION ACT
(16 U.S.C. §§ 4901-4916)

16 U.S.C. § 4901. Findings. The Congress finds the following:

(1) In addition to habitat loss and local use, the international pet trade in wild-caught exotic birds is contributing to the decline of species in the wild, and the mortality associated with the trade remains unacceptably high.

(2) The United States, as the world's largest importer of exotic birds and as a Party to the Convention, should play a substantial role in finding effective solutions to these problems, including assisting countries of origin in implementing programs of wild bird conservation, and ensuring that the market in the United States for exotic birds does not operate to the detriment of the survival of species in the wild.

(3) Sustainable utilization of exotic birds has the potential to create economic value in them and their habitats, which will contribute to their conservation and promote the maintenance of biological diversity generally.

(4) Utilization of exotic birds that is not sustainable should not be allowed.

(5) Broad international attention has focused on the serious conservation and welfare problems which currently exist in the trade in wild-caught animals, including exotic birds.

(6) Many countries have chosen not to export their wild birds for the pet trade. Their decisions should be respected and their efforts should be supported.

(7) Several countries that allow for the export of their wild birds often lack the means to develop or effectively implement scientifically based management plans, and these countries should be assisted in developing and implementing management plans to enable them to ensure that their wild bird trade is conducted humanely and at sustainable levels.

(8) The major exotic bird exporting countries are Parties to the Convention.

(9) The Convention recognizes that trade in species that are threatened with extinction, or that may become so, should be subject to strict regulation.

(10) The necessary population assessments, monitoring programs, and appropriate remedial measures for species listed in Appendix II of the Convention are not always being undertaken in order to maintain species at levels above which they might become eligible for inclusion in Appendix I of the Convention.

(11) Resolutions adopted pursuant to the Convention recommend that the Parties to the Convention take appropriate measures regarding trade in species of exotic birds that have significantly high mortality rates in transport, including suspension of trade for commercial purposes between Parties when appropriate.

(12) Article XIV provides that the Convention in no way affects the right of any Party to the Convention to adopt stricter domestic measures for the regulation of trade in all species, whether or not listed in an Appendix to the Convention.

(13) The United States prohibits the export of all birds native to the United States that are caught in the wild.

(14) This Act [16 U.S.C. §§ 4901 *et seq.*] provides a series of nondiscriminatory measures that are necessary for the conservation of exotic birds, and furthers the obligations of the

United States under the Convention.

[Pub. L. 102-440, Title I, § 102, 106 Stat. 2224 (Oct. 23, 1992)]

16 U.S.C. § 4902. Statement of purpose. The purpose of this Act [16 U.S.C. §§ 4901 *et seq.*] is to promote the conservation of exotic birds by --
(1) assisting wild bird conservation and management programs in the countries of origin of wild birds;
(2) ensuring that all trade in species of exotic birds involving the United States is biologically sustainable and is not detrimental to the species;
(3) limiting or prohibiting imports of exotic birds when necessary to ensure that --
(A) wild exotic bird populations are not harmed by removal of exotic birds from the wild for the trade; or
(B) exotic birds in trade are not subject to inhumane treatment; and
(4) encouraging and supporting effective implementation of the Convention.

[Pub. L. 102-440, Title I, § 103, 106 Stat. 2225 (Oct. 23, 1992)]

16 U.S.C. § 4903. Definitions. In this Act --
(1) The term "Convention" means the Convention on International Trade in Endangered Species of Wild Fauna and Flora, as amended, signed in Washington on March 3, 1973, and the Appendices thereto.
(2) The term "exotic bird" --
(A) means any live or dead member of the class Aves that is not indigenous to the 50 States or the District of Columbia, including any egg or offspring thereof; and
(B) does not include --
(i) domestic poultry, dead sport-hunted birds, dead museum specimens, dead scientific specimens, or products manufactured from such birds; or
(ii) birds in the following families: Phasianidae, Numididae, Cracidae, Meleagrididae, Megapodiidae, Anatidae, Struthionidae, Rheidae, Dromaiinae, and Gruidae.
(3) Each of the terms "import" and "importation" means to land on, bring into, or introduce into, or attempt to land on, bring into, or introduce into, any place subject to the jurisdiction of the United States.
(4) The term "person" means an individual, corporation, partnership, trust, association, or any other private entity; or any officer, employee, agent, department, or instrumentality of the Federal Government, of any State, municipality, or political subdivision of a State, or of any foreign government; any State, municipality, or political subdivision of a State; or any other entity subject to the jurisdiction of the United States.
(5) The term "qualifying facility" means an exotic bird breeding facility that is included in a list published by the Secretary under section 107 [16 U.S.C. § 4906].
(6) The term "Secretary" means the Secretary of the Interior or a designee of the Secretary of the Interior.
(7) The term "species" --
(A) means any species, any subspecies, or any distinct population segment of a species or subspecies; and
(B) includes hybrids of any species or subspecies.

(8) The term "United States" means the 50 States, the District of Columbia, the Commonwealth of Puerto Rico, American Samoa, the Virgin Islands, Guam, the Commonwealth of the Northern Mariana Islands, and the Trust Territory of the Pacific Islands.

[Pub. L. 102-440, Title I, § 104, 106 Stat. 2225 (Oct. 23, 1992)]

16 U.S.C. § 4904. Moratoria on imports of exotic birds covered by Convention. (a) Immediate moratorium.

(1) Establishment of moratorium. The importation of any exotic bird of a species identified as a category B species in the report entitled "Report of the Animals Committee", adopted by the 8th meeting of the Conference of the Parties to the Convention, is prohibited.

(2) Termination of moratorium. A species of exotic birds shall be subject to the prohibition on importation established by paragraph (1) until the Secretary, after notice and an opportunity for public comment --

(A) determines that appropriate remedial measures have been taken in the countries of origin for that species, so as to eliminate the threat of trade to the conservation of the species; and

(B) makes the findings described in section 106(c) [16 U.S.C. § 4905(c)] for the species and includes the species in the list published under section 106(a) [16 U.S.C. § 4905(a)].

(b) Emergency authority to suspend imports of listed species.

(1) Authority to suspend imports. The Secretary is authorized to suspend the importation of exotic birds of any species that is listed in any Appendix to the Convention, and if applicable remove the species from the list under section 106(a) [16 U.S.C. § 4905(a)], if the Secretary determines that --

(A)(i) trade in that species is detrimental to the species,

(ii) there is not sufficient information available on which to base a judgment that the species is not detrimentally affected by trade in that species, or

(iii) remedial measures have been recommended by the Standing Committee of the Convention that have not been implemented; and

(B) the suspension might be necessary for the conservation of the species.

(2) Termination of suspension. A species of exotic birds shall be subject to a suspension of importation under paragraph (1) until the Secretary, after notice and an opportunity for public comment, makes the findings described in section 106(c) [16 U.S.C. § 4905(c)] and includes the species in the list published under section 106(a) [16 U.S.C. § 4905(a)].

(c) Moratorium after one year for other species listed in Appendices. Effective on the date that is one year after October 23, 1992, the importation of any exotic bird of a species that is listed in any Appendix to the Convention is prohibited unless the Secretary makes the findings described in section 106(c) [16 U.S.C. § 4905(c)] and includes the species in the list published under section 106(a) [16 U.S.C. § 4905(a)].

(d) Limitation on number imported during first year. Notwithstanding any other provision of this Act, the Secretary shall prohibit the importation, during the 1-year period beginning on October 23, 1992, of exotic birds of each species that is listed under any Appendix to the Convention in excess of the number of that species that were imported during the most recent year for which the Secretary has complete import data.

[Pub. L. 102-440, Title I, § 105, 106 Stat. 2226 (Oct. 23, 1992)]

16 U.S.C. § 4905. List of approved species. (a) Listing.

(1) In general. One year after October 23, 1992 and periodically thereafter, the Secretary shall, after notice and an opportunity for public comment, publish in the Federal Register a list of species of exotic birds that are listed in an Appendix to the Convention and that are not subject to a prohibition or suspension of importation otherwise applicable under section 105(a), (b), or (c) [16 U.S.C. § 4904(a), (b), or (c)].

(2) Manner of listing. The Secretary shall list a species under paragraph (1) with respect to --

(A) the countries of origin from which the species may be imported; and

(B) if appropriate, the qualifying facilities in those countries from which the species may be imported.

(3) Bases for determinations. In making a determination required under this subsection, the Secretary shall --

(A) use the best scientific information available; and

(B) consider the adequacy of regulatory and enforcement mechanisms in all countries of origin for the species, including such mechanisms for control of illegal trade.

(b) Captive bred species. The Secretary shall include a species of exotic birds in the list under subsection (a) of this section if the Secretary determines that --

(1) the species is regularly bred in captivity and no wild-caught birds of the species are in trade; or

(2) the species is bred in a qualifying facility.

(c) Non-captive bred species. The Secretary shall include in the list under subsection (a) of this section a species of exotic birds that is listed in an Appendix to the Convention if the Secretary finds the Convention is being effectively implemented with respect to that species because of each of the following:

(1) Each country of origin for which the species is listed is effectively implementing the Convention, particularly with respect to --

(A) the establishment of a scientific authority or other equivalent authority;

(B) the requirements of Article IV of the Convention with respect to that species; and

(C) remedial measures recommended by the Parties to the Convention with respect to that species.

(2) A scientifically-based management plan for the species has been developed which --

(A) provides for the conservation of the species and its habitat and includes incentives for conservation;

(B) ensures that the use of the species is biologically sustainable and maintained throughout the range of the species in the country to which the plan applies at a level that is consistent with the role of the species in the ecosystem and is well above the level at which the species might become threatened with extinction; and

(C) addresses factors relevant to the conservation of the species, including illegal trade, domestic trade, subsistence use, disease, and habitat loss.

(3) The management plan is implemented and enforced.

(4) The methods of capture, transport, and maintenance of the species minimizes the risk of injury or damage to health, including inhumane treatment.

[Pub. L. 102-440, Title I, § 106, 106 Stat. 2227 (Oct. 23, 1992)]

16 U.S.C. § 4906. Qualifying facilities. (a) Determination. Upon submission of a petition under section 110 [16 U.S.C. § 4909] by any person, the Secretary shall determine whether an exotic bird breeding facility is a qualifying facility. Such determination shall be effective for a period specified by the Secretary, which may not exceed 3 years. The Secretary shall, from time to time, publish a list of qualifying facilities in the Federal Register.

(b) Criteria. The Secretary shall determine under subsection (a) of this section that a facility is a qualifying facility for a species of exotic birds if the Secretary finds each of the following:

(1) The facility has demonstrated the capability of producing captive bred birds of the species in the numbers to be imported into the United States from that facility.

(2) The facility is operated in a manner that is not detrimental to the survival of the species in the wild.

(3) The facility is operated in a humane manner.

(4) The appropriate governmental authority of the country in which the facility is located has certified in writing, and the Secretary is satisfied, that the facility has the capability of breeding the species in captivity.

(5) The country in which the facility is located is a Party to the Convention.

(6) All birds exported from the facility are bred at the facility.

[Pub. L. 102-440, Title I, § 107, 106 Stat. 2228 (Oct. 23, 1992)]

16 U.S.C. § 4907. Moratoria for species not covered by Convention. (a) In general. The Secretary shall --

(1) review periodically the trade in species of exotic birds that are not listed in any Appendix to the Convention; and

(2) after notice and an opportunity for public comment, establish a moratorium or quota on --

(A) importation of any species of exotic birds from one or more countries of origin for the species, if the Secretary determines that --

(i) the findings described in section 106(c)(2), (3), and (4) [16 U.S.C. § 4905(c)(2), (3), and (4)] cannot be made with respect to the species; and

(ii) the moratorium or quota is necessary for the conservation of the species or is otherwise consistent with the purpose of this Act [16 U.S.C. §§ 4901 *et seq.*]; or

(B) the importation of all species of exotic birds from a particular country, if --
(i) the country has not developed and implemented a management program for exotic birds in trade generally, that ensures both the conservation and the humane treatment of exotic birds during capture, transport, and maintenance; and
(ii) the Secretary finds that the moratorium or quota is necessary for the conservation of the species or is otherwise consistent with the purpose of this Act.

(b) Termination of quota or moratorium. The Secretary shall terminate a quota or moratorium established under subsection (a) of this section if the Secretary finds that the reasons for establishing the quota or moratorium no longer exist.

[Pub. L. 102-440, Title I, § 108, 106 Stat. 2229 (Oct. 23, 1992)]

16 U.S.C. § 4908. Call for information. Within one month after October 23, 1992, the Secretary shall issue a call for information on the wild bird conservation program of each country that exports exotic birds, by --

(1) publishing a notice in the Federal Register requesting submission of such information to the Secretary by all interested persons; and
(2) submitting a written request for such information through the Secretary of State to each country that exports exotic birds.

[Pub. L. 102-440, Title I, § 109, 106 Stat. 2229 (Oct. 23, 1992)]

16 U.S.C. § 4909. Petitions. (a) In general. Any person may at any time submit to the Secretary a petition in writing requesting that the Secretary exercise authority of the Secretary under this Act to --

(1) establish, modify, or terminate any prohibition, suspension, or quota under this Act on importation of any species of exotic bird;
(2) add a species of exotic bird to, or remove such a species from, a list under section 106 [16 U.S.C. § 4905]; or
(3) determine under section 107 [16 U.S.C. § 4906] whether an exotic bird breeding facility is a qualifying facility.

(b) Consideration and ruling. For each petition submitted to the Secretary in accordance with subsection (a) of this section, the Secretary shall --

(1) within 90 days after receiving the petition, issue and publish in the Federal Register a preliminary ruling regarding whether the petition presents sufficient information indicating that the action requested in the petition might be warranted; and
(2) for each petition determined to present such sufficient information --
(A) provide an opportunity for the submission of public comment on the petition; and
(B) issue and publish in the Federal Register a final ruling on the petition, by

not later than 90 days after the end of the period for public comment.

[Pub. L. 102-440, Title I, § 110, 106 Stat. 2229 (Oct. 23, 1992)]

16 U.S.C. § 4910. Prohibited acts. (a) Prohibitions.

(1) In general. Subject to paragraph (2), it is unlawful for any person to --

(A) import any exotic bird in violation of any prohibition, suspension, or quota on importation under section 105 or 108 [16 U.S.C. § 4904 or 4907];

(B) import an exotic bird of a species that pursuant to section 106(a)(2)(B) [16 U.S.C. § 4905(a)(2)(B)] is included in a list under section 106 [16 U.S.C. § 4905], if the bird was not captive bred at a qualifying facility; or

(C) violate any regulation promulgated by the Secretary pursuant to authority provided by this Act [16 U.S.C. §§ 4901 *et seq.*].

(2) Limitation. Paragraph (1)(A) and (B) does not apply to importations made incident to the transit of exotic birds through the United States to foreign countries if the applicable requirements of the Convention have been satisfied with respect to the trade in those exotic birds.

(b) Burden of proof for exemptions. Any person claiming the benefit of any exemption or permit under this Act shall have the burden of proving that the exemption or permit is applicable or has been granted, and was valid and in force at the time of the alleged violation.

[Pub. L. 102-440, Title I, § 111, 106 Stat. 2230 (Oct. 23, 1992)]

16 U.S.C. § 4911. Exemptions. Notwithstanding any prohibition, suspension, or quota under this Act [16 U.S.C. §§ 4901 *et seq.*] on the importation of a species of exotic bird, the Secretary may, through the issuance of import permits, authorize the importation of a bird of the species if the Secretary determines that such importation is not detrimental to the survival of the species and the bird is being imported exclusively for any of the following purposes:

(1) Scientific research.

(2) As a personally owned pet of an individual who is returning to the United States after being continuously out of the country for a minimum of one year, except that an individual may not import more than 2 exotic birds under this paragraph in any year.

(3) Zoological breeding or display programs.

(4) Cooperative breeding programs that are --

(A) designed to promote the conservation of the species and maintain the species in the wild by enhancing the propagation and survival of the species; and

(B) developed and administered by, or in conjunction with, an avicultural, conservation, or zoological organization that meets standards developed by the Secretary.

[Pub. L. 102-440, Title I, § 112, 106 Stat. 2230 (Oct. 23, 1992)]

16 U.S.C. § 4912. Penalties and regulations. (a) Penalties. (1) Civil penalties.

(A) Any person who knowingly violates, and any person engaged in business as an importer of exotic birds who violates, section 111(a)(1)or (2) [4910(a)(1) or (2)] or any permit issued under section 112 [16 U.S.C. § 4911] may be assessed a civil penalty by the Secretary of not more than $25,000 for each violation.

(B) Any person who knowingly violates, and any person engaged in business as an importer of exotic birds who violates, section 111(a)(3) [4910(a)(3)] may be assessed a civil penalty by the Secretary of not more than $12,000 for each such violation.

(C) Any person who otherwise violates section 111(a) [16 U.S.C. § 4910(a)] or any permit issued under section 112 [16 U.S.C. § 4911] may be assessed a civil penalty by the Secretary of not more than $500 for each such violation.

(D) A civil penalty under this section shall be assessed, and may be collected, in the manner in which a civil penalty under the Act of December 28, 1973 (Public Law 93-205) [16 U.S.C. § 1531 *et seq.*], may be assessed and collected under section 111(a) of that Act [16 U.S.C.A. § 1540(a)].

(2) Criminal penalties.

(A) Any person who knowingly violates, and any person engaged in business as an importer of exotic birds who violates, section 111(a)(1) or (2) [16 U.S.C. § 4910(a)(1) or (2)] or any permit issued under section 112 [16 U.S.C. § 4911] shall be fined under Title 18, or imprisoned for not more than 2 years, or both.

(B) Any person who knowingly violates section 11(a)(3) [16 U.S.C. § 4910(a)(3)] shall be fined under Title 18, imprisoned not more than 6 months, or both.

(b) District court jurisdiction. The several district courts of the United States, including the courts enumerated in section 460 of Title 28, United States Code, shall have jurisdiction over any action arising under this Act [16 U.S.C. §§ 4901 *et seq.*]. For the purposes of this Act, American Samoa shall be included in the Judicial District of the District Court of the United States for the District of Hawaii, and the Trust Territory of Palau and the Northern Marianas shall be included in the Judicial District of the District Court of the United States for the District of Guam.

(c) Other enforcement. The importation of an exotic bird is deemed to be transportation of wildlife for purposes of section 3(a) of the Lacey Act Amendments of 1981 (16 U.S.C. 3372(a)).

(d) Regulations. The Secretary shall prescribe regulations that are necessary and appropriate to carry out the purposes of this Act.

(e) Savings provisions. The authority of the Secretary under this Act is in addition to and shall not affect the authority of the Secretary under the Endangered Species Act of 1973 (16 U.S.C. 1531 et seq.) or diminish the authority of the Secretary under the Lacey Act Amendments of 1981 (16 U.S.C. 3371 et seq.). Nothing in this Act shall be construed as repealing, superseding, or modifying any provision of Federal law.

[Pub. L. 102-440, Title I, § 113, 106 Stat. 2231 (Oct. 23, 1992)]

16 U.S.C. § 4913. Exotic bird conservation assistance. (a) Assistance. The Secretary, subject to the availability of appropriations, shall use amounts in the Exotic Bird Conservation Fund established by subsection (b) of this section to provide financial and technical assistance for projects to conserve exotic birds in their native countries. In selecting projects for assistance, the Secretary shall give particular attention to species that are subject to an import moratorium or quota under this Act [16 U.S.C. §§ 4901 *et seq.*], in order to assist those countries in the development and implementation of conservation management programs, or law enforcement, or both.

(b) Fund. (1) Establishment. There is established in the Treasury a separate account, which shall be known as the "Exotic Bird Conservation Fund".

(2) Contents. The Fund shall consist of --

(A) all amounts received by the United States in the form of penalties, fines, or forfeiture of property collected under this Act in excess of the cost of paying rewards under section 113(c) [16 U.S.C. § 4912(c)];

(B) donations received by the Secretary for exotic bird conservation; and

(C) such amounts as are appropriated to the Secretary for conserving exotic birds.

(c) Review and report on other conservation opportunities. The Secretary, in consultation with appropriate representatives of industry, the conservation community, the Secretariat of the Convention, and other national and international bodies, shall --

(1) review opportunities for a voluntary program of labeling exotic birds, certification of exotic bird breeding facilities and retail outlets, and provision of privately organized or funded technical assistance to other nations; and

(2) report to the Congress the results of this review within 2 years after October 23, 1992.

[Pub. L. 102-440, Title I, § 114, 106 Stat. 2232 (Oct. 23, 1992)]

16 U.S.C. § 4914. Marking and recordkeeping. (a) In general. The Secretary is authorized to promulgate regulations to require marking or recordkeeping that the Secretary determines will contribute significantly to the ability of the Secretary to ensure compliance with the prohibitions of section 111 [16 U.S.C. § 4910], for --

(1) any exotic bird that is imported after October 23, 1992; or

(2) any other exotic bird that is --

(A) hatched after October 23, 1992;

(B) offered for sale; and

(C) of a species --

(i) the export of which from any country of origin is prohibited; and

(ii) that is subject to a high level of illegal trade.

(b) Avoiding deterrence of breeding. The Secretary shall seek to ensure that regulations promulgated under this section will not have the effect of deterring captive breeding of exotic birds.

[Pub. L. 102-440, Title I, § 115, 106 Stat. 2232 (Oct. 23, 1992)]

16 U.S.C. § 4915. Authorization of appropriations. ****

16 U.S.C. § 4916. Relationship to State law. Nothing in this Act [16 U.S.C. §§ 4901 *et seq.*] may be construed as precluding the regulation under State law of the sale, transfer, or possession of exotic birds if such regulation --

(1) does not authorize any sale, transfer, or possession of exotic birds that is prohibited under this Act; and

(2) is consistent with the international obligations of the United States.

[Pub. L. 102-440, Title I, § 117, 106 Stat. 2233 (Oct. 23, 1992)]

\- 0 -

Fish and Wildlife Service Enforcement Regulations

The United States Fish and Wildlife Service (FWS) has primary responsibility for enforcing federal wildlife conservation statutes. As noted, the agency has enforcement or management authority under the Lacey Act,[137] the Migratory Bird Treaty Act,[138] the Bald and Golden Eagle Protection Act,[139] the Airborne Hunting Act,[140] the Marine Mammal Protection Act for walruses, otters, manatees, and polar bears,[141] the Endangered Species Act for non-marine species,[142] and the Wild Bird Conservation Act.[143]

The regulatory enforcement system for these is contained in 50 C.F.R. parts 10-24. The excerpts included here outline the basics of that structure: general provisions such as definitions (part 10); the administrative procedures for assessing and contesting penalties (part 11); procedures governing seizures and forfeitures (part 12); and general permit provisions (part 13). Also included are excerpts from the regulations governing hunting of migratory birds (part 20).

Other federal agencies have enforcement responsibilities for some statutes included in this chapter. The National Marine Fisheries Service, for example, is responsible for enforcing the Marine Mammal Protection Act for "the order Cetacea [whales] and members, other than walruses, of the order Pinnipedia [seals],"[144] the Magnuson-Stevens Fishery Conservation and Management Act,[145] and the Endangered Species Act for marine and anadromous species.[146] The Bureau of Land Management enforces the Wild Free-Roaming Horses and Burros Act.[147] The regulations included are similar to the regulatory schemes adopted by other agencies with enforcement and management authority.

United States Fish and Wildlife Service, Department of the Interior

50 C.F.R. PART 10

GENERAL PROVISIONS

Subpart A -- Introduction

Subpart B -- Definitions

Subpart C -- Addresses

AUTHORITY: 18 U.S.C. § 42; 16 U.S.C. §§ 703-712; 16 U.S.C. §§ 668a-d; 19 U.S.C. § 1202; 16 U.S.C. §§ 1531-1543; 16 U.S.C. §§ 1361-1384, 1401-1407; 16 U.S.C. §§ 742a-742j-1; 16 U.S.C. §§ 3371-3378.

SOURCE: 38 FR 22015, Aug. 15, 1973, unless otherwise noted.

SUBPART A -- INTRODUCTION

§ 10.1 Purpose of regulations.

The regulations of this Subchapter B are promulgated to implement the following statutes enforced by the U.S. Fish and Wildlife Service which regulate the taking, possession, transportation, sale, purchase, barter, exportation, and importation of wildlife:

Lacey Act, 18 U.S.C. § 42.

Lacey Act Amendments of 1981, 16 U.S.C. §§ 3371-3378.

Migratory Bird Treaty Act, 16 U.S.C. §§ 703-712.

Bald and Golden Eagle Protection Act, 16 U.S.C. §§ 668a-668d.

Endangered Species Act of 1973, 16 U.S.C. §§ 1531-1543.

Tariff Classification Act of 1962, 19 U.S.C. § 1202, [Schedule 1, Part 15D, Headnote 2(d), T.S.U.S.].

Fish and Wildlife Act of 1956, 16 U.S.C. §§ 742a-742j-l.

Marine Mammal Protection Act of 1972, 16 U.S.C. §§ 1361-1384, 1401-1407.

[53 FR 6649, March 2, 1988]

§ 10.2 Scope of regulations.

The various parts of this Subchapter B [50 C.F.R. parts 10-24] are interrelated, and particular note should be taken that the parts must be construed with reference to each other.

§ 10.3 Other applicable laws.

No statute or regulation of any State shall be construed to relieve a person from the restrictions, conditions, and requirements contained in this Subchapter B [50 C.F.R. parts 10-24]. In addition, nothing in this Subchapter B, nor any permit issued under this Subchapter B, shall be construed to relieve a person from any other requirements imposed by a statute or regulation of any State or of the United States, including any applicable health, quarantine, agricultural, or customs laws or regulations, or other Service enforced statutes or regulations.

§ 10.4 When regulations apply.

The regulations of this Subchapter B shall apply to all matters arising after the effective date of such regulations, with the following exceptions:

(a) *Civil penalty proceedings.* Except as otherwise provided in § 11.25, the civil penalty assessment procedures contained in this Subchapter B shall apply only to any proceeding instituted by notice of violation dated subsequent to the effective date of these regulations, regardless of when the act or omission which is the basis of a civil penalty proceeding occurred.

(b) *Permits.* The regulations in this Subchapter B shall apply to any permit application received after the effective date of the appropriate regulations in this Subchapter B and, insofar as appropriate, to any permit which is renewed after such effective date.

[38 FR 22015, Aug. 15, 1973, as amended at 39 FR 1159, Jan. 4, 1974]

SUBPART B -- DEFINITIONS

§ 10.11 Scope of definitions.

In addition and subject to definitions contained in applicable statutes and subsequent parts or sections of this Subchapter B, words or their variants shall have the meanings ascribed in this subpart. Throughout this Subchapter B words in the singular form shall include the plural, words in the plural form shall include the singular, and words in the masculine form shall include the feminine.

§ 10.12 Definitions.

"Aircraft" means any contrivance used for flight in the air.

"Amphibians" means a member of the class, *Amphibia,* including, but not limited to, frogs, toads, and salamanders; including any part, product, egg, or offspring thereof, or the dead body or parts thereof (excluding fossils), whether or not included in a manufactured product or in a processed food product.

"Animal" means an organism of the animal kingdom, as distinguished from the plant kingdom; including any part, product, egg, or offspring thereof, or the dead body or parts thereof (excluding fossils), whether or not included in a manufactured product or in a processed food product.

"Birds" means a member of the class, *Aves*; including any part, product, egg, or offspring thereof, or the dead body or parts thereof (excluding fossils), whether or not included in a manufactured product or in a processed food product.

"Country of exportation" means the last country from which the animal was exported before importation into the United States.

"Country of origin" means the country where the animal was taken from the wild, or the country of natal origin of the animal.

"Crustacean" means a member of the class, *Crustacea,* including but not limited to, crayfish, lobsters, shrimps, crabs, barnacles, and some terrestrial forms; including any part, product, egg, or offspring thereof, or the dead body or parts thereof (excluding fossils), whether or not included in a manufactured product or in a processed food product.

"Director" means the Director of the United States Fish and Wildlife Service, Department of the Interior, or his authorized representative.

"Endangered wildlife" means any wildlife listed in § 17.11 or § 17.12 of this subchapter.

"Fish" means a member of any of the following classes:

(1) *Cyclostomata,* including, but not limited to, hagfishes and lampreys;

(2) *Elasmobranchii,* including but not limited to, sharks, skates, and rays; and

(3) *Pisces,* including but not limited to trout, perch, bass, minnows, and catfish; including any part, product, egg, or offspring thereof, or the dead body or parts thereof (excluding fossils), whether or not included in a manufactured product or in a processed food product.

"Fish or wildlife" means any wild animal, whether alive or dead, including without limitation any wild mammal, bird, reptile, amphibian, fish, mollusk, crustacean, arthropod, coelenterate, or other invertebrate, whether or not bred, hatched, or born in captivity, and including any part, product, egg, or offspring thereof.

"Foreign commerce" includes, among other things, any transaction (1) between persons within one foreign country, or (2) between persons in two or more foreign countries, or (3) between a person within the United States and a person in one or more foreign countries, or (4) between persons within the United States, where the fish or wildlife in question are moving in any country or countries outside the United States.

"Fossil" means the remains of an animal of past geological ages which has been preserved in the earth's crust through mineralization of the object.

"Import" means to land on, bring into, or introduce into, or attempt to land on, bring into, or introduce into any place subject to the jurisdiction of the United States, whether or not such landing, bringing, or introduction constitutes an importation within the meaning of the tariff laws of the United States.

"Injurious Wildlife" means any wildlife for which a permit is required under Subpart B of Part 16 of this subchapter before being imported into or shipped between the continental United States, the District of Columbia, Hawaii, the Commonwealth of Puerto Rico, or any possession of the United States.

"Mammal" means a member of the class, *Mammalia*; including any part, product, egg, or offspring, or the dead body or parts thereof (excluding fossils), whether or not included in a manufactured product or in a processed food product.

"Migratory bird" means any bird, whatever its origin and whether or not raised in captivity, which belongs to a species listed in § 10.13, or which is a mutation or a hybrid of any such species, including any part, nest, or egg of any such bird, or any product, whether or not manufactured, which consists, or is composed in whole or part, of any such bird or any part, nest, or egg thereof.

"Migratory game birds": See § 20.11 of this subchapter.

"Mollusk" means a member of the phylum, *Mollusca*, including but not limited to, snails, mussels, clams, oysters, scallops, abalone, squid, and octopuses; including any part, product, egg, or offspring thereof, or the dead body or parts thereof (excluding fossils), whether or not included in a manufactured product or in a processed food product.

"Permit" means any document designated as a "permit," "license," "certificate," or any other document issued by the Service to authorize, limit, or describe activity and signed by an authorized official of the Service.

"Person" means any individual, firm, corporation, association, partnership, club, or private body, any one or all, as the context requires.

"Plant" means any member of the plant kingdom, including seeds, roots and other parts thereof.

"Possession" means the detention and control, or the manual or ideal custody of anything which may be the subject of property, for one's use and enjoyment, either as owner or as the proprietor of a qualified right in it, and either held personally or by another who exercises it in one's place and name. Possession includes the act or state of possessing and that condition of facts under which one can exercise his power over a corporeal thing at his pleasure to the exclusion of all other persons. Possession includes constructive possession which means not actual but assumed to exist, where one claims to hold by virtue of some title, without having actual custody.

"Public" as used in referring to museums, zoological parks, and scientific or educational institutions, refers to such as are open to the general public and are either established, maintained, and operated as a governmental service or are privately endowed and organized but not operated for profit.

"Reptile" means a member of the class, *Reptilia*, including but not limited to, turtles, snakes, lizards, crocodiles, and alligators; including any part, product, egg, or offspring thereof, or the dead body or parts thereof, whether or not included in a manufactured product or in a processed food product.

"Secretary" means the Secretary of the Interior or his authorized representative.

"Service" means the United States Fish and Wildlife Service, Department of the Interior.

"Shellfish" means an aquatic invertebrate animal having a shell, including, but not limited to, (a) an oyster, clam, or other mollusk; and (b) a lobster or other crustacean; or any part, product, egg, or offspring thereof, or the dead body or parts thereof (excluding fossils), whether or not included in a manufactured product or in a processed food product.

"State" means any State of the United States, the District of Columbia, the Commonwealth of Puerto Rico, American Samoa, the Virgin Islands, and Guam.

"Take" means to pursue, hunt, shoot, wound, kill, trap, capture, or collect, or attempt to pursue, hunt, shoot, wound, kill, trap, capture, or collect. (With reference to marine mammals, see Part 18 of this subchapter.)

"Transportation" means to ship, convey, carry or transport by any means whatever, and deliver or receive for such shipment, conveyance, carriage, or transportation.

"United States" means the several States of the United States of America, the District of Columbia, the Commonwealth of Puerto Rico, American Samoa, the Virgin Islands, and Guam.

"Whoever" means the same as person.

"Wildlife" means the same as fish or wildlife.

[38 FR 22015, Aug. 15, 1973, as amended at 42 FR 32377, June 24, 1977; 42 FR 59358, Nov. 16, 1977; 45 FR 56673, Aug. 25, 1980; 50 FR 52889, Dec. 26, 1985]

10.13 List of Migratory Birds. ****

50 C.F.R. PART 11
CIVIL PROCEDURES

AUTHORITY. Lacey Act, 83 Stat. 279-81, 18 U.S.C. §§ 42-44; Lacey Act Amendments of 1981, 95 Stat. 1073-1080, 16 U.S.C. §§ 3371 *et seq.*; Bald Eagle Protection Act, § 2, 54 Stat. 251, 16 U.S.C. § 668a; Endangered Species Act of 1973, § 11(f), 87 Stat. 884, 16 U.S.C. § 1540(f); Marine Mammal Protection Act of 1972, § 112(a), 86 Stat. 1042, 16 U.S.C. § 1382.

SOURCE: 39 FR 1159, Jan 4, 1974, unless otherwise noted.

SUBPART A -- INTRODUCTION

§ 11.1 Purpose of regulations.

The regulations contained in this part provide uniform rules and procedures for the assessment of civil penalties in connection with violations of certain laws and regulations enforced by the Service.

§ 11.2 Scope of regulations.

The regulations contained in this part apply only to actions arising under the following laws and regulations issued thereunder:

Lacey Act, 18 U.S.C. 43;
Lacey Act Amendments of 1981, 16 U.S.C. 3371 et seq.;
Bald Eagle Protection Act, 16 U.S.C. 668-668d;
Endangered Species Act of 1973, 87 Stat. 884, 16 U.S.C. 1531 et seq.; and Marine Mammal Protection Act of 1972, 16 U.S.C. 1361-1384 and 1401- 1407.

[39 FR 1159, Jan. 4, 1974, as amended at 39 FR 1445, Jan. 9, 1974; 47 FR 56860, Dec. 21, 1982]

§ 11.3 Filing of documents.

(a) Whenever a document or other paper is required to be filed under this Part within a certain time, such document or paper will be considered filed as of the date of the postmark if mailed, or the date actually delivered to the office where filing is required. The time periods set forth in this Part shall begin to run as of the day following the date of the document or other paper.

(b) If an oral or written application is made to the Director up to 10 calendar days after the expiration of a time period established in this part for the required filing of documents or other papers, the Director may permit a late filing within a fixed period where reasonable grounds are found for an inability or failure to file within the time period required. All such extensions shall be in writing. Except as provided in this subsection, no other requests for an extension of time may be granted.

SUBPART B -- ASSESSMENT PROCEDURE

§ 11.11 Notice of violation.

(a) A notice of violation (hereinafter "notice"), shall be issued by the Director and served personally or by registered or certified mail, return receipt requested, upon the person believed to be subject to a civil penalty (the respondent). The notice shall contain: (1) A concise statement of the facts believed to show a violation, (2) a specific reference to the provisions of the statute or regulation allegedly violated, and (3) the amount of penalty proposed to be assessed. The notice may also contain an initial proposal for compromise or settlement of the case. The notice shall also advise the respondent of his right to file a petition for relief pursuant to § 11.12, or to await the Director's notice of assessment.

(b) The respondent shall have 45 days from the date of the notice of violation in which to respond. During this time he may:

(1) Undertake informal discussions with the Director;

(2) Accept the proposed penalty, or the compromise, if any, offered in the notice;

(3) File a petition for relief; or

(4) Take no action, and await the Director's decision, pursuant to § 11.13.

(c) Acceptance of the proposed penalty or the compromise shall be deemed to be a waiver of the notice of assessment required by § 11.14, and of the opportunity for a hearing. Any counter offer of settlement shall be deemed a rejection of the proposed offer of compromise.

§ 11.12 Petition for relief.

If the respondent so chooses he may ask that no penalty be assessed or that the amount be reduced, and he may admit or contest the legal sufficiency of the charge and the Director's allegations of facts, by filing a petition for relief [hereinafter "petition"] with the Director at the address specified in the notice within 45 days of the date thereof. The petition shall be in writing and signed by the respondent. If the respondent is a corporation, the petition must be signed by an officer authorized to sign such documents. It must set forth in full the legal or other reasons for the relief.

§ 11.13 Decision by the Director.

Upon expiration of the period required or granted for filing of a petition for relief, the Director shall proceed to make an assessment of a civil penalty, taking into consideration information available to him and such showing as may have been made by the respondent, either pursuant to § 11.11 or § 11.12, or upon further request of the Director.

§ 11.14 Notice of assessment.

The Director shall notify the respondent by a written notice of assessment, by personal service or by registered or certified mail, return receipt requested, of his decision pursuant to § 11.13. He shall set forth therein the facts and conclusions upon which he decided that the violation did occur and appropriateness of the penalty assessed.

§ 11.15 Request for a hearing.

Except where a right to request a hearing is deemed to have been waived as provided in § 11.11, the respondent may, within 45 calendar days from the date of the notice of assessment referred to in § 11.14, file a dated, written request for a hearing with the Hearings Division, Office of Hearings and Appeals, U.S. Department of the Interior, 801 North Quincy Street, Arlington, Virginia 22203. The request should state the respondent's preference as to the place and date for a hearing. The request must enclose a copy of the notice of violation and notice of assessment. A copy of the request shall be served upon the Director personally or by registered or certified mail, return receipt requested, at the address specified in the notice.

§ 11.16 Final administrative decision.

(a) Where no request for a hearing is filed as provided in § 11.15 the Director's assessment shall become effective and shall constitute the final administrative decision of the Secretary on the 45th calendar day from the date of the notice of assessment.

(b) If a request for a hearing is timely filed in accordance with § 11.15, the date of the final administrative decision in the matter shall be as provided in Subpart C of this part.

§ 11.17 Payment of final assessment.

When a final administrative decision becomes effective in accordance with this Part 11, the respondent shall have 20 calendar days from the date of the final administrative decision within which to make full payment of the penalty assessed. Payment will be timely only if received in Office of the Director during normal business hours, on or before the 20th day. Upon a failure to pay the penalty, the Solicitor of the Department may request the Attorney General to institute a civil action in the U.S. District Court to collect the penalty.

SUBPART C -- HEARING AND APPEAL PROCEDURES

§ 11.21 Commencement of hearing procedures.

Proceedings under this subpart are commenced upon the timely filing with the Hearings Division of a request for a hearing, as provided in § 11.15 of Subpart B. Upon receipt of a request for a hearing, the Hearings Division will assign an administrative law judge to the case. Notice of assignment will be given promptly to the parties, and thereafter, all pleadings, papers, and other documents in the proceeding shall be filed directly with the administrative law judge, with copies served on the opposing party.

§ 11.22 Appearance and practice.

(a) Subject to the provisions of 43 CFR 1.3, the respondent may appear in person, by representative, or by counsel, and may participate fully in these proceedings.

(b) Department counsel designated by the Solicitor of the Department shall represent the Director in these proceedings. Upon notice to the Director of the assignment of an administrative law judge to the case, said counsel shall enter his appearance on behalf of the Director and shall file all petitions and correspondence exchanged by the Director and the respondent pursuant to Subpart B of this part, which shall become part of the hearing record. Thereinafter, service upon the Director in these proceedings shall be made to his counsel.

§ 11.23 Hearings.

(a) The administrative law judge shall have all powers accorded by law and necessary to preside over the parties and the proceedings and to make decisions in accordance with 5 U.S.C. 554-557. Failure to appear at the time set for hearing shall be deemed a waiver of the right to a hearing and consent to the making of a decision on the record made at the hearing. Copies of the transcript may be inspected or copied.

(b) The transcript of testimony, the exhibits, and all papers, documents, and requests filed in the proceedings, shall constitute the record for decision. The judge will render a written decision upon the record, which shall set forth his findings of fact and conclusions of law, and the reasons and basis therefor, and an assessment of a penalty, if any.

§ 11.24 Final administrative action.

Unless a notice of request for an appeal is filed in accordance with § 11.25 of this Subpart C, the administrative law judge's decision shall constitute the final administrative determination of the Secretary in the matter and shall become effective 30 calendar days from the date of the decision.

§ 11.25 Appeal.

(a) Either the respondent or the Director may seek an appeal from the decision of an administrative law judge rendered subsequent to January 1, 1974, by the filing of a "Notice of Request for Appeal" with the Director, Office of Hearings and Appeals, United States Department of the Interior, 801 North Quincy Street, Arlington, Virginia 22203, within 30 calendar days of the date of the administrative law judge's decision. Such notice shall be accompanied by proof of service on the administrative law judge and the opposing party.

(b) Upon receipt of such a request, the Director, Office of Hearings and Appeals, shall appoint an ad hoc appeals board to determine whether an appeal should be granted, and to hear and decide an appeal. To the extent they are not inconsistent herewith, the provisions of Subpart G of the Department Hearings and Appeals Procedures in 43 CFR Part 4 shall apply to appeal proceedings under this Subpart. The determination of the board to grant or deny an appeal, as well as its decision on the merits of an appeal, shall be in writing and become effective as the final administrative determination of the Secretary in the proceeding on the date it is rendered, unless otherwise specified therein.

50 C.F.R. PART 12
SEIZURE AND FORFEITURE PROCEDURES

Subpart A -- General Provisions

Subpart B -- Preliminary Requirements

Subpart C -- Forfeiture Proceedings

Subpart D -- Disposal of Forfeited or Abandoned Property

AUTHORITY: Act of September 6, 1966, 5 U.S.C. § 301; Bald and Golden Eagle Protection Act, 16 U.S.C. §§ 668-668b; National Wildlife Refuge System Administration Act, 16 U.S.C. § 668dd(e)-(f); Migratory Bird Treaty Act, 16 U.S.C. §§ 704, 706-707; Migratory Bird Hunting and Conservation Stamp Act, 16 U.S.C. §§ 718f-718g; Fish and Wildlife Act of 1956 [Airborne Hunting Amendments], 16 U.S.C. § 742j-1(d)-(f); Black Bass Act, 16 U.S.C. §§ 852d-853; Marine Mammal Protection Act of 1972, 16 U.S.C. §§ 1375-1377; Endangered Species Act of 1973, 16 U.S.C. § 1382; Lacey Act, 18 U.S.C. §§ 43, 44; Lacey Act Amendments of 1981, 95 Stat. 1073-1080, 16 U.S.C. §§ 3371 *et seq.*; Tariff Act of 1930, 19 U.S.C. §§ 1602-1624; Fish and Wildlife Improvement Act of 1978, 16 U.S.C. § 742j; Exotic Organisms, E.O. 11987, 42 FR 26949; American Indian Religious Freedom Act, 42 U.S.C. § 1996.

SOURCE: 45 FR 17864, Mar. 19, 1980, unless otherwise noted.

SUBPART A -- GENERAL PROVISIONS

§ 12.1 Purpose of regulations.

The regulations of this part establish procedures relating to property seized or subject to forfeiture under various laws enforced by the Service.

§ 12.2 Scope of regulations.

Except as hereinafter provided, the regulations of this part apply to all property seized or subject to forfeiture under any of the following laws:

(a) The Eagle Protection Act, 16 U.S.C. §§ 668 *et seq.*;

(b) The National Wildlife Refuge System Administration Act, 16 U.S.C. §§ 668dd *et seq.*;

(c) The Migratory Bird Treaty Act, 16 U.S.C. §§ 703 *et seq.*;

(d) The Migratory Bird Hunting Stamp Act, 16 U.S.C. §§ 718 *et seq.*;

(e) The Airborne Hunting Act, 16 U.S.C. §§ 742j-1;

(f) The Black Bass Act, 16 U.S.C. §§ 851 *et seq.*;

(g) The Marine Mammal Protection Act, 16 U.S.C. §§ 1361 *et seq.*;

(h) The Endangered Species Act, 16 U.S.C. §§ 1531 *et seq.*; and

(i) The Lacey Act, 18 U.S.C. §§ 43-44.

(j) The Lacey Act Amendments of 1981, 16 U.S.C. §§ 3371 *et seq.*

[45 FR 17864, Mar. 19, 1980; 45 FR 31725, May 14, 1980; 47 FR 56860, Dec. 21, 1982]

§ 12.3 Definitions.

(a) As used in this part:

(1) "Attorney General" means the Attorney General of the United States or an authorized representative;

(2) "Disposal" includes, but is not limited to, remission, return to the wild, use by the

Service or transfer to another government agency for official use, donation or loan, sale, or destruction.

(3) "Domestic value" means the price at which the seized property or similar property is freely offered for sale at the time and place of appraisement, in the same quantity or quantities as seized, and in the ordinary course of trade. If there is no market for the seized property at the place of appraisement, such value in the principal market nearest to the place of appraisement shall be reported.

(4) "Solicitor" means the Solicitor of the Department of the Interior or an authorized representative.

(b) The definitions of paragraph (a) of this section are in addition to, and not in lieu of, those contained in § 1.1-1.8 and § 10.12 of this title.

[45 FR 17864, Mar. 19, 1980, as amended at 47 FR 17525, Apr. 23, 1982]

§ 12.4 Filing of documents.

(a) Whenever any document is required by this part to be filed or served within a certain period of time, such document will be considered filed or served as of the date of receipt by the party with or upon whom filing or service is required. The time periods established by this part shall begin to run on the day following the date of filing or service.

(b) If an oral or written application is made before the expiration of a time period established by this part, an extension of such period for a fixed number of days may be granted where there are reasonable grounds for the failure to file or serve the document within the period required. Any such extension shall be in writing. Except as provided in this paragraph, no other requests for an extension shall be granted.

§ 12.5 Seizure by other agencies.

Any authorized employee or officer of any other Federal agency who has seized any wildlife or other property under any of the laws listed in § 12.2 will, if so requested, deliver such seizure to the appropriate Special Agent in Charge designated in § 10.22 of this title, or to an authorized designee, who shall either hold such seized wildlife or other property or arrange for its proper handling and care.

§ 12.6 Bonded release.

(a) Subject to the conditions set forth in paragraph (b) and (c) of this section, and to such additional conditions as may be appropriate, the Service, in its discretion, may accept an appearance bond or other security (including, but not limited to, payment of the value as determined under § 12.12) in place of any property seized under the Endangered Species Act, 16 U.S.C. §§ 1531 *et seq.*; Marine Mammal Protection Act, 16 U.S.C. §§ 1361 *et seq.*; Lacey Act, 18 U.S.C. § 43; Lacey Act Amendments of 1981, 16 U.S.C. §§ 3371 *et seq.*; Airborne Hunting Act, 16 U.S.C. § 742j-1; or Eagle Protection Act, 16 U.S.C. §§ 668 *et seq.*

(b) Property may be released under this section only to the owner or consignee.

(c) Property may be released under this section only if possession thereof will not violate or frustrate the purpose or policy of any applicable law or regulation.

[45 FR 17864, Mar. 19, 1980; 45 FR 31725, May 14, 1980; 47 FR 56860, Dec. 21, 1982]

SUBPART B -- PRELIMINARY REQUIREMENTS

§ 12.11 Notification of seizure.

Except where the owner or consignee is personally notified or seizure is made pursuant to a search warrant, the Service shall, as soon as practicable following the seizure or other receipt of seized wildlife or other property, mail a notification of seizure by registered or certified mail, return receipt requested, to the owner or consignee, if known or easily ascertainable. Such notification shall describe the seized wildlife or other property, and shall state the time, place, and reason for the seizure.

§ 12.12 Appraisement.

The Service shall determine the value of any cargo, of a vessel or other conveyance employed in unlawful taking, seized under the Marine Mammal Protection Act, 16 U.S.C. §§ 1361 *et seq.*, and the value of any property seized under the Endangered Species Act, 16 U.S.C. §§ 1531 *et seq.*; Eagle Protection Act, 16 U.S.C. §§ 668 *et seq.*; Airborne Hunting Act, 16 U.S.C. §§ 742j-1 *et seq.*; or the Lacey Act Amendments of 1981, 16 U.S.C. §§ 3371 *et seq.* If the seized property may lawfully be sold in the United States, its domestic value shall be determined in accordance with § 12.3. If the seized property may not lawfully be sold in the United States, its value shall be determined by other reasonable means.

[47 FR 56860, Dec. 21, 1982]

SUBPART C -- FORFEITURE PROCEEDINGS

§ 12.21 Criminal prosecutions.

If property is subject to criminal forfeiture, such forfeiture will be obtained in accordance with the Federal Rules of Criminal Procedure.

§ 12.22 Civil actions to obtain forfeiture.

The Solicitor may request the Attorney General to file a civil action to obtain forfeiture of any property subject to forfeiture under the Airborne Hunting Act, 16 U.S.C. §§ 742j-1; Lacey Act, 18 U.S.C. §§ 43-44; Lacey Act Amendments of 1981, 16 U.S.C. §§ 3371 *et seq.*; Black Bass Act, 16 U.S.C. §§ 851 *et seq.*; Marine Mammal Protection Act, 16 U.S.C. §§ 1361 *et seq.*; Migratory Bird Treaty Act, 16 U.S.C. §§ 703 *et seq.*; Migratory Bird Hunting Stamp Act, 16 U.S.C. §§ 718 *et seq.*; Eagle Protection Act, 16 U.S.C. §§ 668 *et seq.*; or Endangered Species Act, 16 U.S.C. §§ 1531 *et seq.* Before any such action is filed against property subject to forfeiture under the Lacey Act, 18 U.S.C. 43, or against property, other than the cargo of a vessel or other conveyance employed in unlawful taking, subject to forfeiture under the Marine Mammal Protection Act, 16 U.S.C. 1361 *et seq.*, a civil penalty must first be assessed in accordance with the statute and applicable regulations, and no such action may be filed more than 30 days after the conclusion of civil penalty assessment proceedings.

[47 FR 56860, Dec. 21, 1982]

§ 12.23 Administrative forfeiture proceedings.

(a) *When authorized.* Whenever any property subject to forfeiture under the Eagle Protection Act, 16 U.S.C. 668 *et seq.*, or Airborne Hunting Act, 16 U.S.C. 742j-l, or any wildlife or plant subject to forfeiture under the Endangered Species Act, 16 U.S.C. 1531 *et seq.*, or any fish, wildlife or plant subject to forfeiture under the Lacey Act Amendments of 1981, 16 U.S.C. 3371 *et seq.*, is determined under § 12.12 to have a value not greater than $100,000, the Solicitor may obtain forfeiture of such property in accordance with this section.

(b) *Procedure* --

(1) *Notice of proposed forfeiture.* As soon as practicable following seizure, the Solicitor shall issue a notice of proposed forfeiture.

(A) *Publication.* The notice shall be published once a week for at least three successive weeks in a newspaper of general circulation in the locality where the property was seized. If the value of the seized property as determined under § 12.12 does not exceed $1000, the notice may be published by posting, instead of newspaper publication, for at least three successive weeks in a conspicuous place accessible to the public at the Service's enforcement office, the United States District Court or the United States Customhouse nearest the place of seizure. In cases of posting, the date of initial posting shall be indicated on the notice. In addition to newspaper publication or posting, a reasonable effort shall be made to serve the notice personally or by registered or certified mail, return receipt requested, on each person whose whereabouts and interest in the seized property are known or easily ascertainable.

(B) *Contents.* The notice shall be in substantially the same form as a complaint for forfeiture filed in United States District Court. The notice shall describe the property, including, in the case of motor vehicles, the license, registration, motor, and serial numbers. The notice shall state the time and place of seizure, as well as the reason therefor, and shall specify the value of the property as determined under § 12.12. The notice shall contain a specific reference to the provisions of the laws or regulations allegedly violated and under which the property is subject to forfeiture. The notice shall state that any person desiring to claim the property must file a claim and a bond in accordance with paragraph (b)(2) of this section, and shall state that if a proper claim and bond are not received by the proper office within the time prescribed by such paragraph, the property will be declared forfeited to the United States and disposed of according to law. The notice shall also advise interested persons of their right to file a petition for remission of forfeiture in accordance with § 12.24.

(2) *Filing a claim and bond.* Upon issuance of the notice of proposed forfeiture, any person claiming the seized property may file with the Solicitor's office indicated in the notice a claim to the property and a bond in the penal sum of $5,000, or ten per centum of the value of the claimed property, whichever is lower, but not less than $250. Any claim and bond must be received in such office within 30 days after the date of first publication or posting of the notice of proposed forfeiture. The claim shall state the claimant's interest in the property. The bond filed with the claim shall be on a United States Customs Form 4615 or on a similar form provided by the Department. There shall be endorsed on the bond a list or schedule in substantially the following form which shall be signed by the claimant in the presence of the witnesses to the bond, and attested by the witnesses:

List or schedule containing a particular description of seized article, claim for which is covered by the within bond, to wit:

--- The foregoing list is correct.

Claimant __________

Attest: -----------------

The claim and bond referred to in this paragraph shall not entitle the claimant or any other person to possession of the property.

(3) *Transmittal to Attorney General.* As soon as practicable after timely receipt by the proper office of a proper claim and bond in accordance with paragraph (b)(2) of this section, the Solicitor shall transmit such claim and bond to the Attorney General for institution of forfeiture proceedings in United States District Court.

(4) *Motion for stay.* Upon issuance of the notice of proposed forfeiture, any person claiming the seized property may file with the Solicitor's regional or field office indicated in the notice a motion to stay administrative forfeiture proceedings. Any motion for stay must be filed within 30 days after the date of first publication or posting of the notice of the proposed forfeiture. Each motion must contain:

(i) The claimant's verified statement showing that he or she holds absolute, fee simple title to the seized property, free and clear of all liens, encumbrances, security interests, or other third-party interests, contingent or vested; and

(ii) the claimant's offer to pay in advance all reasonable costs anticipated to be incurred in the storage, care, and maintenance of the seized property for which administrative forfeiture is sought. Where a stay of administrative forfeiture proceedings would not injure or impair the rights of any third parties and where the claimant has agreed to pay in advance anticipated, reasonable storage costs associated with the granting of a stay, the Regional or Field Solicitor as appropriate may, in his discretion, grant the motion for stay and specify reasonable and prudent conditions therefor, including but not limited to the duration of the stay, a description of the factors which would automatically terminate the stay, and any requirement for a bond (including amount) to secure the payment of storage and other maintenance costs. If a motion for stay is denied, or if a stay is terminated for any reason, the claimant must file, if he or she has not already done so, a claim and bond in accordance with paragraph (b)(2) of this section not later than 30 days after receipt of the Solicitor's Office denial or termination order. Failure to file the claim and bond within 30 days will result in summary forfeiture under paragraph (c) of this section.

(c) *Summary forfeiture.* If a proper claim and bond are not received by the proper office within 30 days as specified in paragraph (b)(2) of this section, the Solicitor shall declare the property forfeited. The declaration of forfeiture shall be in writing, and shall be sent by registered or certified mail, return receipt requested, to the Service and to each person whose whereabouts and prior interest in the seized property are known or easily ascertainable. The declaration shall be in substantially the same form as a default judgment of forfeiture entered in United States District Court. The declaration shall describe the property and state the time, place, and reason for its seizure. The declaration shall identify the notice of proposed forfeiture, describing the dates and manner of publication of the notice and any efforts made to serve the notice personally or by mail.

The declaration shall state that in response to the notice a proper claim and bond were not timely received by the proper office from any claimant, and that therefore all potential claimants are deemed to admit the truth of the allegations of the notice. The declaration shall conclude with an order of condemnation and forfeiture of the property to the United States for disposition according to law.

[45 FR 17864, Mar. 19, 1980, as amended at 46 FR 44759, Sept. 8, 1981; 47 FR 56860, Dec. 12, 1982; 50 FR 6350, Feb. 15, 1985]

§ 12.24 Petition for remission of forfeiture.

(a) Any person who has an interest in cargo, of a vessel or other conveyance employed in unlawful taking, subject to forfeiture under the Marine Mammal Protection Act, 16 U.S.C. 1361 *et seq.*, or any person who has an interest in any property subject to forfeiture under the Endangered Species Act, 16 U.S.C. 1531 *et seq.*; Eagle Protection Act, 16 U.S.C. 668 *et seq.*; Airborne Hunting Act, 16 U.S.C. 742j-1; or the Lacey Act Amendments of 1981, 16 U.S.C. 3371 *et seq.*, or any person who has incurred or is alleged to have incurred a forfeiture of any such property, may file with the Solicitor or, when forfeiture proceedings have been brought in United States District Court, the Attorney General, a petition for remission of forfeiture.

(b) A petition filed with the Solicitor need not be in any particular form, but it must be received before disposition of the property and must contain the following:

(1) A description of the property;

(2) The time and place of seizure;

(3) Evidence of the petitioner's interest in the property, including contracts, bills of sale, invoices, security interests, certificates of title, and other satisfactory evidence; and

(4) A statement of all facts and circumstances relied upon by the petitioner to justify remission of the forfeiture.

(c) The petition shall be signed by the petitioner or the petitioner's attorney at law. If the petitioner is a corporation, the petition must be signed by an authorized officer, supervisory employee, or attorney at law, and the corporate seal shall be properly affixed to the signature.

(d) A false statement in the petition may subject the petitioner to prosecution under title 18, United States Code, section 1001.

(e) Upon receiving the petition, the Solicitor shall decide whether or not to grant relief. In making a decision, the Solicitor shall consider the information submitted by the petitioner, as well as any other available information relating to the matter.

(f) If the Solicitor finds the existence of such mitigating circumstances as to justify remission or mitigation of the forfeiture or alleged forfeiture, the Solicitor may remit or mitigate the same upon such terms and conditions as may be reasonable and just or may order discontinuance of any proceeding under § 12.23

(g) If the Solicitor decides that relief should not be granted, the Solicitor shall so notify the petitioner in writing, stating in the notification the reasons for denying relief. The petitioner may then file a supplemental petition, but no supplemental petition shall be considered unless it is received within 60 days from the date of the Solicitor's notification denying the original petition.

[45 FR 17864, Mar. 19, 1980, as amended at 47 FR 56861, Dec. 21, 1982]

§ 12.25 Transfers in settlement of civil penalty claims.

In the discretion of the Solicitor, an owner of wildlife or plants who may be liable for civil penalty under the Endangered Species Act, 16 U.S.C. 1531 *et seq.*; Lacey Act, 18 U.S.C. 43; Lacey Act Amendments of 1981, 16 U.S.C. 3371 *et seq.*; Eagle Protection Act, 16 U.S.C. 668 *et seq.*; or Marine Mammal Protection Act, 16 U.S.C. 1361 *et seq.*, may be given an opportunity to completely or partially settle the civil penalty claim by transferring to the United States all right, title, and interest in any wildlife or plants that are subject to forfeiture. Such transfer may be accomplished by the owner's execution and return of a United States Customs Form 4607 or a similar compromise transfer of property instrument provided by the Department.

[47 FR 56861, Dec. 21, 1982]

SUBPART D -- DISPOSAL OF FORFEITED OR ABANDONED PROPERTY

§ 12.30 Purpose.

Upon forfeiture or abandonment of any property to the United States under this part the Director shall dispose of such property under the provisions of this subpart D.

§ 12.31 Accountability.

All property forfeited or abandoned under this part must be accounted for in official records. These records must include the following information:

(a) A description of the item.
(b) The date and place of the item's seizure (if any) and forfeiture or abandonment.
(c) The investigative case file number with which the item was associated.
(d) The name of any person known to have or to have had an interest in the item.
(e) The date, place, and manner of the item's initial disposal.
(f) Name of the official responsible for the initial disposal.
(g) Domestic value of the property.

§ 12.32 Effect of prior illegality.

The effect of any prior illegality on a subsequent holder of any wildlife or plant disposed of or subject to disposal is terminated upon forfeiture or abandonment, but the prohibitions, restrictions, conditions, or requirements which apply to a particular species of wildlife or plant under the laws or regulations of the United States or any State, including any applicable conservation, health, quarantine, agricultural, or Customs laws or regulations remain in effect as to the conduct of such holder.

§ 12.33 Disposal.

(a) The Director shall dispose of any wildlife or plant forfeited or abandoned under the authority of this part, subject to the restrictions provided in this subpart, by one of the following means, unless the item is the subject of a petition for remission of forfeiture under § 12.24 of this part, or disposed of by court order:

(1) Return to the wild;
(2) Use by the Service or transfer to another government agency for official use;

(3) Donation or loan;

(4) Sale; or

(5) Destruction.

In the exercise of the disposal authority, the Director ordinarily must dispose of any wildlife or plant in the order in which the disposal methods appear in this paragraph (a) of this section.

(b) The Director shall dispose of any other property forfeited or abandoned under the authority of this part (including vehicles, vessels, aircraft, cargo, guns, nets, traps, and other equipment), except wildlife or plants, in accordance with current Federal Property Management Regulations (41 CFR Chapter 101) and Interior Property Management Regulations (41 CFR Chapter 114), unless the item is the subject of a petition for remission of forfeiture under § 12.24 of this part, or disposed of by court order.

(c) The Director shall dispose of property according to the following schedule, unless the property is the subject of a petition for remission of forfeiture under § 12.24 of this part:

(1) Any live wildlife or plant and any wildlife or plant that the Director determines is liable to perish, deteriorate, decay, waste, or greatly decrease in value by keeping, or that the expense of keeping is disproportionate to its value may be disposed of immediately after forfeiture or abandonment; and

(2) All other property may be disposed of no sooner than 60 days after forfeiture or abandonment.

(d) If the property is the subject of a petition for remission of forfeiture under § 12.24 of this part, the Director may not dispose of the property until the Solicitor or Attorney General makes a final decision not to grant relief.

§ 12.34 Return to the wild.

(a) Any live member of a native species of wildlife which is capable of surviving may be released to the wild in suitable habitat within the historical range of the species in the United States with the permission of the landowner, unless release poses an imminent danger to public health or safety.

(b) Any live member of a native species of plant which is capable of surviving may be transplanted in suitable habitat on Federal or other protected lands within the historical range of the species in the United States with the permission of the landowner.

(c) Any live member of an exotic species of wildlife (including injurious wildlife) or plant may not be returned to the wild in the U.S., but may be returned to one of the following countries for return to suitable habitat in accordance with the provisions of § 12.35 of this part if it is capable of surviving:

(1) The country of export (if known) after consultation with and at the expense of the country of export, or

(2) A country within the historic range of the species which is party to the Convention on International Trade in Endangered Species of Wild Fauna and Flora (TIAS 8249) after consultation with and at the expense of such country.

§ 12.35 Use by the Service or transfer to another government agency for official use.

(a) Wildlife and plants may be used by the Service or transferred to another government agency (including foreign agencies) for official use including, but not limited to, one or more of the following purposes:

(1) Training government officials to perform their official duties;

(2) Identifying protected wildlife or plants, including forensic identification or research;

(3) Educating the public concerning the conservation of wildlife or plants;

(4) Conducting law enforcement operations in performance of official duties;

(5) Enhancing the propagation or survival of a species or other scientific purposes;

(6) Presenting as evidence in a legal proceeding involving the wildlife or plant; or

(7) Returning to the wild in accordance with § 12.34 of this part.

(b) Each transfer and the terms of the transfer must be documented.

(c) The agency receiving the wildlife or plants may be required to bear all costs of care, storage, and transportation in connection with the transfer from the date of seizure to the date of delivery.

§ 12.36 Donation or loan.

(a) Except as otherwise provided in this section, wildlife and plants may be donated or loaned for scientific, educational, or public display purposes to any person who demonstrates the ability to provide adequate care and security for the item.

(b) Any donation or loan may be made only after execution of a transfer document between the Director and the donee/borrower, which is subject to the following conditions:

(1) The purpose for which the wildlife or plants are to be used must be stated on the transfer document;

(2) Any attempt by the donee/borrower to use the donation or loan for any other purpose except that stated on the transfer document entitles the Director to immediate repossession of the wildlife or plants;

(3) The donee/borrower must pay an costs associated with the transfer, including the costs of care, storage, transportation, and return to the Service (if applicable);

(4) The donee/borrower may be required to account periodically for the donation or loan;

(5) The donee/borrower is not relieved from the prohibitions, restrictions, conditions, or requirements which may apply to a particular species of wildlife or plant imposed by the laws or regulations of the United States or any State, including any applicable health, quarantine, agricultural, or Customs laws or regulations.

(6) Any attempt by a donee to retransfer the donation during the time period specified in the transfer document within which the donee may not retransfer the donation without the prior authorization of the Director entitles the Director to immediate repossession of the wildlife or plants;

(7) Any attempt by a borrower to retransfer the loan without the prior authorization of the Director entitles the Director to immediate repossession of the wildlife or plants;

(8) Subject to applicable limitations of law, duly authorized Service officers at all reasonable times shall, upon notice, be afforded access to the place where the donation or loan is kept and an opportunity to inspect it;

(9) Any donation is subject to conditions specified in the transfer document, the violation of which causes the property to revert to the United States;

(10) Any loan is for an indefinite period of time unless a date on which the loan must be returned to the Service is stated on the transfer document; and

(11) Any loan remains the property of the United States, and the Director may

demand its return at any time.

(c) Wildlife and plants may be donated to individual American Indians for the practice of traditional American Indian religions. Any donation of the parts of bald or golden eagles to American Indians may only be made to individuals authorized by permit issued in accordance with § 22.22 of this title to possess such items.

(d) Edible wildlife, fit for human consumption, may be donated to a non-profit, tax-exempt charitable organization for use as food, but not for barter or sale.

(e) Wildlife and plants may be loaned to government agencies (including foreign agencies) for official use. Each transfer and the terms of the transfer must be documented.

§ 12.37 Sale.

(a) Wildlife and plants may be sold or offered for sale, except any species which at the time it is to be sold or offered for sale falls into one of the following categories:

(1) Listed in § 10.13 of this title as a migratory bird protected by the Migratory Bird Treaty Act (16 U.S.C. §§ 703-712);

(2) Protected under the Eagle Protection Act (16 U.S.C. §§ 668-668d);

(3) Listed in § 23.33 of this title as "Appendix I" under the Convention on International Trade in Endangered Species of Wild Fauna and Flora;

(4) Listed in § 17.11 of this title as "endangered" or "threatened" under the Endangered Species Act of 1973 (16 U.S.C. § 1533), unless the item or species may be lawfully traded in interstate commerce; and

(5) Protected under the Marine Mammal Protection Act (16 U.S.C. §§ 1361-1407), unless the item or species may be lawfully traded in interstate commerce.

(b) Wildlife and plants must be sold in accordance with current Federal Property Management Regulations (41 CFR Chapter 101) and Interior Property Management Regulations (41 CFR Chapter 114) or U.S. Customs laws and regulations, except the Director may sell any wildlife or plant immediately for its fair market value if the Director determines that it is liable to perish, deteriorate, decay, waste, or greatly decrease in value by keeping, or that the expense of keeping it is disproportionate to its value.

(c) Wildlife or plants which may not be possessed lawfully by purchasers under the laws of the State where held may be moved to a State where possession is lawful and may be sold.

(d) Wildlife or plants purchased at sale are subject to the prohibitions, restrictions, conditions, or requirements which apply to a particular species of wildlife or plant imposed by the laws or regulations of the United States or any State, including any applicable conservation, health, quarantine, agricultural, or Customs laws or regulations, except as provided by § 12.32 of this part.

(e) The Director may use the proceeds of sale to reimburse the Service for any costs which by law the Service is authorized to recover or to pay any rewards which by law may be paid from sums the Service receives.

§ 12.38 Destruction.

(a) Wildlife and plants not otherwise disposed of must be destroyed.

(b) When destroyed, the fact, be certified by the official actually destroying the type and quantity destroyed must be certified by the official actually destroying the items.

§ 12.39 Information on property available for disposal.

Persons interested in obtaining information on property which is available for disposal should contact the appropriate Special Agent in Charge listed in § 10.22 of this title.

50 C.F.R. PART 13
GENERAL PERMIT PROCEDURES

AUTHORITY; 16 U.S.C. §§ 668a, 704, 712, 742j-1, 1382, 1583(d), 3374, 4901-4916; 18 U.S.C. § 42; 19 U.S.C. § 1202; E.O. 11911, 41 FR 15683; 31 U.S.C. § 9701.

SOURCE: 39 FR 1161, Jan 4, 1974, unless otherwise noted.

SUBPART A -- INTRODUCTION

§ 13.1 General.

Each person intending to engage in an activity for which a permit is required by this Subchapter B shall, before commencing such activity, obtain a valid permit authorizing such activity. Each person who desires to obtain the permit privileges authorized by this Subchapter B must make application for such permit in accordance with the requirements of this Part 13 and the other regulations in this Subchapter B which set forth the additional requirements for the specific permits desired. If the activity for which permission is sought is covered by the requirements of more than one part of this Subchapter B, the requirements of each Part must be met. If the information required for each specific permitted activity is included, one application will be accepted for all permits required, and a single permit will be issued.

§ 13.2 Purpose of regulations.

The regulations contained in this part provide uniform rules, conditions, and procedures for the application for and the issuance, denial, suspension, revocation, and general administration of all permits issued pursuant to this subchapter B.

[54 FR 38147, Sept. 14, 1989]

§ 13.3 Scope of regulations.

The provisions in this part are in addition to, and are not in lieu of, other permit regulations of this Subchapter B and apply to all permits issued thereunder, including "Import and Marking" (Part 14), "Feather Imports" (Part 15), "Injurious Wildlife" (Part 16), "Endangered Wildlife and Plants" (Part 17), "Marine Mammals" (Part 18), "Migratory Birds" (Part 21), "Eagles" (Part 22) and "Endangered Species Convention" (Part 23). As used in this Part 13, the term "permit" shall refer to either a license, permit, or certificate as the context may require.

[42 FR 10465, Feb. 22, 1977, as amended at 42 FR 32377, June 24, 1977; 45 FR 56673, Aug. 25, 1980]

§ 13.4 Emergency variation from requirements.

The Director may approve variations from the requirements of this part when he finds that an emergency exists and that the proposed variations will not hinder effective administration of this Subchapter B, and will not be unlawful.

§ 13.5 Information collection requirements.

(a) The Office of Management and Budget approved the information collection requirements contained in this part 13 under 44 U.S.C. and assigned OMB Control Number 1018-0092. The Service may not conduct or sponsor, and you are not required to respond, to a collection of information unless it displays a currently valid OMB control number. We are collecting this information to provide information necessary to evaluate permit applications. We will use this information to review permit applications and make decisions, according to criteria established in various Federal wildlife conservation statutes and regulations, on the issuance, suspension, revocation, or denial permits. You must respond to obtain or retain a permit.

(b) We estimate the public reporting burden for these reporting requirements to vary from 15 minutes to 4 hours per response, with an average of 0.803 hours per response, including time for reviewing instructions, gathering and maintaining data, and completing and reviewing the forms. Direct comments regarding the burden estimate or any other aspect of these reporting requirements to the Service Information Collection Control Officer, MS-222 ARLSQ, U.S. Fish and Wildlife Service, Washington, D.C. 20240, or the Office of Management and Budget, Paperwork Reduction Project (1018-0092), Washington, D.C. 20603.

[47 FR 30785, July 15, 1982; 54 FR 38147, Sept. 14, 1989; 63 FR 52634, Oct. 1, 1998]

SUBPART B -- APPLICATIONS FOR PERMITS

§ 13.11 Application procedures.

The Service may not issue a permit for any activity authorized by this subchapter B unless the applicant has filed an application in accordance with the following procedures. Applicants do not have to submit a separate application for each permit unless otherwise required by this subchapter.

(a) *Forms.* Applications must be submitted in writing on a Federal Fish and Wildlife License/Permit Application (Form 3-200) or as otherwise specifically directed by the Service.

(b) *Forwarding instructions.* Applications for permits in the following categories should be forwarded to the issuing office indicated below.

(1) Migratory bird banding permits (50 CFR 21.22) -- Bird Banding Laboratory, Office of Migratory Bird Management, U.S. Fish and Wildlife Service, Laurel, Maryland 20708. (Special application forms must be used for bird banding permits. They may be obtained by writing to the Bird Banding Laboratory).

(2) Exception to designated port (50 CFR Part 14), import/export license (50 CFR 14.93), migratory bird permit, other than banding (50 CFR Part 21) and Bald or Golden eagle permits (50 CFR Part 22) -- Assistant Regional Director for Law Enforcement District in which the applicant resides (see 50 CFR 10.22 for addresses and boundaries of the Law Enforcement Districts).

(3) Feather quota (50 CFR part 15), injurious wildlife (50 CFR Part 16), endangered and threatened species (50 CFR Part 17), marine mammal (50 CFR Part 18) and permits and certificates for the Convention on International Trade in Endangered Species (CITES) (50 CFR Part 23) -- U.S. Fish and Wildlife Service, Federal Wildlife Permit Office, P.O. Box 3654, Arlington, Virginia 22203.

(c) *Time notice.* The Service will process all applications as quickly as possible. However, it cannot guarantee final action within the time limits the applicant requests. Applicants for endangered species and marine mammal permits should submit applications to the Office of Management Authority which are postmarked at least 90 calendar days prior to the requested effective date. Applicants for all other permits should submit applications to the issuing office which are postmarked at least 60 days prior to the requested effective date.

(d) *Fees.*

(1) Unless otherwise exempted by this paragraph, applicants for issuance or renewal of permits must pay the required permit processing fee at the time of application. Applicants should pay fees by check or money order made payable to "U.S. Fish and Wildlife Service." The Service will not refund any application fee under any circumstances if the Service has processed the application. However, the Service may return the application fee if the applicant withdraws the application before the Service has significantly processed it.

(2) Except as provided in paragraph (d)(4) of this sections the fee for processing any application is $25.00. If regulations in this subchapter require more than one type of permit for an activity, and the permits are issued by the same office, the issuing office may issue one consolidated permit authorizing the activity. The issuing office may charge only the highest single fee for the activity permitted.

(3) A fee shall not be charged to any Federal, State or local government agency, nor to any individual or institution under contract to such agency for the proposed activities. The fee may be waived or reduced for public institutions (see 50 CFR 10.12). Proof of such status must accompany the application.

(4) Nonstandard fees. ****

(e) *Abandoned or incomplete applications.* Upon receipt of an incomplete or improperly executed application, or if the applicant does not submit the proper fees, the issuing office will notify the applicant of the deficiency. If the applicant fails to supply the correct information to complete the application or to pay the required fees within 45 calendar days of the date of notification, the Service will consider the application abandoned. The Service will not refund any fees for an abandoned application.

[39 FR 11611, Jan. 4, 1974, as amended at 45 FR 56673, Aug. 25, 1980; 47 FR 30785, July 15, 1982; 50 FR 52889, Dec. 26, 1985; 54 FR 4031, Jan. 27, 1989; 54 FR 38147, Sept. 14, 1989; 61 FR 31868, June 21, 1996]

§ 13.12 General information requirements on applications for permits.

(a) *General information required for all applications.* All applications must contain the following information:

(1) Applicant's full name, mailing address, telephone number(s), and,

(i) If the applicant is an individual, the date of birth, height, weight, hair color, eye color, sex, and any business or institutional affiliation of the applicant related to the requested permitted activity; or

(ii) If the applicant is a corporation, firm, partnership, association, institution, or public or private agency, the name and address of the president or principal officer and of the registered agent for the service of process;

(2) Location where the requested permitted activity is to occur or be conducted;

(3) Reference to the part(s) and section(s) of this subchapter B as listed in paragraph (b) of this section under which the application is made for a permit or permits, together with any additional justification, including supporting documentation as required by the referenced part(s) and section(s);

(4) If the requested permitted activity involves the import or re-export of wildlife or plants from or to any foreign country, and the country of origin, or the country of export or re-export restricts the taking, possession, transportation, exportation, or sale of wildlife or plants, documentation as indicated in § 14.52(c) of this subchapter B;

(5) Certification in the following language:

I hereby certify that I have read and am familiar with the regulations contained in title 50, part 13, of the Code of Federal Regulations and the other applicable parts in subchapter B of chapter I of title 50, Code of Federal Regulations, and I further certify that the information submitted in this application for a permit is complete and accurate to the best of my knowledge and belief. I understand that any false statement herein may subject me to suspension or revocation of this permit and to the criminal penalties of 18 U.S.C. 1001.

(6) Desired effective date of permit except where issuance date is fixed by the part under which the permit is issued;

(7) Date;

(8) Signature of the applicant; and

(9) Such other information as the Director determines relevant to the processing of the application.

(b) *Additional information required on permit applications.* As stated in paragraph (a)(3) of this section certain additional information is required on all applications. These additional requirements may be found by referring to the section of this Subchapter B cited after the type of permit for which application is being made:

Type of permit	Section
Importation at nondesignated ports:	
Scientific	14.31
Deterioration prevention	14.32
Economic hardship	14.33
Marking of package or container:	
Symbol marking	14.83
Import/export license	14.93
Feather import quota: Importation or entry	15.21
Injurious wildlife: Importation or shipment	16.22
Endangered wildlife and plant permits:	
Similarity of appearance	17.52
Scientific, enhancement of propagation or survival, incidental taking for wildlife	17.22
Scientific, propagation, or survival for plants	17.62
Economic hardship for wildlife	17.23
Economic hardship for plants	17.63
Threatened wildlife and plant permits:	
Similarity of appearance	17.52
General for wildlife	17.32
American alligator-buyer or tanner	17.42(a)
General for plants	17.72
Marine mammals permits:	

[39 FR 1161, Jan. 4, 1974, as amended at 42 FR 10465, Feb. 22, 1977; 42 FR 32377, June 24, 1977; 44 FR 54006, Sept. 17, 1979; 44 FR 59083, Oct. 12, 1979; 45 FR 56673, Aug. 25, 1980; 45 FR 78154, Nov. 25, 1980; 46 FR 42680, Aug. 24, 1981; 48 FR 31607, July 8, 1983; 48 FR 57300, Dec. 29, 1983; 50 FR 39687, Sept. 30, 1985; 50 FR 45408, Oct. 31, 1985; 54 FR 38147, 38148, Sept. 14, 1989]

SUBPART C -- PERMIT ADMINISTRATION

§ 13.21 Issuance of permits.

(a) No permit may be issued prior to the receipt of a written application therefor, unless a written variation from the requirements, as authorized by § 13.4, is inserted into the official file of the Bureau. An oral or written representation of an employee or agent of the United States Government, or an action of such employee or agent, shall not be construed as a permit unless it meets the requirements of a permit as defined in 50 CFR 10.12.

(b) Upon receipt of a properly executed application for a permit, the Director shall issue the appropriate permit unless:

(1) The applicant has been assessed a civil penalty or convicted of any criminal provision of any statute or regulation relating to the activity for which the application is filed, if such assessment or conviction evidences a lack of responsibility.

(2) The applicant has failed to disclose material information required, or has made false statements as to any material fact, in connection with his application;

(3) The applicant has failed to demonstrate a valid justification for the permit and a showing of responsibility;

(4) The authorization requested potentially threatens a wildlife or plant population,

or

(5) The Director finds through further inquiry or investigation, or otherwise, that the applicant is not qualified.

(c) *Disqualifying factors.* Any one of the following will disqualify a person from receiving permits issued under this Part.

(1) A conviction, or entry of a plea of guilty or nolo contendere, for a felony violation of the Lacey Act, the Migratory Bird Treaty Act, or the Bald and Golden Eagle Protection Act disqualifies any such person from receiving or exercising the privileges of a permit, unless such disqualification has been expressly waived by the Director in response to a written petition.

(2) The revocation of a permit for reasons found in § 13.28 (a)(1) or (a)(2) disqualifies any such person from receiving or exercising the privileges of a similar permit for a period of five years from the date of the final agency decision on such revocation.

(3) The failure to pay any required fees or assessed costs and penalties, whether or not reduced to judgement disqualifies such person from receiving or exercising the privileges of a permit as long as such moneys are owed to the United States. This requirement shall not apply to any civil penalty presently subject to administrative or judicial appeal; provided that the pendency of a collection action brought by the United States or its assignees shall not constitute an appeal within the meaning of this subsection.

(4) The failure to submit timely, accurate, or valid reports as required may disqualify such person from receiving or exercising the privileges of a permit as long as the deficiency exists.

(d) *Use of supplemental information.* The issuing officer, in making a determination under this subsection, may use any information available that is relevant to the issue. This may include any prior conviction, or entry of a plea of guilty or nolo contendere, or assessment of civil or criminal penalty for a violation of any Federal or State law or regulation governing the permitted activity. It may also include any prior permit revocations or suspensions, or any reports of State or local officials. The issuing officer shall consider all relevant facts or information available, and may make independent inquiry or investigation to verify information or substantiate qualifications asserted by the applicant.

(e) *Conditions of issuance and acceptance.*

(1) Any permit automatically incorporates within its terms the conditions and requirements of Subpart D of this part and of any part(s) or section(s) specifically authorizing or governing the activity for which the permit is issued.

(2) Any person accepting and holding a permit under this Subchapter B acknowledges the necessity for close regulation and monitoring of the permitted activity by the Government. By accepting such permit, the permittee consents to and shall allow entry by agents or employees of the Service upon premises where the permitted activity is conducted at any reasonable hour. Service agents or employees may enter such premises to inspect the location; any books, records, or permits required to be kept by this Subchapter B; and any wildlife or plants kept under authority of the permit.

(f) *Term of permit.* Unless otherwise modified, a permit is valid during the period specified on the face of the permit. Such period shall include the effective date and the date of expiration.

(g) Denial. The issuing officer may deny a permit to any applicant who fails to meet the issuance criteria set forth in this section or in the part(s) or section(s) specifically governing the activity for which the permit is requested.

[39 FR 1161, Jan. 4, 1974, as amended at 42 FR 32377, June 24, 1977; 47 FR 30785, July 15, 1982; 54 FR 38148, Sept. 14, 1989]

§ 13.22 Renewal of permits.

(a) *Application for renewal.* Applicants for renewal of a permit must submit a written application at least 30 days prior to the expiration date of the permit. Applicants must certify in the form required by § 13.12(a)(5) that all statements and information in the original application remain current and correct, unless previously changed or corrected. If such information is no longer current or correct, the applicant must provide corrected information.

(b) *Renewal criteria.* The Service shall issue a renewal of a permit if the applicant meets the criteria for issuance in § 13.21(b) and is not disqualified under § 13.21(c).

(c) *Continuation of permitted activity.* Any person holding a valid, renewable permit, who has complied with this section, may continue the activities authorized by the expired permit until the Service has acted on such person's application for renewal.

(d) *Denial.* The issuing officer may deny renewal of a permit to any applicant who fails to meet the issuance criteria set forth in § 13.21 of this part, or in the part(s) or section(s) specifically governing the activity for which the renewal is requested.

[54 FR 38148, Sept. 14, 1989]

§ 13.23 Amendment of permits.

(a) *Permittee's request.* Where circumstances have changed so that a permittee desires to have any condition of his permit modified, such permittee must submit a full written justification and supporting information in conformity with this part and the part under which the permit was issued.

(b) The Service reserves the right to amend any permit for just cause at any time during its term, upon written finding of necessity, provided that any such amendment of a permit issued under § 17.22(b) through (d) or § 17.32(b) through (d) of this subchapter shall be consistent with the requirements of § 17.22(b)(5), (c)(5) and (d)(5) or § 17.32(b)(5), (c)(5) and (d)(5) of this subchapter, respectively.

(c) *Change of name or address.* A permittee is not required to obtain a new permit if there is a change in the legal individual or business name, or in the mailing address of the permittee. A permittee is required to notify the issuing office within 10 calendar days of such change. This provision does not authorize any change in location of the conduct of the permitted activity when approval of the location is a qualifying condition of the permit.

[54 FR 38148, Sept. 14, 1989; 64 FR 32711, June 17, 1999]

§ 13.24 Right of succession by certain persons.

(a) Certain persons other than the permittee are authorized to carry on a permitted activity for the remainder of the term of a current permit, provided they comply with the provisions of paragraph (b) of this section. Such persons are the following:

(1) The surviving spouse, child, executor, administrator, or other legal representative of a deceased permittee; or

(2) A receiver or trustee in bankruptcy or a court designated assignee for the benefit

of creditors.

(b) In order to qualify for the authorization provided in this section, the person or persons desiring to continue the activity shall furnish the permit to the issuing officer for endorsement within 90 days from the date the successor begins to carry on the activity.

(c) In the case of permits issued under § 17.22(b) through (d) or § 17.32(b) through (d) of this subchapter B, the successor's authorization under the permit is also subject to a determination by the Service that:

(1) The successor meets all of the qualifications under this part for holding a permit;

(2) The successor has provided adequate written assurances that it will provide sufficient funding for the conservation plan or Agreement and will implement the relevant terms and conditions of the permit, including any outstanding minimization and mitigation requirements; and

(3) The successor has provided such other information as the Service determines is relevant to the processing of the request.

[39 FR 1161, Jan. 4, 1974, as amended at 47 FR 30786, July 15, 1982; 54 FR 38149, Sept. 14, 1989; 64 FR 32711, June 17, 1999]

§ 13.25 Transfer of permits and scope of permit authorization.

(a) Except as otherwise provided for in this section, permits issued under this part are not transferable or assignable.

(b) Permits issued under § 17.22(b) through (d) or § 17.32(b) through (d) of this subchapter B may be transferred in whole or in part through a joint submission by the permittee and the proposed transferee, or in the case of a deceased permittee, the deceased permittee's legal representative and the proposed transferee, provided the Service determines that:

(1) The proposed transferee meets all of the qualifications under this part for holding a permit;

(2) The proposed transferee has provided adequate written assurances that it will provide sufficient funding for the conservation plan or Agreement and will implement the relevant terms and conditions of the permit, including any outstanding minimization and mitigation requirements; and

(3) The proposed transferee has provided such other information as the Service determines is relevant to the processing of the submission.

(c) Except as otherwise stated on the face of the permit, any person who is under the direct control of the permittee, or who is employed by or under contract to the permittee for purposes authorized by the permit, may carry out the activity authorized by the permit.

(d) In the case of permits issued under § 17.22(b)-(d) or § 17.32(b)-(d) of this subchapter to a State or local governmental entity, a person is under the direct control of the permittee where:

(1) The person is under the jurisdiction of the permittee and the permit provides that such person(s) may carry out the authorized activity; or

(2) The person has been issued a permit by the governmental entity or has executed a written instrument with the governmental entity, pursuant to the terms of the implementing agreement.

[54 FR 38149, Sept. 14, 1989; 64 FR 32711, June 17, 1999; 64 FR 52676, Sept. 30, 1999]

§ 13.26 Discontinuance of permit activity.

When a permittee, or any successor to a permittee as provided for by § 13.24, discontinues activities authorized by a permit, the permittee shall within 30 calendar days of the discontinuance return the permit to the issuing office together with a written statement surrendering the permit for cancellation. The permit shall be deemed void and cancelled upon its receipt by the issuing office. No refund of any fees paid for issuance of the permit or for any other fees or costs associated with a permitted activity shall be made when a permit is surrendered for cancellation for any reason prior to the expiration date stated on the face of the permit.

[54 FR 38149, Sept. 14, 1989]

§ 13.27 Permit suspension.

(a) *Criteria for suspension.* The privileges of exercising some or all of the permit authority may be suspended at any time if the permittee is not in compliance with the conditions of the permit, or with any applicable laws or regulations governing the conduct of the permitted activity. The issuing officer may also suspend all or part of the privileges authorized by a permit if the permittee fails to pay any fees, penalties or costs owed to the Government. Such suspension shall remain in effect until the issuing officer determines that the permittee has corrected the deficiencies.

(b) *Procedure for suspension.*

(1) When the issuing officer believes there are valid grounds for suspending a permit the permittee shall be notified in writing of the proposed suspension by certified or registered mail. This notice shall identify the permit to be suspended, the reason(s) for such suspension, the actions necessary to correct the deficiencies, and inform the permittee of the right to object to the proposed suspension. The issuing officer may amend any notice of suspension at any time.

(2) Upon receipt of a notice of proposed suspension the permittee may file a written objection to the proposed action. Such objection must be in writing, must be filed within 45 calendar days of the date of the notice of proposal, must state the reasons why the permittee objects to the proposed suspension, and may include supporting documentation.

(3) A decision on the suspension shall be made within 45 days after the end of the objection period. The issuing officer shall notify the permittee in writing of the Service's decision and the reasons therefore. The issuing officer shall also provide the applicant with the information concerning the right to request reconsideration of the decision under § 13.29 of this part and the procedures for requesting reconsideration.

[54 FR 38149, Sept. 14, 1989]

§ 13.28 Permit revocation.

(a) Criteria for revocation. A permit may be revoked for any of the following reasons:

(1) The permittee willfully violates any Federal or State statute or regulation, or any Indian tribal law or regulation, or any law or regulation of any foreign country, which involves a violation of the conditions of the permit or of the laws or regulations governing

the permitted activity; or

(2) The permittee fails within 60 days to correct deficiencies that were the cause of a permit suspension; or

(3) The permittee becomes disqualified under § 13.21(c) of this part; or

(4) A change occurs in the statute or regulation authorizing the permit that prohibits the continuation of a permit issued by the Service; or

(5) Except for permits issued under § 17.22(b) through (d) or § 17.32(b) through (d) of this subchapter, the population(s) of the wildlife or plant that is the subject of the permit declines to the extent that continuation of the permitted activity would be detrimental to maintenance or recovery of the affected population.

(b) Procedure for revocation.

(1) When the issuing officer believes there are valid grounds for revoking a permit, the permittee shall be notified in writing of the proposed revocation by certified or registered mail. This notice shall identify the permit to be revoked, the reason(s) for such revocation, the proposed disposition of the wildlife, if any, and inform the permittee of the right to object to the proposed revocation. The issuing officer may amend any notice of revocation at any time.

(2) Upon receipt of a notice of proposed revocation the permittee may file a written objection to the proposed action. Such objection must be in writing, must be filed within 45 calendar days of the date of the notice of proposal, must state the reasons why the permittee objects to the proposed revocation, and may include supporting documentation.

(3) A decision on the revocation shall be made within 45 days after the end of the objection period. The issuing officer shall notify the permittee in writing of the Service's decision and the reasons therefore, together with the information concerning the right to request and the procedures for requesting reconsideration.

(4) Unless a permittee files a timely request for reconsideration, any wildlife held under authority of a permit that is revoked must be disposed of in accordance with instructions of the issuing officer. If a permittee files a timely request for reconsideration of a proposed revocation, such permittee may retain possession of any wildlife held under authority of the permit until final disposition of the appeal process.

[54 FR 38149, Sept. 14, 1989; 64 FR 32711, June 17, 1999]

§ 13.29 Review procedures.

(a) *Request for reconsideration.* Any person may request reconsideration of an action under this part if that person is one of the following:

(1) An applicant for a permit who has received written notice of denial;

(2) An applicant for renewal who has received written notice that a renewal is denied;

(3) A permittee who has a permit amended, suspended, or revoked, except for those actions which are required by changes in statutes or regulations, or are emergency changes of limited applicability for which an expiration date is set within 90 days of the permit change; or

(4) A permittee who has a permit issued or renewed but has not been granted authority by the permit to perform all activities requested in the application, except when the activity requested is one for which there is no lawful authority to issue a permit.

(b) *Method of requesting reconsideration.* Any person requesting reconsideration of an action under this part must comply with the following criteria:

(1) Any request for reconsideration must be in writing, signed by the person requesting reconsideration or by the legal representative of that person, and must be submitted to the issuing officer.

(2) The request for reconsideration must be received by the issuing officer within 45 calendar days of the date of notification of the decision for which reconsideration is being requested.

(3) The request for reconsideration shall state the decision for which reconsideration is being requested and shall state the reason(s) for the reconsideration, including presenting any new information or facts pertinent to the issue(s) raised by the request for reconsideration.

(4) The request for reconsideration shall contain a certification in substantially the same form as that provided by § 13.12(a)(5). If a request for reconsideration does not contain such certification, but is otherwise timely and appropriate, it shall be held and the person submitting the request shall be given written notice of the need to submit the certification within 15 calendar days. Failure to submit certification shall result in the request being rejected as insufficient in form and content.

(c) *Inquiry by the Service.* The Service may institute a separate inquiry into the matter under consideration.

(d) *Determination of grant or denial of a request for reconsideration.* The issuing officer shall notify the permittee of the Service's decision within 45 days of the receipt of the request for reconsideration. This notification shall be in writing, shall state the reasons for the decision, and shall contain a description of the evidence which was relied upon by the issuing officer. The notification shall also provide information concerning the right to appeal, the official to whom an appeal may be addressed, and the procedures for making an appeal.

(e) *Appeal.* A person who has received an adverse decision following submission of a request for reconsideration may submit a written appeal to the Regional Director for the region in which the issuing office is located, or to the Director for offices which report directly to the Director. An appeal must be submitted within 45 days of the date of the notification of the decision on the request for reconsideration. The appeal shall state the reason(s) and issue(s) upon which the appeal is based and may contain any additional evidence or arguments to support the appeal.

(f) *Decision on appeal.*

(1) Before a decision is made concerning the appeal the appellant may present oral arguments before the Regional Director or the Director, as appropriate, if such official judges oral arguments are necessary to clarify issues raised in the written record.

(2) The Service shall notify the appellant in writing of its decision within 45 calendar days of receipt of the appeal, unless extended for good cause and the appellant notified of the extension.

(3) The decision of the Regional Director or the Director shall constitute the final administrative decision of the Department of the Interior.

[54 FR 38149, Sept. 14, 1989]

SUBPART D -- CONDITIONS

§ 13.41 Humane conditions.

Any live wildlife possessed under a permit must be maintained under humane and healthful conditions.

[47 FR 30786, July 15, 1982; 54 FR 38150, Sept. 14, 1989]

§ 13.42 Permits are specific.

The authorizations on the face of a permit which set forth specific times, dates, places, methods of taking, numbers and kinds of wildlife or plants, location of activity, authorize certain circumscribed transactions, or otherwise permit a specifically limited matter, are to be strictly construed and shall not be interpreted to permit similar or related matters outside the scope of strict construction.

[39 FR 1161, Jan. 4, 1974, as amended at 42 FR 32377, June 24, 1977]

§ 13.43 Alteration of permits.

Permits shall not be altered, erased, or mutilated, and any permit which has been altered, erased, or mutilated shall immediately become invalid. Unless specifically permitted on the face thereof, no permit shall be copied, nor shall any copy of a permit issued pursuant to this Subchapter B be displayed, offered for inspection, or otherwise used for any official purpose for which the permit was issued.

§ 13.44 Display of permit.

Any permit issued under this part shall be displayed for inspection upon request to the Director or his agent, or to any other person relying upon its existence.

§ 13.45 Filing of reports.

Permittees may be required to file reports of the activities conducted under the permit. Any such reports shall be filed not later than March 31 for the preceding calendar year ending December 31, or any portion thereof, during which a permit was in force, unless the regulations of this Subchapter B or the provisions of the permit set forth other reporting requirements.

§ 13.46 Maintenance of records.

From the date of issuance of the permit, the permittee shall maintain complete and accurate records of any taking, possession, transportation, sale, purchase, barter, exportation, or importation of plants obtained from the wild (excluding seeds) or wildlife pursuant to such permit. Such records shall be kept current and shall include names and addresses of persons with whom any plant obtained from the wild (excluding seeds) or wildlife has been purchased, sold, bartered, or otherwise transferred, and the date of such transaction, and such other information as may be required or appropriate. Such records shall be legibly written or reproducible in English and shall be maintained for five years from the date of expiration of the permit.

[39 FR 1161, Jan. 4, 1974, as amended at 42 FR 32377, June 24, 1977; 54 FR 38150, Sept. 14, 1989]

§ 13.47 Inspection requirement.

Any person holding a permit under this subchapter B shall allow the Director's agent to enter his premises at any reasonable hour to inspect any wildlife or plant held or to inspect, audit, or copy any permits, books, or records required to be kept by regulations of this subchapter B.

[39 FR 1161, Jan. 4, 1974, as amended at 42 FR 32377, June 24, 1977]

§ 13.48 Compliance with conditions of permit.

Any person holding a permit under subchapter B and any person acting under authority of such permit must comply with all conditions of the permit and with all applicable laws and regulations governing the permitted activity.

[54 FR 38150, Sept. 14, 1989]

§ 13.49 Surrender of permit.

Any person holding a permit under subchapter B shall surrender such permit to the issuing officer upon notification that the permit has been suspended or revoked by the Service, and all appeal procedures have been exhausted.

[54 FR 38150, Sept. 14, 1989]

§ 13.50 Acceptance of Liability.

Except as otherwise limited in the case of permits described in § 13.25(d), any person holding a permit under this subchapter B assumes all liability and responsibility for the conduct of any activity conducted under the authority of such permit.

[54 FR 38150, Sept. 14, 1989; 64 FR 32711, June 17, 1999]

50 C.F.R. PART 20
MIGRATORY BIRD HUNTING

Subpart A -- Introduction

Subpart B -- Definitions

Subpart C -- Taking

20.26 Emergency closures.

Subpart D -- Possession

20.31 Prohibited if taken in violation of subpart C.
20.32 During closed season.
20.33 Possession limit.
20.34 Opening day of a season.
20.35 Field possession limit.
20.36 tagging requirement.
20.37 custody of birds of another.
20.38 Possession of live birds.
20.39 Termination of possession.
20.40 Gift of migratory game birds.

Subpart E -- Transportation Within the United States

20.41 Prohibited if taken in violation of subpart C.
20.42 Transportation of birds of another.
20.43 Species identification requirement.
20.44 Marking packages or container.

Subpart F -- Exportation

20.51 Prohibited if taken in violation of subpart C.
20.52 Species identification requirement.
20.53 Marking packages or container.

Subpart G -- Importation

20.61 Importation limits.
20.62 Importation of birds of another.
20.63 Species identification requirement.
20.64 Foreign export permits.
20.65 Processing requirement.
20.66 Marking of package or container.

Subpart H -- Federal, State, and Foreign Law

20.71 Violation of Federal law.
20.72 Violation of State law.
20.73 Violation of foreign law.

Subpart I -- Migratory Bird Preservation Facilities

20.81 Tagging requirement.
20.82 Records required.
20.83 Inspection of premises.

Subpart J -- Feathers and Skins

20.91 Commercial use of feathers.
20.92 Personal use of feathers or skins.

Subpart K -- Annual Seasons, Limits, and Shooting Hours Schedules

****

AUTHORITY: 16 U.S.C. §§ 703-712; 16 U.S.C. §§ 742a-j; Pub. L. No. 106-108.

SOURCE: 38 FR 22021, Aug. 15, 1973, unless otherwise noted.

SUBPART A -- INTRODUCTION

§ 20.1 Scope of regulations.

(a) *In general.* The regulations contained in this part relate only to the hunting of migratory game birds, and crows.

(b) *Procedural and substantive requirements.* Migratory game birds may be taken, possessed, transported, shipped, exported, or imported only in accordance with the restrictions, conditions, and requirements contained in this part. Crows may be taken, possessed, transported, exported, or imported only in accordance with Subpart H of this part and the restrictions, conditions, and requirements prescribed in § 20.133.

§ 20.2 Relation to other provisions.

(a) *Migratory bird permits.* The provisions of this part shall not be construed to alter the terms of any permit or other authorization issued pursuant to part 21 of this subchapter.

(b) *Migratory bird hunting stamps.* The provisions of this part are in addition to the provisions of this part are in addition to the provisions of the Migratory Bird Hunting Stamp Act of 1934 (48 Stat. 451, as amended; 16 U.S.C. 718a).

(c) *National wildlife refuges.* The provisions of this part are in addition to, and are not in lieu of, any other provision of law respecting migratory game birds under the National Wildlife Refuge System Administration Act of 1966 (80 Stat. 927, as amended; 16 U.S.C. 668dd) or any regulation made pursuant thereto.

(d) *State Laws for the protection of migratory birds.* No statute or regulation of any State shall be construed to relieve a person from the restrictions, conditions, and requirements contained in this part, however, nothing in this part shall be construed to prevent the several States from making and enforcing laws or regulations not inconsistent with these regulations and the conventions between the United States and any foreign country for the protection of migratory birds or with the Migratory Bird Treaty Act, or which shall give further protection to migratory game birds.

SUBPART B -- DEFINITIONS

§ 20.11 What terms do I need to understand?

For the purpose of this part, the following terms shall be construed, respectively, to mean and to include:

(a) *Migratory game birds* means those migratory birds included in the terms of conventions between the United States and any foreign country for the protection of migratory birds, for which open seasons are prescribed in this part and belong to the following families:

(1) *Anatidae* (ducks, geese [including brant] and swans);
(2) *Columbidae* (doves and pigeons);
(3) *Gruidae* (cranes);
(4) *Rallidae* (rails, coots and gallinules); and
(5) *Scolopacidae* (woodcock and snipe).

A list of migratory birds protected by the international conventions and the Migratory Bird Treaty Act appears in § 10.13 of this subchapter.

(b) *Seasons* --

(1) *Open season* means the days on which migratory game birds may lawfully be taken. Each period prescribed as an open season shall be construed to include the first and last days thereof.

(2) *Closed season* means the days on which migratory game birds shall not be taken.

(c) *Bag limits* --

(1) *Aggregate bag limit* means a condition of taking in which two or more usually similar species may be bagged (reduced to possession) by the hunter in predetermined or unpredetermined quantities to satisfy a maximum take limit.

(2) *Daily bag limit* means the maximum number of migratory game birds of single species or combination (aggregate) of species permitted to be taken by one person in any one day during the open season in any one specified geographic area for which a daily bag limit is prescribed.

(3) *Aggregate daily bag limit* means the maximum number of migratory game birds permitted to be taken by one person in any one day during the open season when such person hunts in more than one specified geographic area and/or for more than one species for which a combined daily bag limit is prescribed. The aggregate daily bag limit is equal to, but shall not exceed, the largest daily bag limit prescribed for any one species or for any one specified geographic area in which taking occurs.

(4) *Possession limit* means the maximum number of migratory game birds of a single species or a combination of species permitted to be possessed by any one person when lawfully taken in the United States in any one specified geographic area for which a possession limit is prescribed.

(5) *Aggregate possession limit* means the maximum number of migratory game birds of a single species or combination of species taken in the United States permitted to be possessed by any one person when taking and possession occurs in more than one specified geographic area for which a possession limit is prescribed. The aggregate possession limit is equal to, but shall not exceed, the largest possession limit prescribed for any one of the species or specified geographic areas in which taking and possession occurs.

(d) *Personal abode* means one's principal or ordinary home or dwelling place, as distinguished from one's temporary or transient place of abode or dwelling such as a hunting club, or any club house, cabin, tent or trailer house used as a hunting club, or any hotel, motel or rooming house used during a hunting, pleasure or business trip.

(e) *Migratory bird preservation facility* means:

(1) Any person who, at their residence or place of business and for hire or other consideration; or

(2) Any taxidermist, cold-storage facility or locker plant which, for hire or other consideration; or

(3) Any hunting club which, in the normal course of operations; receives, possesses, or has in custody any migratory game birds belonging to another person for purposes of picking, cleaning, freezing, processing, storage or shipment.

(f) *Paraplegic* means an individual afflicted with paralysis of the lower half of the body with involvement of both legs, usually due to disease of or injury to the spinal cord.

(g) *Normal agricultural planting, harvesting, or post-harvest manipulation* means a planting or harvesting undertaken for the purpose of producing and gathering a crop, or manipulation after such harvest and removal of grain, that is conducted in accordance with official recommendations of State Extension Specialists of the Cooperative Extension Service of the U.S. Department of Agriculture.

(h) *Normal agricultural operation* means a normal agricultural planting, harvesting, post-harvest manipulation, or agricultural practice, that is conducted in accordance with official recommendations of State Extension Specialists of the Cooperative Extension Service of the U.S. Department of Agriculture.

(i) *Normal soil stabilization practice* means a planting for agricultural soil erosion control or post-mining land reclamation conducted in accordance with official recommendations of State Extension Specialists of the Cooperative Extension Service of the U.S. Department of Agriculture for agricultural soil erosion control.

(j) *Baited area* means any area on which salt, grain, or other feed has been placed, exposed, deposited, distributed, or scattered, if that salt, grain, or other feed could serve as a lure or attraction for migratory game birds to, on, or over areas where hunters are attempting to take them. Any such area will remain a baited area for ten days following the complete removal of all such salt, grain, or other feed.

(k) *Baiting* means the direct or indirect placing, exposing, depositing, distributing, or scattering of salt, grain, or other feed that could serve as a lure or attraction for migratory game birds to, on, or over any areas where hunters are attempting to take them.

(l) *Manipulation* means the alteration of natural vegetation or agricultural crops by activities that include but are not limited to mowing, shredding, discing, rolling, chopping, trampling, flattening, burning, or herbicide treatments. The term manipulation does not include the distributing or scattering of grain, seed, or other feed after removal from or storage on the field where grown.

(m) *Natural vegetation* means any non-agricultural, native, or naturalized plant species that grows at a site in response to planting or from existing seeds or other propagules. The term natural vegetation does not include planted millet. However, planted millet that grows on its own in subsequent years after the year of planting is considered natural vegetation.

[38 FR 22021, Aug. 15, 1973, as amended at 38 FR 23312, Aug. 29, 1973; 41 FR 31536, July 29, 1976; 42 FR 39667, Aug. 5, 1977; 45 FR 70275, Oct. 23, 1980; 53 FR 24290, June 28, 1988; 64 FR 29804, June 3, 1999]

SUBPART C -- TAKING

§ 20.20 Migratory Bird Harvest Information Program.

(a) *Information collection requirements.* The collections of information contained in § 20.20 have been approved by the Office of Management and Budget under 44 U.S.C. 3501 et seq. and assigned clearance number 1018-0015. An agency may not conduct or sponsor, and a person is not required to respond to a collection of information unless it displays a currently valid OMB control number. The information will be used to provide a sampling frame for the national Migratory Bird Harvest Survey. Response is required from licensed hunters to obtain the benefit of hunting migratory game birds. Public reporting burden for this information is estimated to average 2 minutes per response for 3,300,000 respondents, including the time for reviewing instructions, searching existing data sources, gathering and maintaining the data needed, and completing and reviewing the collection of information. Thus the total annual reporting and record-keeping burden for this collection is estimated to be 112,000 hours. Send comments regarding this burden estimate or any other aspect of this collection of information, including suggestions for reducing the burden, to the Service Information Collection Clearance Officer, ms-224 ARLSQ, Fish and Wildlife Service, Washington, DC 20240, or the Office of Management and Budget, Paperwork Reduction Project 1018-0015, Washington, DC 20503.

(b) *General provisions.* Each person hunting migratory game birds in any State except Hawaii must have identified himself or herself as a migratory bird hunter and given his or her name, address, and date of birth to the respective State hunting licensing authority and must have on his or her person evidence, provided by that State, of compliance with this requirement.

(c) *Tribal exemptions.* Nothing in paragraph (b) of this section shall apply to tribal members on Federal Indian Reservations or to tribal members hunting on ceded lands.

(d) *State exemptions.* Nothing in paragraph (b) of this section shall apply to those hunters who are exempt from State-licensing requirements in the State in which they are hunting.

(e) *State responsibilities.* The State hunting licensing authority will ask each licensed migratory bird hunter in the respective State to report approximately how many ducks, geese, doves, and woodcock he or she bagged the previous year, whether he or she hunted coots, snipe, rails, and/or gallinules the previous year, and, in States that have band-tailed pigeon hunting seasons, whether he or she intends to hunt band-tailed pigeons during the current year.

[58 FR 15098, March 19, 1993; 59 FR 53336, Oct. 21, 1994; 60 FR 43320, Aug. 18, 1995; 61 FR 46352, Aug. 30, 1996; 62 FR 45708, Aug. 28, 1997; 63 FR 46401, Sept. 1, 1998]

§ 20.21 What hunting methods are illegal?

Migratory birds on which open seasons are prescribed in this part may be taken by any method except those prohibited in this section. No person shall take migratory game birds:

(a) With a trap, snare, net, rifle, pistol, swivel gun, shotgun larger than 10 gauge, punt gun, battery gun, machine gun, fish hook, poison, drug, explosive, or stupefying substance;

(b) With a shotgun of any description capable of holding more than three shells, unless it is plugged with a one-piece filler, incapable of removal without disassembling the gun, so its total capacity does not exceed three shells. This restriction does not apply during a light-goose-only season (lesser snow and Ross' geese) when all other waterfowl and crane hunting seasons, excluding falconry, are closed while hunting light geese in Central and Mississippi Flyway portions of Alabama, Arkansas, Colorado, Illinois, Indiana, Iowa, Kansas, Kentucky, Louisiana, Michigan, Minnesota, Mississippi, Missouri, Montana,

Nebraska, New Mexico, North Dakota, Ohio, Oklahoma, South Dakota, Tennessee, Texas, Wisconsin, and Wyoming.

(c) From or by means, aid, or use of a sinkbox or any other type of low floating device, having a depression affording the hunter a means of concealment beneath the surface of the water;

(d) From or by means, aid, or use of any motor vehicle, motor-driven land conveyance, or aircraft of any kind, except that paraplegics and persons missing one or both legs may take from any stationary motor vehicle or stationary motor-driven land conveyance;

(e) From or by means of any motorboat or other craft having a motor attached, or any sailboat, unless the motor has been completely shut off and/or the sails furled, and its progress therefrom has ceased: Provided, That a craft under power may be used to retrieve dead or crippled birds; however, crippled birds may not be shot from such craft under power except in the seaduck area as permitted in Subpart K of this part;

(f) By the use or aid of live birds as decoys; although not limited to, it shall be a violation of this paragraph for any person to take migratory waterfowl on an area where tame or captive live ducks or geese are present unless such birds are and have been for a period of 10 consecutive days prior to such taking, confined within an enclosure which substantially reduces the audibility of their calls and totally conceals such birds from the sight of wild migratory waterfowl;

(g) By the use or aid of recorded or electrically amplified bird calls or sounds, or recorded or electrically amplified imitations of bird calls or sounds. This restriction does not apply during a light-goose-only season (lesser snow and Ross' geese) when all other waterfowl and crane hunting seasons, excluding falconry, are closed while hunting light geese in Central and Mississippi Flyway portions of Alabama, Arkansas, Colorado, Illinois, Indiana, Iowa, Kansas, Kentucky, Louisiana, Michigan, Minnesota, Mississippi, Missouri, Montana, Nebraska, New Mexico, North Dakota, Ohio, Oklahoma, South Dakota, Tennessee, Texas, Wisconsin, and Wyoming.

(h) By means or aid of any motordriven land, water, or air conveyance, or any sailboat used for the purpose of or resulting in the concentrating, driving, rallying, or stirring up of any migratory bird;

(i) By the aid of baiting, or on or over any baited area, where a person knows or reasonably should know that the area is or has been baited. However, nothing in this paragraph prohibits:

(1) the taking of any migratory game bird, including waterfowl, coots, and cranes, on or over the following lands or areas that are not otherwise baited areas--

(i) Standing crops or flooded standing crops (including aquatics); standing, flooded, or manipulated natural vegetation; flooded harvested croplands; or lands or areas where seeds or grains have been scattered solely as the result of a normal agricultural planting, harvesting, post-harvest manipulation or normal soil stabilization practice;

(ii) From a blind or other place of concealment camouflaged with natural vegetation;

(iii) From a blind or other place of concealment camouflaged with vegetation from agricultural crops, as long as such camouflaging does not result in the exposing, depositing, distributing or scattering of grain or other feed; or

(iv) Standing or flooded standing agricultural crops where grain is inadvertently scattered solely as a result of a hunter entering or exiting a hunting area, placing decoys, or retrieving downed birds.

(2) The taking of any migratory game bird, except waterfowl, coots and cranes, on or over lands or areas that are not otherwise baited areas, and where grain or other feed has been distributed or scattered solely as the result of manipulation of an agricultural crop or other feed on the land where grown, or solely as the result of a normal agricultural operation.

(j) While possessing shot (either in shotshells or as loose shot for muzzleloading) other than steel shot, or bismuth-tin (97 parts bismuth: 3 parts tin with <1 percent residual lead) shot, or tungsten-iron (40 parts tungsten: 60 parts iron with <1 percent residual lead) shot, or tungsten- polymer (95.5 parts tungsten: 4.5 parts Nylon 6 or 11 with <1 percent residual lead) shot, or tungsten-matrix (95.9 parts tungsten: 4.1 parts polymer with <1 percent residual lead) shot, or tin (99.9 percent tin with <1 percent residual lead) shot, or tungsten-nickel-iron (50% tungsten: 35% nickel: 15% iron with <1 percent residual lead), or such shot approved as nontoxic by the Director pursuant to procedures set forth in Sec. 20.134, provided that this restriction applies only to the taking of Anatidae (ducks, geese, (including brant) and swans), coots (Fulica americana) and any species that make up aggregate bag limits during concurrent seasons with the former in areas described in Sec. 20.108 as nontoxic shot zones, and further provided that:

(1) Tin shot (99.9 percent tin with 1 percent residual lead) is legal as nontoxic shot for waterfowl and coot hunting for the 2000-2001 hunting season only.

(2) [Reserved]

[38 FR 22021, Aug. 15, 1973, as amended at 38 FR 22896, Aug. 27, 1973; 44 FR 2599, Jan. 12, 1979; 45 FR 70275, Oct. 23, 1980; 49 FR 4079, Feb. 2, 1984; 52 FR 27364, July 21, 1987; 53 FR 24290, June 28, 1988; 60 FR 64, Jan. 3, 1995; 60 FR 43316, Aug. 18, 1995; 61 FR 42494, Aug. 15, 1996; 62 FR 4876, Jan. 31, 1997; 62 FR 43447, Aug. 13, 1997; 63 FR 54019, 54026, Oct. 7, 1998; 63 FR 67624, Dec. 8, 1998; 64 FR 7517, Feb. 16, 1999; 64 FR 29804, June 3, 1999; 64 FR 32780, June 17, 1999; 64 FR 45405, Aug. 19, 1999; 64 FR 71237, Dec. 20, 1999; 65 FR 53940, Sept. 6, 2000; 65 FR 76888, Dec. 7, 2000; 66 FR 742, Jan. 4, 2001; 66 FR 32265, June 14, 2001]

§ 20.22 Closed seasons.

No person shall take migratory game birds during the closed season except as provided in part 21.

[64 FR 7527, Feb. 16, 1999; 64 FR 32780, June 17, 1999; 64 FR 71237, Dec. 20, 1999; 66 FR 32265, June 14, 2001]

§ 20.23 Shooting hours.

No person shall take migratory game birds except during the hours open to shooting as prescribed in Subpart K of this part.

[38 FR 22021, Aug. 15, 1973, as amended at 38 FR 22626, Aug. 23, 1973]

§ 20.24 Daily limit.

No person shall take in any 1 calendar day, more than the daily bag limit or aggregate daily bag limit, whichever applies.

[38 FR 22021, Aug. 15, 1973, as amended at 38 FR 22626, Aug. 23, 1973]

§ 20.25 Wanton waste of migratory game birds.

No person shall kill or cripple any migratory game bird pursuant to this part without making a reasonable effort to retrieve the bird, and retain it in his actual custody, at the place where taken or between that place and either (a) his automobile or principal means of land transportation; or (b) his personal abode or temporary or transient place of lodging; or (c) a migratory bird preservation facility; or (d) a post office; or (e) a common carrier facility.

[41 FR 31536, July 29, 1976]

§ 20.26 Emergency closures.

(a) The Director may close or temporarily suspend any season established under Subpart K of this part:

(1) Upon a finding that a continuation of such a season would constitute an imminent threat to the safety of any endangered or threatened species or other migratory bird populations.

(2) Upon issuance of local public notice by such means as publication in local newspapers of general circulation, posting of the areas affected, notifying the State wildlife conservation agency, and announcement on local radio and television.

(b) Any such closure or temporary suspension shall be announced by publication of a notice to that effect in the Federal Register simultaneous with the local public notice referred to in paragraph (a)(2) of this section. However, in the event that it is impractical to publish a Federal Register notice simultaneously, due to the restriction in time available and the nature of the particular emergency situation, such notice shall follow the steps outlined in paragraph (a) of this section as soon as possible.

(c) Any closure or temporary suspension under this section shall be effective on the date of publication of the Federal Register notice; or if such notice is not published simultaneously, then on the date and at the time specified in the local notification to the public. Every notice of closure shall include the date and time of closing of the season and the area or areas affected. In the case of a temporary suspension, the date and time when the season may be resumed shall be provided by a subsequent local notification to the public, and by publication in the Federal Register.

[41 FR 31536, July 29, 1976]

SUBPART D -- POSSESSION

§ 20.31 Prohibited if taken in violation of Subpart C.

No person shall at any time, by any means, or in any manner, possess or have in custody any migratory game bird or part thereof, taken in violation of any provision of Subpart C of this part.

§ 20.32 During closed season.

No person shall possess any freshly killed migratory game birds during the closed season.

§ 20.33 Possession limit.

No person shall possess more migratory game birds taken in the United States than the possession limit or the aggregate possession limit, whichever applies.

§ 20.34 Opening day of a season.

No person on the opening day of the season shall possess any freshly killed migratory game birds in excess of the daily bag limit, or aggregate daily bag limit, whichever applies.

§ 20.35 Field possession limit.

No person shall possess, have in custody, or transport more than the daily bag limit or aggregate daily bag limit, whichever applies, of migratory game birds, tagged or not tagged, at or between the place where taken and either (a) his automobile or principal means of land transportation; or (b) his personal abode or temporary or transient place of lodging; or (c) a migratory bird preservation facility; or (d) a post office; or (e) a common carrier facility.

[41 FR 31536, July 29, 1976]

§ 20.36 Tagging requirement.

No person shall put or leave any migratory game birds at any place (other than at his personal abode), or in the custody of another person for picking, cleaning, processing, shipping, transportation, or storage (including temporary storage), or for the purpose of having taxidermy services performed, unless such birds have a tag attached, signed by the hunter, stating his address, the total number and species of birds, and the date such birds were killed. Migratory game birds being transported in any vehicle as the personal baggage of the possessor shall not be considered as being in storage or temporary storage.

§ 20.37 Custody of birds of another.

No person shall receive or have in custody any migratory game birds belonging to another person unless such birds are tagged as required by § 20.36.

§ 20.38 Possession of live birds.

Every migratory game bird wounded by hunting and reduced to possession by the hunter shall be immediately killed and become a part of the daily bag limit. No person shall at any time, or by any means, possess or transport live migratory game birds taken under authority of this part.

§ 20.39 Termination of possession.

Subject to all other requirements of this part, the possession of birds taken by any hunter shall be deemed to have ceased when such birds have been delivered by him to another person as a gift; or have been delivered by him to a post office, a common carrier, or a migratory bird preservation facility and consigned for transport by the Postal Service or a common carrier to some person other than the hunter.

[41 FR 31537, July 29, 1976]

§ 20.40 Gift of migratory game birds.

No person may receive, possess, or give to another, any freshly killed migratory game birds as a gift, except at the personal abodes of the donor or donee, unless such birds have a tag attached, signed by the hunter who took the birds, stating such hunter's address, the total number and species of birds and the date such birds were taken.

[42 FR 39668, Aug. 5, 1977]

SUBPART E -- TRANSPORTATION WITHIN THE UNITED STATES

****

SUBPART F -- EXPORTATION

****

SUBPART G -- IMPORTATION

****

SUBPART H -- FEDERAL, STATE, AND FOREIGN LAW

§ 20.71 Violation of Federal law.

No person shall at any time, by any means or in any manner, take, possess, transport, or export any migratory bird, or any part, nest, or egg of any such bird, in violation of any act of Congress or any regulation issued pursuant thereto.

§ 20.72 Violation of State law.

No person shall at any time, by any means or in any manner, take, possess, transport, or export any migratory bird, or any part, nest, or egg of any such bird, in violation of any applicable law or regulation of any State.

§ 20.73 Violation of foreign law.

No person shall at any time, by any means, or in any manner, import, possess, or transport, any migratory bird, or any part, nest, or egg of any such bird taken, bought, sold, transported, possessed, or exported contrary to any applicable law or regulation of any foreign country, or State or province thereof.

- 0 -

CHAPTER 2

STATUTES INTENDED TO CONSERVE WILDLIFE HABITAT

Although there is a long common-law tradition both in England and America of protecting wildlife habitat to conserve wildlife, several factors -- apparent inexhaustibility, naive optimism, comparatively widespread land ownership, and the belief that land was a commodity useful in pursuit of the paramount good of individual wealth -- combined to obscure the importance of habitat. The federal government implemented a policy of disposing of the public domain with no particular attention to its value as wildlife habitat. Indeed, the federal government actively encouraged the destruction of much habitat through initiatives such as the Swamp Lands Acts of 1849, 1850, and 1860 under which the federal government transferred title to swamplands to the states if they agreed to "reclaim" the lands by draining them[1] -- that is, by destroying the wetlands.

Some habitat was protected: California created the first official refuge in 1870[2] and Congress set aside Yellowstone Park in part to protect against "the wanton destruction of the fish and game found within the park."[3] But these refuges are notable primarily for their novelty. And while the "great barbecue"[4] of the post-Civil War generation gave impetus to the conservation movement, the establishment of refuges continued to be an ad hoc process.

Federal statutes seeking to conserve wildlife habitat can be divided into four indistinct categories. The first and most detailed group creates the National Wildlife Refuge System, provides funding and procedures for designating lands for inclusion in the Refuge System, and specifies how lands in the system are to be managed. A second group of statutes funds state acquisition of habitat and imposes restrictions on how lands acquired with federal funds can be used. These two types of statutes are intended to create islands of protected habitat where wildlife is the dominant use.

In addition to conserving habitat directly, two types of federal statutes seek to ensure that wildlife is considered in decisions that potentially alter habitat. The first of these statutes are those that directly mandate consideration of the impact of a proposed action on wildlife; the National Environmental Policy Act[5] is the best-known example of such an approach. Finally, there are a group of statutes that seek to encourage state and federal wildlife agency and land managers to cooperate and to plan for wildlife. These statutes often require federal agencies to consider the recommendations of state fish and game departments.

A. Federal Wildlife Refuges

i. Refuge Acquisition

According to the founding myth of the National Wildlife Refuge System, the first refuge was created by President Theodore Roosevelt in 1903, when he issued an Executive

Order that the federally owned "Pelican Island in Indian River ... State of Florida, be, and it is hereby, reserved and set apart ... as a preserve and breeding ground for native birds."[6] By the time that he left office in 1909, he had created 51 refuges on federal lands.[7] In 1908, Congress appropriated funds to acquire non-federal land for use as a refuge.[8]

The process remained ad hoc, however, until the passage of the Migratory Bird Conservation Act in 1929.

MIGRATORY BIRD CONSERVATION ACT (1929) (16 U.S.C. §§ 715-715r)

The Convention for the Protection of Migratory Birds with Great Britain and the Migratory Bird Treaty Act that implemented it sought to reverse the declining populations of migratory birds by authorizing federally determine bag limits and closed seasons. Neither the Convention nor the Act, however, authorized the acquisition of habitat. When the bag limits and closed seasons failed to stem the decline in waterfowl populations, Congress turned to other approaches and in 1929 enacted the Migratory Bird Conservation Act.[9]

The Act establishes a procedure through which the Secretary of the Interior is authorized to acquire lands and waters "suitable for use as an inviolate sanctuary ... for migratory birds."[10] Since the acquisition of land by the federal government removes it from the tax base and otherwise restricts applicable state and local laws, the Act is solicitous of state and local interests. First, no lands can be acquired in a state unless that state has "consented by law to the acquisition by the United States of lands in that State."[11] Second, if a state has consented in general to federal acquisition of lands, the Secretary is also required to consult with the local government and state before acquiring any specific parcel of land.[12] Following this consultation with state and local officials, the Secretary is required to obtain approval of the Migratory Bird Conservation Commission composed of three cabinet officers (Interior, Transportation, and Agriculture), two senators, two representatives, and an *ex officio* state representative (generally the ranking official from the state's fish and game agency) from the affected state.[13] Finally, the Act also specifically provides that state civil and criminal jurisdiction is not affected by the acquisition of the lands "except so far as the punishment of offenses against the United States is concerned,"[14] and that state game laws are unaffected "in so far as they do not permit what is forbidden by Federal law."[15]

Once lands have been acquired, the Secretary of the Interior is given broad authority to administer the areas "to conserve and protect migratory birds ... and other species of wildlife ... and to restore or develop adequate wildlife habitat."[16] This management authority includes the power "to manage timber, range, and agricultural crops; to manage other species of animals, including but not limited to fenced range animals, with the objectives of perpetuating, distributing, and utilizing the resources."[17] The Act also included an early example of "cooperative federalism": if the state enacted a legislative and regulatory system "adequately to enforce" the federal statutes and regulations, the Secretary of the Interior was to so certify "and thereafter said State may cooperate with the Secretary of the Interior in the enforcement of this Act and the regulations thereunder."[18]

16 U.S.C. § 715. Short title. This Act shall be known by the short title of "Migratory Bird Conservation Act."

[Feb. 18, 1929, ch. 257, § 1, 45 Stat. 1222]

16 U.S.C. § 715a. Migratory Bird Conservation Commission; creation; composition; duties; approval of areas of land and water recommended for purchase or rental. A commission to be known as the Migratory Bird Conservation Commission, consisting of the Secretary of the Interior, as chairman, the Administrator of the Environmental Protection Agency, the Secretary of Agriculture and two Members of the Senate, to be selected by the President of the Senate, and two Members of the House of Representatives to be selected by the Speaker, is created and authorized to consider and pass upon any area of land, water, or land and water that may be recommended by the Secretary of the Interior for purchase or rental under this Act, and to fix the price or prices at which such area may be purchased or rented; and no purchase or rental shall be made of any such area until it has been duly approved for purchase or rental by said commission. Any Member of the House of Representatives who is a member of the commission, if reelected to the succeeding Congress, may serve on the commission notwithstanding the expiration of a Congress. Any vacancy on the commission shall be filled in the same manner as the original appointment. The ranking officer of the branch or department of a State to which is committed the administration of its game laws, or his authorized representative, and in a State having no such branch or department, the governor thereof, or his authorized representative, shall be a member ex officio of said commission for the purpose of considering and voting on all questions relating to the acquisition, under this Act, of areas in his State. For purposes of this Act, the purchase or rental of any area of land, water, or land and water includes the purchase or rental of any interest in any such area of land, water, or land and water.

[Feb. 18, 1929, ch. 257, § 2, 45 Stat. 1222; 1939 Reorg. Plan No. II, § 4(f), (h) (July 1, 1939), 4 Fed. Reg. 2731, 53 Stat. 1433; Pub. L. 90-261, 82 Stat. 39 (Mar. 2, 1968); Pub. L. 94-215, § 4, 90 Stat. 190 (Feb. 17, 1976); Pub. L. 101-233, § 13, 103 Stat. 1977 (Dec. 13, 1989)]

16 U.S.C. § 715b. Annual report. ****

16 U.S.C. § 715c. Areas recommended for approval; character. The Secretary of the Interior may not recommend any area for purchase or rental under the terms of this Act unless the Secretary of the Interior --

(1) has determined that such area is necessary for the conservation of migratory birds; and

(2) has consulted with the county or other unit of local government in which such area is located and with the Governor of the State concerned or the appropriate State

agency.

[Feb. 18, 1929, ch. 257, § 4, 45 Stat. 1223; 1939 Reorg. Plan No. II, § 4(f) (July 1, 1939), 4 Fed. Reg. 2731, 53 Stat. 1433; Pub. L. 89-669, § 7(a), 80 Stat. 929 (Oct. 15, 1966); Pub. L. 95-552, § 2, 92 Stat. 2071 (Oct. 30, 1978)]

16 U.S.C. § 715d. Purchase or rental of approved areas or interests therein; gifts and devises; United States lands. The Secretary of the Interior may --

(1) purchase or rent such areas or interests therein as have been approved for purchase or rental by the Commission at the price or prices fixed by the Commission; and

(2) acquire, by gift or devise, any area or interests therein;

which he determines to be suitable for use as an inviolate sanctuary, or for any other management purpose, for migratory birds. The Secretary may pay, when deemed necessary by him and from moneys authorized to be appropriated for the purposes of this Act (A) the purchase or rental price of any such area or interest therein, and (B) the expenses incident to the location, examination, survey, and acquisition of title (including options) of any such area or interest therein. No lands acquired, held, or used by the United States for military purposes shall be subject to any provisions of this Act.

[Feb. 18, 1929, ch. 257, § 5, 45 Stat. 1223; 1939 Reorg. Plan No. II, § 4(f) (July 1, 1939), 4 Fed. Reg. 2731, 53 Stat. 1433; Pub. L. 95-616, § 5(a), 92 Stat. 3113 (Nov. 8, 1978)]

16 U.S.C. § 715e. Examination of title; easements and reservations. The Secretary of the Interior may do all things and make all expenditures necessary to secure the safe title in the United States to the areas which may be acquired under this Act, but no payment shall be made for any such areas until the title thereto shall be satisfactory to the Attorney General or his designee, but the acquisition of such areas by the United States shall in no case be defeated because of rights-of-way, easements, and reservations which from their nature will in the opinion of the Secretary of the Interior in no manner interfere with the use of the areas so encumbered for the purposes of this Act, but such rights-of-way, easements, and reservations retained by the grantor or lessor from whom the United States receives title under this Act or any other Act for the acquisition by the Secretary of the Interior of areas for wildlife refuges shall be subject to rules and regulations prescribed by the Secretary of the Interior for the occupation, use, operation, protection, and administration of such areas as inviolate sanctuaries for migratory birds or as refuges for wildlife; and it shall be expressed in the deed or lease that the use, occupation, and operation of such rights-of-way, easements, and reservations shall be subordinate to and subject to such rules and regulations as are set out in such deed or lease or, if deemed necessary by the Secretary of the Interior, to such rules and regulations as may be prescribed by him from time to time.

[Feb. 18, 1929, ch. 257, § 6, 45 Stat. 1223; June 15, 1935, ch. 261, Title III, § 301, 49 Stat. 381; 1939 Reorg. Plan No. II, § 4(f) (July 1, 1939), 4 Fed. Reg. 2731, 53 Stat. 1433; Pub. L. 91-393, § 6, 84 Stat. 835 (Sept. 1, 1970)]

16 U.S.C. § 715f. Consent of State to conveyance in fee. No deed or instrument of conveyance in fee shall be accepted by the Secretary of the Interior under this Act unless the State in which the area lies shall have consented by law to the acquisition by the United States of lands in that State.

[Feb. 18, 1929, ch. 257, § 7, 45 Stat. 1223; 1939 Reorg. Plan No. II, § 4(f) (July 1, 1939), 4 Fed. Reg. 2731, 53 Stat. 1433; Pub. L. 103-434, Title XIII, 108 Stat. 4565 (Oct. 31, 1994)]

16 U.S.C. § 715g. Jurisdiction of State over areas acquired. The jurisdiction of the State, both civil and criminal, over persons upon areas acquired under this Act shall not be affected or changed by reason of their acquisition and administration by the United States as migratory-bird reservations, except so far as the punishment of offenses against the United States is concerned.

[Feb. 18, 1929, ch. 257, § 8, 45 Stat. 1224]

16 U.S.C. § 715h. Operation of State game laws. Nothing in this Act is intended to interfere with the operation of the game laws of the several States applying to migratory game birds in so far as they do not permit what is forbidden by Federal law.

[Feb. 18, 1929, ch. 257, § 9, 45 Stat. 1224]

16 U.S.C. § 715i. Administration. (a) Treaty obligations; rules and regulations. Areas of lands, waters, or interests therein acquired or reserved pursuant to this Act shall, unless otherwise provided by law, be administered by the Secretary of the Interior under rules and regulations prescribed by him to conserve and protect migratory birds in accordance with treaty obligations with Mexico, Canada, Japan, and the Union of Soviet Socialist Republics, and other species of wildlife found thereon, including species that are listed pursuant to section 4 of the Endangered Species Act of 1973 [16 U.S.C. § 1533] as endangered species or threatened species, and to restore or develop adequate wildlife habitat.

(b) Management and public and private agency agreements authorization. In administering such areas, the Secretary is authorized to manage timber, range, and agricultural crops; to manage other species of animals, including but not limited to fenced range animals, with the objectives of perpetuating, distributing, and utilizing the resources; and to enter into agreements with public and private agencies.

[Feb. 18, 1929, ch. 257, § 10, 45 Stat. 1224; 1939 Reorg. Plan No. II, § 4(f) (July 1, 1939), 4 Fed. Reg. 2731, 53 Stat. 1433; Pub. L. 89-669, § 7(b), 80 Stat. 929 (Oct. 15, 1966); Pub. L. 93-205, § 13(b), 87 Stat. 902 (Dec. 28, 1973); Pub. L. 95-616, § 5(b), 92 Stat. 3114 (Nov. 8, 1978)]

16 U.S.C. § 715j. "Migratory birds" defined. For the purposes of this Act, and the Migratory Bird Treaty Act (16 U.S.C. §§ 703 *et seq.*), migratory birds are those defined as such by the treaty between the United States and Great Britain for the protection of migratory birds concluded August 16, 1916 (39 Stat. 1702), the treaty between the United States and the United Mexican States for the protection of migratory birds and game mammals concluded February 7, 1936 (50 Stat. 1311), the Convention between the Government of the United States of America and the Government of Japan for the Protection of Migratory Birds and Birds in Danger of Extinction, and their Environment concluded March 4, 1972, and the Convention between the United States and the Union of Soviet Socialist Republics for the Conservation of Migratory Birds and their Environment concluded November 19, 1976.

[Feb. 18, 1929, ch. 257, § 11, 45 Stat. 1224; Pub. L. 89-669, § 7(c), 80 Stat. 930 (Oct. 15, 1966); Pub. L. 95-616, § 5(c), 92 Stat. 3114 (Nov. 8, 1978)]

16 U.S.C. § 715k. Authorization of appropriations for purposes of Act; disposal; reservation protectors. For the acquisition, including the location, examination, and survey, of suitable areas of land, water, or land and water, for use as migratory bird reservations, and necessary expenses incident thereto, and for the administration, maintenance, and development of such areas and other preserves, reservations, or breeding grounds frequented by migratory birds and under the administration of the Secretary of the Interior, including the construction of dams, dikes, ditches, flumes, spillways, buildings, and other necessary improvements, and for the elimination of the loss of migratory birds from alkali poisoning, oil pollution of waters, or other causes, for cooperation with local authorities in wildlife conservation, for investigations and publications relating to North American birds, for personal services, printing, engraving, and issuance of circulars, posters, and other necessary matter and for the enforcement of the provisions of this Act, there are authorized to be appropriated, in addition to all other amounts authorized by law to be appropriated, $200,000 for the fiscal year ending June 30, 1940, and for each fiscal year thereafter. No part of any appropriation authorized by this section shall be used for payment of the salary, compensation, or expenses of any United States protector, except reservation protectors for the administration, maintenance, and protection of such reservations and the birds thereon: *Provided,* That reservation protectors appointed under the provisions of this Act, shall be selected, when practicable, from qualified citizens of the State in which they are to be employed. The Secretary of the Interior is authorized and directed to make such expenditures and to employ such means, including personal services in the District of Columbia and elsewhere, as may be necessary to carry out the foregoing objects.

[Feb. 18, 1929, ch. 257, § 12, 45 Stat. 1224; 1939 Reorg. Plan No. II, § 4(f) (July 1, 1939), 4 Fed. Reg. 2731, 53 Stat. 1433; Pub. L. 89-669, § 7(a), 80 Stat. 929 (Oct. 15, 1966)]

- 0 -

MIGRATORY BIRD HUNTING STAMP ACT (1934) [DUCK STAMP ACT] (16 U.S.C. §§ 718-718j)

Steady funding for migratory bird refuge acquisition was provided five years later when Congress enacted the Migratory Bird Hunting Stamp Act of 1934 -- the "Duck Stamp Act." The Act was enacted

> to supplement and support the Migratory Bird Conservation Act by providing funds for the acquisition of areas for use a migratory-bird sanctuaries, refuges, and breeding grounds, for developing and administering such areas, for the protection of certain

migratory birds, for enforcement of the Migratory Bird Treaty Act ... and for other purposes.[19]

To accomplish these purposes, the Act imposed a license requirement: "No person who has attained the age of sixteen years shall take any migratory waterfowl unless at the time of the taking he carries on his person an unexpired Federal migratory-bird hunting and conservation stamp."[20] Violation of the act subjects the violator to the penalties imposed by the Migratory Bird Treaty Act, including $500 fines, six months imprisonment, and forfeiture of hunting equipment.[21] While possession of a stamp was necessary to hunt, it was itself insufficient: hunters were required to comply both with any federal seasons or bags limits adopted pursuant to any treaty and with the game laws of the individual states.[22]

The stamps are issued and sold by the Postal Service. The cost of the stamp was initially set at $1 and has gradually increased to between $3 and $7.50.[23] All money received from the sale of the stamps is paid into the Migratory Bird Conservation Fund, a special account in the Treasury. After paying the production costs of the stamps, the remaining funds are to be used "for the location, ascertainment, and acquisition of suitable areas for migratory bird refuges under the Migratory Bird Conservation Act" and for the acquisition of "small wetland and pothole areas."[24]

Although the Duck Stamp has provided a source of continuing monies for refuge acquisition, the requirement that the funds be expended on the "acquisition of suitable areas for migratory bird refuges" and "waterfowl production areas"[25] has created a National Wildlife Refuge System that is geared primarily to the production of waterfowl for hunters.

16 U.S.C. § 718. Definitions. (a) Terms defined in the Migratory Bird Treaty Act [16 U.S.C. §§ 703 *et seq.*], or the Migratory Bird Conservation Act [16 U.S.C. §§ 715 *et seq.*], shall, when used in this Act, have the meaning assigned to such terms in such Acts, respectively.

(b) As used in this Act (1) the term "migratory waterfowl" means the species enumerated in paragraph (a) of subdivision 1 of article I of the treaty between the United States and Great Britain for the protection of migratory birds concluded August 16, 1916 (39 Stat. 1702); (2) the term "State" includes the several States and Territories of the United States and the District of Columbia; and (3) the term "take" means pursue, hunt, shoot, capture, collect, kill, or attempt to pursue, hunt, shoot, capture, collect, or kill.

[Mar. 16, 1934, ch. 71, § 9, 48 Stat. 452]

16 U.S.C. § 718a. Hunting and conservation stamp for taking migratory waterfowl. No person who has attained the age of sixteen years shall take any migratory waterfowl unless at the time of such taking he carries on his person an unexpired Federal migratory-bird hunting and conservation stamp validated by his signature written by himself in ink across the face of the stamp prior to his taking such birds; except that no such stamp shall be required for the taking of migratory waterfowl by Federal or State institutions or official agencies, or for propagation, or by the resident owner, tenant, or share cropper of the property or officially designated agencies of the Department of the Interior for the killing, under such restrictions as the Secretary of the Interior may by regulation prescribe, of such waterfowl when found injuring crops or other property. Any person to whom a stamp has been sold under this Act shall upon request exhibit such stamp for inspection to any officer or employee of the Department of the Interior authorized to enforce the provisions of this Act or to any officer of any State or any political subdivision thereof authorized to enforce game laws.

[Mar. 16, 1934, ch. 71, § 1, 48 Stat. 451; June 15, 1935, ch. 261, Title I, § 1, 49 Stat. 378; 1939 Reorg. Plan No. II, § 4(f) (July 1, 1939), 4 Fed. Reg. 2731, 53 Stat. 1433; July 30, 1956, ch. 782, § 1, 70 Stat. 722; Pub. L. 94-215, § 3(a), 90 Stat. 189 (Feb. 17, 1976)]

16 U.S.C. § 718b. Issuance and sale of stamps; deposit of funds in migratory bird conservation fund; fees; validity; expiration; redemption; "retail dealers" and "hunting year" defined. (a) Sales; fund disposition; unsold stamps. The stamps required by section 1 of this Act [16 U.S.C. § 718a] shall be issued and sold by the Postal Service and may be sold by the Department of the Interior, pursuant to regulations prescribed jointly by the Postal Service and the Secretary of the Interior, at (1) each post office of the first- and second-class, and (2) any establishment, facility, or location as the Postal Service and the Secretary of the Interior shall direct or authorize. The funds received from the sale of such stamps by the Department of the Interior shall be deposited in the migratory bird conservation fund in accordance with the provisions of section 4 of this Act [16 U.S.C. § 718d]. Except as provided in subsection (b) of this section, for each stamp sold under the provisions of this section for any hunting year there shall be collected by the Postal Service a sum of not less than $3 and not more than $5 as determined by the Secretary of the Interior after taking into consideration, among other matters, the increased cost of lands needed for the conservation of migratory birds. No such stamp shall be valid under any circumstances to authorize the taking of migratory waterfowl except in compliance with Federal and State laws and regulations and then only when the person so taking such waterfowl shall himself have written his signature in ink across the face of the stamp prior to such taking. Such stamps shall be usable as migratory-bird hunting stamps only during the year for which issued. The Postal Service, pursuant to regulations prescribed by it, shall provide for the redemption, on or before the 30th day of June of each year, of blocks composed of two or more attached unused stamps issued for such year (A) that were sold on consignment to any person, including, but not limited to, retail dealers for resale to their customers, and (B) that have not been resold by any such person. As used in this section, the term "retail dealers" means persons regularly engaged in the business of retailing hunting or fishing equipment, and persons duly authorized to act as agents of a State or political subdivision thereof for the sale of State or county hunting or fishing licenses.

(b) Cost of stamp. The Postal Service shall collect $10.00 for each stamp sold under the provisions of this section for hunting years 1987 and 1988, $12.50 for hunting years 1989 and 1990, and $15.00 for each hunting year thereafter, if the Secretary of the Interior determines, at any time before February 1 of the calendar year in which such hunting year begins, that all sums in the migratory bird conservation fund available for obligation and attributable to --

(1) amounts appropriated pursuant to this Act for the fiscal year ending in the immediately preceding calendar year; and

(2) the sale of stamps under this section during such fiscal year

have been obligated for expenditure. For purposes of this section, the term "hunting year" means the 12-month period beginning on July 1 of any such year.

[Mar. 16, 1934, ch. 71, § 2, 48 Stat. 451; June 15, 1935, ch. 261, Title I, § 2, 49 Stat. 379; Aug. 12, 1949, ch. 421, § 1, 63 Stat. 599; July 30, 1956, ch. 782, §§ 2, 3(b), 70 Stat. 722; Pub. L. 85-585, § 1, 72 Stat. 486 (Aug. 1, 1958); Pub. L. 92-214, §§ 1, 2, 85 Stat. 777 (Dec. 22, 1971); Pub. L. 94-215, § 3(b), (c), 90 Stat. 189 (Feb. 17, 1976); Pub. L. 94-273, § 34, 90 Stat. 380 (Apr. 21, 1976); Pub. L. 95-552, § 1, 92 Stat. 2071 (Oct. 30, 1978); Pub. L. 95-616, § 7(a), 92 Stat. 3114 (Nov. 8, 1978); Pub. L. 99-625, § 3, 100 Stat. 3502 (Nov. 7, 1986); Pub. L. 99-645, Title II, § 202, 100 Stat. 3586 (Nov. 10, 1986)]

16 U.S.C. § 718b-1. Disposition of unsold stamps; collectors' supply; destruction of surplus. On or after the date of enactment of this section [July 30, 1956], such quantity of migratory-bird hunting stamps, not sold at the end of the fiscal year for which issued, as determined by the Postal Service to be (1) required to supply the market for sale to collectors, and (2) in suitable condition for such sale to collectors, shall be turned over to the Philatelic Agency and therein placed on sale. Any surplus stock of such migratory-bird hunting stamps may be destroyed in such manner as the Postal Service shall direct.

[July 30, 1956, ch. 782, § 3(a), 70 Stat. 722; Pub. L. 92-214, § 3, 85 Stat. 777 (Dec. 22, 1971)]

16 U.S.C. § 718c. Compliance with treaty or convention regulations and State game laws. Nothing in this Act shall be construed to authorize any person to take any migratory waterfowl otherwise than in accordance with regulations adopted and approved pursuant to any treaty or convention heretofore or hereafter entered into between the United States and any other country for the protection of migratory birds, nor to exempt any person from complying with the game laws of the several States.

[Mar. 16, 1934, ch. 71, § 3, 48 Stat. 451; Pub. L. 95-616, § 7(b), 92 Stat. 3114 (Nov. 8, 1978)]

16 U.S.C. § 718d. Disposition of receipts from sale of stamps. All moneys received for such stamps shall be accounted for by the Postal Service or the Department of the Interior, whichever is appropriate, and paid into the Treasury of the United States, and shall be reserved and set aside as a special fund to be known as the migratory bird conservation fund, to be administered by the Secretary of the Interior. All moneys received into such fund are appropriated for the following objects and shall be available therefor until expended:

(a) Advance allotments to Postal Service. So much as may be necessary shall be used by the Secretary of the Interior to make advance allotments to the Postal Service at such time and in such amounts as may be mutually agreed upon by the Secretary of the Interior and the Postal Service for direct expenditure by the Postal Service for engraving, printing, issuing, selling, and accounting for migratory bird hunting stamps and moneys received from the sale thereof, in addition to expenses for personal services in the District of Columbia and elsewhere, and such other expenses as may be necessary in executing the duties and functions required of the Postal Service.

(b) Acquisition of bird refuges. Except as authorized in subsections (c) and (d) of this section, the remainder shall be available for the location, ascertainment, and acquisition of suitable areas for migratory bird refuges under the provisions of the Migratory Bird Conservation Act [16 U.S.C. §§ 715 *et seq.*] and for the administrative costs incurred in the acquisition of such areas.

(c) Waterfowl Production Areas. The Secretary of the Interior is authorized to utilize funds made available under subsection (b) of this section for the purposes of such subsection, and such other funds as may be appropriated for the purposes of such subsection, or of this subsection, to acquire, or defray the expense incident to the acquisition by gift, devise, lease, purchase, or exchange of, small wetland and pothole areas, interests therein, and rights-of-way to provide access thereto. Such small areas, to be designated as "Waterfowl Production Areas", may be acquired without regard to the limitations and requirements of the Migratory Bird Conservation Act [16 U.S.C. §§ 715 *et seq.*], but all of the provisions of such Act which govern the administration and protection of lands acquired thereunder, except the inviolate sanctuary provisions of such Act, shall be applicable to areas acquired pursuant to this subsection.

(d) Promotion of stamp sales. (1) The Secretary of the Interior may utilize funds from the sale of migratory bird hunting and conservation stamps, not to exceed $1,000,000 in each of fiscal years 1999, 2000, 2001, 2002, and 2003, for the promotion of additional sales of those stamps, in accordance with a Migratory Bird Conservation Commission approved annual marketing plan. Such promotion shall include the preparation of reports, brochures, or other appropriate materials to be made available to the public that describe the benefits to wildlife derived from stamp sales.

(2) The Secretary of the Interior shall include in each annual report of the Commission under section 3 of the Migratory Bird Conservation Act (16 U.S.C. § 715b) a description of activities conducted under this subsection in the year covered by the report.

[Mar. 16, 1934, ch. 71, § 4, 48 Stat. 451; June 14, 1935, ch. 261, Title I, §§ 3, 4, 49 Stat. 379, 380; 1939 Reorg. Plan. No. II, § 4(f) (July 1, 1939), 4 Fed. Reg. 2731, 53 Stat. 1433; Aug. 12, 1949, ch. 421, § 2, 63 Stat. 600; Oct. 20, 1951, ch. 520, 65 Stat. 451; Pub. L. 85-585, §§ 2, 3, 72 Stat. 486, 487 (Aug. 1, 1958); Pub. L. 89-669, § 6, 80 Stat. 929 (Oct. 15, 1966); Pub. L. 92-214, § 2, 85 Stat. 777 (Dec. 22, 1971); Pub. L. 94-215, § 3(d), 90 Stat. 190 (Feb. 17, 1976); Pub. L. 105-269, § 2, 112 Stat. 2381 (Oct. 19, 1998)]

16 U.S.C. § 718e. Offenses. (a) Loan or transfer of stamp. No person to whom has been sold a migratory-bird hunting stamp, validated as provided in section 1 of this Act [16 U.S.C. § 718a], shall loan or transfer such stamp to any person during the period of its validity; nor shall any person other than the person validating such stamp use it for any purpose during such period.

(b) Alteration and counterfeiting of stamp. Except as provided in clauses (i) and (ii) of section 504(1) of Title 18, no person shall alter, mutilate, imitate, or counterfeit any stamp authorized by this Act, or imitate or counterfeit any die, plate, or engraving therefor, or make, print, or knowingly use, sell, or have in his possession any such counterfeit, die, plate, or engraving.

(c) Reproduction of migratory bird hunting stamps; regulation by Secretary of the Interior; disposition of proceeds. Notwithstanding the provisions of subsection (b) of this section, or the prohibition in section 474 of Title 18, or other provisions of law, the Secretary of the Interior may authorize, with the concurrence of the Secretary of the Treasury,

(1) the color reproduction, or

(2) the black and white reproduction,

of migratory bird hunting stamps authorized by this Act, which otherwise satisfies the requirements of clauses (ii) and (iii) of section 504(1) of Title 18. Any such reproduction shall be subject to those terms and conditions deemed necessary by the Secretary of the Interior by regulation or otherwise and any proceeds received by the Federal Government as a result of such reproduction shall be paid, after deducting expenses for marketing, into the migratory bird conservation fund established under section 4 of this Act [16 U.S.C. § 718d].

[Mar. 16, 1934, ch. 71, § 5, 48 Stat. 452; June 15, 1935, ch. 261, Title I, § 5, 49 Stat. 380; Pub. L. 98-369, Title X, § 1077(a), (b)(3), 98 Stat. 1054, 1055 (July 18, 1984); Pub. L. 100-653, Title III, § 302, 102 Stat. 3827 (Nov. 14, 1988)]

16 U.S.C. § 718f. Enforcement; authority of United States judges, magistrate judges, and employees of Department of the Interior. For the efficient execution of this Act, the judges of the several courts, established under the laws of the United States, United States magistrates, and persons appointed by the Secretary of the Interior to enforce the provisions of this Act, shall have, with respect thereto, like powers and duties as are conferred upon said judges, magistrates, and employees of the Department of the Interior by the Migratory Bird Treaty Act [16 U.S.C. §§ 703 *et seq.*], or any other Act to carry into effect any treaty for the protection of migratory birds with respect to that Act. Any bird or part thereof taken or possessed contrary to this Act shall, when seized, be disposed of by the Secretary in accordance with law.

[Mar. 16, 1934, ch. 71, § 6, 48 Stat. 452; 1939 Reorg. Plan No. II, § 4(f) (July 1, 1939), 4 Fed. Reg. 2731, 53 Stat. 1433; Pub. L. 90-578, Title IV, § 402(b)(2), 82 Stat. 1118 (Oct. 17, 1968); Pub. L. 95-616, § 3(i), 92 Stat. 3112 (Nov. 8, 1978)]

16 U.S.C. § 718g. Penalties. Any person who shall violate any provision of this Act, or who shall violate or fail to comply with any regulation made pursuant thereto shall be subject to the penalties provided in section 6 of the Migratory Bird Treaty Act [16 U.S.C. § 707].

[Mar. 16, 1934, ch. 71, § 7, 48 Stat. 452]

16 U.S.C. § 718h. Cooperation with States and Territories. The Secretary of the Interior is authorized to cooperate with the several States and Territories in the enforcement of the provisions of this Act.

[Mar. 16, 1934, ch. 71, § 8, 48 Stat. 452; 1939 Reorg. Plan No. II, § 4(f) (July 1, 1939), 4 Fed. Reg. 2731, 53 Stat. 1433]

16 U.S.C. § 718i. Repealed.

- 0 -

WETLANDS LOAN ACT (1961)
(16 U.S.C. §§ 715k-3 to 715k-5)

The revenue produced by the Stamp Act failed to keep pace with rising land costs and with the loss of wetlands. Congress responded in 1961 by enacting the Wetlands Loan Act. The Act originally was a loan to the Department of the Interior against future receipts from the sale of Duck Stamps. After increasing the appropriation from $105 to $200 million and extending the repayment date four times,[26] Congress forgave the repayment obligation in 1986.[27]

16 U.S.C. § 715k-3. Authorization of appropriations for the preservation of wetlands and other waterfowl habitat. In order to promote the conservation of migratory waterfowl and to offset or prevent the serious loss of important wetlands and other waterfowl habitat essential to the preservation of such waterfowl, there is authorized to be appropriated for the period beginning on July 1, 1961, and ending when all amounts authorized to be appropriated have been expended, not to exceed $200,000,000.

[Pub. L. 87-383, § 1, 75 Stat. 813 (Oct. 4, 1961); Pub. L. 90-205, § 81 Stat. 612 (Dec. 15, 1967); Pub. L. 94-215, § 2(a), 90 Stat. 189 (Feb. 17, 1976); Pub. L. 98-200, § 1, 97 Stat. 1378 (Dec. 2, 1983); Pub. L. 98-548, Title I, § 101, 98 Stat. 2774 (Oct. 26, 1984); Pub. L. 99-645, Title I, § 101(a), 100 Stat. 3584 (Nov. 10, 1986); Pub. L. 100-653, Title III, § 301, 102 Stat. 3827 (Nov. 14, 1988)]

16 U.S.C. § 715k-4. Accounting and use of appropriations. Funds appropriated each fiscal year pursuant to this Act [16 U.S.C. §§ 715k-3 to 715k-5] shall be accounted for, added to, and used for purposes of the migratory bird conservation fund established pursuant to section 4 the Migratory Bird Hunting Stamp Act of March 16, 1834, as amended [16 U.S.C. § 718d].

[Pub. L. 87-383, § 2, 75 Stat. 813 (Oct. 4, 1961)]

16 U.S.C. § 715k-5. Acquisition of lands. No land shall be acquired with moneys from the migratory bird conservation fund unless the acquisition thereof has been approved by the Governor of the State or appropriate State agency.

[Pub. L. 87-383, § 3, 75 Stat. 813 (Oct. 4, 1961); Pub. L. 90-205, § 1(b), 81 Stat. 612 (Dec. 15, 1967); Pub. L. 94-215, § 2(b), 90 Stat. 189 (Feb. 17, 1976); Pub. L. 98-200, § 2, 97 Stat. 1378 (Dec. 2, 1983); Pub. L. 98-548, Title I, § 102, 98 Stat. 2774 (Oct. 26, 1984); Pub. L. 99-645, Title I, § 101(b), 100 Stat. 3584 (Nov. 10, 1986)]

- 0 -

ii. Refuge Management

Federal lands are often managed through "systems" such as the National Park System and the National Forest System. Such systems share three broad similarities:

*** First, there is a designation process that specifies how lands are added to the system.

*** Second, there is a management standard that specifies how the lands within the system are to be managed.

*** Third, there is often an agency that is given responsibility for managing the lands in the system.

For example, lands may be added to the National Park System, either by Congress or (as National Monuments) by the President under the Antiquities Act.[28] Units of the system are managed pursuant to the schizophrenic use-and-preserve standard of the National Park Service Organic Act as well as the idiosyncratic exceptions, qualifications, and addenda that Congress or the President see fit to annex to the designation document.[29] Finally, the lands in the system are managed by the National Park Service, an agency within the Department of the Interior. Other examples of federal land management systems include the National Forest System, the National Wilderness Preservation System, and the Wild and Scenic River System.

The only federal land management system designated primarily to provide wildlife habitat is the National Wildlife Refuge System. Unlike most federal land management systems, there is no single method for adding lands to the system: lands have been designated as refuges by presidential proclamation, by specific statute, and pursuant to the procedures set out in the Migratory Bird Conservation Act.[30] Similarly, there was no general management standard. Only for lands added to the system under the Conservation Act was there *any* uniform management standard: the Act Migratory Bird Conservation specified that the lands were to be managed "as *inviolate sanctuaries* for migratory birds."[31] Indeed, until recently it was arguably a stretch to consider the federal government's wildlife refuges, wildlife ranges, game ranges, wildlife management areas, and waterfowl production areas to be a "system."

An additional point to note about federal land management systems. They fall along a continuum that can be characterized as stretching between multiple-use and dominant-use. For example, the National Forest System is the paradigm of a multiple-use system: the managing agency is charged with managing the forests to produce a wide range of resources and values ranging from commodities such as timber, forage, mushrooms, and whitewater-rafting days to values such as solitude, off-road vehicle days, and wildlife habitat. At the other extreme are dominant-use systems: lands that are to be used primarily for a single type of activity and where other activities are permitted to the extent that they are compatible with the dominant use. The National Wildlife Refuge System is perhaps the best example of a dominant-use land system.

Refuge Revenue Sharing Act (1935, 1956)
(16 U.S.C. § 715s)

In 1935, Congress provided that 25% "of all money received ... from the sale or other disposition of surplus wildlife, or of timber, hay, grass, or other spontaneous products of the soil ... and from other privileges on refuges established under the Migratory Bird Conservation Act ... shall be paid ... to the county or counties in which such refuge is situated, to be expended for the benefit of the public schools and roads."[32] These provisions were replaced by the current statute in 1964.[33]

The Refuge Revenue Sharing Act undercut the "inviolate sanctuary" conception of refuges by providing that revenues from "the sale or other disposition of animals, salmonoid cascassas [sic], timber, hay, grass, or other produce of the soil, minerals, shells, sand, or gravel ... incidental to but not in conflict with the basic purposes" of the refuge are to be paid to the counties in which refuges are located.[34] Like its predecessor, the current Revenue Sharing Act embodies an assumption that such uses are permissible.

The gradual accretion of non-wildlife uses continued: in 1949, Congress raised the cost of a duck stamp from $1 to $2 and in exchange agreed to allow hunting on up to 25% of each refuge;[35] when the cost of a stamp was increased to $3 in 1958, hunting was allowed on up to 40% of each refuge.[36] Like the Refuge Revenue Sharing Act, the expansion of hunting on refuges increased political pressure to open refuges to such a variety of income-producing activities.

16 U.S.C. § 715s. Participation of local governments in revenue from areas administered by United States Fish and Wildlife Service. (a) Separate fund in United States Treasury; availability of funds until expended; "National Wildlife Refuge System" defined. Beginning with the next full fiscal year and for each fiscal year thereafter, all revenues received by the Secretary of the Interior from the sale or other disposition of animals, salmonoid carcassas [sic], timber, hay, grass, or other products of the soil, minerals, shells, sand, or gravel, from other privileges, or from leases for public accommodations or facilities incidental to but not in conflict with the basic purposes for which those areas of the National Wildlife Refuge System were established, during each fiscal year in connection with the operation and management of those areas of the National Wildlife Refuge System, National Fish Hatcheries, or other areas, that are solely or primarily administered by him, through the United States Fish and Wildlife Service, shall be covered into the United States Treasury and be reserved in a separate fund for disposition as hereafter prescribed. Amounts in the fund shall remain available until expended, and may be expended by the Secretary without further appropriation in the manner hereafter prescribed. The National Wildlife Refuge System (hereafter referred to as the "System") includes those lands and waters administered by the Secretary as wildlife refuges, lands acquired or reserved for the protection and conservation of fish and wildlife that are listed pursuant to section 4 of the Endangered Species Act of 1973 [16 U.S.C. § 1533] as endangered species or threatened species, wildlife ranges, game ranges, wildlife management areas, and waterfowl production areas established under any law, proclamation, Executive, or public land order.

(b) Deduction of expenses. The Secretary may pay from the fund any necessary expenses incurred by him in connection with the revenue-producing and revenue-sharing measures.

(c) Payments to counties. (1) The Secretary shall pay out of the fund, for each fiscal year beginning with the fiscal year ending September 30, 1979, to each county in which is situated any fee area whichever of the following amounts is greater:

(A) An amount equal to the product of 75 cents multiplied by the total acreage of that portion of the fee area which is located within such county.

(B) An amount equal to three-fourths of 1 per centum of the fair market value, as determined by the Secretary, of that portion of the fee area (excluding any improvements thereto made after the date of Federal acquisition) which is located within such county.

(C) An amount equal to 25 per centum of the net receipts collected by the Secretary in connection with the operation and management of such fee area during such fiscal year; but if a fee area is located in two or more counties, the amount each such county is entitled to shall be the amount which bears to such 25 per centum the same ratio as that portion of the fee area acreage which is within such county bears to the total acreage of such fee area.

(2) At the end of each fiscal year the Secretary shall pay out of the fund for such fiscal year to each county in which any reserve area is situated, an amount equal to 25 per centum of the net receipts collected by the Secretary in connection with the operation and management of such area during such fiscal year: *Provided,* That when any such area is situated in more than one county the distributive share to each county from the aforesaid receipts shall be proportional to its acreage of such reserve area.

(3) For purposes of this section, the Commonwealth of Puerto Rico, Guam, and the Virgin Islands shall each be treated as a county.

(4)(A) For purposes of determining the fair market value of fee areas under paragraph (1)(B), the Secretary shall --

(i) appraise before September 30, 1979, all fee areas for which payments under this section were not authorized for fiscal years occurring before October 1, 1977; and

(ii) appraise all other fee areas, within five years after October 17, 1978, in the order in which such areas were first established by the Service.

After initial appraisal under clause (i) or (ii), each fee area shall thereafter be reappraised by the Secretary at least once during each five-year period occurring after the date of the initial appraisal. Until any fee area referred to in clause (ii) is initially appraised under this subparagraph, the fair market value of such area shall be deemed to be that adjusted cost of the area which was used to determine payments under this subsection for fiscal year 1977; and in no case may the amount of any payment to any local government under paragraph (1)(B) with respect to any fee area be less than the amount paid under paragraph (2)(A) of this subsection (as in effect on September 30, 1977) with respect to such area.

(B) The Secretary shall make the determinations required under this subsection in such manner as the Secretary considers to be equitable and in the public interest. All such determinations shall be final and conclusive.

(5)(A) Each county which receives payments under paragraphs (1) and (2) with respect to any fee area or reserve area shall distribute, under guidelines established by the Secretary, such payments on a proportional basis to those units of local government (including, but not limited to, school districts and the county itself in appropriate cases) which have incurred the loss or reduction of real property tax revenues by reason of the existence of such area. In any case in which a unit of local government other than the county acts as the collecting and distributing agency for real property taxes, the payments under paragraphs (1) and (2) shall be made to such other unit which shall distribute the payments in accordance with the guidelines.

(B) The Secretary may prescribe regulations under which payments under this paragraph may be made to units of local government in cases in which subparagraph (A) will not effect the purposes of this paragraph.

(C) Payments received by units of local government under this subsection may be used by such units for any governmental purpose.

(d) Authorization of appropriations equal to difference between amount of net receipts and aggregate amount of required payments. If the net receipts in the fund which are attributable to revenue collections for any fiscal year do not equal the aggregate amount of payments required to be made for such fiscal year under subsection (c) of this section to counties, there are authorized to be appropriated to the fund an amount equal to the difference between the total amount of net receipts and such aggregate amount of payments.

(e) Transfer and use of excess of net receipts over aggregate amount of required payments. If the net receipts in the fund which are attributable to revenue collections for any fiscal year exceed the aggregate amount of payments required to be made for such fiscal year under subsection (c) of this section to counties, the amount of such excess shall be transferred to the Migratory Bird Conservation Fund for use in the acquisition of suitable areas for migratory bird refuges under the provisions of the Migratory Bird Conservation Act (16 U.S.C. 715 to 715r).

(f) Terms, conditions, and regulations for execution of revenue producing activities; disposal of animals. The Secretary shall carry out any revenue producing activity referred to in subsection (a)(1), (2), and (3) of this section within any fee area or reserve area subject to such terms, conditions, or regulations, including sales in the open markets, as the Secretary determines to be in the best interest of the United States. The Secretary may, in accordance with such regulations as the Secretary may prescribe, dispose of animals which are surplus to any such area by exchange of the same or other kinds, gift or loan to public institutions for exhibition or propagation purposes, and for the advancement of knowledge and the dissemination of information relating to the conservation of wildlife.

(g) Definitions. As used in this section --

(1) The term "Secretary" means the Secretary of the Interior.

(2) The term "fee area" means any area which was acquired in fee by the United

States and is administered, either solely or primarily, by the Secretary through the Service.
(3) The term "reserve area" means any area of land withdrawn from the public domain and administered, either solely or primarily, by the Secretary through the Service.
(4) The term "Service" means the United States Fish and Wildlife Service.
(5) The term "county" means any county, parish, or organized or unorganized borough.

[June 15, 1935, ch. 261, Title IV, § 401, 49 Stat. 383; 1939 Reorg. Plan No. II, § 4(f) (July 1, 1939), 4 Fed. Reg. 2731, 53 Stat. 1433; 1940 Reorg. Plan No. III, § 3 (June 30, 1940), 5 Fed. Reg. 2108, 54 Stat. 1232; Oct. 31, 1951, ch. 654, § 2(13), 65 Stat. 707; Pub. L. 88-523, 78 Stat. 701 (Aug. 30, 1964); Pub. L. 89-669, § 8(b), 80 Stat. 930 (Oct. 15, 1966); Pub. L. 93-205, § 13(b), 87 Stat. 902 (Dec. 28, 1973); Pub. L. 93-509, § 4, 88 Stat. 1603 (Dec. 3, 1974); Pub. L. 95-469, § 1(a), 92 Stat. 1319 (Oct. 17, 1978); Pub. L. 97-258, § 5(b), 96 Stat. 1068 (Sept. 13, 1982)]

- 0 -

REFUGE TRESPASS ACT (1948)
(18 U.S.C. § 41)

In 1948, Congress consolidated the penalty provisions of the various acts it had adopted from 1905 through 1934 that had established federal wildlife areas.[37] The statute restated Congress' intent to protect all wildlife within federal sanctuaries. The Act imposed a fine of not more than $500 and imprisonment of not more than 6 months.

The statute was largely superseded -- though not repealed --by a 1988 statute that subjected violators of the Refuge System Administration Act and its implementing regulations to the penalties provided by the uniform sentencing provisions of title 18.[38]

18 U.S.C. § 41. Hunting, fishing, trapping; disturbance or injury on wildlife refuges. Whoever, except in compliance with rules and regulations promulgated by authority of law, hunts, traps, captures, willfully disturbs or kills any bird, fish, or wild animal of any kind whatever, or takes or destroys the eggs or nest of any such bird or fish, on any lands or waters which are set apart or reserved as sanctuaries, refuges or breeding grounds for such birds, fish, or animals under any law of the United States or willfully injures, molests, or destroys any property of the United States on any such lands or waters, shall be fined under this title or imprisoned not more than six months, or both.

[June 25, 1948, ch. 645, 62 Stat. 686; Pub. L. 103-322, Title XXXIII, § 330016(1)(G), 108 Stat. 2147 (Sept. 13, 1994)]

- 0 -

REFUGE RECREATION ACT (1962)
(16 U.S.C. §§ 460k to 460k-1)

In 1962, Congress enacted the first general administrative standards for the refuges.[39] The Refuge Recreation Act of 1962 authorized the Secretary to permit "public recreation" if it is "compatible with, and will not prevent the accomplishment of, the primary purposes" for which the refuge was acquired, "*Provided*, That such public recreation use shall be permitted only to the extent that is practicable and not inconsistent with ... the primary objectives for which each particular area is established."[40]

Although the Recreation Act marked a significant step away from the "inviolate sanctuaries" standard of the Conservation Act, it introduced an important concept: "compatibility." By specifying that the agency was required to manage refuges in a manner compatible with the purposes of the refuge, those purposes became the dominant use of the land. The management uniformity produced by the compatibility standard is, however, often more apparent than real. In 1966, the system included some 300 refuges totalling 28 million acres and containing a diverse range of habitat types from dwarf tundra in arctic Alaska to sub-tropical forests in Hawaii and Puerto Rico.[41] Since "compatibility" focuses on the purposes for which the *unit* was established, there remains the potential for substantial differences between units: a refuge that was acquired to protect an endangered species, for example, is likely to have a different set of compatible uses than is a migratory waterfowl refuge.

16 U.S.C. § 460k. Public recreation use of fish and wildlife conservation areas; compatibility with conservation purposes; appropriate incidental or secondary use; consistency with other Federal operations and primary objectives of particular areas; curtailment; forms of recreation not directly related to primary purposes of individual areas; repeal or amendment of provisions for particular areas. In recognition of mounting public demands for recreational opportunities on areas within the National Wildlife Refuge System, national fish hatcheries, and other conservation areas administered by the Secretary of the Interior for fish and wildlife purposes; and in recognition also of the resulting imperative need, if such recreational opportunities are provided, to assure that any present or future recreational use will be compatible with, and will not prevent accomplishment of, the primary purposes for which the said conservation areas were acquired or established, the Secretary of the Interior is authorized, as an appropriate incidental or secondary use, to administer such areas or parts thereof for public recreation when in his judgment public recreation can be an appropriate incidental or secondary use: *Provided,* That such public recreation use shall be permitted only to the extent that is practicable and not inconsistent with other previously authorized Federal operations or with the primary objectives for which each particular area is established: *Provided further,* That in order to insure accomplishment of such primary objectives, the Secretary, after consideration of all authorized uses, purposes, and other pertinent factors relating to individual areas, shall curtail public recreation use generally or certain types of public recreation use within individual areas or in portions thereof whenever he considers such action to be necessary: *And provided further,* That none of the aforesaid refuges,

hatcheries, game ranges, and other conservation areas shall be used during any fiscal year for those forms of recreation that are not directly related to the primary purposes and functions of the individual areas until the Secretary shall have determined --
(a) that such recreational use will not interfere with the primary purposes for which the areas were established, and
(b) that funds are available for the development, operation, and maintenance of these permitted forms of recreation. This section shall not be construed to repeal or amend previous enactments relating to particular areas.

[Pub. L. 87-714, § 1, 76 Stat. 653 (Sept. 28, 1962); Pub. L. 89-669, § 9, 80 Stat. 930 (Oct. 15, 1966)]

16 U.S.C. § 460k-1. Acquisition of lands for recreational development; funds. The Secretary is authorized to acquire areas of land, or interests therein, which are suitable for --

(1) incidental fish and wildlife-oriented recreational development,
(2) the protection of natural resources,
(3) the conservation of endangered species or threatened species listed by the Secretary pursuant to section 4 of the Endangered Species Act of 1973 [16 U.S.C. § 1533], or
(4) carrying out two or more of the purposes set forth in paragraphs (1) through (3) of this section, and are adjacent to, or within, the said conservation areas, except that the acquisition of any land or interest therein pursuant to this section shall be accomplished only with such funds as may be appropriated therefor by the Congress or donated for such purposes, but such property shall not be acquired with funds obtained from the sale of Federal migratory bird hunting stamps.

Lands acquired pursuant to this section shall become a part of the particular conservation area to which they are adjacent.

[Pub. L. 87-714, § 2, 76 Stat. 653 (Sept. 28, 1962); Pub. L. 92-534, Oct. 23, 1972, 86 Stat. 1063; Pub. L. 93-205, § 13(d), Dec. 28, 1973, 87 Stat. 902.)

16 U.S.C. § 460k-2. Cooperation with agencies, organizations and individuals; acceptance of donations; restrictive covenants. In furtherance of the purposes of this Act [16 U.S.C. §§ 460k *et seq.*], the Secretary is authorized to cooperate with public and private agencies, organizations, and individuals, and he may accept and use, without further authorization, donations of funds and real and personal property. Such acceptance may be accomplished under the terms and conditions of restrictive covenants imposed by donors when such covenants are deemed by the Secretary to be compatible with the purposes of the wildlife refuges, games ranges, fish hatcheries, and other fish and wildlife conservation areas.

[Pub. L. 87-714, § 3, 76 Stat. 653 (Sept. 28, 1962)]

16 U.S.C. § 460k-3. Charges and fees; permits; regulations; penalties; enforcement. The Secretary may establish reasonable charges and fees and issue permits for public use of national wildlife refuges, game ranges, national fish hatcheries, and other conservation areas administered by the Department of the Interior for fish and wildlife purposes. The

Secretary may issue regulations to carry out the purposes of this Act [16 U.S.C. §§ 460k *et seq.*]. A violation of such regulations shall be a misdemeanor with maximum penalties of imprisonment for not more than six months, or a fine of not more than $500, or both. The provisions of this Act [16 U.S.C. §§ 460k *et seq.*] and any such regulation shall be enforced by any officer or employee of the United States Fish and Wildlife Service designated by the Secretary of the Interior.

[Pub. L. 87-714, § 4, 76 Stat. 654 (Sept. 28, 1962); Pub. L. 95-616, § 3(e), 92 Stat. 3111 (Nov. 8, 1978); Pub. L. 98-473, Title II, § 221, 98 Stat. 2028 (Oct. 12, 1984)]

16 U.S.C. § 460k-4. Authorization of appropriations. There is authorized to be appropriated such funds as may be necessary to carry out the purposes of this Act [16 U.S.C. §§ 460k *et seq.*], including the construction and maintenance of public recreational facilities.

[Pub. L. 87-714, § 5, 76 Stat. 654 (Sept. 28, 1962)]

\- 0 -

REFUGE ADMINISTRATION ACT (1966)
NATIONAL WILDLIFE REFUGE SYSTEM IMPROVEMENT ACT (1997)
(16 U.S.C. 16 U.S.C. §§ 668dd-668ee)

The Refuge Administration Act of 1966[42] was Congress' initial attempt to fashion a National Wildlife Refuge System out of the five types of areas that had been set aside for wildlife conservation purposes -- wildlife refuges, wildlife ranges, game ranges, wildlife management areas, and waterfowl production areas.[43] Compounding the variety of land designations were the variety of methods of designating lands for wildlife conservation: by executive withdrawal; through an exchange or purchase funded by statutes such as the Migratory Bird Conservation Act, the Land and Water Conservation Fund, or the Endangered Species Act; through an independent act of Congress; by transfers from other land managing agencies such as the Army Corps of Engineers; and by donation.[44] The ad hoc nature of the various procedures used to designate refuges produced wide variation in the management standards applicable to individual units. The Refuge Recreation Act had introduced the concept of "consistency" as a dominant management criterion,[45] but that Act's focus on recreation left many types of activities unaffected.

The Administration Act sought to rectify this problem by "consolidat[ing] and clarif[ying]" the agency's authority[46] to manage the units within the refuge system. The Act did so by prohibiting most activities unless they were permitted "under the express provisions of some other law, proclamation, Executive order, or public land order establishing the area,"[47] or they were found "to be compatible with the purposes for which such areas were established."[48] Thus, all activities were either required to be expressly authorized or found to be compatible with the wildlife conservation purposes of the system. But neither the Recreation Act nor the Administration Act contained any definition of "compatible."

In 1997, Congress revisited the management requirements when it enacted the National Wildlife Refuge System Improvement Act (RIA).[49] The RIA sought to remedy the perceived shortcomings in the existing management structure. First, existing law did not "include a mission or a definition of 'compatible use'" and this "lack of an overall mission and management procedures had allowed numerous incompatible uses to be tolerated on wildlife refuges."[50] The Act therefore includes "an overarching mission statement ... to guide overall management of the System and to supplement the purposes for which individual refuges have been established"[51] -- "to administer a national network of lands and waters for the conservation, management, and where appropriate, restoration of the fish, wildlife, and plant resources and their habitats within the United States for the benefit of present and future generations of Americans."[52]

The Act addressed the lack of a definition of "compatible use" both by defining the term -- "a wildlife-dependent recreational use or any other use of a refuge that, in the sound professional judgment of the Director, will not materially interfere with or detract from the fulfillment of the mission of the System or the purposes of the refuge"[53] -- and by specifying procedures for making compatibility determinations.[54]

The Act also sought to address the lack of planning by requiring the Fish and Wildlife Service to develop "comprehensive conservation plans" for the refuges. A recurrent theme in the management of federal land systems has been an increasing emphasis on land-use planning. The National Forest Management Act requires the National Forest Service to prepare land management plans for each forest.[55] The Federal Land Policy and Management Act imposed similar planning obligations on the Bureau of Land Management.[56] The Refuge Improvement Act requires FWS to develop plans for each refuge or complex of refuges.[57] The Plans are important because the agency is required to manage the refuges "in a manner consistent with the plan."[58]

Finally, the Act provided penalties and enforcement provisions.[59]

16 U.S.C. § 668dd. National Wildlife Refuge System. (a) Designation; administration; continuance of resources-management-programs for refuge lands in Alaska; disposal of acquired lands; proceeds.

(1) For the purpose of consolidating the authorities relating to the various categories of areas that are administered by the Secretary for the conservation of fish and wildlife, including species that are threatened with extinction, all lands, waters, and interests therein administered by the Secretary as wildlife refuges, areas for the protection and conservation of fish and wildlife that are threatened with extinction, wildlife ranges, game ranges, wildlife management areas, or waterfowl production areas are hereby designated as the "National Wildlife Refuge System" (referred to herein as the "System"), which shall be subject to the provisions of this section, and shall be administered by the Secretary through the United States Fish and Wildlife Service. With respect to refuge lands in the State of Alaska, those programs relating to the management of resources for which any other agency of the Federal Government exercises administrative responsibility through cooperative agreement shall remain in effect, subject to the direct supervision of the United States Fish and

Wildlife Service, as long as such agency agrees to exercise such responsibility.

(2) The mission of the System is to administer a national network of lands and waters for the conservation, management, and where appropriate, restoration of the fish, wildlife, and plant resources and their habitats within the United States for the benefit of present and future generations of Americans.

(3) With respect to the System, it is the policy of the United States that --

(A) each refuge shall be managed to fulfill the mission of the System, as well as the specific purposes for which that refuge was established;

(B) compatible wildlife-dependent recreation is a legitimate and appropriate general public use of the System, directly related to the mission of the System and the purposes of many refuges, and which generally fosters refuge management and through which the American public can develop an appreciation for fish and wildlife;

(C) compatible wildlife-dependent recreational uses are the priority general public uses of the System and shall receive priority consideration in refuge planning and management; and

(D) when the Secretary determines that a proposed wildlife-dependent recreational use is a compatible use within a refuge, that activity should be facilitated, subject to such restrictions or regulations as may be necessary, reasonable, and appropriate.

(4) In administering the System, the Secretary shall --

(A) provide for the conservation of fish, wildlife, and plants, and their habitats within the System;

(B) ensure that the biological integrity, diversity, and environmental health of the System are maintained for the benefit of present and future generations of Americans;

(C) plan and direct the continued growth of the System in a manner that is best designed to accomplish the mission of the System, to contribute to the conservation of the ecosystems of the United States, to complement efforts of States and other Federal agencies to conserve fish and wildlife and their habitats, and to increase support for the System and participation from conservation partners and the public;

(D) ensure that the mission of the System described in paragraph (2) and the purposes of each refuge are carried out, except that if a conflict exists between the purposes of a refuge and the mission of the System, the conflict shall be resolved in a manner that first protects the purposes of the refuge, and, to the extent practicable, that also achieves the mission of the System;

(E) ensure effective coordination, interaction, and cooperation with owners of land adjoining refuges and the fish and wildlife agency of the States in which the units of the System are located;

(F) assist in the maintenance of adequate water quantity and water quality to fulfill the mission of the System and the purposes of each refuge;

(G) acquire, under State law, water rights that are needed for refuge purposes;

(H) recognize compatible wildlife-dependent recreational uses as the priority general public uses of the System through which the American public can develop an appreciation for fish and wildlife;

(I) ensure that opportunities are provided within the System for compatible wildlife-dependent recreational uses;

(J) ensure that priority general public uses of the System receive enhanced consideration over other general public uses in planning and management within the System;

(K) provide increased opportunities for families to experience compatible wildlife-dependent recreation, particularly opportunities for parents and their children to safely engage in traditional outdoor activities, such as fishing and hunting;

(L) continue, consistent with existing laws and interagency agreements, authorized or permitted uses of units of the System by other Federal agencies, including those necessary to facilitate military preparedness;

(M) ensure timely and effective cooperation and collaboration with Federal agencies and State fish and wildlife agencies during the course of acquiring and managing refuges; and

(N) monitor the status and trends of fish, wildlife, and plants in each refuge.

(5) No acquired lands which are or become a part of the System may be transferred or otherwise disposed of under any provision of law (except by exchange pursuant to subsection (b)(3) of this section) unless --

(A) the Secretary determines with the approval of the Migratory Bird Conservation Commission that such lands are no longer needed for the purposes for which the System was established; and

(B) such lands are transferred or otherwise disposed of for an amount not less than --

(i) the acquisition costs of such lands, in the case of lands of the System which were purchased by the United States with funds from the migratory bird conservation fund, or fair market value, whichever is greater; or

(ii) the fair market value of such lands (as determined by the Secretary as of the date of the transfer or disposal), in the case of lands of the System which were donated to the System.

The Secretary shall pay into the migratory bird conservation fund the aggregate amount of the proceeds of any transfer or disposal referred to in the preceding sentence.

(6) Each area which is included within the System on January 1, 1975, or thereafter, and which was or is --

(A) designated as an area within such System by law, Executive order, or secretarial order; or

(B) so included by public land withdrawal, donation, purchase, exchange, or pursuant to a cooperative agreement with any State or local government, any Federal department or agency, or any other governmental entity,

shall continue to be a part of the System until otherwise specified by Act of Congress, except that nothing in this paragraph shall be construed as precluding --

(i) the transfer or disposal of acquired lands within any such area pursuant to paragraph (5) of this subsection;

(ii) the exchange of lands within any such area pursuant to subsection (b)(3) of this section; or

(iii) the disposal of any lands within any such area pursuant to the terms of any cooperative agreement referred to in subparagraph (B) of this paragraph.

(b) Administration; public accommodations contracts; acceptance and use of funds; exchange of properties; cash equalization payments. In administering the System, the Secretary is authorized to take the following actions:

(1) Enter into contracts with any person or public or private agency through negotiation for the provision of public accommodations when, and in such locations, and to the extent that the Secretary determines will not be inconsistent with the primary purpose for which the affected area was established.

(2) Accept donations of funds and to use such funds to acquire or manage lands or interests therein.

(3) Acquire lands or interests therein by exchange (A) for acquired lands or public lands, or for interests in acquired or public lands, under his jurisdiction which he finds to be suitable for disposition, or (B) for the right to remove, in accordance with such terms and conditions as he may prescribe, products from the acquired or public lands within the System. The values of the properties so exchanged either shall be approximately equal, or if they are not approximately equal the values shall be equalized by the payment of cash to the grantor or to the Secretary as the circumstances require.

(4) Subject to standards established by and the overall management oversight of the Director, and consistent with standards established by this Act, to enter into cooperative agreements with State fish and wildlife agencies for the management of programs on a refuge.

(5) Issue regulations to carry out this Act.

(c) Prohibited and permitted activities; application of mining and mineral leasing laws, hunting or fishing regulations, and State laws or regulations. No person shall disturb, injure, cut, burn, remove, destroy, or possess any real or personal property of the United States, including natural growth, in any area of the System; or take or possess any fish, bird, mammal, or other wild vertebrate or invertebrate animals or part or nest or egg thereof within any such area; or enter, use, or otherwise occupy any such area for any purpose; unless such activities are performed by persons authorized to manage such area, or unless such activities are permitted either under subsection (d) of this section or by express provision of the law, proclamation, Executive order, or public land order establishing the area, or amendment thereof: *Provided,* That the United States mining and mineral leasing laws shall continue to apply to any lands within the System to the same extent they apply prior to October 15, 1966, unless subsequently withdrawn under other authority of law. With the exception of endangered species and threatened species listed by the Secretary pursuant to section 4 of the Endangered Species Act of 1973 [16 U.S.C. § 1533] in States wherein a cooperative agreement does not exist pursuant to section 4(c) of the Endangered Species Act of 1973 [16 U.S.C. § 1535(c)], nothing in this Act shall be construed to authorize the Secretary to control or regulate hunting or fishing of resident fish and wildlife on lands not within the system. The regulations permitting hunting and fishing of resident fish and wildlife within the System shall be, to the extent practicable, consistent with State fish and wildlife laws and regulations.

(d) Use of areas; administration of migratory bird sanctuaries as game taking areas; rights of way, easements, and reservations; payment of fair market value.

(1) The Secretary is authorized, under such regulations as he may prescribe, to --

(A) permit the use of any area within the System for any purpose, including but not limited to hunting, fishing, public recreation and accommodations, and access whenever he determines that such uses are compatible with the major purposes for which such areas were established: *Provided,* That not to exceed 40 per centum at any one time of any area that has been, or hereafter may be acquired, reserved, or set apart as an inviolate sanctuary for migratory birds, under any law, proclamation, Executive order, or public land order may be administered by the Secretary as an area within which the taking of migratory game birds may be permitted under such regulations as he may prescribe unless the Secretary finds that the taking of any species of migratory game birds in more than 40 percent of such area would be beneficial to the species; and

(B) permit the use of, or grant easements in, over, across, upon, through, or under any areas within the System for purposes such as but not necessarily limited to, powerlines, telephone lines, canals, ditches, pipelines, and roads, including the construction, operation, and maintenance thereof, whenever he determines that such uses are compatible with the purposes for which these areas are established.

(2) Notwithstanding any other provision of law, the Secretary may not grant to any Federal, State, or local agency or to any private individual or organization any right-of-way, easement, or reservation in, over, across, through, or under any area within the system in connection with any use permitted by him under paragraph (1)(B) of this subsection unless the grantee pays to the Secretary, at the option of the Secretary, either (A) in lump sum the fair market value (determined by the Secretary as of the date of conveyance to the grantee) of the right-of-way, easement, or reservation; or (B) annually in advance the fair market rental value (determined by the Secretary) of the right-of-way, easement, or reservation. If any Federal, State, or local agency is exempted from such payment by any other provision of Federal law, such agency shall otherwise compensate the Secretary by any other means agreeable to the Secretary, including, but not limited to, making other land available or the loan of equipment or personnel; except that (A) any such compensation shall relate to, and be consistent with, the objectives of the National Wildlife Refuge System, and (B) the Secretary may waive such requirement for compensation if he finds such requirement impracticable or unnecessary. All sums received by the Secretary of the Interior pursuant to this paragraph shall, after payment of any necessary expenses incurred by him in administering this paragraph, be deposited into the Migratory Bird Conservation Fund and shall be available to carry out the provisions for land acquisition of the Migratory Bird Conservation Act (16 U.S.C. § 715 *et seq.*) and the Migratory Bird Hunting Stamp Act (16 U.S.C. § 718 *et seq.*).

(3)(A)(i) Except as provided in clause (iv), the Secretary shall not initiate or permit a new use of a refuge or expand, renew, or extend an existing use of a refuge, unless the Secretary has determined that the use is a compatible use and that the use is not inconsistent with public safety. The Secretary may make the determinations referred to in this paragraph for a refuge concurrently with development of a conservation plan under subsection (e).

(ii) On lands added to the System after March 25, 1996, the Secretary shall identify, prior to acquisition, withdrawal, transfer, reclassification, or donation of any such lands, existing compatible wildlife-dependent recreational uses that the Secretary determines shall be permitted to continue on an interim basis pending completion of the comprehensive conservation plan for the refuge.

(iii) Wildlife-dependent recreational uses may be authorized on a refuge when they are compatible and not inconsistent with public safety. Except for consideration of consistency with State laws and regulations as provided for in subsection (m), no other determinations or findings are required to be made by the refuge official under this Act or the Refuge Recreation Act for wildlife-dependent recreation to occur.

(iv) Compatibility determinations in existence on October 9, 1997 shall remain in effect until and unless modified.

(B) Not later than 24 months after the date of the enactment of the National Wildlife Refuge System Improvement Act of 1997 [October 9, 1997], the Secretary shall issue final regulations establishing the process for determining under subparagraph (A) whether a use of a refuge is a compatible use. These regulations shall --

(i) designate the refuge official responsible for making initial compatibility determinations;

(ii) require an estimate of the timeframe, location, manner, and purpose of each use;

(iii) identify the effects of each use on refuge resources and purposes of each refuge;

(iv) require that compatibility determinations be made in writing;

(v) provide for the expedited consideration of uses that will likely have no detrimental effect on the fulfillment of the purposes of a refuge or the mission of the System;

(vi) provide for the elimination or modification of any use as expeditiously as practicable after a determination is made that the use is not a compatible use;

(vii) require, after an opportunity for public comment, reevaluation of each existing use, other than those uses specified in clause (viii), if conditions under which the use is permitted change significantly or if there is significant new information regarding the effects of the use, but not less frequently than once every 10 years, to ensure that the use remains a compatible use, except that, in the case of any use authorized for a period longer than 10 years (such as an electric utility right-of-way), the reevaluation required by this clause shall examine compliance with the terms and conditions of the authorization, not examine the authorization itself;

(viii) require, after an opportunity for public comment, reevaluation of each compatible wildlife-dependent recreational use when conditions under which the use is permitted change significantly or if there is significant new information regarding the effects of the use, but not less frequently than in conjunction with each preparation or revision of a conservation plan under subsection (e) of this section or at least every 15 years, whichever is earlier; and

(ix) provide an opportunity for public review and comment on each evaluation of a use, unless an opportunity for public review and comment on the evaluation of the use has already been provided during the development or revision of a conservation plan for the refuge under subsection (e) of this section or has otherwise been provided during routine, periodic determinations of compatibility for wildlife-dependent recreational uses.

(4) The provisions of this Act relating to determinations of the compatibility of a use shall not apply to --

(A) overflights above a refuge; and

(B) activities authorized, funded, or conducted by a Federal agency (other than the United States Fish and Wildlife Service) which has primary jurisdiction over a refuge or a portion of a refuge, if the management of those activities is in accordance with a memorandum of understanding between the Secretary or the Director and the head of the Federal agency with primary jurisdiction over the refuge governing the use of the refuge.

(e) Refuge conservation planning program for non-Alaskan refuge lands.

(1)(A) Except with respect to refuge lands in Alaska (which shall be governed by the refuge planning provisions of the Alaska National Interest Lands Conservation Act (16 U.S.C. §§ 3101 *et seq.*)), the Secretary shall --

(i) propose a comprehensive conservation plan for each refuge or related complex of refuges (referred to in this subsection as a "planning unit") in the System;

(ii) publish a notice of opportunity for public comment in the Federal Register on each proposed conservation plan;

(iii) issue a final conservation plan for each planning unit consistent with the provisions of this Act and, to the extent practicable, consistent with fish and wildlife conservation plans of the State in which the refuge is located; and

(iv) not less frequently than 15 years after the date of issuance of a conservation plan under clause (iii) and every 15 years thereafter, revise the conservation plan as may be necessary.

(B) The Secretary shall prepare a comprehensive conservation plan under this subsection for each refuge within 15 years of the date of the enactment of the National Wildlife Refuge System Improvement Act of 1997 [October 9, 1997].

(C) The Secretary shall manage each refuge or planning unit under plans in effect on the date of the enactment of the National Wildlife Refuge System Improvement Act of 1997 [October 9, 1997], to the extent such plans are consistent with this Act, until such plans are revised or superseded by new comprehensive conservation plans issued under this subsection.

(D) Uses or activities consistent with this Act may occur on any refuge or planning unit before existing plans are revised or new comprehensive conservation plans are issued under this subsection.

(E) Upon completion of a comprehensive conservation plan under this subsection for a refuge or planning unit, the Secretary shall manage the refuge or planning unit in a manner consistent with the plan and shall revise the plan at any time if the Secretary determines that conditions that affect the refuge or planning unit have changed significantly.

(2) In developing each comprehensive conservation plan under this subsection for a planning unit, the Secretary, acting through the Director, shall identify and describe --

(A) the purposes of each refuge comprising the planning unit;

(B) the distribution, migration patterns, and abundance of fish, wildlife, and plant populations and related habitats within the planning unit;

(C) the archaeological and cultural values of the planning unit;

(D) such areas within the planning unit that are suitable for use as administrative sites or visitor facilities;

(E) significant problems that may adversely affect the populations and habitats of fish, wildlife, and plants within the planning unit and the actions necessary to correct or mitigate such problems; and

(F) opportunities for compatible wildlife-dependent recreational uses.

(3) In preparing each comprehensive conservation plan under this subsection, and any revision to such a plan, the Secretary, acting through the Director, shall, to the maximum extent practicable and consistent with this Act --

(A) consult with adjoining Federal, State, local, and private landowners and affected State conservation agencies; and

(B) coordinate the development of the conservation plan or revision with relevant State conservation plans for fish and wildlife and their habitats.

(4)(A) In accordance with subparagraph (B), the Secretary shall develop and implement a process to ensure an opportunity for active public involvement in the preparation and revision of comprehensive conservation plans under this subsection. At a minimum, the Secretary shall require that publication of any final plan shall include a summary of the comments made by States, owners of adjacent or potentially affected land, local governments, and any other affected persons, and a statement of the disposition of concerns expressed in those comments.

(B) Prior to the adoption of each comprehensive conservation plan under this subsection, the Secretary shall issue public notice of the draft proposed plan, make copies of the plan available at the affected field and regional offices of the United States Fish and Wildlife Service, and provide opportunity for public comment.

(f) Penalties. (1) Knowing violations. Any person who knowingly violates or fails to comply with any of the provisions of this Act or any regulations issued thereunder shall be fined under Title 18, or imprisoned for not more than 1 year, or both.

(2) Other violations. Any person who otherwise violates or fails to comply with any of the provisions of this Act (including a regulation issued under this Act) shall be fined under Title 18, or imprisoned not more than 180 days, or both.

(g) Enforcement of provisions; arrest, search, and seizure; custody of property; forfeiture upon conviction; use of other Federal or State agency personnel and services. Any person authorized by the Secretary to enforce the provisions of this Act or any regulations issued thereunder, may, without a warrant, arrest any person violating this Act or regulations in his presence or view, and may execute any warrant or other process issued by an officer or court of competent jurisdiction to enforce the provisions of this Act or regulations, and may with a search warrant search for and seize any property, fish, bird, mammal, or other wild vertebrate or invertebrate animals or part or nest or egg thereof, taken or possessed in violation of this Act or the regulations issued thereunder. Any property, fish, bird, mammal, or other wild vertebrate or invertebrate animals or part or egg thereof seized with or without a search warrant shall be held by such person or by a United States marshal, and upon conviction, shall be forfeited to the United States and disposed of by the Secretary, in accordance with law. The Director of the United States Fish and Wildlife Service is authorized to utilize by agreement, with or without reimbursement, the personnel and services of any other Federal or State agency for purposes of enhancing the enforcement of this Act.

(h) Regulations; continuation, modification, or rescission. Regulations applicable to areas of the System that are in effect on October 15, 1966, shall continue in effect until modified or rescinded.

(i) National conservation recreational area provisions; amendment, repeal, or modification. Nothing in this section shall be construed to amend, repeal, or otherwise modify the provision of the Act of September 28, 1962 [Refuge Recreation Act, 76 Stat. 653, 16 U.S.C. §§ 460k to 460k-4] which authorizes the Secretary to administer the areas within the System for public recreation. The provisions of this section relating to recreation shall be administered in accordance with the provisions of said sections.

(j) Exemption from State water laws. Nothing in this Act shall constitute an express or implied claim or denial on the part of the Federal Government as to exemption from State water laws.

(k) Emergency power. Notwithstanding any other provision of this Act, the Secretary may temporarily suspend, allow, or initiate any activity in a refuge in the System if the Secretary determines it is necessary to protect the health and safety of the public or any fish or wildlife population.

(l) Hunting and fishing on lands and waters not within the System. Nothing in this Act shall be construed to authorize the Secretary to control or regulate hunting or fishing of fish and resident wildlife on lands or waters that are not within the System.

(m) State authority. Nothing in this Act shall be construed as affecting the authority, jurisdiction, or responsibility of the several States to manage, control, or regulate fish and resident wildlife under State law or regulations in any area within the System. Regulations permitting hunting or fishing of fish and resident wildlife within the System shall be, to the extent practicable, consistent with State fish and wildlife laws, regulations, and management plans.

(n) Water rights. (1) Nothing in this Act shall --

(A) create a reserved water right, express or implied, in the United States for any purpose;

(B) affect any water right in existence on the date of the enactment of the National Wildlife Refuge System Improvement Act of 1997 [October 9, 1997]; or

(C) affect any Federal or State law in existence on the date of the enactment of the National Wildlife Refuge System Improvement Act of 1997 [October 9, 1997], regarding water quality or water quantity.

(2) Nothing in this Act shall diminish or affect the ability to join the United States in the adjudication of rights to the use of water pursuant to the McCarran Act (43 U.S.C. 666).

(o) Coordination with State agencies. Coordination with State fish and wildlife agency personnel or with personnel of other affected State agencies pursuant to this Act shall not be subject to the Federal Advisory Committee Act (5 U.S.C. App.).

[Pub. L. 89-669, § 4, 80 Stat. 927 (Oct. 15, 1966); Pub. L. 90-404, § 1, 82 Stat. 359 (July 18, 1968); Pub. L. 93-205, § 13(a), 87 Stat. 902 (Dec. 28, 1973); Pub. L. 93-509, § 2, 88 Stat. 1603 (Dec. 3, 1974); Pub. L. 94- 215, § 5, 90 Stat. 190 (Feb. 17, 1976); Pub. L. 94-223, 90 Stat. 199 (Feb. 27, 1976); Pub. L. 95-616, §§ 3(f), 6, 92 Stat. 3111, 3114 (Nov. 8, 1978); Pub. L. 100-226, § 4, 101 Stat. 1551 (Dec. 31, 1987); Pub. L. 100-653, Title IX, § 904, 102 Stat. 3834 (Nov. 14, 1988); Pub. L. 105-57, §§ 3(b) to 8, 111 Stat. 1254 (Oct. 9, 1997); Pub. L. 105-312, Title II, § 206, 112 Stat. 2958 (Oct. 30, 1998)]

[Pub. L. 105-312, Title II, § 201, 112 Stat. 2957 (Oct. 30, 1998), provided that: "This title [Title II of Pub. L. 105-312, 112 Stat. 2957 (Oct. 30, 1998), amending this section, and sections 721 and 722 of this title, amending section 564w-1 of Title 25, and enacting provisions set out as a note under section 722 of this title] may be cited as the 'National Wildlife Refuge System Improvement Act of 1998.'"]

16 U.S.C. § 668ee. Definitions. For purposes of this Act:

(1) The term "compatible use" means a wildlife-dependent recreational use or any other use of a refuge that, in the sound professional judgment of the Director, will not materially interfere with or detract from the fulfillment of the mission of the System or the purposes of the refuge.

(2) The terms "wildlife-dependent recreation" and "wildlife-dependent recreational use" means a use of a refuge involving hunting, fishing, wildlife observation and photography, or environmental education and interpretation.

(3) The term "sound professional judgment" means a finding, determination, or decision that is consistent with principles of sound fish and wildlife management and administration, available science and resources, and adherence to the requirements of this Act and other applicable laws.

(4) The terms "conserving", "conservation", "manage", "managing", and "management", mean to sustain and, where appropriate, restore and enhance, healthy populations of fish, wildlife, and plants utilizing, in accordance with applicable Federal and State laws, methods and procedures associated with modern scientific resource programs. Such methods and procedures include, consistent with the provisions of this Act, protection, research, census, law enforcement, habitat management, propagation, live trapping and transplantation, and regulated taking.

(5) The term "Coordination Area" means a wildlife management area that is made

available to a State --

(A) by cooperative agreement between the United States Fish and Wildlife Service and a State agency having control over wildlife resources pursuant to section 4 of the Fish and Wildlife Coordination Act (16 U.S.C. § 664); or

(B) by long-term leases or agreements pursuant to title III of the Bankhead-Jones Farm Tenant Act (50 Stat. 525, 7 U.S.C. §§ 1010 *et seq.*).

(6) The term "Director" means the Director of the United States Fish and Wildlife Service or a designee of that Director.

(7) The terms "fish", "wildlife", and "fish and wildlife" mean any wild member of the animal kingdom whether alive or dead, and regardless of whether the member was bred, hatched, or born in captivity, including a part, product, egg, or offspring of the member.

(8) The term "person" means any individual, partnership, corporation, or association.

(9) The term "plant" means any member of the plant kingdom in a wild, unconfined state, including any plant community, seed, root, or other part of a plant.

(10) The terms "purposes of the refuge" and "purposes of each refuge" mean the purposes specified in or derived from the law, proclamation, executive order, agreement, public land order, donation document, or administrative memorandum establishing, authorizing, or expanding a refuge, refuge unit, or refuge subunit.

(11) The term "refuge" means a designated area of land, water, or an interest in land or water within the System, but does not include Coordination Areas.

(12) The term "Secretary" means the Secretary of the Interior.

(13) The terms "State" and "United States" mean the several States of the United States, Puerto Rico, American Samoa, the Virgin Islands, Guam, and the territories and possessions of the United States.

(14) The term "System" means the National Wildlife Refuge System designated under section 4(a)(1) [16 U.S.C. § 668dd(a)(1)].

(15) The terms "take", "taking", and "taken" mean to pursue, hunt, shoot, capture, collect, or kill, or to attempt to pursue, hunt, shoot, capture, collect, or kill.

[Pub. L. 89-669, § 5, 80 Stat. 929 (Oct. 15, 1966); Pub. L. 105-57, § 3(a), 111 Stat. 1253 (Oct. 9, 1997)]

- 0 -

Fish and Wildlife Service Refuge Management Regulations

The FWS has implemented the management authority delegated to it in these statutes in a groups of regulations in 50 C.F.R. parts 25-38. The regulations included here set to the basic administrative provisions, 50 C.F.R. part 25; the entry and use restrictions, *id.* part 26, and the accompanying statement of prohibited acts, *id.* part 27, and the applicable penalty provisions, *id.* part 28. The regulations are extremely broad and general -- a fact that reflects the importance of the provisions in the document establishing the individual refuge in determining the use of the refuge. The breadth of the regulations also accord the managers of individual refuges substantial administrative discretion.

50 C.F.R. PART 25
ADMINISTRATIVE PROVISIONS

AUTHORITY: 5 U.S.C. § 301; 16 U.S.C. §§ 460k, 664,, 668dd, and 715i, 3901 *et seq.*; and Pub. L. 102-402, 106 Stat. 1961.

SOURCE: 41 FR 9166, Mar. 3, 1976, unless otherwise noted.

SUBPART A -- INTRODUCTION

§ 25.11 Purpose of regulations.

(a) The regulations in this subchapter govern general administration of units of the National Wildlife Refuge System, public notice of changes in U.S. Fish and Wildlife Service policy regarding Refuge System units, issuance of permits required on Refuge System units and other administrative aspects involving the management of various units of the National Wildlife Refuge System. The regulations in this subchapter apply to areas of land and water held by the United States in fee title and to property interests in such land and water in less than fee, including but not limited to easements. For areas held in less than fee, the regulations in this subchapter apply only to the extent that the property interest held by the United States may be affected. The regulations in this subchapter also apply to and govern those areas of the Rocky Mountain Arsenal over which management responsibility has been transferred to the U.S. Fish and Wildlife Service under the Rocky Mountain Arsenal Act of 1992 (Pub. L. 102-402, 106 Stat. 1961), before their establishment as a refuge and inclusion in the National Wildlife Refuge System.

(b) All national wildlife refuges are maintained for the primary purpose of developing a national program of wildlife and ecological conservation and rehabilitation. These refuges are established for the restoration, preservation, development and management of wildlife and wildlands habitat; for the protection and preservation of endangered or threatened species and their habitat; and for the management of wildlife and wildlands to obtain the maximum benefits from these resources.

[51 FR 7574, March 5, 1986; 62 FR 47375, Sept. 9, 1997]

§ 25.12 What do these terms mean?

(a) As used in the rules and regulations in this subchapter:

Authorized official means any Federal, State or local official empowered to enforce provisions of this subchapter C.

Big game means large game animals, including moose, elk, caribou, reindeer, musk ox, deer, bighorn sheep, mountain goat, pronghorn, bear, and peccary, or such species as the separate States may so classify within their boundaries.

Compatibility determination means a written determination signed and dated by the Refuge Manager and Regional Chief, signifying that a proposed or existing use of a national wildlife refuge is a compatible use or is not a compatible use. The Director makes this delegation through the Regional Director.

Compatible use means a proposed or existing wildlife-dependent recreational use or any other use of a national wildlife refuge that, based on sound professional judgment, will not materially interfere with or detract from the fulfillment of the National Wildlife Refuge System mission or the purpose(s) of the national wildlife refuge.

Comprehensive conservation plan means a document that describes the desired future conditions of a refuge or planning unit and provides long-range guidance and management direction to achieve the purposes of the refuge; helps fulfill the mission of the Refuge System; maintains and, where appropriate, restores the ecological integrity of each refuge and the Refuge System; helps achieve the goals of the National Wilderness Preservation System; and meets other mandates.

Conservation, and Management mean to sustain and, where appropriate, restore and enhance, healthy populations of fish, wildlife, and plants utilizing, in accordance with applicable Federal and State laws, methods and procedures associated with modern scientific resource programs. Such methods and procedures include, consistent with the provisions of the National Wildlife Refuge System Administration Act of 1966 (16 U.S.C. 668dd-668ee), protection, research, census, law enforcement, habitat management, propagation, live trapping and transplantation, and regulated taking.

Coordination area means a wildlife management area made available to a State by cooperative agreement between the U.S. Fish and Wildlife Service and a State agency having control over wildlife resources pursuant to section 4 of the Fish and Wildlife Coordination Act (16 U.S.C. 664 or by long-term leases or agreements pursuant to title III of the Bankhead-Jones Farm Tenant Act (7 U.S.C. 1010 et seq.). The States manage coordination areas but they are part of the National Wildlife Refuge System. The compatibility standard does not apply to coordination areas.

Director means the Director, U.S. Fish and Wildlife Service or the authorized representative of such official.

Easement means a less than fee interest in land or water acquired and administered by the U.S. Fish and Wildlife Service for the purpose of maintaining fish and wildlife habitat.

Fish, Wildlife, and Fish and *wildlife* mean any member of the animal kingdom in a wild, unconfined state, whether alive or dead, including a part, product, egg, or offspring of the member.

Migratory bird means and refers to those species of birds listed under § 10.13 of this chapter.

National wildlife refuge, and *Refuge* mean a designated area of land, water, or an interest in land or water located within the National Wildlife Refuge System but does not include coordination areas.

National Wildlife Refuge System, and *System* mean all lands, waters, and interests therein administered by the U.S. Fish and Wildlife Service as wildlife refuges, wildlife ranges, wildlife management areas, waterfowl production areas, coordination areas, and other areas for the protection and conservation of fish and wildlife including those that are threatened with extinction as determined in writing by the Director or so directed by Presidential or Secretarial order. The determination by the Director may not be delegated.

National Wildlife Refuge System mission, and *System mission* mean to administer a national network of lands and waters for the conservation, management, and where appropriate, restoration of the fish, wildlife, and plant resources and their habitats within the United States for the benefit of present and future generations of Americans.

Nontoxic shot means steel shot or other shot approved pursuant to 50 CFR 20.134.

Plant means any member of the plant kingdom in a wild, unconfined state, including any plant community, seed, root, or other part of a plant.

Purpose(s) of the refuge means the purposes specified in or derived from the law, proclamation, executive order, agreement, public land order, donation document, or administrative memorandum establishing, authorizing, or expanding a national wildlife refuge, national wildlife refuge unit, or national wildlife refuge subunit. For refuges that encompass Congressionally designated wilderness, the purposes of the Wilderness Act are additional purposes of the wilderness portion of the refuge.

Refuge management activity means an activity conducted by the Service or a Service-authorized agent to fulfill one or more purposes of the national wildlife refuge, or the National Wildlife Refuge System mission. Service- authorized agents include contractors, cooperating agencies, cooperating associations, refuge support groups, and volunteers.

Refuge management economic activity means a refuge management activity on a national wildlife refuge which results in generation of a commodity which is or can be sold for income or revenue or traded for goods or services. Examples include: Farming, grazing, haying, timber harvesting, and trapping.

Refuge Manager means the official directly in charge of a national wildlife refuge or the authorized representative of such official. In the case of a national wildlife refuge complex, this refers to the official directly in charge of the complex.

Regional Chief means the official in charge of the National Wildlife Refuge System within a Region of the U.S. Fish and Wildlife Service or the authorized representative of such official.

Refuge use, and *Use of a refuge* mean a recreational use (including refuge actions associated with a recreational use or other general public use), refuge management economic activity, or other use of a national wildlife refuge by the public or other non-National Wildlife Refuge System entity.

Regional Director means the official in charge of a Region of the U.S. Fish and Wildlife Service or the authorized representative of such official.

Secretary means the Secretary of the Interior or the authorized representative of such official.

Service, We, and *Us* mean the U.S. Fish and Wildlife Service, Department of the Interior.

Sound professional judgment means a finding, determination, or decision that is consistent with principles of sound fish and wildlife management and administration, available science and resources, and adherence to the requirements of the National Wildlife Refuge System Administration Act of 1966 (16 U.S.C. 668dd-668ee), and other applicable laws. Included in this finding, determination, or decision is a refuge manager's field experience and knowledge of the particular refuge's resources.

State, and *United States* mean one or more of the States of the United States, Puerto Rico, American Samoa, the Virgin Islands, Guam, and the territories and possessions of the United States.

Waterfowl production area means any wetland or pothole area acquired pursuant to section 4(c) of the amended Migratory Bird Hunting Stamp Act (72 Stat. 487; 16 U.S.C. 718d(c)), owned or controlled by the United States and administered by the U.S. Fish and Wildlife Service as a part of the National Wildlife Refuge System.

Wildlife-dependent recreational use, and *Wildlife-dependent recreation* mean a use of a national wildlife refuge involving hunting, fishing, wildlife observation and photography, or environmental education and interpretation. The National Wildlife Refuge System Administration Act of 1966 (16 U.S.C. 668dd-668ee), specifies that these are the six priority general public uses of the National Wildlife Refuge System.

Wildlife management area means a general term used in describing a variety of areas that are managed for wildlife purposes which may be included in the National Wildlife Refuge System.

You means the public.

(b) Unless otherwise stated the definitions found in 50 CFR 10.12 also apply to all of subchapter C of this title 50.

[51 FR 7574, March 5, 1986; 60 FR 62040, Dec. 4, 1995; 64 FR 14150, March 24, 1999; 65 FR 62480, Oct. 18, 2000]

§ 25.13 Other applicable laws.

Nothing in this subchapter shall be construed to relieve a person from any other applicable requirements imposed by a local ordinance or by a statute or regulation of any State or of the United States.

SUBPART B -- ADMINISTRATIVE PROVISIONS

§ 25.21 When and how do we open and close areas of the National Wildlife Refuge System to public access and use or continue a use?

(a) Except as provided below, all areas included in the National Wildlife Refuge System are closed to public access until and unless we open the area for a use or uses in accordance with the National Wildlife Refuge System Administration Act of 1966 (16 U.S.C. 668dd-668ee), the Refuge Recreation Act of 1962 (16 U.S.C. 460k-460k-4) and this subchapter C. See 50 CFR 36 for details on use and access restrictions, and the public participation and closure process established for Alaska national wildlife refuges. We may open an area by regulation, individual permit, or public notice, in accordance with § 25.31 of this subchapter.

(b) We may open a national wildlife refuge for any refuge use, or expand, renew, or extend an existing refuge use only after the Refuge Manager determines that it is a compatible use and not inconsistent with any applicable law. Lands subject to the patent restrictions imposed by Section 22(g) of the Alaska Native Claims Settlement Act are subject to the compatibility requirements of Parts 25 and 26 of 50 CFR except as otherwise provided in paragraph (b)(1) of this section.

(1) We will complete compatibility determinations for uses of Alaska Native Claims Settlement Act 22(g) lands in compliance with the following requirements:

(i) Refuge managers will work with 22(g) landowners in implementation of these regulations. The landowners should contact the Refuge Manager in advance of initiating a use and request a compatibility determination. After a compatibility determination is requested, refuge managers have no longer than ninety (90) days to complete the compatibility determination and notify the landowner of the finding by providing a copy of the compatibility determination or to inform the landowner of the specific reasons for delay. If a refuge manager believes that a finding of not compatible is likely, the Refuge Manager will notify the landowner prior to rendering a decision to encourage dialog on how the proposed use might be modified to be compatible.

(ii) Refuge managers will allow all uses proposed by 22(g) landowners when the Refuge Manager determines the use to be compatible with refuge purposes.

(iii) Compatibility determinations will include only evaluations of how the proposed use would affect the ability of the refuge to meet its mandated purposes. The National Wildlife Refuge System mission will not be considered in the evaluation. Refuge purposes will include both pre-ANILCA purposes and those established by ANILCA, so long as they do not conflict. If conflicts arise, ANILCA purposes will take precedence.

(iv) A determination that a use is not compatible may be appealed by the landowner to the Regional Director. The appeal must be submitted in writing within forty-five (45) days of receipt of the determination. The appeals process provided for in 50 CFR 36.41(i)(3) through (5) will apply.

(v) Compatibility determinations for proposed uses of 22(g) lands will only evaluate the effects of the use on the adjacent refuge lands, and the ability of that refuge to achieve its purposes, not on the effects of the proposed use to the 22(g) lands.

(vi) Compatibility determinations for 22(g) lands that a use is compatible are not subject to re-evaluation unless the use changes significantly, significant new information is made available that could affect the compatibility determination, or if requested by the landowner.

(vii) Refuge comprehensive conservation plans will not include 22(g) lands, and compatibility determinations affecting such lands will not to be automatically re-evaluated when the plans are routinely updated.

(viii) Refuge special use permits will not be required for compatible uses of 22(g) lands. Special conditions necessary to ensure a proposed use is compatible may be included in the compatibility determination and must be complied with for the use to be considered compatible.

(c) The Refuge Manager may temporarily allow or initiate any refuge use without making a compatibility determination if necessary to protect the health and safety of the public or any fish or wildlife population.

(d) When we add lands to the National Wildlife Refuge System, the Refuge Manager will identify, prior to acquisition, withdrawal, transfer, reclassification, or donation of those lands, existing wildlife-dependent recreational public uses (if any) determined to be compatible that we will permit to continue on an interim basis, pending completion of the comprehensive conservation plan for the national wildlife refuge. We will make these compatibility determinations in accordance with procedures in § 26.41 of this subchapter.

(e) In the event of a threat or emergency endangering the health and safety of the public or property or to protect the resources of the area, the Refuge Manager may close or curtail refuge uses of all or any part of an opened area to public access and use in accordance with the provisions in § 25.31, without advance notice. See 50 CFR 36.42 for procedures on closing Alaska national wildlife refuges.

(f) We will re-evaluate compatibility determinations for existing wildlife-dependent recreational uses when conditions under which the use is permitted change significantly, or if there is significant new information regarding the effects of the use, or concurrently with the preparation or revision of a comprehensive conservation plan, or at least every 15 years, whichever is earlier. In addition, a refuge manager always may re-evaluate the compatibility of a use at any time.

(g) Except for uses specifically authorized for a period longer than 10 years (such as right-of-ways), we will re-evaluate compatibility determinations for all existing uses other than wildlife-dependent recreational uses when conditions under which the use is permitted change significantly, or if there is significant new information regarding the effects of the use, or at least every 10 years, whichever is earlier. In addition, a refuge manager always may re-evaluate the compatibility of a use at any time.

(h) For uses in existence on November 17, 2000 that were specifically authorized for a period longer than 10 years (such as right-of-ways), our compatibility re-evaluation will examine compliance with the terms and conditions of the authorization, not the authorization itself. We will frequently monitor and review the activity to ensure that the permittee carries out all permit terms and conditions. However, the Service will request modifications to the terms and conditions of these permits from the permittee if the Service determines that such changes are necessary to ensure that the use remains compatible. After November 17, 2000 no uses will be permitted or re-authorized, for a period longer than 10 years, unless the terms and conditions for such long-term permits specifically allows for modifications to the terms and conditions, if necessary to ensure compatibility. We will make a new compatibility determination prior to extending or renewing such long-term uses at the expiration of the authorization. When we prepare a compatibility determination for re-authorization of an existing right-of-way, we will base our analysis on the existing conditions with the use in place, not from a pre-use perspective.

(i) When we re-evaluate a use for compatibility, we will take a fresh look at the use and prepare a new compatibility determination following the procedure outlined in 50 CFR 26.41.

[65 FR 62481, Oct. 18, 2000]

§ 25.22 Lost and found articles.

Lost articles or money found on a national wildlife refuge are to be immediately turned in to the nearest refuge office.

§ 25.23 What are the general regulations and information collection requirements?

The Office of Management and Budget has approved the information collection requirements contained in subchapter C, parts 25, 32, and 36 under 44 U.S.C. 3501 et seq. and assigned the following clearance numbers: Special Use Permit Applications on National Wildlife Refuges in Alaska (SUP-AK), clearance number 1018-0014; Special Use Permit Applications on National Wildlife Refuges Outside Alaska (SUP), clearance number 1018-0102. See § 36.3 of this subchapter for further information on Special Use Permit Applications on National Wildlife Refuges in Alaska. We are collecting the information to assist us in administering these programs in accordance with statutory authorities that require that recreational uses be compatible with the primary purposes for which the areas were established. We require the information requested in the application form for the applicant to obtain a benefit. We estimate the public reporting burden for the SUP application form to be 30 minutes per response. This includes time for reviewing instructions, gathering and maintaining data, and completing and reviewing the form. Direct comments on the burden estimate or any other aspect of this form to the Information Collection Clearance Officer, U.S. Fish and Wildlife Service, MS 222 ARLSQ, Washington, DC 20240 (1018-0014 or 1018-0102).

[56 FR 66795, Dec. 26, 1991; 65 FR 56400, Sept. 18, 2000]

SUBPART C -- PUBLIC NOTICE

§ 25.31 General provisions.

Whenever a particular public access, use or recreational activity of any type whatsoever, not otherwise expressly permitted under this subchapter, is permitted on a national wildlife refuge or where public access, use, or recreational or other activities previously permitted are curtailed, the public may be notified by any of the following methods, all of which supplement this Subchapter C:

(a) Official signs posted conspicuously at appropriate intervals and locations;

(b) Special regulations issued under the provisions of § 26.33 of this Subchapter C.

(c) Maps available in the office of the refuge manager, regional director, or area director, or

(d) Other appropriate methods which will give the public actual or constructive notice of the permitted or curtailed public access, use, or recreational activity.

SUBPART D -- PERMITS

§ 25.41 General provisions.

Permits required by this Subchapter C can be obtained from the administrative office responsible for the refuge where the activity is to take place. If the applicant is required to obtain the applicable permit from the Director or Secretary, the refuge manager will so inform the applicant, giving the applicant all the necessary information as to how and where to apply.

§ 25.42 Permits required to be exhibited on request.

Any person on a national wildlife refuge shall upon request by any authorized official exhibit the required Federal or State permit or license authorizing their presence and activity on the area and shall furnish such other information for identification purposes as may be requested.

§ 25.43 Revocation of permits.

A permit may be terminated or revoked at any time for noncompliance with the terms thereof or of the regulations in this Subchapter C, for nonuse, for violation of any law, regulation or order applicable to the refuge, or to protect public health or safety or the resources of a national wildlife refuge.

§ 25.44 How do we grant permits for easement area uses?

(a) The provisions of this subsection shall govern the regulation of activities that affect easement interests acquired by the United States. All other provisions of Subchapter C shall apply to activities within such easement areas, but only to the extent that those provisions are directly or indirectly related to the protection of those easement interests expressly acquired by the United States which are specified in the easement agreement itself, and are not inconsistent with the provisions of this subsection.

(b) We require permits for use of easement areas administered by us where proposed activities may affect the property interest acquired by the United States. Applications for permits will be submitted in writing to the Regional Director or a designee. We may grant special use permits to owners of servient estates, or to third parties with the owner's agreement, by the Regional Director or a designee, upon written determination that such permitted use is compatible. If we ultimately determine that the requested use will not affect the United States' interest, the Regional Director will issue a letter of non-objection.

(c) In instances where the third applicant is a governmental entity which has acquired a partial interest in the servient estate by subsequent condemnation, a special use permit may be granted to the governmental entity without the servient estate owner's agreement if the regional director or his or her designee determines:

(1) The permitted use is compatible; and

(2) The permitted use is consistent with the partial property interests obtained through condemnation.

(d) Regulations pertaining to rights-of-way in easement areas are contained in 50 CFR part 29.21.

[51 FR 7575, March 5, 1986; 65 FR 62482, Oct. 18, 2000]

§ 25.45 Appeals procedure.

(a) *Who may appeal.* Any person who is adversely affected by a refuge manager's decision or order relating to the person's permit granted by the Service, or application for permit, within the National Wildlife Refuge System. This section does not apply to permits or applications for rights-of-way. See § 29.22 for the hearing and appeals procedure on rights-of-way.

(b) *Preliminary Procedure.* Prior to making any adverse decision or order on a permit or application for permit, the refuge manager shall notify the permittee or applicant orally or in writing of the proposed action and its effective date. The permittee or applicant shall have twenty (20) days after notification in which to present to the refuge manager, orally or in writing, a statement in opposition to the proposed action or date. The permittee or applicant shall be notified in writing within twenty (20) days after receipt of the statement in opposition, of the refuge manager's final decision or order.

(c) *Appeals, how taken.* If the refuge manager still intends to proceed with the proposed action, the permittee or applicant shall have thirty (30) days from the postmarked date of the refuge manager's final decision or order in which to file a written appeal to the appropriate area manager. The appellant (permittee or applicant) shall be notified in writing within thirty (30) days from the postmarked date of the appeal of the area manager's decision. The appellant shall have (30) days from the postmarked date of the area manager's decision to further appeal in writing to the appropriate regional director.

(d) *Decision of regional director.* The regional director's decision shall be final and issued in writing to the appellant within thirty (30) days from the postmarked date of the appeal.

(e) *Oral presentation.* The appellant shall be provided an opportunity for oral presentation before the area manager or the regional director within the respective thirty (30) day appeal periods.

(f) *Addresses.* The addresses of the appropriate officials to whom appeals may be taken shall be furnished in each decision or order.

(g) *Suspension pending appeal.* Compliance with any decision or order of a refuge manager shall not be suspended by reason of an appeal having been taken unless such suspension is authorized in writing by the area manager or regional director (depending upon the official before whom the appeal is pending), and then only upon a determination by these officials that such suspension will not be detrimental to the interests of the United States or upon submission and acceptance of a bond deemed adequate to indemnify the United States from loss or damage.

[42 FR 64120, Dec. 22, 1977; 51 FR 7575, March 5, 1986

SUBPART E -- FEES AND CHARGES

§ 25.51 General provisions.

Reasonable charges and fees may be established for public recreational use of and, except in Alaska, entrance onto national wildlife refuges. Regulations regarding recreational use fees are contained in 36 CFR Part 71. Regulations regarding entrance fees are contained in this subpart E.

§ 25.52 Designation.

To be designated as an "Entrance Fee Area", a unit of the National Wildlife Refuge System must be found to demonstrate that:

(a) The level of visitation for recreational purposes is high enough to justify the collection of fees for admission permits for economic reasons;

(b) There is a practical mechanism in existence for implementing and operating a system of collecting fees for admission permits; and

(c) Imposition of a fee for admission permits is not likely to result in undue economic hardship for a significant number of visitors to the unit.

§ 25.53 Establishment of single visit entrance fees.

Entrance fees established for single visit permits at a designated Entrance Fee Area shall consider the following criteria with regard to the local area within which the refuge is located:

(a) The direct and indirect cost to the Government.

(b) The benefits to the permit holder.

(c) The public policy or interest served.

(d) The comparable fees charged by non-Federal public agencies.

(e) The economic and administrative feasibility of fee collection.

§ 25.54 Posting and public notification.

The public shall be notified that an entrance fee is charged through refuge publications and posted designation signs in accordance with § 25.31 of this part.

§ 25.55 Refuge admission permits.

(a) Unless otherwise provided, persons entering an Entrance Fee Area shall obtain and be in possession of a valid admission permit.

(b) The following five types of permits allowing entrance onto an Entrance Fee Area will be available for issue or purchase at such area and, except for refuge-specific permits, at Fish and Wildlife Service Regional and Washington, DC Offices, and at other locations as may be designated.

(1) Single visit permit with a charge not to exceed $3 per person or $7.50 per noncommercial vehicle (single visit can be defined as 1-15 days, dependent upon a determination of the period of time reasonably and ordinarily necessary for such a visit at a particular refuge unit).

(2) Golden Eagle Passport.

(3) Golden Age Passport.

(4) Golden Access Passport.

(5) Federal Migratory Bird Hunting and Conservation (Duck) Stamp. To be valid, the Duck Stamp must be current and bear the signature of the holder on the front.

§ 25.56 Enforcement.

Permits issued or used for entrance onto Entrance Fee Areas are nontransferable. Failure to pay the entrance fee, to display upon request of an authorized official a valid permit, or to comply with other entrance fee provisions, rules or regulations, will be subject to the penalties prescribed in 50 CFR 28.31.

§ 25.57 Exceptions and exemptions.

At Entrance Fee Areas:

(a) Special admission permits for uses, such as group activities, may be issued.

(b) No entrance fee shall be charged for persons under 16 years of age.

(c) No entrance fee shall be charged for travel by private noncommercial vehicle over any road or highway established as part of the National Federal Aid System (defined in 23 U.S.C. 101), which is commonly used by the public as a means of travel between two places which are outside the Entrance Fee Area.

(d) No entrance fee shall be charged for travel by private noncommercial vehicle over any road or highway to any land in which such person has a property interest if such land is within any Entrance Fee Area.

(e) Persons accompanying the holder of a valid single visit permit, Federal Duck Stamp or Golden Eagle, Age, or Access Passport in a single, private, noncommercial vehicle shall be entitled to general entrance.

(f) Where entry is by any means other than single, private, noncommercial vehicle, the spouse, children, or parents accompanying the holder of a valid single visit permit, Federal Duck Stamp or Golden Eagle, Age, or Access Passport shall be entitled to general entrance.

50 C.F.R. PART 26
PUBLIC ENTRY AND USE

Subpart A -- Introduction

Subpart B -- Public Entry

Subpart C -- Public Use and Recreation

AUTHORITY: 5 U.S.C. § 301; 16 U.S.C. §§ 460k, 664, 668dd, 715i; Pub. L. No. 96-315 (94 Stat. 958) and Pub. L. No. 98-146 (97 Stat. 955).

SOURCE: 41 FR 9167, Mar. 3, 1976, unless otherwise noted.

SUBPART A -- INTRODUCTION

§ 26.11 Purpose of regulations.

The regulations in this part govern the circumstances under which the public can enter and use a national wildlife refuge.

SUBPART B -- PUBLIC ENTRY

§ 26.21 General trespass provision.

(a) No person shall trespass, including but not limited to entering, occupying, using, or being upon, any national wildlife refuge, except as specifically authorized in this Subchapter C or in other applicable Federal regulations.

(b) No unconfined domestic animals, including but not limited to dogs, hogs, cats, horses, sheep and cattle, shall be permitted to enter upon any national wildlife refuge or to roam at large upon such an area, except as specifically authorized under the provisions of § 26.34, § 27.91 or § 29.2 of this subchapter C.

§ 26.22 General exception for entry.

(a) Any person entering or using any national wildlife refuge will comply with the regulations in this Subchapter C, the provisions of any special regulations and any other official notification as is appropriate under § 25.31.

(b) A permit shall be required for any person entering a national wildlife refuge, unless otherwise provided under the provisions of subchapter C. The permittee will abide by all the terms and conditions set forth in the permit.

§ 26.23 Exception for entry to the headquarters office.

The headquarters office of any national wildlife refuge is open to public access and admission during regularly established business hours.

§ 26.24 Exception for entry when accompanied by refuge personnel.

A permit is not required for access to any part of a national wildlife refuge by a person when accompanied by refuge personnel.

§ 26.25 Exception for entry to persons with an economic use privilege.

Access to and travel upon a national wildlife refuge by a person granted economic use privileges on that national wildlife refuge should be restricted to a specified area in accordance with the provisions of their agreement, lease, or permit.

§ 26.26 Exception for entry for use of emergency shelter.

A permit is not required for access to any national wildlife area for temporary shelter or temporary protection in the event of emergency conditions.

§ 26.27 Exception for entry on designated routes of travel.

A permit is not required to enter, travel on, and exit from any national wildlife refuge on public waters and roads, and such roads, trails, footpaths, walkways, or other routes and areas which are designated for public use under the provisions of this subchapter C.

SUBPART C -- PUBLIC USE AND RECREATION

§ 26.31 General provisions.

Public recreation will be permitted on national wildlife refuges as an appropriate incidental or secondary use, only after it has been determined that such recreational use is practicable and not inconsistent with the primary objectives for which each particular area was established or with other authorized Federal operations.

§ 26.32 Recreational uses.

Recreational uses such as, but not limited to, sightseeing, nature observation and photography, interpretive centers and exhibits, hunting and fishing, bathing, boating, camping, ice skating, picnicking, swimming, water skiing, and other similar activities may be permitted on national wildlife refuges. When such uses are permitted the public will be notified under the provisions of this subchapter C.

§ 26.33 Special regulations.

(a) Special regulations shall be issued for public use, access, and recreation within certain individual national wildlife refuges where there is a need to amend, modify, relax or make more stringent the regulations contained in this subchapter C. The issued special regulations will supplement the provisions in this part 26.

(b) Special recreational use regulations may contain the following items:

(1) Recreational uses authorized.

(2) Seasons, period, or specific time of use.

(3) Description of areas open to recreation.

(4) Specific conditions or requirements.

(5) Other provisions.

(6) Special regulations for public use, access, and recreation are published in the daily issue of the Federal Register and may be codified in the Code of Federal

Regulations. They shall be issued in compliance with procedures contained in the Departmental Manual.

§ 26.34 Special regulations concerning public access, use and recreation for individual national wildlife refuges.

****

§ 26.35 Cabin sites.

(a) There shall be no new private cabin site permits issued for national wildlife refuges. All appropriate provisions of 43 CFR Part 21 apply to the phaseout of existing permits on national wildlife refuges.

(b) No new government owned cabin site permits for private recreational purposes shall be issued nor shall existing permits be renewed.

§ 26.36 Public assemblies and meetings.

(a) Public meetings, assemblies, demonstrations, parades and other public expressions of view may be permitted within a national wildlife refuge open to public use, provided a permit therefore has been issued by the refuge manager.

(b) Any application for such permit shall set forth the name of the applicant, the date, time, duration, nature and place of the proposed event, an estimate of the number of persons expected to attend, and a statement of equipment and facilities to be used in connection therewith.

(c) The refuge manager may issue a permit on proper application unless:

(1) A prior application for the same time and place has been made which has been or will be granted; or

(2) The activity will present a clear and present danger to public health or safety, or undue disturbance to the other users or resources of the area; or

(3) The activity is of such nature that it cannot be reasonably accommodated in the particular national wildlife refuge; or

(4) The activity conflicts with the purposes of the national wildlife refuge.

(d) The permit may contain such conditions as are reasonably consistent with protection and use of the national wildlife refuge for the purpose for which it is maintained. It may also contain reasonable limitations on the time and area within which the activity is permitted.

§ 26.41 What is the process for determining if a use of a national wildlife refuge is a compatible use?

The Refuge Manager will not initiate or permit a new use of a national wildlife refuge or expand, renew, or extend an existing use of a national wildlife refuge, unless the Refuge Manager has determined that the use is a compatible use. This section provides guidelines for making compatibility determinations, and procedures for documenting compatibility determinations and for periodic review of compatibility determinations. We will usually complete compatibility determinations as part of the comprehensive conservation plan or step-down management plan process for individual uses, specific use programs, or groups of related uses described in the plan. We will make all compatibility determinations in writing.

(a) What information do we include in a compatibility determination? All compatibility determinations will include the following information:

(1) The proposed or existing use;

(2) The name of the national wildlife refuge;

(3) The authorities used to establish the national wildlife refuge;

(4) The purpose(s) of the national wildlife refuge;

(5) The National Wildlife Refuge System mission;

(6) The nature and extent of the use including the following:

(i) What is the use? Is the use a priority public use?;

(ii) Where would the use be conducted?;

(iii) When would the use be conducted?;

(iv) How would the use be conducted?; and

(v) Why is the use being proposed?.

(7) An analysis of costs for administering and managing each use;

(8) The anticipated impacts of the use on the national wildlife refuge's purposes and the National Wildlife Refuge System mission;

(9) The amount of opportunity for public review and comment provided;

(10) Whether the use is compatible or not compatible (does it or will it materially interfere with or detract from the fulfillment of the National Wildlife Refuge System mission or the purpose(s) of the national wildlife refuge);

(11) Stipulations necessary to ensure compatibility;

(12) A logical explanation describing how the proposed use would, or would not, materially interfere with or detract from the fulfillment of the National Wildlife Refuge System mission or the purpose(s) of the national wildlife refuge;

(13) The Refuge Manager's signature and date signed; and

(14) The Regional Chief's concurrence signature and date signed.

(15) The mandatory 10- or 15-year re-evaluation date.

(b) Making a use compatible through replacement of lost habitat values or other compensatory mitigation. We will not allow compensatory mitigation to make a proposed refuge use compatible, except by replacement of lost habitat values as provided in paragraph (c) of this section. If we cannot make the proposed use compatible with stipulations we cannot allow the use.

(c) Existing right-of-ways. We will not make a compatibility determination and will deny any request for maintenance of an existing right-of-way which will affect a unit of the National Wildlife Refuge System, unless: the design adopts appropriate measures to avoid resource impacts and includes provisions to ensure no net loss of habitat quantity and quality; restored or replacement areas identified in the design are afforded permanent protection as part of the national wildlife refuge or wetland management district affected by the maintenance; and all restoration work is completed by the applicant prior to any title transfer or recording of the easement, if applicable. Maintenance of an existing right-of-way includes minor expansion or minor realignment to meet safety standards.

(d) Termination of uses that are not compatible. When we determine an existing use is not compatible, we will expeditiously terminate or modify the use to make it compatible. Except with written authorization by the Director, this process of termination or modification will not exceed 6 months from the date that the compatibility determination is signed.

[65 FR 62482, Oct. 18, 2000]

50 C.F.R. PART 27
PROHIBITED ACTS

AUTHORITY: Sec. 2, 33 Stat. 614, as amended (16 U.S.C. 685); Sec. 5, 43 Stat. 651 (16 U.S.C. 725); Sec. 5, Stat. 449 (16 U.S.C. 690d); Sec. 10, 45 Stat. 1224 (16 U.S.C. 715i); Sec. 4, 48 Stat. 402, as amended (16 U.S.C. 664); Sec. 2, 48 Stat. 1270 (43 U.S.C. 315a); 49 Stat. 383 as amended; Sec. 4, 76 Stat. (16 U.S.C. 460k); Sec. 4, 80 Stat. 927 (16 U.S.C. 668dd) p (5 U.S.C. 685, 752, 690d); 16 U.S.C. 715s).

SOURCE: 41 FR 9168, Mar. 3, 1976, unless otherwise noted.

SUBPART A -- INTRODUCTION

§ 27.11 Purpose of regulations.

The regulations in this Part 27 govern those acts by the public which are prohibited at all times except as permitted in this part, Part 26, and Part 25, subpart D--Permits.

[42 FR 56954, Oct. 31, 1977]

SUBPART B -- TAKING VIOLATIONS

§ 27.21 General provisions.

No person shall take any animal or plant on any national wildlife refuge, except as authorized under 50 CFR 27.51 and Parts 31, 32, and 33 of this subchapter C.

SUBPART C -- DISTURBING VIOLATIONS: WITH VEHICLES

§ 27.31 General provisions regarding vehicles.

Travel in or use of any motorized or other vehicles, including those used on air, water, ice, snow, is prohibited on national wildlife refuges except on designated routes of travel, as indicated by the appropriate traffic control signs or signals and in designated areas posted or delineated on maps by the refuge manager and subject to the following requirements and limitations:

(a) Unless specifically covered by the general and special regulations set forth in this chapter, the laws and regulations of the State within whose exterior boundaries a national wildlife refuge or portion thereof is located shall govern traffic and the operation and use of vehicles. Such State laws and regulations which are now or may hereafter be in effect are hereby adopted and made a part of the regulations in this part.

(b) No operator of a vehicle shall be under the influence of intoxicating beverages or controlled substances.

(c) Driving or operating any vehicle carelessly or heedlessly, or in willful or wanton disregard for the rights or safety of other persons, or without due care or at a speed greater than is reasonable and prudent under prevailing conditions, having regard to traffic, weather, wildlife, road, and light conditions, and surface, width, and character of the travel way is prohibited. Every operator shall maintain such control of the vehicle as may be necessary to avoid danger to persons or property or wildlife.

(d) The vehicle speed limit shall not exceed 25 m.p.h. except as otherwise legally posted.

(e)(1) Every motor vehicle shall at all time be equipped with a muffler in good working order, and which cannot be removed or otherwise altered while the vehicle is being operated on a national wildlife refuge. To prevent excessive or unusual noise no person shall use a muffler cut-out, bypass, or similar device upon a motor vehicle. A vehicle that produces unusual or excessive noise or visible pollutants is prohibited.

(2) A refuge manager, by posting of appropriate signs or by marking on a map which shall be available at the refuge headquarters, may require that any motor vehicle operating in the designated area shall be equipped with a spark arrestor that meets Standard 5100-1a of the United States Forest Service, Department of Agriculture which standard includes the requirements that such spark arrestor shall have an efficiency to retain or destroy at least 80 percent of carbon particles, for all flow rates, and that such spark arrestor has been warranted by its manufacturer as meeting the above mentioned efficiency requirement for at least 1,000 hours, subject to normal use, with maintenance and mounting in accordance with the manufacturers recommendations.

(f) The operation of a vehicle which does not bear valid license plates and is not properly certified, registered, or inspected in accordance with applicable State laws is prohibited.

(g) Driving or permitting another person to drive a vehicle without valid license is prohibited. A valid driver's or operator's license must be displayed upon the request of any authorized official.

(h) Stopping, parking or leaving any vehicle, whether attended or unattended, upon any road, trail, or fire lane so as to obstruct the free movement of other vehicles is prohibited, except in the event of accident or other conditions beyond the immediate control of the operator, or as otherwise directed by an authorized official.

(i) All persons shall obey the lawful order or signal of any authorized official directing, controlling, or regulating the movement of traffic.

(j) Load, weight and width limitations, as may be necessary, shall be prescribed and the public advised under provisions of § 25.31. Such limitations must be complied with by the operators of all vehicles.

(k) A motor vehicle involved in an accident is not to be moved until an authorized official arrives at the scene of the accident, unless such vehicle constitutes a traffic or safety hazard.

(l) A motor vehicle shall not be operated at anytime without proper brakes and brake lights, or from sunset to sunrise without working headlights and taillights which comply with the regulations for operation on the roads of the State within whose boundaries the refuge is located.

(m) Such other requirements which are established under the provisions of this subchapter C.

§ 27.32 Boats.

(a) The use of boats in national wildlife refuges is prohibited except as may be authorized under and subject to the requirements set forth below.

(b) When the use of boats is permitted on any national wildlife refuge, the public will be notified under the provisions of this Subchapter C and the following operational requirements and limitations will apply:

(1)(i) In addition to the regulations contained in this part, the U.S. Coast Guard Regulations, Titles 33 and 46, Code of Federal Regulations, are applicable on navigable waters of the United States.

(ii) Unless specifically covered by the general and special regulations set forth in this chapter, the laws and regulations of the State within whose exterior boundaries a national wildlife refuge or portion thereof is located shall govern boating and the operation and use of boats. Such laws and regulations which are now or may hereafter be in effect are hereby adopted and made a part of the regulations in this part.

(2) No operator or person in charge of any boat shall operate or knowingly permit any other person to operate a boat in a reckless or negligent manner, or in a manner so as to endanger or be likely to endanger any person, property or wildlife.

(3) No person shall operate or be in actual physical control of a boat while under the influence of intoxicating beverages or controlled substances.

(4) No person shall operate a boat in a manner which will unreasonably interfere with other boats or with free and proper navigation of the waterways of the areas. Anchoring in heavily traveled channels or main thoroughfares shall constitute such interference if unreasonable in the prevailing circumstances.

(5) No person shall operate a boat on refuge waters that has a marine head (toilet) unless it conforms to Environmental Protection Agency regulations regarding sewage discharge.

(6) Every sailboat when underway from sunset to sunrise shall carry and exhibit a bright white light visible all around the horizon for a distance of two miles.

(7) Leaving any boat unattended, outside of designated mooring or beaching areas, for a period in excess of 72 hours without written permission of the refuge manager is prohibited and any boat so left may be impounded by the refuge manager.

(8) Government-owned docks, piers, and floats are not to be used for loading and unloading of boats, except in emergencies or unless specifically authorized by the refuge manager.

§ 27.33 Water skiing.

When water skiing is permitted upon national wildlife refuge waters, the public will be notified under the provisions of this Subchapter C and the following requirements and limitations will apply:

(a) Water skiing is permitted only during daylight hours and during periods posted or otherwise designated under the provisions of this Subchapter C.

(b) When a skier is in "tow" there must be two persons in the boat at all times, with one person not operating the boat, acting as an observer of the skier in tow.

(c) The direction of a tow boat when circling will be counter clockwise.

(d) Skiers must wear U.S. Coast Guard approved ski belts, life jackets or buoyant vests.

(e) Water skiing is prohibited within 300 feet of harbors, swimming beaches, and mooring areas, and within 100 feet of any designated swimming area.

§ 27.34 Aircraft.

The unauthorized operation of aircraft, including sail planes, and hang gliders, at altitudes resulting in harassment of wildlife, or the unauthorized landing or take-off on a national wildlife refuge, except in an emergency, is prohibited. National wildlife refuge boundaries are designated on up-date FAA aeronautical charts.

SUBPART D -- DISTURBING VIOLATIONS: WITH WEAPONS

§ 27.41 General provisions.

Carrying, possessing, or discharging firearms, fireworks, or explosives on national wildlife refuges is prohibited unless specifically authorized under the provisions of this subchapter C.

§ 27.42 Firearms.

Only the following persons may possess, use, or transport firearms on national wildlife refuges in accordance with this section and applicable Federal and State law:

(a) Persons using firearms for public hunting under the provisions of 50 CFR part 32.

(b) Persons carrying unloaded firearms, that are dismantled or cased, in vehicles and boats over routes of travel designated under the provision of subchapter C.

(c) Persons authorized to use firearms for the taking of specimens of wildlife for scientific purposes.

(d) Persons authorized by special regulations or permits to possess or use firearms for the protection of property, for field trials, and other special purposes.

[46 FR 47230, Sept. 25, 1981]

§ 27.43 Weapons other than firearms.

The use or possession of cross bows, bows and arrows, air guns, spears, gigs, or other weapons on national wildlife refuges is prohibited except as may be authorized under the provision of this subchapter C.

[46 FR 47230, Sept. 25, 1981]

SUBPART E -- DISTURBING VIOLATIONS: AGAINST PLANTS AND ANIMALS

§ 27.51 Disturbing, injuring, and damaging plants and animals.

(a) Disturbing, injuring, spearing, poisoning, destroying, collecting or attempting to disturb, injure, spear, poison, destroy or collect any plant or animal on any national wildlife refuge is prohibited except by special permit unless otherwise permitted under this subchapter C.

(b) [Reserved]

§ 27.52 Introduction of plants and animals.

Plants and animals or their parts taken elsewhere shall not be introduced, liberated, or placed on any national wildlife refuge except as authorized.

SUBPART F -- DISTURBING VIOLATIONS: AGAINST NONWILDLIFE PROPERTY

§ 27.61 Destruction or removal of property.

The destruction, injury, defacement, disturbance, or the unauthorized removal of any public property including natural objects or private property on or from any national wildlife refuge is prohibited.

§ 27.62 Search for and removal of objects of antiquity.

No person shall search for or remove from national wildlife refuges objects of antiquity except as may be authorized by 43 CFR part 3.

§ 27.63 Search for and removal of other valued objects.

(a) No person shall search for buried treasure, treasure trove, valuable semi-precious rocks, stones, or mineral specimens on national wildlife refuges unless authorized by permit or by provision of this subchapter C.

(b) Permits are required for archeological studies on national wildlife refuges in accordance with the provisions of this subchapter C.

§ 27.64 Prospecting and mining.

Prospecting, locating, or filing mining claims on national wildlife refuges is prohibited unless otherwise provided by law. See § 29.31 for provisions concerning mineral leasing.

§ 27.65 Tampering with vehicles and equipment.

Tampering with, entering, or starting any motor vehicle, boat, equipment or machinery or attempting to tamper with, enter, or start any motor vehicle, boat, equipment or machinery on any national wildlife refuge without proper authorization is prohibited.

SUBPART G -- DISTURBING VIOLATIONS: LIGHT AND SOUND EQUIPMENT

§ 27.71 Motion or sound pictures.

The taking or filming of any motion or sound pictures on a national wildlife refuge for subsequent commercial use is prohibited except as may be authorized under the provisions of 43 CFR part 5.

§ 27.72 Audio equipment.

The operation or use of audio devices including radios, recording and playback devices, loudspeakers, television sets, public address systems and musical instruments so as to cause unreasonable disturbance to others in the vicinity is prohibited.

§ 27.73 Artificial lights.

No unauthorized person shall use or direct the rays of a spotlight or other artificial light, or automotive headlights for the purpose of spotting, locating, or taking any animal within the boundaries of any national wildlife refuge or along rights-of-way for public or private roads within a national wildlife refuge.

SUBPART H -- DISTURBING VIOLATIONS: PERSONAL CONDUCT

§ 27.81 Alcoholic beverages.

Entering or remaining in any national wildlife refuge when under the influence of alcohol, to a degree that may endanger oneself or other persons or property or unreasonably annoy persons in the vicinity, is prohibited.

§ 27.82 Possession and delivery of controlled substances.

(a) Definitions for the purpose of this section:

(1) The term "controlled substance" means a drug or other substance, or immediate precursor, included in Schedules I, II, III, IV, or V of Part B of the Controlled Substance Act (21 U.S.C. 812) or any drug or substance added to these schedules pursuant to the terms of the Controlled Substance Act.

(2) The term "practitioner" means a physician, dentist, veterinarian, scientific investigator, pharmacist, or other person licensed, registered, or otherwise permitted by the United States or the jurisdiction in which he practices to distribute or possess a controlled substance in the course of professional practice.

(3) The term "delivery" means the actual, attempted or constructive transfer and/or distribution of a controlled substance, whether or not there exists an agency relationship.

(b) Offenses.

(1) The delivery of any controlled substance on a national wildlife refuge is prohibited, except that distributed by a practitioner in accordance with applicable law.

(2) The possession of a controlled substance on a national wildlife refuge is prohibited unless such substance was obtained by the possessor directly, or pursuant to a valid prescription or order, from a practitioner acting in the course of his professional practice, or except as otherwise authorized by applicable law.

(3) Presence in a national wildlife refuge when under the influence of a controlled substance to a degree that may endanger oneself, or another person, or property, or may cause unreasonable interference with another person's enjoyment of a national wildlife refuge is prohibited.

§ 27.83 Indecency and disorderly conduct.

Any act of indecency or disorderly conduct as defined by State or local laws is prohibited on any national wildlife refuge.

§ 27.85 Gambling.

Gambling in any form, or the operation of gambling devices, for money or otherwise, on any national wildlife refuge is prohibited.

§ 27.86 Begging.

Begging on any national wildlife refuge is prohibited. Soliciting of funds for the support or assistance of any cause or organization is also prohibited unless properly authorized.

SUBPART I -- OTHER DISTURBING VIOLATIONS

§ 27.91 Field trials.

The conducting or operation of field trials for dogs on national wildlife refuges is prohibited except as may be authorized by special permit.

§ 27.92 Private structures.

No person shall without proper authority construct, install, occupy, or maintain any building, log boom, pier, dock, fence, wall, pile, anchorage, or other structure or obstruction in any national wildlife refuge.

§ 27.93 Abandonment of property.

Abandoning, discarding, or otherwise leaving any personal property in any national wildlife refuge is prohibited.

§ 27.94 Disposal of waste.

(a) The littering, disposing, or dumping in any manner of garbage, refuse sewage, sludge, earth, rocks, or other debris on any national wildlife refuge except at points or locations designated by the refuge manager, or the draining or dumping of oil, acids, pesticide wastes, poisons, or any other types of chemical wastes in, or otherwise polluting any waters, water holes, streams or other areas within any national wildlife refuge is prohibited.

(b) Persons using a national wildlife refuge shall comply with the sanitary requirements established under the provisions of this Subchapter C for each individual refuge; the sanitation provisions which may be included in leases, agreements, or use permits, and all applicable Federal and State laws.

§ 27.95 Fires.

On all national wildlife refuges persons are prohibited from the following:

(a) Setting on fire or causing to be set on fire any timber, brush, grass, or other inflammable material including camp or cooking fires, except as authorized by the refuge manager or at locations designated for that purpose or as provided for under § 26.33(c) of this subchapter C.

(b) Leaving a fire unattended or not completely extinguished;

(c) Throwing a burning cigarette, match, or other lighted substance from any moving conveyance or throwing of same in any place where it may start a fire; and

(d) Smoking on any lands, including roads, or in any buildings which have been designated and/or posted with no smoking signs.

§ 27.96 Advertising.

Except as may be authorized, posting, distributing, or otherwise displaying private or public notices, advertisements, announcements, or displays of any kind in any national wildlife refuge, other than business designations on private vehicles or boats is prohibited.

§ 27.97 Private operations.

Soliciting business or conducting a commercial enterprise on any national wildlife refuge is prohibited except as may be authorized by special permit.

50 C.F.R. PART 28
ENFORCEMENT, PENALTY, AND PROCEDURAL REQUIREMENTS FOR VIOLATIONS OF PARTS 25, 26, AND 27

AUTHORITY: Sec. 2, 33 Stat. 614, as amended (16 U.S.C. 685); Sec. 5, 43 Stat. 651 (16 U.S.C. 725); Sec. 5, 45 Stat. 449 (16 U.S.C. 690d); Sec. 10, 45 Stat. 1224 (16 U.S.C. 715i); Sec. 4, 48 Stat. 402, as amended (16 U.S.C. 664); Sec. 2, 48 Stat. 1270 (43 U.S.C. 315a); Sec. 4, 76 Stat. 654 (16 U.S.C. 460k); Sec. 4, 80 Stat. 927 (16 U.S.C. 668dd)(5 U.S.C. 301).

SOURCE: 41 FR 9171, Mar. 3, 1976, unless otherwise noted.

SUBPART A -- INTRODUCTION

§ 28.11 Purpose of regulations.

The regulations in this part govern the enforcement, penalty and procedural requirements for violations of Parts 25, 26, and 27.

SUBPART B -- ENFORCEMENT AUTHORITY

§ 28.21 General provisions.

Refuge managers and other authorized personnel are authorized pursuant to authority delegated from the Secretary and which has been published in the Federal Register (Administrative Manual 4 AM 4.2) to protect fish and wildlife and their habitat and prevent their disturbance, to protect Service lands, property, facilities, or interests therein, and to insure the safety of the using public to the fullest degree possible. The control of recreational use will be enforced to meet these purposes pursuant to Federal, State, and local laws and regulations: The provisions of this Subchapter C and any special regulations issued pursuant thereto; and the prohibitions and restrictions as posted.

[41 FR 9171, Mar. 3, 1976, as amended at 44 FR 42976, July 23, 1979; 51 FR 7575, March 5, 1986]

SUBPART C -- PENALTY PROVISIONS

§ 28.31 General penalty provisions.

(a) Any person who violates any of the provisions, rules, regulations, posted signs, or special regulations of this Subchapter C, or any items, conditions or restrictions in a permit, license, grant, privilege, or any other limitation established under the Subchapter C shall be subject to the penalty provisions of this section.

(b) Failure of any person, utilizing the resources of any national wildlife refuge or enjoying any privilege of use thereon for any purpose whatsoever, to comply with any of the provisions, conditions, restrictions, or requirements of this Subchapter C or to comply with any applicable provisions of Federal or State law may render such person liable to:

(1) The penalties as prescribed by law. (Sec. 4, 76 Stat. 654, 16 U.S.C. 460k-3; Sec. 4, 80 Stat. 927, as amended, 16 U.S.C. 668dd(e); Sec. 7, 60 Stat. 1080, 16 U.S.C. 666a; Sec. 6, 40 Stat. 756, as amended, 16 U.S.C. 707; Sec. 7, 48 Stat. 452, 16 U.S.C. 718g; Sec. 2, 33 Stat. 614, as amended, 18 U.S.C. 41.)

§ 28.32 Penalty provisions concerning fires and timber.

(a) Any person violating sections 1855-1856 of the Criminal Code (18 U.S.C. 1855-1856) as they pertain to fires on national wildlife refuge lands of the United States shall be subject to civil action and to the penalty provisions of the law.

(b) Any person violating sections 1852-1853 of the Criminal Code (18 U.S.C. 1852-1853) as they pertain to timber on national wildlife refuge lands of the United States shall be subject to civil action and to the penalty provisions of the law.

SUBPART D -- IMPOUNDMENT PROCEDURES

§ 28.41 Impoundment of abandoned property.

Any property abandoned or left unattended without authority on any national wildlife refuge for a period in excess of 72 hours is subject to removal. The expense of the removal shall be borne by the person owning or claiming ownership of the property. Such property is subject to sale or other disposal after 3 months, in accordance with section 203m of the Federal Property and Administrative Services Act of 1959, as amended (40 U.S.C. 484m), and regulations issued thereunder. Former owners may apply within 3 years for reimbursement for such property, subject to disposal and storage costs and similar expenses, upon sufficient proof of ownership.

§ 28.42 Impounding of domestic animals.

(a) Any animal trespassing on the lands of any national wildlife refuge may be impounded and disposed of in accordance with State statutes insofar as they may be applicable. In the absence of such State statutes, the animals shall be disposed of in accordance with this section.

(b) If the owner is known, prompt written notice of the impounding will be served in person with written receipt obtained or delivery by certified mail with return receipt requested. In the event of his failure to remove the impounded animal within five (5) days from receipt of such notice, it will be sold or otherwise disposed of as prescribed in this section.

(c) If the owner is unknown, no disposition of the animal shall be made until at least fifteen (15) days have elapsed from the date of a legal notice of the impounding has been posted at the county courthouse and 15 days after the second notice published in a newspaper in general circulation in the county in which the trespass took place.

(d) The notice shall state when and where the animal was impounded and shall describe it by brand or earmark or distinguishing marks or by other reasonable identification. The notice shall specify the time and place the animal will be offered at public sale to the highest bidder, in the event it is not claimed or redeemed. The notice shall reserve the right of the official conducting the sale to reject any and all bids so received.

(e) Prior to such sale, the owner may redeem the animal by submitting proof of ownership and paying all expenses of the United States for, capturing, impounding, advertising, care, forage, and damage claims.

(f) If an animal impounded under this section is offered at public sale and no bid is received or if the highest bid received is an amount less than the claim of the United States, the animal may be sold at private sale for the highest amount obtainable, or be condemned and destroyed or converted to the use of the United States. Upon the sale of any animal in accordance with this section, the buyer shall be issued a certificate of sale.

(g) In determining the claim of the Federal Government in all livestock trespass cases on national wildlife refuges, the value of forage consumed shall be computed at the commercial unit rate prevailing in the locality for that class of livestock. In addition, the claim shall include damages to national wildlife refuge property injured or destroyed, and all the related expenses incurred in the impounding, caring for and disposing of the animal. The salary of Service employees for the time spent in and about the investigations, reports, and settlement or prosecution of the case shall be prorated in computing the expense. Payment of claims due the United States shall be made by certified check or postal money order payable to the U.S. Fish and Wildlife Service.

§ 28.43 Destruction of dogs and cats.

Dogs and cats running at large on a national wildlife refuge and observed by an authorized official in the act of killing, injuring, harassing or molesting humans or wildlife may be disposed of in the interest of public safety and protection of the wildlife.

- 0 -

NATIONAL MARINE SANCTUARIES ACT (1972, 1992)
(16 U.S.C. §§ 1431-1445b)

The National Wildlife Refuge System is not the only federal land management system intended specifically to preserve habitat. The Refuge System's less well-known sibling is the Marine Sanctuary System. Not only is the Marine Sanctuary System less well-known, it is also much smaller: there are only thirteen marine sanctuaries.[60]

The Marine Sanctuary System was established under the Marine Research and Sanctuaries Act of 1972,[61] a statute that was focused primarily on ocean dumping. The statute was significantly amended in 1992 and renamed the National Marine Sanctuaries Act.[62]

The Act authorizes the Secretary of Commerce to "designate any discrete area of the marine environment as a national marine sanctuary" by promulgating a regulation.[63] The designation is predicated upon a finding that it will fulfill the purposes of the Act, including which includes "to maintain the natural biological communities in the national marine sanctuaries, and to protect, and, where appropriate, restore and enhance natural habitats, populations, and ecological processes."[64] In making this finding, the Secretary is to consider a lengthy list of factors -- including "the area's natural resource and ecological qualities, including its contribution to biological productivity, maintenance of ecosystem structure, maintenance of ecologically or commercially important or threatened species or species assemblages, maintenance of critical habitat of endangered species, and the biogeographic representation of the site."[65] These findings are to be made in the context of an elaborate procedural process that includes consultations with congressional committees, the heads of several federal agencies, officials of state and local governments, the regional fishery management council, and "other interested persons";[66] preparation of an environmental impact statement and maps of the proposed area;[67] publication of notice in the *Federal Register* and local newspapers.[68] The Secretary is required to publish notice of this decision to designate or not and must provide Congress with time to review his decision. Given the procedure, it is hardly surprising that so few sanctuaries have been designated.

Designation of an area as a sanctuary gives the Secretary the power to regulate activities that are inconsistent with resource conservation.[69] This includes a consultation provision applicable to federal agencies undertaking or authorizing activities that are likely to injure any sanctuary resource.[70] The Act also makes it unlawful to

(1) destroy, cause the loss of, or injure any sanctuary resource managed under law or regulations for that sanctuary;

(2) possess, sell, offer for sale, purchase, import, export, deliver, carry, transport, or ship by any means any sanctuary resource taken in violation of this section;

(3) interfere with the enforcement of this title [16 U.S.C. §§ 1431 *et seq.*] ...; or

(4) violate any provision of this title or any regulation or permit issued pursuant to this title.[71]

Violations are punishable by fines up to $100,000,[72] forfeiture of the vessel involved,[73] and liability for damages to sanctuary resources.[74]

Regulations implementing the Act and listing the existing sanctuaries are in 15 C.F.R. part 922.

16 U.S.C. § 1431. Findings, purposes, and policies; establishment of System. (a) Findings. The Congress finds that --

(1) this Nation historically has recognized the importance of protecting special areas of its public domain, but these efforts have been directed almost exclusively to land areas above the high-water mark;

(2) certain areas of the marine environment possess conservation, recreational, ecological, historical, scientific, educational, cultural, archeological, or esthetic qualities which give them special national, and in some cases international, significance;

(3) while the need to control the effects of particular activities has led to enactment of resource-specific legislation, these laws cannot in all cases provide a coordinated and comprehensive approach to the conservation and management of special areas of the marine environment; and

(4) a Federal program which establishes areas of the marine environment which have special conservation, recreational, ecological, historical, cultural, archeological, scientific, educational, or esthetic qualities as national marine sanctuaries managed as the National Marine Sanctuary System will--

(A) improve the conservation, understanding, management, and wise and sustainable use of marine resources;

(B) enhance public awareness, understanding, and appreciation of the marine environment; and

(C) maintain for future generations the habitat, and ecological services, of the natural assemblage of living resources that inhabit these areas.

(5), (6) [deleted]

(b) Purposes and policies. The purposes and policies of this title [16 U.S.C. §§ 1431 *et seq.*] are (1) to identify and designate as national marine sanctuaries areas of the marine environment which are of special national significance and to manage these areas as the National Marine Sanctuary System;

(2) to provide authority for comprehensive and coordinated conservation and management of these marine areas, and activities affecting them, in a manner which complements existing regulatory authorities;

(3) to maintain the natural biological communities in the national marine sanctuaries, and to protect, and, where appropriate, restore and enhance natural habitats, populations, and ecological processes;

(4) to enhance public awareness, understanding, appreciation, and wise and sustainable use of the marine environment, and the natural, historical, cultural, and archeological resources of the National Marine Sanctuary System;

(5) to support, promote, and coordinate scientific research on, and long-term monitoring of, the resources of these marine areas;

(6) to facilitate to the extent compatible with the primary objective of resource protection, all public and private uses of the resources of these marine areas not prohibited pursuant to other authorities;

(7) to develop and implement coordinated plans for the protection and management of these areas with appropriate Federal agencies, State and local governments, Native American tribes and organizations, international organizations, and other public and private interests concerned with the continuing health and resilience of these marine areas;

(8) to create models of, and incentives for, ways to conserve and manage these areas, including the application of innovative management techniques; and

(9) to cooperate with global programs encouraging conservation of marine resources.

(c) Establishment of system. There is established the National Marine Sanctuary System, which shall consist of national marine sanctuaries designated by the Secretary in accordance with this title.

[Pub. L. 92-532, Title III, § 301, 86 Stat. 1061 (Oct. 23, 1972); Pub. L. 96-332, § 1, 94 Stat. 1057 (Aug. 29, 1980); Pub. L. 98-498, Title I, § 102, 98 Stat. 2296 (Oct. 19, 1984); Pub. L. 102-587, Title II, § 2101, 106 Stat. 5039 (Nov. 4, 1992); Pub. L. 104-283, § 9(a), 110 Stat. 3367 (Oct. 11, 1996)]

16 U.S.C. § 1432. Definitions. As used in this title, the term --

(1) "draft management plan" means the plan described in section 304(a)(1)(C)(v) [16 U.S.C. § 1434(a)(1)(C)(v)];

(2) "Magnuson-Stevens Act" means the Magnuson-Stevens Fishery Conservation and Management Act (16 U.S.C. §§ 1801 *et seq.*);

(3) "marine environment" means those areas of coastal and ocean waters, the Great Lakes and their connecting waters, and submerged lands over which the United States exercises jurisdiction, including the exclusive economic zone, consistent with international law;

(4) "Secretary" means the Secretary of Commerce;

(5) "State" means each of the several States, the District of Columbia, the Commonwealth of Puerto Rico, the Commonwealth of the Northern Mariana Islands, American Samoa, the Virgin Islands, Guam, and any other commonwealth, territory, or possession of the United States;

(6) "damages" includes --

(A) compensation for --

(i)(I) the cost of replacing, restoring, or acquiring the equivalent of a sanctuary resource; and

(II) the value of the lost use of a sanctuary resource pending its restoration or replacement or the acquisition of an equivalent sanctuary resource; or

(ii) the value of a sanctuary resource if the sanctuary resource cannot be restored or replaced or if the equivalent of such resource cannot be acquired;

(B) the cost of damage assessments under section 312(b)(2);

(C) the reasonable cost of monitoring appropriate to the injured, restored, or replaced resources;

(D) the cost of curation and conservation of archeological, historical, and cultural sanctuary resources; and

(E) the cost of enforcement actions undertaken by the Secretary in response to the destruction or loss of, or injury to, a sanctuary resource;

(7) "response costs" means the costs of actions taken or authorized by the Secretary to minimize destruction or loss of, or injury to, sanctuary resources, or to minimize the imminent risks of such destruction, loss, or injury, including costs related to seizure, forfeiture, storage, or disposal arising from liability under section 312 [16 U.S.C. § 1443];

(8) "sanctuary resource" means any living or nonliving resource of a national marine sanctuary that contributes to the conservation, recreational, ecological, historical, educational, cultural, archeological, scientific, or aesthetic value of the sanctuary;

(9) "exclusive economic zone" means the exclusive economic zone as defined in the Magnuson-Stevens Act [16 U.S.C.A. § 1801 *et seq.*]; and

(10) "System" means the National Marine Sanctuary System established by section 301 [16 U.S.C. § 1431].

[Pub. L. 92-532, Title III, § 302, 86 Stat. 1061 (Oct. 23, 1972); Pub. L. 96-332, § 2, 94 Stat. 1057 (Aug. 29, 1980); Pub. L. 97-375, Title II, § 202(a), 96 Stat. 1822 (Dec. 21, 1982); Pub. L. 98-498, Title I, § 102, 98 Stat. 2297 (Oct. 19, 1984); Pub. L. 100-627, Title II, § 204(b), 102 Stat. 3217 (Nov. 7, 1988); Pub. L. 102-587, Title II, § 2102, 106 Stat. 5040 (Nov. 4, 1992); Pub. L. 104-208, Div. A, Title I, § 101(a) [Title II, § 211(b)], 110 Stat. 3009-41 (Sept. 30, 1996); Pub. L. 104-283, § 9(b), 110 Stat. 3367 (Oct. 11, 1996)]

16 U.S.C. § 1433. Sanctuary designation standards. (a) Standards. The Secretary may designate any discrete area of the marine environment as a national marine sanctuary and promulgate regulations implementing the designation if the Secretary determines that --

(1) the designation will fulfill the purposes and policies of this title;

(2) the area is of special national significance due to--

(A) its conservation, recreational, ecological, historical, scientific, cultural, archaeological, educational, or esthetic qualities;

(B) the communities of living marine resources it harbors; or

(C) its resource or human-use values;

(3) existing State and Federal authorities are inadequate or should be supplemented to ensure coordinated and comprehensive conservation and management of the area, including resource protection, scientific research, and public education;

(4) designation of the area as a national marine sanctuary will facilitate the objectives stated in paragraph (3); and

(5) the area is of a size and nature that will permit comprehensive and coordinated conservation and management.

(b) Factors and consultations required in making determinations and findings. (1) Factors. For purposes of determining if an area of the marine environment meets the standards set forth in subsection (a) of this section, the Secretary shall consider--

(A) the area's natural resource and ecological qualities, including its contribution to biological productivity, maintenance of ecosystem structure, maintenance of ecologically or commercially important or threatened species or species assemblages, maintenance of critical habitat of endangered species, and the biogeographic representation of the site;

(B) the area's historical, cultural, archaeological, or paleontological significance;

(C) the present and potential uses of the area that depend on maintenance of the area's resources, including commercial and recreational fishing, subsistence uses, other commercial and recreational activities, and research and education;

(D) the present and potential activities that may adversely affect the factors identified in subparagraphs (A), (B), and (C);

(E) the existing State and Federal regulatory and management authorities applicable to the area and the adequacy of those authorities to fulfill the purposes and policies of this title [16 U.S.C. §§ 1431 *et seq.*];

(F) the manageability of the area, including such factors as its size, its ability to be identified as a discrete ecological unit with definable boundaries, its accessibility, and its suitability for monitoring and enforcement activities;

(G) the public benefits to be derived from sanctuary status, with emphasis on the benefits of long-term protection of nationally significant resources, vital habitats, and resources which generate tourism;

(H) the negative impacts produced by management restrictions on income-generating activities such as living and nonliving resources development;

(I) the socioeconomic effects of sanctuary designation;

(J) the area's scientific value and value for monitoring the resources and natural processes that occur there;

(K) the feasibility, where appropriate, of employing innovative management approaches to protect sanctuary resources or to manage compatible uses; and

(L) the value of the area as an addition to the System.

(2) Consultation. In making determinations and findings, the Secretary shall consult with--

(A) the Committee on Resources of the House of Representatives and the Committee on Commerce, Science, and Transportation of the Senate;

(B) the Secretaries of State, Defense, Transportation, and the Interior, the Administrator, and the heads of other interested Federal agencies;

(C) the responsible officials or relevant agency heads of the appropriate State and local government entities, including coastal zone management agencies, that will or are likely to be affected by the establishment of the area as a national marine sanctuary;

(D) the appropriate officials of any Regional Fishery Management Council established by section 302 of the Magnuson-Stevens Act [16 U.S.C. § 1852] that may be affected by the proposed designation; and

(E) other interested persons.

(3) Repealed. Pub. L. 106-513, § 5(b)(2), Nov. 13, 2000, 114 Stat. 2383.

[Pub. L. 92-532, Title III, § 303, 86 Stat. 1062 (Oct. 23, 1972); Pub. L. 98-498, Title I, § 102, 98 Stat. 2297 (Oct. 19, 1984); Pub. L. 102-587, Title II, § 2103, 106 Stat. 5041 (Nov. 4, 1992)]

16 U.S.C. § 1434. Procedures for designation and implementation. (a) Sanctuary proposal. (1) In proposing to designate a national marine sanctuary, the Secretary shall--

(A) issue, in the Federal Register, a notice of the proposal, proposed regulations that may be necessary and reasonable to implement the proposal, and a summary of the draft management plan;

(B) provide notice of the proposal in newspapers of general circulation or electronic media in the communities that may be affected by the proposal; and

(C) no later than the day on which the notice required under subparagraph (A) is submitted to the Office of the Federal Register, submit a copy of that notice and the draft sanctuary designation documents prepared pursuant to section 304(a)(2) [16 U.S.C. § 1434(a)(2)], including an executive summary, to the Committee on Resources of the House of Representatives, the Committee on Commerce, Science, and Transportation of the Senate, and the Governor of each State in which any part of the proposed sanctuary would be located.

(2) Sanctuary designation documents. The Secretary shall prepare and make available to the public sanctuary designation documents on the proposal that include the following:

(A) A draft environmental impact statement pursuant to the National Environmental Policy Act of 1969 (42 U.S.C. 4321 *et seq.*).

(B) A resource assessment that documents --

(i) present and potential uses of the area, including commercial and recreational fishing, research and education, minerals and energy development, subsistence uses, and other commercial, governmental, or recreational uses;

(ii) after consultation with the Secretary of the Interior, any commercial, governmental, or recreational resource uses in the areas that are subject to the primary jurisdiction of the Department of the Interior; and

(iii) information prepared in consultation with the Secretary of Defense, the Secretary of Energy, and the Administrator of the Environmental Protection Agency, on any past, present, or proposed future disposal or discharge of materials in the vicinity of the proposed sanctuary.

Public disclosure by the Secretary of such information shall be consistent with national security regulations.

(C) A draft management plan for the proposed national marine sanctuary that includes the following:

(i) The terms of the proposed designation.

(ii) Proposed mechanisms to coordinate existing regulatory and management authorities within the area.

(iii) The proposed goals and objectives, management responsibilities, resource studies, and appropriate strategies for managing sanctuary resources of the proposed sanctuary, including interpretation and education, innovative management strategies, research, monitoring and assessment, resource protection, restoration, enforcement, and surveillance activities.

(iv) An evaluation of the advantages of cooperative State and Federal management if all or part of the proposed sanctuary is within the territorial limits of any State or is superjacent to the subsoil and seabed within the seaward boundary of a State, as that boundary is established under the

Submerged Lands Act (43 U.S.C. §§ 1301 *et seq.*).

(v) An estimate of the annual cost to the Federal Government of the proposed designation, including costs of personnel, equipment and facilities, enforcement, research, and public education.

(vi) The proposed regulations referred to in paragraph (1)(A).

(D) Maps depicting the boundaries of the proposed sanctuary.

(E) The basis for the determinations made under section 303(a) [16 U.S.C. § 1433(a)] with respect to the area.

(F) An assessment of the considerations under section 303(b)(1) [16 U.S.C. § 1433(b)(1)].

(3) Public hearing. No sooner than thirty days after issuing a notice under this subsection, the Secretary shall hold at least one public hearing in the coastal area or areas that will be most affected by the proposed designation of the area as a national marine sanctuary for the purpose of receiving the views of interested parties.

(4) Terms of designation. The terms of designation of a sanctuary shall include the geographic area proposed to be included within the sanctuary, the characteristics of the area that give it conservation, recreational, ecological, historical, research, educational, or esthetic value, and the types of activities that will be subject to regulation by the Secretary to protect those characteristics. The terms of designation may be modified only by the same procedures by which the original designation is made.

(5) Fishing regulations. The Secretary shall provide the appropriate Regional Fishery Management Council with the opportunity to prepare draft regulations for fishing within the Exclusive Economic Zone as the Council may deem necessary to implement the proposed designation. Draft regulations prepared by the Council, or a Council determination that regulations are not necessary pursuant to this paragraph, shall be accepted and issued as proposed regulations by the Secretary unless the Secretary finds that the Council's action fails to fulfill the purposes and policies of this title [16 U.S.C. §§ 1431 *et seq.*] and the goals and objectives of the proposed designation. In preparing the draft regulations, a Regional Fishery Management Council shall use as guidance the national standards of section 301(a) of the Magnuson Act [16 U.S.C. § 1851(a)] to the extent that the standards are consistent and compatible with the goals and objectives of the proposed designation. The Secretary shall prepare the fishing regulations, if the Council declines to make a determination with respect to the need for regulations, makes a determination which is rejected by the Secretary, or fails to prepare the draft regulations in a timely manner. Any amendments to the fishing regulations shall be drafted, approved, and issued in the same manner as the original regulations. The Secretary shall also cooperate with other appropriate fishery management authorities with rights or responsibilities within a proposed sanctuary at the earliest practicable stage in drafting any sanctuary fishing regulations.

(6) Committee action. After receiving the documents under subsection (a)(1)(C) of this section, the Committee on Resources of the House of Representatives and the Committee on Commerce, Science, and Transportation of the Senate may each hold hearings on the proposed designation and on the matters set forth in the documents. If within the forty-five day period of continuous session of Congress beginning on the date of submission of the documents, either Committee issues a report concerning

matters addressed in the documents, the Secretary shall consider this report before publishing a notice to designate the national marine sanctuary.

(b) Taking effect of designations. (1) Notice. In designating a national marine sanctuary, the Secretary shall publish in the Federal Register notice of the designation together with final regulations to implement the designation and any other matters required by law, and submit such notice to the Congress. The Secretary shall advise the public of the availability of the final management plan and the final environmental impact statement with respect to such sanctuary. The Secretary shall issue a notice of designation with respect to a proposed national marine sanctuary site not later than 30 months after the date a notice declaring the site to be an active candidate for sanctuary designation is published in the Federal Register under regulations issued under this Act, or shall publish not later than such date in the Federal Register findings regarding why such notice has not been published. No notice of designation may occur until the expiration of the period for Committee action under subsection (a)(6) of this section. The designation (and any of its terms not disapproved under this subsection) and regulations shall take effect and become final after the close of a review period of forty-five days of continuous session of Congress beginning on the day on which such notice is published unless, in the case of a national marine sanctuary that is located partially or entirely within the seaward boundary of any State, the Governor affected certifies to the Secretary that the designation or any of its terms is unacceptable, in which case the designation or the unacceptable term shall not take effect in the area of the sanctuary lying within the seaward boundary of the State.
(2) Withdrawal of designation. If the Secretary considers that actions taken under paragraph (1) will affect the designation of a national marine sanctuary in a manner that the goals and objectives of the sanctuary or System cannot be fulfilled, the Secretary may withdraw the entire designation. If the Secretary does not withdraw the designation, only those terms of the designation not certified under paragraph (1) shall take effect.
(3) Procedures in computing the forty-five-day periods of continuous session of Congress pursuant to subsection (a)(6) of this section and paragraph (1) of this subsection--

(A) continuity of session is broken only by an adjournment of Congress sine die; and

(B) the days on which either House of Congress is not in session because of an adjournment of more than three days to a day certain are excluded.

(c) Access and valid rights. (1) Nothing in this title [16 U.S.C. §§ 1431 *et seq.*] shall be construed as terminating or granting to the Secretary the right to terminate any valid lease, permit, license, or right of subsistence use or of access that is in existence on the date of designation of any national marine sanctuary.
(2) The exercise of a lease, permit, license, or right is subject to regulation by the Secretary with the purposes for which the sanctuary is designated.

(d) Interagency cooperation. (1) Review of agency actions. (A) In general. Federal agency actions internal or external to a national marine sanctuary, including private activities authorized by licenses, leases, or permits, that are likely to destroy, cause the loss of, or injure any sanctuary resource are subject to consultation with the Secretary.

(B) Agency statements required. Subject to any regulations the Secretary may establish each Federal agency proposing an action described in subparagraph (A) shall provide the Secretary with a written statement describing the action and its potential effects on sanctuary resources at the earliest practicable time, but in no case later than 45 days before the final approval of the action unless such Federal agency and the Secretary agree to a different schedule.

(2) Secretary's recommended alternatives. If the Secretary finds that a Federal agency action is likely to destroy, cause the loss of, or injure a sanctuary resource, the Secretary shall (within 45 days of receipt of complete information on the proposed agency action) recommend reasonable and prudent alternatives, which may include conduct of the action elsewhere, which can be taken by the Federal agency in implementing the agency action that will protect sanctuary resources.

(3) Response to recommendations. The agency head who receives the Secretary's recommended alternatives under paragraph (2) shall promptly consult with the Secretary on the alternatives. If the agency head decides not to follow the alternatives, the agency head shall provide the Secretary with a written statement explaining the reasons for that decision.

(4) Failure to follow alternative. If the head of a Federal agency takes an action other than an alternative recommended by the Secretary and such action results in the destruction of, loss of, or injury to a sanctuary resource, the head of the agency shall promptly prevent and mitigate further damage and restore or replace the sanctuary resource in a manner approved by the Secretary.

(e) Review of management plans. Not more than five years after the date of designation of any national marine sanctuary, and thereafter at intervals not exceeding five years, the Secretary shall evaluate the substantive progress toward implementing the management plan and goals for the sanctuary, especially the effectiveness of site-specific management techniques and strategies, and shall revise the management plan and regulations as necessary to fulfill the purposes and policies of this title [16 U.S.C. §§ 1431 *et seq.*]. This review shall include a prioritization of management objectives.

(f) Limitation on designation of new sanctuaries. (1) Finding required. The Secretary may not publish in the Federal Register any sanctuary designation notice or regulations proposing to designate a new sanctuary, unless the Secretary has published a finding that --

(A) the addition of a new sanctuary will not have a negative impact on the System; and

(B) sufficient resources were available in the fiscal year in which the finding is made to --

(i) effectively implement sanctuary management plans for each sanctuary in the System; and

(ii) complete site characterization studies and inventory known sanctuary resources, including cultural resources, for each sanctuary in the System within 10 years after the date that the finding is made if the resources available for those activities are maintained at the same level for each fiscal year in that 10 year period.

(2) Deadline. If the Secretary does not submit the findings required by paragraph (1) before February 1, 2004, the Secretary shall submit to the Congress before October 1, 2004, a finding with respect to whether the requirements of subparagraphs (A) and (B) of paragraph (1) have been met by all existing sanctuaries.

(3) Limitation on application. Paragraph (1) does not apply to any sanctuary designation documents for --

(A) a Thunder Bay National Marine Sanctuary; or

(B) a Northwestern Hawaiian Islands National Marine Sanctuary.

[Pub. L. 92-532, Title III, § 304, 86 Stat. 1063 (Oct. 23, 1972); Pub. L. 94-62, § 4, July 25, 1975, 89 Stat. 303; Pub. L. 94-326, § 4, 90 Stat. 725 (June 30, 1976); Pub. L. 95-153, § 3, 91 Stat. 1255 (Nov. 4, 1977); Pub. L. 96-332, § 3, 94 Stat. 1059 (Aug. 29, 1980); Pub. L. 97-109, 95 Stat. 1512 (Dec. 26, 1981); Pub. L. 98-498, Title I, § 102, 98 Stat. 2298 (Oct. 19, 1984); Pub. L. 100-627, Title II, § 202, 102 Stat. 3214 (Nov. 7, 1988); Pub. L. 102-587, Title II, § 2104, 106 Stat. 5041 (Nov. 4, 1992); Pub. L. 104-283, § 9(h), 110 Stat. 3368 (Oct. 11, 1996)]

16 U.S.C. § 1435. Application of regulations; international negotiations and cooperation. (a) Regulations. This title and the regulations issued under section 304 [16 U.S.C. § 1434] shall be applied in accordance with generally recognized principles of international law, and in accordance with treaties, conventions, and other agreements to which the United States is a party. No regulation shall apply to or be enforced against a person who is not a citizen, national, or resident alien of the United States, unless in accordance with --

(1) generally recognized principles of international law;

(2) an agreement between the United States and the foreign state of which the person is a citizen; or

(3) an agreement between the United States and the flag state of a foreign vessel, if the person is a crewmember of the vessel.

(b) Negotiations. The Secretary of State, in consultation with the Secretary, shall take appropriate action to enter into negotiations with other governments to make necessary arrangements for the protection of any national marine sanctuary and to promote the purposes for which the sanctuary is established.

(c) International cooperation. The Secretary, in consultation with the Secretary of State and other appropriate Federal agencies, shall cooperate with other governments and international organizations in furtherance of the purposes and policies of this title [16 U.S.C. §§ 1431 *et seq.*] and consistent with applicable regional and multilateral arrangements for the protection and management of special marine areas.

[Pub. L. 98-498, Title I, § 102, 98 Stat. 2302 (Oct. 19, 1984); Pub. L. 102-587, Title II, § 2105, 106 Stat. 5043 (Nov. 4, 1992)]

16 U.S.C. § 1436. Prohibited activities. It is unlawful for any person to --

(1) destroy, cause the loss of, or injure any sanctuary resource managed under law or regulations for that sanctuary;

(2) possess, sell, offer for sale, purchase, import, export, deliver, carry, transport, or ship by any means any sanctuary resource taken in violation of this section;

(3) interfere with the enforcement of this title [16 U.S.C. §§ 1431 *et seq.*] by --

(A) refusing to permit any officer authorized to enforce this title to board a vessel, other than a vessel operated by the Department of Defense or United States Coast Guard, subject to such person's control for the purposes of conducting any search or inspection in connection with the enforcement of this title;

(B) resisting, opposing, impeding, intimidating, harassing, bribing, interfering with, or forcibly assaulting any person authorized by the Secretary to implement this title or any such authorized officer in the conduct of any search or inspection performed under this title; or

(C) knowingly and willfully submitting false information to the Secretary or any officer authorized to enforce this title in connection with any search or inspection conducted under this title; or

(4) violate any provision of this title or any regulation or permit issued pursuant to this title.

[Pub. L. 98-498, Title I, § 102, 98 Stat. 2302 (Oct. 19, 1984); Pub. L. 102-587, Title II, § 2106, 106 Stat. 5043 (Nov. 4, 1992)]

16 U.S.C. § 1437. Enforcement. (a) In general. The Secretary shall conduct such enforcement activities as are necessary and reasonable to carry out this title [16 U.S.C. §§ 1431 *et seq.*].

(b) Powers of authorized officers. Any person who is authorized to enforce this title [16 U.S.C. may --

(1) board, search, inspect, and seize any vessel suspected of being used to violate this title or any regulation or permit issued under this title and any equipment, stores, and cargo of such vessel;

(2) seize wherever found any sanctuary resource taken or retained in violation of this title [16 U.S.C. or any regulation or permit issued under this title;

(3) seize any evidence of a violation of this title or of any regulation or permit issued under this title;

(4) execute any warrant or other process issued by any court of competent jurisdiction;

(5) exercise any other lawful authority; and

(6) arrest any person, if there is reasonable cause to believe that such person has committed an act prohibited by section 306(3) [16 U.S.C. § 1436(3)].

(c) Criminal offenses. (1) Offenses. A person is guilty of an offense under this subsection if the person commits any act prohibited by section 306(3) [16 U.S.C. § 1436(3)].

(2) Punishment. Any person that is guilty of an offense under this subsection --

(A) except as provided in subparagraph (B), shall be fined under Title 18, imprisoned for not more than 6 months, or both; or

(B) in the case of a person who in the commission of such an offense uses a dangerous weapon, engages in conduct that causes bodily injury to any person authorized to enforce this title or any person authorized to implement the provisions of this title, or places any such person in fear of imminent bodily injury, shall be fined under Title 18, imprisoned for not more than 10 years, or both.

(d) Civil penalties. (1) Civil penalty. Any person subject to the jurisdiction of the United States who violates this chapter or any regulation or permit issued under this title shall be liable to the United States for a civil penalty of not more than $100,000 for each such violation, to be assessed by the Secretary. Each day of a continuing violation shall constitute a separate violation.

(2) Notice. No penalty shall be assessed under this subsection until after the person charged has been given notice and an opportunity for a hearing.

(3) In rem jurisdiction. A vessel used in violating this title or any regulation or permit issued under this title shall be liable in rem for any civil penalty assessed for such violation. Such penalty shall constitute a maritime lien on the vessel and may be recovered in an action in rem in the district court of the United States having jurisdiction over the vessel.

(4) Review of civil penalty. Any person against whom a civil penalty is assessed under this subsection may obtain review in the United States district court for the appropriate district by filing a complaint in such court not later than 30 days after the date of such order.

(5) Collection of penalties. If any person fails to pay an assessment of a civil penalty under this section after it has become a final and unappealable order, or after the appropriate court has entered final judgment in favor of the Secretary, the Secretary shall refer the matter to the Attorney General, who shall recover the amount assessed in any appropriate district court of the United States. In such action, the validity and appropriateness of the final order imposing the civil penalty shall not be subject to review.

(6) Compromise or other action by Secretary. The Secretary may compromise, modify, or remit, with or without conditions, any civil penalty which is or may be imposed under this section.

(e) Forfeiture. (1) In general. Any vessel (including the vessel's equipment, stores, and cargo) and other item used, and any sanctuary resource taken or retained, in any manner, in connection with or as a result of any violation of this title or of any regulation or permit issued under this title shall be subject to forfeiture to the United States pursuant to a civil proceeding under this subsection. The proceeds from forfeiture actions under this subsection shall constitute a separate recovery in addition to any amounts recovered as civil penalties under this section or as civil damages under section 312 [16 U.S.C. § 1443]. None of those proceeds shall be subject to set-off.

(2) Application of the customs laws. The Secretary may exercise the authority of any United States official granted by any relevant customs law relating to the seizure, forfeiture, condemnation, disposition, remission, and mitigation of property in enforcing this chapter.

(3) Disposal of sanctuary resources. Any sanctuary resource seized pursuant to this title may be disposed of pursuant to an order of the appropriate court, or, if perishable, in a manner prescribed by regulations promulgated by the Secretary. Any

proceeds from the sale of such sanctuary resource shall for all purposes represent the sanctuary resource so disposed of in any subsequent legal proceedings.

(4) Presumption. For the purposes of this section there is a rebuttable presumption that all sanctuary resources found on board a vessel that is used or seized in connection with a violation of this title or of any regulation or permit issued under this title were taken or retained in violation of this title or of a regulation or permit issued under this title.

(f) Payment of storage, care, and other costs. (1) Expenditures. (A) Notwithstanding any other law, amounts received by the United States as civil penalties, forfeitures of property, and costs imposed under paragraph (2) shall be retained by the Secretary in the manner provided for in section 9607(f)(1) of Title 42.

(B) Amounts received under this section for forfeitures and costs imposed under paragraph (2) shall be used to pay the reasonable and necessary costs incurred by the Secretary to provide temporary storage, care, maintenance, and disposal of any sanctuary resource or other property seized in connection with a violation of this title or any regulation or permit issued under this title.

(C) Amounts received under this section as civil penalties and any amounts remaining after the operation of subparagraph (B) shall be used, in order of priority, to--

(i) manage and improve the national marine sanctuary with respect to which the violation occurred that resulted in the penalty or forfeiture;

(ii) pay a reward to any person who furnishes information leading to an assessment of a civil penalty, or to a forfeiture of property, for a violation of this title or any regulation or permit issued under this title; and

(iii) manage and improve any other national marine sanctuary.

(2) Liability for costs. Any person assessed a civil penalty for a violation of this title or of any regulation or permit issued under this title, and any claimant in a forfeiture action brought for such a violation, shall be liable for the reasonable costs incurred by the Secretary in storage, care, and maintenance of any sanctuary resource or other property seized in connection with the violation.

(g) Subpoenas. In the case of any hearing under this section which is determined on the record in accordance with the procedures provided for under section 554 of Title 5, the Secretary may issue subpoenas for the attendance and testimony of witnesses and the production of relevant papers, books, electronic files, and documents, and may administer oaths.

(h) Use of resources of State and other Federal agencies. The Secretary shall, whenever appropriate, use by agreement the personnel, services, and facilities of State and other Federal departments, agencies, and instrumentalities, on a reimbursable or nonreimbursable basis, to carry out the Secretary's responsibilities under this section.

(i) Coast Guard authority not limited. Nothing in this section shall be considered to limit the authority of the Coast Guard to enforce this or any other Federal law under section 89 of Title 14.

(j) Injunctive relief. If the Secretary determines that there is an imminent risk of destruction or loss of or injury to a sanctuary resource, or that there has been actual destruction or loss of, or injury to, a sanctuary resource which may give rise to liability under section 312 [16 U.S.C. § 1443], the Attorney General, upon request of the Secretary, shall seek to obtain such relief as may be necessary to abate such risk or actual destruction, loss, or injury, or to restore or replace the sanctuary resource, or both. The district courts of the United States shall have jurisdiction in such a case to order such relief as the public interest and the equities of the case may require.

(k) Area of application and enforceability. The area of application and enforceability of this title includes the territorial sea of the United States, as described in Presidential Proclamation 5928 of December 27, 1988, which is subject to the sovereignty of the United States, and the United States exclusive economic zone, consistent with international law.

(l) Nationwide service of process. In any action by the United States under this title, process may be served in any district where the defendant is found, resides, transacts business, or has appointed an agent for the service of process.

[Pub. L. Pub. L. 98-498, Title I, § 102, 98 Stat. 2302 (Oct. 19, 1984); Pub. L. 100-627, Title II, § 207, 102 Stat. 3219 (Nov. 7, 1988); Pub. L. 102-587, Title II, § 2107(a)-(c), (e), 106 Stat. 5043 (Nov. 4, 1992), 5044; Pub. L. 104-283, § 9(c), 110 Stat. 3367 (Oct. 11, 1996)]

16 U.S.C. § 1438. Repealed. Pub. L. 100-627, Title II, § 203(1), Nov. 7, 1988, 102 Stat. 3214.

16 U.S.C. § 1439. Regulations. The Secretary may issue such regulations as may be necessary to carry out this title.

[Pub. L. 98-498, Title I, § 102, 98 Stat. 2303 (Oct. 19, 1984); renumbered Pub. L. 100-627, Title II, § 203(2), 102 Stat. 3214 (Nov. 7, 1988)]

16 U.S.C. § 1440. Research, monitoring, and education. ****

§ 1441. Special use permits. (a) Issuance of permits. The Secretary may issue special use permits which authorize the conduct of specific activities in a national marine sanctuary if the Secretary determines such authorization is necessary --

(1) to establish conditions of access to and use of any sanctuary resource; or
(2) to promote public use and understanding of a sanctuary resource.

(b) Public notice required. The Secretary shall provide appropriate public notice before identifying any category of activity subject to a special use permit under subsection (a).

(c) Permit terms. A permit issued under this section --

(1) shall authorize the conduct of an activity only if that activity is compatible with the purposes for which the sanctuary is designated and with protection of sanctuary resources;
(2) shall not authorize the conduct of any activity for a period of more than 5 years

unless renewed by the Secretary;

(3) shall require that activities carried out under the permit be conducted in a manner that does not destroy, cause the loss of, or injure sanctuary resources; and

(4) shall require the permittee to purchase and maintain comprehensive general liability insurance, or post an equivalent bond, against claims arising out of activities conducted under the permit and to agree to hold the United States harmless against such claims.

(d) Fees. (1) Assessment and collection. The Secretary may assess and collect fees for the conduct of any activity under a permit issued under this section.

(2) Amount. The amount of a fee under this subsection shall be equal to the sum of --

(A) costs incurred, or expected to be incurred, by the Secretary in issuing the permit;

(B) costs incurred, or expected to be incurred, by the Secretary as a direct result of the conduct of the activity for which the permit is issued, including costs of monitoring the conduct of the activity; and

(C) an amount which represents the fair market value of the use of the sanctuary resource.

(3) Use of fees. Amounts collected by the Secretary in the form of fees under this section may be used by the Secretary --

(A) for issuing and administering permits under this section; and

(B) for expenses of managing national marine sanctuaries.

(4) Waiver or reduction of fees. The Secretary may accept in-kind contributions in lieu of a fee under paragraph (2)(C), or waive or reduce any fee assessed under this subsection for any activity that does not derive profit from the access to or use of sanctuary resources.

(e) Violations. Upon violation of a term or condition of a permit issued under this section, the Secretary may --

(1) suspend or revoke the permit without compensation to the permittee and without liability to the United States;

(2) assess a civil penalty in accordance with section 307 [16 U.S.C. § 1436]; or

(3) both.

(f) Reports. Each person issued a permit under this section shall submit an annual report to the Secretary not later than December 31 of each year which describes activities conducted under that permit and revenues derived from such activities during the year.

(g) Fishing. Nothing in this section shall be considered to require a person to obtain a permit under this section for the conduct of any fishing activities in a national marine sanctuary.

[Pub. L. 100-627, Title II, § 203(3), 102 Stat. 3214 (Nov. 7, 1988)]

16 U.S.C. § 1442. Cooperative agreements, donations, and acquisitions. ****

16 U.S.C. § 1443. Destruction or loss of, or injury to, sanctuary resources. (a) Liability. (1) Liability to United States. Any person who destroys, causes the loss of, or injures any sanctuary resource is liable to the United States for an amount equal to the sum of--

(A) the amount of response costs and damages resulting from the destruction, loss, or injury; and

(B) interest on that amount calculated in the manner described under section 2705 of Title 33.

(2) Liability in rem. Any vessel used to destroy, cause the loss of, or injure any sanctuary resource shall be liable in rem to the United States for response costs and damages resulting from such destruction, loss, or injury. The amount of that liability shall constitute a maritime lien on the vessel and may be recovered in an action in rem in any district court of the United States that has jurisdiction over the vessel.

(3) Defenses. A person is not liable under this subsection if that person establishes that--

(A) the destruction or loss of, or injury to, the sanctuary resource was caused solely by an act of God, an act of war, or an act or omission of a third party, and the person acted with due care;

(B) the destruction, loss, or injury was caused by an activity authorized by Federal or State law; or

(C) the destruction, loss, or injury was negligible.

(4) Limits to liability. Nothing in sections 175, 181 to 183, and 183b to 188 of the Appendix to Title 46 or section 192 of the Appendix to Title 46 shall limit the liability of any person under this title.

(b) Response actions and damage assessment. (1) Response actions. The Secretary may undertake or authorize all necessary actions to prevent or minimize the destruction or loss of, or injury to, sanctuary resources, or to minimize the imminent risk of such destruction, loss, or injury.

(2) Damage assessment. The Secretary shall assess damages to sanctuary resources in accordance with section 302(6) [16 U.S.C. § 1432(6)].

(c) Civil actions for response costs and damages. (1) Commencement. The Attorney General, upon request of the Secretary, may commence a civil action against any person or vessel who may be liable under subsection (a) for response costs and damages. The Secretary, acting as trustee for sanctuary resources for the United States, shall submit a request for such an action to the Attorney General whenever a person may be liable for such costs or damages.

(2) Venue. An action under this subsection may be brought in the United States district court for any district in which --

(A) the defendant is located, resides, or is doing business, in the case of an action against a person;

(B) the vessel is located, in the case of an action against a vessel; or

(C) the destruction of, loss of, or injury to a sanctuary resource occurred.

(d) Use of recovered amounts. Response costs and damages recovered by the Secretary under this section shall be retained by the Secretary in the manner provided for in section 9607(f)(1) of Title 42 and used as follows:

(1) Response costs. Amounts recovered by the United States for costs of response actions and damage assessments under this section shall be used, as the Secretary considers appropriate --

(A) to reimburse the Secretary or any other Federal or State agency that conducted those activities; and

(B) after reimbursement of such costs, to restore, replace, or acquire the equivalent of any sanctuary resource.

(2) Other amounts. All other amounts recovered shall be used, in order of priority --

(A) to restore, replace, or acquire the equivalent of the sanctuary resources that were the subject of the action, including for costs of monitoring and the costs of curation and conservation of archeological, historical, and cultural sanctuary resources;

(B) to restore degraded sanctuary resources of the national marine sanctuary that was the subject of the action, giving priority to sanctuary resources and habitats that are comparable to the sanctuary resources that were the subject of the action; and

(C) to restore degraded sanctuary resources of other national marine sanctuaries.

(3) Federal-State coordination. Amounts recovered under this section with respect to sanctuary resources lying within the jurisdiction of a State shall be used under paragraphs (2)(A) and (B) in accordance with the court decree or settlement agreement and an agreement entered into by the Secretary and the Governor of that State.

(e) Statute of limitations. An action for response costs or damages under subsection (c) shall be barred unless the complaint is filed within 3 years after the date on which the Secretary completes a damage assessment and restoration plan for the sanctuary resources to which the action relates.

[Pub. L. 100-627, Title II, § 204(a), 102 Stat. 3215 (Nov. 7, 1988); Pub. L. 102-587, Title II, §§ 2107(d), 2110, 106 Stat. 5044 (Nov. 4, 1992), 5045; Pub. L. 104-283, § 9(e), 110 Stat. 3367 (Oct. 11, 1996)]

16 U.S.C. § 1444. Authorization of appropriations. ****

16 U.S.C. § 1445. U.S.S. Monitor artifacts and materials. ****

16 U.S.C. § 1445a. Advisory Councils. (a) Establishment. The Secretary may establish one or more advisory councils (in this section referred to as an "Advisory Council") to advise and make recommendations to the Secretary regarding the designation and management of national marine sanctuaries. The Advisory Councils shall be exempt from the Federal Advisory Committee Act.

(b) Membership. Members of the Advisory Councils may be appointed from among --

(1) persons employed by Federal or State agencies with expertise in management of natural resources;

(2) members of relevant Regional Fishery Management Councils established under

section 302 of the Magnuson-Stevens Act [16 U.S.C. § 1852]; and

(3) representatives of local user groups, conservation and other public interest organizations, scientific organizations, educational organizations, or others interested in the protection and multiple use management of sanctuary resources.

(c) Limits on membership. For sanctuaries designated after November 4, 1992, the membership of Advisory Councils shall be limited to no more than 15 members.

(d) Staffing and assistance. ****

(e) Public participation and procedural matters. The following guidelines apply with respect to the conduct of business meetings of an Advisory Council:

(1) Each meeting shall be open to the public, and interested persons shall be permitted to present oral or written statements on items on the agenda.

(2) Emergency meetings may be held at the call of the chairman or presiding officer.

(3) Timely notice of each meeting, including the time, place, and agenda of the meeting, shall be published locally and in the Federal Register, except that in the case of a meeting of an Advisory Council established to provide assistance regarding any individual national marine sanctuary the notice is not required to be published in the Federal Register.

(4) Minutes of each meeting shall be kept and contain a summary of the attendees and matters discussed.

[Pub. L. 102-587, Title II, § 2112, 106 Stat. 5046 (Nov. 4, 1992); Pub. L. 104-208, Div. A, Title I, § 101(a) [Title II, § 211(b)], Sept. 30, 1996, 110 Stat. 3009-41; Pub. L. 104-283, § 5, 110 Stat. 3363 (Oct. 11, 1996)]

16 U.S.C. § 1445b. Enhancing support for national marine sanctuaries. ****

- 0 -

B. Funding State Acquisition of Wildlife Habitat

The constitutional jurisprudence embodied in *Geer v. Connecticut*[75] and the state ownership doctrine envisioned two mutually exclusive spheres. When this "dual federalism" perspective began to collapse under the weight of its increasingly formalistic and untenable distinctions,[76] it was gradually replaced with an understanding of federalism that acknowledged that the powers of the national and state governments overlapped to a substantial degree. Rather than separate spheres of powers, the operative metaphor was a "rainbow or marble cake, characterized by an inseparable mingling of differently colored ingredients, the colors appearing in vertical and diagonal strands and unexpected swirls. As colors are mixed in a marble cake, so functions are mixed in the American federal system."[77] The courts abandoned their futile attempt to draw lines: the states were protected by the structure of Congress; federalism became a question of politics.

Apart from migratory birds and a few symbolic species such as the bald eagle,[78] the shifting understanding of federalism had little effect on wildlife issues. In part, this reflected the fact that "wildlife" was a synonym for "game" and there was no political pressure on Congress to federalize the regulation of hunting and fishing. Once migratory birds were protected, the transboundary problems created by hunting game species generally were trivial.

As overharvesting became less a problem, attention shifted to the other major cause of population decline, habitat destruction. Congress addressed habitat loss by authorizing the acquisition of federal wildlife refuges through the Migratory Bird Conservation Act.[79] It also sought to encourage states to protect habitat by providing economic incentives to do so. This approach is an example of what came to be known as "cooperative federalism": a system in which states are authorized to manage a program and spend federal dollars if their statutes and regulations meet minimum national standards. Over the past 60 years, the national government has provided substantial funds to allow states to acquire wildlife management areas and other islands of protected habitat. The result was that, during a period when the constitutional universe shifted dramatically,[80] congressional deference to state prerogatives led to remarkably little change in state fish and game law.

FEDERAL AID IN WILDLIFE RESTORATION ACT [PITTMAN-ROBERTSON ACT] (16 U.S.C. §§ 669-669i; 26 U.S.C. §§ 4161, 4181)

The Federal Aid in Wildlife Restoration Act[81] -- more commonly known as the Pittman-Robertson Act -- is the primary program of federal assistance to states for "the selection, restoration, rehabilitation, and improvement" of wildlife habitat.[82] As with many federal programs funding state activities, the Pittman-Robertson Act has been used to encourage states to act consistently with a national perspective on an issue. Initially, the Act was designed to ensure that state funding of wildlife programs was insulated from the political vagaries of the appropriation process. To that end, the Act provided:

> no money apportioned under this Act to any State shall be expended therein until its legislature, or other State agency authorized by the State constitution to make laws governing the conservation of wildlife, shall have assented to the provision of this Act and shall have passed laws for the conservation of wildlife which shall include a prohibition against the diversion of license fees paid by hunters for any other purpose than the administration of said State fish and game department.[83]

In 1970, increasing federal emphasis on land-use planning led Congress to amend the Act to allow states to participate either by submitting "projects" or "programs."[84] Prior to the 1970 amendment, states were required to "submi[t] to the Secretary of the Interior full and detailed statements of any wildlife restoration projects" for which it was seeking funding.[85] The term "wildlife-restoration project" is defined to "include the selection, restoration, rehabilitation, and improvement of areas of land or water adaptable as feeding, resting, or breeding places for wildlife, including [acquisition] of such areas ... and the construction ... of such works as may be necessary to make them available" for wildlife.[86]

In addition to such project-by-project approach, the 1970 amendment allowed states to submit "a comprehensive fish and wildlife resource management plan which shall insure the perpetuation of these resources"; the plan is to cover not less than five years.[87]

Under either alternative, the Secretary is authorized to fund up to 75% of the proposal.[88] After allowances for certain federal administrative costs, funds are apportioned among the states based on geographic area, paid hunting-license holders, and total population.[89] The monies are drawn from taxes imposed on firearms, shells, and cartridges.[90]

16 U.S.C. § 669. Cooperation of Secretary of the Interior with States; conditions. The Secretary of the Interior is authorized to cooperate with the States, through their respective State fish and game departments, in wildlife- restoration projects as hereinafter in this Act set forth; but no money apportioned under this Act to any State shall be expended therein until its legislature, or other State agency authorized by the State constitution to make laws governing the conservation of wildlife, shall have assented to the provision of this Act and shall have passed laws for the conservation of wildlife which shall include a prohibition against the diversion of license fees paid by hunters for any other purpose than the administration of said State fish and game department, except that, until the final adjournment of the first regular session of the legislature held after September 2, 1937, the assent of the Governor of the State shall be sufficient. The Secretary of the Interior and the State fish and game department of each State accepting the benefits of this Act, shall agree upon the wildlife-restoration projects to be aided in such State under the terms of this Act and all projects shall conform to the standards fixed by the Secretary of the Interior.

[Sept. 2, 1937, ch. 899, § 1, 50 Stat. 917; 1939 Reorg. Plan No. II, § 4(f) (July 1, 1939), 4 Fed. Reg. 2731, 53 Stat. 1433]

16 U.S.C. § 669a. Definitions. As used in this Act --

(1) the term "conservation" means the use of methods and procedures necessary or desirable to sustain healthy populations of wildlife, including all activities associated with scientific resources management such as research, census, monitoring of populations, acquisition, improvement and management of habitat, live trapping and transplantation, wildlife damage management, and periodic or total protection of a species or population, as well as the taking of individuals within wildlife stock or population if permitted by applicable State and Federal law;

(2) the term "Secretary" means the Secretary of the Interior;

(3) the term "State fish and game department" or "State fish and wildlife department" means any department or division of department of another name, or commission, or official or officials, of a State empowered under its laws to exercise the functions ordinarily exercised by a State fish and game department or State fish and wildlife department.

(4) the term "wildlife" means any species of wild, free-ranging fauna including fish, and also fauna in captive breeding programs the object of which is to reintroduce individuals of a depleted indigenous species into previously occupied range;

(5) the term "wildlife-associated recreation" means projects intended to meet the demand for outdoor activities associated with wildlife including, but not limited to, hunting and fishing, wildlife observation and photography, such projects as construction or restoration of wildlife viewing areas, observation towers, blinds, platforms, land and water trails, water access, field trialing, trail heads, and access for such projects;

(6) the term "wildlife conservation and restoration program" means a program developed by a State fish and wildlife department and approved by the Secretary under section 4(d) [16 U.S.C. § 669c(d)], the projects that constitute such a program, which may be implemented in whole or part through grants and contracts by a State to other State, Federal, or local agencies (including those that gather, evaluate, and disseminate information on wildlife and their habitats), wildlife conservation organizations, and outdoor recreation and conservation education entities from funds apportioned under this Act, and maintenance of such projects;

(7) the term "wildlife conservation education" means projects, including public outreach, intended to foster responsible natural resource stewardship; and

(8) the term "wildlife-restoration project' includes the wildlife conservation and restoration program and means the selection, restoration, rehabilitation, and improvement of areas of land or water adaptable as feeding, resting, or breeding places for wildlife, including acquisition of such areas or estates or interests therein as are suitable or capable of being made suitable therefor, and the construction thereon or therein of such works as may be necessary to make them available for such purposes and also including such research into problems of wildlife management as may be necessary to efficient administration affecting wildlife resources, and such preliminary or incidental costs and expenses as may be incurred in and about such projects.

[Sept. 2, 1937, ch. 899, § 2, 50 Stat. 917; July 2, 1956, ch. 489, § 1, 70 Stat. 473; Pub. L. 86-624, § 10, 74 Stat. 412 (July 12, 1960); as rewritten, Pub. L. 106-553, § 1(a)(2), 114 Stat. 2762 (Dec. 21, 2000)]

16 U.S.C. § 669b. Authorization of appropriations; disposition of unexpended funds.

(a)(1) An amount equal to all revenues accruing each fiscal year (beginning with the fiscal year 1975) from any tax imposed on specified articles by sections 4161(b) and 4181 of Title 26, shall, subject to the exemptions in section 4182 of such Title, be covered into the Federal aid to wildlife restoration fund in the Treasury (hereinafter referred to as the "fund") and is authorized to be appropriated and made available until expended to carry out the purposes of this Act. So much of such appropriation apportioned to any State for any fiscal year as remains unexpended at the close thereof is authorized to be made available for expenditure in that State until the close of the succeeding fiscal year. Any amount apportioned to any State under the provisions of this Act which is unexpended or unobligated at the end of the period during which it is available for expenditure on any project is authorized to be made available for expenditure by the Secretary of the Interior in carrying out the provisions of the Migratory Bird Conservation Act [16 U.S.C. §§ 715 *et seq.*].

(2) There is established in the Federal aid to wildlife restoration fund a subaccount to be known as the "Wildlife Conservation and Restoration Account." There are authorized to be appropriated for the purposes of the Wildlife Conservation and

Restoration Account $50,000,000 in fiscal year 2001 for apportionment in accordance with this Act to carry out State wildlife conservation and restoration programs.***

****

(c) (1) Amounts transferred to the Wildlife Conservation and Restoration Account shall supplement, but not replace, existing funds available to the States from the sport fish restoration account and wildlife restoration account and shall be used for the development, revision, and implementation of wildlife conservation and restoration programs and should be used to address the unmet needs for a diverse array of wildlife and associated habitats, including species that are not hunted or fished, for wildlife conservation, wildlife conservation education, and wildlife-associated recreation projects. Such funds may be used for new programs and projects as well as to enhance existing programs and projects.

(2) Funds may be used by a State or an Indian tribe for the planning and implementation of its wildlife conservation and restoration program and wildlife conservation strategy, as provided in sections 4(d) and (e) of this Act [16 U.S.C. §§ 669c(d), (e)], including wildlife conservation, wildlife conservation education, and wildlife-associated recreation projects. Such funds may be used for new programs and projects as well as to enhance existing programs and projects.

(3) Priority for funding from the Wildlife Conservation and Restoration Account shall be for those species with the greatest conservation need as defined by the State wildlife conservation and restoration program.

****

[Sept. 2, 1937, ch. 899, § 3, 50 Stat. 917; 1939 Reorg. Plan No. II, § 4(f) (July 1, 1939), 4 Fed. Reg. 2731, 53 Stat. 1433; Pub. L. 91-503, Title I, § 101, 84 Stat. 1097 (Oct. 23, 1970); Pub. L. 92-558, Title I, § 101(a), 86 Stat. 1172 (Oct. 25, 1972); Pub. L. 101-233, § 7(a)(1), 103 Stat. 1974 (Dec. 13, 1989); as amended, Pub. L. 106-553, § 1(a)(2) [Title IX, § 902(d)], 114 Stat. 2762, 2762A-120 (Dec. 21, 2000)]

16 U.S.C. § 669c. Allocation and apportionment of available amounts. (a) Set-aside for expenses for administration of the Pittman-Robertson Wildlife Restoration Act.

****

(b) Apportionment to States. The Secretary of the Interior, after [making several deductions] shall apportion the remainder of the revenue in said fund for each fiscal year among the several States in the following manner: One-half in the ratio which the area of each State bears to the total area of all the States, and one-half in the ratio which the number of paid hunting-license holders of each State in the second fiscal year preceding the fiscal year for which such apportionment is made, as certified to said Secretary by the State fish and game departments, bears to the total number of paid hunting-license holders of all the States. Such apportionments shall be adjusted equitably so that no State shall receive less than one-half of 1 per centum nor more than 5 per centum of the total amount apportioned. The term fiscal year as used in this Act shall be a period of twelve consecutive months from October 1 through the succeeding September 30, except that the period for enumeration of paid hunting-license holders shall be a State's fiscal or license year.

****

(d) Wildlife conservation and restoration programs. (1) Any State, through its fish and wildlife department, may apply to the Secretary of the Interior for approval of a wildlife conservation and restoration program, or for funds from the Wildlife Conservation and Restoration Account, to develop a program. To apply, a State shall submit a comprehensive plan that includes --

(A) provisions vesting in the fish and wildlife department of the State overall responsibility and accountability for the program;

(B) provisions for the development and implementation of --

(i) wildlife conservation projects that expand and support existing wildlife programs, giving appropriate consideration to all wildlife;

(ii) wildlife-associated recreation projects; and

(iii) wildlife conservation education projects pursuant to programs under section 8(a) [16 U.S.C. § 669g(a)]; and

(C) provisions to ensure public participation in the development, revision, and implementation of projects and programs required under this paragraph.

(D) Wildlife conservation strategy. Within five years of the date of the initial apportionment, develop and begin implementation of a wildlife conservation strategy based upon the best available and appropriate scientific information and data that --

(i) uses such information on the distribution and abundance of species of wildlife, including low population and declining species as the State fish and wildlife department deems appropriate, that are indicative of the diversity and health of wildlife of the State;

(ii) identifies the extent and condition of wildlife habitats and community types essential to conservation of species identified under paragraph (1);

(iii) identifies the problems which may adversely affect the species identified under paragraph (1) or their habitats, and provides for priority research and surveys to identify factors which may assist in restoration and more effective conservation of such species and their habitats;

(iv) determines those actions which should be taken to conserve the species identified under paragraph (1) and their habitats and establishes priorities for implementing such conservation actions;

(v) provides for periodic monitoring of species identified under paragraph (1) and their habitats and the effectiveness of the conservation actions determined under paragraph (4), and for adapting conservation actions as appropriate to respond to new information or changing conditions;

(vi) provides for the review of the State wildlife conservation strategy and, if appropriate, revision at intervals of not more than ten years;

(vii) provides for coordination to the extent feasible the State fish and wildlife department, during the development, implementation, review, and revision of the wildlife conservation strategy, with Federal, State, and local agencies and Indian tribes that manage significant areas of land or water within the State, or administer programs that significantly affect the conservation of species identified under paragraph (1) or their habitats.

(2) A State shall provide an opportunity for public participation in the development

of the comprehensive plan required under paragraph (1).

(3) If the Secretary finds that the comprehensive plan submitted by a State complies with paragraph (1), the Secretary shall approve the wildlife conservation and restoration program of the State and set aside from the apportionment to the State *** an amount that shall not exceed 75 percent of the estimated cost of developing and implementing the program.

[Sept. 2, 1937, ch. 899, § 4, 50 Stat. 918; 1939 Reorg. Plan No. II, § 4(f) (July 1, 1939), 4 Fed. Reg. 2731, 53 Stat. 1433; July 24, 1946, ch. 605, § 1, 60 Stat. 656; Pub. L. 91-503, Title I, § 102, 84 Stat. 1098 (Oct. 23, 1970); Pub. L. 92-558, Title I, § 101(b), 86 Stat. 1172 (Oct. 25, 1972); Pub. L. 94-273, § 4(1), 90 Stat. 377 (Apr. 21, 1976); Pub. L. 99-396, § 8(b), 100 Stat. 839 (Aug. 27, 1986); Pub. L. 101-233, § 7(a)(2), 103 Stat. 1975 (Dec. 13, 1989); as amended, Pub. L. 106-408, Title I, § 111(a), 114 Stat. 1763 (Nov. 1, 2000); Pub. L. 106-553, § 1(a)(2) [Title IX, § 902(e)], 114 Stat. 2762, 2762A-121 (Dec. 21, 2000)]

16 U.S.C. § 669e. Submission and approval of plans and projects. (a) Setting aside funds. Any State desiring to avail itself of the benefits of this Act shall, by its State fish and game department, submit programs or projects for wildlife restoration in either of the following two ways:

(1) The State shall prepare and submit to the Secretary of the Interior a comprehensive fish and wildlife resource management plan which shall insure the perpetuation of these resources for the economic, scientific, and recreational enrichment of the people. Such plan shall be for a period of not less than five years and be based on projections of desires and needs of the people for a period of not less than fifteen years. It shall include provisions for updating at intervals of not more than three years and be provided in a format as may be required by the Secretary of the Interior. If the Secretary of the Interior finds that such plans conform to standards established by him and approves such plans, he may finance up to 75 per centum of the cost of implementing segments of those plans meeting the purposes of this Act from funds apportioned under this Act upon his approval of an annual agreement submitted to him.

(2) A State may elect to avail itself of the benefits of this Act by its State fish and game department submitting to the Secretary of the Interior full and detailed statements of any wildlife-restoration project proposed for that State. If the Secretary of the Interior finds that such project meets with the standards set by him and approves said project, the State fish and game department shall furnish to him such surveys, plans, specifications, and estimates therefor as he may require. If the Secretary of the Interior approves the plans, specifications, and estimates for the project, he shall notify the State fish and game department and immediately set aside so much of said fund as represents the share of the United States payable under this Act on account of such project, which sum so set aside shall not exceed 75 per centum of the total estimated cost thereof.

The Secretary of the Interior shall approve only such comprehensive plans or projects as may be substantial in character and design and the expenditure of funds hereby authorized shall be applied only to such approved comprehensive wildlife plans or projects and if otherwise applied they shall be replaced by the State before it may participate in any further apportionment under this Act. No payment of any money apportioned under this Act shall be made on any comprehensive wildlife plan or project until an agreement to participate therein shall have been submitted to and approved by the Secretary of the Interior.

(b) "Project" defined. If the State elects to avail itself of the benefits of this Act by preparing a comprehensive fish and wildlife plan under option (1) of subsection (a) of this section, then the term "project" may be defined for the purposes of this Act as a wildlife program, all other definitions notwithstanding.

****

[Sept. 2, 1937, ch. 899, § 6, 50 Stat. 918; 1939 Reorg. Plan No. II, § 4(f) (July 1, 1939), 4 Fed. Reg. 2731, 53 Stat. 1433; Pub. L. 91-503, Title I, § 102, 84 Stat. 1099 (Oct. 23, 1970)]

16 U.S.C. § 669f. Payment of funds to States; laws governing construction and labor. ****

16 U.S.C. § 669g. Maintenance of projects; expenditures for management of wildlife areas and resources. (a) Maintenance of wildlife-restoration projects established under the provisions of this Act [16 U.S.C. §§ 669 *et seq.*] shall be the duty of the States in accordance with their respective laws. Beginning July 1, 1945, the term "wildlife-restoration project," as defined in section 2 of this Act [16 U.S.C. § 669a], shall include maintenance of completed projects. Notwithstanding any other provisions of this Act [16 U.S.C. §§ 669 *et seq.*], funds apportioned to a State under this Act may be expended by the State for management (exclusive of law enforcement and public relations) of wildlife areas and resources. Funds from the Wildlife Conservation and Restoration Account may be used for a wildlife conservation education program, except that no such funds may be used for education efforts, projects, or programs that promote or encourage opposition to the regulated taking of wildlife.

(b) Each State may use the funds apportioned to it *** to pay up to 75 per centum of the costs of a hunter safety program and the construction, operation, and maintenance of public target ranges, as a part of such program. The non-Federal share of such costs may be derived from license fees paid by hunters, but not from other Federal grant programs.***

[Sept. 2, 1937, ch. 899, § 8, 50 Stat. 919; July 24, 1946, ch. 605, § 2, 60 Stat. 656; Aug. 12, 1955, ch. 861, § 2, 69 Stat. 698; Pub. L. 91-503, Title I, § 102, 84 Stat. 1100 (Oct. 23, 1970); Pub. L. 92-558, Title I, § 102(a), 86 Stat. 1173 (Oct. 25, 1972); as amended, Pub. L. 106-408, Title I, § 111(c), 114 Stat. 1766 (Nov. 1, 2000); Pub. L. 106-553, § 1(a)(2) [Title IX, § 902(g)], 114 Stat. 2762, 2762A-124 (Dec. 21, 2000)]

16 U.S.C. § 669h. Requirements and restrictions concerning use of amounts for expenses for administration. ****

16 U.S.C. § 669h-1. Firearm and bow hunter education and safety program grants. ****

16 U.S.C. § 669h-2. Multistate conservation grant program. (a) In general. (1) Amount for grants. Not more than $3,000,000 of the revenues covered into the fund for a fiscal year shall be available to the Secretary of the Interior for making multistate conservation project grants in accordance with this section.

****

(b) Selection of projects. (1) States or entities to be benefited. A project shall not be eligible for a grant under this section unless the project will benefit --

(A) at least 26 States;

(B) a majority of the States in a region of the United States Fish and Wildlife Service; or

(C) a regional association of State fish and game departments.

(2) Use of submitted priority list of projects. The Secretary of the Interior may make grants under this section only for projects identified on a priority list of wildlife restoration projects described in paragraph (3).

(3) Priority list of projects. A priority list referred to in paragraph (2) is a priority list of wildlife restoration projects that the International Association of Fish and Wildlife Agencies --

(A) prepares through a committee comprised of the heads of State fish and game departments (or their designees), in consultation with --

(i) nongovernmental organizations that represent conservation organizations;

(ii) sportsmen organizations; and

(iii) industries that support or promote hunting, trapping, recreational shooting, bow hunting, or archery;

(B) approves by vote of a majority of the heads of State fish and game departments (or their designees); and

(C) not later than October 1 of each fiscal year, submits to the Assistant Director for Wildlife and Sport Fish Restoration Programs.

(4) Publication. The Assistant Director for Wildlife and Sport Fish Restoration Programs shall publish in the Federal Register each priority list submitted under paragraph (3)(C).

(c) Eligible grantees. (1) In general. The Secretary of the Interior may make a grant under this section only to --

(A) a State or group of States;

(B) the United States Fish and Wildlife Service, or a State or group of States, for the purpose of carrying out the National Survey of Fishing, Hunting, and Wildlife-Associated Recreation; and

(C) subject to paragraph (2), a nongovernmental organization.

(2) Nongovernmental organizations.

(A) In general. Any nongovernmental organization that applies for a grant under this section shall submit with the application to the International Association of Fish and Wildlife Agencies a certification that the organization --

(i) will not use the grant funds to fund, in whole or in part, any activity of the organization that promotes or encourages opposition to the regulated hunting or trapping of wildlife; and

(ii) will use the grant funds in compliance with subsection (d).

(B) Penalties for certain activities. Any nongovernmental organization that is found to use grant funds in violation of subparagraph (A) shall return all funds received under this section and be subject to any other applicable penalties under law.

(d) Use of grants. A grant under this section shall not be used, in whole or in part, for an activity, project, or program that promotes or encourages opposition to the regulated hunting or trapping of wildlife.

****

[Pub. L. 106-408, Title I, § 113, 114 Stat. 1767 (Nov. 1, 2000)]

16 U.S.C. § 669i. Rules and regulations. The Secretary of the Interior is authorized to make rules and regulations for carrying out the provisions of this Act.

[Sept. 2, 1937, ch. 899, § 12, formerly § 10, 50 Stat. 919; 1939 Reorg. Plan No. II, § 4(f) (July 1, 1939), 4 Fed. Reg. 2731, 53 Stat. 1433]

26 U.S.C. § 4161. Imposition of tax. (a) Sport fishing equipment. (1) Imposition of tax. There is hereby imposed on the sale of any article of sport fishing equipment by the manufacturer, producer, or importer a tax equal to 10 percent of the price for which so sold.

(2) 3 percent rate of tax for electric outboard motors and sonar devices suitable for finding fish.

(A) In general. In the case of an electric outboard motor or a sonar device suitable for finding fish, paragraph (1) shall be applied by substituting "3 percent" for "10 percent".

(B) $30 limitation on tax imposed on sonar devices suitable for finding fish. The tax imposed by paragraph (1) on any sonar device suitable for finding fish shall not exceed $30.

(3) Parts or accessories sold in connection with taxable sale. In the case of any sale by the manufacturer, producer, or importer of any article of sport fishing equipment, such article shall be treated as including any parts or accessories of such article sold on or in connection therewith or with the sale thereof.

(b) Bows and arrows, etc. (1) Bows. (A) In general. There is hereby imposed on the sale by the manufacturer, producer, or importer of any bow which has a draw weight of 10 pounds or more, a tax equal to 11 percent of the price for which so sold.

(B) Parts and accessories. There is hereby imposed upon the sale by the manufacturer, producer, or importer --

(i) of any part of accessory suitable for inclusion in or attachment to a bow described in subparagraph (A), and

(ii) of any quiver suitable for use with arrows described in paragraph (2),

a tax equivalent to 11 percent of the price for which so sold.

(2) Arrows. There is hereby imposed on the sale by the manufacturer, producer, or importer of any shaft, point, nock, or vane of a type used in the manufacture of any arrow which after its assembly --

(A) measures 18 inches overall or more in length, or

(B) measures less than 18 inches overall in length but is suitable for use with a bow described in paragraph (1)(A),

a tax equal to 12.4 percent of the price for which so sold.

(3) Coordination with subsection (a). No tax shall be imposed under this subsection with respect to any article taxable under subsection (a).

[Aug. 16, 1954, ch. 736, 68A Stat. 489; Pub. L. 89-44, Title II, § 205(a), 79 Stat. 140 (June 21, 1965); Pub. L. 92-558, Title II, § 201(a), 86 Stat. 1173 (Oct. 25, 1972); Pub. L. 98-369, Div.A, Title X, §§ 1015(a), 1017(a), (b), 98 Stat. 1017, 1021 (July 18, 1984); Pub. L. 99-514, Title XVIII, § 1899A (48), 100 Stat. 2961 (Oct. 22, 1986); Pub. L. 105-34, Title XIV, § 1433(a), 111 Stat. 1051 (Aug. 5, 1997)]

26 U.S.C. § 4181. Imposition of tax. There is hereby imposed upon the sale by the manufacturer, producer, or importer of the following articles a tax equivalent to the specified percent of the price for which so sold:

Articles taxable at 10 percent --

Pistols.

Revolvers.

Articles taxable at 11 percent --

Firearms (other than pistols and revolvers).

Shells, and cartridges.

[Aug. 16, 1954, ch. 736, 68A Stat. 490]

- 0 -

FEDERAL AID IN FISH RESTORATION ACT [DINGELL-JOHNSON ACT] (16 U.S.C. §§ 777-777*l*; 26 U.S.C. § 9504(a).)

The Dingell-Johnson Act[91] -- the Federal Aid in Fish Restoration Act -- is a statute essentially identical to the Pittman-Robertson Act that applies to fish. Funding comes from a federal excise tax on fishing equipment and baits.

§ 777. Federal-State relationships. (a) Cooperation between Federal Government and State fish and game departments; expenditure of funds. The Secretary of the Interior is authorized and directed to cooperate with the States through their respective State fish and game departments in fish restoration and management projects as hereinafter set forth: No money apportioned under this Act [16 U.S.C. §§ 777 *et seq.*] to any State, except as hereinafter provided, shall be expended therein until its legislature, or other State agency authorized by the State constitution to make laws governing the conservation of fish, shall have assented to the provisions of this Act and shall have passed laws for the conservation of fish, which shall include a prohibition against the diversion of license fees paid by fishermen for any other purpose than the administration of said State fish and game department, except that, until the final adjournment of the first regular session of the legislature held after passage of this Act [August 9, 1950], the assent of the governor of the State shall be sufficient. The Secretary of the Interior and the State fish and game department of each State accepting the benefits of this Act shall agree upon the fish restoration and management projects to be aided in such State under the terms of this Act, and all projects shall conform to the standards fixed by the Secretary of the Interior.

(b) Allocation of amounts by coastal States between marine fish projects and freshwater fish projects. (1) In general. Subject to paragraph (2), each coastal State, to the extent practicable, shall equitably allocate amounts apportioned to such State under this Act between marine fish projects and freshwater fish projects in the same proportion as the estimated number of resident marine anglers and the estimated number of resident freshwater anglers, respectively, bear to the estimated number of all resident anglers in that State.

(2) Preservation of freshwater project allocation at 1988 level. (A) Subject to subparagraph (B), the amount allocated by a State pursuant to this subsection to freshwater fish projects for each fiscal year shall not be less than the amount allocated by such State to such projects for fiscal year 1988.

(B) Subparagraph (A) shall not apply to a State with respect to any fiscal year for which the amount apportioned to the State under this Act is less than the amount apportioned to the State under this Act for fiscal year 1988.

(3) "Coastal State" defined. As used in this subsection, the term "coastal State" means any one of the States of Alabama, Alaska, California, Connecticut, Delaware, Florida, Georgia, Hawaii, Louisiana, Maine, Maryland, Massachusetts, Mississippi, New Hampshire, New Jersey, New York, North Carolina, Oregon, Rhode Island, South Carolina, Texas, Virginia, and Washington. The term also includes the Commonwealth of Puerto Rico, the United States Virgin Islands, Guam, American Samoa, and the Commonwealth of the Northern Mariana Islands.

[Aug. 9, 1950, ch. 658, § 1, 64 Stat. 430; Pub. L. 98-369, Title X, § 1014(a)(1), 98 Stat. 1015 (July 18, 1984); Pub. L. 100-448, § 6(c)(1), 102 Stat 1840 (Sept. 28, 1988)]

16 U.S.C. § 777a. Definitions. For purposes of this Act [16 U.S.C. §§ 777 *et seq.*] --

(1) the term "fish restoration and management projects" shall be construed to mean projects designed for the restoration and management of all species of fish which have material value in connection with sport or recreation in the marine and/or fresh waters of the United States and include --

(A) such research into problems of fish management and culture as may be necessary to efficient administration affecting fish resources;

(B) the acquisition of such facts as are necessary to guide and direct the regulation of fishing by law, including the extent of the fish population, the drain on the fish supply from fishing and/or natural causes, the necessity of legal regulation of fishing, and the effects of any measures of regulation that are applied;

(C) the formulation and adoption of plans of restocking waters with food and game fishes according to natural areas or districts to which such plans are applicable, together with the acquisition of such facts as are necessary to the formulation, execution, and testing the efficacy of such plans;

(D) the selection, restoration, rehabilitation, and improvement of areas of water or land adaptable as hatching, feeding, resting, or breeding places for fish, including acquisition by purchase, condemnation, lease, or gift of such areas or estates or interests therein as are suitable or capable of being made suitable therefor, and the construction thereon or therein of such works as may be necessary to make them available for such purposes, and such preliminary or incidental costs and expenses as may be incurred in and about such works; the term "State fish and game department" shall be construed to mean and include any department or division of department of another name, or commission, or official or officials, of a State empowered under its laws to exercise the functions ordinarily exercised by a State fish and game department;

(2) the term "outreach and communications program" means a program to improve communications with anglers, boaters, and the general public regarding angling and boating opportunities, to reduce barriers to participation in these activities, to advance adoption of sound fishing and boating practices, to promote conservation and the responsible use of the Nation's aquatic resources, and to further safety in fishing and boating; and

(3) the term "aquatic resource education program" means a program designed to enhance the public's understanding of aquatic resources and sportfishing, and to promote the development of responsible attitudes and ethics toward the aquatic environment.

[Aug. 9, 1950, ch. 658, § 2, 64 Stat. 431; July 2, 1956, ch. 489, § 3, 70 Stat. 473; Pub. L. 86-624, § 12, 74 Stat. 413 (July 12, 1960); Pub. L. 105-178, Title VII, § 7402(a), 112 Stat. 483 (June 9, 1998)]

16 U.S.C. § 777b. Authorization of appropriations. ****

16 U.S.C. § 777c. Division of annual appropriations. ****

16 U.S.C. § 777d. Certification of funds deducted for expenses and amounts apportioned to States. ****

16 U.S.C. § 777e. Submission and approval of plans and projects. (a) Apportionment of funds. Any State desiring to avail itself of the benefits of this Act [16 U.S.C. §§ 777 *et seq.*] shall, by its State fish and game department, submit programs or projects for fish restoration in either of the following two ways:

(1) The State shall prepare and submit to the Secretary of the Interior a comprehensive fish and wildlife resource management plan which shall insure the perpetuation of these resources for the economic, scientific, and recreational enrichment of the people. Such plan shall be for a period of not less than five years and be based on projections of desires and needs of the people for a period of not less than fifteen years. It shall include provisions for updating at intervals of not more than three years and be provided in a format as may be required by the Secretary of the Interior. If the Secretary of the Interior finds that such plans conform to standards established by him and approves such plans, he may finance up to 75 per centum of the cost of implementing segments of those plans meeting the purposes of this Act from funds apportioned under this Act upon his approval of an annual agreement submitted to him.

(2) A State may elect to avail itself of the benefits of this Act by its State fish and game department submitting to the Secretary of the Interior full and detailed

statements of any fish restoration and management project proposed for that State. If the Secretary of the Interior finds that such project meets with the standards set by him and approves said project, the State fish and game department shall furnish to him such surveys, plans, specifications, and estimates therefor as he may require. If the Secretary of the Interior approves the plans, specifications, and estimates for the project, he shall notify the State fish and game department and immediately set aside so much of said appropriation as represents the share of the United States payable under this Act on account of such project, which sum so set aside shall not exceed 75 per centum of the total estimated cost thereof.

The Secretary of the Interior shall approve only such comprehensive plans or projects as may be substantial in character and design and the expenditure of funds hereby authorized shall be applied only to such approved comprehensive fishery plan or projects and if otherwise applied they shall be replaced by the State before it may participate in any further apportionment under this Act. No payment of any money apportioned under this Act shall be made on any comprehensive fishery plan or project until an agreement to participate therein shall have been submitted to and approved by the Secretary of the Interior.

(b) "Project" defined. If the State elects to avail itself of the benefits of this Act by preparing a comprehensive fish and wildlife plan under option (1) of subsection (a) of this section, then the term "project" may be defined for the purpose of this Act as a fishery program, all other definitions notwithstanding.

(c) Costs. Administrative costs in the form of overhead or indirect costs for services provided by State central service activities outside of the State fish and game department charged against programs or projects supported by funds made available under this Act shall not exceed in any one fiscal year 3 per centum of the annual apportionment to the State.

(d) Agreements to finance initial costs of acquisition of lands and construction of structures. The Secretary of the Interior may enter into agreements to finance up to 75 per centum of the initial costs of the acquisition of lands or interests therein and the construction of structures or facilities [from] appropriations currently available for the purposes of this Act; and to agree to finance up to 75 per centum of the remaining costs over such a period of time as the Secretary may consider necessary. The liability of the United States in any such agreement is contingent upon the continued availability of funds for the purposes of this Act.

[Aug. 9, 1950, ch. 658, § 6, 64 Stat. 432; Pub. L. 91-503, Title II, § 202, 84 Stat. 1102 (Oct. 23, 1970); Pub. L. 98-369, Title X, § 1014(a)(5), 98 Stat. 1016 (July 18, 1984)]

16 U.S.C. § 777e-1. New England Fishery Resources Restoration Act of 1990. (a) Short title. This section may be cited as the "New England Fishery Resources Restoration Act of 1990".

(b) Purposes. The purposes of this section are to --

(1) ensure timely and effective implementation of restoration plans and programs

for Atlantic salmon and other fishery resources of selected river systems in New England;

(2) complete a study of fish passage impediments and requirements on small streams and rivers in New England; and

(3) develop an inventory of important fish and wildlife habitat and other natural areas of river basins in New England.

(c) Implementation of fishery resource restoration plans. The Director of the United States Fish and Wildlife Service, hereinafter referred to as the Director, in consultation with the Assistant Administrator for Fisheries of the National Oceanic and Atmospheric Administration shall formulate, establish and implement programs to restore and maintain nationally significant, interjurisdictional fishery resources originating in New England river systems, including the Connecticut, Thames, Pawcatuck, Merrimack, Saco, Androscoggin, Kennebec, Sheepscot, Duck Trap, St. George, Penobscot, Union, Narraguagus, Pleasant, Machias, Dennys, St. Croix, Meduxnekeag and Aroostock and their tributaries. These programs shall be in accordance with the schedule and responsibilities established in comprehensive basin-wide restoration plans prepared by the Director in cooperation with State, local, and other entities involved and interested in the conservation and management of the affected fishery resources. Preparation and periodic revision of restoration plans, and their implementation, shall be based on a Memorandum of Agreement for each restoration program which shall be entered into by the Director and cooperating entities. The Director shall prepare and submit to the House Committee on Merchant Marine and Fisheries and the Senate Committee on Environment and Public Works an annual report documenting activities undertaken and accomplishments achieved in fulfillment of this section, including an assessment of the prognosis for restoration of each of the stocks and species involved.

(d) Fish passage study. The Director shall conduct a study to identify impediments to upstream and downstream passage of fish in rivers and streams in the New England States due to dams that are not licensed by the Federal Energy Regulatory Commission or other human-caused obstructions. In addition, the study shall identify actions needed to alleviate those impediments where desirable and feasible. The study shall include, but not be limited to, identifying --

(1) all dams not licensed by the Federal Energy Regulatory Commission and other human-caused obstructions on New England rivers and streams where construction of upstream or downstream fish passage facilities or their removal would benefit fishery resources, including an estimate of the degree of benefits expected; and

(2) the proposed nature and size and estimated cost of appropriate fish passage facilities or other actions determined to be necessary and feasible or each dam or other obstruction identified in response to paragraph (1).

The Director shall provide notice to the public of the extent and nature of the study by publication of such information in major newspapers in the region and by other appropriate means. Within three years of November 16, 1990, the Director shall submit a report containing the findings, conclusions and recommendations of the study to the House Committee on Merchant Marine and Fisheries and the Senate Committee on Environment and Public Works.

(e) New England rivers fish and wildlife inventory. The Director shall inventory the natural values of river basins in New England, including the Connecticut, Pawcatuck, Acushnet, North and South (in Plymouth County, Massachusetts), Charles, Merrimack, Saco, Androscoggin, Kennebec, Penobscot, Union, St. Croix, and Aroostock Rivers and their tributaries, and identify fish and wildlife habitat in most need of protection or where public access to the rivers should be provided. In addition, the Director shall, in cooperation with appropriate State agencies and local governments and after providing notice and opportunity for public comment, identify appropriate public or private measures for providing the necessary protection or access for each area included in the inventory. Within two years of November 16, 1990, the Director shall submit a report containing the findings, conclusions, and recommendations of the inventory and assessment to the House Committee on Merchant Marine and Fisheries and the Senate Committee on Environment and Public Works.

(f) Authorization of appropriations. ****

[Pub. L. 101-593, Title I, § 111, 104 Stat. 2960 (Nov. 16, 1990)]

16 U.S.C. § 777f. Payments by United States. ****

16 U.S.C. § 777g. Maintenance of projects. (a) Duty of States; status of projects; title to property. To maintain fish-restoration and management projects established under the provisions of this Act [16 U.S.C. §§ 777 *et seq.*] shall be the duty of the States according to their respective laws. Beginning July 1, 1953, maintenance of projects heretofore completed under the provisions of this Act may be considered as projects under this Act. Title to any real or personal property acquired by any State, and to improvements placed on State-owned lands through the use of funds paid to the State under the provisions of this Act, shall be vested in such State.

(b) Funding requirements. (1) Each State shall allocate 15 percent of the funds apportioned to it for each fiscal year under section 4 of this Act [16 U.S.C. § 777c] for the payment of up to 75 per centum of the costs of the acquisition, development, renovation, or improvement of facilities (and auxiliary facilities necessary to insure the safe use of such facilities) that create, or add to, public access to the waters of the United States to improve the suitability of such waters for recreational boating purposes. Notwithstanding this provision, States within a United States Fish and Wildlife Service Administrative Region may allocate more or less than 15 percent in a fiscal year, provided that the total regional allocation averages 15 percent over a 5 year period.

(2) So much of the funds that are allocated by a State under paragraph (1) in any fiscal year that remained unexpended or unobligated at the close of such year are authorized to be made available for the purposes described in paragraph (1) during the succeeding four fiscal years, but any portion of such funds that remain unexpended or unobligated at the close of such period are authorized to be made available for expenditure by the Secretary of the Interior in carrying out the research program of the Fish and Wildlife Service in respect to fish of material value for sport or recreation.

(c) Aquatic resource education program; funding, etc. Each State may use not to exceed 15 percent of the funds apportioned to it under section 4 of this Act [16 U.S.C. § 777c] to pay up to 75 per centum of the costs of an aquatic resource education and outreach and communications program for the purpose of increasing public understanding of the Nation's water resources and associated aquatic life forms. The non-Federal share of such costs may not be derived from other Federal grant programs. The Secretary shall issue not later than the one hundred and twentieth day after the effective date of this subsection such regulations as he deems advisable regarding the criteria for such programs.

(d) National outreach and communications program. (1) Implementation. Within 1 year after June 9, 1998, the Secretary of the Interior shall develop and implement, in cooperation and consultation with the Sport Fishing and Boating Partnership Council, a national plan for outreach and communications.

(2) Content. The plan shall provide --

(A) guidance, including guidance on the development of an administrative process and funding priorities, for outreach and communications programs; and

(B) for the establishment of a national program.

(3) Secretary may match or fund programs. Under the plan, the Secretary may obligate amounts available under subsection (c) or (d) of section 4 of this Act [16 U.S.C. § 777c(c) or (d)] --

(A) to make grants to any State or private entity to pay all or any portion of the cost of carrying out any outreach and communications program under the plan; or

(B) to fund contracts with States or private entities to carry out such a program.

(4) Review. The plan shall be reviewed periodically, but not less frequently than once every 3 years.

(e) State outreach and communications program. Within 12 months after the completion of the national plan under subsection (d)(1) of this section, a State shall develop a plan for an outreach and communications program and submit it to the Secretary. In developing the plan, a State shall --

(1) review the national plan developed under subsection (d) of this section;

(2) consult with anglers, boaters, the sportfishing and boating industries, and the general public; and

(3) establish priorities for the State outreach and communications program proposed for implementation.

(f) Pumpout stations and waste reception facilities. Amounts apportioned to States under section 4 of this Act [16 U.S.C. § 777c] may be used to pay not more than 75 percent of the costs of constructing, renovating, operating, or maintaining pumpout stations and waste reception facilities (as those terms are defined in the Clean Vessel Act of 1992).

(g) Surveys. (1) National framework. Within 6 months after June 8, 1998, the Secretary, in consultation with the States, shall adopt a national framework for a public boat access needs assessment which may be used by States to conduct surveys to determine the adequacy, number, location, and quality of facilities providing access to recreational waters for all sizes of recreational boats.

(2) State surveys. Within 18 months after June 8, 1998, each State that agrees to conduct a public boat access needs survey following the recommended national framework shall report its findings to the Secretary for use in the development of a comprehensive national assessment of recreational boat access needs and facilities.

(3) Exception. Paragraph (2) does not apply to a State if, within 18 months after June 8, 1998, the Secretary certifies that the State has developed and is implementing a plan that ensures there are and will be public boat access adequate to meet the needs of recreational boaters on its waters.

(4) Funding. A State that conducts a public boat access needs survey under paragraph (2) may fund the costs of conducting that assessment out of amounts allocated to it as funding dedicated to motorboat access to recreational waters under subsection (b)(1) of this section.

[Aug. 9, 1950, ch. 658, § 8, 64 Stat. 433; Pub. L. 91-503, Title II, § 202, 84 Stat. 1103 (Oct. 23, 1970); Pub. L. 98-369, Title X, § 1014(a)(6), 98 Stat. 1016 (July 18, 1984); Pub. L. 102-587, Title V, § 5604(b), 106 Stat. 5088 (Nov. 4, 1992); Pub. L. 105-178, Title VII, §§ 7402(c), 7404(b), 112 Stat. 484, 486 (June 9, 1998), Pub. L. 105-206, Title IX, § 9012(c), 112 Stat. 864 (July 22, 1998)]

16 U.S.C. § 777g-1. Boating infrastructure. (a) Purpose. The purpose of this section is to provide funds to States for the development and maintenance of facilities for transient nontrailerable recreational vessels.

(b) Omitted.

(c) Plan. Within 6 months after submitting a survey to the Secretary under section 8(g) of the Act entitled "An Act to provide that the United States shall aid the States in fish restoration and management projects, and for other purposes," approved August 9, 1950 [16 U.S.C. § 777g(g)], a State may develop and submit to the Secretary a plan for the construction, renovation, and maintenance of facilities for transient nontrailerable recreational vessels, and access to those facilities, to meet the needs of nontrailerable recreational vessels operating on navigable waters in the State.

(d) Grant program. (1) Matching grants. The Secretary of the Interior shall obligate amounts made available under section 4(b)(3)(B) of the Act entitled "An Act to provide that the United States shall aid the States in fish restoration and management projects, and for other purposes," approved August 9, 1950 [16 U.S.C. § 777c(b)(3)(B)] to make grants to any State to pay not more than 75 percent of the cost to a State of constructing, renovating, or maintaining facilities for transient nontrailerable recreational vessels.

(2) Priorities. In awarding grants under paragraph (1), the Secretary shall give priority to projects that --

(A) consist of the construction, renovation, or maintenance of facilities for transient nontrailerable recreational vessels in accordance with a plan submitted by a State under subsection (c) of this section;

(B) provide for public/private partnership efforts to develop, maintain, and operate facilities for transient nontrailerable recreational vessels; and

(C) propose innovative ways to increase the availability of facilities for transient nontrailerable recreational vessels.

(e) Definitions. For purposes of this section, the term --

(1) "nontrailerable recreational vessel" means a recreational vessel 26 feet in length or longer --

(A) operated primarily for pleasure; or

(B) leased, rented, or chartered to another for the latter's pleasure;

(2) "facilities for transient nontrailerable recreational vessels" includes mooring buoys, day-docks, navigational aids, seasonal slips, safe harbors, or similar structures located on navigable waters, that are available to the general public (as determined by the Secretary of the Interior) and designed for temporary use by nontrailerable recreational vessels; and

(3) "State" means each of the several States of the United States, the District of Columbia, the Commonwealth of Puerto Rico, Guam, American Samoa, the Virgin Islands, and the Commonwealth of the Northern Mariana Islands.

[Pub. L. 105-178, Title VII, § 7404(a), (c) to (e), 112 Stat. 486, 487 (June 9, 1998); Pub. L. 105-206, Title IX, § 9012(c), 112 Stat. 864 (July 22, 1998)].

16 U.S.C. § 777h. Requirements and restrictions concerning use of amounts for expenses for administration. (a) Authorized expenses for administration. Except as provided in subsection (b), the Secretary of the Interior may use available amounts under section 4(d)(1) [16 U.S.C. § 777c(d)(1)] only for expenses for administration that directly support the implementation of this Act [16 U.S.C §§ 777 *et seq.*] that consist of --

(1) personnel costs of employees who directly administer this Act on a full-time basis;

(2) personnel costs of employees who directly administer this Act on a part-time basis for at least 20 hours each week, not to exceed the portion of those costs incurred with respect to the work hours of the employee during which the employee directly administers this Act, as those hours are certified by the supervisor of the employee;

(3) support costs directly associated with personnel costs authorized under paragraphs (1) and (2), excluding costs associated with staffing and operation of regional offices of the United States Fish and Wildlife Service and the Department of the Interior other than for the purposes of this Act;

(4) costs of determining under section 6(a) [16 U.S.C. § 777e(a)] whether State comprehensive plans and projects are substantial in character and design;

(5) overhead costs, including the costs of general administrative services, that are directly attributable to administration of this Act and are based on --

(A) actual costs, as determined by a direct cost allocation methodology approved by the Director of the Office of Management and Budget for use by Federal agencies; and

(B) in the case of costs that are not determinable under subparagraph (A), an amount per full-time equivalent employee authorized under paragraphs (1) and

(2) that does not exceed the amount charged or assessed for costs per full-time equivalent employee for any other division or program of the United States Fish and Wildlife Service;

(6) costs incurred in auditing, every 5 years, the wildlife and sport fish activities of each State fish and game department and the use of funds under section 6 [16 U.S.C. § 777e] by each State fish and game department;

(7) costs of audits under subsection (d);

(8) costs of necessary training of Federal and State full-time personnel who administer this Act to improve administration of this Act;

(9) costs of travel to States, territories, and Canada by personnel who --

(A) administer this Act on a full-time basis for purposes directly related to administration of State programs or projects; or

(B) administer grants under section 6 or 14 [16 U.S.C. § 777e or 777m];

(10) costs of travel outside the United States (except travel to Canada), by personnel who administer this Act on a full-time basis, for purposes that directly relate to administration of this Act and that are approved directly by the Assistant Secretary for Fish and Wildlife and Parks;

(11) relocation expenses for personnel who, after relocation, will administer this Act on a full-time basis for at least 1 year, as certified by the Director of the United States Fish and Wildlife Service at the time at which the relocation expenses are incurred; and

(12) costs to audit, evaluate, approve, disapprove, and advise concerning grants under sections 6 and 14 [16 U.S.C. §§ 777e, 777m].

(b) Reporting of other uses. (1) In general. Subject to paragraph (2), if the Secretary of the Interior determines that available amounts under section 4(d)(1) [16 U.S.C. § 777c(d)(1)] should be used for an expense for administration other than an expense for administration described in subsection (a), the Secretary--

(A) shall submit to the Committee on Environment and Public Works of the Senate and the Committee on Resources of the House of Representatives a report describing the expense for administration and stating the amount of the expense; and

(B) may use any such available amounts for the expense for administration only after the end of the 30-day period beginning on the date of submission of the report under subparagraph (A).

(2) Maximum amount. For any fiscal year, the Secretary of the Interior may use under paragraph (1) not more than $25,000.

(c) Restriction on use to supplement general appropriations. The Secretary of the Interior shall not use available amounts under subsection (b) to supplement the funding of any function for which general appropriations are made for the United States Fish and Wildlife Service or any other entity of the Department of the Interior.

(d) Audit requirement. (1) In general. The Inspector General of the Department of the Interior shall procure the performance of biennial audits, in accordance with generally accepted accounting principles, of expenditures and obligations of amounts used by the Secretary of the Interior for expenses for administration incurred in implementation of this Act.

(2) Auditor. (A) In general. An audit under this subsection shall be performed under a contract that is awarded under competitive procedures (as defined in section 403 of Title 41) by a person or entity that is not associated in any way with the Department of the Interior (except by way of a contract for the performance of an audit or other review).

(B) Supervision of auditor. The auditor selected under subparagraph (A) shall report to, and be supervised by, the Inspector General of the Department of the Interior, except that the auditor shall submit a copy of the biennial audit findings to the Secretary of the Interior at the time at which the findings are submitted to the Inspector General of the Department of the Interior.

(3) Report to Congress. The Inspector General of the Department of the Interior shall promptly submit to the Committee on Resources of the House of Representatives and the Committee on Environment and Public Works of the Senate --

(A) a report on the results of each audit under this subsection; and

(B) a copy of each audit under this subsection.

[Aug. 9, 1950, ch. 658, § 9, 64 Stat. 433; Pub. L. 106-408, Title I, § 121(b), 114 Stat. 1770 (Nov. 1, 2000)]

16 U.S.C. § 777i. Rules and regulations. The Secretary of the Interior is authorized to make rules and regulations for carrying out the provisions of this Act [16 U.S.C. §§ 777 *et seq.*].

[Aug. 9, 1950, ch. 658, § 10, 64 Stat. 434]

§ 777j. Repealed.

§ 777k. Payments of funds to and cooperation with Puerto Rico, the District of Columbia, Guam, American Samoa, Commonwealth of the Northern Mariana Islands, and Virgin Islands. ****

16 U.S.C. § 777l. State use of contributions. A State may use contributions of funds, real property, materials, and services to carry out an activity under this Act [16 U.S.C. §§ 777 *et seq.*] in lieu of payment by the State of the State share of the cost of such activity. Such a State share shall be considered to be paid in an amount equal to the fair market value of any contribution so used.

[Pub. L. 100-448, § 6(c)(2), 102 Stat. 1841 (Sept. 28, 1988)]

26 U.S.C. § 9504. Aquatic Resources Trust Fund. (a) Creation of trust fund. --

(1) In general. There is hereby established in the Treasury of the United States a trust fund to be known as the "Aquatic Resources Trust Fund."

(2) Accounts in trust fund. The Aquatic Resources Trust Fund shall consist of --

(A) a Sport Fish Restoration Account, and

(B) a Boat Safety Account.

Each such Account shall consist of such amounts as may be appropriated, credited, or paid to it as provided in this section, section 9503(c)(4),[1] section 9503(c)(5),[2] or section 9602(b).[3]

(b) Sport Fish Restoration Account. (1) Transfer of certain taxes to Account. There is hereby appropriated to the Sport Fish Restoration Account amounts equivalent to the following amounts received in the Treasury on or after October 1, 1984 --

(A) the taxes imposed by section 4161(a) (relating to sport fishing equipment), and

(B) the import duties imposed on fishing tackle under heading 9507 of the Harmonized Tariff Schedule of the United States (19 U.S.C. 1202) and on yachts and pleasure craft under chapter 89 of the Harmonized Tariff Schedule of the United States.

(2) Expenditures from account. Amounts in the Sport Fish Restoration Account shall be available, as provided by appropriation Acts, for making expenditures --

(A) to carry out the purposes of the Act entitled "An Act to provide that the United States shall aid the States in fish restoration and management projects, and for other purposes", approved August 9, 1950 (as in effect on the date of the enactment of the Wildlife and Sport Fish Restoration Programs Improvement Act of 2000), and

(B) to carry out the purposes of section 7404(d) of the Transportation Equity Act for the 21st Century (as in effect on the date of the enactment of the TEA 21 Restoration Act), and

(C) to carry out the purposes of the Coastal Wetlands Planning, Protection and Restoration Act (as in effect on the date of the enactment of the TEA 21 Restoration Act).

Amounts transferred to such account under section 9503(c)(5) may be used only for making expenditures described in subparagraph (B) of this paragraph.

(c) Expenditures from Boat Safety Account. Amounts in the Boat Safety Account shall be available, as provided by appropriation Acts, for making expenditures before October 1, 2003, to carry out the purposes of section 13106 of title 46, United States Code (as in effect on the date of the enactment of the TEA 21 Restoration Act).

(d) Limitation on transfers to Aquatic Resources Trust Fund. (1) In general.--Except as provided in paragraph (2), no amount may be appropriated or paid to any Account in the Aquatic Resources Trust Fund on and after the date of any expenditure from any such Account which is not permitted by this section. The determination of whether an expenditure is so permitted shall be made without regard to --

(A) any provision of law which is not contained or referenced in this title or in

---

[1] 26 U.S.C. § 9503 creates the "Highway Trust Fund." Subsection (c)(4) provides for transfers of (1) up to $70,000,000 in motorboat fuel taxes from the Trust Fund into a "Boat Safety Account"; (2) of up to $1,000,000 into the Land and Water Conservation Fund; and (3) of all excess funds into the Sport Fish Restoration Account.

[2] Subsection (c)(5) provides for transfers of small-engine fuel taxes from the Highway Trust Fund into the Sport Fish Restoration Account.

[3] 26 U.S.C. § 9602(b) provides for the investment of the monies in the trust fund and requires that all interest received be credited to the fund.

a revenue Act, and

(B) whether such provision of law is a subsequently enacted provision or directly or indirectly seeks to waive the application of this subsection.

(2) Exception for prior obligations. Paragraph (1) shall not apply to any expenditure to liquidate any contract entered into (or for any amount otherwise obligated) before October 1, 2003, in accordance with the provisions of this section.

(e) Cross reference. ****

[Pub. L. 98-369, Div. A, Title X, § 1016(a), 98 Stat. 1019 (July 18, 1984); Pub. L. 100-418, Title I, § 1214(p)(2), 102 Stat. 1159 (Aug. 23, 1988); Pub. L. 100-448, § 6(a)(2), (c)(3), 102 Stat. 1839, 1841 (Sept. 28, 1988); Pub. L. 101-508, Title XI, § 11211(i)(2), (3), 104 Stat. 1388-428 (Nov. 5, 1990); Pub. L. 102-240, Title VIII, § 8002(d)(2)(C), (i), 105 Stat. 2204, 2205 (Dec. 18, 1991); Pub. L. 105-130, § 9(b), 111 Stat. 2561 (Dec. 1, 1997); Pub. L. 105-178, Title IX, §§ 9005(b) to (d), (f), 112 Stat. 505 (June 9, 1998); Pub. L. 105-206, Title IX, § 9015(b), 112 Stat. 867 (July 22, 1998); Pub. L. 106-408, Title I, § 126, 114 Stat. 1775 (Nov. 1, 2000)]

26 U.S.C. § 4161. Imposition of tax. (a) Sport fishing equipment. (1) Imposition of tax. There is hereby imposed on the sale of any article of sport fishing equipment by the manufacturer, producer, or importer a tax equal to 10 percent of the price for which so sold.

(2) 3 percent rate of tax for electric outboard motors and sonar devices suitable for finding fish.

(A) In general. In the case of an electric outboard motor or a sonar device suitable for finding fish, paragraph (1) shall be applied by substituting "3 percent" for "10 percent".

(B) $30 limitation on tax imposed on sonar devices suitable for finding fish.--The tax imposed by paragraph (1) on any sonar device suitable for finding fish shall not exceed $30.

(3) Parts or accessories sold in connection with taxable sale.--In the case of any sale by the manufacturer, producer, or importer of any article of sport fishing equipment, such article shall be treated as including any parts or accessories of such article sold on or in connection therewith or with the sale thereof.

[Aug. 16, 1954, ch. 736, 68A Stat. 489; Pub. L. 89-44, Title II, § 205(a), 79 Stat. 140 (June 21, 1965); Pub. L. 92-558, Title II, § 201(a), 86 Stat. 1173 (Oct. 25, 1972); Pub. L. 98-369, Div.A, Title X, §§ 1015(a), 1017(a), (b), 98 Stat. 1017, 1021 (July 18, 1984); Pub. L. 99-514, Title XVIII, § 1899A (48), 100 Stat. 2961 (Oct. 22, 1986); Pub. L. 105-34, Title XIV, § 1433(a), 111 Stat. 1051 (Aug. 5, 1997)]

- 0 -

LAND & WATER CONSERVATION FUND ACT (1963)
(16 U.S.C. §§ 460*l* to 460*l*-11)

The Land and Water Conservation Fund Act[92] was enacted in 1964 to assure "adequate outdoor recreation resources."[93] Like Pittman-Robertson[94] and Dingell-Johnson,[95] the Conservation Fund Act is drawn from earmarked licenses and taxes. The range of sources is, however, far broader than under either of the fish and game acts:

surplus property sales, a motorboat fuels tax, and miscellaneous receipts under the Outer Continental Shelf Lands Act are all funding sources.[96]

Although the Conservation Fund Act preceded any federal endangered species legislation, the Act is the first congressional response to growing concern for protecting endangered wildlife. Recognizing that species loss was due largely to habitat loss, Congress included a provision in the Conservation Fund Act allowing monies to be used in "the acquisition of land, waters, or interests in land or waters ... [f]or any national area which may be authorized for the preservation of species of fish or wildlife that are threatened with extinction."[97]

Though it was not designed primarily to acquire wildlife habitat, Michael Bean has concluded that the Fund "has been an important device for generating and distributing revenues for outdoor recreation purposes, including many of substantial direct or indirect benefit to wildlife."[98]

16 U.S.C. § 460*l*. Congressional findings and declaration of policy. The Congress finds and declares it to be desirable that all American people of present and future generations be assured adequate outdoor recreation resources, and that it is desirable for all levels of government and private interests to take prompt and coordinated action to the extent practicable without diminishing or affecting their respective powers and functions to conserve, develop, and utilize such resources for the benefit and enjoyment of the American people.

[Pub. L. 88-29, § 1, 77 Stat. 49 (May 28, 1963)]

16 U.S.C. § 460*l*-1. Powers and duties of Secretary of the Interior. In order to carry out the purposes of this Act, the Secretary of the Interior is authorized to perform the following functions and activities:

(a) Inventory and evaluation of needs and resources. Prepare and maintain a continuing inventory and evaluation of outdoor recreation needs and resources of the United States.

(b) Classification of resources. Prepare a system for classification of outdoor recreation resources to assist in the effective and beneficial use and management of such resources.

(c) Nationwide plan; contents; problems, solutions and actions; initial plan; revisions of plan; transmittal to Congress and Governors. Formulate and maintain a comprehensive nationwide outdoor recreation plan, taking into consideration the plans of the various Federal agencies, States, and their political subdivisions. The plan shall set forth the needs and demands of the public for outdoor recreation and the current and foreseeable availability in the future of outdoor recreation resources to meet those needs. The plan shall identify critical outdoor recreation problems, recommend solutions, and recommend desirable actions to be taken at each level of government and by private interests. The Secretary shall transmit the initial plan, which shall be prepared as soon as practicable within five years on and after to the President for transmittal to the Congress. Future revisions of the plan shall be similarly transmitted at succeeding five-year intervals. When a plan or revision is transmitted to the Congress, the Secretary shall transmit copies to the Governors of the several States.

(d) Technical assistance and advice; cooperation with States and private interests. Provide technical assistance and advice to and cooperate with States, political subdivisions, and private interests, including nonprofit organizations, with respect to outdoor recreation.

(e) Interstate and regional cooperation. Encourage interstate and regional cooperation in the planning, acquisition, and development of outdoor recreation resources.

(f) Research and education. (1) Sponsor, engage in, and assist in research relating to outdoor recreation, directly or by contract or cooperative agreements, and make payments for such purposes without regard to the limitations of section 3324(a) and (b) of Title 31 concerning advances of funds when he considers such action in the public interest, (2) undertake studies and assemble information concerning outdoor recreation, directly or by contract or cooperative agreement, and disseminate such information without regard to the provisions of section 3204 of Title 39, and (3) cooperate with educational institutions and others in order to assist in establishing education programs and activities and to encourage public use and benefits from outdoor recreation.

(g) Federal interdepartmental cooperation; coordination of Federal plans and activities; expenditures; reimbursement. (1) Cooperate with and provide technical assistance to Federal departments and agencies and obtain from them information, data, reports, advice, and assistance that are needed and can reasonably be furnished in carrying out the purposes of this Act, and (2) promote coordination of Federal plans and activities generally relating to outdoor recreation. Any department or agency furnishing advice or assistance hereunder may expend its own funds for such purposes, with or without reimbursement, as may be agreed to by that agency.

(h) Donations. Accept and use donations of money, property, personal services, or facilities for the purposes of this Act.

[Pub. L. 88-29, § 2, 77 Stat. 49 (May 28, 1963); Pub. L. 91-375, § 6(h), 84 Stat. 776 (Aug. 12, 1970); Pub. L. 97-258, § 4(b), 96 Stat. 1067 (Sept. 13, 1982)]

16 U.S.C. § 460*l*-2. Consultations of Secretary of the Interior with administrative officers; execution of administrative responsibilities in conformity with nationwide plan. In order further to carry out the policy declared in section 1 of this Act [16 U.S.C. § 460*l*] of this title, the heads of Federal departments and independent agencies having administrative responsibility over activities or resources the conduct or use of which is pertinent to fulfillment of that policy shall, either individually or as a group, (a) consult with and be consulted by the Secretary from time to time both with respect to their conduct of those activities and their use of those resources and with respect to the activities which the

Secretary of the Interior carries on under authority of this Act which are pertinent to their work, and (b) carry out such responsibilities in general conformance with the nationwide plan authorize

[Pub. L. 88-29, § 3, 77 Stat. 50 (May 28, 1963)]

16 U.S.C. § 460*l*-3. Definitions. ****

16 U.S.C. § 460*l*-4. Land and water conservation provisions; statement of purposes. The purposes of this Act are to assist in preserving, developing, and assuring accessibility to all citizens of the United States of America of present and future generations and visitors who are lawfully present within the boundaries of the United States of America such quality and quantity of outdoor recreation resources as may be available and are necessary and desirable for individual active participation in such recreation and to strengthen the health and vitality of the citizens of the United States by (1) providing funds for and authorizing Federal assistance to the States in planning, acquisition, and development of needed land and water areas and facilities and (2) providing funds for the Federal acquisition and development of certain lands and other areas.

[Pub. L. 88-578, Title I, § 1(b), 78 Stat. 897 (Sept. 3, 1964)]

16 U.S.C. § 460*l*-5. Land and water conservation fund; establishment; covering certain revenues and collections into fund. During the period ending September 30, 2015, there shall be covered into the land and water conservation fund in the Treasury of the United States, which fund is hereby established and is hereinafter referred to as the "fund", the following revenues and collections:

(a) Surplus property sales. All proceeds (except so much thereof as may be otherwise obligated, credited, or paid under authority of those provisions of law set forth in section 485(b)-(e), Title 40, or the Independent Offices Appropriation Act, 1963 (76 Stat. 725) or in any later appropriation Act) hereafter received from any disposal of surplus real property and related personal property under the Federal Property and Administrative Services Act of 1949, as amended [40 U.S.C. §§ 471 *et seq.*], notwithstanding any provision of law that such proceeds shall be credited to miscellaneous receipts of the Treasury. Nothing in this Act shall affect existing laws or regulations concerning disposal of real or personal surplus property to schools, hospitals, and States and their political subdivisions.

(b) Motorboat fuels tax. The amounts provided for in section 460*l*-11 of this title.

(c) Other revenues. (1) In addition to the sum of the revenues and collections estimated by the Secretary of the Interior to be covered into the fund pursuant to this section, as amended, there are authorized to be appropriated annually to the fund out of any money in the Treasury not otherwise appropriated such amounts as are necessary to make the income of the fund not less than $300,000,000 for fiscal year 1977, and $900,000,000 for fiscal year 1978 and for each fiscal year thereafter through September 30, 2015.

(2) To the extent that any such sums so appropriated are not sufficient to make the

total annual income of the fund equivalent to the amounts provided in clause (1), an amount sufficient to cover the remainder thereof shall be credited to the fund from revenues due and payable to the United States for deposit in the Treasury as miscellaneous receipts under the Outer Continental Shelf Lands Act, as amended (43 U.S.C. §§ 1331 *et seq.*): *Provided,* That notwithstanding the provisions of section 460*l*-6 of this title, moneys covered into the fund under this paragraph shall remain in the fund until appropriated by the Congress to carry out the purpose of this Act.

[Pub. L. 88-578, Title I, § 2, 78 Stat. 897 (Sept. 3, 1964); Pub. L. 89-72, § 11, 79 Stat. 218 (July 9, 1965); Pub. L. 90-401, §§ 1(a), 2, 82 Stat. 354, 355 (July 15, 1968); Pub. L. 91-308, § 2, 84 Stat. 410 (July 7, 1970); Pub.L. 91-485, § 1, 84 Stat. 1084 (Oct. 22, 1970); Pub. L. 94-273, § 2(7), 90 Stat. 375 (Apr. 21, 1976); Pub. L. 94-422, Title I, § 101(1), 90 Stat. 1313 (Sept. 28, 1976); Pub. L. 95-42, § 1(1), 91 Stat. 210 (June 10, 1977); Pub.L. 100-203, Title V, § 5201(f)(1), 101 Stat. 1330-267 (Dec. 22, 1987)]

16 U.S.C. § 460*l*-7. Allocation of land and water conservation fund for State and Federal purposes. There shall be submitted with the annual budget of the United States a comprehensive statement of estimated requirements during the ensuing fiscal year for appropriations from the fund. Not less than 40 per centum of such appropriations shall be available for Federal purposes. Those appropriations from the fund up to and including $600,000,000 in fiscal year 1978 and up to and including $750,000,000 in fiscal year 1979 shall continue to be allocated in accordance with this section. There shall be credited to a special account within the fund $300,000,000 in fiscal year 1978 and $150,000,000 in fiscal year 1979 from the amounts authorized by section 460*l*-5 of this title. Amounts credited to this account shall remain in the account until appropriated. Appropriations from the special account shall be available only with respect to areas existing and authorizations enacted prior to the convening of the Ninety- fifth Congress, for acquisition of lands, waters, or interests in lands or waters within the exterior boundaries, as aforesaid, of --

(1) the national park system;

(2) national scenic trails;

(3) the national wilderness preservation system;

(4) federally administered components of the National Wild and Scenic Rivers System; and

(5) national recreation areas administered by the Secretary of Agriculture.

[Pub. L. 88-578, Title I, § 5, formerly § 4, 78 Stat. 900 (Sept. 3, 1964); Pub. L. 90-401, § 3, 82 Stat. 355 (July 15, 1968), renumbered § 5, Pub. L. 92-347, § 2, 86 Stat. 459 (July 11, 1972), and amended Pub. L. 94-273, § 3(4), 90 Stat. 376 (Apr. 21, 1976); Pub. L. 94-422, Title I, § 101(2), 90 Stat. 1314 (Sept. 28, 1976); Pub. L. 95-42, § 1(2), 91 Stat. 210 (June 10, 1977)]

16 U.S.C. § 460*l*-8. Financial assistance to States. (a) Authority of Secretary of the Interior; payments to carry out purposes of land and water conservation provisions. The Secretary of the Interior (hereinafter referred to as the "Secretary") is authorized to provide financial assistance to the States from moneys available for State purposes. Payments may be made to the States by the Secretary as hereafter provided, subject to such terms and conditions as he considers appropriate and in the public interest to carry out the purposes of this Act, for outdoor recreation: (1) planning, (2) acquisition of land, waters, or interests in land or waters, or (3) development.

(b) Apportionment among States; finality of administrative determination; formula; notification; reapportionment of unobligated amounts; definition of State. ****

(d) Comprehensive State plan; necessity; adequacy; contents; correlation with other plans; factors for formulation of Housing and Home Finance Agency financed plans; planning projects; wetlands consideration; wetlands priority plan. A comprehensive statewide outdoor recreation plan shall be required prior to the consideration by the Secretary of financial assistance for acquisition or development projects. The plan shall be adequate if, in the judgment of the Secretary, it encompasses and will promote the purposes of this Act: *Provided,* That no plan shall be approved unless the Governor of the respective State certifies that ample opportunity for public participation in plan development and revision has been accorded. The Secretary shall develop, in consultation with others, criteria for public participation, which criteria shall constitute the basis for the certification by the Governor. The plan shall contain --

(1) the name of the State agency that will have authority to represent and act for the State in dealing with the Secretary for purposes of this Act;

(2) an evaluation of the demand for and supply of outdoor recreation resources and facilities in the State;

(3) a program for the implementation of the plan; and

(4) other necessary information, as may be determined by the Secretary.

The plan shall take into account relevant Federal resources and programs and shall be correlated so far as practicable with other State, regional, and local plans. ****

For fiscal year 1988 and thereafter each comprehensive statewide outdoor recreation plan shall specifically address wetlands within that State as an important outdoor recreation resource as a prerequisite to approval, except that a revised comprehensive statewide outdoor recreation plan shall not be required by the Secretary, if a State submits, and the Secretary, acting through the Director of the National Park Service, approves, as a part of and as an addendum to the existing comprehensive statewide outdoor recreation plan, a wetlands priority plan developed in consultation with the State agency with responsibility for fish and wildlife resources and consistent with the national wetlands priority conservation plan developed under section 3921 of this title or, if such national plan has not been completed, consistent with the provisions of that section[.]

(e) Projects for land and water acquisition; development. In addition to assistance for planning projects, the Secretary may provide financial assistance to any State for the following types of projects or combinations thereof if they are in accordance with the State comprehensive plan:

(1) For the acquisition of land, waters, or interests in land or waters, or wetland areas and interests therein as identified in the wetlands provisions of the comprehensive plan (other than land, waters, or interests in land or waters acquired from the United States for less than fair market value), but not including incidental costs relating to acquisition.

****

(f) Requirements for project approval; conditions; progress payments; payments

to Governors or State officials or agencies; State transfer of funds to public agencies; conversion of property to other uses; reports to Secretary; accounting; records; audit; discrimination prohibited. ****

(3) No property acquired or developed with assistance under this section shall, without the approval of the Secretary, be converted to other than public outdoor recreation uses. The Secretary shall approve such conversion only if he finds it to be in accord with the then existing comprehensive statewide outdoor recreation plan and only upon such conditions as he deems necessary to assure the substitution of other recreation properties of at least equal fair market value and of reasonably equivalent usefulness and location: *Provided,* That wetland areas and interests therein as identified in the wetlands provisions of the comprehensive plan and proposed to be acquired as suitable replacement property within that same State that is otherwise acceptable to the Secretary, acting through the Director of the National Park Service, shall be considered to be of reasonably equivalent usefulness with the property proposed for conversion.

****

[Pub. L. 88-578, Title I, § 6, formerly § 5, 78 Stat. 900 (Sept. 3, 1964), renumbered § 6, Pub. L. 92-347, § 2, 86 Stat. 459 (July 11, 1972), and amended Pub. L. 93-303, § 2, June 7, 1974, 88 Stat. 194; Pub. L. 94-422, Title I, § 101(3), 90 Stat. 1314 (Sept. 28, 1976); Pub. L. 95-625, Title VI, § 606, 92 Stat. 3519 (Nov. 10, 1978); Pub. L. 99-645, Title III, § 303, 100 Stat. 3587 (Nov. 10, 1986); Pub. L. 103-322, Title IV, § 40133, 108 Stat. 1918 (Sept. 13, 1994); Pub. L. 103-437, § 6(p)(2), 108 Stat. 4586 (Nov. 2, 1994); Pub. L. 104-333, Div. I, Title VIII, § 814(d)(1)(H), 110 Stat. 4196 (Nov. 12, 1996)]

16 U.S.C. § 460*l*-9. Allocation of land and water conservation fund moneys for Federal purposes. (a) Allowable purposes and subpurposes; acquisition of land and waters and interests therein; offset for specified capital costs. Moneys appropriated from the fund for Federal purposes shall, unless otherwise allotted in the appropriation Act making them available, be allotted by the President to the following purposes and subpurposes:

(1) For the acquisition of land, waters, or interests in land or waters as follows:

National Park System; recreation areas -- Within the exterior boundaries of areas of the National Park System now or hereafter authorized or established and of areas now or hereafter authorized to be administered by the Secretary of the Interior for outdoor recreation purposes.

National Forest System -- Inholdings within (a) wilderness areas of the National Forest System, and (b) other areas of national forests ****

National Wildlife Refuge System -- Acquisition for (a) endangered species and threatened species authorized under section 5(a) of the Endangered Species Act of 1973 [16 U.S.C. § 1534(a)]; (b) areas authorized by section 2 of the Act of September 28, 1962, as amended (16 U.S.C. § 460k-1) [Refuge Recreation Act]; (c) national wildlife refuge areas under section 7(a)(4) of the Fish and Wildlife Act of 1956 (16 U.S.C. § 742f(a)(4)) and wetlands acquired under section 304 of the Emergency

Wetlands Resources Act of 1986 [16 U.S.C. § 3922]; (d) any areas authorized for the National Wildlife Refuge System by specific Acts.

(2) For payment into miscellaneous receipts of the Treasury as a partial offset for those capital costs, if any, of Federal water development projects hereafter authorized to be constructed by or pursuant to an Act of Congress which are allocated to public recreation and the enhancement of fish and wildlife values and financed through appropriations to water resource agencies.

****

[Pub. L. 88-578, Title I, § 7, formerly § 6, 78 Stat. 903 (Sept. 3, 1964); Pub. L. 90-401, § 1(c), 82 Stat. 355 (July 15, 1968); renumbered § 7, Pub. L. 92-347, § 2, 86 Stat. 459 (July 11, 1972), and amended Pub. L. 93-205, § 13(c), 87 Stat. 902 (Dec. 28, 1973); Pub. L. 94-422, Title I, § 101(4), 90 Stat. 1317 (Sept. 28, 1976); Pub. L. 95-42, § 1(3)-(5), 91 Stat. 210 (June 10, 1977), 211; Pub. L. 96-203, § 2, 94 Stat. 81 (Mar. 10, 1980); Pub. L. 99-645, Title III, § 302, 100 Stat. 3587 (Nov. 10, 1986); Pub. L. 103-437, § 6(p)(3), 108 Stat. 4586 (Nov. 2, 1994); Pub. L. 104-333, Div. I, Title VIII, § 814(b), (d)(2)(C), 110 Stat. 4194, 4196 (Nov. 12, 1996); Pub. L. 106-176, Title I, §§ 120(b), 129, 114 Stat. 28, 30 (Mar. 10, 2000)]

16 U.S.C. § 460*l*-10. Availability of land and water conservation fund for publicity purposes; standardized temporary signing; standards and guidelines. ****

16 U.S.C. § 460*l*-11. Transfers to and from land and water conservation fund. (a) Motorboat fuel taxes from highway trust fund into conservation fund. There shall be set aside in the land and water conservation fund in the Treasury of the United States provided for in this Act the amounts specified in section 9503(c)(4)(B) of Title 26 (relating to special motor fuels and gasoline used in motorboats).

(b) Refunds of gasoline taxes for certain nonhighway purposes or used by local transit systems and motorboat fuel taxes from conservation fund into general fund of Treasury. There shall be paid from time to time from the land and water conservation fund into the general fund of the Treasury amounts estimated by the Secretary of the Treasury as equivalent to --

(1) the amounts paid before October 1, 2004, under section 6421 of Title 26 (relating to amounts paid in respect of gasoline used for certain nonhighway purposes or by local transit systems) with respect to gasoline used after December 31, 1964, in motorboats, on the basis of claims filed for periods ending before October 1, 2003; and

(2) 80 percent of the floor stocks refunds made before October 1, 2004, under section 6412(a)(2) of Title 26 with respect to gasoline to be used in motorboats.

[Pub. L. 88-578, Title II, § 201, 78 Stat. 904 (Sept. 3, 1964); Pub. L. 91-605, Title III, § 302, 84 Stat. 1743 (Dec. 31, 1970); Pub. L. 94-273, § 3(4), 90 Stat. 376 (Apr. 21, 1976); Pub. L. 94-280, Title III, § 302, 90 Stat. 456 (May 5, 1976); Pub. L. 95-599, Title V, § 503(b), 92 Stat. 2757 (Nov. 6, 1978); Pub. L. 97-424, Title V, § 531(c), 96 Stat. 2191 (Jan. 6, 1983); Pub. L. 99-514, § 2, Title XVIII, § 1875(e), 100 Stat. 2095, 2897 (Oct. 22, 1986); Pub. L. 100-17, Title V, § 503(c), 101 Stat. 258 (Apr. 2, 1987); Pub. L. 101-508, Title XI, § 11211(g)(2), 104 Stat. 1388-427 (Nov. 5, 1990); Pub. L. 102-240, Title VIII, § 8002(d)(2)(B), 105 Stat. 2204 (Dec. 18, 1991); Pub. L. 105-178, Title IX, § 9002(c)(2)(B), 112 Stat. 500 (June 9, 1998)]

THE FISH & WILDLIFE CONSERVATION ACT (1980)
(16 U.S.C. §§ 2901-2911)

Both Pittman-Robertson[99] and Dingell-Johnson[100] focus on games species. In 1980, Congress enacted the Fish and Wildlife Conservation Act[101] -- commonly known as the Non-game Act. The Act actually has a broader reach than its common name might indicate: it emphasizes comprehensive planning for all wildlife species. It is a complicated statute with ten requirements for conservation plans, a multi-step process for approving the state conservation plans, and five federal reimbursement options. States were to inventory the nongame fish and wildlife within the state, to determine "the size, range, and distribution" of populations and the "extent, condition, and location" of "significant habitat," evaluate potential problems facing the species and their habitat, and determine the steps to conserve the species in the face of those problems.[102]

The Act's broad definition of "conservation,"[103] and its emphasis on habitat echo the Endangered Species Act -- in fact, the Act is designed to operate as a pre-Endangered Species Act: the conservation plans are to identify species at risk and take steps to prevent their slide toward endangerment.

There is, however, one problem: the Act does not include independent funding provisions like those found in Pittman-Robertson, Dingell-Johnson, and the Conservation Fund Act -- and Congress has never appropriated funds to reimburse the states.

16 U.S.C. § 2901. Congressional findings and declaration of purpose. (a) Findings. The Congress finds and declares the following:

(1) Fish and wildlife are of ecological, educational, esthetic, cultural, recreational, economic, and scientific value to the Nation.

(2) The improved conservation and management of fish and wildlife, particularly nongame fish and wildlife, will assist in restoring and maintaining fish and wildlife and in assuring a productive and more esthetically pleasing environment for all citizens.

(3) Many citizens, particularly those residing in urban areas, have insufficient opportunity to participate in recreational and other programs designed to foster human interaction with fish and wildlife and thereby are unable to have a greater appreciation and awareness of the environment.

(4) Historically, fish and wildlife conservation programs have been focused on the more recreationally and commercially important species within any particular ecosystem. As a consequence such programs have been largely financed by hunting and fishing license revenues or excise taxes on certain hunting and fishing equipment. These traditional financing mechanisms are neither adequate nor fully appropriate to meet the conservation needs of nongame fish and wildlife.

(5) Each State should be encouraged to develop, revise, and implement, in consultation with appropriate Federal, State, and local and regional agencies, a plan for the conservation of fish and wildlife, particularly those species which are indigenous to the State.

(b) Purpose. It is the purpose of this Act [16 U.S.C. §§ 2901 *et. seq.*] --

(1) to provide financial and technical assistance to the States for the development, revision, and implementation of conservation plans and programs for nongame fish and wildlife; and

(2) to encourage all Federal departments and agencies to utilize their statutory and administrative authority, to the maximum extent practicable and consistent with each agency's statutory responsibilities, to conserve and to promote conservation of nongame fish and wildlife and their habitats, in furtherance of the provisions of this Act.

[Pub. L. 96-366, § 2, 94 Stat. 1322 (Sept. 29, 1980)]

16 U.S.C. § 2902. Definitions. As used in this Act --

(1) The term "approved conservation plan" means the conservation plan of a State approved by the Secretary pursuant to section 5(a) of this Act [16 U.S.C. § 2904(a)].

(2) The term "conservation plan" means a plan developed by a State for the conservation of fish and wildlife which meets the requirements set forth in section 4 [16 U.S.C. § 2903].

(3) The terms "conserve", "conserving", and "conservation" mean to use, and the use of, such methods and procedures which are necessary to ensure, to the maximum extent practicable, the well being and enhancement of fish and wildlife and their habitats for the ecological, educational, esthetic, cultural, recreational, and scientific enrichment of the public. Such methods and procedures may include, but are not limited to, any activity associated with scientific resources management, such as research, census, law enforcement, habitat acquisition, maintenance, development, information, education, population manipulation, propagation, technical assistance to private landowners, live trapping, and transplantation.

(4) The term "designated State agency" means the commission, department, division, or other agency of a State which has primary legal authority for the conservation of fish and wildlife. If any State has placed such authority in more than one agency, such term means each such agency acting with respect to its assigned responsibilities but such agencies, for purposes of this chapter, shall submit a single conservation plan.

(5) The term "fish and wildlife" means wild vertebrate animals that are in an unconfined state, including, but not limited to, nongame fish and wildlife.

(6) The term "nongame fish and wildlife" means wild vertebrate animals that are in an unconfined state and that --

(A) are not ordinarily taken for sport, fur, or food, except that if under applicable State law, any of such animals may be taken for sport, fur, or food in some, but not all, areas of the State, any of such animals within any area of the State in which such taking is not permitted may be deemed to be nongame fish and wildlife;

(B) are not listed as endangered species or threatened species under the Endangered Species Act of 1973 (16 U.S.C. §§1531-1543); and

(C) are not marine mammals within the meaning of section 3(5) of the Marine Mammal Protection Act of 1972 (16 U.S.C. § 1362(5)).

Such term does not include any domesticated species that has reverted to a feral existence.

(7) The term "Secretary" means the Secretary of the Interior.

(8) The term "State" means any of the several States, the District of Columbia, the Commonwealth of Puerto Rico, American Samoa, the Virgin Islands, Guam, the Trust Territory of the Pacific Islands, and the Commonwealth of the Northern Mariana Islands.

[Pub. L. 96-366, § 3, 94 Stat. 1323 (Sept. 29, 1980)]

16 U.S.C. § 2903. Conservation plans. The conservation plan for any State must --

(1) provide for the vesting in the designated State agency of the overall responsibility for the development and revision of the conservation plan;

(2) provide for an inventory of the nongame fish and wildlife, and such other fish and wildlife as the designated State agency deems appropriate, that are within the State and are valued for ecological, educational, esthetic, cultural, recreational, economic, or scientific benefits by the public;

(3) with respect to those species identified under paragraph (2) (hereinafter in this section referred to as "plan species"), provide for --

(A) the determination of the size, range, and distribution of their populations, and

(B) the identification of the extent, condition, and location of their significant habitats;

(4) identify the significant problems which may adversely affect the plan species and their significant habitats;

(5) determine those actions which should be taken to conserve the plan species and their significant habitats;

(6) establish priorities for implementing the conservation actions determined under paragraph (5);

(7) provide for the monitoring, on a regular basis, of the plan species and the effectiveness of the conservation actions determined under paragraph (5);

(8) provide for plan review and revision, if appropriate, at intervals of not more than 3 years;

(9) ensure that the public be given opportunity to make its views known and considered during the development, revision, and implementation of the plan; and

(10) provide that the designated State agency consult, as appropriate, with Federal agencies, and other State agencies during the development, revision, and implementation of the plan, in order to minimize duplication of efforts and to ensure that the best information is available to all such agencies.

[Pub. L. 96-366, § 4, 94 Stat. 1323 (Sept. 29, 1980)]

16 U.S.C. § 2904. Approval of conservation plans and certain nongame fish and wildlife conservation actions. (a) Approval by Secretary of plans. (1) Any State may apply to the Secretary for approval of a conservation plan.

(2) Applications for the approval of conservation plans shall be made and reviewed by the Secretary in such manner as the Secretary shall by regulation prescribe.

(3) As soon as practicable, but not later than 180 days, after the date on which a

State submits (or resubmits in the case of prior disapproval) an application for the approval of a conservation plan the Secretary shall --

(A) approve the conservation plan, and designate it as an approved conservation plan, if he determines that the plan --

(i) meets the requirements set forth in section 4 [16 U.S.C. § 2903], and

(ii) is substantial in character and design; or

(B) disapprove the conservation plan if he determines that --

(i) the plan does not meet the requirements set forth in section 4 [16 U.S.C. § 2903], or

(ii) to implement any part of the plan on the basis of the specifications, determinations, identifications, or priorities therein would threaten the natural stability and continued viability of any of the plan species concerned.

If the Secretary disapproves a plan, he shall give the State concerned a written statement of the reasons for disapproval and provide the State opportunity for consultation with respect to deficiencies in the plan and the modifications required for approval.

(b) Effect of approval of plans. If the Secretary approves the conservation plan of any State under subsection (a) of this section --

(1) that portion of such plan that pertains to wildlife conservation shall be deemed to be an approved plan for purposes of section 6(a)(1) of the Act of September 2, 1937 (16 U.S.C. 669e(a)(1)), commonly referred to as the Pittman-Robertson Wildlife Restoration Act [16 U.S.C. § 669 *et seq.*]; and

(2) that portion of such plan that pertains to fish conservation shall be deemed to be an approved plan for the purposes of section 6(a)(1) of the Act of August 9, 1950 (16 U.S.C. 777c(a)(1)), commonly referred to as the Dingell-Johnson Sport Fish Restoration Act [16 U.S.C. § 777 *et seq.*].

(c) Conservation actions. If the Secretary approves the conservation plan of any State under subsection (a) of this section, those conservation actions set forth in the plan which pertain to nongame fish and wildlife shall be deemed to be eligible as nongame fish and wildlife projects for which reimbursement is available under section 6 [16 U.S.C. § 2905].

(d) Nongame conservation actions in the absence of an approved plan. In the absence of an approved conservation plan, and on a showing of need by the State, the Secretary may deem certain conservation actions to be nongame fish and wildlife projects for which reimbursement is available under section 6(a)(3) [16 U.S.C. § 2905(a)(3)] if they --

(1) are consistent with such of the requirements set forth in section 4 [16 U.S.C. § 2903] as may be appropriate, including, but not limited to, the requirements in paragraphs (3), (4), (5), and (7) of such section; and

(2) are substantial in character and design.

[Pub. L. 96-366, § 5, 94 Stat. 1324 (Sept. 29, 1980)]

16 U.S.C. § 2905. Reimbursement of State costs for developing, revising, and

implementing conservation plans and implementing certain nongame fish and wildlife conservation actions. (a) In general. Any State may apply to the Secretary for reimbursement under this section for costs incurred by the State for the following:

(1) The development of a conservation plan.

(2) The revision of an approved conservation plan.

(3) The implementation of nongame fish and wildlife conservation actions approved under section 5(c) and (d) [16 U.S.C. § 2904(c) and (d)].

(4) The implementation of conservation actions specified in an approved conservation plan.

(5) The coordination, consolidation, or implementation of the conservation plan or conservation actions approved under this chapter with other related plans or actions developed pursuant to the Act of September 2, 1937 (16 U.S.C. 669e(a)(1)), commonly referred to as the Pittman-Robertson Wildlife Restoration Act [16 U.S.C. § 669 *et seq.*] and the Act of August 9, 1950 (16 U.S.C. 777c(a)(1)), commonly referred to as the Dingell-Johnson Sport Fish Restoration Act [16 U.S.C. § 777 *et seq.*].

(b) Applications. Application for reimbursement under this section shall be made in such manner as the Secretary shall by regulation prescribe and shall contain such information as is necessary to enable the Secretary to determine whether the State meets the eligibility requirements set forth in subsection (c) of this section.

(c) Eligibility. No State is eligible for reimbursement under this section unless the Secretary finds that the costs, for which reimbursement is sought, have been incurred by the State as follows:

(1) If reimbursement is sought under subsection (a)(1) of this section, such costs have been incurred in developing a conservation plan that meets the requirements set forth in section 4 [16 U.S.C. § 2903].

(2) If reimbursement is sought under subsection (a)(2) of this section, such costs have been incurred in revising the plan in a manner consistent with such requirements.

(3) If reimbursement is sought under subsection (a)(3) of this section, such costs have been incurred in implementing the conservation actions as approved by the Secretary.

(4) If reimbursement is sought under subsection (a)(4) of this section, such costs have been incurred in implementing conservation actions specified in, and in a manner consistent with, the approved conservation plan.

(5) If reimbursement is sought under subsection (a)(5) of this section, such costs have been incurred in consolidating, coordinating or implementing conservation plans and actions approved under this chapter with approved plans and acticns under the Act of August 9, 1950 (16 U.S.C. 777c(a)(1)), commonly referred to as the Dingell-Johnson Sport Fish Restoration Act [16 U.S.C. § 777 *et seq.*] and the Act of September 2, 1937 (16 U.S.C. 669e(a) (1)), commonly referred to as the Pittman-Robertson Wildlife Restoration Act [16 U.S.C. § 669 *et seq.*] in a manner consistent with sections 2 and 4 [16 U.S.C. §§ 2901 and 2903].

(d) Reimbursement. Subject to the limitations in subsection (c) of this section and the terms and conditions imposed under section 7 [16 U.S.C. § 2906], and to the availability of funds appropriated under section 11 [16 U.S.C. § 2910], the Secretary shall reimburse each State which the Secretary finds to be eligible therefor under subsection (c) of this section.

(e) Limitations. (1) The total amount of the reimbursement paid to any State under this section with respect to any fiscal year may not exceed the allocation available to the State under section 8 [16 U.S.C. § 2907] for such year.

(2) No reimbursement may be paid under this section to any State for any cost incurred by the State during any fiscal year --

(A) after September 30, 1991, in developing a conservation plan;

(B) after September 30, 1986, for costs incurred in implementing certain nongame fish and wildlife actions approved under section 5(d) [16 U.S.C. § 2904(d)];

(C) in which less than 80 percent of the costs to be reimbursed are for the principal benefit of nongame fish and wildlife or the users of nongame fish and wildlife;

(D) in implementing an approved conservation plan, unless the cost was incurred in implementing actions approved under section 5(c) or (d) [16 U.S.C. § 2904(c) or (d)];

(E) in implementing an approved conservation plan covering only nongame fish and wildlife, or any nongame fish and wildlife conservation action approved under 5(c) or (d) [16 U.S.C. § 2904(c) or (d)], to the extent that more than 10 percent of such costs are paid for with moneys collected during such year by the State --

(i) from the sale of hunting, fishing, and trapping licenses, and

(ii) as penalties (including forfeitures) for violations of the hunting, fishing, and trapping laws of the State; or

(F) in implementing an approved conservation plan or any nongame fish and wildlife conservation action approved under section 5(c) or (d) [16 U.S.C. § 2904(c) or (d)], to the extent that --

(i) more than 10 percent of such costs are applied for purposes of conservation law enforcement under any such plan or action, and

(ii) more than 10 percent of such costs in any such year are accounted for by personal service or other in-kind contributions.

(3) The amount of the reimbursement paid to any State under this section with respect to any fiscal year --

****

[Pub. L. 96-366, § 6, 94 Stat. 1325 (Sept. 29, 1980)]

16 U.S.C. § 2906. Terms and conditions of reimbursement. ****

16 U.S.C. § 2907. Allocation of funds for administration and reimbursement of States. ****

16 U.S.C. § 2908. Other Federal assistance and actions. The Secretary and the chief executive officer of any other appropriate Federal department or agency may loan to any State such personnel and equipment of the department or agency, share such scientific or other appropriate information, and provide such other assistance as the Secretary or officer determines appropriate for purposes of assisting any State to develop or revise conservation plans.

[Pub. L. 96-366, § 9, 94 Stat. 1329 (Sept. 29, 1980)]

16 U.S.C. § 2909. Disclaimers. Nothing in this Act [16 U.S.C. §§ 2901 *et seq.*] shall be construed as affecting --

(1) the authority, jurisdiction, or responsibility of the States to manage, control, or regulate fish and resident wildlife under State law;

(2) any requirement under State law that lands, waters, and interests therein may only be acquired for conservation purposes if the owner thereof is a willing seller; and

(3) the authority of the Secretary of Agriculture under the Act of March 2, 1931 (46 Stat. 1468-1469, 7 U.S.C. §§ 426-426b).

[Pub. L. 96-366, § 10, 94 Stat. 1329 (Sept. 29, 1980)]

16 U.S.C. § 2910. Authorization of appropriations. ****

16 U.S.C. § 2911. Study on most equitable and effective mechanism for funding State conservation plans; report to Congressional committees. The Director of the United States Fish and Wildlife Service, in consultation with affected parties, shall conduct a comprehensive study to determine the most equitable and effective mechanism for funding State conservation plans and actions under this chapter, including, but not limited to, funding by means of an excise tax on appropriate items. On or before December 31, 1984, the Director shall report to the Committee on Environment and Public Works of the Senate and to the Committee on Merchant Marine and Fisheries of the House of Representatives the results of such study, together with his recommendations with respect thereto.

[Pub. L. 96-366, § 12, 94 Stat. 1330 (Sept. 29, 1980); Pub. L. 97-396, § 6, 96 Stat. 2006 (Dec. 31, 1982)]

- 0 -

C. Consideration of the Effect of Federal Actions on Wildlife Habitat

With the Fish & Wildlife Coordination Act, Congress adopted a different approach to conserving wildlife species and habitats. Rather than prohibiting the take of species or providing for the acquisition of habitat, Congress chose to require federal agencies to evaluate the impact of their proposed actions on wildlife. The statute thus was an early attempt to incorporate the conservation of wildlife into the working environment. The statute thus is the forerunner of a number of federal statutes that mandate consideration of the effects of development activities on wildlife and its habitat.[104] The Coordination Act is not only the classic example of such statutes, it is an equally classic example of the failures of a purely procedural approach: single-focus agencies often fail to appreciate other resources and values.[105]

FISH & WILDLIFE COORDINATION ACT (1934, 1946, 1958)
(16 U.S.C. §§ 661-666c)

The original version of the Coordination Act called for the "development of a program for the maintenance of an adequate supply of wildlife" and for state and federal cooperation in "developing a Nation-wide program of wildlife conservation and rehabilitation."[106] More mundanely, the Act also required consultation with the Bureau of Fisheries before the construction of any dam to determine whether fish ladders were "necessary."[107] The Act, however, included a significant qualification: if consultation produced suggestions for modifications to proposed water-development projects, modifications were to be made "if economically practicable."[108] As the House Report on the bill noted, "there is nothing but a spirit of cooperation which is insisted on in this bill. There is nothing mandatory about the bill."[109]

In 1946, Congress recognized that the Act had "proved to be inadequate in many respects,"[110] and amended it to require consultation between the federal action agency, the Fish and Wildlife Service (FWS), and the state wildlife agency.[111] Consultation was to produce results: the action agency was to "make adequate provision consistent with the primary purposes of such impoundment ... for the conservation ... of wildlife."[112] The amendment also expanded the Act's coverage by extending the consultation and conservation requirements to include non-federal actions subject to federal permit requirements.[113]

A dozen years later Congress again noted that implementation of the Act "had fallen far short of the results anticipated."[114] The Act was again substantially amended, most significantly by requiring that wildlife be given "equal consideration" with other features of the project.[115]

The current version of the Act states its objective to be "to provide that wildlife conservation shall receive equal consideration ... with other features of water-resource development."[116] To that end,

> whenever the waters of any stream ... are proposed ... to be ... modified for any purpose whatever ... by any ... agency of the United States, or by any public or private agency under Federal permit ... such agency shall first consult with the United States Fish and Wildlife Service .... [T]he Federal agencies shall give full consideration to the ... recommendations of the [FWS].[117]

The statute thus reaches two types of federal actions: (1) federal water projects and (2) public and private water-related activities that require a federal permit.

Despite Congress' repeated attempts to force water development and development-permitting agencies to conserve fish and wildlife, the Act has proved a failure. While the initial judicial construction of the 1958 amendments suggested that Congress had finally found the language necessary to give the statute teeth,[118] the Coordination Act was quickly swallowed up by the National Environmental Policy Act. Its consultation and equal consideration mandates becoming simply procedural requirements: the action agency must only "giv[e] serious consideration to the views expressed by the USFWS."[119]

16 U.S.C. § 661. Declaration of purpose; cooperation of agencies; surveys and investigations; donations. For the purpose of recognizing the vital contribution of our wildlife resources to the Nation, the increasing public interest and significance thereof due to expansion of our national economy and other factors, and to provide that wildlife conservation shall receive equal consideration and be coordinated with other features of water-resource development programs through the effectual and harmonious planning, development, maintenance, and coordination of wildlife conservation and rehabilitation for the purposes of this Act [16 U.S.C. §§ 661 to 666c] in the United States, its Territories and possessions, the Secretary of the Interior is authorized (1) to provide assistance to, and cooperate with, Federal, State, and public or private agencies and organizations in the development, protection, rearing, and stocking of all species of wildlife, resources thereof, and their habitat, in controlling losses of the same from disease or other causes, in minimizing damages from overabundant species, in providing public shooting and fishing areas, including easements across public lands for access thereto, and in carrying out other measures necessary to effectuate the purposes of said sections; (2) to make surveys and investigations of the wildlife of the public domain, including lands and waters or interests therein acquired or controlled by any agency of the United States; and (3) to accept donations of land and contributions of funds in furtherance of the purposes of said sections.

[Mar. 10, 1934, ch. 55, § 1, 48 Stat. 401; 1939 Reorg. Plan No. II, § 4(e), (f), (July 1, 1939), 4 Fed. Reg. 2731, 53 Stat. 1433; Aug. 14, 1946, ch. 965, 60 Stat. 1080; Pub. L. 85-624, § 2, 72 Stat. 563 (Aug. 12, 1958)]

16 U.S.C. § 662. Impounding, diverting, or controlling of waters. (a) Consultations between agencies. Except as hereafter stated in subsection (h) of this section, whenever the waters of any stream or other body of water are proposed or authorized to be impounded, diverted, the channel deepened, or the stream or other body of water otherwise controlled or modified for any purpose whatever, including navigation and drainage, by any department or agency of the United States, or by any public or private agency under Federal permit or license, such department or agency first shall consult with the United States Fish and Wildlife Service, Department of the Interior, and with the head of the agency exercising administration over the wildlife resources of the particular State wherein the impoundment, diversion, or other control facility is to be constructed, with a view to the conservation of wildlife resources by preventing loss of and damage to such resources as well as providing for the development and improvement thereof in connection with such water-resource development.

(b) Reports and recommendations; consideration. In furtherance of such purposes, the reports and recommendations of the Secretary of the Interior on the wildlife aspects of such projects, and any report of the head of the State agency exercising administration over the wildlife resources of the State, based on surveys and investigations conducted by the United States Fish and Wildlife Service and such State agency for the purpose of determining the possible damage to wildlife resources and for the purpose of determining means and measures that should be adopted to prevent the loss of or damage to such wildlife resources, as well as to provide concurrently for the development and improvement of such resources, shall be made an integral part of any report prepared or submitted by any agency of the Federal Government responsible for engineering surveys and construction of such projects when such reports are presented to the Congress or to any agency or person having the authority or the power, by administrative action or otherwise, (1) to authorize the construction of water-resource development projects or (2) to approve a report on the modification or supplementation of plans for previously authorized projects, to which this Act [16 U.S.C. §§ 661 to 666c] applies. Recommendations of the Secretary of the Interior shall be as specific as is practicable with respect to features recommended for wildlife conservation and development, lands to be utilized or acquired for such purposes , the results expected, and shall describe the damage to wildlife attributable to the project and the measures proposed for mitigating or compensating for these damages. The reporting officers in project reports of the Federal agencies shall give full consideration to the report and recommendations of the Secretary of the Interior and to any report of the State agency on the wildlife aspects of such projects, and the project plan shall include such justifiable means and measures for wildlife purposes as the reporting agency finds should be adopted to obtain maximum overall project benefits.

(c) Modification of projects; acquisition of lands. Federal agencies authorized to construct or operate water-control projects are authorized to modify or add to the structures and operations of such projects, the construction of which has not been substantially completed on the date of enactment of the Fish and Wildlife Coordination Act, and to acquire lands in accordance with section 3 of this Act [16 U.S.C. § 663], in order to accommodate the means and measures for such conservation of wildlife resources as an integral part of such projects: *Provided,* That for projects authorized by a specific Act of Congress before the date of enactment of the Fish and Wildlife Coordination Act (1) such modification or land acquisition shall be compatible with the purposes for which the project was authorized; (2) the cost of such modifications or land acquisition, as means and measures to prevent loss of and damage to wildlife resources to the extent justifiable, shall be an integral part of the cost of such projects; and (3) the cost of such modifications or land acquisition for the development or improvement of wildlife resources may be included to the extent justifiable, and an appropriate share of the cost of any project may be allocated for this purpose with a finding as to the part of such allocated cost, if any, to be reimbursed by non-Federal interests.

(d) Project costs. The cost of planning for and the construction or installation and maintenance of such means and measures adopted to carry out the conservation purposes of this section shall constitute an integral part of the cost of such projects: *Provided,* That such cost attributable to the development and improvement of wildlife shall not extend beyond that necessary for (1) land acquisition, (2) facilities as specifically recommended in water resource project reports, (3) modification of the project, and (4) modification of project operations, but shall not include the operation of wildlife facilities.

(e) Transfer of funds. In the case of construction by a Federal agency, that agency is authorized to transfer to the United States Fish and Wildlife Service, out of appropriations or other funds made available for investigations, engineering, or construction, such funds as may be necessary to conduct all or part of the investigations required to carry out the purposes of this section.

(f) Estimation of wildlife benefits or losses. In addition to other requirements, there shall be included in any report submitted to Congress supporting a recommendation for authorization of any new project for the control or use of water as described herein (including any new division of such project or new supplemental works on such project) an estimation of the wildlife benefits or losses to be derived therefrom including benefits to be derived from measures recommended specifically for the development and improvement of wildlife resources, the cost of providing wildlife benefits (including the cost of additional facilities to be installed or lands to be acquired specifically for that particular phase of wildlife conservation relating to the development and improvement of wildlife), the part of the cost of joint-use facilities allocated to wildlife, and the part of such costs, if any, to be reimbursed by non-Federal interests.

(g) Applicability to projects. The provisions of this section shall be applicable with respect to any project for the control or use of water as prescribed herein, or any unit of such project authorized before or after the date of enactment of the Fish and Wildlife Coordination Act for planning or construction, but shall not be applicable to any project or unit thereof authorized before the date of enactment of the Fish and Wildlife Coordination Act if the construction of the particular project or unit thereof has been substantially completed. A project or unit thereof shall be considered to be substantially completed when sixty percent or more of the estimated construction cost has been obligated for expenditure.

(h) Exempt projects and activities. The provisions of this Act [16 U.S.C. §§ 661 to 666c] shall not be applicable to those projects for the impoundment of water where the maximum surface area of such impoundments is less than ten acres, nor to activities for or in connection with programs primarily for land management and use carried out by Federal agencies with respect to Federal lands under their jurisdiction.

[Mar. 10, 1934, ch. 55, § 2, 48 Stat. 401; 1939 Reorg. Plan No. II, § 4(e), (f) (July 1, 1939), 4 Fed. Reg. 2731, 53 Stat. 1433; Aug. 14, 1946, ch. 965, 60 Stat. 1080; Pub. L. 85-624, § 2, 72 Stat. 564 (Aug. 12, 1958); Pub. L. 89-72, § 6(b), 79 Stat. 216 (July 9, 1965)]

16 U.S.C. § 663. Impoundment or diversion of waters. (a) Conservation, maintenance, and management of wildlife resources; development and improvement. Subject to the exceptions prescribed in section 2(h) of this Act [16 U.S.C. § 662(h)], whenever the waters of any stream or other body of water are impounded, diverted, the channel deepened, or the stream or other body of water otherwise controlled or modified for any purpose whatever, including navigation and drainage, by any department or agency of the United States, adequate provision, consistent with the primary purposes of such impoundment, diversion, or other control, shall be made for the use thereof, together with any areas of land, water, or interests therein, acquired or administered by a Federal agency in connection therewith, for the conservation, maintenance, and management of wildlife resources thereof, and its habitat thereon, including the development and improvement of such wildlife resources pursuant to the provisions of section 2 of this Act [16 U.S.C. § 662].

(b) Use and availability of waters, land, or interests therein. The use of such waters, land, or interests therein for wildlife conservation purposes shall be in accordance with general plans approved jointly (1) by the head of the particular department or agency exercising primary administration in each instance, (2) by the Secretary of the Interior, and (3) by the head of the agency exercising the administration of the wildlife resources of the particular State wherein the waters and areas lie. Such waters and other interests shall be made available, without cost for administration, by such State agency, if the management of the properties relate to the conservation of wildlife other than migratory birds, or by the Secretary of the Interior, for administration in such manner as he may deem advisable, where the particular properties have value in carrying out the national migratory bird management program: *Provided,* That nothing in this section shall be construed as affecting the authority of the Secretary of Agriculture to cooperate with the States or in making lands available to the States with respect to the management of wildlife and wildlife habitat on lands administered by him.

(c) Acquisition of land, waters, and interests therein; report to Congress. When consistent with the purposes of this Act [16 U.S.C. §§ 661 to 666c] and the reports and findings of the Secretary of the Interior prepared in accordance with section 2 [16 U.S.C. § 662], land, waters, and interests therein may be acquired by Federal construction agencies for the wildlife conservation and development purposes of this Act [16 U.S.C. §§ 661 to 666c] in connection with a project as reasonably needed to preserve and assure for the public benefit the wildlife potentials of the particular project area: *Provided,* That before properties are acquired for this purpose, the probable extent of such acquisition shall be set forth, along with other data necessary for project authorization, in a report submitted to the Congress, or in the case of a project previously authorized, no such properties shall be acquired unless specifically authorized by Congress, if specific authority for such acquisition is recommended by the construction agency.

(d) Use of acquired properties. Properties acquired for the purposes of this section shall continue to be used for such purposes, and shall not become the subject of exchange or other transactions if such exchange or other transaction would defeat the initial purpose of their acquisition.

(e) Availability of Federal lands acquired or withdrawn for Federal water-resource purposes. Federal lands acquired or withdrawn for Federal water-resource purposes and made available to the States or to the Secretary of the Interior for wildlife management purposes, shall be made available for such purposes in accordance with this Act [16 U.S.C. §§ 661 to 666c], notwithstanding other provisions of law.

(f) National forest lands. Any lands acquired pursuant to this section by any Federal agency within the exterior boundaries of a national forest shall, upon acquisition, be added to and become national forest lands, and shall be administered as a part of the forest within which they are situated, subject to all laws applicable to lands acquired under the provisions of the Act of March 1, 1911 (36 Stat. 961), unless such lands are acquired to carry out the National Migratory Bird Management Program.

[Mar. 10, 1934, ch. 55, § 3, 48 Stat. 401; 1940 Reorg. Plan No. III, § 3 (June 30, 1940), 5 Fed. Reg. 2108, 54 Stat. 1232; Aug. 14, 1946, ch. 965, 60 Stat. 1080; Pub. L. 85-624, § 2, 72 Stat. 566 (Aug. 12, 1958)]

16 U.S.C. § 664. Administration; rules and regulations; availability of lands to State agencies. Such areas as are made available to the Secretary of the Interior for the purposes of this Act, pursuant to sections 1 and 3 [16 U.S.C. §§ 661 to 666c], or pursuant to any other authorization, shall be administered by him directly or in accordance with cooperative agreements entered into pursuant to the provisions of the first section of this Act [16 U.S.C. § 661] and in accordance with such rules and regulations for the conservation, maintenance, and management of wildlife, resources thereof, and its habitat thereon, as may be adopted by the Secretary in accordance with general plans approved jointly by the Secretary of the Interior and the head of the department or agency exercising primary administration of such areas: *Provided,* That such rules and regulations shall not be inconsistent with the laws for the protection of fish and game of the States in which such area is situated: *Provided further,* That lands having value to the National Migratory Bird Management Program may, pursuant to general plans, be made available without cost directly to the State agency having control over wildlife resources, if it is jointly determined by the Secretary of the Interior and such State agency that this would be in the public interest: *And provided further,* That the Secretary of the Interior shall have the right to assume the management and administration of such lands in behalf of the National Migratory Bird Management Program if the Secretary finds that the State agency has withdrawn from or otherwise relinquished such management and administration.

[Mar. 10, 1934, ch. 55, § 4, 48 Stat. 402; 1939 Reorg. Plan No. II, § 4(e), (f) (July 1, 1939), 4 Fed. Reg. 2731, 53 Stat. 1433; 1940 Reorg. Plan No. III, § 3 (June 30, 1940), 5 Fed. Reg. 2108, 54 Stat. 1232; Aug. 14, 1946, ch. 965, 60 Stat. 1080; Pub. L. 85-624, § 2, 72 Stat. 567 (Aug. 12, 1958)]

16 U.S.C. § 665. Investigations as to effect of sewage, industrial wastes; reports. The Secretary of the Interior, through the Fish and Wildlife Service and the United States Bureau of Mines, is authorized to make such investigations as he deems necessary to determine the effects of domestic sewage, mine, petroleum, and industrial wastes, erosion silt, and other polluting substances on wildlife, and to make reports to the Congress concerning such investigations and of recommendations for alleviating dangerous and undesirable effects of such pollution. These investigations shall include (1) the determination of standards of water quality for the maintenance of wildlife; (2) the study of methods of abating and preventing pollution, including methods for the recovery of useful or marketable products and byproducts of wastes; and (3) the collation and distribution of data on the progress and results of such investigations for the use of Federal, State, municipal, and private agencies, individuals, organizations, or enterprises.

[Mar. 10, 1934, ch. 55, § 5, 48 Stat. 402; 1940 Reorg. Plan No. III, § 3 (June 30, 1940), 5 Fed. Reg. 2108, 54 Stat. 1232; Aug. 14, 1946, ch. 965, 60 Stat. 1081; Pub. L. 102-285, § 10(b), 106 Stat. 172 (May 18, 1992)]

16 U.S.C. § 666. Authorization of appropriations. ****

16 U.S.C. § 666a. Penalties. Any person who shall violate any rule or regulation promulgated in accordance with this Act [16 U.S.C. §§ 661 to 666c] shall be guilty of a misdemeanor and upon conviction thereof shall be fined not more than $500 or imprisoned for not more than one year, or both.

[Aug. 14, 1946, ch. 965, 60 Stat. 1082]

16 U.S.C. § 666b. Definitions. The terms "wildlife" and "wildlife resources" as used herein include birds, fishes, mammals, and all other classes of wild animals and all types of aquatic and land vegetation upon which wildlife is dependent.

[Aug. 14, 1946, ch. 965, 60 Stat. 1082]

- 0 -

NATIONAL ENVIRONMENTAL POLICY ACT (1969)
(42 U.S.C. §§ 4321, 4331-4335)

The National Environmental Policy Act[120] -- NEPA to nearly the entire nation -- is among the most important federal statutes for the conservation of wildlife -- despite the fact that the term "wildlife" does not appear in the statute. "[R]ecognizing the profound impact of man's activity on the interrelations of all components of the natural environment,"[121] Congress enacted NEPA "to promote efforts which will prevent or eliminate damage to the environment and biosphere"[122] by requiring federal agencies to evaluate "major Federal actions significantly affecting the quality of the human environment" through the preparation of an environmental impact statement.[123] Although the Supreme Court has held that NEPA has no substantive effect,[124] requiring agencies to consider the impact of their proposed actions on wildlife is a salutary step.

42 U.S.C. § 4321. Congressional declaration of purpose. The purposes of this Act [42 U.S.C. §§ 4321 *et seq.*] are: To declare a national policy which will encourage productive and enjoyable harmony between man and his environment; to promote efforts which will prevent or eliminate damage to the environment and biosphere and stimulate the health and welfare of man; to enrich the understanding of the ecological systems and natural resources important to the Nation; and to establish a Council on Environmental Quality.

[Pub. L. 91-190, § 2, 83 Stat. 852 (Jan. 1, 1970)]

42 U.S.C. § 4331. Congressional declaration of national environmental policy. (a) The Congress, recognizing the profound impact of man's activity on the interrelations of all components of the natural environment, particularly the profound influences of population growth, high-density urbanization, industrial expansion, resource exploitation, and new and expanding technological advances and recognizing further the critical importance of restoring and maintaining environmental quality to the overall welfare and development of man, declares that it is the continuing policy of the Federal Government, in cooperation with State and local governments, and other concerned public and private organizations, to use all practicable means and measures, including financial and technical assistance, in a manner calculated to foster and promote the general welfare, to create and maintain conditions under which man and nature can exist in productive harmony, and fulfill the social, economic, and other requirements of present and future generations of Americans.

(b) Continuing responsibility of Federal Government to use all practicable means to improve and coordinate Federal plans, functions, programs, and resources. In order to carry out the policy set forth in this Act [42 U.S.C. §§ 4321 *et seq.*], it is the continuing responsibility of the Federal Government to use all practicable means, consistent with other essential considerations of national policy, to improve and coordinate Federal plans, functions, programs, and resources to the end that the Nation may --

(1) fulfill the responsibilities of each generation as trustee of the environment for succeeding generations;

(2) assure for all Americans safe, healthful, productive, and esthetically and culturally pleasing surroundings;

(3) attain the widest range of beneficial uses of the environment without degradation, risk to health or safety, or other undesirable and unintended consequences;

(4) preserve important historic, cultural, and natural aspects of our national heritage, and maintain, wherever possible, an environment which supports diversity and variety of individual choice;

(5) achieve a balance between population and resource use which will permit high standards of living and a wide sharing of life's amenities; and

(6) enhance the quality of renewable resources and approach the maximum attainable recycling of depletable resources.

(c) Responsibility of each person to contribute to preservation and enhancement of environment. The Congress recognizes that each person should enjoy a healthful environment and that each person has a responsibility to contribute to the preservation and enhancement of the environment.

[Pub. L. 91-190, Title I, § 101, 83 Stat. 852 (Jan. 1, 1970)]

42 U.S.C. § 4332. Cooperation of agencies; reports; availability of information;

recommendations; international and national coordination of efforts. The Congress authorizes and directs that, to the fullest extent possible: (1) the policies, regulations, and public laws of the United States shall be interpreted and administered in accordance with the policies set forth in this Act [42 U.S.C. §§ 4321 *et seq.*], and (2) all agencies of the Federal Government shall --

(A) utilize a systematic, interdisciplinary approach which will insure the integrated use of the natural and social sciences and the environmental design arts in planning and in decisionmaking which may have an impact on man's environment;

(B) identify and develop methods and procedures, in consultation with the Council on Environmental Quality established by title II of this Act [42 U.S.C. §§ 4341 *et seq.*], which will insure that presently unquantified environmental amenities and values may be given appropriate consideration in decisionmaking along with economic and technical considerations;

(C) include in every recommendation or report on proposals for legislation and other major Federal actions significantly affecting the quality of the human environment, a detailed statement by the responsible official on --

(i) the environmental impact of the proposed action,

(ii) any adverse environmental effects which cannot be avoided should the proposal be implemented,

(iii) alternatives to the proposed action,

(iv) the relationship between local short-term uses of man's environment and the maintenance and enhancement of long-term productivity, and

(v) any irreversible and irretrievable commitments of resources which would be involved in the proposed action should it be implemented.

Prior to making any detailed statement, the responsible Federal official shall consult with and obtain the comments of any Federal agency which has jurisdiction by law or special expertise with respect to any environmental impact involved. Copies of such statement and the comments and views of the appropriate Federal, State, and local agencies, which are authorized to develop and enforce environmental standards, shall be made available to the President, the Council on Environmental Quality and to the public as provided by section 552 of Title 5, and shall accompany the proposal through the existing agency review processes;

(D) Any detailed statement required under subparagraph (C) after January 1, 1970, for any major Federal action funded under a program of grants to States shall not be deemed to be legally insufficient solely by reason of having been prepared by a State agency or official, if:

(i) the State agency or official has statewide jurisdiction and has the responsibility for such action,

(ii) the responsible Federal official furnishes guidance and participates in such preparation,

(iii) the responsible Federal official independently evaluates such statement prior to its approval and adoption, and

(iv) after January 1, 1976, the responsible Federal official provides early notification to, and solicits the views of, any other State or any Federal land management entity of any action or any alternative thereto which may have significant impacts upon such State or affected Federal land management entity and, if there is any disagreement on such impacts, prepares a written assessment of such impacts and views for incorporation into such detailed statement.

The procedures in this subparagraph shall not relieve the Federal official of his responsibilities for the scope, objectivity, and content of the entire statement or of any other responsibility under this Act [42 U.S.C. §§ 4321 *et seq.*]; and further, this subparagraph does not affect the legal sufficiency of statements prepared by State agencies with less than statewide jurisdiction[;]

(E) study, develop, and describe appropriate alternatives to recommended courses of action in any proposal which involves unresolved conflicts concerning alternative uses of available resources;

(F) recognize the worldwide and long-range character of environmental problems and, where consistent with the foreign policy of the United States, lend appropriate support to initiatives, resolutions, and programs designed to maximize international cooperation in anticipating and preventing a decline in the quality of mankind's world environment;

(G) make available to States, counties, municipalities, institutions, and individuals, advice and information useful in restoring, maintaining, and enhancing the quality of the environment;

(H) initiate and utilize ecological information in the planning and development of resource-oriented projects; and

(I) assist the Council on Environmental Quality established by title II of this Act [42 U.S.C. §§ 4341 *et seq.*]

[Pub. L. 91-190, Title I, § 102, 83 Stat. 853 (Jan. 1, 1970); Pub. L. 94-83, 89 Stat. 424 (Aug. 9, 1975)]

42 U.S.C. § 4333. Conformity of administrative procedures to national environmental policy. All agencies of the Federal Government shall review their present statutory authority, administrative regulations, and current policies and procedures for the purpose of determining whether there are any deficiencies or inconsistencies therein which prohibit full compliance with the purposes and provisions of this chapter and shall propose to the President not later than July 1, 1971, such measures as may be necessary to bring their authority and policies into conformity with the intent, purposes, and procedures set forth in this chapter.

[Pub. L. 91-190, Title I, § 103, 83 Stat. 854 (Jan. 1, 1970)]

42 U.S.C. § 4334. Other statutory obligations of agencies. Nothing in section 4332 or 4333 of this title shall in any way affect the specific statutory obligations of any Federal agency (1) to comply with criteria or standards of environmental quality, (2) to coordinate or consult with any other Federal or State agency, or (3) to act, or refrain from acting contingent upon the recommendations or certification of any other Federal or State agency.

[Pub. L. 91-190, Title I, § 104, 83 Stat. 854 (Jan. 1, 1970)]

42 U.S.C. § 4335. Efforts supplemental to existing authorizations. The policies and goals set forth in this chapter are supplementary to those set forth in existing authorizations of Federal agencies.

[Pub. L. 91-190, Title I, § 105, 83 Stat. 854 (Jan. 1, 1970)]

- 0 -

D. Planning and Coordination

Federalism, with its division of power between different governments operating in the same geographical area, was designed in part to produce some friction. The unfortunate result often is a loss of wildlife habitat caused by the lack of coordination among land managers. A final category of statutes are those that seek to remedy this problem by establishing planning and coordination requirements. Such statutes often seek to encourage state involvement by providing federal funding.

ANADROMOUS FISH ACT (1965)
(16 U.S.C. §§ 757a-757g)

Anadromous fish such as salmon spawn in freshwater, migrate to saltwater where they mature before returning to their natal streams to spawn. Such a life cycle allows them to escape the limits of freshwater habitats -- generally a seasonally limited food supply -- while also allowing the species to take advantage of the habitat's relatively low number of predators.[125] The life cycle, however, also exposed the species to the human-caused alterations to the habitats through which the species must migrate -- most significantly hydro-electric and irrigation dams and reservoirs.

The Anadromous Fish Act[126] seeks to address these problems by authorizing the Secretary of the Interior "to enter into cooperative agreements with one or more States, acting jointly or severally, that are concerned with the development, conservation, and enhancement" of anadromous fisheries.[127] Under these agreements, the Secretary is authorized to conduct studies, clear streams, construct fish passage facilities and fish hatcheries.[128]

The Act is an example of three recurrent themes. First, with its emphasis on fish passage facilities and fish hatcheries, it embodies a technological approach to a biological problem.[129] Second, it is a classic example of what might be called "pork-barrel conservation." Third, the Act is essentially toothless: the Secretary is "authorized" to act, but not required to do so; he is empowered to study and make recommendations, but not required to do so.

16 U.S.C. § 757a. Anadromous, Great Lakes, and Lake Champlain fisheries. (a) Conservation, development, and enhancement; cooperative agreements; costs. For the purpose of conserving, developing, and enhancing within the several States the anadromous fishery resources of the Nation that are subject to depletion from water resources developments and other causes, or with respect to which the United States has made conservation commitments by international agreements, and for the purpose of conserving, developing, and enhancing the fish in the Great Lakes and Lake Champlain that ascend streams to spawn, the Secretary of the Interior is authorized to enter into cooperative agreements with one or more States, acting jointly or severally, that are concerned with the development, conservation, and enhancement of such fish, and, whenever he deems it appropriate, with other non-Federal interests. Such agreements shall describe (1) the actions to be taken by the Secretary and the cooperating parties, (2) the benefits that are expected to be derived by the States and other non-Federal interests, (3) the estimated costs of these actions, (4) the share of such costs to be borne by the Federal Government and by the States and other non-Federal interests: *Provided,* That, except as provided in subsection (c) of this section, the Federal share, including the operation and maintenance costs of any facilities constructed by the Secretary pursuant to this Act [16 U.S.C. §§ 757a to 757g], which he annually determines to be a proper Federal cost, shall not exceed 50 per centum of such costs exclusive of the value of any Federal land involved: *Provided further,* That the non-Federal share may be in the form of real or personal property, the value of which will be determined by the Secretary, as well as money, (5) the term of the agreement, (6) the terms and conditions for disposing of any real or personal property acquired by the Secretary during or at the end of the term of the agreement, and (7) such other terms and conditions as he deems desirable.

(b) Operation, management, and administration of property. The Secretary may also enter into agreements with the States for the operation of any facilities and management and administration of any lands or interests therein acquired or facilities constructed pursuant to this Act [16 U.S.C. §§ 757a to 757g].

(c) Increase of Federal share. (1) Whenever two or more States having a common interest in any basin jointly enter into a cooperative agreement with the Secretary under subsection (a) of this section to carry out a research and development program to conserve, develop, and enhance anadromous fishery resources of the Nation, or fish in the Great Lakes and Lake Champlain that ascend streams to spawn, the Federal share of the program costs shall be increased to a maximum of 66 2/3 per centum. For the purpose of this subsection, the term "basin" includes rivers and their tributaries, lakes, and other bodies of water or portions thereof.

(2) In the case of any State that has implemented an interstate fisheries management plan for anadromous fishery resources, prepared by an interstate commission, the Federal share of any grant made under this section to carry out activities required by such plan shall be up to 90 percent. For purposes of this paragraph, the term "interstate commission" means --

(A) the commission established by the Atlantic States Marine Fisheries Compact (as consented to and approved by Public Law 80-77), approved May 4, 1942 (56 Stat. 267);

(B) the commission established by the Pacific Marine Fisheries Compact (as consented to and approved by Public Law 80-232), approved July 24, 1947 ([61] Stat. 419); and

(C) the commission established by the Gulf States Marine Fisheries Compact (as consented to and approved by Public Law 81-66), approved May 19, 1949 (63 Stat. 70).

[Pub. L. 89-304, § 1, 79 Stat. 1125 (Oct. 30, 1965); Pub. L. 91-249, § 1, 84 Stat. 214 (May 14, 1970); Pub. L. 93-362, § 3(a), 88 Stat. 398 (July 30, 1974); Pub. L. 95-464, 92 Stat. 1278 (Oct. 17, 1978); Pub. L. 96-118, § 1, 93 Stat. 859 (Nov. 16, 1979); Pub. L. 97-453, § 14(b)(1), 96 Stat. 2492 (Jan. 12, 1983); Pub. L. 98-44, Title I, § 104, 97 Stat. 216 (July 12, 1983)]

16 U.S.C. § 757b. Authority of the Secretary with regards to Anadromous and Great Lakes fisheries; development and management. The Secretary, in accordance with any agreements entered into pursuant to section 1(a) of this Act [16 U.S.C. § 757a(a)], is authorized (1) to conduct such investigations, engineering and biological surveys, and research as may be desirable to carry out the program; (2) to carry out stream clearance activities; (3) to construct, install, maintain, and operate devices and structures for the improvement of feeding and spawning conditions, for the protection of fishery resources, and for facilitating the free migration of the fish, and for the control of the sea lamprey; (4) to construct, operate, and maintain fish hatcheries wherever necessary to accomplish the purposes of this Act [16 U.S.C. §§ 757a to 757g]; (5) to conduct such studies and make such recommendations as the Secretary determines to be appropriate regarding the development and management of any stream or other body of water for the conservation and enhancement of anadromous fishery resources and the fish in the Great Lakes and Lake Champlain that ascend streams to spawn: *Provided,* That the reports on such studies and the recommendations of the Secretary shall be transmitted to the States, the Congress, and the Federal water resources construction agencies for their information: *Provided further,* That this Act [16 U.S.C. §§ 757a to 757g] shall not be construed as authorizing the formulation or construction of water resources projects, except that water resources projects which are determined by the Seretary [sic] to be needed solely for the conservation, protection, and enhancement of such fish may be planned and constructed by the Bureau of Reclamation in its currently authorized geographic area of responsibility, or by the Corps of Engineers, or by the Department of Agriculture, or by the States, with funds made available by the Secretary under this Act [16 U.S.C. §§ 757a to 757g] and subject to the cost-sharing and appropriations provisions of this Act [16 U.S.C. §§ 757a to 757g]; (6) to acquire lands or interests therein by purchase, lease, donation, or exchange for acquired lands or public lands under his jurisdiction which he finds suitable for disposition: *Provided,* That the lands or interests therein so exchanged shall involve approximately equal values, as determined by the Secretary: *Provided further,* That the Secretary may accept cash from, or pay cash to, the grantor in such an exchange in order to equalize the values of the properties exchanged; (7) to accept donations of funds and to use such funds to acquire or manage lands or interests therein; and (8) to administer such lands or interests therein for the purposes of this Act [16 U.S.C. §§ 757a to 757g]. Title to lands or interests therein acquired pursuant to this Act [16 U.S.C. §§ 757a to 757g] shall be in the cooperating States or other non-Federal interests.

[Pub. L. 89-304, § 2, 79 Stat. 1125 (Oct. 30, 1965); Pub. L. 93-362, § 1, 88 Stat. 398 (July 30, 1974); Pub. L. 95-464, 92 Stat. 1278 (Oct. 17, 1978); Pub. L. 96-118, § 2, 93 Stat. 859 (Nov. 16, 1979)]

16 U.S.C. § 757c. Approval for activities on land administered by other Federal

departments or agencies. Activities authorized by this Act [16 U.S.C. §§ 757a to 757g] to be performed on lands administered by other Federal departments or agencies shall be carried out only with the prior approval of such departments or agencies.

[Pub. L. 89-304, § 3, 79 Stat. 1126 (Oct. 30, 1965)]

16 U.S.C. § 757d. Funding. (a) Authorization of appropriations. ****

(b) Limitation on obligation of funds in any one State. Not more than $625,000 of the funds appropriated under this section in any one fiscal year shall be obligated in any one State.

[Pub. L. 89-304, § 4, 79 Stat. 1126 (Oct. 30, 1965); Pub. L. 91-249, § 2, 84 Stat. 214 (May 14, 1970); Pub. L. 93-362, §§ 2, 3(b), 88 Stat. 398 (July 30, 1974); Pub. L. 96-118, § 3, 93 Stat. 859 (Nov. 16, 1979); Pub. L. 97-453, § 14(b)(2), 96 Stat. 2492 (Jan. 12, 1983); Pub. L. 99-659, Title IV, § 402, 100 Stat. 3737 (Nov. 14, 1986); Pub. L. 101-627, Title IV, § 401, 104 Stat. 4462 (Nov. 28, 1990); Pub. L. 104-297, Title IV, § 403, 110 Stat. 3619 (Oct. 11, 1996)]

16 U.S.C. § 757e. Application to Columbia River basin. This Act [16 U.S.C. §§ 757a to 757g] shall not be construed to affect, modify, or apply to the same area as the provisions of the Act of May 11, 1938 [16 U.S.C. §§ 755 to 757].[1] The State of Idaho shall be eligible on an equal standing with other States for Federal funding for purposes authorized by sections 757a to 757f of this title.

[Pub. L. 89-304, § 5, 79 Stat. 1126 (Oct. 30, 1965); Pub. L. 98-146, Title I, § 100, 97 Stat. 922 (Nov. 4, 1983)]

16 U.S.C. § 757f. Studies on pollution; recommendations to Secretary of Health and Human Services. The Secretary of the Interior shall, on the basis of studies carried out pursuant to this Act [16 U.S.C. §§ 757a to 757g] and section 5 of the Fish and Wildlife Coordination Act (48 Stat. 402), as amended [16 U.S.C. § 665], make recommendations to the Secretary of Health and Human Services concerning the elimination or reduction of polluting substances detrimental to fish and wildlife in interstate or navigable waters or the tributaries thereof. Such recommendations and any enforcement measures initiated pursuant thereto by the Secretary of Health and Human Services shall be designed to enhance the quality of such waters, and shall take into consideration all other legitimate uses of such waters.

[Pub. L. 89-304, § 6, 79 Stat. 1126 (Oct. 30, 1965); Pub. L. 96-88, Title V, § 509(b), 93 Stat. 695 (Oct. 17, 1979)]

16 U.S.C. § 757g. Repealed.

[Pub. L. 105-146, § 3(a), 111 Stat. 2677 (Dec. 16, 1997)]

- 0 -

---

[1] 16 U.S.C. §§ 755-757 provide for the establishment of "salmon-cultural stations" [hatcheries] in the three regional states using funds appropriated in 1930.

SIKES ACT EXTENSION (1974)
(16 U.S.C. §§ 670g-670o)

In 1960, Congress authorized the Secretary of Defense in cooperation with the Secretary of the Interior and the appropriate state agency "to carry out a program of planning for ... fish and game conservation" on military installations.[130] In 1970, the Public Land Law Review Commission recommended that federal and state wildlife programs be coordinated through formal cooperative agreements.[131] This recommendation was enacted into law as an extension of the Sikes Act.[132]

The Act states that the Secretaries of the Interior and Agriculture "shall develop, in consultation with the State agencies, a comprehensive plan for conservation and rehabilitation programs to be implemented on public land under" their respective jurisdictions.[133] The Secretaries are also directed, "in cooperation with the State agencies and in accordance with comprehensive plans ..., [to] plan, develop, maintain, and coordinate programs for the conservation and rehabilitation of wildlife, fish, and game[, including] specific habitat improvement projects."[134]

Although the Act is a seemingly significant statutory requirement for coordination and planning between state and federal entities, the leading examination of the Forest Service concludes that the Act's impact "on Forest Service authority and policy is difficult to assess."[135] The Act is short on detail and long on discretion.

16 U.S.C. § 670g. Wildlife, fish, and game conservation and rehabilitation programs; cooperation between Secretary of the Interior, Secretary of Agriculture, and State agencies in planning, etc., in accordance with comprehensive plans; scope and implementation of programs. (a) Conservation and rehabilitation programs. The Secretary of the Interior and the Secretary of Agriculture shall each, in cooperation with the State agencies and in accordance with comprehensive plans developed pursuant to section 202 of this title [16 U.S.C. § 670h], plan, develop, maintain, and coordinate programs for the conservation and rehabilitation of wildlife, fish, and game. Such conservation and rehabilitation programs shall include, but not be limited to, specific habitat improvement projects and related activities and adequate protection for species of fish, wildlife, and plants considered threatened or endangered.

(b) Implementation of programs. The Secretary of the Interior shall implement the conservation and rehabilitation programs required under subsection (a) of this section on public land under his jurisdiction. The Secretary of the Interior shall adopt, modify, and implement the conservation and rehabilitation programs required under subsection (a) of this section on public land under the jurisdiction of the Chairman, but only with the prior written approval of the Atomic Energy Commission, and on public land under the jurisdiction of the Administrator, but only with the prior written approval of the Administrator. The Secretary of Agriculture shall implement such conservation and rehabilitation programs on public land under his jurisdiction.

[Pub. L. 93-452, § 2, 88 Stat. 1369 (Oct. 18, 1974); Pub. L. 97-396, § 3, 96 Stat. 2005 (Dec. 31, 1982)]

16 U.S.C. § 670h. Comprehensive plans for conservation and rehabilitation programs. (a) Development by Secretary of the Interior and Secretary of Agriculture; consultation with State agencies; prior written approval of concerned Federal agencies.

(1) The Secretary of the Interior shall develop, in consultation with the State agencies, a comprehensive plan for conservation and rehabilitation programs to be implemented on public land under his jurisdiction and the Secretary of Agriculture shall do the same in connection with public land under his jurisdiction.

(2) The Secretary of the Interior shall develop, with the prior written approval of the Atomic Energy Commission, a comprehensive plan for conservation and rehabilitation programs to be implemented on public land under the jurisdiction of the Chairman and develop, with the prior written approval of the Administrator, a comprehensive plan for such programs to be implemented on public land under the jurisdiction of the Administrator. Each such plan shall be developed after the Secretary of the Interior makes, with the prior written approval of the Chairman or the Administrator, as the case may be, and in consultation with the State agencies, necessary studies and surveys of the land concerned to determine where conservation and rehabilitation programs are most needed.

(b) Development consistent with overall land use and management plans; hunting, trapping, and fishing authorized in accordance with applicable State laws and regulations. Each comprehensive plan developed pursuant to this section shall be consistent with any overall land use and management plans for the lands involved. In any case in which hunting, trapping, or fishing (or any combination thereof) of resident fish and wildlife is to be permitted on public land under a comprehensive plan, such hunting, trapping, and fishing shall be conducted in accordance with applicable laws and regulations of the State in which such land is located.

(c) Cooperative agreements by State agencies for implementation of programs; modification; contents; hunting, trapping and fishing authorized in accordance with applicable State laws and regulations; regulations.

(1) Each State agency may enter into a cooperative agreement with --

(A) the Secretary of the Interior with respect to those conservation and rehabilitation programs to be implemented under this Act within the State on public land which is under his jurisdiction;

(B) the Secretary of Agriculture with respect to those conservation and rehabilitation programs to be implemented under this Act within the State on public land which is under his jurisdiction; and

(C) the Secretary of the Interior and the Chairman or the Administrator, as the case may be, with respect to those conservation and rehabilitation programs to be implemented under this Act within the State on public land under the jurisdiction of the Chairman or the Administrator; except that before entering into any cooperative agreement which affects public land under the jurisdiction of the Chairman, the Secretary of the Interior shall obtain the prior written approval of the Atomic Energy Commission and before entering into any cooperative agreement which affects public lands under the jurisdiction of the Administrator, the Secretary of the Interior shall obtain the prior written approval of the Administrator.

Conservation and rehabilitation programs developed and implemented pursuant to this Act shall be deemed as supplemental to wildlife, fish, and game- related programs conducted by the Secretary of the Interior and the Secretary of Agriculture pursuant to other provisions of law. Nothing in this Act shall be construed as limiting the authority of the Secretary of the Interior or the Secretary of Agriculture, as the case may be, to manage the national forests or other public lands for wildlife and fish and other purposes in accordance with the Multiple-Use Sustained-Yield Act of 1960 (74 Stat. 215, 16 U.S.C. 528 to 531) or other applicable authority.

(2) Any conservation and rehabilitation program included within a cooperative agreement entered into under this subsection may be modified in a manner mutually agreeable to the State agency and the Secretary concerned (and the Chairman or the Administrator, as the case may be, if public land under his jurisdiction is involved). Before modifying any cooperative agreement which affects public land under the jurisdiction of the Chairman, the Secretary of the Interior shall obtain the prior written approval of the Atomic Energy Commission and before modifying any cooperative agreement which affects public land under the jurisdiction of the Administrator, the Secretary of the Interior shall obtain the prior written approval of the Administrator.

(3) Each cooperative agreement entered into under this subsection shall --

(A) specify those areas of public land within the State on which conservation and rehabilitation programs will be implemented;

(B) provide for fish and wildlife habitat improvements or modifications, or both;

(C) provide for range rehabilitation where necessary for support of wildlife;

(D) provide adequate protection for fish and wildlife officially classified as threatened or endangered pursuant to section 4 of the Endangered Species Act of 1973 [16 U.S.C. § 1533] or considered to be threatened, rare, or endangered by the State agency;

(E) require the control of off-road vehicle traffic;

(F) if the issuance of public land area management stamps is agreed to pursuant to section 203(a) of this title [16 U.S.C. § 670i(a)] --

(i) contain such terms and conditions as are required under section 203(b) of this title [16 U.S.C. § 670i(b)];

(ii) require the maintenance of accurate records and the filing of annual reports by the State agency to the Secretary of the Interior or the Secretary of Agriculture, or both, as the case may be, setting forth the amount and disposition of the fees collected for such stamps; and

(iii) authorize the Secretary concerned and the Comptroller General of the United States, or their authorized representatives, to have access to such records for purposes of audit and examination; and

(G) contain such other terms and conditions as the Secretary concerned and the State agency deem necessary and appropriate to carry out the purposes of this Act.

A cooperative agreement may also provide for arrangements under which the Secretary concerned may authorize officers and employees of the State agency to enforce, or to assist in the enforcement of, section 204(a) of this title [16 U.S.C. §

670j(a)].

(4) Except where limited under a comprehensive plan or pursuant to cooperative agreement, hunting, fishing, and trapping shall be permitted with respect to resident fish and wildlife in accordance with applicable laws and regulations of the State in which such land is located on public land which is the subject of a conservation and rehabilitation program implemented under this Act.

(5) The Secretary of the Interior and the Secretary of Agriculture, as the case may be, shall prescribe such regulations as are deemed necessary to control, in a manner consistent with the applicable comprehensive plan and cooperative agreement, the public use of public land which is the subject of any conservation and rehabilitation program implemented by him under this Act.

(d) State agency agreements not cooperative agreements under other provisions. Agreements entered into by State agencies under the authority of this section shall not be deemed to be, or treated as, cooperative agreements to which chapter 63 of Title 31 applies.

[Pub. L. 93-452, § 2, 88 Stat. 1369 (Oct. 18, 1974); Pub. L. 97-396, § 4, 96 Stat. 2005 (Dec. 31, 1982)]

16 U.S.C. § 670i. Public land management area stamps; agreement between State agencies and Secretary of the Interior and Secretary of Agriculture requiring stamps for hunting, trapping, and fishing on public lands subject to programs; conditions of agreement. (a) Any State agency may agree with the Secretary of the Interior and the Secretary of Agriculture (or with the Secretary of the Interior or the Secretary of Agriculture, as the case may be, if within the State concerned all conservation and rehabilitation programs under this Act will be implemented by him) that no individual will be permitted to hunt, trap, or fish on any public land within the State which is subject to a conservation and rehabilitation program implemented under this Act unless at the time such individual is engaged in such activity he has on his person a valid public land management area stamp issued pursuant to this section.

(b) Any agreement made pursuant to subsection (a) of this section to require the issuance of public land management area stamps shall be subject to the following conditions:

(1) Such stamps shall be issued, sold, and the fees therefor collected, by the State agency or by the authorized agents of such agency.

(2) Notice of the requirement to possess such stamps shall be displayed prominently in all places where State hunting, trapping, or fishing licenses are sold. To the maximum extent practicable, the sale of such stamps shall be combined with the sale of such State hunting, trapping, and fishing licenses.

(3) Except for expenses incurred in the printing, issuing, or selling of such stamps, the fees collected for such stamps by the State agency shall be utilized in carrying out conservation and rehabilitation programs implemented under this Act in the State concerned. Such fees may be used by the State agency to acquire lands or interests therein from willing sellers or donors to provide public access to program lands that have no existing public access for enhancement of outdoor recreation and wildlife conservation: *Provided,* That the Secretary of Agriculture and the Secretary of the

Interior maintain such access, or ensure that maintenance is provided for such access, through or to lands within their respective jurisdiction.
(4) The purchase of any such stamp shall entitle the purchaser thereof to hunt, trap, and fish on any public land within such State which is the subject of a conservation or rehabilitation program implemented under this Act except to the extent that the public use of such land is limited pursuant to a comprehensive plan or cooperative agreement; but the purchase of any such stamp shall not be construed as (A) eliminating the requirement for the purchase of a migratory bird hunting stamp as set forth in the first section of the Act of March 16, 1934, commonly referred to as the Migratory Bird Hunting Stamp Act [16 U.S.C. § 718a], or (B) relieving the purchaser from compliance with any applicable State game and fish laws and regulations.
(5) The amount of the fee to be charged for such stamps, the age at which the individual is required to acquire such a stamp, and the expiration date for such stamps shall be mutually agreed upon by the State agency and the Secretary or Secretaries concerned; except that each such stamp shall be void not later than one year after the date of issuance.
(6) Each such stamp must be validated by the purchaser thereof by signing his name across the face of the stamp.
(7) Any individual to whom a stamp is sold pursuant to this section shall upon request exhibit such stamp for inspection to any officer or employee of the Department of the Interior or the Department of Agriculture, or to any other person who is authorized to enforce section 204(a) of this title [16 U.S.C. § 670j(a)].

[Pub. L. Pub. L. 93-452, § 2, 88 Stat. 1371 (Oct. 18, 1974); Pub. L. 100-653, Title II, § 201, 102 Stat. 3826 (Nov. 14, 1988)]

16 U.S.C. § 670j. Enforcement provisions. (a) Violations and penalties. (1) Any person who hunts, traps, or fishes on any public land which is subject to a conservation and rehabilitation program implemented under this Act without having on his person a valid public land management area stamp, if the possession of such a stamp is required, shall be fined not more than $1,000, or imprisoned for not more than six months, or both.
(2) Any person who knowingly violates or fails to comply with any regulations prescribed under section 205(c)(5) [16 U.S.C. § 670h(c)(5)] shall be fined not more than $500, or imprisoned not more than six months, or both.

(b) Designation of enforcement personnel powers; issuance of arrest warrants; trial and sentencing by United States magistrate judges. (1) For the purpose of enforcing subsection (a) of this section, the Secretary of the Interior and the Secretary of Agriculture may designate any employee of their respective departments, and any State officer or employee authorized under a cooperative agreement to enforce subsection (a) of this section, to (i) carry firearms; (ii) execute and serve any warrant or other process issued by a court or officer of competent jurisdiction; (iii) make arrests without warrant or process for a misdemeanor he has reasonable grounds to believe is being committed in his presence or view; (iv) search without warrant or process any person, place, or conveyance as provided by law; and (v) seize without warrant or process any evidentiary item as provided by law.

(2) Upon the sworn information by a competent person, any United States magistrate judge or court of competent jurisdiction may issue process for the arrest of any person charged with committing any offense under subsection (a) of this section.

(3) Any person charged with committing any offense under subsection (a) of this section may be tried and sentenced by any United States magistrate judge designated for that purpose by the court by which he was appointed, in the same manner and subject to the same conditions as provided for in section 3401 of Title 18.

(c) Seizure and forfeiture of equipment and vessels. All guns, traps, nets, and other equipment, vessels, vehicles, and other means of transportation used by any person when engaged in committing an offense under subsection (a) of this section shall be subject to forfeiture to the United States and may be seized and held pending the prosecution of any person arrested for committing such offense. Upon conviction for such offense, such forfeiture may be adjudicated as a penalty in addition to any other provided for committing such offense.

(d) Applicability of customs laws to seizures and forfeitures; exceptions. All provisions of law relating to the seizure, forfeiture, and condemnation of a vessel for violation of the customs laws, the disposition of such vessel or the proceeds from the sale thereof, and the remission or mitigation of such forfeitures, shall apply to the seizures and forfeitures incurred, or alleged to have been incurred, under the provisions of this section, insofar as such provisions of law are applicable and not inconsistent with the provisions of this section; except that all powers, rights, and duties conferred or imposed by the customs laws upon any officer or employee of the Department of the Treasury shall, for the purposes of this section, be exercised or performed by the Secretary of the Interior or the Secretary of Agriculture, as the case may be, or by such persons as he may designate.

[Pub. L. 93-452, § 2, 88 Stat. 1372 (Oct. 18, 1974); Pub. L. 101-650, Title III, § 321, 104 Stat. 5117 (Dec. 1, 1990)]

16 U.S.C. § 670k. Definitions. As used in this Act --

(1) The term "Administrator" means the Administrator of the National Aeronautics and Space Administration.

(2) The term "Chairman" means the Chairman of the Atomic Energy Commission.

(3) The term "off-road vehicle" means any motorized vehicle designed for, or capable of, cross-country travel on or immediately over land, water, sand, snow, ice, marsh, swampland, or other natural terrain; but such term does not include --

(A) any registered motorboat at the option of each State;

(B) any military, fire, emergency, or law enforcement vehicle when used for emergency purposes; and

(C) any vehicle the use of which is expressly authorized by the Secretary of the Interior or the Secretary of Agriculture under a permit, lease, license, or contract.

(4) The term "public land" means all lands under the respective jurisdiction of the Secretary of the Interior, the Secretary of Agriculture, the Chairman, and the Administrator, except land which is, or hereafter may be, within or designated as --

(A) a military reservation;

(B) a unit of the National Park System;

(C) an area within the national wildlife refuge system;

(D) an Indian reservation; or

(E) an area within an Indian reservation or land held in trust by the United States for an Indian or Indian tribe.

(5) The term "State agency" means the agency or agencies of a State responsible for the administration of the fish and game laws of the State.

(6) The term "conservation and rehabilitation programs" means to utilize those methods and procedures which are necessary to protect, conserve, and enhance wildlife, fish, and game resources to the maximum extent practicable on public lands subject to this Act consistent with any overall land use and management plans for the lands involved. Such methods and procedures shall include, but shall not be limited to, all activities associated with scientific resources management such as protection, research, census, law enforcement, habitat management, propagation, live trapping and transplantation, and regulated taking in conformance with the provisions of this Act. Nothing in this term shall be construed as diminishing the authority or jurisdiction of the States with respect to the management of resident species of fish, wildlife, or game, except as otherwise provided by law.

[Pub. L. 93-452, § 2, 88 Stat. 1373 (Oct. 18, 1974)]

16 U.S.C. § 670l. Applicability to Forest Service and Bureau of Land Management lands of public land management area stamp requirements; authorized fees. Notwithstanding any other provision in this Act, section 203 of this tittle [16 U.S.C. § 670i] shall not apply to land which is, or hereafter may be, within or designated as Forest Service land or as Bureau of Land Management land of any State in which all Federal lands therein comprise 60 percent or more of the total area of such State; except that in any such State, any appropriate State agency may agree with the Secretary of Agriculture or the Secretary of the Interior, or both, as the case may be, to collect a fee as specified in such agreement at the point of sale of regular licenses to hunt, trap, or fish in such State, the proceeds of which shall be utilized in carrying out conservation and rehabilitation programs implemented under this Act in the State concerned and for no other purpose.

[Pub. L. 93-452, § 2, 88 Stat. 1374 (Oct. 18, 1974)]

16 U.S.C. § 670m. Indian rights unaffected; State or Federal jurisdiction regulating Indian rights preserved. Nothing in this Act shall enlarge or diminish or in any way affect (1) the rights of Indians or Indian tribes to the use of water or natural resources or their rights to fish, trap, or hunt wildlife as secured by statute, agreement, treaty, Executive order, or court decree; or (2) existing State or Federal jurisdiction to regulate those rights either on or off reservations.

[Pub. L. 93-452, § 2, 88 Stat. 1374 (Oct. 18, 1974)]

16 U.S.C. § 670n. Omitted.

16 U.S.C. § 670o. Authorization of appropriations. ****

(c). Use of other conservation or rehabilitation authorities. The Secretary of the Interior and the Secretary of Agriculture may each use any authority available to him under other laws relating to fish, wildlife, or plant conservation or rehabilitation for purposes of carrying out the provisions of this Act.

****

[Pub. L. 93-452, § 2, 88 Stat. 1374 (Oct. 18, 1974); Pub. L. 95-420, § 3, 92 Stat. 921 (Oct. 5, 1978); Pub. L. 97-396, § 5, 96 Stat. 2005 (Dec. 31, 1982); Pub. L. 99-561, § 1(b), 100 Stat. 3149 (Oct. 27, 1986); Pub. L. 100-653, Title II, § 202(b), 102 Stat. 3827 (Nov. 14, 1988); Pub. L. 105-85, Div. B, Title XXIX, § 2914(b), 111 Stat. 2023 (Nov. 18, 1997)]

- 0 -

CHAPTER 3

CONSERVING BIODIVERSITY

Biodiversity is not simply a question of numbers. Although numbers are important on a global scale, quality is more important than quantity at local scales. Checker-boarded tracts of old growth and clearcuts, for example, may have a larger number of species at the local level as cowbirds and starlings move into the area, but such fragmentation of habitat actually decreases biodiversity at larger scales as sensitive, old-growth species such as spotted owls are lost. Species richness thus is only part of the story. Biologists recognize at least three types of biodiversity: *genetic diversity*, the variations in each individual's genes that allow species to evolve and hence adapt to changing conditions; *species diversity*, the variation in the number, type, and distribution of species within ecosystems; and *ecosystem diversity*, the variation in habitats and communities. Preserving biodiversity requires the preservation of all three.

There is no United States statute that broadly seeks to conserve biodiversity. The closest is the Endangered Species Act (ESA) of 1973. Although the Act is often presented as focusing exclusively on species (albeit broadly defined to include subspecies and populations),

> The purposes of this Act are to provide a means whereby the ecosystems upon which endangered species and threatened species depend may be conserved, [and] to provide a program for the conservation of such endangered species and threatened species.[1]

The snail darter case[2] demonstrated the Act's ability to protect habitat -- until it was legislatively reversed by Congress. But the ESA remains limited by its focus on species at risk of extinction.

To the extent that biodiversity is protected, that protection comes from a crazy-quilt of statutes that address parts of the puzzle -- the Clean Water Act, conservation reserve planting, forest service timber harvesting regulations.

A. Conserving Endangered Species

In 1962, the Committee on Rare and Endangered Wildlife Species was established within the Department of the Interior's Bureau of Sport Fisheries and Wildlife.[3] In 1964, the Committee compiled a preliminary list of 63 species of fish, amphibians, reptiles, birds, and mammals that it considered to be threatened with extinction.[4] The final list -- commonly known as the "Redbook" -- lacked any legal status; indeed, it contained one species, the Utah prairie dog, that Animal Damage Control (a sibling agency in the Department of the Interior) was trying to eradicate. The Redbook did, however, increase awareness of the loss of species[5] at a time when a broadly based environmental consciousness was beginning to stir.

The first legal response to increasing public concern for protecting endangered wildlife came in 1964. Recognizing that species loss was due largely to habitat loss, Congress included a provision in the Land and Water Conservation Fund Act allowing monies to be used in "the acquisition of land, waters, or interests in land or waters ... [f]or any national area which may be authorized for the preservation of species of fish or wildlife that are threatened with extinction."[6] This statutory beginning reflected two fundamental changes that grew out of the increased scientific and popular awareness of ecosystems: it provided for the *protection* of wildlife rather than the *management* of game species and that protection was to be accomplished through *habitat* preservation rather than *taking* restrictions. Zoo specimens -- like the Victorian curio cabinet -- were no longer sufficient: wildlife was to be protected in the wild.

i. Endangered Species Preservation Act of 1966

Habitat protection was also the core element of the Endangered Species Preservation Act of 1966 [ESPA],[7] the "first major congressional [demonstration of] concern for the preservation of the endangered species."[8] Acknowledging that "one of the unfortunate consequences of growth and development" is the extermination of native species of fish and wildlife, Congress declared a national policy for the "conservation, protection, restoration, and propagation" of native fish and wildlife "that are threatened with extinction."[9]

As is often the case, the grand sweep of the Act's policy statement gave way to a more modest implementation scheme. Congress established only a modest program of habitat acquisition. It authorized the Secretary of the Interior to acquire lands "to carry out a program ... of conserving, protecting, restoring, and propagating selected species of native fish and wildlife that are threatened with extinction."[10] Even here, however, the Act's objectives were modest. It sanctioned the use of funds available under the Land and Water Conservation Fund Act and authorized the expenditure of a largely symbolic amount -- no more than an additional $15,000,000 over the succeeding three years.[11]

Although Michael Bean is correct in noting that "[b]eyond the land acquisition authority, the contents of the new endangered species program were vague and imprecise,"[12] the Act did contain four seed ideas that were to prove fruitful. First, it directed the Secretary of the Interior to publish a list of endangered "species of native fish and wildlife";[13] the creation of an endangered species list became a powerful symbol. Second, the Act directed the Secretaries of Interior, Agriculture, and Defense to protect endangered fish and wildlife and, "insofar as is practicable and consistent with the[ir] primary purposes ... [to] preserve the habitats of such threatened species on lands under their jurisdiction."[14] Although the where-practicable and when-consistent-with-their-primary-purposes qualifications gave the statute a largely hortatory effect, it did reinforce other federal land management laws requiring wildlife to be considered in land use decisionmaking.

The final two points reflect recognition of the sensitivity of state concerns for their traditional prerogatives in regulating the taking of resident wildlife. As with other statutes asserting a federal regulatory presence in wildlife management, Congress repeatedly emphasized the need for state involvement in the endangered species program.[15] Finally -- and more importantly -- the Act contained only a very limited and qualified prohibition on the taking of listed species. As with numerous other resource statutes,[16] the ESPA specifically provided that "[n]othing in this Act shall be construed to authorize the Secretary to control or regulate hunting or fishing of resident fish and wildlife, including endangered species thereof, on lands not within the [National Wildlife Refuge] System."[17] As the House Report specifically noted, "nothing in this legislation would authorize the Secretary to control or regulate hunting or fishing of resident species of fish and wildlife, *including endangered species,* on lands not within the system."[18]

ii. Endangered Species Conservation Act of 1969

The ESPA's focus on habitat slighted the impact commercial activity can have on wildlife. The failure to regulate commerce was partially remedied in 1969 when Congress extensively supplemented the ESPA and named the combined provisions the Endangered Species Conservation Act [ESCA].[19] The ESCA provided a more comprehensive but still limited program that emphasized the regulation of interstate and foreign commerce in species listed as endangered.

The 1969 Act's provisions on interstate commerce amended the Lacey Act by expanding the type of wildlife that fell within the Act's proscription interstate shipment of wildlife[20] but did not itself impose any additional restrictions on commerce in listed species. The ESCA thus marked no fundamental shift in federal policy on the regulation of interstate commerce.

Although the Act's provisions on interstate commerce were largely symbolic, its provisions on international commerce introduced major changes. The Act prohibited the importation of any species listed by the Secretary of the Interior as "threatened with worldwide extinction."[21] The prohibition was backed by stiff civil and criminal sanctions, and forfeiture provisions.[22] Because of the new importance of the endangered species list, 1969 Act introduced significant procedural and substantive changes to the process for listing a species[23] as endangered.

The ESCA -- the combination of the provisions contained in the 1966 and 1969 endangered species legislation -- was neither comprehensive nor entirely coherent. The latent incongruity is best demonstrated by the two lists of species facing extinction -- one for domestic and the other for foreign species -- that the Secretary of the Interior was to publish. The lists were created through different procedures and had very different legal effects. Protection of domestic species continued to be based almost exclusively upon state law: it was legal to kill a listed species if the taking did not violate state law. Federal law also did not independently prohibit interstate commerce in listed species: it remained legal not only to kill a species listed by the federal government as endangered but also to ship the body to another state for sale unless it violated the law of one of the states involved. The federal role in the protection of domestic endangered species was limited to the acquisition of land -- and here the amount of money appropriated demonstrated the largely symbolic nature of the federal role. While the ESCA accorded domestic endangered species little protection and the federal government could not directly control the taking of foreign species, the Act did prohibit access to the American market and thus affect the economics of endangerment. But the import prohibition negatively impacted domestic commercial interests, and the provisions governing international commerce reflect the balancing of preservation and economics. The procedural and substantive requirements for listing a species as endangered were increased and the public was given a role in the process.

The 1969 Act contained one final international component of future importance. It directed the Secretaries of the Interior and State to "seek the convening of an international ministerial meeting on fish and wildlife" to prepare "a binding international convention on the conservation of endangered species."[24]

iii. Convention on International Trade in Endangered Species of Wild Fauna & Flora (CITES)

The international meeting that 1969 Act instructed the Secretaries of Interior and State to call finally met February of 1973 when representatives from some eighty nations convened in Washington, D.C. The conference reflected a convergence of interests between wildlife-exporting and -importing nations. Exporting states had increasingly recognized that conservation measures were necessary to prevent the extermination of an economically valuable resource; many importing nations, on the other hand, were responding to public opinion that favored protection of wildlife and utilitarian concerns for maintenance of genetic resources for potential exploitation.[25] The result was a multilateral treaty -- the Convention on International Trade in Endangered Species of Wild Fauna and Flora (CITES) -- that was signed in March 1973.[26] The United States ratified the Convention in September, 1973.

CITES embodies a system of import and export permits that provide the basis for a control structure to regulate international commerce in species designated for protection in one of the Convention's three appendices. Wildlife and plants in need of protection are listed in three appendices. Appendix I includes "all species threatened with extinction, which are, or may be affected by trade" and therefore may not be traded for commercial purposes.[27] Appendix II species are those that may become threatened with extinction "unless trade in specimens of such species is subject to strict regulation" or species that closely resemble other Appendix II species; these species may be traded subject to restrictions.[28] Appendix III includes all species that have been identified by a party to CITES as subject to regulation within its jurisdiction.[29]

Since CITES is not self-executing, enforcement is the responsibility of party states.[30] The need for legislation to implement CITES was a primary impetus for the process that led to the enactment of the Endangered Species Act in 1973.[31]

iv. The Endangered Species Act of 1973 (The First Endangered Species Act of 1973)

The Act's central substantive and procedural requirements are found in five sections:

- *** *section 4,* which establishes procedures for listing species as either threatened or endangered, for designating critical habitat, and for preparing recovery plans for listed species;
- *** *section 7,* which requires federal agencies to "insure that actions authorized, funded or carried out by them do not jeopardize the continued existence" of the species;
- *** *section 9,* which prohibits any person from taking or engaging in commerce in endangered species;
- *** *section 11,* which specifies the civil and criminal penalties applicable to the violations set out in section 9; and
- *** *section 10,* which provides specific exemptions, permits, and exceptions to the prohibitions in section 9.

The ESA thus envisions a linear process: when a species is listed as endangered or threatened under section 4, the FWS prepares a recovery plan for the species that specifies how the threat to the species continued existence will be removed and mitigated; the plan is implemented and the species recovers to the point that it no longer requires protection under the ESA. In the interim, the species is protected by the provisions of sections 7 and 9 unless the activity is exempted or permitted pursuant to section 10.

ENDANGERED SPECIES ACT (1973)
(16 U.S.C. §§ 1531-1544)

16 U.S.C. § 1531. Congressional findings and declaration of purposes and policy.

(a) Findings. The Congress finds and declares that --

(1) various species of fish, wildlife, and plants in the United States have been rendered extinct as a consequence of economic growth and development untempered by adequate concern and conservation;

(2) other species of fish, wildlife, and plants have been so depleted in numbers that they are in danger of or threatened with extinction;

(3) these species of fish, wildlife, and plants are of esthetic, ecological, educational, historical, recreational, and scientific value to the Nation and its people;

(4) the United States has pledged itself as a sovereign state in the international community to conserve to the extent practicable the various species of fish or wildlife and plants facing extinction, pursuant to--

(A) migratory bird treaties with Canada and Mexico;

(B) the Migratory and Endangered Bird Treaty with Japan;

(C) the Convention on Nature Protection and Wildlife Preservation in the Western Hemisphere;

(D) the International Convention for the Northwest Atlantic Fisheries;

(E) the International Convention for the High Seas Fisheries of the North Pacific Ocean;

(F) the Convention on International Trade in Endangered Species of Wild Fauna and Flora; and

(G) other international agreements; and

(5) encouraging the States and other interested parties, through Federal financial

assistance and a system of incentives, to develop and maintain conservation programs which meet national and international standards is a key to meeting the Nation's international commitments and to better safeguarding, for the benefit of all citizens, the Nation's heritage in fish, wildlife, and plants.

(b) Purposes. The purposes of this Act are to provide a means whereby the ecosystems upon which endangered species and threatened species depend may be conserved, to provide a program for the conservation of such endangered species and threatened species, and to take such steps as may be appropriate to achieve the purposes of the treaties and conventions set forth in subsection (a) of this section.

(c) Policy. (1) It is further declared to be the policy of Congress that all Federal departments and agencies shall seek to conserve endangered species and threatened species and shall utilize their authorities in furtherance of the purposes of this Act.

(2) It is further declared to be the policy of Congress that Federal agencies shall cooperate with State and local agencies to resolve water resource issues in concert with conservation of endangered species.

[Pub. L. 93-205, § 2, 87 Stat. 884 (Dec.28, 1973); Pub. L. 96-159, § 1, 93 Stat. 1225 (Dec. 28, 1979; Pub. L. 97-304, § 9(a), 96 Stat. 1426 (Oct. 13, 1982); Pub. L. 100-478, Title I, § 1013(a), 102 Stat. 2315 (Oct. 7, 1988)]

16 U.S.C. § 1532. Definitions. For the purposes of this Act --

(1) The term "alternative courses of action" means all alternatives and thus is not limited to original project objectives and agency jurisdiction.

(2) The term "commercial activity" means all activities of industry and trade, including, but not limited to, the buying or selling of commodities and activities conducted for the purpose of facilitating such buying and selling: *Provided, however,* That it does not include exhibition of commodities by museums or similar cultural or historical organizations.

(3) The terms "conserve", "conserving", and "conservation" mean to use and the use of all methods and procedures which are necessary to bring any endangered species or threatened species to the point at which the measures provided pursuant to this Act are no longer necessary. Such methods and procedures include, but are not limited to, all activities associated with scientific resources management such as research, census, law enforcement, habitat acquisition and maintenance, propagation, live trapping, and transplantation, and, in the extraordinary case where population pressures within a given ecosystem cannot be otherwise relieved, may include regulated taking.

(4) The term "Convention" means the Convention on International Trade in Endangered Species of Wild Fauna and Flora, signed on March 3, 1973, and the appendices thereto.

(5)(A) The term "critical habitat" for a threatened or endangered species means --

(i) the specific areas within the geographical area occupied by the species, at the time it is listed in accordance with the provisions of section 4 of this Act [16 U.S.C. § 1533], on which are found those physical or biological features (I) essential to the conservation of the species and (II) which may require special management considerations or protection; and

(ii) specific areas outside the geographical area occupied by the species at the time it is listed in accordance with the provisions of section 4 of this Act [16 U.S.C. § 1533], upon a determination by the Secretary that such areas are essential for the conservation of the species.

(B) Critical habitat may be established for those species now listed as threatened or endangered species for which no critical habitat has heretofore been established as set forth in subparagraph (A) of this paragraph.

(C) Except in those circumstances determined by the Secretary, critical habitat shall not include the entire geographical area which can be occupied by the threatened or endangered species.

(6) The term "endangered species" means any species which is in danger of extinction throughout all or a significant portion of its range other than a species of the Class Insecta determined by the Secretary to constitute a pest whose protection under the provisions of this Act would present an overwhelming and overriding risk to man.

(7) The term "Federal agency" means any department, agency, or instrumentality of the United States.

(8) The term "fish or wildlife" means any member of the animal kingdom, including without limitation any mammal, fish, bird (including any migratory, nonmigratory, or endangered bird for which protection is also afforded by treaty or other international agreement), amphibian, reptile, mollusk, crustacean, arthropod or other invertebrate, and includes any part, product, egg, or offspring thereof, or the dead body or parts thereof.

(9) The term "foreign commerce" includes, among other things, any transaction --

(A) between persons within one foreign country;

(B) between persons in two or more foreign countries;

(C) between a person within the United States and a person in a foreign country; or

(D) between persons within the United States, where the fish and wildlife in question are moving in any country or countries outside the United States.

(10) The term "import" means to land on, bring into, or introduce into, or attempt to land on, bring into, or introduce into, any place subject to the jurisdiction of the United States, whether or not such landing, bringing, or introduction constitutes an importation within the meaning of the customs laws of the United States.

(11) [Repealed.]

(12) The term "permit or license applicant" means, when used with respect to an action of a Federal agency for which exemption is sought under section 7 of this Act [16 U.S.C. § 1536], any person whose application to such agency for a permit or license has been denied primarily because of the application of section 7(a) of this Act [16 U.S.C. § 1536(a)] to such agency action.

(13) The term "person" means an individual, corporation, partnership, trust, association, or any other private entity; or any officer, employee, agent, department, or instrumentality of the Federal Government, of any State, municipality, or political subdivision of a State, or of any foreign government; any State, municipality, or political subdivision of a State; or any other entity subject to the jurisdiction of the

United States.

(14) The term "plant" means any member of the plant kingdom, including seeds, roots and other parts thereof.

(15) The term "Secretary" means, except as otherwise herein provided, the Secretary of the Interior or the Secretary of Commerce as program responsibilities are vested pursuant to the provisions of Reorganization Plan Numbered 4 of 1970 [5 U.S.C. § 903 note]; except that with respect to the enforcement of the provisions of this Act and the Convention which pertain to the importation or exportation of terrestrial plants, the term also means the Secretary of Agriculture.

(16) The term "species" includes any subspecies of fish or wildlife or plants, and any distinct population segment of any species of vertebrate fish or wildlife which interbreeds when mature.

(17) The term "State" means any of the several States, the District of Columbia, the Commonwealth of Puerto Rico, American Samoa, the Virgin Islands, Guam, and the Trust Territory of the Pacific Islands.

(18) The term "State agency" means any State agency, department, board, commission, or other governmental entity which is responsible for the management and conservation of fish, plant, or wildlife resources within a State.

(19) The term "take" means to harass, harm, pursue, hunt, shoot, wound, kill, trap, capture, or collect, or to attempt to engage in any such conduct.

(20) The term "threatened species" means any species which is likely to become an endangered species within the foreseeable future throughout all or a significant portion of its range.

(21) The term "United States", when used in a geographical context, includes all States.

[Pub. L. 93-205, § 3, 87 Stat. 885 (Dec.28, 1973); Pub. L. 94-359, § 5, 90 Stat. 913 (July 12, 1976); Pub. L. 95-632, § 2, 92 Stat. 3751 (Nov. 10, 1978); Pub. L. 96-159, § 2, 93 Stat. 1225 (Dec. 28, 1979); Pub. L. 97-304, § 4(b), 96 Stat. 1420 (Oct. 13, 1982); Pub. L. 100-478, Title I, § 1001, 102 Stat. 2306 (Oct. 7, 1988)]

16 U.S.C. § 1533. Determination of endangered species and threatened species.

(a) Generally.

(1) The Secretary shall by regulation promulgated in accordance with subsection (b) of this section determine whether any species is an endangered species or a threatened species because of any of the following factors:

(A) the present or threatened destruction, modification, or curtailment of its habitat or range;

(B) overutilization for commercial, recreational, scientific, or educational purposes;

(C) disease or predation;

(D) the inadequacy of existing regulatory mechanisms; or

(E) other natural or manmade factors affecting its continued existence.

(2) With respect to any species over which program responsibilities have been vested in the Secretary of Commerce pursuant to Reorganization Plan Numbered 4 of 1970 [5 U.S.C. § 903 note] --

(A) in any case in which the Secretary of Commerce determines that such species should --

(i) be listed as an endangered species or a threatened species, or

(ii) be changed in status from a threatened species to an endangered species,

he shall so inform the Secretary of the Interior, who shall list such species in accordance with this section;

(B) in any case in which the Secretary of Commerce determines that such species should --

(i) be removed from any list published pursuant to subsection (c) of this section, or

(ii) be changed in status from an endangered species to a threatened species,

he shall recommend such action to the Secretary of the Interior, and the Secretary of the Interior, if he concurs in the recommendation, shall implement such action; and

(C) the Secretary of the Interior may not list or remove from any list any such species, and may not change the status of any such species which are listed, without a prior favorable determination made pursuant to this section by the Secretary of Commerce.

(3) The Secretary, by regulation promulgated in accordance with subsection (b) of this section and to the maximum extent prudent and determinable --

(A) shall, concurrently with making a determination under paragraph (1) that a species is an endangered species or a threatened species, designate any habitat of such species which is then considered to be critical habitat; and

(B) may, from time-to-time thereafter as appropriate, revise such designation.

(b) Basis for determinations. (1)(A) The Secretary shall make determinations required by subsection (a)(1) of this section solely on the basis of the best scientific and commercial data available to him after conducting a review of the status of the species and after taking into account those efforts, if any, being made by any State or foreign nation, or any political subdivision of a State or foreign nation, to protect such species, whether by predator control, protection of habitat and food supply, or other conservation practices, within any area under its jurisdiction, or on the high seas.

(B) In carrying out this section, the Secretary shall give consideration to species which have been--

(i) designated as requiring protection from unrestricted commerce by any foreign nation, or pursuant to any international agreement; or

(ii) identified as in danger of extinction, or likely to become so within the foreseeable future, by any State agency or by any agency of a foreign nation that is responsible for the conservation of fish or wildlife or plants.

(2) The Secretary shall designate critical habitat, and make revisions thereto, under subsection (a)(3) of this section on the basis of the best scientific data available and after taking into consideration the economic impact, and any other relevant impact, of specifying any particular area as critical habitat. The Secretary may exclude any area from critical habitat if he determines that the benefits of such exclusion outweigh the benefits of specifying such area as part of the critical habitat, unless he determines, based on the best scientific and commercial data available, that the

failure to designate such area as critical habitat will result in the extinction of the species concerned.

(3)(A) To the maximum extent practicable, within 90 days after receiving the petition of an interested person under section 553(e) of Title 5 to add a species to, or to remove a species from, either of the lists published under subsection (c) of this section, the Secretary shall make a finding as to whether the petition presents substantial scientific or commercial information indicating that the petitioned action may be warranted. If such a petition is found to present such information, the Secretary shall promptly commence a review of the status of the species concerned. The Secretary shall promptly publish each finding made under this subparagraph in the Federal Register.

(B) Within 12 months after receiving a petition that is found under subparagraph (A) to present substantial information indicating that the petitioned action may be warranted, the Secretary shall make one of the following findings:

(i) The petitioned action is not warranted, in which case the Secretary shall promptly publish such finding in the Federal Register.

(ii) The petitioned action is warranted, in which case the Secretary shall promptly publish in the Federal Register a general notice and the complete text of a proposed regulation to implement such action in accordance with paragraph (5).

(iii) The petitioned action is warranted, but that--

(I) the immediate proposal and timely promulgation of a final regulation implementing the petitioned action in accordance with paragraphs (5) and (6) is precluded by pending proposals to determine whether any species is an endangered species or a threatened species, and

(II) expeditious progress is being made to add qualified species to either of the lists published under subsection (c) of this section and to remove from such lists species for which the protections of this Act are no longer necessary,

in which case the Secretary shall promptly publish such finding in the Federal Register, together with a description and evaluation of the reasons and data on which the finding is based.

(C)(i) A petition with respect to which a finding is made under subparagraph (B)(iii) shall be treated as a petition that is resubmitted to the Secretary under subparagraph (A) on the date of such finding and that presents substantial scientific or commercial information that the petitioned action may be warranted.

(ii) Any negative finding described in subparagraph (A) and any finding described in subparagraph (B)(i) or (iii) shall be subject to judicial review.

(iii) The Secretary shall implement a system to monitor effectively the status of all species with respect to which a finding is made under subparagraph (B)(iii) and shall make prompt use of the authority under paragraph 7 to prevent a significant risk to the well being of any such species.

(D)(i) To the maximum extent practicable, within 90 days after receiving the petition of an interested person under section 553(e) of Title 5, to revise a critical habitat designation, the Secretary shall make a finding as to whether the petition presents substantial scientific information indicating that the revision may be warranted. The Secretary shall promptly publish such finding in the Federal Register.

(ii) Within 12 months after receiving a petition that is found under clause (i) to present substantial information indicating that the requested revision may be warranted, the Secretary shall determine how he intends to proceed with the requested revision, and shall promptly publish notice of such intention in the Federal Register.

(4) Except as provided in paragraphs (5) and (6) of this subsection, the provisions of section 553 of Title 5 (relating to rulemaking procedures), shall apply to any regulation promulgated to carry out the purposes of this Act.

(5) With respect to any regulation proposed by the Secretary to implement a determination, designation, or revision referred to in subsection (a)(1) or (3) of this section, the Secretary shall--

(A) not less than 90 days before the effective date of the regulation --

(i) publish a general notice and the complete text of the proposed regulation in the Federal Register, and

(ii) give actual notice of the proposed regulation (including the complete text of the regulation) to the State agency in each State in which the species is believed to occur, and to each county or equivalent jurisdiction in which the species is believed to occur, and invite the comment of such agency, and each such jurisdiction, thereon;

(B) insofar as practical, and in cooperation with the Secretary of State, give notice of the proposed regulation to each foreign nation in which the species is believed to occur or whose citizens harvest the species on the high seas, and invite the comment of such nation thereon;

(C) give notice of the proposed regulation to such professional scientific organizations as he deems appropriate;

(D) publish a summary of the proposed regulation in a newspaper of general circulation in each area of the United States in which the species is believed to occur; and

(E) promptly hold one public hearing on the proposed regulation if any person files a request for such a hearing within 45 days after the date of publication of general notice.

(6)(A) Within the one-year period beginning on the date on which general notice is published in accordance with paragraph (5)(A)(i) regarding a proposed regulation, the Secretary shall publish in the Federal Register--

(i) if a determination as to whether a species is an endangered species or a threatened species, or a revision of critical habitat, is involved, either--

(I) a final regulation to implement such determination,

(II) a final regulation to implement such revision or a finding that such revision should not be made,

(III) notice that such one-year period is being extended under subparagraph (B)(i), or

(IV) notice that the proposed regulation is being withdrawn under subparagraph (B)(ii), together with the finding on which such withdrawal is based; or

(ii) subject to subparagraph (C), if a designation of critical habitat is involved, either--

(I) a final regulation to implement such designation, or

(II) notice that such one-year period is being extended under such subparagraph.

(B)(i) If the Secretary finds with respect to a proposed regulation referred to in subparagraph (A)(i) that there is substantial disagreement regarding the sufficiency or accuracy of the available data relevant to the determination or revision concerned, the Secretary may extend the one-year period specified in subparagraph (A) for not more than six months for purposes of soliciting additional data.

(ii) If a proposed regulation referred to in subparagraph (A)(i) is not promulgated as a final regulation within such one-year period (or longer period if extension under clause (i) applies) because the Secretary finds that there is not sufficient evidence to justify the action proposed by the regulation, the Secretary shall immediately withdraw the regulation. The finding on which a withdrawal is based shall be subject to judicial review. The Secretary may not propose a regulation that has previously been withdrawn under this clause unless he determines that sufficient new information is available to warrant such proposal.

(iii) If the one-year period specified in subparagraph (A) is extended under clause (i) with respect to a proposed regulation, then before the close of such extended period the Secretary shall publish in the Federal Register either a final regulation to implement the determination or revision concerned, a finding that the revision should not be made, or a notice of withdrawal of the regulation under clause (ii), together with the finding on which the withdrawal is based.

(C) A final regulation designating critical habitat of an endangered species or a threatened species shall be published concurrently with the final regulation implementing the determination that such species is endangered or threatened, unless the Secretary deems that--

(i) it is essential to the conservation of such species that the regulation implementing such determination be promptly published; or

(ii) critical habitat of such species is not then determinable, in which case the Secretary, with respect to the proposed regulation to designate such habitat, may extend the one-year period specified in subparagraph (A) by not more than one additional year, but not later than the close of such additional year the Secretary must publish a final regulation, based on such data as may be available at that time, designating, to the maximum extent prudent, such habitat.

(7) Neither paragraph (4), (5), or (6) of this subsection nor section 553 of Title 5 shall apply to any regulation issued by the Secretary in regard to any emergency posing a significant risk to the well-being of any species of fish or wildlife or plants, but only if --

(A) at the time of publication of the regulation in the Federal Register the Secretary publishes therein detailed reasons why such regulation is necessary;

and

(B) in the case such regulation applies to resident species of fish or wildlife, or plants, the Secretary gives actual notice of such regulation to the State agency in each State in which such species is believed to occur.

Such regulation shall, at the discretion of the Secretary, take effect immediately upon the publication of the regulation in the Federal Register. Any regulation promulgated under the authority of this paragraph shall cease to have force and effect at the close of the 240-day period following the date of publication unless, during such 240-day period, the rulemaking procedures which would apply to such regulation without regard to this paragraph are complied with. If at any time after issuing an emergency regulation the Secretary determines, on the basis of the best appropriate data available to him, that substantial evidence does not exist to warrant such regulation, he shall withdraw it.

(8) The publication in the Federal Register of any proposed or final regulation which is necessary or appropriate to carry out the purposes of this Act shall include a summary by the Secretary of the data on which such regulation is based and shall show the relationship of such data to such regulation; and if such regulation designates or revises critical habitat, such summary shall, to the maximum extent practicable, also include a brief description and evaluation of those activities (whether public or private) which, in the opinion of the Secretary, if undertaken may adversely modify such habitat, or may be affected by such designation.

(c) Lists.

(1) The Secretary of the Interior shall publish in the Federal Register a list of all species determined by him or the Secretary of Commerce to be endangered species and a list of all species determined by him or the Secretary of Commerce to be threatened species. Each list shall refer to the species contained therein by scientific and common name or names, if any, specify with respect to each such species over what portion of its range it is endangered or threatened, and specify any critical habitat within such range. The Secretary shall from time to time revise each list published under the authority of this subsection to reflect recent determinations, designations, and revisions made in accordance with subsections (a) and (b) of this section.

(2) The Secretary shall --

(A) conduct, at least once every five years, a review of all species included in a list which is published pursuant to paragraph (1) and which is in effect at the time of such review; and

(B) determine on the basis of such review whether any such species should - -

(i) be removed from such list;

(ii) be changed in status from an endangered species to a threatened species; or

(iii) be changed in status from a threatened species to an endangered species.

Each determination under subparagraph (B) shall be made in accordance with the provisions of subsections (a) and (b) of this section.

(d) Protective regulations. Whenever any species is listed as a threatened species pursuant to subsection (c) of this section, the Secretary shall issue such regulations as he deems necessary and advisable to provide for the conservation of such species. The Secretary may by regulation prohibit with respect to any threatened species any act prohibited under section 9(a)(1) of this Act [16 U.S.C. § 1538(a)(1)], in the case of fish or wildlife, or section 9(a)(2) of this Act [16 U.S.C. § 1538(a)(2)], in the case of plants, with respect to endangered species; except that with respect to the taking of resident species of fish or wildlife, such regulations shall apply in any State which has entered into a cooperative agreement pursuant to section 6(c) of this Act [16 U.S.C. § 1535(c)] only to the extent that such regulations have also been adopted by such State.

(e) Similarity of appearance cases. The Secretary may, by regulation of commerce or taking, and to the extent he deems advisable, treat any species as an endangered species or threatened species even though it is not listed pursuant to this section if he finds that -

(A) such species so closely resembles in appearance, at the point in question, a species which has been listed pursuant to such section that enforcement personnel would have substantial difficulty in attempting to differentiate between the listed and unlisted species;
(B) the effect of this substantial difficulty is an additional threat to an endangered or threatened species; and
(C) such treatment of an unlisted species will substantially facilitate the enforcement and further the policy of this Act.

(f) Recovery plans.

(1) The Secretary shall develop and implement plans (hereinafter in this subsection referred to as "recovery plans") for the conservation and survival of endangered species and threatened species listed pursuant to this section, unless he finds that such a plan will not promote the conservation of the species. The Secretary, in developing and implementing recovery plans, shall, to the maximum extent practicable --

(A) give priority to those endangered species or threatened species, without regard to taxonomic classification, that are most likely to benefit from such plans, particularly those species that are, or may be, in conflict with construction or other development projects or other forms of economic activity;
(B) incorporate in each plan --
(i) a description of such site-specific management actions as may be necessary to achieve the plan's goal for the conservation and survival of the species;
(ii) objective, measurable criteria which, when met, would result in a determination, in accordance with the provisions of this section, that the species be removed from the list; and
(iii) estimates of the time required and the cost to carry out those measures needed to achieve the plan's goal and to achieve intermediate steps toward that goal.

(2) The Secretary, in developing and implementing recovery plans, may procure the services of appropriate public and private agencies and institutions, and other qualified persons. Recovery teams appointed pursuant to this subsection shall not

be subject to the Federal Advisory Committee Act.

(3) The Secretary shall report every two years to the Committee on Environment and Public Works of the Senate and the Committee on Merchant Marine and Fisheries of the House of Representatives on the status of efforts to develop and implement recovery plans for all species listed pursuant to this section and on the status of all species for which such plans have been developed.

(4) The Secretary shall, prior to final approval of a new or revised recovery plan, provide public notice and an opportunity for public review and comment on such plan. The Secretary shall consider all information presented during the public comment period prior to approval of the plan.

(5) Each Federal agency shall, prior to implementation of a new or revised recovery plan, consider all information presented during the public comment period under paragraph (4).

(g) Monitoring. (1) The Secretary shall implement a system in cooperation with the States to monitor effectively for not less than five years the status of all species which have recovered to the point at which the measures provided pursuant to this Act are no longer necessary and which, in accordance with the provisions of this section, have been removed from either of the lists published under subsection (c) of this section.

(2) The Secretary shall make prompt use of the authority under paragraph 7 of subsection (b) of this section to prevent a significant risk to the well being of any such recovered species.

(h) Agency guidelines; publication in Federal Register; scope; proposals and amendments: notice and opportunity for comments. The Secretary shall establish, and publish in the Federal Register, agency guidelines to insure that the purposes of this section are achieved efficiently and effectively. Such guidelines shall include, but are not limited to --

(1) procedures for recording the receipt and the disposition of petitions submitted under subsection (b)(3) of this section;

(2) criteria for making the findings required under such subsection with respect to petitions;

(3) a ranking system to assist in the identification of species that should receive priority review under subsection (a)(1) of this section; and

(4) a system for developing and implementing, on a priority basis, recovery plans under subsection (f) of this section.

The Secretary shall provide to the public notice of, and opportunity to submit written comments on, any guideline (including any amendment thereto) proposed to be established under this subsection.

(i) Submission to State agency of justification for regulations inconsistent with State agency's comments or petition. If, in the case of any regulation proposed by the Secretary under the authority of this section, a State agency to which notice thereof was given in accordance with subsection (b)(5)(A)(ii) of this section files comments disagreeing with all or part of the proposed regulation, and the Secretary issues a final regulation which is in conflict with such comments, or if the Secretary fails to adopt a regulation pursuant to an action petitioned by a State agency under subsection (b)(3) of this section, the Secretary shall submit to the State agency a written justification for his failure to adopt regulations consistent with the agency's comments or petition.

[Pub. L. 93-205, § 4, 87 Stat. 886 (Dec. 28, 1973); Pub. L. 94-359, § 1, 90 Stat. 911 (July 12, 1976); Pub. L. 95-632, §§ 11, 13, 92 Stat. 3764, 3766 (Nov. 10, 1978); Pub. L. 96-159, § 3, 93 Stat. 1225 (Dec. 28, 1979); Pub. L. 97-304, § 2(a), 96 Stat. 1411 (Oct. 13, 1982); Pub. L. 100-478, Title I, §§ 1002-1004, 102 Stat. 2306-2307 (Oct. 7, 1988)]

16 U.S.C. § 1534. Land acquisition.

(a) Implementation of conservation program; authorization of Secretary and Secretary of Agriculture. The Secretary, and the Secretary of Agriculture with respect to the National Forest System, shall establish and implement a program to conserve fish, wildlife, and plants, including those which are listed as endangered species or threatened species pursuant to section 4 of this Act of this Act [16 U.S.C. § 1533]. To carry out such a program, the appropriate Secretary --

(1) shall utilize the land acquisition and other authority under the Fish and Wildlife Act of 1956, as amended [16 U.S.C. § 742a *et seq.*], the Fish and Wildlife Coordination Act, as amended [16 U.S.C. § 661 *et seq.*], and the Migratory Bird Conservation Act [16 U.S.C. § 715 *et seq.*], as appropriate; and

(2) is authorized to acquire by purchase, donation, or otherwise, lands, waters, or interest therein, and such authority shall be in addition to any other land acquisition authority vested in him.

(b) Availability of funds for acquisition of lands, waters, etc. Funds made available pursuant to the Land and Water Conservation Fund Act of 1965, as amended [16 U.S.C. §§ 460l-4 *et seq.*], may be used for the purpose of acquiring lands, waters, or interests therein under subsection (a) of this section.

[Pub. L. 93-205, § 5, 87 Stat. 889 (Dec. 28, 1973); Pub. L. 95-632, § 12, 92 Stat. 3766 (Nov. 10, 1978)]

16 U.S.C. § 1535. Cooperation with States.

(a) Generally. In carrying out the program authorized by this Act, the Secretary shall cooperate to the maximum extent practicable with the States. Such cooperation shall include consultation with the States concerned before acquiring any land or water, or interest therein, for the purpose of conserving any endangered species or threatened species.

(b) Management agreements. The Secretary may enter into agreements with any State for the administration and management of any area established for the conservation of endangered species or threatened species. Any revenues derived from the administration of such areas under these agreements shall be subject to the provisions of [16 U.S.C. § 715s].

(c) Cooperative agreements. (1) In furtherance of the purposes of this Act, the Secretary is authorized to enter into a cooperative agreement in accordance with this section with any State which establishes and maintains an adequate and active program for the conservation of endangered species and threatened species. Within one hundred and twenty days after the Secretary receives a certified copy of such a proposed State program, he shall make a determination whether such program is in accordance with this Act. Unless he determines, pursuant to this paragraph, that the State program is not in accordance with this Act, he shall enter into a cooperative agreement with the State for the purpose of assisting in implementation of the State program. In order for a State program to be deemed an adequate and active program for the conservation of endangered species and threatened species, the Secretary must find, and annually thereafter reconfirm such finding, that under the State program --

(A) authority resides in the State agency to conserve resident species of fish or wildlife determined by the State agency or the Secretary to be endangered or threatened;

(B) the State agency has established acceptable conservation programs, consistent with the purposes and policies of this Act, for all resident species of fish or wildlife in the State which are deemed by the Secretary to be endangered or threatened, and has furnished a copy of such plan and program together with all pertinent details, information, and data requested to the Secretary;

(C) the State agency is authorized to conduct investigations to determine the status and requirements for survival of resident species of fish and wildlife;

(D) the State agency is authorized to establish programs, including the acquisition of land or aquatic habitat or interests therein, for the conservation of resident endangered or threatened species of fish or wildlife; and

(E) provision is made for public participation in designating resident species of fish or wildlife as endangered or threatened; or

that under the State program --

(i) the requirements set forth in subparagraphs (C), (D), and (E) of this paragraph are complied with, and

(ii) plans are included under which immediate attention will be given to those resident species of fish and wildlife which are determined by the Secretary or the State agency to be endangered or threatened and which the Secretary and the State agency agree are most urgently in need of conservation programs; except that a cooperative agreement entered into with a State whose program is deemed adequate and active pursuant to clause (i) and this clause shall not affect the applicability of prohibitions set forth in or authorized pursuant to section 4(d) of this Act [16 U.S.C. § 1533(d)] or section 7(a)(1) [16 U.S.C. § 1538(a)(1)] with respect to the taking of any resident endangered or threatened species.

(2) In furtherance of the purposes of this Act, the Secretary is authorized to enter into a cooperative agreement in accordance with this section with any State which establishes and maintains an adequate and active program for the conservation of endangered species and threatened species of plants. Within one hundred and twenty days after the Secretary receives a certified copy of such a proposed State program, he shall make a determination whether such program is in accordance with this Act. Unless he determines, pursuant to this paragraph, that the State program is not in accordance with this Act, he shall enter into a cooperative agreement with

the State for the purpose of assisting in implementation of the State program. In order for a State program to be deemed an adequate and active program for the conservation of endangered species of plants and threatened species of plants, the Secretary must find, and annually thereafter reconfirm such finding, that under the State program --

(A) authority resides in the State agency to conserve resident species of plants determined by the State agency or the Secretary to be endangered or threatened;

(B) the State agency has established acceptable conservation programs, consistent with the purposes and policies of this Act, for all resident species of plants in the State which are deemed by the Secretary to be endangered or threatened, and has furnished a copy of such plan and program together with all pertinent details, information, and data requested to the Secretary;

(C) the State agency is authorized to conduct investigations to determine the status and requirements for survival of resident species of plants; and

(D) provision is made for public participation in designating resident species of plants as endangered or threatened; or

that under the State program --

(i) the requirements set forth in subparagraphs (C) and (D) of this paragraph are complied with, and

(ii) plans are included under which immediate attention will be given to those resident species of plants which are determined by the Secretary or the State agency to be endangered or threatened and which the Secretary and the State agency agree are most urgently in need of conservation programs; except that a cooperative agreement entered into with a State whose program is deemed adequate and active pursuant to clause (i) and this clause shall not affect the applicability of prohibitions set forth in or authorized pursuant to section 7(d) or section 9(a)(1) [16 U.S.C. § 1533(d) or § 1538(a)(1)] with respect to the taking of any resident endangered or threatened species.

(d) Allocation of funds. (1) The Secretary is authorized to provide financial assistance to any State, through its respective State agency, which has entered into a cooperative agreement pursuant to subsection (c) of this section to assist in development of programs for the conservation of endangered and threatened species or to assist in monitoring the status of candidate species pursuant to subparagraph (C) of section 4(b)(3) of this Act [16 U.S.C. § 1533(b)(3)] and recovered species pursuant to section 4(g) of this Act [16 U.S.C. § 1533(g)]. The Secretary shall allocate each annual appropriation made in accordance with the provisions of subsection (i) of this section to such States based on consideration of --

(A) the international commitments of the United States to protect endangered species or threatened species;

(B) the readiness of a State to proceed with a conservation program consistent with the objectives and purposes of this Act;

(C) the number of endangered species and threatened species within a State;

(D) the potential for restoring endangered species and threatened species within a State;

(E) the relative urgency to initiate a program to restore and protect an endangered species or threatened species in terms of survival of the species;
(F) the importance of monitoring the status of candidate species within a State to prevent a significant risk to the well being of any such species; and
(G) the importance of monitoring the status of recovered species within a State to assure that such species do not return to the point at which the measures provided pursuant to this Act are again necessary.

So much of the annual appropriation made in accordance with provisions of subsection (i) of this section allocated for obligation to any State for any fiscal year as remains unobligated at the close thereof is authorized to be made available to that State until the close of the succeeding fiscal year. Any amount allocated to any State which is unobligated at the end of the period during which it is available for expenditure is authorized to be made available for expenditure by the Secretary in conducting programs under this section.

(2) Such cooperative agreements shall provide for
(A) the actions to be taken by the Secretary and the States;
(B) the benefits that are expected to be derived in connection with the conservation of endangered or threatened species;
(C) the estimated cost of these actions; and
(D) the share of such costs to be borne by the Federal Government and by the States; except that--
(i) the Federal share of such program costs shall not exceed 75 percent of the estimated program cost stated in the agreement; and
(ii) the Federal share may be increased to 90 percent whenever two or more States having a common interest in one or more endangered or threatened species, the conservation of which may be enhanced by cooperation of such States, enter jointly into an agreement with the Secretary.

The Secretary may, in his discretion, and under such rules and regulations as he may prescribe, advance funds to the State for financing the United States pro rata share agreed upon in the cooperative agreement. For the purposes of this section, the non-Federal share may, in the discretion of the Secretary, be in the form of money or real property, the value of which will be determined by the Secretary, whose decision shall be final.

(e) Review of State programs. Any action taken by the Secretary under this section shall be subject to his periodic review at no greater than annual intervals.

(f) Conflicts between Federal and State laws. Any State law or regulation which applies with respect to the importation or exportation of, or interstate or foreign commerce in, endangered species or threatened species is void to the extent that it may effectively (1) permit what is prohibited by this Act or by any regulation which implements this Act, or (2) prohibit what is authorized pursuant to an exemption or permit provided for in this Act or in any regulation which implements this Act. This Act shall not otherwise be construed to void any State law or regulation which is intended to conserve migratory, resident, or introduced fish or wildlife, or to permit or prohibit sale of such fish or wildlife. Any State law or regulation respecting the taking of an endangered species or threatened species may be more restrictive than the exemptions or permits provided for in this Act or in any regulation which implements this Act but not less restrictive than the prohibitions so defined.

(g) Transition. (1) For purposes of this subsection, the term "establishment period" means, with respect to any State, the period beginning on December 28, 1973 and ending on whichever of the following dates first occurs: (A) the date of the close of the 120-day period following the adjournment of the first regular session of the legislature of such State which commences after December 28, 1973, or (B) the date of the close of the 15-month period following December 28, 1973.

(2) The prohibitions set forth in or authorized pursuant to sections 4(d) and 9(a)(1)(B) [16 U.S.C. §§ 1533(d) and 1538(a)(1)(B)] shall not apply with respect to the taking of any resident endangered species or threatened species (other than species listed in Appendix I to the Convention or otherwise specifically covered by any other treaty or Federal law) within any State --

(A) which is then a party to a cooperative agreement with the Secretary pursuant to subsection (c) of this section (except to the extent that the taking of any such species is contrary to the law of such State); or (B) except for any time within the establishment period when --

(i) the Secretary applies such prohibition to such species at the request of the State, or

(ii) the Secretary applies such prohibition after he finds, and publishes his finding, that an emergency exists posing a significant risk to the well-being of such species and that the prohibition must be applied to protect such species. The Secretary's finding and publication may be made without regard to the public hearing or comment provisions of section 553 of Title 5 or any other provision of this Act; but such prohibition shall expire 90 days after the date of its imposition unless the Secretary further extends such prohibition by publishing notice and a statement of justification of such extension.

(h) Regulations. The Secretary is authorized to promulgate such regulations as may be appropriate to carry out the provisions of this section relating to financial assistance to States.

(i) Appropriations. (1) To carry out the provisions of this section for fiscal years after September 30, 1988, there shall be deposited into a special fund known as the cooperative endangered species conservation fund, to be administered by the Secretary, an amount equal to 5 percent of the combined amounts covered each fiscal year into the Federal aid to wildlife restoration fund under [16 U.S.C. § 669b], and paid, transferred, or otherwise credited each fiscal year to the Sport Fishing Restoration Account established under 1016 of the Act of July 18, 1984.

(2) Amounts deposited into the special fund are authorized to be appropriated annually and allocated in accordance with subsection (d) of this section.

[Pub. L. 93-205, § 6, 87 Stat. 884 (Dec.28, 1973); Pub. L. 95-212, § 1, 91 Stat. 1493 (Dec. 19, 1977); Pub. L. 95-632, § 10, 92 Stat. 3762 (Nov. 10, 1978); Pub. L. 96-246, 94 Stat. 348 (May 23, 1980); Pub. L. 97-304, §§ 3,

8(b), 96 Stat. 1416, 1426 (Oct. 13, 1982); Pub. L. 100-478, Title I, § 1005, 102 Stat. 2307 (Oct. 7, 1988)]

16 U.S.C. § 1536. Interagency cooperation.

(a) Federal agency actions and consultations. (1) The Secretary shall review other programs administered by him and utilize such programs in furtherance of the purposes of this Act. All other Federal agencies shall, in consultation with and with the assistance of the Secretary, utilize their authorities in furtherance of the purposes of this Act by carrying out programs for the conservation of endangered species and threatened species listed pursuant to section 4 of this Act [16 U.S.C. § 1533].

(2) Each Federal agency shall, in consultation with and with the assistance of the Secretary, insure that any action authorized, funded, or carried out by such agency (hereinafter in this section referred to as an "agency action") is not likely to jeopardize the continued existence of any endangered species or threatened species or result in the destruction or adverse modification of habitat of such species which is determined by the Secretary, after consultation as appropriate with affected States, to be critical, unless such agency has been granted an exemption for such action by the Committee pursuant to subsection (h) of this section. In fulfilling the requirements of this paragraph each agency shall use the best scientific and commercial data available.

(3) Subject to such guidelines as the Secretary may establish, a Federal agency shall consult with the Secretary on any prospective agency action at the request of, and in cooperation with, the prospective permit or license applicant if the applicant has reason to believe that an endangered species or a threatened species may be present in the area affected by his project and that implementation of such action will likely affect such species.

(4) Each Federal agency shall confer with the Secretary on any agency action which is likely to jeopardize the continued existence of any species proposed to be listed under section 4 of this Act [16 U.S.C. § 1533] or result in the destruction or adverse modification of critical habitat proposed to be designated for such species. This paragraph does not require a limitation on the commitment of resources as described in subsection (d) of this section.

(b) Opinion of Secretary. (1)(A) Consultation under subsection (a)(2) of this section with respect to any agency action shall be concluded within the 90-day period beginning on the date on which initiated or, subject to subparagraph (B), within such other period of time as is mutually agreeable to the Secretary and the Federal agency.

(B) In the case of an agency action involving a permit or license applicant, the Secretary and the Federal agency may not mutually agree to conclude consultation within a period exceeding 90 days unless the Secretary, before the close of the 90th day referred to in subparagraph (A)--

(i) if the consultation period proposed to be agreed to will end before the 150th day after the date on which consultation was initiated, submits to the applicant a written statement setting forth--

(I) the reasons why a longer period is required,

(II) the information that is required to complete the consultation, and

(III) the estimated date on which consultation will be completed; or

(ii) if the consultation period proposed to be agreed to will end 150 or more days after the date on which consultation was initiated, obtains the consent of the applicant to such period.

The Secretary and the Federal agency may mutually agree to extend a consultation period established under the preceding sentence if the Secretary, before the close of such period, obtains the consent of the applicant to the extension.

(2) Consultation under subsection (a)(3) of this section shall be concluded within such period as is agreeable to the Secretary, the Federal agency, and the applicant concerned.

(3) (A) Promptly after conclusion of consultation under paragraph (2) or (3) of subsection (a) of this section, the Secretary shall provide to the Federal agency and the applicant, if any, a written statement setting forth the Secretary's opinion, and a summary of the information on which the opinion is based, detailing how the agency action affects the species or its critical habitat. If jeopardy or adverse modification is found, the Secretary shall suggest those reasonable and prudent alternatives which he believes would not violate subsection (a)(2) of this section and can be taken by the Federal agency or applicant in implementing the agency action.

(B) Consultation under subsection (a)(3) of this section, and an opinion issued by the Secretary incident to such consultation, regarding an agency action shall be treated respectively as a consultation under subsection (a)(2) of this section, and as an opinion issued after consultation under such subsection, regarding that action if the Secretary reviews the action before it is commenced by the Federal agency and finds, and notifies such agency, that no significant changes have been made with respect to the action and that no significant change has occurred regarding the information used during the initial consultation.

(4) If after consultation under subsection (a)(2) of this section, the Secretary concludes that --

(A) the agency action will not violate such subsection, or offers reasonable and prudent alternatives which the Secretary believes would not violate such subsection;

(B) the taking of an endangered species or a threatened species incidental to the agency action will not violate such subsection; and

(C) if an endangered species or threatened species of a marine mammal is involved, the taking is authorized pursuant to [16 U.S.C. § 1371(a)(5)];

the Secretary shall provide the Federal agency and the applicant concerned, if any, with a written statement that --

(i) specifies the impact of such incidental taking on the species,

(ii) specifies those reasonable and prudent measures that the Secretary considers necessary or appropriate to minimize such impact,

(iii) in the case of marine mammals, specifies those measures that are necessary to comply with [16 U.S.C. § 1371(a)(5)] with regard to such taking, and

(iv) sets forth the terms and conditions (including, but not limited to, reporting requirements) that must be complied with by the Federal agency or applicant (if any), or both, to implement the measures specified under clauses (ii) and (iii).

(c) Biological assessment. (1) To facilitate compliance with the requirements of subsection (a)(2) of this section, each Federal agency shall, with respect to any agency action of such agency for which no contract for construction has been entered into and for which no construction has begun on November 10, 1978, request of the Secretary information whether any species which is listed or proposed to be listed may be present in the area of such proposed action. If the Secretary advises, based on the best scientific and commercial data available, that such species may be present, such agency shall conduct a biological assessment for the purpose of identifying any endangered species or threatened species which is likely to be affected by such action. Such assessment shall be completed within 180 days after the date on which initiated (or within such other period as is mutually agreed to by the Secretary and such agency, except that if a permit or license applicant is involved, the 180-day period may not be extended unless such agency provides the applicant, before the close of such period, with a written statement setting forth the estimated length of the proposed extension and the reasons therefor) and, before any contract for construction is entered into and before construction is begun with respect to such action. Such assessment may be undertaken as part of a Federal agency's compliance with the requirements of section 102 of the National Environmental Policy Act of 1969 (42 U.S.C. § 4332).

(2) Any person who may wish to apply for an exemption under subsection (g) of this section for that action may conduct a biological assessment to identify any endangered species or threatened species which is likely to be affected by such action. Any such biological assessment must, however, be conducted in cooperation with the Secretary and under the supervision of the appropriate Federal agency.

(d) Limitation on commitment of resources. After initiation of consultation required under subsection (a)(2) of this section, the Federal agency and the permit or license applicant shall not make any irreversible or irretrievable commitment of resources with respect to the agency action which has the effect of foreclosing the formulation or implementation of any reasonable and prudent alternative measures which would not violate subsection (a)(2) of this section.

(e) Endangered Species Committee. (1) There is established a committee to be known as the Endangered Species Committee (hereinafter in this section referred to as the "Committee").

(2) The Committee shall review any application submitted to it pursuant to this section and determine in accordance with subsection (h) of this section whether or not to grant an exemption from the requirements of subsection (a)(2) of this section for the action set forth in such application.

(3) The Committee shall be composed of seven members as follows:

(A) The Secretary of Agriculture.

(B) The Secretary of the Army.

(C) The Chairman of the Council of Economic Advisors.

(D) The Administrator of the Environmental Protection Agency.

(E) The Secretary of the Interior.

(F) The Administrator of the National Oceanic and Atmospheric Administration.

(G) The President, after consideration of any recommendations received pursuant to subsection (g)(2)(B) of this section shall appoint one individual from each affected State, as determined by the Secretary, to be a member of the Committee for the consideration of the application for exemption for an agency action with respect to which such recommendations are made, not later than 30 days after an application is submitted pursuant to this section.

(4)(A) Members of the Committee shall receive no additional pay on account of their service on the Committee.

(B) While away from their homes or regular places of business in the performance of services for the Committee, members of the Committee shall be allowed travel expenses, including per diem in lieu of subsistence, in the same manner as persons employed intermittently in the Government service are allowed expenses under section 5703 of Title 5.

(5)(A) Five members of the Committee or their representatives shall constitute a quorum for the transaction of any function of the Committee, except that, in no case shall any representative be considered in determining the existence of a quorum for the transaction of any function of the Committee if that function involves a vote by the Committee on any matter before the Committee.

(B) The Secretary of the Interior shall be the Chairman of the Committee.

(C) The Committee shall meet at the call of the Chairman or five of its members.

(D) All meetings and records of the Committee shall be open to the public.

(6) Upon request of the Committee, the head of any Federal agency is authorized to detail, on a nonreimbursable basis, any of the personnel of such agency to the Committee to assist it in carrying out its duties under this section.

(7)(A) The Committee may for the purpose of carrying out its duties under this section hold such hearings, sit and act at such times and places, take such testimony, and receive such evidence, as the Committee deems advisable.

(B) When so authorized by the Committee, any member or agent of the Committee may take any action which the Committee is authorized to take by this paragraph.

(C) Subject to the Privacy Act [5 U.S.C. § 552a], the Committee may secure directly from any Federal agency information necessary to enable it to carry out its duties under this section. Upon request of the Chairman of the Committee, the head of such Federal agency shall furnish such information to the Committee.

(D) The Committee may use the United States mails in the same manner and upon the same conditions as a Federal agency.

(E) The Administrator of General Services shall provide to the Committee on a reimbursable basis such administrative support services as the Committee may request.

(8) In carrying out its duties under this section, the Committee may promulgate and amend such rules, regulations, and procedures, and issue and amend such orders as it deems necessary.

(9) For the purpose of obtaining information necessary for the consideration of an application for an exemption under this section the Committee may issue subpoenas for the attendance and testimony of witnesses and the production of relevant papers, books, and documents.

(10) In no case shall any representative, including a representative of a member designated pursuant to paragraph (3)(G) of this subsection, be eligible to cast a vote on behalf of any member.

(f) Promulgation of regulations; form and contents of exemption application. Not later than 90 days after November 10, 1978, the Secretary shall promulgate regulations which set forth the form and manner in which applications for exemption shall be submitted to the Secretary and the information to be contained in such applications. Such regulations shall require that information submitted in an application by the head of any Federal agency with respect to any agency action include, but not be limited to --

(1) a description of the consultation process carried out pursuant to subsection (a)(2) of this section between the head of the Federal agency and the Secretary; and

(2) a statement describing why such action cannot be altered or modified to conform with the requirements of subsection (a)(2) of this section.

(g) Application for exemption; report to Committee. (1) A Federal agency, the Governor of the State in which an agency action will occur, if any, or a permit or license applicant may apply to the Secretary for an exemption for an agency action of such agency if, after consultation under subsection (a)(2) of this section, the Secretary's opinion under subsection (b) of this section indicates that the agency action would violate subsection (a)(2) of this section. An application for an exemption shall be considered initially by the Secretary in the manner provided for in this subsection, and shall be considered by the Committee for a final determination under subsection (h) of this section after a report is made pursuant to paragraph (5). The applicant for an exemption shall be referred to as the "exemption applicant" in this section.

(2)(A) An exemption applicant shall submit a written application to the Secretary, in a form prescribed under subsection (f) of this section, not later than 90 days after the completion of the consultation process; except that, in the case of any agency action involving a permit or license applicant, such application shall be submitted not later than 90 days after the date on which the Federal agency concerned takes final agency action with respect to the issuance of the permit or license. For purposes of the preceding sentence, the term "final agency action" means (i) a disposition by an agency with respect to the issuance of a permit or license that is subject to administrative review, whether or not such disposition is subject to judicial review; or (ii) if administrative review is sought with respect to such disposition, the decision resulting after such review. Such application shall set forth the reasons why the exemption applicant considers that the agency action meets the requirements for an exemption under this subsection.

(B) Upon receipt of an application for exemption for an agency action under paragraph (1), the Secretary shall promptly (i) notify the Governor of each affected State, if any, as determined by the Secretary, and request the Governors so notified to recommend individuals to be appointed to the Endangered Species Committee for consideration of such application; and (ii) publish notice of receipt of the application in the Federal Register, including a summary of the information contained in the application and a description of the agency action with respect to which the application for exemption has been filed.

(3) The Secretary shall within 20 days after the receipt of an application for exemption, or within such other period of time as is mutually agreeable to the exemption applicant and the Secretary --

(A) determine that the Federal agency concerned and the exemption applicant have --

(i) carried out the consultation responsibilities described in subsection (a) of this section in good faith and made a reasonable and responsible effort to develop and fairly consider modifications or reasonable and prudent alternatives to the proposed agency action which would not violate subsection (a)(2) of this section;

(ii) conducted any biological assessment required by subsection (c) of this section; and

(iii) to the extent determinable within the time provided herein, refrained from making any irreversible or irretrievable commitment of resources prohibited by subsection (d) of this section; or

(B) deny the application for exemption because the Federal agency concerned or the exemption applicant have not met the requirements set forth in subparagraph (A)(i), (ii), and (iii).

The denial of an application under subparagraph (B) shall be considered final agency action for purposes of chapter 7 of Title 5.

(4) If the Secretary determines that the Federal agency concerned and the exemption applicant have met the requirements set forth in paragraph (3)(A)(i), (ii), and (iii) he shall, in consultation with the Members of the Committee, hold a hearing on the application for exemption in accordance with sections 554, 555, and 556 (other than subsection (b)(1) and (2) thereof) of Title 5 and prepare the report to be submitted pursuant to paragraph (5).

(5) Within 140 days after making the determinations under paragraph (3) or within such other period of time as is mutually agreeable to the exemption applicant and the Secretary, the Secretary shall submit to the Committee a report discussing --

(A) the availability of reasonable and prudent alternatives to the agency action, and the nature and extent of the benefits of the agency action and of alternative courses of action consistent with conserving the species or the critical habitat;

(B) a summary of the evidence concerning whether or not the agency action is in the public interest and is of national or regional significance;

(C) appropriate reasonable mitigation and enhancement measures which should be considered by the Committee; and

(D) whether the Federal agency concerned and the exemption applicant refrained from making any irreversible or irretrievable commitment of resources prohibited by subsection (d) of this section.

(6) To the extent practicable within the time required for action under subsection (g) of this section, and except to the extent inconsistent with the requirements of this section, the consideration of any application for an exemption under this section and the conduct of any hearing under this subsection shall be in accordance with sections 554, 555, and 556 (other than subsection (b)(3) of section 556) of Title 5.

(7) Upon request of the Secretary, the head of any Federal agency is authorized

to detail, on a nonreimbursable basis, any of the personnel of such agency to the Secretary to assist him in carrying out his duties under this section.

(8) All meetings and records resulting from activities pursuant to this subsection shall be open to the public.

(h) Grant of exemption. (1) The Committee shall make a final determination whether or not to grant an exemption within 30 days after receiving the report of the Secretary pursuant to subsection (g)(5) of this section. The Committee shall grant an exemption from the requirements of subsection (a)(2) of this section for an agency action if, by a vote of not less than five of its members voting in person --

(A) it determines on the record, based on the report of the Secretary, the record of the hearing held under subsection (g)(4) of this section and on such other testimony or evidence as it may receive, that --

(i) there are no reasonable and prudent alternatives to the agency action;

(ii) the benefits of such action clearly outweigh the benefits of alternative courses of action consistent with conserving the species or its critical habitat, and such action is in the public interest;

(iii) the action is of regional or national significance; and

(iv) neither the Federal agency concerned nor the exemption applicant made any irreversible or irretrievable commitment of resources prohibited by subsection (d) of this section; and

(B) it establishes such reasonable mitigation and enhancement measures, including, but not limited to, live propagation, transplantation, and habitat acquisition and improvement, as are necessary and appropriate to minimize the adverse effects of the agency action upon the endangered species, threatened species, or critical habitat concerned.

Any final determination by the Committee under this subsection shall be considered final agency action for purposes of chapter 7 of Title 5.

(2)(A) Except as provided in subparagraph (B), an exemption for an agency action granted under paragraph (1) shall constitute a permanent exemption with respect to all endangered or threatened species for the purposes of completing such agency action --

(i) regardless whether the species was identified in the biological assessment; and

(ii) only if a biological assessment has been conducted under subsection (c) of this section with respect to such agency action.

(B) An exemption shall be permanent under subparagraph (A) unless --

(i) the Secretary finds, based on the best scientific and commercial data available, that such exemption would result in the extinction of a species that was not the subject of consultation under subsection (a)(2) of this section or was not identified in any biological assessment conducted under subsection (c) of this section, and

(ii) the Committee determines within 60 days after the date of the Secretary's finding that the exemption should not be permanent.

If the Secretary makes a finding described in clause (i), the Committee shall meet with respect to the matter within 30 days after the date of the finding.

(i) Review by Secretary of State; violation of international treaty or other international obligation of United States. Notwithstanding any other provision of this Act, the Committee shall be prohibited from considering for exemption any application made to it, if the Secretary of State, after a review of the proposed agency action and its potential implications, and after hearing, certifies, in writing, to the Committee within 60 days of any application made under this section that the granting of any such exemption and the carrying out of such action would be in violation of an international treaty obligation or other international obligation of the United States. The Secretary of State shall, at the time of such certification, publish a copy thereof in the Federal Register.

(j) Exemption for national security reasons. Notwithstanding any other provision of this Act, the Committee shall grant an exemption for any agency action if the Secretary of Defense finds that such exemption is necessary for reasons of national security.

(k) Exemption decision not considered major Federal action; environmental impact statement. An exemption decision by the Committee under this section shall not be a major Federal action for purposes of the National Environmental Policy Act of 1969 [42 U.S.C. § 4321 *et seq.*]: *Provided,* That an environmental impact statement which discusses the impacts upon endangered species or threatened species or their critical habitats shall have been previously prepared with respect to any agency action exempted by such order.

(l) Committee order granting exemption; cost of mitigation and enhancement measures; report by applicant to Council on Environmental Quality.

(1) If the Committee determines under subsection (h) of this section that an exemption should be granted with respect to any agency action, the Committee shall issue an order granting the exemption and specifying the mitigation and enhancement measures established pursuant to subsection (h) of this section which shall be carried out and paid for by the exemption applicant in implementing the agency action. All necessary mitigation and enhancement measures shall be authorized prior to the implementing of the agency action and funded concurrently with all other project features.

(2) The applicant receiving such exemption shall include the costs of such mitigation and enhancement measures within the overall costs of continuing the proposed action. Notwithstanding the preceding sentence the costs of such measures shall not be treated as project costs for the purpose of computing benefit-cost or other ratios for the proposed action. Any applicant may request the Secretary to carry out such mitigation and enhancement measures. The costs incurred by the Secretary in carrying out any such measures shall be paid by the applicant receiving the exemption. No later than one year after the granting of an exemption, the exemption applicant shall submit to the Council on Environmental Quality a report describing its compliance with the mitigation and enhancement measures prescribed by this section. Such a report shall be submitted annually until all such mitigation and enhancement measures have been completed. Notice of the public availability of such reports shall be published in the Federal Register by the Council on Environmental Quality.

(m) Notice requirement for citizen suits not applicable. The 60-day notice requirement of section 11(g) of this Act [16 U.S.C. § 1540(g)] shall not apply with respect to review of any final determination of the Committee under subsection (h) of this section granting an exemption from the requirements of subsection (a)(2) of this section.

(n) Judicial review. Any person, as defined by section 3(13) of this Act [16 U.S.C. § 1532(13)] may obtain judicial review, under chapter 7 of Title 5, of any decision of the Endangered Species Committee under subsection (h) of this section in the United States Court of Appeals for (1) any circuit wherein the agency action concerned will be, or is being, carried out, or (2) in any case in which the agency action will be, or is being, carried out outside of any circuit, the District of Columbia, by filing in such court within 90 days after the date of issuance of the decision, a written petition for review. A copy of such petition shall be transmitted by the clerk of the court to the Committee and the Committee shall file in the court the record in the proceeding, as provided in section 2112, of Title 28. Attorneys designated by the Endangered Species Committee may appear for, and represent the Committee in any action for review under this subsection.

(o) Exemption as providing exception on taking of endangered species. Notwithstanding sections 4(d) and 9(a)(1)(B) and (C) of this Act [16 U.S.C.§ 1533(d) and 1538(a)(1)(B) and (C)], [16 U.S.C. §§ 1371 and 1372], or any regulation promulgated to implement any such section --

(1) any action for which an exemption is granted under subsection (h) of this section shall not be considered to be a taking of any endangered species or threatened species with respect to any activity which is necessary to carry out such action; and

(2) any taking that is in compliance with the terms and conditions specified in a written statement provided under subsection (b)(4)(iv) of this section shall not be considered to be a prohibited taking of the species concerned.

(p) Exemptions in Presidentially declared disaster areas. In any area which has been declared by the President to be a major disaster area under the Disaster Relief and Emergency Assistance Act [42 U.S.C. § 5121 *et seq.*], the President is authorized to make the determinations required by subsections (g) and (h) of this section for any project for the repair or replacement of a public facility substantially as it existed prior to the disaster under section 405 or 406 of the Disaster Relief and Emergency Assistance Act [42 U.S.C. §§ 5171 or 5172], and which the President determines (1) is necessary to prevent the recurrence of such a natural disaster and to reduce the potential loss of human life, and (2) to involve an emergency situation which does not allow the ordinary procedures of this section to be followed. Notwithstanding any other provision of this section, the Committee shall accept the determinations of the President under this subsection.

[Pub. L. 93-205, § 7, 87 Stat. 892 (Dec. 28, 1973); Pub. L. 95-632, § 3, 92 Stat. 3752 (Nov. 10, 1978); Pub. L. 96-159, § 4, 93 Stat. 1226 (Dec. 28, 1979); Pub. L. 97-304, §§ 4(a), 8(b), 96 Stat. 1417, 1426 (Oct. 13, 1982); Pub. L. 99-659, Title IV, § 411(b), (c), 100 Stat. 3742 (Nov. 14, 1986); Pub. L. 100-707, Title I, § 109(g), 102 Stat. 4709 (Nov. 23, 1988)]

16 U.S.C. § 1537. International cooperation. (a) Financial assistance. As a demonstration of the commitment of the United States to the worldwide protection of endangered species and threatened species, the President may, subject to the provisions of section 1306 of Title 31, use foreign currencies accruing to the United States

Government under the Agricultural Trade Development and Assistance Act of 1954 [7 U.S.C. § 1691 *et seq.*] or any other law to provide to any foreign country (with its consent) assistance in the development and management of programs in that country which the Secretary determines to be necessary or useful for the conservation of any endangered species or threatened species listed by the Secretary pursuant to section 4 of this Act [16 U.S.C. § 1533]. The President shall provide assistance (which includes, but is not limited to, the acquisition, by lease or otherwise, of lands, waters, or interests therein) to foreign countries under this section under such terms and conditions as he deems appropriate. Whenever foreign currencies are available for the provision of assistance under this section, such currencies shall be used in preference to funds appropriated under the authority of section 13 of this Act [16 U.S.C. § 1542].

(b) Encouragement of foreign programs. In order to carry out further the provisions of this Act, the Secretary, through the Secretary of State, shall encourage --

(1) foreign countries to provide for the conservation of fish or wildlife and plants including endangered species and threatened species listed pursuant to section 4 of this Act [16 U.S.C. § 1533];

(2) the entering into of bilateral or multilateral agreements with foreign countries to provide for such conservation; and

(3) foreign persons who directly or indirectly take fish or wildlife or plants in foreign countries or on the high seas for importation into the United States for commercial or other purposes to develop and carry out with such assistance as he may provide, conservation practices designed to enhance such fish or wildlife or plants and their habitat.

(c) Personnel. After consultation with the Secretary of State, the Secretary may --

(1) assign or otherwise make available any officer or employee of his department for the purpose of cooperating with foreign countries and international organizations in developing personnel resources and programs which promote the conservation of fish or wildlife or plants; and

(2) conduct or provide financial assistance for the educational training of foreign personnel, in this country or abroad, in fish, wildlife, or plant management, research and law enforcement and to render professional assistance abroad in such matters.

(d) Investigations. After consultation with the Secretary of State and the Secretary of the Treasury, as appropriate, the Secretary may conduct or cause to be conducted such law enforcement investigations and research abroad as he deems necessary to carry out the purposes of this Act.

[Pub. L. 93-205, § 8, 87 Stat. 892 (Dec. 28, 1973); Pub. L. 96-159, § 5, 93 Stat. 1228 (Dec. 28, 1979)]

16 U.S.C. § 1538. Prohibited acts.

(a) Generally. (1) Except as provided in sections 6(g)(2) and 10 of this Act [16 U.S.C. §§ 1535(g)(2) and 1539], with respect to any endangered species of fish or wildlife listed pursuant to section 4 of this Act [16 U.S.C. § 1533] it is unlawful for any person subject to the jurisdiction of the United States to --

(A) import any such species into, or export any such species from the United

States;

(B) take any such species within the United States or the territorial sea of the United States;

(C) take any such species upon the high seas;

(D) possess, sell, deliver, carry, transport, or ship, by any means whatsoever, any such species taken in violation of subparagraphs (B) and (C);

(E) deliver, receive, carry, transport, or ship in interstate or foreign commerce, by any means whatsoever and in the course of a commercial activity, any such species;

(F) sell or offer for sale in interstate or foreign commerce any such species; or

(G) violate any regulation pertaining to such species or to any threatened species of fish or wildlife listed pursuant to section 4 of this Act [16 U.S.C. § 1533] and promulgated by the Secretary pursuant to authority provided by this Act.

(2) Except as provided in sections 6(g)(2) and 10 [16 U.S.C. §§ 1535(g)(2) and 1539], with respect to any endangered species of plants listed pursuant to section 4 of this Act [16 U.S.C. § 1533] it is unlawful for any person subject to the jurisdiction of the United States to --

(A) import any such species into, or export any such species from, the United States;

(B) remove and reduce to possession any such species from areas under Federal jurisdiction; maliciously damage or destroy any such species on any such area; or remove, cut, dig up, or damage or destroy any such species on any other area in knowing violation of any law or regulation of any State or in the course of any violation of a State criminal trespass law;

(C) deliver, receive, carry, transport, or ship in interstate or foreign commerce, by any means whatsoever and in the course of a commercial activity, any such species;

(D) sell or offer for sale in interstate or foreign commerce any such species; or

(E) violate any regulation pertaining to such species or to any threatened species of plants listed pursuant to section 4 of this Act [16 U.S.C. § 1533] and promulgated by the Secretary pursuant to authority provided by this Act.

(b) Species held in captivity or controlled environment. (1) The provisions of subsections (a)(1)(A) and (a)(1)(G) of this section shall not apply to any fish or wildlife which was held in captivity or in a controlled environment on (A) December 28, 1973, or (B) the date of the publication in the Federal Register of a final regulation adding such fish or wildlife species to any list published pursuant to subsection (c) of section 4 of this Act [16 U.S.C. § 1533]: *Provided,* That such holding and any subsequent holding or use of the fish or wildlife was not in the course of a commercial activity. With respect to any act prohibited by subsections (a)(1)(A) and (a)(1)(G) of this section which occurs after a period of 180 days from (i) December 28, 1973, or (ii) the date of publication in the Federal Register of a final regulation adding such fish or wildlife species to any list published pursuant to subsection (c) of section 4 of this Act [16 U.S.C. § 1533], there shall be a rebuttable presumption that the fish or wildlife involved in such act is not entitled to the exemption contained in this subsection.

(2) (A) The provisions of subsection (a)(1) of this section shall not apply to --

(i) any raptor legally held in captivity or in a controlled environment on November 10, 1978; or

(ii) any progeny of any raptor described in clause (i);

until such time as any such raptor or progeny is intentionally returned to a wild state.

(B) Any person holding any raptor or progeny described in subparagraph (A) must be able to demonstrate that the raptor or progeny does, in fact, qualify under the provisions of this paragraph, and shall maintain and submit to the Secretary, on request, such inventories, documentation, and records as the Secretary may by regulation require as being reasonably appropriate to carry out the purposes of this paragraph. Such requirements shall not unnecessarily duplicate the requirements of other rules and regulations promulgated by the Secretary.

(c) Violation of Convention. (1) It is unlawful for any person subject to the jurisdiction of the United States to engage in any trade in any specimens contrary to the provisions of the Convention, or to possess any specimens traded contrary to the provisions of the Convention, including the definitions of terms in article I thereof.

(2) Any importation into the United States of fish or wildlife shall, if --

(A) such fish or wildlife is not an endangered species listed pursuant to section 4 of this Act [16 U.S.C. § 1533] but is listed in Appendix II to the Convention,

(B) the taking and exportation of such fish or wildlife is not contrary to the provisions of the Convention and all other applicable requirements of the Convention have been satisfied,

(C) the applicable requirements of subsections (d), (e), and (f) of this section have been satisfied, and

(D) such importation is not made in the course of a commercial activity,

be presumed to be an importation not in violation of any provision of this Act or any regulation issued pursuant to this Act.

(d) Imports and exports. (1) In general. It is unlawful for any person, without first having obtained permission from the Secretary, to engage in business --

(A) as an importer or exporter of fish or wildlife (other than shellfish and fishery products which (i) are not listed pursuant to section 4 of this Act [16 U.S.C. § 1533] as endangered species or threatened species, and (ii) are imported for purposes of human or animal consumption or taken in waters under the jurisdiction of the United States or on the high seas for recreational purposes) or plants; or

(B) as an importer or exporter of any amount of raw or worked African elephant ivory.

(2) Requirements. Any person required to obtain permission under paragraph (1) of this subsection shall --

(A) keep such records as will fully and correctly disclose each importation or exportation of fish, wildlife, plants, or African elephant ivory made by him and the subsequent disposition made by him with respect to such fish, wildlife, plants, or ivory;

(B) at all reasonable times upon notice by a duly authorized representative of the Secretary, afford such representative access to his place of business, an opportunity to examine his inventory of imported fish, wildlife, plants, or African elephant ivory and the records required to be kept under subparagraph (A) of this paragraph, and to copy such records; and

(C) file such reports as the Secretary may require.

(3) Regulations. The Secretary shall prescribe such regulations as are necessary and appropriate to carry out the purposes of this subsection.

(4) Restriction on consideration of value or amount of African elephant ivory imported or exported. In granting permission under this subsection for importation or exportation of African elephant ivory, the Secretary shall not vary the requirements for obtaining such permission on the basis of the value or amount of ivory imported or exported under such permission.

(e) Reports. It is unlawful for any person importing or exporting fish or wildlife (other than shellfish and fishery products which (1) are not listed pursuant to section 4 of this Act [16 U.S.C. § 1533] as endangered or threatened species, and (2) are imported for purposes of human or animal consumption or taken in waters under the jurisdiction of the United States or on the high seas for recreational purposes) or plants to fail to file any declaration or report as the Secretary deems necessary to facilitate enforcement of this Act or to meet the obligations of the Convention.

(f) Designation of ports. (1) It is unlawful for any person subject to the jurisdiction of the United States to import into or export from the United States any fish or wildlife (other than shellfish and fishery products which (A) are not listed pursuant to section 4 of this Act [16 U.S.C. § 1533] as endangered species or threatened species, and (B) are imported for purposes of human or animal consumption or taken in waters under the jurisdiction of the United States or on the high seas for recreational purposes) or plants, except at a port or ports designated by the Secretary of the Interior. For the purpose of facilitating enforcement of this Act and reducing the costs thereof, the Secretary of the Interior, with approval of the Secretary of the Treasury and after notice and opportunity for public hearing, may, by regulation, designate ports and change such designations. The Secretary of the Interior, under such terms and conditions as he may prescribe, may permit the importation or exportation at nondesignated ports in the interest of the health or safety of the fish or wildlife or plants, or for other reasons if, in his discretion, he deems it appropriate and consistent with the purpose of this subsection.

(2) Any port designated by the Secretary of the Interior under the authority of [16 U.S.C. § 668cc-4(d)], shall, if such designation is in effect on December 27, 1973, be deemed to be a port designated by the Secretary under paragraph (1) of this subsection until such time as the Secretary otherwise provides.

(g) Violations. It is unlawful for any person subject to the jurisdiction of the United States to attempt to commit, solicit another to commit, or cause to be committed, any offense defined in this section.

[Pub. L. 93-205, § 9, 87 Stat. 893 (Dec. 28, 1973); Pub. L. 95-632, § 4, 92 Stat. 3760 (Nov. 10, 1978); Pub. L. 97-304, § 9(b), 96 Stat. 1426 (Oct. 13, 1982); Pub. L. 100-478, Title I, § 1006, Title II, § 2301, 102 Stat. 2308, 2321 (Oct. 7, 1988); Pub. L. 100-653, Title IX, § 905, 102 Stat. 3835 (Nov. 14, 1988)]

16 U.S.C. § 1539. Exceptions. (a) Permits. (1) The Secretary may permit, under such terms and conditions as he shall prescribe --

(A) any act otherwise prohibited by section 9 of this Act [16 U.S.C. § 1538] for scientific purposes or to enhance the propagation or survival of the affected species, including, but not limited to, acts necessary for the establishment and maintenance of experimental populations pursuant to subsection (j) of this section; or

(B) any taking otherwise prohibited by section 9(a)(1)(B) of this Act [16 U.S.C. § 1538(a)(1)(B)] if such taking is incidental to, and not the purpose of, the carrying out of an otherwise lawful activity.

(2)(A) No permit may be issued by the Secretary authorizing any taking referred to in paragraph (1)(B) unless the applicant therefor submits to the Secretary a conservation plan that specifies --

(i) the impact which will likely result from such taking;

(ii) what steps the applicant will take to minimize and mitigate such impacts, and the funding that will be available to implement such steps;

(iii) what alternative actions to such taking the applicant considered and the reasons why such alternatives are not being utilized; and

(iv) such other measures that the Secretary may require as being necessary or appropriate for purposes of the plan.

(B) If the Secretary finds, after opportunity for public comment, with respect to a permit application and the related conservation plan that--

(i) the taking will be incidental;

(ii) the applicant will, to the maximum extent practicable, minimize and mitigate the impacts of such taking;

(iii) the applicant will ensure that adequate funding for the plan will be provided;

(iv) the taking will not appreciably reduce the likelihood of the survival and recovery of the species in the wild; and

(v) the measures, if any, required under subparagraph (A)(iv) will be met;

and he has received such other assurances as he may require that the plan will be implemented, the Secretary shall issue the permit. The permit shall contain such terms and conditions as the Secretary deems necessary or appropriate to carry out the purposes of this paragraph, including, but not limited to, such reporting requirements as the Secretary deems necessary for determining whether such terms and conditions are being complied with.

(C) The Secretary shall revoke a permit issued under this paragraph if he finds that the permittee is not complying with the terms and conditions of the permit.

(b) Hardship exemptions. (1) If any person enters into a contract with respect to a species of fish or wildlife or plant before the date of the publication in the Federal Register of notice of consideration of that species as an endangered species and the subsequent listing of that species as an endangered species pursuant to section 4 of this Act [16 U.S.C. § 1533] will cause undue economic hardship to such person under the contract, the Secretary, in order to minimize such hardship, may exempt such person from the application of section 9(a) of this Act [16 U.S.C. § 1538(a)] to the extent the Secretary deems appropriate if such person applies to him for such exemption and includes with such application such information as the Secretary may require to prove such hardship; except that (A) no such exemption shall be for a duration of more than one year from the date of publication in the Federal Register of notice of consideration of the species concerned, or shall apply to a quantity of fish or wildlife or plants in excess of that specified by the Secretary; (B) the one-year period for those species of fish or wildlife listed by the Secretary as endangered prior to December 28, 1973 shall expire in accordance with the terms of [16 U.S.C. § 668cc-3]; and (C) no such exemption may be granted for the importation or exportation of a specimen listed in Appendix I of the Convention which is to be used in a commercial activity.

(2) As used in this subsection, the term "undue economic hardship" shall include, but not be limited to.

(A) substantial economic loss resulting from inability caused by this Act to perform contracts with respect to species of fish and wildlife entered into prior to the date of publication in the Federal Register of a notice of consideration of such species as an endangered species;

(B) substantial economic loss to persons who, for the year prior to the notice of consideration of such species as an endangered species, derived a substantial portion of their income from the lawful taking of any listed species, which taking would be made unlawful under this Act; or (C) curtailment of subsistence taking made unlawful under this Act by persons (i) not reasonably able to secure other sources of subsistence; and (ii) dependent to a substantial extent upon hunting and fishing for subsistence; and (iii) who must engage in such curtailed taking for subsistence purposes.

(3) The Secretary may make further requirements for a showing of undue economic hardship as he deems fit. Exceptions granted under this section may be limited by the Secretary in his discretion as to time, area, or other factor of applicability.

(c) Notice and review. The Secretary shall publish notice in the Federal Register of each application for an exemption or permit which is made under this section. Each notice shall invite the submission from interested parties, within thirty days after the date of the notice, of written data, views, or arguments with respect to the application; except that such thirty-day period may be waived by the Secretary in an emergency situation where the health or life of an endangered animal is threatened and no reasonable alternative is available to the applicant, but notice of any such waiver shall be published by the Secretary in the Federal Register within ten days following the issuance of the exemption or permit. Information received by the Secretary as a part of any application shall be available to the public as a matter of public record at every stage of the proceeding.

(d) Permit and exemption policy. The Secretary may grant exceptions under subsections (a)(1)(A) and (b) of this section only if he finds and publishes his finding in the Federal Register that (1) such exceptions were applied for in good faith, (2) if granted and exercised will not operate to the disadvantage of such endangered species, and (3) will be consistent with the purposes and policy set forth in section 2 of this Act [16 U.S.C. § 1531].

(e) Alaska natives. (1) Except as provided in paragraph (4) of this subsection the provisions of this Act shall not apply with respect to the taking of any endangered species or threatened species, or the importation of any such species taken pursuant to this section, by --

(A) any Indian, Aleut, or Eskimo who is an Alaskan Native who resides in Alaska; or

(B) any non-native permanent resident of an Alaskan native village;

if such taking is primarily for subsistence purposes. Non-edible byproducts of species taken pursuant to this section may be sold in interstate commerce when made into authentic native articles of handicrafts and clothing; except that the provisions of this subsection shall not apply to any non-native resident of an Alaskan native village found by the Secretary to be not primarily dependent upon the taking of fish and wildlife for consumption or for the creation and sale of authentic native articles of handicrafts and clothing.

(2) Any taking under this subsection may not be accomplished in a wasteful manner.

(3) As used in this subsection --

(i) The term "subsistence" includes selling any edible portion of fish or wildlife in native villages and towns in Alaska for native consumption within native villages or towns; and

(ii) The term "authentic native articles of handicrafts and clothing" means items composed wholly or in some significant respect of natural materials, and which are produced, decorated, or fashioned in the exercise of traditional native handicrafts without the use of pantographs, multiple carvers, or other mass copying devices. Traditional native handicrafts include, but are not limited to, weaving, carving, stitching, sewing, lacing, beading, drawing, and painting.

(4) Notwithstanding the provisions of paragraph (1) of this subsection, whenever the Secretary determines that any species of fish or wildlife which is subject to taking under the provisions of this subsection is an endangered species or threatened species, and that such taking materially and negatively affects the threatened or endangered species, he may prescribe regulations upon the taking of such species by any such Indian, Aleut, Eskimo, or non-Native Alaskan resident of an Alaskan native village. Such regulations may be established with reference to species, geographical description of the area included, the season for taking, or any other factors related to the reason for establishing such regulations and consistent with the policy of this Act. Such regulations shall be prescribed after a notice and hearings in the affected judicial districts of Alaska and as otherwise required by [16 U.S.C. § 1373], and shall be removed as soon as the Secretary determines that the need for their impositions has disappeared.

(f) Pre-Act endangered species parts exemption; application and certification; regulation; validity of sales contract; separability of provisions; renewal of exemption; expiration of renewal certification. (1) As used in this subsection --

(A) The term "pre-Act endangered species part" means --

(i) any sperm whale oil, including derivatives thereof, which was lawfully held within the United States on December 28, 1973, in the course of a commercial activity; or

(ii) any finished scrimshaw product, if such product or the raw material for such product was lawfully held within the United States on December 28, 1973, in the course of a commercial activity.

(B) The term "scrimshaw product" means any art form which involves the substantial etching or engraving of designs upon, or the substantial carving of figures, patterns, or designs from, any bone or tooth of any marine mammal of the order Cetacea. For purposes of this subsection, polishing or the adding of minor superficial markings does not constitute substantial etching, engraving, or carving.

(2) The Secretary, pursuant to the provisions of this subsection, may exempt, if such exemption is not in violation of the Convention, any pre-Act endangered species part from one or more of the following prohibitions:

(A) The prohibition on exportation from the United States set forth in section 9(a)(1)(A) of this Act [16 U.S.C. § 1538(a)(1)(A)].

(B) Any prohibition set forth in section 9(a)(1)(E) or (F) of this Act [16 U.S.C. §§ 1538(a)(1)(E) or (F)].

(3) Any person seeking an exemption described in paragraph (2) of this subsection shall make application therefor to the Secretary in such form and manner as he shall prescribe, but no such application may be considered by the Secretary unless the application --

(A) is received by the Secretary before the close of the one-year period beginning on the date on which regulations promulgated by the Secretary to carry out this subsection first take effect;

(B) contains a complete and detailed inventory of all pre-Act endangered species parts for which the applicant seeks exemption;

(C) is accompanied by such documentation as the Secretary may require to prove that any endangered species part or product claimed by the applicant to be a pre-Act endangered species part is in fact such a part; and

(D) contains such other information as the Secretary deems necessary and appropriate to carry out the purposes of this subsection.

(4) If the Secretary approves any application for exemption made under this subsection, he shall issue to the applicant a certificate of exemption which shall specify --

(A) any prohibition in section 9(a) of this Act [16 U.S.C. § 1538(a)] which is exempted;

(B) the pre-Act endangered species parts to which the exemption applies;

(C) the period of time during which the exemption is in effect, but no exemption made under this subsection shall have force and effect after the close of the three-year period beginning on the date of issuance of the certificate unless such exemption is renewed under paragraph (8); and

(D) any term or condition prescribed pursuant to paragraph (5)(A) or (B), or both, which the Secretary deems necessary or appropriate.

(5) The Secretary shall prescribe such regulations as he deems necessary and appropriate to carry out the purposes of this subsection. Such regulations may set

forth --

(A) terms and conditions which may be imposed on applicants for exemptions under this subsection (including, but not limited to, requirements that applicants register inventories, keep complete sales records, permit duly authorized agents of the Secretary to inspect such inventories and records, and periodically file appropriate reports with the Secretary); and

(B) terms and conditions which may be imposed on any subsequent purchaser of any pre-Act endangered species part covered by an exemption granted under this subsection;

to insure that any such part so exempted is adequately accounted for and not disposed of contrary to the provisions of this Act. No regulation prescribed by the Secretary to carry out the purposes of this subsection shall be subject to section 4(f)(2)(A)(i) of this Act [16 U.S.C. § 1533(f)(2)(A)(i)].

(6) (A) Any contract for the sale of pre-Act endangered species parts which is entered into by the Administrator of General Services prior to the effective date of this subsection and pursuant to the notice published in the Federal Register on January 9, 1973, shall not be rendered invalid by virtue of the fact that fulfillment of such contract may be prohibited under section 9(a)(1)(F) of this Act [16 U.S.C. § 1538(a)(1)(F)].

(B) In the event that this paragraph is held invalid, the validity of the remainder of this Act, including the remainder of this subsection, shall not be affected.

(7) Nothing in this subsection shall be construed to --

(A) exonerate any person from any act committed in violation of paragraphs (1)(A), (1)(E), or (1)(F) of section 9(a) of this Act [16 U.S.C. § 1538(a)] prior to July 12, 1976; or

(B) immunize any person from prosecution for any such act.

(8)(A) Any valid certificate of exemption which was renewed after October 13, 1982, and was in effect on March 31, 1988, shall be deemed to be renewed for a six-month period beginning on October 7, 1988. Any person holding such a certificate may apply to the Secretary for one additional renewal of such certificate for a period not to exceed 5 years beginning on October 7, 1988.[1]

(B) If the Secretary approves any application for renewal of an exemption under this paragraph, he shall issue to the applicant a certificate of renewal of such exemption which shall provide that all terms, conditions, prohibitions, and other regulations made applicable by the previous certificate shall remain in effect during the period of the renewal.

(C) No exemption or renewal of such exemption made under this subsection shall have force and effect after the expiration date of the certificate of renewal of such exemption issued under this paragraph.

---

[1] This provision was amended by section 18 of the Marine Mammal Protection Act Amendments of 1994: Notwithstanding any other provision of law, any valid certificate of exemption renewed by the Secretary (or deemed to be renewed) under section 10(f)(8) of the Endangered Species Act of 1973 (16 U.S.C. 1539(f)(8)) for any person holding such a certificate with respect to the possession of pre-Act finished scrimshaw products or raw material for such products shall remain valid for a period not to exceed 5 years beginning on the date of enactment of this Act.

Marine Mammal Protection Act Amendments of 1994, Pub. L. No. 103-238, § 18, 108 Stat. 532

(D) No person may, after January 31, 1984, sell or offer for sale in interstate or foreign commerce, any pre-Act finished scrimshaw product unless such person holds a valid certificate of exemption issued by the Secretary under this subsection, and unless such product or the raw material for such product was held by such person on October 13, 1982.

(9) [Repealed.]

(g) Burden of proof. In connection with any action alleging a violation of section 9 of this Act [16 U.S.C. § 1538], any person claiming the benefit of any exemption or permit under this Act shall have the burden of proving that the exemption or permit is applicable, has been granted, and was valid and in force at the time of the alleged violation.

(h) Certain antique articles; importation; port designation; application for return of articles. (1) Sections 4(d) and 9(a) and (c) [16 U.S.C. §§ 1533(d) and 1538(a) and (c)] do not apply to any article which --

(A) is not less than 100 years of age;

(B) is composed in whole or in part of any endangered species or threatened species listed under section 4 of this Act [16 U.S.C. § 1533];

(C) has not been repaired or modified with any part of any such species on or after December 28, 1973; and

(D) is entered at a port designated under paragraph (3).

(2) Any person who wishes to import an article under the exception provided by this subsection shall submit to the customs officer concerned at the time of entry of the article such documentation as the Secretary of the Treasury, after consultation with the Secretary of the Interior, shall by regulation require as being necessary to establish that the article meets the requirements set forth in paragraph (1)(A), (B), and (C).

(3) The Secretary of the Treasury, after consultation with the Secretary of the Interior, shall designate one port within each customs region at which articles described in paragraph (1)(A), (B), and (C) must be entered into the customs territory of the United States.

(4) Any person who imported, after December 27, 1973, and on or before November 10, 1978, any article described in paragraph (1) which --

(A) was not repaired or modified after the date of importation with any part of any endangered species or threatened species listed under section 4 of this Act [16 U.S.C. § 1533];

(B) was forfeited to the United States before November 10, 1978, or is subject to forfeiture to the United States on such date of enactment, pursuant to the assessment of a civil penalty under section 11 of this Act [16 U.S.C. § 1540]; and

(C) is in the custody of the United States on November 10, 1978;

may, before the close of the one-year period beginning on November 10, 1978, make application to the Secretary for return of the article. Application shall be made in such form and manner, and contain such documentation, as the Secretary prescribes. If on the basis of any such application which is timely filed, the Secretary is satisfied that the requirements of this paragraph are met with respect to the article concerned, the Secretary shall return the article to the applicant and the importation of such article shall, on and after the date of return, be deemed to be a lawful importation under this Act.

(i) Noncommercial transshipments. Any importation into the United States of fish or wildlife shall, if --

(1) such fish or wildlife was lawfully taken and exported from the country of origin and country of reexport, if any;

(2) such fish or wildlife is in transit or transshipment through any place subject to the jurisdiction of the United States en route to a country where such fish or wildlife may be lawfully imported and received;

(3) the exporter or owner of such fish or wildlife gave explicit instructions not to ship such fish or wildlife through any place subject to the jurisdiction of the United States, or did all that could have reasonably been done to prevent transshipment, and the circumstances leading to the transshipment were beyond the exporter's or owner's control;

(4) the applicable requirements of the Convention have been satisfied; and

(5) such importation is not made in the course of a commercial activity,

be an importation not in violation of any provision of this Act or any regulation issued pursuant to this Act while such fish or wildlife remains in the control of the United States Customs Service.

(j) Experimental populations. (1) For purposes of this subsection, the term "experimental population" means any population (including any offspring arising solely therefrom) authorized by the Secretary for release under paragraph (2), but only when, and at such times as, the population is wholly separate geographically from nonexperimental populations of the same species.

(2)(A) The Secretary may authorize the release (and the related transportation) of any population (including eggs, propagules, or individuals) of an endangered species or a threatened species outside the current range of such species if the Secretary determines that such release will further the conservation of such species.

(B) Before authorizing the release of any population under subparagraph (A), the Secretary shall by regulation identify the population and determine, on the basis of the best available information, whether or not such population is essential to the continued existence of an endangered species or a threatened species.

(C) For the purposes of this Act, each member of an experimental population shall be treated as a threatened species; except that --

(i) solely for purposes of section 7 of this Act [16 U.S.C. § 1536] (other than subsection (a)(1) thereof), an experimental population determined under subparagraph (B) to be not essential to the continued existence of a species shall be treated, except when it occurs in an area within the National Wildlife Refuge System or the National Park System, as a species proposed to be listed under section 4 of this Act [16 U.S.C. § 1533]; and

(ii) critical habitat shall not be designated under this Act for any experimental population determined under subparagraph (B) to be not essential to the continued existence of a species.

(3) The Secretary, with respect to populations of endangered species or threatened species that the Secretary authorized, before October 13, 1982, for release in geographical areas separate from the other populations of such species, shall determine by regulation which of such populations are an experimental population for the purposes of this subsection and whether or not each is essential to the continued existence of an endangered species or a threatened species.

[Pub. L. 93-205, § 10, 87 Stat. 896 (Dec. 28, 1973); Pub. L. 94-359, §§ 2, 3, 90 Stat. 911, 912 (July 12, 1976); Pub. L. 95-632, § 5, 92 Stat. 3760 (Nov. 10, 1978); Pub. L. 96-159, § 7, 93 Stat. 1230 (Dec. 28, 1979); Pub. L. 97-304, § 6(1) to (3), (4)(A), (5), (6), 96 Stat. 1422-1424 (Oct. 13, 1982); Pub. L. 100-478, Title I, §§ 1011, 1013(b), (c), 102 Stat. 2314-2315 (Oct. 7, 1988)]

16 U.S.C. § 1540. Penalties and enforcement. (a) Civil penalties. (1) Any person who knowingly violates, and any person engaged in business as an importer or exporter of fish, wildlife, or plants who violates, any provision of this Act, or any provision of any permit or certificate issued hereunder, or of any regulation issued in order to implement subsection (a)(1)(A), (B), (C), (D), (E), or (F), (a)(2)(A), (B), (C), or (D), (c), (d) (other than regulation relating to recordkeeping or filing of reports), (f) or (g) of section 9 of this Act [16 U.S.C. § 1538], may be assessed a civil penalty by the Secretary of not more than $25,000 for each violation. Any person who knowingly violates, and any person engaged in business as an importer or exporter of fish, wildlife, or plants who violates, any provision of any other regulation issued under this Act may be assessed a civil penalty by the Secretary of not more than $12,000 for each such violation. Any person who otherwise violates any provision of this Act, or any regulation, permit, or certificate issued hereunder, may be assessed a civil penalty by the Secretary of not more than $500 for each such violation. No penalty may be assessed under this subsection unless such person is given notice and opportunity for a hearing with respect to such violation. Each violation shall be a separate offense. Any such civil penalty may be remitted or mitigated by the Secretary. Upon any failure to pay a penalty assessed under this subsection, the Secretary may request the Attorney General to institute a civil action in a district court of the United States for any district in which such person is found, resides, or transacts business to collect the penalty and such court shall have jurisdiction to hear and decide any such action. The court shall hear such action on the record made before the Secretary and shall sustain his action if it is supported by substantial evidence on the record considered as a whole.

(2) Hearings held during proceedings for the assessment of civil penalties authorized by paragraph (1) of this subsection shall be conducted in accordance with section 554 of Title 5. The Secretary may issue subpoenas for the attendance and testimony of witnesses and the production of relevant papers, books, and documents, and administer oaths. Witnesses summoned shall be paid the same fees and mileage that are paid to witnesses in the courts of the United States. In case of contumacy or refusal to obey a subpena served upon any person pursuant to this paragraph, the district court of the United States for any district in which such person is found or resides or transacts business, upon application by the United States and after notice to such person, shall have jurisdiction to issue an order requiring such

person to appear and give testimony before the Secretary or to appear and produce documents before the Secretary, or both, and any failure to obey such order of the court may be punished by such court as a contempt thereof.

(3) Notwithstanding any other provision of this Act, no civil penalty shall be imposed if it can be shown by a preponderance of the evidence that the defendant committed an act based on a good faith belief that he was acting to protect himself or herself, a member of his or her family, or any other individual from bodily harm, from any endangered or threatened species.

(b) Criminal violations. (1) Any person who knowingly violates any provision of this Act, of any permit or certificate issued hereunder, or of any regulation issued in order to implement subsection (a)(1)(A), (B), (C), (D), (E), or (F); (a)(2)(A), (B), (C), or (D), (c), (d)(other than a regulation relating to recordkeeping, or filing of reports), (f), or (g) of section 9 of this Act [16 U.S.C. § 1538] shall, upon conviction, be fined not more than $50,000 or imprisoned for not more than one year, or both. Any person who knowingly violates any provision of any other regulation issued under this Act shall, upon conviction, be fined not more than $25,000 or imprisoned for not more than six months, or both.

(2) The head of any Federal agency which has issued a lease, license, permit, or other agreement authorizing a person to import or export fish, wildlife, or plants, or to operate a quarantine station for imported wildlife, or authorizing the use of Federal lands, including grazing of domestic livestock, to any person who is convicted of a criminal violation of this Act or any regulation, permit, or certificate issued hereunder may immediately modify, suspend, or revoke each lease, license, permit, or other agreement. The Secretary shall also suspend for a period of up to one year, or cancel, any Federal hunting or fishing permits or stamps issued to any person who is convicted of a criminal violation of any provision of this Act or any regulation, permit, or certificate issued hereunder. The United States shall not be liable for the payments of any compensation, reimbursement, or damages in connection with the modification, suspension, or revocation of any leases, licenses, permits, stamps, or other agreements pursuant to this section.

(3) Notwithstanding any other provision of this Act, it shall be a defense to prosecution under this subsection if the defendant committed the offense based on a good faith belief that he was acting to protect himself or herself, a member of his or her family, or any other individual, from bodily harm from any endangered or threatened species.

(c) District court jurisdiction. The several district courts of the United States, including the courts enumerated in section 460 of Title 28, shall have jurisdiction over any actions arising under this Act. For the purpose of this Act, American Samoa shall be included within the judicial district of the District Court of the United States for the District of Hawaii.

(d) Rewards and certain incidental expenses. The Secretary or the Secretary of the Treasury shall pay, from sums received as penalties, fines, or forfeitures of property for any violation of this Act or any regulation issued hereunder (1) a reward to any person who furnishes information which leads to an arrest, a criminal conviction, civil penalty assessment, or forfeiture of property for any violation of this Act or any regulation issued hereunder, and (2) the reasonable and necessary costs incurred by any person in providing temporary care for any fish, wildlife, or plant pending the disposition of any civil or criminal proceeding alleging a violation of this Act with respect to that fish, wildlife, or plant. The amount of the reward, if any, is to be designated by the Secretary or the Secretary of the Treasury, as appropriate. Any officer or employee of the United States or any State or local government who furnishes information or renders service in the performance of his official duties is ineligible for payment under this subsection. Whenever the balance of sums received under this section and [16 U.S.C. § 3375(d)], as penalties or fines, or from forfeitures of property, exceed $500,000, the Secretary of the Treasury shall deposit an amount equal to such excess balance in the cooperative endangered species conservation fund established under section 6(i) of this Act [16 U.S.C. § 1535(i)].

(e) Enforcement. (1) The provisions of this Act and any regulations or permits issued pursuant thereto shall be enforced by the Secretary, the Secretary of the Treasury, or the Secretary of the Department in which the Coast Guard is operating, or all such Secretaries. Each such Secretary may utilize by agreement, with or without reimbursement, the personnel, services, and facilities of any other Federal agency or any State agency for purposes of enforcing this Act.

(2) The judges of the district courts of the United States and the United States magistrates may, within their respective jurisdictions, upon proper oath or affirmation showing probable cause, issue such warrants or other process as may be required for enforcement of this Act and any regulation issued thereunder.

(3) Any person authorized by the Secretary, the Secretary of the Treasury, or the Secretary of the Department in which the Coast Guard is operating, to enforce this Act may detain for inspection and inspect any package, crate, or other container, including its contents, and all accompanying documents, upon importation or exportation. Such person may make arrests without a warrant for any violation of this Act if he has reasonable grounds to believe that the person to be arrested is committing the violation in his presence or view, and may execute and serve any arrest warrant, search warrant, or other warrant or civil or criminal process issued by any officer or court of competent jurisdiction for enforcement of this Act. Such person so authorized may search and seize, with or without a warrant, as authorized by law. Any fish, wildlife, property, or item so seized shall be held by any person authorized by the Secretary, the Secretary of the Treasury, or the Secretary of the Department in which the Coast Guard is operating pending disposition of civil or criminal proceedings, or the institution of an action in rem for forfeiture of such fish, wildlife, property, or item pursuant to paragraph (4) of this subsection; except that the Secretary may, in lieu of holding such fish, wildlife, property, or item, permit the owner or consignee to post a bond or other surety satisfactory to the Secretary, but upon forfeiture of any such property to the United States, or the abandonment or waiver of any claim to any such property, it shall be disposed of (other than by sale to the general public) by the Secretary in such a manner, consistent with the purposes of this Act, as the Secretary shall by regulation prescribe.

(4)(A) All fish or wildlife or plants taken, possessed, sold, purchased, offered for sale or purchase, transported, delivered, received, carried, shipped, exported, or imported contrary to the provisions of this Act, any regulation made pursuant thereto, or any permit or certificate issued hereunder shall be subject to forfeiture to the United States.

(B) All guns, traps, nets, and other equipment, vessels, vehicles, aircraft, and other means of transportation used to aid the taking, possessing, selling, purchasing, offering for sale or purchase, transporting, delivering, receiving, carrying, shipping, exporting, or importing of any fish or wildlife or plants in violation of this Act, any regulation made pursuant thereto, or any permit or certificate issued thereunder shall be subject to forfeiture to the United States upon conviction of a criminal violation pursuant to subsection (b)(1) of this section.

(5) All provisions of law relating to the seizure, forfeiture, and condemnation of a vessel for violation of the customs laws, the disposition of such vessel or the proceeds from the sale thereof, and the remission or mitigation of such forfeiture, shall apply to the seizures and forfeitures incurred, or alleged to have been incurred, under the provisions of this Act, insofar as such provisions of law are applicable and not inconsistent with the provisions of this Act; except that all powers, rights, and duties conferred or imposed by the customs laws upon any officer or employee of the Treasury Department shall, for the purposes of this Act, be exercised or performed by the Secretary or by such persons as he may designate.

(6) The Attorney General of the United States may seek to enjoin any person who is alleged to be in violation of any provision of this Act or regulation issued under authority thereof.

(f) Regulations. The Secretary, the Secretary of the Treasury, and the Secretary of the Department in which the Coast Guard is operating, are authorized to promulgate such regulations as may be appropriate to enforce this Act, and charge reasonable fees for expenses to the Government connected with permits or certificates authorized by this Act including processing applications and reasonable inspections, and with the transfer, board, handling, or storage of fish or wildlife or plants and evidentiary items seized and forfeited under this Act. All such fees collected pursuant to this subsection shall be deposited in the Treasury to the credit of the appropriation which is current and chargeable for the cost of furnishing the services. Appropriated funds may be expended pending reimbursement from parties in interest.

(g) Citizen suits. (1) Except as provided in paragraph (2) of this subsection any person may commence a civil suit on his own behalf--

(A) to enjoin any person, including the United States and any other governmental instrumentality or agency (to the extent permitted by the eleventh amendment to the Constitution), who is alleged to be in violation of any provision of this Act or regulation issued under the authority thereof; or

(B) to compel the Secretary to apply, pursuant to section 6(g)(2)(B)(ii) of this Act [16 U.S.C. § 1535(g)(2)(B)(ii)], the prohibitions set forth in or authorized pursuant to section 4(d) or 9(a)(1)(B) of this Act [16 U.S.C. §§ 1533(d) or 1538(a)(1)(B)] with respect to the taking of any resident endangered species or threatened species within any State; or

(C) against the Secretary where there is alleged a failure of the Secretary to perform any act or duty under section 4 of this Act [16 U.S.C. § 1533] which is not discretionary with the Secretary.

The district courts shall have jurisdiction, without regard to the amount in controversy or the citizenship of the parties, to enforce any such provision or regulation, or to order the Secretary to perform such act or duty, as the case may be. In any civil suit commenced under subparagraph (B) the district court shall compel the Secretary to apply the prohibition sought if the court finds that the allegation that an emergency exists is supported by substantial evidence.

(2)(A) No action may be commenced under subparagraph (1)(A) of this section --

(i) prior to sixty days after written notice of the violation has been given to the Secretary, and to any alleged violator of any such provision or regulation;

(ii) if the Secretary has commenced action to impose a penalty pursuant to subsection (a) of this section; or

(iii) if the United States has commenced and is diligently prosecuting a criminal action in a court of the United States or a State to redress a violation of any such provision or regulation.

(B) No action may be commenced under subparagraph (1)(B) of this section --

(i) prior to sixty days after written notice has been given to the Secretary setting forth the reasons why an emergency is thought to exist with respect to an endangered species or a threatened species in the State concerned; or

(ii) if the Secretary has commenced and is diligently prosecuting action under section 6(g)(2)(B)(ii) of this Act [16 U.S.C. § 1535(g)(2)(B)(ii)] to determine whether any such emergency exists.

(C) No action may be commenced under subparagraph (1)(C) of this section prior to sixty days after written notice has been given to the Secretary; except that such action may be brought immediately after such notification in the case of an action under this section respecting an emergency posing a significant risk to the well-being of any species of fish or wildlife or plants.

(3)(A) Any suit under this subsection may be brought in the judicial district in which the violation occurs.

(B) In any such suit under this subsection in which the United States is not a party, the Attorney General, at the request of the Secretary, may intervene on behalf of the United States as a matter of right.

(4) The court, in issuing any final order in any suit brought pursuant to paragraph (1) of this subsection, may award costs of litigation (including reasonable attorney and expert witness fees) to any party, whenever the court determines such award is appropriate.

(5) The injunctive relief provided by this subsection shall not restrict any right which any person (or class of persons) may have under any statute or common law to seek enforcement of any standard or limitation or to seek any other relief (including relief against the Secretary or a State agency).

(h) Coordination with other laws. The Secretary of Agriculture and the Secretary shall provide for appropriate coordination of the administration of this Act with the administration of the animal quarantine laws (21 U.S.C. § 101-105, 111-135b, and 612-614) and section

306 of the Tariff Act of 1930 (19 U.S.C. § 1306). Nothing in this Act or any amendment made by this Act shall be construed as superseding or limiting in any manner the functions of the Secretary of Agriculture under any other law relating to prohibited or restricted importations or possession of animals and other articles and no proceeding or determination under this Act shall preclude any proceeding or be considered determinative of any issue of fact or law in any proceeding under any Act administered by the Secretary of Agriculture. Nothing in this Act shall be construed as superseding or limiting in any manner the functions and responsibilities of the Secretary of the Treasury under the Tariff Act of 1930 [19 U.S.C. § 1202 *et seq.*], including, without limitation, section 527 of that Act (19 U.S.C. § 1527), relating to the importation of wildlife taken, killed, possessed, or exported to the United States in violation of the laws or regulations of a foreign country.

[Pub. L. 93-205, § 11, 87 Stat. 897 (Dec. 28, 1973); Pub. L. 94-359, § 4, 90 Stat. 913 (July 12, 1976); Pub. L. 95-632, §§ 6 to 8, 92 Stat. 3761 (Nov. 10, 1978), 3762; Pub. L. 97-79, § 9(e), 95 Stat. 1079 (Nov. 16, 1981); Pub. L. 97-304, §§ 7, 9(c), 96 Stat. 1425 (Oct. 13, 1982), 1427; Pub. L. 98-327, § 4, 98 Stat. 271 (June 25, 1984); Pub. L. 100-478, Title I, § 1007, 102 Stat. 2309 (Oct. 7, 1988); Pub. L. 101-650, Title III, § 321, 104 Stat. 5117 (Dec. 1, 1990)]

16 U.S.C. § 1541. Endangered plants. The Secretary of the Smithsonian Institution, in conjunction with other affected agencies, is authorized and directed to review (1) species of plants which are now or may become endangered or threatened and (2) methods of adequately conserving such species, and to report to Congress, within one year after December 28, 1973, the results of such review including recommendations for new legislation or the amendment of existing legislation.

[Pub. L. 93-205, § 12, 87 Stat. 901 (Dec. 28, 1973)]

16 U.S.C. § 1542. Authorization of appropriations. ****

16 U.S.C. § 1543. Construction with marine mammal protection act of 1972. Except as otherwise provided in this Act, no provision of this Act shall take precedence over any more restrictive conflicting provision of the Marine Mammal Protection Act of 1972 [16 U.S.C. § 1361 *et seq.*].

[Pub. L. 93-205, § 17, 87 Stat. 903 (Dec. 28, 1973)]

- 0 -

Regulations Implementing the Endangered Species Act

The Endangered Species Act (ESA) is implemented in regulations promulgated independently by the Fish and Wildlife Service (FWS) and the National Marine Fisheries Service (NMFS) as well as jointly by the FWS and the NMFS. In general, FWS has been more conscientious in promulgating regulations.

The independent FWS regulations are in Part 17. They include the list of endangered and threatened species for which the Secretary of the Interior is responsible, 50 C.F.R. §§

17.11, 17.12, as well as the regulations governing prohibitions, permits for taking, and special rules for listed species, *id.* §§ 17.21-.23, 17.31-48; regulations governing similarity-of-appearance species, *id.* §§ 17.50-.52; regulations governing the reintroduction of experimental populations, *id.* §§ 17.80-.85; and regulations on critical habitats, *id.* §§ 17.94-.96. The agency's regulations covering incidental take permits, no surprises, and safe harbor provisions are found in §§ 17.22, 17.32.

The independent NMFS regulations in Parts 222-224. The listed species subject tot he jurisdiction of the Secretary of Commerce are enumerated in 50 C.F.R. parts 223 (threatened species) and 224 (endangered species). Part 222 contains permitting provisions.

In addition, there are joint FWS-NMFS regulations in Chapter IV of title 50. These include regulations on consultation under § 7 of the ESA, *id.* §§ 402.01-.16; listing under § 4, *id.* §§ 424.01-.02, 424.10-.21; and the endangered species exemption (the "God Squad") process, *id.* §§ 450.01, 451.01-.03, 452.01-.09, 453.01-.06.

The division of responsibility between the two agencies means that the regulations are not set out in the Code sequentially. For example, the listing procedures -- which include delisting and reclassification -- are at 50 C.F.R. §§ 424.01-.02, 424.10-.21; the list of endangered and threatened species as well as the special regulations applicable to individual species are 50 C.F.R. §§ 17.11-.12, 17.21-.23, 17.31-48 for the Department of the Interior and at 50 C.F.R. parts 223-224 for the Department of Commerce. Critical habitat provisions are located in 50 C.F.R. §§ 17.95-.96 and 50 C.F.R. part 226.

United States Fish and Wildlife Service, Department of the Interior

50 C.F.R. PART 17
ENDANGERED AND THREATENED WILDLIFE AND PLANTS

Subpart A -- Introduction and General Provisions

sec.

Subpart B -- Lists

Subpart C -- Endangered Wildlife

17.21 Prohibitions.
17.22 Permits for scientific purposes, enhancement of propagation or survival, or for incidental taking.
17.23 Economic hardship permits.

Subpart D -- Threatened Wildlife

17.31 Prohibitions.
17.32 Permits -- general.
17.40 Special Rules -- mammals.
17.41 Special Rules -- birds.
17.42 Special Rules -- reptiles.
17.43 Special Rules -- amphibians.
17.44 Special Rules -- fishes.
17.45 Special Rules -- snails and clams. [Reserved]
17.46 Special Rules -- crustaceans.
17.47 [Reserved]
17.48 Special Rules -- common sponges and other forms. [Reserved]

Subpart E -- Similarity of Appearance

17.50 General.
17.51 Treatment as endangered or threatened.
17.52 Permits -- similarity of appearance.

Subpart F -- Endangered Plants

17.61 Prohibitions.
17.62 Permits for scientific purposes or for the enhancement of propagation or survival.
17.63 Economic hardship permits.

Subpart G -- Threatened Plants

17.71 Prohibitions.
17.72 Permits -- general.
17.73-17.78 [Reserved]

Subpart H -- Experimental Populations

17.80 Definitions.
17.81 Listing.
17.82 Prohibitions.
17.83 Special rules -- vertebrates.
17.84 Special rules -- invertebrates.
17.85 Special rules -- plants. [Reserved]

Subpart I -- Interagency Cooperation

17.94 Critical habitats.
17.95 Critical habitat -- fish and wildlife.

17.96 Critical habitat -- plants.

Subpart J -- Manatee Protection Areas

****

AUTHORITY: 16 U.S.C. §§ 1361-1407; 16 U.S.C. §§ 1531-1544; 16 U.S.C. §§ 4201-4245; Pub. L. No. 99-625, 100 Stat. 3500; unless otherwise noted.

SOURCE: 40 FR 44415, Sept. 26, 1975, unless otherwise noted.

SUBPART A -- INTRODUCTION AND GENERAL PROVISIONS

§ 17.1 Purpose of regulations.

(a) The regulations in this part implement the Endangered Species Act of 1973, 87 Stat. 884, 16 U.S.C. 1531-1543, except for those provisions in the Act concerning the Convention on International Trade in Endangered Species of Wild Fauna and Flora, for which regulations are provided in Part 23 of this subchapter.

(b) The regulations identify those species of wildlife and plants determined by the Director to be endangered or threatened with extinction under section 4(a) of the Act and also carry over the species and subspecies of wildlife designated as endangered under the Endangered Species Conservation Act of 1969 (83 Stat. 275, 16 U.S.C. 668cc-1 to 6) which are deemed endangered species under section 4(c)(3) of the Act.

[40 FR 44415, Sept. 26, 1975, as amended at 42 FR 10465, Feb. 22, 1977]

§ 17.2 Scope of regulations.

(a) The regulations of this part apply only to endangered and threatened wildlife and plants.

(b) By agreement between the Service and the National Marine Fisheries Service, the jurisdiction of the Department of Commerce has been specifically defined to include certain species, while jurisdiction is shared in regard to certain other species. Such species are footnoted in Subpart B of this part, and reference is given to special rules of the National Marine Fisheries Service for those species.

(c) The provisions in this part are in addition to, and are not in lieu of, other regulations of this Subchapter B which may require a permit or prescribe additional restrictions or conditions for the importation, exportation, and interstate transportation of wildlife.

(d) The examples used in this part are provided solely for the convenience of the public, and to explain the intent and meaning of the regulation to which they refer. They have no legal significance.

(e) Certain of the wildlife and plants listed in § 17.11 and § 17.12 as endangered or threatened are included in Appendix I, II or III to the Convention on International Trade in Endangered Species of Wild Fauna and Flora. The importation, exportation and reexportation of such species are subject to additional regulations provided in Part 23 of this subchapter.

[40 FR 44415, Sept. 26, 1975, as amended at 42 FR 10465, Feb. 22, 1977]

§ 17.3 Definitions.

In addition to the definitions contained in Part 10 of this subchapter, and unless the context otherwise requires, in this Part 17:

Act means the Endangered Species Act of 1973 (16 U.S.C. 1531-1543; 87 Stat. 884);

Adequately covered means, with respect to species listed pursuant to section 4 of the ESA, that a proposed conservation plan has satisfied the permit issuance criteria under section 10(a)(2)(B) of the ESA for the species covered by the plan, and, with respect to unlisted species, that a proposed conservation plan has satisfied the permit issuance criteria under section 10(a)(2)(B) of the ESA that would otherwise apply if the unlisted species covered by the plan were actually listed. For the Services to cover a species under a conservation plan, it must be listed on the section 10(a)(1)(B) permit.

Alaskan Native means a person defined in the Alaska Native Claims Settlement Act [43 U.S.C. section 1603(b) (85 Stat. 588)] as a citizen of the United States who is of one-fourth degree or more Alaska Indian (including Tsimshian Indians enrolled or not enrolled in the Metlaktla Indian Community), Eskimo, or Aleut blood, or combination thereof. The term includes any Native, as so defined, either or both of whose adoptive parents are not Natives. It also includes, in the absence of proof of a minimum blood quantum, any citizen of the United States who is regarded as an Alaska Native by the Native village or town of which he claims to be a member and whose father or mother is (or, if deceased, was) regarded as Native by any Native village or Native town. Any citizen enrolled by the Secretary pursuant to section 5 of the Alaska Native Claims Settlement Act shall be conclusively presumed to be an Alaskan Native for purposes of this part;

Authentic native articles of handicrafts and clothing means items made by an Indian, Aleut, or Eskimo which (a) were commonly produced on or before December 28, 1973, and (b) are composed wholly or in some significant respect of natural materials, and (c) are significantly altered from their natural form and which are produced, decorated, or fashioned in the exercise of traditional native handicrafts without the use of pantographs, multiple carvers, or similar mass copying devices. Improved methods of production utilizing modern implements such as sewing machines or modern techniques at a tannery registered pursuant to § 18.23(c) of this subchapter (in the case of marine mammals) may be used so long as no large scale mass production industry results. Traditional native handicrafts include, but are not limited to, weaving, carving, stitching, sewing, lacing, beading, drawing, and painting. The formation of traditional native groups such as cooperatives, is permitted so long as no large scale mass production results;

Bred in captivity or *captive-bred* refers to wildlife, including eggs, born or otherwise produced in captivity from parents that mated or otherwise transferred gametes in captivity, if reproduction is sexual, or from parents that were in captivity when development of the progeny began, if development is asexual.

Captivity means that living wildlife is held in a controlled environment that is intensively manipulated by man for the purpose of producing wildlife of the selected species, and that has boundaries designed to prevent animal, eggs or gametes of the selected species from entering or leaving the controlled environment. General characteristics of captivity may include but are not limited to artificial housing, waste removal, health care, protection from predators, and artificially supplied food.

Changed circumstances means changes in circumstances affecting a species or geographic area covered by a conservation plan that can reasonably be anticipated by plan developers and the Service and that can be planned for (*e.g.,* the listing of new species, or a fire or other natural catastrophic event in areas prone to such events).

Conservation plan means the plan required by section 10(a)(2)(A) of the ESA that an applicant must submit when applying for an incidental take permit. Conservation plans also are known as "habitat conservation plans" or "HCPs."

Conserved habitat areas means areas explicitly designated for habitat restoration, acquisition, protection, or other conservation purposes under a conservation plan.

Convention means the Convention on International Trade in Endangered Species of Wild Fauna and Flora, TIAS 8249.

Enhance the propagation or survival, when used in reference to wildlife in captivity, includes but is not limited to the following activities when it can be shown that such activities would not be detrimental to the survival of wild or captive populations of the affected species:

(a) Provision of health care, management of populations by culling, contraception, euthanasia, grouping or handling of wildlife to control survivorship and reproduction, and similar normal practices of animal husbandry needed to maintain captive populations that are self-sustaining and that possess as much genetic vitality as possible;

(b) Accumulation and holding of living wildlife that is not immediately needed or suitable for propagative or scientific purposes, and the transfer of such wildlife between persons in order to relieve crowding or other problems hindering the propagation or survival of the captive population at the location from which the wildlife would be removed; and

(c) Exhibition of living wildlife in a manner designed to educate the public about the ecological role and conservation needs of the affected species.

Endangered means a species of wildlife listed in § 17.11 or a species of plant listed in § 17.12 and designated as endangered.

Harass in the definition of "take" in the Act means an intentional or negligent act or omission which creates the likelihood of injury to wildlife by annoying it to such an extent as to significantly disrupt normal behavioral patterns which include, but are not limited to, breeding, feeding, or sheltering. This definition, when applied to captive wildlife, does not include generally accepted:

(1) Animal husbandry practices that meet or exceed the minimum standards for facilities and care under the Animal Welfare Act,

(2) Breeding procedures, or

(3) Provisions of veterinary care for confining, tranquilizing, or anesthetizing, when such practices, procedures, or provisions are not likely to result in injury to the wildlife.

Harm in the definition of "take" in the Act means an act which actually kills or injures wildlife. Such act may include significant habitat modification or degradation where it actually kills or injures wildlife by significantly impairing essential behavioral patterns, including breeding, feeding or sheltering.

Incidental taking means any taking otherwise prohibited, if such taking is incidental to, and not the purpose of, the carrying out of an otherwise lawful activity.

Industry or trade in the definition of "commercial activity" in the Act means the actual or intended transfer of wildlife or plants from one person to another person in the pursuit of gain or profit;

Native village or town means any community, association, tribe, clan or group;

Operating conservation program means those conservation management activities which are expressly agreed upon and described in a conservation plan or its Implementing Agreement, if any, and which are to be undertaken for the affected species when implementing an approved conservation plan, including measures to respond to changed circumstances.

Population means a group of fish or wildlife in the same taxon below the subspecific level, in common spatial arrangement that interbreed when mature;

Properly implemented conservation plan means any conservation plan, Implementing Agreement and permit whose commitments and provisions have been or are being fully implemented by the permittee.

Specimen means any animal or plant, or any part, product, egg, seed or root of any animal or plant;

Subsistence means the use of endangered or threatened wildlife for food, clothing, shelter, heating, transportation and other uses necessary to maintain the life of the taker of the wildlife, or those who depend upon the taker to provide them with such subsistence, and includes selling any edible portions of such wildlife in native villages and towns in Alaska for native consumption within native villages and towns;

Threatened means a species of wildlife listed in § 17.11 or plant listed in § 17.12 and designated as threatened.

Unforeseen circumstances means changes in circumstances affecting a species or geographic area covered by a conservation plan that could not reasonably have been anticipated by plan developers and the Service at the time of the conservation plan's negotiation and development, and that result in a substantial and adverse change in the status of the covered species.

Wasteful manner means any taking or method of taking which is likely to result in the killing or injury of endangered or threatened wildlife beyond those needed for subsistence purposes, or which results in the waste of a substantial portion of the wildlife, and includes without limitation the employment of a method of taking which is not likely to assure the capture or killing of the wildlife, or which is not immediately followed by a reasonable effort to retrieve the wildlife.

[40 FR 44415, Sept. 26, 1975, as amended at 42 FR 28056, June 1, 1977; 44 FR 54006, Sept. 17, 1979; 46 FR 54750, Nov. 4, 1981; 47 FR 31387, July 20, 1982; 50 FR 39687, Sept. 30, 1985; 63 FR 8870, Feb. 23, 1998; 63 FR 48639, Sept. 11, 1998]

§ 17.4 Pre-Act wildlife.

(a) The prohibitions defined in Subparts C and D of this Part 17 shall not apply to any activity involving endangered or threatened wildlife which was held in captivity or in a controlled environment on December 28, 1973: *Provided,*

(1) That the purposes of such holding were not contrary to the purposes of the Act; and

(2) That the wildlife was not held in the course of a commercial activity.

Example 1. On January 25, 1974, a tourist buys a stuffed hawksbill turtle (an endangered species listed since June, 1970), in a foreign country. On December 28, 1973, the stuffed turtle had been on display for sale. The tourist imports the stuffed turtle into the United States on January 26, 1974. This is a violation of the Act since the stuffed turtle was held for commercial purposes on December 28, 1973.

Example 2. On December 27, 1973 (or earlier), a tourist buys a leopard skin coat (the leopard has been listed as endangered since March 1972) for his wife in a foreign country. On January 5, he imports it into the United States. He has not committed a violation since on December 28, 1973, he was the owner of the coat, for personal purposes, and the chain of commerce had ended with the sale on the 27th. Even if he did not finish paying for the coat for another year, as long as he had possession of it, and he was not going to resell it, but was using it for personal purposes, the Act does not apply to that coat.

Example 3. On or before December 28, 1973, a hunter kills a leopard legally in Africa. He has the leopard mounted and imports it into the United States in March 1974. The importation is not subject to the Act. The hunter has not engaged in a commercial activity, even though he bought the services of a guide, outfitters, and a taxidermist to help him take, preserve, and import the leopard. This applies even if the trophy was in the possession of the taxidermist on December 28, 1973.

Example 4. On January 15, 1974, a hunter kills a leopard legally in Africa. He has the leopard mounted and imports it into the United States in June 1974. This importation is a violation of the Act since the leopard was not in captivity or a controlled environment on December 28, 1973.

(b) Service officers or Customs officers may refuse to clear endangered or threatened wildlife for importation into or exportation from the United States, pursuant to § 14.53 of this subchapter, until the importer or exporter can demonstrate that the exemption referred to in this section applies. Exempt status may be established by any sufficient evidence, including an affidavit containing the following:

(1) The affiant's name and address;

(2) Identification of the affiant;

(3) Identification of the endangered or threatened wildlife which is the subject of the affidavit;

(4) A statement by the affiant that to the best of his knowledge and belief, the endangered or threatened wildlife which is the subject of the affidavit was in captivity or in a controlled environment on December 28, 1973, and was not being held for purposes contrary to the Act or in the course of a commercial activity;

(5) A statement by the affiant in the following language:

The foregoing is principally based on the attached exhibits which, to the best of my knowledge and belief, are complete, true and correct. I understand that this affidavit is being submitted for the purpose of inducing the Federal Government to recognize an exempt status regarding (insert description of wildlife), under the Endangered Species Act of 1973 (16 U.S.C. 1531- 1543), and regulations promulgated thereunder, and that any false statements may subject me to the criminal penalties of 18 U.S.C. 1001.

(6) As an attachment, records or other available evidence to show:

(i) That the wildlife in question was being held in captivity or in a controlled environment on December 28, 1973;

(ii) The purpose for which the wildlife was being held; and

(iii) The nature of such holding (to establish that no commercial activity was involved).

(c) This section applies only to wildlife born on or prior to December 28, 1973. It does not apply to the progeny of any such wildlife born after December 28, 1973.

§ 17.5 Alaska natives.

****

§ 17.6 State cooperative agreements. [Reserved]

§ 17.7 Raptor exemption.

(a) The prohibitions found in §§ 17.21 and 17.31 do not apply to any raptor [a live migratory bird of the Order Falconiformes or the Order Strigiformes, other than a bald eagle (*Haliaeetus leucocephalus*) or a golden eagle (*Aquila chrysaetos*)] legally held in captivity or in a controlled environment on November 10, 1978, or to any of its progeny, which is:

(1) Possessed and banded in compliance with the terms of a valid permit issued under Part 21 of this chapter; and

(2) Identified in the earliest applicable annual report required to be filed by a permittee under Part 21 of this chapter as in a permittee's possession on November 10, 1978, or as the progeny of such a raptor.

(b) This section does not apply to any raptor intentionally returned to the wild.

[48 FR 31607, July 8, 1983]

§ 17.8 Permit applications and information collection requirements.

(a) Address permit applications for activities affecting species listed under the Endangered Species Act, as amended, as follows:

(1) Address activities affecting endangered and threatened species that are native to the United States to the Regional Director for the Region in which the activity is to take place. You can find addresses for the Regional Directors in 50 CFR 2.2. Send applications for interstate commerce in native endangered and threatened species to the Regional Director with lead responsibility for the species. To determine the appropriate region, call the nearest Regional Office:

****

(2) Submit permit applications for activities affecting native endangered and threatened species in international movement or commerce, and all activities affecting nonnative endangered and threatened species to the Director, U.S. Fish and Wildlife Service, (Attention Office of Management Authority), 4401 N. Fairfax Drive, Room 700, Arlington, VA 22203.

(b) The Office of Management and Budget approved the information collection requirements contained in this part 17 under 44 U.S.C. 3507 and assigned OMB Control Numbers 1018-0093 and 1018-0094. The Service may not conduct or sponsor, and you are not required to respond to, a collection of information unless it displays a currently valid OMB control number. We are collecting this information to provide information necessary to evaluate permit applications. We will use this information to review permit applications and make decisions, according to criteria established in various Federal wildlife conservation statutes and regulations, on the issuance, suspension, revocation, or denial of permits. You must respond to obtain or retain a permit. We estimate the public reporting burden for these reporting requirements to vary from 2 to 2 1/2 hours per response, including time for reviewing instructions, gathering and maintaining data, and completing and reviewing the forms. Direct comments regarding the burden estimate or any other aspect of these reporting requirements to the Service Information Collection Control Officer, MS-222 ARLSQ, U.S. Fish and Wildlife Service, Washington, D.C. 20240, or the Office of Management and Budget, Paperwork Reduction Project (1018-0093/0094), Washington, D.C. 20603.

[63 FR 52635, Oct. 1, 1998]

SUBPART B -- LISTS

§ 17.11 Endangered and threatened wildlife.

(a) The list in this section contains the names of all species of wildlife which have been determined by the Services to be Endangered or Threatened. It also contains the names of species of wildlife treated as Endangered or Threatened because they are sufficiently similar in appearance to Endangered or Threatened species (see § 17.50 et seq.).

(b) The columns entitled "Common Name," "Scientific Name," and "Vertebrate Population Where Endangered or Threatened" define the species of wildlife within the meaning of the Act. Thus, differently classified geographic populations of the same vertebrate subspecies or species shall be identified by their differing geographic boundaries, even though the other two columns are identical. The term "Entire" means that all populations throughout the present range of a vertebrate species are listed. Although common names are included, they cannot be relied upon for identification of any specimen, since they may vary greatly in local usage. The Services shall use the most recently accepted scientific name. In cases in which confusion might arise, a synonym(s) will be provided in parentheses. The Services shall rely to the extent practicable on the International Code of Zoological Nomenclature.

****

§ 17.12 Endangered and threatened plants.

****

SUBPART C -- ENDANGERED WILDLIFE

§ 17.21 Prohibitions.

(a) Except as provided in Subpart A of this part, or under permits issued pursuant to § 17.22 or § 17.23, it is unlawful for any person subject to the jurisdiction of the United States to commit, to attempt to commit, to solicit another to commit or to cause to be committed, any of the acts described in paragraphs (b) through (f) of this section in regard to any endangered wildlife.

(b) *Import or export.* It is unlawful to import or to export any endangered wildlife. Any shipment in transit through the United States is an importation and an exportation, whether or not it has entered the country for customs purposes.

(c) *Take.* (1) It is unlawful to take endangered wildlife within the United States, within the territorial sea of the United States, or upon the high seas. The high seas shall be all waters seaward of the territorial sea of the United States, except waters officially recognized by the United States as the territorial sea of another country, under international law.

(2) Notwithstanding paragraph (c)(1) of this section, any person may take endangered wildlife in defense of his own life or the lives of others.

(3) Notwithstanding paragraph (c)(1) of this section, any employee or agent of the

Service, any other Federal land management agency, the National Marine Fisheries Service, or a State conservation agency, who is designated by his agency for such purposes, may, when acting in the course of his official duties, take endangered wildlife without a permit if such action is necessary to:

(i) Aid a sick, injured or orphaned specimen; or

(ii) Dispose of a dead specimen; or

(iii) Salvage a dead specimen which may be useful for scientific study; or

(iv) Remove specimens which constitute a demonstrable but nonimmediate threat to human safety, provided that the taking is done in a humane manner; the taking may involve killing or injuring only if it has not been reasonably possible to eliminate such threat by live-capturing and releasing the specimen unharmed, in a remote area.

(4) Any taking pursuant to paragraphs (c)(2) and (3) of this section must be reported in writing to the United States Fish and Wildlife Service, Division of Law Enforcement, P.O. Box 19183, Washington, D.C. 20036, within 5 days. The specimen may only be retained, disposed of, or salvaged in accordance with directions from Service.

(5) Notwithstanding paragraph (c)(1) of this section, any qualified employee or agent of a State Conservation Agency which is a party to a Cooperative Agreement with the Service in accordance with section 6(c) of the Act, who is designated by his agency for such purposes, may, when acting in the course of his official duties take those endangered species which are covered by an approved cooperative agreement for conservation programs in accordance with the Cooperative Agreement, provided that such taking is not reasonably anticipated to result in:

(i) The death or permanent disabling of the specimen;

(ii) The removal of the specimen from the State where the taking occurred;

(iii) The introduction of the specimen so taken, or of any progeny derived from such a specimen, into an area beyond the historical range of the species; or

(iv) The holding of the specimen in captivity for a period of more than 45 consecutive days.

(d) *Possession and other acts with unlawfully taken wildlife.* (1) It is unlawful to possess, sell, deliver, carry, transport, or ship, by any means whatsoever, any endangered wildlife which was taken in violation of paragraph (c) of this section.

> *Example.* A person captures a whooping crane in Texas and gives it to a second person, who puts it in a closed van and drives thirty miles, to another location in Texas. The second person then gives the whooping crane to a third person, who is apprehended with the bird in his possession. All three have violated the law -- the first by illegally taking the whooping crane; the second by transporting an illegally taken whooping crane; and the third by possessing an illegally taken whooping crane.

(2) Notwithstanding paragraph (d)(1) of this section, Federal and State law enforcement officers may possess, deliver, carry, transport or ship any endangered wildlife taken in violation of the Act as necessary in performing their official duties.

(e) *Interstate or foreign commerce.* It is unlawful to deliver, receive, carry transport, or ship in interstate or foreign commerce, by any means whatsoever, and in the course of a commercial activity, any endangered wildlife.

(f) *Sale or offer for sale.* (1) It is unlawful to sell or to offer for sale in interstate or foreign commerce any endangered wildlife.

(2) An advertisement for the sale of endangered wildlife which carries a warning to

the effect that no sale may be consummated until a permit has been obtained from the U.S. Fish and Wildlife Service shall not be considered an offer for sale within the meaning of this section.

(g) *Captive-bred wildlife.* (1) Notwithstanding paragraphs (b), (c), (e) and (f) of this section, any person may take; export or re-import; deliver, receive, carry, transport or ship in interstate or foreign commerce, in the course of a commercial activity; or sell or offer for sale in interstate or foreign commerce any endangered wildlife that is bred in captivity in the United States provided either that the wildlife is of a taxon listed in paragraph (g)(6) of this section, or that the following conditions are met:

(i) The wildlife is of a species having a natural geographic distribution not including any part of the United States, or the wildlife is of a species that the Director has determined to be eligible in accordance with paragraph (g)(5) of this section;

(ii) The purpose of such activity is to enhance the propagation or survival of the affected species;

(iii) Such activity does not involve interstate or foreign commerce, in the course of a commercial activity, with respect to non-living wildlife;

(iv) Each specimen of wildlife to be re-imported is uniquely identified by a band, tattoo or other means that was reported in writing to an official of the Service at a port of export prior to export from the United States; and

(v) Any person subject to the jurisdiction of the United States who engages in any of the activities authorized by this paragraph does so in accordance with paragraphs (g)(2), (3) and (4) of this section, and with all other applicable regulations in this Subchapter B.

(2) Any person subject to the jurisdiction of the United States seeking to engage in any of the activities authorized by this paragraph must first register with the Service (Office of Management Authority, U.S. Fish and Wildlife Service, 4401 N. Fairfax Drive, Arlington, Virginia 22203). Requests for registration must be submitted on an official application form (Form 3-200- 41) provided by the Service, and must include the following information:

(i) The types of wildlife sought to be covered by the registration, identified by common and scientific name to the taxonomic level of family, genus or species;

(ii) A description of the applicant's experience in maintaining and propagating the types of wildlife sought to be covered by the registration, and when appropriate, in conducting research directly related to maintaining and propagating such wildlife;

(iii) Photograph(s) or other evidence clearly depicting the facilities where such wildlife will be maintained; and

(iv) A copy of the applicant's license or registration, if any, under the animal welfare regulations of the U.S. Department of Agriculture (9 CFR part 2).

(3) Upon receiving a complete application, the Director will decide whether or not the registration will be approved. In making this decision, the Director will consider, in addition to the general criteria in § 13.21(b) of this subchapter, whether the expertise, facilities or other resources available to the applicant appear adequate to enhance the propagation or survival of the affected wildlife. Public education activities may not be the sole basis to justify issuance of a registration or to otherwise establish eligibility for the exception granted in paragraph (g)(1) of this section. Each person so registered must maintain accurate written records of activities conducted under the registration, and allow reasonable access to Service agents for inspection purposes as set forth in §§ 13.46 and 13.47. Each person registered must submit to the Director an individual written annual report of activities, including all births, deaths and transfers of any type.

(4) Any person subject to the jurisdiction of the United States seeking to export or conduct foreign commerce in captive-bred endangered wildlife that will not remain under the care of that person must first obtain approval by providing written evidence to satisfy the Director that the proposed recipient of the wildlife has expertise, facilities or other resources adequate to enhance the propagation or survival of such wildlife and that the proposed recipient will use such wildlife for purposes of enhancing the propagation or survival of the affected species.

(5)(i) The Director will use the following criteria to determine if wildlife of any species having a natural geographic distribution that includes any part of the United States is eligible for the provisions of this paragraph:

(A) Whether there is a low demand for taking of the species from wild populations, either because of the success of captive breeding or because of other reasons, and

(B) Whether the wild populations of the species are effectively protected from unauthorized taking as a result of the inaccessibility of their habitat to humans or as a result of the effectiveness of law enforcement.

(ii) The Director will follow the procedures set forth in the Act and in the regulations thereunder with respect to petitions and notification of the public and governors of affected States when determining the eligibility of species for purposes of this paragraph.

(iii) In accordance with the criteria in paragraph (g)(5)(i) of this section, the Director has determined the following species to be eligible for the provisions of this paragraph:

Laysan duck (*Anas laysanensis*).

(6) Any person subject to the jurisdiction of the United States seeking to engage in any of the activities authorized by paragraph (g)(1) of this section may do so without first registering with the Service with respect to the bar-tailed pheasant (*Syrmaticus humiae*), Elliot's pheasant (*S. ellioti*), Mikado pheasant (*S. mikado*), brown eared pheasant (*Crossoptilon mantchuricum*), white eared pheasant (*C. crossoptilon*), cheer pheasant (*Catreus wallichii*), Edward's pheasant (*Lophura edwardsi*), Swinhoe's pheasant (*L. swinhoii*), Chinese monal (*Lophophorus lhuysii*), and Palawan peacock pheasant (*Polyplectron emphanum*); parakeets of the species *Neophema pulchella* and *N. splendida*; the Laysan duck (*Anas laysanensis*); the white-winged wood duck (*Cairina scutulata*); and the inter-subspecific crossed or "generic" tiger (*Panthera tigris*) (*i.e.*, specimens not identified or identifiable as members of the Bengal, Sumatran, Siberian or Indochinese subspecies (*Panthera tigris tigris, P.t. sumatrae, P.t. altaica and P.t. corbetti*, respectively) provided:

(i) The purpose of such activity is to enhance the propagation or survival of the affected exempted species;

(ii) Such activity does not involve interstate or foreign commerce, in the course of a commercial activity, with respect to non-living wildlife;

(iii) Each specimen to be re-imported is uniquely identified by a band, tattoo or other means that was reported in writing to an official of the Service at a port of export prior to export of the specimen from the United States;

(iv) No specimens of the taxa in this paragraph (g)(6) of this section that were taken from the wild may be imported for breeding purposes absent a definitive showing that the need for new bloodlines can only be met by wild specimens, that suitable foreign-bred, captive individuals are unavailable, and that wild populations can sustain limited taking, and an import permit is issued under § 17.22;

(v) Any permanent exports of such specimens meet the requirements of paragraph (g)(4) of this section; and

(vi) Each person claiming the benefit of the exception in paragraph (g)(1) of this section must maintain accurate written records of activities, including births, deaths and transfers of specimens, and make those records accessible to Service agents for inspection at reasonable hours as set forth in §§ 13.46 and 13.47.

[40 FR 44415, Sept. 26, 1975, as amended at 40 FR 53400, Nov. 18, 1975; 41 FR 19226, May 11, 1976; 44 FR 31580, May 31, 1979; 44 FR 54007, Sept. 17, 1979; 58 FR 68325, Dec. 27, 1993; 63 FR 48640, Sept. 11, 1998]

§ 17.22 Permits for scientific purposes, enhancement of propagation or survival, or for incidental taking.

Upon receipt of a complete application, the Director may issue a permit authorizing any activity otherwise prohibited by § 17.21, in accordance with the issuance criteria of this section, for scientific purposes, for enhancing the propagation or survival, or for the incidental taking of endangered wildlife. Such permits may authorize a single transaction, a series of transactions, or a number of activities over a specific period of time. (See § 17.32 for permits for threatened species.) The Director shall publish notice in the Federal Register of each application for a permit that is made under this section. Each notice shall invite the submission from interested parties, within 30 days after the date of the notice, of written data, views, or arguments with respect to the application. The 30-day period may be waived by the Director in an emergency situation where the life or health of an endangered animal is threatened and no reasonable alternative is available to the applicant. Notice of any such waiver shall be published in the Federal Register within 10 days following issuance of the permit.

(a)(1) *Application requirements for permits for scientific purposes or for the enhancement of propagation or survival.* A person wishing to get a permit for an activity prohibited by § 17.21 submits an application for activities under this paragraph. The Service provides Form 3-200 for the application to which all of the following must be attained:

(i) The common and scientific names of the species sought to the covered by the permit, as well as the number, age, and sex of such species, and the activity sought to be authorized (such as taking, exporting, selling in interstate commerce);

(ii) A statement as to whether, at the time of application, the wildlife sought to be covered by the permit (A) is still in the wild, (B) has already been removed from the wild, or (C) was born in captivity;

(iii) A resume of the applicant's attempts to obtain the wildlife sought to be covered by the permit in a manner which would not cause the death or removal from the wild of such wildlife;

(iv) If the wildlife sought to be covered by the permit has already been removed from the wild, the country and place where such removal occurred; if the wildlife sought to be covered by the permit was born in captivity, the country and place where such wildlife was born;

(v) A complete description and address of the institution or other facility where the wildlife sought to be covered by the permit will be used, displayed, or maintained;

(vi) If the applicant seeks to have live wildlife covered by the permit, a complete description, including photographs or diagrams, of the facilities to house and/or care for the wildlife and a resume of the experience of those person who will be caring for the wildlife;

(vii) A full statement of the reasons why the applicant is justified in obtaining a permit including the details of the activities sought to be authorized by the permit;

(viii) If the application is for the purpose of enhancement of propagation, a statement of the applicant's willingness to participate in a cooperative breeding program and to maintain or contribute data to a studbook;

(2) *Issuance criteria.* Upon receiving an application completed in accordance with paragraph (a)(1) of this section, the Director will decide whether or not a permit should be issued. In making this decision, the Director shall consider, in addition to the general criteria in § 13.21(b) of this subchapter, the following factors:

(i) Whether the purpose for which the permit is required is adequate to justify removing from the wild or otherwise changing the status of the wildlife sought to be covered by the permit;

(ii) The probable direct and indirect effect which issuing the permit would have on the wild populations of the wildlife sought to be covered by the permit;

(iii) Whether the permit, if issued, would in any way, directly or indirectly, conflict with any known program intended to enhance the survival probabilities of the population from which the wildlife sought to be covered by the permit was or would be removed;

(iv) Whether the purpose for which the permit is required would be likely to reduce the threat of extinction facing the species of wildlife sought to be covered by the permit;

(v) The opinions or views of scientists or other persons or organizations having expertise concerning the wildlife or other matters germane to the application; and

(vi) Whether the expertise, facilities, or other resources available to the applicant appear adequate to successfully accomplish the objectives stated in the application.

(3) *Permit conditions.* In addition to the general conditions set forth in Part 13 of this subchapter, every permit issued under this paragraph shall be subject to the special condition that the escape of living wildlife covered by the permit shall be immediately reported to the Service office designated in the permit.

(4) *Duration of permits.* The duration of permits issued under this paragraph shall be designated on the face of the permit.

(b)(1) *Application requirements for permits for incidental taking.* A person wishing to get a permit for an activity prohibited by § 17.21(c) submits an application for activities under this paragraph. The Service provides Form 3-200 for the application to which all of the following must be attached:

(i) A complete description of the activity sought to be authorized;

(ii) The common and scientific names of the species sought to be covered by the permit, as well as the number, age, and sex of such species, if known;

(iii) A conservation plan that specifies:

(A) The impact that will likely result from such taking;

(B) What steps the applicant will take to monitor, minimize, and mitigate such impacts, the funding that will be available to implement such steps, and the procedures to be used to deal with unforeseen circumstances;

(C) What alternative actions to such taking the applicant considered and the reasons why such alternatives are not proposed to be utilized; and

(D) Such other measures that the Director may require as being necessary or appropriate for purposes of the plan;

(2) *Issuance criteria.* (i) Upon receiving an application completed in accordance with paragraph (b)(1) of this section, the Director will decide whether or not a permit should be issued. The Director shall consider the general issuance criteria in § 13.21(b) of this subchapter, except for § 13.21(b)(4), and shall issue the permit if he or she finds that:

(A) The taking will be incidental;

(B) The applicant will, to the maximum extent practicable, minimize and mitigate the impacts of such takings;

(C) The applicant will ensure that adequate funding for the conservation plan and procedures to deal with unforeseen circumstances will be provided;

(D) The taking will not appreciably reduce the likelihood of the survival and recovery of the species in the wild;

(E) The measures, if any, required under paragraph (b)(1)(iii)(D) of this section will be met; and

(F) He or she has received such other assurances as he or she may require that the plan will be implemented.

(ii) In making his or her decision, the Director shall also consider the anticipated duration and geographic scope of the applicant's planned activities, including the amount of listed species habitat that is involved and the degree to which listed species and their habitats are affected.

(3) *Permit conditions.* In addition to the general conditions set forth in Part 13 of this subchapter, every permit issued under this paragraph shall contain such terms and conditions as the Director deems necessary or appropriate to carry out the purposes of the permit and the conservation plan including, but not limited to, monitoring and reporting requirements deemed necessary for determining whether such terms and conditions are being complied with. The Director shall rely upon existing reporting requirements to the maximum extent practicable.

(4) *Duration of permits.* The duration of permits issued under this paragraph shall be sufficient to provide adequate assurances to the permittee to commit funding necessary for the activities authorized by the permit, including conservation activities and land use restrictions. In determining the duration of a permit, the Director shall consider the duration of the planned activities, as well as the possible positive and negative effects associated with permits of the proposed duration on listed species, including the extent to which the conservation plan will enhance the habitat of listed species and increase the long-term survivability of such species.

(5) *Assurances provided to permittee in case of changed or unforeseen circumstances.* The assurances in this paragraph (b)(5) apply only to incidental take permits issued in accordance with paragraph (b)(2) of this section where the conservation plan is being properly implemented, and apply only with respect to species adequately covered by the conservation plan. These assurances cannot be provided to Federal agencies. This rule does not apply to incidental take permits issued prior to March 25, 1998. The assurances provided in incidental take permits issued prior to March 25, 1998 remain in effect, and those permits will not be revised as a result of this rulemaking.

(i) *Changed circumstances provided for in the plan.* If additional conservation and mitigation measures are deemed necessary to respond to changed circumstances and were provided for in the plan's operating conservation program, the permittee will implement the measures specified in the plan.

(ii) *Changed circumstances not provided for in the plan.* If additional conservation and mitigation measures are deemed necessary to respond to changed circumstances and such measures were not provided for in the plan's operating conservation program, the Director will not require any conservation and mitigation measures in addition to those provided for in the plan without the consent of the permittee, provided the plan is being properly implemented.

(iii) *Unforeseen circumstances.* (A) In negotiating unforeseen circumstances, the Director will not require the commitment of additional land, water, or financial compensation or additional restrictions on the use of land, water, or other natural resources beyond the level otherwise agreed upon for the species covered by the conservation plan without the consent of the permittee.

(B) If additional conservation and mitigation measures are deemed necessary to respond to unforeseen circumstances, the Director may require additional measures of the permittee where the conservation plan is being properly implemented, but only if such measures are limited to modifications within conserved habitat areas, if any, or to the conservation plan's operating conservation program for the affected species, and maintain the original terms of the conservation plan to the maximum extent possible. Additional conservation and mitigation measures will not involve the commitment of additional land, water or financial compensation or additional restrictions on the use of land, water, or other natural resources otherwise available for development or use under the original terms of the conservation plan without the consent of the permittee.

(C) The Director will have the burden of demonstrating that unforeseen circumstances exist, using the best scientific and commercial data available. These findings must be clearly documented and based upon reliable technical information regarding the status and habitat requirements of the affected species. The Director will consider, but not be limited to, the following factors:

(1) Size of the current range of the affected species;

(2) Percentage of range adversely affected by the conservation plan;

(3) Percentage of range conserved by the conservation plan;

(4) Ecological significance of that portion of the range affected by the conservation plan;

(5) Level of knowledge about the affected species and the degree of specificity of the species' conservation program under the conservation plan; and

(6) Whether failure to adopt additional conservation measures would appreciably reduce the likelihood of survival and recovery of the affected species in the wild.

(6) Nothing in this rule will be construed to limit or constrain the Director, any Federal, State, local, or Tribal government agency, or a private entity, from taking additional actions at its own expense to protect or conserve a species included in a conservation plan.

(7) *Discontinuance of permit activity.* Notwithstanding the provisions of § 13.26 of this subchapter, a permittee under this paragraph (b) remains responsible for any outstanding minimization and mitigation measures required under the terms of the permit for take that occurs prior to surrender of the permit and such minimization and mitigation measures as may be required pursuant to the termination provisions of an implementing agreement, habitat conservation plan, or permit even after surrendering the permit to the Service pursuant to § 13.26 of this subchapter. The permit shall be deemed canceled only upon a determination by the Service that such minimization and mitigation measures have

been implemented. Upon surrender of the permit, no further take shall be authorized under the terms of the surrendered permit.

(8) *Criteria for Revocation.* A permit issued under this paragraph (b) may not be revoked for any reason except those set forth in § 13.28(a)(1) through (4) of this subchapter or unless continuation of the permitted activity would be inconsistent with the criterion set forth in 16 U.S.C. 1539(a)(2)(B)(iv) and the inconsistency has not been remedied in a timely fashion.

(c)(1) *Application requirements for permits for the enhancement of survival through Safe Harbor Agreements.* The applicant must submit an application for a permit under this paragraph (c) to the appropriate Regional Director, U.S. Fish and Wildlife Service, for the Region where the applicant resides or where the proposed activity is to occur (for appropriate addresses, see 50 CFR 10.22), if the applicant wishes to engage in any activity prohibited by § 17.21. The applicant must submit an official Service application form (3-200.54) that includes the following information:

(i) The common and scientific names of the listed species for which the applicant requests incidental take authorization;

(ii) A description of the land use or water management activity for which the applicant requests incidental take authorization; and

(iii) A Safe Harbor Agreement that complies with the requirements of the Safe Harbor policy available from the Service.

(2) *Issuance criteria.* Upon receiving an application completed in accordance with paragraph (c)(1) of this section, the Director will decide whether or not to issue a permit. The Director shall consider the general issuance criteria in § 13.21(b) of this subchapter, except for § 13.21(b)(4), and may issue the permit if he or she finds:

(i) The take will be incidental to an otherwise lawful activity and will be in accordance with the terms of the Safe Harbor Agreement;

(ii) The implementation of the terms of the Safe Harbor Agreement will provide a net conservation benefit to the affected listed species by contributing to the recovery of listed species included in the permit and the Safe Harbor Agreement otherwise complies with the Safe Harbor policy available from the Service;

(iii) The probable direct and indirect effects of any authorized take will not appreciably reduce the likelihood of survival and recovery in the wild of any listed species;

(iv) Implementation of the terms of the Safe Harbor Agreement is consistent with applicable Federal, State, and Tribal laws and regulations;

(v) Implementation of the terms of the Safe Harbor Agreement will not be in conflict with any ongoing conservation or recovery programs for listed species covered by the permit; and

(vi) The applicant has shown capability for and commitment to implementing all of the terms of the Safe Harbor Agreement.

(3) *Permit conditions.* In addition to any applicable general permit conditions set forth in part 13 of this subchapter, every permit issued under this paragraph (c) is subject to the following special conditions:

(i) A requirement for the participating property owner to notify the Service of any transfer of lands subject to a Safe Harbor Agreement;

(ii) A requirement for the property owner to notify the Service at least 30 days in advance, but preferably as far in advance as possible, of when he or she expects to incidentally take any listed species covered under the permit. Such notification will provide the Service with an opportunity to translocate affected individuals of the species, if possible and appropriate; and

(iii) Any additional requirements or conditions the Director deems necessary or appropriate to carry out the purposes of the permit and the Safe Harbor Agreement.

(4) *Permit effective date.* Permits issued under this paragraph (c) become effective the day of issuance for species covered by the Safe Harbor Agreement.

(5) *Assurances provided to permittee.* (i) The assurances in paragraph (c)(5)(ii) of this section (c)(5) apply only to Safe Harbor permits issued in accordance with paragraph (c)(2) of this section where the Safe Harbor Agreement is being properly implemented, and apply only with respect to species covered by the Agreement and permit. These assurances cannot be provided to Federal agencies. The assurances provided in this section apply only to Safe Harbor permits issued after July 19, 1999.

(ii) If additional conservation and mitigation measures are deemed necessary, the Director may require additional measures of the permittee, but only if such measures are limited to modifications within conserved habitat areas, if any, for the affected species and maintain the original terms of the Safe Harbor Agreement to the maximum extent possible. Additional conservation and mitigation measures will not involve the commitment of additional land, water or financial compensation or additional restrictions on the use of land, water, or other natural resources otherwise available for development or use under the original terms of the Safe Harbor Agreement without the consent of the permittee.

(6) *Additional actions.* Nothing in this rule will be construed to limit or constrain the Director, any Federal, State, local or Tribal government agency, or a private entity, from taking additional actions at its own expense to protect or conserve a species included in a Safe Harbor Agreement.

(7) *Criteria for revocation.* A permit issued under this paragraph (c) may not be revoked for any reason except those set forth in § 13.28(a)(1) through (4) of this subchapter or unless continuation of the permitted activity would be inconsistent with the criterion set forth in § 17.22(c)(2)(iii) and the inconsistency has not been remedied in a timely fashion.

(8) *Duration of permits.* The duration of permits issued under this paragraph (c) must be sufficient to provide a net conservation benefit to species covered in the enhancement of survival permit. In determining the duration of a permit, the Director will consider the duration of the planned activities, as well as the positive and negative effects associated with permits of the proposed duration on covered species, including the extent to which the conservation activities included in the Safe Harbor Agreement will enhance the survival and contribute to the recovery of listed species included in the permit.

(d)(1) *Application requirements for permits for the enhancement of survival through Candidate Conservation Agreements with Assurances.* The applicant must submit an application for a permit under this paragraph (d) to the appropriate Regional Director, U.S. Fish and Wildlife Service, for the Region where the applicant resides or where the proposed activity is to occur (for appropriate addresses, see 50 CFR 10.22). When a species covered by a Candidate Conservation Agreement with Assurances is listed as endangered and the applicant wishes to engage in activities identified in the Agreement and otherwise prohibited by § 17.31, the applicant must apply for an enhancement of survival permit for species covered by the Agreement. The permit will become valid if and when covered proposed, candidate or other unlisted species is listed as an endangered species. The applicant must submit an official Service application form (3-200.54) that includes the following information:

(i) The common and scientific names of the species for which the applicant requests incidental take authorization;

(ii) A description of the land use or water management activity for which the applicant requests incidental take authorization; and

(iii) A Candidate Conservation Agreement that complies with the requirements of the Candidate Conservation Agreement with Assurances policy available from the Service.

(2) *Issuance criteria.* Upon receiving an application completed in accordance with paragraph (d)(1) of this section, the Director will decide whether or not to issue a permit. The Director shall consider the general issuance criteria in § 13.21(b) of this subchapter, except for § 13.21(b)(4), and may issue the permit if he or she finds:

(i) The take will be incidental to an otherwise lawful activity and will be in accordance with the terms of the Candidate Conservation Agreement;

(ii) The Candidate Conservation Agreement complies with the requirements of the Candidate Conservation Agreement with Assurances policy available from the Service;

(iii) The probable direct and indirect effects of any authorized take will not appreciably reduce the likelihood of survival and recovery in the wild of any species;

(iv) Implementation of the terms of the Candidate Conservation Agreement is consistent with applicable Federal, State, and Tribal laws and regulations;

(v) Implementation of the terms of the Candidate Conservation Agreement will not be in conflict with any ongoing conservation programs for species covered by the permit; and

(vi) The applicant has shown capability for and commitment to implementing all of the terms of the Candidate Conservation Agreement.

(3) *Permit conditions.* In addition to any applicable general permit conditions set forth in part 13 of this subchapter, every permit issued under this paragraph (d) is subject to the following special conditions:

(i) A requirement for the property owner to notify the Service of any transfer of lands subject to a Candidate Conservation Agreement;

(ii) A requirement for the property owner to notify the Service at least 30 days in advance, but preferably as far in advance as possible, of when he or she expects to incidentally take any species covered under the permit. Such notification will provide the Service with an opportunity to translocate affected individuals of the species, if possible and appropriate; and

(iii) Any additional requirements or conditions the Director deems necessary or appropriate to carry out the purposes of the permit and the Candidate Conservation Agreement.

(4) *Permit effective date.* Permits issued under this paragraph (d) become effective for a species covered by a Candidate Conservation Agreement on the effective date of a final rule that lists a covered species as endangered.

(5) *Assurances provided to permittee in case of changed or unforeseen circumstances.* The assurances in this paragraph (d)(5) apply only to permits issued in accordance with paragraph (d)(2) where the Candidate Conservation with Assurances Agreement is being properly implemented, and apply only with respect to species adequately covered by the Candidate Conservation with Assurances Agreement. These assurances cannot be provided to Federal agencies.

(i) *Changed circumstances provided for in the Agreement.* If additional conservation and mitigation measures are deemed necessary to respond to changed circumstances and were provided for in the Agreement's operating conservation program, the permittee will implement the measures specified in the Agreement.

(ii) *Changed circumstances not provided for in the Agreement.* If additional conservation and mitigation measures are deemed necessary to respond to changed circumstances and such measures were not provided for in the Agreement's operating conservation program, the Director will not require any conservation and mitigation measures in addition to those provided for in the Agreement without the consent of the permittee, provided the Agreement is being properly implemented.

(iii) *Unforeseen circumstances.* (A) In negotiating unforeseen circumstances, the Director will not require the commitment of additional land, water, or financial compensation or additional restrictions on the use of land, water, or other natural resources beyond the level otherwise agreed upon for the species covered by the Agreement without the consent of the permittee.

(B) If additional conservation and mitigation measures are deemed necessary to respond to unforeseen circumstances, the Director may require additional measures of the permittee where the Agreement is being properly implemented, but only if such measures are limited to modifications within conserved habitat areas, if any, or to the Agreement's operating conservation program for the affected species, and maintain the original terms of the Agreement to the maximum extent possible. Additional conservation and mitigation measures will not involve the commitment of additional land, water or financial compensation or additional restrictions on the use of land, water, or other natural resources otherwise available for development or use under the original terms of the Agreement without the consent of the permittee.

(C) The Director will have the burden of demonstrating that unforeseen circumstances exist, using the best scientific and commercial data available. These findings must be clearly documented and based upon reliable technical information regarding the status and habitat requirements of the affected species. The Director will consider, but not be limited to, the following factors:

(1) Size of the current range of the affected species;

(2) Percentage of range adversely affected by the Agreement;

(3) Percentage of range conserved by the Agreement;

(4) Ecological significance of that portion of the range affected by the Agreement;

(5) Level of knowledge about the affected species and the degree of specificity of the species' conservation program under the Agreement; and

(6) Whether failure to adopt additional conservation measures would appreciably reduce the likelihood of survival and recovery of the affected species in the wild.

(6) *Additional actions.* Nothing in this rule will be construed to limit or constrain the Director, any Federal, State, local or Tribal government agency, or a private entity, from taking additional actions at its own expense to protect or conserve a species included in a Candidate Conservation with Assurances Agreement.

(7) *Criteria for revocation.* A permit issued under this paragraph (d) may not be revoked for any reason except those set forth in § 13.28(a)(1) through (4) of this subchapter or unless continuation of the permitted activity would be inconsistent with the criterion set forth in paragraph (d)(2)(iii) of this section and the inconsistency has not been remedied in a timely fashion.

(8) *Duration of the Candidate Conservation Agreement.* The duration of a

Candidate Conservation Agreement covered by a permit issued under this paragraph (d) must be sufficient to enable the Director to determine that the benefits of the conservation measures in the Agreement, when combined with those benefits that would be achieved if it is assumed that the conservation measures would also be implemented on other necessary properties, would preclude or remove any need to list the species covered by the Agreement.

(e) *Objection to permit issuance.* (1) In regard to any notice of a permit application published in the Federal Register, any interested party that objects to the issuance of a permit, in whole or in part, may, during the comment period specified in the notice, request notification of the final action to be taken on the application. A separate written request shall be made for each permit application. Such a request shall specify the Service's permit application number and state the reasons why that party believes the applicant does not meet the issuance criteria contained in §§ 13.21 and 17.22 of this subchapter or other reasons why the permit should not be issued.

(2) If the Service decides to issue a permit contrary to objections received pursuant to paragraph (c)(1) of this section, then the Service shall, at least ten days prior to issuance of the permit, make reasonable efforts to contact by telephone or other expedient means, any party who has made a request pursuant to paragraph (c)(1) of this section and inform that party of the issuance of the permit. However, the Service may reduce the time period or dispense with such notice if it determines that time is of the essence and that delay in issuance of the permit would: (i) Harm the specimen or population involved; or (ii) unduly hinder the actions authorized under the permit.

(3) The Service will notify any party filing an objection and request for notice under paragraph (c)(1) of this section of the final action taken on the application, in writing. If the Service has reduced or dispensed with the notice period referred to in paragraph (c)(2) of this section, it will include its reasons therefore in such written notice.

[40 FR 44415, Sept. 26, 1975, as amended at 40 FR 53400, Nov. 18, 1975; 41 FR 19926, May 11, 1976; 47 FR 30786, July 15, 1982; 50 FR 39687, Sept. 30, 1985; 63 FR 8871, Feb. 23, 1998; 63 FR 52635, Oct. 1, 1998; 64 FR 32711, June 17, 1999; 64 FR 52676, Sept. 30, 1999]

§ 17.23 Economic hardship permits.

Upon receipt of a complete application, the Director may issue a permit authorizing any activity otherwise prohibited by § 17.21, in accordance with the issuance criteria of this section in order to prevent undue economic hardship. The Director shall publish notice in the Federal Register of each application for a permit that is made under this section. Each notice shall invite the submission from interested parties, within 30 days after the date of the notice, of written data, views, or arguments with respect to the application. The 30-day period may be waived by the Director in an emergency situation where the life or health of an endangered animal is threatened and no reasonable alternative is available to the applicant. Notice of any such waiver shall be published in the Federal Register within 10 days following issuance of the permit.

(a) *Application requirements.* Applications for permits under this section must be submitted to the Director by the person allegedly suffering undue economic hardship because his desired activity is prohibited by § 17.21. Each application must be submitted on an official application form (Form 3-200) provided by the Service, and must include, as an attachment, all of the information required in § 17.22 plus the following additional information:

(1) The possible legal, economic or subsistence alternatives to the activity sought to be authorized by the permit;

(2) A full statement, accompanied by copies of all relevant contracts and correspondence, showing the applicant's involvement with the wildlife sought to be covered by the permit (as well as his involvement with similar wildlife), including, where applicable, that portion of applicant's income derived from the taking of such wildlife, or the subsistence use of such wildlife, during the calendar year immediately preceding either the notice in the Federal Register of review of the status of the species or of the proposal to list such wildlife as endangered, whichever is earliest;

(3) Where applicable, proof of a contract or other binding legal obligation which:

(i) Deals specifically with the wildlife sought to be covered by the permit;

(ii) Became binding prior to the date when the notice of a review of the status of the species or the notice of proposed rulemaking proposing to list such wildlife as endangered was published in the Federal Register, whichever is earlier; and

(iii) Will cause monetary loss of a given dollar amount if the permit sought under this section is not granted.

(b) *Issuance criteria.* Upon receiving an application completed in accordance with paragraph (a) of this section, the Director will decide whether or not a permit should be issued under any of the three categories of economic hardship, as defined in section 10(b)(2) of the Act. In making his decisions, the Director shall consider, in addition to the general criteria in § 13.21(b) of this subchapter, the following factors:

(1) Whether the purpose for which the permit is being requested is adequate to justify removing from the wild or otherwise changing the status of the wildlife sought to be covered by the permit;

(2) The probable direct and indirect effect which issuing the permit would have on the wild populations of the wildlife sought to be covered by the permit;

(3) The economic, legal, subsistence, or other alternatives or relief available to the applicant;

(4) The amount of evidence that the applicant was in fact party to a contract or other binding legal obligation which;

(i) Deals specifically with the wildlife sought to be covered by the permit; and

(ii) Became binding prior to the date when the notice of a review of the status of the species or the notice of proposed rulemaking proposing to list such wildlife as endangered was published in the Federal Register, whichever is earlier.

(5) The severity of economic hardship which the contract or other binding legal obligation referred to in paragraph (b)(4) of this section would cause if the permit were denied;

(6) Where applicable, the portion of the applicant's income which would be lost if the permit were denied, and the relationship of that portion to the balance of his income;

(7) Where applicable, the nature and extent of subsistence taking generally by the applicant; and

(8) The likelihood that applicant can reasonably carry out his desired activity within one year from the date a notice is published in the Federal Register to review status of such wildlife, or to list such wildlife as endangered, whichever is earlier.

(c) *Permit conditions.* In addition to the general conditions set forth in Part 13 of this subchapter, every permit issued under this section shall be subject to the following special conditions:

(1) In addition to any reporting requirements contained in the permit itself, the permittee shall also submit to the Director a written report of his activities pursuant to the permit. Such report must be postmarked or actually delivered no later than 10 days after completion of the activity.

(2) The death or escape of all living wildlife covered by the permit shall be immediately reported to the Service's office designated in the permit.

(d) Duration of permits issued under this section shall be designated on the face of the permit. No permit issued under this section, however, shall be valid for more than one year from the date a notice is published in the Federal Register to review status of such wildlife, or to list such wildlife as endangered, whichever is earlier.

[40 FR 44415, Sept. 26, 1975, as amended at 40 FR 53400, Nov. 18, 1975; 40 FR 58307, Dec. 16, 1975; 50 FR 39688, Sept. 30, 1985]

SUBPART D -- THREATENED WILDLIFE

§ 17.31 Prohibitions.

(a) Except as provided in subpart A of this Part, or in a permit issued under this subpart, all of the provisions in § 17.21 shall apply to threatened wildlife, except § 17.21(c)(5).

(b) In addition to any other provisions of this Part 17, any employee or agent of the Service, of the National Marine Fisheries Service, or of a State conservation agency which is operating a conservation program pursuant to the terms of a Cooperative Agreement with the Service in accordance with section 6(c) of the Act, who is designated by his agency for such purposes, may, when acting in the course of his official duties, take those threatened species of wildlife which are covered by an approved cooperative agreement to carry out conservation programs.

(c) Whenever a special rule in §§ 17.40 to 17.48 applies to a threatened species, none of the provisions of paragraphs (a) and (b) of this section will apply. The special rule will contain all the applicable prohibitions and exceptions.

[43 FR 18181, Apr. 28, 1978, as amended at 44 FR 31580, May 31, 1979]

§ 17.32 Permits -- general.

Upon receipt of a complete application the Director may issue a permit for any activity otherwise prohibited with regard to threatened wildlife. Such permit shall be governed by the provisions of this section unless a special rule applicable to the wildlife, appearing in § 17.40 to 17.48, of this part provides otherwise. Permits issued under this section must be for one of the following purposes: Scientific purposes, or the enhancement of propagation or survival, or economic hardship, or zoological exhibition, or educational purposes, or incidental taking, or special purposes consistent with the purposes of the Act. Such permits may authorize a single transaction, a series of transactions, or a number of activities over a specific period of time.

(a)(1) *Application requirements for permits for scientific purposes, or the enhancement of propagation or survival, or economic hardship, or zoological exhibition, or educational purposes, or special purposes consistent with the purposes of the Act.* A person wishing to get a permit for an activity prohibited by § 17.31 submits an application for activities under this paragraph. The Service provides Form 3-200 for the application to which as much of the following information relating to the purpose of the permit must be attached:

(i) The Common and scientific names of the species sought to be covered by the permit, as well as the number, age, and sex of such species, and the activity sought to be authorized (such as taking, exporting, selling in interstate commerce);

(ii) A statement as to whether, at the time of application, the wildlife sought to be covered by the permit (A) is still in the wild, (B) has already been removed from the wild, or (C) was born in captivity;

(iii) A resume of the applicant's attempts to obtain the wildlife sought to be covered by the permit in a manner which would not cause the death or removal from the wild of such wildlife;

(iv) If the wildlife sought to be covered by the permit has already been removed from the wild, the country and place where such removal occurred; if the wildlife sought to be covered by permit was born in captivity, the country and place where such wildlife was born;

(v) A complete description and address of the institution or other facility where the wildlife sought to be covered by the permit will be used, displayed, or maintained;

(vi) If the applicant seeks to have live wildlife covered by the permit, a complete description, including photographs or diagrams, of the facilities to house and/or care for the wildlife and a resume of the experience of those persons who will be caring for the wildlife;

(vii) A full statement of the reasons why the applicant is justified in obtaining a permit including the details of the activities sought to be authorized by the permit;

(viii) If the application is for the purpose of enhancement of propagation, a statement of the applicant's willingness to participate in a cooperative breeding program and to maintain or contribute data to a studbook;

(2) *Issuance criteria.* Upon receiving an application completed in accordance with paragraph (a)(1) of this section, the Director will decide whether or not a permit should be issued. In making this decision, the Director shall consider, in addition to the general criteria in § 13.21(b) of this subchapter, the following factors:

(i) Whether the purpose for which the permit is required is adequate to justify removing from the wild or otherwise changing the status of the wildlife sought to be covered by the permit;

(ii) The probable direct and indirect effect which issuing the permit would have on the wild populations of the wildlife sought to be covered by the permit;

(iii) Whether the permit, if issued, would in any way, directly or indirectly, conflict with any known program intended to enhance the survival probabilities of the population from which the wildlife sought to be covered by the permit was or would be removed;

(iv) Whether the purpose for which the permit is required would be likely to reduce the threat of extinction facing the species of wildlife sought to be covered by the permit;

(v) The opinions or views of scientists or other persons or organizations having expertise concerning the wildlife or other matters germane to the application; and

(vi) Whether the expertise, facilities, or other resources available to the applicant appear adequate to successfully accomplish the objectives stated in the application.

(3) *Permit conditions.* In addition to the general conditions set forth in Part 13 of this subchapter, every permit issued under this paragraph shall be subject to the special condition that the escape of living wildlife covered by the permit shall be immediately reported to the Service office designated in the permit.

(4) *Duration of permits.* The duration of permits issued under this paragraph shall be designated on the face of the permit.

(b)(1) Application requirements for permits for incidental taking.

(i) A person wishing to get a permit for an activity prohibited by § 17.31 submits an application for activities under this paragraph.

(ii) The director shall publish notice in the Federal Register of each application for a permit that is made under this section. Each notice shall invite the submission from interested parties, within 30 days after the date of the notice, of written data, views, or arguments with respect to the application.

(iii) Each application must be submitted on an official application (Form 3- 200) provided by the Service, and must include as an attachment, all of the following information:

(A) A complete description of the activity sought to be authorized;

(B) The common and scientific names of the species sought to be covered by the permit, as well as the number, age, and sex of such species, if known;

(C) A conservation plan that specifies:

(1) The impact that will likely result from such taking;

(2) What steps the applicant will take to monitor, minimize, and mitigate such impacts, the funding that will be available to implement such steps, and the procedures to be used to deal with unforeseen circumstances;

(3) What alternative actions to such taking the applicant considered and the reasons why such alternatives are not proposed to be utilized; and

(4) Such other measures that the Director may require as being necessary or appropriate for purposes of the plan.

(2) Issuance criteria.

(i) Upon receiving an application completed in accordance with paragraph (b)(1) of this section, the Director will decide whether or not a permit should be issued. The Director shall consider the general issuance criteria in 13.21(b) of this subchapter, except for 13.21(b)(4), and shall issue the permit if he or she finds that:

(A) The taking will be incidental;

(B) The applicant will, to the maximum extent practicable, minimize and mitigate the impacts of such takings;

(C) The applicant will ensure that adequate funding for the conservation plan and procedures to deal with unforeseen circumstances will be provided;

(D) The taking will not appreciably reduce the likelihood of the survival and recovery of the species in the wild;

(E) The measures, if any, required under paragraph (b)(1)(iii)(D) of this section will be met; and

(F) He or she has received such other assurances as he or she may require that the plan will be implemented.

(ii) In making his or her decision, the Director shall also consider the anticipated duration and geographic scope of the applicant's planned activities, including the amount of listed species habitat that is involved and the degree to which listed species and their habitats are affected.

(3) Permit conditions. In addition to the general conditions set forth in part 13 of this subchapter, every permit issued under this paragraph shall contain such terms and conditions as the Director deems necessary or appropriate to carry out the purposes of the permit and the conservation plan including, but not limited to, monitoring and reporting requirements deemed necessary for determining whether such terms and conditions are being complied with. The Director shall rely upon existing reporting requirements to the maximum extent practicable.

(4) Duration of permits. The duration of permits issued under this paragraph shall be sufficient to provide adequate assurances to the permittee to commit funding necessary for the activities authorized by the permit, including conservation activities and land use restrictions. In determining the duration of a permit, the Director shall consider the duration of the planned activities, as well as the possible positive and negative effects associated with permits of the proposed duration on listed species, including the extent to which the conservation plan will enhance the habitat of listed species and increase the long-term survivability of such species.

(5) *Assurances provided to permittee in case of changed or unforeseen circumstances.* The assurances in this paragraph (b)(5) apply only to incidental take permits issued in accordance with paragraph (b)(2) of this section where the conservation plan is being properly implemented, and apply only with respect to specifies adequately covered by the conservation plan. These assurances cannot be provided to Federal agencies. This rule does not apply to incidental take permits issued prior to [insert 30 days after the date of publication in the Federal Register]. The assurances provided in incidental take permits issued prior to [insert 30 days after the date of publication in the Federal Register] remain in effect, and those permits will not be revised as a result of this rulemaking.

(i) *Changed circumstances provided for in the plan.* If additional conservation and mitigation measures are deemed necessary to respond to changed circumstances and were provided for in the plan's operating conservation program, the permittee will implement the measures specified in the plan.

(ii) *Changed circumstances not provided for in the plan.* If additional conservation and mitigation measures are deemed necessary to respond to changed circumstances and such measures were not provided for in the plan's operating conservation program, the Director will not require any conservation and mitigation measures in addition to those provided for in the plan without the consent of the permittee, provided the plan is being properly implemented.

(iii) *Unforeseen circumstances.*

(A) In negotiating unforeseen circumstances, the Director will not require the commitment of additional land, water, or financial compensation or additional restrictions on the use of land, water, or other natural resources beyond the level otherwise agreed upon for the species covered by the conservation plan without the consent of the permittee.

(B) If additional conservation and mitigation measures are deemed necessary to respond to unforeseen circumstances, the Director may require additional measures of the permittee where the conservation plan is being properly implemented, but only if such measures are limited to modifications within conserved habitat areas, if any, or to the conservation plan's operating conservation program for the affected species, and maintain the original terms of the conservation plan to the maximum extent possible. Additional conservation and mitigation measures will not involve the commitment of additional land, water or financial compensation or additional restrictions on the use of land, water, or other natural resources otherwise available for development or use under the original terms of the conservation plan without the consent of the permittee.

(C) The Director will have the burden of demonstrating that such unforeseen circumstances exist, using the best scientific and commercial data available. These findings must be clearly documented and based upon reliable technical information regarding the status and habitat requirements of the affected species. The Director will consider, but not be limited to, the following factors:

(1) Size of the current range of the affected species;

(2) Percentage of range adversely affected by the conservation plan;

(3) Percentage of range conserved by the conservation plan;

(4) Ecological significance of that portion of the range affected by the conservation plan;

(5) Level of knowledge about the affected species and the degree of specificity of the species' conservation program under the conservation plan; and

(6) Whether failure to adopt additional conservation measures would appreciably reduce the likelihood of survival and recovery of the affected species in the wild.

(6) *Additional actions.* Nothing in this rule will be construed to limit or constrain the Director, any Federal, State, local, or Tribal government agency, or a private entity, from taking additional actions at its own expense to protect or conserve a species included in a conservation plan.

(7) *Discontinuance of permit activity.* Notwithstanding the provisions of § 13.26 of this subchapter, a permittee under this paragraph (b) remains responsible for any outstanding minimization and mitigation measures required under the terms of the permit for take that occurs prior to surrender of the permit and such minimization and mitigation measures as may be required pursuant to the termination provisions of an implementing agreement, habitat conservation plan, or permit even after surrendering the permit to the Service pursuant to § 13.26 of this subchapter. The permit shall be deemed canceled only upon a determination by the Service that such minimization and mitigation measures have been implemented. Upon surrender of the permit, no further take shall be authorized under the terms of the surrendered permit.

(8) *Criteria for revocation.* A permit issued under this paragraph (b) may not be revoked for any reason except those set forth in § 13.28(a)(1) through (4) of this subchapter or unless continuation of the permitted activity would be inconsistent with the criterion set forth in 16 U.S.C. 1539(a)(2)(B)(iv) and the inconsistency has not been remedied in a timely fashion.

(c)(1) *Application requirements for permits for the enhancement of survival through Safe Harbor Agreements.* The applicant must submit an application for a permit under this paragraph (c) to the appropriate Regional Director, U.S. Fish and Wildlife Service, for the Region where the applicant resides or where the proposed action is to occur (for appropriate addresses, see 50 CFR 10.22), if the applicant wishes to engage in any activity prohibited by § 17.31. The applicant must submit an official Service application form (3-200.54) that includes the following information:

(i) The common and scientific names of the listed species for which the applicant requests incidental take authorization;

(ii) A description of the land use or water management activity for which the applicant requests incidental take authorization;

(iii) A Safe Harbor Agreement that complies with the requirements of the Safe Harbor policy available from the Service; and

(iv) The Director must publish notice in the Federal Register of each application for a permit that is made under this paragraph (c). Each notice must invite the submission from interested parties within 30 days after the date of the notice of written data, views, or arguments with respect to the application. The procedures included in § 17.22(e) for permit objection apply to any notice published by the Director under this paragraph (c).

(2) *Issuance criteria.* Upon receiving an application completed in accordance with paragraph (c)(1) of this section, the Director will decide whether or not to issue a permit. The Director shall consider the general issuance criteria in § 13.21(b) of this subchapter, except for § 13.21(b)(4), and may issue the permit if he or she finds:

(i) The take will be incidental to an otherwise lawful activity and will be in accordance with the terms of the Safe Harbor Agreement;

(ii) The implementation of the terms of the Safe Harbor Agreement will provide a net conservation benefit to the affected listed species by contributing to the recovery of listed species included in the permit and the Safe Harbor Agreement otherwise complies with the Safe Harbor policy available from the Service;

(iii) The probable direct and indirect effects of any authorized take will not appreciably reduce the likelihood of survival and recovery in the wild of any listed species;

(iv) Implementation of the terms of the Safe Harbor Agreement is consistent with applicable Federal, State, and Tribal laws and regulations;

(v) Implementation of the terms of the Safe Harbor Agreement will not be in conflict with any ongoing conservation or recovery programs for listed species covered by the permit; and

(vi) The applicant has shown capability for and commitment to implementing all of the terms of the Safe Harbor Agreement.

(3) *Permit conditions.* In addition to any applicable general permit conditions set forth in part 13 of this subchapter, every permit issued under this paragraph (c) is subject to the following special conditions:

(i) A requirement for the participating property owner to notify the Service of any transfer of lands subject to a Safe Harbor Agreement;

(ii) A requirement for the property owner to notify the Service at least 30 days in advance, but preferably as far in advance as possible, of when he or she expects to incidentally take any listed species covered under the permit. Such notification will provide the Service with an opportunity to translocate affected individuals of the species, if possible and appropriate; and

(iii) Any additional requirements or conditions the Director deems necessary or appropriate to carry out the purposes of the permit and the Safe Harbor Agreement.

(4) *Permit effective date.* Permits issued under this paragraph (c) become effective the day of issuance for species covered by the Safe Harbor Agreement.

(5) *Assurances provided to permittee.*

(i) The assurances in subparagraph (ii) of this paragraph (c)(5) apply only to Safe Harbor permits issued in accordance with paragraph (c)(2) of this section where the Safe Harbor Agreement is being properly implemented, and apply only with respect to species covered by the Agreement and permit. These assurances cannot be provided to Federal agencies. The assurances provided in this section apply only to Safe Harbor permits issued after July 19, 1999.

(ii) If additional conservation and mitigation measures are deemed necessary, the Director may require additional measures of the permittee, but only if such measures are limited to modifications within conserved habitat areas, if any, for the affected species and maintain the original terms of the Safe Harbor Agreement to the maximum extent possible. Additional conservation and mitigation measures will not involve the commitment of additional land, water or financial compensation or additional restrictions on the use of land, water, or other natural resources otherwise available for development or use under the original terms of the Safe Harbor Agreement without the consent of the permittee.

(6) *Additional actions.* Nothing in this rule will be construed to limit or constrain the Director, any Federal, State, local or Tribal government agency, or a private entity, from taking additional actions at its own expense to protect or conserve a species included in a Safe Harbor Agreement.

(7) *Criteria for revocation.* A permit issued under this paragraph (c) may not be revoked for any reason except those set forth in § 13.28(a)(1) through (4) of this subchapter or unless continuation of the permitted activity would be inconsistent with the criterion set forth in 17.22(c)(2)(iii) and the inconsistency has not been remedied in a timely fashion.

(8) *Duration of permits.* The duration of permits issued under this paragraph (c) must be sufficient to provide a net conservation benefit to species covered in the enhancement of survival permit. In determining the duration of a permit, the Director will consider the duration of the planned activities, as well as the positive and negative effects associated with permits of the proposed duration on covered species, including the extent to which the conservation activities included in the Safe Harbor Agreement will enhance the survival and contribute to the recovery of listed species included in the permit.

(d)(1) *Application requirements for permits for the enhancement of survival through Candidate Conservation Agreements with Assurances.* The applicant must submit an application for a permit under this paragraph (d) to the appropriate Regional Director, U.S. Fish and Wildlife Service, for the Region where the applicant resides or where the proposed activity is to occur (for appropriate addresses, see 50 CFR 10.22). When a species covered by a Candidate Conservation Agreement with Assurances is listed as threatened and the applicant wishes to engage in activities identified in the Agreement and otherwise prohibited by § 17.31, the applicant must apply for an enhancement of survival permit for species covered by the Agreement. The permit will become valid if and when covered proposed, candidate or other unlisted species is listed as a threatened species. The applicant must submit an official Service application form (3-200.54) that includes the following information:

(i) The common and scientific names of the species for which the applicant requests incidental take authorization;

(ii) A description of the land use or water management activity for which the applicant requests incidental take authorization; and

(iii) A Candidate Conservation Agreement that complies with the requirements of the Candidate Conservation Agreement with Assurances policy available from the Service.

(iv) The Director must publish notice in the Federal Register of each application for a permit that is made under this paragraph (d). Each notice must invite the submission from interested parties within 30 days after the date of the notice of written data, views, or arguments with respect to the application. The procedures included in § 17.22(e) for permit objection apply to any notice published by the Director under this paragraph (d).

(2) *Issuance criteria.* Upon receiving an application completed in accordance with paragraph (d)(1) of this section, the Director will decide whether or not to issue a permit. The Director shall consider the general issuance criteria in § 13.21(b) of this subchapter, except for § 13.21(b)(4), and may issue the permit if he or she finds:

(i) The take will be incidental to an otherwise lawful activity and will be in accordance with the terms of the Candidate Conservation Agreement;

(ii) The Candidate Conservation Agreement complies with the requirements of the Candidate Conservation Agreement with Assurances policy available from the Service;

(iii) The probable direct and indirect effects of any authorized take will not appreciably reduce the likelihood of survival and recovery in the wild of any species;

(iv) Implementation of the terms of the Candidate Conservation Agreement is consistent with applicable Federal, State, and Tribal laws and regulations;

(v) Implementation of the terms of the Candidate Conservation Agreement will not be in conflict with any ongoing conservation programs for species covered by the permit; and

(vi) The applicant has shown capability for and commitment to implementing all of the terms of the Candidate Conservation Agreement.

(3) *Permit conditions.* In addition to any applicable general permit conditions set forth in part 13 of this subchapter, every permit issued under this paragraph (d) is subject to the following special conditions:

(i) A requirement for the property owner to notify the Service of any transfer of lands subject to a Candidate Conservation Agreement;

(ii) A requirement for the property owner to notify the Service at least 30 days in advance, but preferably as far in advance as possible, of when he or she expects to incidentally take any species covered under the permit. Such notification will provide the Service with an opportunity to translocate affected individuals of the species, if possible and appropriate; and

(iii) Any additional requirements or conditions the Director deems necessary or appropriate to carry out the purposes of the permit and the Candidate Conservation Agreement.

(4) *Permit effective date.* Permits issued under this paragraph (d) become effective for a species covered by a Candidate Conservation Agreement on the effective date of a final rule that lists a covered species as threatened.

(5) *Assurances provided to permittee in case of changed or unforeseen circumstances.* The assurances in this paragraph (d)(5) apply only to permits issued in accordance with paragraph (d)(2) where the Candidate Conservation with Assurances Agreement is being properly implemented, and apply only with respect to species adequately covered by the Candidate Conservation with Assurances Agreement. These assurances cannot be provided to Federal agencies.

(i) *Changed circumstances provided for in the Agreement.* If additional conservation and mitigation measures are deemed necessary to respond to changed circumstances and were provided for in the Agreement's operating conservation program, the permittee will implement the measures specified in the Agreement.

(ii) *Changed circumstances not provided for in the Agreement.* If additional conservation and mitigation measures are deemed necessary to respond to changed circumstances and such measures were not provided for in the Agreement's operating conservation program, the Director will not require any conservation and mitigation measures in addition to those provided for in the Agreement without the consent of the permittee, provided the Agreement is being properly implemented.

(iii) *Unforeseen circumstances.*

(A) In negotiating unforeseen circumstances, the Director will not require the commitment of additional land, water, or financial compensation or additional restrictions on the use of land, water, or other natural resources beyond the level otherwise agreed upon for the species covered by the Agreement without the consent of the permittee.

(B) If additional conservation and mitigation measures are deemed necessary to respond to unforeseen circumstances, the Director may require additional measures of the permittee where the Agreement is being properly implemented, but only if such measures are limited to modifications within conserved habitat areas, if any, or to the Agreement's operating conservation program for the affected species, and maintain the original terms of the Agreement to the maximum extent possible. Additional conservation and mitigation measures will not involve the commitment of additional land, water or financial compensation or additional restrictions on the use of land, water, or other natural resources otherwise available for development or use under the original terms of the Agreement without the consent of the permittee.

(C) The Director will have the burden of demonstrating that unforeseen circumstances exist, using the best scientific and commercial data available. These findings must be clearly documented and based upon reliable technical information regarding the status and habitat requirements of the affected species. The Director will consider, but not be limited to, the following factors:

(1) Size of the current range of the affected species;

(2) Percentage of range adversely affected by the Agreement;

(3) Percentage of range conserved by the Agreement;

(4) Ecological significance of that portion of the range affected by the Agreement;

(5) Level of knowledge about the affected species and the degree of specificity of the species' conservation program under the Agreement; and

(6) Whether failure to adopt additional conservation measures would appreciably reduce the likelihood of survival and recovery of the affected species in the wild.

(6) *Additional actions.* Nothing in this rule will be construed to limit or constrain the Director, any Federal, State, local or Tribal government agency, or a private entity, from taking additional actions at its own expense to protect or conserve a species included in a Candidate Conservation with Assurances Agreement.

(7) *Criteria for revocation.* A permit issued under this paragraph (d) may not be revoked for any reason except those set forth in § 13.28(a)(1) through (4) of this subchapter or unless continuation of the permitted activity would be inconsistent with the criterion set forth in paragraph (d)(2)(iii) of this section and the inconsistency has not been remedied in a timely fashion.

(8) *Duration of the Candidate Conservation Agreement.* The duration of a Candidate Conservation Agreement covered by a permit issued under this paragraph (d) must be sufficient to enable the Director to determine that the benefits of the conservation measures in the Agreement, when combined with those benefits that would be achieved if it is assumed that the conservation measures would also be implemented on other necessary properties, would preclude or remove any need to list the species covered by

the Agreement.

[40 FR 44415, Sept. 26, 1975, as amended at 41 FR 19226, May 11, 1976; 47 FR 30787, July 15, 1982; 50 FR 39689, Sept. 30, 1985; 63 FR 8871, Feb. 23, 1998; 63 FR 52635, Oct. 1, 1998; 64 FR 32714, June 17, 1999; 64 FR 52676, Sept. 30, 1999]

****

SUBPART E -- SIMILARITY OF APPEARANCE

SOURCE: 42 FR 32377, June 24, 1977, unless otherwise noted.

§ 17.50 General.

(a) Whenever a species which is not Endangered or Threatened closely resembles an Endangered or Threatened species, such species may be treated as either Endangered or Threatened if the director makes such determination in accordance with section 4(e) of the Act and the criteria of paragraph (b) of this section. After the Director has made such determination in accordance with the notification procedures specified in the Act, such species shall appear in the list in § 17.11 (Wildlife) or § 17.12 (Plants) with the notation "(S/A)" (similarity of appearance) in the "Status" column, following either a letter "E" or a letter "T" to indicate whether the species is being treated as Endangered or Threatened.

(b) In determining whether to treat a species as Endangered or Threatened due to similarity of appearance, the Director shall consider the criteria in section 4(e) of the Act, as indicated below:

(1) The degree of difficulty enforcement personnel would have in distinguishing the species, at the point in question, from an Endangered or Threatened species (including those cases where the criteria for recognition of a species are based on geographical boundaries);

(2) The additional threat posed to the Endangered or Threatened species by the loss of control occasioned because of the similarity of appearance; and

(3) The probability that so designating a similar species will substantially facilitate enforcement and further the purposes and policy of the Act.

****

§ 17.51 Treatment as endangered or threatened.

(a) Any species listed in § 17.11 or § 17.12, pursuant to § 17.50, shall be treated as endangered or threatened, as indicated in the "Status" column.

(b) All of the provisions of Subparts C (Endangered Wildlife), D (Threatened Wildlife), F (Endangered Plants) or G (Threatened Plants), as appropriate, shall apply to any such species.

§ 17.52 Permits -- similarity of appearance.

Upon receipt of a complete application and unless otherwise indicated in a special rule, the Director may issue permits for any activity otherwise prohibited with a species designated as endangered or threatened due to its similarity of appearance. Such a permit may authorize a single transaction, a series of transactions, or a number of activities over a specified period of time.

(a) *Application requirements.* An application for a permit under this section must be submitted to the Director by the person who wishes to engage in the prohibited activity. The permit for activities involving interstate commerce of plants must be obtained by the seller; in the case of wildlife, the permit must be obtained by the buyer. The application must be submitted on an official application form (Form 3-200) provided by the Service, or must contain the general information and certification required by § 13.12(a) of this subchapter. It must include, as an attachment, all of the following information: Documentary evidence, sworn affidavits, or other information to show species identification and the origin of the wildlife or plant in question. This information may be in the form of hunting licenses, hide seals, official stamps, export documents, bills of sales, certification, expert opinion, or other appropriate information.

(b) *Issuance criteria.* Upon receiving an application completed in accordance with paragraph (a) of this section, the Director will decide whether or not a permit should be issued. In making his decision, the Director shall consider, in addition to the general criteria, in § 13.21(b) of this subchapter, the following factors:

(1) Whether the information submitted by the applicant appears reliable;

(2) Whether the information submitted by the applicant adequately identifies the wildlife or plant in question so as to distinguish it from any Endangered or Threatened wildlife or plant.

(c) *Permit conditions.* In addition to the general conditions set forth in Part 13 of this subchapter, every permit issued under this section shall be subject to the following special conditions:

(1) If indicated in the permit, a special mark, to be specified in the permit, must be applied to the wildlife or plant, and remain for the time designated in the permit;

(2) A copy of the permit or an identification label, which includes the scientific name and the permit number, must accompany the wildlife or plant or its container during the course of any activity subject to these regulations.

(d) *Duration of permits.* The duration of a permit issued under this section shall be designated on the face of the permit.

****

SUBPART H -- EXPERIMENTAL POPULATIONS

SOURCE: 49 FR 33893, Aug. 27, 1984, unless otherwise noted.

§ 17.80 Definitions.

(a) The term *experimental population* means an introduced and/or designated population (including any off-spring arising solely therefrom) that has been so designated in accordance with the procedures of this subpart but only when, and at such times as the population is wholly separate geographically from nonexperimental populations of the same species. Where part of an experimental population overlaps with natural populations of the same species on a particular occasion, but is wholly separate at other times, specimens of the experimental population will not be recognized as such while in the area of overlap. That is, experimental status will only be recognized outside the areas of overlap. Thus, such a population shall be treated as experimental only when the times of geographic separation are reasonably predictable; *e.g.,* fixed migration patterns, natural or man-made barriers. A population is not treated as experimental if total separation will occur solely as a result of random and unpredictable events.

(b) The term *essential experimental population* means an experimental population whose loss would be likely to appreciably reduce the likelihood of the survival of the species in the wild. All other experimental populations are to be classified as *nonessential.*

§ 17.81 Listing.

(a) The Secretary may designate as an experimental population a population of endangered or threatened species that has been or will be released into suitable natural habitat outside the species' current natural range (but within its probable historic range, absent a finding by the Director in the extreme case that the primary habitat of the species has been unsuitably and irreversibly altered or destroyed), subject to the further conditions specified in this section; *provided,* that all designations of experimental populations must proceed by regulation adopted in accordance with 5 U.S.C. 553 and the requirements of this subpart.

(b) Before authorizing the release as an experimental population of any population (including eggs, propagules, or individuals) of an endangered or threatened species, and before authorizing any necessary transportation to conduct the release, the Secretary must find by regulation that such release will further the conservation of the species. In making such a finding the Secretary shall utilize the best scientific and commercial data available to consider:

(1) Any possible adverse effects on extant populations of a species as a result of removal of individuals, eggs, or propagules for introduction elsewhere;

(2) The likelihood that any such experimental population will become established and survive in the foreseeable future;

(3) The relative effects that establishment of an experimental population will have on the recovery of the species; and

(4) The extent to which the introduced population may be affected by existing or anticipated Federal or State actions or private activities within or adjacent to the experimental population area.

The Secretary may issue a permit under section 10(a)(1)(A) of the Act, if appropriate under the standards set out in subsections 10(d) and (j) of the Act, to allow acts necessary for the establishment and maintenance of an experimental population.

(c) Any regulation promulgated under paragraph (a) of this section shall provide:

(1) Appropriate means to identify the experimental population, including, but not limited to, its actual or proposed location, actual or anticipated migration, number of specimens released or to be released, and other criteria appropriate to identify the experimental population(s);

(2) A finding, based solely on the best scientific and commercial data available, and the supporting factual basis, on whether the experimental population is, or is not, essential to the continued existence of the species in the wild;

(3) Management restrictions, protective measures, or other special management concerns of that population, which may include but are not limited to, measures to isolate and/or contain the experimental population designated in the regulation from natural populations; and

(4) A process for periodic review and evaluation of the success or failure of the

release and the effect of the release on the conservation and recovery of the species.

(d) The Fish and Wildlife Service shall consult with appropriate State fish and wildlife agencies, local governmental entities, affected Federal agencies, and affected private landowners in developing and implementing experimental population rules. When appropriate, a public meeting will be conducted with interested members of the public. Any regulation promulgated pursuant to this section shall, to the maximum extent practicable, represent an agreement between the Fish and Wildlife Service, the affected State and Federal agencies and persons holding any interest in land which may be affected by the establishment of an experimental population.

(e) Any population of an endangered species or a threatened species determined by the Secretary to be an experimental population in accordance with this subpart shall be identified by special rule in § 17.84-§ 17.86 as appropriate and separately listed in § 17.11(h) (wildlife) or § 17.12(h) (plants) as appropriate.

(f) The Secretary may designate critical habitat as defined in section (3)(5)(A) of the Act for an essential experimental population as determined pursuant to paragraph (c)(2) of this section. Any designation of critical habitat for an essential experimental population will be made in accordance with section 4 of the Act. No designation of critical habitat will be made for nonessential populations. In those situations where a portion or all of an essential experimental population overlaps with a natural population of the species during certain periods of the year, no critical habitat shall be designated for the area of overlap unless implemented as a revision to critical habitat of the natural population for reasons unrelated to the overlap itself.

§ 17.82 Prohibitions.

Any population determined by the Secretary to be an experimental population shall be treated as if it were listed as a threatened species for purposes of establishing protective regulations under section 4(d) of the Act with respect to such population. The Special rules (protective regulations) adopted for an experimental population under § 17.81 will contain applicable prohibitions, as appropriate, and exceptions for that population.

****

SUBPART I -- INTERAGENCY COOPERATION

§ 17.94 Critical habitats.

(a) The areas listed in § 17.95 (fish and wildlife) and § 17.96 (plants) and referred to in the lists at §§ 17.11 and 17.12 have been determined by the Director to be Critical Habitat. All Federal agencies must insure that any action authorized, funded, or carried out by them is not likely to result in the destruction or adverse modification of the constituent elements essential to the conservation of the listed species within these defined Critical Habitats. (See Part 402 for rules concerning this prohibition; see also Part 424 for rules concerning the determination of Critical Habitat).

(b) The map provided by the Director does not, unless otherwise indicated, constitute the definition of the boundaries of a Critical Habitat. Such maps are provided for reference purposes to guide Federal agencies and other interested parties in locating the general boundaries of the Critical Habitat. Critical Habitats are described by reference to surveyable landmarks found on standard topographic maps of the area and to the

States and county(ies) within which all or part of the Critical Habitat is located. Unless otherwise indicated within the Critical Habitat description, the State and county(ies) names are provided for informational purposes only.

(c) Critical Habitat management focuses only on the biological or physical constituent elements within the defined area of Critical Habitat that are essential to the conservation of the species. Those major constituent elements that are known to require special management considerations or protection will be listed with the description of the Critical Habitat.

(d) The sequence of species within each list of Critical Habitats in §§ 17.95 and 17.96 will follow the sequences in the lists of Endangered and Threatened wildlife (§ 17.11) and plants (§ 17.12). Multiple entries for each species will be alphabetic by State.

[45 FR 13021, Feb. 27, 1980]

****

National Marine Fisheries Service, National Oceanic and Atmospheric Administration, Department of Commerce

50 C.F.R. PART 222
GENERAL ENDANGERED AND THREATENED MARINE SPECIES

Subpart A -- Introduction and General Provisions

sec.

222.101 Purpose and scope of regulations.
222.102 Definitions.
222.103 Federal/state cooperation in the conservation of endangered and threatened species.

Subpart B -- Certificate of Exemption for Pre-Act Endangered Species Parts

222.201 General requirements.
222.202 Certificate renewal.
222.203 Modification, amendment, suspension, and revocation of certificates.
222.204 Administration of certificates.
222.205 Import and export requirements.

Subpart C -- General Permit Procedures

222.301 General requirements.
222.302 Procedure for obtaining permits.
222.303 Issuance of permits.
222.304 Renewal of permits.
222.305 Rights of succession and transfer of permits.
222.306 Modification, amendment, suspension, and revocation of permits.
222.307 Permits for incidental taking of species.

AUTHORITY: 16 U.S.C. §§ 1531 *et seq.*; 16 U.S.C. §§ 742a *et seq.*; 16 U.S.C. § 9701.

SOURCE: 64 FR 14054, Mar. 23, 1999, unless otherwise noted.

SUBPART A -- INTRODUCTION AND GENERAL PROVISIONS

§ 222.101 Purpose and scope of regulations.

(a) The regulations of parts 222, 223, and 224 of this chapter implement the Endangered Species Act (Act), and govern the taking, possession, transportation, sale, purchase, barter, exportation, importation of, and other requirements pertaining to wildlife and plants under the jurisdiction of the Secretary of Commerce and determined to be threatened or endangered pursuant to section 4(a) of the Act. These regulations are implemented by the National Marine Fisheries Service, National Oceanic and Atmospheric Administration, U.S. Department of Commerce, This part pertains to general provisions and definitions. Specifically, parts 223 and 224 pertain to provisions to threatened species and endangered species, respectively. Part 226 enumerates designated critical habitat for endangered and threatened species. Certain of the endangered and threatened marine species enumerated in §§ 224.102 and 223.102 are included in Appendix I or II to the Convention on International Trade of Endangered Species of Wild Fauna and Flora. The importation, exportation, and re-exportation of such species are subject to additional regulations set forth at 50 CFR part 23, chapter I.

(b) For rules and procedures relating to species determined to be threatened or endangered under the jurisdiction of the Secretary of the Interior, see 50 CFR parts 10 through 17. For rules and procedures relating to the general implementation of the Act jointly by the Departments of the Interior and Commerce and for certain species under the joint jurisdiction of both the Secretaries of the Interior and Commerce, see 50 CFR Chapter IV. Marine mammals listed as endangered or threatened and subject to these regulations may also be subject to additional requirements pursuant to the Marine Mammal Protection Act (for regulations implementing that act, see 50 CFR part 216).

(c) No statute or regulation of any state shall be construed to relieve a person from the restrictions, conditions, and requirements contained in parts 222, 223, and 224 of this chapter. In addition, nothing in parts 222, 223, and 224 of this chapter, including any permit issued pursuant thereto, shall be construed to relieve a person from any other requirements imposed by a statute or regulation of any state or of the United States, including any applicable health, quarantine, agricultural, or customs laws or regulations, or any other National Marine Fisheries Service enforced statutes or regulations.

§ 222.102 Definitions.

Accelerator funnel means a device used to accelerate the flow of water through a shrimp trawl net.

Act means the Endangered Species Act of 1973, as amended, 16 U.S.C. 1531 et seq.

Adequately covered means, with respect to species listed pursuant to section 4 of the Act, that a proposed conservation plan has satisfied the permit issuance criteria under section 10(a)(2)(B) of the Act for the species covered by the plan and, with respect to unlisted species, that a proposed conservation plan has satisfied the permit issuance criteria under section 10(a)(2)(B) of the Act that would otherwise apply if the unlisted species covered by the plan were actually listed. For the Services to cover a species under a conservation plan, it must be listed on the section 10(a)(1)(B) permit.

Alaska Regional Administrator means the Regional Administrator for the Alaska Region of the National Marine Fisheries Service, National Oceanic and Atmospheric Administration, U.S. Department of Commerce, or their authorized representative. Mail sent to the Alaska Regional Administrator should be addressed: Alaska Regional Administrator, F/AK, Alaska Regional Office, National Marine Fisheries Service, NOAA, P.O. Box 21668 Juneau, AK 99802-1668.

Approved turtle excluder device (TED) means a device designed to be installed in a trawl net forward of the cod end for the purpose of excluding sea turtles from the net, as described in 50 CFR 223.207.

Assistant Administrator means the Assistant Administrator for Fisheries of the National Marine Fisheries Service, National Oceanic and Atmospheric Administration, U.S. Department of Commerce, or his authorized representative. Mail sent to the Assistant Administrator should be addressed: Assistant Administrator for Fisheries, National Marine Fisheries Service, NOAA, 1315 East-West Highway, Silver Spring, MD 20910.

Atlantic Area means all waters of the Atlantic Ocean south of 36<<degrees>> 33'00.8" N. lat. (the line of the North Carolina/Virginia border) and adjacent seas, other than waters of the Gulf Area, and all waters shoreward thereof (including ports).

Atlantic Shrimp Fishery -- Sea Turtle Conservation Area (Atlantic SFSTCA) means the inshore and offshore waters extending to 10 nautical miles (18.5 km) offshore along the coast of the States of Georgia and South Carolina from the Georgia-Florida border (defined as the line along 30<<degrees>> 42'45.6" N. lat.) to the North Carolina-South Carolina border (defined as the line extending in a direction of 135<<degrees>> 34'55" from true north from the North Carolina-South Carolina land boundary, as marked by the border station on Bird Island at 33d<<degrees>> 51'07.9" N. lat., 078<<degrees>> 32'32.6" W. long.).

Authorized officer means:

(1) Any commissioned, warrant, or petty officer of the U.S. Coast Guard;

(2) Any special agent or enforcement officer of the National Marine Fisheries Service;

(3) Any officer designated by the head of a Federal or state agency that has entered into an agreement with the Secretary or the Commandant of the Coast Guard to enforce the provisions of the Act; or

(4) Any Coast Guard personnel accompanying and acting under the direction of any person described in paragraph (1) of this definition.

Bait shrimper means a shrimp trawler that fishes for and retains its shrimp catch alive for the purpose of selling it for use as bait.

Beam trawl means a trawl with a rigid frame surrounding the mouth that is towed from a vessel by means of one or more cables or ropes.

Certificate of exemption means any document so designated by the National Marine Fisheries Service and signed by an authorized official of the National Marine Fisheries

Service, including any document which modifies, amends, extends or renews any certificate of exemption.

Changed circumstances means changes in circumstances affecting a species or geographic area covered by a conservation plan that can reasonably be anticipated by plan developers and NMFS and that can be planned for (e.g., the listing of new species, or a fire or other natural catastrophic event in areas prone to such events).

Commercial activity means all activities of industry and trade, including, but not limited to, the buying or selling of commodities and activities conducted for the purpose of facilitating such buying and selling: Provided, however, that it does not include the exhibition of commodities by museums or similar cultural or historical organizations.

Conservation plan means the plan required by section 10(a)(2)(A) of the Act that an applicant must submit when applying for an incidental take permit. Conservation plans also are known as "habitat conservation plans" or "HCPs."

Conserved habitat areas means areas explicitly designated for habitat restoration, acquisition, protection, or other conservation purposes under a conservation plan.

Cooperative Agreement means an agreement between a state(s) and the National Marine Fisheries Service, NOAA, Department of Commerce, which establishes and maintains an active and adequate program for the conservation of resident species listed as endangered or threatened pursuant to section 6(c)(1) of the Endangered Species Act.

Fishing, or *to fish,* means:

(1) The catching, taking, or harvesting of fish or wildlife;

(2) The attempted catching, taking, or harvesting of fish or wildlife;

(3) Any other activity that can reasonably be expected to result in the catching, taking, or harvesting of fish or wildlife; or

(4) Any operations on any waters in support of, or in preparation for, any activity described in paragraphs (1) through (3) of this definition.

Footrope means a weighted rope or cable attached to the lower lip (bottom edge) of the mouth of a trawl net along the forward most webbing.

Footrope length means the distance between the points at which the ends of the footrope are attached to the trawl net, measured along the forward-most webbing.

Foreign commerce includes, among other things, any transaction between persons within one foreign country, or between persons in two or more foreign countries, or between a person within the United States and a person in one or more foreign countries, or between persons within the United States, where the fish or wildlife in question are moving in any country or countries outside the United States.

Four-seam, straight-wing trawl means a design of shrimp trawl in which the main body of the trawl is formed from a top panel, a bottom panel, and two side panels of webbing. The upper and lower edges of the side panels of webbing are parallel over the entire length.

Four-seam, tapered-wing trawl means a design of shrimp trawl in which the main body of the trawl is formed from a top panel, a bottom panel, and two side panels of webbing. The upper and lower edges of the side panels of webbing converge toward the rear of the trawl.

[Text of definition effective until Nov. 10, 2002.]

Gillnet means a panel of netting, suspended vertically in the water by floats along the top and weights along the bottom, to entangle fish that attempt to pass through it.

Gulf Area means all waters of the Gulf of Mexico west of 81<<degrees>> W. long.

(the line at which the Gulf Area meets the Atlantic Area) and all waters shoreward thereof (including ports).

Gulf Shrimp Fishery-Sea Turtle Conservation Area (Gulf SFSTCA) means the offshore waters extending to 10 nautical miles (18.5 km) offshore along the coast of the States of Texas and Louisiana from the South Pass of the Mississippi River (west of 89<<degrees>> 08.5' W. long.) to the U.S.-Mexican border.

Habitat restoration activity means an activity that has the sole objective of restoring natural aquatic or riparian habitat conditions or processes.

Harm in the definition of "take" in the Act means an act which actually kills or injures fish or wildlife. Such an act may include significant habitat modification or degradation which actually kills or injures fish or wildlife by significantly impairing essential behavioral patterns, including, breeding, spawning, rearing, migrating, feeding or sheltering.

Headrope means a rope that is attached to the upper lip (top edge) of the mouth of a trawl net along the forward-most webbing.

Headrope length means the distance between the points at which the ends of the headrope are attached to the trawl net, measured along the forward-most webbing.

Import means to land on, bring into, or introduce into, or attempt to land on, bring into, or introduce into any place subject to the jurisdiction of the United States, whether or not such landing, bringing, or introduction constitutes an importation within the meaning of the tariff laws of the United States.

Inshore means marine and tidal waters landward of the 72 COLREGS demarcation line (International Regulations for Preventing Collisions at Sea, 1972), as depicted or noted on nautical charts published by the National Oceanic and Atmospheric Administration (Coast Charts, 1:80,000 scale) and as described in 33 CFR part 80.

Leatherback conservation zone means that portion of the Atlantic Area lying north of a line along 28<<degrees>> 24.6' N. lat. (Cape Canaveral, FL).

Northeast Regional Administrator means the Regional Administrator for the Northeast Region of the National Marine Fisheries Service, National Oceanic and Atmospheric Administration, U.S. Department of Commerce, or their authorized representative. Mail sent to the Northeast Regional Administrator should be addressed: Northeast Regional Administrator, F/NE, Northeast Regional Office, National Marine Fisheries Service, NOAA, One Blackburn Drive, Gloucester, MA 01930-2298.

Northwest Regional Administrator means the Regional Administrator for the Northwest Region of the National Marine Fisheries Service, National Oceanic and Atmospheric Administration, U.S. Department of Commerce, or their authorized representative. Mail sent to the Northwest Regional Administrator should be addressed: Northwest Regional Administrator, F/NW, Northwest Regional Office, National Marine Fisheries Service, NOAA, 7600 Sand Point Way NE, Seattle, WA 98115-0070.

Office of Enforcement means the national fisheries enforcement office of the National Marine Fisheries Service. Mail sent to the Office of Enforcement should be addressed: Office of Enforcement, F/EN, National Marine Fisheries Service, NOAA, 8484 Suite 415, Georgia Ave., Silver Spring, MD 20910.

Office of Protected Resources means the national program office of the endangered species and marine mammal programs of the National Marine Fisheries Service. Mail sent to the Office of Protected Resources should be addressed: Office of Protected Resources, F/PR, National Marine Fisheries Service, NOAA, 1315 East West Highway, Silver Spring, MD 20910.

Offshore means marine and tidal waters seaward of the 72 COLREGS demarcation line (International Regulations for Preventing Collisions at Sea, 1972), as depicted or noted on nautical charts published by the National Oceanic and Atmospheric Administration (Coast Charts, 1:80,000 scale) and as described in 33 CFR part 80.

Operating conservation program means those conservation management activities which are expressly agreed upon and described in a Conservation Plan or its Implementing Agreement. These activities are to be undertaken for the affected species when implementing an approved Conservation Plan, including measures to respond to changed circumstances.

Permit means any document so designated by the National Marine Fisheries Service and signed by an authorized official of the National Marine Fisheries Service, including any document which modifies, amends, extends, or renews any permit.

Person means an individual, corporation, partnership, trust, association, or any other private entity, or any officer, employee, agent, department, or instrumentality of the Federal government of any state or political subdivision thereof or of any foreign government.

Possession means the detention and control, or the manual or ideal custody of anything that may be the subject of property, for one's use and enjoyment, either as owner or as the proprietor of a qualified right in it, and either held personally or by another who exercises it in one's place and name. Possession includes the act or state of possessing and that condition of facts under which persons can exercise their power over a corporeal thing at their pleasure to the exclusion of all other persons. Possession includes constructive possession that which means not an actual but an assumed existence one claims to hold by virtue of some title, without having actual custody.

Pre-Act endangered species part means any sperm whale oil, including derivatives and products thereof, which was lawfully held within the United States on December 28, 1973, in the course of a commercial activity; or any finished scrimshaw product, if such product or the raw material for such product was lawfully held within the United States on December 28, 1973, in the course of a commercial activity.

Properly implemented conservation plan means any conservation plan, implementing agreement, or permit whose commitments and provisions have been or are being fully implemented by the permittee.

Pusher-head trawl (chopsticks) means a trawl that is spread by two poles suspended from the bow of the trawler in an inverted "V" configuration.

Resident species means, for purposes of entering into cooperative agreements with any state pursuant to section 6(c) of the Act, a species that exists in the wild in that state during any part of its life.

Right whale means, as used in part 224 of this chapter, any whale that is a member of the western North Atlantic population of the northern right whale species (Eubalaena glacialis).

Roller trawl means a variety of beam trawl that is used, usually by small vessels, for fishing over uneven or vegetated sea bottoms.

Scrimshaw product means any art form which involves the substantial etching or engraving of designs upon, or the substantial carving of figures, patterns, or designs from any bone or tooth of any marine mammal of the order Cetacea. For purposes of this part, polishing or the adding of minor superficial markings does not constitute substantial etching, engraving, or carving.

Secretary means the Secretary of Commerce or an authorized representative.

Shrimp means any species of marine shrimp (Order *Crustacea*) found in the Atlantic Area or the Gulf Area, including, but not limited to:

(1) Brown shrimp (*Penaeus aztecus*).
(2) White shrimp (*Penaeus setiferus*).
(3) Pink shrimp (*Penaeus duorarum*).
(4) Rock shrimp (*Sicyonia brevirostris*).
(5) Royal red shrimp (*Hymenopenaeus robustus*).
(6) Seabob shrimp (*Xiphopenaeus kroyeri*).

Shrimp trawler means any vessel that is equipped with one or more trawl nets and that is capable of, or used for, fishing for shrimp, or whose on-board or landed catch of shrimp is more than 1 percent, by weight, of all fish comprising its on-board or landed catch.

Skimmer trawl means a trawl that is fished along the side of the vessel and is held open by a rigid frame and a lead weight. On its outboard side, the trawl is held open by one side of the frame extending downward and, on its inboard side, by a lead weight attached by cable or rope to the bow of the vessel.

Southeast Regional Administrator means the Regional Administrator for the Southeast Region of the National Marine Fisheries Service, National Oceanic and Atmospheric Administration, U.S. Department of Commerce, or their authorized representative. Mail sent to the Southeast Regional Administrator should be addressed: Southeast Regional Administrator, F/SE, Southeast Regional Office, National Marine Fisheries Service, NOAA, 9721 Executive Center Drive N., St. Petersburg, FL 33702-2432.

Southwest Regional Administrator means the Regional Administrator for the Southwest Region of the National Marine Fisheries Service, National Oceanic and Atmospheric Administration, U.S. Department of Commerce, or their authorized representative. Mail sent to the Southwest Regional Administrator should be addressed: Southwest Regional Administrator, F/SW, Southwest Regional Office, National Marine Fisheries Service, NOAA, 501 West Ocean Blvd, Suite 4200, Long Beach, CA 90802-4213.

Stretched mesh size means the distance between the centers of the two opposite knots in the same mesh when pulled taut.

Summer flounder means the species *Paralichthys dentatus.*

Summer flounder fishery-sea turtle protection area means all offshore waters, bounded on the north by a line along 37<<degrees>> 05' N. lat. (Cape Charles, VA) and bounded on the south by a line extending in a direction of 135<<degrees>> 34'55" from true north from the North Carolina-South Carolina land boundary, as marked by the border station on Bird Island at 33<<degrees>> 51'07.9" N. lat., 078<<degrees>> 32'32.6" W. long. (the North Carolina-South Carolina border).

Summer flounder trawler means any vessel that is equipped with one or more bottom trawl nets and that is capable of, or used for, fishing for flounder or whose on-board or landed catch of flounder is more than 100 lb (45.4 kg).

Take means to harass, harm, pursue, hunt, shoot, wound, kill, trap, capture, or collect, or to attempt to harass, harm, pursue, hunt, shoot, wound, kill, trap, capture, or collect.

Taper, in reference to the webbing used in trawls, means the angle of a cut used to shape the webbing, expressed as the ratio between the cuts that reduce the width of the webbing by cutting into the panel of webbing through one row of twine (bar cuts) and the cuts that extend the length of the panel of webbing by cutting straight aft through two adjoining rows of twine (point cuts). For example, sequentially cutting through the lengths of twine on opposite sides of a mesh, leaving an uncut edge of twines all lying in the same line, produces a relatively strong taper called "all-bars"; making a sequence of 4-bar cuts followed by 1-point cut produces a more gradual taper called "4 bars to 1 point" or "4b1p"; similarly, making a sequence of 2-bar cuts followed by 1- point cut produces a still more gradual taper called "2b1p"; and making a sequence of cuts straight aft does not reduce the width of the panel and is called a "straight" or "all-points" cut.

Taut means a condition in which there is no slack in the net webbing.

Test net, or *try net,* means a net pulled for brief periods of time just before, or during, deployment of the primary net(s) in order to test for shrimp concentrations or determine fishing conditions (*e.g.,* presence or absence of bottom debris, jellyfish, bycatch, seagrasses, etc.).

Tongue means any piece of webbing along the top, center, leading edge of a trawl, whether lying behind or ahead of the headrope, to which a towing bridle can be attached for purposes of pulling the trawl net and/or adjusting the shape of the trawl.

Transportation means to ship, convey, carry or transport by any means whatever, and deliver or receive for such shipment, conveyance, carriage, or transportation.

Triple-wing trawl means a trawl with a tongue on the top, center, leading edge of the trawl and an additional tongue along the bottom, center, leading edge of the trawl.

Two-seam trawl means a design of shrimp trawl in which the main body of the trawl is formed from a top and a bottom panel of webbing that are directly attached to each other down the sides of the trawl.

Underway with respect to a vessel, means that the vessel is not at anchor, or made fast to the shore, or aground.

Unforeseen circumstances means changes in circumstances affecting a species or geographic area covered by a conservation plan that could not reasonably have been anticipated by plan developers and NMFS at the time of the conservation plan's negotiation and development, and that result in a substantial and adverse change in the status of the covered species.

Vessel means a vehicle used, or capable of being used, as a means of transportation on water which includes every description of watercraft, including nondisplacement craft and seaplanes.

Vessel restricted in her ability to maneuver has the meaning specified for this term at 33 U.S.C. 2003(g).

Wildlife means any member of the animal kingdom, including without limitation any mammal, fish, bird (including any migratory, nonmigratory, or endangered bird for which protection is also afforded by treaty or other international agreement), amphibian, reptile, mollusk, crustacean, arthropod or other invertebrate, and includes any part, product, egg, or offspring thereof, or the dead body or parts thereof.

Wing net (butterfly trawl) means a trawl that is fished along the side of the vessel and that is held open by a four-sided, rigid frame attached to the outrigger of the vessel.

[64 FR 60731, Nov. 8, 1999; 67 FR 13101, March 21, 2002]

§ 222.103 Federal/state cooperation in the conservation of endangered and threatened species.

(a) Application for and renewal of cooperative agreements.

(1) The Assistant Administrator may enter into a Cooperative Agreement with any

state that establishes and maintains an active and adequate program for the conservation of resident species listed as endangered or threatened. In order for a state program to be deemed an adequate and active program, the Assistant Administrator must find, and annually reconfirm that the criteria of either sections 6(c)(1)(A) through (E) or sections 6(c)(1)(i) and (ii) of the Act have been satisfied.

(2) Following receipt of an application by a state for a Cooperative Agreement with a copy of a proposed state program, and a determination by the Assistant Administrator that the state program is adequate and active, the Assistant Administrator shall enter into an Agreement with the state.

(3) The Cooperative Agreement, as well as the Assistant Administrator's finding upon which it is based, must be reconfirmed annually to ensure that it reflects new laws, species lists, rules or regulations, and programs and to demonstrate that it is still adequate and active.

(b) Allocation and availability of funds.

(1) The Assistant Administrator shall allocate funds, appropriated for the purpose of carrying out section 6 of the Act, to various states using the following as the basis for the determination:

(i) The international commitments of the United States to protect endangered or threatened species;

(ii) The readiness of a state to proceed with a conservation program consistent with the objectives and purposes of the Act;

(iii) The number of federally listed endangered and threatened species within a state;

(iv) The potential for restoring endangered and threatened species within a state; and

(v) The relative urgency to initiate a program to restore and protect an endangered or threatened species in terms of survival of the species.

(2) Funds allocated to a state are available for obligation during the fiscal year for which they are allocated and until the close of the succeeding fiscal year. Obligation of allocated funds occurs when an award or contract is signed by the Assistant Administrator.

(c) Financial assistance and payments.

(1) A state must enter into a Cooperative Agreement before financial assistance is approved by the Assistant Administrator for endangered or threatened species projects. Specifically, the Agreement must contain the actions that are to be taken by the Assistant Administrator and/or by the state, the benefits to listed species expected to be derived from these actions, and the estimated cost of these actions.

(2) Subsequent to such Agreement, the Assistant Administrator may further agree with a state to provide financial assistance in the development and implementation of acceptable projects for the conservation of endangered and threatened species. Documents to provide financial assistance will consist of an application for Federal assistance and an award or a contract. The availability of Federal funds shall be contingent upon the continued existence of the Cooperative Agreement and compliance with all applicable Federal regulations for grant administration and cost accounting principles.

(3)(i) The payment of the Federal share of costs incurred when conducting activities included under a contract or award shall not exceed 75 percent of the program costs as stated in the agreement. However, the Federal share may be increased to 90 percent when two or more states having a common interest in one or more endangered or threatened resident species, the conservation of which may be enhanced by cooperation of such states, jointly enter into an agreement with the Assistant Administrator.

(ii) The state share of program costs may be in the form of cash or in-kind contributions, including real property, subject to applicable Federal regulations.

(4) Payments of funds, including payment of such preliminary costs and expenses as may be incurred in connection with projects, shall not be made unless all necessary or required documents are first submitted to and approved by the Assistant Administrator. Payments shall only be made for expenditures reported and certified by the state agency. Payments shall be made only to the state office or official designated by the state agency and authorized under the laws of the state to receive public funds for the state.

SUBPART B -- CERTIFICATES OF EXEMPTION FOR PRE-ACT ENDANGERED SPECIES PARTS

§ 222.201 General requirements.

(a) The Assistant Administrator may exempt any pre-Act endangered species part from the prohibitions of sections 9(a)(1)(A), 9(a)(1)(E), or 9(a)(1)(F) of the Act.

(1) No person shall engage in any activities identified in such sections of the Act that involve any pre-Act endangered species part without a valid Certificate of Exemption issued pursuant to this subpart B.

(2) No person may export, deliver, receive, carry, transport or ship in interstate or foreign commerce in the course of a commercial activity; or sell or offer for sale in interstate or foreign commerce any pre-Act finished scrimshaw product unless that person has been issued a valid Certificate of Exemption and the product or the raw material for such product was held by such certificate holder on October 13, 1982.

(3) Any person engaged in activities otherwise prohibited under the Act or regulations shall bear the burden of proving that the exemption or certificate is applicable, was granted, and was valid and in force at the time of the otherwise prohibited activity.

(b) Certificates of Exemption issued under this subpart are no longer available to new applicants. However, the Assistant Administrator may renew or modify existing Certificates of Exemptions as authorized by the provisions set forth in this subpart.

(c) Any person granted a Certificate of Exemption, including a renewal, under this subpart, upon a sale of any exempted pre-Act endangered species part, must provide the purchaser in writing with a description (including full identification number) of the part sold and must inform the purchaser in writing of the purchaser's obligation under paragraph (b) of this section, including the address given in the certificate to which the purchaser's report is to be sent.

(d) Any purchaser of pre-Act endangered species parts included in a valid Certificate of Exemption, unless an ultimate user, within 30 days after the receipt of such parts, must submit a written report to the address given in the certificate. The report must specify the quantity of such parts or products received, the name and address of the seller, a copy of the invoice or other document showing the serial numbers, weight, and descriptions of the parts or products received, the date on which such parts or products were received, and the intended use of such parts by the purchaser. The term "ultimate user", for purposes of this paragraph, means any person who acquired such endangered species part or product for his or her own consumption or for other personal use (including gifts) and not for resale.

§ 222.202 Certificate renewal.

(a) Any person to whom a Certificate of Exemption has been issued by the National Marine Fisheries Service may apply to the Assistant Administrator for renewal of such certificate. Any person holding a valid Certificate of Exemption which was renewed after October 13, 1982, and was in effect on March 31, 1988, may apply to the Secretary for one renewal for a period not to exceed 5 years.

(b) The sufficiency of the application shall be determined by the Assistant Administrator in accordance with the requirements of paragraph (c) of this section. At least 15 days should be allowed for processing. When an application for a renewal has been received and deemed sufficient, the Assistant Administrator shall issue a Certificate of Renewal to the applicant as soon as practicable.

(c) The following information will be used as the basis for determining whether an application for renewal of a Certificate of Exemption is complete:

(1) Title: Application for Renewal of Certificate of Exemption.

(2) The date of application.

(3) The identity of the applicant, including complete name, original Certificate of Exemption number, current address, and telephone number. If the applicant is a corporation, partnership, or association, set forth the details.

(4) The period of time for which a renewal of the Certificate of Exemption is requested. However, no renewal of Certificate of Exemption, or right claimed thereunder, shall be effective after the close of the 5-year period beginning on the date of the expiration of the previous renewal of the certificate of exemption.

(5)(i) A complete and detailed updated inventory of all pre-Act endangered species parts for which the applicant seeks exemption. Each item on the inventory must be identified by the following information: A unique serial number; the weight of the item to the nearest whole gram; and a detailed description sufficient to permit ready identification of the item. Small lots, not exceeding five pounds (2,270 grams), of scraps or raw material, which may include or consist of one or more whole raw whale teeth, may be identified by a single serial number and total weight. All finished scrimshaw items subsequently made from a given lot of scrap may be identified by the lot serial number plus additional digits to signify the piece number of the individual finished item. Identification numbers will be in the following format: 00-000000-0000. The first two digits will be the last two digits of the appropriate certificate of exemption number; the next six digits, the serial number of the individual piece or lot of scrap or raw material; and the last four digits, where applicable, the piece number of an item made from a lot of scrap or raw material. The serial numbers for each certificate holder's inventory must begin with 000001, and piece numbers, where applicable, must begin with 0001 for each separate lot.

(ii) Identification numbers may be affixed to inventory items by any means, including, but not limited to, etching the number into the item, attaching a label or tag bearing the number to the item, or sealing the item in a plastic bag, wrapper or other container bearing the number. The number must remain affixed to the item until the item is sold to an ultimate user, as defined in § 222.201(d).

(iii) No renewals will be issued for scrimshaw products in excess of any quantities declared in the original application for a Certificate of Exemption.

(6) A Certification in the following language: I hereby certify that the foregoing information is complete, true, and correct to the best of my knowledge and belief. I understand that this information is submitted for the purpose of obtaining a renewal of my Certificate of Exemption under the Endangered Species Act, as amended, and the Department of Commerce regulations issued thereunder, and that any false statement may subject me to the criminal penalties of 18 U.S.C. 1001, or to the penalties under the Act.

(7) Signature of the applicant.

(d) Upon receipt of an incomplete or improperly executed application for renewal, the applicant shall be notified of the deficiency in the application for renewal. If the application for renewal is not corrected and received by the Assistant Administrator within 30 days following the date of receipt of notification, the application for renewal shall be considered abandon.

§ 222.203 Modification, amendment, suspension, and revocation of certificates.

(a) When circumstances have changed so that an applicant or certificate holder desires to have any material, term, or condition of the application or certificate modified, the applicant or certificate holder must submit in writing full justification and supporting information in conformance with the provisions of this part.

(b) All certificates are issued subject to the condition that the Assistant Administrator reserves the right to amend the provisions of a Certificate of Exemption for just cause at any time. Such amendments take effect on the date of notification, unless otherwise specified.

(c) Any violation of the applicable provisions of parts 222, 223, or 224 of this chapter, or of the Act, or of a condition of the certificate may subject the certificate holder to penalties provided in the Act and to suspension, revocation, or modification of the Certificate of Exemption, as provided in subpart D of 15 CFR part 904.

§ 222.204 Administration of certificates.

(a) The Certificate of Exemption covers the business or activity specified in the Certificate of Exemption at the address described therein. No Certificate of Exemption is required to cover a separate warehouse facility used by the certificate holder solely for storage of pre-Act endangered species parts, if the records required by this subpart are maintained at the address specified in the Certificate of Exemption served by the warehouse or storage facility.

(b) Certificates of Exemption issued under this subpart are not transferable. However, in the event of the lease, sale, or other transfer of the operations or activity authorized by the Certificate of Exemption, the successor is not required to obtain a new Certificate of Exemption prior to commencing such operations or activity. In such case, the successor will be treated as a purchaser and must comply with the record and reporting requirements set forth in § 222.201(d).

(c) The Certificate of Exemption holder must notify the Assistant Administrator, in writing, of any change in address, in trade name of the business, or in activity specified in the certificate. The Assistant Administrator must be notified within 10 days of a change of address, and within 30 days of a change in trade name. The certificate with the change of address or in trade name must be endorsed by the Assistant Administrator, who shall provide an amended certificate to the person to whom it was issued. A certificate holder who seeks amendment of a certificate may continue all authorized activities while awaiting action by the Assistant Administrator.

(d) A Certificate of Exemption issued under this subpart confers no right or privilege to conduct a business or an activity contrary to state or other law. Similarly, compliance with the provisions of any state or other law affords no immunity under any Federal laws or regulations of any other Federal agency.

(e) Any person authorized to enforce the Act may enter the premises of any Certificate of Exemption holder or of any purchaser during business hours, including places of storage, for the purpose of inspecting or of examining any records or documents and any endangered species parts.

(f) The records pertaining to pre-Act endangered species parts prescribed by this subpart shall be in permanent form and shall be retained at the address shown on the Certificate of Exemption or at the principal address of a purchaser in the manner prescribed by this subpart.

(g)(1) Holders of Certificates of Exemption must maintain records of all pre- Act endangered species parts they receive, sell, transfer, distribute or dispose of otherwise. Purchasers of pre-Act endangered species parts, unless ultimate users, as defined in § 222.201(d), must similarly maintain records of all such parts or products they receive.

(2) Such records referred to in paragraph (g)(1) of this section may consist of invoices or other commercial records, which must be filed in an orderly manner separate from other commercial records maintained and be readily available for inspection. Such records must show the name and address of the purchaser, seller, or other transferor; show the type, quantity, and identity of the part or product; show the date of such sale or transfer; and be retained, in accordance with the requirements of this subpart, for a period of not less than 3 years following the date of sale or transfer. Each pre-Act endangered species part will be identified by its number on the updated inventory required to renew a Certificate of Exemption.

(i) Each Certificate of Exemption holder must submit a quarterly report (to the address given in the certificate) containing all record information required by paragraph (g)(2) of this section, on all transfers of pre-Act endangered species parts made in the previous calendar quarter, or such other record information the Assistant Administrator may specify from time to time.

(ii) Quarterly reports are due on January 15, April 15, July 15, and October 15.

(3) The Assistant Administrator may authorize the record information to be submitted in a manner other than that prescribed in paragraph (g)(2) of this section when the record holder demonstrates that an alternate method of reporting is reasonably necessary and will not hinder the effective administration or enforcement of this subpart.

§ 222.205 Import and export requirements.

(a) Any fish and wildlife subject to the jurisdiction of the National Marine Fisheries Service and is intended for importation into or exportation from the United States, shall not be imported or exported except at a port(s) designated by the Secretary of the Interior. Shellfish and fishery products that are neither endangered nor threatened species and that are imported for purposes of human or animal consumption or taken in waters under the jurisdiction of the United States or on the high seas for recreational purposes are excluded from this requirement. The Secretary of the Interior may permit the importation or exportation at nondesignated ports in the interest of the health or safety of the species for other reasons if the Secretary deems it appropriate and consistent with the purpose of facilitating enforcement of the Act and reducing the costs thereof. Importers and exporters are advised to see 50 CFR part 14 for importation and exportation requirements and information.

(b) No pre-Act endangered species part shall be imported into the United States. A Certificate of Exemption issued in accordance with the provisions of this subpart confers no right or privilege to import into the United States any such part.

(c)(1) Any person exporting from the United States any pre-Act endangered species part must possess a valid Certificate of Exemption issued in accordance with the provisions of this subpart. In addition, the exporter must provide to the Assistant Administrator, in writing, not less than 10 days prior to shipment, the following information: The name and address of the foreign consignee, the intended port of exportation, and a complete description of the parts to be exported. No shipment may be made until these requirements are met by the exporter.

(2) The exporter must send a copy of the Certificate of Exemption, and any endorsements thereto, to the District Director of Customs at the port of exportation, which must precede or accompany the shipment in order to permit the appropriate inspection prior to lading. Upon receipt, the District Director may order such inspection, as deemed necessary; the District will clear the merchandise for export, prior to the lading of the merchandise. If they are satisfied that the shipment is proper and complies with the information contained in the certificate and any endorsement thereto. The certificate, and any endorsements, will be forwarded to the Chief of the Office of Enforcement for NMFS.

(3) No pre-Act endangered species part in compliance with the requirements of this subpart may be exported except at a port or ports designated by the Secretary of the Interior, pursuant to § 222.103.

(4) Notwithstanding any provision of this subpart, it shall not be required that the Assistant Administrator authorizes the transportation in interstate or foreign commerce of pre-Act endangered species parts.

SUBPART C -- GENERAL PERMIT PROCEDURES

§ 222.301 General requirements.

(a)(1) The regulations in this subpart C provide uniform rules and procedures for application, issuance, renewal, conditions, and general administration of permits issuable pursuant to parts 222, 223, and 224 of this chapter. While this section provides generic rules and procedures applicable to all permits, other sections may provide more specific rules and procedures with respect to certain types of permits. In such cases, the requirements in all applicable sections must be satisfied.

(2) Notwithstanding paragraph (a)(1) of this section, the Assistant Administrator may approve variations from the requirements of parts 222, 223, and 224 of this chapter when the Assistant Administrator finds that an emergency exists and that the proposed variations will not hinder effective administration of those parts and will not be unlawful. Other sections within parts 222, 223, and 224 of this chapter may allow for a waiver or variation of specific requirements for emergency situations, upon certain conditions. In such cases, those conditions must be satisfied in order for the waiver or variation to be lawful.

(b) No person shall take, import, export or engage in any other prohibited activity involving any species of fish or wildlife under the jurisdiction of the Secretary of Commerce that has been determined to be endangered under the Act, or that has been determined to be threatened and for which the prohibitions of section 9(a)(1) of the Act have been applied by regulation, without a valid permit issued pursuant to these regulations. The permit shall entitle the person to whom it is issued to engage in the activity specified in the permit, subject to the limitations of the Act and the regulations in parts 222, 223, and 224 of this chapter, for the period stated on the permit, unless sooner modified, suspended or revoked.

(c) Each person intending to engage in an activity for which a permit is required by parts 222, 223, and 224 of this chapter or by the Act shall, before commencing such activity, obtain a valid permit authorizing such activity. Any person who desires to obtain permit privileges authorized by parts 222, 223, and 224 of this chapter must apply for such permit in accordance with the requirements of these sections. If the information required for each specific, permitted activity is included, one application may be accepted for all permits required, and a single permit may be issued.

(d)(1) Any permit issued under these regulations must be in the possession of the person to whom it is issued (or of an agent of such person) while any animal subject to the permit is in the possession of such person or agent. Specifically, a person or his/her agent must be in possession of a permit during the time of the authorized taking, importation, exportation, or of any other act and during the period of any transit incident to such taking, importation, exportation, or to any other act.

(2) A duplicate copy of the issued permit must be physically attached to the tank, container, package, enclosure, or other means of containment, in which the animal is placed for purposes of storage, transit, supervision, or care.

(e) The authorizations on the face of a permit setting forth specific times, dates, places, methods of taking, numbers and kinds of fish or wildlife, location of activity, authorize certain circumscribed transactions, or otherwise permit a specifically limited matter, are to be strictly construed and shall not be interpreted to permit similar or related matters outside the scope of strict construction.

(f) Permits shall not be altered, erased, or mutilated, and any permit which has been altered, erased, or mutilated shall immediately become invalid.

(g) Any permit issued under parts 222, 223, and 224 of this chapter shall be displayed for inspection, upon request, to an authorized officer, or to any other person relying upon its existence.

(h) Permittees may be required to file reports of the activities conducted under the permit. Any such reports shall be filed not later than March 31 for the preceding calendar year ending December 31, or any portion thereof, during which a permit was in force, unless the regulations of parts 222, 223, or 224 of this chapter or the provisions of the permit set forth other reporting requirements.

(i) From the date of issuance of the permit, the permittee shall maintain complete and accurate records of any taking, possession, transportation, sale, purchase, barter, exportation, or importation of fish or wildlife pursuant to such permit. Such records shall be kept current and shall include the names and addresses of persons with whom any fish or wildlife has been purchased, sold, bartered, or otherwise transferred, and the date of such transaction, and such other information as may be required or appropriate. Such records, unless otherwise specified, shall be entered in books, legibly written in the English language. Such records shall be retained for 5 years from the date of issuance of the permit.

(j) Any person holding a permit pursuant to parts 222, 223, and 224 of this chapter shall allow the Assistant Administrator to enter the permit holder's premises at any reasonable hour to inspect any fish or wildlife held or to inspect, audit, or copy any permits, books, or records required to be kept by these regulations or by the Act. Such person shall display any permit issued pursuant to these regulations or to the Act upon request by an authorized officer or by any other person relying on its existence.

§ 222.302 Procedure for obtaining permits.

(a) Applications must be submitted to the Assistant Administrator, by letter containing all necessary information, attachments, certification, and signature, as specified by the regulations in parts 222, 223, and 224 of this chapter, or by the Act. In no case, other than for emergencies pursuant to § 222.301(a)(2), will applications be accepted either orally or by telephone.

(b) Applications must be received by the Assistant Administrator at least 90 calendar days prior to the date on which the applicant desires to have the permit made effective, unless otherwise specified in the regulations or guidelines pertaining to a particular permit. The National Marine Fisheries Service will attempt to process applications deemed sufficient in the shortest possible time, but does not guarantee that the permit will be issued 90 days after notice of receipt of the application is published in the Federal Register.

(c)(1) Upon receipt of an insufficiently or improperly executed application, the applicant shall be notified of the deficiency in the application. If the applicant fails to supply the deficient information or otherwise fails to correct the deficiency within 60 days following the date of notification, the application shall be considered abandoned.

(2) The sufficiency of the application shall be determined by the Assistant Administrator in accordance with the requirements of this part. The Assistant Administrator, however, may waive any requirement for information or require any elaboration or further information deemed necessary.

§ 222.303 Issuance of permits.

(a)(1) No permit may be issued prior to the receipt of a written application unless an emergency pursuant to § 222.301(a)(2) exists, and a written variation from the requirements is recorded by the National Marine Fisheries Service.

(2) No representation of an employee or agent of the United States shall be construed as a permit unless it meets the requirements of a permit defined in § 222.102.

(3) Each permit shall bear a serial number. Upon renewal, such a number may be reassigned to the permittee to whom issued so long as the permittee maintains continuity of renewal.

(b) When an application for a permit received by the Assistant Administrator is deemed sufficient, the Assistant Administrator shall, as soon as practicable, publish a notice in the Federal Register. Information received by the Assistant Administrator as a part of the application shall be available to the public as a matter of public record at every stage of the proceeding. An interested party, within 30 days after the date of publication of such notice, may submit to the Assistant Administrator written data, views, or arguments with respect to the taking, importation, or to other action proposed in the application, and may request a hearing in connection with the action to be taken thereon.

(c) If a request for a hearing is made within the 30-day period referred to in paragraph (b) of this section, or if the Assistant Administrator determines that a hearing would otherwise be advisable, the Assistant Administrator may, within 60 days after the date of publication of the notice referred to in paragraph (b) of this section, afford to such requesting party or parties an opportunity for a hearing. Such hearing shall also be open to participation by any interested members of the public. Notice of the date, time, and place of such hearing shall be published in the Federal Register not less than 15 days in advance of such hearing. Any interested person may appear at the hearing in person or through a representative and may submit any relevant material, data, views, comments, arguments, or exhibits. A summary record of the hearing shall be kept.

(d) Except as provided in subpart D to 15 CFR part 904, as soon as practicable but not later than 30 days after the close of the hearing. If no hearing is held, as soon as practicable but not later than 30 days from the publication of the notice in the Federal Register, the Assistant Administrator shall issue or deny issuance of the permit. Notice of the decision of the Assistant Administrator shall be published in the Federal Register within 10 days after the date of the issuance or denial and indicate where copies of the permit, if issued, may be obtained.

(e)(1) The Assistant Administrator shall issue the permit unless:

(i) Denial of the permit has been made pursuant to subpart D to 15 CFR part 904;

(ii) The applicant has failed to disclose material or information required, or has made false statements as to any material fact, in connection with the application;

(iii) The applicant has failed to demonstrate a valid justification for the permit or a showing of responsibility;

(iv) The authorization requested potentially threatens a fish or wildlife population; or

(v) The Assistant Administrator finds through further inquiry or investigation, or otherwise, that the applicant is not qualified.

(2) The applicant shall be notified in writing of the denial of any permit request, and the reasons thereof. If authorized in the notice of denial, the applicant may submit further information or reasons why the permit should not be denied. Such further information shall not be considered a new application. The final action by the Assistant Administrator shall be considered the final administrative decision of the Department of Commerce.

(f) If a permit is issued under § 222.308, the Assistant Administrator shall publish notice thereof in the Federal Register, including the Assistant Administrator's finding that such permit--

(1) Was applied for in good faith;

(2) Will not operate to the disadvantage of such endangered species; and

(3) Will be consistent with the purposes and policy set forth in section 2 of the Act.

(g) The Assistant Administrator may waive the 30-day period in an emergency situation where the health or life of an endangered animal is threatened and no reasonable alternative is available to the applicant. Notice of any such waiver shall be published by the Assistant Administrator in the Federal Register within 10 days following the issuance of the permit.

§ 222.304 Renewal of permits.

When the permit is renewable and a permittee intends to continue the activity described in the permit during any portion of the year ensuing its expiration, the permittee shall, unless otherwise notified in writing by the Assistant Administrator, file a request for permit renewal, together with a certified statement, verifying that the information in the original application is still currently correct. If the information is incorrect the permittee shall file a statement of all changes in the original application, accompanied by any required fee at least 30 days prior to the expiration of the permit. Any person holding a valid renewable permit, who has complied with the foregoing provision of this section, may continue such activities as were authorized by the expired permit until the renewal application is acted upon.

§ 222.305 Rights of succession and transfer of permits.

(a)(1) Permits issued pursuant to parts 222, 223, and 224 of this chapter are not transferable or assignable. In the event that a permit authorizes certain activities in connection with a business or commercial enterprise, which is then subject to any subsequent lease, sale or transfer, the successor to that enterprise must obtain a permit prior to continuing the permitted activity, with the exceptions provided in paragraph (a)(2) of this section.

(2) Certain persons, other than the permittee, are granted the right to carry on a permitted activity for the remainder of the term of a current permit, provided that they furnish the permit to the issuing officer for endorsement within 90 days from the date the successor begins to carry on the activity. Such persons are the following:

(i) The surviving spouse, child, executor, administrator, or other legal representative of a deceased permittee, and

(ii) The receiver or trustee in bankruptcy or a court designated assignee for the benefit of creditors.

(b) Except as otherwise stated on the face of the permit, any person who is under the direct control of the permittee, or who is employed by or under contract to the permittee for purposes authorized by the permit, may carry out the activity authorized by the permit.

§ 222.306 Modification, amendment, suspension, cancellation, and revocation of permits.

(a) When circumstances have changed so that an applicant or a permittee desires to have any term or condition of the application or permit modified, the applicant or permittee must submit in writing full justification and supporting information in conformance with the provisions of this part and the part under which the permit has been issued or requested. Such applications for modification are subject to the same issuance criteria as original applications.

(b) Notwithstanding the requirements of paragraph (a) of this section, a permittee may change the mailing address or trade name under which business is conducted without obtaining a new permit or being subject to the same issuance criteria as original permits. The permittee must notify the Assistant Administrator, in writing within 30 days, of any change in address or of any change in the trade name for the business or activity specified in the permit. The permit with the change of address or in trade name must be endorsed by the Assistant Administrator, who shall provide an amended permit to the person to whom it was issued.

(c) All permits are issued subject to the condition that the National Marine Fisheries Service reserves the right to amend the provisions of a permit for just cause at any time during its term. Such amendments take effect on the date of notification, unless otherwise specified.

(d) When any permittee discontinues the permitted activity, the permittee shall, within 30 days thereof, mail the permit and a request for cancellation to the Issuing officer, and the permit shall be deemed void upon receipt. No refund of any part of an amount paid as a permit fee shall be made when the operations of the permittee are, for any reason, discontinued during the tenure of an issued permit.

(e) Any violation of the applicable provisions of parts 222, 223, or 224 of this chapter, or of the Act, or of a term or condition of the permit may subject the permittee to both the penalties provided in the Act and suspension, revocation, or amendment of the permit, as provided in subpart D to 15 CFR part 904.

§ 222.307 Permits for incidental taking of species.

(a) *Scope.*

(1) The Assistant Administrator may issue permits to take endangered and threatened species incidentally to an otherwise lawful activity under section 10(a)(1)(B) of the Act. The regulations in this section apply to all endangered species, and those threatened species for which the prohibitions of section 9(a)(1) of the Act, under the jurisdiction of the Secretary of Commerce, apply.

(2) If the applicant represents an individual or a single entity, such as a corporation, the Assistant Administrator will issue an individual incidental take permit. If the applicant represents a group or organization whose members conduct the same or a similar activity in the same geographical area with similar impacts on listed species for which a permit is required, the Assistant Administrator will issue a general incidental take permit. To be covered by a general incidental take permit, each individual conducting the activity must have a certificate of inclusion issued under paragraph (f) of this section.

(b) *Permit application procedures.* Applications should be sent to the Assistant Administrator. The Assistant Administrator shall determine the sufficiency of the application in accordance with the requirements of this section. At least 120 days should be allowed for processing. Each application must be signed and dated and must include the following:

(1) The type of application, either:

(i) Application for an Individual Incidental Take Permit under the Act; or

(ii) Application for a General Incidental Take Permit under the Act;

(2) The name, address, and telephone number of the applicant. If the applicant is a partnership or a corporate entity or is representing a group or an organization, the applicable details;

(3) The species or stocks, by common and scientific name, and a description of the status, distribution, seasonal distribution, habitat needs, feeding habits and other biological requirements of the affected species or stocks;

(4) A detailed description of the proposed activity, including the anticipated dates, duration, and specific location. If the request is for a general incidental take permit, an estimate of the total level of activity expected to be conducted;

(5) A conservation plan, based on the best scientific and commercial data available, which specifies the following:

(i) The anticipated impact (*i.e.,* amount, extent, and type of anticipated taking) of the proposed activity on the species or stocks;

(ii) The anticipated impact of the proposed activity on the habitat of the species or stocks and the likelihood of restoration of the affected habitat;

(iii) The steps (specialized equipment, methods of conducting activities, or other means) that will be taken to monitor, minimize, and mitigate such impacts, and the funding available to implement such measures;

(iv) The alternative actions to such taking that were considered and the reasons why those alternatives are not being used; and

(v) A list of all sources of data used in preparation of the plan, including reference reports, environmental assessments and impact statements, and personal communications with recognized experts on the species or activity who may have access to data not published in current literature.

(c) *Issuance criteria.*

(1) In determining whether to issue a permit, the Assistant Administrator will consider the following:

(i) The status of the affected species or stocks;

(ii) The potential severity of direct, indirect, and cumulative impacts on the species or stocks and habitat as a result of the proposed activity;

(iii) The availability of effective monitoring techniques;

(iv) The use of the best available technology for minimizing or mitigating impacts; and

(v) The views of the public, scientists, and other interested parties knowledgeable of the species or stocks or other matters related to the application.

(2) To issue the permit, the Assistant Administrator must find that--

(i) The taking will be incidental;

(ii) The applicant will, to the maximum extent practicable, monitor, minimize, and mitigate the impacts of such taking;

(iii) The taking will not appreciably reduce the likelihood of the survival and recovery of the species in the wild;

(iv) The applicant has amended the conservation plan to include any measures (not originally proposed by the applicant) that the Assistant Administrator determines are necessary or appropriate; and

(v) There are adequate assurances that the conservation plan will be funded and implemented, including any measures required by the Assistant Administrator.

(d) *Permit conditions.* In addition to the general conditions set forth in this part, every permit issued under this section will contain such terms and conditions as the Assistant Administrator deems necessary and appropriate, including, but not limited to the following:

(1) Reporting requirements or rights of inspection for determining whether the terms and conditions are being complied with;

(2) The species and number of animals covered;

(3) The authorized method of taking;

(4) The procedures to be used to handle or dispose of any animals taken; and

(5) The payment of an adequate fee to the National Marine Fisheries Service to process the application.

(e) *Duration of permits.* The duration of permits issued under this section will be such as to provide adequate assurances to the permit holder to commit funding necessary for the activities authorized by the permit, including conservation activities. In determining the duration of a permit, the Assistant Administrator will consider the duration of the proposed activities, as well as the possible positive and negative effects on listed species associated with issuing a permit of the proposed duration, including the extent to which the conservation plan is likely to enhance the habitat of the endangered species or to increase the long-term survivability of the species.

(f) *Certificates of inclusion.*

(1) Any individual who wishes to conduct an activity covered by a general incidental take permit must apply to the Assistant Administrator for a Certificate of Inclusion. Each application must be signed and dated and must include the following:

(i) The general incidental take permit under which the applicant wants coverage;

(ii) The name, address, and telephone number of the applicant. If the applicant is a partnership or a corporate entity, the applicable details;

(iii) A description of the activity the applicant seeks to have covered under the general incidental take permit, including the anticipated dates, duration, and specific location; and

(iv) A signed certification that the applicant has read and understands the general incidental take permit and the conservation plan, will comply with their terms and conditions, and will fund and implement applicable measures of the conservation plan.

(2) To issue a Certificate of Inclusion, the Assistant Administrator must find that:

(i) The applicant will be engaged in the activity covered by the general permit, and

(ii) The applicant has made adequate assurances that the applicable measures of the conservation plan will be funded and implemented.

(g) *Assurances provided to permittee in case of changed or unforeseen circumstances.* The assurances in this paragraph (g) apply only to incidental take permits issued in accordance with paragraph (c) of this section where the conservation plan is being properly implemented, and apply only with respect to species adequately covered by the conservation plan. These assurances cannot be provided to Federal agencies. This rule does not apply to incidental take permits issued prior to March 25, 1998. The assurances provided in incidental take permits issued prior to March 25, 1998, remain in effect, and those permits will not be revised as a result of this rulemaking.

(1) *Changed circumstances provided for in the plan.* If additional conservation and mitigation measures are deemed necessary to respond to changed circumstances and were provided for in the plan's operating conservation program, the permittee will implement the measures specified in the plan.

(2) *Changed circumstances not provided for in the plan.* If additional conservation and mitigation measures are deemed necessary to respond to changed circumstances and such measures were not provided for in the plan's operating conservation program, NMFS will not require any conservation and mitigation measures in addition to those provided for in the plan without the consent of the permittee, provided the plan is being properly implemented.

(3) *Unforeseen circumstances.*

(i) In negotiating unforeseen circumstances, NMFS will not require the commitment of additional land, water, or financial compensation or additional restrictions on the use of land, water, or other natural resources beyond the level otherwise agreed upon for the species covered by the conservation plan without the consent of the permittee.

(ii) If additional conservation and mitigation measures are deemed necessary to respond to unforeseen circumstances, NMFS may require additional measures of the permittee where the conservation plan is being properly implemented. However, such additional measures are limited to modifications within any conserved habitat areas or to the conservation plan's operating conservation program for the affected species. The original terms of the conservation plan will be maintained to the maximum extent possible. Additional conservation and mitigation measures will not involve the commitment of additional land, water, or financial compensation or additional restrictions on the use of land, water, or other natural resources otherwise available for development or use under the original terms of the conservation plan without the consent of the permittee.

(iii) NMFS has the burden of demonstrating that unforeseen circumstances exist, using the best scientific and commercial data available. These findings must be clearly documented and based upon reliable technical information regarding the status and habitat requirements of the affected species. NMFS will consider, but not be limited to, the following factors:

(A) Size of the current range of the affected species;

(B) Percentage of range adversely affected by the conservation plan;

(C) Percentage of range conserved by the conservation plan;

(D) Ecological significance of that portion of the range affected by the conservation plan;

(E) Level of knowledge about the affected species and the degree of specificity of the species' conservation program under the conservation plan; and

(F) Whether failure to adopt additional conservation measures would appreciably reduce the likelihood of survival and recovery of the affected species in the wild.

(h) Nothing in this rule will be construed to limit or constrain the Assistant Administrator, any Federal, State, local, or Tribal government agency, or a private entity, from taking additional actions at his or her own expense to protect or conserve a species included in a conservation plan.

§ 222.308 Permits for scientific purposes or for the enhancement of propagation or survival of species.

(a) *Scope.* The Assistant Administrator may issue permits for scientific purposes or for the enhancement of the propagation or survival of the affected endangered or threatened species in accordance with the regulations in parts 222, 223, and 224 of this chapter and under such terms and conditions as the Assistant Administrator may prescribe, authorizing the taking, importation, or other acts otherwise prohibited by section 9 of the Act. Within the jurisdiction of a State, more restrictive state laws or regulations in regard to endangered species shall prevail in regard to taking. Proof of compliance with applicable state laws will be required before a permit will be issued.

(b) *Application procedures.* Any person desiring to obtain such a permit may make application therefor to the Assistant Administrator. Permits for marine mammals shall be issued in accordance with the provisions of part 216, subpart D of this chapter. Permits relating to sea turtles may involve the Fish and Wildlife Service, in which case the applicant shall follow the procedures set out in § 222.309. The following information will be used as the basis for determining whether an application is complete and whether a permit for scientific purposes or for enhancement of propagation or survival of the affected species should be issued by the Assistant Administrator. An application for a permit shall provide the following information and such other information that the Assistant Administrator may require:

(1) Title, as applicable, either--

(i) Application for permit for scientific purposes under the Act; or

(ii) Application for permit for the enhancement of the propagation or survival of the endangered species Under the Act.

(2) The date of the application.

(3) The identity of the applicant including complete name, address, and telephone number. If the applicant is a partnership or a corporate entity, set forth the details. If the endangered species is to be utilized by a person other than the applicant, set forth the name of that person and such other information as would be required if such person were an applicant.

(4) A description of the purpose of the proposed acts, including the following:

(i) A detailed justification of the need for the endangered species, including a discussion of possible alternatives, whether or not under the control of the applicant; and

(ii) A detailed description of how the species will be used.

(5) A detailed description of the project, or program, in which the endangered species is to be used, including the following:

(i) The period of time over which the project or program will be conducted;

(ii) A list of the names and addresses of the sponsors or cooperating institutions and the scientists involved;

(iii) A copy of the formal research proposal or contract if one has been prepared;

(iv) A statement of whether the proposed project or program has broader significance than the individual researcher's goals. For example, does the proposed project or program respond directly or indirectly to recommendation of any national or international scientific body charged with research or management of the endangered species? If so, how?; and

(v) A description of the arrangements, if any, for the disposition of any dead specimen or its skeleton or other remains in a museum or other institutional collection for the continued benefit to science.

(6) A description of the endangered species which is the subject of the application, including the following:

(i) A list of each species and the number of each, including the common and scientific name, the subspecies (if applicable), population group, and range;

(ii) A physical description of each animal, including the age, size, and sex;

(iii) A list of the probable dates of capture or other taking, importation, exportation, and other acts which require a permit for each animal and the location of capture or other taking, importation, exportation, and other acts which require a permit, as specifically as possible;

(iv) A description of the status of the stock of each species related insofar as possible to the location or area of taking;

(v) A description of the manner of taking for each animal, including the gear to be used;

(vi) The name and qualifications of the persons or entity which will capture or otherwise take the animals; and

(vii) If the capture or other taking is to be done by a contractor, a statement as to whether a qualified member of your staff (include name(s) and qualifications) will supervise or observe the capture or other taking. Accompanying such statement shall be a copy of the proposed contract or a letter from the contractor indicating agreement to capture or otherwise take the animals, should a permit be granted.

(7) A description of the manner of transportation for any live animal taken, imported,

exported, or shipped in interstate commerce, including the following:

(i) Mode of transportation;

(ii) Name of transportation company;

(iii) Length of time in transit for the transfer of the animal(s) from the capture site to the holding facility;

(iv) Length of time in transit for any planned future move or transfer of the animals;

(v) The qualifications of the common carrier or agent used for transportation of the animals;

(vi) A description of the pen, tank, container, cage, cradle, or other devices used to hold the animal at both the capture site and during transportation;

(vii) Special care before and during transportation, such as salves, antibiotics, moisture; and

(viii) A statement as to whether the animals will be accompanied by a veterinarian or by another similarly qualified person, and the qualifications of such person.

(8) Describe the contemplated care and maintenance of any live animals sought, including a complete description of the facilities where any such animals will be maintained including:

(i) The dimensions of the pools or other holding facilities and the number, sex, and age of animals by species to be held in each;

(ii) The water supply, amount, and quality;

(iii) The diet, amount and type, for all animals;

(iv) Sanitation practices used;

(v) Qualifications and experience of the staff;

(vi) A written certification from a licensed veterinarian or from a recognized expert who are knowledgeable on the species (or related species) or group covered in the application. The certificate shall verify that the veterinarian has personally reviewed the amendments for transporting and maintaining the animal(s) and that, in the veterinarian's opinion, they are adequate to provide for the well-being of the animal; and

(vii) The availability in the future of a consulting expert or veterinarian meeting paragraph requirements of (b)(8)(vi) in this section.

(9) A statement of willingness to participate in a cooperative breeding program and maintain or contribute data to a stud book.

(10) A statement of how the applicant's proposed project or program will enhance or benefit the wild population.

(11) For the 5 years preceding the date of application, the applicant shall provide a detailed description of all mortalities involving species under the control of or utilized by the applicant and are either presently listed as endangered species or are taxonomically related within the Order to the species which is the subject of this application, including:

(i) A list of all endangered species and related species that are the subject of this application that have been captured, transported, maintained, or utilized by the applicant for scientific purposes or for the enhancement of propagation or survival of the affected species, and/or of related species that are captured, transported, maintained, or utilized by the applicant for scientific purposes or for enhancement of propagation or survival of the affected species;

(ii) The numbers of mortalities among such animals by species, by date, by location of capture, i.e., from which population, and the location of such mortalities;

(iii) The cause(s) of any such mortality; and

(iv) The steps which have been taken by applicant to avoid or decrease any such mortality.

(12) A certification in the following language: I hereby certify that the foregoing information is complete, true, and correct to the best of my knowledge and belief. I understand that this information is submitted for the purpose of obtaining a permit under the Endangered Species Act, as amended, and regulations promulgated thereunder, and that any false statement may subject me to the criminal penalties of 18 U.S.C. 1001, or to penalties under the Act.

(13) The applicant and/or an officer thereof must sign the application.

(14) Assistance in completing this application may be obtained by writing Chief, Endangered Species Division, Office of Protected Resources, NMFS, 1315 East-West Highway, Silver Spring, MD 20910 or calling the Office of Protected Resources at 301-713-1401. Allow at least 90 days for processing.

(c) *Issuance criteria.* In determining whether to issue a permit for scientific purposes or to enhance the propagation or survival of the affected endangered species, the Assistant Administrator shall specifically consider, among other application criteria, the following:

(1) Whether the permit was applied for in good faith;

(2) Whether the permit, if granted and exercised, will not operate to the disadvantage of the endangered species;

(3) Whether the permit would be consistent with the purposes and policy set forth in section 2 of the Act;

(4) Whether the permit would further a bona fide and necessary or desirable scientific purpose or enhance the propagation or survival of the endangered species, taking into account the benefits anticipated to be derived on behalf of the endangered species;

(5) The status of the population of the requested species and the effect of the proposed action on the population, both direct and indirect;

(6) If a live animal is to be taken, transported, or held in captivity, the applicant's qualifications for the proper care and maintenance of the species and the adequacy of the applicant's facilities;

(7) Whether alternative non-endangered species or population stocks can and should be used;

(8) Whether the animal was born in captivity or was (or will be) taken from the wild;

(9) Provision for disposition of the species if and when the applicant's project or program terminates;

(10) How the applicant's needs, program, and facilities compare and relate to proposed and ongoing projects and programs;

(11) Whether the expertise, facilities, or other resources available to the applicant appear adequate to successfully accomplish the objectives stated in the application; and

(12) Opinions or views of scientists or other persons or organizations knowledgeable about the species which is the subject of the application or of other matters germane to the application.

(d) *Terms and conditions.* Permits applied for under this section shall contain terms and conditions as the Assistant Administrator may deem appropriate, including but not limited to the following:

(1) The number and kind of species covered;

(2) The location and manner of taking;

(3) Port of entry or export;

(4) The methods of transportation, care, and maintenance to be used with live species;

(5) Any requirements for reports or rights of inspections with respect to any activities carried out pursuant to the permit;

(6) The transferability or assignability of the permit;

(7) The sale or other disposition of the species, its progeny, or the species product; and

(8) A reasonable fee covering the costs of issuance of such permit, including reasonable inspections and an appropriate apportionment of overhead and administrative expenses of the Department of Commerce. All such fees will be deposited in the Treasury to the credit of the appropriation which is current and chargeable for the cost of furnishing the service.

§ 222.309 Permits for listed species of sea turtles involving the Fish and Wildlife Service.

(a) This section establishes specific procedures for issuance of the following permits: scientific purposes or to enhance the propagation or survival of endangered or threatened species of sea turtles; zoological exhibition or educational purposes for threatened species of sea turtles; and permits that requires coordination with the Fish and Wildlife Service. The National Marine Fisheries Service maintains jurisdiction for such species in the marine environment. The Fish and Wildlife Service maintains jurisdiction for such species of sea turtles in the land environment.

(b) For permits relating to any activity in the marine environment exclusively, permit applicants and permittees must comply with the regulations in parts 222, 223, and 224 of this chapter.

(c) For permits relating to any activity in the land environment exclusively, permit applicants must submit applications to the Wildlife Permit Office (WPO) of the U.S. Fish and Wildlife Service in accordance with either 50 CFR 17.22(a), if the species is endangered, or 50 CFR 17.32(a), if the species is threatened.

(d) For permits relating to any activity in both the land and marine environments, applicants must submit applications to the WPO. WPO will forward the application to NMFS for review and processing of those activities under its jurisdiction. Based on this review and processing, WPO will issue either a permit or a letter of denial in accordance with its own regulations.

(e) For permits relating to any activity in a marine environment and that also requires a permit under the Convention on International Trade in Endangered Species of Wild Fauna and Flora (CITES) (TIAS 8249, July 1, 1975) (50 CFR part 23), applicants must submit applications to the WPO. WPO will forward the application to NMFS for review and processing, after which WPO will issue a combination ESA/CITES permit or a letter of denial.

50 C.F.R. PART 223
THREATENED MARINE AND ANADROMOUS SPECIES

SUBPART A -- GENERAL PROVISIONS

§ 223.101 Purpose and scope.

(a) The regulations contained in this part identify the species under the jurisdiction of the Secretary of Commerce that have been determined to be threatened species pursuant to section 4(a) of the Act, and provide for the conservation of such species by establishing rules and procedures to governing activities involving the species.

(b) The regulations contained in this part apply only to the threatened species enumerated in § 223.102.

(c) The provisions of this part are in addition to, and not in lieu of, other regulations of parts 222 through 226 of this chapter which prescribe additional restrictions or conditions governing threatened species.

[64 FR 14068, March 23, 1999]

§ 223.102 Enumeration of threatened marine and anadromous species.

The species determined by the Secretary of Commerce to be threatened pursuant to section 4(a) of the Act, as well as species listed under the Endangered Species Conservation of Act of 1969 by the Secretary of the Interior and currently under the jurisdiction of the Secretary of Commerce, are the following:

(a) Marine and anadromous fish. ****
(b) Marine plants. ****
(c) Marine mammals. ****
(d) Sea turtles. ****

[64 FR 14068, March 23, 1999; 64 FR 14328, March 24, 1999; 64 FR 14517, 14528, 14536, March 25, 1999; 64 FR 50415, Sept. 16, 1999; 65 FR 36094, June 7, 2000; 65 FR 60383, Oct. 11, 2000]

SUBPART B -- RESTRICTIONS

APPLICABLE TO THREATENED MARINE AND ANADROMOUS SPECIES

****

50 C.F.R. PART 224
ENDANGERED MARINE AND ANADROMOUS SPECIES

§ 224.101 Enumeration of endangered marine and anadromous species.

The marine and anadromous species determined by the Secretary of Commerce to be endangered pursuant to section 4(a) of the Act, as well as species listed under the Endangered Species Conservation Act of 1969 by the Secretary of the Interior and currently under the jurisdiction of the Secretary of Commerce, are the following:

(a) *Marine and anadromous fish.* ****
(b) *Marine mammals.* ****
(c) *Sea turtles.* ****
(d) *Marine invertebrates.*

[64 FR 14328, March 24, 1999; 65 FR 20918, April 19, 2000; 65 FR 69481, Nov. 17, 2000; 66 FR 29055, May 29, 2001; 67 FR 21598, May 1, 2002]

§ 224.102 Permits for endangered marine and anadromous species.

No person shall take, import, export, or engage in any activity prohibited by section 9 of the Act involving any marine species that has been determined to be endangered under the Endangered Species Conservation Act of 1969 or the Act, and that is under the jurisdiction of the Secretary, without a valid permit issued pursuant to part 222, subpart C of this chapter.

§ 224.103 Special prohibitions for endangered marine mammals.

(a) Approaching humpback whales in Hawaii. ****
(b) Approaching humpback whales in Alaska ****
(c) Approaching North Atlantic right whales ****
(d) Special prohibitions relating to endangered Steller sea lion protection. ****

[66 FR 29509, May 31, 2001]

§ 224.104 Special requirements for fishing activities to protect endangered sea turtles.

(a) Shrimp fishermen in the southeastern United States and the Gulf of Mexico who comply with rules for threatened sea turtles specified in § 223.206 of this chapter will not be subject to civil penalties under the Act for incidental captures of endangered sea turtles by shrimp trawl gear.

(b) Summer flounder fishermen in the Summer flounder fishery-sea turtle protection area who comply with rules for threatened sea turtles specified in § 223.206 of this chapter will not be subject to civil penalties under the Act for incidental captures of endangered sea turtles by summer flounder gear.

(c) Special prohibitions relating to leatherback sea turtles are provided at § 223.206(d)(2)(iv) and § 223.206(d)(6) of this chapter.

(d) Special handling and resuscitation requirements are specified at § 223.206(d)(1).

[66 FR 44552, Aug. 24, 2001; 66 FR 67496, Dec. 31, 2001]

Joint Regulations of the United States Fish and Wildlife Service, Department of the Interior, and National Marine Fisheries Service, National Oceanic and Atmospheric Administration, Department of Commerce

50 C.F.R. PART 402 INTERAGENCY COOPERATION

Subpart A -- General

Subpart B -- Consultation Procedures

SUBPART A -- GENERAL

§ 402.01 Scope.

(a) This Part interprets and implements sections 7(a)-(d) [16 U.S.C. 1536(a)-(d)] of the Endangered Species Act of 1973, as amended ("Act"). Section 7(a) grants authority to and imposes requirements upon Federal agencies regarding endangered or threatened species of fish, wildlife, or plants ("listed species") and habitat of such species that has been designated as critical ("critical habitat"). Section 7(a)(1) of the Act directs Federal agencies, in consultation with and with the assistance of the Secretary of the Interior or of Commerce, as appropriate, to utilize their authorities to further the purposes of the Act by carrying out conservation programs for listed species. Such affirmative conservation programs must comply with applicable permit requirements (50 CFR Parts 17, 220, 222, and 227) for listed species and should be coordinated with the appropriate Secretary. Section 7(a)(2) of the Act requires every Federal agency, in consultation with and with the assistance of the Secretary, to insure that any action it authorizes, funds, or carries out, in the United States or upon the high seas, is not likely to jeopardize the continued existence of any listed species or results in the destruction or adverse modification of critical habitat. Section 7(a)(3) of the Act authorizes a prospective permit or license applicant to request the issuing Federal agency to enter into early consultation with the Service on a proposed action to determine whether such action is likely to jeopardize the continued existence of listed species or result in the destruction or adverse modification of critical habitat. Section 7(a)(4) of the Act requires Federal agencies to confer with the Secretary on any action that is likely to jeopardize the continued existence of proposed species or result in the destruction or adverse modification of proposed critical habitat. Section 7(b) of the Act requires the Secretary, after the conclusion of early or formal consultation, to issue a written statement setting forth the Secretary's opinion detailing how the agency action affects listed species or critical habitat Biological assessments are required under section 7(c) of the Act if listed species or critical habitat may be present in the area affected by any major construction activity as defined in § 404.02. Section 7(d) of the Act prohibits Federal agencies and applicants from making any irreversible or irretrievable commitment of resources which has the effect of foreclosing the formulation or implementation of reasonable and prudent alternatives which would avoid jeopardizing the continued existence of listed species or resulting in the destruction or adverse modification of critical habitat. Section 7(e)-(o)(1) of the Act provide procedures for granting exemptions from the requirements of section 7(a)(2). Regulations governing the submission of exemption applications are found at 50 CFR Part 451, and regulations governing the exemption process are found at 50 CFR Parts 450, 452, and 453.

(b) The U.S. Fish and Wildlife Service (FWS) and the National Marine Fisheries Service (NMFS) share responsibilities for administering the Act. The Lists of Endangered and Threatened Wildlife and Plants are found in 50 CFR 17.11 and 17.12 and the designated critical habitats are found in 50 CFR 17.95 and 17.96 and 50 CFR Part 226. Endangered or threatened species under the jurisdiction of the NMFS are located in 50 CFR 222.23(a) and 227.4. If the subject species is cited in 50 CFR 222.23(a) or 227.4, the Federal agency shall contact the NMFS. For all other listed species the Federal Agency shall contact the FWS.

§ 402.02 Definitions.

Act means the Endangered Species Act of 1973, as amended, 16 U.S.C. 1531 et seq.

Action means all activities or programs of any kind authorized, funded, or carried out, in whole or in part, by Federal agencies in the United States or upon the high seas. Examples include, but are not limited to: (a) actions intended to conserve listed species or their habitat; (b) the promulgation of regulations; (c) the granting of licenses, contracts, leases, easements, rights-of-way, permits, or grants-in-aid; or (d) actions directly or indirectly causing modifications to the land, water, or air.

Action area means all areas to be affected directly or indirectly by the Federal action and not merely the immediate area involved in the action.

Applicant refers to any person, as defined in section 3(13) of the Act, who requires formal approval or authorization from a Federal agency as a prerequisite to conducting the action.

Biological assessment refers to the information prepared by or under the direction of the Federal agency concerning listed and proposed species and designated and proposed critical habitat that may be present in the action area and the evaluation potential effects of the action on such species and habitat.

Biological opinion is the document that states the opinion of the Service as to whether or not the Federal action is likely to jeopardize the continued existence of listed species or result in the destruction or adverse modification of critical habitat.

Conference is a process which involves informal discussions between a Federal agency and the Service under section 7(a)(4) of the Act regarding the impact of an action on proposed species or proposed critical habitat and recommendations to minimize or avoid the adverse effects.

Conservation recommendations are suggestions of the Service regarding discretionary measures to minimize or avoid adverse effects of a proposed action on listed species or critical habitat or regarding the development of information.

Critical habitat refers to an area designated as critical habitat listed in 50 CFR Parts 17 or 226.

Cumulative effects are those effects of future State or private activities, not involving Federal activities, that are reasonably certain to occur within the action area of the Federal action subject to consultation.

Designated non-Federal representative refers to a person designated by the Federal agency as its representative to conduct informal consultation and/or to prepare any biological assessment.

Destruction or adverse modification means a direct or indirect alteration that appreciably diminishes the value of critical habitat for both the survival and recovery of a listed species. Such alterations include, but are not limited to, alterations adversely modifying any of those physical or biological features that were the basis for determining the habitat to be critical.

Director refers to the Assistant Administrator for Fisheries for the National Oceanic and Atmospheric Administration, or his authorized representative; or the Fish and Wildlife Service regional director, or his authorized representative, for the region where the action would be carried out.

Early consultation is a process requested by a Federal agency on behalf of a prospective applicant under section 7(a)(3) of the Act.

Effects of the action refers to the direct and indirect effects of an action on the species or critical habitat, together with the effects of other activities that are interrelated or interdependent with that action, that will be added to the environmental baseline. The environmental baseline includes the past and present impacts of all Federal, State, or private actions and other human activities in the action area, the anticipated impacts of all proposed Federal projects in the action area that have already undergone formal or early section 7 consultation, and the impact of State or private actions which are contemporaneous with the consultation in process. Indirect effects are those that are caused by the proposed action and are later in time, but still are reasonably certain to occur. Interrelated actions are those that are part of a larger action and depend on the larger action for their justification. Interdependent actions are those that have no independent utility apart from the action under consideration.

Formal consultation is a process between the Service and the Federal agency that commences with the Federal agency's written request for consultation under section 7(a)(2) of the Act and concludes with the Service's issuance of the biological opinion under section 7(b)(3) of the Act.

Incidental take refers to takings that result from, but are not the purpose of, carrying out an otherwise lawful activity conducted by the Federal agency or applicant.

Informal consultation is an optional process that includes all discussions, correspondence, etc., between the Service and the Federal agency or the designated non-Federal representative prior to formal consultation, if required.

Jeopardize the continued existence of means to engage in an action that reasonably would be expected, directly or indirectly, to reduce appreciably the likelihood of both the survival and recovery of a listed species in the wild by reducing the reproduction, numbers, or distribution of that species.

Listed species means any species of fish, wildlife, or plant which has been determined to be endangered or threatened under section 4 of the Act. Listed species are found in 50 CFR 17.11-17.12.

Major construction activity is a construction project (or other undertaking having similar physical impacts) which is a major Federal action significantly affecting the quality of the human environment as referred to in the National Environmental Policy Act [NEPA, 42 U.S.C. 4332(2)(C)].

Preliminary biological opinion refers to an opinion issued as a result of early consultation.

Proposed critical habitat means habitat proposed in the Federal Register to be designated or revised as critical habitat under section 4 of the Act for any listed or proposed species.

Proposed species means any species of fish, wildlife, or plant that is proposed in the Federal Register to be listed under section 4 of the Act.

Reasonable and prudent alternatives refer to alternative actions identified during formal consultation that can be implemented in a manner consistent with the intended purpose of the action, that can be implemented consistent with the scope of the Federal agency's legal authority and jurisdiction, that is economically and technologically feasible, and that the Director believes would avoid the likelihood of jeopardizing the continued existence of listed species or resulting in the destruction or adverse modification of critical habitat.

Reasonable and prudent measures refer to those actions the Director believes necessary or appropriate to minimize the impacts, i.e., amount or extent, of incidental take.

Recovery means improvement in the status of listed species to the point at which listing is no longer appropriate under the criteria set out in section 4(a)(1) of the Act.

Service means the U.S. Fish and Wildlife Service or the National Marine Fisheries Service, as appropriate.

§ 402.03 Applicability.

Section 7 and the requirements of this Part apply to all actions in which there is discretionary Federal involvement or control.

§ 402.04 Counterpart regulations.

The consultation procedures set forth in this Part may be superseded for a particular Federal agency by joint counterpart regulations among that agency, the Fish and Wildlife Service, and the National Marine Fisheries Service. Such counterpart regulations shall be published in the Federal Register in proposed form and shall be subject to public comment for at least 60 days before final rules are published.

§ 402.05 Emergencies.

(a) Where emergency circumstances mandate the need to consult in an expedited manner, consultation may be conducted informally through alternative procedures that the Director determines to be consistent with the requirements of sections 7(a)-(d) of the Act. This provision applies to situations involving acts of God, disasters, casualties, national defense or security emergencies, etc.

(b) Formal consultation shall be initiated as soon as practicable after the emergency is under control. The Federal agency shall submit information on the nature of the emergency action(s), the justification for the expedited consultation, and the impacts to endangered or threatened species and their habitats. The Service will evaluate such information and issue a biological opinion including the information and recommendations given during the emergency consultation.

§ 402.06 Coordination with other environmental reviews.

(a) Consultation, conference, and biological assessment procedures under section 7 may be consolidated with interagency cooperation procedures required by other statutes, such as the National Environmental Policy Act (NEPA) (42 U.S.C. 4321 et seq., implemented at 40 CFR Parts 1500-1508) or the Fish and Wildlife Coordination Act (FWCA) (16 U.S.C. 661 et seq.). Satisfying the requirements of these other statutes, however, does not in itself relieve a Federal agency of its obligations to comply with the procedures set forth in this Part or the substantive requirements of section 7. The Service will attempt to provide a coordinated review and analysis of all environmental requirements.

(b) Where the consultation or conference has been consolidated with the interagency cooperation procedures required by other statutes such as NEPA or FWCA, the results should be included in the documents required by those statutes.

§ 402.07 Designation of lead agency.

When a particular action involves more than one Federal agency, the consultation and conference responsibilities may be fulfilled through a lead agency. Factors relevant in determining an appropriate lead agency include the time sequence in which the agencies would become involved, the magnitude of their respective involvement, and their relative expertise with respect to the environmental effects of the action. The Director shall be notified of the designation in writing by the lead agency.

§ 402.08 Designation of non-Federal representative.

A Federal agency may designate a non-Federal representative to conduct informal consultation or prepare a biological assessment by giving written notice to the Director of such designation. If a permit or license applicant is involved and is not the designated non-Federal representative, then the applicant and Federal agency must agree on the choice of the designated non- Federal representative. If a biological assessment is prepared by the designated non-Federal representative, the Federal agency shall furnish guidance and supervision and shall independently review and evaluate the scope and contents of the biological assessment. The ultimate responsibility for compliance with section 7 remains with the Federal agency.

§ 402.09 Irreversible or irretrievable commitment of resources.

After initiation or reinitiation of consultation required under section 7(a)(2) of the Act, the Federal agency and any applicant shall make no irreversible or irretrievable commitment of resources with respect to the agency action which has the effect of foreclosing the formulation or implementation of any reasonable and prudent alternatives which would avoid violating section 7(a)(2). This prohibition is in force during the consultation process and continues until the requirements of section 7(a)(2) are satisfied. This provision does not apply to the conference requirement for proposed species or proposed critical habitat under section 7(a)(4) of the Act.

§ 402.10 Conference on proposed species or proposed critical habitat.

(a) Each Federal agency shall confer with the Service on any action which is likely to jeopardize the continued existence of any proposed species or result in the destruction or adverse modification of proposed critical habitat. The conference is designed to assist the Federal agency and any applicant in identifying and resolving potential conflicts at an early stage in the planning process.

(b) The Federal agency shall initiate the conference with the Director. The Service may request a conference if, after a review of available information, it determines that a conference is required for a particular action.

(c) A conference between a Federal agency and the Service shall consist of informal discussions concerning an action that is likely to jeopardize the continued existence of the proposed species or result in the destruction or adverse modification of the proposed critical habitat at issue. Applicants may be involved in these informal discussions to the greatest extent practicable. During the conference, the Service will make advisory recommendations, if any, on ways to minimize or avoid adverse effects. If the proposed species is subsequently listed or the proposed critical habitat is designated prior to completion of the action, the Federal agency must review the action to determine whether formal consultation is required.

(d) If requested by the Federal agency and deemed appropriate by the Service, the conference may be conducted in accordance with the procedures for formal consultation in § 402.14. An opinion issued at the conclusion of the conference may be adopted as the biological opinion when the species is listed or critical habitat is designated, but only if no significant new information is developed (including that developed during the rulemaking process on the proposed listing or critical habitat designation) and no significant changes to the Federal action are made that would alter the content of the opinion. An incidental take statement provided with a conference opinion does not become effective unless the Service adopts the opinion once the listing is final.

(e) The conclusions reached during a conference and any recommendations shall be documented by the Service and provided to the Federal agency and to any applicant. The style and magnitude of this document will vary with the complexity of the conference. If formal consultation also is required for a particular action, then the Service will provide the results of the conference with the biological opinion.

§ 402.11 Early consultation.

(a) *Purpose.* Early consultation is designed to reduce the likelihood of conflicts between listed species or critical habitat and proposed actions and occurs prior to the filing of an application for a Federal permit or license. Although early consultation is conducted between the Service and the Federal agency, the prospective applicant should be involved throughout the consultation process.

(b) *Request by prospective applicant.* If a prospective applicant has reason to believe that the prospective action may affect listed species or critical habitat, it may request the Federal agency to enter into early consultation with the Service. The prospective applicant must certify in writing to the Federal agency that (1) it has a definitive proposal outlining the action and its effects and (2) it intends to implement its proposal, if authorized.

(c) *Initiation of early consultation.* If the Federal agency receives the prospective applicant's certification in paragraph (b) of this section, then the Federal agency shall initiate early consultation with the Service. This request shall be in writing and contain the information outlined in § 402.14(c) and, if the action is a major construction activity, the biological assessment as outlined in § 402.12.

(d) *Procedures and responsibilities.* The procedures and responsibilities for early consultation are the same as outlined in § 402.14(c)-(j) for formal consultation, except that all references to the "applicant" shall be treated as the "prospective applicant" and all references to the "biological opinion" or the "opinion" shall be treated as the "preliminary biological opinion" for the purpose of this section.

(e) *Preliminary biological opinion.* The contents and conclusions of a preliminary biological opinion are the same as for a biological opinion issued after formal consultation except that the incidental take statement provided with a preliminary biological opinion does not constitute authority to take listed species.

(f) *Confirmation of preliminary biological opinion as final biological opinion.* A preliminary biological opinion may be confirmed as a biological opinion issued after formal consultation if the Service reviews the proposed action and finds that there have been no significant changes in the action as planned or in the information used during the early consultation. A written request for confirmation of the preliminary biological opinion should be submitted after the prospective applicant applies to the Federal agency for a permit or license but prior to the issuance of such permit or license. Within 45 days of receipt of the Federal agency's request, the Service shall either:

(1) Confirm that the preliminary biological opinion stands as a final biological opinion; or

(2) If the findings noted above cannot be made, request that the Federal agency

initiate formal consultation.

§ 402.12 Biological assessments.

(a) *Purpose.* A biological assessment shall evaluate the potential effects of the action on listed and proposed species and designated and proposed critical habitat and determine whether any such species or habitat are likely to be adversely affected by the action and is used in determining whether formal consultation or a conference is necessary.

(b) *Preparation requirement.*

(1) The procedures of this section are required for Federal actions that are "major construction activities"; provided that a contract for construction was not entered into or actual construction was not begun on or before November 10, 1978. Any person, including those who may wish to apply for an exemption from section 7(a)(2) of the Act, may prepare a biological assessment under the supervision of the Federal agency and in cooperation with the Service consistent with the procedures and requirements of this section. An exemption from the requirements of section 7(a)(2) is not permanent unless a biological assessment has been prepared.

(2) The biological assessment shall be completed before any contract for construction is entered into and before construction is begun.

(c) *Request for information.* The Federal agency or the designated non-Federal representative shall convey to the Director either (1) a written request for a list of any listed or proposed species or designated or proposed critical habitat that may be present in the action area; or (2) a written notification of the species and critical habitat that are being included in the biological assessment.

(d) *Director's response.* Within 30 days of receipt of the notification of, or the request for, a species list, the Director shall either concur with or revise the list or, in those cases where no list has been provided, advise the Federal agency or the designated non-Federal representative in writing whether, based on the best scientific and commercial data available, any listed or proposed species or designated or proposed critical habitat may be present in the action area. In addition to listed and proposed species, the Director will provide a list of candidate species that may be present in the action area. Candidate species refers to any species being considered by the Service for listing as endangered or threatened species but not yet the subject of a proposed rule. Although candidate species have no legal status and are accorded no protection under the Act, their inclusion will alert the Federal agency of potential proposals or listings.

(1) If the Director advises that no listed species or critical habitat may be present, the Federal agency need not prepare a biological assessment and further consultation is not required. If only proposed species or proposed critical habitat may be present in the action area, then the Federal agency must confer with the Service if required under § 402.10, but preparation of a biological assessment is not required unless the proposed listing and/or designation becomes final.

(2) If a listed species or critical habitat may be present in the action area, the Director will provide a species list or concur with the species list provided. The Director also will provide available information (or references thereto) regarding these species and critical habitat, and may recommend discretionary studies or surveys that may provide a better information base for the preparation of an assessment. Any recommendation for

studies or surveys is not to be construed as the Service's opinion that the Federal agency has failed to satisfy the information standard of section 7(a)(2) of the Act.

(e) *Verification of current accuracy of species list.* If the Federal agency or the designated non-Federal representative does not begin preparation of the biological assessment within 90 days of receipt of (or concurrence with) the species list, the Federal agency or the designated non-Federal representative must verify (formally or informally) with the Service the current accuracy of the species list at the time the preparation of the assessment is begun.

(f) *Contents.* The contents of a biological assessment are at the discretion of the Federal agency and will depend on the nature of the Federal action. The following may be considered for inclusion:

(1) The results of an on-site inspection of the area affected by the action to determine if listed or proposed species are present or occur seasonally.

(2) The views of recognized experts on the species at issue.

(3) A review of the literature and other information.

(4) An analysis of the effects of the action on the species and habitat, including consideration of cumulative effects, and the results of any related studies.

(5) An analysis of alternate actions considered by the Federal agency for the proposed action.

(g) *Incorporation by reference.* If a proposed action requiring the preparation of a biological assessment is identical, or very similar, to a previous action for which a biological assessment was prepared, the Federal agency may fulfill the biological assessment requirement for the proposed action by incorporating by reference the earlier biological assessment, plus any supporting data from other documents that are pertinent to the consultation, into a written certification that:

(1) The proposed action involves similar impacts to the same species in the same geographic area;

(2) No new species have been listed or proposed or no new critical habitat designated or proposed for the action area; and

(3) The biological assessment has been supplemented with any relevant changes in information.

(h) *Permit requirements.* If conducting a biological assessment will involve the taking of a listed species, a permit under section 10 of the Act (16 U.S.C. 1539) and part 17 of this title (with respect to species under the jurisdiction of the FWS) or parts 220, 222, and 227 of this title (with respect to species under the jurisdiction of the NMFS) is required.

(i) Completion time. The Federal agency or the designated non- Federal representative shall complete the biological assessment within 180 days after its initiation (receipt of or concurrence with the species list) unless a different period of time is agreed to by the Director and the Federal agency. If a permit or license applicant is involved, the 180-day period may not be extended unless the agency provides the applicant, before the close of the 180- day period, with a written statement setting forth the estimated length of the proposed extension and the reasons why such an extension is necessary.

(j) *Submission of biological assessment.* The Federal agency shall submit the completed biological assessment to the Director for review. The Director will respond in writing within 30 days as to whether or not he concurs with the findings of the biological assessment. At the option of the Federal agency, formal consultation may be initiated under § 402.14(c) concurrently with the submission of the assessment.

(k) *Use of the biological assessment.*

(1) The Federal agency shall use the biological assessment in determining whether formal consultation or a conference is required under § 402.14 or § 402.10, respectively. If the biological assessment indicates that there are no listed species or critical habitat present that are likely to be adversely affected by the action and the Director concurs as specified in paragraph (j) of this section, then formal consultation is not required. If the biological assessment indicates that the action is not likely to jeopardize the continued existence of proposed species or result in the destruction or adverse modification of proposed critical habitat, and the Director concurs, then a conference is not required.

(2) The Director may use the results of the biological assessment in (i) determining whether to request the Federal agency to initiate formal consultation or a conference, (ii) formulating a biological opinion, or (iii) formulating a preliminary biological opinion.

§ 402.13 Informal consultation.

(a) Informal consultation is an optional process that includes all discussions, correspondence, etc., between the Service and the Federal agency or the designated non-Federal representative, designed to assist the Federal agency in determining whether formal consultation or a conference is required. If during informal consultation it is determined by the Federal agency, with the written concurrence of the Service, that the action is not likely to adversely affect listed species or critical habitat, the consultation process is terminated, and no further action is necessary.

(b) During informal consultation, the Service may suggest modifications to the action that the Federal agency and any applicant could implement to avoid the likelihood of adverse effects to listed species or critical habitat.

§ 402.14 Formal consultation.

(a) *Requirement for formal consultation.* Each Federal agency shall review its actions at the earliest possible time to determine whether any action may affect listed species or critical habitat. If such a determination is made, formal consultation is required, except as noted in paragraph (b) of this section. The Director may request a Federal agency to enter into consultation if he identifies any action of that agency that may affect listed species or critical habitat and for which there has been no consultation. When such a request is made, the Director shall forward to the Federal agency a written explanation of the basis for the request.

(b) *Exceptions.*

(1) A Federal agency need not initiate formal consultation if, as a result of the preparation of a biological assessment under § 402.12 or as a result of informal consultation with the Service under § 402.13, the Federal agency determines, with the written concurrence of the Director, that the proposed action is not likely to adversely affect any listed species or critical habitat.

(2) A Federal agency need not initiate formal consultation if a preliminary biological opinion, issued after early consultation under § 402.11, is confirmed as the final biological opinion.

(c) *Initiation of formal consultation.* A written request to initiate formal consultation shall be submitted to the Director and shall include:

(1) A description of the action to be considered;

(2) A description of the specific area that may be affected by the action;

(3) A description of any listed species or critical habitat that may be affected by the action;

(4) A description of the manner in which the action may affect any listed species or critical habitat and an analysis of any cumulative effects;

(5) Relevant reports, including any environmental impact statement, environmental assessment, or biological assessment prepared; and

(6) Any other relevant available information on the action, the affected listed species, or critical habitat.

Formal consultation shall not be initiated by the Federal agency until any required biological assessment has been completed and submitted to the Director in accordance with § 402.12. Any request for formal consultation may encompass, subject to the approval of the Director, a number of similar individual actions within a given geographical area or a segment of a comprehensive plan. This does not relieve the Federal agency of the requirements for considering the effects of the action as a whole.

(d) *Responsibility to provide best scientific and commercial data available.* The Federal agency requesting formal consultation shall provide the Service with the best scientific and commercial data available or which can be obtained during the consultation for an adequate review of the effects that an action may have upon listed species or critical habitat. This information may include the results of studies or surveys conducted by the Federal agency or the designated non-Federal representative. The Federal agency shall provide any applicant with the opportunity to submit information for consideration during the consultation.

(e) *Duration and extension of formal consultation.* Formal consultation concludes within 90 days after its initiation unless extended as provided below. If an applicant is not involved, the Service and the Federal agency may mutually agree to extend the consultation for a specific time period. If an applicant is involved, the Service and the Federal agency may mutually agree to extend the consultation provided that the Service submits to the applicant, before the close of the 90 days, a written statement setting forth:

(1) The reasons why a longer period is required,

(2) The information that is required to complete the consultation, and

(3) The estimated date on which the consultation will be completed.

A consultation involving an applicant cannot be extended for more than 60 days without the consent of the applicant. Within 45 days after concluding formal consultation, the Service shall deliver a biological opinion to the Federal agency and any applicant.

(f) *Additional data.* When the Service determines that additional data would provide a better information base from which to formulate a biological opinion, the Director may request an extension of formal consultation and request that the Federal agency obtain additional data to determine how or to what extent the action may affect listed species or critical habitat. If formal consultation is extended by mutual agreement according to § 402.14(e), the Federal agency shall obtain, to the extent practicable, that data which can be developed within the scope of the extension. The responsibility for conducting and funding any studies belongs to the Federal agency and the applicant, not the Service. The Service's request for additional data is not to be construed as the Service's opinion that the Federal agency has failed to satisfy the information standard of section 7(a)(2) of the Act. If no extension of formal consultation is agreed to, the Director will issue a biological opinion using the best scientific and commercial data available.

(g) *Service responsibilities.* Service responsibilities during formal consultation are as follows:

(1) Review all relevant information provided by the Federal agency or otherwise available. Such review may include an on-site inspection of the action area with representatives of the Federal agency and the applicant.

(2) Evaluate the current status of the listed species or critical habitat.

(3) Evaluate the effects of the action and cumulative effects on the listed species or critical habitat.

(4) Formulate its biological opinion as to whether the action, taken together with cumulative effects, is likely to jeopardize the continued existence of listed species or result in the destruction or adverse modification of critical habitat.

(5) Discuss with the Federal agency and any applicant the Service's review and evaluation conducted under paragraphs (g)(1)-(3) of this section, the basis for any finding in the biological opinion, and the availability of reasonable and prudent alternatives (if a jeopardy opinion is to be issued) that the agency and the applicant can take to avoid violation of section 7(a)(2). The Service will utilize the expertise of the Federal agency and any applicant in identifying these alternatives. If requested, the Service shall make available to the Federal agency the draft biological opinion for the purpose of analyzing the reasonable and prudent alternatives. The 45-day period in which the biological opinion must be delivered will not be suspended unless the Federal agency secures the written consent of the applicant to an extension to a specific date. The applicant may request a copy of the draft opinion from the Federal agency. All comments on the draft biological opinion must be submitted to the Service through the Federal agency, although the applicant may send a copy of its comments directly to the Service. The Service will not issue its biological opinion prior to the 45-day or extended deadline while the draft is under review by the Federal agency. However, if the Federal agency submits comments to the Service regarding the draft biological opinion within 10 days of the deadline for issuing the opinion, the Service is entitled to an automatic 10-day extension on the deadline.

(6) Formulate discretionary conservation recommendations, if any, which will assist the Federal agency in reducing or eliminating the impacts that its proposed action may have on listed species or critical habitat.

(7) Formulate a statement concerning incidental take, if such take may occur.

(8) In formulating its biological opinion, any reasonable and prudent alternatives, and any reasonable and prudent measures, the Service will use the best scientific and commercial data available and will give appropriate consideration to any beneficial actions taken by the Federal agency or applicant, including any actions taken prior to the initiation of consultation.

(h) *Biological opinions.* The biological opinion shall include:

(1) A summary of the information on which the opinion is based;

(2) A detailed discussion of the effects of the action on listed species or critical habitat; and

(3) The Service's opinion on whether the action is likely to jeopardize the continued existence of a listed species or result in the destruction or adverse modification of critical habitat (a "jeopardy biological opinion"); or, the action is not likely to jeopardize the continued existence of a listed species or result in the destruction or adverse modification of critical habitat (a "no jeopardy" biological opinion). A "jeopardy" biological opinion shall

include reasonable and prudent alternatives, if any. If the Service is unable to develop such alternatives, It will indicato that to the best of its knowledge there are no reasonable and prudent alternatives.

(i) *Incidental take.*

(1) In those cases where the Service concludes that an action (or the implementation of any reasonable and prudent alternatives) and the resultant incidental take of listed species will not violate section 7(a)(2), and, in the case of marine mammals, where the taking is authorized pursuant to section 101(a)(5) of the Marine Mammal Protection Act of 1972, the Service will provide with the biological opinion a statement concerning incidental take that:

(i) Specifies the impact, i.e., the amount or extent, of such incidental taking on the species;

(ii) Specifies those reasonable and prudent measures that the Director considers necessary or appropriate to minimize such impact;

(iii) In the case of marine mammals, specifies those measures that are necessary to comply with section 101(a)(5) of the Marine Mammal Protection Act of 1972 and applicable regulations with regard to such taking;

(iv) Sets forth the terms and conditions (including, but not limited to, reporting requirements) that must be complied with by the Federal agency or any applicant to implement the measures specified under paragraph (i)(1)(ii) and (i)(1)(iii) of this section; and

(v) Specifies the procedures to be used to handle or dispose of any individuals of a species actually taken.

(2) Reasonable and prudent measures, along with the terms and conditions that implement them, cannot alter the basic design, location, scope, duration, or timing of the action and may involve only minor changes.

(3) In order to monitor the impacts of incidental take, the Federal agency or any applicant must report the progress of the action and its impact on the species to the Service as specified in the incidental take statement. The reporting requirements will be established in accordance with 50 CFR 13.45 and 18.27 for FWS and 50 CFR 220.45 and 228.5 for NMFS.

(4) If during the course of the action the amount or extent of incidental taking, as specified under paragraph (i)(1)(i) of this Section, is exceeded, the Federal agency must reinitiate consultation immediately.

(5) Any taking which is subject to a statement as specified in paragraph (i)(1) of this section and which is in compliance with the terms and conditions of that statement is not a prohibited taking under the Act, and no other authorization or permit under the Act is required.

(j) *Conservation recommendations.* The Service may provide with the biological opinion a statement containing discretionary conservation recommendations. Conservation recommendations are advisory and are not intended to carry any binding legal force.

(k) *Incremental steps.* When the action is authorized by a statute that allows the agency to take incremental steps toward the completion of the action, the Service shall, if requested by the Federal agency, issue a biological opinion on the incremental step being considered, including its views on the entire action. Upon the issuance of such a biological opinion, the Federal agency may proceed with or authorize the incremental steps of the action if:

(1) The biological opinion does not conclude that the incremental step would violate section 7(a)(2);

(2) The Federal agency continues consultation with respect to the entire action and obtains biological opinions, as required, for each incremental step;

(3) The Federal agency fulfills its continuing obligation to obtain sufficient data upon which to base the final biological opinion on the entire action;

(4) The incremental step does not violate section 7(d) of the Act concerning irreversible or irretrievable commitment of resources; and

(5) There is a reasonable likelihood that the entire action will not violate section 7(a)(2) of the Act.

(l) *Termination of consultation.*

(1) Formal consultation is terminated with the issuance of the biological opinion.

(2) If during any stage of consultation a Federal agency determines that its proposed action is not likely to occur, the consultation may be terminated by written notice to the Service.

(3) If during any stage of consultation a Federal agency determines, with the concurrence of the Director, that its proposed action is not likely to adversely affect any listed species or critical habitat, the consultation is terminated.

[54 FR 40350, Sept. 29, 1989]

§ 402.15 Responsibilities of Federal agency following issuance of a biological opinion.

(a) Following the issuance of a biological opinion, the Federal agency shall determine whether and in what manner to proceed with the action in light of its section 7 obligations and the Service's biological opinion.

(b) If a jeopardy biological opinion is issued, the Federal agency shall notify the Service of its final decision on the action.

(c) If the Federal agency determines that it cannot comply with the requirements of section 7(a)(2) after consultation with the Service, it may apply for an exemption. Procedures for exemption applications by Federal agencies and others are found in 50 CFR part 451.

§ 402.16 Reinitiation of formal consultation.

Reinitiation of formal consultation is required and shall be requested by the Federal agency or by the Service, where discretionary Federal involvement or control over the action has been retained or is authorized by law and:

(a) If the amount or extent of taking specified in the incidental take statement is exceeded;

(b) If new information reveals effects of the action that may affect listed species or critical habitat in a manner or to an extent not previously considered;

(c) If the identified action is subsequently modified in a manner that causes an effect to the listed species or critical habitat that was not considered in the biological opinion; or

(d) If a new species is listed or critical habitat designated that may be affected by the identified action.

50 C.F.R. PART 424
LISTING ENDANGERED AND THREATENED SPECIES AND DESIGNATING CRITICAL HABITAT

Subpart A -- General Provisions

Subpart B -- Revision of the Lists

AUTHORITY: Pub. L. No. 93-205, 87 Stat. 884; Pub. L. No. 95-632, 92 Stat. 3751; Pub. L. No. 96-159, 93 Stat. 1225; Pub. L. No. 97-304, 96 Stat. 1411 (16 U.S.C. §§ 1531 *et seq.*]

SOURCE: 49 FR 38908, Oct. 1, 1984, unless otherwise noted

SUBPART A -- GENERAL PROVISIONS

§ 424.01 Scope and purpose.

(a) Part 424 provides rules for revising the Lists of Endangered and Threatened Wildlife and Plants and, where appropriate, designating or revising their critical habitats. Criteria are provided for determining species to be endangered or threatened and for designating critical habitats. Procedures for receiving and considering petitions to revise the lists and for conducting periodic reviews of listed species also are established.

(b) The purpose of these rules is to interpret and implement those portions of the Endangered Species Act of 1973, as amended (16 U.S.C. 1531 et seq.), that pertain to the listing of species and the determination of critical habitats.

[45 FR 13022, Feb. 27, 1980; 45 FR 64195, Sept. 29, 1980]

§ 424.02 Definitions.

(a) The definitions of terms in 50 CFR 402.02 shall apply to this Part 424, except as otherwise stated.

(b) *Candidate* means any species being considered by the Secretary for listing as an endangered or a threatened species, but not yet the subject of a proposed rule.

(c) *Conservation, conserve,* and *conserving* mean to use and the use of all methods and procedures that are necessary to bring any endangered or threatened species to the point at which the measures provided pursuant to the Act are no longer necessary. Such methods and procedures include, but are not limited to, all activities associated with scientific resources management such as research, census, law enforcement, habitat acquisition and maintenance, propagation, live trapping, and transplantation, and, in the extraordinary case where population pressures within a given ecosystem cannot be otherwise relieved, may include regulated taking.

(d) *Critical habitat* means (1) the specific areas within the geographical area currently occupied by a species, at the time it is listed in accordance with the Act, on which are found those physical or biological features (i) essential to the conservation of the species and (ii) that may require special management considerations or protection, and (2) specific areas outside the geographical area occupied by a species at the time it is listed upon a determination by the Secretary that such areas are essential for the conservation of the species.

(e) *Endangered species* means a species that is in danger of extinction throughout all or a significant portion of its range.

(f) *List* or *lists* means the Lists of Endangered and Threatened Wildlife and Plants found at 50 CFR 17.11(h) or 17.12(h).

(g) *Plant* means any member of the plant kingdom, including, without limitation, seeds, roots, and other parts thereof.

(h) *Public hearing* means an informal hearing to provide the public with the opportunity to give comments and to permit an exchange of information and opinion on a proposed rule.

(i) *Secretary* means the Secretary of the Interior or the Secretary of Commerce, as appropriate, or their authorized representatives.

(j) *Special management considerations or protection* means any methods or procedures useful in protecting physical and biological features of the environment for the conservation of listed species.

(k) *Species* includes any species or subspecies of fish, wildlife, or plant, and any distinct population segment of any vertebrate species that interbreeds when mature. Excluded is any species of the Class Insecta determined by the Secretary to constitute a pest whose protection under the provisions of the Act would present an overwhelming and overriding risk to man.

(l) *State agency* means any State agency, department, board, commission, or other governmental entity that is responsible for the management and conservation of fish, plant, or wildlife resources within a State.

(m) *Threatened species* means any species that is likely to become an endangered species within the foreseeable future throughout all or a significant portion of its range.

(n) *Wildlife* or *fish and wildlife* means any member of the animal kingdom, including without limitation, any vertebrate, mollusk, crustacean, arthropod, or other invertebrate, and includes any part, product, egg, or offspring thereof, or the dead body or parts thereof.

[45 FR 13022, Feb. 27, 1980; 45 FR 64195, Sept. 29, 1980]]

SUBPART B -- REVISIONS OF THE LISTS

§ 424.10 General.

The Secretary may add a species to the lists or designate critical habitat, delete a species or critical habitat, change the listed status of a species, revise the boundary of an area designated as critical habitat, or adopt or modify special rules (see 50 CFR 17.40-17.48 and Parts 222 and 227) applied to a threatened species only in accordance with the procedures of this Part.

§ 424.11 Factors for listing, delisting, or reclassifying species.

(a) Any species or taxonomic group of species (*e.g.*, genus, subgenus) as defined in § 424.02(k) is eligible for listing under the Act. A taxon of higher rank than species may be listed only if all included species are individually found to be endangered or threatened. In determining whether a particular taxon or population is a species for the purposes of the Act, the Secretary shall rely on standard taxonomic distinctions and the biological expertise of the Department and the scientific community concerning the relevant taxonomic group.

(b) The Secretary shall make any determination required by paragraphs (c) and (d) of this section solely on the basis of the best available scientific and commercial information regarding a species' status, without reference to possible economic or other impacts of such determination.

(c) A species shall be listed or reclassified if the Secretary determines, on the basis of the best scientific and commercial data available after conducting a review of the species' status, that the species is endangered or threatened because of any one or a combination of the following factors:

(1) The present or threatened destruction, modification, or curtailment of its habitat or range;

(2) Overutilization for commercial, recreational, scientific, or educational purposes;

(3) Disease or predation;

(4) The inadequacy of existing regulatory mechanisms; or

(5) Other natural or manmade factors affecting its continued existence.

(d) The factors considered in delisting a species are those in paragraph (c) of this section as they relate to the definitions of endangered or threatened species. Such removal must be supported by the best scientific and commercial data available to the Secretary after conducting a review of the status of the species. A species may be delisted only if such data substantiate that it is neither endangered nor threatened for one or more of the following reasons:

(1) *Extinction.* Unless all individuals of the listed species had been previously identified and located, and were later found to be extirpated from their previous range, a sufficient period of time must be allowed before delisting to indicate clearly that the species is extinct.

(2) *Recovery.* The principal goal of the U.S. Fish and Wildlife Service and the National Marine Fisheries Service is to return listed species to a point at which protection under the Act is no longer required. A species may be delisted on the basis of recovery only if the best scientific and commercial data available indicate that it is no longer endangered or threatened.

(3) *Original data for classification in error.* Subsequent investigations may show that the best scientific or commercial data available when the species was listed, or the

interpretation of such data, were in error.

(e) The fact that a species of fish, wildlife, or plant is protected by the Convention on International Trade in Endangered Species of Wild Fauna and Flora (see Part 23 of this Title 50) or a similar international agreement on such species, or has been identified as requiring protection from unrestricted commerce by any foreign nation, or to be in danger of extinction or likely to become so within the foreseeable future by any State agency or by any agency of a foreign nation that is responsible for the conservation of fish, wildlife, or plants, may constitute evidence that the species is endangered or threatened. The weight given such evidence will vary depending on the international agreement in question, the criteria pursuant to which the species is eligible for protection under such authorities, and the degree of protection afforded the species. The Secretary shall give consideration to any species protected under such an international agreement, or by any State or foreign nation, to determine whether the species is endangered or threatened.

(f) The Secretary shall take into account, in making determinations under paragraph (c) or (d) of this section, those efforts, if any, being made by any State or foreign nation, or any political subdivision of a State or foreign nation, to protect such species, whether by predator control, protection of habitat and food supply, or other conservation practices, within any area under its jurisdiction, or on the high seas.

§ 424.12 Criteria for designating Critical Habitat.

(a) Critical habitat shall be specified to the maximum extent prudent and determinable at the time a species is proposed for listing. If designation of critical habitat is not prudent or if critical habitat is not determinable, the reasons for not designating critical habitat will be stated in the publication of proposed and final rules listing a species. A final designation of critical habitat shall be made on the basis of the best scientific data available, after taking into consideration the probable economic and other impacts of making such a designation in accordance with § 424.19.

(1) A designation of critical habitat is not prudent when one or both of the following situations exist:

(i) The species is threatened by taking or other human activity, and identification of critical habitat can be expected to increase the degree of such threat to the species, or

(ii) Such designation of critical habitat would not be beneficial to the species.

(2) Critical habitat is not determinable when one or both of the following situations exist:

(i) Information sufficient to perform required analyses of the impacts of the designation is lacking, or

(ii) The biological needs of the species are not sufficiently well known to permit identification of an area as critical habitat.

(b) In determining what areas are critical habitat, the Secretary shall consider those physical and biological features that are essential to the conservation of a given species and that may require special management considerations or protection. Such requirements include, but are not limited to the following:

(1) Space for individual and population growth, and for normal behavior;

(2) Food, water, air, light, minerals, or other nutritional or physiological requirements;

(3) Cover or shelter;

(4) Sites for breeding, reproduction, rearing of offspring, germination, or seed

dispersal; and generally,

(5) Habitats that are protected from disturbance or are representative of the historic geographical and ecological distributions of a species.

When considering the designation of critical habitat, the Secretary shall focus on the principal biological or physical constituent elements within the defined area that are essential to the conservation of the species. Known primary constituent elements shall be listed with the critical habitat description. Primary constituent elements may include, but are not limited to, the following: roost sites, nesting grounds, spawning sites, feeding sites, seasonal wetland or dryland, water quality or quantity, host species or plant pollinator, geological formation, vegetation type, tide, and specific soil types.

(c) Each critical habitat will be defined by specific limits using reference points and lines as found on standard topographic maps of the area. Each area will be referenced to the State(s), county(ies), or other local governmental units within which all or part of the critical habitat is located. Unless otherwise indicated within the critical habitat descriptions, the names of the State(s) and county(ies) are provided for information only and do not constitute the boundaries of the area. Ephemeral reference points (*e.g.,* trees, sand bars) shall not be used in defining critical habitat.

(d) When several habitats, each satisfying the requirements for designation as critical habitat, are located in proximity to one another, an inclusive area may be designated as critical habitat.

Example: Several dozen or more small ponds, lakes, and springs are found in a small local area. The entire area could be designated critical habitat if it were concluded that the upland areas were essential to the conservation of an aquatic species located in the ponds and lakes.

(e) The Secretary shall designate as critical habitat areas outside the geographical area presently occupied by a species only when a designation limited to its present range would be inadequate to ensure the conservation of the species.

(f) Critical habitat may be designated for those species listed as threatened or endangered but for which no critical habitat has been previously designated.

(g) Existing critical habitat may be revised according to procedures in this section as new data become available to the Secretary.

(h) Critical habitat shall not be designated within foreign countries or in other areas outside of United States jurisdiction.

[45 FR 13022, Feb. 27, 1980; 45 FR 64195, Sept. 29, 1980]

§ 424.13 Sources of information and relevant data.

When considering any revision of the lists, the Secretary shall consult as appropriate with affected States, interested persons and organizations, other affected Federal agencies, and, in cooperation with the Secretary of State, with the country or countries in which the species concerned are normally found or whose citizens harvest such species from the high seas. Data reviewed by the Secretary may include, but are not limited to scientific or commercial publications, administrative reports, maps or other graphic materials, information received from experts on the subject, and comments from interested parties.

§ 424.14 Petitions.

(a) General. Any interested person may submit a written petition to the Secretary requesting that one of the actions described in § 424.10 be taken. Such a document must clearly identify itself as a petition and be dated. It must contain the name, signature, address, telephone number, if any, and the association, institution, or business affiliation, if any, of the petitioner. The Secretary shall acknowledge in writing receipt of such a petition within 30 days.

(b) Petitions to list, delist, or reclassify species.

(1) To the maximum extent practicable, within 90 days of receiving a petition to list, delist, or reclassify a species, the Secretary shall make a finding as to whether the petition presents substantial scientific or commercial information indicating that the petitioned action may be warranted. For the purposes of this section, "substantial information" is that amount of information that would lead a reasonable person to believe that the measure proposed in the petition may be warranted. The Secretary shall promptly publish such finding in the Federal Register and so notify the petitioner.

(2) In making a finding under paragraph (b)(1) of this section, the Secretary shall consider whether such petition --

(i) Clearly indicates the administrative measure recommended and gives the scientific and any common name of the species involved;

(ii) Contains detailed narrative justification for the recommended measure, describing, based on available information, past and present numbers and distribution of the species involved and any threats faced by the species;

(iii) Provides information regarding the status of the species over all or a significant portion of its range; and

(iv) Is accompanied by appropriate supporting documentation in the form of bibliographic references, reprints of pertinent publications, copies of reports or letters from authorities, and maps.

The petitioner may provide information that describes any recommended critical habitat as to boundaries and physical features, and indicates any benefits and/or adverse effects on the species that would result from such designation. Such information, however, will not be a basis for the determination of the substantiality of a petition.

(3) Upon making a positive finding under paragraph (b)(1) of this section, the Secretary shall commence a review of the status of the species concerned and shall make, within 12 months of receipt of such petition, one of the following findings:

(i) The petitioned action is not warranted, in which case the Secretary shall promptly publish such finding in the Federal Register and so notify the petitioner.

(ii) The petitioned action is warranted, in which case the Secretary shall promptly publish in the Federal Register a proposed regulation to implement the action pursuant to § 424.16 of this Part, or

(iii) The petitioned action is warranted, but that --

(A) The immediate proposal and timely promulgation of a regulation to implement the petitioned action is precluded because of other pending proposals to list, delist, or reclassify species, and

(B) Expeditious progress is being made to list, delist, or reclassify qualified species,

in which case, such finding shall be promptly published in the Federal Register together with a description and evaluation of the reasons and data on which the finding is based.

(4) If a finding is made under paragraph (b)(3)(iii) of this Section with regard to any petition, the Secretary shall, within 12 months of such finding, again make one of the findings described in paragraph (b)(3) with regard to such petition, but no further finding of substantial information will be required.

(c) Petitions to revise critical habitat.

(1) To the maximum extent practicable, within 90 days of receiving a petition to revise a critical habitat designation, the Secretary shall make a finding as to whether the petition presents substantial scientific information indicating that the revision may be warranted. The Secretary shall promptly publish such finding in the Federal Register and so notify the petitioner.

(2) In making the finding required by paragraph (c)(1) of this section, the Secretary shall consider whether a petition contains --

(i) Information indicating that areas petitioned to be added to critical habitat contain physical and biological features essential to, and that may require special management to provide for, the conservation of the species involved; or

(ii) Information indicating that areas designated as critical habitat do not contain resources essential to, or do not require special management to provide for, the conservation of the species involved.

(3) Within 12 months after receiving a petition found under paragraph (c)(1) of this section to present substantial information indicating that revision of a critical habitat may be warranted, the Secretary shall determine how he intends to proceed with the requested revision, and shall promptly publish notice of such intention in the Federal Register.

(d) Petitions to designate critical habitat or adopt special rules. Upon receiving a petition to designate critical habitat or to adopt a special rule to provide for the conservation of a species, the Secretary shall promptly conduct a review in accordance with the Administrative Procedure Act (5 U.S.C. 553) and applicable Departmental regulations, and take appropriate action.

§ 424.15 Notices of review.

(a) If the Secretary finds that one of the actions described in § 424.10 may be warranted, but that the available evidence is not sufficiently definitive to justify proposing the action at that time, a notice of review may be published in the Federal Register. The notice will describe the measure under consideration, briefly explain the reasons for considering the action, and solicit comments and additional information on the action under consideration.

(b) The Secretary from time to time also may publish notices of review containing the names of species that are considered to be candidates for listing under the Act and indicating whether sufficient scientific or commercial information is then available to warrant proposing to list such species, the names of species no longer being considered for listing, or the names of listed species being considered for delisting or reclassification. However, none of the substantive or procedural provisions of the Act apply to a species that is designated as a candidate for listing.

(c) Such notices of review will invite comment from all interested parties regarding the status of the species named. At the time of publication of such a notice, notification in writing will be sent to State agencies in any affected States, known affected Federal agencies, and, to the greatest extent practicable, through the Secretary of State, to the governments of any foreign countries in which the subject species normally occur.

§ 424.16 Proposed rules.

(a) *General.* Based on the information received through §§ 424.13, 424.14, 424.15, and 424.21, or through other available avenues, the Secretary may propose revising the lists as described in § 424.10.

(b) *Contents.* A notice of a proposed rule to carry out one of the actions described in § 424.10 shall contain the complete text of the proposed rule, a summary of the data on which the proposal is based (including, as appropriate, citation of pertinent information sources), and shall show the relationship of such data to the rule proposed. If such a rule designates or revises critical habitat, such summary shall, to the maximum extent practicable, include a brief description and evaluation of those activities (whether public or private) that, in the opinion of the Secretary, if undertaken, may adversely modify such habitat, or may be affected by such designation. Any proposed rule to designate or revise critical habitat shall contain a map of such habitat. Any such notice proposing the listing, delisting, or reclassification of a species or the designation or revision of critical habitat shall also include a summary of factors affecting the species and/or critical habitat.

(c) *Procedures.* --

(1) *Notifications.* In the case of any proposed rule to list, delist, or reclassify a species, or to designate or revise critical habitat, the Secretary shall--

(i) Publish notice of the proposal in the Federal Register;

(ii) Give actual notice of the proposed regulation (including the complete text of the regulation) to the State agency in each State in which the species is believed to occur, and to each county or equivalent jurisdiction therein in which the species is believed to occur, and invite the comment of each such agency and jurisdiction;

(iii) Give notice of the proposed regulation to any Federal agencies, local authorities, or private individuals or organizations known to be affected by the rule;

(iv) Insofar as practical, and in cooperation with the Secretary of State, give notice of the proposed regulation to list, delist, or reclassify a species to each foreign nation in which the species is believed to occur or whose citizens harvest the species on the high seas, and invite the comment of such nation;

(v) Give notice of the proposed regulation to such professional scientific organizations as the Secretary deems appropriate; and

(vi) Publish a summary of the proposed regulation in a newspaper of general circulation in each area of the United States in which the species is believed to occur.

(2) *Period of public comments.* At least 60 days shall be allowed for public comment following publication in the Federal Register of a rule proposing the listing, delisting, or reclassification of a species, or the designation or revision of critical habitat. All other proposed rules shall be subject to a comment period of at least 30 days following publication in the Federal Register. The Secretary may extend or reopen the period for public comment on a proposed rule upon a finding that there is good cause to do so. A notice of any such extension or reopening shall be published in the Federal Register, and shall specify the basis for so doing.

(3) *Public hearings.* The Secretary shall promptly hold at least one public hearing if any person so requests within 45 days of publication of a proposed regulation to list, delist, or reclassify a species, or to designate or revise critical habitat. Notice of the location and time of any such hearing shall be published in the Federal Register not less

than 15 days before the hearing is held.

§ 424.17 Time limits and required actions.

(a) *General.*

(1) Within 1 year of the publication of a rule proposing to determine whether a species is an endangered or threatened species, or to designate or revise critical habitat, the Secretary shall publish one of the following in the Federal Register:

(i) A final rule to implement such determination or revision,

(ii) A finding that such revision should not be made,

(iii) A notice withdrawing the proposed rule upon a finding that available evidence does not justify the action proposed by the rule, or

(iv) A notice extending such 1-year period by an additional period of not more than 6 months because there is substantial disagreement among scientists knowledgeable about the species concerned regarding the sufficiency or accuracy of the available data relevant to the determination or revision concerned.

(2) If an extension is made under paragraph (a)(1)(iv) of this section, the Secretary shall, within the extended period, take one of the actions described in paragraphs (a)(1) (i), (ii), or (iii) of this section.

(3) If a proposed rule is withdrawn under paragraph (a)(1)(iii) of this section, the notice of withdrawal shall set forth the basis upon which the proposed rule has been found not to be supported by available evidence. The Secretary shall not again propose a rule withdrawn under such provision except on the basis of sufficient new information that warrants a reproposal.

(b) *Critical habitat designations.* A final rule designating critical habitat of an endangered or a threatened species shall to the extent permissible under § 424.12 be published concurrently with the final rule listing such species, unless the Secretary deems that --

(1) It is essential to the conservation of such species that it be listed promptly; or

(2) Critical habitat of such species is not then determinable,

in which case, the Secretary, with respect to the proposed regulation to designate such habitat, may extend the 1-year period specified in paragraph (a) of this section by not more than one additional year. Not later than the close of such additional year the Secretary must publish a final regulation, based on such data as may be available at that time, designating, to the maximum extent prudent, such habitat.

[45 FR 13022, Feb. 27, 1980; 45 FR 64195, Sept. 29, 1980]

§ 424.18 Final rules -- general.

(a) *Contents.* A final rule promulgated to carry out the purposes of the Act will be published in the Federal Register. This publication will contain the complete text of the rule, a summary of the comments and recommendations received in response to the proposal (including applicable public hearings), summaries of the data on which the rule is based and the relationship of such data to the final rule, and a description of any conservation measures available under the rule. Publication of a final rule to list, delist, or reclassify a species or designate or revise critical habitat shall also provide a summary of factors affecting the species. A rule designating or revising critical habitat will also contain a description of the boundaries and a map of such habitat and will, to the maximum extent practicable, be accompanied by a brief description and evaluation of those activities (whether public or private) that might occur in the area and which, in the opinion of the Secretary, may adversely modify such habitat or be affected by such designation.

(b) *Effective date.* A final rule shall take effect --

(1) Not less than 30 days after it is published in the Federal Register, except as otherwise provided for good cause found and published with the rule; and

(2) Not less than 90 days after (i) publication in the Federal Register of the proposed rule, and (ii) actual notification of any affected State agencies and counties or equivalent jurisdictions in accordance with § 424.16(c)(1)(ii).

(c) *Disagreement with State agency.* If a State agency, given notice of a proposed rule in accordance with § 424.16(c)(1)(ii), submits comments disagreeing in whole or in part with a proposed rule, and the Secretary issues a final rule that is in conflict with such comments, or if the Secretary fails to adopt a regulation for which a State agency has made a petition in accordance with § 424.14, the Secretary shall provide such agency with a written justification for the failure to adopt a rule consistent with the agency's comments or petition.

[45 FR 13022, Feb. 27, 1980; 45 FR 64195, Sept. 29, 1980]

§ 424.19 Final rules -- impact analysis of critical habitat.

The Secretary shall identify any significant activities that would either affect an area considered for designation as critical habitat or be likely to be affected by the designation, and shall, after proposing designation of such an area, consider the probable economic and other impacts of the designation upon proposed or ongoing activities. The Secretary may exclude any portion of such an area from the critical habitat if the benefits of such exclusion outweigh the benefits of specifying the area as part of the critical habitat. The Secretary shall not exclude any such area if, based on the best scientific and commercial data available, he determines that the failure to designate that area as critical habitat will result in the extinction of the species concerned.

§ 424.20 Emergency rules.

(a) Sections 424.16, 424.17, 424.18, and 424.19 notwithstanding, the Secretary may at any time issue a regulation implementing any action described in § 424.10 in regard to any emergency posing a significant risk to the well-being of a species of fish, wildlife, or plant. Such rules shall, at the discretion of the Secretary, take effect immediately on publication in the Federal Register. In the case of any such action that applies to a resident species, the Secretary shall give actual notice of such regulation to the State agency in each State in which such species is believed to occur. Publication in the Federal Register of such an emergency rule shall provide detailed reasons why the rule is necessary. An emergency rule shall cease to have force and effect after 240 days unless the procedures described in §§ 424.16, 424.17, 424.18, and 424.19 (as appropriate) have been complied with during that period.

(b) If at any time after issuing an emergency rule, the Secretary determines, on the basis of the best scientific and commercial data available, that substantial evidence does not then exist to warrant such rule, it shall be withdrawn.

[45 FR 13022, Feb. 27, 1980; 45 FR 64195, Sept. 29, 1980]

§ 424.21 Periodic review.

At least once every 5 years, the Secretary shall conduct a review of each listed species to determine whether it should be delisted or reclassified. Each such determination shall be made in accordance with §§ 424.11, 424.16, and 424.17 of this Part, as appropriate. A notice announcing those species under active review will be published in the Federal Register. Notwithstanding this section's provisions, the Secretary may review the status of any species at any time based upon a petition (see § 424.14) or upon other data available to the Service.

SUBCHAPTER C
ENDANGERED SPECIES EXEMPTION PROCESS

50 C.F.R. PART 450
GENERAL PROVISIONS

AUTHORITY: Endangered Species Act of 1973, 16 U.S.C. §§ 1531 *et seq.*, as amended

450.01 Definitions.

The following definitions apply to terms used in this subchapter.

Act means the Endangered Species Act of 1973, as amended, 16 U.S.C. 1531, et seq.

Agency action means all actions of any kind authorized, funded or carried out, in whole or in part by Federal agencies, including, in the instance of an application for a permit or license, the underlying activity for which the permit or license is sought.

Alternative courses of action means all reasonable and prudent alternatives, including both no action and alternatives extending beyond original project objectives and acting agency jurisdiction.

Benefits means all benefits of an agency action, both tangible and intangible, including but not limited to economic, environmental and cultural benefits.

Biological assessment means the report prepared pursuant to section 7(c) of the Act, 16 U.S.C. 1536(c).

Biological opinion means the written statement prepared pursuant to section 7(b) of the Act, 16 U.S.C. 1536(b).

Chairman means the Chairman of the Endangered Species Committee, who is the Secretary of the Interior.

Committee means the Endangered Species Committee established pursuant to section 7(e) of the Act, 16 U.S.C. 1536(e).

Critical Habitat refers to those areas listed as Critical Habitat in 50 CFR Parts 17 and 226.

Destruction or adverse modification is defined at 50 CFR 402.02.

Federal agency means any department, agency or instrumentality of the United States.

Irreversible or irretrievable commitment of resources means any commitment of resources which has the effect of foreclosing the formulation or implementation of any reasonable or prudent alternatives which would not violate section 7(a)(2) of the Act.

Jeopardize the continued existence of is defined at 50 CFR 402.02.

Mitigation and enhancement measures means measures, including live propagation, transplantation, and habitat acquisition and improvement, necessary and appropriate (a) to minimize the adverse effects of a proposed action on listed species or their critical habitats and/or (b) to improve the conservation status of the species beyond that which would occur without the action. The measures must be likely to protect the listed species or the critical habitat, and be reasonable in their cost, the availability of the technology required to make them effective, and other considerations deemed relevant by the Committee.

Permit or license applicant means any person whose application to an agency for a permit or license has been denied primarily because of the application of section 7(a)(2) of the Act, 16 U.S.C. 1536(a)(2).

Person means an individual, corporation, partnership, trust, association, or any other private entity, or any public body or officer, employee, agent, department, or instrumentality of the Federal government, of any State or political subdivision thereof, or of any foreign government.

Proposed action means the action proposed by the Federal agency or by a permit or license applicant, for which exemption is sought.

Secretary means the Secretary of the Interior or the Secretary of Commerce, or his or her delegate, depending upon which Secretary has responsibility for the affected species as determined pursuant to 50 CFR 402.01.

Service means the United States Fish and Wildlife Service or the National Marine Fisheries Service, as appropriate.

To the extent that such information is available to the applicant means all pertinent information the applicant has on the subject matter at the time the application is submitted, and all other pertinent information obtainable from the appropriate Federal agency pursuant to a Freedom of Information Act request.

[45 FR 23357, Apr. 4, 1980]

50 C.F.R. PART 451
APPLICATION PROCEDURE

sec.

AUTHORITY: Endangered Species Act of 1973, 16 U.S.C. §§ 1531 *et seq.*, as amended

SOURCE: 50 FR 8127, Feb. 28, 1985, unless otherwise noted.

§ 451.01 Definitions.

All definitions contained in 50 CFR 450.01 are applicable to this part.

§ 451.02 Applications for exemptions.

(a) *Scope.* This section prescribes the application procedures for applying for an exemption from the requirements of section 7(a)(2) of the Endangered Species Act, as amended.

(b) *Where to apply.* Applications should be made to the appropriate Secretary(ies) by writing:

(1) The Secretary, Attention: Endangered Species Committee, Department of the Interior, 18th and C Street, NW., Washington, D.C. 20240.

(2) The Secretary, Department of Commerce, 14th Street and Constitution Avenue NW., Washington, D.C. 20030.

(c) *Who may apply.* (1) A Federal agency, (2) the Governor of the State in which an agency action will occur, if any, or (3) a permit or license applicant may apply to the Secretary for an exemption for an agency action if, after consultation under section 7(a)(2) of the Act, the Secretary's opinion indicates that the agency action would violate section 7(a)(2) of the Act.

(d) *When to apply.*

(1) Except in the case of agency action involving a permit or license application, an application for an exemption must be submitted to the Secretary within 90 days following the termination of the consultation process.

(2) In the case of agency action involving a permit or license application, an application for an exemption may be submitted after the Federal agency concerned formally denies the permit or license. An applicant denied a permit or license may not simultaneously seek administrative review within the permitting or licensing agency and apply for an exemption. If administrative review is sought, an application for an exemption may be submitted if that review results in a formal denial of the permit or license. For an exemption application to be considered, it must be submitted within 90 days after the date of a formal denial of a permit or license.

(e) *Contents of the application when submitted.* Exemption applicants must provide the following information at the time the application is submitted.

(1) Name, mailing address, and phone number, including the name and telephone number of an individual to be contacted regarding the application.

(2) If the applicant is a Federal agency:

(i) A comprehensive description of the proposed agency action and if a license or permit denial is involved, a comprehensive description of the license or permit applicant's proposed action.

(ii) In the case of a denial of a license or permit, a description of the permit or license sought, including a statement of who in the Federal agency denied the permit or license, the grounds for the denial, and a copy of the permit or license denial.

(iii) A description of all permit(s), license(s) or other legal requirements which have been satisfied or obtained, or which must still be satisfied or obtained, before the proposed action can proceed.

(iv) A description of the consultation process carried out pursuant to section 7(a) of the Act.

(v) A copy of the biological assessment, if one was prepared.

(vi) A copy of the biological opinion.

(vii) A description of each alternative to the proposed action considered by the Federal agency, by the licensing or permitting agency, and by the permit or license applicant, to the extent known.

(viii) A statement describing why the proposed agency action cannot be altered or modified to avoid violating section 7(a)(2) of the Act.

(ix) A description of resources committed by the Federal agency, or the permit or license applicant, if any, to the proposed action subsequent to the initiation of consultation.

(3) If the applicant is a permit or license applicant other than a Federal agency:

(i) A comprehensive description of the applicant's proposed action.

(ii) A description of the permit or license sought from the Federal agency, including a statement of who in that agency denied the permit or license and the grounds for the denial.

(iii) A description of all permit(s), license(s) or other legal requirements which have been satisfied or obtained, or which must still be satisfied or obtained, before it can proceed with the proposed action.

(iv) A copy of the permit or license denial.

(v) A copy of the biological assessment, if one was prepared.

(vi) A copy of the biological opinion.

(vii) A description of the consultation process carried out pursuant to section 7(a) of the Act, to the extent that such information is available to the applicant.

(viii) A description of each alternative to the proposed action considered by the applicant, and to the extent that such information is available to the applicant, a description of each alternative to the proposed action considered by the Federal agency.

(ix) A statement describing why the applicant's proposed action cannot be altered or modified to avoid violating section 7(a)(2) of the Act.

(x) A description of resources committed to the proposed action by the permit or license applicant subsequent to the initiation of consultation.

(4) If the applicant is the Governor of a State in which the proposed agency action may occur:

(i) A comprehensive description of the proposed agency action and if a license or permit denial is involved, a comprehensive description of the license or permit applicant's proposed action.

(ii) A description of the permit or license, if any, sought from the Federal agency, including a statement of who in that agency denied the permit or license and the grounds for the denial, to the extent that such information is available to the Governor.

(iii) A description of all permit(s), license(s) or other legal requirements which have been satisfied or obtained, or which must still be satisfied or obtained before the agency can proceed with the proposed action, to the extent that such information is available to the Governor.

(iv) A copy of the biological assessment, if one was prepared.

(v) A copy of the biological opinion.

(vi) A description of the consultation process carried out pursuant to section 7(a) of the Act, to the extent that such information is available to the Governor.

(vii) A description of all alternatives considered by the Federal agency, by the licensing or permitting agency, and by the permit or license applicant, to the extent that such information is available to the Governor.

(viii) A statement describing why the proposed agency action cannot be altered or modified to avoid violating section 7(a)(2) of the Act.

(ix) A description of resources committed to the proposed action subsequent to the initiation of consultation, to the extent that such information is available to the Governor.

(5) Each applicant, whether a Federal agency, a permit or license applicant, or a Governor, must also submit the following:

(i) A complete statement of the nature and the extent of the benefits of the proposed action.

(ii) A complete discussion of why the benefits of the proposed action clearly outweigh the benefits of each considered alternative course of action.

(iii) A complete discussion of why none of the considered alternatives are reasonable and prudent.

(iv) A complete statement explaining why the proposed action is in the public interest.

(v) A complete explanation of why the action is of regional or national significance.

(vi) A complete discussion of mitigation and enhancement measures proposed to be undertaken if an exemption is granted

(6) When the exemption applicant is a license or permit applicant or a Governor, a copy of the application shall be provided by the exemption applicant at the time the application is filed, to the Federal agency which denied the license or permit.

(f) *Review of the application by the Secretary.*

(1) Upon receiving the application, the Secretary shall review the contents thereof and consider whether the application complies with the requirements set forth in paragraphs (c), (d) and (e) of this section.

(2) The Secretary shall reject an application within 10 days of receiving it if he determines that it does not comply with paragraphs (c), (d) and (e) of this section. If the Secretary rejects an application because it does not contain the information required by paragraph (e) of this section, the applicant may resubmit a revised application so long as the applicant does so during the 90 day period specified in paragraph (d) of this section.

(3) If the Secretary finds that the application meets the requirements of paragraphs (c), (d), and (e) of this section, he will consider the application in accordance with Part 452.

(g) *Notification of the Secretary of State.* The Secretary will promptly transmit to the Secretary of State a copy of all applications submitted in accordance with § 451.02.

(h) *Public notification.* Upon receipt of an application for exemption, the Secretary shall promptly publish a notice in the Federal Register (1) announcing that an application has been filed, (2) stating the applicant's name, (3) briefly describing the proposed agency action and the result of the consultation process, (4) summarizing the information contained in the application, (5) designating the place where copies of the application can be obtained and (6) specifying the name of the person to contact for further information. The Secretary will promptly notify each member of the Committee upon receipt of an application for exemption.

(i) The information collection requirements contained in Part 451 do not require approval by the Office of Management and Budget under 44 U.S.C. 3501 et seq., because it is anticipated there will be fewer than ten respondents annually.

§ 451.03 Endangered Species Committee.

(a) *Scope.* This section contains provisions governing the relationship between the

Secretary and the Endangered Species Committee.

(b) *Appointment of State member.*

(1) Upon receipt of an application for exemption, the Secretary shall promptly notify the Governors of each affected State, if any, as determined by the Secretary, and request the Governors to recommend individuals to be appointed to the Endangered Species Committee for consideration of the application. Written recommendations of these Governors must be received by the Secretary within 10 days of receipt of notification. The Secretary will transmit the Governors' recommendations to the President and will request that the President appoint a State resident to the Endangered Species Committee from each affected State within 30 days after the application for exemption was submitted.

(2) When no State is affected, the Secretary will submit to the President a list of individuals with expertise relevant to the application and will request the President to appoint, within 30 days after the application for exemption was submitted, an individual to the Endangered Species Committee.

50 C.F.R. PART 452
CONSIDERATION OF APPLICATION BY THE SECRETARY

sec.

AUTHORITY: Endangered Species Act of 1973, 16 U.S.C. §§ 1531 *et seq.*, as amended

SOURCE: 50 FR 8129, Feb. 28, 1985, unless otherwise noted.

§ 452.01 Purpose and scope.

This part prescribes the procedures to be used by the Secretary when examining applications for exemption from section 7(a)(2) of the Endangered Species Act.

§ 452.02 Definitions.

Definitions applicable to this part are contained in 50 CFR 450.01.

§ 452.03 Threshold review and determinations.

(a) *Threshold determinations.* Within 20 days after receiving an exemption application, or a longer time agreed upon between the exemption applicant and the Secretary, the Secretary shall conclude his review and determine:

(1) Whether any required biological assessment was conducted;

(2) To the extent determinable within the time period provided, whether the Federal agency and permit or license applicant, if any, have refrained from making any irreversible or irretrievable commitment of resources, and

(3) Whether the Federal agency and permit or license applicant, if any, have carried out consultation responsibilities in good faith and have made a reasonable and responsible effort to develop and fairly consider modifications or reasonable and prudent alternatives to the proposed action which would not violate section 7(a)(2) of the Act.

(b) *Burden of proof.* The exemption applicant has the burden of proving that the requirements of § 452.(a) have been met.

(c) *Negative finding.* If the Secretary makes a negative finding on any threshold determination, the Secretary shall deny the application and notify the exemption applicant in writing of his finding and grounds therefor. The exemption process shall terminate when the applicant receives such written notice. The Secretary's denial shall constitute final agency action for purposes of judicial review under Chapter 7 of Title 5 of the United States Code.

(d) *Positive finding.* If the Secretary makes a positive finding on each of the threshold determinations, he shall notify the exemption applicant in writing that the application qualifies for consideration by the Endangered Species Committee.

(e) *Secretary of State opinion.* The Secretary shall terminate the exemption process immediately if the Secretary of State, pursuant to his obligations under section 7(i) of the Act, certifies in writing to the Committee that granting an exemption and carrying out the proposed action would violate an international treaty obligation or other international obligation of the United States.

§ 452.04 Secretary's report.

(a) *Contents of the report.* If the Secretary has made a positive finding on each of the threshold determinations, he shall proceed to gather information and prepare a report for the Endangered Species Committee:

(1) Discussing the availability of reasonable and prudent alternatives to the proposed action;

(2) Discussing the nature and extent of the benefits of the proposed action;

(3) Discussing the nature and extent of the benefits of alternative courses of action consistent with conserving the species or the critical habitat;

(4) Summarizing the evidence concerning whether the proposed action is of national or regional significance;

(5) Summarizing the evidence concerning whether the proposed action is in the public interest;

(6) Discussing appropriate and reasonable mitigation and enhancement measures which should be considered by the Committee in granting an exemption; and

(7) Discussing whether the Federal agency and permit or license applicant, if any, have refrained from making any irreversible or irretrievable commitment of resources.

(b) *Preparation of the report.* The report shall be prepared in accordance with procedures set out in § 452.05 and § 452.09.

§ 452.05 Hearings.

(a) *Hearings.*

(1) To develop the record for the report under § 452.04, the Secretary, in

consultation with the members of the Committee, shall hold a hearing in accordance with 5 U.S.C. 554, 555, and 556.

(2) The Secretary shall designate an Administrative Law Judge to conduct the hearing. The Secretary shall assign technical staff to assist the Administrative Law Judge.

(3) When the Secretary designates the Administrative Law Judge, the Secretary may establish time periods for conducting the hearing and closing the record.

(4) The Secretary may require the applicant to submit further discussions of the information required by § 451.02(e)(5). This information will be made part of the record.

(b) *Prehearing conferences.*

(1) The Administrative Law Judge may, on his own motion or the motion of a party or intervenor, hold a prehearing conference to consider: (i) The possibility of obtaining stipulations, admissions of fact or law and agreement to the introduction of documents; (ii) the limitation of the number of witnesses; (iii) questions of law which may bear upon the course of the hearings; (iv) prehearing motions, including motions for discovery; and (v) any other matter which may aid in the disposition of the proceedings.

(2) If time permits and if necessary to materially clarify the issues raised at the prehearing conference, the Administrative Law Judge shall issue a statement of the actions taken at the conference and the agreements made. Such statement shall control the subsequent course of the hearing unless modified for good cause by a subsequent statement.

(c) *Notice of hearings.* Hearings and prehearing conferences will be announced by a notice in the Federal Register stating: (1) The time, place and nature of the hearing or prehearing conference; and (2) the matters of fact and law to be considered. Such notices will ordinarily be published at least 15 days before the scheduled hearings.

(d) *Conduct of hearings.* --

(1) *Admissibility of evidence.* Relevant, material, and reliable evidence shall be admitted. Immaterial, irrelevant, unreliable, or unduly repetitious parts of an admissible document may be segregated and excluded so far as practicable.

(2) *Motions, objections, rebuttal and cross-examination.* Motions and objections may be filed with the Administrative Law Judge, rebuttal evidence may be submitted, and cross-examination may be conducted, as required for a full and true disclosure of the facts, by parties, witnesses under subpoena, and their respective counsel.

(i) *Objections.* Objections to evidence shall be timely, and the party making them may be required to state briefly the grounds relied upon.

(ii) *Offers of proof.* When an objection is sustained, the examining party may make a specific offer of proof and the Administrative Law Judge may receive the evidence in full. Such evidence, adequately marked for identification, shall be retained in the record for consideration by any reviewing authority.

(iii) *Motions.* Motions and petitions shall state the relief sought, the basis for relief and the authority relied upon. If made before or after the hearing itself, these matters shall be in writing and shall be filed and served on all parties. If made at the hearing, they may be stated and responded to orally, but the Administrative Law Judge may require that they be reduced to writing. Oral argument on motions and deadlines by which to file responses to written motions will be at the discretion of the Administrative Law Judge.

(e) *Applicant responsibility.* In proceedings conducted pursuant to this section, the exemption applicant has the burden of going forward with evidence concerning the criteria for exemption.

(f) *Open meetings and record.* All hearings and all hearing records shall be open to the public.

(g) *Requests for information, subpoenas.*

(1) The Administrative Law Judge is authorized to exercise the authority of the Committee to request, subject to the Privacy Act of 1974, that any person provide information necessary to enable the Committee to carry out its duties. Any Federal agency or the exemption applicant shall furnish such information to the Administrative Law Judge. (2) The Administrative Law Judge may exercise the authority of the Committee to issue subpoenas for the attendance and testimony of witnesses and the production of relevant papers, books, and documents.

(h) *Information Collection.* The information collection requirements contained in § 452.05 do not require approval by the Office of Management and Budget under 44 U.S.C. 3501 et seq., because it is anticipated there will be fewer than ten respondents annually.

§ 452.06 Parties and intervenors.

(a) *Parties.* The parties shall consist of the exemption applicant, the Federal agency responsible for the agency action in question, the Service, and intervenors whose motions to intervene have been granted.

(b) *Intervenors.*

(1) The Administrative Law Judge shall provide an opportunity for intervention in the hearing. A motion to intervene must state the petitioner's name and address, identify its representative, if any, set forth the interest of the petitioner in the proceeding and show that the petitioner's participation would assist in the determination of the issues in question.

(2) The Administrative Law Judge shall grant leave to intervene if he determines that an intervenor's participation would contribute to the fair determination of issues. In making this determination, the Administrative Law Judge may consider whether an intervenor represents a point of view not adequately represented by a party or another intervenor.

§ 452.07 Separation of functions and ex parte communications.

(a) *Separation of functions.*

(1) The Administrative Law Judge and the technical staff shall not be responsible for or subject to the supervision or direction of any person who participated in the endangered species consultation at issue;

(2) The Secretary shall not allow an agency employee or agent who participated in the endangered species consultation at issue or a factually related matter to participate or advise in a determination under this part except as a witness or counsel in public proceedings.

(b) *Ex parte communications.* The provisions of 5 U.S.C. 557(d) apply to the hearing and the preparation of the report.

§ 452.08 Submission of Secretary's report.

(a) Upon closing of the record, the Administrative Law Judge shall certify the record and transmit it to the Secretary for preparation of the Secretary's report which shall be based on the record. The Secretary may direct the Administrative Law Judge to reopen the record and obtain additional information if he determines that such action is necessary.

(b) The Secretary shall submit his report and the record of the hearing to the

Committee within 140 days after making his threshold determinations under § 452.03(a) or within such other period of time as is mutually agreeable to the applicant and the Secretary.

§ 452.09 Consolidated and joint proceedings.

(a) When the Secretary is considering two or more related exemption applications, the Secretary may consider them jointly and prepare a joint report if doing so would expedite or simplify consideration of the issues.

(b) When the Secretaries of the Interior and Commerce are considering two or more related exemption applications, they may consider them jointly and prepare a joint report if doing so would expedite or simplify consideration of the issues.

50 C.F.R. PART 453
ENDANGERED SPECIES COMMITTEE

AUTHORITY: Endangered Species Act of 1973, 16 U.S.C. §§ 1531 *et seq.*, as amended

SOURCE: 50 FR 8129, Feb. 28, 1985, unless otherwise noted.

§ 453.01 Purpose.

This part prescribes the procedures to be used by the Endangered Species Committee when examining applications for exemption from section 7(a)(2) of the Endangered Species Act of 1973, as amended.

§ 453.02 Definitions.

Definitions applicable to this part are contained in 50 CFR 450.01.

§ 453.03 Committee review and final determinations.

(a) *Final determinations.* Within 30 days of receiving the Secretary's report and record, the Committee shall grant an exemption from the requirements of section 7(a)(2) of the Act for an agency action if, by a vote in which at least five of its members concur:

(1) It determines that based on the report to the Secretary, the record of the hearing held under § 452.05, and on such other testimony or evidence as it may receive:

(i) There are no reasonable and prudent alternatives to the proposed action;

(ii) The benefits of such action clearly outweigh the benefits of alternative courses of action consistent with conserving the species or its critical habitat, and such action is in the public interest;

(iii) The action is of regional or national significance; and

(iv) Neither the Federal agency concerned nor the exemption applicant made any irreversible or irretrievable commitment of resources prohibited by section 7(d) of the Act; and,

(2) It establishes such reasonable mitigation and enhancement measures, including, but not limited to, live propagation, transplantation, and habitat acquisition and improvement, as are necessary and appropriate to minimize the adverse effects of the proposed action upon the endangered species, threatened species, or critical habitat concerned. Any required mitigation and enhancement measures shall be carried out and paid for by the exemption applicant.

(b) *Decision and order.* The Committee's final determinations shall be documented in a written decision. If the Committee determines that an exemption should be granted, the Committee shall issue an order granting the exemption and specifying required mitigation and enhancement measures. The Committee shall publish its decision and order in the Federal Register as soon as practicable.

(c) *Permanent exemptions.* Under section 7(h)(2) of the Act, an exemption granted by the Committee shall constitute a permanent exemption with respect to all endangered or threatened species for the purposes of completing such agency action (1) regardless of whether the species was identified in the biological assessment, and (2) only if a biological assessment has been conducted under section 7(c) of the Act with respect to such agency action. Notwithstanding the foregoing, an exemption shall not be permanent if (i) the Secretary finds, based on the best scientific and commercial data available, that such exemption would result in the extinction of a species that was not the subject of consultation under section 7(a)(2) of the Act or was not identified in any biological assessment conducted under section 7(c) of the Act, and (ii) the Committee determines within 60 days after the date of the Secretary's finding that the exemption should not be permanent. If the Secretary makes a finding that the exemption would result in the extinction of a species, as specified above, the Committee shall meet with respect to the matter within 30 days after the date of the finding. During the 60 day period following the Secretary's determination, the holder of the exemption shall refrain from any action which would result in extinction of the species.

(d) *Finding by the Secretary of Defense.* If the Secretary of Defense finds in writing that an exemption for the agency action is necessary for reasons of national security, the Committee shall grant the exemption notwithstanding any other provision in this part.

§ 453.04 Committee information gathering.

(a) *Written submissions.* When the Chairman or four Committee members decide that written submissions are necessary to enable the Committee to make its final determinations, the Chairman shall publish a notice in the Federal Register inviting written submissions from interested persons. The notice shall include: (1) The address to which such submissions are to be sent; (2) the deadline for such submissions; and (3) a statement of the type of information needed.

(b) *Public hearing.*

(1) When the Chairman or four Committee members decide that oral presentations are necessary to enable the Committee to make its final determinations, a public hearing shall be held.

(2) The public hearing shall be conducted by (i) the Committee or (ii) a member of

the Committee or other person, designated by the Chairman or by four members of the Committee.

(3) *Notice.* The Chairman shall publish in the Federal Register a general notice of a public hearing, stating the time, place and nature of the public hearing.

(4) *Procedure.* The public hearing shall be open to the public and conducted in an informal manner. All information relevant to the Committee's final determinations shall be admissible, subject to the imposition of reasonable time limitations on oral testimony.

(5) *Transcript.* Public hearings will be recorded verbatim and a transcript thereof will be available for public inspection.

§ 453.05 Committee meetings.

(a) The committee shall meet at the call of the Chairman or five of its members.

(b) Five members of the Committee or their representatives shall constitute a quorum for the transaction of any function of the Committee, except that in no case shall any representative be considered in determining the existence of a quorum for the transaction of a Committee function which involves a vote by the Committee on the Committee's final determinations.

(c) Only members of the Committee may cast votes. In no case shall any representative cast a vote on behalf of a member.

(d) Committee members appointed from the affected States shall collectively have one vote. They shall determine among themselves how it will be cast.

(e) All meetings and records of the Committee shall be open to the public.

(f) The Chairman shall publish a notice of all Committee meetings in the Federal Register. The notice will ordinarily be published at least 15 days prior to the meeting.

§ 453.06 Additional committee powers.

(a) *Secure information.* Subject to the Privacy Act, the Committee may secure information directly from any Federal agency when necessary to enable it to carry out its duties.

(b) *Subpoenas.* For the purpose of obtaining information necessary for the consideration of an application for an exemption, the Committee may issue subpoenas for the attendance and testimony of witnesses and the production of relevant papers, books, and documents.

(c) *Rules and orders.* The Committee may issue and amend such rules and orders as are necessary to carry out its duties.

(d) *Delegate authority.* The Committee may delegate its authority under paragraphs (a) and (b) of this section to any member.

- 0 -

B. Cobbling Together the Conservation of both Species *and* Habitat

i. Federal Lands

The federal government owns nearly one-third of the land in the United States -- most of it located in eleven Western states and Alaska. Most of this land is managed by four federal agencies: the Bureau of Land Management (267 million acres), the National Forest Service (192 million acres), the Fish and Wildlife Service (87 million acres), and the National Park Service (77 million acres). Although much of this land is nominally managed for "conservation," conservation of biological resources has seldom been the dominant concern. As Bob Keiter has noted, "The fact is that few, if any, of the principal laws governing public land management are modeled upon contemporary ecological principles."[32]

The statutes in this section demonstrate the accuracy of this statement. Wildlife conservation is seldom an explicit concern much less a limit on agency discretion --the land-managing agencies generally have sufficient discretion to conserve wildlife habitat but are seldom mandated to do so.

a. The National Park Service: National Parks and Monuments

The National Park Service was created by the National Park Service Act of 1916.[33] The Act provides the organic authority for the Service, defining its basic preservation/recreation mission.[34] The agency's planning obligations are set out in the National Parks and Recreation Act of 1978.[35]

Parks are added to the National Park System by act of Congress; each of the nearly 400 units thus has its own place in title 16 of the United States Code. In addition, the President has been authorized to designate National Monuments under the Antiquities Act.[36] Monuments are also managed by the Park Service.

ANTIQUITIES ACT (1906)
(16 U.S.C. §§ 431-33)

The Antiquities Act authorizes the President "to declare by public proclamation ... objects of ... scientific interest that are situated upon the lands owned or controlled by the Government of the United States to be national monuments."[37] This power encompasses authority to reserve lands to protect wildlife habitat. For example, President Franklin Roosevelt's decision to designate Jackson Hole in Wyoming as a national monument was upheld because the areas was "a biological field for research of wild life in its particular habitat within the area."[38]

16 U.S.C. § 431. National monuments; reservation of lands; relinquishment of private claims. The President of the United States is authorized, in his discretion, to declare by public proclamation historic landmarks, historic and prehistoric structures, and other objects of historic or scientific interest that are situated upon the lands owned or controlled by the Government of the United States to be national monuments, and may reserve as a part thereof parcels of land, the limits of which in all cases shall be confined to the smallest area compatible with the proper care and management of the objects to be protected. When such objects are situated upon a tract covered by a bona fide unperfected claim or held in private ownership, the tract, or so much thereof as may be necessary for the proper care and management of the object, may be relinquished to the Government, and the Secretary of the Interior is authorized to accept the relinquishment of such tracts in behalf of the Government of the United States.

[June 8, 1906, ch. 3060, § 2, 34 Stat. 225]

16 U.S.C. § 432. Permits to examine ruins, excavations, and gathering of objects; regulations. Permits for the examination of ruins, the excavation of archaeological sites, and the gathering of objects of antiquity upon the lands under their respective jurisdictions may be granted by the Secretaries of the Interior, Agriculture, and Army to institutions which they may deem properly qualified to conduct such examination, excavation, or gathering, subject to such rules and regulations as they may prescribe: *Provided,* That the examinations, excavations, and gatherings are undertaken for the benefit of reputable museums, universities, colleges, or other recognized scientific or educational institutions, with a view to increasing the knowledge of such objects, and that the gatherings shall be made for permanent preservation in public museums. The Secretaries of the departments aforesaid shall make and publish from time to time uniform rules and regulations for the purpose of carrying out the provisions of this Act [16 U.S.C. §§ 431-433].

[June 8, 1906, ch. 3060, §§ 3, 4, 34 Stat. 225]

16 U.S.C. § 433. American antiquities. Any person who shall appropriate, excavate, injure, or destroy any historic or prehistoric ruin or monument, or any object of antiquity, situated on lands owned or controlled by the Government of the United States, without the permission of the Secretary of the Department of the Government having jurisdiction over the lands on which said antiquities are situated, shall, upon conviction, be fined in a sum of not more than $500 or be imprisoned for a period of not more than ninety days, or shall suffer both fine and imprisonment, in the discretion of the court.

[June 8, 1906, ch. 3060, § 1, 34 Stat. 225]

- 0 -

NATIONAL PARK SERVICE ORGANIC ACT
GENERAL AUTHORITIES ACT
(16 U.S.C. §§ 1-20g)

In 1872, Congress took the first step in creating what came to be the National Park System by reserving a tract of land "lying near the head-waters of the Yellowstone River" and setting it aside "as a public park and pleasuring-ground for the benefit and enjoyment of the people."[39] The lands that became Sequoia and Yosemite parks were set aside in 1890.[40]

> The National Park Service was established in 1916[41] and given a mission to promote and regulate the use of the Federal areas known as national parks, monuments, and reservations hereinafter specified ... by such means and measures as conform to the fundamental purpose of the said parks, monuments, and reservations, which purpose is to conserve the scenery and the natural and historic objects and the wild life therein and to provide for the enjoyment of the same in such manner and by such means as will leave them unimpaired for the enjoyment of future generations.[42]

This expansive delegation has provided the Service with substantial discretion -- and the agency's treatment of wildlife and wildlife habitat has varied widely.[43] Perhaps the most telling bit of anecdotal information is the simple fact that the agency has always employed more landscape architects than biologists -- and didn't hire its first biologist until 1929.[44]

16 U.S.C. § 1. Service created; director; other employees. There is created in the Department of the Interior a service to be called the National Park Service, which shall be under the charge of a director, who shall be appointed by the President, by and with the advice and consent of the Senate. The Director shall have substantial experience and demonstrated competence in land management and natural or cultural resource conservation. The Director shall select two Deputy Directors. The first Deputy Director shall have responsibility for National Park Service operations, and the second Deputy Director shall have responsibility for other programs assigned to the National Park Service. The service thus established shall promote and regulate the use of the Federal areas known as national parks, monuments, and reservations hereinafter specified, except such as are under the jurisdiction of the Secretary of the Army, as provided by law, by such means and measures as conform to the fundamental purpose of the said parks, monuments, and reservations, which purpose is to conserve the scenery and the natural and historic objects and the wild life therein and to provide for the enjoyment of the same in such manner and by such means as will leave them unimpaired for the enjoyment of future generations.

[Aug. 25, 1916, ch. 408, § 1, 39 Stat. 535; E.O. No. 6166, § 2, June 10, 1933; Mar. 2, 1934, ch. 38, § 1, 48 Stat. 389; Pub. L. 104- 333, Div. I, Title VIII, § 814(e)(1), 110 Stat. 4197 (Nov. 12, 1996)]

16 U.S.C. § 1a-1. National Park System: administration; declaration of findings and purpose. Congress declares that the national park system, which began with establishment of Yellowstone National Park in 1872, has since grown to include superlative natural, historic, and recreation areas in every major region of the United States, its territories and island possessions; that these areas, though distinct in character, are united through their inter-related purposes and resources into one national park system as cumulative expressions of a single national heritage; that, individually and collectively, these areas derive increased national dignity and recognition of their superb environmental quality through their inclusion jointly with each other in one national park system preserved and managed for the benefit and inspiration of all the people of the United States; and that it is the purpose of this Act to include all such areas in the System and to clarify the authorities applicable to the system. Congress further reaffirms, declares, and directs that the promotion and regulation of the various areas of the National Park System, as defined in section 2 of this Act [16 U.S.C. § 1c], shall be consistent with and founded in the purpose established by the first section of the Act of August 25, 1916 [National Park Service Organic Act, 16 U.S.C. § 1], to the common benefit of all the people of the United States. The authorization of activities shall be construed and the protection, management, and administration of these areas shall be conducted in light of the high public value and integrity of the National Park System and shall not be exercised in derogation of the values and purposes for which these various areas have been established, except as may have been or shall be directly and specifically provided by Congress.

[Pub. L. 91-383, § 1, 84 Stat. 825 (Aug. 18, 1970); Pub. L. 95-250, Title I, § 101(b), 92 Stat. 166 (Mar. 27, 1978)]

16 U.S.C. § 1c. General administration provisions; system defined; particular area.
(a) "National park system" defined. The "national park system" shall include any area of land and water now or hereafter administered by the Secretary of the Interior through the National Park Service for park, monument, historic, parkway, recreational, or other purposes.

(b) Specific provisions applicable to area; uniform application of sections 1b to 1d and other provisions of this title to all areas when not in conflict with specific provisions; references in other provisions to national parks, monuments, recreation areas, historic monuments, or parkways not a limitation of such other provisions to those areas. Each area within the national park system shall be administered in accordance with the provisions of any statute made specifically applicable to that area. In addition, the provisions of this Act [16 U.S.C. §§ 1b to 1d], and the various authorities relating to the administration and protection of areas under the administration of the Secretary of the Interior through the National Park Service, including but not limited to the Act of August 25, 1916 (39 Stat. 535), as amended (16 U.S.C. §§ 1, 2-4), the Act of March 4, 1911 (36 Stat. 1253), as amended (16 U.S.C. § 5) relating to rights-of-way, the Act of June 5, 1920 (41 Stat. 917), as amended (16 U.S.C. § 6), relating to donation of land and money, sections 1, 4, 5, and 6 of the Act of April 9, 1924 (43 Stat. 90), as amended (16 U.S.C. §§ 8 and 8a-8c), relating to roads and trails, the Act of March 4, 1931 (46 Stat. 1570, 16 U.S.C. § 8d) relating to approach roads to national monuments, the Act of June 3, 1948 (62 Stat. 334), as amended (16 U.S.C. §§ 8e-8f), relating to conveyance of roads to States, the Act of August 31, 1954 (68 Stat. 1037), as amended (16 U.S.C. § 452a), relating to acquisitions of inholdings, section 1 of the Act of July 3, 1926 (44 Stat. 900), as amended (16 U.S.C. § 12), relating to aid to visitors in emergencies, the Act of March 3,

1905 (33 Stat. 873, 16 U.S.C. § 10), relating to arrests, sections 3, 4, 5, and 6 of the Act of May 26, 1930 (46 Stat. 381), as amended (16 U.S.C. §§ 17b, 17c, 17d, and 17e), relating to services or other accommodations for the public, emergency supplies and services to concessioners, acceptability of travelers checks, care and removal of indigents, the Act of October 9, 1965 (79 Stat. 696, 16 U.S.C. §§ 20-20g), relating to concessions, the Land and Water Conservation Fund Act of 1965, as amended [16 U.S.C. § 406l-4 *et seq.*], and the Act of July 15, 1968 (82 Stat. 355), shall, to the extent such provisions are not in conflict with any such specific provision, be applicable to all areas within the national park system and any reference in such Act to national parks, monuments, recreation areas, historic monuments, or parkways shall hereinafter not be construed as limiting such Acts to those areas.

[Aug. 8, 1953, ch. 384, § 2, 67 Stat. 496; Pub. L. 91-383, § 2(b), 84 Stat. 826 (Aug. 18, 1970)]

16 U.S.C. § 2. National parks, reservations, and monuments; supervision. The director shall, under the direction of the Secretary of the Interior, have the supervision, management, and control of the several national parks and national monuments which on August 25, 1916, were under the jurisdiction of the Department of the Interior, and of the Hot Springs National Park in the State of Arkansas, and of such other national parks and reservations of like character as may be created by Congress. In the supervision, management, and control of national monuments contiguous to national forests the Secretary of Agriculture may cooperate with said National Park Service to such extent as may be requested by the Secretary of the Interior.

[Aug. 25, 1916, ch. 408, § 2, 39 Stat. 535; Mar. 4, 1921, ch. 161, § 1, 41 Stat. 1407]

16 U.S.C. § 3. Rules and regulations of national parks, reservations, and monuments; timber; leases. The Secretary of the Interior shall make and publish such rules and regulations as he may deem necessary or proper for the use and management of the parks, monuments, and reservations under the jurisdiction of the National Park Service, and any violation of any of the rules and regulations authorized by this Act shall be punished by a fine of not more than $500 or imprisonment for not exceeding six months, or both, and be adjudged to pay all costs of the proceedings. He may also, upon terms and conditions to be fixed by him, sell or dispose of timber in those cases where in his judgment the cutting of such timber is required in order to control the attacks of insects or diseases or otherwise conserve the scenery or the natural or historic objects in any such park, monument, or reservation. He may also provide in his discretion for the destruction of such animals and of such plant life as may be detrimental to the use of any of said parks, monuments, or reservations. No natural, curiosities, wonders, or objects of interest shall be leased, rented, or granted to anyone on such terms as to interfere with free access to them by the public: *Provided, however,* That the Secretary of the Interior may, under such rules and regulations and on such terms as he may prescribe, grant the privilege to graze livestock within any national park, monument, or reservation herein referred to when in his judgment such use is not detrimental to the primary purpose for which such park, monument, or reservation was created, except that this provision shall not apply to the Yellowstone National Park: *And provided further,* That the Secretary of the Interior may grant said privileges, leases, and permits and enter into contracts relating to the same with responsible persons, firms, or corporations without advertising and without securing competitive bids: *And provided further,* That no contract, lease, permit, or privilege granted shall be assigned or transferred by such grantees, permittees, or licensees without the approval of the Secretary of the Interior first obtained in writing.

[Aug. 25, 1916, ch. 408, § 3, 39 Stat. 535; June 2, 1920, ch. 218, § 5, 41 Stat. 732; Mar. 7, 1928, ch. 137, § 1, 45 Stat. 235; Pub. L. 85-434, 72 Stat. 152 (May 29, 1958); Pub. L. 105-391, Title IV, § 415(b)(1), 112 Stat. 3515 (Nov. 13, 1998)]

- 0 -

b. The National Forest Service: The National Forest System

The National Forest Service is the first federal land management agency to have its mission defined in an organic act. Indeed, the act is known simply as The Organic Act of 1897.[45] The Organic Act delegated the agency very broad management discretion.[46] The agency's multiple-use management style was confirmed in The Multiple-Use, Sustained-Yield Act of 1960 (MUSYA).[47] In MUSYA, Congress specifically noted that wildlife was a valid purpose for managing the forests:

> It is the policy of the Congress that the national forests are established and shall be administered for outdoor recreation, range, timber, watershed, and wildlife and fish purposes.[48]

The agency's discretion was substantially restricted and a new management system was introduced in the National Forest Management Act of 1976 (NFMA).[49] The NFMA governs forest management practices from land-use planning to clearcutting standards. It also includes the most specific biodiversity requirements applicable to any federal agency.[50]

NATIONAL FOREST SERVICE ORGANIC ACT (1897) (16 U.S.C. § 475)

16 U.S.C. § 475. Purposes for which national forests may be established and administered. All public lands heretofore [before June 4, 1897] designated and reserved by the President of the United States under the provisions of the Act approved March third, eighteen hundred and ninety-one, the orders for which shall be and remain in full force and effect, unsuspended and unrevoked, and all public lands that may hereafter be set aside and reserved as public forest reserves [national forests] under said Act, shall be as far as practicable controlled and administered in accordance with the following provisions. No public forest reservation [national forest] shall be established, except to improve and protect the forest within the reservation [national forest] or for the purpose of securing favorable conditions of water flows, and to furnish a continuous supply of timber for the use and necessities of citizens of the United States; but it is not the purpose or intent of these provisions, or of said section, to authorize the inclusion therein of lands more valuable for the mineral therein, or for agricultural purposes, than for forest purposes.

[June 4, 1897, ch. 2, § 1, 30 Stat. 34]

MULTIPLE-USE SUSTAINED-YIELD ACT (1960)
(16 U.S.C. §§ 528-531)

16 U.S.C. § 528. Development and administration of renewable surface resources for multiple use and sustained yield of products and services; Congressional declaration of policy and purpose. It is the policy of the Congress that the national forests are established and shall be administered for outdoor recreation, range, timber, watershed, and wildlife and fish purposes. The purposes of this Act [16 U.S.C. §§ 528-531] are declared to be supplemental to, but not in derogation of, the purposes for which the national forests were established as set forth in the Act of June 4, 1897 (16 U.S.C. § 475). Nothing herein shall be construed as affecting the jurisdiction or responsibilities of the several States with respect to wildlife and fish on the national forests. Nothing herein shall be construed so as to affect the use or administration of the mineral resources of national forest lands or to affect the use or administration of Federal lands not within national forests.

[Pub. L. 86-517, § 1, 74 Stat. 215 (June 12, 1960)]

16 U.S.C. § 529. Authorization of development and administration; consideration to relative values of resources; areas of wilderness. The Secretary of Agriculture is authorized and directed to develop and administer the renewable surface resources of the national forests for multiple use and sustained yield of the several products and services obtained therefrom. In the administration of the national forests due consideration shall be given to the relative values of the various resources in particular areas. The establishment and maintenance of areas of wilderness are consistent with the purposes and provisions of this Act [16 U.S.C. §§ 528-531].

[Pub. L. 86-517, § 2, 74 Stat. 215 (June 12, 1960)]

16 U.S.C. § 530. Cooperation for purposes of development and administration with State and local governmental agencies and others. In the effectuation of this Act [16 U.S.C. §§ 528-531] the Secretary of Agriculture is authorized to cooperate with interested State and local governmental agencies and others in the development and management of the national forests.

[Pub. L. 86-517, § 3, 74 Stat. 215 (June 12, 1960)]

16 U.S.C. § 531. Definitions. As used in this Act [16 U.S.C. §§ 528-531] the following terms shall have the following meanings:

(a) "Multiple use" means: The management of all the various renewable surface resources of the national forests so that they are utilized in the combination that will best meet the needs of the American people; making the most judicious use of the

land for some or all of these resources or related services over areas large enough to provide sufficient latitude for periodic adjustments in use to conform to changing needs and conditions; that some land will be used for less than all of the resources; and harmonious and coordinated management of the various resources, each with the other, without impairment of the productivity of the land, with consideration being given to the relative values of the various resources, and not necessarily the combination of uses that will give the greatest dollar return or the greatest unit output.
(b) "Sustained yield of the several products and services" means the achievement and maintenance in perpetuity of a high-level annual or regular periodic output of the various renewable resources of the national forests without impairment of the productivity of the land.

[Pub. L. 86-517, § 4, 74 Stat. 215 (June 12, 1960)]

NATIONAL FOREST MANAGEMENT ACT (1976)
(16 U.S.C. §§ 1600-1616)

16 U.S.C. § 1600. Congressional findings. The Congress finds that --

(1) the management of the Nation's renewable resources is highly complex and the uses, demand for, and supply of the various resources are subject to change over time;

(2) the public interest is served by the Forest Service, Department of Agriculture, in cooperation with other agencies, assessing the Nation's renewable resources, and developing and preparing a national renewable resource program, which is periodically reviewed and updated;

(3) to serve the national interest, the renewable resource program must be based on a comprehensive assessment of present and anticipated uses, demand for, and supply of renewable resources from the Nation's public and private forests and rangelands, through analysis of environmental and economic impacts, coordination of multiple use and sustained yield opportunities as provided in the Multiple-Use Sustained-Yield Act of 1960 (74 Stat. 215; 16 U.S.C. 528-531), and public participation in the development of the program;

(4) the new knowledge derived from coordinated public and private research programs will promote a sound technical and ecological base for effective management, use, and protection of the Nation's renewable resources;

(5) inasmuch as the majority of the Nation's forests and rangeland is under private, State, and local governmental management and the Nation's major capacity to produce goods and services is based on these nonfederally managed renewable resources, the Federal Government should be a catalyst to encourage and assist these owners in the efficient long-term use and improvement of these lands and their renewable resources consistent with the principles of sustained yield and multiple use;

(6) the Forest Service, by virtue of its statutory authority for management of the National Forest System, research and cooperative programs, and its role as an agency in the Department of Agriculture, has both a responsibility and an opportunity to be a leader in assuring that the Nation maintains a natural resource conservation posture that will meet the requirements of our people in perpetuity; and

(7) recycled timber product materials are as much a part of our renewable forest resources as are the trees from which they originally came, and in order to extend our timber and timber fiber resources and reduce pressures for timber production from Federal lands, the Forest Service should expand its research in the use of recycled and waste timber product materials, develop techniques for the substitution of these secondary materials for primary materials, and promote and encourage the use of recycled timber product materials.

[Pub. L. 93-378, § 2, as added Pub. L. 94-588, § 2, 90 Stat. 2949 (Oct. 22, 1976)]

16 U.S.C. § 1601. Renewable Resource Assessment. (a) Preparation by Secretary of Agriculture; time of preparation, updating and contents. In recognition of the vital importance of America's renewable resources of the forest, range, and other associated lands to the Nation's social and economic well-being, and of the necessity for a long term perspective in planning and undertaking related national renewable resource programs administered by the Forest Service, the Secretary of Agriculture shall prepare a Renewable Resource Assessment (hereinafter called the "Assessment"). The Assessment shall be prepared not later than December 31, 1975, and shall be updated during 1979 and each tenth year thereafter, and shall include but not be limited to --

(1) an analysis of present and anticipated uses, demand for, and supply of the renewable resources, with consideration of the international resource situation, and an emphasis of pertinent supply and demand and price relationship trends;

(2) an inventory, based on information developed by the Forest Service and other Federal agencies, of present and potential renewable resources, and an evaluation of opportunities for improving their yield of tangible and intangible goods and services, together with estimates of investment costs and direct and indirect returns to the Federal Government;

(3) a description of Forest Service programs and responsibilities in research, cooperative programs and management of the National Forest System, their interrelationships, and the relationship of these programs and responsibilities to public and private activities;

(4) a discussion of important policy considerations, laws, regulations, and other factors expected to influence and affect significantly the use, ownership, and management of forest, range, and other associated lands;

(5) an analysis of the potential effects of global climate change on the condition of renewable resources on the forests and rangelands of the United States; and

(6) an analysis of the rural and urban forestry opportunities to mitigate the buildup of atmospheric carbon dioxide and reduce the risk of global climate change[.]

(b) Omitted.

(c) Contents of Assessments. The Secretary shall report in the 1979 and subsequent Assessments on:

(1) the additional fiber potential in the National Forest System including, but not restricted to, forest mortality, growth, salvage potential, potential increased forest products sales, economic constraints, alternate markets, contract considerations, and other multiple use considerations;

(2) the potential for increased utilization of forest and wood product wastes in the National Forest System and on other lands, and of urban wood wastes and wood product recycling, including recommendations to the Congress for actions which would lead to increased utilization of material now being wasted both in the forests and in manufactured products; and

(3) the milling and other wood fiber product fabrication facilities and their location in the United States, noting the public and private forested areas that supply such facilities, assessing the degree of utilization into product form of harvested trees by such facilities, and setting forth the technology appropriate to the facilities to improve utilization either individually or in aggregate units of harvested trees and to reduce wasted wood fibers. The Secretary shall set forth a program to encourage the adoption by these facilities of these technologies for improving wood fiber utilization.

(d) Public involvement; consultation with governmental departments and agencies.

****

(d) Congressional policy of multiple use sustained yield management; examination and certification of lands; estimate of appropriations necessary for reforestation and other treatment; budget requirements; authorization of appropriations. (1) It is the policy of the Congress that all forested lands in the National Forest System shall be maintained in appropriate forest cover with species of trees, degree of stocking, rate of growth, and conditions of stand designed to secure the maximum benefits of multiple use sustained yield management in accordance with land management plans. Accordingly, the Secretary is directed to identify and report to the Congress annually at the time of submission of the President's budget together with the annual report provided for under section 8(c) of this Act [16 U.S.C. § 1606(c)], beginning with submission of the President's budget for fiscal year 1978, the amount and location by forests and States and by productivity class, where practicable, of all lands in the National Forest System where objectives of land management plans indicate the need to reforest areas that have been cut-over or otherwise denuded or deforested, and all lands with stands of trees that are not growing at their best potential rate of growth. All national forest lands treated from year to year shall be examined after the first and third growing seasons and certified by the Secretary in the report provided for under this subsection as to stocking rate, growth rate in relation to potential and other pertinent measures. Any lands not certified as satisfactory shall be returned to the backlog and scheduled for prompt treatment. The level and types of treatment shall be those which secure the most effective mix of multiple use benefits.

(2) Notwithstanding the provisions of section 9 of this Act [16 U.S.C. § 1607], the Secretary shall annually for eight years following the enactment of this subsection [October 22, 1976], transmit to the Congress in the manner provided in this subsection an estimate of the sums necessary to be appropriated, in addition to the funds available from other sources, to replant and otherwise treat an acreage equal to the acreage to be cut over that year, plus a sufficient portion of the backlog of lands found to be in need of treatment to eliminate the backlog within the eight-year period. After such eight-year period, the Secretary shall transmit annually to the Congress an estimate of the sums necessary to replant and otherwise treat all lands

being cut over and maintain planned timber production on all other forested lands in the National Forest System so as to prevent the development of a backlog of needed work larger than the needed work at the beginning of the fiscal year. The Secretary's estimate of sums necessary, in addition to the sums available under other authorities, for accomplishment of the reforestation and other treatment of National Forest System lands under this section shall be provided annually for inclusion in the President's budget and shall also be transmitted to the Speaker of the House and the President of the Senate together with the annual report provided for under section 8(c) of this Act [16 U.S.C. § 1606(c)] at the time of submission of the President's budget to the Congress beginning with the budget for fiscal year 1978. The sums estimated as necessary for reforestation and other treatment shall include moneys needed to secure seed, grow seedlings, prepare sites, plant trees, thin, remove deleterious growth and underbrush, build fence to exclude livestock and adverse wildlife from regeneration areas and otherwise establish and improve growing forests to secure planned production of trees and other multiple use values.

****

(e) Report on herbicides and pesticides. ****

[Pub. L. 93-378, § 3, formerly § 2, 88 Stat. 476 (Aug. 17, 1974); renumbered § 3 and amended Pub. L. 94-588, §§ 2-4, 90 Stat. 2949, 2950 (Oct. 22, 1976); Pub. L. 101-624, Title XXIV, § 2408(a), 104 Stat. 4061 (Nov. 28, 1990)]

16 U.S.C. § 1602. Renewable Resource Program; preparation by Secretary of Agriculture and transmittal to President; purpose and development of program; time of preparation, updating and contents. In order to provide for periodic review of programs for management and administration of the National Forest System, for research, for cooperative State and private Forest Service programs, and for conduct of other Forest Service activities in relation to the findings of the Assessment, the Secretary of Agriculture, utilizing information available to the Forest Service and other agencies within the Department of Agriculture, including data prepared pursuant to section 302 of the Rural Development Act of 1972 [7 U.S.C. § 1010a], shall prepare and transmit to the President a recommended Renewable Resource Program (hereinafter called the "Program"). The Program transmitted to the President may include alternatives, and shall provide in appropriate detail for protection, management, and development of the National Forest System, including forest development roads and trails; for cooperative Forest Service programs; and for research. The Programs shall be developed in accordance with principles set forth in the Multiple-Use Sustained-Yield Act of June 12, 1960 (74 Stat. 215; 16 U.S.C. 528-531), and the National Environmental Policy Act of 1969 (83 Stat. 852) [42 U.S.C. § 4321 *et seq.*]. The Program shall be prepared not later than December 31, 1975, to cover the four-year period beginning October 1, 1976, and at least each of the four fiscal decades next following such period, and shall be updated no later than during the first half of the fiscal year ending September 30, 1980, and the first half of each fifth fiscal year thereafter to cover at least each of the four fiscal decades beginning next after such updating. The Program shall include, but not be limited to --

(1) an inventory of specific needs and opportunities for both public and private program investments. The inventory shall differentiate between activities which are

of a capital nature and those which are of an operational nature;

(2) specific identification of Program outputs, results anticipated, and benefits associated with investments in such a manner that the anticipated costs can be directly compared with the total related benefits and direct and indirect returns to the Federal Government;

(3) a discussion of priorities for accomplishment of inventoried Program opportunities, with specified costs, outputs, results, and benefits;

(4) a detailed study of personnel requirements as needed to implement and monitor existing and ongoing programs; and

(5) Program recommendations which --

(A) evaluate objectives for the major Forest Service programs in order that multiple-use and sustained-yield relationships among and within the renewable resources can be determined;

(B) explain the opportunities for owners of forests and rangeland to participate in programs to improve and enhance the condition of the land and the renewable resource products therefrom;

(C) recognize the fundamental need to protect and, where appropriate, improve the quality of soil, water, and air resources;

(D) state national goals that recognize the interrelationships between and interdependence within the renewable resources;

(E) evaluate the impact of the export and import of raw logs upon domestic timber supplies and prices; and

(F) account for the effects of global climate change on forest and rangeland conditions, including potential effects on the geographic ranges of species, and on forest and rangeland products.

[Pub. L. 93-378, § 4, formerly § 3, 88 Stat. 477 (Aug. 17, 1974), renumbered and amended Pub. L. 94-588, §§ 2, 5, 90 Stat. 2949, 2951 (Oct. 22, 1976); Pub. L. 101-624, Title XXIV, § 2408(b), 104 Stat. 4061 (Nov. 28, 1990)]

16 U.S.C. § 1603. National Forest System resource inventories; development, maintenance, and updating by Secretary of Agriculture as part of Assessment. As a part of the Assessment, the Secretary of Agriculture shall develop and maintain on a continuing basis a comprehensive and appropriately detailed inventory of all National Forest System lands and renewable resources. This inventory shall be kept current so as to reflect changes in conditions and identify new and emerging resources and values.

[Pub. L. 93-378, § 5, formerly § 4, 88 Stat. 477 (Aug. 17, 1974), renumbered Pub.L. 94-588, § 2, 90 Stat. 2949 (Oct. 22, 1976)]

16 U.S.C. § 1604. National Forest System land and resource management plans. (a) Development, maintenance, and revision by Secretary of Agriculture as part of program; coordination. As a part of the Program provided for by section 4 of this Act [16 U.S.C. § 1602], the Secretary of Agriculture shall develop, maintain, and, as appropriate, revise land and resource management plans for units of the National Forest System, coordinated with the land and resource management planning processes of State and local governments and other Federal agencies.

(b) Criteria. In the development and maintenance of land management plans for use on units of the National Forest System, the Secretary shall use a systematic interdisciplinary approach to achieve integrated consideration of physical, biological, economic, and other sciences.

(c) Incorporation of standards and guidelines by Secretary; time of completion; progress reports; existing management plans. ****

(d) Public participation in management plans; availability of plans; public meetings. The Secretary shall provide for public participation in the development, review, and revision of land management plans including, but not limited to, making the plans or revisions available to the public at convenient locations in the vicinity of the affected unit for a period of at least three months before final adoption, during which period the Secretary shall publicize and hold public meetings or comparable processes at locations that foster public participation in the review of such plans or revisions.

(e) Required assurances. In developing, maintaining, and revising plans for units of the National Forest System pursuant to this section, the Secretary shall assure that such plans --

(1) provide for multiple use and sustained yield of the products and services obtained therefrom in accordance with the Multiple-Use Sustained-Yield Act of 1960 [16 U.S.C. §§ 528-531], and, in particular, include coordination of outdoor recreation, range, timber, watershed, wildlife and fish, and wilderness; and

(2) determine forest management systems, harvesting levels, and procedures in the light of all of the uses set forth in subsection (c)(1) of this section, the definition of the terms "multiple use" and "sustained yield" as provided in the Multiple-Use Sustained-Yield Act of 1960, and the availability of lands and their suitability for resource management.

(f) Required provisions. Plans developed in accordance with this section shall --

(1) form one integrated plan for each unit of the National Forest System, incorporating in one document or one set of documents, available to the public at convenient locations, all of the features required by this section;

(2) be embodied in appropriate written material, including maps and other descriptive documents, reflecting proposed and possible actions, including the planned timber sale program and the proportion of probable methods of timber harvest within the unit necessary to fulfill the plan;

(3) be prepared by an interdisciplinary team. Each team shall prepare its plan based on inventories of the applicable resources of the forest;

(4) be amended in any manner whatsoever after final adoption after public notice, and, if such amendment would result in a significant change in such plan, in accordance with the provisions of subsections (e) and (f) of this section and public involvement comparable to that required by subsection (d) of this section; and

(5) be revised (A) from time to time when the Secretary finds conditions in a unit have significantly changed, but at least every fifteen years, and (B) in accordance with the provisions of subsections (e) and (f) of this section and public involvement

comparable to that required by subsection (d) of this section.

(g) Promulgation of regulations for development and revision of plans; environmental considerations; resource management guidelines; guidelines for land management plans. As soon as practicable, but not later than two years after the enactment of this subsection [October 22, 1976], the Secretary shall in accordance with the procedures set forth in section 553 of Title 5 promulgate regulations, under the principles of the Multiple-Use Sustained-Yield Act of 1960 [16 U.S.C. §§ 528-531], that set out the process for the development and revision of the land management plans, and the guidelines and standards prescribed by this subsection. The regulations shall include, but not be limited to --

(1) specifying procedures to insure that land management plans are prepared in accordance with the National Environmental Policy Act of 1969 [42 U.S.C. § 4321 *et seq.*], including, but not limited to, direction on when and for what plans an environmental impact statement required under section 102(2)(C) of that Act [42 U.S.C. § 4332(2)(C)] shall be prepared;

(2) specifying guidelines which --

(A) require the identification of the suitability of lands for resource management;

(B) provide for obtaining inventory data on the various renewable resources, and soil and water, including pertinent maps, graphic material, and explanatory aids; and

(C) provide for methods to identify special conditions or situations involving hazards to the various resources and their relationship to alternative activities;

(3) specifying guidelines for land management plans developed to achieve the goals of the Program which --

(A) insure consideration of the economic and environmental aspects of various systems of renewable resource management, including the related systems of silviculture and protection of forest resources, to provide for outdoor recreation (including wilderness), range, timber, watershed, wildlife, and fish;

(B) provide for diversity of plant and animal communities based on the suitability and capability of the specific land area in order to meet overall multiple-use objectives, and within the multiple-use objectives of a land management plan adopted pursuant to this section, provide, where appropriate, to the degree practicable, for steps to be taken to preserve the diversity of tree species similar to that existing in the region controlled by the plan;

(C) insure research on and (based on continuous monitoring and assessment in the field) evaluation of the effects of each management system to the end that it will not produce substantial and permanent impairment of the productivity of the land;

(D) permit increases in harvest levels based on intensified management practices, such as reforestation, thinning, and tree improvement if (i) such practices justify increasing the harvests in accordance with the Multiple-Use Sustained-Yield Act of 1960, and (ii) such harvest levels are decreased at the end of each planning period if such practices cannot be successfully implemented or funds are not received to permit such practices to continue substantially as planned;

(E) insure that timber will be harvested from National Forest System lands only where --

(i) soil, slope, or other watershed conditions will not be irreversibly damaged;

(ii) there is assurance that such lands can be adequately restocked within five years after harvest;

(iii) protection is provided for streams, streambanks, shorelines, lakes, wetlands, and other bodies of water from detrimental changes in water temperatures, blockages of water courses, and deposits of sediment, where harvests are likely to seriously and adversely affect water conditions or fish habitat; and

(iv) the harvesting system to be used is not selected primarily because it will give the greatest dollar return or the greatest unit output of timber; and

(F) insure that clearcutting, seed tree cutting, shelterwood cutting, and other cuts designed to regenerate an even-aged stand of timber will be used as a cutting method on National Forest System lands only where --

(i) for clearcutting, it is determined to be the optimum method, and for other such cuts it is determined to be appropriate, to meet the objectives and requirements of the relevant land management plan;

(ii) the interdisciplinary review as determined by the Secretary has been completed and the potential environmental, biological, esthetic, engineering, and economic impacts on each advertised sale area have been assessed, as well as the consistency of the sale with the multiple use of the general area;

(iii) cut blocks, patches, or strips are shaped and blended to the extent practicable with the natural terrain;

(iv) there are established according to geographic areas, forest types, or other suitable classifications the maximum size limits for areas to be cut in one harvest operation, including provision to exceed the established limits after appropriate public notice and review by the responsible Forest Service officer one level above the Forest Service officer who normally would approve the harvest proposal: *Provided,* That such limits shall not apply to the size of areas harvested as a result of natural catastrophic conditions such as fire, insect and disease attack, or windstorm; and

(v) such cuts are carried out in a manner consistent with the protection of soil, watershed, fish, wildlife, recreation, and esthetic resources, and the regeneration of the timber resource.

(h) Scientific committee to aid in promulgation of regulations; termination; revision committees; clerical and technical assistance; compensation of committee members. (1) In carrying out the purposes of subsection (g) of this section, the Secretary of Agriculture shall appoint a committee of scientists who are not officers or employees of the Forest Service. The committee shall provide scientific and technical advice and counsel on proposed guidelines and procedures to assure that an effective interdisciplinary approach is proposed and adopted. The committee shall terminate upon promulgation of the regulations, but the Secretary may, from time to time, appoint similar committees when considering revisions of the regulations. The views of the committees shall be included in the public information supplied when the regulations are proposed for adoption.

****

(i) Consistency of resource plans, permits, contracts, and other instruments with land management plans; revision. Resource plans and permits, contracts, and other instruments for the use and occupancy of National Forest System lands shall be consistent with the land management plans. ****

(j) Effective date of land management plans and revisions. ****

(k) Development of land management plans. In developing land management plans pursuant to this Act, the Secretary shall identify lands within the management area which are not suited for timber production, considering physical, economic, and other pertinent factors to the extent feasible, as determined by the Secretary, and shall assure that, except for salvage sales or sales necessitated to protect other multiple-use values, no timber harvesting shall occur on such lands for a period of 10 years. Lands once identified as unsuitable for timber production shall continue to be treated for reforestation purposes, particularly with regard to the protection of other multiple-use values. The Secretary shall review his decision to classify these lands as not suited for timber production at least every 10 years and shall return these lands to timber production whenever he determines that conditions have changed so that they have become suitable for timber production.

(l) Program evaluation; process for estimating long-term costs and benefits; summary of data included in annual report. ****

(m) Establishment of standards to ensure culmination of mean annual increment of growth; silvicultural practices; salvage harvesting; exceptions. The Secretary shall establish --

(1) standards to insure that, prior to harvest, stands of trees throughout the National Forest System shall generally have reached the culmination of mean annual increment of growth (calculated on the basis of cubic measurement or other methods of calculation at the discretion of the Secretary): *Provided,* That these standards shall not preclude the use of sound silvicultural practices, such as thinning or other stand improvement measures: *Provided further,* That these standards shall not preclude the Secretary from salvage or sanitation harvesting of timber stands which are substantially damaged by fire, windthrow or other catastrophe, or which are in imminent danger from insect or disease attack; and

(2) exceptions to these standards for the harvest of particular species of trees in management units after consideration has been given to the multiple uses of the forest including, but not limited to, recreation, wildlife habitat, and range and after completion of public participation processes utilizing the procedures of subsection (d) of this section.

[Pub. L. 93-378, § 6, formerly § 5, 88 Stat. 477 (Aug. 17, 1974); renumbered § 6 and amended Pub. L. 94-588, §§ 2, 6, 12(a), 90 Stat. 2949, 2952, 2958 (Oct. 22, 1976)]

16 U.S.C. § 1605. Protection, use and management of renewable resources on non-Federal lands; utilization of Assessment, surveys and Program by Secretary of Agriculture to assist States, etc. ****

16 U.S.C. § 1606. Budget requests by President for Forest Service activities. ****

16 U.S.C. § 1607. National Forest System renewable resources; development and administration by Secretary of Agriculture in accordance with multiple use and sustained yield concepts for products and services; target year for operational posture of resources; budget requests. The Secretary of Agriculture shall take such action as will assure that the development and administration of the renewable resources of the National Forest System are in full accord with the concepts for multiple use and sustained yield of products and services as set forth in the Multiple-Use Sustained-Yield Act of 1960 [16 U.S.C. §§ 528-531]. To further these concepts, the Congress hereby sets the year 2000 as the target year when the renewable resources of the National Forest System shall be in an operating posture whereby all backlogs of needed treatment for their restoration shall be reduced to a current basis and the major portion of planned intensive multiple-use sustained-yield management procedures shall be installed and operating on an environmentally-sound basis. The annual budget shall contain requests for funds for an orderly program to eliminate such backlogs: *Provided,* That when the Secretary finds that (1) the backlog of areas that will benefit by such treatment has been eliminated, (2) the cost of treating the remainder of such area exceeds the economic and environmental benefits to be secured from their treatment, or (3) the total supplies of the renewable resources of the United States are adequate to meet the future needs of the American people, the budget request for these elements of restoration may be adjusted accordingly.

[Pub. L. 93-378, § 9, formerly § 8, 88 Stat. 479 (Aug. 17, 1974), renumbered Pub. L. 94-588, § 2, 90 Stat. 2949 (Oct. 22, 1976)]

16 U.S.C. § 1608. National Forest Transportation System. (a) Congressional declaration of policy; time for development; method of financing; financing of forest development roads. ****

(b) Construction of temporary roadways in connection with timber contracts, and other permits or leases. Unless the necessity for a permanent road is set forth in the forest development road system plan, any road constructed on land of the National Forest System in connection with a timber contract or other permit or lease shall be designed with the goal of reestablishing vegetative cover on the roadway and areas where the vegetative cover has been disturbed by the construction of the road, within ten years after the termination of the contract, permit, or lease either through artificial or natural means. Such action shall be taken unless it is later determined that the road is needed for use as a part of the National Forest Transportation System.

(c) Standards of roadway construction. ****

[Pub. L. 93-378, § 10, formerly § 9, 88 Stat. 479 (Aug. 17, 1974), renumbered and amended Pub. L. 94-588, §§ 2, 8, 90 Stat. 2949, 2956 (Oct. 22, 1976); Pub. L. 97-100, Title II, § 201, 95 Stat. 1405 (Dec. 23, 1981)]

16 U.S.C. § 1609. National Forest System. ****

16 U.S.C. § 1610. Implementation of provisions by Secretary of Agriculture; utilization of information and data of other organizations; avoidance of duplication of planning, etc.; "renewable resources" defined. ****

16 U.S.C. § 1611. Timber. (a) Limitations on removal; variations in allowable sale quantity; public participation. The Secretary of Agriculture shall limit the sale of timber from each national forest to a quantity equal to or less than a quantity which can be removed from such forest annually in perpetuity on a sustained-yield basis: *Provided,* That, in order to meet overall multiple-use objectives, the Secretary may establish an allowable sale quantity for any decade which departs from the projected long-term average sale quantity that would otherwise be established: *Provided further,* That any such planned departure must be consistent with the multiple-use management objectives of the land management plan. Plans for variations in the allowable sale quantity must be made with public participation as required by section 6(d) of this Act [16 U.S.C. § 1604(d)]. In addition, within any decade, the Secretary may sell a quantity in excess of the annual allowable sale quantity established pursuant to this section in the case of any national forest so long as the average sale quantities of timber from such national forest over the decade covered by the plan do not exceed such quantity limitation. In those cases where a forest has less than two hundred thousand acres of commercial forest land, the Secretary may use two or more forests for purposes of determining the sustained yield.

(b) Salvage harvesting. Nothing in subsection (a) of this section shall prohibit the Secretary from salvage or sanitation harvesting of timber stands which are substantially damaged by fire, windthrow, or other catastrophe, or which are in imminent danger from insect or disease attack. The Secretary may either substitute such timber for timber that would otherwise be sold under the plan or, if not feasible, sell such timber over and above the plan volume.

[Pub. L. 93-378, § 13, as added Pub. L. 94-588, § 11, 90 Stat. 2957 (Oct. 22, 1976)]

16 U.S.C. § 1612. Public participation. ****

16 U.S.C. § 1613. Promulgation of regulations. The Secretary of Agriculture shall prescribe such regulations as he determines necessary and desirable to carry out the provisions of this Act.

[Pub. L. 93-378, § 15, as added Pub. L. 94-588, § 11, 90 Stat. 2958 (Oct. 22, 1976)]

16 U.S.C. § 1614. Severability. ****

\- 0 -

c. The Bureau of Land Management: The Remnants of the Public Domain

The Bureau of Land Management is the successor of the General Land Office and the Grazing Service. It is the agency that is responsible for managing the remnants of the public domain -- all of the lands not otherwise reserved as forests, refuges, monuments, and parks. There are hundreds of statutes applicable to this residue.

Traditionally, the BLM had two primary "missions": grazing and mining -- hence the derisive appellation, the "Bureau of Livestock and Mining." Range resources are managed pursuant to the Taylor Grazing Act of 1934[51] and the Public Rangelands Improvement Act of 1978.[52] Mineral resources are subject to disposition under the General Mining Law of 1872,[53] the Mineral Lands Leasing Act of 1920,[54] the Acquired Lands Leasing Act of 1947,[55] and the Geothermal Steam Act of 1970.[56]

The BLM did not have an organic act until 1976 when Congress enacted the Federal Land Policy and Management Act (FLPMA).[57] FLPMA was enacted the day before the NFMA. Although the two statutes do share several principles -- for example, both impose land-use planning requirements on the land-managing agency -- for wildlife it is the differences that seem most notable. Unlike the biodiversity provisions included in NFMA's land use planning requirements, wildlife appears only marginally in FLPMA. The Act does delegate sufficient discretion to permit the agency to conserve wildlife habitat -- it does not, however, explicitly mandate such conservation. Similarly, in the subsequently enacted Public Rangelands Improvement Act of 1978[58] Congress noted wildlife and habitat concerns[59] but did not mandate any specific conservation measures.

FEDERAL LAND POLICY & MANAGEMENT ACT (1976)
(43 U.S.C. §§ 1701-1784)

43 U.S.C. § 1701. Congressional declaration of policy. (a) The Congress declares that it is the policy of the United States that --

(1) the public lands be retained in Federal ownership, unless as a result of the land use planning procedure provided for in this Act, it is determined that disposal of a particular parcel will serve the national interest;

(2) the national interest will be best realized if the public lands and their resources are periodically and systematically inventoried and their present and future use is projected through a land use planning process coordinated with other Federal and State planning efforts;

(3) public lands not previously designated for any specific use and all existing classifications of public lands that were effected by executive action or statute before the date of enactment of this statute [October 21, 1976], be reviewed in accordance with the provisions of this Act;

(4) the Congress exercise its constitutional authority to withdraw or otherwise designate or dedicate Federal lands for specified purposes and that Congress delineate the extent to which the Executive may withdraw lands without legislative action;

(5) in administering public land statutes and exercising discretionary authority granted by them, the Secretary be required to establish comprehensive rules and regulations after considering the views of the general public; and to structure adjudication procedures to assure adequate third party participation, objective administrative review of initial decisions, and expeditious decisionmaking;
(6) judicial review of public land adjudication decisions be provided by law;
(7) goals and objectives be established by law as guidelines for public land use planning, and that management be on the basis of multiple use and sustained yield unless otherwise specified by law;
(8) the public lands be managed in a manner that will protect the quality of scientific, scenic, historical, ecological, environmental, air and atmospheric, water resource, and archeological values; that, where appropriate, will preserve and protect certain public lands in their natural condition; that will provide food and habitat for fish and wildlife and domestic animals; and that will provide for outdoor recreation and human occupancy and use;
(9) the United States receive fair market value of the use of the public lands and their resources unless otherwise provided for by statute;
(10) uniform procedures for any disposal of public land, acquisition of non- Federal land for public purposes, and the exchange of such lands be established by statute, requiring each disposal, acquisition, and exchange to be consistent with the prescribed mission of the department or agency involved, and reserving to the Congress review of disposals in excess of a specified acreage;
(11) regulations and plans for the protection of public land areas of critical environmental concern be promptly developed;
(12) the public lands be managed in a manner which recognizes the Nation's need for domestic sources of minerals, food, timber, and fiber from the public lands including implementation of the Mining and Minerals Policy Act of 1970 (84 Stat. 1876, 30 U.S.C. 21a) as it pertains to the public lands; and
(13) the Federal Government should, on a basis equitable to both the Federal and local taxpayer, provide for payments to compensate States and local governments for burdens created as a result of the immunity of Federal lands from State and local taxation.

(b) The policies of this Act shall become effective only as specific statutory authority for their implementation is enacted by this Act or by subsequent legislation and shall then be construed as supplemental to and not in derogation of the purposes for which public lands are administered under other provisions of law.

[Pub. L. 94-579, Title I, § 102, 90 Stat. 2744 (Oct. 21, 1976)]

43 U.S.C. § 1702. Definitions. Without altering in any way the meaning of the following terms as used in any other statute, whether or not such statute is referred to in, or amended by, this Act, as used in this Act --

(a) The term "areas of critical environmental concern" means areas within the public lands where special management attention is required (when such areas are developed or used or where no development is required) to protect and prevent irreparable damage to important historic, cultural, or scenic values, fish and wildlife resources or other natural systems or processes, or to protect life and safety from natural hazards.

(b) The term "holder" means any State or local governmental entity, individual, partnership, corporation, association, or other business entity receiving or using a right-of-way under title V of this Act [43 U.S.C. §§ 1761 *et seq.*].

(c) The term "multiple use" means the management of the public lands and their various resource values so that they are utilized in the combination that will best meet the present and future needs of the American people; making the most judicious use of the land for some or all of these resources or related services over areas large enough to provide sufficient latitude for periodic adjustments in use to conform to changing needs and conditions; the use of some land for less than all of the resources; a combination of balanced and diverse resource uses that takes into account the long-term needs of future generations for renewable and nonrenewable resources, including, but not limited to, recreation, range, timber, minerals, watershed, wildlife and fish, and natural scenic, scientific and historical values; and harmonious and coordinated management of the various resources without permanent impairment of the productivity of the land and the quality of the environment with consideration being given to the relative values of the resources and not necessarily to the combination of uses that will give the greatest economic return or the greatest unit output.

(d) The term "public involvement" means the opportunity for participation by affected citizens in rulemaking, decisionmaking, and planning with respect to the public lands, including public meetings or hearings held at locations near the affected lands, or advisory mechanisms, or such other procedures as may be necessary to provide public comment in a particular instance.

(e) The term "public lands" means any land and interest in land owned by the United States within the several States and administered by the Secretary of the Interior through the Bureau of Land Management, without regard to how the United States acquired ownership, except--

(1) lands located on the Outer Continental Shelf; and

(2) lands held for the benefit of Indians, Aleuts, and Eskimos.

(f) The term "right-of-way" includes an easement, lease, permit, or license to occupy, use, or traverse public lands granted for the purpose listed in title V of this Act [43 U.S.C. §§ 1761 *et seq.*].

(g) The term "Secretary", unless specifically designated otherwise, means the Secretary of the Interior.

(h) The term "sustained yield" means the achievement and maintenance in perpetuity of a high-level annual or regular periodic output of the various renewable resources of the public lands consistent with multiple use.

(i) The term "wilderness" as used in section 603 [43 U.S.C. § 1782] shall have the same meaning as it does in section 2(c) of the Wilderness Act [16 U.S.C. § 1131(c)].

(j) The term "withdrawal" means withholding an area of Federal land from settlement, sale, location, or entry, under some or all of the general land laws, for the purpose of limiting activities under those laws in order to maintain other public values in the area or reserving the area for a particular public purpose or program; or transferring jurisdiction over an area of Federal land, other than "property" governed by the Federal Property and Administrative Services Act, as amended (40 U.S.C. § 472) from one department, bureau or agency to another department, bureau or agency.

(k) An "allotment management plan" means a document prepared in consultation with the lessees or permittees involved, which applies to livestock operations on the public lands or on lands within National Forests in the eleven contiguous Western States and which:

(1) prescribes the manner in, and extent to, which livestock operations will be conducted in order to meet the multiple-use, sustained-yield, economic and other needs and objectives as determined for the lands by the Secretary concerned; and

(2) describes the type, location, ownership, and general specifications for the range improvements to be installed and maintained on the lands to meet the livestock grazing and other objectives of land management; and

(3) contains such other provisions relating to livestock grazing and other objectives found by the Secretary concerned to be consistent with the provisions of this Act and other applicable law.

(l) The term "principal or major uses" includes, and is limited to, domestic livestock grazing, fish and wildlife development and utilization, mineral exploration and production, rights-of-way, outdoor recreation, and timber production.

(m) The term "department" means a unit of the executive branch of the Federal Government which is headed by a member of the President's Cabinet and the term "agency" means a unit of the executive branch of the Federal Government which is not under the jurisdiction of a head of a department.

(n) The term "Bureau" means the Bureau of Land Management.

(o) The term "eleven contiguous Western States" means the States of Arizona, California, Colorado, Idaho, Montana, Nevada, New Mexico, Oregon, Utah, Washington, and Wyoming.

(p) The term "grazing permit and lease" means any document authorizing use of public lands or lands in National Forests in the eleven contiguous western States for the purpose of grazing domestic livestock.

[Pub. L. 94-579, Title I, § 103, 90 Stat. 2745 (Oct. 21, 1976)]

Title II -- LAND USE PLANNING AND LAND ACQUISITION AND DISPOSITION

43 U.S.C. § 1711. Continuing inventory and identification of public lands; preparation and maintenance. (a) The Secretary shall prepare and maintain on a continuing basis an inventory of all public lands and their resources and other values (including, but not limited to, outdoor recreation and scenic values), giving priority to areas of critical environmental concern. This inventory shall be kept current so as to reflect changes in conditions and to identify new and emerging resource and other values. The preparation and maintenance of such inventory or the identification of such areas shall not, of itself, change or prevent change of the management or use of public lands.

****

[Pub. L. 94-579, Title II, § 201, 90 Stat. 2746 (Oct. 21, 1976)]

43 U.S.C. § 1712. Land use plans. (a) Development, maintenance, and revision by Secretary. The Secretary shall, with public involvement and consistent with the terms and conditions of this Act, develop, maintain, and, when appropriate, revise land use plans which provide by tracts or areas for the use of the public lands. Land use plans shall be developed for the public lands regardless of whether such lands previously have been classified, withdrawn, set aside, or otherwise designated for one or more uses.

(b) Coordination of plans for National Forest System lands with Indian land use planning and management programs for purposes of development and revision. In the development and revision of land use plans, the Secretary of Agriculture shall coordinate land use plans for lands in the National Forest System with the land use planning and management programs of and for Indian tribes by, among other things, considering the policies of approved tribal land resource management programs.

(c) Criteria for development and revision. In the development and revision of land use plans, the Secretary shall --

(1) use and observe the principles of multiple use and sustained yield set forth in this and other applicable law;

(2) use a systematic interdisciplinary approach to achieve integrated consideration of physical, biological, economic, and other sciences;

(3) give priority to the designation and protection of areas of critical environmental concern;

(4) rely, to the extent it is available, on the inventory of the public lands, their resources, and other values;

(5) consider present and potential uses of the public lands;

(6) consider the relative scarcity of the values involved and the availability of alternative means (including recycling) and sites for realization of those values;

(7) weigh long-term benefits to the public against short-term benefits;

(8) provide for compliance with applicable pollution control laws, including State and Federal air, water, noise, or other pollution standards or implementation plans; and

(9) to the extent consistent with the laws governing the administration of the public lands, coordinate the land use inventory, planning, and management activities of or for such lands with the land use planning and management programs of other Federal departments and agencies and of the States and local governments within which the lands are located, including, but not limited to, the statewide outdoor recreation plans

developed under the Act of September 3, 1964 (78 Stat. 897), as amended [16 U.S.C.A. § 460l-4 et seq.], and of or for Indian tribes by, among other things, considering the policies of approved State and tribal land resource management programs. In implementing this directive, the Secretary shall, to the extent he finds practical, keep apprised of State, local, and tribal land use plans; assure that consideration is given to those State, local, and tribal plans that are germane in the development of land use plans for public lands; assist in resolving, to the extent practical, inconsistencies between Federal and non- Federal Government plans, and shall provide for meaningful public involvement of State and local government officials, both elected and appointed, in the development of land use programs, land use regulations, and land use decisions for public lands, including early public notice of proposed decisions which may have a significant impact on non-Federal lands. Such officials in each State are authorized to furnish advice to the Secretary with respect to the development and revision of land use plans, land use guidelines, land use rules, and land use regulations for the public lands within such State and with respect to such other land use matters as may be referred to them by him. Land use plans of the Secretary under this section shall be consistent with State and local plans to the maximum extent he finds consistent with Federal law and the purposes of this Act.

(d) Review and inclusion of classified public lands; review of existing land use plans; modification and termination of classifications. Any classification of public lands or any land use plan in effect on October 21, 1976, is subject to review in the land use planning process conducted under this section, and all public lands, regardless of classification, are subject to inclusion in any land use plan developed pursuant to this section. The Secretary may modify or terminate any such classification consistent with such land use plans.

(e) Management decisions for implementation of developed or revised plans. The Secretary may issue management decisions to implement land use plans developed or revised under this section in accordance with the following:

(1) Such decisions, including but not limited to exclusions (that is, total elimination) of one or more of the principal or major uses made by a management decision shall remain subject to reconsideration, modification, and termination through revision by the Secretary or his delegate, under the provisions of this section, of the land use plan involved.

(2) Any management decision or action pursuant to a management decision that excludes (that is, totally eliminates) one or more of the principal or major uses for two or more years with respect to a tract of land of one hundred thousand acres or more shall be reported by the Secretary to the House of Representatives and the Senate. If within ninety days from the giving of such notice (exclusive of days on which either House has adjourned for more than three consecutive days), the Congress adopts a concurrent resolution of nonapproval of the management decision or action, then the management decision or action shall be promptly terminated by the Secretary. If the committee to which a resolution has been referred during the said ninety day period, has not reported it at the end of thirty calendar days after its referral, it shall be in order to either discharge the committee from further consideration of such resolution or to discharge the committee from consideration of any other resolution with respect

to the management decision or action. A motion to discharge may be made only by an individual favoring the resolution, shall be highly privileged (except that it may not be made after the committee has reported such a resolution), and debate thereon shall be limited to not more than one hour, to be divided equally between those favoring and those opposing the resolution. An amendment to the motion shall not be in order, and it shall not be in order to move to reconsider the vote by which the motion was agreed to or disagreed to. If the motion to discharge is agreed to or disagreed to, the motion may not be made with respect to any other resolution with respect to the same management decision or action. When the committee has reprinted, or has been discharged from further consideration of a resolution, it shall at any time thereafter be in order (even though a previous motion to the same effect has been disagreed to) to move to proceed to the consideration of the resolution. The motion shall be highly privileged and shall not be debatable. An amendment to the motion shall not be in order, and it shall not be in order to move to reconsider the vote by which the motion was agreed to or disagreed to.

(3) Withdrawals made pursuant to section 204 [43 U.S.C. § 1714] may be used in carrying out management decisions, but public lands shall be removed from or restored to the operation of the Mining Law of 1872, as amended (R.S. 2318-2352; 30 U.S.C. § 21 *et seq.*) or transferred to another department, bureau, or agency only by withdrawal action pursuant to section 204 [43 U.S.C. § 1714] or other action pursuant to applicable law: *Provided*, That nothing in this section shall prevent a wholly owned Government corporation from acquiring and holding rights as a citizen under the Mining Law of 1872.

(f) Procedures applicable to formulation of plans and programs for public land management. The Secretary shall allow an opportunity for public involvement and by regulation shall establish procedures, including public hearings where appropriate, to give Federal, State, and local governments and the public, adequate notice and opportunity to comment upon and participate in the formulation of plans and programs relating to the management of the public lands.

[Pub. L. 94-579, Title II, § 202, 90 Stat. 2747 (Oct. 21, 1976)]

****

Title III -- ADMINISTRATION

43 U.S.C. § 1731. Bureau of Land Management. (a) Director; appointment, qualifications, functions, and duties. ****

43 U.S.C. § 1732. Management of use, occupancy, and development of public lands. (a) Multiple use and sustained yield requirements applicable; exception. The Secretary shall manage the public lands under principles of multiple use and sustained yield, in accordance with the land use plans developed by him under section 202 of this Act [43 U.S.C. § 1712] when they are available, except that where a tract of such public land has been dedicated to specific uses according to any other provisions of law it shall be managed in accordance with such law.

(b) Easements, permits, etc., for utilization through habitation, cultivation, and development of small trade or manufacturing concerns; applicable statutory requirements. In managing the public lands, the Secretary shall, subject to this Act and other applicable law and under such terms and conditions as are consistent with such law, regulate, through easements, permits, leases, licenses, published rules, or other instruments as the Secretary deems appropriate, the use, occupancy, and development of the public lands, including, but not limited to, long-term leases to permit individuals to utilize public lands for habitation, cultivation, and the development of small trade or manufacturing concerns: *Provided,* That unless otherwise provided for by law, the Secretary may permit Federal departments and agencies to use, occupy, and develop public lands only through rights-of-way under section 507 of this Act [43 U.S.C. § 1767], withdrawals under section 204 of this Act [43 U.S.C. § 1714], and, where the proposed use and development are similar or closely related to the programs of the Secretary for the public lands involved, cooperative agreements under section 307 of this Act [43 U.S.C. § 1737(b)]: *Provided further,* That nothing in this Act shall be construed as authorizing the Secretary concerned to require Federal permits to hunt and fish on public lands or on lands in the National Forest System and adjacent waters or as enlarging or diminishing the responsibility and authority of the States for management of fish and resident wildlife. However, the Secretary concerned may designate areas of public land and of lands in the National Forest System where, and establish periods when, no hunting or fishing will be permitted for reasons of public safety, administration, or compliance with provisions of applicable law. Except in emergencies, any regulations of the Secretary concerned relating to hunting and fishing pursuant to this section shall be put into effect only after consultation with the appropriate State fish and game department. Nothing in this Act shall modify or change any provision of Federal law relating to migratory birds or to endangered or threatened species. Except as provided in section 314, section 603, and subsection (f) of section 601 of this Act [43 U.S.C. §§ 1744, 1782, and 1781(f)] and in the last sentence of this paragraph, no provision of this section or any other section of this Act shall in any way amend the Mining Law of 1872 or impair the rights of any locators or claims under that Act, including, but not limited to, rights of ingress and egress. In managing the public lands the Secretary shall, by regulation or otherwise, take any action necessary to prevent unnecessary or undue degradation of the lands.

(c) Revocation or suspension provision in instrument authorizing use, occupancy or development; violation of provision; procedure applicable. The Secretary shall insert in any instrument providing for the use, occupancy, or development of the public lands a provision authorizing revocation or suspension, after notice and hearing, of such instrument upon a final administrative finding of a violation of any term or condition of the instrument, including, but not limited to, terms and conditions requiring compliance with regulations under Acts applicable to the public lands and compliance with applicable State or Federal air or water quality standard or implementation plan: *Provided,* That such violation occurred on public lands covered by such instrument and occurred in connection with the exercise of rights and privileges granted by it: *Provided further,* That the Secretary shall terminate any such suspension no later than the date upon which he determines the cause of said violation has been rectified: *Provided further,* That the Secretary may order an immediate temporary suspension prior to a hearing or final administrative finding if he determines that such a suspension is necessary to protect health or safety or the environment: *Provided further,* That, where other applicable law contains specific provisions for suspension, revocation, or cancellation of a permit, license, or other authorization to use, occupy, or develop the public lands, the specific provisions of such law shall prevail.

(d)(1) The Secretary of the Interior, after consultation with the Governor of Alaska, may issue to the Secretary of Defense or to the Secretary of a military department within the Department of Defense or to the Commandant of the Coast Guard a nonrenewable general authorization to utilize public lands in Alaska (other than within a conservation system unit or the Steese National Conservation Area or the White Mountains National Recreation Area) for purposes of military maneuvering, military training, or equipment testing not involving artillery firing, aerial or other gunnery, or other use of live ammunition or ordnance.

(2) Use of public lands pursuant to a general authorization under this subsection shall be limited to areas where such use would not be inconsistent with the plans prepared pursuant to section 202 [43 U.S.C. § 1712]. Each such use shall be subject to a requirement that the using department shall be responsible for any necessary cleanup and decontamination of the lands used, and to such other terms and conditions (including but not limited to restrictions on use of off-road or all-terrain vehicles) as the Secretary of the Interior may require to --

(A) minimize adverse impacts on the natural, environmental, scientific, cultural, and other resources and values (including fish and wildlife habitat) of the public lands involved; and

(B) minimize the period and method of such use and the interference with or restrictions on other uses of the public lands involved.

(3)(A) A general authorization issued pursuant to this subsection shall not be for a term of more than three years and shall be revoked in whole or in part, as the Secretary of the Interior finds necessary, prior to the end of such term upon a determination by the Secretary of the Interior that there has been a failure to comply with its terms and conditions or that activities pursuant to such an authorization have had or might have a significant adverse impact on the resources or values of the affected lands.

(B) Each specific use of a particular area of public lands pursuant to a general authorization under this subsection shall be subject to specific authorization by the Secretary and to appropriate terms and conditions, including such as are described in paragraph (2) of this subsection.

(4) Issuance of a general authorization pursuant to this subsection shall be subject to the provisions of section 202(f) [43 U.S.C. § 1712(f)], section 810 of the Alaska National Interest Lands Conservation Act [16 U.S.C. § 3120], and all other applicable provisions of law. The Secretary of a military department (or the commandant of the Coast Guard) requesting such authorization shall reimburse the Secretary of the Interior for the costs of implementing this paragraph. An authorization pursuant to this subsection shall not authorize the construction of permanent structures or facilities on the public lands.

(5) To the extent that public safety may require closure to public use of any portion of the public lands covered by an authorization issued pursuant to this subsection, the Secretary of the military department concerned or the Commandant of the Coast

Guard shall take appropriate steps to notify the public concerning such closure and to provide appropriate warnings of risks to public safety.

(6) For purposes of this subsection, the term "conservation system unit" has the same meaning as specified in section 102 of the Alaska National Interest Lands Conservation Act [16 U.S.C. § 3102].

[Pub. L. 94-579, Title III, § 302, 90 Stat. 2762 (Oct. 21, 1976)]

43 U.S.C. § 1733. Enforcement authority. (a) Regulations for implementation of management, use, and protection requirements; violations; criminal penalties. The Secretary shall issue regulations necessary to implement the provisions of this Act with respect to the management, use, and protection of the public lands, including the property located thereon. Any person who knowingly and willfully violates any such regulation which is lawfully issued pursuant to this Act shall be fined no more than $1,000 or imprisoned no more than twelve months, or both. Any person charged with a violation of such regulation may be tried and sentenced by any United States magistrate judge designated for that purpose by the court by which he was appointed, in the same manner and subject to the same conditions and limitations as provided for in section 3401 of Title 18.

****

(g) Unlawful activities. The use, occupancy, or development of any portion of the public lands contrary to any regulation of the Secretary or other responsible authority, or contrary to any order issued pursuant to any such regulation, is unlawful and prohibited.

[Pub. L. 94-579, Title III, § 303, 90 Stat. 2763 (Oct. 21, 1976)]

- 0 -

PUBLIC RANGELANDS IMPROVEMENT ACT (1978)
(43 U.S.C. §§ 1901-1908)

43 U.S.C. § 1901. Congressional findings and declaration of policy. (a) The Congress finds and declares that --

(1) vast segments of the public rangelands are producing less than their potential for livestock, wildlife habitat, recreation, forage, and water and soil conservation benefits, and for that reason are in an unsatisfactory condition;

(2) such rangelands will remain in an unsatisfactory condition and some areas may decline further under present levels of, and funding for, management;

(3) unsatisfactory conditions on public rangelands present a high risk of soil loss, desertification, and a resultant underproductivity for large acreages of the public lands; contribute significantly to unacceptable levels of siltation and salinity in major western watersheds including the Colorado River; negatively impact the quality and availability of scarce western water supplies; threaten important and frequently critical fish and wildlife habitat; prevent expansion of the forage resource and resulting

benefits to livestock and wildlife production; increase surface runoff and flood danger; reduce the value of such lands for recreational and esthetic purposes; and may ultimately lead to unpredictable and undesirable long-term local and regional climatic and economic changes;

(4) the above-mentioned conditions can be addressed and corrected by an intensive public rangelands maintenance, management, and improvement program involving significant increases in levels of rangeland management and improvement funding for multiple-use values;

(5) to prevent economic disruption and harm to the western livestock industry, it is in the public interest to charge a fee for livestock grazing permits and leases on the public lands which is based on a formula reflecting annual changes in the costs of production;

(6) the Act of December 15, 1971 [the Wild Free-Roaming Horses and Burros Act, 16 U.S.C. §§ 1331 *et seq.*], continues to be successful in its goal of protecting wild free-roaming horses and burros from capture, branding, harassment, and death, but that certain amendments are necessary thereto to avoid excessive costs in the administration of the Act, and to facilitate the humane adoption or disposal of excess wild free-roaming horses and burros which because they exceed the carrying capacity of the range, pose a threat to their own habitat, fish, wildlife, recreation, water and soil conservation, domestic livestock grazing, and other rangeland values;

(b) The Congress therefore hereby establishes and reaffirms a national policy and commitment to:

(1) inventory and identify current public rangelands conditions and trends as a part of the inventory process required by section 201(a) of the Federal Land Policy and Management Act of 1976 [43 U.S.C. § 1711(a)];

(2) manage, maintain and improve the condition of the public rangelands so that they become as productive as feasible for all rangeland values in accordance with management objectives and the land use planning process established pursuant to section 202 of the Federal Land Policy and Management Act of 1976 [43 U.S.C. § 1712];

(3) charge a fee for public grazing use which is equitable and reflects the concerns addressed in paragraph (a)(5) above;

(4) continue the policy of protecting wild free-roaming horses and burros from capture, branding, harassment, or death, while at the same time facilitating the removal and disposal of excess wild free-roaming horses and burros which pose a threat to themselves and their habitat and to other rangeland values;

(c) The policies of this chapter shall become effective only as specific statutory authority for their implementation is enacted by this chapter or by subsequent legislation, and shall be construed as supplemental to and not in derogation of the purposes for which public rangelands are administered under other provisions of law.

[Pub. L. 95-514, § 2, 92 Stat. 1803 (Oct. 25, 1978)]

43 U.S.C. § 1902. Definitions. As used in this Act --

(a) The terms "rangelands" or "public rangelands" means lands administered by the

Secretary of the Interior through the Bureau of Land Management or the Secretary of Agriculture through the Forest Service in the sixteen contiguous Western States on which there is domestic livestock grazing or which the Secretary concerned determines may be suitable for domestic livestock grazing.

(b) The term "allotment management plan" is the same as defined in section 103(k) of the Federal Land Policy and Management Act of 1976 [43 U.S.C. § 1702(k)], except that as used in this Act such term applies to the sixteen contiguous Western States.

(c) The term "grazing permit and lease" means any document authorizing use of public lands or lands in national forests in the sixteen contiguous Western States for the purpose of grazing domestic livestock.

(d) The term "range condition" means the quality of the land reflected in its ability in specific vegetative areas to support various levels of productivity in accordance with range management objectives and the land use planning process, and relates to soil quality, forage values (whether seasonal or year round), wildlife habitat, watershed and plant communities, the present state of vegetation of a range site in relation to the potential plant community for that site, and the relative degree to which the kinds, proportions, and amounts of vegetation in a plant community resemble that of the desired community for that site.

(e) The term "native vegetation" means those plant species, communities, or vegetative associations which are endemic to a given area and which would normally be identified with a healthy and productive range condition occurring as a result of the natural vegetative process of the area.

(f) The term "range improvement" means any activity or program on or relating to rangelands which is designed to improve production of forage; change vegetative composition; control patterns of use; provide water; stabilize soil and water conditions; and provide habitat for livestock and wildlife. The term includes, but is not limited to, structures, treatment projects, and use of mechanical means to accomplish the desired results.

(g) The term "court ordered environmental impact statement" means any environmental statements which are required to be prepared by the Secretary of the Interior pursuant to the final judgment or subsequent modification thereof as set forth on June 18, 1975, in the matter of Natural Resources Defense Council against Andrus.

(h) The term "Secretary" unless specifically designated otherwise, means the Secretary of the Interior.

(i) The term "sixteen contiguous Western States" means the States of Arizona, California, Colorado, Idaho, Kansas, Montana, Nebraska, Nevada, New Mexico, North Dakota, Oklahoma, Oregon, South Dakota, Utah, Washington, and Wyoming.

[Pub. L. 95-514, § 3, 92 Stat. 1804 (Oct. 25, 1978)]

43 U.S.C. § 1903. Rangelands inventory and management; public availability. (a) Following enactment of this Act [October 25, 1978], the Secretary of the Interior and the Secretary of Agriculture shall update, develop (where necessary) and maintain on a continuing basis thereafter, an inventory of range conditions and record of trends of range conditions on the public rangelands, and shall categorize or identify such lands on the basis of the range conditions and trends thereof as they deem appropriate. Such inventories shall be conducted and maintained by the Secretary as a part of the inventory process required by section 201(a) of the Federal Land Policy and Management Act [43 U.S.C. § 1711], and by the Secretary of Agriculture in accordance with section 5 of the Forest and Rangeland Renewable Resources Planning Act of 1974 [16 U.S.C. § 1603]; shall be kept current on a regular basis so as to reflect changes in range conditions; and shall be available to the public.

(b) The Secretary shall manage the public rangelands in accordance with the Taylor Grazing Act [43 U.S.C. §§ 315-315(o)], the Federal Land Policy and Management Act of 1976 [43 U.S.C. §§ 1701-1782], and other applicable law consistent with the public rangelands improvement program pursuant to this chapter. Except where the land use planning process required pursuant to section 202 of the Federal Land Policy and Management Act [43 U.S.C. § 1712] determines otherwise or the Secretary determines, and sets forth his reasons for this determination, that grazing uses should be discontinued (either temporarily or permanently) on certain lands, the goal of such management shall be to improve the range conditions of the public rangelands so that they become as productive as feasible in accordance with the rangeland management objectives established through the land use planning process, and consistent with the values and objectives listed in sections 2(a) and (b)(2) of this Act [43 U.S.C. §§ 1901(a), (b)(2)].

[Pub. L. 95-514, § 4, 92 Stat. 1805 (Oct. 25, 1978)]

43 U.S.C. § 1904. Range improvement funding. ****

\- 0 -

d. Military Lands

SIKES ACT (1960, 1997)
(16 U.S.C. §§ 670-670f)

The military manages some 25 million acres of land. Much of it is in large tracts of land, a significant amount of which is used as buffer around restricted areas.

In 1960, Congress "authorized" the Secretary of Defense in cooperation with the Secretary of the Interior and the appropriate state agency "to carry out a program of planning for ... fish and game conservation" on military installations.[60] The focus of the Act was on providing hunters with access to military reservations.[61] In 1997, the discretionary "is authorized" was replaced with the mandatory "shall carry out a program to provide for the conservation and rehabilitation of natural resources on military installations."[61] The Act mandates cooperative preparation of a management plan for "conservation, protection, and management of fish and wildlife resources" on each military installation with the "United States Fish and Wildlife Service, and the head of each appropriate State fish and wildlife agency for the State in which the military installation concerned is located."[62] The 1997 amendments also increased the emphasis on habitat conservation.

Not surprisingly, the management plan is to be "[c]onsistent with the use of military installations to ensure the preparedness of the Armed Forces."[63]

16 U.S.C. § 670. Definitions. In this title [16 U.S.C. §§ 670 *et seq.*]:

(1) Military installation. The term "military installation" --

(A) means any land or interest in land owned by the United States and administered by the Secretary of Defense or the Secretary of a military department, except land under the jurisdiction of the Assistant Secretary of the Army having responsibility for civil works;

(B) includes all public lands withdrawn from all forms of appropriation under public land laws and reserved for use by the Secretary of Defense or the Secretary of a military department; and

(C) does not include any land described in subparagraph (A) or (B) that is subject to an approved recommendation for closure under the Defense Base Closure and Realignment Act of 1990 (part A of title XXIX of Public Law 101-510; 10 U.S.C. 2687 note).

(2) State fish and wildlife agency. The term "State fish and wildlife agency" means the one or more agencies of State government that are responsible under State law for managing fish or wildlife resources.

(3) United States. The term "United States" means the States, the District of Columbia, and the territories and possessions of the United States.

[Pub. L. 105-85, Div. B, Title XXIX, § 2911, Nov. 18, 1997, 111 Stat. 2021, 2022.)

16 U.S.C. § 670a. Cooperative plan for wildlife conservation and rehabilitation. (a) Authority of Secretary of Defense. (1) Program. (A) In general. The Secretary of Defense shall carry out a program to provide for the conservation and rehabilitation of natural resources on military installations.

(B) Integrated natural resources management plan. To facilitate the program, the Secretary of each military department shall prepare and implement an integrated natural resources management plan for each military installation in the United States under the jurisdiction of the Secretary, unless the Secretary determines that the absence of significant natural resources on a particular installation makes preparation of such a plan inappropriate.

(2) Cooperative preparation. The Secretary of a military department shall prepare each integrated natural resources management plan for which the Secretary is responsible in cooperation with the Secretary of the Interior, acting through the

Director of the United States Fish and Wildlife Service, and the head of each appropriate State fish and wildlife agency for the State in which the military installation concerned is located. Consistent with paragraph (4), the resulting plan for the military installation shall reflect the mutual agreement of the parties concerning conservation, protection, and management of fish and wildlife resources.

(3) Purposes of program. Consistent with the use of military installations to ensure the preparedness of the Armed Forces, the Secretaries of the military departments shall carry out the program required by this subsection to provide for --

(A) the conservation and rehabilitation of natural resources on military installations;

(B) the sustainable multipurpose use of the resources, which shall include hunting, fishing, trapping, and nonconsumptive uses; and

(C) subject to safety requirements and military security, public access to military installations to facilitate the use.

(4) Effect on other law. Nothing in this title [16 U.S.C. §§ 670 *et seq.*] --

(A)(i) affects any provision of a Federal law governing the conservation or protection of fish and wildlife resources; or

(ii) enlarges or diminishes the responsibility and authority of any State for the protection and management of fish and resident wildlife; or

(B) except as specifically provided in the other provisions of this section and in section 670b of this title, authorizes the Secretary of a military department to require a Federal license or permit to hunt, fish, or trap on a military installation.

(b) Required elements of plans. Consistent with the use of military installations to ensure the preparedness of the Armed Forces, each integrated natural resources management plan prepared under subsection (a) of this section --

(1) shall, to the extent appropriate and applicable, provide for --

(A) fish and wildlife management, land management, forest management, and fish- and wildlife-oriented recreation;

(B) fish and wildlife habitat enhancement or modifications;

(C) wetland protection, enhancement, and restoration, where necessary for support of fish, wildlife, or plants;

(D) integration of, and consistency among, the various activities conducted under the plan;

(E) establishment of specific natural resource management goals and objectives and time frames for proposed action;

(F) sustainable use by the public of natural resources to the extent that the use is not inconsistent with the needs of fish and wildlife resources;

(G) public access to the military installation that is necessary or appropriate for the use described in subparagraph (F), subject to requirements necessary to ensure safety and military security;

(H) enforcement of applicable natural resource laws (including regulations);

(I) no net loss in the capability of military installation lands to support the military mission of the installation; and

(J) such other activities as the Secretary of the military department determines appropriate;

(2) must be reviewed as to operation and effect by the parties thereto on a regular

basis, but not less often than every 5 years; and

(3) may stipulate the issuance of special State hunting and fishing permits to individuals and require payment of nominal fees therefor, which fees shall be utilized for the protection, conservation, and management of fish and wildlife, including habitat improvement and related activities in accordance with the integrated natural resources management plan; except that --

(A) the Commanding Officer of the installation or persons designated by that Officer are authorized to enforce such special hunting and fishing permits and to collect, spend, administer, and account for fees for the permits, acting as agent or agents for the State if the integrated natural resources management plan so provides, and

(B) the fees collected under this paragraph may not be expended with respect to other than the military installation on which collected, unless the military installation is subsequently closed, in which case the fees may be transferred to another military installation to be used for the same purposes.

(c) Prohibitions on sale and lease of lands unless effects compatible with plan. After an integrated natural resources management plan is agreed to under subsection (a) of this section --

(1) no sale of land, or forest products from land, that is within a military installation covered by that plan may be made under section 2665(a) or (b) of Title 10; and

(2) no leasing of land that is within the installation may be made under section 2667 of such Title 10;

unless the effects of that sale or leasing are compatible with the purposes of the plan.

(d) Implementation and enforcement of cooperative plans. With regard to the implementation and enforcement of integrated natural resources management plans agreed to under subsection (a) of this section --

(1) neither Office of Management and Budget Circular A-76 nor any successor circular thereto applies to the procurement of services that are necessary for that implementation and enforcement; and

(2) priority shall be given to the entering into of contracts for the procurement of such implementation and enforcement services with Federal and State agencies having responsibility for the conservation or management of fish or wildlife.

(e) Applicability of other laws. Integrated natural resources management plans agreed to under the authority of this section and section 670b of this title shall not be deemed to be, nor treated as, cooperative agreements to which chapter 63 of Title 31 applies.

(f) Reviews and reports. (1) Secretary of Defense. Not later than March 1 of each year, the Secretary of Defense shall review the extent to which integrated natural resources management plans were prepared or were in effect and implemented in accordance with this title in the preceding year, and submit a report on the findings of the review to the committees. Each report shall include --

(A) the number of integrated natural resources management plans in effect in the year covered by the report, including the date on which each plan was issued in final form or most recently revised;

(B) the amounts expended on conservation activities conducted pursuant to the plans in the year covered by the report; and

(C) an assessment of the extent to which the plans comply with this title.

(2) Secretary of the Interior. Not later than March 1 of each year and in consultation with the heads of State fish and wildlife agencies, the Secretary of the Interior shall submit a report to the committees on the amounts expended by the Department of the Interior and the State fish and wildlife agencies in the year covered by the report on conservation activities conducted pursuant to integrated natural resources management plans.

(3) Definition of committees. In this subsection, the term "committees" means --

(A) the Committee on Resources and the Committee on Armed Services of the House of Representatives; and

(B) the Committee on Armed Services and the Committee on Environment and Public Works of the Senate.

[Pub. L. 86-797, Title I, § 101, formerly § 1, 74 Stat. 1052 (Sept. 15, 1960); renumbered § 101 and amended Pub. L. 93-452, §§ 1(1), 3(1), (2), 88 Stat. 1369, 1375 (Oct. 18, 1974); Pub. L. 97-396, § 1, 96 Stat. 2005 (Dec. 31, 1982); Pub. L. 99-561, § 3(a)(1), 100 Stat. 3150 (Oct. 27, 1986); Pub. L. 105-85, Div. B, Title XXIX, §§ 2904(a), (b)(1), (2), (3), (4), (c), 2906, 2907, 2913(2), (3), (4), 111 Stat. 2017 to 2019, 2020 to 2022 (Nov. 18, 1997); Pub. L. 106-65, Div. A, Title X, § 1067(19), 113 Stat. 775 (Oct. 5, 1999)]

16 U.S.C. § 670b. Migratory game birds; permits; fees; Stamp Act and State law requirements. The Secretary of Defense in cooperation with the Secretary of the Interior and the appropriate State agency is authorized to carry out a program for the conservation, restoration and management of migratory game birds on military installations, including the issuance of special hunting permits and the collection of fees therefor, in accordance with an integrated natural resources management plan mutually agreed upon by the Secretary of Defense, the Secretary of the Interior and the appropriate State agency: Provided, That possession of a special permit for hunting migratory game birds issued pursuant to this subchapter shall not relieve the permittee of the requirements of the Migratory Bird Hunting Stamp Act as amended [16 U.S.C. § 718 *et seq.*] nor of the requirements pertaining to State law set forth in Public Law 85-337.

[Pub. L. 86-797, Title I, § 102, formerly § 2, 74 Stat. 1053 (Sept. 15, 1960); renumbered § 102 and amended Pub. L. 93-452, § 3(1), (3), 88 Stat. 1375 (Oct. 18, 1974); Pub. L. 105-85, Div. B, Title XXIX, §§ 2904(b)(5), 2913(5), 111 Stat. 2018 (Nov. 18, 1997)]

16 U.S.C. § 670c. Program for public outdoor recreation. (a) Program authorized. The Secretary of Defense is also authorized to carry out a program for the development, enhancement, operation, and maintenance of public outdoor recreation resources at military installations in accordance with an integrated natural resources management plan mutually agreed upon by the Secretary of Defense and the Secretary of the Interior, in consultation with the appropriate State agency designated by the State in which the installations are located.

(b) Access for disabled veterans, military dependents with disabilities, and other persons with disabilities. (1) In developing facilities and conducting programs for public outdoor recreation at military installations, consistent with the primary military mission of the installations, the Secretary of Defense shall ensure, to the extent reasonably practicable, that outdoor recreation opportunities (including fishing, hunting, trapping, wildlife viewing, boating, and camping) made available to the public also provide access for persons described in paragraph (2) when topographic, vegetative, and water resources allow access for such persons without substantial modification to the natural environment.

(2) Persons referred to in paragraph (1) are the following:

(A) Disabled veterans.

(B) Military dependents with disabilities.

(C) Other persons with disabilities, when access to a military installation for such persons and other civilians is not otherwise restricted.

(3) The Secretary of Defense shall carry out this subsection in consultation with the Secretary of Veterans Affairs, national service, military, and veterans organizations, and sporting organizations in the private sector that participate in outdoor recreation projects for persons described in paragraph (2).

(c) Acceptance of donations. ****

(d) Treatment of volunteers. ****

[Pub. L. 86-797, Title I, § 103, formerly § 3, 74 Stat. 1053 (Sept. 15, 1960); Pub. L. 90-465, § 1, Aug. 8, 1968, 82 Stat. 661; renumbered § 103, Pub. L. 93-452, § 3(1), 88 Stat. 1375 (Oct. 18, 1974); Pub. L. 105-85, Div. B, Title XXIX, §§ 2904(b)(6), 2913(6), 111 Stat. 2018 (Nov. 18, 1997); Pub. L. 105-261, Div. B, Title XXVIII, § 2813, 112 Stat. 2206 (Oct. 17, 1998)]

16 U.S.C. § 670c-1. Cooperative agreements for land management on Department of Defense installations. (a) Authority of Secretary of a military department. The Secretary of a military department may enter into cooperative agreements with States, local governments, nongovernmental organizations, and individuals to provide for the maintenance and improvement of natural resources on, or to benefit natural and historic research on, Department of Defense installations.

(b) Multiyear agreements. Funds appropriated to the Department of Defense for a fiscal year may be obligated to cover the cost of goods and services provided under a cooperative agreement entered into under subsection (a) or through an agency agreement under section 1535 of title 31, United States Code, during any 18-month period beginning in that fiscal year, without regard to whether the agreement crosses fiscal years.

(c) Availability of funds; agreements under other laws. Cooperative agreements entered into under this section shall be subject to the availability of funds and shall not be considered, nor be treated as, cooperative agreements to which chapter 63 of Title 31 applies.

[Pub. L. 101-189, Div. C, Title XXVIII, § 2845(a), 103 Stat. 1664 (Nov. 29, 1989); Pub. L. 105-85, Div. B, Title XXIX, § 2908, 111 Stat. 2021 (Nov. 18, 1997)]

16 U.S.C. § 670d. Liability for funds; accounting to Comptroller General. ****

16 U.S.C. § 670e. Applicability to other laws; national forest lands. ****

16 U.S.C. § 670e-1. Federal enforcement of other laws. All Federal laws relating to the management of natural resources on Federal land may be enforced by the Secretary of Defense with respect to violations of the laws that occur on military installations within the United States.

[Pub. L. 105-85, Div. B, Title XXIX, § 2909(2), 111 Stat. 2021 (Nov. 18, 1997)]

16 U.S.C. § 670e-2. Natural resources management services. To the extent practicable using available resources, the Secretary of each military department shall ensure that sufficient numbers of professionally trained natural resources management personnel and natural resources law enforcement personnel are available and assigned responsibility to perform tasks necessary to carry out this title, including the preparation and implementation of integrated natural resources management plans.

[Pub. L. 105-85, Div. B, Title XXIX, § 2910, 111 Stat. 2021 (Nov. 18, 1997)]

16 U.S.C. § 670f. Appropriations and expenditures. ****

\- 0 -

e. Preservation Land Systems: Wild Lands and Rivers

Most federal land management systems are managed by a single agency. The National Wildlife Refuge System, for example, is managed by the Fish and Wildlife Service. Two land systems that indirectly conserve wildlife habitat deviate from this pattern. Units of both the National Wilderness Preservation System and the National Wild and Scenic River System are managed by the agency that managed the lands before their inclusion in the system. Thus, the National Park Service, the Fish and Wildlife Service, the Bureau of Land Management, and the Forest Service each manage part of their lands pursuant to the Wilderness Act.

THE WILDERNESS ACT (1964)
(16 U.S.C. §§ 1131-1136)

Wilderness as a waste and desolate place and wilderness as the preservation of man have uneasily coexisted in the collective psyche at least since the nineteenth century. In 1964, Congress enacted the Wilderness Act[64] establishing the National Wilderness Preservation System. The statute established a procedure for designating wilderness areas that begins with an evaluation by the land-managing agency of roadless areas under their jurisdiction for their "wilderness values."[65] The agency makes a recommendation to the President who forwards it with his additional recommendation to Congress.[66] Congress alone has the power to designate wilderness areas.

While wildlife habitat is an only implicitly a factor in the designation process,[67] the size[68] and relatively undisturbed status make such areas important habitat -- particularly for large carnivores.

16 U.S.C. § 1131. National Wilderness Preservation System. (a) Establishment; Congressional declaration of policy; wilderness areas; administration for public use and enjoyment, protection, preservation, and gathering and dissemination of information; provisions for designation as wilderness areas. In order to assure that an increasing population, accompanied by expanding settlement and growing mechanization, does not occupy and modify all areas within the United States and its possessions, leaving no lands designated for preservation and protection in their natural condition, it is hereby declared to be the policy of the Congress to secure for the American people of present and future generations the benefits of an enduring resource of wilderness. For this purpose there is hereby established a National Wilderness Preservation System to be composed of federally owned areas designated by Congress as "wilderness areas", and these shall be administered for the use and enjoyment of the American people in such manner as will leave them unimpaired for future use and enjoyment as wilderness, and so as to provide for the protection of these areas, the preservation of their wilderness character, and for the gathering and dissemination of information regarding their use and enjoyment as wilderness; and no Federal lands shall be designated as "wilderness areas" except as provided for in this Act or by a subsequent Act.

(b) Management of area included in System; appropriations. The inclusion of an area in the National Wilderness Preservation System notwithstanding, the area shall continue to be managed by the Department and agency having jurisdiction thereover immediately before its inclusion in the National Wilderness Preservation System unless otherwise provided by Act of Congress. No appropriation shall be available for the payment of expenses or salaries for the administration of the National Wilderness Preservation System as a separate unit nor shall any appropriations be available for additional personnel stated as being required solely for the purpose of managing or administering areas solely because they are included within the National Wilderness Preservation System.

(c) "Wilderness" defined. A wilderness, in contrast with those areas where man and his own works dominate the landscape, is hereby recognized as an area where the earth and its community of life are untrammeled by man, where man himself is a visitor who does not remain. An area of wilderness is further defined to mean in this Act an area of undeveloped Federal land retaining its primeval character and influence, without permanent improvements or human habitation, which is protected and managed so as to preserve its natural conditions and which (1) generally appears to have been affected primarily by the forces of nature, with the imprint of man's work substantially unnoticeable; (2) has outstanding opportunities for solitude or a primitive and unconfined type of recreation; (3) has at least five thousand acres of land or is of sufficient size as to make practicable its preservation and use in an unimpaired condition; and (4) may also contain ecological, geological, or other features of scientific, educational, scenic, or historical value.

[Pub. L. 88-577, § 2, 78 Stat. 890 (Sept. 3, 1964)]

16 U.S.C. § 1132. Extent of System. (a) Designation of wilderness areas; filing of maps and descriptions with Congressional committees; correction of errors; public records; availability of records in regional offices. All areas within the national forests classified at least 30 days before the effective date of this Act [September 3, 1964] by the Secretary of Agriculture or the Chief of the Forest Service as "wilderness", "wild", or "canoe" are hereby designated as wilderness areas. The Secretary of Agriculture shall --

(1) Within one year after the effective date of this Act [September 3, 1964], file a map and legal description of each wilderness area with the Interior and Insular Affairs Committees of the United States Senate and the House of Representatives, and such descriptions shall have the same force and effect as if included in this Act: *Provided, however,* That correction of clerical and typographical errors in such legal descriptions and maps may be made.

(2) Maintain, available to the public, records pertaining to said wilderness areas, including maps and legal descriptions, copies of regulations governing them, copies of public notices of, and reports submitted to Congress regarding pending additions, eliminations, or modifications. Maps, legal descriptions, and regulations pertaining to wilderness areas within their respective jurisdictions also shall be available to the public in the offices of regional foresters, national forest supervisors, and forest rangers.

(b) Review by Secretary of Agriculture of classifications as primitive areas; Presidential recommendations to Congress; approval of Congress; size of primitive areas; Gore Range-Eagles Nest Primitive Area, Colorado. The Secretary of Agriculture shall, within ten years after the effective date of this Act [September 3, 1964], review, as to its suitability or nonsuitability for preservation as wilderness, each area in the national forests classified on September 3, 1964 by the Secretary of Agriculture or the Chief of the Forest Service as "primitive" and report his findings to the President. The President shall advise the United States Senate and House of Representatives of his recommendations with respect to the designation as "wilderness" or other reclassification of each area on which review has been completed, together with maps and a definition of boundaries. **** Nothing herein contained shall limit the President in proposing, as part of his recommendations to Congress, the alteration of existing boundaries of primitive areas or recommending the addition of any contiguous area of national forest lands predominantly of wilderness value. ****

(c) Review by Secretary of the Interior of roadless areas of national park system and national wildlife refuges and game ranges and suitability of areas for preservation as wilderness; authority of Secretary of the Interior to maintain roadless areas in national park system unaffected. Within ten years after the effective date of this Act [September 3, 1964], the Secretary of the Interior shall review every roadless area of five thousand contiguous acres or more in the national parks, monuments and other units of the national park system and every such area of, and every roadless island within, the national wildlife refuges and game ranges, under his jurisdiction on September 3, 1964 and shall report to the President his recommendation as to the suitability or nonsuitability of each such area or island for preservation as wilderness. The

President shall advise the President of the Senate and the Speaker of the House of Representatives of his recommendation with respect to the designation as wilderness of each such area or island on which review has been completed, together with a map thereof and a definition of its boundaries. **** A recommendation of the President for designation as wilderness shall become effective only if so provided by an Act of Congress. Nothing contained herein shall, by implication or otherwise, be construed to lessen the present statutory authority of the Secretary of the Interior with respect to the maintenance of roadless areas within units of the national park system.

(d) Conditions precedent to administrative recommendations of suitability of areas for preservation as wilderness; publication in Federal Register; public hearings; views of State, county, and Federal officials; submission of views to Congress.
(1) The Secretary of Agriculture and the Secretary of the Interior shall, prior to submitting any recommendations to the President with respect to the suitability of any area for preservation as wilderness --

(A) give such public notice of the proposed action as they deem appropriate, including publication in the Federal Register and in a newspaper having general circulation in the area or areas in the vicinity of the affected land;

(B) hold a public hearing or hearings at a location or locations convenient to the area affected. The hearings shall be announced through such means as the respective Secretaries involved deem appropriate, including notices in the Federal Register and in newspapers of general circulation in the area: *Provided,* That if the lands involved are located in more than one State, at least one hearing shall be held in each State in which a portion of the land lies;

(C) at least thirty days before the date of a hearing advise the Governor of each State and the governing board of each county, or in Alaska the borough, in which the lands are located, and Federal departments and agencies concerned, and invite such officials and Federal agencies to submit their views on the proposed action at the hearing or by no later than thirty days following the date of the hearing.

(2) Any views submitted to the appropriate Secretary under the provisions of (1) of this subsection with respect to any area shall be included with any recommendations to the President and to Congress with respect to such area.

(e) Modification or adjustment of boundaries; public notice and hearings; administrative and executive recommendations to Congress; approval of Congress.
****

[Pub. L. 88-577, § 3, 78 Stat. 891 (Sept. 3, 1964)]

16 U.S.C. § 1133. Use of wilderness areas. (a) Purposes of national forests, national park system, and national wildlife refuge system; other provisions applicable to national forests, Superior National Forest, and national park system. The purposes of this chapter are hereby declared to be within and supplemental to the purposes for which national forests and units of the national park and national wildlife refuge systems are established and administered and --

(1) Nothing in this Act shall be deemed to be in interference with the purpose for

which national forests are established as set forth in the Act of June 4, 1897 [Forest Service Organic Act, 16 U.S.C. §§ 475 *et seq.*], and the Multiple-Use Sustained-Yield Act of June 12, 1960 [16 U.S.C. §§ 528-531].

****

(3) Nothing in this Act shall modify the statutory authority under which units of the national park system are created. Further, the designation of any area of any park, monument, or other unit of the national park system as a wilderness area pursuant to this Act shall in no manner lower the standards evolved for the use and preservation of such park, monument, or other unit of the national park system in accordance with the Act of August 25, 1916 [the National Park Service Organic Act, 16 U.S.C. 1-4], the statutory authority under which the area was created, or any other Act of Congress which might pertain to or affect such area, including, but not limited to, the Act of June 8, 1906 (34 Stat. 225; 16 U.S.C. §§ 432 *et seq.*); section 3(2) of the Federal Power Act (16 U.S.C. § 796(2)); and the Act of August 21, 1935 (49 Stat. 666; 16 U.S.C. § 461 *et seq.*).

(b) Agency responsibility for preservation and administration to preserve wilderness character; public purposes of wilderness areas. Except as otherwise provided in this Act, each agency administering any area designated as wilderness shall be responsible for preserving the wilderness character of the area and shall so administer such area for such other purposes for which it may have been established as also to preserve its wilderness character. Except as otherwise provided in this Act, wilderness areas shall be devoted to the public purposes of recreational, scenic, scientific, educational, conservation, and historical use.

(c) Prohibition provisions: commercial enterprise, permanent or temporary roads, mechanical transports, and structures or installations; exceptions: area administration and personal health and safety emergencies. Except as specifically provided for in this Act, and subject to existing private rights, there shall be no commercial enterprise and no permanent road within any wilderness area designated by this Act and, except as necessary to meet minimum requirements for the administration of the area for the purpose of this Act (including measures required in emergencies involving the health and safety of persons within the area), there shall be no temporary road, no use of motor vehicles, motorized equipment or motorboats, no landing of aircraft, no other form of mechanical transport, and no structure or installation within any such area.

(d) Special provisions. The following special provisions are hereby made:

(1) Aircraft or motorboats; fire, insects, and diseases. Within wilderness areas designated by this Act the use of aircraft or motorboats, where these uses have already become established, may be permitted to continue subject to such restrictions as the Secretary of Agriculture deems desirable. In addition, such measures may be taken as may be necessary in the control of fire, insects, and diseases, subject to such conditions as the Secretary deems desirable.

(2) Mineral activities, surveys for mineral value. Nothing in this Act shall prevent within national forest wilderness areas any activity, including prospecting, for the purpose of gathering information about mineral or other resources, if such activity is carried on in a manner compatible with the preservation of the wilderness

environment. Furthermore, in accordance with such program as the Secretary of the Interior shall develop and conduct in consultation with the Secretary of Agriculture, such areas shall be surveyed on a planned, recurring basis consistent with the concept of wilderness preservation by the United States Geological Survey and the United States Bureau of Mines to determine the mineral values, if any, that may be present; and the results of such surveys shall be made available to the public and submitted to the President and Congress.

(3) Mining and mineral leasing laws; leases, permits, and licenses; withdrawal of minerals from appropriation and disposition. Notwithstanding any other provisions of this Act, until midnight December 31, 1983, the United States mining laws and all laws pertaining to mineral leasing shall, to the same extent as applicable prior to the effective date of this Act [September 3, 1964], extend to those national forest lands designated by this Act as "wilderness areas"; subject, however, to such reasonable regulations governing ingress and egress as may be prescribed by the Secretary of Agriculture consistent with the use of the land for mineral location and development and exploration, drilling, and production, and use of land for transmission lines, waterlines, telephone lines, or facilities necessary in exploring, drilling, producing, mining, and processing operations, including where essential the use of mechanized ground or air equipment and restoration as near as practicable of the surface of the land disturbed in performing prospecting, location, and, in oil and gas leasing, discovery work, exploration, drilling, and production, as soon as they have served their purpose. Mining locations lying within the boundaries of said wilderness areas shall be held and used solely for mining or processing operations and uses reasonably incident thereto; and hereafter, subject to valid existing rights, all patents issued under the mining laws of the United States affecting national forest lands designated by this Act as wilderness areas shall convey title to the mineral deposits within the claim, together with the right to cut and use so much of the mature timber therefrom as may be needed in the extraction, removal, and beneficiation of the mineral deposits, if needed timber is not otherwise reasonably available, and if the timber is cut under sound principles of forest management as defined by the national forest rules and regulations, but each such patent shall reserve to the United States all title in or to the surface of the lands and products thereof, and no use of the surface of the claim or the resources therefrom not reasonably required for carrying on mining or prospecting shall be allowed except as otherwise expressly provided in this Act: *Provided,* That, unless hereafter specifically authorized, no patent within wilderness areas designated by this Act shall issue after December 31, 1983, except for the valid claims existing on or before December 31, 1983. Mining claims located after the effective date of this Act [September 3, 1964], within the boundaries of wilderness areas designated by this Act shall create no rights in excess of those rights which may be patented under the provisions of this subsection. Mineral leases, permits, and licenses covering lands within national forest wilderness areas designated by this Act shall contain such reasonable stipulations as may be prescribed by the Secretary of Agriculture for the protection of the wilderness character of the land consistent with the use of the land for the purposes for which they are leased, permitted, or licensed. Subject to valid rights then existing, effective January 1, 1984, the minerals in lands designated by this Act as wilderness areas are withdrawn from all forms of appropriation under the mining laws and from disposition

under all laws pertaining to mineral leasing and all amendments thereto.

(4) Water resources, reservoirs, and other facilities; grazing. Within wilderness areas in the national forests designated by this Act, (1) the President may, within a specific area and in accordance with such regulations as he may deem desirable, authorize prospecting for water resources, the establishment and maintenance of reservoirs, water-conservation works, power projects, transmission lines, and other facilities needed in the public interest, including the road construction and maintenance essential to development and use thereof, upon his determination that such use or uses in the specific area will better serve the interests of the United States and the people thereof than will its denial; and (2) the grazing of livestock, where established prior to the effective date of this Act [September 3, 1964], shall be permitted to continue subject to such reasonable regulations as are deemed necessary by the Secretary of Agriculture.

(5) Commercial services. Commercial services may be performed within the wilderness areas designated by this Act to the extent necessary for activities which are proper for realizing the recreational or other wilderness purposes of the areas.

(6) State water laws exemption. Nothing in this Act shall constitute an express or implied claim or denial on the part of the Federal Government as to exemption from State water laws.

(7) State jurisdiction of wildlife and fish in national forests. Nothing in this Act shall be construed as affecting the jurisdiction or responsibilities of the several States with respect to wildlife and fish in the national forests.

[Pub. L. 88-577, § 4, 78 Stat. 893 (Sept. 3, 1964); Pub. L. 95-495, § 4(b), 92 Stat. 1650 (Oct. 21, 1978); Pub. L. 102-154, Title I, 105 Stat. 1000 (Nov. 13, 1991); Pub. L. 102-285, § 10, 106 Stat. 171 (May 18, 1992)]

16 U.S.C. § 1134. State and private lands within wilderness areas. (a) Access; exchange of lands; mineral interests restriction. In any case where State-owned or privately owned land is completely surrounded by national forest lands within areas designated by this Act as wilderness, such State or private owner shall be given such rights as may be necessary to assure adequate access to such State-owned or privately owned land by such State or private owner and their successors in interest, or the State-owned land or privately owned land shall be exchanged for federally owned land in the same State of approximately equal value under authorities available to the Secretary of Agriculture: *Provided, however,* That the United States shall not transfer to a State or private owner any mineral interests unless the State or private owner relinquishes or causes to be relinquished to the United States the mineral interest in the surrounded land.

(b) Customary means for ingress and egress to wilderness areas subject to mining claims or other occupancies. In any case where valid mining claims or other valid occupancies are wholly within a designated national forest wilderness area, the Secretary of Agriculture shall, by reasonable regulations consistent with the preservation of the area as wilderness, permit ingress and egress to such surrounded areas by means which have been or are being customarily enjoyed with respect to other such areas similarly situated.

(c) Acquisition of lands. Subject to the appropriation of funds by Congress, the Secretary of Agriculture is authorized to acquire privately owned land within the perimeter of any area designated by this Act as wilderness if (1) the owner concurs in such acquisition or (2) the acquisition is specifically authorized by Congress.

[Pub. L. 88-577, § 5, 78 Stat. 896 (Sept. 3, 1964)]

16 U.S.C. § 1135. Gifts, bequests, and contributions. ****

16 U.S.C. § 1136. Annual reports to Congress. ****

- 0 -

WILD AND SCENIC RIVERS ACT (1968)
(16 U.S.C. §§ 1271-1287)

In addition to preserving wild lands, Congress has created a management system to provide species protection for free-flowing river segments. The Wild and Scenic Rivers Act of 1968 (WSRA)[70] resembles the Wilderness Act in some details and differs in others.

Like wilderness areas, river segments are added to the system by Congress.[71] Unlike wilderness, rivers can be included in the system through state action with the Secretary of the Interior's approval.[72] Also unlike wilderness, the management standards for river segments differ depending upon whether the segment is "wild," "scenic," or "recreational."[73] Furthermore, although wilderness is a designation of federal lands, river segments may include state and private land as well.

The WSRA also is more explicitly concerned with wildlife than is the Wilderness Act. Fish and wildlife are one of the outstandingly remarkable values (ORVs) that can lead to the inclusion of a river segment in the system.[74] As such, the managing agency is required to prepare a comprehensive management plan[75] to guide the management of the river segment "to protect and enhance the values which caused it to be included" in the system.[76] The Act thus empowers the agency to manage the segment to protect fish and wildlife values and requires it to do so when such values were among the outstandingly remarkable values that caused the segment to be designated.

Although the WSRA was enacted in 1968 and currently includes more than 160 rivers totalling thousands of river miles, the litigation potential of the statute has only recently been recognized by wildlife advocates.

16 U.S.C. § 1271. Congressional declaration of policy. It is hereby declared to be the policy of the United States that certain selected rivers of the Nation which, with their immediate environments, possess outstandingly remarkable scenic, recreational, geologic, fish and wildlife, historic, cultural, or other similar values, shall be preserved in free-flowing condition, and that they and their immediate environments shall be protected for the benefit and enjoyment of present and future generations. The Congress declares that the established national policy of dam and other construction at appropriate sections of the rivers of the United States needs to be complemented by a policy that would preserve other selected rivers or sections thereof in their free-flowing condition to protect the water quality of such rivers and to fulfill other vital national conservation purposes.

[Pub. L. 90-542, § 1(b), 82 Stat. 906 (Oct. 2, 1968)]

16 U.S.C. § 1272. Congressional declaration of purpose. The purpose of this Act is to implement this policy [16 U.S.C. § 1271] by instituting a national wild and scenic rivers system, by designating the initial components of that system, and by prescribing the methods by which and standards according to which additional components may be added to the system from time to time.

[Pub. L. 90-542, § 1(c), 82 Stat. 906 (Oct. 2, 1968)]

16 U.S.C. § 1273. National wild and scenic rivers system. (a) Composition; application; publication in Federal Register; expense; administration of federally owned lands. The national wild and scenic rivers system shall comprise rivers (i) that are authorized for inclusion therein by Act of Congress, or (ii) that are designated as wild, scenic or recreational rivers by or pursuant to an act of the legislature of the State or States through which they flow, that are to be permanently administered as wild, scenic or recreational rivers by an agency or political subdivision of the State or States concerned, that are found by the Secretary of the Interior, upon application of the Governor of the State or the Governors of the States concerned, or a person or persons thereunto duly appointed by him or them, to meet the criteria established in this Act and such criteria supplementary thereto as he may prescribe, and that are approved by him for inclusion in the system .... Upon receipt of an application under clause (ii) of this subsection, the Secretary shall notify the Federal Energy Regulatory Commission and publish such application in the Federal Register. Each river designated under clause (ii) shall be administered by the State or political subdivision thereof without expense to the United States other than for administration and management of federally owned lands. For purposes of the preceding sentence, amounts made available to any State or political subdivision under the Land and Water Conservation Act of 1965 [16 U.S.C. §§ 460l-4 *et seq.*] or any other provision of law shall not be treated as an expense to the United States. Nothing in this subsection shall be construed to provide for the transfer to, or administration by, a State or local authority of any federally owned lands which are within the boundaries of any river included within the system under clause (ii).

(b) Classification, designation, and administration of rivers. A wild, scenic or recreational river area eligible to be included in the system is a free-flowing stream and the related adjacent land area that possesses one or more of the values referred to in section 1(b) of this Act [16 U.S.C. § 1271]. Every wild, scenic or recreational river in its free-flowing condition, or upon restoration to this condition, shall be considered eligible for inclusion in the national wild and scenic rivers system and, if included, shall be classified, designated, and administered as one of the following:

(1) Wild river areas -- Those rivers or sections of rivers that are free of impoundments and generally inaccessible except by trail, with watersheds or shorelines essentially primitive and waters unpolluted. These represent vestiges of

primitive America.

(2) Scenic river areas -- Those rivers or sections of rivers that are free of impoundments, with shorelines or watersheds still largely primitive and shorelines largely undeveloped, but accessible in places by roads.

(3) Recreational river areas -- Those rivers or sections of rivers that are readily accessible by road or railroad, that may have some development along their shorelines, and that may have undergone some impoundment or diversion in the past.

[Pub. L. 90-542, § 2, 82 Stat. 906 (Oct. 2, 1968); Pub. L. 94-407, § 1(1), 90 Stat. 1238 (Sept. 11, 1976); Pub. L. 95-625, Title VII, § 761, 92 Stat. 3533 (Nov. 10, 1978)]

16 U.S.C. § 1274. Component rivers and adjacent lands. (a) Designation. The following rivers and the land adjacent thereto are hereby designated as components of the national wild and scenic rivers system:

****

(b) Establishment of boundaries; classification. The agency charged with the administration of each component of the national wild and scenic rivers system designated by subsection (a) of this section shall, within one year from the date of designation of such component under subsection (a) (except where a different date [is] provided in subsection (a)), establish detailed boundaries therefor (which boundaries shall include an average of not more than 320 acres of land per mile measured from the ordinary high water mark on both sides of the river); and determine which of the classes outlined in section 2(b) of this Act [16 U.S.C. § 1273(b)] best fit the river or its various segments.

Notice of the availability of the boundaries and classification, and of subsequent boundary amendments shall be published in the Federal Register and shall not become effective until ninety days after they have been forwarded to the President of the Senate and the Speaker of the House of Representatives.

(c) Public inspection of maps and descriptions. Maps of all boundaries and descriptions of the classifications of designated river segments, and subsequent amendments to such boundaries, shall be available for public inspection in the offices of the administering agency in the District of Columbia and in locations convenient to the designated river.

(d) Comprehensive management plan for protection of river values; review of boundaries, classifications, and plans. (1) For rivers designated on or after January 1, 1986, the Federal agency charged with the administration of each component of the National Wild and Scenic Rivers System shall prepare a comprehensive management plan for such river segment to provide for the protection of the river values. The plan shall address resource protection, development of lands and facilities, user capacities, and other management practices necessary or desirable to achieve the purposes of this Act. The plan shall be coordinated with and may be incorporated into resource management planning for affected adjacent Federal lands. The plan shall be prepared, after consultation with State and local governments and the interested public within 3 full fiscal years after the date of designation. Notice of the completion and availability of such plans shall be published in the Federal Register.

(2) For rivers designated before January 1, 1986, all boundaries, classifications, and plans shall be reviewed for conformity within the requirements of this subsection within 10 years through regular agency planning processes.

[Pub. L. 90-542, § 3, 82 Stat. 907 (Oct. 2, 1968); ****]

16 U.S.C. § 1275. Additions to national wild and scenic rivers system. (a) Reports by Secretaries of the Interior and Agriculture; recommendations to Congress; contents of reports. The Secretary of the Interior or, where national forest lands are involved, the Secretary of Agriculture or, in appropriate cases, the two Secretaries jointly shall study and submit to the President reports on the suitability or nonsuitability for addition to the national wild and scenic rivers system of rivers which are designated herein or hereafter by the Congress as potential additions to such system. The President shall report to the Congress his recommendations and proposals with respect to the designation of each such river or section thereof under this Act.... In conducting these studies the Secretary of the Interior and the Secretary of Agriculture shall give priority to those rivers (i) with respect to which there is the greatest likelihood of developments which, if undertaken, would render the rivers unsuitable for inclusion in the national wild and scenic rivers system, and (ii) which possess the greatest proportion of private lands within their areas. Every such study and plan shall be coordinated with any water resources planning involving the same river which is being conducted pursuant to the Water Resources Planning Act [42 U.S.C. §§ 1962 *et seq.*].

Each report, including maps and illustrations, shall show among other things the area included within the report; the characteristics which do or do not make the area a worthy addition to the system; the current status of land ownership and use in the area; the reasonably foreseeable potential uses of the land and water which would be enhanced, foreclosed, or curtailed if the area were included in the national wild and scenic rivers system; the Federal agency (which in the case of a river which is wholly or substantially within a national forest, shall be the Department of Agriculture) by which it is proposed the area, should it be added to the system, be administered; the extent to which it is proposed that such administration, including the costs thereof, be shared by State and local agencies; and the estimated cost to the United States of acquiring necessary lands and interests in land and of administering the area, should it be added to the system. Each such report shall be printed as a Senate or House document.

(b) Study of report by affected Federal and State officials; recommendations and comments; transmittal to President and Congress. Before submitting any such report to the President and the Congress, copies of the proposed report shall, unless it was prepared jointly by the Secretary of the Interior and the Secretary of Agriculture, be submitted by the Secretary of the Interior to the Secretary of Agriculture or by the Secretary of Agriculture to the Secretary of the Interior, as the case may be, and to the Secretary of the Army, the Secretary of Energy, the head of any other affected Federal department or agency and, unless the lands proposed to be included in the area are already owned by the United States or have already been authorized for acquisition by Act of Congress, the Governor of the State or States in which they are located or an officer designated by the Governor to receive the same. Any recommendations or comments on the proposal which the said officials furnish the Secretary or Secretaries who prepared the report within ninety days of the date on which the report is submitted to them, together with the Secretary's or Secretaries' comments thereon, shall be included with the transmittal to the President and the Congress.

(c) Publication in Federal Register. Before approving or disapproving for inclusion in the national wild and scenic rivers system any river designated as a wild, scenic or recreational river by or pursuant to an act of a State legislature, the Secretary of the Interior shall submit the proposal to the Secretary of Agriculture, the Secretary of the Army, the Secretary of Energy, and the head of any other affected Federal department or agency and shall evaluate and give due weight to any recommendations or comments which the said officials furnish him within ninety days of the date on which it is submitted to them. If he approves the proposed inclusion, he shall publish notice thereof in the Federal Register.

(d) Areas comprised by boundaries; scope of study report. The boundaries of any river proposed in section 5(a) of this Act [16 U.S.C. § 1276(a)] for potential addition to the National Wild and Scenic Rivers System shall generally comprise that area measured within one-quarter mile from the ordinary high water mark on each side of the river. In the case of any designated river, prior to publication of boundaries pursuant to section 3(b) of this Act [16 U.S.C. § 1274(b)], the boundaries also shall comprise the same area. This subsection shall not be construed to limit the possible scope of the study report to address areas which may lie more than one-quarter mile from the ordinary high water mark on each side of the river.

[Pub. L. 90-542, § 4, 82 Stat. 909 (Oct. 2, 1968); Pub. L. 93-279, § 1(b)(1), 88 Stat. 122 (May 10, 1974); Pub. L. 93-621, § 1(d), 88 Stat. 2096 (Jan. 3, 1975); Pub. L. 94-486, Title V, § 501, 90 Stat. 2330 (Oct. 12, 1976); Pub. L. 95-91, Title III, § 301(b), 91 Stat. 577 (Aug. 4, 1977); Pub. L. 99-590, Title V, § 502, 100 Stat. 3335 (Oct. 30, 1986)]

16 U.S.C. § 1276. Rivers constituting potential additions to national wild and scenic rivers system. (a) Enumeration of designated rivers. The following rivers are hereby designated for potential addition to the national wild and scenic rivers system:

****

(c) State participation. The study of any of said rivers shall be pursued in as close cooperation with appropriate agencies of the affected State and its political subdivisions as possible, shall be carried on jointly with such agencies if request for such joint study is made by the State, and shall include a determination of the degree to which the State or its political subdivisions might participate in the preservation and administration of the river should it be proposed for inclusion in the national wild and scenic rivers system.

(d) Continuing consideration by Federal agencies to potential national, wild, scenic and recreational river areas. (1) In all planning for the use and development of water and related land resources, consideration shall be given by all Federal agencies involved to potential national wild, scenic and recreational river areas, and all river basin and project plan reports submitted to the Congress shall consider and discuss any such potentials. The Secretary of the Interior and the Secretary of Agriculture shall make specific studies and investigations to determine which additional wild, scenic and recreational river areas within the United States shall be evaluated in planning reports by all Federal agencies as potential alternative uses of the water and related land resources involved.

****

[Pub. L. 90-542, § 5, 82 Stat. 910 (Oct. 2, 1968); ****]

16 U.S.C. § 1277. Land acquisition. (a) Grant of authority to acquire; State and Indian lands; use of appropriated funds; acquisition of tracts partially outside component boundaries; disposition of lands. (1) The Secretary of the Interior and the Secretary of Agriculture are each authorized to acquire lands and interest in land within the authorized boundaries of any component of the national wild and scenic rivers system designated in section 3 of this Act [16 U.S.C. § 1274], or hereafter designated for inclusion in the system by Act of Congress, which is administered by him, but he shall not acquire fee title to an average of more than 100 acres per mile on both sides of the river. Lands owned by a State may be acquired only by donation or by exchange in accordance with subsection (d) of this section. Lands owned by an Indian tribe or a political subdivision of a State may not be acquired without the consent of the appropriate governing body thereof as long as the Indian tribe or political subdivision is following a plan for management and protection of the lands which the Secretary finds protects the land and assures its use for purposes consistent with this Act. Money appropriated for Federal purposes from the land and water conservation fund shall, without prejudice to the use of appropriations from other sources, be available to Federal departments and agencies for the acquisition of property for the purposes of this Act.

****

(e) Transfer of jurisdiction over federally owned property to appropriate Secretary. The head of any Federal department or agency having administrative jurisdiction over any lands or interests in land within the authorized boundaries of any federally administered component of the national wild and scenic rivers system designated in section 3 of this Act [16 U.S.C. § 1274] or hereafter designated for inclusion in the system by Act of Congress is authorized to transfer to the appropriate secretary jurisdiction over such lands for administration in accordance with the provisions of this Act. Lands acquired by or transferred to the Secretary of Agriculture for the purposes of this Act within or adjacent to a national forest shall upon such acquisition or transfer become national forest lands.

****

[Pub. L. 90-542, § 6, 82 Stat. 912 (Oct. 2, 1968); Pub. L. 95-625, Title VII, § 763(b), 92 Stat. 3533 (Nov. 10, 1978); Pub. L. 99-590, Title V, § 504, 100 Stat. 3336 (Oct. 30, 1986)]

16 U.S.C. § 1278. Restrictions on water resources projects. (a) Construction

projects licensed by Federal Energy Regulatory Commission. The Federal Energy Regulatory Commission shall not license the construction of any dam, water conduit, reservoir, powerhouse, transmission line, or other project works under the Federal Power Act (41 Stat. 1063), as amended (16 U.S.C. 791a et seq.), on or directly affecting any river which is designated in section 3 of this Act [16 U.S.C. § 1274] as a component of the national wild and scenic rivers system or which is hereafter designated for inclusion in that system, and no department or agency of the United States shall assist by loan, grant, license, or otherwise in the construction of any water resources project that would have a direct and adverse effect on the values for which such river was established, as determined by the Secretary charged with its administration. Nothing contained in the foregoing sentence, however, shall preclude licensing of, or assistance to, developments below or above a wild, scenic or recreational river area or on any stream tributary thereto which will not invade the area or unreasonably diminish the scenic, recreational, and fish and wildlife values present in the area on the date of designation of a river as a component of the National Wild and Scenic Rivers System. No department or agency of the United States shall recommend authorization of any water resources project that would have a direct and adverse effect on the values for which such river was established, as determined by the Secretary charged with its administration, or request appropriations to begin construction of any such project, whether heretofore or hereafter authorized, without advising the Secretary of the Interior or the Secretary of Agriculture, as the case may be, in writing of its intention so to do at least sixty days in advance, and without specifically reporting to the Congress in writing at the time it makes its recommendation or request in what respect construction of such project would be in conflict with the purposes of this Act and would affect the component and the values to be protected by it under this Act. Any license heretofore or hereafter issued by the Federal Energy Regulatory Commission affecting the New River of North Carolina shall continue to be effective only for that portion of the river which is not included in the National Wild and Scenic Rivers System pursuant to section 2 of this Act [16 U.S.C. § 1273] and no project or undertaking so licensed shall be permitted to invade, inundate or otherwise adversely affect such river segment.

(b) Construction projects on rivers designated for potential addition to system. The Federal Energy Regulatory Commission shall not license the construction of any dam, water conduit, reservoir, powerhouse, transmission line, or other project works under the Federal Power Act, as amended [16 U.S.C. §§ 791a *et seq.*], on or directly affecting any river which is listed in section 1276(a) of this title, and no department or agency of the United States shall assist by loan, grant, license, or otherwise in the construction of any water resources project that would have a direct and adverse effect on the values for which such river might be designated, as determined by the Secretary responsible for its study or approval --

(i) during the ten-year period following enactment of this Act [October 2, 1968] or for a three complete fiscal year period following any Act of Congress designating any river for potential addition to the national wild and scenic rivers system, whichever is later, unless, prior to the expiration of the relevant period, the Secretary of the Interior and, where national forest lands are involved, the Secretary of Agriculture, on the basis of study, determine that such river should not be included in the national wild and scenic rivers system and notify the Committee on Energy and Natural Resources of the Senate and the Committee on Natural Resources of the House of

Representatives, in writing, including a copy of the study upon which the determination was made, at least one hundred and eighty days while Congress is in session prior to publishing notice to that effect in the Federal Register: *Provided,* That if any Act designating any river or rivers for potential addition to the national wild and scenic rivers system provides a period for the study or studies which exceeds such three complete fiscal year period the period provided for in such Act shall be substituted for the three complete fiscal year period in the provisions of this clause (i); and

(ii) during such interim period from the date a report is due and the time a report is actually submitted to the Congress; and

(iii) during such additional period thereafter as, in the case of any river the report for which is submitted to the President and the Congress, is necessary for congressional consideration thereof or, in the case of any river recommended to the Secretary of the Interior for inclusion in the national wild and scenic rivers system under section 2(a)(ii) of this Act [16 U.S.C. § 1273(a)(ii)], is necessary for the Secretary's consideration thereof, which additional period, however, shall not exceed three years in the first case and one year in the second.

Nothing contained in the foregoing sentence, however, shall preclude licensing of, or assistance to, developments below or above a potential wild, scenic or recreational river area or on any stream tributary thereto which will not invade the area or diminish the scenic or recreational, and fish and wildlife values present in the potential wild, scenic or recreational river area on the date of designation of a river for study as provided for in section 5 of this Act [16 U.S.C. § 1276]. No department or agency of the United States shall, during the periods hereinbefore specified, recommend authorization of any water resources project on any such river or request appropriations to begin construction of any such project, whether heretofore or hereafter authorized, without advising the Secretary of the Interior and, where national forest lands are involved, the Secretary of Agriculture in writing of its intention so to do at least sixty days in advance of doing so and without specifically reporting to the Congress in writing at the time it makes its recommendation or request in what respect construction of such project would be in conflict with the purposes of this Act and would affect the component and the values to be protected by it under this Act.

(c) Activities in progress affecting river of system; notice to Secretary. The Federal Energy Regulatory Commission and all other Federal agencies shall, promptly upon enactment of this Act, inform the Secretary of the Interior and, where national forest lands are involved, the Secretary of Agriculture, of any proceedings, studies, or other activities within their jurisdiction which are now in progress and which affect or may affect any of the rivers specified in section 5(a) of this Act [16 U.S.C. § 1276(a)]. They shall likewise inform him of any such proceedings, studies, or other activities which are hereafter commenced or resumed before they are commenced or resumed.

(d) Grants under Land and Water Conservation Fund Act of 1965. Nothing in this section with respect to the making of a loan or grant shall apply to grants made under the Land and Water Conservation Fund Act of 1965 [16 U.S.C. §§ 460l-4 *et seq.*].

[Pub. L. 90-542, § 7, 82 Stat. 913 (Oct. 2, 1968); Pub. L. 93-279, § 1(b)(3), (4), 88 Stat. 123 (May 10, 1974); Pub.

L. 93-621, § 1(c), 88 Stat. 2096 (Jan. 3, 1975); Pub. L. 94-407, § 1(2), 90 Stat. 1238 (Sept. 11, 1976); Pub. L. 95-91, Title IV, § 402(a)(1)(A), 91 Stat. 583 (Aug. 4, 1977); Pub. L. 99-590, Title V, § 505, 100 Stat. 3336 (Oct. 30, 1986); Pub. L. 103-437, § 6(a)(7), 108 Stat. 4583 (Nov. 2, 1994)]

16 U.S.C. § 1279. Withdrawal of public lands from entry, sale, or other disposition under public land laws. (a) Lands within authorized boundaries of components of system. All public lands within the authorized boundaries of any component of the national wild and scenic rivers system which is designated in section 3 of this Act [16 U.S.C. § 1274] or which is designated after October 2, 1968, for inclusion in that system are hereby withdrawn from entry, sale, or other disposition under the public land laws of the United States. This subsection shall not be construed to limit the authorities granted in section 6(d) [16 U.S.C. § 1277(d)] or 14A [16 U.S.C. § 1285a] of this Act.

(b) Lands constituting bed or bank of river; lands within bank area. All public lands which constitute the bed or bank, or are within one-quarter mile of the bank, of any river which is listed in section 5(a) of this Act [16 U.S.C. § 1276(a)] are hereby withdrawn from entry, sale, or other disposition under the public land laws of the United States for the periods specified in section 7(b) of this Act [16 U.S.C. § 1278(b)]. ***

[Pub. L. 90-542, § 8, 82 Stat. 915 (Oct. 2, 1968); Pub. L. 96-487, Title VI, § 606(c), 94 Stat. 2417 (Dec. 2, 1980); Pub. L. 99-590, Title V, § 506, 100 Stat. 3336 (Oct. 30, 1986)]

16 U.S.C. § 1280. Federal mining and mineral leasing laws. (a) Applicability to components of system. Nothing in this Act shall affect the applicability of the United States mining and mineral leasing laws within components of the national wild and scenic rivers system except that --

(i) all prospecting, mining operations, and other activities on mining claims which, in the case of a component of the system designated in section 3 of this Act [16 U.S.C. § 1274], have not heretofore been perfected or which, in the case of a component hereafter designated pursuant to this Act or any other Act of Congress, are not perfected before its inclusion in the system and all mining operations and other activities under a mineral lease, license, or permit issued or renewed after inclusion of a component in the system shall be subject to such regulations as the Secretary of the Interior or, in the case of national forest lands, the Secretary of Agriculture may prescribe to effectuate the purposes of this Act;

(ii) subject to valid existing rights, the perfection of, or issuance of a patent to, any mining claim affecting lands within the system shall confer or convey a right or title only to the mineral deposits and such rights only to the use of the surface and the surface resources as are reasonably required to carrying on prospecting or mining operations and are consistent with such regulations as may be prescribed by the Secretary of the Interior or, in the case of national forest lands, by the Secretary of Agriculture; and

(iii) subject to valid existing rights, the minerals in Federal lands which are part of the system and constitute the bed or bank or are situated within one-quarter mile of the bank of any river designated a wild river under this Act or any subsequent Act are hereby withdrawn from all forms of appropriation under the mining laws and from operation of the mineral leasing laws including, in both cases, amendments thereto.

Regulations issued pursuant to paragraphs (i) and (ii) of this subsection shall, among other things, provide safeguards against pollution of the river involved and unnecessary impairment of the scenery within the component in question.

(b) Withdrawal from appropriation of minerals in Federal river beds or bank areas; prospecting, leases, licenses, and permits. The minerals in any Federal lands which constitute the bed or bank or are situated within one-quarter mile of the bank of any river which is listed in section 5(a) of this Act [16 U.S.C. § 1276(a)] are hereby withdrawn from all forms of appropriation under the mining laws during the periods specified in section 7(b) of this Act [16 U.S.C. § 1278(b)]. Nothing contained in this subsection shall be construed to forbid prospecting or the issuance of leases, licenses, and permits under the mineral leasing laws subject to such conditions as the Secretary of the Interior and, in the case of national forest lands, the Secretary of Agriculture find appropriate to safeguard the area in the event it is subsequently included in the system. ***

[Pub. L. 90-542, § 9, 82 Stat. 915 (Oct. 2, 1968); Pub. L. 96-487, Title VI, § 606(b), 94 Stat. 2416 (Dec. 2, 1980); Pub. L. 99-590, Title V, § 507, 100 Stat. 3336 (Oct. 30, 1986)]

16 U.S.C. § 1281. Administration. (a) Public use and enjoyment of components; protection of features; management plans. Each component of the national wild and scenic rivers system shall be administered in such manner as to protect and enhance the values which caused it to be included in said system without, insofar as is consistent therewith, limiting other uses that do not substantially interfere with public use and enjoyment of these values. In such administration primary emphasis shall be given to protecting its esthetic, scenic, historic, archaeologic, and scientific features. Management plans for any such component may establish varying degrees of intensity for its protection and development, based on the special attributes of the area.

(b) Wilderness areas. Any portion of a component of the national wild and scenic rivers system that is within the national wilderness preservation system, as established by or pursuant to the Wilderness Act [16 U.S.C. § 1131 et seq.], shall be subject to the provisions of both the Wilderness Act and this Act with respect to preservation of such river and its immediate environment, and in case of conflict between the provisions of the Wilderness Act and this Act the more restrictive provisions shall apply.

(c) Areas administered by National Park Service and Fish and Wildlife Service. Any component of the national wild and scenic rivers system that is administered by the Secretary of the Interior through the National Park Service shall become a part of the national park system, and any such component that is administered by the Secretary through the Fish and Wildlife Service shall become a part of the national wildlife refuge system. The lands involved shall be subject to the provisions of this Act and the Acts under which the national park system or national wildlife system, as the case may be, is administered, and in case of conflict between the provisions of this Act and such Acts, the more restrictive provisions shall apply. The Secretary of the Interior, in his administration of any component of the national wild and scenic rivers system, may utilize such general statutory authorities relating to areas of the national park system and such general statutory authorities otherwise available to him for recreation and preservation purposes and for the conservation and management of natural resources as he deems appropriate to carry out the purposes of this Act.

(d) Statutory authorities relating to national forests. The Secretary of Agriculture, in his administration of any component of the national wild and scenic rivers system area, may utilize the general statutory authorities relating to the national forests in such manner as he deems appropriate to carry out the purposes of this Act.

(e) Cooperative agreements with State and local governments. The Federal agency charged with the administration of any component of the national wild and scenic rivers system may enter into written cooperative agreements with the Governor of a State, the head of any State agency, or the appropriate official of a political subdivision of a State for State or local governmental participation in the administration of the component. The States and their political subdivisions shall be encouraged to cooperate in the planning and administration of components of the system which include or adjoin State- or county-owned lands.

[Pub. L. 90-542, § 10, 82 Stat. 916 (Oct. 2, 1968)]

16 U.S.C. § 1282. Assistance to State and local projects. ****

16 U.S.C. § 1283. Management policies. (a) Action of Secretaries and heads of agencies; cooperative agreements. The Secretary of the Interior, the Secretary of Agriculture, and the head of any other Federal department or agency having jurisdiction over any lands which include, border upon, or are adjacent to, any river included within the National Wild and Scenic Rivers System or under consideration for such inclusion, in accordance with section 2(a)(ii), 3(a), or 5(a) [16 U.S.C. § 1273(a)(ii), 1274(a), or 1276(a)], shall take such action respecting management policies, regulations, contracts, plans, affecting such lands, following November 10, 1978, as may be necessary to protect such rivers in accordance with the purposes of this Act. Such Secretary or other department or agency head shall, where appropriate, enter into written cooperative agreements with the appropriate State or local official for the planning, administration, and management of Federal lands which are within the boundaries of any rivers for which approval has been granted under section 2(a)(ii) [16 U.S.C. § 1273(a)(ii)]. Particular attention shall be given to scheduled timber harvesting, road construction, and similar activities which might be contrary to the purposes of this Act.

(b) Existing rights, privileges, and contracts affecting Federal lands. Nothing in this section shall be construed to abrogate any existing rights, privileges, or contracts affecting Federal lands held by any private party without the consent of said party.

(c) Water pollution. The head of any agency administering a component of the national wild and scenic rivers system shall cooperate with the Administrator, Environmental Protection Agency and with the appropriate State water pollution control agencies for the purpose of eliminating or diminishing the pollution of waters of the river.

[Pub. L. 90-542, § 12, 82 Stat. 917 (Oct. 2, 1968); Pub. L. 95-625, Title VII, § 762, 92 Stat. 3533 (Nov. 10, 1978);

Pub. L. 99-590, Title V, § 509, 100 Stat. 3337 (Oct. 30, 1986)]

16 U.S.C. § 1284. Existing State jurisdiction and responsibilities. (a) Fish and wildlife. Nothing in this Act shall affect the jurisdiction or responsibilities of the States with respect to fish and wildlife. Hunting and fishing shall be permitted on lands and waters administered as parts of the system under applicable State and Federal laws and regulations unless, in the case of hunting, those lands or waters are within a national park or monument. The administering Secretary may, however, designate zones where, and establish periods when, no hunting is permitted for reasons of public safety, administration, or public use and enjoyment and shall issue appropriate regulations after consultation with the wildlife agency of the State or States affected.

(b) Compensation for water rights. The jurisdiction of the States and the United States over waters of any stream included in a national wild, scenic or recreational river area shall be determined by established principles of law. Under the provisions of this Act, any taking by the United States of a water right which is vested under either State or Federal law at the time such river is included in the national wild and scenic rivers system shall entitle the owner thereof to just compensation. Nothing in this Act shall constitute an express or implied claim or denial on the part of the Federal Government as to exemption from State water laws.

(c) Reservation of waters for other purposes or in unnecessary quantities prohibited. Designation of any stream or portion thereof as a national wild, scenic or recreational river area shall not be construed as a reservation of the waters of such streams for purposes other than those specified in this Act, or in quantities greater than necessary to accomplish these purposes.

(d) State jurisdiction over included streams. The jurisdiction of the States over waters of any stream included in a national wild, scenic or recreational river area shall be unaffected by this Act to the extent that such jurisdiction may be exercised without impairing the purposes of this Act or its administration.

(e) Interstate compacts. Nothing contained in this Act shall be construed to alter, amend, repeal, interpret, modify, or be in conflict with any interstate compact made by any States which contain any portion of the national wild and scenic rivers system.

(f) Rights of access to streams. Nothing in this Act shall affect existing rights of any State, including the right of access, with respect to the beds of navigable streams, tributaries, or rivers (or segments thereof) located in a national wild, scenic or recreational river area.

(g) Easements and rights-of-way. The Secretary of the Interior or the Secretary of Agriculture, as the case may be, may grant easements and rights-of-way upon, over, under, across, or through any component of the national wild and scenic rivers system in accordance with the laws applicable to the national park system and the national forest system, respectively: *Provided,* That any conditions precedent to granting such easements and rights-of-way shall be related to the policy and purpose of this Act.

[Pub. L. 90-542, § 13, 82 Stat. 917 (Oct. 2, 1968)]

16 U.S.C. § 1285. Claim and allowance of charitable deduction for contribution or gift of easement. ****

16 U.S.C. § 1286. Definitions. As used in this Act, the term --

(a) "River" means a flowing body of water or estuary or a section, portion, or tributary thereof, including rivers, streams, creeks, runs, kills, rills, and small lakes.

(b) "Free-flowing", as applied to any river or section of a river, means existing or flowing in natural condition without impoundment, diversion, straightening, rip-rapping, or other modification of the waterway. The existence, however, of low dams, diversion works, and other minor structures at the time any river is proposed for inclusion in the national wild and scenic rivers system shall not automatically bar its consideration for such inclusion: *Provided,* That this shall not be construed to authorize, intend, or encourage future construction of such structures within components of the national wild and scenic rivers system.

(c) "Scenic easement" means the right to control the use of land (including the air space above such land) within the authorized boundaries of a component of the wild and scenic rivers system, for the purpose of protecting the natural qualities of a designated wild, scenic or recreational river area, but such control shall not affect, without the owner's consent, any regular use exercised prior to the acquisition of the easement. For any designated wild and scenic river, the appropriate Secretary shall treat the acquisition of fee title with the reservation of regular existing uses to the owner as a scenic easement for purposes of this Act. Such an acquisition shall not constitute fee title ownership for purposes of section 6(b) [16 U.S.C. § 1277(b)].

[Pub. L. 90-542, § 16, formerly § 15, 82 Stat. 918 (Oct. 2, 1968); Pub. L. 93-279, § 1(c), 88 Stat. 123 (May 10, 1974); renumbered Pub. L. 96-487, Title VI, § 606(a), 94 Stat. 2416 (Dec. 2, 1980); Pub. L. 99-590, Title V, § 510, 100 Stat. 3337 (Oct. 30, 1986)]

16 U.S.C. § 1287. Authorization of appropriations. ****

- 0 -

ii. Federal Waters

The Supreme Court's early emphasis on water-borne commerce as a basis for federal power under the Commerce Clause[76] has tied a large body of regulatory law to "navigable" waters. While the conflation of the two has been laid to rest[77] so that regulation is tied to effects on interstate commerce rather than navigability, many federal statutes continue to tie federal involvement to "navigability" variously defined.[78]

FEDERAL POWER ACT (1920)
(16 U.S.C. §§ 791a-823b)

The Federal Power Act was the culmination of the Progressive Conservation Movement that began as a response to the waste that characterized the 1890's Robber Baron era, a period of unbridled greed and unregulated markets. The Progressives believed that experts could manage resources for the public benefit; centralized planning by impartial experts, they urged, would insure that natural resources were used to provide the greatest good for the greatest number.[79] As applied to river basins, these beliefs led Progressives to advocate an active federal role that included planning, regulating, and developing water projects. The Federal Power Act was an imperfect embodiment of these objectives. The most significant deviation was the dilution of planning -- the Act substituted federal regulation of private development for comprehensive planning.[80]

To license and regulate nonfederal projects, the Act created the Federal Power Commission (FPC).[81] Congress asserted jurisdiction of four categories of private hydroelectric projects:[82] those projects that (1) are located on "the navigable waters of the United States," (2) are located on other waters "over which Congress has jurisdiction under its authority to regulate commerce with foreign nations and among the several States ... if ... the interests of interstate or foreign commerce would be affected by" the project,[83] (3) are located "upon any part of the public lands or reservations of the United States," or (4) use surplus waterpower from a federal dam. The first two bases of jurisdiction are predicated upon the Commerce Clause; the latter two upon the Property Clause.

Although fish and game -- at least economically valuable species -- were among the resources that the Progressives sought to manage sustainably, the Federal Power Act did not initially contain any reference to wildlife. The FPC's willingness to devalue wildlife in its drive to maximize hydroelectric development led initially to the enactment of the Fish & Wildlife Coordination Act in 1934;[84] when the statute produced no change in agency action, Congress amended the Act in 1946[85] and again in 1958.[86] When the Coordination Act alone proved insufficient, Congress amended the Federal Power Act to mandate that the Commission "shall give equal consideration to ... the protection, mitigation of damage to, and enhancement of, fish and wildlife (including related spawning grounds and habitat)."[87] "[T]o ensure that the project adopted" will provide for the protection of wildlife and habitat, the Act establishes a procedure under which the Commission is required to solicit and consider recommendations from federal, state, and tribal fish and wildlife agencies.[88] If the Commission does not include conditions in the license to protect fish and wildlife, it is required to find that the proposed conditions are inconsistent with the Act and that the conditions that it is instead imposing meet the wildlife and habitat protection mandate "together with a statement of the basis for each of the findings."[89]

Despite such changes, FERC's actions raise questions about forcing single-use agencies to consider multiple values.

16 U.S.C. § 791a. Short title. This Act may be cited as the "Federal Power Act."

[Aug. 26, 1935, ch. 687, Title II, § 213, 49 Stat. 863; Pub. L. 95-617, Title II, § 201, 92 Stat. 3134 (Nov. 9, 1978)]

16 U.S.C. § 796. Definitions. The words defined in this section shall have the following meanings for purposes of this Act, to wit:

(1) "public lands" means such lands and interest in lands owned by the United States as are subject to private appropriation and disposal under public land laws. It shall not include "reservations", as hereinafter defined;

(2) "reservations" means national forests, tribal lands embraced within Indian reservations, military reservations, and other lands and interests in lands owned by the United States, and withdrawn, reserved, or withheld from private appropriation and disposal under the public land laws; also lands and interests in lands acquired and held for any public purposes; but shall not include national monuments or national parks;

(3) "corporation" means any corporation, joint-stock company, partnership, association, business trust, organized group of persons, whether incorporated or not, or a receiver or receivers, trustee or trustees of any of the foregoing. It shall not include "municipalities" as hereinafter defined;

(4) "person" means an individual or a corporation;

(5) "licensee" means any person, State, or municipality licensed under the provisions of section 4 of this Act [16 U.S.C. § 797], and any assignee or successor in interest thereof;

(6) "State" means a State admitted to the Union, the District of Columbia, and any organized Territory of the United States;

(7) "municipality" means a city, county, irrigation district, drainage district, or other political subdivision or agency of a State competent under the laws thereof to carry on the business of developing, transmitting, utilizing, or distributing power;

(8) "navigable waters" means those parts of streams or other bodies of water over which Congress has jurisdiction under its authority to regulate commerce with foreign nations and among the several States, and which either in their natural or improved condition notwithstanding interruptions between the navigable parts of such streams or waters by falls, shallows, or rapids compelling land carriage, are used or suitable for use for the transportation of persons or property in interstate or foreign commerce, including therein all such interrupting falls, shallows, or rapids, together with such other parts of streams as shall have been authorized by Congress for improvement by the United States or shall have been recommended to Congress for such improvement after investigation under its authority;

(9) "municipal purposes" means and includes all purposes within municipal powers as defined by the constitution or laws of the State or by the charter of the municipality;

(10) "Government dam" means a dam or other work constructed or owned by the United States for Government purposes with or without contribution from others;

(11) "project" means complete unit of improvement or development, consisting of a power house, all water conduits, all dams and appurtenant works and structures (including navigation structures) which are a part of said unit, and all storage, diverting, or forebay reservoirs directly connected therewith, the primary line or lines transmitting power therefrom to the point of junction with the distribution system or

with the interconnected primary transmission system, all miscellaneous structures used and useful in connection with said unit or any part thereof, and all water-rights, rights-of-way, ditches, dams, reservoirs, lands, or interest in lands the use and occupancy of which are necessary or appropriate in the maintenance and operation of such unit;

(12) "project works" means the physical structures of a project;

****

[June 10, 1920, ch. 285, § 3, 41 Stat. 1063; Aug. 26, 1935, ch. 687, Title II, § 201, 49 Stat. 838; Pub. L. 95-617, Title II, § 201, 92 Stat. 3134 (Nov. 9, 1978); Pub. L. 96-294, Title VI, § 643(a)(1), 94 Stat. 770 [June 30, 1980); Pub. L. 101-575, § 3, 104 Stat. 2834 (Nov. 15, 1990); Pub. L. 102-46, 105 Stat. 249 (May 17, 1991); Pub. L. 102-486, Title VII, § 726, 106 Stat. 2921 (Oct. 24, 1992)]

16 U.S.C. § 797. General powers of Commission. The Commission is authorized and empowered --

****

(e) Issue of licenses for construction, etc., of dams, conduits, reservoirs, etc. To issue licenses to citizens of the United States, or to any association of such citizens, or to any corporation organized under the laws of the United States or any State thereof, or to any State or municipality for the purpose of constructing, operating, and maintaining dams, water conduits, reservoirs, power houses, transmission lines, or other project works necessary or convenient for the development and improvement of navigation and for the development, transmission, and utilization of power across, along, from, or in any of the streams or other bodies of water over which Congress has jurisdiction under its authority to regulate commerce with foreign nations and among the several States, or upon any part of the public lands and reservations of the United States (including the Territories), or for the purpose of utilizing the surplus water or water power from any Government dam, except as herein provided: *Provided,* That licenses shall be issued within any reservation only after a finding by the Commission that the license will not interfere or be inconsistent with the purpose for which such reservation was created or acquired, and shall be subject to and contain such conditions as the Secretary of the department under whose supervision such reservation falls shall deem necessary for the adequate protection and utilization of such reservation: *Provided further,* That no license affecting the navigable capacity of any navigable waters of the United States shall be issued until the plans of the dam or other structures affecting the navigation have been approved by the Chief of Engineers and the Secretary of the Army. Whenever the contemplated improvement is, in the judgment of the Commission, desirable and justified in the public interest for the purpose of improving or developing a waterway or waterways for the use or benefit of interstate or foreign commerce, a finding to that effect shall be made by the Commission and shall become a part of the records of the Commission: *Provided further,* That in case the Commission shall find that any Government dam may be advantageously used by the United States for public purposes in addition to navigation, no license therefor shall be issued until two years after it shall have reported to Congress the facts and conditions relating thereto, except that this provision shall not apply to any Government dam constructed prior to June 10, 1920: *And provided further,* that upon the filing of any application for a license which has not been preceded by a preliminary permit under subsection (f) of this section, notice shall be given and published as required by the proviso of said subsection. In deciding whether to issue any license under this Part [16 U.S.C. §§ 792 *et seq.*] for any project, the Commission, in addition to the power and development purposes for which licenses are issued, shall give equal consideration to the purposes of energy conservation, the protection, mitigation of damage to, and enhancement of, fish and wildlife (including related spawning grounds and habitat), the protection of recreational opportunities, and the preservation of other aspects of environmental quality.

(f) Preliminary permits; notice of application. To issue preliminary permits for the purpose of enabling applicants for a license hereunder to secure the data and to perform the acts required by section 9 hereof [16 U.S.C. § 802]: *Provided,* however, That upon the filing of any application for a preliminary permit by any person, association, or corporation the Commission, before granting such application, shall at once give notice of such application in writing to any State or municipality likely to be interested in or affected by such application; and shall also publish notice of such application once each week for four weeks in a daily or weekly newspaper published in the county or counties in which the project or any part hereof or the lands affected thereby are situated.

****

[June 10, 1920, ch. 285, § 4, 41 Stat. 1065; June 23, 1930, ch. 572, § 2, 46 Stat. 798; Aug. 26, 1935, ch. 687, Title II, § 202, 49 Stat. 839; Pub. L. 97-375, Title II, § 212, 96 Stat. 1826 (Dec. 21, 1982); Pub. L. 99-495, § 3(a), 100 Stat. 1243 (Oct. 16, 1986)]

16 U.S.C. § 799. License; duration, conditions, revocation, alteration, or surrender. Licenses under this Part [16 U.S.C. §§ 792 *et seq.*] shall be issued for a period not exceeding fifty years. Each such license shall be conditioned upon acceptance by the licensee of all the terms and conditions of this Act and such further conditions, if any, as the Commission shall prescribe in conformity with this Act, which said terms and conditions and the acceptance thereof shall be expressed in said license. Licenses may be revoked only for the reasons and in the manner prescribed under the provisions of this Act, and may be altered or surrendered only upon mutual agreement between the licensee and the Commission after thirty days' public notice.

[June 10, 1920, ch. 285, § 6, 41 Stat. 1067; Aug. 26, 1935, ch. 687, Title II, § 204, 49 Stat. 841; Pub. L. 104-106, Div. D, Title XLIII, § 4321(i)(6), 110 Stat. 676 (Feb. 10, 1996); Pub. L. 104-316, Title I, § 108(a), 110 Stat. 3832 (Oct. 19, 1996); Pub. L. 105-192, § 2, 112 Stat. 625 (July 14, 1998)]

16 U.S.C. § 800. Issuance of preliminary permits or licenses. (a) Preference. In issuing preliminary permits hereunder or original licenses where no preliminary permit has been issued, the Commission shall give preference to applications therefor by States and municipalities, provided the plans for the same are deemed by the Commission equally well adapted, or shall within a reasonable time to be fixed by the Commission be made equally well adapted, to conserve and utilize in the public interest the water resources of the region; and as between other applicants, the Commission may give preference to the applicant the plans of which it finds and determines are best adapted to develop, conserve, and utilize in the public interest the water resources of the region, if it be satisfied as to the ability of the applicant to carry out such plans.

(b) Development of water resources by United States; reports. Whenever, in the judgment of the Commission, the development of any water resources for public purposes should be undertaken by the United States itself, the Commission shall not approve any application for any project affecting such development, but shall cause to be made such examinations, surveys, reports, plans, and estimates of the cost of the proposed development as it may find necessary, and shall submit its findings to Congress with such recommendations as it may find appropriate concerning such development.

(c) Assumption of project by United States after expiration of license. Whenever, after notice and opportunity for hearing, the Commission determines that the United States should exercise its right upon or after the expiration of any license to take over any project or projects for public purposes, the Commission shall not issue a new license to the original licensee or to a new licensee but shall submit its recommendation to Congress together with such information as it may consider appropriate.

[June 10, 1920, ch. 285, § 7, 41 Stat. 1067; Aug. 26, 1935, ch. 687, Title II, § 205, 49 Stat. 842; Pub. L. 90-451, § 1, 82 Stat. 616 (Aug. 3, 1968); Pub. L. 99-495, § 2, 100 Stat. 1243 (Oct. 16, 1986)]

16 U.S.C. § 803. Conditions of license generally. All licenses issued under this Part [16 U.S.C. §§ 792 *et seq.*] shall be on the following conditions:

(a) Modification of plans; factors considered to secure adaptability of project; recommendations for proposed terms and conditions. (1) That the project adopted, including the maps, plans, and specifications, shall be such as in the judgment of the Commission will be best adapted to a comprehensive plan for improving or developing a waterway or waterways for the use or benefit of interstate or foreign commerce, for the improvement and utilization of water-power development, for the adequate protection, mitigation, and enhancement of fish and wildlife (including related spawning grounds and habitat), and for other beneficial public uses, including irrigation, flood control, water supply, and recreational and other purposes referred to in section 4(e) [16 U.S.C. § 797(e); and] if necessary in order to secure such plan the Commission shall have authority to require the modification of any project and of the plans and specifications of the project works before approval.

(2) In order to ensure that the project adopted will be best adapted to the comprehensive plan described in paragraph (1), the Commission shall consider each of the following:

(A) The extent to which the project is consistent with a comprehensive plan (where one exists) for improving, developing, or conserving a waterway or waterways affected by the project that is prepared by --

(i) an agency established pursuant to Federal law that has the authority to prepare such a plan; or

(ii) the State in which the facility is or will be located.

(B) The recommendations of Federal and State agencies exercising administration over flood control, navigation, irrigation, recreation, cultural and other relevant resources of the State in which the project is located, and the recommendations (including fish and wildlife recommendations) of Indian tribes affected by the project.

(C) In the case of a State or municipal applicant, or an applicant which is primarily engaged in the generation or sale of electric power (other than electric power solely from cogeneration facilities or small power production facilities), the electricity consumption efficiency improvement program of the applicant, including its plans, performance and capabilities for encouraging or assisting its customers to conserve electricity cost-effectively, taking into account the published policies, restrictions, and requirements of relevant State regulatory authorities applicable to such applicant.

(3) Upon receipt of an application for a license, the Commission shall solicit recommendations from the agencies and Indian tribes identified in subparagraphs (A) and (B) of paragraph (2) for proposed terms and conditions for the Commission's consideration for inclusion in the license.

****

(e) **Annual charges payable by licensees; maximum rates; application; review and report to Congress.** (1) That the licensee shall pay to the United States reasonable annual charges in an amount to be fixed by the Commission for the purpose of reimbursing the United States for the costs of the administration of this Part [16 U.S.C. §§ 792 *et seq.*], including any reasonable and necessary costs incurred by Federal and State fish and wildlife agencies and other natural and cultural resource agencies in connection with studies or other reviews carried out by such agencies for purposes of administering their responsibilities under this Part; for recompensing it for the use, occupancy, and enjoyment of its lands or other property; ****

****

(j) **Fish and wildlife protection, mitigation and enhancement; consideration of recommendations; findings.** (1) That in order to adequately and equitably protect, mitigate damages to, and enhance, fish and wildlife (including related spawning grounds and habitat) affected by the development, operation, and management of the project, each license issued under this Part [16 U.S.C. §§ 792 *et seq.*] shall include conditions for such protection, mitigation, and enhancement. Subject to paragraph (2), such conditions shall be based on recommendations received pursuant to the Fish and Wildlife Coordination Act (16 U.S.C. § 661 *et seq.*) from the National Marine Fisheries Service, the United States Fish and Wildlife Service, and State fish and wildlife agencies.

(2) Whenever the Commission believes that any recommendation referred to in paragraph (1) may be inconsistent with the purposes and requirements of this Part or other applicable law, the Commission and the agencies referred to in paragraph (1) shall attempt to resolve any such inconsistency, giving due weight to the recommendations, expertise, and statutory responsibilities of such agencies. If, after such attempt, the Commission does not adopt in whole or in part a recommendation of any such agency, the Commission shall publish each of the following findings (together with a statement of the basis for each of the findings):

(A) A finding that adoption of such recommendation is inconsistent with the purposes and requirements of this Part or with other applicable provisions of law.

(B) A finding that the conditions selected by the Commission comply with the requirements of paragraph (1).

[June 10, 1920, ch. 285, § 10, 41 Stat. 1068; Aug. 26, 1935, ch. 687, Title II, § 206, 49 Stat. 842; Sept. 7, 1962, Pub. L. 87-647, 76 Stat. 447; Pub. L. 90-451, § 4, 82 Stat. 617 (Aug. 3, 1968); Pub. L. 99-495, §§ 3(b), (c), 9(a), 13, 100 Stat. 1244, 1252, 1257 (Oct. 16, 1986); Pub. L. 99-546, Title IV, § 401, 100 Stat. 3056 (Oct. 27, 1986); Pub. L. 102-486, Title XVII, § 1701(a), 106 Stat. 3008 (Oct. 24, 1992)]

16 U.S.C. § 817. Projects not affecting navigable waters; necessity for Federal license, permit or right-of-way; unauthorized activities. (1) It shall be unlawful for any person, State, or municipality, for the purpose of developing electric power, to construct, operate, or maintain any dam, water conduit, reservoir, power house, or other works incidental thereto across, along, or in any of the navigable waters of the United States, or upon any part of the public lands or reservations of the United States (including the Territories), or utilize the surplus water or water power from any Government dam, except under and in accordance with the terms of a permit or valid existing right-of-way granted prior to June 10, 1920, or a license granted pursuant to this Act. Any person, association, corporation, State, or municipality intending to construct a dam or other project works across, along, over, or in any stream or part thereof, other than those defined in this Act as navigable waters, and over which Congress has jurisdiction under its authority to regulate commerce with foreign nations and among the several States shall before such construction file declaration of such intention with the Commission, whereupon the Commission shall cause immediate investigation of such proposed construction to be made, and if upon investigation it shall find that the interests of interstate or foreign commerce would be affected by such proposed construction, such person, association, corporation, State, or municipality shall not construct, maintain, or operate such dam or other project works until it shall have applied for and shall have received a license under the provisions of this Act. If the Commission shall not so find, and if no public lands or reservations are affected, permission is granted to construct such dam or other project works in such stream upon compliance with State laws.

(2) No person may commence any significant modification of any project licensed under, or exempted from, this Act unless such modification is authorized in accordance with terms and conditions of such license or exemption and the applicable requirements of this Part [16 U.S.C. §§ 792 *et seq.*]. As used in this paragraph, the term "commence" refers to the beginning of physical on-site activity other than surveys or testing.

[June 10, 1920, ch. 285, § 23(b), 41 Stat. 1075; Aug. 26, 1935, ch. 687, Title II, § 210, 49 Stat. 846; Pub. L. 99-495, § 6, 100 Stat. 1248 (Oct. 16, 1986)]

16 U.S.C. § 818. Public lands included in project; reservation of lands from entry. Any lands of the United States included in any proposed project under the provisions of this Part [16 U.S.C. §§ 792 *et seq.*] shall from the date of filing of application therefor be reserved from entry, location, or other disposal under the laws of the United States until otherwise directed by the Commission or by Congress. Notice that such application has been made, together with the date of filing thereof and a description of the lands of the United States affected thereby, shall be filed in the local land office for the district in which such lands are located. Whenever the Commission shall determine that the value of any lands of the United States so applied for, or heretofore or hereafter reserved or classified as power sites, will not be injured or destroyed for the purposes of power development by location, entry, or selection under the public-land laws, the Secretary of the Interior, upon notice of such determination, shall declare such lands open to location, entry, or selection, for such purpose or purposes and under such restrictions as the Commission may determine, subject to and with a reservation of the right of the United States or its permittees or licensees to enter upon, occupy, and use any part or all of said lands necessary, in the judgment of the Commission, for the purposes of this Part, which right shall be expressly reserved in every patent issued for such lands; and no claim or right to compensation shall accrue from the occupation or use of any of said lands for said purposes. The United States or any licensee for any such lands hereunder may enter thereupon for the purposes of this Part, upon payment of any damages to crops, buildings, or other improvements caused thereby to the owner thereof, or upon giving a good and sufficient bond to the United States for the use and benefit of the owner to secure the payment of such damages as may be determined and fixed in an action brought upon the bond in a court of competent jurisdiction, said bond to be in the form prescribed by the Commission: *Provided,* That locations, entries, selections, or filings heretofore made for lands reserved as water-power sites, or in connection with water-power development, or electrical transmission may proceed to approval or patent under and subject to the limitations and conditions in this section contained: *Provided further,* That before any lands applied for, or heretofore or hereafter reserved, or classified as power sites, are declared open to location, entry, or selection by the Secretary of the Interior, notice of intention to make such declaration shall be given to the Governor of the State within which such lands are located, and such State shall have ninety days from the date of such notice within which to file, under any statute or regulation applicable thereto, an application for the reservation to the State, or any political subdivision thereof, of any lands required as a right-of-way for a public highway or as a source of materials for the construction and maintenance of such highways, and a copy of such application shall be filed with the Federal Power Commission; and any location, entry, or selection of such lands, or subsequent patent thereof, shall be subject to any rights granted the State pursuant to such application.

[June 10, 1920, ch. 285, § 24, 41 Stat. 1075; Aug. 26, 1935, ch. 687, Title II, § 211, 49 Stat. 846; May 28, 1948, ch. 351, 62 Stat. 275]

16 U.S.C. § 823a. Conduit hydroelectric facilities. (a) Exemption qualifications. Except as provided in subsection (b) or (c) of this section, the Commission may grant an exemption in whole or in part from the requirements of this Part [16 U.S.C. §§ 792 *et seq.*], including any license requirements contained in this Part, to any facility (not including any dam or other impoundment) constructed, operated, or maintained for the generation of electric power which the Commission determines, by rule or order --

(1) is located on non-Federal lands, and

(2) utilizes for such generation only the hydroelectric potential of a manmade

conduit, which is operated for the distribution of water for agricultural, municipal, or industrial consumption and not primarily for the generation of electricity.

(b) Maximum installation capacity for exemption. The Commission may not grant any exemption under subsection (a) of this section to any facility the installed capacity of which exceeds 15 megawatts (40 megawatts in the case of a facility constructed, operated, and maintained by an agency or instrumentality of a State or local government solely for water supply for municipal purposes).

(c) Consultation with Federal and State agencies. In making the determination under subsection (a) of this section the Commission shall consult with the United States Fish and Wildlife Service, National Marine Fisheries Service, and the State agency exercising administration over the fish and wildlife resources of the State in which the facility is or will be located, in the manner provided by the Fish and Wildlife Coordination Act (16 U.S.C. § 661 *et seq.*), and shall include in any such exemption --

(1) such terms and conditions as the Fish and Wildlife Service, National Marine Fisheries Service, and the State agency each determine are appropriate to prevent loss of, or damage to, such resources and to otherwise carry out the purposes of such Act, and

(2) such terms and conditions as the Commission deems appropriate to insure that such facility continues to comply with the provisions of this section and terms and conditions included in any such exemption.

(d) Violation of terms of exemption. Any violation of a term or condition of any exemption granted under subsection (a) of this section shall be treated as a violation of a rule or order of the Commission under this Act.

(e) Fees for studies. The Commission, in addition to the requirements of section 10(e) [16 U.S.C. § 803(e)], shall establish fees which shall be paid by an applicant for a license or exemption for a project that is required to meet terms and conditions set by fish and wildlife agencies under subsection (c) of this section. Such fees shall be adequate to reimburse the fish and wildlife agencies referred to in subsection (c) of this section for any reasonable costs incurred in connection with any studies or other reviews carried out by such agencies for purposes of compliance with this section. The fees shall, subject to annual appropriations Acts, be transferred to such agencies by the Commission for use solely for purposes of carrying out such studies and shall remain available until expended.

[Pub. L. 95-617, Title II, § 213, 92 Stat. 3148 (Nov. 9, 1978); Pub. L. 99-495, § 7, 100 Stat. 1248 (Oct. 16, 1986)]

\- 0 -

RIVERS AND HARBORS ACT OF 1899
(33 U.S.C. § 407)

THE FEDERAL WATER POLLUTION CONTROL ACT
[CLEAN WATER ACT]
(33 U.S.C. §§ 1251-1387)

The Federal Water Pollution Control Act (FWPCA) was enacted in 1948.[91] The original version was so solicitous of state sensibilities as to be ineffective. In 1961, the statute was amended to apply to all navigable waters;[92] it was amended again in 1965 to require the states to establish water quality standards for interstate streams.[93]

Although the FWPCA's enforcement provisions and the federal role were strengthened by the 1961 and 1965 amendments, significant change to the water pollution-control regime came from the rediscovery and reformulation of an earlier statute. Section 13 of the Rivers and Harbors Act of 1899 made it unlawful to "throw, discharge, or deposit, or cause, suffer, or procure to be thrown, discharged, or deposited ... any refuse matter of any kind or description whatever."[94] The prohibition had traditionally been applied only to discharges that impeded navigation. In 1970, however, the Act was applied to all industrial discharges under guidelines developed by the Environmental Protection Agency.

Increasing concern with water pollution led to the Federal Water Pollution Control Amendments of 1972.[95] The "Amendments" rewrote the Act and fundamentally altered the previous federal policy. Most significantly, the previous law had mandated abatement of water pollution when it "endanger[ed] the health or welfare of persons in a state other than that in which the ... discharges .. originate"[96] or when the "discharge ... reduces the quality of such ["receiving"] waters below the water quality standards."[97] The Amendments enunciated a new policy: "it is the national goal that the discharge of pollutants into the navigable waters be eliminated."[98] Departures from this objective were to be permitted only when it was technologically impossible to eliminate the discharge. Coupled with this shift is a new focus on pollutants rather than on their impact on human health. To this end, "effluent limitations" are imposed on all "point source" discharges.[99] Finally, the Amendments largely federalized water pollution control.

The FWPCA's regulatory scheme has three important components:

*** *point source pollution* -- the Act has been most successful in remedying "point resource pollution," that is, discharges from "any discernible, confined and discrete conveyance, including but not limited to any pipe, ditch, channel, tunnel, conduit, well, discrete fissure, container, rolling stock, concentrated animal feeding operation, or vessel or other floating craft."[100] It is illegal to discharge pollutants from a point source without a permit obtained under the National Pollution Discharge Elimination System (NPDES).[101]

*** *nonpoint source pollution* -- water pollution that comes from all other sources -- land use activities such as agricultural and silvicultural operations, road construction, land clearing, streets, and the like -- have proved (politically, at least) more difficult to control. The Amendments adopted a planning process to address nonpoint source pollution. The mandated plan is to identify nonpoint sources of pollution and methods for controlling such sources.[102]

*** *water quality standards* -- although effluent limitations are the primary vehicle for eliminating pollution, the Amendments retained water quality standards in a secondary role.[103] States are required to identify waters for which effluent limitations are insufficiently stringent to satisfy water quality standards. For such "water quality limited segments," the state is to establish applicable the "total maximum daily load" (TMDL) for pollutants. TMDLs -- unlike the NPDES process -- focus on the cumulative effect of all sources -- both point and nonpoint -- of pollution on the waterbody.

Finally, although FWPCA defines "navigable" as "the waters of the United States,"[104] the legislative history states specifically that the intent behind the definition was that the term "be given the broadest possible constitutional interpretation."[105] *All* waters in the United States thus are subject to federal regulatory authority to control water pollution.

Rivers and Harbors Act of 1899

33 U.S.C. § 407. Deposit of refuse in navigable waters generally. It shall not be lawful to throw, discharge, or deposit, or cause, suffer, or procure to be thrown, discharged, or deposited either from or out of any ship, barge, or other floating craft of any kind, or from the shore, wharf, manufacturing establishment, or mill of any kind, any refuse matter of any kind or description whatever other than that flowing from streets and sewers and passing therefrom in a liquid state, into any navigable water of the United States, or into any tributary of any navigable water from which the same shall float or be washed into such navigable water; and it shall not be lawful to deposit, or cause, suffer, or procure to be deposited material of any kind in any place on the bank of any navigable water, or on the bank of any tributary of any navigable water, where the same shall be liable to be washed into such navigable water, either by ordinary or high tides, or by storms or floods, or otherwise, whereby navigation shall or may be impeded or obstructed: *Provided,* That nothing herein contained shall extend to, apply to, or prohibit the operations in connection with the improvement of navigable waters or construction of public works, considered necessary and proper by the United States officers supervising such improvement or public work: *And provided further,* That the Secretary of the Army, whenever in the judgment of the Chief of Engineers anchorage and navigation will not be injured thereby, may permit the deposit of any material above mentioned in navigable waters, within limits to be defined and under conditions to be prescribed by him, provided application is made to him prior to depositing such material; and whenever any permit is so granted the conditions thereof shall be strictly complied with, and any violation thereof shall be unlawful.

Federal Water Pollution Control Act

33 U.S.C. § 1251. Congressional declaration of goals and policy. (a) Restoration and maintenance of chemical, physical and biological integrity of Nation's waters; national goals for achievement of objective. The objective of this Act is to restore and maintain the chemical, physical, and biological integrity of the Nation's waters. In order to achieve this objective it is hereby declared that, consistent with the provisions of this Act

--

(1) it is the national goal that the discharge of pollutants into the navigable waters be eliminated by 1985;
(2) it is the national goal that wherever attainable, an interim goal of water quality which provides for the protection and propagation of fish, shellfish, and wildlife and provides for recreation in and on the water be achieved by July 1, 1983;
(3) it is the national policy that the discharge of toxic pollutants in toxic amounts be prohibited;
(4) it is the national policy that Federal financial assistance be provided to construct publicly owned waste treatment works;
(5) it is the national policy that areawide waste treatment management planning processes be developed and implemented to assure adequate control of sources of pollutants in each State;
(6) it is the national policy that a major research and demonstration effort be made to develop technology necessary to eliminate the discharge of pollutants into the navigable waters, waters of the contiguous zone, and the oceans; and
(7) it is the national policy that programs for the control of nonpoint sources of pollution be developed and implemented in an expeditious manner so as to enable the goals of this Act to be met through the control of both point and nonpoint sources of pollution.

(b) Congressional recognition, preservation, and protection of primary responsibilities and rights of States. It is the policy of the Congress to recognize, preserve, and protect the primary responsibilities and rights of States to prevent, reduce, and eliminate pollution, to plan the development and use (including restoration, preservation, and enhancement) of land and water resources, and to consult with the Administrator in the exercise of his authority under this Act. ***

****

(d) Administrator of Environmental Protection Agency to administer Act. Except as otherwise expressly provided in this Act, the Administrator of the Environmental Protection Agency (hereinafter in this Act called "Administrator") shall administer this Act.

(e) Public participation in development, revision, and enforcement of any regulation, etc. Public participation in the development, revision, and enforcement of any regulation, standard, effluent limitation, plan, or program established by the Administrator or any State under this Act shall be provided for, encouraged, and assisted by the Administrator and the States. The Administrator, in cooperation with the States, shall develop and publish regulations specifying minimum guidelines for public participation in such processes.

****

(g) Authority of States over water. It is the policy of Congress that the authority of each State to allocate quantities of water within its jurisdiction shall not be superseded, abrogated or otherwise impaired by this Act. It is the further policy of Congress that nothing in this Act shall be construed to supersede or abrogate rights to quantities of water which have been established by any State. Federal agencies shall co-operate with State and local agencies to develop comprehensive solutions to prevent, reduce and eliminate pollution in concert with programs for managing water resources.

[Pub. L. 92-500, § 2, 86 Stat. 816 (Oct. 18, 1972); Pub. L. 95-217, §§ 5(a), 26(b), 91 Stat. 1567, 1575 (Dec. 27, 1977); Pub. L. 100-4, Title III, § 316(b), 101 Stat. 60 (Feb. 4, 1987)]

33 U.S.C. § 1252. Comprehensive programs for water pollution control. (a) Preparation and development. The Administrator shall, after careful investigation, and in cooperation with other Federal agencies, State water pollution control agencies, interstate agencies, and the municipalities and industries involved, prepare or develop comprehensive programs for preventing, reducing, or eliminating the pollution of the navigable waters and ground waters and improving the sanitary condition of surface and underground waters. In the development of such comprehensive programs due regard shall be given to the improvements which are necessary to conserve such waters for the protection and propagation of fish and aquatic life and wildlife, recreational purposes, and the withdrawal of such waters for public water supply, agricultural, industrial, and other purposes. For the purpose of this section, the Administrator is authorized to make joint investigations with any such agencies of the condition of any waters in any State or States, and of the discharges of any sewage, industrial wastes, or substance which may adversely affect such waters.

****

[Pub. L. 92-500, § 2, 86 Stat. 817 (Oct. 18, 1972); Pub. L. 95-91, Title IV, § 402(a)(1)(A), 91 Stat. 583 (Aug. 4, 1977); Pub. L. 95-217, § 5(b), 91 Stat. 1567 (Dec. 27, 1977); Pub. L. 104-66, Title II, § 2021(a), 109 Stat. 726 (Dec. 21, 1995)]

33 U.S.C. § 1311. Effluent limitations. (a) Illegality of pollutant discharges except in compliance with law. Except as in compliance with this section and sections 302, 306, 307, 318, 402, and 404 of this Act [33 U.S.C. §§ 1312, 1316, 1317, 1328, 1342, and 1344], the discharge of any pollutant by any person shall be unlawful.

(b) Timetable for achievement of objectives. In order to carry out the objective of this Act there shall be achieved --

(1)(A) not later than July 1, 1977, effluent limitations for point sources, other than publicly owned treatment works, (i) which shall require the application of the best practicable control technology currently available as defined by the Administrator pursuant to section 304(b) of this Act [33 U.S.C. § 1314(b)], or (ii) in the case of a discharge into a publicly owned treatment works which meets the requirements of subparagraph (B) of this paragraph, which shall require compliance with any applicable pretreatment requirements and any requirements under section 307 of this Act [33 U.S.C. § 1317]; and

(B) for publicly owned treatment works ***;

(2)(A) for pollutants identified in subparagraphs (C), (D), and (F) of this paragraph ***;

(B) Repealed.

(C) with respect to all toxic pollutants referred to in table 1 of Committee Print Numbered 95-30 of the Committee on Public Works and Transportation of the House of Representatives ***;

(D) for all toxic pollutants listed under paragraph (1) of subsection (a) of section 307 of this Act [33 U.S.C. § 1317] ***;

(E) *** in the case of pollutants [that] require application of the best conventional pollutant control technology ***; and

(F) for all pollutants (other than those subject to subparagraphs (C), (D), or (E) of this paragraph) compliance with effluent limitations in accordance with subparagraph (A) of this paragraph as expeditiously as practicable but in no case later than 3 years after the date such limitations are established, and in no case later than March 31, 1989.

****

(d) Review and revision of effluent limitations. Any effluent limitation required by paragraph (2) of subsection (b) of this section shall be reviewed at least every five years and, if appropriate, revised pursuant to the procedure established under such paragraph.

****

(g) Modifications for certain nonconventional pollutants. (1) General authority. The Administrator, with the concurrence of the State, may modify the requirements of subsection (b)(2)(A) of this section with respect to the discharge from any point source of ammonia, chlorine, color, iron, and total phenols (4AAP) (when determined by the Administrator to be a pollutant covered by subsection (b)(2)(F) of this section) and any other pollutant which the Administrator lists under paragraph (4) of this subsection.

(2) Requirements for granting modifications. A modification under this subsection shall be granted only upon a showing by the owner or operator of a point source satisfactory to the Administrator that --

****

(C) such modification will not interfere with the attainment or maintenance of that water quality which shall assure protection of public water supplies, and the protection and propagation of a balanced population of shellfish, fish, and wildlife, and allow recreational activities, in and on the water and such modification will not result in the discharge of pollutants in quantities which may reasonably be anticipated to pose an unacceptable risk to human health or the environment because of bioaccumulation, persistency in the environment, acute toxicity, chronic toxicity (including carcinogenicity, mutagenicity or teratogenicity), or synergistic propensities.

****

(h) Modification of secondary treatment requirements. The Administrator, with the concurrence of the State, may issue a permit under section 402 of this Act [33 U.S.C. § 1342] which modifies the requirements of subsection (b)(1)(B) of this section with respect to the discharge of any pollutant from a publicly owned treatment works into marine waters, if the applicant demonstrates to the satisfaction of the Administrator that --

****

(2) the discharge of pollutants in accordance with such modified requirements will not interfere, alone or in combination with pollutants from other sources, with the attainment or maintenance of that water quality which assures protection of public water supplies and the protection and propagation of a balanced, indigenous population of shellfish, fish and wildlife, and allows recreational activities, in and on the water;

(3) the applicant has established a system for monitoring the impact of such discharge on a representative sample of aquatic biota, to the extent practicable, and the scope of such monitoring is limited to include only those scientific investigations which are necessary to study the effects of the proposed discharge;

****

(m) Modification of effluent limitation requirements for point sources. (1) The Administrator, with the concurrence of the State, may issue a permit under section 402 [33 U.S.C. § 1342] which modifies the requirements of subsections (b)(1)(A) and (b)(2)(E) of this section, and of section 403 [33 U.S.C. § 1343], with respect to effluent limitations to the extent such limitations relate to biochemical oxygen demand and pH from discharges by an industrial discharger in such State into deep waters of the territorial seas, if the applicant demonstrates and the Administrator finds that --

****

(2) The effluent limitations established under a permit issued under paragraph (1) shall be sufficient to implement the applicable State water quality standards, to assure the protection of public water supplies and protection and propagation of a balanced, indigenous population of shellfish, fish, fauna, wildlife, and other aquatic organisms, and to allow recreational activities in and on the water. In setting such limitations, the Administrator shall take into account any seasonal variations and the need for an adequate margin of safety, considering the lack of essential knowledge concerning the relationship between effluent limitations and water quality and the lack of essential knowledge of the effects of discharges on beneficial uses of the receiving waters.

****

[Pub. L. 92-500, § 2, 86 Stat. 844 (Oct. 18, 1972); Pub. L. 95-217, §§ 42-47, 53(c), 91 Stat. 1582-1586, 1590 (Dec. 27, 1977); Pub. L. 97-117, §§ 21, 22(a)-(d), 95 Stat. 1631, 1632 (Dec. 29, 1981); Pub. L. 97-440, 96 Stat. 2289 (Jan. 8, 1983); Pub. L. 100-4, Title III, §§ 301(a) to (e), 302(a) to (d), 303(a), (b)(1), (c) to (f), 304(a), 305, 306(a), (b), 307, 101 Stat. 29-37 (Feb. 4, 1987); Pub. L. 100-688, Title III, § 3202(b), 102 Stat. 4154 (Nov. 18, 1988); Pub. L. 103-431, § 2, 108 Stat. 4396 (Oct. 31, 1994); Pub. L. 104-66, Title II, § 2021(b), 109 Stat. 727 (Dec. 21, 1995)]

33 U.S.C. § 1312. Water quality related effluent limitations. (a) Establishment. Whenever, in the judgment of the Administrator or as identified under section 304(l) [33 U.S.C. § 1314(l)], discharges of pollutants from a point source or group of point sources, with the application of effluent limitations required under section 301(b)(2) of this Act [33 U.S.C. § 1311(b)(2)], would interfere with the attainment or maintenance of that water quality in a specific portion of the navigable waters which shall assure protection of public health, public water supplies, agricultural and industrial uses, and the protection and propagation of a balanced population of shellfish, fish and wildlife, and allow recreational activities in and on the water, effluent limitations (including alternative effluent control strategies) for such point source or sources shall be established which can reasonably be expected to contribute to the attainment or maintenance of such water quality.

****

[Pub. L. 92-500, § 2, 86 Stat. 846 (Oct. 18, 1972); Pub. L. 100-4, Title III, § 308(e), 101 Stat. 39 (Feb. 4, 1987)]

33 U.S.C. § 1313. Water quality standards and implementation plans. (a) Existing water quality standards. ****

(b) Proposed regulations. (1) The Administrator shall promptly prepare and publish proposed regulations setting forth water quality standards for a State in accordance with the applicable requirements of this Act as in effect immediately prior to October 18, 1972, if --

(A) the State fails to submit water quality standards within the times prescribed in subsection (a) of this section.
(B) a water quality standard submitted by such State under subsection (a) of this section is determined by the Administrator not to be consistent with the applicable requirements of [this Act as in effect immediately prior to October 18, 1972.]

(c) Review; revised standard; publication. ****

(2)(A) Whenever the State revises or adopts a new standard, such revised or new standard shall be submitted to the Administrator. Such revised or new water quality standard shall consist of the designated uses of the navigable waters involved and the water quality criteria for such waters based upon such uses. Such standards shall be such as to protect the public health or welfare, enhance the quality of water and serve the purposes of this Act. Such standards shall be established taking into consideration their use and value for public water supplies, propagation of fish and wildlife, recreational purposes, and agricultural, industrial, and other purposes, and also taking into consideration their use and value for navigation.

****

(3) If the Administrator, within sixty days after the date of submission of the revised or new standard, determines that such standard meets the requirements of this Act, such standard shall thereafter be the water quality standard for the applicable waters of that State. If the Administrator determines that any such revised or new standard is not consistent with the applicable requirements of this Act, he shall not later than the ninetieth day after the date of submission of such standard notify the State and specify the changes to meet such requirements. If such changes are not adopted by the State within ninety days after the date of notification, the Administrator shall promulgate such standard pursuant to paragraph (4) of this subsection.

****

(d) Identification of areas with insufficient controls; maximum daily load; certain effluent limitations revision. (1)(A) Each State shall identify those waters within its boundaries for which the effluent limitations required by section 301(b)(1)(A) and section 301(b)(1)(B) [33 U.S.C. §§ 1311(b)(1)(A) and 1311(b)(1)(B)] are not stringent enough to implement any water quality standard applicable to such waters. The State shall establish a priority ranking for such waters, taking into account the severity of the pollution and the uses to be made of such waters.

(B) Each State shall identify those waters or parts thereof within its boundaries for which controls on thermal discharges under section 301 [33 U.S.C. § 1311] are not stringent enough to assure protection and propagation of a balanced indigenous population of shellfish, fish, and wildlife.

(C) Each State shall establish for the waters identified in paragraph (1)(A) of this subsection, and in accordance with the priority ranking, the total maximum daily load, for those pollutants which the Administrator identifies under section 304(a)(2) [33 U.S.C. § 1314(a)(2)] as suitable for such calculation. Such load shall be established at a level necessary to implement the applicable water quality standards with seasonal variations and a margin of safety which takes into account any lack of knowledge concerning the relationship between effluent limitations and water quality.

(D) Each State shall estimate for the waters identified in paragraph (1)(B) of this subsection the total maximum daily thermal load required to assure protection and propagation of a balanced, indigenous population of shellfish, fish and wildlife. Such estimates shall take into account the normal water temperatures, flow rates, seasonal variations, existing sources of heat input, and the dissipative capacity of the identified waters or parts thereof. Such estimates shall include a calculation of the maximum heat input that can be made into each such part and shall include a margin of safety which takes into account any lack of knowledge concerning the development of thermal water quality criteria for such protection and propagation in the identified waters or parts thereof.

(2) Each State shall submit to the Administrator from time to time, with the first such submission not later than one hundred and eighty days after the date of publication of the first identification of pollutants under section 304(a)(2)(D) [33 U.S.C. § 1314(a)(2)(D)], for his approval the waters identified and the loads established under paragraphs (1)(A), (1)(B), (1)(C), and (1)(D) of this subsection. The Administrator shall either approve or disapprove such identification and load not later than thirty days after the date of submission. If the Administrator approves such identification and load, such State shall incorporate them into its current plan under subsection (e) of this section. If the Administrator disapproves such identification and load, he shall not later than thirty days after the date of such disapproval identify such waters in such State and establish such loads for such waters as he determines necessary to implement the water quality standards applicable to such waters and upon such identification and establishment the State shall incorporate them into its current plan under subsection (e) of this section.

(3) For the specific purpose of developing information, each State shall identify all waters within its boundaries which it has not identified under paragraph (1)(A) and

(1)(B) of this subsection and estimate for such waters the total maximum daily load with seasonal variations and margins of safety, for those pollutants which the Administrator identifies under section 304(a)(2) [33 U.S.C. § 1314(a)(2)] as suitable for such calculation and for thermal discharges, at a level that would assure protection and propagation of a balanced indigenous population of fish, shellfish and wildlife.

(4) Limitations on revision of certain effluent limitations. (A) Standard not attained. For waters identified under paragraph (1)(A) where the applicable water quality standard has not yet been attained, any effluent limitation based on a total maximum daily load or other waste load allocation established under this section may be revised only if (i) the cumulative effect of all such revised effluent limitations based on such total maximum daily load or waste load allocation will assure the attainment of such water quality standard, or (ii) the designated use which is not being attained is removed in accordance with regulations established under this section.

(B) Standard attained. For waters identified under paragraph (1)(A) where the quality of such waters equals or exceeds levels necessary to protect the designated use for such waters or otherwise required by applicable water quality standards, any effluent limitation based on a total maximum daily load or other waste load allocation established under this section, or any water quality standard established under this section, or any other permitting standard may be revised only if such revision is subject to and consistent with the antidegradation policy established under this section.

****

[Pub. L. 92-500, § 2, 86 Stat. 846 (Oct. 18, 1972); Pub. L. 100-4, Title III, § 308(d), Title IV, § 404(b), 101 Stat. 39, 68 (Feb. 4, 1987); Pub. L. 106-284, § 2, 114 Stat. 870 (Oct. 10, 2000)]

33 U.S.C. § 1329. Nonpoint source management programs. (a) State assessment reports. (1) Contents. The Governor of each State shall, after notice and opportunity for public comment, prepare and submit to the Administrator for approval, a report which --

(A) identifies those navigable waters within the State which, without additional action to control nonpoint sources of pollution, cannot reasonably be expected to attain or maintain applicable water quality standards or the goals and requirements of this Act;

(B) identifies those categories and subcategories of nonpoint sources or, where appropriate, particular nonpoint sources which add significant pollution to each portion of the navigable waters identified under subparagraph (A) in amounts which contribute to such portion not meeting such water quality standards or such goals and requirements;

(C) describes the process, including intergovernmental coordination and public participation, for identifying best management practices and measures to control each category and subcategory of nonpoint sources and, where appropriate, particular nonpoint sources identified under subparagraph (B) and to reduce, to the maximum extent practicable, the level of pollution resulting from such category, subcategory, or source; and

(D) identifies and describes State and local programs for controlling pollution added from nonpoint sources to, and improving the quality of, each such portion of the navigable waters, including but not limited to those programs which are receiving Federal assistance under subsections (h) and (i) of this section.

(2) Information used in preparation. In developing the report required by this section, the State (A) may rely upon information developed pursuant to sections 208, 303(e), 304(f), 305(b), and 314 [33 U.S.C. §§ 1288, 1313(e), 1314(f), 1315(b), and 1324], and other information as appropriate, and (B) may utilize appropriate elements of the waste treatment management plans developed pursuant to sections 208(b) and 303 [33 U.S.C. § 1288(b) and 1313], to the extent such elements are consistent with and fulfill the requirements of this section.

(b) State management programs. (1) In general. The Governor of each State, for that State or in combination with adjacent States, shall, after notice and opportunity for public comment, prepare and submit to the Administrator for approval a management program which such State proposes to implement in the first four fiscal years beginning after the date of submission of such management program for controlling pollution added from nonpoint sources to the navigable waters within the State and improving the quality of such waters.

(2) Specific contents. Each management program proposed for implementation under this subsection shall include each of the following:

(A) An identification of the best management practices and measures which will be undertaken to reduce pollutant loadings resulting from each category, subcategory, or particular nonpoint source designated under paragraph (1)(B), taking into account the impact of the practice on ground water quality.

(B) An identification of programs (including, as appropriate, nonregulatory or regulatory programs for enforcement, technical assistance, financial assistance, education, training, technology transfer, and demonstration projects) to achieve implementation of the best management practices by the categories, subcategories, and particular nonpoint sources designated under subparagraph (A).

(C) A schedule containing annual milestones for (i) utilization of the program implementation methods identified in subparagraph (B), and (ii) implementation of the best management practices identified in subparagraph (A) by the categories, subcategories, or particular nonpoint sources designated under paragraph (1)(B). Such schedule shall provide for utilization of the best management practices at the earliest practicable date.

(D) A certification of the attorney general of the State or States (or the chief attorney of any State water pollution control agency which has independent legal counsel) that the laws of the State or States, as the case may be, provide adequate authority to implement such management program or, if there is not such adequate authority, a list of such additional authorities as will be necessary to implement such management program. A schedule and commitment by the State or States to seek such additional authorities as expeditiously as practicable.

(E) Sources of Federal and other assistance and funding (other than assistance provided under subsections (h) and (i) of this section) which will be available in each of such fiscal years for supporting implementation of such practices and measures and the purposes for which such assistance will be used in each of such fiscal years.

(F) An identification of Federal financial assistance programs and Federal development projects for which the State will review individual assistance applications or development projects for their effect on water quality pursuant to the procedures set forth in Executive Order 12372 as in effect on September 17, 1983, to determine whether such assistance applications or development projects would be consistent with the program prepared under this subsection; for the purposes of this subparagraph, identification shall not be limited to the assistance programs or development projects subject to Executive Order 12372 but may include any programs listed in the most recent Catalog of Federal Domestic Assistance which may have an effect on the purposes and objectives of the State's nonpoint source pollution management program.

(3) Utilization of local and private experts. In developing and implementing a management program under this subsection, a State shall, to the maximum extent practicable, involve local public and private agencies and organizations which have expertise in control of nonpoint sources of pollution.

(4) Development on watershed basis. A State shall, to the maximum extent practicable, develop and implement a management program under this subsection on a watershed-by-watershed basis within such State.

(c) Administrative provisions. (1) Cooperation requirement. Any report required by subsection (a) of this section and any management program and report required by subsection (b) of this section shall be developed in cooperation with local, substate regional, and interstate entities which are actively planning for the implementation of nonpoint source pollution controls and have either been certified by the Administrator in accordance with section 208 [33 U.S.C. § 1288], have worked jointly with the State on water quality management planning under section 205(j) [33 U.S.C. § 1285(j)], or have been designated by the State legislative body or Governor as water quality management planning agencies for their geographic areas.

(2) Time period for submission of reports and management programs. Each report and management program shall be submitted to the Administrator during the 18-month period beginning on February 4, 1987.

(d) Approval or disapproval of reports and management programs. (1) Deadline. Subject to paragraph (2), not later than 180 days after the date of submission to the Administrator of any report or management program under this section (other than subsections (h), (i), and (k) of this section), the Administrator shall either approve or disapprove such report or management program, as the case may be. The Administrator may approve a portion of a management program under this subsection. If the Administrator does not disapprove a report, management program, or portion of a management program in such 180-day period, such report, management program, or portion shall be deemed approved for purposes of this section.

(2) Procedure for disapproval. If, after notice and opportunity for public comment and consultation with appropriate Federal and State agencies and other interested

persons, the Administrator determines that --

(A) the proposed management program or any portion thereof does not meet the requirements of subsection (b)(2) of this section or is not likely to satisfy, in whole or in part, the goals and requirements of this Act;

(B) adequate authority does not exist, or adequate resources are not available, to implement such program or portion;

(C) the schedule for implementing such program or portion is not sufficiently expeditious; or

(D) the practices and measures proposed in such program or portion are not adequate to reduce the level of pollution in navigable waters in the State resulting from nonpoint sources and to improve the quality of navigable waters in the State;

the Administrator shall within 6 months of the receipt of the proposed program notify the State of any revisions or modifications necessary to obtain approval. The State shall thereupon have an additional 3 months to submit its revised management program and the Administrator shall approve or disapprove such revised program within three months of receipt.

(3) Failure of State to submit report. If a Governor of a State does not submit the report required by subsection (a) of this section within the period specified by subsection (c)(2) of this section, the Administrator shall, within 30 months after February 4, 1987, prepare a report for such State which makes the identifications required by paragraphs (1)(A) and (1)(B) of subsection (a) of this section. Upon completion of the requirement of the preceding sentence and after notice and opportunity for comment, the Administrator shall report to Congress on his actions pursuant to this section.

(e) Local management programs; technical assistance. If a State fails to submit a management program under subsection (b) of this section or the Administrator does not approve such a management program, a local public agency or organization which has expertise in, and authority to, control water pollution resulting from nonpoint sources in any area of such State which the Administrator determines is of sufficient geographic size may, with approval of such State, request the Administrator to provide, and the Administrator shall provide, technical assistance to such agency or organization in developing for such area a management program which is described in subsection (b) of this section and can be approved pursuant to subsection (d) of this section. After development of such management program, such agency or organization shall submit such management program to the Administrator for approval. If the Administrator approves such management program, such agency or organization shall be eligible to receive financial assistance under subsection (h) of this section for implementation of such management program as if such agency or organization were a State for which a report submitted under subsection (a) of this section and a management program submitted under subsection (b) of this section were approved under this section. Such financial assistance shall be subject to the same terms and conditions as assistance provided to a State under subsection (h) of this section.

(f) Technical assistance for States. Upon request of a State, the Administrator may provide technical assistance to such State in developing a management program approved under subsection (b) of this section for those portions of the navigable waters requested by such State.

****

[Pub. L. 100-4, Title III, § 316(a), 101 Stat. 52 (Feb. 4, 1987); Pub. L. 105-362, Title V, § 501(c), 112 Stat. 3283 (Nov. 10, 1998)]

33 U.S.C. § 1341. Certification. (a) Compliance with applicable requirements; application; procedures; license suspension. (1) Any applicant for a Federal license or permit to conduct any activity including, but not limited to, the construction or operation of facilities, which may result in any discharge into the navigable waters, shall provide the licensing or permitting agency a certification from the State in which the discharge originates or will originate, or, if appropriate, from the interstate water pollution control agency having jurisdiction over the navigable waters at the point where the discharge originates or will originate, that any such discharge will comply with the applicable provisions of sections 301, 302, 303, 306, and 307 of this Act [33 U.S.C. §§ 1311, 1312, 1313, 1316, and 1317]. In the case of any such activity for which there is not an applicable effluent limitation or other limitation under sections 301(b) and 302 [33 U.S.C. §§ 1311(b) and 1312], and there is not an applicable standard under sections 306 and 307 [33 U.S.C. §§ 1316 and 1317], the State shall so certify, except that any such certification shall not be deemed to satisfy section 511(c) of this Act [33 U.S.C. § 1371(c)]. Such State or interstate agency shall establish procedures for public notice in the case of all applications for certification by it and, to the extent it deems appropriate, procedures for public hearings in connection with specific applications. In any case where a State or interstate agency has no authority to give such a certification, such certification shall be from the Administrator. If the State, interstate agency, or Administrator, as the case may be, fails or refuses to act on a request for certification, within a reasonable period of time (which shall not exceed one year) after receipt of such request, the certification requirements of this subsection shall be waived with respect to such Federal application. No license or permit shall be granted until the certification required by this section has been obtained or has been waived as provided in the preceding sentence. No license or permit shall be granted if certification has been denied by the State, interstate agency, or the Administrator, as the case may be.

****

[Pub. L. 92-500, § 2, 86 Stat. 877 (Oct. 18, 1972); Pub. L. 95-217, §§ 61(b), 64, 91 Stat. 1598, 1599 (Dec. 27, 1977)]

33 U.S.C. § 1342. National pollutant discharge elimination system. (a) Permits for discharge of pollutants. (1) Except as provided in sections 318 and 404 of this Act [33 U.S.C. §§ 1328 and 1344], the Administrator may, after opportunity for public hearing, issue a permit for the discharge of any pollutant, or combination of pollutants, notwithstanding section 301(a) of this Act [33 U.S.C. § 1311(a)], upon condition that such discharge will meet either (A) all applicable requirements under sections 301,

302, 306, 307, 308, and 403 of this Act [33 U.S.C. §§ 1311, 1312, 1316, 1317, 1318, and 1343], or (B) prior to the taking of necessary implementing actions relating to all such requirements, such conditions as the Administrator determines are necessary to carry out the provisions of this Act.

(2) The Administrator shall prescribe conditions for such permits to assure compliance with the requirements of paragraph (1) of this subsection, including conditions on data and information collection, reporting, and such other requirements as he deems appropriate.

****

(4) All permits for discharges into the navigable waters issued pursuant to section 13 of the Act of March 3, 1899 [33 U.S.C. § 407], shall be deemed to be permits issued under this title [33 U.S.C. §§ 1341 *et seq.*], and permits issued under this title shall be deemed to be permits issued under section 407 of this title, and shall continue in force and effect for their term unless revoked, modified, or suspended in accordance with the provisions of this Act.

(5) No permit for a discharge into the navigable waters shall be issued under section 13 of the Act of March 3, 1899 [33 U.S.C. § 407] after the date of enactment of this title [October 18, 1972]. ****

(b) State permit programs. At any time after the promulgation of the guidelines required by subsection (i)(2) of section 304 of this Act [33 U.S.C. § 1314(i)(2)], the Governor of each State desiring to administer its own permit program for discharges into navigable waters within its jurisdiction may submit to the Administrator a full and complete description of the program it proposes to establish and administer under State law or under an interstate compact. **** The Administrator shall approve each such submitted program unless he determines that adequate authority does not exist:

(1) To issue permits which --

(A) apply, and insure compliance with, any applicable requirements of sections 301, 302, 306, 307, and 403 [33 U.S.C. §§ 1311, 1312, 1316, 1317, and 1343];

(B) are for fixed terms not exceeding five years; and

(C) can be terminated or modified for cause including, but not limited to, the following:

(i) violation of any condition of the permit;

(ii) obtaining a permit by misrepresentation, or failure to disclose fully all relevant facts;

(iii) change in any condition that requires either a temporary or permanent reduction or elimination of the permitted discharge;

(D) control the disposal of pollutants into wells;

(2)(A) To issue permits which apply, and insure compliance with, all applicable requirements of section 308 of this Act [33 U.S.C. § 1318]; ****

(c) Suspension of Federal program upon submission of State program; withdrawal of approval of State program; return of State program to Administrator. (1) Not later than ninety days after the date on which a State has submitted a program (or revision thereof) pursuant to subsection (b) of this section, the Administrator shall suspend the issuance of permits under subsection (a) of this section as to those discharges subject to such program unless he determines that the State permit program does not meet the requirements of subsection (b) of this section or does not conform to the guidelines issued under section 304(i)(2) of this Act [33 U.S.C. § 1314(i)(2)]. If the Administrator so determines, he shall notify the State of any revisions or modifications necessary to conform to such requirements or guidelines.

****

(i) Federal enforcement not limited. Nothing in this section shall be construed to limit the authority of the Administrator to take action pursuant to section 309 of this Act [33 U.S.C. § 1319].

****

[Pub. L. 92-500, § 2, 86 Stat. 880 (Oct. 18, 1972); Pub. L. 95-217, §§ 33(c), 50, 54(c)(1), 65, 66, 91 Stat. 1577, 1588, 1591, 1599, 1600 (Dec. 27, 1977); Pub. L. 100-4, Title IV, §§ 401 to 404(a), (c), formerly (d), 405, 101 Stat. 65 to 67, 69 (Feb. 4, 1987); Pub. L. 102-580, Title III, § 364, 106 Stat. 4862 (Oct. 31, 1992); Pub. L. 104-66, Title II, § 2021(e)(2), 109 Stat. 727 (Dec. 21, 1995); Pub. L. 106-554, § 1(a)(4) [Div. B, Title I, § 112(a)], 114 Stat. 2763, 2763A-224 (Dec. 21, 2000)]

33 U.S.C. § 1362 Definitions. Except as otherwise specifically provided, when used in this Act:

****

(6) The term "pollutant" means dredged spoil, solid waste, incinerator residue, sewage, garbage, sewage sludge, munitions, chemical wastes, biological materials, radioactive materials, heat, wrecked or discarded equipment, rock, sand, cellar dirt and industrial, municipal, and agricultural waste discharged into water. This term does not mean (A) "sewage from vessels or a discharge incidental to the normal operation of a vessel of the Armed Forces" within the meaning of section 312 of this Act [33 U.S.C. § 1322]; or (B) water, gas, or other material which is injected into a well to facilitate production of oil or gas, or water derived in association with oil or gas production and disposed of in a well, if the well used either to facilitate production or for disposal purposes is approved by authority of the State in which the well is located, and if such State determines that such injection or disposal will not result in the degradation of ground or surface water resources.

(7) The term "navigable waters" means the waters of the United States, including the territorial seas.

(8) The term "territorial seas" means the belt of the seas measured from the line of ordinary low water along that portion of the coast which is in direct contact with the open sea and the line marking the seaward limit of inland waters, and extending seaward a distance of three miles.

****

(11) The term "effluent limitation" means any restriction established by a State or the Administrator on quantities, rates, and concentrations of chemical, physical, biological, and other constituents which are discharged from point sources into navigable waters, the waters of the contiguous zone, or the ocean, including schedules of compliance.

(12) The term "discharge of a pollutant" and the term "discharge of pollutants" each means (A) any addition of any pollutant to navigable waters from any point source,

(B) any addition of any pollutant to the waters of the contiguous zone or the ocean from any point source other than a vessel or other floating craft.

(13) The term "toxic pollutant" means those pollutants, or combinations of pollutants, including disease-causing agents, which after discharge and upon exposure, ingestion, inhalation or assimilation into any organism, either directly from the environment or indirectly by ingestion through food chains, will, on the basis of information available to the Administrator, cause death, disease, behavioral abnormalities, cancer, genetic mutations, physiological malfunctions (including malfunctions in reproduction) or physical deformations, in such organisms or their offspring.

(14) The term "point source" means any discernible, confined and discrete conveyance, including but not limited to any pipe, ditch, channel, tunnel, conduit, well, discrete fissure, container, rolling stock, concentrated animal feeding operation, or vessel or other floating craft, from which pollutants are or may be discharged. This term does not include agricultural stormwater discharges and return flows from irrigated agriculture.

(15) The term "biological monitoring" shall mean the determination of the effects on aquatic life, including accumulation of pollutants in tissue, in receiving waters due to the discharge of pollutants (A) by techniques and procedures, including sampling of organisms representative of appropriate levels of the food chain appropriate to the volume and the physical, chemical, and biological characteristics of the effluent, and (B) at appropriate frequencies and locations.

(16) The term "discharge" when used without qualification includes a discharge of a pollutant, and a discharge of pollutants.

****

(19) The term "pollution" means the man-made or man-induced alteration of the chemical, physical, biological, and radiological integrity of water.

****

[Pub. L. 92-500, § 2, 86 Stat. 886 (Oct. 18, 1972); Pub. L. 95-217, § 33(b), 91 Stat. 1577 (Dec. 27, 1977); Pub. L. 100-4, Title V, §§ 502(a), 503, 101 Stat. 75 (Feb. 4, 1987); Pub. L. 100-688, Title III, § 3202(a), 102 Stat. 4154 (Nov. 18, 1988); Pub. L. 104-106, Div. A, Title III, § 325(c)(3), 110 Stat. 259 (Feb. 10, 1996); Pub. L. 106-284, § 5, 114 Stat. 875 (Oct. 10, 2000)]

- 0 -

iii. Private Lands

Perhaps the most important federal statute restricting a landowner's ability to alter land uses and thereby adversely modify wildlife habitat is the Endangered Species Act. The ESA prohibits any person -- including private individuals -- from conduct that "takes" a species listed as endangered.[105] Since "take" is defined to include "harm"[106] and "harm" is in turn defined to include "significant habitat modification or degradation where it actually kills or injures wildlife by significantly impairing essential behavioral patterns, including breeding, feeding, or sheltering,"[107] a landowner generally may not alter the use of land by adversely modifying its habitat qualities.[108] Similarly, the ESA may effect private development activities that require federal permits since this triggers the Act's consultation requirements.[109] But the ESA applies only to lands that harbor listed species -- a reach that is far short of conserving most remaining habitat.

To conserve this habitat requires a more expansive and more localized approach. But the regulation of the use of private property in land has traditionally been performed by state and local governments. Although this division is not constitutionally mandated,[110] Congress has generally been reticent to regulate land uses on a wholesale basis. Instead -- as was the case with wildlife conservation measures at the beginning of the twentieth century -- Congress has chosen to become involved selectively and through a variety of approaches that are less intrusive than traditional regulatory approaches.

The conservation of wetlands demonstrates the range of legal instruments that Congress has available.

a. Wetlands

Federal law once encouraged the "reclamation" of "swamps" by providing incentives to drain them. Increasing ecological knowledge has led to a reversal of that policy. Wetlands are now recognized as invaluable for their pollution control and water purification services, as flood control mechanisms, and as habitat for fish and wildlife.[111] Despite their values, the loss of wetlands has been dramatic: less than half of the wetlands that were present when Europeans began settling the continent remain. Nearly 60% of the species listed as threatened or endangered depend upon wetlands during at least part of their life cycle.

Direct regulation of actions adversely affecting wetlands falls under § 404 of the Federal Water Pollution Control Act.

THE FEDERAL WATER POLLUTION CONTROL ACT [CLEAN WATER ACT] (33 U.S.C. § 1344)

Section 404 of the Clean Water Act is the primary federal proscription of draining or filling wetlands. The section authorizes the Secretary of the Army acting through the Army Corps of Engineers to "issue permits ... for the discharge of dredged or fill material into the navigable waters at specified disposal sites."[112] This simple statement is more importantly read in the negative: the Secretary may also deny permits.

The Corps issues permits under guidelines promulgated by the Environmental Protection Agency.[113] The EPA guidelines and the Corps permitting regulations explicitly provide for ecosystem-level conservation of biodiversity[114] and contain a general presumption against granting permits.[115]

33 U.S.C. § 1344. Permits for dredged or fill material. (a) Discharge into navigable waters at specified disposal sites. The Secretary may issue permits, after notice and opportunity for public hearings for the discharge of dredged or fill material into the navigable waters at specified disposal sites. Not later than the fifteenth day after the date an applicant submits all the information required to complete an application for a permit under this subsection, the Secretary shall publish the notice required by this subsection.

(b) Specification for disposal sites. Subject to subsection (c) of this section, each such disposal site shall be specified for each such permit by the Secretary (1) through the application of guidelines developed by the Administrator, in conjunction with the Secretary, which guidelines shall be based upon criteria comparable to the criteria applicable to the territorial seas, the contiguous zone, and the ocean under section 403(c) of this Act [33 U.S.C. § 1343(c)], and (2) in any case where such guidelines under clause (1) alone would prohibit the specification of a site, through the application additionally of the economic impact of the site on navigation and anchorage.

(c) Denial or restriction of use of defined areas as disposal sites. The Administrator is authorized to prohibit the specification (including the withdrawal of specification) of any defined area as a disposal site, and he is authorized to deny or restrict the use of any defined area for specification (including the withdrawal of specification) as a disposal site, whenever he determines, after notice and opportunity for public hearings, that the discharge of such materials into such area will have an unacceptable adverse effect on municipal water supplies, shellfish beds and fishery areas (including spawning and breeding areas), wildlife, or recreational areas. Before making such determination, the Administrator shall consult with the Secretary. The Administrator shall set forth in writing and make public his findings and his reasons for making any determination under this subsection.

(d) "Secretary" defined. The term "Secretary" as used in this section means the Secretary of the Army, acting through the Chief of Engineers.

(e) General permits on State, regional, or nationwide basis. (1) In carrying out his functions relating to the discharge of dredged or fill material under this section, the Secretary may, after notice and opportunity for public hearing, issue general permits on a State, regional, or nationwide basis for any category of activities involving discharges of dredged or fill material if the Secretary determines that the activities in such category are similar in nature, will cause only minimal adverse environmental effects when performed separately, and will have only minimal cumulative adverse effect on the environment. Any general permit issued under this subsection shall (A) be based on the guidelines described in subsection (b)(1) of this section, and (B) set forth the requirements and standards which shall apply to any activity authorized by such general permit.

(2) No general permit issued under this subsection shall be for a period of more than five years after the date of its issuance and such general permit may be revoked or modified by the Secretary if, after opportunity for public hearing, the Secretary determines that the activities authorized by such general permit have an adverse

impact on the environment or such activities are more appropriately authorized by individual permits.

(f) Non-prohibited discharge of dredged or fill material. (1) Except as provided in paragraph (2) of this subsection, the discharge of dredged or fill material --

(A) from normal farming, silviculture, and ranching activities such as plowing, seeding, cultivating, minor drainage, harvesting for the production of food, fiber, and forest products, or upland soil and water conservation practices;

(B) for the purpose of maintenance, including emergency reconstruction of recently damaged parts, of currently serviceable structures such as dikes, dams, levees, groins, riprap, breakwaters, causeways, and bridge abutments or approaches, and transportation structures;

(C) for the purpose of construction or maintenance of farm or stock ponds or irrigation ditches, or the maintenance of drainage ditches;

(D) for the purpose of construction of temporary sedimentation basins on a construction site which does not include placement of fill material into the navigable waters;

(E) for the purpose of construction or maintenance of farm roads or forest roads, or temporary roads for moving mining equipment, where such roads are constructed and maintained, in accordance with best management practices, to assure that flow and circulation patterns and chemical and biological characteristics of the navigable waters are not impaired, that the reach of the navigable waters is not reduced, and that any adverse effect on the aquatic environment will be otherwise minimized;

(F) resulting from any activity with respect to which a State has an approved program under section 208(b)(4) of this Act [33 U.S.C. § 1288(b)(4)] which meets the requirements of subparagraphs (B) and (C) of such section,

is not prohibited by or otherwise subject to regulation under this section or section 301(a) or 402 of this Act [33 U.S.C. § 1311(a) or 1342] (except for effluent standards or prohibitions under section 1317 of this title).

(2) Any discharge of dredged or fill material into the navigable waters incidental to any activity having as its purpose bringing an area of the navigable waters into a use to which it was not previously subject, where the flow or circulation of navigable waters may be impaired or the reach of such waters be reduced, shall be required to have a permit under this section.

(g) State administration. (1) The Governor of any State desiring to administer its own individual and general permit program for the discharge of dredged or fill material into the navigable waters (other than those waters which are presently used, or are susceptible to use in their natural condition or by reasonable improvement as a means to transport interstate or foreign commerce shoreward to their ordinary high water mark, including all waters which are subject to the ebb and flow of the tide shoreward to their mean high water mark, or mean higher high water mark on the west coast, including wetlands adjacent thereto) within its jurisdiction may submit to the Administrator a full and complete description of the program it proposes to establish and administer under State law or under an interstate compact. In addition, such State shall submit a statement from the attorney general (or the attorney for those State agencies which have independent legal counsel), or from the chief legal officer in the case of an interstate agency, that the laws of such State, or the interstate compact, as the case may be, provide adequate authority to carry out the described program.

(2) Not later than the tenth day after the date of the receipt of the program and statement submitted by any State under paragraph (1) of this subsection, the Administrator shall provide copies of such program and statement to the Secretary and the Secretary of the Interior, acting through the Director of the United States Fish and Wildlife Service.

(3) Not later than the ninetieth day after the date of the receipt by the Administrator of the program and statement submitted by any State, under paragraph (1) of this subsection, the Secretary and the Secretary of the Interior, acting through the Director of the United States Fish and Wildlife Service, shall submit any comments with respect to such program and statement to the Administrator in writing.

(h) Determination of State's authority to issue permits under State program; approval; notification; transfers to State program. (1) Not later than the one-hundred-twentieth day after the date of the receipt by the Administrator of a program and statement submitted by any State under paragraph (1) of this subsection, the Administrator shall determine, taking into account any comments submitted by the Secretary and the Secretary of the Interior, acting through the Director of the United States Fish and Wildlife Service, pursuant to subsection (g) of this section, whether such State has the following authority with respect to the issuance of permits pursuant to such program:

(A) To issue permits which --

(i) apply, and assure compliance with, any applicable requirements of this section, including, but not limited to, the guidelines established under subsection (b)(1) of this section, and sections 307 and 403 of this Act [33 U.S.C. §§ 1317 and 1343];

(ii) are for fixed terms not exceeding five years; and

(iii) can be terminated or modified for cause including, but not limited to, the following:

(I) violation of any condition of the permit;

(II) obtaining a permit by misrepresentation, or failure to disclose fully all relevant facts;

(III) change in any condition that requires either a temporary or permanent reduction or elimination of the permitted discharge.

(B) To issue permits which apply, and assure compliance with, all applicable requirements of section 308 of this Act [33 U.S.C. § 1318], or to inspect, monitor, enter, and require reports to at least the same extent as required in section 308 of this Act [33 U.S.C. § 1318].

(C) To assure that the public, and any other State the waters of which may be affected, receive notice of each application for a permit and to provide an opportunity for public hearing before a ruling on each such application.

(D) To assure that the Administrator receives notice of each application (including a copy thereof) for a permit.

(E) To assure that any State (other than the permitting State), whose waters may be affected by the issuance of a permit may submit written recommendations to the permitting State (and the Administrator) with respect to any permit application and, if any part of such written recommendations are not accepted by the permitting State, that the permitting State will notify such affected State (and the Administrator) in writing of its failure to so accept such recommendations together with its reasons for so doing.

(F) To assure that no permit will be issued if, in the judgment of the Secretary, after consultation with the Secretary of the department in which the Coast Guard is operating, anchorage and navigation of any of the navigable waters would be substantially impaired thereby.

(G) To abate violations of the permit or the permit program, including civil and criminal penalties and other ways and means of enforcement.

(H) To assure continued coordination with Federal and Federal-State water-related planning and review processes.

****

(n) Enforcement authority not limited. Nothing in this section shall be construed to limit the authority of the Administrator to take action pursuant to section 309 of this Act [33 U.S.C. § 1319].

****

(s) Violation of permits. (1) Whenever on the basis of any information available to him the Secretary finds that any person is in violation of any condition or limitation set forth in a permit issued by the Secretary under this section, the Secretary shall issue an order requiring such person to comply with such condition or limitation, or the Secretary shall bring a civil action in accordance with paragraph (3) of this subsection.

****

(3) The Secretary is authorized to commence a civil action for appropriate relief, including a permanent or temporary injunction for any violation for which he is authorized to issue a compliance order under paragraph (1) of this subsection. Any action under this paragraph may be brought in the district court of the United States for the district in which the defendant is located or resides or is doing business, and such court shall have jurisdiction to restrain such violation and to require compliance. Notice of the commencement of such action shall be given immediately to the appropriate State.

(4) Any person who violates any condition or limitation in a permit issued by the Secretary under this section, and any person who violates any order issued by the Secretary under paragraph (1) of this subsection, shall be subject to a civil penalty not to exceed $25,000 per day for each violation. In determining the amount of a civil penalty the court shall consider the seriousness of the violation or violations, the economic benefit (if any) resulting from the violation, any history of such violations, any good-faith efforts to comply with the applicable requirements, the economic impact of the penalty on the violator, and such other matters as justice may require.

[Pub. L. 92-500, § 2, 86 Stat. 884 (Oct. 18, 1972); Pub. L. 95-217, § 67(a), (b), 91 Stat. 1600 (Dec. 27, 1977); Pub. L. 100-4, Title III, § 313(d), 101 Stat. 45 (Feb. 4, 1987)]

- 0 -

"SWAMPBUSTER" PROVISIONS
(16 U.S.C. §§ 3801, 3821-23)

Section 404 expressly exempts "the discharge of ... fill material ... from normal farming, silviculture, and ranching activities" from its permit requirement.[116] The exemption is qualified by the subsequent prohibition against bringing lands "into a use to which it was not previously subject" without a permit.[117] Thus, while normal agricultural activities do not require a 404 permit, one is required to bring wetlands into production. The "Swampbuster" provisions of the 1985,[118] 1990,[119] and 1996[120] farm bills remove some of the incentive that farmers and ranchers might have to do so. These provisions deny all federal farm subsidies to anyone who "drained, dredged, filled, leveled, or otherwise manipulated (including any activity that results in impairing or reducing the flow, circulation, or reach of water) for the purpose or to have the effect of making the production of an agricultural commodity possible."[121] The ineligibility applies to the person and is permanent: "any person who ... converts a wetland ... shall be ineligible for [specified] payments, loans, or programs ... for that crop year and all subsequent crop years."[122] To regain eligibility, the person must restore the wetland.[123]

16 U.S.C. § 3801. Definitions. (a) For purposes of subtitles A through E:

(1) The term "agricultural commodity" means --

(A) any agricultural commodity planted and produced in a State by annual tilling of the soil, including tilling by one-trip planters; or

(B) sugarcane planted and produced in a State.

****

(6)(A) The term "converted wetland" means wetland that has been drained, dredged, filled, leveled, or otherwise manipulated (including any activity that results in impairing or reducing the flow, circulation, or reach of water) for the purpose or to have the effect of making the production of an agricultural commodity possible if --

(i) such production would not have been possible but for such action; and

(ii) before such action --

(I) such land was wetland; and

(II) such land was neither highly erodible land nor highly erodible cropland.

(B) Wetland shall not be considered converted wetland if production of an agricultural commodity on such land during a crop year --

(i) is possible as a result of a natural condition, such as drought; and

(ii) is not assisted by an action of the producer that destroys natural wetland characteristics.

****

(10) The term "hydric soil" means soil that, in its undrained condition, is saturated,

flooded, or ponded long enough during a growing season to develop an anaerobic condition that supports the growth and regeneration of hydrophytic vegetation.

(11) The term "hydrophytic vegetation" means a plant growing in --

(A) water; or

(B) a substrate that is at least periodically deficient in oxygen during a growing season as a result of excessive water content.

****

(14) The term "Secretary" means the Secretary of Agriculture.

****

(18) The term "wetland", except when such term is part of the term "converted wetland", means land that --

(A) has a predominance of hydric soils;

(B) is inundated or saturated by surface or groundwater at a frequency and duration sufficient to support a prevalence of hydrophytic vegetation typically adapted for life in saturated soil conditions; and

(C) under normal circumstances does support a prevalence of such vegetation.

For purposes of this Act, and any other Act, this term shall not include lands in Alaska identified as having high potential for agricultural development which have a predominance of permafrost soils.

(b) The Secretary shall develop --

(1) criteria for the identification of hydric soils and hydrophytic vegetation; and

(2) lists of such soils and such vegetation.

[Pub. L. 99-198, Title XII, § 1201, 99 Stat. 1504 (Dec. 23, 1985); Pub. L. 99-349, Title I, c. I, 100 Stat. 714 (July 2, 1986); Pub. L. 101-624, Title XIV, § 1421(a), 104 Stat. 3572 (Nov. 28, 1990); Pub. L. 104-127, Title III, § 301(a) to (c), 110 Stat. 980 (Apr. 4, 1996)]

16 U.S.C. § 3821. Program ineligibility. (a) Production on converted wetland. Except as provided in this subtitle [16 U.S.C. §§ 3811 *et seq.*] and notwithstanding any other provision of law, any person who in any crop year produces an agricultural commodity on converted wetland, as determined by the Secretary, shall be --

(1) in violation of this section; and

(2) ineligible for loans or payments in an amount determined by the Secretary to be proportionate to the severity of the violation.

(b) Ineligibility for certain loans and payments. If a person is determined to have committed a violation under subsection (a) of this section during a crop year, the Secretary shall determine which of, and the amount of, the following loans and payments for which the person shall be ineligible:

(1) Contract payments under a production flexibility contract, marketing assistance loans, and any type of price support or payment made available under the Agricultural Market Transition Act [7 U.S.C. §§ 7201 *et seq.*], the Commodity Credit Corporation Charter Act [15 U.S.C. §§ 714 *et seq.*), or any other Act.

(2) A loan made or guaranteed under the Consolidated Farm and Rural Development Act [7 U.S.C. §§ 1921 *et seq.*] or any other provision of law

administered by the Consolidated Farm Service Agency, if the Secretary determines that the proceeds of the loan will be used for a purpose that will contribute to conversion of a wetland (other than as provided in this subtitle [16 U.S.C. §§ 3821 *et seq.*]) to produce an agricultural commodity.

(3) During the crop year:

(A) A payment made pursuant to a contract entered into under the environmental quality incentives program under chapter 4 of subtitle D [16 U.S.C. §§ 3839aa *et seq.*].

(B) A payment under any other provision of subtitle D [16 U.S.C. §§ 3830 *et seq.*].

(C) A payment under section 401 or 402 of the Agricultural Credit Act of 1978 [16 U.S.C. § 2201 or 2202].

(D) A payment, loan, or other assistance under section 3 or 8 of the Watershed Protection and Flood Prevention Act [16 U.S.C. § 1003 or 1006a].

(c) Wetland conversion. Except as provided in section 1222 [16 U.S.C. § 3822] and notwithstanding any other provision of law, any person who in any crop year beginning after November 28, 1990, converts a wetland by draining, dredging, filling, leveling, or any other means for the purpose, or to have the effect, of making the production of an agricultural commodity possible on such converted wetland shall be ineligible for those payments, loans, or programs specified in subsection (b) of this section for that crop year and all subsequent crop years.

****

[Pub. L. 99-198, Title XII, § 1221, 99 Stat. 1507 (Dec. 23, 1985); Pub. L. 101-624, § 1421(b), 104 Stat. 3572 (Nov. 28, 1990); Pub. L. 102-237, Title II, § 204(3), 105 Stat. 1855 (Dec. 13, 1991); Pub. L. 102-552, Title III, § 308(a), 106 Stat. 4116 (Oct. 28, 1992); Pub. L. 104-127, Title III, § 321, 110 Stat. 986 (Apr.4, 1996)]

16 U.S.C. § 3822. Delineation of wetlands; exemptions. (a) Delineation by the Secretary. (1) In general. Subject to subsection (b) of this section and paragraph (6), the Secretary shall delineate, determine, and certify all wetlands located on subject land on a farm.

(2) Wetland delineation maps. The Secretary shall delineate wetlands on wetland delineation maps. On the request of a person, the Secretary shall make a reasonable effort to make an on-site wetland determination prior to delineation.

(3) Certification. On providing notice to affected persons, the Secretary shall --

(A) certify whether a map is sufficient for the purpose of making a determination of ineligibility for program benefits under section 1221 [16 U.S.C. § 3821]; and

(B) provide an opportunity to appeal the certification prior to the certification becoming final.

(4) Duration of certification. A final certification made under paragraph (3) shall remain valid and in effect as long as the area is devoted to an agricultural use or until such time as the person affected by the certification requests review of the certification by the Secretary.

(5) Review of mapping on appeal. In the case of an appeal of the Secretary's certification, the Secretary shall review and certify the accuracy of the mapping of all

land subject to the appeal to ensure that the subject land has been accurately delineated. Prior to rendering a decision on the appeal, the Secretary shall conduct an on-site inspection of the subject land on a farm.

(6) Reliance on prior certified delineation. No person shall be adversely affected because of having taken an action based on a previous certified wetland delineation by the Secretary. The delineation shall not be subject to a subsequent wetland certification or delineation by the Secretary, unless requested by the person under paragraph (4).

(b) Exemptions. No person shall become ineligible under section 1221 [16 U.S.C. § 3821] for program loans or payments under the following circumstances:

(1) As the result of the production of an agricultural commodity on the following lands:

(A) A converted wetland if the conversion of the wetland was commenced before December 23, 1985.

(B) Land that is a nontidal drainage or irrigation ditch excavated in upland.

(C) A wet area created by a water delivery system, irrigation, irrigation system, or application of water for irrigation.

(D) A wetland on which the owner or operator of a farm or ranch uses normal cropping or ranching practices to produce an agricultural commodity in a manner that is consistent for the area where the production is possible as a result of a natural condition, such as drought, and is without action by the producer that destroys a natural wetland characteristic.

(E) Land that is an artificial lake or pond created by excavating or diking land (that is not a wetland) to collect and retain water and that is used primarily for livestock watering, fish production, irrigation, wildlife, fire control, flood control, cranberry growing, or rice production, or as a settling pond.

(F) A wetland that is temporarily or incidentally created as a result of adjacent development activity.

(G) A converted wetland if the original conversion of the wetland was commenced before December 23, 1985, and the Secretary determines the wetland characteristics returned after that date as a result of --

(i) the lack of maintenance of drainage, dikes, levees, or similar structures;

(ii) a lack of management of the lands containing the wetland; or

(iii) circumstances beyond the control of the person.

(H) A converted wetland, if --

(i) the converted wetland was determined by the Natural Resources Conservation Service to have been manipulated for the production of an agricultural commodity or forage prior to December 23, 1985, and was returned to wetland conditions through a voluntary restoration, enhancement, or creation action subsequent to that determination;

(ii) technical determinations regarding the prior site conditions and the restoration, enhancement, or creation action have been adequately documented by the Natural Resources Conservation Service;

(iii) the proposed conversion action is approved by the Natural Resources Conservation Service prior to implementation; and

(iv) the extent of the proposed conversion is limited so that the conditions will be at least equivalent to the wetland functions and values that existed prior to implementation of the voluntary wetland restoration, enhancement, or creation action.

(2) For the conversion of the following:

(A) An artificial lake or pond created by excavating or diking land that is not a wetland to collect and retain water and that is used primarily for livestock watering, fish production, irrigation, wildlife, fire control, flood control, cranberry growing, rice production, or as a settling pond.

(B) A wetland that is temporarily or incidentally created as a result of adjacent development activity.

(C) A wetland on which the owner or operator of a farm or ranch uses normal cropping or ranching practices to produce an agricultural commodity in a manner that is consistent for the area where the production is possible as a result of a natural condition, such as drought, and is without action by the producer that destroys a natural wetland characteristic.

(D) A wetland previously identified as a converted wetland (if the original conversion of the wetland was commenced before December 23, 1985), but that the Secretary determines returned to wetland status after that date as a result of --

(i) the lack of maintenance of drainage, dikes, levees, or similar structures;

(ii) a lack of management of the lands containing the wetland; or

(iii) circumstances beyond the control of the person.

(E) A wetland, if --

(i) the wetland was determined by the Natural Resources Conservation Service to have been manipulated for the production of an agricultural commodity or forage prior to December 23, 1985, and was returned to wetland conditions through a voluntary restoration, enhancement, or creation action subsequent to that determination;

(ii) technical determinations regarding the prior site conditions and the restoration, enhancement, or creation action have been adequately documented by the Natural Resources Conservation Service;

(iii) the proposed conversion action is approved by the Natural Resources Conservation Service prior to implementation; and

(iv) the extent of the proposed conversion is limited so that the conditions will be at least equivalent to the wetland functions and values that existed prior to implementation of the voluntary wetland restoration, enhancement, or creation action.

(c) On-site inspection requirement. No program lcans, payments, or benefits shall be withheld from a person under this subchapter unless the Secretary has conducted an on-site visit of the subject land.

(d) Identification of minimal effect exemptions. For purposes of applying the minimal effect exemption under subsection (f)(1) of this section, the Secretary shall identify by regulation categorical minimal effect exemptions on a regional basis to assist persons in avoiding a violation of the ineligibility provisions of section 1221 [16 U.S.C. § 3821]. The Secretary shall ensure that employees of the Department of Agriculture who administer this subchapter receive appropriate training to properly apply the minimal effect exemptions determined by the Secretary.

(e) Nonwetlands. The Secretary shall exempt from the ineligibility provisions of section 1221 [16 U.S.C. § 3821] any action by a person upon lands in any case in which the Secretary determines that any one of the following does not apply with respect to such lands:

(1) Such lands have a predominance of hydric soils.

(2) Such lands are inundated or saturated by surface or groundwater at a frequency and duration sufficient to support a prevalence of hydrophytic vegetation typically adapted for life in saturated soil conditions.

(3) Such lands, under normal circumstances, support a prevalence of such vegetation.

(f) Minimal effect; mitigation. The Secretary shall exempt a person from the ineligibility provisions of section 1221 [16 U.S.C. § 3821] for any action associated with the production of an agricultural commodity on a converted wetland, or the conversion of a wetland, if 1 or more of the following conditions apply, as determined by the Secretary:

(1) The action, individually and in connection with all other similar actions authorized by the Secretary in the area, will have a minimal effect on the functional hydrological and biological value of the wetlands in the area, including the value to waterfowl and wildlife.

(2) The wetland and the wetland values, acreage, and functions are mitigated by the person through the restoration of a converted wetland, the enhancement of an existing wetland, or the creation of a new wetland, and the restoration, enhancement, or creation is --

(A) in accordance with a wetland conservation plan;

(B) in advance of, or concurrent with, the action;

(C) not at the expense of the Federal Government;

(D) in the case of enhancement or restoration of wetlands, on not greater than a 1-for-1 acreage basis unless more acreage is needed to provide equivalent functions and values that will be lost as a result of the wetland conversion to be mitigated;

(E) in the case of creation of wetlands, on greater than a 1-for-1 acreage basis if more acreage is needed to provide equivalent functions and values that will be lost as a result of the wetland conversion that is mitigated;

(F) on lands in the same general area of the local watershed as the converted wetland; and

(G) with respect to the restored, enhanced, or created wetland, made subject to an easement that --

(i) is recorded on public land records;

(ii) remains in force for as long as the converted wetland for which the restoration, enhancement, or creation to be mitigated remains in agricultural use or is not returned to its original wetland classification with equivalent functions and values; and

(iii) prohibits making alterations to the restored, enhanced, or created wetland that lower the wetland's functions and values.

(3) The wetland was converted after December 23, 1985, but before November 28, 1990, and the wetland values, acreage, and functions are mitigated by the producer through the requirements of subparagraphs (A), (B), (C), (D), (F), and (G) of paragraph (2).

(4) The action was authorized by a permit issued under section 1344 of Title 33 and the wetland values, acreage, and functions of the converted wetland were adequately mitigated for the purposes of this subchapter.

(g) Mitigation appeals. A person shall be afforded the right to appeal, under section 1243 [16 U.S.C. § 3843], the imposition of a mitigation agreement requiring greater than one-to- one acreage mitigation to which the person is subject.

(h) Good faith exemption. (1) Exemption described. The Secretary may waive a person's ineligibility under section 1221 [16 U.S.C. § 3821] for program loans, payments, and benefits as the result of the conversion of a wetland subsequent to November 28, 1990, or the production of an agricultural commodity on a converted wetland, if the Secretary determines that the person has acted in good faith and without intent to violate this subchapter.

(2) Period for compliance. The Secretary shall provide a person who the Secretary determines has acted in good faith and without intent to violate this subchapter with a reasonable period, but not to exceed 1 year, during which to implement the measures and practices necessary to be considered to [be] actively restoring the subject wetland.

(i) Restoration. Any person who is determined to be ineligible for program benefits under section 1221 [16 U.S.C. § 3821] for any crop year shall not be ineligible for such program benefits under such section for any subsequent crop year if, prior to the beginning of such subsequent crop year, the person has fully restored the characteristics of the converted wetland to its prior wetland state or has otherwise mitigated for the loss of wetland values, as determined by the Secretary, through the restoration, enhancement, or creation of wetland values in the same general area of the local watershed as the converted wetland.

(j) Determinations; restoration and mitigation plans; monitoring activities. Technical determinations, the development of restoration and mitigation plans, and monitoring activities under this section shall be made by the [Natural] Resources Conservation Service;

(k) Mitigation banking program. Using authorities available to the Secretary, the Secretary may operate a pilot program for mitigation banking of wetlands to assist persons to increase the efficiency of agricultural operations while protecting wetland functions and values. Subsection (f)(2)(C) of this section shall not apply to this subsection.

[Pub. L. 99-198, Title XII, § 1222, 99 Stat. 1508 (Dec. 23, 1985); Pub. L. 101-624, Title XIV, § 1422, 104 Stat. 3573 (Nov. 28, 1990); Pub. L. 104-127, Title III, § 322, 110 Stat. 987 (Apr. 4, 1996)]

16 U.S.C. § 3823. Affiliated persons. If a person is affected by a reduction in benefits under section 1221 [16 U.S.C. § 3821] and the affected person is affiliated with other persons for the purpose of receiving the benefits, the benefits of each affiliated person shall be reduced under section 3821 of this title in proportion to the interest held by the affiliated person.

[Pub. L. 104-127, Title III, § 324, 110 Stat. 992 (Apr. 4, 1996)]

- 0 -

There are other federal statutes that seek to conserve wetland habitats:

*** the Wetlands Loan Act[124] was enacted in 1961 "to offset or prevent the serious loss of important wetlands and other waterfowl habitat essential to the preservation of such waterfowl" when the revenue produced by the Duck Stamp Act failed to keep pace with rising land costs. As discussed above, the statute authorized additional funds for the acquisition of wildlife refuges and waterfowl production areas.

*** the Water Bank Act[125] authorized the Secretary of Agriculture to "bank" wetlands by entering into "agreements with landowners [of] important migratory waterfowl nesting and breeding areas for the conservation of ... wetlands."[126] The agreements had a ten-year duration[127] and obligated the landowner "not to drain, burn, fill, or otherwise destroy the wetland character" of the area.[128]

*** the Wetlands Reserve Program[129] authorizes the Secretary of Agriculture to enroll up to 975,000 acres in the program through the purchase of permanent easements, 30-year easements, and restoration cost-share agreements.[130] Enrolled lands are to be maintained or restored as wetlands and can be used for "such activities as hunting and fishing, managed timber harvest, or periodic haying or grazing" if the use is "consistent with the long-term protection and enhancement of the wetlands resources."[131]

*** the Emergency Wetlands Resources Act of 1986[132] requires Secretary of the Interior to establish a national wetlands priority conservation plan "which shall specify ... the types of wetlands and interests in wetlands which should be given priority with respect to Federal and State acquisition" based on wildlife habitat and similar considerations.[133]

*** the North American Wetlands Conservation Act[134] establishes a North American Wetlands Conservation Council that is empowered to approve conservation projects based in part on the project's consistency with the national wetlands priority conservation plan developed under the Emergency Wetlands Resources Act of 1986 and the suitability of the wetland as wildlife habitat.[135] The statute provides for federal funding for the acquisition of lands and interests in lands; the funding is through the Federal Aid in Wildlife Restoration Act of 1937 [The Pittman-Robertson Act].[136] Wetland conservation projects in Canada and Mexico may also be funded through the Act.

*** the Coastal Wetlands Planning, Protection, and Restoration Act[137] provides matching grants to coastal states to conserve wetlands.

The federal wetlands statutes thus highlight the range of approaches available to conserve wildlife habitat:[138]

- *** Section 404 of the Federal Water Pollution Control Act is a traditional regulatory approach that prohibits the destruction of wetlands unless the landowner has obtained a permit from the appropriate federal agency.
- *** The "Swampbuster" provisions of the farm bills do not prohibit conversion of wetlands but they do remove much of the incentive to do so by denying all federal farm subsidies to anyone who has done so.
- *** The Emergency Wetlands Resources Act of 1986 establishes a planning and educational program designed to assist federal and state officials in monitoring wetlands and to guide acquisition decisions.
- *** The Wetlands Reserve Program is a voluntary program that provides for the acquisition of interests in land that protect the wetlands values while also allowing the landowner to exclude others and to contain some economic uses of the land.
- *** the North American Wetlands Conservation Act provides a funding and acquisition mechanism for interests in wetlands and transferring those lands in the National Wildlife Refuge System.
- *** And there are other possibilities as well: for example, the Tax Reform Act of 1976 provides a tax deduction for the value of an conservation easement if it is donated to a private land trust.[139]

- 0 -

COASTAL BARRIER RESOURCES ACT (1982)
(16 U.S.C. §§ 3501-3510)

Straddling the line between wetlands and dry uplands are coastal lands where the tides move the line back and forth twice daily. Such lands are particularly valuable for wildlife: the "coastal barriers ... and adjacent wetlands, marshes, estuaries, inlets and nearhsore water provide ... habitats for migratory birds and other wildlife; and habitats which are essential spawning, nursery, nesting, and feeding areas for commercially and recreationally important species of finfish and shellfish, as well as other aquatic organisms such as sea turtles."[140] Such coastal areas, however, are also popular with tourists and often support a thriving second-home market. Historically, the federal government has assisted in developing coastal areas through a series of subsidies such as insurance, mortgages and loans, disaster assistance, and the like. To remove this perverse incentive to destroy crucial habitat, Congress enacted the Coastal Barrier Resources Act in 1982.[141] Like the Swampbuster provisions of the farm bills that seek to discourage the loss of wetlands by denying subsidy payments to individuals that drain wetlands, the Coastal Barrier Resources Act prohibits new "expenditures or ... financial assistance" for nearly all habitat-destroying activities[142] within a "Coastal Barrier Resource System."[143] Unlike other federal land "systems," the Coastal Barrier Resource System applies to all lands that meet the statutory criteria regardless of land ownership.

As with the Swampbuster provisions, the Coast Act does not prevent development, but it does remove some of the economic incentive to do so.

16 U.S.C. § 3501. Congressional statement of findings and purpose. (a) The Congress finds that --

(1) coastal barriers along the Atlantic and Gulf coasts and along the shore areas of the Great Lakes of the United States and the adjacent wetlands, marshes, estuaries, inlets and nearshore waters provide --

(A) habitats for migratory birds and other wildlife; and

(B) habitats which are essential spawning, nursery, nesting, and feeding areas for commercially and recreationally important species of finfish and shellfish, as well as other aquatic organisms such as sea turtles;

(2) coastal barriers contain resources of extraordinary scenic, scientific, recreational, natural, historic, archeological, cultural, and economic importance; which are being irretrievably damaged and lost due to development on, among, and adjacent to, such barriers;

(3) coastal barriers serve as natural storm protective buffers and are generally unsuitable for development because they are vulnerable to hurricane and other storm damage and because natural shoreline recession and the movement of unstable sediments undermine manmade structures;

(4) certain actions and programs of the Federal Government have subsidized and permitted development on coastal barriers and the result has been the loss of barrier resources, threats to human life, health, and property, and the expenditure of millions of tax dollars each year; and

(5) a program of coordinated action by Federal, State, and local governments is critical to the more appropriate use and conservation of coastal barriers.

(b) The Congress declares that it is the purpose of this chapter to minimize the loss of human life, wasteful expenditure of Federal revenues, and the damage to fish, wildlife, and other natural resources associated with the coastal barriers along the Atlantic and Gulf Coasts and along the shore areas of the Great Lakes by restricting future Federal expenditures and financial assistance which have the effect of encouraging development of coastal barriers, by establishing the John H. Chafee Coastal Barrier Resources System, and by considering the means and measures by which the long-term conservation of these fish, wildlife, and other natural resources may be achieved.

[Pub. L. 97-348, § 2, 96 Stat. 1653 (Oct. 18, 1982); Pub. L. 100-707, Title II, § 204(c)(1), 102 Stat. 4714 (Nov. 23, 1988); Pub. L. 106-167, § 3(c)(1), 113 Stat. 1804 (Dec. 9, 1999)]

16 U.S.C. § 3502. Definitions. For purposes of this Act --

(1) The term "undeveloped coastal barrier" means --

(A) a depositional geologic feature (such as a bay barrier, tombolo, barrier spit, or barrier island) that --

(i) is subject to wave, tidal, and wind energies, and

(ii) protects landward aquatic habitats from direct wave attack; and

(B) all associated aquatic habitats, including the adjacent wetlands, marshes, estuaries, inlets, and nearshore waters;

but only if such feature and associated habitats contain few manmade structures and these structures, and man's activities on such feature and within such habitats, do not significantly impede geomorphic and ecological processes.

(2) The term "Committees" means the Committee on Resources of the House of Representatives and the Committee on Environment and Public Works of the Senate.

(3) The term "financial assistance" means any form of loan, grant, guaranty, insurance, payment, rebate, subsidy, or any other form of direct or indirect Federal assistance other than --

(A) deposit or account insurance for customers of banks, savings and loan associations, credit unions, or similar institutions;

(B) the purchase of mortgages or loans by the Government National Mortgage Association, the Federal National Mortgage Association, or the Federal Home Loan Mortgage Corporation;

(C) assistance for environmental studies, planning, and assessments that are required incident to the issuance of permits or other authorizations under Federal law; and

(D) assistance pursuant to programs entirely unrelated to development, such as any Federal or federally assisted public assistance program or any Federal old-age survivors or disability insurance program.

Such term includes flood insurance described in section 4028 of Title 42.

(4) The term "Great Lakes" means Lake Ontario, Lake Erie, Lake Huron, Lake St. Clair, Lake Michigan, and Lake Superior, to the extent that those lakes are subject to the jurisdiction of the United States.

(5) The term "Secretary" means the Secretary of the Interior.

(6) The term "System" means the John H. Chafee Coastal Barrier Resources System established by section 4(a) [16 U.S.C. § 3503(a)].

(7) The term "System unit" means any undeveloped coastal barrier, or combination of closely-related undeveloped coastal barriers, included within the John H. Chafee Coastal Barrier Resources System established by 4 [16 U.S.C. § 3503].

[Pub. L. 97-348, § 3, 96 Stat. 1653 (Oct. 18, 1982); Pub. L. 99-272, Title XIV, § 14001(b)(5), 100 Stat. 329 (Apr. 7, 1986); Pub. L. 100-707, Title II, § 204(c)(2), 102 Stat. 4714 (Nov. 23, 1988); Pub. L. 101-591, § 2, 104 Stat. 2931 (Nov. 16, 1990); Pub. L. 106-167, § 3(c)(2), 113 Stat. 1804 (Dec. 9, 1999)]

16 U.S.C. § 3503. Establishment of John H. Chafee Coastal Barrier Resources System. (a) Establishment. There is established the John H. Chafee Coastal Barrier Resources System, which shall consist of those undeveloped coastal barriers and other areas located on the coasts of the United States that are identified and generally depicted on the maps on file with the Secretary entitled 'Coastal Barrier Resources System', dated October 24, 1990, as those maps may be modified, revised, or corrected under --

(1) subsection (f)(3);

(2) section 4 of the Coastal Barrier Improvement Act of 1990 (16 U.S.C . 3503 note; Public Law 101-591); or

(3) any other provision of law enacted on or after November 16, 1990, that specifically authorizes the modification, revision, or correction.".

(b) System maps. The Secretary shall keep the maps referred to in subsection (a) of this section on file and available for public inspection in the Office of the Director of the United States Fish and Wildlife Service, and in such other offices of that service as the

Director considers appropriate.

(c) Boundary review and modification. At least once every 5 years, the Secretary shall review the maps referred to in subsection (a) of this section and shall make, in consultation with the appropriate State, local, and Federal officials, such minor and technical modifications to the boundaries of System units as are necessary solely to reflect changes that have occurred in the size or location of any System unit as a result of natural forces.

(d) Additions to System. The Secretary may add a parcel of real property to the System, if --

(1) the owner of the parcel requests, in writing, that the Secretary add the parcel to the System; and

(2) the parcel is an undeveloped coastal barrier.

(e) Addition of excess Federal property. (1) Consultation and determination. Prior to transfer or disposal of excess property under the Federal Property and Administrative Services Act of 1949 (40 U.S.C. § 471 *et seq.*) that may be an undeveloped coastal barrier, the Administrator of General Services shall consult with and obtain from the Secretary a determination as to whether and what portion of the property constitutes an undeveloped coastal barrier. Not later than 180 days after the initiation of such consultation, the Secretary shall make and publish notice of such Immediately upon issuance of a positive determination, the Secretary shall--

(A) prepare a map depicting the undeveloped coastal barrier portion of such property; and

(B) publish in the Federal Register notice of the addition of such property to the System.

(2) Effective date of inclusion. An area to be added to the System under this subsection shall be part of the System effective on the date on which the Secretary publishes notice in the Federal Register under paragraph (1)(B) with respect to that area.

(f) Maps. The Secretary shall --

(1) keep a map showing the location of each boundary modification made under subsection (c) and of each parcel of real property added to the System under subsection (d) or (e) on file and available for public inspection in the Office of the Director of the United States Fish and Wildlife Service and in such other offices of the Service as the Director considers appropriate;

(2) provide a copy of the map to --

(A) the State and unit of local government in which the property is located;

(B) the Committees; and

(C) the Federal Emergency Management Agency; and

(3) revise the maps referred to in subsection (a) to reflect each boundary modification under subsection (c) and each addition of real property to the System under subsection (d) or (e), after publishing in the Federal Register a notice of any such proposed revision.

(g) Guidelines for certain recommendations and determinations. (1) In general. In making any recommendation to the Congress regarding the addition of any area to the System or in determining whether, at the time of the inclusion of a System unit within the System, a coastal barrier is undeveloped, the Secretary shall consider whether within the area--

(A) the density of development is less than 1 structure per 5 acres of land above mean high tide; and

(B) there is existing infrastructure consisting of --

(i) a road, with a reinforced road bed, to each lot or building site in the area;

(ii) a wastewater disposal system sufficient to serve each lot or building site in the area;

(iii) electric service for each lot or building site in the area; and

(iv) a fresh water supply for each lot or building site in the area.

(2) Structure defined. In paragraph (1), the term "structure" means a walled and roofed building, other than a gas or liquid storage tank, that --

(A) is principally above ground and affixed to a permanent site, including a manufactured home on a permanent foundation; and

(B) covers an area of at least 200 square feet.

(3) Savings clause. Nothing in this subsection supersedes the official maps referred to in subsection (a).

[Pub. L. 97-348, § 4, 96 Stat. 1654 (Oct. 18, 1982); Pub. L. 97-396, § 8, 96 Stat. 2007 (Dec. 31, 1982); Pub. L. 100-707, Title II, § 204(b), 102 Stat. 4713 (Nov. 23, 1988); Pub. L. 101-591, §§ 3, 4(d), 104 Stat. 2931, 2933 (Nov. 16, 1990); Pub. L. 106-167, § 3(c)(3), 113 Stat. 1804 (Dec. 9, 1999); Pub. L. 106-514, §§ 2, 3(a), (b)(1), (c), (d), 114 Stat. 2394, 2395 (Nov. 13, 2000)]

16 U.S.C. § 3504. Limitations on Federal expenditures affecting the System. (a) Construction or purchase of structure, facility, road, airport, etc.; projects to prevent erosion; exceptions. Except as provided in section 6 [16 U.S.C. § 3505], no new expenditures or new financial assistance may be made available under authority of any Federal law for any purpose within the System, including, but not limited to --

(1) the construction or purchase of any structure, appurtenance, facility, or related infrastructure;

(2) the construction or purchase of any road, airport, boat landing facility, or other facility on, or bridge or causeway to, any System unit; and

(3) the carrying out of any project to prevent the erosion of, or to otherwise stabilize, any inlet, shoreline, or inshore area, except that such assistance and expenditures may be made available on units designated pursuant to 6 [16 U.S.C. § 3505] on maps numbered S01 through S08 and LA07 for purposes other than encouraging development and, in all units, in cases where an emergency threatens life, land, and property immediately adjacent to that unit.

(b) New expenditures or new financial assistance. An expenditure or financial assistance made available under authority of Federal law shall, for purposes of this chapter, be a new expenditure or new financial assistance if --

(1) in any case with respect to which specific appropriations are required, no money

for construction or purchase purposes was appropriated before the date on which the relevant System unit or portion of the System unit was included within the System under this chapter or the Coastal Barrier Improvement Act of 1990; or

(2) no legally binding commitment for the expenditure or financial assistance was made before such date.

[Pub. L. 97-348, § 5, 96 Stat. 1656 (Oct. 18, 1982); Pub. L. 101-591, §§ 2(b)(2), 5(c), 104 Stat. 2931, 2936 (Nov. 16, 1990)]

16 U.S.C. § 3505. Exceptions to limitations on expenditures. (a) In general. Notwithstanding section 3504 of this title, the appropriate Federal officer, after consultation with the Secretary, may make Federal expenditures and may make financial assistance available within the System for the following:

(1) Any use or facility necessary for the exploration, extraction, or transportation of energy resources which can be carried out only on, in, or adjacent to a coastal water area because the use or facility requires access to the coastal water body.

(2) The maintenance or construction of improvements of existing Federal navigation channels (including the Intracoastal Waterway) and related structures (such as jetties), including the disposal of dredge materials related to such maintenance or construction.

(3) The maintenance, replacement, reconstruction, or repair, but not the expansion, of publicly owned or publicly operated roads, structures, or facilities that are essential links in a larger network or system.

(4) Military activities essential to national security.

(5) The construction, operation, maintenance, and rehabilitation of Coast Guard facilities and access thereto.

(6) Any of the following actions or projects, if a particular expenditure or the making available of particular assistance for the action or project is consistent with the purposes of this chapter:

(A) Projects for the study, management, protection, and enhancement of fish and wildlife resources and habitats, including acquisition of fish and wildlife habitats and related lands, stabilization projects for fish and wildlife habitats, and recreational projects.

(B) Establishment, operation, and maintenance of air and water navigation aids and devices, and for access thereto.

(C) Projects under the Land and Water Conservation Fund Act of 1965 (16 U.S.C. 4601-4 through 11) and the Coastal Zone Management Act of 1972 (16 U.S.C. 1451 et seq.).

(D) Scientific research, including aeronautical, atmospheric, space, geologic, marine, fish and wildlife, and other research, development, and applications.

(E) Assistance for emergency actions essential to the saving of lives and the protection of property and the public health and safety, if such actions are performed pursuant to sections 5170a, 5170b, and 5192 of Title 42 and section 1362 of the National Flood Insurance Act of 1968 (42 U.S.C. § 4103) and are limited to actions that are necessary to alleviate the emergency.

(F) Maintenance, replacement, reconstruction, or repair, but not the expansion (except with respect to United States route 1 in the Florida Keys), of publicly owned or publicly operated roads, structures, and facilities.

(G) Nonstructural projects for shoreline stabilization that are designed to mimic, enhance, or restore a natural stabilization system.

(b) Existing Federal navigation channels. For purposes of subsection (a)(2) of this section, a Federal navigation channel or a related structure is an existing channel or structure, respectively, if it was authorized before the date on which the relevant System unit or portion of the System unit was included within the System.

(c) Expansion of highways in Michigan. The limitations on the use of Federal expenditures or financial assistance within the System under subsection (a)(3) of this section shall not apply to a highway--

(1) located in a unit of the System in Michigan; and

(2) in existence on November 16, 1990.

(d) Services and facilities outside system. (1) In general. Except as provided in paragraphs (2) and (3) of this subsection, limitations on the use of Federal expenditures or financial assistance within the System under section 3504 of this title shall not apply to expenditures or assistance provided for services or facilities and related infrastructure located outside the boundaries of unit T-11 of the System (as depicted on the maps referred to in section 3503(a) of this title) which relate to an activity within that unit.

(2) Prohibition of flood insurance coverage. No new flood insurance coverage may be provided under the National Flood Insurance Act of 1968 (42 U.S.C. 4001 et seq.) for any new construction or substantial improvements relating to services or facilities and related infrastructure located outside the boundaries of unit T-11 of the System that facilitate an activity within that unit that is not consistent with the purposes of this chapter.

(3) Prohibition of HUD Assistance. (A) In general. No financial assistance for acquisition, construction, or improvement purposes may be provided under any program administered by the Secretary of Housing and Urban Development for any services or facilities and related infrastructure located outside the boundaries of unit T-11 of the System that facilitate an activity within that unit that is not consistent with the purposes of this chapter.

(B) "Financial assistance" defined. For purposes of this paragraph, the term "financial assistance" includes any contract, loan, grant, cooperative agreement, or other form of assistance, including the insurance or guarantee of a loan, mortgage, or pool of mortgages.

[Pub. L. 97-348, § 6, 96 Stat. 1656 (Oct. 18, 1982); Pub. L. 100-707, Title I, § 109(h), 102 Stat. 4709 (Nov. 23, 1988); Pub. L. 101-591, § 5(a), 104 Stat. 2934 (Nov. 16, 1990)]

- 0 -

b. Uplands

Wetlands are unusual both because their ecological values are widely acknowledged and -- despite the difficulty of drawing precise boundaries -- because they are relatively easy to identify. Identification of other categories of lands with significant habitat values is more difficult in part because it requires local knowledge. This difficulty can be ameliorated by relying upon local officials -- and the federal agency with the most local agents is the Department of Agriculture (USDA), which has a history over the past 70 years of providing assistance based upon local conditions. The Department's presence is also particularly helpful because agriculture is among the most ecologically destructive land uses.[145] As was the case with many of the wetland conservation statutes, the upland conservation statutes focus on agricultural operations.

The range of approaches applicable to the conservation of biodiversity on privately uplands is similar to that employed to conserve wetlands. The Internal Revenue Code provisions, for example, are applicable to all conservation easements; the Wetlands Reserve Program was based upon the Conservation Reserve Program.

CONSERVATION RESERVE PROGRAM (1985)
(16 U.S.C. §§ 3831-3836a)

When it was established in 1985, the Conservation Reserve Program was initially established to remove "highly erodible land" from agricultural production and planted in permanent cover such as grasses or trees.[146] Participation in the program is voluntary. Farmers with eligible lands[147] submit contract offers and a proposed conservation plan; the Natural Resources Conservation Service -- an agency in the USDA -- selects offers taking into consideration "the extent to which enrollment of the land ... would improve soil resources, water quality, wildlife habitat, or provide other environmental benefits."[148]

Contracts run for at least ten and not more than fifteen years.[149] Participants receive annual rental payments. In addition, the Secretary shares the cost of the conservation measures.

16 U.S.C. § 3801. Definitions. (a) For purposes of subtitles A through E:

(1) The term "agricultural commodity" means --

(A) any agricultural commodity planted and produced in a State by annual tilling of the soil, including tilling by one-trip planters; or

(B) sugarcane planted and produced in a State.

(2) The term "conservation plan" means the document that --

(A) applies to highly erodible cropland;

(B) describes the conservation system applicable to the highly erodible cropland and describes the decisions of the person with respect to location, land use, tillage systems, and conservation treatment measures and schedule; and

(C) is approved by the local soil conservation district, in consultation with the local committees established under section 8(b)(5) of the Soil Conservation and Domestic Allotment Act [16 U.S.C. § 590h(b)(5)] and the Secretary, or by the

Secretary.

(3) The term "conservation system" means a combination of 1 or more conservation measures or management practices that --

(A) are based on local resource conditions, available conservation technology, and the standards and guidelines contained in the Natural Resources Conservation Service field office technical guides; and

(B) are designed to achieve, in a cost effective and technically practicable manner, a substantial reduction in soil erosion or a substantial improvement in soil conditions on a field or group of fields containing highly erodible cropland when compared to the level of erosion or soil conditions that existed before the application of the conservation measures and management practices.

(4) The term "conservation district" means any district or unit of State or local government formed under State or territorial law for the express purpose of developing and carrying out a local soil and water conservation program. Such district or unit of government may be referred to as a "conservation district", "soil conservation district", "soil and water conservation district", "resource conservation district", "natural resource district", "land conservation committee", or a similar name.

(5) The term "cost sharing payment" means a payment made by the Secretary to an owner or operator of a farm or ranch containing highly erodible cropland under the provisions of section 1234(b) of this Act [16 U.S.C. § 3834(b)].

****

(8) The term "highly erodible cropland" means highly erodible land that is in cropland use, as determined by the Secretary.

(9)(A) The term "highly erodible land" means land--

(i) that is classified by the Soil Conservation Service as class IV, VI, VII, or VIII land under the land capability classification system in effect on December 23, 1985; or

(ii) that has, or that if used to produce an agricultural commodity, would have an excessive average annual rate of erosion in relation to the soil loss tolerance level, as established by the Secretary, and as determined by the Secretary through application of factors from the universal soil loss equation and the wind erosion equation, including factors for climate, soil erodibility, and field slope.

(B) For purposes of this paragraph, the land capability class or rate of erosion for a field shall be that determined by the Secretary to be the predominant class or rate of erosion under regulations issued by the Secretary.

(C) Not later than 60 days after the date of the enactment of this subparagraph [April 4, 1996], the Secretary shall publish in the Federal Register the universal soil loss equation and wind erosion equation used by the Department of Agriculture as of that date. The Secretary may not change the equations after that date except following notice and comment in a manner consistent with section 553 of Title 5.

****

(13) The term "rental payment" means a payment made by the Secretary to an owner or operator of a farm or ranch containing highly erodible cropland to compensate the owner or operator for retiring such land from crop production and placing such land in the conservation reserve in accordance with subtitle D [16 U.S.C.

§ 3831 *et seq.*].

(14) The term "Secretary" means the Secretary of Agriculture.

(15) The term "shelterbelt" means a vegetative barrier with a linear configuration composed of trees, shrubs, and other approved perennial vegetation.

****

(17) The term "vegetative cover" means --

(A) perennial grasses, legumes, forbs, or shrubs with an expected life span of 5 or more years; or

(B) trees.

****

[Pub. L. 99-198, Title XII, § 1201, 99 Stat. 1504 (Dec. 23, 1985); Pub. L. 99-349, Title I, c. I, 100 Stat. 714 (July 2, 1986); Pub. L. 101-624, Title XIV, § 1421(a), 104 Stat. 3572 (Nov. 28, 1990); Pub. L. 104-127, Title III, § 301(a) to (c), 110 Stat. 980 (Apr. 4, 1996)]

16 U.S.C. § 3831. Conservation reserve. (a) In general. Through the 2002 calendar year, the Secretary shall formulate and carry out the enrollment of lands in a conservation reserve program through the use of contracts to assist owners and operators of lands specified in subsection (b) of this section to conserve and improve the soil and water resources of such lands.

(b) Eligible lands. The Secretary may include in the program established under this subchapter [16 U.S.C. § 3831 *et seq.*] --

(1) highly erodible croplands that --

(A) if permitted to remain untreated could substantially reduce the production capability for future generations; or

(B) can not be farmed in accordance with a plan under section 1212 [16 U.S.C. § 3812];

(2) marginal pasture lands converted to wetland or established as wildlife habitat prior to the enactment of the Food, Agriculture, Conservation, and Trade Act of 1990 [November 28, 1990];

(3) marginal pasture lands to be devoted to trees in or near riparian areas or for similar water quality purposes, not to exceed 10 percent of the number of acres of land that is placed in the conservation reserve under this subchapter [16 U.S.C. § 3831 *et seq.*]in each of the 1991 through 2002 calendar years;

(4) croplands that are otherwise not eligible --

(A) if the Secretary determines that (i) such lands contribute to the degradation of water quality or would pose an on-site or off-site environmental threat to water quality if permitted to remain in agricultural production, and (ii) water quality objectives with respect to such land cannot be achieved under the water quality incentives program established under chapter 2 [16 U.S.C. §§ 1238 *et seq.*];

(B) if such croplands are newly-created, permanent grass sod waterways, or are contour grass sod strips established and maintained as part of an approved conservation plan;

(C) that will be devoted to newly established living snow fences, permanent wildlife habitat, windbreaks, shelterbelts, or filterstrips devoted to trees or shrubs; or

(D) if the Secretary determines that such lands pose an off-farm environmental threat, or pose a threat of continued degradation of productivity due to soil salinity, if permitted to remain in production.

(c) Certain land affected by secretarial action. For purposes of determining the eligibility of land to be placed in the conservation reserve established under this subchapter [16 U.S.C. § 3831 *et seq.*], land shall be considered planted to an agricultural commodity during a crop year if an action of the Secretary prevented land from being planted to the commodity during the crop year.

(d) Maximum enrollment. The Secretary may maintain up to 36,400,000 acres in the conservation reserve at any one time during the 1986 through 2002 calendar years (including contracts extended by the Secretary pursuant to section 1437(c) of the Food, Agriculture, Conservation, and Trade Act of 1990 (Public Law 101-624, 16 U.S.C. § 3831 note)).

(e) Duration of contract. (1) In general. For the purpose of carrying out this subchapter [16 U.S.C. § 3831 *et seq.*], the Secretary shall enter into contracts of not less than 10, nor more than 15, years.

(2) Certain lands. In the case of land devoted to hardwood trees, shelterbelts, windbreaks, or wildlife corridors under a contract entered into under this subchapter after October 1, 1990, and land devoted to such uses under contracts modified under section 1235A [16 U.S.C. § 3535A], the owner or operator of such land may, within the limitations prescribed under this section, specify the duration of the contract. The Secretary may, in the case of land that is devoted to hardwood trees under a contract entered into under this subchapter prior to October 1, 1990, extend such contract for not to exceed 5 years, as agreed to by the owner or operator of such land and the Secretary.

(f) Conservation priority areas. (1) Designation. Upon application by the appropriate State agency, the Secretary shall designate watershed areas of the Chesapeake Bay Region (Pennsylvania, Maryland, and Virginia), the Great Lakes Region, the Long Island Sound Region, and other areas of special environmental sensitivity as conservation priority areas.

(2) Eligible watersheds. Watersheds eligible for designation under this subsection shall include areas with actual and significant adverse water quality or habitat impacts related to agricultural production activities.

(3) Expiration. Conservation priority area designation under this subsection shall expire after 5 years, subject to redesignation, except that the Secretary may withdraw a watershed's designation --

(A) upon application by the appropriate State agency; or

(B) in the case of areas specified in this subsection, if the Secretary finds that such areas no longer contain actual and significant adverse water quality or habitat impacts related to agricultural production activities.

(4) Duty of Secretary. In utilizing the authority granted under this subsection, the Secretary shall attempt to maximize water quality and habitat benefits in such

watersheds by promoting a significant level of enrollment of lands within such watersheds in the program under this subchapter by whatever means the Secretary determines appropriate and consistent with the purposes of this subchapter [16 U.S.C. § 3831 *et seq.*].

(g) Multi-year grasses and legumes. For purposes of this subchapter [16 U.S.C. § 3831 *et seq.*], alfalfa and other multi-year grasses and legumes in a rotation practice, approved by the Secretary, shall be considered agricultural commodities.

(h) Pilot program for enrollment of wetland and buffer acreage in conservation reserve. (1) In general. During the 2001 and 2002 calendar years, the Secretary shall carry out a pilot program in the States of Iowa, Minnesota, Montana, Nebraska, North Dakota, and South Dakota under which the Secretary shall include eligible acreage described in paragraph (3) in the program established under this subchapter [16 U.S.C. § 3831 *et seq.*].

(2) Participation among States. The Secretary shall ensure, to the maximum extent practicable, that owners and operators in each of the States referred to in paragraph (1) have an equitable opportunity to participate in the pilot program established under this subsection.

(3) Eligible acreage. (A) In general. Subject to subparagraphs (B) through (D), an owner or operator may enroll in the conservation reserve under this subsection--

(i) a wetland (including a converted wetland described in section 122(b)(1)(A) [16 U.S.C. § 3822(b)(1)(A)]) that was cropped during at least 3 of the immediately preceding 10 crop years; and

(ii) Buffer acreage that

(I) is contiguous to the wetland described in clause (i);

(II) is used to protect the wetland; and

(III) is of such width as the Secretary determines is necessary to protect the wetland, taking into consideration and accommodating the farming practices (including the straightening of boundaries to accommodate machinery) used with respect to the cropland that surrounds the wetland.

(B) Exclusions. An owner or operator may not enroll in the conservation reserve under this subsection --

(i) any wetland, or land on a floodplain, that is, or is adjacent to, a perennial riverine system wetland identified on the final national wetland inventory map of the Secretary of the Interior; or

(ii) in the case of an area that is not covered by the final national inventory map, any wetland, or land on a floodplain, that is adjacent to a perennial stream identified on a 1-24,000 scale map of the United States Geological Survey.

(C) Program limitations. (i) In general. The Secretary may enroll in the conservation reserve under this subsection --

(I) not more than 500,000 acres in all States referred to in paragraph (1); and

(II) not more than 150,000 acres in any 1 State referred to in paragraph (1).

(ii) Relationship to program maximum. Subject to clause (iii), for the purposes of subsection (d), any acreage enrolled in the conservation reserve under this subsection shall be considered acres maintained in the conservation reserve.

(iii) Relationship to other enrolled acreage. Acreage enrolled under this subsection shall not affect for any fiscal year the quantity of --

(I) acreage enrolled to establish conservation buffers as part of the program announced on March 24, 1998 (63 Fed. Reg. 14109); or

(II) acreage enrolled into the conservation reserve enhancement program announced on May 27, 1998 (63 Fed. Reg. 28965).

(D) Owner or operator limitations. (i) Wetland. The maximum size of any wetland described in subparagraph (A)(i) of an owner or operator enrolled in the conservation reserve under this subsection shall be 5 contiguous acres.

(ii) Buffer acreage. The maximum size of any buffer acreage described in subparagraph (A)(ii) of an owner or operator enrolled in the conservation reserve under this subsection shall be the greater of --

(I) 3 times the size of any wetland described in subparagraph (A)(i) to which the buffer acreage is contiguous; or

(II) 150 feet on either side of the wetland.

(iii) Tracts. The maximum size of any eligible acreage described in subparagraph (A) in a tract (as determined by the Secretary) of an owner or operator enrolled in the conservation reserve under this subsection shall be 40 acres.

(4) Duties of owners and operators. Under a contract entered into under this subsection, during the term of the contract, an owner or operator of a farm or ranch must agree --

(A) to restore the hydrology of the wetland within the eligible acreage to the maximum extent practicable, as determined by the Secretary;

(B) to establish vegetative cover (which may include emerging vegetation in water) on the eligible acreage, as determined by the Secretary; and

(C) to carry out other duties described in section 1232 [16 U.S.C. § 3832].

(5) Duties of the Secretary. (A) In general. Except as provided in subparagraphs (B) and (C), in return for a contract entered into by an owner or operator under this subsection, the Secretary shall make payments and provide assistance to the owner or operator in accordance with sections 1233 and 1234 [16 U.S.C. §§ 3833 and 3834].

(B) Continuous signup. The Secretary shall use continuous signup under section 1234(c)(2)(B) [16 U.S.C. § 3834(c)(2)(B)] to determine the acceptability of contract offers and the amount of rental payments under this subsection.

(C) Incentives. The amounts payable to owners and operators in the form of rental payments under contracts entered into under this subsection shall reflect incentives that are provided to owners and operators to enroll filterstrips in the conservation reserve under section 1234 [16 U.S.C. § 3834].

[Pub. L. 99-198, Title XII, § 1231, 99 Stat. 1509 (Dec. 23, 1985); Pub. L. 99-500, Title I, § 101(a), [Title VI, § 643], 100 Stat. 3341-36 (Oct. 18, 1986); Pub. L. 99-591, Title I, § 101(a), [Title VI, § 643], 100 Stat. 3341-36 (Oct. 30,

1986); Pub. L. 99-641, Title II, § 205, 100 Stat. 3563 (Nov. 10, 1986); Pub. L. 101-624, Title XIV, §§ 1432(2), 1447(a), 104 Stat. 3577, 3605 (Nov. 28, 1990); Pub. L. 102-324, § 1(a), 106 Stat. 447 (July 22, 1992); Pub. L. 103-66, Title I, § 1402(b), 107 Stat. 332 (Aug. 10, 1993); Pub. L. 104-127, Title III, § 332(a)(1), (b), 110 Stat. 994 (Apr. 4, 1996)]

16 U.S.C. § 3832. Duties of owners and operators. (a) Terms of contract. Under the terms of a contract entered into under this subchapter [16 U.S.C. § 3831 *et seq.*], during the term of such contract, an owner or operator of a farm or ranch must agree --

(1) to implement a plan approved by the local conservation district (or in an area not located within a conservation district, a plan approved by the Secretary) for converting eligible lands normally devoted to the production of an agricultural commodity on the farm or ranch to a less intensive use (as defined by the Secretary), such as pasture, permanent grass, legumes, forbs, shrubs, or trees, substantially in accordance with a schedule outlined in the plan;

(2) to place highly erodible cropland subject to the contract in the conservation reserve established under this subchapter [16 U.S.C. § 3831 *et seq.*];

(3) not to use such land for agricultural purposes, except as permitted by the Secretary;

(4) to establish approved vegetative cover (which may include emerging vegetation in water), or water cover for the enhancement of wildlife, on such land, except that --

(A) such water cover shall not include ponds for the purpose of watering livestock, irrigating crops, or raising fish for commercial purposes; and

(B) The Secretary shall not terminate the contract for failure to establish approved vegetative or water cover on the land if

(i) the failure to plant such cover was due to excessive rainfall or flooding;

(ii) the land subject to the contract that could practicably be planted to such cover is planted to such cover; and

(iii) the land on which the owner or operator was unable to plant such cover is planted to such cover after the wet conditions that prevented the planting subsides;

(5) in addition to the remedies provided under section 1236(c) [16 U.S.C. § 3836(c)], on the violation of a term or condition of the contract at any time the owner or operator has control of such land --

(A) to forfeit all rights to receive rental payments and cost sharing payments under the contract and to refund to the Secretary any rental payments and cost sharing payments received by the owner or operator under the contract, together with interest thereon as determined by the Secretary, if the Secretary, after considering the recommendations of the soil conservation district and the Soil Conservation Service, determines that such violation is of such nature as to warrant termination of the contract; or

(B) to refund to the Secretary, or accept adjustments to, the rental payments and cost sharing payments provided to the owner or operator, as the Secretary considers appropriate, if the Secretary determines that such violation does not warrant termination of the contract;

(6) on the transfer of the right and interest of the owner or operator in land subject to the contract --

(A) to forfeit all rights to rental payments and cost sharing payments under the contracts; and

(B) to refund to the United States all rental payments and cost sharing payments received by the owner or operator, or accept such payment adjustments or make such refunds as the Secretary considers appropriate and consistent with the objectives of this subchapter,

unless the transferee of such land agrees with the Secretary to assume all obligations of the contract, or the transferee and the Secretary agree to modifications to such contract, where such modifications are consistent with the objectives of the program as determined by the Secretary; *Provided however,* no refund of rental payments and cost sharing payments shall be required when the land is purchased by or for the United States Fish and Wildlife Service;

(7) not to conduct any harvesting or grazing, nor otherwise make commercial use of the forage, on land that is subject to the contract, nor adopt any similar practice specified in the contract by the Secretary as a practice that would tend to defeat the purposes of the contract, except that the Secretary --

(A) may permit --

(i) harvesting or grazing or other commercial use of the forage on land that is subject to the contract in response to a drought or other similar emergency; and

(ii) limited grazing on such land where such grazing is incidental to the gleaning of crop residues on the fields in which such land is located and occurs --

(I) in the case of land other than eligible acreage enrolled under section 1231(h) [16 U.S.C. § 3831(h)], during the 7-month period in which grazing of conserving use acreage is allowed in a State under the Agricultural Act of 1949 (7 U.S.C. § 1421 *et seq.*) or after the producer harvests the grain crop of the surrounding field for a reduction in rental payment commensurate with the limited economic value of such incidental grazing; and

(II) in the case of eligible acreage enrolled under section 1231(h) [16 U.S.C. § 3831(h)], at any time other than during the period beginning May 1 and ending August 1 of each year for a reduction in rental payment commensurate with the limited economic value of such incidental grazing; and

(B) shall approve not more than six projects, no more than one of which may be in any State, under which land subject to the contract may be harvested for recovery of biomass used in energy production if --

(i) no acreage subject to the contract is harvested more than once every other year;

(ii) not more than 25 percent of the total acreage enrolled in the program under this subchapter in any crop reporting district (as designated by the Secretary), is harvested in any 1 year;

(iii) no portion of the crop is used for any commercial purpose other than energy production from biomass;

(iv) no wetland, or acreage of any type enrolled in a partial field conservation practice (including riparian forest buffers, filter strips, and buffer strips), is harvested;

(v) the owner or operator agrees to a payment reduction under this section in an amount determined by the Secretary.

(C) the total acres for all of the projects shall not exceed 250,000 acres.

(8) not to conduct any planting of trees on land that is subject to the contract unless the contract specifies that the harvesting and commercial sale of trees such as Christmas trees are prohibited, nor otherwise make commercial use of trees on land that is subject to the contract unless it is expressly permitted in the contract, nor adopt any similar practice specified in the contract by the Secretary as a practice that would tend to defeat the purposes of the contract, except that no contract shall prohibit activities consistent with customary forestry practice, such as pruning, thinning, or stand improvement of trees, on lands converted to forestry use;

(9) not to adopt any practice specified by the Secretary in the contract as a practice that would tend to defeat the purposes of this subchapter [16 U.S.C. § 3831 *et seq.*]; and

(10) to comply with such additional provisions as the Secretary determines are desirable and are included in the contract to carry out this subchapter [16 U.S.C. § 3831 *et seq.*] or to facilitate the practical administration thereof.

(11) Repealed.

(b) Conversion plan provisions. The plan referred to in subsection (a)(1) of this section --

(1) shall set forth --

(A) the conservation measures and practices to be carried out by the owner or operator during the term of the contract; and

(B) the commercial use, if any, to be permitted on the land during such term; and

(2) may provide for the permanent retirement of any existing cropland base and allotment history for the land.

(c) Environmental use. To the extent practicable, not less than one-eighth of land that is placed in the conservation reserve under this subchapter [16 U.S.C. § 3831 *et seq.*] during the 1991 through 2002 calendar years shall be devoted to trees, or devoted to shrubs or other noncrop vegetation or water that may provide a permanent habitat for wildlife including migratory waterfowl.

(d) Alley cropping. (1) The Secretary may permit alley cropping of agricultural commodities on land that is subject to contracts entered into under this subchapter [16 U.S.C. § 3831 *et seq.*], if --

(A) such land is planted to hardwood trees;

(B) such agricultural commodities will be produced in conjunction with, and in close proximity to, such hardwood trees; and

(C) the owner or operator of such land agrees to implement appropriate conservation practices concerning such land.

(2) The Secretary shall develop a bid system by which owners and operators may offer to reduce their annual rental payments in exchange for permission to produce agricultural commodities on such land in accordance with this subsection. The Secretary shall not accept offers under this paragraph that provide for less than a 50 percent reduction in such annual payments.

(3) The Secretary shall ensure that the total annual rental payments over the term of any contract modified under this subsection are not in excess of that specified in the original contract.

(4) For the purposes of this subsection, the term "alley cropping" means the practice of planting rows of trees bordered on each side by a narrow strip of groundcover, alternated with wider strips of row crops or grain.

****

[Pub. L. 99-198, Title XII, § 1232, 99 Stat. 1509 (Dec. 23, 1985); Pub. L. 101-512, Title I, 104 Stat. 1919 (Nov. 5, 1990); Pub. L. 101-624, Title XIV, §§ 1433, 1447(a), 104 Stat. 3579, 3605 (Nov. 28, 1990); Pub. L. 102-237, Title II, § 204(5), 105 Stat. 1855 (Dec. 13, 1991); Pub. L. 102-552, Title V, § 516(a), 106 Stat. 4136 (Oct. 28, 1992); Pub. L. 104-127, Title III, § 332(a)(2), 110 Stat. 994 (Apr. 4, 1996); Pub. L. 106-78, Title VII, §§ 763, 769, 113 Stat. 1173, 1174 (Oct. 22, 1999)]

16 U.S.C. § 3833. Duties of Secretary. In return for a contract entered into by an owner or operator under section 3832 of this title, the Secretary shall --

(1) share the cost of carrying out the conservation measures and practices set forth in the contract for which the Secretary determines that cost sharing is appropriate and in the public interest;

(2) For a period of years not in excess of the term of the contract, pay an annual rental payment in an amount necessary to compensate for --

(A) the conversion of highly erodible cropland normally devoted to the production of an agricultural commodity on a farm or ranch to a less intensive use; and

(B) the retirement of any cropland base and allotment history that the owner or operator agrees to retire permanently; and

(3) provide conservation technical assistance to assist the owner or operator in carrying out the contract.

[Pub. L. 99-198, Title XII, § 1233, 99 Stat. 1511 (Dec. 23, 1985)]

16 U.S.C. § 3834. Payments. ****

(c) Annual rental payments; encouragement factor; method of determination; acceptance of contract offers. (1) In determining the amount of annual rental payments to be paid to owners and operators for converting highly erodible cropland normally devoted to the production of an agricultural commodity to less intensive use, the Secretary may consider, among other things, the amount necessary to encourage owners or operators of highly erodible cropland to participate in the program established by this subtitle [16 U.S.C. §§ 3831 *et seq.*].

(2) The amounts payable to owners or operators in the form of rental payments under contracts entered into under this subtitle [16 U.S.C. §§ 3831 *et seq.*] may be determined through --

(A) the submission of bids for such contracts by owners and operators in such manner as the Secretary may prescribe; or

(B) such other means as the Secretary determines are appropriate.

(3) In determining the acceptability of contract offers, the Secretary may --

(A) take into consideration the extent to which enrollment of the land that is the subject of the contract offer would improve soil resources, water quality, wildlife habitat, or provide other environmental benefits; and

(B) establish different criteria in various States and regions of the United States based upon the extent to which water quality or wildlife habitat may be improved or erosion may be abated.

[Pub. L. 99-198, Title XII, § 1234, 99 Stat. 1511 (Dec. 23, 1985); Pub. L. 100-387, Title III, § 322, 102 Stat. 951 (Aug. 11, 1988); Pub. L. 101-624, Title XIV, §§ 1434, 1447(a), 104 Stat. 3581, 3605 (Nov. 28, 1990)]

16 U.S.C. § 3835. Contracts. ****

16 U.S.C. § 3835a. Conversion of land subject to contract to other conserving fees.

(a) Conversion to trees. (1) In general. The Secretary shall permit an owner or operator who has entered into a contract under this subchapter [16 U.S.C. § 3831 *et seq.*] that is in effect on the date of enactment of this section [November 28, 1990] to convert areas of highly erodible cropland that are subject to such contract, and that are devoted to vegetative cover, from such use to hardwood trees, windbreaks, shelterbelts, or wildlife corridors.

(2) Terms. (A) Extension of contract. With respect to a contract that is modified under this section that provides for the planting of hardwood trees, windbreaks, shelterbelts, or wildlife corridors, if the original term of the contract was less than 15 years, the owner or operator may extend the contract to a term of not to exceed 15 years.

(B) Cost share assistance. The Secretary shall pay 50 percent of the cost of establishing conservation measures and practices authorized under this subsection for which the Secretary determines the cost sharing is appropriate and in the public interest.

(b) Conversion to wetlands. The Secretary shall permit an owner or operator who has entered into a contract under this subchapter [16 U.S.C. § 3831 *et seq.*] that is in effect on November 28, 1990 to restore areas of highly erodible cropland that are devoted to vegetative cover under such contract to wetlands if --

(1) such areas are prior converted wetlands;

(2) the owner or operator of such areas enters into an agreement to provide the Secretary with a long-term or permanent easement under subpart C of part I of this subchapter covering such areas;

(3) there is a high probability that the prior converted area can be successfully restored to wetland status; and

(4) the restoration of such areas otherwise meets the requirements of subpart C of part I of this subchapter.

(c) Limitation. The Secretary shall not incur, through a conversion under this section, any additional expense on such acres, including the expense involved in the original establishment of the vegetative cover, that would result in cost share for costs in excess of the costs that would have been subject to cost share for the new practice had that practice been the original practice.

(d) Condition of contract. An owner or operator shall as a condition of entering into a contract under subsection (a) of this section participate in the Forest Stewardship Program established under section 2103a of this title.

[Pub. L. 101-624, Title XIV, § 1435, 104 Stat. 3582 (Nov. 28, 1990); Pub. L. 102-324, § 1(b), 106 Stat. 447 (July 22, 1992)]

16 U.S.C. § 3836. Base history. ****

16 U.S.C. § 3836a. Wildlife Habitat Incentive Program. (a) In general. The Secretary of Agriculture, in consultation with the State technical committees established under section 1261 of the Food Security Act of 1985 (16 U.S.C. § 3861), shall establish a program under the Natural Resources Conservation Service to be known as the "Wildlife Habitat Incentive Program".

(b) Cost-share payments. Under the program, the Secretary shall make cost-share payments to landowners to develop upland wildlife, wetland wildlife, threatened and endangered species, fish, and other types of wildlife habitat approved by the Secretary.

(c) Funding. To carry out this section, a total of $50,000,000 shall be made available for fiscal years 1996 through 2002 from funds made available to carry out subchapter B of chapter 1 of subtitle D of title XII of the Food Security Act of 1985 (16 U.S.C. § 3831 *et seq.*).

[Pub. L. 104-127, Title III, § 387, 110 Stat. 1020 (Apr. 4, 1996)]

\- 0 -

ENVIRONMENTAL EASEMENT PROGRAM (1990)
(16 U.S.C. §§ 3839-38339d)

The Environmental Easement Program was established in 1990[149] "to ensure the continued long-term protection of environmentally sensitive lands or reduction in the degradation of water quality" by acquiring easements from the owners of eligible farms and ranches.[150] Land is eligible for the program if it "contains riparian corridors, is an area of critical habitat for wildlife, especially threatened or endangered species, or contains other environmentally sensitive areas."[151] In part, the program is designed to secure protection beyond that available under the Conservation Reserve Program.[152]

16 U.S.C. § 3839. Environmental easement program. (a) Establishment. The

Secretary shall, during the 1991 through 1995 calendar years, formulate and carry out an environmental easement program (hereafter in this chapter [16 U.S.C. §§ 3839 *et seq.*] referred to as the "easement program") in accordance with this chapter, through the acquisition of permanent easements or easements for the maximum term permitted under applicable State law from willing owners of eligible farms or ranches in order to ensure the continued long-term protection of environmentally sensitive lands or reduction in the degradation of water quality on such farms or ranches through the continued conservation and improvement of soil and water resources.

(b) Eligibility; termination. (1) In general. The Secretary may acquire easements under this section on land placed in the conservation reserve under this subtitle [16 U.S.C. §§ 3831 *et seq.*] (other than such land that is likely to continue to remain out of production and that does not pose an off-farm environmental threat), land under the Water Bank Act (16 U.S.C. 1301), or other cropland that --

(A) contains riparian corridors;

(B) is an area of critical habitat for wildlife, especially threatened or endangered species; or

(C) contains other environmentally sensitive areas, as determined by the Secretary, that would prevent a producer from complying with other Federal, State, or local environmental goals if commodities were to be produced on such land.

(2) Ineligible land. The Secretary may not acquire easements on --

(A) land that contains timber stands established under the conservation reserve under subtitle D [16 U.S.C. §§ 3831 *et seq.*]; or

(B) pasture land established to trees under the conservation reserve under this subtitle D [16 U.S.C. §§ 3831 *et seq.*].

(3) Termination of existing contract. The Secretary may terminate or modify any existing contract entered into under section 1231(a) [16 U.S.C. § 3831(a)] if eligible land that is subject to such contract is transferred into the program established by this part.

[Pub. L. 101-624, Title XIV, § 1440, 104 Stat. 3597 (Nov. 28, 1990); Pub. L. 102-237, Title II, § 204(7), 105 Stat. 1855 (Dec. 13, 1991)]

16 U.S.C. § 3839a. Duties of owners; components of plan. (a) Duties of owners. (1) Plan. In conjunction with the creation of an easement on any lands under this chapter [16 U.S.C. §§ 3839 *et seq.*], the owner of the farm or ranch wherein such lands are located must agree to implement a natural resource conservation management plan under subsection (b) of this section approved by the Secretary in consultation with the Secretary of the Interior.

(2) Agreement. In return for the creation of an easement on any lands under this chapter [16 U.S.C. §§ 3839 *et seq.*], the owner of the farm or ranch wherein such lands are located must agree to the following:

(A) To the creation and recordation of an appropriate deed restriction in accordance with applicable State law to reflect the easement agreed to under this chapter [16 U.S.C. §§ 3839 *et seq.*] with respect to such lands.

(B) To provide a written statement of consent to such easement signed by those holding a security interest in the land.

(C) To comply with such additional provisions as the Secretary determines are desirable and are included in the easement to carry out this chapter [16 U.S.C. §§ 3839 *et seq.*] or to facilitate the practical administration thereof.

(D) To specify the location of any timber harvesting on land subject to the easement. Harvesting and commercial sales of Christmas trees and nuts shall be prohibited on such land, except that no such easement or related agreement shall prohibit activities consistent with customary forestry practices, such as pruning, thinning, or tree stand improvement on lands converted to forestry uses.

(E) To limit the production of any agricultural commodity on such lands only to production for the benefit of wildlife.

(F) Not to conduct any harvesting or grazing, nor otherwise make commercial use of the forage, on land that is subject to the easement unless specifically provided for in the easement or related agreement.

(G) Not to adopt any other practice that would tend to defeat the purposes of this chapter [16 U.S.C. §§ 3839 *et seq.*], as determined by the Secretary.

(3) Violation. On the violation of the terms or conditions of the easement or related agreement entered into under this section, the easement shall remain in force and the Secretary may require the owner to refund all or part of any payments received by the owner under this chapter [16 U.S.C. §§ 3839 *et seq.*], together with interest thereon as determined appropriate by the Secretary.

(b) Components of plan. The natural resource conservation management plan referred to in subsection (a)(1) of this section (hereafter referred to as the "plan") --

(1) shall set forth --

(A) the conservation measures and practices to be carried out by the owner of the land subject to the easement; and

(B) the commercial use, if any, to be prohibited on such land during the term of the easement; and

(2) shall provide for the permanent retirement of any existing cropland base and allotment history for such land under any program administered by the Secretary.

[Pub. L. 101-624, Title XIV, § 1440, 104 Stat. 3597 (Nov. 28, 1990)]

16 U.S.C. § 3839b. Duties of Secretary. In return for the granting of an easement by an owner under this part, the Secretary shall --

(1) share the cost of carrying out the establishment of conservation measures and practices set forth in the plan for which the Secretary determines that cost sharing is appropriate and in the public interest;

(2) pay for a period not to exceed 10 years annual easement payments in the aggregate not to exceed the lesser of --

(A) $250,000; or

(B) the difference in the value of the land with and without an easement;

(3) provide necessary technical assistance to assist owners in complying with the terms and conditions of the easement and the plan; and

(4) permit the land to be used for wildlife activities, including hunting and fishing, if

such use is permitted by the owner.

[Pub. L. 101-624, Title XIV, § 1440, 104 Stat. 3598 (Nov. 28, 1990)]

16 U.S.C. § 3839c. Payments. ****

- 0 -

FOREST LEGACY PROGRAM (1990)
(16 U.S.C. § 2103c)

The Forest Legacy Program was established in 1990[154] and is similar to the Wetland Reserve Program and the Environmental Easement Program. It is designed to conserve "environmentally important forest areas that are threatened by conversion to nonforest uses."[155] The Program authorizes the Secretary of Agriculture to acquire easements and other interests in land to protect "important scenic, cultural, fish, wildlife, and recreational resources, riparian areas, and other ecological values."[156]

16 U.S.C. § 2103c. Forest Legacy Program. (a) Establishment and purpose. The Secretary shall establish a program, to be known as the Forest Legacy Program, in cooperation with appropriate State, regional, and other units of government for the purposes of ascertaining and protecting environmentally important forest areas that are threatened by conversion to nonforest uses and, through the use of conservation easements and other mechanisms, for promoting forest land protection and other conservation opportunities. Such purposes shall also include the protection of important scenic, cultural, fish, wildlife, and recreational resources, riparian areas, and other ecological values.

(b) State and regional forest legacy programs. The Secretary shall exercise the authority under subsection (a) of this section in conjunction with State or regional programs that the Secretary deems consistent with this section.

(c) Interests in land. In addition to the authorities granted under section 6 of the Act of March 1, 1911 [16 U.S.C. § 515] and section 11(a) of the Department of Agriculture Organic Act [7 U.S.C. § 428a(a)], the Secretary may acquire from willing landowners lands and interests therein, including conservation easements and rights of public access, for Forest Legacy Program purposes. The Secretary shall not acquire conservation easements with title held in common ownership with any other entity.

(d) Implementation. (1) In general. Lands and interests therein acquired under subsection (c) of this section may be held in perpetuity for program and easement administration purposes as the Secretary may provide. In administering lands and interests therein under the program, the Secretary shall identify the environmental values to be protected by entry of the lands into the program, management activities which are planned and the manner in which they may affect the values identified, and obtain from the landowner other information determined appropriate for administration and management purposes.

(2) Initial programs. Not later than November 28, 1991, the Secretary shall establish a regional program in furtherance of the Northern Forest Lands Study in the States of New York, New Hampshire, Vermont, and Maine under Public Law 100-446. The Secretary shall establish additional programs in each of the Northeast, Midwest, South, and Western regions of the United States, and the Pacific Northwest (including the State of Washington), on the preparation of an assessment of the need for such programs.

(e) Eligibility. Not later than November 28, 1991, and in consultation with State Forest Stewardship Coordinating Committees established under section 19(b) [16 U.S.C. § 2113(b)] and similar regional organizations, the Secretary shall establish eligibility criteria for the designation of forest areas from which lands may be entered into the Forest Legacy Program and subsequently select such appropriate areas. To be eligible, such areas shall have significant environmental values or shall be threatened by present or future conversion to nonforest uses. Of land proposed to be included in the Forest Legacy Program, the Secretary shall give priority to lands which can be effectively protected and managed, and which have important scenic or recreational values; riparian areas; fish and wildlife values, including threatened and endangered species; or other ecological values.

(f) Application. For areas included in the Forest Legacy Program, an owner of lands or interests in lands who wishes to participate may prepare and submit an application at such time in such form and containing such information as the Secretary may prescribe. The Secretary shall give reasonable advance notice for the submission of all applications to the State forester, equivalent State official, or other appropriate State or regional natural resource management agency. If applications exceed the ability of the Secretary to fund them, priority shall be given to those forest areas having the greatest need for protection pursuant to the criteria described in subsection (e) of this section.

(g) State consent. Where a State has not approved the acquisition of land under section 6 of the Act of March 1, 1911 [16 U.S.C. § 515], the Secretary shall not acquire lands or interests therein under authority granted by this section outside an area of that State designated as a part of a program established under subsection (b) of this section.

(h) Forest management activities. (1) In general. Conservation easements or deed reservations acquired or reserved pursuant to this section may allow forest management activities, including timber management, on areas entered in the Forest Legacy Program insofar as the Secretary deems such activities consistent with the purposes of this section.

(2) Assignment of responsibilities. For Forest Legacy Program areas, the Secretary may delegate or assign management and enforcement responsibilities over federally owned lands and interests in lands only to another governmental entity.

(i) Duties of owners. Under the terms of a conservation easement or other property interest acquired under subsection (b) of this section, the landowner shall be required to manage property in a manner that is consistent with the purposes for which the land was entered in the Forest Legacy Program and shall not convert such property to other uses. Hunting, fishing, hiking, and similar recreational uses shall not be considered inconsistent with the purposes of this program.

(j) Compensation and cost sharing. (1) Compensation. The Secretary shall pay the fair market value of any property interest acquired under this section. Payments under this section shall be in accordance with Federal appraisal and acquisition standards and procedures.
(2) Cost sharing. In accordance with terms and conditions that the Secretary shall prescribe, costs for the acquisition of lands or interests therein or project costs shall be shared among participating entities including regional organizations, State and other governmental units, landowners, corporations, or private organizations. Such costs may include, but are not limited to, those associated with planning, administration, property acquisition, and property management. To the extent practicable, the Federal share of total program costs shall not exceed 75 percent, including any in-kind contribution.

(k) Easements. (1) Reserved interest deeds. As used in this section, the term "conservation easement" includes an easement utilizing a reserved interest deed where the grantee acquires all rights, title, and interests in a property, except those rights, title, and interests that may run with the land that are expressly reserved by a grantor.
(2) Prohibitions on limitations. Notwithstanding any provision of State law, no conservation easement held by the United States or its successors or assigns under this section shall be limited in duration or scope or be defeasible by --
(A) the conservation easement being in gross or appurtenant;
(B) the management of the conservation easement having been delegated or assigned to a non-Federal entity;
(C) any requirement under State law for re-recordation or renewal of the easement; or
(D) any future disestablishment of a Forest Legacy Program area or other Federal project for which the conservation easement was originally acquired.
(3) Construction. Notwithstanding any provision of State law, conservation easements shall be construed to effect the Federal purposes for which they were acquired and, in interpreting their terms, there shall be no presumption favoring the conservation easement holder or fee owner.

****

[Pub. L. 101-624, Title XII, § 1217, 104 Stat. 3528 (Nov. 28, 1990); Pub. L. 102-237, Title X, § 1018(a)(2), 105 Stat. 1905 (Dec. 13, 1991); Pub. L. 104-127, Title III, § 374, 110 Stat. 1015 (Apr. 4, 1996)]

- 0 -

CHAPTER 4

PROBLEM WILDLIFE

Not all wildlife is beneficial. Historically, among the first wildlife measures adopted in this country were bounties on predators such as wolves and mountain lions. In 1630, Massachusetts Bay Colony offered the first bounty: one penny per wolf.[1] Virginia subsequently sought to combine a number of goals by offering Native Americans a cow for every eight wolves they killed, thus "introducing among them the idea of separate property" as a "step to civilizing them and to making them Christians."[2]

A second category of problematic wildlife are "exotics" -- those species introduced into North America either intentionally (as was the case with starlings and house sparrows) or inadvertently (as was the case with the zebra mussel). Such species often have substantial economic impact. They are also a major cause of extinction of indigenous species: a recent review of the causes of endangerment among imperiled species in the United States found that "[c]ompetition with or predation by alien species is the second-ranked threat ... affecting 49% of imperiled species."[3]

LACEY ACT (1900)
(18 U.S.C. § 42)

As noted, the Lacey Act was the first federal wildlife statute with a national scope. The original version of the Act prohibited the importation of "any foreign wild animal or bird except under special permit" from the Department of Agriculture and specifically prohibited the importation of fruit bats, mongooses, English sparrows, starlings, and "other birds and animals as the Secretary of Agriculture may from time to time declare injurious to the interest of agriculture or horticulture."[4] The statutory language has since been expanded substantially. The most important change for wildlife conservation was the inclusion of the authority to ban the importation of wildlife that is "injurious ... to wildlife or the wildlife resources of the United States."[5]

Violation of the importation ban is subject to imposition of a fine, imprisonment of up to six months, or both.[6] The statute does not contain a scienter requirement; all that is required is the "importation" of the prohibited species.

18 U.S.C. § 42. Importation or shipment of injurious mammals, birds, fish (including mollusks and crustacea), amphibia, and reptiles; permits, specimens for museums; regulations.

(a)(1) The importation into the United States, any territory of the United States, the District of Columbia, the Commonwealth of Puerto Rico, or any possession of the United States, or any shipment between the continental United States, the District of Columbia, Hawaii, the Commonwealth of Puerto Rico, or any possession of the United States, of the mongoose of the species *Herpestes auropunctatus*; of the species of so-called "flying foxes" or fruit bats of the genus *Pteropus*; of the zebra mussel of the species *Dreissena polymorpha*; and such other species of wild mammals, wild birds, fish (including mollusks and crustacea), amphibians, reptiles, brown tree snakes, or the offspring or eggs of any of the foregoing which the Secretary of the Interior may prescribe by regulation to be injurious to human beings, to the interests of agriculture, horticulture, forestry, or to wildlife or the wildlife resources of the United States, is hereby prohibited. All such prohibited mammals, birds, fish (including mollusks and crustacea), amphibians, and reptiles, and the eggs or offspring therefrom, shall be promptly exported or destroyed at the expense of the importer or consignee. Nothing in this section shall be construed to repeal or modify any provision of the Public Health Service Act or Federal Food, Drug, and Cosmetic Act. Also, this section shall not authorize any action with respect to the importation of any plant pest as defined in the Federal Plant Pest Act, insofar as such importation is subject to regulation under that Act.

(2) As used in this subsection, the term "wild" relates to any creatures that, whether or not raised in captivity, normally are found in a wild state; and the terms "wildlife" and "wildlife resources" include those resources that comprise wild mammals, wild birds, fish (including mollusks and crustacea), and all other classes of wild creatures whatsoever, and all types of aquatic and land vegetation upon which such wildlife resources are dependent.

(3) Notwithstanding the foregoing, the Secretary of the Interior, when he finds that there has been a proper showing of responsibility and continued protection of the public interest and health, shall permit the importation for zoological, educational, medical, and scientific purposes of any mammals, birds, fish (including mollusks and crustacea), amphibia, and reptiles, or the offspring or eggs thereof, where such importation would be prohibited otherwise by or pursuant to this Act, and this Act shall not restrict importations by Federal agencies for their own use.

(4) Nothing in this subsection shall restrict the importation of dead natural-history specimens for museums or for scientific collections, or the importation of domesticated canaries, parrots (including all other species of *psittacine* birds), or such other cage birds as the Secretary of the Interior may designate.

(5) The Secretary of the Treasury and the Secretary of the Interior shall enforce the provisions of this subsection, including any regulations issued hereunder, and, if requested by the Secretary of the Interior, the Secretary of the Treasury may require the furnishing of an appropriate bond when desirable to insure compliance with such provisions.

(b) Whoever violates this section, or any regulation issued pursuant thereto, shall be fined under this Act or imprisoned not more than six months, or both.

(c) The Secretary of the Interior within one hundred and eighty days of the enactment of the Lacey Act Amendments of 1981 shall prescribe such requirements and issue such permits as he may deem necessary for the transportation of wild animals and birds under humane and healthful conditions, and it shall be unlawful for any person, including any importer, knowingly to cause or permit any wild animal or bird to be transported to the United States, or any Territory or district thereof, under inhumane or unhealthful conditions or in violation of such requirements. In any criminal prosecution for violation of this subsection and in any administrative proceeding for the suspension of the issuance of further permits --

(1) the condition of any vessel or conveyance, or the enclosures in which wild animals or birds are confined therein, upon its arrival in the United States, or any Territory or district thereof, shall constitute relevant evidence in determining whether the provisions of this subsection have been violated; and

(2) the presence in such vessel or conveyance at such time of a substantial ratio of dead, crippled, diseased, or starving wild animals or birds shall be deemed prima facie evidence of the violation of the provisions of this subsection.

[June 25, 1948, ch. 645, 62 Stat. 687; May 24, 1949, ch. 139, § 2, 63 Stat. 89; Pub. L. 86-702, § 1, 74 Stat. 753 (Sept. 2, 1960); Pub. L. 97-79, § 9(d), 95 Stat. 1079 (Nov. 16, 1981); Pub. L. 101-646, § 1208, 104 Stat. 4772 (Nov. 29, 1990); Pub. L. 102-237, Title X, § 1013(e), 105 Stat. 1901 (Dec. 13, 1991); Pub. L. 103-322, Title XXXIII, § 330016(1)(G), 108 Stat. 2147 (Sept. 13, 1994); Pub. L. 104-332, § 2(h)(1), 110 Stat. 4091 (Oct. 26, 1996)]

- 0 -

ANIMAL DAMAGE CONTROL
(7 U.S.C. § 426)

Attempts to eradicate animals -- primarily predators -- began almost simultaneously with the arrival of Europeans in North America. The federal government did not become involved in predator control programs until 1909 when Congress enacted a statute appropriating money for "experiments and demonstrations in destroying noxious animals."[7] The program was given permanent status in 1931 when Congress directed the Secretary of Agriculture to "promulgate the best methods of eradication ... mountain lions, wolves, coyotes, bobcats, prairie dogs, gophers, ground squirrels, jack rabbits, and other animals injurious to agriculture, horticulture, forestry, animal husbandry, wild game animals, fur-bearing animals, and birds."[8] Despite strong scientific challenges to the program in reports to Secretary in 1964, 1971, and 1978, Animal Damage Control (ADC) was reinvigorated by the Reagan administration.[9]

The success of ADC has contributed several species to the current endangered species list: the gray wolf, the grizzly bear, the Utah prairie dog, and the black-footed ferret have all been direct or indirect targets of animal damage control programs.

7 U.S.C. § 426. Predatory and other wild animals. The Secretary of Agriculture may conduct a program of wildlife services with respect to injurious animal species and take any action the Secretary considers necessary in conducting the program. The Secretary shall administer the program in a manner consistent with all of the wildlife services authorities in effect on the day before October 28, 2000.

[Mar. 2, 1931, ch. 370, § 1, 46 Stat. 1468; Pub. L. 102-237, Title X, § 1013(d), 105 Stat. 1901 (Dec. 13, 1991); Pub. L. 106-387, § 1(a) [Title VII, § 767], 114 Stat. 1549, 1549A-44 (Oct. 28, 2000)]

NONINDIGENOUS AQUATIC NUISANCE CONTROL & PREVENTION ACT (1990)
NATIONAL INVASIVE SPECIES ACT (1996)
(16 U.S.C. §§ 4701-4741)

Finding that "the potential economic disruption to communities affected by the zebra mussel due to its colonization of water pipes, boat hulls and other hard surfaces has been estimated at $5,000,000,000 by the year 2000, and the potential disruption to diversity and abundance of native fish and other species ... could be severe," Congress in 1990 enacted The Nonindigenous Aquatic Nuisance Prevention and Control Act.[10] The Act's coverage is extremely broad: "nonindigenous species" is defined as "any species or other viable biological material that enters an ecosystem beyond its historic range."[11] The definition thus includes HIV/AIDS and the West Nile Virus since both are "viable biological material." The species must, however, also be a "nuisance," which the Act implicitly and ambiguously defines as a species that "threatens the diversity or abundance of native species or the ecological stability of infested waters, or commercial, agricultural, aquacultural or recreational activities dependent upon such waters."[12]

While acknowledging the potential economic and ecological costs of introduced species, the Act itself does not detail any specific steps to be taken to deal with the threat. Rather, it establishes a task force -- the Aquatic Nuisance Species Task Force -- co-chaired by the Director of the Fish and Wildlife Service and the Undersecretary of Commerce for Oceans and Atmosphere with the Administrator of the Environmental Protection Agency, the Commandant of the Coast Guard, the Assistant Secretary of the Army, and the Secretary of Agriculture as members.[13] The Task Force is to develop and implement a program to "identify the goals, priorities, and approaches" for preventing introduction of aquatic nuisance species and "describe the specific prevention, monitoring, control, education and research activities" to accomplish these goals.[14]

16 U.S.C. § 4701. Findings and purposes. (a) Findings. The Congress finds that --

(1) the discharge of untreated water in the ballast tanks of vessels and through other means results in unintentional introductions of nonindigenous species to fresh, brackish, and saltwater environments;

(2) when environmental conditions are favorable, nonindigenous species become established, may compete with or prey upon native species of plants, fish, and wildlife, may carry diseases or parasites that affect native species, and may disrupt the aquatic environment and economy of affected near-shore areas;

(3) the zebra mussel was unintentionally introduced into the Great Lakes and has infested --

(A) waters south of the Great Lakes, into a good portion of the Mississippi River drainage;

(B) waters west of the Great Lakes, into the Arkansas River in Oklahoma; and

(C) waters east of the Great Lakes, into the Hudson River and Lake Champlain;

(4) the potential economic disruption to communities affected by the zebra mussel due to its colonization of water pipes, boat hulls and other hard surfaces has been

estimated at $5,000,000,000 by the year 2000, and the potential disruption to the diversity and abundance of native fish and other species by the zebra mussel and ruffe, round goby, and other nonindigenous species could be severe;

(5) the zebra mussel was discovered on Lake Champlain during 1993 and the opportunity exists to act quickly to establish zebra mussel controls before Lake Champlain is further infested and management costs escalate;

(6) in 1992, the zebra mussel was discovered at the northernmost reaches of the Chesapeake Bay watershed;

(7) the zebra mussel poses an imminent risk of invasion in the main waters of the Chesapeake Bay;

(8) since the Chesapeake Bay is the largest recipient of foreign ballast water on the East Coast, there is a risk of further invasions of other nonindigenous species;

(9) the zebra mussel is only one example of thousands of nonindigenous species that have become established in waters of the United States and may be causing economic and ecological degradation with respect to the natural resources of waters of the United States;

(10) since their introduction in the early 1980's in ballast water discharges, ruffe --

(A) have caused severe declines in populations of other species of fish in Duluth Harbor (in Minnesota and Wisconsin);

(B) have spread to Lake Huron; and

(C) are likely to spread quickly to most other waters in North America if action is not taken promptly to control their spread;

(11) examples of nonindigenous species that, as of the date of enactment of the National Invasive Species Act of 1996 [October 26, 1996], infest coastal waters of the United States and that have the potential for causing adverse economic and ecological effects include --

(A) the mitten crab (*Eriocher sinensis*) that has become established on the Pacific Coast;

(B) the green crab (*Carcinus maenas*) that has become established in the coastal waters of the Atlantic Ocean;

(C) the brown mussel (*Perna perna*) that has become established along the Gulf of Mexico; and

(D) certain shellfish pathogens;

(12) many aquatic nuisance vegetation species, such as Eurasian watermilfoil, hydrilla, water hyacinth, and water chestnut, have been introduced to waters of the United States from other parts of the world causing or having a potential to cause adverse environmental, ecological, and economic effects;

(13) if preventive management measures are not taken nationwide to prevent and control unintentionally introduced nonindigenous aquatic species in a timely manner, further introductions and infestations of species that are as destructive as, or more destructive than, the zebra mussel or the ruffe infestations may occur;

(14) once introduced into waters of the United States, aquatic nuisance species are unintentionally transported and introduced into inland lakes and rivers by recreational boaters, commercial barge traffic, and a variety of other pathways; and

(15) resolving the problems associated with aquatic nuisance species will require the participation and cooperation of the Federal Government and State governments, and investment in the development of prevention technologies.

(b) Purposes. The purposes of this Act are --

(1) to prevent unintentional introduction and dispersal of nonindigenous species into waters of the United States through ballast water management and other requirements;

(2) to coordinate federally conducted, funded or authorized research, prevention, control information dissemination and other activities regarding the zebra mussel and other aquatic nuisance species;

(3) to develop and carry out environmentally sound control methods to prevent, monitor and control unintentional introductions of nonindigenous species from pathways other than ballast water exchange;

(4) to understand and minimize economic and ecological impacts of nonindigenous aquatic nuisance species that become established, including the zebra mussel; and

(5) to establish a program of research and technology development and assistance to States in the management and removal of zebra mussels.

[Pub. L. 101-646, Title I, § 1002, 104 Stat. 4761 (Nov. 29, 1990); Pub. L. 104-182, Title III, § 308(a), 110 Stat. 1689 (Aug. 6, 1996); Pub. L. 104-332, § 2(a)(1), (h)(1), Oct. 26, 1996, 110 Stat. 4073, 4091.)

16 U.S.C. § 4702. Definitions. As used in this Act, the term --

(1) "aquatic nuisance species" means a nonindigenous species that threatens the diversity or abundance of native species or the ecological stability of infested waters, or commercial, agricultural, aquacultural or recreational activities dependent on such waters;

(2) "Assistant Secretary" means the Assistant Secretary of the Army (Civil Works);

(3) "ballast water" means any water and associated sediments used to manipulate the trim and stability of a vessel;

(4) "Director" means the Director of the United States Fish and Wildlife Service;

(5) "exclusive economic zone" means the Exclusive Economic Zone of the United States established by Proclamation Number 5030, dated March 10, 1983 [16 U.S.C. § 1453 note], and the equivalent zone of Canada;

(6) "environmentally sound" methods, efforts, actions or programs means methods, efforts, actions or programs to prevent introductions or control infestations of aquatic nuisance species that minimize adverse impacts to the structure and function of an ecosystem and adverse effects on non-target organisms and ecosystems and emphasize integrated pest management techniques and nonchemical measures;

(7) "Great Lakes" means Lake Ontario, Lake Erie, Lake Huron (including Lake St. Clair), Lake Michigan, Lake Superior, and the connecting channels (Saint Mary's River, Saint Clair River, Detroit River, Niagara River, and Saint Lawrence River to the Canadian Border), and includes all other bodies of water within the drainage basin of such lakes and connecting channels.

(8) "Great Lakes region" means the 8 States that border on the Great Lakes;

(9) "Indian tribe" means any Indian tribe, band, nation, or other organized group or community, including any Alaska Native village or regional corporation (as defined in or established pursuant to the Alaska Native Claims Settlement Act (43 U.S.C. § 1601 *et seq.*)) that is recognized as eligible for the special programs and services provided by the United States to Indians because of their status as Indians;

(10) "interstate organization" means an entity --

(A) established by --

(i) an interstate compact that is approved by Congress;

(ii) a Federal statute; or

(iii) a treaty or other international agreement with respect to which the United States is a party; and

(B)(i) that represents 2 or more --

(I) States or political subdivisions thereof; or

(II) Indian tribes; or

(ii) that represents --

(I) 1 or more States or political subdivisions thereof; and

(II) 1 or more Indian tribes; or

(iii) that represents the Federal Government and 1 or more foreign governments; and

(C) has jurisdiction over, serves as forum for coordinating, or otherwise has a role or responsibility for the management of, any land or other natural resource;

(11) "nonindigenous species" means any species or other viable biological material that enters an ecosystem beyond its historic range, including any such organism transferred from one country into another;

(12) "Secretary" means the Secretary of the department in which the Coast Guard is operating;

(13) "Task Force" means the Aquatic Nuisance Species Task Force established under section 1201 of this Act [16 U.S.C. § 4721];

(14) "territorial sea" means the belt of the sea measured from the baseline of the United States determined in accordance with international law, as set forth in Presidential Proclamation Number 5928, dated December 27, 1988 [43 U.S.C. § 1331 note];

(15) "Under Secretary" means the Under Secretary of Commerce for Oceans and Atmosphere;

(16) "waters of the United States" means the navigable waters and the territorial sea of the United States; and

(17) "unintentional introduction" means an introduction of nonindigenous species that occurs as the result of activities other than the purposeful or intentional introduction of the species involved, such as the transport of nonindigenous species in ballast or in water used to transport fish, mollusks or crustaceans for aquaculture or other purposes.

[Pub. L. 101-646, Title I, § 1003, 104 Stat. 4762 (Nov. 29, 1990); Pub. L. 102-580, Title III, § 302(b)(2), Oct. 31, 1992, 106 Stat. 4839; Pub. L. 104- 332, § 2(a)(2), (h)(1), (3), Oct. 26, 1996, 110 Stat. 4075, 4091.)

16 U.S.C. § 4711. Aquatic nuisance species in waters of the United States. (a) Great Lakes guidelines. (1) In general. Not later than 6 months after the date of enactment of this Act [November 29, 1990], the Secretary shall issue voluntary guidelines to prevent the introduction and spread of aquatic nuisance species into the Great Lakes through the exchange of ballast water of vessels prior to entering those waters.

(2) Content of guidelines. The guidelines issued under this subsection shall --

(A) ensure to the maximum extent practicable that ballast water containing aquatic nuisance species is not discharged into the Great Lakes;

(B) protect the safety of --

(i) each vessel; and

(ii) the crew and passengers of each vessel;

(C) take into consideration different vessel operating conditions; and

(D) be based on the best scientific information available.

(b) Regulations. (1) In general. Not later than 2 years after the date of enactment of this Act [November 29, 1990], the Secretary, in consultation with the Task Force, shall issue regulations to prevent the introduction and spread of aquatic nuisance species into the Great Lakes through the ballast water of vessels.

(2) Content of regulations. The regulations issued under this subsection shall --

(A) apply to all vessels equipped with ballast water tanks that enter a United States port on the Great Lakes after operating on the waters beyond the exclusive economic zone;

(B) require a vessel to --

(i) carry out exchange of ballast water on the waters beyond the exclusive economic zone prior to entry into any port within the Great Lakes;

(ii) carry out an exchange of ballast water in other waters where the exchange does not pose a threat of infestation or spread of aquatic nuisance species in the Great Lakes and other waters of the United States, as recommended by the Task Force under section 4712(a)(1) of this title; or

(iii) use environmentally sound alternative ballast water management methods if the Secretary determines that such alternative methods are as effective as ballast water exchange in preventing and controlling infestations of aquatic nuisance species;

(C) not affect or supersede any requirements or prohibitions pertaining to the discharge of ballast water into waters of the United States under the Federal Water Pollution Control Act (33 U.S.C. §§ 1251 *et seq.*);

(D) provide for sampling procedures to monitor compliance with the requirements of the regulations;

(E) prohibit the operation of a vessel in the Great Lakes if the master of the vessel has not certified to the Secretary or the Secretary's designee by not later than the departure of that vessel from the first lock in the St. Lawrence Seaway that the vessel has complied with the requirements of the regulations;

(F) protect the safety of --

(i) each vessel; and

(ii) the crew and passengers of each vessel;

(G) take into consideration different operating conditions; and

(H) be based on the best scientific information available.

(3) Additional regulations. In addition to promulgating regulations under paragraph (1), the Secretary, in consultation with the Task Force, shall, not later than November

4, 1994, issue regulations to prevent the introduction and spread of aquatic nuisance species into the Great Lakes through ballast water carried on vessels that enter a United States port on the Hudson River north of the George Washington Bridge.

(4) Education and technical assistance programs. The Secretary may carry out education and technical assistance programs and other measures to promote compliance with the regulations issued under this subsection.

(c) Voluntary national guidelines. (1) In general. Not later than 1 year after the date of enactment of the National Invasive Species Act of 1996 [October 26, 1996], and after providing notice and an opportunity for public comment, the Secretary shall issue voluntary guidelines to prevent the introduction and spread of nonindigenous species in waters of the United States by ballast water operations and other operations of vessels equipped with ballast water tanks.

(2) Content of guidelines. The voluntary guidelines issued under this subsection shall --

(A) ensure to the maximum extent practicable that aquatic nuisance species are not discharged into waters of the United States from vessels;

(B) apply to all vessels equipped with ballast water tanks that operate in waters of the United States;

(C) protect the safety of --

(i) each vessel; and

(ii) the crew and passengers of each vessel;

(D) direct a vessel that is carrying ballast water into waters of the United States after operating beyond the exclusive economic zone to --

(i) carry out the exchange of ballast water of the vessel in waters beyond the exclusive economic zone;

(ii) exchange the ballast water of the vessel in other waters where the exchange does not pose a threat of infestation or spread of nonindigenous species in waters of the United States, as recommended by the Task Force under section 4712(a)(1) of this title; or

(iii) use environmentally sound alternative ballast water management methods, including modification of the vessel ballast water tanks and intake systems, if the Secretary determines that such alternative methods are at least as effective as ballast water exchange in preventing and controlling infestations of aquatic nuisance species;

(E) direct vessels to carry out management practices that the Secretary determines to be necessary to reduce the probability of unintentional nonindigenous species transfer resulting from --

(i) ship operations other than ballast water discharge; and

(ii) ballasting practices of vessels that enter waters of the United States with no ballast water on board;

(F) provide for the keeping of records that shall be submitted to the Secretary, as prescribed by the guidelines, and that shall be maintained on board each vessel and made available for inspection, upon request of the Secretary and in a manner consistent with subsection (i) of this section, in order to enable the Secretary to determine compliance with the guidelines, including --

(i) with respect to each ballast water exchange referred to in clause (ii),

reporting on the precise location and thoroughness of the exchange; and
(ii) any other information that the Secretary considers necessary to assess the rate of effective compliance with the guidelines;

(G) provide for sampling procedures to monitor compliance with the guidelines;

(H) take into consideration --

(i) vessel types;

(ii) variations in the characteristics of point of origin and receiving water bodies;

(iii) variations in the ecological conditions of waters and coastal areas of the United States; and

(iv) different operating conditions;

(I) be based on the best scientific information available;

(J) not affect or supersede any requirements or prohibitions pertaining to the discharge of ballast water into waters of the United States under the Federal Water Pollution Control Act (33 U.S.C. §§ 1251 *et seq.*); and

(K) provide an exemption from ballast water exchange requirements to passenger vessels with operating ballast water systems that are equipped with treatment systems designed to kill aquatic organisms in ballast water, unless the Secretary determines that such treatment systems are less effective than ballast water exchange at reducing the risk of transfers of invasive species in the ballast water of passenger vessels; and

(L) not apply to crude oil tankers engaged in the coastwise trade.

(3) Education and technical assistance programs. Not later than 1 year after the date of enactment of the National Invasive Species Act of 1996 [October 26, 1996], the Secretary shall carry out education and technical assistance programs and other measures to encourage compliance with the guidelines issued under this subsection.

(d) Report to Congress. Not sooner than 24 months after the date of issuance of guidelines pursuant to subsection (c) of this section and not later than 30 months after such date, and after consultation with interested and affected persons, the Secretary shall prepare and submit to Congress a report containing the information required pursuant to paragraphs (1) and (2) of subsection (e) of this section.

(e) Periodic review and revision. (1) In general. Not later than 3 years after the date of issuance of guidelines pursuant to subsection (c) of this section, and not less frequently than every 3 years thereafter, the Secretary shall, in accordance with criteria developed by the Task Force under paragraph (3) --

(A) assess the compliance by vessels with the voluntary guidelines issued under subsection (c) of this section and the regulations promulgated under this Act;

(B) establish the rate of compliance that is based on the assessment under subparagraph (A);

(C) assess the effectiveness of the voluntary guidelines and regulations referred to in subparagraph (A) in reducing the introduction and spread of aquatic nuisance species by vessels; and

(D) as necessary, on the basis of the best scientific information available --

(i) revise the guidelines and regulations referred to in subparagraph (A);

(ii) promulgate additional regulations pursuant to subsection (f)(1) of this section; or

(iii) carry out each of clauses (i) and (ii).

(2) Special review and revision. Not later than 90 days after the Task Force makes a request to the Secretary for a special review and revision for coastal and inland waterways designated by the Task Force, the Secretary shall --

(A) conduct a special review of guidelines and regulations applicable to those waterways in accordance with the review procedures under paragraph (1); and

(B) as necessary, in the same manner as provided under paragraph (1)(D) --

(i) revise those guidelines;

(ii) promulgate additional regulations pursuant to subsection (f)(1) of this section; or

(iii) carry out each of clauses (i) and (ii).

(3) Criteria for effectiveness. Not later than 18 months after the date of enactment of the National Invasive Species Act of 1996 [October 26, 1996], the Task Force shall submit to the Secretary criteria for determining the adequacy and effectiveness of the voluntary guidelines issued under subsection (c) of this section.

(f) Authority of Secretary. (1) General regulations. If, on the basis of a periodic review conducted under subsection (e)(1) of this section or a special review conducted under subsection (e)(2) of this section, the Secretary determines that --

(A) the rate of effective compliance (as determined by the Secretary) with the guidelines issued pursuant to subsection (c) of this section is inadequate; or

(B) the reporting by vessels pursuant to those guidelines is not adequate for the Secretary to assess the compliance with those guidelines and provide a rate of compliance of vessels, including the assessment of the rate of compliance of vessels under subsection (e)(2) of this section,

the Secretary shall promptly promulgate regulations that meet the requirements of paragraph (2).

(2) Requirements for regulations. The regulations promulgated by the Secretary under paragraph (1) --

(A) shall --

(i) not be promulgated sooner than 180 days following the issuance of the report to Congress submitted pursuant to subsection (d) of this section;

(ii) make mandatory the requirements included in the voluntary guidelines issued under subsection (c) of this section; and

(iii) provide for the enforcement of the regulations; and

(B) may be regional in scope.

(3) International regulations. The Secretary shall revise regulations promulgated under this subsection to the extent required to make such regulations consistent with the treatment of a particular matter in any international agreement, agreed to by the United States, governing management of the transfer of nonindigenous aquatic species by vessel.

(g) Sanctions. (1) Civil penalties. Any person who violates a regulation promulgated under subsection (b) or (f) of this section shall be liable for a civil penalty in an amount not to exceed $25,000. Each day of a continuing violation constitutes a separate violation. A vessel operated in violation of the regulations is liable in rem for any civil penalty assessed under this subsection for that violation.

(2) Criminal penalties. Any person who knowingly violates the regulations promulgated under subsection (b) or (f) of this section is guilty of a class C felony.

(3) Revocation of clearance. Upon request of the Secretary, the Secretary of the Treasury shall withhold or revoke the clearance of a vessel required by section 91 of the Appendix to Title 46, if the owner or operator of that vessel is in violation of the regulations issued under subsection (b) or (f) of this section.

(4) Exception to sanctions. This subsection does not apply to a failure to exchange ballast water if --

(A) the master of a vessel, acting in good faith, decides that the exchange of ballast water will threaten the safety or stability of the vessel, its crew, or its passengers; and

(B) the recordkeeping and reporting requirements of this Act are complied with.

(h) Coordination with other agencies. In carrying out the programs under this section, the Secretary is encouraged to use, to the maximum extent practicable, the expertise, facilities, members, or personnel of established agencies and organizations that have routine contact with vessels, including the Animal and Plant Health Inspection Service of the Department of Agriculture, the National Cargo Bureau, port administrations, and ship pilots' associations.

(i) Consultation with Canada, Mexico, and other foreign governments. In developing the guidelines issued and regulations promulgated under this section, the Secretary is encouraged to consult with the Government of Canada, the Government of Mexico, and any other government of a foreign country that the Secretary, in consultation with the Task Force, determines to be necessary to develop and implement an effective international program for preventing the unintentional introduction and spread of nonindigenous species.

(j) International cooperation. The Secretary, in cooperation with the International Maritime Organization of the United Nations and the Commission on Environmental Cooperation established pursuant to the North American Free Trade Agreement, is encouraged to enter into negotiations with the governments of foreign countries to develop and implement an effective international program for preventing the unintentional introduction and spread of nonindigenous species.

(k) Safety exemption. (1) Master discretion. The master of a vessel is not required to conduct a ballast water exchange if the master decides that the exchange would threaten the safety or stability of the vessel, its crew, or its passengers because of adverse weather, vessel architectural design, equipment failure, or any other extraordinary conditions.

(2) Other requirements. (A) In general. Except as provided in subparagraph (B), a vessel that does not exchange ballast water on the high seas under paragraph (1) shall not be restricted from discharging ballast water in any

harbor.

(B) Great Lakes. Subparagraph (A) shall not apply in a case in which a vessel is subject to the regulations issued by the Secretary under subsection (b) of this section.

(3) Crude oil tanker ballast facility study. (A) Within 60 days of the date of enactment of the National Invasive Species Act of 1996 [October 26, 1996], the Secretary of the department in which the Coast Guard is operating, in consultation with the Under Secretary of Commerce for Oceans and Atmosphere, affected shoreside ballast water facility operators, affected crude oil tanker operators, and interested parties, shall initiate a study of the effectiveness of existing shoreside ballast water facilities used by crude oil tankers in the coastwise trade off Alaska in preventing the introduction of nonindigenous aquatic species into the waters off Alaska, as well as the cost and feasibility of modifying such facilities to improve such effectiveness.

(B) The study required under subparagraph (A) shall be submitted to the Congress by no later than October 1, 1997.

(l) Non-discrimination. The Secretary shall ensure that vessels registered outside of the United States do not receive more favorable treatment than vessels registered in the United States when the Secretary performs studies, reviews compliance, determines effectiveness, establishes requirements, or performs any other responsibilities under this chapter.

[Pub. L. 101-646, Title I, § 1101, 104 Stat. 4763 (Nov. 29, 1990); Pub. L. 102-580, Title III, § 302(b)(1), Oct. 31, 1992, 106 Stat. 4839; Pub. L. 102- 587, Title IV, § 4002, Nov. 4, 1992, 106 Stat. 5068; Pub. L. 104-332, § 2(b)(2), (h)(1), Oct. 26, 1996, 110 Stat. 4075, 4091.)

16 U.S.C. § 4712. National ballast water management information. (a) Studies on introduction of aquatic nuisance species by vessels. (1) Ballast exchange study. The Task Force, in cooperation with the Secretary, shall conduct a study --

(A) to assess the environmental effects of ballast water exchange on the diversity and abundance of native species in receiving estuarine, marine, and fresh waters of the United States; and

(B) to identify areas within the waters of the United States and the exclusive economic zone, if any, where the exchange of ballast water does not pose a threat of infestation or spread of aquatic nuisance species in the Great Lakes and other waters of the United States.

(2) Biological study. The Task Force, in cooperation with the Secretary, shall conduct a study to determine whether aquatic nuisance species threaten the ecological characteristics and economic uses of Lake Champlain and other waters of the United States other than the Great Lakes.

(3) Shipping study. The Secretary shall conduct a study to determine the need for controls on vessels entering waters of the United States, other than the Great Lakes, to minimize the risk of unintentional introduction and dispersal of aquatic nuisance species in those waters. The study shall include an examination of --

(A) the degree to which shipping may be a major pathway of transmission of

aquatic nuisance species in those waters;
(B) possible alternatives for controlling introduction of those species through shipping; and
(C) the feasibility of implementing regional versus national control measures.

(b) Ecological and ballast water discharge surveys. (1) Ecological surveys. (A) In general. The Task Force, in cooperation with the Secretary, shall conduct ecological surveys of the Chesapeake Bay, San Francisco Bay, and Honolulu Harbor and, as necessary, of other estuaries of national significance and other waters that the Task Force determines --

(i) to be highly susceptible to invasion by aquatic nuisance species resulting from ballast water operations and other operations of vessels; and
(ii) to require further study.

(B) Requirements for surveys. In conducting the surveys under this paragraph, the Task Force shall, with respect to each such survey --

(i) examine the attributes and patterns of invasions of aquatic nuisance species; and
(ii) provide an estimate of the effectiveness of ballast water management and other vessel management guidelines issued and regulations promulgated under this subtitle in abating invasions of aquatic nuisance species in the waters that are the subject of the survey.

(2) Ballast water discharge surveys. (A) In general. The Secretary, in cooperation with the Task Force, shall conduct surveys of ballast water discharge rates and practices in the waters referred to in paragraph (1)(A) on the basis of the criteria under clauses (i) and (ii) of such paragraph.

(B) Requirements for surveys. In conducting the surveys under this paragraph, the Secretary shall --

(i) examine the rate of, and trends in, ballast water discharge in the waters that are the subject of the survey; and
(ii) assess the effectiveness of voluntary guidelines issued, and regulations promulgated, under this subchapter in altering ballast water discharge practices to reduce the probability of accidental introductions of aquatic nuisance species.

(3) Columbia River. The Secretary, in cooperation with the Task Force and academic institutions in each of the States affected, shall conduct an ecological and ballast water discharge survey of the Columbia River system consistent with the requirements of paragraphs (1) and (2).

(c) Reports. ****

(d) Negotiations. The Secretary, working through the International Maritime Organization, is encouraged to enter into negotiations with the governments of foreign countries concerning the planning and implementation of measures aimed at the prevention and control of unintentional introductions of aquatic nuisance species in coastal waters.

****

[Pub. L. 101-646, Title I, § 1102, 104 Stat. 4764 (Nov. 29, 1990); Pub. L. 104-332, § 2(c), (g), (h)(1), Oct. 26, 1996, 110 Stat. 4081, 4091; Pub. L. 105-362, Title XV, § 1502(d), Nov. 10 1998, 112 Stat. 3295.)

16 U.S.C. § 4713. Armed Services ballast water programs. (a) Department of Defense vessels. Subject to operational conditions, the Secretary of Defense, in consultation with the Secretary, the Task Force, and the International Maritime Organization, shall implement a ballast water management program for seagoing vessels of the Department of Defense to minimize the risk of introduction of nonindigenous species from releases of ballast water.

(b) Coast Guard vessels. Subject to operational conditions, the Secretary, in consultation with the Task Force and the International Maritime Organization, shall implement a ballast water management program for seagoing vessels of the Coast Guard to minimize the risk of introduction of nonindigenous species from releases of ballast water.

[Pub. L. 101-646, Title I, § 1103, as added Pub. L. 104-332, § 2(d), Oct. 26, 1996, 110 Stat. 4083.)

16 U.S.C. § 4714. Ballast water management demonstration program. ****

16 U.S.C. § 4721. Establishment of Task Force. (a) Task Force. There is hereby established an "Aquatic Nuisance Species Task Force."

(b) Membership. Membership of the Task Force shall consist of --

(1) the Director;
(2) the Under Secretary;
(3) the Administrator of the Environmental Protection Agency;
(4) the Commandant of the United States Coast Guard;
(5) the Assistant Secretary;
(6) the Secretary of Agriculture; and
(7) the head of any other Federal agency that the chairpersons designated under subsection (d) of this section deem appropriate.

****

[Pub. L. 101-646, Title I, § 1201, 104 Stat. 4765 (Nov. 29, 1990); Pub. L. 104-182, Title III, § 308(b), 110 Stat. 1689 (Aug. 6, 1996); Pub. L. 104-332, § 2(e)(2), (h)(1), 110 Stat. 4085, 4091 (Oct. 26, 1996)]

16 U.S.C. § 4722. Aquatic nuisance species program. (a) In general. The Task Force shall develop and implement a program for waters of the United States to prevent introduction and dispersal of aquatic nuisance species; to monitor, control and study such species; and to disseminate related information.

(b) Content. The program developed under subsection (a) of this section shall --

(1) identify the goals, priorities, and approaches for aquatic nuisance species

prevention, monitoring, control, education and research to be conducted or funded by the Federal Government;

(2) describe the specific prevention, monitoring, control, education and research activities to be conducted by each Task Force member;

(3) coordinate aquatic nuisance species programs and activities of Task Force members and affected State agencies;

(4) describe the role of each Task Force member in implementing the elements of the program as set forth in this subtitle;

(5) include recommendations for funding to implement elements of the program; and

(6) develop a demonstration program of prevention, monitoring, control, education and research for the zebra mussel, to be implemented in the Great Lakes and any other waters infested, or likely to become infested in the near future, by the zebra mussel.

(c) Prevention. (1) In general. The Task Force shall establish and implement measures, within the program developed under subsection (a) of this section, to minimize the risk of introduction of aquatic nuisance species to waters of the United States, including --

(A) identification of pathways by which aquatic organisms are introduced to waters of the United States;

(B) assessment of the risk that an aquatic organism carried by an identified pathway may become an aquatic nuisance species; and

(C) evaluation of whether measures to prevent introductions of aquatic nuisance species are effective and environmentally sound.

(2) Implementation. Whenever the Task Force determines that there is a substantial risk of unintentional introduction of an aquatic nuisance species by an identified pathway and that the adverse consequences of such an introduction are likely to be substantial, the Task Force shall, acting through the appropriate Federal agency, and after an opportunity for public comment, carry out cooperative, environmentally sound efforts with regional, State and local entities to minimize the risk of such an introduction.

(d) Monitoring. The Task Force shall establish and implement monitoring measures, within the program developed under subsection (a) of this section, to --

(1) detect unintentional introductions of aquatic nuisance species;

(2) determine the dispersal of aquatic nuisance species after introduction; and

(3) provide for the early detection and prevention of infestations of aquatic nuisance species in unaffected drainage basins.

(e) Control. (1) In general. The Task Force may develop cooperative efforts, within the program established under subsection (a) of this section, to control established aquatic nuisance species to minimize the risk of harm to the environment and the public health and welfare. For purposes of this chapter, control efforts include eradication of infestations, reductions of populations, development of means of adapting human activities and public facilities to accommodate infestations, and prevention of the spread of aquatic nuisance species from infested areas. Such control efforts shall be developed in consultation with affected Federal agencies, States, Indian Tribes, local governments, interjurisdictional organizations, and other appropriate entities. Control actions authorized by this section shall be based on the best available scientific information and shall be conducted in an environmentally sound manner.

(2) Decisions. The Task Force or any other affected agency or entity may recommend that the Task Force initiate a control effort. In determining whether a control program is warranted, the Task Force shall evaluate the need for control (including the projected consequences of no control and less than full control); the technical and biological feasibility and cost-effectiveness of alternative control strategies and actions; whether the benefits of control, including costs avoided, exceed the costs of the program; the risk of harm to non-target organisms and ecosystems, public health and welfare; and such other considerations the Task Force determines appropriate. The Task Force shall also determine the nature and extent of control of target aquatic nuisance species that is feasible and desirable.

(3) Programs. If the Task Force determines in accordance with paragraph (2) that control of an aquatic nuisance species is warranted, the Task Force shall develop a proposed control program to achieve the target level of control. A notice summarizing the proposed action and soliciting comments shall be published in the Federal Register, in major newspapers in the region affected, and in principal trade publications of the industries affected. Within 180 days of proposing a control program, and after consultation with affected governmental and other appropriate entities and taking into consideration other comments received, the Task Force shall complete development of the proposed control program.

(f) Research. (1) Priorities. The Task Force shall, within the program developed under subsection (a) of this section, conduct research concerning --

(A) the environmental and economic risks and impacts associated with the introduction of aquatic nuisance species into the waters of the United States;

(B) the principal pathways by which aquatic nuisance species are introduced and dispersed;

(C) possible methods for the prevention, monitoring and control of aquatic nuisance species; and

(D) the assessment of the effectiveness of prevention, monitoring and control methods.

(2) Protocol. Within 90 days of the date of enactment of this Act [November 29, 1990], the Task Force shall establish and follow a protocol to ensure that research activities carried out under this subchapter do not result in the introduction of aquatic nuisance species to waters of the United States.

(3) Grants for research. The Task Force shall allocate funds authorized under this chapter for competitive research grants to study all aspects of aquatic nuisance species, which shall be administered through the National Sea Grant College Program and the Cooperative Fishery and Wildlife Research Units. Grants shall be conditioned to ensure that any recipient of funds follows the protocol established under paragraph (2) of this subsection.

****

[Pub. L. 101-646, Title I, § 1202, 104 Stat. 4766 (Nov. 29, 1990); Pub. L. 104-332, § 2(e)(3), (4), (g), (h)(1), 110 Stat. 4085, 4087, 4091 (Oct. 26, 1996)]

16 U.S.C. § 4723. Regional coordination. (a) Great Lakes panel. ****

(b) Western regional panel. ****

(c) Additional regional panels. ****

16 U.S.C. § 4724. State aquatic nuisance species management plans. (a) State or interstate invasive species management plans. (1) In general. After providing notice and opportunity for public comment, the Governor of each State may prepare and submit, or the Governors of the States and the governments of the Indian tribes involved in an interstate organization, may jointly prepare and submit --

(A) a comprehensive management plan to the Task Force for approval which identifies those areas or activities within the State or within the interstate region involved, other than those related to public facilities, for which technical, enforcement, or financial assistance (or any combination thereof) is needed to eliminate or reduce the environmental, public health, and safety risks associated with aquatic nuisance species, particularly the zebra mussel; and

(B) a public facility management plan to the Assistant Secretary for approval which is limited solely to identifying those public facilities within the State or within the interstate region involved for which technical and financial assistance is needed to reduce infestations of zebra mussels.

(2) Content. Each plan shall, to the extent possible, identify the management practices and measures that will be undertaken to reduce infestations of aquatic nuisance species. Each plan shall --

(A) identify and describe State and local programs for environmentally sound prevention and control of the target aquatic nuisance species;

(B) identify Federal activities that may be needed for environmentally sound prevention and control of aquatic nuisance species and a description of the manner in which those activities should be coordinated with State and local government activities;

(C) identify any authority that the State (or any State or Indian tribe involved in the interstate organization) does not have at the time of the development of the plan that may be necessary for the State (or any State or Indian tribe involved in the interstate organization) to protect public health, property, and the environment from harm by aquatic nuisance species; and

(D) a schedule of implementing the plan, including a schedule of annual objectives, and enabling legislation.

(3) Consultation. (A) In developing and implementing a management plan, the State or interstate organization should, to the maximum extent practicable, involve local governments and regional entities, Indian tribes, and public and private organizations that have expertise in the control of aquatic nuisance species.

(B) Upon the request of a State or the appropriate official of an interstate organization, the Task Force or the Assistant Secretary, as appropriate under paragraph (1), may provide technical assistance in developing and implementing a management plan.

(4) Plan approval. Within 90 days after the submission of a management plan, the Task Force or the Assistant Secretary in consultation with the Task Force, as appropriate under paragraph (1), shall review the proposed plan and approve it if it meets the requirements of this subsection or return the plan to the Governor or the interstate organization with recommended modifications.

(b) Grant program. (1) State grants. The Director may, at the recommendation of the Task Force, make grants to States with management plans approved under subsection (a) of this section for the implementation of those plans.

****

(c) Enforcement assistance. Upon request of a State or Indian tribe, the Director or the Under Secretary, to the extent allowable by law and in a manner consistent with section 141 of Title 14, may provide assistance to a State or Indian tribe in enforcing an approved State or interstate invasive species management plan.

[Pub. L. 101-646, Title I, § 1204, 104 Stat. 4770 (Nov. 29, 1990); Pub. L. 104-332, § 2(e)(6), (h)(1), 110 Stat. 4089, 4091 (Oct. 26, 1996)]

16 U.S.C. § 4725. Relationship to other laws. All actions taken by Federal agencies in implementing the provisions of section 4722 of this title shall be consistent with all applicable Federal, State, and local environmental laws. Nothing in this chapter shall affect the authority of any State or political subdivision thereof to adopt or enforce control measures for aquatic nuisance species, or diminish or affect the jurisdiction of any State over species of fish and wildlife. Compliance with the control and eradication measures of any State or political subdivision thereof regarding aquatic nuisance species shall not relieve any person of the obligation to comply with the provisions of this subtitle.

[Pub. L. 101-646, Title I, § 1205, 104 Stat. 4771 (Nov. 29, 1990); Pub. L. 104-332, § 2(h)(1), 110 Stat. 4091 (Oct. 26, 1996)]

16 U.S.C. § 4726. International cooperation. (a) Advice. The Task Force shall provide timely advice to the Secretary of State concerning aquatic nuisance species that infest waters shared with other countries.

(b) Negotiations. The Secretary of State, in consultation with the Task Force, is encouraged to initiate negotiations with the governments of foreign countries concerning the planning and implementation of prevention, monitoring, research, education, and control programs related to aquatic nuisance species infesting shared water resources.

[Pub. L. 101-646, Title I, § 1206, 104 Stat. 4771 (Nov. 29, 1990); Pub. L. 104-332, § 2(h)(1), 110 Stat. 4091 (Oct. 26, 1996)]

16 U.S.C. § 4728. Brown tree snake control program. The Task Force shall, within the program developed under section [4722](a), undertake a comprehensive, environmentally sound program in coordination with regional, territorial, State and local entities to control the brown tree snake (*Boiga irregularis*) in Guam and other areas where the species is established outside of its historic range.

[Pub. L. 101-646, Title I, § 1209, 104 Stat. 4772 (Nov. 29, 1990); Pub. L. 104-332, § 2(h)(1), 110 Stat. 4091 (Oct. 26, 1996)]

- 0 -

Fish and Wildlife Service Regulations on Injurious Wildlife

50 C.F.R. PART 16
INJURIOUS WILDLIFE

Subpart A -- Introduction

Subpart B -- Importation or Shipment of Injurious Wildlife

Subpart C -- Permits

Subpart D -- Additional Exemptions

AUTHORITY: 18 U.S.C. § 42.

SOURCE: 39 FR 1169, Jan 4, 1974, unless otherwise noted.

SUBPART A -- INTRODUCTION

§ 16.1 Purpose of regulations.

The regulations contained in this part implement the Lacey Act (18 U.S.C. § 42).

§ 16.2 Scope of regulations.

The provisions of this part are in addition to, and are not in lieu of, other regulations of this Subchapter B which may require a permit or prescribe additional restrictions or conditions for the importation, exportation, and interstate transportation of wildlife (see also part 13).

§ 16.3 General restrictions.

Any importation or transportation of live wildlife or eggs thereof, or dead fish or eggs or salmonids of the fish family Salmonidae into the United States or its territories or possessions is deemed to be injurious or potentially injurious to the health and welfare of human beings, to the interest of forestry, agriculture, and horticulture, and to the welfare and survival of the wildlife or wildlife resources of the United States; and any such importation into or the transportation of live wildlife or eggs thereof between the continental United States, the District of Columbia, Hawaii, the Commonwealth of Puerto Rico, or any territory or possession of the United States by any means whatsoever, is prohibited except for certain purposes and under certain conditions as hereinafter provided in this part: *Provided,* That the provisions of this section shall not apply to psittacine birds (see also §§ 16.32 and 16.33 for other exemptions).

SUBPART B -- IMPORTATION OR SHIPMENT OF INJURIOUS WILDLIFE

§ 16.11 Importation of live wild mammals.

(a) The importation, transportation, or acquisition is prohibited of live specimens of: (1) Any species of so-called "flying fox" or fruit bat of the genus *Pteropus*; (2) any species of mongoose or meerkat of the genera *Atilax, Cynictis, Helogale, Herpestes, Ichneumia, Mungos, and Suricata*; (3) any species of European rabbit of the genus *Oryctolagus*; (4) any species of Indian wild dog, red dog, or dhole of the genus *Cuon*; (5) any species of multimammate rat or mouse of the genus *Mastomys*; and (6) any raccoon dog, *Nyctereutes procyonoides*: *Provided,* that the Director shall issue permits authorizing the importation, transportation, and possession of such mammals under the terms a conditions set forth in § 16.22.

(b) Upon the filing of a written declaration with the District Director of Customs at the port of entry as required under § 14.61, all other species of live wild mammals may be imported, transported, and possessed in captivity, without a permit, for scientific, medical, educational, exhibition, or propagating purposes, but no such live wild mammals or any progeny thereof may be released into the wild except by the State wildlife conservation agency having jurisdiction over the area of release or by persons having prior written permission for release from such agency: *Provided,* That the provisions of this paragraph shall not apply to live game mammals from Mexico, the importation of which is governed by regulations under Part 14 of this chapter.

[39 FR 1169, Jan. 4, 1974, as amended at 47 FR 56362, Dec. 16, 1982]

§ 16.12 Importation of live wild birds or their eggs.

(a) The importation, transportation, or acquisition is prohibited of any live specimen or egg of (1) the species of so-called "pink starling" or "rosy pastor" *Sturnus roseus*; (2) the species of dioch (including the subspecies black-fronted, red-billed, or Sudan dioch) *Quelea quelea;* (3) any species of Java sparrow, *Padda oryzivora*; (4) the species of red-whiskered bul-bul, *Pycnonotus jocosus*: *Provided,* That the Director shall issue permits authorizing the importation, transportation, and possession of such live birds under the terms and conditions set forth in § 16.22.

(b) Upon the filing of a written declaration with the District Director of Customs at the port of entry as required under § 14.61, all species of live wild game, birds may be imported, transported, and possessed in captivity, without a permit, for scientific, medical, educational, exhibition, or propagating purposes, and the eggs of such birds may be imported, transported, and possessed, without a permit, for propagating or scientific collection purposes, but no such live wild game birds or any progeny thereof may be released into the wild except by the State wildlife conservation agency having jurisdiction over the area of release or by persons having prior written permission for release from such agency.

(c) Upon the filing of a written declaration with the District Director of Customs at the port of entry as required under § 14.61, all species of live, wild nongame birds (other than those listed in paragraph (a) of this section) may be imported, transported, and possessed in captivity, without a permit, for scientific, medical, educational, exhibition, or propagating purposes, but no such live, wild nongame birds or any progeny thereof may be released into the wild except by or under the direction of State wildlife conservation agencies when such agencies have received prior written permission from the Director for such release: *Provided,* That the provisions of this paragraph shall not apply to live bald and golden eagles or to live migratory birds, the importation of which is governed by regulations under Parts 22 and 21 of this chapter, respectively, or to birds of the Family Psittacidae (parrots, macaws, cockatoos, parakeets, lories, lovebirds, etc.), the importation and transportation of which is governed by U.S. Public Health Service regulations under 42 CFR Parts 71 and 72.

(d) The importation of the eggs of wild nongame birds is prohibited except as permitted under § 16.33.

§ 16.13 Importation of live or dead fish, mollusks, and crustaceans, or their eggs.

(a) Upon an exporter filing a written declaration with the District Director of Customs at the port of entry as required under § 14.61 of this chapter, live or dead fish, mollusks, and crustaceans, or parts thereof, or their gametes or fertilized eggs, may be imported, transported, and possessed in captivity without a permit except as follows:

(1) No such live fish, mollusks, crustacean, or any progency or eggs thereof may be released into the wild except by the State wildlife conservation agency having jurisdiction over the area of release or by persons having prior written permission from such agency.

(2) The importation, transportation, or acquisition of any live fish or viable eggs of the walking catfish, family *Clariidae*; live mitten crabs, genus *Eriochei*, or their viable eggs; and live mollusks, veligers, or viable eggs of zebra mussels, genus *Dreissena,* are proibited except as provided under the terms and conditions set forth in § 16.22.

(3) Notwithstanding § 16.32, all Federal agencies shall be subject to the requirements stated within this section. Live or dead uneviscerated salmonid fish (family Salmonidae), live fertilized eggs, or gametes of salmonid fish are prohibited entry into the United States for any purpose except by direct shipment accompanied by a certification that: as defined in paragraph (e)(1) of this section, the fish lots, from which the shipments originated, have been sampled; virus assays have been conducted on the samples according to methods described in paragraphs (e)(2) through (4); of this section; and

Oncorhynchus masou virus and the viruses causing viral hemorrhagic septicemia, infectious hematopoietic necrosis, and infectious pancreatic necrosis have not been detected in the fish stocks from which the samples were taken. In addition, live salmonid fish can be imported into the United States only upon written approval from the Director of the U.S. Fish and Wildlife Service.

(4) All live fish eggs of salmonid fish must be disinfected within 24 hours prior to shipment to the United States.***

(b)(1) The certification to accompany importations as required by this section shall consist of a statement in the English language, printed or typewritten, stating that this shipment of dead uneviscerated salmonid fish, live salmonid fish, or live, disinfected fertilized eggs or gametes of salmonid fish has been tested, by the methods outlined in this section, and none of the listed viruses were detected. The certification shall be signed in the country of origin by a qualified fish pathologist designated as a certifying official by the Director.

(2) The certification must contain:

(i) The date and port of export in the country of origin and the anticipated date of arrival in the United States and port of entry;

(ii) Surface vessel name or number or air carrier and flight number;

(iii) Bill of lading number or airway bill number;

(iv) The date and location where fish, tissue, or fluid samples were collected;

(v) The date and location where virus assays were completed; and

(vi) The original handwritten signature, in ink, of the certifying official and his or her address and telephone number.

(3) Certification may be substantially in the following form:

> I, ____, designated by the Director of the U.S. Fish and Wildlife Service on ____(date), as a certifying official for ____ (country), as required by Title 50, CFR 16.13, do hereby certify that the fish lot(s) of origin for this shipment of ____ (weight in kilograms) dead uneviscerated salmonid fish, live salmonid fish, live salmonid fish eggs disinfected as described in § 16.13, or live salmonid gametes to be shipped under ____(bill of lading number or airway bill number), were sampled at ____(location of fish facility) on ____ (sampling date) and the required viral assays were completed on ____(date assays were completed) at ____(location where assays were conducted) using the methodology described in § 16.13. I further certify that Oncorhynchus masou virus and the viruses causing viral hemorrhagic septicemia, infectious hematopoietic necrosis, and infectious pancreatic necrosis have not been detected in viral assays of the fish lot(s) of origin.
>
> The shipment is scheduled to depart ____(city and country) on ____(date), via ____ (name of carrier) with anticipated arrival at the port of ____ (city), U.S.A., on ____ (date).
>
> ****

(c) Nothing in this part shall restrict the importation and transportation of dead salmonid fish when such fish have been eviscerated (all internal organs removed, gills may remain) or filleted or when such fish or eggs have been processed by canning, pickling, smoking, or otherwise prepared in a manner whereby the Oncorhynchus masou virus and the viruses causing viral hemorrhagic septicemia, infectious hematopoietic necrosis, and infectious pancreatic necrosis have been killed.

(d) Any fish caught in the wild in North America under a valid sport or commercial fishing license shall be exempt from sampling and certification requirements and from filing the Declaration for Importation of Wildlife. The Director may enter into formal agreements allowing the importation of gametes, fertilized eggs, live fish, or dead, uneviscerated fish without inspection and certification of pathogen status, if the exporting Nation has an acceptable program of inspection and pathogen control in operation, can document the occurrence and distribution of fish pathogens within its boundaries, and can demonstrate that importation of salmonid fishes into the United States from that National will not pose a substantial risk to the public and private fish stocks of the United States.

(e) *Fish sampling requirements, sample processing, and methods for virus assays.*

(1) *Fish sampling requirements.* ****

(2) *General sample processing requirements.* ****

(3) *Cell culture procedures.* ****

(f) Information concerning the importation requirements of this section and application requirements for designation as a certifying official for purposes of this section may be obtained by contacting: U.S. Department of the Interior, U.S. Fish and Wildlife Service, Division of Fish Hatcheries (820 Arlington Square), 1849 C Street, NW., Washington, DC 20240. Telephone 703- 358-1878.

(g) The information collection requirements contained in this part have been approved by the Office of Management and Budget under 44 U.S.C. § 3501 *et seq.* and assigned clearance number 1018-0078. The information is being collected to inform U.S. Customs and USFWS inspectors of the contents, origin, routing, and destination of fish and eggs shipments and to certify that the fish lots were inspected for listed pathogens. The information will be used to protect the health of the fishery resource. Response is required to obtain a benefit.

[54 FR 22289, May 23, 1989; 56 FR 56942, Nov. 7, 1991; 58 FR 58979, Nov. 5, 1993; 65 FR 37063, June 13, 2000]

§ 16.14 Importation of live amphibians or their eggs.

Upon the filing of a written declaration with the District Director of Customs at the port of entry as required under § 14.61, all species of live amphibians or their eggs may be imported, transported, and possessed in captivity, without a permit, for scientific, medical, education, exhibition, or propagating purposes, but no such live amphibians or any progeny or eggs thereof may be released into the wild except by the State wildlife conservation agency having jurisdiction over the area of release or by persons having prior written permission for release from such agency.

§ 16.15 Importation of live reptiles or their eggs.

(a) The importation, transportation, or acquisition is prohibited of any live specimen or egg of the brown tree snake (*Boiga irregularis*): *Provided,* that the Director shall issue permits authorizing the importation, transportation, and possession of such live snakes or viable eggs under the terms and conditions set forth in § 16.22.

(b) Upon the filing of a written declaration with the District Director of Customs at the port of entry as required under § 14.61, all other species of live reptiles or their eggs may be imported, transported, and possessed in captivity, without a permit, for scientific, medical, educational, exhibitional or propagating purposes, but no such live reptiles or any progency or eggs thereof may be released into the wild except by the State wildlife conservation agency having jurisdiction over the area of release or by persons having prior written permission for release from such agency.

[55 17441, April 25, 1990]

SUBPART C -- PERMITS

§ 16.22 Injurious wildlife permits.

The Director may, upon receipt of an application and in accordance with the issuance criteria of this section, issue a permit authorizing the importation into or shipment between the continental United States, the District of Columbia, Hawaii, the Commonwealth of Puerto Rico, or any possession of the United States of injurious wildlife (See subpart B of this part) for zoological, educational, medical, or scientific purposes.

(a) *Application requirements.* Submit applications for permits to import, transport or acquire injurious wildlife for such purposes to the Director, U.S. Fish and Wildlife Service, (Attention: Office of Management Authority), 4401 N. Fairfax Drive, Room 700, Arlington, VA 22203. Submit applications in writing on a Federal Fish and Wildlife License/Permit application (Form 3-200) and attach all of the following information:

(1) The number of specimens and the common and scientific names (genus and species) of each species of live wildlife proposed to be imported or otherwise acquired, transported and possessed;

(2) The purpose of such importation or other acquisition, transportation and possession;

(3) The address of the premises where such live wildlife will be kept in captivity;

(4) A statement of the applicant's qualifications and previous experience in caring for and handling captive wildlife.

(b) *Additional permit conditions.* In addition to the general conditions set forth in Part 13 of this Subchapter B, permits to import or ship injurious wildlife for zoological, educational, medical, or scientific purposes shall be subject to the following conditions:

(1) All live wildlife acquired under permit and all progeny thereof, must be confined in the approved facilities on the premises authorized in the permit.

(2) No live wildlife, acquired under permit, or any eggs or progeny thereof, may be sold, donated, traded, loaned, or transferred to any other person unless such person has a permit issued by the Director under § 16.22 authorizing him to acquire and possess such wildlife or the eggs or progeny thereof.

(3) Permittees shall notify the nearest Special Agent-in-Charge (see § 10.22 of this chapter) by telephone or other expedient means within 24 hours following the escape of any wildlife imported or transported under authority of a permit issued under this section, or the escape of any progeny of such wildlife, unless otherwise specifically exempted by terms of the permit.

(c) *Issuance criteria.* The Director shall consider the following in determining whether to issue a permit to import or ship injurious wildlife for zoological, educational, medical, or scientific purposes:

(1) Whether the wildlife is being imported or otherwise acquired for a bona fide scientific, medical, educational, or zoological exhibition purpose;

(2) Whether the facilities for holding the wildlife in captivity have been inspected and approved, and consist of a basic cage or structure of a design and material adequate to prevent escape which is maintained inside a building or other facility of such structure that the wildlife could not escape from the building or other facility after escaping from the cage or structure maintained therein;

(3) Whether the applicant is a responsible person who is aware of the potential dangers to public interests posed by such wildlife, and who by reason of his knowledge, experience, and facilities reasonably can be expected to provide adequate protection for such public interests; and

(4) If such wildlife is to be imported or otherwise acquired for zoological or aquarium exhibition purposes, whether such exhibition or display will be open to the public during regular appropriate hours.

(d) The Office of Management and Budget approved the information collection requirements contained in this part 16 under 44 U.S.C. § 3507 and assigned OMB Control Number 1018-0093. The Service may not conduct or sponsor, and you are not required to respond to, a collection of information unless it displays a currently valid OMB control number. We are collecting this information to provide information necessary to evaluate permit applications. We will use this information to review permit applications and make decisions, according to criteria established in various Federal wildlife conservation statutes and regulations, on the issuance, suspension, revocation, or denial of permits. You must respond to obtain or retain a permit. We estimate the public reporting burden for these reporting requirements to average 2 hours per response, including time for reviewing instructions, gathering and maintaining data, and completing and reviewing the forms. Direct comments regarding the burden estimate or any other aspect of these reporting requirements to the Service Information Collection Control Officer, MS-222 ARLSQ, U.S. Fish and Wildlife Service, Washington, D.C. 20240, or the Office of Management and Budget, Paperwork Reduction Project (1018-0093), Washington, D.C. 20603.

[39 FR 1169, Jan. 4, 1974, as amended at 47 FR 30786, July 15, 1982; 63 FR 52634, Oct. 1, 1998]

SUBPART D -- ADDITIONAL EXEMPTIONS

§ 16.32 Importation by Federal agencies.

Nothing in this part shall restrict the importation and transportation, without a permit, of any live wildlife by Federal agencies solely for their own use, upon the filing of a written declaration with the District Director of Customs at the port of entry as required under § 14.61: *Provided,* That the provisions of this section shall not apply to bald and golden eagles or their eggs, or to migratory birds or their eggs, the importations of which are governed by regulations under Parts 22 and 21 of this chapter, respectively.

§ 16.33 Importation of natural-history specimens.

Nothing in this part shall restrict the importation and transportation, without a permit, of dead natural-history specimens of wildlife or their eggs for museum or scientific collection purposes: *Provided,* That the provisions of this section shall not apply to dead migratory birds, the importation of which is governed by regulations under Parts 20 and 21 of this chapter; to dead game mammals from Mexico, the importation of which is governed by regulations under Part 14 of this chapter; or to dead bald and golden eagles or their eggs, the importation of which is governed by regulations under Part 22 of this chapter.

50 C.F.R. PART 21
MIGRATORY BIRD PERMITS

Subpart A -- Introduction

Subpart B -- General Requirements and Exceptions

Subpart C -- Specific Permit Provisions

****

Subpart D -- Control of Depredating Birds

Subpart E -- Control of Overabundant Migratory Bird Populations

AUTHORITY: Pub. L. No. 95-616; 92 Stat. 3112 (16 U.S.C. 712(2)); Pub. L. No. 106-108.

SOURCE: 39 FR 1178, Jan. 4, 1974; 54 FR 38150, Sept. 14, 1989; 64 FR 71237, Dec. 20, 1999, unless otherwise noted.

SUBPART A -- INTRODUCTION

§ 21.1 Purpose of regulations.

The regulations contained in this part supplement the general permit regulations of part 13 of this subchapter with respect to permits for the taking, possession, transportation, sale, purchase, barter, importation, exportation, and banding or marking of migratory birds. This part also provides certain exceptions to permit requirements for public, scientific, or educational institutions, and establishes depredation orders which provide limited exceptions to the Migratory Bird Treaty Act (16 U.S.C. 703-712).

[39 FR 1178, Jan. 4, 1974, as amended at 46 FR 42680, Aug. 24, 1981; 54 FR 38150, Sept. 14, 1989]

§ 21.2 Scope of regulations.

(a) Migratory birds, their parts, nests, or eggs, lawfully acquired prior to the effective date of Federal protection under the Migratory Bird Treaty Act (16 U.S.C. 703-712) may be possessed or transported without a permit, but may not be imported, exported, purchased, sold, bartered, or offered for purchase, sale or barter, and all shipments of such birds must be marked as provided by part 14 of this subchapter: Provide, no exemption from any statute or regulation shall accrue to any offspring of such migratory birds.

(b) This part 21, except for § 21.22 (banding or marking permits), does not apply to the bald eagle (*Haliaeetus leucocephalus*) or the golden eagle (*Aquila chrysaetos*) for which regulations are provided in Part 22 of this subchapter.

(c) The provisions of this part are in addition to, and are not in lieu of other regulations of this Subchapter B which may require a permit or prescribe additional restrictions or conditions for the importation, exportation, and interstate transportation of wildlife (see also part 13.)

[39 FR 1178, Jan. 4, 1974, as amended at 46 FR 42680, Aug. 24, 1981; 54 FR 38150, Sept. 14, 1989]

§ 21.3 Definitions.

In addition to definitions contained in Part 10 of this chapter, and unless the context requires otherwise, as used in this part:

Bred in captivity or *captive-bred* refers to raptors, including eggs, hatched in captivity from parents that mated or otherwise transferred gametes in captivity.

Captivity means that a live raptor is held in a controlled environment that is intensively manipulated by man for the purpose of producing raptors of selected species, and that has boundaries designed to prevent raptors, eggs or gametes of the selected species from entering or leaving the controlled environment. General characteristics of captivity may include, but are not limited to, artificial housing, waste removal, health care, protection from predators, and artificially supplied food.

Falconry means the sport of taking quarry by means of a trained raptor.

Raptor means a live migratory bird of the Order Falconiformes or the Order Strigiformes, other than a bald eagle (*Haliaeetus leucocephalus*) or a golden eagle (*Aquila chrysaetos*).

Resident Canada geese means Canada geese that nest within the conterminous United States and/or Canada geese which reside within the conterminous United States during the months of June, July, or August.

Service or *we* means the U.S. Fish and Wildlife Service, Department of the Interior.

[48 FR 31607, July 8, 1983; 64 FR 32774, June 17, 1999]

§ 21.4 Information collection requirements.

****

SUBPART B -- GENERAL REQUIREMENTS AND EXCEPTIONS

§ 21.11 General permit requirements.

No person shall take, possess, import, export, transport, sell, purchase, barter, or offer for sale, purchase or barter, any migratory bird, or the parts, nests, or eggs of such bird except as may be permitted under the terms of a valid permit issued pursuant to the provisions of this part and part 13, or as permitted by regulations in this part or part 20 (the hunting regulations).

[39 FR 1178, Jan. 4, 1974, as amended at 46 FR 42680, Aug. 24, 1981; 54 FR 38151, Sept. 14, 1989]

§ 21.12 General exceptions to permit requirements.

The following exceptions to the permit requirement are allowed.

(a) Employees of the Department of the Interior authorized to enforce the provisions of the Migratory Bird Treaty Act of July 3, 1918, as amended (40 Stat. 755; 16 U.S.C. 703-711), may, without a permit, take or otherwise acquire, hold in custody, transport, and dispose of migratory birds or their parts, nests, or eggs as necessary in performing their official duties.

(b) State game departments, municipal game farms or parks, and public museums, public zoological parks, accredited institutional members of the American Association of Zoological Parks and Aquariums (AAZPA) and public scientific or educational institutions may acquire by gift or purchase, possess, transport, and by gift or sale dispose of lawfully acquired migratory birds or their progeny, parts, nests, or eggs without a permit: Provided, That such birds may be acquired only from persons authorized by this paragraph or by a permit issued pursuant to this part to possess and dispose of such birds, or from Federal or State game authorities by the gift of seized, condemned, or sick or injured birds. Any such birds, acquired without a permit, and any progeny therefrom may be disposed of only to persons authorized by this paragraph to acquire such birds without a permit. Any person exercising a privilege granted by this paragraph must keep accurate records of such operations showing the species and number of birds acquired, possessed, and disposed of; the names and addresses of the persons from whom such birds were acquired or to whom such birds were donated or sold; and the dates of such transactions. Records shall be maintained or reproducible in English on a calendar year basis and shall be retained for a period of five (5) years following the end of the calendar year covered by the records.

[50 FR 8638, March 4, 1985; 54 FR 38151, Sept. 14, 1989]

§ 21.13 Permit exceptions for captive-reared mallard ducks.

****

§ 21.14 Permit exceptions for captive-reared migratory waterfowl other than mallard ducks.

****

SUBPART C -- SPECIFIC PERMIT PROVISIONS

****

SUBPART D -- CONTROL OF DEPREDATING BIRDS

§ 21.41 Depredation permits.

(a) *Permit requirement.* Except as provided in §§ 21.42 through 21.46, a depredation permit is required before any person may take, possess, or transport migratory birds for depredation control purposes. No permit is required merely to scare or herd depredating migratory birds other than endangered or threatened species or bald or golden eagles.

(b) *Application procedures.* Submit application for depredation permits to the appropriate Regional Director (Attention: Migratory bird permit office). You can find addresses for the Regional Directors in 50 CFR 2.2. Each application must contain the general information and certification required in § 13.12(a) of this subchapter, and the following additional information:

(1) A description of the area where depredations are occurring;

(2) The nature of the crops or other interests being injured;

(3) The extent of such injury; and

(4) The particular species of migratory birds committing the injury.

(c) *Additional permit conditions.* In addition to the general conditions set forth in Part 13 of this Subchapter B, depredation permits shall be subject to requires, in this section:

(1) Permittees may not kill migratory birds unless specifically authorized on the permit.

(2) Unless otherwise specifically authorized, when permittees are authorized to kill migratory birds they may do so only with a shotgun not larger than No. 10 gauge fired from the shoulder, and only on or over the threatened area or area described on the permit.

(3) Permittees may not use blinds, pits, or other means of concealment, decoys, duck calls, or other devices to lure or entice birds within gun range.

(4) All migratory birds killed shall be retrieved by the permittee and turned over to a Bureau representative or his designee for disposition to charitable or other worthy institutions for use as food, or otherwise disposed of as provided by law.

(5) Only persons named on the permit are authorized to act as agents of the permittee under authority of the permit.

(d) *Tenure of permits.* The tenure of depredation permits shall be limited to the dates which appear on its face, but in no case shall be longer than one year.

[39 FR 1178, Jan. 4, 1974, as amended at 42 FR 17122, March 31, 1977; 63 FR 52637, Oct. 1, 1998]

§ 21.42 Authority to issue depredating orders to permit the killing of migratory game birds.

Upon the receipt of evidence clearly showing that migratory game birds have accumulated in such numbers in a particular area as to cause or about to cause serious damage to agricultural, horticultural, and fish cultural interests, the Director is authorized to issue by publication in the Federal Register a depredation order to permit the killing of such birds under the following conditions:

(a) That such birds may only be killed by shooting with a shotgun not larger than No. 10 gauge fired from the shoulder, and only on or over the threatened area or areas;

(b) That shooting shall be limited to such time as may be fixed by the Director on the basis of all circumstances involved. If prior to termination of the period fixed for such shooting, the Director receives information that there no longer exists a serious threat to the area or areas involved, he shall without delay cause to be published in the Federal Register an order of revocation;

(c) That such migratory birds as are killed under the provisions of any depredation order may be used for food or donated to public museums or public scientific and educational institutions for exhibition, scientific, or educational purposes, but shall not be sold, offered for sale, bartered, or shipped for purpose of sale or barter, or be wantonly wasted or destroyed: Provided, That any migratory game birds which cannot be so utilized shall be disposed of as prescribed by the Director;

(d) That any order issued pursuant to this section shall not authorize the killing of the designated species of depredating birds contrary to any State laws or regulations. The order shall specify that it is issued as an emergency measure designed to relieve depredations only and shall not be construed as opening, reopening, or extending any open hunting season contrary to any regulations promulgated pursuant to section 3 of the Migratory Bird Treaty Act.

§ 21.43 Depredation order for blackbirds, cowbirds, grackles, crows and magpies.

A Federal permit shall not be required to control yellow-headed, red-winged, rusty, and Brewer's blackbirds, cowbirds, all grackles, crows, and magpies, when found committing or about to commit depredations upon ornamental or shade trees, agricultural crops, livestock, or wildlife, or when concentrated in such numbers and manner as to constitute a health hazard or other nuisance: Provided:

(a) That none of the birds killed pursuant to this section, nor their plumage, shall be sold or offered for sale, but may be possessed, transported, and otherwise disposed of or utilized.

(b) That any person exercising any of the privileges granted by this section shall permit at all reasonable times including during actual operations, any Federal or State game or deputy game agent, warden, protector, or other game law enforcement officer free and unrestricted access over the premises on which such operations have been or are being conducted; and shall furnish promptly to such officer whatever information he may require, concerning said operations.

(c) That nothing in this section shall be construed to authorize the killing of such birds contrary to any State laws or regulations; and that none of the privileges granted under this section shall be exercised unless the person possesses whatever permit as may be required for such activities by the State concerned.

[39 FR 1178, Jan. 4, 1974, as amended at 42 FR 17122, Mar. 31, 1977; 54 FR 47525, Nov. 15, 1989]

§ 21.44 Depredation order for designated species of depredating birds in California.

****

§ 21.45 Depredation order for depredating purple gallinules in Louisiana.

****

§ 21.46 Depredation order for depredating scrub jays and Steller's jays in Washington and Oregon.

****

§ 21.47 Depredation order for double-crested cormorants at aquaculture facilities.

****

SUBPART E -- CONTROL OF OVERABUNDANT MIGRATORY BIRD POPULATIONS

§ 21.60 Conservation Order for Mid-continent light geese.

(a) *Which waterfowl species are covered by this order?* This conservation order addresses management of lesser snow (*Anser c. caerulescens*) and Ross' (*Anser rossii*) geese that breed, migrate, and winter in the mid-continent portion of North America, primarily in the Central and Mississippi Flyways (mid-continent light geese).

(b) *In what areas can the conservation order be implemented?*

(1) The following States, or portions of States, that are contained within the boundaries of the Central and Mississippi Flyways: Alabama, Arkansas, Colorado, Illinois, Indiana, Iowa, Kansas, Kentucky, Louisiana, Michigan, Minnesota, Mississippi, Missouri, Montana, Nebraska, New Mexico, North Dakota, Ohio, Oklahoma, South Dakota, Tennessee, Texas, Wisconsin, and Wyoming.

(2) Tribal lands within the geographic boundaries in paragraph (b)(1) of this section.

(3) The following areas within the boundaries in paragraph (b)(1) of this section are closed to the conservation order after 10 March of each year: Monte Vista National Wildlife Refuge (CO); Bosque del Apache National Wildlife Refuge (NM); the area within 5 miles of the Platte River from Lexington, Nebraska to Grand Island, Nebraska; the following area in and around Aransas National Wildlife Refuge; those portions of Refugio, Calhoun, and Aransas counties that lie inside a line extending from 5 nautical miles offshore to and including Pelican Island, thence to Port O'Conner, thence northwest along State Highway 185 and southwest along State Highway 35 to Aransas Pass, thence southeast along State Highway 361 to Port Aransas, thence east along the Corpus Christi Channel, thence southeast along the Aransas Channel, extending to 5 nautical miles offshore; except that it is lawful to take mid-continent light geese after 10 March of each year within the Guadalupe WMA. If at any time we receive evidence that a need to close the areas in this paragraph (b)(3) no longer exists, we will publish a proposal to remove the closures in the Federal Register.

(c) *What is required in order for State/Tribal governments to participate in the conservation order?* Any State or Tribal government responsible for the management of wildlife and migratory birds may, without permit, kill or cause to be killed under its general supervision, mid-continent light geese under the following conditions:

(1) Activities conducted under this section may not affect endangered or threatened species as designated under the Endangered Species Act.

(2) Control activities must be conducted clearly as such and are intended to relieve pressures on migratory birds and habitat essential to migratory bird populations only and are not to be construed as opening, re-opening, or extending any open hunting season

contrary to any regulations promulgated under section 3 of the Migratory Bird Treaty Act.

(3) Control activities may be conducted only when all waterfowl and crane hunting seasons, excluding falconry, are closed.

(4) Control measures employed through this section may be implemented only between the hours of one-half hour before sunrise to one-half hour after sunset.

(5) Nothing in this section may limit or initiate management actions on Federal land without concurrence of the Federal Agency with jurisdiction.

(6) States and Tribes must designate participants who must operate under the conditions of this section.

(7) States and Tribes must inform participants of the requirements/conditions of this section that apply.

(8) States and Tribes must keep records of activities carried out under the authority of this section, including the number of mid-continent light geese taken under this section, the methods by which they were taken, and the dates they were taken. The States and Tribes must submit an annual report summarizing activities conducted under this section on or before August 30 of each year, to the Chief, Division of Migratory Bird Management, U.S. Fish and Wildlife Service, ms 634--ARLSQ, 1849 C Street NW., Washington, DC 20240.

(d) *What is required in order for individuals to participate in the conservation order?* Individual participants in State or tribal programs covered by this section are required to comply with the following requirements:

(1) Nothing in this section authorizes the take of mid-continent light geese contrary to any State or Tribal laws or regulations; and none of the privileges granted under this section may be exercised unless persons acting under the authority of the conservation order possesses whatever permit or other authorization(s) required for such activities by the State or Tribal government concerned.

(2) Participants who take mid-continent light geese under this section may not sell or offer for sale those birds nor their plumage, but may possess, transport, and otherwise properly use them.

(3) Participants acting under the authority of this section must permit at all reasonable times, including during actual operations, any Federal or State game or deputy game agent, warden, protector, or other game law enforcement officer free and unrestricted access over the premises on which such operations have been or are being conducted, and must promptly furnish whatever information an officer requires concerning the operation.

(4) Participants acting under the authority of this section may take mid- continent light geese by any method except those prohibited as follows:

(i) With a trap, snare, net, rifle, pistol, swivel gun, shotgun larger than 10 gauge, punt gun, battery gun, machine gun, fish hook, poison, drug, explosive, or stupefying substance;

(ii) From or by means, aid, or use of a sinkbox or any other type of low floating device, having a depression affording the person a means of concealment beneath the surface of the water;

(iii) From or by means, aid, or use of any motor vehicle, motor-driven land conveyance, or aircraft of any kind, except that paraplegics and persons missing one or both legs may take from any stationary motor vehicle or stationary motor-driven land conveyance;

(iv) From or by means of any motorboat or other craft having a motor attached, or any sailboat, unless the motor has been completely shut off and the sails furled, and its progress therefrom has ceased. A craft under power may be used only to retrieve dead or crippled birds; however, the craft may not be used under power to shoot any crippled birds;

(v) By the use or aid of live birds as decoys; although not limited to, it shall be a violation of this paragraph for any person to take mid-continent light geese on an area where tame or captive live geese are present unless such birds are and have been for a period of 10 consecutive days before the taking, confined within an enclosure that substantially reduces the audibility of their calls and totally conceals the birds from the sight of mid-continent light geese;

(vi) By means or aid of any motor-driven land, water, or air conveyance, or any sailboat used for the purpose of or resulting in the concentrating, driving, rallying, or stirring up of mid-continent light geese;

(vii) By the aid of baiting, or on or over any baited area. As used in this paragraph, "baiting" means the placing, exposing, depositing, distributing, or scattering of shelled, shucked, or unshucked corn, wheat or other grain, salt, or other feed so as to constitute for such birds a lure, attraction or enticement to, on, or over any areas where hunters are attempting to take them; and "baited area" means any area where shelled, shucked, or unshucked corn, wheat or other grain, salt, or other feed capable of luring, attracting, or enticing such birds is directly or indirectly placed, exposed, deposited, distributed, or scattered; and such area shall remain a baited area for 10 days following complete removal of all such corn, wheat or other grain, salt, or other feed. However, nothing in this paragraph prohibits the taking of mid- continent light geese on or over standing crops, flooded standing crops (including aquatics), flooded harvested croplands, grain crops properly shucked on the field where grown, or grains found scattered solely as the result of normal agricultural planting or harvesting; or

(viii) Participants may not possess shot (either in shotshells or as loose shot for muzzleloading) other than steel shot, or bismuth-tin, or other shots that are authorized in 50 CFR 20.21(j). Season limitations in that section do not apply to participants acting under this order.

(e) *Under what conditions would the conservation order be revoked?* The Service will annually assess the overall impact and effectiveness of the conservation order to ensure compatibility with long-term conservation of this resource. If at any time we receive that clearly demonstrates a serious threat of injury to the area or areas involved no longer exists, we will initiate action to revoke the conservation order.

(f) *Will information concerning the conservation order be collected?* The information collection requirements of the conservation order have been approved by OMB and assigned clearance number 1018-0103. Agencies may not conduct or sponsor, and a person is not required to respond to, a collection of information unless it displays a currently valid OMB control number. The recordkeeping and reporting requirements imposed under regulations established in this subpart E will be utilized to administer this program, particularly in the assessment of impacts alternative regulatory strategies may have on mid- continent light geese and other migratory bird populations. The information collected will be required to authorize State and Tribal governments responsible for migratory bird management to take mid-continent light geese within the guidelines provided by the Service.

APPENDIX

CHRONOLOGY OF FEDERAL WILDLIFE STATUTES

1897
National Forest Service Organic Act, 16 U.S.C. § 475

1900
Lacey Act, ch. 553, 31 Stat. 187 (May 25, 1900) [repealed in part] (currently codified at 16 U.S.C. § 701; 16 U.S.C. § 42)

1906
Antiquities Act, 16 U.S.C. §§ 431-433

1913
Weeks-McLean Migratory Bird Act, ch. 145, 37 Stat. 828, 847 (Mar. 3, 1913)

1916
National Park Service Organic Act, 16 U.S.C. §§ 1, 2-4

1918
Migratory Bird Treaty Act, 16 U.S.C. §§ 703-711

1926
Black Bass Act, ch. 346, 44 Stat. 576 (May 20, 1926) [repealed]

1929
Migratory Bird Conservation Act, 16 U.S.C. §§ 715-715k

1930
Tariff Act of 1930, 19 U.S.C. § 1527

1931
Animal Damage Control, 7 U.S.C. § 426

1934
Fish & Wildlife Coordination Act, 16 U.S.C. §§ 661-666c
Migratory Bird Stamp Act [Duck Stamp Act], 16 U.S.C. §§ 718-718j

1935
Refuge Revenue Sharing Act, ch. 261, § 401, 49 Stat. 383 (June 15, 1935) [repealed]

1937
Federal Aid in Wildlife Restoration Act [The Pittman-Robertson Act], 16 U.S.C. §§ 669-669i; 26 U.S.C. §§ 4161(b), 4181

1940

Bald Eagle Protection Act, 16 U.S.C. §§ 668-668d

1946

Fish & Wildlife Coordination Act Amendments, ch. 965, § 2, 60 Stat. 1080 (Aug. 14, 1946)

1948

Refuge Trespass Act, 18 U.S.C. § 41

1949

Migratory Bird Stamp Act Amendments [Duck Stamp Act], ch. 421, 63 Stat. 599 (Aug. 12, 1949)

1950

Federal Aid in Fish Restoration Act [Dingell-Johnson Act], 16 U.S.C. §§ 777-777*l*; 26 U.S.C. § 9504(a)

1958

Fish & Wildlife Coordination Act Amendments, Pub. L. No. 85-624, 72 Stat. 563 (Aug. 12, 1958)

Migratory Bird Stamp Act Amendments [Duck Stamp Act], Pub. L. No. 85-585, 72 Stat. 486 (Aug. 1, 1958)

1959

Act Prohibiting the Use of Aircraft & Motor Vehicles to Hunt Feral Horse & Burros, 18 U.S.C. § 47

1960

Multiple-Use Sustained-Yield Act, 16 U.S.C. §§ 528-531

Sikes Act, 16 U.S.C. §§ 670a-670f

1961

Wetlands Loan Act, 16 U.S.C. §§ 715k-3 to 715k-5

1962

Refuge Recreation Act, 16 U.S.C. §§ 460k to 460k-4

Bald and Golden Eagle Protection Act Amendments, Pub. L. No. 87-884, 76 Stat. 1246 (Oct. 24, 1962)

1963

Land and Water Conservation Fund Act, 16 U.S.C. §§ 460*l* to 460*l*-11

1964

Wilderness Act, 16 U.S.C. §§ 1131-1136

Refuge Revenue Sharing Act, 16 U.S.C. § 715s

1965

The Anadromous Fish Act, 16 U.S.C. §§ 757a-757b

1966

Refuge Administration Act, 16 U.S.C. 16 U.S.C. §§ 668dd-668ee
Endangered Species Preservation Act, Pub. L. No. 89-669, 80 Stat. 926 [repealed]
Migratory Bird Conservation Act Amendments, 16 U.S.C. § 715i(a)

1968

Wild and Scenic River Act, 16 U.S.C. §§ 1271-1287

1969

National Environmental Policy Act of 1969, 42 U.S.C. §§ 4321, 4331-4335
Endangered Species Conservation Act, Pub. L. No. 91-135, 83 Stat. 275 [repealed]

1970

General Authorities Act [Park Service], 16 U.S.C. §§ 1a-1, 1c
Federal Aid in Wildlife Restoration Act Amendments [The Pittman-Robertson Act], Pub. L. No. 91-503, §§ 101-102, 84 Stat. 1097 (Oct. 23, 1970)

1971

Airborne Hunting Act, 16 U.S.C. § 742j-1
Wild Free-Roaming Horses and Burros Act, 16 U.S.C. §§ 1331-1340

1972

Marine Mammal Protection Act, 16 U.S.C. §§ 1361-1407
Bald and Golden Eagle Protection Act Amendments, Pub. L. No. 82-535, 86 Stat. 1064 (Oct. 23, 1972)
Federal Water Pollution Control Act, 33 U.S.C. §§ 1251-1387

1973

Endangered Species Act, 16 U.S.C. §§ 1531-1544

1974

Sikes Act Extension, 16 U.S.C. §§ 670g-670o

1976

Magnuson Fisheries Conservation & Management Act of 1976, 16 U.S.C. §§ 1801-1883
National Forest Management Act, 16 U.S.C. §§ 1600-1614
Federal Land Policy and Management Act, 43 U.S.C. §§ 1701-1784

1978

Public Rangelands Improvement Act, 43 U.S.C. §§ 1901-1908

1980

Fish and Wildlife Conservation Act of 1980 [Non-Game Act], 16 U.S.C. §§ 2901-2911
The Pacific Northwest Electric Power Planning & Conservation Act, 16 U.S.C. §§ 839-839h

1981

Lacey Act Amendments, 16 U.S.C. §§ 3371-3378

1985

"Swampbuster" Provisions [Food Security Act of 1985], 16 U.S.C. §§ 3801, 3821-23
Conservation Reserve Program, 16 U.S.C. §§ 3801, 3831-3836a

1986
Emergency Wetlands Resources Act of 1986, 16 U.S.C. §§ 3901-3932

1989
North American Wetlands Conservation Act, 16 U.S.C. §§ 4401-4414

1990
Coastal Wetlands Planning, Protection, and Restoration Act, 16 U.S.C. §§ 3951-3956
Nonindigenous Aquatic Nuisance Prevention and Control Act, 16 U.S.C. §§ 4701-4751
"Swampbuster" Amendments [Food, Agriculture, Conservation, and Trade Act of 1990], Pub. L. No. 101-624, 104 Stat. 3359
Environmental Easement Program, 16 U.S.C. §§ 3839-3839d
Wetlands Reserve Program, 16 U.S.C. §§ 3837a-3837f
Forest Legacy Program, 16 U.S.C. § 2103c

1992
Wild Bird Conservation Act, 16 U.S.C. §§ 4901-4916

1996
Magnuson Fishery Conservation and Management Act Amendments
"Swampbuster" Amendments [Federal Agriculture Improvement and Reform Act of 1996], Pub. L. No. 104-127, 110 Stat. 888

1997
National Wildlife Refuge System Improvement Act, 16 U.S.C. §§ 668dd-668ee
National Defense Authorization Act of 1998, Pub. L. 105-85, Div. B, Title XXIX, § 2904(a), 111 Stat. 1629, 2017 (Nov. 18, 1997) (amending Sikes Act, 16 U.S.C. § 670a-670f)

1999
Neotropical Bird Conservation Act, 16 U.S.C. § 6101-6109

INTRODUCTION

1) JOHN MANWOOD, A TREATISE AND DISCOURSE OF THE LAWES OF THE FOREST cap. iv, §§ 1-2 (Thomas Wright & Bonham Wright, London 1598).

2) John Manwood defined the forest as

> a certen Territorie of woody grounds & fruitfull pastures, privileged for wild beasts and fowles ... to rest and abide in, in the safe protectio[n] of the King, for his princely delight and pleasure, which Territorie of grou[n]d ... is [legally defined] ... for the preservation and continuance of which said place ... there are certen particuler Lawes, Priviledges and Officers.

Id. cap. I, § 1. *See also* E.P. THOMPSON, WHIGS AND HUNTERS 28-32 (1975); G.J. Turner, *Introduction* to SELECT PLEAS OF THE FOREST (G.J. Turner ed. & trans., 1901) (vol. 13 Selden Soc'y Pubs.).

3) RICHARD, FITZ NIGEL, DIALOGUS DE SCACCARIO [THE COURSE OF THE EXCHEQUER] bk. I, ch. XI-XII (Charles Johnson ed. & trans. 1983) (ca. 1176).

4) JOHN MANWOOD, *supra* note 1, at cap. I, § 1. The "vert" -- "every plant, that doth growe within the Forest and beare greene leafe" -- was protected to preserve the "Venison" -- a term that at the time meant flesh of any of the animals of the chase: in Manwood's flowery phrasing, "therefore you shall understand, that even as the old Foresters & good Woodmen, do ... by this generall woord *Venison,* understand every beast of Forest and Chase, as a woord of art proper to beasts of Forest, & beasts of Chase, and to none other." *Id.* at cap. vi, § 1; cap. v, § 1.

5) *Id.* at cap. 8, § 2. *See also* Thomas A. Lund, *British Wildlife Law Before the American Revolution: Lessons from the Past,* 74 MICH. L. REV. 49, 60-62 (1975) (arguing that the forest laws were intended at least in part to create "wildlife rights").

6) JOHN MANWOOD, *supra* note 1, at cap. xviii, § 1.

7) Statute of Westminister II, cap. 47 (1285). The statute is not unique. *See, e.g.,* The Penalty for Unlawfully Hunting the Hare, 14 & 15 Hen. 8, ch. 10 (1523); To Avoid Destroying of Wild-Fowl, 25 Hen. 8, ch. 11, § 2 (1533); An Act ... for the Preservation of the Game in Pheasants and Partridges, and against the Destroying of Hares with Hare-Pipes and Tracing Hares in the Snow, 2 Jac. 1, ch. 27, § 6 (1604).

8) Justices of the Peace Shall be Conservators of the Statutes Made Touching Salmons, 17 Rich. 2, ch. 9 (1393).

9) An Act for the More Easy Discovery and Conviction of Such as Shall Destroy the Game of this Kingdom, 3 & 4 Wm. & M., ch. 23, § 11 (1692). When the statute prohibiting the burning of heath proved insufficient to deter illegal habitat destruction, Parliament prohibited unlicensed persons from selling fern ashes. An Act for the Better Preservation of the Game, 5 Anne ch. 14, § 5 (1706). *See also* An Act for the Preventing the Burning or Destroying of Goss, Furze or Ferne, in Forests or Chaces, 28 Geo. 2, ch. 19, § 3 (1755).

10) *E.g.,* An Act for Preservation of Spawn and Fry of Fish, 1 Eliz., ch. 17, § 2 (1558).

11) *E.g.,* No Man Shall Fasten Nets to Any Thing over Rivers, 2 Hen. 6, ch. 15 (1423); An Act for the Preservation of Fishing in the River Severn, 30 Car. 2, ch. 9 (1678).

12) *E.g.,* 32 Hen. 8, ch. 8 (1540); An Act for the Better Preservation of the Game, 5 Anne, ch. 14, § 2 (1706).

13) A statute enacted in 1390 -- None Shall Hunt but They Who Have a Sufficient Living, 13 Rich. 2, ch. 13 (1390) -- was the first in a series of increasingly comprehensive statutes restricting hunting of game to the landed gentry. These statutes culminated in An Act for the Better Preservation of the Game, and for Securing Warrens not Inclosed, and the Several Fishings of the Realm, 22 & 23 Car. 2, ch. 25 (1671). This statute formed the

basis of the game system until 1831.

14) Beginning in 1275, Parliament passed a series of statutes imposing both criminal and civil penalties. *See* Statute of Westminister I, ch. 20 (1275) (providing three years imprisonment for "trespassers in parks and ponds"). This group of statutes led to the Waltham Black Act, 9 Geo. I, ch. 22, § 1 (1723). The Black Act was a truly remarkable statute: it imposed capital punishment on various categories of individuals and offenses totalling between 200 and 250 separate offenses. On the Act and it social context, see E.P. THOMPSON, WHIGS AND HUNTERS (1975); L. Radzinowicz, *The Waltham Black Act: A Study of the Legislative Attitude Towards Crime in the Eighteenth Century,* 9 CAMB. L.J. 56 (1945); Pat Rogers, *The Waltham Blacks and the Black Act,* 17 HIST. J. 465 (1974).

15) JAMES A. TOBER, WHO OWNS THE WILDLIFE? 4 (1981).

16) *See* Thomas A. Lund, *Early American Wildlife Law,* 51 N.Y.U.L. REV. 703, 719-21 (1976).

17) *E.g.,* John F. Hart, *Colonial Land Use Law and Its Significance for Modern Takings Doctrine,* 109 HARV. L. REV. 1252 (1996).

18) *E.g., Curtis v. Hurlburt,* 2 Conn. 309 (1817); *Eastman v. Curtis,* 1 Conn. 323 (1815); *Cottrill v. Myrick,* 12 Me. 222 (1835); *Vinton v. Walsh,* 26 Mass. (9 Pick.) 87 (1829); *Stoughton v. Baker,* 4 Mass. 522 (1808); *Sickles v. Sharp,* 13 Johns. 497 (N.Y. Sup. Ct. 1816); *State v. Glen,* 52 N.C. 321 (1859); *Fagan v. Armistead,* 33 N.C. 433 (1850); *Hart v. Hill,* 1 Whart. 124 (Pa. 1835); *Boatwright v. Bookman,* 24 S.C.L. (Rice) 447 (1839).

19) THEODORE STEINBERG, NATURE INCORPORATED 83-84 (1991). *See also* Peter M. Molloy, *Nineteenth Century-Hydropower: Design and Construction of Lawrence Dam, 1845-1848,* 15 WINTERTHUR PORTFOLIO 315 (1980).

20) CHARLES E. POTTER, THE HISTORY OF MANCHESTER, FORMERLY DERRYFIELD IN NEW-HAMPSHIRE 651 (1856).

21) LAWRENCE M. FRIEDMAN, A HISTORY OF AMERICAN LAW 187 (2d ed. 1985). In wildlife law, this basic fact is reflected in the most common cases was a *qui tam* action -- effectively placing a bounty on bad guys -- rather than a criminal prosecution for poaching. And since many of the informers were identified as fish wardens, it appears that the wardens salary was dependent upon these actions -- an obvious incentive to bribery. CHARLES E. POTTER, *supra* note 20, at 651 ("The methods resorted to by the fishermen to elude the fish-wardens were various, the most common one doubtless being that of bribery."). Furthermore, reliance on *qui tam* actions was also ineffective in areas where most of the population was engaged in the activity: "It was found that in the neighborhood of large fishing-places, all were more or less interested in the fishing-rights; as a consequence, the statute remained a dead letter." *Id.* at 650.

22)

> The fish clandestinely obtained seemed to possess a peculiar flavor ... that legal restraint was impossible. On one occasion, as the disciples of Walton were playing an unlawful business on Long Island ... an obnoxious and officious official from Haverhill ... with his posse, pounced upon them, and the scene that ensued may be imagined. Donneybrook was outdone, the official and his party were repeatedly fished out of the river, after unceremonious baptisms by the faithful, and soon as possible beat a precipitate retreat without making any arrests, but with a wholesome lesson in prudence to guide them in the future enforcement of obnoxious laws.

J.W. MEADER, THE MERRIMACK RIVER 248-49 (1869).

23) LAWRENCE M. FRIEDMAN, *supra* note 21, at 284 (2d ed. 1985).

24) THEODORE STEINBERG, *supra* note 19, at 174.

25) *The Legislature and the Fish-way of the Essex Company,* LAWRENCE COURIER, May 20, 1856, quoted in THEODORE STEINBERG, *supra* note 19, at 179.

26) *See, e.g.*, HELENETTE SILVER, A HISTORY OF NEW HAMPSHIRE GAME AND FURBEARERS 195 (1957) (overhunting was the prime cause of the extermination of white-tailed deer in New Hampshire).

27) KURKPATRICK DORSEY, THE DAWN OF CONSERVATION DIPLOMACY 165-237 (1998). *See generally* SAMUEL P. HAYS, CONSERVATION AND THE GOSPEL OF EFFICIENCY (1959); Henry Clepper, *The Conservation Movement: Birth and Infancy, in* ORIGINS OF AMERICAN CONSERVATION 3 (Henry Clepper, ed. 1966).

28) George C. Coggins, *Grizzly Bears Don't Stop at Customs: A Preface to Transboundary Problems in Natural Resources Law,* 32 KAN. L. REV. 1 (1983); Dale D. Goble, *The Compact Clause and Transboundary Problems: "a Federal remedy for the disease most incident to a Federal Government,* 17 ENVTL. L. 785 (1987).

29) 161 U.S. 519 (1896). The earlier cases included *Martin v. Waddell,* 41 U.S. (16 Pet.) 367 (1842), *Smith v. Maryland,* 59 U.S. (18 How.) 71 (1855), *McCready v. Virginia,* 94 U.S. 391 (1876), and *Manchester v. Massachusetts,* 139 U.S. 240 (1890).

30) Act of Mar. 4, 1913, ch. 145, 37 828, 847 (commonly known as the Weeks-McLean Migratory Bird Act).

31) *E.g., United States v. Shauver,* 214 F. 154 (E.D. Ark. 1914), *dismissed as moot,* 248 U.S. 594 (1919).

32) JOHN H. INGHAM, THE LAW OF ANIMALS (1900).

33) *Id.* at § 128.

34) 6 N.J.L. 1 (1821).

35) *Id.* at 71-72.

36) *Corfield v. Coryell,* 6 F. Ca. 546, 547-48 (C.C.E.D. Pa. 1823) (No. 3,230). Subsequent developments can be traced in *Martin v. Waddell,* 41 U.S. (16 Pet.) 367 (1842), *Pollard v. Hagan,* 44 U.S. (3 How.) 212 (1845), *Smith v. Maryland,* 59 U.S. (18 How.) 71, 73 (1855), *McCready v. Virginia,* 94 U.S. 391 (1876), and *Manchester v. Massachusetts,* 139 U.S. 240 (1890).

37) *Geer v. Connecticut,* 161 U.S. 519, 527-28 (1896), *overruled on other grounds by Hushes v. Oklahoma,* 441 U.S. 322 (1979).

38) *Geer,* 161 U.S. at 534 (quoting *Magner v. The People,* 97 Illinois, 320, 333 (1881)).

39) Proponents of the state ownership doctrine ignored the Court's careful qualification that the state power extended only "so far as its exercise may not be incompatible with, or restrained by, the rights [sic] conveyed to the Federal government by the Constitution." *Geer v. Connecticut,* 161 U.S. at 528.

40) *See generally* MICHAEL J. BEAN, THE EVOLUTION OF NATIONAL WILDLIFE LAW 12-17 (rev. & expanded ed. 1983); JAMES A. TOBER, *supra* note 15, at 148-51 (discussion of state ownership doctrine).

41) Act of May 25, 1900, ch. 553, 31 Stat. 187. On the political battles leading to the enactment of the Lacey Act, see Theodore W. Cart, *The Lacey Act: America's First Nationwide Wildlife Statute,* FOREST HIST., Oct. 1973, at 4.

42) Act of 1913, ch. 145, 37 Stat. 828, 847-48.

43) OLIVER W. HOLMES, THE COMMON LAW 5 (Mark DeW. Howe ed., 1963) (1st ed. Boston, 1881).

44) *See Laurel Hill Cemetery v. City & County of San Francisco,* 216 U.S. 358, 366 (1910) ("the extent to which legislation may modify and restrict the uses of property consistently with the Constitution is not a question for pure abstract theory alone. Tradition and the habits of the community count for more than logic."). Holmes also made passing reference to the idea in his most famous wildlife law decision, *Missouri v. Holland,* writing that "[w]e must consider what this country has become in deciding what [the Tenth] Amendment has reserved." 252 U.S. 416, 434 (1920).

NOTES

45) *E.g.*, Andrew L. Kaufman, *Judges or Scholars: To Whom Shall We Look for Our Constitutional Law,* 37 J. LEGAL EDUC. 184 (1987); Laurence H. Tribe, *The Idea of the Constitution: A Metaphor-morphosis,* 37 J. LEGAL EDUC. 170 (1987).

46) JAMES B. TREFETHEN, AN AMERICAN CRUSADE FOR WILDLIFE 148 (1975). In the more politic -- and bloodless -- language of a contemporaneous Senate Report, the "strong temptation pressing upon every state to secure its full share of edible game birds during the spring and fall migrations ... rendered harmonious and effective State supervision impossible." S. REP. NO. 675, 62 Cong., 2d Sess. 1 (1912).

47) *See* STEPHEN FOX, THE AMERICAN CONSERVATION MOVEMENT 148-82 (1981); WILLIAM T. HORNADAY, THIRTY YEARS WAR FOR WILD LIFE 161-66 (1931).

48) Act of 1913, ch. 145, 37 Stat. 828, 847-48.

49) *E.g., United States v. Shauver,* 214 F. 154 (E.D. Ark. 1914), *appeal dismissed,* 248 U.S. 594 (1919); *United States v. McCullagh,* 221 F. 288 (D. Kan. 1915).

50) Convention with Great Britain for the Protection of Migratory Birds, art. I, 39 Stat. 1702, T.S. No. 628 (1916).

51) Act of July 3, 1918, ch. 128, 40 Stat. 755 (codified as amended at 16 U.S.C. §§ 703-704).

52) *Missouri v. Holland,* 252 U.S. 416, 435 (1920). *See generally* Charles A. Lofgren, *Missouri v. Holland in Historical Perspective,* 1975 SUP. CT. REV. 77.

53) *Missouri v. Holland,* 252 U.S. at 432. Article II, § 2, is the Treaty Making Power and delegates the President "Power, by and with the Advice and Consent of the Senate, to make Treaties, provided two-thirds of the Senate present shall concur." U.S. CONST. art. II, § 2, cl. 2. Article VI is the Supremacy Clause, which provides that "[t]his Constitution, and the Laws of the United States which shall be made in Pursuance thereof; and all Treaties made, or which shall be made, under the Authority of the United States, shall be the supreme Law of the Land." *Id.* art. VI. Article I, § 8, provides in part that "[t]he Congress shall have Power ... To make all Laws which shall be necessary and proper for carrying into Execution the foregoing Powers, and all other Powers vested by this Constitution in the Government of the United States, or in any Department or Officer thereof." *Id.* art. I, § 8, cl. 18.

54) The original treaty has been supplemented by treaties with Mexico, Japan, and the Soviet Union. *See* Convention for the Protection of Migratory Birds and Game Mammals, Feb. 7, 1936, U.S.-Mex., 50 Stat. 1311, T.S. No. 912; Convention for the Protection of Migratory Birds and Birds in Danger of Extinction, and their Environment, Mar. 4, 1972, U.S.-Japan, 25 U.S.T. 3329; Convention Concerning the Conservation of Migratory Birds and their Environment, Nov. 19, 1976, U.S.-U.S.S.R., 29 U.S.T. 4647, T.I.A.S. No. 9073. Other treaties on wildlife include: Treaty for the Preservation and Protection of Fur Seals, July 7, 1911, 37 Stat. 1542, T.S. No. 564; the International Convention for the Regulation of Whaling, Dec. 2, 1946, 62 Stat. 1716, T.I.A.S. 1849; Agreement on the Conservation of Polar Bears, Nov. 15, 1973, T.I.A.S. No. 8409. *See generally* DALE D. GOBLE & ERIC T. FREYFOGLE, WILDLIFE LAW 675-761 (2002).

55) *Missouri v. Holland,* 252 U.S. at 434.

56) The Property Clause provides that "Congress shall have Power to dispose of and make all needful Rules and Regulations respecting the Territory or other Property belonging to the United States." U.S. CONST. art. IV, § 3, cl. 2.

57) The story of the Kaibab deer herd can be found in THOMAS R. DUNLAP, SAVING AMERICA'S WILDLIFE 65-70 (1988); PETER MATTHIESSEN, WILDLIFE IN AMERICA 197-98 (1959).

58) ALDO LEOPOLD, *Thinking like a Mountain, in* SAND COUNTY ALMANAC 129, 130-32 (1968).

59) *Hunt v. United States,* 278 U.S. 96, 100 (1928).

60) *See New Mexico State Game Comm'n v. Udall,* 410 F.2d 1197 (10th Cir.), *cert. denied sub nom. New Mexico State Game Comm'n v. Hickel,* 396 U.S. 961 (1969); *Chalk v. United States,* 114 F.2d 207 (4th Cir. 1940).

61) 426 U.S. 529 (1976).

62) Pub. L. No. 92-195, 85 Stat. 649 (codified as amended 16 U.S.C. §§ 1331-1340 (1988)).

63) 16 U.S.C. § 1333(a).

64) *Kleppe v. New Mexico,* 426 U.S. at 540-41 (quoting *United States v. San Francisco,* 310 U.S. 16, 30 (1940)).

65) "We hold today that the Property Clause also gives Congress the power to protect wildlife on the public lands, state law notwithstanding." *Id.* at 546.

66) *Id.*

67) *Id.* at 539.

68) 167 U.S. 518 (1897). *See also McKelvey v. United States,* 260 U.S. 353, 359 (1922).

69) *See, e.g., Minnesota ex rel. Alexander v. Block,* 660 F.2d 1240, 1249 (8th Cir. 1981), *cert. denied,* 455 U.S. 1007 (1982).

70) *United States v. Brown,* 552 F.2d 817, 822 (8th Cir.), *cert. denied,* 431 U.S. 949 (1977); *see also Stupak-Thrall v. United States,* 843 F. Supp. 327 (W.D. Mich. 1994) (Forest Service may prohibit the use of such mechanical devices as fish-finders on lake where lake is boundary of wilderness ares and where plaintiffs are riparian owners on the lake).

71) *United States v. Brown,* 552 F.2d at 817.

72) *Organized Fishermen v. Andrus,* 488 F. Supp. 1351, 1355-56 (S.D. Fla. 1980).

73) *Nevada v. United States,* 547 F. Supp. 777, 777-78 (D. Nev. 1982), *aff'd,* 731 F.2d 633, 636 (9th Cir. 1984). A final point worth noting is the comment by the Court in *Kleppe* that "it is far from clear ... that Congress cannot assert a property interest in the regulated horses and burros superior to that of the State." *Kleppe v. New Mexico,* 426 U.S. at 537. The suggestion was echoed in a subsequent case involving an endangered species of Hawaiian honeycreeper, the Palila, where the district court noted that the "importance of preserving such a natural resource may be of such magnitude to rise to the level of a federal property interest." *Palila v. Hawaii Dept. of Land & Natural Resources,* 471 F. Supp. 985, 995 n.40 (D. Hawaii 1979), *aff'd,* 639 F.2d 495 (9th Cir. 1981).

74) U.S. CONST. art. I, § 8, cl. 3 ("The Congress shall have Power ... To regulate Commerce with foreign Nations, and among the several States, and with the Indian Tribes.").

75) A classic statement of the principles at work in the Commerce Clause cases is *United States v. E.C. Knight Co.,* 156 U.S. 1 (1895). Preservation of the states required the Court to ignore reality by crafting artificial and ultimately untenable constructions. *See generally* GEOFFREY R. STONE ET AL., CONSTITUTIONAL LAW 151-67 (2d ed. 1991).

76) *E.g., Hudson County Water Co. v. McCarter,* 209 U.S. 349, 357-58 (1908); *Geer v. Connecticut,* 161 U.S. 519 (1896).

77) The formalistic lines led to distinctions that in retrospect can only be seen as absurd. *E.g.,* Note, *Limitation by a State of Exportation of Its Natural Resources,* 24 COLUM. L. REV. 64 (1924) (discussing *Pennsylvania v. West Virginia,* 262 U.S. 553 (1923)).

78) *E.g., Pennsylvania v. West Virginia,* 262 U.S. 553 (1923); *West v. Kansas Natural Gas Co.,* 221 U.S. 229 (1911).

79) *E.g., Toomer v. Witsell,* 334 U.S. 385, 405-06 (1948) (*Geer* did not save state statute requiring shrimp to be unloaded within state; statute violated dormant Commerce Clause); *Foster Packing v. Haydel,* 278 U.S. 1, 16 (1928) (same conclusion on state statute holding that shrimp had to be processed within state).

80) *Douglas v. Seacoast Products, Inc.,* 431 U.S. 265, 284 (1977).

81) 441 U.S. 322 (1979).

NOTES

82) *Cf. Maine v. Taylor,* 477 U.S. 131 (1986) (upholding state statute prohibiting the importation of live baitfish based on finding that the statute protected resident wild species from parasites and unpredictable ecological impacts); *see also Baldwin v. Fish & Game Comm'n,* 436 U.S. 371, 390 (1978) (substantially higher non-resident hunting and fishing license fees violate neither the Privileges and Immunities Clause nor the Equal Protection Clause of the Fourteenth Amendment because it is a "legislative choice [that] was an economic means not unreasonably related to the preservation of a finite resource and a substantial regulatory interest to the State.").

83) 22 U.S. (9 Wheat.) 1 (1824).

84) *E.g., Geer v. Connecticut,* 161 U.S. 519, 528 (1896) (power to regulate the taking of game held by the states "in so far as its exercise may not be incompatible with, or restrained by, the rights conveyed to the Federal government by the Constitution."); *McCready v. Virginia,* 94 U.S. 391, 394 (1876) (state title "is held subject to the paramount right of navigation, the regulation of which, in respect to foreign and inter-state commerce, has been granted to the United States.).

85) 431 U.S. 265 (1977).

86) *Id.* at 281-82 (footnote omitted).

87) *Id.* at 282.

88) 444 U.S. 51, 63 n.19 (1979).

89) 130 F.3d 1041 (D.C. Cir. 1997), *cert. denied,* 524 U.S. 937 (1998).

90) 417 U.S. 111, 125 (1942).

91) *See also Gibbs v. Babbitt,* 214 F.3d 483 (4th Cir. 2000), *cert. denied sub nom., Gibbs v. Norton,* 531 U.S. 1135 (2001); *United States v. Bramble,* 103 F.3d 1475 (9th Cir. 1996); *GDF Realty Investments, Ltd. v. Norton,* 169 F. Supp. 2d 648 (W.D. Tex. 2001).

92) *See* 5 U.S.C. § 903 note.

93) The Secretary of Commerce's functions "relating to the protection of fur seals and other fur-bearing animals, to the supervision of the Pribilof Islands ... and to the Whaling Treaty Act" were also transferred to the Secretary of the Interior.

94) *See* 5 U.S.C. § 903 note.

95) Act of Aug. 8, 1956, ch. 1036, 70 Stat. 1119.

96) *See* 84 Stat. 2090 (effective Oct. 3, 1970).

97) Fish & Wildlife Service, Department of the Interior, & National Oceanic & Atmospheric Administration, Department of Commerce, *Interagency Cooperation,* 51 Fed. Reg. 19,926, 19,926 (June 3, 1986).

98) 16 U.S.C. 3373.

99) *Id.* §§ 706-707.

100) *Id.* § 668.

101) *Id.* § 742j-1.

102) *Id.* § 1362(12)(A).

103) *Id.* § 1532(15).

104) *Id.* § 4702(4).

105) *Id.* § 4903(6).

106) *Id.* § 6103(3).

107) *Id.* § 1362(12)(A)(1).

108) 16 U.S.C. § 1802(34).

109) *Id.* § 1532(15).

CHAPTER 1: Species Conservation

1) Ch. 273, § 6, 15 Stat. 240, 241 (repealed 1944).

2) Act of July 1, 1870, ch. 189, 16 Stat. 180.

3) *See* GUY A. BALDASSARRE & ERIC G. BOLEN, WATERFOWL ECOLOGY AND MANAGEMENT 517-20 (1994).

4) *See generally* WILLIAM CRONON, NATURE'S METROPOLIS 55-93, 230-35 (1991); A.W. SCHORGER, THE PASSENGER PIGEON 144 (1955).

5) *See generally* KURKPATRICK DORSEY, THE DAWN OF CONSERVATION DIPLOMACY (1998); ROBIN W. DOUGHTY, FEATHER FASHIONS AND BIRD PRESERVATION (1975); THOMAS R. DUNLAP, SAVING AMERICA'S WILDLIFE (1988); STEPHEN FOX, THE AMERICAN CONSERVATION MOVEMENT (1981); SAMUEL P. HAYS, CONSERVATION AND THE GOSPEL OF EFFICIENCY (1959); JOHN F. REIGER, AMERICAN SPORTSMEN AND THE ORIGIN OF CONSERVATION 3d ed. 2001); Theodore Whaley Cart, *The Lacey Act: America's First Nationwide Wildlife Statute,* FOREST. HIST., Oct. 1973, at 4; Dale D. Goble, *Salmon in the Columbia Basin: From Abundance to Extinction, in* NORTHWEST LANDS, NORTHWEST PEOPLES 229 (Dale D. Goble & Paul W. Hirt eds., 1999).

6) The Act was predicated upon the constitutional jurisprudence that had developed under the then-politically sensitive question of temperance. In *Bowman v. Chicago & Nw. Ry.,* 125 U.S. 465 (1888), the Court held that a statute prohibiting the transportation of intoxicating liquors into the state was unconstitutional because it regulated interstate commerce: "the right to prohibit sales ... arises only after the act of transportation has terminated." *Id.* at 499. Two years later, it extended the holding in *Bowman* to include the first sale after transportation into the state as long as that sale was of an unopened packages: "Under our decision in *Bowman* [defendants] had the right to import this beer into that State, and ... they had the right to sell it, by which act alone it would become mingled in the common mass of property within the State." *Leisy v. Hardin,* 135 U.S. 100, 124 (1890). The Court qualified this conclusion by noting that it applied "in the absence of congressional permission" to prohibit the importation. *Id.* Congress responded by enacting a statute making intoxicating liquors "subject to the operation and effect of the laws" of the importing state "upon arrival in such State." Act of Aug. 8, 1890, ch. 728, 26 Stat. 313. The Court upheld the constitutionality of the federal statute. *In re Rahrer,* 140 U.S. 545 (1891).

7) *Quoted in* John C. Phillips, *Migratory Bird Protection in North America* 7 (American Committee for International Wild Life Protection, Special Pub. No. 4, 1934).

8) Act of 1913, ch. 145, 37 Stat. 828, 847-48.

9) *E.g., United States v. Shauver,* 214 F. 154 (E.D. Ark. 1914), *appeal dismissed,* 248 U.S. 594 (1919); *United States v. McCullagh,* 221 F. 288 (D. Kan. 1915).

10) Convention with Great Britain for the Protection of Migratory Birds, art. I, 39 Stat. 1702, T.S. No. 628 (1916).

11) 252 U.S. 416 (1920).

12) Ch. 128, 40 Stat. 755.

13) Act of May 20, 1926, ch. 346, 44 Stat. 576.

14) June 17, 1930, ch. 497, Title IV, § 527, 46 Stat. 741.

15) 16 U.S.C. § 668 note.

16) Act of June 8, 1940, ch. 278, 54 Stat. 250. Congress had considered protecting the bald eagles during the 1930s, but the livestock industry managed to prevent the adoption of a statute until 1940.

17) *Cf. The Case of Swans,* 7 Co. Rep. 15b, 77 Eng. Rep. 435 (K.B. 1592) (the king owns swans -- and thus can regulate access to them -- because they are regal birds).

18) Act of Oct. 15, 1966, Pub. L. No. 89-669, §§ 1-3, 80 Stat. 926, *repealed by* Endangered Species Act of 1973, Pub. L. No. 93-205, § 14, 87 Stat. 884, 903 (1973).

19) Act of Oct. 15, 1966, Pub. L. No. 89-669, §§ 4-5, 80 Stat. 926 (codified as amended at 16 U.S.C. §§ 668ddd-668ee).

20) Endangered Species Preservation Act of 1966, Pub. L. No. 89-669, § 1(a), 80 Stat. 926, 926; *see also* S. REP. NO. 1463, 89th Cong., 2d Sess. 2, (1966), *reprinted in* 1966 U.S.C.C.A.N. 3342, 3343, 3344; H.R. REP. NO. 1168, 89th Cong., 1st Sess. 2-3, 4 (1965).

21) Pub. L. No. 91-135, § 12(d), 83 Stat. 275, 283, *repealed by* Endangered Species Act of 1973, Pub. L. No. 93-205, § 14, 87 Stat. 884, 903 (1973).

22) Act of Dec. 15, 1971, Pub. L. No. 86-234, 73 Stat. 470 (codified as amended at 16 U.S.C. 1331-1340).

23) 16 U.S.C. § 1331.

24) Act of Oct. 21, 1972, Pub. L. 92-522, 86 Stat. 1027 (codified as amended at 16 U.S.C. §§ 1361-1407).

25) Act of Apr. 13, 1976, Pub. L. 94-265, 90 Stat. 331 (codified as amended at 16 U.S.C. § 1801-1883).

26) 426 U.S. 529 (1976).

27) Under the Reorganization Plan No. II of 1939, these functions were transferred to the Secretary of the Interior.

28) The text of 18 U.S.C. § 42 is set out in Chapter 4.

29) The current version is at 16 U.S.C. § 3372(a).

30) The current version is at 16 U.S.C. § 3372(b).

31) Act of Mar. 4, 1909, ch. 321, § 341, 35 Stat. 1153.

32) Section 5's provisions were repealed by the Lacey Act Amendments of 1981, Pub. L. No. 97-79, § 9(b)(2), 95 Stat. 1073, 1079 (formerly codified at 16 U.S.C. § 667e and 18 U.S.C. § 43). The repeal of section 5 had no effect following the Supreme Court's decision in *New York ex rel. Silz v. Hesterberg,* 211 U.S. 31 (1908), that the receiving state had the constitutional power to criminalize possession of game out of season regardless of its origin and independent of the Lacey Act.

33) Lacey Act Amendments of 1981, Pub. L. No. 97-79, 95 Stat. 1073.

34) Ch. 128, 40 Stat. 755.

35) Convention with Great Britain for the Protection of Migratory Birds, art. I, 39 Stat. 1702, T.S. No. 628 (1916).

36) *Id.* art. II, ¶¶ 2, 3. The Convention created an exception for scientific research "under permits issued by proper authorities," *id.*, and for native subsistence hunting of migratory nongame birds, *id.* ¶ 3.

37) *Id.* ¶ 1.

38) Convention for the Protection of Migratory Birds and Game Mammals, Feb. 7, 1936, U.S.-Mex., 50 Stat. 1311, T.S. No. 912.

39) Convention for the Protection of Migratory Birds and Birds in Danger of Extinction, and their Environment, Mar. 4, 1972, U.S.-Japan, 25 U.S.T. 3329.

40) Convention Concerning the Conservation of Migratory Birds and Their Environment, Nov. 19, 1976, U.S.-U.S.S.R., 29 U.S.T. 4647, T.I.A.S. No. 9073.

41) Following the negotiation of the Convention between the United States of America and Mexico for the Protection of Migratory Birds and Game Mammals, Feb. 7, 1936, U.S.-Mex., 50 Stat. 1311, T.S. No. 912, Congress did amend the MBTA by adding "at any time, by any means or in any manner" to its description of prohibited conduct. Act of June 20, 1936, ch. 634, § 3, 49 Stat. 1555, 1556 (codified at 16 U.S.C. § 703.

42) Act of July 3, 1918, ch. 128, § 2, 40 Stat. 755, 755.

43) 16 U.S.C. § 703.

44) *Id.* § 704.

45) June 17, 1930, ch. 497, Title IV, § 527, 46 Stat. 741.

46) 16 U.S.C. § 668 note. *Cf. The Case of Swans,* 7 Co. Rep. 15b, 77 Eng. Rep. 435 (K.B. 1592).

47) Act of Oct. 24, 1962, Pub. L. No. 87-884, 76 Stat. 1246.
48) Act of Oct. 23, 1972, Pub. L. No. 82-535, § 1, 86 Stat. 1064.
49) *Andrus v. Allard,* 444 U.S. 51, 56 (1979).
50) *See* 32 Fed. Reg. 4001 (Mar. 11, 1967).
51) Velma B. Johnston, *Review: The Fight to Save A Memory,* 50 TEX. L. REV. 1055, 1057 (1972).
52) *See* Kenneth P. Pitt, *The Wild Free-Roaming Horses and Burros Act: A Western Melodrama,* 15 ENVTL L. 503 (1985).
53) Act of Sept. 8, 1959, Pub. L. No. 86-234, § 1(a), 73 Stat. 470.
54) Act of Nov. 18, 1971, Pub. L. No. 92-159, § 1, 85 Stat. 481. The Act was held to be unconstitutional as an invasion of the Tenth Amendment in a strange decision by the Federal District Court of Montana. *United States v. Helsey,* 463 F. Supp. 1111 (D. Mont 1979). The decision was subsequently reversed in an acerbic Ninth Circuit decision. *United States v. Helsley,* 615 F.2d 784 (9th Cir. 1979).
55) 16 U.S.C. § 742j-1(b)(1).
56) Velma B. Johnston, *supra* note 51, at 1059-62.
57) Act of Dec. 15, 1971, Pub. L. No. 86-234, 73 Stat. 470 (codified as amended at 16 U.S.C. 1331-1340).
58) S. Rep. 242, 92d Cong., 1st Sess. 1 (1971).
59) 16 U.S.C. § 1331.
60) 16 U.S.C. § 1338(a)(1)-(5).
61) 16 U.S.C. § 1331.
62) *Id.* § 1333(a).
63) *Id.* § 1633 note (repealed in 1978).
64) *Compare American Horse Protection Ass'n, Inc. v. Frizzell,* 403 F. Supp. 1206 (D. Nev. 1975) (rejecting argument that wild horses were to be accorded higher priority than other grazers), *with American Horse Protection Ass'n v. Kleppe,* 6 Envtl. L. Rep. (Envtl. L. Inst.) 20802 (D.D.C. 1976) (holding an agency decision to round up horses to be arbitrary and capricious because it failed to consider all alternatives that would have less of an impact on horse populations).
65) *Id.* § 1633(b)(2).
66) *Id.* § 1332(f). *See American Horse Protection Ass'n v. Watt,* 694 1310, 1315 (D.C. Cir. 1982); *see generally* DALE D. GOBLE & ERIC T.. FREYFOGLE, WILDLIFE LAW 893-94 (2002).
67) *Cf.* Susan M. Schectman, *The "Bambi Syndrome": How NEPA's Public Participation in Wildlife Management is Hurting the Environment,* 8 ENVTL. L. 611 (1978).
68) Act of July 1, 1870, ch. 189, 16 Stat. 180.
69) Treaty for the Preservation and Protection of Fur Seals, July 7, 1911, 37 Stat. 1542, T.S. No. 564. *See generally* KURKPATRICK DORSEY, *supra* note 5, at 105-64.
70) The Interim Convention on the Conservation of North Pacific Fur Seals, Feb. 9, 1957, 8 U.S.T. 2283, T.I.A.S. No. 3948, 314 U.N.T.S. 105.
71) Act of Oct. 21, 1972, Pub. L. 92-522, 86 Stat. 1027 (codified as amended at 16 U.S.C. §§ 1361-1407). *But see* 16 U.S.C. §§ 1151-1175 (regulations applicable to fur seal rookeries on federal land in the Pribilof Island).
72) George C. Coggins, *Federal Wildlife Law Achieves Adolescence: Developments in the 1970s,* 1978 DUKE L.J. 753, 786.
73) 16 U.S.C. § 1379(a).
74) *Id.* § 1379.
75) *Id.* §§ 1372, 1362(10).
76) *Id.* § 1371(a).
77) *Id.* §§ 1373, 1374.

78) "Maximum sustained yield" is an economic rather than an ecological concept that focuses on the harvest the species, *i.e.*, "the maximization of production." *See, e.g.*, FRANCIS T. CHRISTY & ANTHONY SCOTT, THE COMMON WEALTH IN OCEAN FISHERIES 7-15, 215-21 (1965).

79) Marine Mammal Protection Act of 1972, Pub. L. No. 95-522, § 3(9), 86 Stat. 1027, 1029 (codified as amended at 16 U.S.C. § 1362(8)0.

80) *See, e.g., id.* § 1371(a)(3)(A).

81) *See id.* §§ 1362(19), (20), (24), 1386, 1387.

82) *Id.* § 1387(f).

83) The best short introduction to the MMPA is MICHAEL J. BEAN & MELANIE J. ROWLAND, THE EVOLUTION OF NATIONAL WILDLIFE LAW 108-37 (3d ed. 1997).

84) Act of Feb. 9, 1871, 16 Stat. 593. *See generally* MICHAEL J. BEAN & MELANIE J. ROWLAND, *supra* note 83, at 148; DALE D. GOBLE & ERIC T. FREYFOGLE, *supra* note 66, at 924-27; Eldon V.C. Greenberg, *Ocean Fisheries, in* ENVIRONMENTAL LAW 258 (Celia Campbell-Mohn ed., 1993); EDWARD MILES *ET AL.*, THE MANAGEMENT OF MARINE REGIONS 52-82 (1982); Wilbert M. Chapman, *The Theory and Practice of International Fishery Development-Management,* 7 SAN DIEGO L. REV. 408 (1970).

85) *Pollard v. Hagan,* 44 U.S. (3 How.) 212 (1845); *Martin v. Waddell,* 41 U.S. (16 Pet.) 367 (1842).

86) *See Manchester v. Massachusetts,* 139 U.S. 240 (1890) (mackerel); *McCready v. Virginia,* 94 U.S. 391 (1876) (oysters); *Smith v. Maryland,* 59 U.S. (18 How.) 71 (1855) (oysters).

87) Federal regulation of fishing by United States citizens beyond the territorial limits of the states was permissible but uncommon. *See* 16 U.S.C. §§ 781-785 (regulating the taking of commercial sponges "by any citizen of the United States, or person owing duty of obedience to the laws of the United States ... outside of state territorial limits"). *See also The Abby Dodge,* 223 U.S. 166 (1912).

88) 3 Cai. 175 (N.Y. 1805).

89) The states were, however, happy to accept federal funding for fisheries projects such as fish hatcheries. *See, e.g.,* Act of May 11, 1938, ch. 193, 52 Stat. 345 (codified at 16 U.S.C. § 755) (authorizing the establishment of a salmon "cultural" station). *See generally* 16 U.S.C. §§ 755-760g (various hatchery statutes).

90) As noted in the Introduction, state regulatory authority -- particularly over nonresidents -- was limited over the course of the twentieth century under the dormant Commerce Clause, *Toomer v. Witsell,* 334 U.S. 365 (1948); the Privileges and Immunities Clause, *id.*; the Equal Protection Clause, *Takahashi v. Fish & Game Commission,* 334 U.S. 410 (1948); and the Affirmative Commerce Clause, *Douglas v. Seacoast Products,* 431 U.S. 265 (1977).

91) *E.g.,* Convention on the Sockeye Salmon Fisheries, May 26, 1930, Canada-United States, 50 Stat. 1355, T.S. No. 918. For representative statutes implementing high-seas fishery treaties, see Tuna Conventions Act of 1950, 16 U.S.C. §§ 951-962; Atlantic Tuna Conventions Act of 1975, 16 U.S.C. §§ 971-971k; Eastern Pacific Tuna Licensing Act of 1984, 16 U.S.C. §§ 972-972h; South Pacific Tuna Act of 1988, 16 U.S.C. §§ 973-973r.

92) *See* Bartlett Act, Pub. L. No. 88-308, 78 Stat. 194 (1964) (repealed 1977); Contiguous Fisheries Zone Act, Pub. L. No. 89-658, 80 Stat. 908 (1966) (repealed 1977).

93) Warren Magnuson, *The Fishery Conservation and Management Act of 1976: First Step Toward Improved Management of Marine Fisheries,* 52 WASH. L. REV. 427, 431 (1977).

94) Act of Apr. 13, 1976, Pub. L. 94-265, 90 Stat. 331 (codified as amended at 16 U.S.C. § 1801-1883).

95) 16 U.S.C. § 1811. The EEZ was initially the "*fishery* conservation zone." The term was expanded following conclusion of the United National Law of the Sea Convention established the EEZ concept. Law of the Sea Convention, arts. 55, 61, 62, U.N. Doc. No A/Conf. 62/122 (Dec. 10, 1982). The United States has never signed the Convention.

96) 16 U.S.C. § 1821(a).

97) NATIONAL ACADEMY OF SCIENCES, SHARING THE FISH 13-14 (1999).

98) *Id.* §§ 1801(b)(3), (6).

99) *Id.* § 1801(b)(1). The Act defines "conservation" and "management" to be synonymous. *Id.* § 1802(5).

100) Those species such as salmon that spawn in fresh water and then migrate to the sea.

101) 16 U.S.C. § 1811(b)(1).

102) *Id.* § 1811(b)(2).

103) *Id.* § 1802(7).

104) *Id.* § 1802(20).

105) *Id.* § 1852(a).

106) *Id.* § 1852(h)(1).

107) *Id.* §§ 1851(a)(1)-(10).

108) *Id.* § 1851(a)(2).

109) *Id.* § 1851(a)(1).

110) *Id.* § 1802(28).

111) "Overfishing" is "a rate or level of fishing mortality that jeopardizes the capacity of a fishery to produce the maximum sustainable yield on a continuing basis." *Id.* § 1802(29). "Maximum sustainable yield" is the harvest level that can be consistently taken without reducing stocks; it thus ensures perpetually sustainable level. While it is a beguiling concept, it has proven remarkably unsuccessful as a wildlife management strategy. *See, e.g.,* DALE D. GOBLE & ERIC T. FREYFOGLE, *supra* note 66, at 894-96.

112) *Id.* §§ 1854, 1857.

113) 16 U.S.C. § 6101(1).

114) Act of July 20, 2000, Pub. L. No. 106-247, 114 Stat. 593 (codified at 16 U.S.C. §§ 6101-6109.

115) 16 U.S.C. § 6108.

116) *Id.* § 6104(a).

117) Act of Oct. 23, 1992, Pub. L. No. 102-440 (codified at 16 U.S.C. §§ 4901-4916).

118) That is, birds that are "not indigenous to the 50 States or the District of Columbia." 16 U.S.C. § 4903(2)(A).

119) African Elephant Conservation Act, 16 U.S.C. §§ 4201-4246; Asian Elephant Conservation Fund, 4261-4266.

120) Rhinoceros and Tiger Conservation Act of 1998, 16 U.S.C. §§ 5301-5306.

121) Great Ape Conservation Act of 2000, 16 U.S.C. §§ 6301-6305.

122) H.R. Rep. No. 102-749(II), 102d Cong., 2d Sess. 7, *reprinted in* 1992 U.S.C.C.A.N. 1610, 1610.

123) H.R. Rep. No. 102-749(I), 102d Cong., 2d Sess. 9, *reprinted in* 1992 U.S.C.C.A.N. 1592, 1594.

124) 27 U.S.T. 1087, T.I.A.S. No. 8249 (Mar. 3, 1973).

125) *Id.*

126) 16 U.S.C. § 4904.

127) *Id.* § 4907

128) *Id.* § 4905(b).

129) *Id.* § 4905(c).

130) *Id.* §§ 4910, 4912.

131) *Id.* § 4913.

132) *Id.*

133) *Id.* § 4212. The Rhinoceros and Tiger Conservation Act established a similar fund. *Id.* § 5305. In 1998, Congress created the Multinational Species Conservation Fund to house donations and penalties received under the two statutes as well as the Asian Elephant Conservation Act. Act of Oct. 21, 1998, Pub. L. No. 105-277, Div. A, § 101(e), 112 Stat. 2681-237 (currently codified at 16 U.S.C. § 4246).

134) *Id.* § 4211. *See also* The Rhinoceros and Tiger Conservation Act, *id.* § 5304.

135) 16 U.S.C. §§ 4223-4224. *See also* The Rhinoceros and Tiger Conservation Act, *id.* § 5305a.

136) Asian Elephant Conservation Act, *id.* §§ 4264-4265; Great Apes Conservation Act, *id.* §§ 6303-6304.

137) 16 U.S.C. 3373.

138) *Id.* §§ 706-707.

139) *Id.* § 668.

140) *Id.* § 742j-1.

141) *Id.* § 1362(12)(A).

142) *Id.* § 1532(15).

143) *Id.* § 4903(6).

144) *Id.* § 1362(12)(A)(1).

145) 16 U.S.C. § 1802(34).

146) *Id.* § 1532(15).

147) Act of Dec. 15, 1971, Pub. L. No. 86-234, 73 Stat. 470 (codified as amended at 16 U.S.C. 1331-1340).

CHAPTER 2: Habitat Conservation

1) *See* PAUL W. GATES, HISTORY OF PUBLIC LAND LAW DEVELOPMENT 321-32 (photo reprint 1979) (1968).

2) IRA N. GABRIELSON, WILDLIFE REFUGES 6 (1943).

3) Yellowstone Park Act, 17 Stat. 32 (Mar. 1, 1872) [currently codified at 30 U.S.C. §§ 21-22).

4)

> Congress had riches to bestow -- in lands, tariffs, subsidies, favors of all sorts; and when influential citizens made their wishes known to the reigning statesmen, the sympathetic politicians were quick to turn the government into the fairy godmother the voters wanted it to be. A huge barbecue was spread to which all presumably were invited. Not quite all, to be sure; inconspicuous persons, those who were at home on the farm or at work in the mills and offices, were overlooked; a good many indeed out of the total number of the America people. But all the important persons, leading bankers and promoters and business men, received invitations. There wasn't room for everybody and these were presumed to represent the whole. It was a splendid feast. If the waiters saw to it that the choicest portions were served to favored guests, they were not unmindful of their numerous homespun constituency and they loudly proclaimed the fine democratic principle that what belongs to the people should be enjoyed by the people -- not with petty bureaucratic restrictions, not as a social body, but as individuals, each free citizen using what came to hand for his own private ends, with no questions asked.
>
> It was sound Gilded Age doctrine. To a frontier people what was more democratic than barbecue, and to a paternalistic age what was more fitting than

that the state should provide the beeves for roasting.

VERNON L. PARRINGTON, BEGINNINGS OF CRITICAL REALISM IN AMERICA: 1860-1920, at 23 (1958).

5) 42 U.S.C. §§ 4321, 4331-4335.

6) Quoted in NATHANIEL P. REED & DENNIS DRABELLE, THE UNITED STATES FISH AND WILDLIFE SERVICE 7 (1984). The agency's founding myth is set out by Reed and Drabelle, *id.* at 5-8, and in Lynn Greenwalt, *The National Wildlife Refuge System, in* WILDLIFE IN AMERICA 399 (Howard P. Brokaw ed., 1978). As Michael Bean has noted, the first refuge might in fact be the reservation of Afognak Island in Alaska by President Benjamin Harrison in 1892 "in order that salmon fisheries in the waters of the Island, and salmon and other fish and sea animals, and other animals and birds ... may be protected and preserved unimpaired." Proclamation No. 39, 27 Stat. 1052 (1892); MICHAEL J. BEAN, THE EVOLUTION OF NATIONAL WILDLIFE LAW 22 n.59 (rev. & expanded ed. 1983). Benjamin Harrison, however, lacks the romantic cache of Teddy Roosevelt.

7) U.S. FISH & WILDLIFE SERVICE, U.S. DEPARTMENT OF THE INTERIOR, REFUGES 2003 at 1-2 (Draft Environmental Impact Statement, 1993).

8) Act of May 23, 1908, ch. 192, 35 Stat. 267 (National Bison Range in Montana) (codified as amended at 16 U.S.C. § 671 (1988)). The following year, Congress appropriated funds to acquire unspecified lands for refuges. Act of Mar. 4, 1909, ch. 301, 35 Stat. 1051.

9) Act of Feb. 18, 1929, ch. 257, 45 Stat. 1222. *See generally* THOMAS R. DUNLAP, SAVING AMERICA'S WILDLIFE 65-83 (1988).

10) 16 U.S.C. 715d.

11) *Id.* § 715f.

12) *Id.* § 715c. The Act also prohibits the designation of "any part of any national forest or power site" as a migratory bird reserve "except by and with the consent of the legislature of the State wherein such forest or power site is located." 16 U.S.C. § 715*o*.

13) *Id.* § 715a.

14) *Id.* § 715g.

15) *Id.* § 715h.

16) *Id.* § 715i(a).

17) *Id.* § 715i(b).

18) *Id.* § 715p.

19) Act of March 16, 1934, ch. 71, 48 Stat. 452.

20) 16 U.S.C. § 718a.

21) *Id.* §§ 718g, 707.

22) *Id.* § 718c.

23) The Act authorizes the Secretary of the Interior to set the price at "not less than $3 and not more than $5" unless the Secretary determines that all sums either appropriated by Congress or derived from the sale of stamps "have been obligated for expenditure." If the Secretary so determines, the stamps cost $7.50. *Id.* § 718(b).

24) *Id.* § 718d. These "small wetland and pothole areas" are to be known as "Waterfowl Production Areas" and "may be acquired without regard to the limitations and requirements of the Migratory Bird Conservation Act." *Id.* § 718d(c).

25) *Id.* §§ 718d(b), (c).

26) Funding was increased in 1976 (Act of Feb. 17, 1976, Pub. L. No. 94-215, § 2(a), 90 Stat. 189), and repayment was extended in 1967 (Act of Dec. 15, 1967, Pub. L. No. 90-205, § 1(b), 81 Stat. 612), 1976 (Act of Feb. 17, 1976, Pub. L. No. 94-215, § 2(b), 90 Stat. 189), 1983 (Act of Dec. 2, 1983, Pub. L. No. 98-200, § 2, 97 Stat. 1378), and 1984 (Act of Oct. 26, 1984, Pub. L. No. 98-548, § 102, 98 Stat. 2774).

27) Act of Nov. 10, 1986, Pub. L. No. 99-645, § 101(b), 100 Stat. 3584.

NOTES

28) 16 U.S.C. §§ 431-433.

29) An important point to note is that even within a "system" there is likely to be a high degree of individualized management requirements.

30) Migratory Bird Conservation Act of 1929, ch. 257, § 5, 45 Stat. 1223 (codified as amended at 16 U.S.C. §§ 715a-715r (1988)).

31) *Id.* § 5.

32) Act of June 15, 1935, ch. 261, § 401, 49 Stat. , 383.

33) Act of Aug. 30, 1964, Pub. L. No. 88-523, 78 Stat. 701.

34) Act of Aug. 30, 1964, Pub. L. No. 88-523, 78 Stat. 701 (codified as amended at 16 U.S.C. § 715s (1988)).

35) Act of Aug. 12, 1949, ch. 421, 63 Stat. 599.

36) Act of Aug. 1, 1958, Pub. L. No. 85-585, 72 Stat. 486.

37) Act of June 25, 1948, ch. , 62 Stat. 686 (codified at 18 U.S.C. § 41).

38) Act of Nov. 14, 1988, Pub. L. No. 100-653, § 904, 102 Stat. 3825, 3834.

39) Act of Sept. 28, 1962, Pub. L. No. 87-714, 76 Stat. 653 (codified as amended at 16 U.S.C. §§ 460k through 460k-4 (1988)).

40) 16 U.S.C. § 460k.

41) H.R. Rep. No. 106, 105th Cong., 1st Sess. 2 (1997), *reprinted at* 1997 U.S.C.C.A.N. 1798-5, 1798-6.

42) Act of Oct. 15, 1966 Pub. L. No. 89-669, §§ 4-5, 80 Stat. 926, 927 (currently codified as amended at 16 U.S.C. §§ 668dd-668ee). The Refuge Administration Act was initially sections 4 and 5 of a statute that was subsequently named the Endangered Species Preservation Act of 1966. It was not denominated the National Wildlife Refuge System Administration Act until the Endangered Species Conservation Act of 1969. *See* Endangered Species Conservation Act of 1969, Pub. L. No. 91-137, § 12(f), 83 Stat. 275, 283.

Congress established the United States Fish and Wildlife in the Fish and Wildlife Act of 1956, ch. 1036, 70 Stat. 1120 (Aug. 8, 1956) (codified as amended at 16 U.S.C. §§ 742a-754a). The Act gave the agency a variety of administrative powers but provided only incidental directives on managing the lands under the agency's jurisdiction.

43) *See* 16 U.S.C. § 668dd(a)(1).

44) *See, e.g.*, NATHANIEL P. REED & D. DRABELLE, THE UNITED STATES FISH AND WILDLIFE SERVICE (1984).

45) 16 U.S.C. § 460k.

46) S. Rep. 1463, 89th Cong., 2d Sess. (1966), *reprinted in* 1966 U.S.C.C.A.N. 3342, 3346.

47) *Id.* at 3347.

48) 16 U.S.C. § 66bdd(d)(1)(A).

49) Act of Oct. 9, 1997, Pub. L. No. 105-57, 111 Stat. 1252 (codified at 16 U.S.C. §§ 668dd-668ee).

50) H.R. Rep. No. 106, 105th Cong., 1st Sess. 3 (1997), *reprinted at* 1997 U.S.C.C.A.N. 1798-5, 1798-7.

51) *Id.* at 8, *reprinted in* 1997 U.S.C.C.A.N. at 198-12.

52) 16 U.S.C. § 668dd(a)(2).

53) *Id.* § 668ee(1).

54) 16 U.S.C. § 668bb(d)(3).

55) 16 U.S.C. §§ 1600-1614.

56) 43 U.S.C. §§ 1701-1781.

57) 16 U.S.C. § 668dd(e).

58) *Id.* § 668dd(e)(1)(E).

59) *Id.* § 668dd(f)-(g).

60) *See* 15 C.F.R. part 922 (listing the sanctuaries and the regulation applicable to each).

61) Act of Oct. 23, 1972, Pub. L. No. 92-532, Title. III, 86 Stat. 1052, 1061 (currently codified as amended at 16 U.S.C. §§ 1431-1445b).
62) Oceans Act of 1992, Pub. L. No. 102-587, Title II, 106 Stat. 5039, 5039.
63) 16 U.S.C. § 1433(a).
64) *Id.* § 1431(b)(3).
65) *Id.* § 4133(b)(1)(A).
66) *Id.* § 1433(b)(2).
67) *Id.* § 1434(a)(2).
68) *Id.* § 1434(a).
69) *Id.* § 1431(b)(5).
70) *Id.* § 1434(d)(1)(A).
71) *Id.* § 1436.
72) *Id.* § 1437(c)(1).
73) *Id.* § 1437(d)(1).
74) *Id.* § 1443(a)(1).
75) 161 U.S. 519 (1896).
76) *See, e.g., United States v. E.C. Knight Co.*, 156 U.S. 1 (1895) (company that controlled 98% of sugar refining in the United States was not part of interstate commerce and could not be regulated as a monopoly).
77) Morton Grodzins, *The Federal System, in* GOALS FOR AMERICANS 265, 265 (The American Assembly ed., 1965).
78) In 1940, Congress enacted the Bald Eagle Protection Act protect the "symbol of American ideals of freedom." *See* 16 U.S.C. §§ 668-668d.
79) 16 U.S.C. §§ 715-715r.
80) *See, e.g., Hughes v. Oklahoma*, 441 U.S. 322 (1979) (overruling *Geer* and holding that Commerce Clause prevents state from prohibiting export of game when it permits commercial exploitation within the state); *Douglas v. Seacoast Products, Inc.*, 431 U.S. 265 (1977) (state prohibition on commercial fishing by nonresidents preempted by federal statute providing for licensing of commercial fishing vessels); *Kleppe v. New Mexico*, 426 U.S. 529 (1976) (under Property Clause, the federal government may protect wildlife located on federal lands despite state law); *Toomer v. Witsell*, 334 U.S. 385 (1948) (Privileges and Immunities Clause prohibit state discrimination against non-state residents engaged in commercial fishing); *Takahashi v. Fish & Game Commission*, 334 U.S. 410 (1948) (Equal Protection Clause prohibits states from barring aliens from commercial fishing); *Hunt v. United States*, 278 U.S. 96 (1928) (under the Property Clause, the federal government may authorizing killing of deer in violation of state law to protect its land). *But see Maine v. Taylor*, 477 U.S. 131 (1986) (Commerce Clause does not prevent state from prohibiting importation of wildlife that might introduce parasites into wild populations); *Baldwin v. Fish & Game Commission*, 436 U.S. 371 (1978) (neither Privileges and Immunities Clause nor Equal Protection Clause prohibit state from charging higher fee for non-resident recreational hunting license).
81) Act of Sept. 2, 1937, ch. 899, § 1, 50 Stat. 917 (codified as amended at 16 U.S.C. §§ 669-669i).
82) 16 U.S.C. § 669a.
83) *Id.* § 669.
84) Act of Oct. 23, 1970, Pub. L. No. 91-503, §§ 101-102, 84 Stat. 1097.
85) 16 U.S.C. § 669e(2).
86) *Id.* § 669a.
87) *Id.* § 669e(a).
88) *Id.* § 669e(a), (b).
89) *Id.* § 669c.

90) 16 U.S.C. § 669b(a); 26 U.S.C. §§ 4161(b), 4181.

91) Act of Aug. 9, 1950, ch. 658, § 1, 64 Stat. 430 (codified as amended at 16 U.S.C. §§ 777-777*l*).

92) Act of May 28, 1963, Pub. L. 88-29, 77 Stat. 49.

93) 16 U.S.C. § 460*l*.

94) Although Pittman-Robertson contains the undefined term "wildlife" that is not limited to game species, the Fish & Wildlife Service has long restricted the term to birds and mammals of benefit to hunters. *See* 43 C.F.R. pt. 17.

95) Dingell-Johnson applies only to "fish which have material value in connection with sport or recreation in the marine and/or fresh waters of the United States." 16 U.S.C. § 777a.

96) 16 U.S.C. § 460*l*-11.

97) Land & Water Conservation Fund of 1965, Pub. L. No. 88-578, § 6(a)(1), 78 Stat. 897, 903 (1964) (current version at 16 U.S.C. § 460*l*-9(a)(1)). The Endangered Species Preservation Act of 1966 authorized appropriations of up to $15 million from the fund. Act of Oct. 15, 1966, Pub. L. No. 89-669, § 2, 80 Stat. 926. The Endangered Species Conservation Act of 1969 increased the maximum amount that could be spent on a single area. Act of Dec. 5, 1969, Pub. L. No. 91-135, § 12(b), 83 Stat. 282. The Endangered Species Act of 1973 removed all funding limitations. 16 U.S.C. § 1534(b).

98) MICHAEL J. BEAN, *supra* note 6, at 233.

99) Although Pittman-Robertson contains the undefined term "wildlife" that is not limited to game species, the Fish & Wildlife Service has long restricted the term to birds and mammals of benefit to hunters. *See* 43 C.F.R. pt. 17.

100) Dingell-Johnson applies only to "fish which have material value in connection with sport or recreation in the marine and/or fresh waters of the United States." 16 U.S.C. § 777a.

101) Act of Sept. 29, 1980, Pub. L. 96-366, 94 Stat. 1322 (codified as amended at 16 U.S.C. §§ 2901-2911).

102) 16 U.S.C. § 2903.

103) *Id.* § 2902(3).

104) The National Environmental Policy Act, 42 U.S.C. §§ 4321, 4331-4335, is the best-known example of this approach.

105) For a more recent attempt to force water-management agencies to manage their systems "in a manner that provides equitable treatment for ... fish and wildlife," see Pacific Northwest Electric Power Planning and Conservation Act, 16 U.S.C. § 839-839g. The "equitable treatment" requirement is found at *id.* § 839b(h)(11)(A)(i). Most of the anadromous fish runs covered by this provision were listed under the Endangered Species Act subsequent to the imposition of this requirement.

106) Act of Mar. 10, 1934, ch. 55, §§ 5, 1, 48 Stat. 401, 402, 401.

107) *Id.* § 3(b).

108) *Id.*

109) H.R. REP. NO. 850, 73d Cong., 2d Sess. 1 (1934).

110) H.R. REP. NO. 1944, 79th Cong., 2d Sess. 1 (1946).

111) Act of Aug. 14, 1946, ch. 965, § 2, 60 Stat. 1080 (codified at 16 U.S.C. § 662(a) (1988)).

112) *Id.* § 3.

113) *Id.* § 2.

114) S. Rep. No. 1981, 85th Cong., 2d Sess. 4 (1958), *reprinted in* 1958 U.S.C.C.A.N. 3446, 3449.

115) Act of Aug. 12, 1958, Pub. L. No. 85-624, 72 Stat. 563.

116) 16 U.S.C. § 661.

117) *Id.* § 662.
118) *Udall v. FPC,* 387 U.S. 428 (1967).
119) *Texas Committee on Natural Resources v. Marsh,* 736 F.2d 262, 269 (5th Cir. 1984); *see also Missouri ex rel. Ashcroft v. Army Corps of Engineers,* 526 F. Supp. 660 (W.D. Mo. 1980).
120) Act of Jan. 1, 1970, Pub. L. 91-190, 83 Stat. 852 (codified at 42 U.S.C. §§ 4321, 4331-4335).
121) 42 U.S.C. § 4331(a).
122) *Id.* § 4321.
123) *Id.* § 4332(2)(c).
124) *Strycker's Bay Neighborhood Council v. Karlen,* 444 U.S. 223 (1980) (*per curiam*).
125) Dale D. Goble, *Salmon in the Columbia Basin: From Abundance to Extinction, in* NORTHWEST LANDS, NORTHWEST PEOPLES 229, 232-33 (Dale. D. Goble & Paul W. Hirt eds. 1999).
126) Act of Oct. 30, 1965, Pub. L. 89-304, 79 Stat. 1125 (codified as amended at 16 U.S.C. §§ 757a-757g).
127) 16 U.S.C. § 757a.
128) *Id.* § 757b.
129) *See, e.g.,* Gary K. Meffe, *Techno-Arrogance and Halfway Measures: Salmon Hatcheries on the Pacific Coast of North America,* 6 CONSERVATION BIO. 351 (1992).
130) Act of Sept. 15, 1960, Pub. L. No. 86-797, §§ 1, 2, 74 Stat. 1052, 1052-53 (formerly codified at 16 U.S.C. § 670a) (repealed 1997).
131) *See* Charles F. Wilkinson & H. Michael Anderson, *Land and Resource Planning int he National Forests,* 64 OREGON L. REV. 1, 309 (1985).
132) Act of Oct. 18, 1974, Pub. L. 93-452, 88 Stat. 1369 (codified at 16 U.S.C. §§ 670g-670o).
133) 16 U.S.C. § 670h(1)(a). The Act defines "state agency" as "the agency or agencies of a State responsible for the administration of the fish and game laws of the State." *Id.* § 670k(5).
134) *Id.* § 670g(a).
135) Charles F. Wilkinson & H. Michael Anderson, *supra* note 114, at 310.

CHAPTER 3: Conserving Biodiversity

1) 16 U.S.C. § 1531(b).
2) *Tennessee Valley Authority v. Hill,* 437 U.S. 153 (1978).
3) *See* THOMAS R. DUNLAP, SAVING AMERICA'S WILDLIFE 142-44 (1988); STEVEN L. YAFFEE, PROHIBITIVE POLICY 33-34 (1982).
4) COMMITTEE ON RARE & ENDANGERED WILDLIFE SPECIES, BUREAU OF SPORT FISHERIES & WILDLIFE, U.S. DEPT. OF THE INTERIOR, RARE AND ENDANGERED FISH AND WILDLIFE OF THE UNITED STATES introduction at i (Resource Pub. No. 34, July 1966).
5) The Redbook's authors stated that this was their intention: "Compilation of the list of rare and endangered wildlife is intended to focus attention on these species -- to stimulate corrective actions whenever possible." *Id.* at iii.
6) Land & Water Conservation Fund of 1965, Pub. L. No. 88-578, § 6(a)(1), 78 Stat. 897, 903 (1964).
7) Endangered Species Preservation Act of 1966, Pub. L. No. 89-669, 80 Stat. 926, *repealed by* Endangered Species Act of 1973, Pub. L. No. 93-205, § 14, 87 Stat. 884, 903 (1973).
8) *Tennessee Valley Authority v. Hill,* 437 U.S. 153, 174 (1978).

9) Endangered Species Preservation Act of 1966, Pub. L. No. 89-669, § 1(a), 80 Stat. 926, 926; *see also* S. REP. NO. 1463, 89th Cong., 2d Sess. 2, (1966), *reprinted in* 1966 U.S.C.C.A.N. 3342, 3343, 3344; H.R. REP. NO. 1168, 89th Cong., 1st Sess. 2-3, 4 (1965).

10) *Id.* §§ 3(a), (b).

11) *Id.* § 2(c).

12) MICHAEL J. BEAN, THE EVOLUTION OF NATIONAL WILDLIFE LAW 320 (rev. & expanded ed. 1983).

13) *Id.* § 1(c).

14) *Id.* § 1(b).

15) Thus, species were to be listed by the Secretary only "after consultation with the affected States." *Id.* § 1(c). Similarly, the Secretary was to cooperate "to the maximum extent practicable with the several States," including consultation before the acquisition of land to protect wildlife habitat. *Id.* §§ 3(a), (b).

16) Despite the increasingly pervasive federal role in wildlife conservation since the Lacey Act, the national government has retained a formal policy of deference to traditional state prerogatives. Congress has repeatedly sought to reassure the states that it is they who have the responsibility and authority to manage resident wildlife. *E.g.,* Migratory Bird Conservation Act, 16 U.S.C. §§ 715h (state may set bag limits more restrictive than federal limits), 718c (state may require hunting license); the Multiple Use-Sustained Yield Act of 1960, 16 U.S.C. § 528 (1988) ("Nothing herein shall be construed as affecting the jurisdiction or responsibilities of the several States with respect to wildlife and fish on the national forests."); National Wildlife Refuge System Administration Act, 16 U.S.C. § 668dd(c) (1988) ("The Provisions of this Act shall not be construed as affecting the authority, jurisdiction, or responsibility of the several States to manage, control, or regulate fish and resident wildlife under State law or regulations in any area within the System."); National Wild & Scenic Rivers Act, 16 U.S.C. § 1284(a) (1988) ("Nothing in this Act shall affect the jurisdiction or responsibilities of the States with respect to fish and wildlife."); Federal Land Policy & Management Act, 43 U.S.C. § 1732(b) (1988) ("[N]othing in this Act shall be construed as authorizing the Secretary concerned to require Federal permits to hunt and fish ion public lands or on lands in the National Forest System and adjacent waters or as enlarging or diminishing the responsibility and authority of the States for management of fish and resident wildlife.").

17) Endangered Species Preservation Act of 1966, Pub. L. No. 89-669, § 4(c), 80 Stat. 926, 928.

18) H.R. REP. NO. 1168, 89th Cong., 1st Sess. 7 (1965).

19) Pub. L. No. 91-135, § 12(d), 83 Stat. 275, 283, *repealed by* Endangered Species Act of 1973, Pub. L. No. 93-205, § 14, 87 Stat. 884, 903 (1973).

20) *Id.* § 7(a).

21) *Id.* § 3(a).

22) The Act provided for civil penalties of up to $5,000 and criminal penalties of $10,000 and/or 1 year in prison; the wildlife or property was forfeited. *Id.* § 4.

23) The Act covered both species and subspecies. *Id.* § 3(a). This was an extension of the ESPA, which had applied only to "species."

24) *Id.* § 5(b).

25) *See* Alan Schonfeld, *International Trade in Wildlife: How Effective is the Endangered Species Treaty?,* 15 CAL. W. INT'L L.J. 111, 114-17 (1985).

26) Convention on International Trade in Endangered Species of Wild Fauna & Flora, Mar. 3, 1973, 27 U.S.T. 1087, T.I.A.S. No. 8249.

27) *Id.* art. II, § 1.

28) *Id.* art. II, § 2.

29) *Id.* art. II, § 3.
30) *Id.* art. VIII, § 1.
31) Act of Dec. 28, 1973, Pub. L. No. 93-205, 87 Stat. 884 (codified at 16 U.S.C. §§ 5131-1544).
32) Robert B. Keiter, *Beyond the Boundary Line: Constructing a Law of Ecosystem Management,* 65 U.COLO. L. REV. 293, 314 (1994).
33) Act of Aug. 25, 1916, ch. 408, 39 Stat. 535 (codified as amended at 16 U.S.C. §§ 1-20g).
34) 16 U.S.C. § 1.
35) Act of Mar. 27, 1978, Pub. L. No. 95-250, 92 Stat. 166 (codified at 16 U.S.C. §§ 1a-1 to 1a-8).
36) Act of June 8, 1906, ch. 3060, § 2, 34 Stat. 225 (codified at 16 U.S.C. §§ 431-433).
37) 16 U.S.C. § 431.
38) *Wyoming v. Franks,* 58 F. Supp. 890 (D. Wyo. 1945). *See also Cappaert v. United States,* 426 U.S. 128 (1976) (Devil's Hole National Monument intended to protect remnant of pleistocene lakes system and its indigenous pupfish population).
39) Act of Mar. 1, 1872, ch. 24, § 1, 17 Stat. 32 (codified at 16 U.S.C. § 21).
40) Act of Sept. 25, 1890, ch. 926, 26 Stat. 478 (codified at 16 U.S.C. § 41).
41) Act of Aug. 25, 1916, ch. 408, 39 Stat. 535 (codified as amended at 16 U.S.C. §§ 1-20g).
42) 16 U.S.C. § 1.
43) *E.g.,* JAMES A. PRITCHARD, PRESERVING YELLOWSTONE'S NATURAL CONDITIONS (1999).
44) *See* RICHARD WEST SELLARS, PRESERVING NATURE IN THE NATIONAL PARKS 91 (1997).
45) Act of June 4, 1897, ch. 2, 30 Stat. 34 (codified at 16 U.S.C. §§ 475, 477-482; partially repealed).
46) The United States Supreme Court gave the delegation a narrow interpretation in the context of reserved water rights in *United States v. New Mexico,* 438 U.S. 696 (1978).
47) Act of June 12, 1960, Pub. L. 86-517, 74 Stat. 215 (codified at 16 U.S.C. 528-531).
48) 16 U.S.C. § 528.
49) Act of Oct. 22, 1976, Pub. L. 94-588, 90 Stat. 2949 (codified as amended at 16 U.S.C. §§ 1600-1616).
50) 16 U.S.C. § 1604(g)(3)(B).
51) Act of June 28, 1934, ch. 865, 48 Stat. 1269 (codified as amended at 43 U.S.C. §§ 315-315r).
52) Act of Oct. 25, 1978, Pub. L. No. 95-514, 92 Stat. 1803 (codified at 43 U.S.C. §§ 1901-1908).
53) 30 U.S.C. §§ 22-47.
54) Act of Feb. 25, 1920, ch. 85, 41 Stat. 437 (codified as amended at 30 U.S.C. §§ 181-287).
55) Act of Aug. 7, 1947, ch. 513, 61 Stat. 913 (codified as amended at 30 U.S.C. §§ 351-359).
56) Act of Dec. 24, 1970, Pub. L. No. 91-581, 84 Stat. 1566 (codified as amended at 30 U.S.C. 1001-1025).
57) Act of Oct. 21, 1976, Pub. L. No. 94-579, 90 Stat. 2744 (codified as amended at 43 U.S.C. §§ 1701-1784).
58) Act of Oct. 25, 1978, Pub. L. 95-514, 92 Stat. 1803 (codified at 43 U.S.C. §§ 1901-1908).
59) 43 U.S.C. §§ 1901(a)(1), (3), (6), (b)(4).
60) Act of Sept. 15, 1960, Pub. L. No. 86-797, §§ 1, 2, 74 Stat. 1052, 1052-53 (formerly codified at 16 U.S.C. § 670a) (repealed 1997).
61) *Id.*
62) National Defense Authorization Act of 1998, Pub. L. 105-85, Div. B, Title XXIX, § 2904(a), 111 Stat. 1629, 2017 (Nov. 18, 1997) (codified at 16 U.S.C. § 670a).
63) 16 U.S.C. § 670a(a)(2).

64) *Id.* § 670a(b).
65) Act of Sept. 3, 1964, Pub. L. 88-577, 78 Stat. 890 (codified at 16 U.S.C. §§ 1131-1136).
66) 16 U.S.C. § 1131(c).
67) *Id.* §§ 1132(b)-(c).
68) The definition of "wilderness" states that it "may also contain ecological, geological, or other features of scientific, educational, scenic, or historical value." *Id.* § 1131(c)(4).
69) Wilderness areas are generally at least 5000 contiguous, roadless acres. *Id.* § 1132(c).
70) Act of Oct. 2, 1968, Pub. L. 90-542, 82 Stat. 906 (codified as amended at 16 U.S.C. §§ 1271-1287).
71) 16 U.S.C. § 1273(a).
72) *Id.*
73) *Id.* §§ 1273(b), 1280(a)(iii), 1281(a).
74) *Id.* § 1271.
75) *Id.* § 1274(d).
76) *Id.* § 1281(a).
77) *E.g., Gibbons v. Ogden,* 22 U.S. (9 Wheat.) 1 (1824).
78) *E.g., Kaiser Aetna v. United States,* 444 U.S. 164 (1979).
79) *E.g., Solid Waste Agency of Northern Cook County v. United States Army Corps of Engineers,* 531 U.S. 159 (2001).
80) SAMUEL P. HAYS, CONSERVATION AND THE GOSPEL OF EFFICIENCY 261-76 (1959).
81) *See* Michael C. Blumm, *The Northwest's Hydroelectric Heritage, in* NORTHWEST LANDS, NORTHWEST PEOPLES 264 (Dale D. Goble & Paul W. Hirt eds., 1999).
82) In 1977, the FPC was abolished and its licensing functions became the Federal Energy Regulatory Commission -- FERC. *See* Department of Energy Organization Act, Pub. L. No. 95-91, 91 Stat. 565 (Aug. 4, 1977).
83) 16 U.S.C. § 817.
84) For the scope of this delegation, see *FPC v. Union Electric Co.,* 381 U.S. 90 (1965). The effect-on-interstate-commerce basis for jurisdiction is met if the project will have a substantial effect on anadromous fish. *U.S. Department of Commerce v. FERC,* 36 F.3d 893 (9th Cir. 1994).
85) Act of Mar. 10, 1934, ch. 55, 48 Stat. 401.
86) Act of Aug. 14, 1946, ch. 965, 60 Stat. 1080.
87) Act of Aug. 12, 1958, Pub. L. No. 85-624, 72 Stat. 563 (currently codified at 16 U.S.C. §§ 661-666c).
88) 16 U.S.C. 797(e).
89) *Id.* § 803(a).
90) *Id.* § 803(j).
91) Act of June 30, 1948, ch. 758, 62 Stat. 1155.
92) Act of July 20, 1961, Pub. L. No. 87-88, § 7, 75 Stat. 204, 207-10.
93) Act of Oct. 2, 1965, Pub. L. No. 89-234, § 5, 79 Stat. 903, 907-09.
94) Act of Mar. 3, 1899, ch. 425, § 13, 30 Stat. 1152.
95) Act of Oct. 18, 1972, Pub. L. No. 92-500, 86 Stat. 816.
96) Act of July 20, 1961, Pub. L. No. 87-88, § 7, 75 Stat. 204, 207-10.
97) Act of Oct. 2, 1965, Pub. L. No. 89-234, § 5, 79 Stat. 903, 909. Although water quality standards were to be set following "consideration" of the waterbody's "value for public water supplies, propagation of fish and wildlife, recreational purposes, and agricultural, industrial, and other legitimate uses," the focus remained on "protect[ing] the public health and welfare." *Id.* at 908.
98) 33 U.S.C. § 1251(a)(1).
99) *Id.* § 1311(a).
100) *Id.* § 1362(14).

101) *Id.* §§ 1311, 1342.
102) *Id.* § 1288.
103) *Id.* § 1313.
104) *Id.* § 1362(7).
105) S. Rep. No. 1236, 92d Cong., 2d Sess. 144 (1972). *Cf. United States v. Riverside Bayview Homes, Inc.*, 474 U.S. 121 (1985).
106) 16 U.S.C. § 1538(a)(1)(B). This protection has been extended by regulation to species listed as threatened under the Act unless the listing document provides otherwise. 50 C.F.R. §§ 17.31(a), 17.71.
107) *Id.* § 1532(19).
108) 50 C.F.R. § 17.3
109) These statements are qualified by the availability of incidental take permits when the landowner develops a habitat conservation plan. 16 U.S.C. § 1539(a)(1)-(2).
110) Federal agency that authorize or fund private actions are subject to the consultation requirements, including the proscription on "jeopardiz[ing] the continued existence of any [listed] species" or "adversely modif[ying critical] habitat of such species." *Id.* § 1536(a)(2).
111) *E.g., Hodel v. Indiana,* 452 U.S. 314 (1981); *National Association of Home Builders v. Babbitt,* 130 F.3d 1041 (D.C. Cir. 1997), *cert. denied,* 524 U.S. 937 (1998).
112) *See generally* Oliver A. Houck & Michael Rolland, *Federalism in Wetlands Regulation: A Consideration of Delegation of Clean Water Act Section 404 and Related Programs to the States,* 52 MD. L. REV. 1241, 1244-1251 (1995).
113) 16 U.S.C. § 1344(a).
114) *Id.* § 1344(b)(1).
115) 40 C.F.R. §§ 230.10(c), 230.11(e), 230.41(b). *See also* 33 C.F.R. § 320.4(a)(1) (Corps regulations requiring a "public interest review" that includes consideration of "fish and wildlife values.").
116) *Id.* § 230.10.
117) 33 U.S.C. § 1344(f)(1)(A).
118) *Id.* § 1344(f)(2). *See, e.g., Avoyelles Sportsmen's League, Inc. v. Marsh,* 715 F.2d 897 (5th Cir. 1983).
119) Food Security Act of 1985, Pub. L. No. 99-198, 99 Stat. 1504.
120) Food, Agriculture, Conservation, and Trade Act of 1990, Pub. L. No. 101-624, 104 Stat. 3359.
121) Federal Agriculture Improvement and Reform Act of 1996, Pub. L. No. 104-127, 110 Stat. 888.
122) 16 U.S.C. §§ 3801(6)(A), 3821(a).
123) *Id.*
124) *Id.* § 3822(f)(2).
125) 16 U.S.C. §§ 715k–3 to 715k–5.
126) Act of Dec. 19, 1970, Pub. L. No. 91–559, 84 Stat. 1468 (Codified at 16 U.S.C. §§ 1301–1311).
127) *Id.* § 1302.
128) *Id.*
129) *Id.* § 1301(2).
130) *See* 16 U.S.C. §§ 3837a-3837f.
131) *Id.* § 3837a.
132) *Id.* § 3837a(d).
133) *Id.* §§ 3901-3932.
134) *Id.* § 3921(a), (c).
135) *Id.* §§ 4401-4414.

136) *Id.* § 4404(a)(4), (5).
137) *Id.* § 4405.
138) *See* 16 U.S.C. §§ 3951-3956. The statute is focused on Louisiana.
139) *See generally* Barton H. Thompson, Jr., *Providing Biodiversity Through Policy Diversity,* 38 IDAHO L. REV. 355 (2002).
140) *See* I.R.C. § 170(f)(3)(B), (h).
141) Coastal Barrier Resource Act, Pub. L. No. § 1, 96 Stat. 1653, 1653 (codified as amended at 16 U.S.C. § 3501(a)(1)).
142) Act of Oct. 18, 1982, Pub. L. No. 97-348, 96 Stat. 1653 (codified as amended at 16 U.S.C. §§ 3501-3510).
143) *Id.* § 3504(a).
144) *Id.* § 3503.
145) *E.g.,* DONALD WORSTER, *Transformations of the Earth, in* THE WEALTH OF NATURE 45 (1993).
146) Food Security Act, Pub. L. 99-198, Title XII, §§ 1231-1236, 99 Stat. 1509 (Dec. 23, 1985) (currently codified as amended at 16 U.S.C. §§ 3831-3836).
147) 16 U.S.C. § 3831(b).
148) *Id.* § 3834(c)(3)(A).
149) *Id.* § 3831(e).
150) Food, Agriculture, Conservation, and Trade Act of 1990, Pub. L. 101-624, Title XIV, § 1440, 104 Stat. 3597 (Nov. 28, 1990) (codified as amended at 16 U.S.C. §§ 3839-38339d).
151) 16 U.S.C. § 3839(a).
152) *Id.* § 3839(b).
153) *See* MICHAEL J. BEAN & MELANIE J. ROWLAND, THE EVOLUTION OF NATIONAL WILDLIFE LAW 437 (3d ed. 1997).
154) Food, Agriculture, Conservation, and Trade Act of 1990, Pub. L. 101-624, Title XIV, § 1217, 104 Stat. 3597 (Nov. 28, 1990) (codified as amended at 16 U.S.C. § 2103c).
155) 16 U.S.C. § 2103c(a).
156) *Id.*

CHAPTER 4: Problem Wildlife

1) *See* 1 RECORDS OF THE GOVERNOR AND COMPANY OF MASSACHUSETTS BAY IN NEW ENGLAND 81 (Nathaniel B. Shurtleff ed., Boston, William White 1853).
2) The Act of Mar. 10, 1656, 1 Va. Stat. 393 (W. Hening, ed., New York, N.Y. 1823).
3) David S. Wilcove *et al., Quantifying Threats to Imperiled Species in the United States,* 48 BIOSCI. 607, 609 (1998).
4) Act of May 25, 1900, ch. 533, § 2, 31 Stat. 187 (codified as amended at 18 U.S.C. § 42).
5) 18 U.S.C. § 42(a)(1).
6) 18 U.S.C. § 42(b).
7) Act of Mar. 4, 1909, ch. 301, 35 Stat. 1051.
8) Act of Mar. 2, 1931, ch. 370, § 1, 46 Stat. 1468 (codified as amended at 7 U.S.C. § 426).
9) *See* MICHAEL J. BEAN, THE EVOLUTION OF NATIONAL WILDLIFE LAW 236-39 (rev. & expanded ed. 1983).
10) Act of Nov. 29, 1990, Pub. L. 101-646, Title I, § 1002, 104 Stat. 4761 (codified as amended at 16 U.S.C. § 4701-4751).
11) 16 U.S.C. § 4702(11).
12) *Id.* § 4702(1).
13) *Id.* § 4721(b).
14) *Id.* § 4722(b).